THE

ENCYCLOPEDIA

OF

PROTESTANTISM

THE
ENCYCLOPEDIA
OF
PROTESTANTISM

VOLUME 3
L–R

HANS J. HILLERBRAND

EDITOR

Routledge
New York   London

Published in 2004 by

Routledge
29 West 35th Street
New York, NY 10001-2299
www.routledge-ny.com

Published in Great Britain by
Routledge
11 New Fetter Lane
London EC4P 4EE
www.routledge.co.uk

Routledge is an imprint of Taylor & Francis Books, Inc.

10   9   8   7   6   5   4   3   2   1

Printed on acid-free, 250-year-life paper
Manufactured in the United States of America

Library of Congress Cataloging-in-Publication Data

Encyclopedia of Protestantism / Hans J. Hillerbrand, editor.
   p. cm.
Includes bibliographical references and index.
  ISBN 0-415-92472-3 (set)
  1. Protestantism—Encyclopedias. I. Hillerbrand, Hans Joachim.
BX4811.3.E53 2003
280′.4′03—dc21

                                 2003011582

Contents

A to Z List of Articles   vii

Thematic List of Articles   xvii

Preface   xxvii

Volume 1, Entries A–C   1

Volume 2, Entries D–K   549

Volume 3, Entries L–R   1047

Volume 4, Entries S–Z   1633

Appendix   2087

List of Contributors   2095

Index   2117

L

LAESTADIUS, LARS LEVI (1800–1861)

Swedish reformer. Laestadius was born January 10, 1800, in Jakkvik, in the northern region of SWEDEN. His father was a Lutheran pastor. While still in high school (Gymnasium), he showed his interest in THEOLOGY and philosophy as well as in botany, the latter triggered by his half-brother Carl Erik. His industrious collection of specimen plants in Lapland during his summer vacations soon earned him a reputation as an outstanding botanist. A published report of one of his first field trips earned him the recognition of the Swedish Academy of Sciences and Letters, which supported his subsequent research.

In 1820 he matriculated at the University of Uppsala, where he studied theology, languages, and botany. He was ordained in 1825 and was appointed pastor in Kaaresuvando, where he continued until 1849. On the occasion of a ministerial visitation to Lapland he met a Sami woman after church on New Year's Day 1844 who not only impressed him with the need for personal religious regeneration as the hallmark of authentic Christian existence but also was instrumental in triggering Laestadius's own CONVERSION. From then on, Laestadius's PREACHING included similar exhortations to repent and be converted. He gained converts and worshippers from other towns and villages flocked to hear his sermons. A revival began to sweep over northern Sweden and, before long, over neighboring FINLAND as well. To deal with the consequences of an increasingly widespread awakening, Laestadius commissioned laymen to assist him in his work (see REVIVALS; AWAKENINGS).

Laestadius always affirmed his Lutheran orientation. The awakening, brought about by his preaching, therefore focused not so much on theology as on personal commitment, sobriety, temperance, devotional meetings, and Bible study—all hallmarks of eighteenth-century German Lutheran PIETISM.

Immigrants brought the Laestadian Lutheran revival to the UNITED STATES; the first Laestadian worship was held in Cokato, Minnesota, in 1863, among immigrants from northern NORWAY. Given the ethnic bifurcation of religious immigrant traditions in North America, the Laestadian immigrants to the United States soon evolved their own separate church structures, something that had not occurred in Finland. In North America the Apostolic Lutheran Church stands in the Laestadian tradition.

The use of the term "apostolic" denotes the principle that only the BIBLE is the source of AUTHORITY and that the Apostle's Creed—that is, the belief of the Apostles—summarizes the teachings of the Bible. The Lutheran confessional documents of the sixteenth century, such as the Formula of Concord or the AUGSBURG CONFESSION, are not rejected but seen as belonging to a different category of authoritative sources. Laestadian theology is conservative, assumes the inerrancy of the Bible, stresses conversion, and insists on the sanctified way of life for believers who confess their sins to one another. This is understood as the faithful application of MARTIN LUTHER's teaching on the PRIESTHOOD OF ALL BELIEVERS. In addition, again in close adherence to Luther's notions, Laestadians see the local congregation as the place of SALVATION and the living fellowship of believers. Laestadians emphasize missionary activity, education, and music, usually sung *a capella*.

See also Biblical Inerrancy; Sanctification

References and Further Reading

Hallencreutz, Carl F. "Lars Levi Laestadius' Attitude to Saami Religion," in *Saami Religion*. Åbo, Finland: Donner Inst, 1987.

Esala, Philip J. "American Laestadianism Schismatic." *Concordia Historical Institute Quarterly* 58 (1985): 183–189.

Gothóni, René, and Kirsti Suolinna. "The Religious Message in Action: A Case Study," in *New Religions*. Stockkholm: Almquist and Wiksell, 1975.

Heikkinen, Jacob W. "Lars Levi Laestadius." *Lutheran Quarterly* 8 (1956): 360–362.

Laestadius, L. L. *The new postilla of Lars Levi Laestadius*. Hancock, MI: Finnish Luteran Book Concern, 1925.

———. *Evangeliepostilla*. Stockholm: Svenska Kyrkans Diakonistyrelses Bokförlag, 1957.

HANS J. HILLERBRAND

LAGARDE, PAUL ANTON DE (1827–1891)

German theologian. Lagarde was born Paul Botticher, the son of a classical secondary school teacher in Berlin on November 2, 1827. He studied THEOLOGY in Berlin and HALLE and received a doctoral degree in 1849 and the universal teaching license in oriental languages at the philosophical faculty. While he was a student Lagarde escaped the piety of his parents and became estranged from traditional Protestantism, which he would later criticize fundamentally. After research stays in London and Paris, where he copied particularly Eastern manuscripts, he worked for many years as a teacher in Berlin schools. After several attempts he became professor for Eastern languages in Göttingen in 1869.

Lagarde's most important field of work was in critical editions. He edited Coptic, Greek, Latin, and Arab texts of the church fathers and the BIBLE. His special attention was the publication of a critical edition of the Septuagint. Theological questions engaged Lagarde his entire life. He required a strict separation of state and church and an abolishing of theological faculties at state universities.

His ideal was a national church (*nationale Kirche*) and a national religion, in which the traditional denominations and theological disputes are removed. Lagarde was particularly critical of Pauline theology. Lagarde's opinion was that Paul had falsified the message of Jesus with the help of the Old Testament. His conceptions of a national church, the result of an exaggerated sense of nationalism, were connected with his ANTI-SEMITISM. Even if he was not a racial anti-Semite, his speeches and publications, which placed before the Jews the alternatives of complete assimilation or the deprivation of citizenship, exerted a long-term influence on the anti-Semitic movement. Lagarde asserted that JUDAISM prevented the internal unification of GERMANY. Thus the Nazis, *Nationalsozialisten* engaged the writings of Paul de Lagarde.

See also Church and State, Overview; Education, Theology: Europe

References and Further Reading

Gottheil, Richard J. H. *Bibliography of the Works of Paul Anton de Lagarde*. Washington, D.C.: reprinted from the Proceedings of the American Oriental Society, 1892.

Heiligenthal, Roman. "Paul de Lagarde." In *Theologische Realenzyklopädie*, edited by Gerhard Müller. Vol. 20, 375–378. Berlin/New York: de Gruyter, 1990.

Lougee, Robert Wayne. *Paul de Lagarde, 1827–1891. A Study of Radical Conservatism in Germany*. Cambridge, MA: Harvard University Press, 1962.

Rahlfs, Alfred. *Paul de Lagardes wissenschaftliches Lebenswerk im Rahmen einer Geschichte seines Lebens*. Berlin: Weidmann, 1928 [with bibliography].

Stern, Fritz. *The Politics of Cultural Despair. A Study in the Rise of the Germanic Ideology*. Berkeley: University of California, 1974.

NORBERT FRIEDRICH

LAITY

Biblical Origins

The term *laity* is a collective description commonly applied to those church members who are not part of the ordained CLERGY. Unlike the Greek noun *laos*, meaning "people," the derivative term *laïkos* (Lat. *laicus*, "laity") is not found in the New Testament. Where the Greek Septuagint version of the Old Testament uses *laos* to refer to Israel as the chosen people of God, the New Testament applies the term to the New Israel, the community of Christian believers. Although both uses presuppose a theocratic context, the New Testament term, at least in its early, Pauline form, lacks the institutional and cultic overtones found in Israelite worship. Instead the early Christians as the people of God constitute the CHURCH, which is regarded as an organic rather than an institutional entity. In the Apostle Paul's teaching (I Corinthians 12), the metaphor of the human body is used to demonstrate the conviction that each believer has a distinct yet essential function to exercise within the community of faith for the good of the whole and under the headship of Christ. The human leadership of this new community is found within the *laos*. Its rudimentary distinctions appear to center more on functional matters than issues of status.

Both in the Pauline figure of Jesus as the heavenly intercessor and, more explicitly, in the image of the eternal high priest of the New Covenant presented by the Epistle to the Hebrews, the theology of some of the earliest Christian writings depicts Christ as the perfect fulfillment of the Israelite priesthood. Recalling the words of Jeremiah, all members of the new *laos* are seen as enjoying direct, personal knowledge of God. The new people of God, the *adelphoi* ("brothers") or *kletoi* ("called ones"), whom Christ represents in heaven, are collectively called to act as prophets, priests, and kings in the service of God irrespective of whether they have a specific ministerial designation. As a redeemed and forgiven company of people they proclaim the gospel of Jesus Christ to the world by means of word and deed, they intercede for mankind through prayer and self-sacrifice, and they exercise the privileges of royal status as sons and daughters of the living God.

The quintessential expression of early DOCTRINE concerning the laity is found in the Petrine epistles (I Peter 2:9–10) in the concept of the royal priesthood, or as it is more commonly known, the PRIESTHOOD OF ALL BELIEVERS. This doctrine of the corporate priesthood of the laity was carried decisively into the sphere of Protestant thought by the early theological writings of MARTIN LUTHER. In his 1520 address *To the Christian Nobility of the German Nation* he argued passionately against the prevailing understanding within the church of the laity as being restricted to a subordinate role in relation to the ordained priesthood.

Historical Development: Early and Medieval Church

The seeds of the subordination of the laity can be traced, even within the canonical writings, because the Pastoral Epistles afford evidence of an incipient hierarchy, although at that stage ecclesiastical leadership is still firmly located within the all-embracing concept of the *laos*. The earliest use of the more specialized term "laity" is found outside the future canon of scripture (c.96 A.D.) in the First Epistle of Clement (40:5). Writing from Rome, the author of Clement accepts an organizational pattern for the church that mirrors the religious structures of Israel, with a differentiated clergy analogous to the Old Testament priesthood. One hundred and fifty years later the correspondence of Cyprian, bishop of Carthage, reveals the church in North Africa operating with a clear hierarchy of BISHOPS, presbyters, and DEACONS. Although the laity were still participating in church councils their contribution was rapidly being eroded. By the Middle Ages the emphasis had switched from the original common inheritance and calling of believers, including those with particular leadership responsibilities, to an understanding of the church where a strong juridical distinction was drawn between clergy and laity. Unlike the Eastern church, which maintained the possibility of an active and significant role for the nonordained, the Western church from the fall of the Roman Empire relegated its ordinary members to a position of marginal importance. As the function and status of the clergy became formalized so the laity came to be regarded in an increasingly negative light, defined more by the areas from which they were proscribed, especially PREACHING and the administration of the SACRAMENTS, than by anything positive.

From the twelfth century the fortunes of the laity began to change with the growth of civic pride and the wider availability of education. Popular piety deepened, partly in response to the work of the newly founded mendicant orders. In this changing climate a mood of assertiveness appeared among sections of the laity encouraged by new theological ideas. In 1324 Marsiglio of Padua challenged the professional exclusivity of the priesthood, arguing that discipline and spirituality belonged to the whole church, not simply to the clergy, and that the claim of the latter to a hierarchical AUTHORITY had no scriptural basis. Fifty years later John Wycliffe went even further, rejecting the traditional feudal understanding of relationships within the church and arguing that by virtue of God's GRACE to the individual believer all Christians were equal, whether pope or layman, prince or peasant. Over the following century his lay followers, the "Poor Preachers," put this principle to the test by taking to themselves the right to propagate the teachings of the Bible read in the vernacular and publicly to attack those aspects of the late medieval priesthood that appeared to contradict scripture. By the dawn of the REFORMATION the laity were showing that they were no longer prepared meekly to accept their traditional passive role within the church. Their resistance took various forms, but was expressed most notably in the spread of lay-led HERESY, the general growth of dissatisfaction with the clergy, and the popular sense of grievance against tithe and other ecclesiastical exactions.

The Reformation

When Martin Luther launched his assault on the traditional distinction between the clergy and the laity his words resonated with this popular anticlericalism. With considerable adroitness he sought to enlist the support of the German princes, building on a rivalry between the secular and spiritual leaders of Western society that had troubled the Holy Roman Empire in varying degrees since the Lay Investiture Controversy of the eleventh and twelfth centuries. The essence of Luther's complaint against the church was that under papal leadership the Roman clergy had erected three defensive walls around themselves, thereby protecting the so-called spiritual estate against reform. These protective measures robbed the members of the temporal estate, whether prince or peasant, of any spiritual role, and reserved to the papacy the rights of pronouncing on the interpretation of scripture and of summoning a general council of the church. None of these measures in Luther's opinion had any justification. Appealing to scripture he insisted that all Christians belonged to the spiritual estate by virtue of their BAPTISM. Consequently all were consecrated priests and in the absence of ordained clergy could elect one of their number to preach and administer the SACRAMENTS. By the same token where the papacy was itself the cause of offense the temporal rulers as fellow Christians had a duty to convene a true reforming council of the church. Luther's 1520 analysis of the true position of the Christian laity was confirmed in still more striking terms the following year by the high degree of spiritual autonomy claimed for the individual believer in his famous appeal to the scriptures before the imperial Diet at Worms. Yet within four years he had begun to realize the less-attractive social implications of the new doctrine of the laity, as popular unrest spread across GERMANY using ideas uncomfortably similar to his own. Although the mature Luther did not renege on the universal priesthood, preserving the new emphasis implicitly in his encouragement of lay understanding of FAITH and WORSHIP through popular hymns, vernacular preaching and LITURGY, and full participation in the sacraments, it no longer constituted a subject for discussion and was modified to suit the structures and norms of German princely and civic society. Elsewhere within the Reformation the role and status of the laity received varying degrees of attention. In general the Magisterial Reformers, HULDRYCH ZWINGLI, MARTIN BUCER, and JOHN CALVIN, did not address the subject with the same directness as Luther, but they showed by their emphasis on assurance of faith, the work of Christ as sole mediator between the individual and God, and the centrality of the vernacular scriptures a similar concern to develop the spiritual life of all believers.

It was left to the Radical Reformers to implement most fully the essential equality of all Christians. In a conscious attempt to refashion the church according to a literal reading of the New Testament, the barriers created by sacramental theology disappeared and the concept of Christian leadership underwent a fundamental revision. In the most typical ecclesiological statement produced by the moderate wing of the Radical Reformation, the SCHLEITHEIM CONFESSION of 1527, the division between clergy and laity was virtually eradicated. Article 5 of the CONFESSION depicts the pastor as a person of good repute chosen and supported by the congregation to teach, discipline, and conduct prayer and the breaking of bread "for the advancement of all the brethren and sisters." Such a leader would be subject to discipline by the congregation if necessary (see CHURCH DISCIPLINE) and if he were removed by banishment or martyrdom another would immediately be ordained in his place for the preservation of the group of believers.

The direction taken by the Swiss and South German Anabaptists at Schleitheim and by other contemporary Radicals by no means indicated a dramatic change for most early Protestants. The Radicals were a small and largely ephemeral force because of their social attitudes and the strength of the persecution that befell them. For the non-Radical majority the survival of the term "laity" into the post-Reformation era gives some indication of the power of theological conservatism when it came to the relationship between the Protestant communities of northern Europe and their religious leaders. It is perfectly possible to argue that the term "laity" as a juridical concept, which flourished under medieval Catholicism, had no place in the Reformation reconstruction of the church. However, the historical manifestation of Protestantism was broad-ranging, extending from the modified Catholicism of Luther and the CHURCH OF ENGLAND, through the broad spectrum of Reformed churchmanship, which traced its origins to Zürich and Geneva, and arriving ultimately at the relatively simple congregational structure of ANABAPTISM and the later Separatists. In churches possessing an episcopal or quasi-episcopal structure and a relatively high sacramental doctrine, the separation between clergy and laity, although diminished, continued to have practical substance. In the remainder the term "laity" was retained with varying degrees of emphasis as a convenient shorthand indicating differences in function within the overall body of church members.

Although the changes in the status and role of the laity proposed by Luther were by no means reversed, they were implemented only gradually over the succeeding centuries. Many strands of continuity can be found between late medieval Catholicism and Magisterial Protestantism, especially in the century of religious upheaval after the Reformation. Many aspects of the former clerical mentality survived within the new ecclesiastical structures, to the extent that the new Reformed presbyters often appeared surprisingly similar to their medieval priestly counterparts as far as their relationship to the laity was concerned. According to the 1587 English "Book of Discipline" printed in 1644, active involvement in the church was a wholly clerical matter, with ruling elders and deacons counted as part of the body of ministers. Ecclesiastical hierarchy may have disappeared among the Reformed leadership but old professional attitudes appeared to be flourishing.

When the clerical leadership of sixteenth- and seventeenth-century scholastic CALVINISM is subjected to careful scrutiny, however, a different picture begins to emerge. In areas such as ENGLAND and SCOTLAND, where Calvinist ideas had begun to shape territorial churches, the empowerment of the individual believer was certainly subordinate to the need to fill the void left by the Roman clergy. A new and purified leadership had to be found—one that was confident of its calling and capable of arresting any slide into SECTARIANISM. From the outset the Reformed tradition set great store by clerical EDUCATION. Within the universities the continuation of the scholastic approach to theological studies reflected the need of the emerging national churches for ministers adequately trained in the skills of reasoning vital to the defense of Protestantism. Yet the availability of university-educated clergy, able to read the scriptures in their original languages and to expound them from a sound theological basis, was intended to aid the spiritual development of the laity rather than foster elitism. A succession of leaders like WILLIAM PERKINS and RICHARD BAXTER in England and Gisbertus Voetius in Holland combined significant scholarship with a strong pastoral concern for lay piety. Not only did the spiritual writings of Perkins and Baxter affect generations of English readers but, in translation along with the works of other Puritan writers (see PURITANISM), they provided a rich stimulus to lay development in Germany during the following century. More locally, individual Puritan ministers in England and in the early American colonies encouraged members of their congregations to keep journals in which they charted their own personal process of CONVERSION. These early signs of lay expression also manifested themselves in less conventional ways. Groups of Quakers (see FRIENDS, SOCIETY OF) began to appear: men and women who pursued simplicity and truthfulness, and who sought guidance from the Inner Light rather than the customary authorities of scripture or church. With their egalitarianism and rejection of the ministry and sacraments they established considerable local influence in parts of England as well as the eastern seaboard of America.

In the Lutheran Church the impetus toward scholasticism had a less favorable outcome. After the Peace of Westphalia (1648) and the end of the bitter three-sided religious conflict in Germany, many Lutheran clergy became entrenched in a formal professionalism whose fashion was to impress the largely passive congregations under their care with pedantic theological discourses. Against this trend the Pietist movement under the leadership of PHILIPP JAKOB SPENER began from the 1660s to discover a more active role for the laity. Spener's *collegia pietatis,* his groups for private devotion, together with the Christian Institute founded by his disciple AUGUST HERMANN FRANCKE at Glauchau near HALLE transformed the situation for the Lutheran laity. The latter were encouraged in their active form of Christianity by a stream of Pietist clergy, which began to emerge after 1692 from the new University of Halle.

Popular Evangelism

In the English-speaking world the first appearance of an active lay leadership is widely, if not entirely accurately, associated with the work of the eighteenth-century clergyman JOHN WESLEY. Early METHODISM drew on Reformation, Puritan, and Anglican influences as well as the contemporary example of German PIETISM. Its cellular structure, which owed a strong organizational debt to Moravianism, provided an ideal setting for the employment of considerable numbers of lay Christians and for the development of their skills. As a movement outside conventional religion and directed at the neglected sectors of society it offered the freedom to experiment with new forms of lay leadership. Laymen and women became class leaders, exhorters, and SUNDAY SCHOOL teachers. Individual believers were expected to offer spiritual counsel to their peers. Still more revolutionary was the widespread use of men as lay preachers who had received neither seminary education nor ordination. During Wesley's lifetime the social scandal created by these novelties was made even worse by his willingness to overlook the crossing of the preaching boundary by certain gifted WOMEN such as Sarah Crosby and Mary Bosanquet. Wesley's friend and contemporary GEORGE WHITEFIELD showed a similar inclination to ignore the traditional barrier established by ordination in the interests of missionary religion, but in his case his relative disinterest in creating organizational structures among his converts meant that his empowerment of the laity was less obvious.

As opportunities for lay leadership began to diminish among British Methodists in the climate of conservatism that followed the death of Wesley, the rapid expansion of the movement in newly independent America created new scope for the gifted layperson. In the UNITED STATES the Methodist circuit system created by FRANCIS ASBURY soon employed hundreds of young unmarried men but the call of women to public ministry was not recognized (see CIRCUIT RIDERS; ITINERACY). Of the small number of white women deeply involved in the spread of early American Methodism most confined their activities to the semiprivate sphere of the class meeting. Yet for one small but significant group of black African American women, the coming of Methodism created an unprecedented opportunity for leadership. A handful of emancipated slaves and free-born women entered into a public itinerant ministry that defied the conventions of nineteenth-century society, challenging existing denominational structures and attesting to the dangerous and unpredictable force of a vocation attributed to the Holy Spirit. Although the focus in the new ecclesiastical structures created by EVANGELICALISM may have remained with the community of believers, increasingly the traditional practices of corporate Christianity appeared to be at variance with the expectations of post-Enlightenment INDIVIDUALISM.

Social Action

The increasing opportunities for lay involvement can also be seen in the church's handling of matters that extended beyond the narrowly religious. In the *Franckesche Stiftungen,* the network of facilities built around the orphanage at Halle, lay Pietists as well as theological students worked together to a degree unprecedented in earlier Protestantism, caring for widows and the poor, educating children across the social spectrum, printing and circulating a wide range of improving literature, and producing medicines. This German example provided a model for features that were subsequently reproduced elsewhere on both sides of the Atlantic.

A second great social impetus issued from JOHN WOOLMAN and his fellow American Quakers during the eighteenth century in their determined opposition to the institution of SLAVERY. In the British context the leadership of this struggle, initially directed against the degrading and cruel trade in human beings that operated between West Africa and the New World, was in the hands of a small but formidable group of lay Anglicans known derogatorily as the CLAPHAM SECT, whose parliamentary spokesman was WILLIAM WILBERFORCE. In this ultimately successful campaign, an interdenominational lay-led Christian movement pitted itself against entrenched economic interests, national policies, deep-seated social conservatism, and, in many cases, clerical complacency.

The third significant strand of lay action came with the massive expansion of the voluntary society system seen in Britain and America during the Second Evangelical Awakening (see VOLUNTARY SOCIETIES; AWAKENINGS). In both countries during the first three decades of the nineteenth century a host of national and regional societies came into being as an expression of the contemporary concern that EVANGELISM would be ineffective if practical action were not taken to alleviate prominent social ills. As single-issue agencies they addressed a range of serious deficiencies including extreme poverty, PROSTITUTION, exploitive employment practices, and lack of basic education. At all structural levels they used a range of lay talent in a way that permanently transformed expectations concerning the role of the ordinary church member. In America, building on Calvinist ideas derived from

JONATHAN EDWARDS and SAMUEL HOPKINS as well as more general considerations of the nature of virtue, the influential evangelist CHARLES FINNEY taught a generation of converts to believe that the sincerity of their Christian conversion would prove itself in subsequent commitment to practical "benevolence."

Church Administration

Increasingly, involvement in the wider moral and practical issues of society led to a desire for a greater say in the administration of the church. The growth of this desire accompanied both extensions to the political franchise and the development of universal systems of education across the Western world. At the level of civic and political leadership, interference by the laity in the affairs of the church was as old as Christendom. Nor did this change with the coming of the Reformation. Not only did Luther base his defiance of Rome on the baptized status of his princely supporters, and Zwingli require the consent of the Zürich burghers to introduce his *Sixty-Seven Articles* of religion, but also Calvin, as a second generation reformer, still found himself circumscribed in important ecclesiastical matters by what the city councils in Geneva were prepared to allow. In general, territorial Protestant churches had to accept their livings and pulpits being treated as tools of the social and political hierarchy, and the funds necessary for the maintenance of church and ministry being subjected to lay depredations and meanness. In the Reformed churches from the outset elders cooperated with the clergy in ecclesiastical government but, even if that eldership can be regarded as part of the laity, its presence within the higher courts until comparatively modern times was scarcely representative of the general membership.

By the nineteenth century lay ambitions began to extend beyond control of the church for selfish or essentially secular purposes. Nonordained members increasingly sought an active voice in policy determination and administration. Among the nonterritorial connexional churches the process of change was set in motion by the small Methodist New Connexion established in 1797, which, more than half a century before the mainstream Methodist denominations in either America or Britain, insisted that at every level its governing bodies should be composed of equal numbers of ministers and lay representatives, the latter being chosen freely by the membership. Within the bodies constituting the Anglican Communion the initiative was seized most boldly by the Church of Ireland, which from its unsought disestablishment in 1869 created a General Synod composed of twice as many lay as clerical representatives. Elsewhere within the Episcopal communion lay representation proceeded more cautiously. The mother church acquired a properly constituted House of Laity only in 1919 with the passing of parliamentary legislation that created a National Assembly for the Church of England.

Overseas Missions

In one final aspect the nineteenth century was to prove decisive for the laity: the expansion of the faith into parts of the world not previously exposed to Christianity. Protestant overseas interest had begun a century earlier with the establishment of Pietist and MORAVIAN CHURCH missionary groups in places as widely separated as Tranquebar, Surinam, and Georgia. The main phase of missionary growth commenced with the founding of a wave of new societies in Britain and America during the Second Evangelical Awakening. One of the earliest, the London Missionary Society, launched its South Seas operations using lay personnel from a predominantly artisan background but as the movement developed the general focus shifted toward a requirement for college or seminary training linked to ordination. Not until the rise of specialized medical MISSIONS after 1843 did absolute clerical dominance begin to lessen. As medicine became professionalized, staff in the new missionary hospitals became increasingly unwilling to defer to nonmedical missionaries whose principal claim to leadership was the possession of ordination. By the end of the century lay participation had been broadened still further by the appearance of female doctors and by the widening of the professional presence within missionary ranks to include teachers, engineers, and other young people drawn from the burgeoning student volunteer movement. Through the subsequent influence of ecumenical cooperation this trend toward a full and active role for the laity has become a permanent feature of modern international Christianity.

Controversy: Absence of Major Conflict

Over the centuries few important aspects of THEOLOGY or ECCLESIOLOGY have remained untouched by disagreement. History is littered with religious debates that have proved serious and intractable. Yet, at first sight, the developing theory of the laity seems to offer a notable exception. Since the Reformation there have been no disputes in this area to match the divisiveness of the Sacramentarian Controversy between Luther and Zwingli. There has been nothing to approach the deep philosophical differences of the Deist debate within early Hanoverian Anglicanism, or the hatred that characterized the Fundamentalist–Modernist

struggle in early twentieth-century America. Nevertheless until comparatively modern times the doctrine of the laity has afforded one of the most fertile breeding grounds within Protestantism for low-level tensions and undercurrents. In most cases the hostility generated has been limited to ridicule, polemical overstatement, and manipulation of influence. However, in one notorious period, that of the English Restoration, those who wielded ecclesiastical power applied a policy of penal legislation and imprisonment. During the reign of Charles II one of the most famous lay preachers of the seventeenth century, JOHN BUNYAN, spent much of the period 1660 to 1672 incarcerated in a Bedford jail. The same years also witnessed the deaths of perhaps as many as 450 Quakers. In parts of Germany and in SWEDEN, where Lutheran ORTHODOXY was strong, the early eighteenth century saw a similar if less severe pattern of repression and expulsion directed at groups of lower-class laypeople who sought to practice their own biblically based understanding of the Christian community. Although the punishments meted out in Restoration England, as later in Germany, stemmed from the unacceptability of religious DISSENT, the changing character of lay religion constituted an additional factor. The more the issue was debated, the more it exposed the complex relationship that existed between clergy, laity, institutional church, and Christian society. The debate ceased to have meaning only when organized Christianity was compelled for the sake of survival to come to terms with the secular, pluralist, and democratic forces of the new industrial age (see INDUSTRIALIZATION).

Hermeneutical Debate

Almost every historical dispute about the role of the laity has resorted at some point to New Testament hermeneutics. Not only did Luther justify his opposition to the Roman hierarchy in August 1520 with a general denial of scriptural support for its exclusivist pretensions and an appeal to the Petrine text concerning the royal priesthood, but also in his later tract entitled *The Freedom of a Christian* he expounded more fully the scriptural obligations laid on the individual believer. The Christian was both the perfectly free lord of all, who was subject to no other person, and at the same time the servant of all, who was, therefore, subject to everyone. Referring to various Pauline passages, Luther argued that the believer's kingly freedom belonged like his priesthood to the spiritual sphere and consequently did not impinge on the province of kings, princes, and those set in positions of civil authority. Nor did the functions of true Christian priesthood—"to pray for others and to teach one another divine things"—trespass on the rights of the so-called clergy. Such titles as "priest," "cleric," "spiritual," "ecclesiastic," when they were erroneously applied to a minority within the Christian community, were manifestly unscriptural. The New Testament terms for the Christian leadership—"ministers," "servants," "stewards" (cf. I Corinthians 4:1)—all indicated a differentiation based on function rather than status. Although Luther's argument struck deep roots within Protestantism, some aspects of the medieval division between clergy and laity remained, and subsequent adjustments to this mode of thinking prompted further reference to the biblical text. As late as the nineteenth century opponents of lay evangelism argued from the Acts of the Apostles and the Pastoral Epistles for the absolute necessity of ordination. By way of contrast, those who advocated greater freedom in the deployment of lay personnel pointed to other scriptural passages that seemed to indicate the primary importance of spiritual gifts. As a means of resolving debates, appeals to scripture tended to be inconclusive and merely served to reinforce existing prejudices. Resolution came if anything from more practical considerations such as the need to bring greater flexibility into the ministry of the church.

Social Conservatism

Behind the allegedly scriptural resistance to an active laity there often lay considerable social conservatism: a concern that laypeople who found an independent voice would threaten the natural hierarchy based on birth, education, and wealth. Luther appears not to have been concerned about this possibility because of the clear distinction he drew between the Christian's spiritual realm and the temporal sphere where the normal conventions of social leadership operated; however, later spokesmen for mainstream Protestantism were not so sanguine. To the Lutheran consistorial authorities of the Electorate of Hanover during the 1730s the groups of radical Pietists, who publicly criticized their establishment pastors, blaming them for a lack of humility and brotherly love, and depicting them as spiritually unregenerate, far exceeded the liberty allowed by Luther's priesthood of all believers. The bounding self-confidence of these lower-class laymen offended the Lutheran hierarchy, eliciting condemnation and repression. Their popular restiveness also spilled over into the civil sphere where they found themselves in many cases struggling against their employers.

In Britain the public ministry of Methodists and other unauthorized lay preachers and catechists aroused the indignation and fury of those who sought to defend eighteenth-century patterns of deference. The interlopers were seen as manifestly unsuited to their self-appointed religious tasks, a point that often seemed to be supported by their relatively humble origins. Drawn predominantly from the ranks of tradesmen, they lacked significant education and were, their critics argued, forced to rely on a dangerous mixture of novelty and anticlericalism to attract attention. The parish clergy by contrast were trained in scriptural exegesis and the biblical languages and were charged with the welfare of every person within their bounds. The natural alliance between landowner and resident clergyman was seen to place the temporal and spiritual care of the general population into the hands of those whose social position best fitted them to offer sound leadership.

In the spread of American popular religion during the same period the challenge to existing social conventions was extended still further by the issues of GENDER and race. The appearance of women in unauthorized leadership roles from the 1750s onward by no means proved generally acceptable, even among the independent churches to which many belonged. Some were seen as troublemakers: their work appeared to lead to scandal and division. Although many were praised for the quality of their prayers and testimonies, even at times by ordained clergymen, ambivalence remained. Despite the existence of considerable numbers of female preachers and exhorters at the end of the eighteenth century, the trend in the infant republic was away from female leadership. Similar problems arose in connection with race. In the context of reviving economic fortunes for the institution of slavery, the American churches in the pre–Civil War period enshrined leadership values that, although softening the old rigid boundary between clergy and laity, nevertheless reflected the contemporary secular focus on citizenship as something essentially white and Anglo-Saxon.

Political Fears

At certain strategic points in modern history the continuance of a stable Christian society has appeared to be threatened politically by the activities of the laity. In Luther's reforming career that point was reached very quickly. As early as the period of concealment in the Wartburg after the Diet of Worms it became obvious that some of his followers were steering the ecclesiastical reforms in dangerous directions. Armed rioting took place in Wittenberg in December 1521 in an attempt to enforce the new practices. Subsequent acts of ICONOCLASM coincided with the arrival of a group of lay prophets from Zwickau who claimed direct inspiration by the Holy Spirit and preached about the coming millennium. When Luther realized that these developments were threatening the stability of the infant reform process and were compromising the position of his own protector, the elector Frederick, he emerged from hiding and sought to end the violence. Part of the reason, however, for the success of Luther's church-reforming message lay in its resonance with deeper political aspirations among the German populace. Although he was able to calm the immediate circumstances in Wittenberg, he was powerless to stop the spreading wave of political unrest over the following months. He could neither restrain the maverick clergyman THOMAS MÜNTZER, who used apocalyptic passages from scripture to incite popular revolution, nor could he prevent a gathering such as the "Parliament" at Memmingen from incorporating biblical ideas into the *Twelve Articles of the Swabian Peasants,* which it issued in March 1525 against the unreasonable exactions of the landowners. When gentle rebuke failed, Luther resorted to a violent condemnation of the mounting popular rebellion in his notorious tract *Against the Robbing and Murdering Hordes of Peasants.* With the appearance of this work in May 1525 calling for draconian measures by rulers, even by those who would not "tolerate the gospel," he acknowledged the political dangers implicit in the popular appropriation of religious ideas and drew a veil of silence over his own earlier emphasis on the laity.

Later crises tended to revive this specter of the politicized layman. During the English Interregnum of the 1640s and 1650s the agents of several independent sects promulgated their innovatory ideas, challenging what remained of political stability in the wake of the Civil Wars (see CIVIL WAR, ENGLAND). Even in the comparatively tolerant climate created by Cromwell, where alternative religious ideas and lay initiative were able to flourish and there was an absence of strong clerical supervision, the behavior of groups such as the LEVELLERS and Fifth Monarchists was treated as being subversive of an orderly Christian society. With the return of the monarchy and the established church at the Restoration any such opportunity for lay improvisation disappeared entirely.

In Britain the FRENCH REVOLUTION and the threat of invasion produced one final period of tension in which the religious activities of laymen again aroused in establishment minds the fear of political machinations. Given the ideological potency of republicanism and the apparent willingness of Revolutionary FRANCE to export its values and institutions, the apparent threat was all too credible. The unfortunate individuals who were tried and punished for taking part in secular republican gatherings and demonstrations seemed to many church leaders in the 1790s to have their counterparts in the wave of unknown individuals who at much the same time began to conduct religious meetings in barns and cottages, to organize children into unauthorized Sunday schools, and to penetrate even the remotest villages. For a year or two political paranoia gripped the bench of English bishops as well as the General Assembly of the CHURCH OF SCOTLAND but, when the leading politicians declined to act and the threat of invasion began to recede, this final political crisis involving the laity evaporated.

Heterodoxy and Ecclesiastical Order

The other major area in which arguments arose was that of religious belief and order. In the eighteenth century accusations against the laity ranged from heterodoxy to enthusiasm, but the latter caused particular concern to those who espoused the values of the ENLIGHTENMENT. With the decline of interest in formal theology the charge of heterodoxy was not widely employed against the emerging laity, but in orthodox LUTHERANISM the older preoccupations seem to have lingered longer than elsewhere. In a catalog of heresies compiled and published by Samuel Schelwig, a senior clergyman at Dantzig, the erroneous teachings of the Pietists, both moderate and radical, clerical and lay, were classified in the clear conviction that they formed a natural and interdependent corpus of error. More common, however, was the offense caused to contemporary clerical sensibilities by the pretensions of the new generation of publicly active laymen to "an extraordinary measure of the Holy Spirit's influence." To most critical observers of the evangelical Awakenings the dangerous and unseemly combination of enthusiasm and the uneducated mind was the inevitable outcome of laxity in the official control of popular religion.

Whereas the concept of ministry inherited from the medieval church centered on the sacraments, Protestantism was altogether more equivocal, emphasizing from the outset the fundamental importance of preaching. Traditionally the Christian sacraments had conveyed a powerful sense of mystery. Their celebration by the clergy had been surrounded by a mystique that was inseparably connected with ordination. Preaching by contrast belonged to the realm of explanation and understanding, and as such was accessible to clergy and laity alike. The Protestant flexing of lay muscles in areas such as group leadership, exhortation, catechizing, and even preaching itself raised serious questions about the nature and distinctness of the church's ministry. Few if any of those who favored these developments wanted to see unsupervised activity; most emphasized the importance of careful selection based on the requisite spiritual and moral qualities as well as the recognition of God-given abilities. However, for those sections of Protestant opinion that were closest to the Catholic traditions of the past, any widening of the ministry to include individuals who lacked regular ordination endangered their belief in the sacramental basis of Christianity. Such actions threatened the unity of the church and raised the destructive possibility of schism. In practice mere encroachment on clerical prerogatives did not give rise to serious and lasting divisions within Protestantism. When schism came to a number of established churches in the nineteenth century its causes lay in the growing secularism and indifference of the modern state.

Rejection of the Clergy

One important response to changing circumstances was the development of entirely lay movements such as the Brethren, which—like the Quakers before them—rejected the concept of a professional and ordained ministry. The Brethren appeared in the late 1820s as a breakaway from Irish Episcopalianism. In their early polemic they accused the Irish clergy of opposing the work of God by refusing to work with laymen in the task of EVANGELISM. As an alternative to the complex structures of the traditional church, the new movement embraced a primitivist ecclesiology in a conscious attempt to re-create the forms of worship and relationship found in the New Testament. Yet even this restorationist approach was not immune from the natural tendencies toward elitism that the need for leadership encouraged. After the movement split into two wings in 1848, the Exclusive Brethren developed a structure that allowed for collective decision making at the level of the local assembly but at the same time looked to guidance from a leader who achieved overall prominence within the movement. Ultimately this led the Exclusives into the dictatorial period of leadership under James Taylor Jr. during the 1960s. Although the movement as a whole, both in Europe and America, resisted such blatant distortions of the democratic impulse, it relied on a system of eldership that, especially in its most developed form within the Churches of God, subordinated the original concern for the priesthood of all believers to the needs of a nonordained but nevertheless self-perpetuating oligarchy.

The Laity in Modern Protestantism

In the changing ecclesiastical landscape of the present day one of the most significant features affecting almost all traditional denominations is the general decline apparent in vocations to the ordained ministry. In some of the longer-established bodies the shortage of clergy is beginning to threaten the future viability of congregations and to prompt both the pooling of ministerial expertise and the creation of permanent teams that combine lay talent of various types with that of ordained personnel. In some of the youngest and most rapidly growing churches the scarcity of trained ministers has reached the point where it threatens the ability to teach converts effectively.

Elsewhere in modern Protestantism other factors are eroding the traditional importance of the clergy. Within America's vast Southern Baptist community the theological emphasis on "soul competency" and belief in the spiritual autonomy of the individual has produced a climate where the Christian believer stands essentially alone in his relationship to God. The implications of this spiritual INDIVIDUALISM are various and far-reaching. Not only has the scriptural doctrine of the priesthood of all believers, with its appreciation of the corporate action of the Christian community, metamorphosed into the strikingly different concept of the "priesthood of the believer," but important challenges to ecclesiology have also ensued. The rise of the self-sufficient soul has been accompanied by a rejection of any form of mediation, whether human or divine. The new outlook has little place for a ministry concerned with anything beyond preaching and its related functions; nor are the corporate intercessions of the church given the importance once assigned to them. Most serious of all has been its challenge to historical orthodoxy in the practical relegation of Christ from his unique role as the mediator between man and God. In this strikingly individualistic vision of Christianity the lay believer seems finally to have come of age.

Since the 1960s the existence of the Charismatic Movement has appeared to challenge the hitherto subordinate position of the laity. Just as the moving frontier of charismatic practice has militated against other ecclesiastical conventions, so the centrality of the individual's encounter with the Holy Spirit seems to have rendered customary distinctions between clergy and laity irrelevant. Yet analysis of the movement by no means supports this conclusion. Although the charismatic approach has dramatically widened participation in worship and ministry, there is little evidence to suggest that professional leadership has declined in importance. On the contrary, the movement is well known for its propensity to throw up strong leadership figures who enjoy among their following an authority that is virtually episcopal. Charismatic worship may have given greater scope to the laity but any fundamental change to their status is probably more imaginary than real.

What then does the future hold for the laity? In an age when secondary education is almost universal and large numbers of citizens have access to university, the effect on the church is necessarily profound.

Within its ranks the clergy no longer constitute the principal repository of educated opinion and this in itself raises important questions about the lay–clerical relationship. No longer can it be assumed that the leadership of the church is better equipped or more able than the general membership. Even in respect of theological expertise educated lay opinion is making an important contribution to many congregations. Although these trends are clear and the former state of impotence has disappeared for good, the nonordained majority of believers seems likely to retain its differentiation from the ordained leadership for as long as organized Christianity exists.

See also Ecumenism; Education, Theology: Europe/United States/Asia; Higher Education; Missionary Organizations

References and Further Reading

Bulley, C. *The Priesthood of Some Believers: Developments from the General to the Special Priesthood in the Christian Literature of the First Three Centuries.* Carlisle, UK: Paternoster, 2000.

Christensen, Michael J. and Carl E. Savage. *Equipping the Saints: Mobilizing Laity for Ministry.* Nashville: Abingdon Press, 2000.

Eastwood, C. *The Royal Priesthood of the Faithful: An Investigation of the Doctrine from Biblical Times to the Reformation.* London: Epworth, 1963.

———. *The Priesthood of All Believers: An Examination of the Doctrine from the Reformation to the Present Day.* London: Epworth, 1960.

Jacob, W. M. *Lay People and Religion in the Early Eighteenth Century.* New York: Cambridge University Press, 1996.

Laici in ecclesia. An ecumenical bibliography on the role of the laity in the life and mission of the church. Geneva, Switzerland: World Council of Churches, 1961.

Lovegrove, D. W., ed. *The Rise of the Laity in Evangelical Protestantism.* London: Routledge, 2002.

Weber, Hans Ruedi. *Living in the Image of Christ: The Laity in Ministry.* Geneva: WCC Publications, 1986.

DERYCK W. LOVEGROVE

LAMBETH CONFERENCE

The Lambeth Conference is an international conference of the bishops of the Anglican Communion that meets approximately every ten years. The first such conference was called by Archbishop C. T. Longley, the archbishop of Canterbury, in 1867, and met at Lambeth Palace, the London residence of the archbishop, from which the conference takes its name. The 1867 conference included seventy-six Anglican bishops principally from ENGLAND, IRELAND, CANADA, and the UNITED STATES.

The desire for establishing the conference first emerged in North America more than a decade before the first meeting. The original impetus for such a conference came from the need for regular consultation among the bishops of an increasingly diverse, international church with very little centralized AUTHORITY. Before such a conference could be organized, the Canadian bishops appealed to the archbishop of Canterbury to convene the bishops to deal with the crisis precipitated by Bishop JOHN WILLIAM COLENSO, an English priest who had been appointed bishop of Natal. Serious concern developed over what was perceived to be the laxity with which Colenso dealt with ecclesiastical discipline in the cultural context of Natal, especially with respect to DIVORCE in a polygamist CULTURE (see CHURCH DISCIPLINE). Colenso's critical biblical scholarship also made many uneasy. Attempts to establish the conference as an Anglican magisterial authority to establish and judge the DOCTRINE and practice of the member churches met with strong opposition, however, and the conference adjourned after only four days.

A second conference was held in 1878, and a third conference met in 1888 at the call of Archbishop Edward White Benson. This third conference focused its conversations largely on matters of church unity both within ANGLICANISM and with respect to Anglicanism's role in the reunion of the churches. The major document that emerged from the 1888 conference is the LAMBETH QUADRILATERAL, more generally referred to as the Chicago-Lambeth Quadrilateral, one of the defining documents in the history of Anglicanism.

The four articles were first formulated and agreed upon by the General Convention of the Protestant Episcopal Church in the United States (see EPISCOPAL CHURCH, UNITED STATES) meeting in Chicago in 1886, and were slightly revised and promulgated by the bishops at Lambeth two years later. The articles set forth the Anglican-Episcopal position on the nonnegotiable requirements for church union: "(1) The Holy Scriptures of the Old and New Testaments, as containing all things necessary to salvation, and as being the rule and ultimate standard of faith; (2) the Apostles' Creed, as the Baptismal Symbol; and the Nicene Creed, as the sufficient statement of the Christian faith; (3) the two Sacraments ordained by Christ Himself—Baptism and the Supper of the Lord—ministered with unfailing use of Christ's Words of Institution, and of the elements ordained by Him; (4) the Historical Episcopate, locally adapted in the methods of its administration to the varying needs of the nations and peoples called of God into the Unity of His Church." The Quadrilateral remains the definitive Anglican position statement with respect to ecumenical conversations (see ECUMENISM; DIALOGUE, INTERCONFESSIONAL).

Church unity was among the major topics of consultation at all succeeding conferences to the present day. The early conferences of the twentieth century (1908, 1920, 1930) generally engaged the topic from the perspective of Anglicanism's role in world Christianity, while more recent conferences have been concerned with the unity of Anglicanism itself. Social issues began to take center stage in the conferences that followed World War II. MARRIAGE and Divorce, family planning, racism, WAR and peace, women's ordination (see WOMEN CLERGY), and SEXUALITY, particularly HOMOSEXUALITY, have been among the major issues considered.

A particularly important Lambeth Conference was that of 1968 when, in the wake of the Second Vatican Council of the Roman Catholic Church, the world's Anglican bishops turned their attention to the renewal of the life and faith of the church and to new initiatives in ecumenical relations. By 1968, the number of bishops at the conference had grown to 462. Among the more important initiatives of the meeting was the establishment of the Anglican Consultative Council, a representative body of BISHOPS, CLERGY, and lay persons from the member churches of the Anglican Communion that acts as a source of communication, consultation, and mutual support among Anglicans worldwide.

The Anglican Communion is composed of 38 self-governing churches that share a common Anglican heritage and recognize the archbishop of Canterbury as the symbol of its unity. Because the member churches of the Anglican Communion are fully autonomous and have the full authority to establish their own WORSHIP, doctrine, and canon law, the Lambeth Conference, the Anglican Consultative Council, and the archbishop of Canterbury serve as important sources of Anglican unity but have no legislative or executive authority to exercise over member churches. Resolutions and decisions of the Lambeth Conference are not binding on the member churches of the Communion, but are generally received as having significant moral and spiritual weight, because they originate from the bishops of the church.

A total of 749 bishops attended the 1998 Lambeth Conference. Although many important topics were before the assembly, the conference was deeply divided over issues of human sexuality. This conference also represented a turning point in the makeup of the Anglican Communion because of the large number of bishops from parts of the world other than Western Europe and North America. Reflecting the evolving realities of the Anglican Communion is a proposal that the 2008 Lambeth Conference be held not in England, but in Cape Town, South Africa, in conjunction with an international Anglican Gathering of clergy and laity.

References and Further Reading

Lytle, G. F. *Lambeth Conferences Past and Present.* Austin, TX: Historical Society of the Episcopal Church, 1989.
Stephenson, A. M. G. *Anglicanism and the Lambeth Conferences.* London: SPCK, 1978.

J. NEIL ALEXANDER

LAMBETH QUADRILATERAL

Part of the LAMBETH CONFERENCES, the periodic meetings of the bishops of the Anglican Church, the term refers specifically to the statement endorsed by the conference of the bishops of the Anglican Communion, held at Lambeth (the official residence of the archbishop of Canterbury in London) in 1888. At that conference the Anglican involvements in conversations with other churches about possible fellowship and union were discussed. A statement made two years earlier by the convention of the Protestant Episcopal Church in North America was adopted in revised form and is known as the Lambeth Quadrilateral. It expressed the fundamental commitments of the Anglican Church under four headings. The Scriptures of the Old and the New Testament are declared to contain everything necessary for salvation and declared the rule and standard of the faith. The Apostles Creed and the Nicene Creed are affirmed as the sufficient statement of the Christian faith. Two sacraments are affirmed—baptism and the Lord's Supper—accompanied by the words of institution and the elements of water, bread, and wine. Finally, the Lambeth Quadrilateral affirmed the historic episcopacy, that is, the unbroken succession of bishops from apostolic times to the present, albeit with the proviso that there may be local adaptations of how this historic succession is expressed.

See also Anglicanism

References and Further Reading

Communion and Episcopacy: Essays to Mark the Centenary of the Chicago-Lambeth Quadrilateral. Oxford, UK: Ripon College Cuddesdon, 1988.
Haskell, C. W. (Charles Williams). *The Plan and the Lambeth Quadrilateral.* Nelson: Selwyn Publications, 1973.
Morris, Edwin (Alfred Edwin). *The Lambeth Quadrilateral and Reunion.* [London]: Faith Press, 1969.

HANS J. HILLERBRAND

LASKI, JAN (JOANNES A LASCO, JOHN A LASCO) (1499–1560)

Religious reformer. Laski was born in 1499 to an aristocratic family in POLAND. His father Stanislas was palatine of Sieradz, while his uncle Jan was chancellor, archbishop of Gniezno, and primate of Poland. Destined to occupy a high position in the clerical hierarchy—his uncle obtained numerous advantages for him—Laski studied in Bologna between 1515 and 1518, and in Padova between 1518 and 1519. In 1524 he stayed in Paris and in 1525 traveled to Basel, where he came to know the philosopher Erasmus of Rotterdam. Erasmus exerted a great influence on Laski who helped him materially and even purchased his library, which he gave to Erasmus for lifelong use.

After his return to Poland in summer 1526, Laski occupied clerical positions. At that time he became close to the reformer PHILIPP MELANCHTHON, whom he met in April 1537.

In the second half of 1539 he left Poland, probably disaffected with Catholicism. During a stay in Louvain he approached the Brethren of the Common Life. Early in 1540 he married and moved to Emden in Eastern Friesland. The news about his MARRIAGE quickly reached Poland and led to his forced resignation from his clerical functions (see CLERGY, MARRIAGE OF). He returned to Poland in 1542 because of his brother's terminal illness, and on February 6 he abjured his Protestant beliefs. As a result, he was restored to his clerical functions. However, in May 1542 Laski returned to Friesland, definitively ending his relation with the Catholic Church. Probably his abjuration was a tactical maneuver that enabled him to take care of his interests in Poland.

In 1543 Laski was appointed head of the Eastern churches that were reorganized in the Reformed mode. At that time he gave evidence of his organizational skills and his irenic attitude toward MENNONITES and Spiritualists (see SPIRITUALISM).

In London King Edward VI appointed Laski superintendent of the churches of foreign communities, the latter being organizationally independent from the English churches. The development of this well-organized and managed international community came to an end with the death of Edward VI and the effort to reinstitute Catholicism in ENGLAND by Mary Tudor. The adherents of the foreign church—including Laski—were expelled from England and left in September 1553.

Whereas in DENMARK exiles were not given asylum because of the resistance of orthodox Lutherans, Laski managed to obtain asylum in Eastern Friesland. He again obtained his old office as superintendent, although his position was unstable because of Spanish pressures on one side and the attacks of orthodox Lutherans on the other. Laski was finally dismissed and left for Frankfurt am Main in 1555, where many English exiles resided. Here Laski vigorously quarreled with Lutherans, particularly with Joachim Westphal. In Frankfurt he published one of his main works: *Forma ac ratio tota ecclesiastici ministerii in peregrinorum . . . ecclesia, instituta Londini in Anglia . . .*, 1555 (*The Form and Principle of the Ecclesiastic Service in the Church for Foreigners Established in London, England*).

Invited to return to Poland by the leaders of the Calvinist church being established there, Laski arrived on December 3, 1556. Realizing that King Sigmund August did not actively support reform, Laski wanted to unify all Polish Protestants in order to efficiently oppose Catholicism. He counted on a victory during the next national diet to persuade the king to establish Protestantism formally as the religion in Poland.

His intentions were not realized because of the resistance of both Lutherans and the Czech Brethren to his unification plan and because of the lack of visible threats to the Reformed confession in Poland. Finally Laski's stay in Poland was too short to have enabled him to have a great impact. Laski died on January 8, 1560.

Laski was the only Polish figure of lasting significance in the history of the classical REFORMATION. Outstanding organizer, practical theologian, and efficient polemicist, he enjoyed the esteem and friendship of the leaders of the European Reformation, such as MARTIN BUCER, THOMAS CRANMER, JOHN CALVIN, and PHILIPP MELANCHTHON.

See also Calvinism; Catholic Reactions to Protestantism; Catholicism, Protestant Reactions; Church of England; Lutheranism;

References and Further Reading

Primary Source:

Lasco, Joannes a. *Opera tam edita quam inedita.* Edited by Abraham Kuyper. T I–II. Amsterdam: Frederic. Muller: 1866.

Secondary Sources:

Bartel, Oskar. *Jan Laski.* Berlin: 1981.
Dalton, Hermann. *John a Lasco. His Earlier Life and Labours: A Contribution to the History of Reformation in Poland, Germany and England.* London: 1886.
Hall, Basil. *John a Lasco 1499–1560. A Pole in Reformation England.* London: 1971.
Kowalska, Halina. *Dzialalnosc reformatorska Jana Laskiego w Polsce 1556–1560 (Jan Laski's Activity in Poland 1556–1560).* Warsaw: 1999.
Rodgers, Dirk Wayne. *John a Lasco in England.* New York: Peter Lang, 1994.

LECH SZCZUCKI

LATIMER, HUGH (C.1485–1555)

English reformer. Latimer, a leading figure of the English Reformation, is best known not so much for his theological writings but for the sermons he preached between his CONVERSION to the Protestant cause around 1524 and his martyrdom in 1555. Latimer was born at Thurcaston in Leicestershire, the son of a yeoman farmer, and the plight of that class became a topic of his later sermons. Trained at Cambridge and ordained in 1515, Latimer was initially opposed to Lutheran ideas. Under the influence of Thomas Bilney, however, Latimer was converted around 1524 to the Protestant cause and began PREACHING in support of an English BIBLE and against the veneration of the SAINTS.

Latimer's fortunes over the next two decades rose and fell with the changing religious and political landscape in England. He was appointed bishop of Worcester in 1535 but had to resign in 1539. After the death of HENRY VIII in 1547 Latimer returned to prominence as a preacher at the court of Edward VI until 1550. Many of his best-known sermons stem from this period, during which Latimer also took a more distinctly Protestant position on matters of DOCTRINE, rejecting TRANSUBSTANTIATION in 1548. Latimer's lifelong interest in social welfare and economic injustice surfaced again in his later sermons, for which he has been counted among the "commonwealth" thinkers of his generation in ENGLAND. After the accession of Queen Mary, a Catholic, in 1553, Latimer became a target of the new regime and in 1555 was burned at the stake along with Nicholas Ridley. Immortalized by JOHN FOXE for his martyrdom, Latimer is widely acknowledged as the foremost preacher of his generation in the English Reformation.

See also Acts and Monuments; Bible Translation; Martyrs and Martyrologies

References and Further Reading

Primary Source:

Corrie, G. E. *The Works of Hugh Latimer* (1844–1845). Reprint, New York, Cambridge, UK: Printed at The University Press, 1144–45: 1968.

Secondary Sources:

Chester, A. G. *Hugh Latimer*. Reprint, New York: Octagon Books, 1978.
Loades, David. *The Oxford Martyrs*. London: B.T. Batsford, 1970.

DEBORAH K. MARCUSE

LATIN AMERICA

At the beginning of the twenty-first century, the religiosity of Latin America was in flux. The Catholic monopoly of colonial and early postindependence times, and even the secure hegemony of the early twentieth century, were under threat in most countries. The traditional Catholic claim to be an essential part of Latin American identity had lost plausibility as pluralism increased and Protestantism became deeprooted. Catholic structures were too tied to a rural Christendom mentality. The chronic shortage of national priests in most countries highlighted the gap between "official" churchly Catholicism and "popular" or "folk" Catholicism. LIBERATION THEOLOGY and Base Communities were important from the 1960s to 1980s but were then overtaken by phenomena such as the Catholic Charismatic Renewal. In many countries Afro-Latin American religions (far from limited to blacks) or revived indigenous Amerindian religions also competed for followers, whereas the main new phenomenon among the middle-class was esoterical and extrainstitutional.

In this context Protestantism rose to prominence, marked by a strongly "oppositional" identity in relation to Catholicism (see CATHOLICISM, PROTESTANT REACTIONS). It had entered Latin America in the nineteenth century as an effectively sectarian variant of the dominant religion, but in tandem with the political and economic liberalism brought by the Anglo-Saxon powers. Except in BRAZIL, growth was slow until the mid-twentieth century, but by the 1980s it was possible to talk of a regionwide phenomenon, attracting the interest of academics, the concern of Catholic hierarchs, and the puzzlement of the media.

In colonial times Protestantism was excluded from Spanish and Portuguese America by the Inquisition. The exceptions were temporary: failed colonization projects, whether reluctantly tolerated by the Iberian powers (German Lutherans in Venezuela from 1529 to 1546, linked to Spanish indebtedness to the Welser banking house) or in opposition to them (French HUGUENOTS in Rio de Janeiro, 1555–1567; the Dutch in North-Eastern Brazil, 1624–1654); and the occasional presence of individual Protestant laymen (pirates, merchants). A permanent presence was established only around or after independence in the early nineteenth century.

The first tolerated Protestant communities were composed of foreigners linked to the commercial interests of Protestant countries. To break the closed colonial system Britain had supported independence and made commercial treaties with the new republics (or, in Brazil, initially with the exiled Portuguese monarchy), which included freedom of WORSHIP for its citizens. Anglican churches were built in Rio de Janeiro in 1819 and in Buenos Aires in 1825.

More important than these tiny trading communities were the Protestant immigrants who arrived in several countries from the 1820s. Immigration as a means of peopling territories and Protestant immigration as a means of bringing progress and weakening Catholic political power were defended by liberal anticlerical elites. Brazil, the Southern Cone, and Costa Rica received such immigrants; the largest group were the German Lutherans of southern Brazil. Although Latin American constitutions still recognized Catholicism, Protestant churches could not have the external appearance of a temple and their services could not be in the vernacular. The religious impact of immigrants was therefore minimal, but their presence created a precedent that later helped the introduction of missionary churches. Although immigrant churches now represent a small minority of Protestants in Latin America, they are still important in areas such as southern Brazil; now using the national language and sometimes attracting members from outside their ethnic group (see ETHNICITY), they contribute to the Protestant world with their solid institutions.

The first Protestant organizations to see Latin America as a mission field were the BIBLE SOCIETIES. The creation of mission churches was often preceded by circulation of the Scriptures; sometimes churches were founded autonomously, before the arrival of missionaries. The colporteur (itinerant Bible-seller) sometimes made no attempt at founding churches; mere BIBLE distribution was either seen as all that was politically possible, or was a strategy aimed at a reformation of the national church, with separation from Rome and doctrinal reform. Colporteurs were often initially well received by elites and even Catholic clergy, but this changed as the nineteenth century wore on.

Churches for Latin Americans appeared only from the 1850s onward, as a late fruit of the worldwide Protestant missionary effort. The delay was partly attributed to the legally dubious status of such churches, and also to the feeling among some Protestant sectors that Latin America had already been Christianized. Even at the famous MISSIONS conference at Edinburgh in 1910 (see WORLD MISSIONARY CONFERENCE), the region was regarded as off-limits. (The reply to this was a congress in Panama in 1916, which defended the validity of Protestant missions in Latin America and planned their advance.) Thus, most missions were not European but American, and were linked to the PIETISM of FRONTIER RELIGION in the UNITED STATES. Denominations from the U.S. South predominated: revivalist, anti-intellectualist, and individualist. Protestant missions have often been regarded as carriers of a liberal critique of traditional Latin society, associated with Anglo-American economic interests and a civilizing pathos. However, some missionaries defended the rights of Latin American countries, as in the Mexican Revolution; and the belief that Protestantism meant EDUCATION and

progress was common to many liberals among the Latin American elites. Protestants allied with liberals and Freemasons in many countries to gain freedom of religion and diminish Catholic political power.

The relative intellectual poverty of the missions made it difficult to win converts among the elite, even though many put their children in the considerable number of Protestant schools that sprang up (often with educational methods that were innovative in the region).

In Brazil the first Protestant church (Congregational) using Portuguese was opened in 1855. Presbyterians (1859), Methodists (1867), and BAPTISTS (1882) followed (see BAPTIST MISSIONS). Presbyterian work in Spanish began in Chile in 1868 (see PRESBYTERIANISM); METHODISM reached Argentina by 1867. Protestantism was only effectively introduced to Bolivia and Ecuador after the liberals gained power in the 1890s. As late as 1900 the only denomination working in Colombia were the Presbyterians. In Nicaragua, although the Moravians had worked on the Atlantic Coast among indigenous and blacks since 1847 (see MORAVIAN CHURCH), the rest of the country saw Protestant churches only after the liberals took power in 1894.

In a few countries liberal governments went further than TOLERATION. To restrict the enormous influence of the Catholic Church, the Juárez government in Mexico went beyond anticlericalism and encouraged a religious revolution in the 1860s, at first by supporting an independent national church and then by encouraging Protestant missions and Mexican non-Catholic groups. In Guatemala the first missionaries from the United States were invited and escorted by the president in 1882. They were showered with privileges, but growth was slow.

Historical Protestantism (as the first mission churches are known) remained distant from the masses and achieved modest success only in Brazil. Protestantism became truly "popular" (numerically successful among the lower classes) only with the advent of PENTECOSTALISM. The rapid international expansion of pentecostalism was attributed to American missionaries in contact with home, and immigrants in the United States in contact with their homelands and with compatriots elsewhere. Chile, MEXICO, and Brazil illustrate these routes.

In 1907 a Methodist missionary in Chile, informed of the novelty by friends in the States and elsewhere, began to teach pentecostal DOCTRINE. His followers were expelled from the Methodist Church two years later and founded a denomination that later became Chile's largest Protestant group. The same year saw conversions in Argentina through an Italian artisan from Chicago. In Brazil the same man inaugurated in

1910 the Christian Congregation among Italians in São Paulo. The early 1910s saw beginnings in Central America (through independent U.S. or Canadian missionaries) and in Mexico (partly by returning emigrants). The remaining republics were slower off the mark, the last being Ecuador (1956). Initial fortunes were modest, but by the 1950s Brazil and Chile had rapid growth, which by the 1980s covered virtually the whole of Latin America.

Latin American pentecostalism today is organized in a huge number of denominations, a few of which originated abroad (such as the ASSEMBLIES OF GOD), whereas the majority are homegrown (such as Brazil for Christ and the Universal Church of the Kingdom of God, from Brazil; or the Pentecostal Methodist Church and the Pentecostal Evangelical Church in Chile).

Pentecostalism shows regional diversity in denominational composition and degree of nationalization. Brazil's first historical churches did fairly well, and some bred early movements for autonomy. The subsequent historical/pentecostal divide did not correspond to a missionary/nationalist one, although Chilean historicals never made a serious impact. The pentecostal schism in the Methodist Church of Chile marked the break between missionaries and nationals, between middle class cultural forms and the popular classes. Chilean pentecostalism is accentuatedly national in origin. Chile's Protestantism is more pentecostal, and its pentecostalism more national, than anywhere else in Latin America.

Peru is different. Pentecostalism is a minority within Protestantism, and only really took off in the 1970s. It is dominated by the Assemblies of God, which resulted from American missionary work.

El Salvador differs again. Its large pentecostalism is divided between two large churches (Assemblies of God [AG] and Church of God) and a plethora of neo-pentecostal groups of American or Guatemalan origin. It was almost totally rural until recently. The main groups illustrate a pattern. The AG's origins go back to an independent Canadian missionary in the 1910s; the American church took over in 1930. The Church of God began in 1940 by a similar process. This pattern, of groups started by independent missionaries or breakaway nationals later seeking affiliation to a U.S. DENOMINATION, is typical of countries where Protestantism was weak, but is unknown in Chile or Brazil.

The general picture is that most pentecostal churches (unlike historical ones) were founded by Latin Americans or by independent missionaries, and only rarely by a foreign pentecostal denomination. A different phenomenon is that of middle-class pentecostalized groups (known in some countries as "neo-pentecostals" and in others as "charismatics"). There were charismatic breakaways from historical denominations in the 1960s, although recent Protestant expansion in middle and even upper classes has been mainly attributable to charismatic "communities," part of an international trend in which traditional denominations lose importance. They have been especially successful in Guatemala. A significant minority of the Guatemalan elite has converted to such churches (whether of U.S. origin, such as the Church of the Word, or local initiatives such as El Shaddai).

In the last decades of the twentieth century, Protestantism (especially in pentecostal forms) made considerable headway among Amerindian peoples in southern Mexico, Central America, and the Andes. Its initial context is often the breakdown of communities. It may deepen existing divisions or create new ones, or it may help to reconstitute community (voluntary, rather than ascribed). It is too early to say what new ecclesiastical and doctrinal forms may emerge from this large-scale adoption of Protestantism by indigenous peoples.

By 2000, Protestantism was the religion of perhaps 12 percent of Latin Americans. In the largest country, Brazil, the 2000 census showed 15.5 percent Protestant; growth in the 1990s had been especially quick. However, the highest percentage is probably in Guatemala (20 percent plus), although growth seems to have stagnated in the 1990s. The 2002 census in Chile showed 15.1 percent Protestant, up from 12.4 percent in 1992. At the other end of the scale, Uruguay is still below 5 percent. The middle range embraces the Andean countries at the top end and Argentina, Mexico, and Colombia at the lower end. David Martin gives as a rule of thumb that Protestantism's chances of growth have been higher where the Catholic Church was politically weakened by liberalism in the nineteenth century but the culture remained unsecularized. Where secularization took hold, or where the Catholic Church retained great political power, growth has been slower.

Although studies have revealed a considerable number of nonpracticing pentecostals in Chile, in Brazil levels of practice among Protestants remain high (over three-quarters attend church weekly). With variations, one can say that Latin American Protestantism is characterized by being highly practicing and fast-growing, predominantly lower class, and organized in a plethora of nationally run and even nationally created denominations. Perhaps 60 to 70 percent of Latin American Protestants are pentecostals, and this percentage is increasing. Protestantism is most pentecostalized in Chile (perhaps 80 percent) and least in the Andean countries (under half).

In some countries there is still discrimination at certain social levels against Protestants as individuals, as well as legal discrimination against churches. Although official separation of CHURCH AND STATE, effectuated in some countries in the nineteenth century and in others only in the 1990s, is now almost universal (only Bolivia, Argentina, and Costa Rica still have an official religion), there are countries where Protestant churches do not enjoy the same legal rights as the Catholic Church. Even where tolerance and freedom of worship are secure, there is often some way still to go before full equality takes hold in public life and civil society.

In social composition, Protestants in most countries are disproportionately from the poorer, less educated, and darker sectors of society. However, there is growing social diversification (greater presence among, for example, entrepreneurs, sportsmen, artists, and policemen). Membership is predominantly female, although leadership positions are largely male (some pentecostal denominations, however (see WOMEN CLERGY), were founded by WOMEN and accept female pastors). Some recent authors have spoken of pentecostalism's reconciliation of GENDER values that serves the interests of poor women, resocializing men away from machismo.

Another focus of recent study has been the economic effects of CONVERSION. Latin American pentecostalism does not have the classic Protestant work ethic, and operates in a different economic context. Evidence for mobility is scarce, and for a macroeffect on economies, even scarcer (see ECONOMICS). At the individual level, however, the transformative effect on the disorganized lives of many poor (and not so poor) people is evident.

Political involvement by Protestants is not recent (they were disproportionately active in the Mexican Revolution), but since the 1980s this trend has increased, especially with the involvement of many previously apolitical pentecostal denominations. Two Protestant presidents have governed Guatemala, and there have been large Protestant congressional caucuses in several countries, notably Brazil. Over twenty political parties of Protestant inspiration have been founded in the Spanish-speaking republics, although none has achieved great success. Much Protestant political activity has been conservative and/or oriented to institutional aggrandizement, leading to a worsening of the public image of Protestants as a whole in some countries. Another factor in this is the lack, in most countries, of a strong representative Protestant body; an exception is in Peru, where the National Evangelical Council (CONEP) has had a notable role in the defense of HUMAN RIGHTS since the 1980s.

In the early twenty-first century, the multiple and highly fragmented Protestantisms of Latin America seem destined for further numerical growth and deeper penetration of their national societies. The social and political implications of this are debatable, as is the extent to which Latin America will eventually become Protestant. In Brazil and Chile, for which reliable data are available, only half of all those who cease regarding themselves as Catholics become Protestants. This suggests the region is becoming religiously pluralist rather than Protestant, and it may be hard for Protestants to become the majority in any Latin American country.

References and Further Reading

Boudewijnse, Barbara, André Droogers, and Frank Kamsteeg, eds. *More Than Opium: An Anthropological Approach to Latin American and Caribbean Pentecostal Praxis.* Lanham, MD. and London: Scarecrow Press, 1998.

Cleary, Edward, and Hannah Stewart-Gambino, eds. *Power, Politics and Pentecostals in Latin America.* Boulder, CO: Westview, 1997.

Corten, André, and Ruth Marshall-Fratani, eds. *Between Babel and Pentecost: Transnational Pentecostalism in Africa and Latin America.* Part II. London: Hurst, 2001.

D'Epinay, Christian Lalive. *Haven of the Masses.* London: Lutterworth Press, 1969.

Freston, Paul. *Evangelicals and Politics in Asia, Africa and Latin America.* Cambridge: Cambridge University Press, 2001.

———. "Pentecostalism in Latin America: Characteristics and Controversies." *Social Compass* 45 (September 1998): 335–358.

Garrard-Burnett, Virginia, and David Stoll. *Rethinking Protestantism in Latin America.* Philadelphia, PA: Temple University Press, 1993.

Martin, David. *Tongues of Fire: The Explosion of Protestantism in Latin America.* Oxford, UK: Blackwell, 1990.

———. *Pentecostalism: The World Their Parish.* chaps. 3 and 4. Oxford, UK: Blackwell, 2002.

Stoll, David. *Is Latin America Turning Protestant?* Berkeley: University of California Press, 1990.

PAUL FRESTON

LATITUDINARIANISM

Latitudinarianism is the term used to describe a collection of certain values held by seventeenth- and eighteenth-century clerics within the CHURCH OF ENGLAND. The term "Latitude-men" was first employed by one of their number, Simon Patrick, in his "Brief Account of the new sect of Latitude-men" (1662), to describe some theologian-philosophers at CAMBRIDGE UNIVERSITY, later termed the "CAMBRIDGE PLATONISTS." Such "latitude men," claimed Patrick, stressed the importance of Reason, "a deduction from the light of nature, and those principles which are the candle of the lord, set up in the soul of every man that hath not wilfully extinguished it . . ." (Patrick 1662:10). The Latitudinarian Gilbert Burnet (1643–1715), a theologian and historian, in his famous "History of His Own Time," claimed that the early latitude men "studied to assert and examine the principles of religion and morality on clear grounds and in a philosophical way . . ." (Burnet 1991:45). A belief in liberty of conscience along with an emphasis on virtue and a stress on the complementary nature of FAITH and works gave Latitudinarian THEOLOGY a strongly Arminian tendency.

However, the term "Latitudinarian" was in no sense complimentary. An affronted Edward Fowler (1632–1714) wrote that "very lovely" and "moderate divines" were "abusively" termed Latitudinarians (Fowler 1671:37). Such clerics were often criticized by their Anglican contemporaries for placing too much emphasis on morality in religion at the expense of GRACE and for their tolerant attitude toward other Christian denominations and relaxed, liberal outlook regarding "indifferent" rites and ceremonies.

The rational ARMINIANISM of RICHARD HOOKER (1553/4–1600) was a significant early influence on the formation of Latitudinarianism. His antivoluntarist "Laws of Ecclesiastical Polity" (1604) had proclaimed the glorious light of reason as a necessary aid to deciphering the truths inherent in Scripture. Other significant ideas originated from the Great Tew group, the pre–English Civil War Oxfordshire movement stressing reason and tolerant unity of Reformed Protestantism. Among the Great Tew group's members were such early preachers of rational tolerance as John Hales (1584–1656) and WILLIAM CHILLINGWORTH (1602–1644), whose "Religion of Protestants" (1638) was an important influence on Latitudinarian thought.

There appear to have been two distinct phases of Latitudinarianism. The first was that of the Cambridge Latitude men, the second was that of those "BROAD CHURCH" Anglicans whose influence reached a zenith during the 1690s when JOHN TILLOTSON (1630–1694) was appointed archbishop of Canterbury in 1691. Significantly the later group of Latitudinarians incurred royal favor because they were closely involved in the replacement of the Roman Catholic James II as king with William of Orange. Gilbert Burnet even acted as William's chaplain on his journey to ENGLAND in November 1688. The earlier Latitudinarians, the more mystical Cambridge Platonists, are not always considered as fully part of the movement. However, Benjamin Whichcote (1609–1683) in particular, often described as the leader of the Cambridge Platonists and with his strong emphasis on reason, clearly displays many of the intellectual qualities strongly characteristic of Latitudinarianism.

Key Latitudinarian Tenets

Perhaps the belief most associated with the Latitudinarians is that of the role of reason in religion. All the Latitudinarians, and particularly the Cambridge Platonists of the mid-seventeenth century, considered it vital to highlight the complementary nature of reason and revelation. The contemporary background was one of extremes regarding reason; during the turbulent days of the English CIVIL WAR and Interregnum there existed on the one hand an irrational, spiritual "enthusiasm," as expressed by the many radical sects such as the Ranters, and on the other hand the atheistic, calculative reasoning as espoused in THOMAS HOBBES's "Leviathan" (1651). Hobbesian reasoning was particularly attacked by the Latitudinarians for its relativism rather than being anchored in the unchanging, objective reason of God. Therefore the Latitudinarians attempted to use reason to confront both extreme (sometimes heretical and antinomian) Protestantism as well as Hobbesian "atheism" (see HERESY; ANTINOMIANISM). HENRY MORE (1614–1687) confronted the former in his "Enthusiasmus Triumphatus" (1656), as did Simon Patrick in his "Friendly Debate betwixt . . . a Conformist (and) a Nonconformist" (1669), whereas Edward Stillingfleet's "Origines Sacrae" focused on attacking the atheist threat he saw in the work of Hobbes and others.

The later Latitudinarians were especially conscious of the threat provided by DEISM. Ever since the publication of HERBERT OF CHERBURY's (1583–1645) precursor to deism, "De Veritate" (1625), the deist idea of human reason as contrary to Christian revelation had become more and more prevalent as the century went on and as the eighteenth century dawned. Works by Latitudinarians, such as Edward Stillingfleet's "Letter to a Deist" (1675), argued in reply to such beliefs the case for the compatibility of reason and Christian DOCTRINE. Reason, the Latitudinarians claimed, was of divine origin, and in fact was, in the words of Proverbs 20:27, the "candle of the Lord." It was Benjamin Whichcote who most frequently employed this favorite phrase and also most impressively argued for the rationality of religion, claiming that "to go against Reason is to go against God" (Whichcote 1930:11). The candle of the Lord was the divine spark within one, through which it was possible to become united with God. Humans were fallen, but the candle's spiritual reason enabled something of God to be discerned. The very fact that this divine reason was in all people fitted with the unchanging law of morality, the universal tenets of which are known as a result of this NATURAL LAW from God. Therefore even rational "heathens" such as Plato and Socrates saw something of the divine, thanks to the "candle of the Lord" within them leading them toward God. In this way not only faith and reason, but also theology and philosophy became complementary.

The idea of the "candle of the Lord" within each person naturally led to the Latitudinarians' espousal of human free will. This belief in the divine rationality in all complements the notion of individual free will. Such an Arminian view can therefore be contrasted with Calvinist PREDESTINATION.

During the latter half of the seventeenth century TOLERATION became a pressing issue confronting the English Church. The persecution of DISSENT in the early days of the Restoration was officially ended in 1689 by the Toleration Act, which applied to all Trinitarian Protestants. The Latitudinarians are considered to be a group espousing a tolerant stance in religious matters, but they would have held mixed feelings regarding this Act. Therefore it would be most accurate to describe the Latitudinarians as being in favor of comprehension, in which the church was broadened to accommodate various doctrines, instead of favoring the toleration of all dissenting groups outside the church. The 1668 Bill for Comprehension was unsuccessful, but it had been prepared by a group including the Latitudinarians John Tillotson (the future archbishop of Canterbury) and Edward Stillingfleet. Additionally Gilbert Burnet's 1699 work "Exposition of the THIRTY-NINE ARTICLES" defended the idea of comprehension. For the most part then, Latitudinarians stressed the unity of orthodox, Trinitarian Christians within the Church of England, rather than the toleration of the many religious groups outside it. However, the Latitudinarian clerics were opposed to Roman Catholicism on the grounds of its "super-additions" as they saw it, to the plain Gospel truth, and because of its still-perceived political threat as a consequence of its allegiance to the pope.

The issue of ADIAPHORA was a significant one, and closely tied to toleration; were such "things indifferent" within religious rites and ceremonies to be prescribed by the state, or instead left to individual congregations to decide? Earlier in the century the Cambridge Platonists had witnessed much conflict and disagreement over matters such as bowing at the name of Jesus, kneeling at communion, and the wearing of VESTMENTS, during the widely unpopular and strict decrees by Archbishop WILLIAM LAUD. As a whole the Latitudinarians believed that such matters should not be prescribed, given that they had not been specifically appointed by God, but left to the individual conscience, for what was most important for them was the unity and moral goodness of Christians, rather than petty squabbling over outward affairs.

In the same attitude of simplicity the Latitudinarians considered that the Christian message should be presented in as plain and comprehensible style as possible, for the Christian faith as presented in Scripture was plain and sufficient for all people to gain SALVATION. Therefore Latitudinarian sermons were distinctive for their commonsense approach and application of images familiar to their congregations. Christianity's saving message could be expounded simply in a few key doctrines, clear enough for all people to understand.

The third earl of Shaftsbury declared Whichcote to advocate good morals. Whichcote maintained religion to involve a "good mind, and a good life" (Whichcote 1930:50). All the Latitudinarians stressed the importance of morality and living a virtuous life in their PREACHING, to such an extent that they were sometimes criticized for downplaying the importance of grace and revelation. However, in a somewhat Platonic vein, they believed that to know God one should try to be Godlike, or "deiform." For them, grace was intricately entwined with virtue because there could never truly be one without the other. Therefore faith was entirely inseparable from works.

Gilbert Burnet reminded clergymen that the Christian religion called one to "great purity and virtue . . . humility and self denial, to a contempt of the world and heavenly mindedness, to a patient resignation to the will of God. . . ." Christian clergy should be able to "state right the grounds of our hope, and the terms of our salvation . . ." (Burnet 1997:150–162).

Key Latitudinarians

Of all the Cambridge Platonists it was Whichcote who is most easily aligned with the Latitudinarians, given that he lacked the mystical strain found in Cambridge Platonist colleagues such as More and John Smith (1618–1652). Although he wrote nothing during his lifetime, some sermons were published posthumously, and his collections of "Aphorisms" clearly convey his rational, tolerant spirit. Whichcote entered the Puritan Emmanuel College, Cambridge, in 1626 where he became a fellow. His hugely popular lecture series at Holy Trinity Church, Cambridge, began in 1636 and flourished for many years. Whichcote became provost of King's College in 1645, and in 1650 he became vice chancellor of the University of Cambridge. After his ejection from King's at the Restoration, and brief spells as a clergyman in Somerset, his career again flourished in London where he was vicar of St. Lawrence Jewry from 1668 to 1683. St. Lawrence Jewry was a highly significant center of Latitudinarianism, and Latitudinarians such as Tillotson and Stillingfleet were among Whichcote's congregation there. Interestingly, the philosopher JOHN LOCKE (1632–1704), who himself had Latitudinarian tendencies, was a member of the church from 1667 to 1675.

Simon Patrick (1626–1707), a friend and contemporary at Queens' College, Cambridge, of the Cambridge Platonist John Smith, was an early chronicler of Latitudinarianism, and he excellently displays the rational, spiritual, moral nature of the movement. In his "Sermon preached on St. Mark's Day, 1646" he stressed reason's importance, yet not merely as a natural, human faculty but as dependent on divine grace. After the Restoration in 1660 Patrick became the much-loved rector of St. Paul's, Covent Garden, London where his unselfish dedication was particularly noted when he continued to minister to his congregation even during the Great Plague of 1665, when many other clergy left the city. His various PRAYER manuals, which contained special prayers for a variety of occasions, were widely read and highly useful aids in the furthering of private devotion.

Stillingfleet (1635–1699) was a key leader of Latitudinarianism during the latter half of the seventeenth century and was renowned for his learning. He entered St. John's College, Cambridge, in 1649, and spent many years as a clergyman in London before eventually becoming bishop of Worcester in 1689. Stillingfleet's "Irenicon" (1659), which stressed the need for a strong, united national church in which Anglicans and Presbyterians could worship in harmony, apparently contributed in the following century to persuading JOHN WESLEY to remain in the Church of England. Work such as "Origines Sacrae" (1662) also highlighted the significance of universal, natural theology as a common TRADITION shared by all. Stillingfleet's well-known criticisms of John Locke's so-called unorthodoxy and Locke's possible influence on the deist JOHN TOLAND (1670–1722), highlight his own ORTHODOXY regarding reason and revelation. Reason may be important, as his "Rational Account of the Grounds of Protestant Religion" (1665) showed, but it must never be elevated to the extent as to cast doubt on divine revelation and miracles.

Assessment

It is often considered that John Locke was a Latitudinarian. Certainly he had many links with the movement, was a friend of Tillotson and an admirer of Whichcote, and owned a considerable number of Latitudinarian works. However, his thought differed from that of the movement. In his "Reasonableness of Christianity" (1695), Locke called reason the "candle of the Lord" and wrote that the Gospel was full of clear, easily intelligible truths, and yet he cast Christ's incarnation, resurrection, and miracles in a Socinian light (which discounted the divinity of Jesus Christ, see SOCINIANISM).

Latitudinarians have been variously attacked by their own contemporaries and in subsequent years for being teachers of morality instead of preachers of Christ's incarnation and ATONEMENT. Association with men such as Locke and the Latitudinarians' emphasis on reason led some Anglicans and Nonconformists (see NONCONFORMITY) to condemn Latitudinarianism for ANTI-TRINITARIANISM. Such charges are inaccurate. The Latitudinarians were not Socinians because their message was an orthodox Christian one. Their emphasis on reason and the moral life went hand in hand with a constant appreciation of God's divine grace and Christ's revelation and consequent gift of Salvation. Therefore reason and revelation, faith and works all coexisted in harmony, with problems arising only when one aspect was exalted too highly above the other.

Religion and SCIENCE were seen by the Latitudinarians to be mutually supportive, and many Latitudinarians had links with the emerging scientific interests of the day. Men such as Henry More and Ralph Cudworth (1617–1688) were fellows of the young Royal Society. John Wilkins's (1614–1672) study on the classification system was published by the Society in 1668. EDUCATION was important too; later Latitudinarians, such as Thomas Tenison (1636–1715), became interested in furthering education particularly among the poor, and Tenison founded a number of schools.

During the eighteenth century the Church of England arguably lost the vital spirit and moral power of the latitude men amid dry High Church rationalism and emphasis on the beauty, ceremony, and rites of holiness. However, it seems that the irenic and spiritual candle of the Lord burned on in significant areas of theological thought, particularly that of JOSEPH BUTLER, bishop of Durham (1692–1752), and in the work of the natural scientist and archdeacon of Carlisle WILLIAM PALEY (1743–1805). The influence of the Latitudinarians on later ANGLICANISM has been on the whole underestimated, yet undoubtedly it is there.

References and Further Reading

Beiser, Frederick C. *The Sovereignty of Reason: The Defense of Rationality in the Early English Enlightenment.* Princeton, NJ: Princeton University Press, 1996.

Burnet, Gilbert. *Discourse of the Pastoral Care.* Lewiston, NY: E. Mellen Press, 1997.

———. *History of my Own Time.* Abridged by Thomas Stackhouse, introduced by David Allen. London: J. M. Dent, 1991.

Fowler, Edward. *The Principles and Practices of certain moderate Divines of the Church of England, abusively called Latitudinarians . . . In A Free Discourse between two Intimate Friends.* London: 1671.

George, Edward Augustus. *Seventeenth-century Men of Latitude*. New York: Charles Scribner's Sons, 1908.

Gibson, William. *The Church of England 1688–1832: Unity and Accord*. London: Routledge, 2001.

Griffin, Martin I. J. *Latitudinarianism in the Seventeenth-Century Church of England*. Leiden/New York: E. J. Brill, 1992.

Kroll, Richard, Richard Ashcraft, and Perez Zagorin. *Philosophy, Science and Religion in England 1640–1700*. Cambridge: Cambridge University Press, 1992.

Patrick, Simon. *A Brief Account of the new sect of Latitude-men*. London: 1662.

Rivers, Isabel. *Reason, Grace and Sentiment—A Study of the Language of Religion and Ethics in England, 1660–1780*. vol. I, *Whichcote to Wesley*. Cambridge: Cambridge University Press, 1991.

Spellman, W. M. *The Latitudinarians and the Church of England 1660–1700*. Athens: University of Georgia Press, 1993.

Whichcote, Benjamin. *Moral and Religious Aphorisms*. Introduced by W. R. Inge. London: E. Mathews and Marrot, 1930.

ALISON J. TEPLY

LATTER RAIN REVIVAL

The Latter Rain Revival was a phrase frequently used to describe the pentecostal movement during the early twentieth century. The term was found attractive because it linked PENTECOSTALISM both to the New Testament account of Pentecost and to the end-time revival that many American Protestants believed would precede the return of Jesus Christ. The phrase was drawn from the Old Testament, which mentioned two wet periods in the climate cycle of ancient Palestine. Interpreted prophetically, those two rainy periods were identified by pentecostal theologians with the original charismatic outburst on the day of Pentecost and with the reappearance of the baptism of the Spirit and spiritual gifts in the modern pentecostal movement.

Of the many pentecostal spokespersons who used the phrase, the most articulate was David Wesley Myland. His *The Latter Rain Covenant and Pentecostal Power* (1910) argued that, in addition to the symbolic foreshadowing of the pentecostal latter rain revival in the Old Testament, climate changes in Palestine during the late nineteenth century also paralleled the return of the Spirit's latter rain to the church. For him, the physical history of the world mimicked spiritual developments. Myland was also attracted to latter rain imagery because it preached so well. He implored non-pentecostal Christians to put down their old umbrellas of theological ORTHODOXY and human inhibition and to let God's new cloudburst of Holy Ghost power soak them to the bone.

The use of latter rain imagery declined somewhat after the mid-century. About 1950 a spiritual protest movement emerged within pentecostalism that called

itself the New Order of the Latter Rain—a title often shortened to simply the Latter Rain. The more well established pentecostal denominations, especially the ASSEMBLIES OF GOD, denounced this new movement and since then the use of latter rain terminology has fallen into relative disuse within mainstream pentecostalism.

See also Assemblies of God

References and Further Reading

Faupel, D. William. *The Everlasting Gospel: The Significance of Eschatology in the Development of Pentecostal Thought*. Sheffield, UK: Sheffield Academic Press, 1996.

Myland, D. Wesley. *The Latter Rain Covenant and Pentecostal Power, with Testimony of Healings and Baptism*. Chicago, IL: Evangel Publishing House, 1910.

Riss, Richard Michael. *A Survey of 20th Century Revival Movements in North America*. Peabody, MA.: Hendrickson, 1988.

DOUGLAS JACOBSEN

LATVIA

Latvia's location between East and West has made it geopolitically a natural battleground, and thus, determined its fate. So has its situation between the Roman and Orthodox churches. The REFORMATION introduced a third force of Protestantism, creating a three-point religious struggle.

By the twelfth century the Baltic was the only pagan region left in all Europe. The Christianization of Latvia occurred in three periods. The first, the eleventh-century Danish mission, had no enduring success. Second, the Orthodox mission accompanying Russian invasion in the eleventh and twelfth centuries was likewise short-lived. Lasting influence was established with a German invasion in the twelfth century. Augustinian Meinhard of Holstein arrived in 1180, built a church in Ikšķile on the Daugava, consecrated a bishop in 1186, and set up a mission for the Livs. His successor Bishop Berthold employed a policy of militant proselytism and persuaded Pope Innocent III to mount a crusade against pagan Balts. The third bishop, Albert (1165–1229), consecrated March 29, 1199, an energetic leader, founded Rīga, made it his episcopal see in 1201, and persuaded Innocent to proclaim a crusade against Livonia. The pope established the Order of the Brothers of the Sword (1202) to help missionize the Baltic people. By 1230 the Roman curia decided to establish an ecclesiastical state in Livonia under papal jurisdiction. As the largest Roman church state, under the archbishop of Riga, Livonia was plagued by civil war among the archbishop, the city of Riga, and the Order. The Christianization of the Latvians was superficial, formal, and slow, with minimum catechization, attributed to language and cultural barriers and the incompetence of the clergy, as well as the Germanization of local Christianity as a part of colonial efforts (*Drang nach Osten*). The result was a syncretistic mix of previous pagan practice with medieval Christianity. This colonization introduced a new socioeconomic structure and integrated the Balts into the western European civilization.

The violent Christianization allowed nineteenth- and twentieth-century Latvian authors and Marxists to criticize Christianity in tendentious ways for usurping political power and colonizing the people. Only after 1918 did Latvian history emerge as a history of the Latvian people and its church, not as a province of occupying cultures (mainly German).

Ecclesiastical Latin provided the basis for the Latvian alphabet. The Livonian state guarded Latvians against the Russian expansion, abolished tribal strife, and forcefully promoted the consolidation of the Latvian nation by a policy of not assimilating into the German upper classes so primitive in Latvia.

The Reformation

Latvia was the first country to accept the Reformation outside of GERMANY. It began in Rīga, more through converted priests than through MARTIN LUTHER's writings. The chaplain at St. Peter's church, Andreas Knopken (1468–1539), studied Luther's teachings in Germany. He soon found followers among the city councilors. A public debate on June 12, 1522, over twenty-four theses prepared by Knopken at St. Peter's focused on JUSTIFICATION by FAITH and the critique of medieval ecclesiastical practices. The city council appointed him archdeacon of St. Peter's October 23, 1522, effectively introducing the Reformation among German merchants and artisans. Knopken published a commentary on Romans in 1524.

Sylvester Tegetmayer (d. 1552) arrived in Rīga in September 1522 and was placed in St. James' church. Luther wrote *To the Christians in Riga, Revell, and Dorpat* (1523), *Exposition of Psalm 127 for the Christians of Riga and Livonia* (1524), *A Christian Exhortation to the Livonians Concerning Public Worship and Concord* (1525), and fourteen letters to support his Livonian followers. Latvian preachers Nicolaus Ramm and Johan Eck established a Latvian Lutheran congregation in 1524; Riga's workers were the first Latvians to accept the Reformation. Wolter von Plettenberg, the master of the Livonian Order guaranteed toleration of the reform in 1525, which was reaffirmed by the Diet of Valmiera in 1554. In 1538 Rīga joined the German Protestant SCHMALKALDIC LEAGUE. Representatives of the Order signed the Religious Peace of Augsburg (1555).

Johan Briessmann (1488–1549), superintendent and pastor at the Rīga cathedral, composed a *Brief Order of Divine Worship* (1530). The first widespread book in Latvian was Luther's *Small Catechism,* published in 1586. Twenty-eight of his hymns were included in the first Latvian hymnal (1587). Apart from city dwellers, however, Latvians were little touched by the Reformation. From the partition of Livonia (1562), Courland and Semigallia in the west and Vidzeme in the north (after 1629) remained Lutheran under Swedish suzerainty; Latgallia under Poland became Roman Catholic.

The Counter-Reformation and Lutheran Orthodoxy

The last master of the Order, Gothard Kettler (1559–1563) abolished the Order, giving Vidzeme to the Poles (1562) and becoming a Polish vassal. King Stephan Batory gave two of Rīga's churches to the Jesuits, who arrived in great numbers, learned Latvian, and actively converted people. The Livonian constitution of 1582 tolerated LUTHERANISM but gave Roman Catholicism a superior position. In 1585 Canisius's Catechism was translated into Latvian. Germans in Rīga revolted in the "Calendar Rebellion" (1587–1591).

Kettler cultivated Lutheranism in Courland and Semigallia, restoring or rebuilding churches, building schools, teaching pastors Latvian, and publishing *Small Catechism* in Latvian. Georg Mancelius (1593–1654) edited it with supplements (1631) and composed a Postil (sermon book) in Latvian (1654). A notable Orthodox theologian and superintendent was Paul Einhorn (1636–1655). Christofer Fürecker (died c.1681) composed rhythmically accurate Latvian hymns.

Swedish Times

During the Polish–Swedish War, in 1621, GUSTAVUS ADOLPHUS took Rīga. Catholic services were forbidden. Swedish rule, considered the "brightest times" in Latvian history, supported Latvian peasants against the landlords and improved their legal and social situation and their education. Energetic Herman Samson (1579–1643) was placed in the position of superintendent of Vidzeme (1622). Swedish church law was introduced (1686). Pastors vigorously combatted Latvian pagan traditions. Ernst Glück (1652–1705) translated the Bible into Latvian (New Testament 1685; entire Bible 1689).

Russian Times

The Swedish–Russian "Great Northern" War (1700–1720) destroyed Vidzeme. Peter the Great invaded Rīga in 1710; the peace of Niestadt (1721) awarded Vidzeme to Russia. The privileges of the German nobility were recognized, continuing peasant dependency on them. Swedish traditions and church law, which continued in force until 1832, helped perpetuate church life.

Both PIETISM and RATIONALISM spread their influence from the universities of Rostock and Königsberg. The faculty of theology at the University of Dorpat (founded 1632) was dominated by Rationalism from 1802. Latvians studied there but clergy had difficulty obtaining parishes within Latvia.

Pietism and the Brethren Movement (Hernhuter)

The clericalism, intellectualism, didacticism, and harsh discipline of the Orthodox period failed to foster peasant piety. The German pastor and the Latvian peasant were separated socially and ethnically. The old mixture of Christianity and paganism lay barely below the surface.

The Brethren Movement among Latvians grew from the Teacher's College founded by Magdalen von Hallart (1738) and visitors from HALLE (Christian David, 1729–1730, 1738–1740; Count NIKOLAUS VON ZINZENDORF, 1736), creating renewal in Valmiera and environs in 1739. The diet attempted suppression (1742); Empress Elizabeth's ban (1743) interrupted the progress of the movement, but ultimately its adherents multiplied, led by Latvians Šķestera Pēteris (1702–1787) and Ķišu Pēteris (c.1698–1771).

The Hernhuter (see HERRNHUT) movement brought Latvians into the evangelical faith through Pietism, strengthened Christian morality, promoted diligence, taught management skills, welfare, literacy, and a sense of nationhood but also produced sanctimoniousness. The Christianization of the Latvians was completed by the mid-nineteenth century.

The Nineteenth and Early Twentieth Centuries

By 1890 Courland, Vidzeme, and Rīga each had its own CONSISTORY and its own specific traditions (e.g., hymnals: Courland's in 1836, Vidzeme's in 1846; a common Agenda in 1843 and 1900). In 1839 a Teachers Seminary was established in Valmiera under Jānis Cimze. Native pastors were educated at Dorpat. Bishop K. Kr. Ullmann, vice-president of the general consistory, organized evangelical social help through Russia (1859). In 1897, 1,009,994 Latvians in 189 congregations and 113,011 Germans in eighteen congregations composed the Lutheran church in Latvia. Very few Latvian pastors filled higher offices, and the number of Latvians placed within Latvian congregations was limited.

Conversion to Russian Orthodoxy was seen as a way for peasants to eliminate the pressure of German nobility; in 1846–1847 some 120,000–125,000 Latvians converted, against the opposition of German nobles and pastors, who were in turn severely punished by the Russian government.

Nineteenth-century Latvian households had religious books, practiced daily prayer, and attended worship regularly. Christian upbringing of children and moral life became an organic part of Latvian life. Economic consolidation and an increase in the educational level of peasants and burghers created tensions with the German governing class. A nascent Latvian intelligentsia urged Latvians to move up the social ladder through education and cultivate their own culture. Awakened national consciousness demanded native pastors; however, the church remained the possession of the nobility, eliciting attacks on the nobility during the Revolution of 1905. The deep social and ethnic breach between Germans and Latvians was incurable.

The Latvian National Church

The conditions after World War I were difficult. The "nobility's church" disappeared with the collapse of the Russian Empire and the abolition of the nobility's privileges. A theological faculty was begun in 1920 and followed prewar currents in German theology, leading to tensions between faculty and church leadership, which founded its own Theological Institute under Ādams Mačulāns (1923). In 1922 a synod elected a supreme Consistory, its president, and a bishop, Kārlis Irbe (1861–1934). A new hymnal appeared in 1922, a choral book in 1924, and an order of worship in 1928. The Foreign Mission started in 1924, with the work of Anna Irbe (1890–1973), daughter of K. Irbe, in South India; and in 1939 with the support of secretary Roberts Feldmanis (1910–) expanded through all of Latvia. In 1934 Teodors Grīnbergs (1870–1962) succeeded Irbe. In 1936 the church had 272 Latvian and 52 German congregations. The twenty years of Latvian independence (1920–1940) were a period of a productive work and a success in many respects.

The War and Occupations

The "Year of Horror"—1940—brought invasion and active sovietization of the nation and the churches, and deportation of 15,424 people on June 14. German invasion (June 22, 1941) prevented a second round of Soviet deportations aimed at destroying the nation's spiritual and intellectual leadership. National Socialist (Nazi) control of the church limited theological studies and acted against those, like Rīga Dean Pauls Rozenbergs, who protested anti-Semitic policies. Archbishop Grīnbergs also publicly opposed the killing of Gypsies before his forced deportation to Germany (1944), although church life continued during the Nazi occupation.

Renewed Soviet occupation eliminated the leadership of the church, headed by Dean Kārlis Irbe, a nephew of the former archbishop, in 1946. One hundred five pastors were serving 305 congregations, and only sixty churches of 190 remained undamaged by the war. March 24, 1949, saw the deportation of 47,332 Latvians to Siberia, including many Lutheran laity. Thirty pastors were arrested and deported. Local Soviets took over twenty-two church buildings; in 1959 the Rīga cathedral was seized. By 1961 the church claimed 24 percent of the population (214 congregations, 115 pastors) and had twenty theological students. From 1963 oppressive taxation further undermined the church's ownership of property.

Archbishop Gustavs Turs, known as the "red bishop" skillfully accommodated Soviet wishes while striving to maintain the integrity of the church against harsh oppression. In 1954 permission to conduct theological training was obtained; the academic standing of the program of the Theological Seminary was confirmed in 1969. The "Decree on Religious Associations" of 1975 reconfirmed all previous Soviet restrictions, depriving churches of all rights and limited their activities to public worship.

In 1987 a group of pastors organized "Rebirth and Renewal," demanding that the church be made self-governing. One pastor was killed and two exiled. However, members were elected to the Consistory, and one, Kārlis Gailītis (1936–1992), was elected archbishop in 1989. In 1990 the seminary program became a faculty of theology at the University of Riga.

Throughout the Soviet period a significant church in exile had continued Latvian church life in Germany, Sweden, Australia, Canada, Latin America, and the United States. In 2002 it had 89 pastors in 132 congregations.

The Latvian Lutheran Church elected Archbishop Jānis Vanags, D.D., in 1993. One hundred twenty-seven pastors served in 295 congregations. A Diaconia Center was started in 1994, St. Gregor's Christian Ministry School in 1995 (thirty students), Luther Academy in 1997 (sixty pastoral, forty-five pedagogical students), under Rector Dr. Hab. Reinhard Slen-czka (as of 2002). Other denominations, such as Baptist congregations, first organized in 1860, currently united in the Union of Baptist Congregations of Latvia (seventy-six congregations, 6,200 members), under Bishop Jānis Šmits. Adventist churches have existed since 1896 (currently forty-four congregations, 4,000 members in the Union of Adventists of the Seventh Day, President Viesturs Reķis). The Union of Pentecostal Congregations, organized 1931, has seventy-three congregations (6,000 members) under Bishop Jānis Ozolinkēvics. The Lutherans of the Augsburg Confession, organized in 1997, have nine congregations with 400 members. The United Methodist Church began work in 1910 and has ten congregations with 480 members under Superintendent Ārijs Vīksna (as of 2002).

References and Further Reading

Adamovičs, A. *Raksti par Latvijas Baznīcas Vēsturi. Latviešu ev.-lut. Baznīca Amerikā.* 1978.

Andersons, E. *Latvijas Vēsture, 1914–1920.* Stockholm, 1967.

Arbusow, L. Jr. *Die Einführung der Reformation in Liv-, Est-, und Kurland.* 1921. Reprint, Aalen, Germany: Scientia Verlag Daugava, 1964.

Dunsdorfs, E. *Latvijas Vēsture, 1600–1710.* Uppsala, 1962.

———. *Latvijas Vēsture, 1710–1800.* Sundbyberg, 1973.

———, and A. Spekke. *Latvijas Vēsture, 1500–1600.* Stockholm, 1964.

Grislis, E. "Recent Trends in the Study of the Reformation in the City of Riga, Livonia." *Journal of Baltic Studies* 7 (1976): 145–169.

Hoerschelmann, D. F. *Andreas Knopken, der Reformator Rigas: Ein Beitrag zur Kirchengeschichte Livlands.* Leipzig, 1896.

Johansons, A. *Latvijas Kultūras Vēsture, 1710–1800.* Stockholm, 1975.

Ķiploks, E. *Latvijas ev.-lut. Baznīca 1918–1968, Cęla Biedrs* 1968, vol. 9, 1970.

Plakans, A. *The Latvians. A Short History.* Stanford, CA.: Hoover Institution, Stanford University Press, 1995.

Šilde, A. *Latvijas Vēsture, 1914–1940.* Stockholm, Daugava 1976.

Spekke, A. *History of Latvia: An Outline.* Stockholm: M. Goppers 1951.

Švābe, A. *Latvijas Vēsture, 1800–1914.* Uppsala: 1958.

Talonenen, J. *Church Under the Pressure of Stalinism.* Jyväskylä, Finland: Historical Society of Northern Finland, 1997.

Wittram, R., ed. *Baltische Kirchengeschichte.* Göttingen, Germany, Vandenhoeck & Ruprecht 1956.

GUNTIS CALME

LAUD, WILLIAM (1573–1645)

Archbishop of Canterbury. Laud is probably the most controversial archbishop of Canterbury in the history of the Anglican Church. A favorite of King Charles I, he was hated by Puritans who opposed his religious policies. In later years he was admired by leaders of the OXFORD MOVEMENT like JOHN HENRY NEWMAN, who respected his attempts to restore Catholic liturgies and practices abandoned at the time of the REFORMATION, but denounced by such twentieth-century historians as Patrick Collinson, who called him "the greatest calamity visited upon the English church" (1984: 90). He is the only archbishop to have been tried for treason and publicly executed.

Early Life

Laud was born on October 7, 1573, in the town of Reading, west of London. His father was a member of the merchant class, a relatively well-off clothier; because of this ancestry Laud was sometimes ridiculed in later life because he was not a member of the gentry. His mother's relatives, the Webbs, were also clothiers, but several of them prospered and married into prominent families. One became a lord mayor of London.

Laud was educated at Reading Grammar School and at the age of sixteen proceeded to St. John's College, Oxford, which had ties with the Grammar School. He became a fellow of the College in 1593, a year before he completed the B.A. In 1601 he was named a senior fellow and soon became a lecturer in divinity and a university proctor. In 1611 he was elected president of St. John's, a position he held until being appointed a bishop. As president he beautified the college chapel, commissioned anthems from such composers as Orlando Gibbons, and took steps to improve the college finances. In later years he was responsible for the addition of a beautiful new quadrangle to the college. While at Oxford, Laud was greatly influenced by the distinguished scholar and theologian LANCELOT ANDREWES.

Preferment in the church came during the later years of the reign of James I (d. 1625). In 1621 Laud was named dean of Gloucester cathedral. The king had told Laud that "there was scarce ever a church in England so ill governed, and so much out of order." Laud immediately undertook the repair of the edifice and "the redress of other things amiss" (*Works*, VI, Pt. 1, 239). It was at Gloucester that Laud's concern for medieval TRADITION became manifest because he restored the high ALTAR to its original place at the east end of the church. During the reign of Edward VI stone altars had been removed from many cathedrals and other churches—smashed up or hidden away—on the grounds that they were superstitious reminders of the doctrine of the mass as a sacrifice, a Catholic view no longer accepted in the reformed church. Instead "honest wooden tables" had been set up "table-wise" (east and west), not "altar-wise" (north and south), and placed in the main body of the church, so that worshipers might see the actions of the minister and participate more directly in the service. The more moderate Elizabethan Injunctions of 1559 returned the table to its traditional position against the east wall. Canons promulgated in 1604 anticipated Laud's insistence on traditional altars; in fact he was enforcing them, not bringing forth a novelty.

In 1621 Laud was appointed a prebend of Westminster Abbey. His hopes of becaming dean of the Abbey were thwarted, but in 1621 the king named him bishop of the Welsh diocese of St. David's. Here again he reinstated a stone altar.

The Reign of Charles I

With the accession of Charles I in 1625 Laud became the recognized leader of the English church because Charles respected his abilities and shared many of his views. In 1626 Laud became dean of the Chapel Royal and was translated to the English bishopric of Bath and Wells. In 1627 he was designated a member of the king's Privy Council. A year later he was named bishop of London; to make this place available the king promoted the previous bishop to the archbishopric of York. Here Laud worked with the dean of St. Paul's, JOHN DONNE, and the architect Inigo Jones to repair and restore the fabric of the cathedral, which had become ruinous. He also issued orders prohibiting the use of the cathedral for secular purposes, demanding that no business be transacted there and that children not be allowed to play in the church.

When the see of CANTERBURY became vacant through the death of George Abbot in 1633 Laud gained the position of archbishop and primate, a recognition of the influence that he had been exercising for nearly a decade. At Canterbury Cathedral he again refitted the choir with a high altar adorned with candlesticks and a rich carpet. Some other specific matters that concerned him were the buildings that encroached on the church, the fair that was held in the churchyard, and the necessity for multiple locks to the muniment room, as specified in the statutes. The archbishop's relations with members of the staff were not always pleasant; as he said, "one peevish difference or another" always seemed to be arising, generally caused by mere "spleen" (*Works*, VII, 215–216, 349–352).

Both Laud and Charles I are often referred to as Arminians. In fact they were not true followers of the Dutch theologian JACOBUS ARMINIUS, who is best known for his opposition to the doctrine of PREDESTINATION and his belief in free will (see ARMINIANISM). They did, however, agree that a number of meaningful beliefs and practices of the medieval church had been abandoned in England after the Reformation, at the urging of Archbishop THOMAS CRANMER and as a result of the influence of Continental Calvinists and English Puritans. As Laud often said, he loved the beauty of holiness and the solemnity of church buildings and liturgies. In addition to restoring stone altars to their traditional locations and railing them in so that they could not be defiled by dogs, he favored elaborate music provided by trained choirs, genuflecting and kneeling, stained glass windows, and traditional VESTMENTS with a white linen chasuble as the minimum garb for the priest. He regarded the SACRAMENTS as being more important than PREACHING. He once complained that " 'tis superstition now-a-days for any man to come with more reverence into a church, than a tinker and his bitch come into an ale-house" (*Works*, VI, Pt. I, 57). He curtailed the activities of the so-called Stranger Churches that ministered to Protestant immigrants to ENGLAND, especially the group of French HUGUENOTS that met in the crypt of Canterbury cathedral, evidently because he thought, erroneously, that they were allied with the Puritan nonconformists. He was also concerned to improve church finances so that the clergy might receive reasonable stipends. He attempted to see that tithes were properly collected, especially in London, although his efforts were not very successful.

During the years of Charles I's personal rule without Parliament (1629–1640), Laud worked with the king and his chief minister, the earl of Strafford, to enforce a policy often characterized as "Thorough." Laud sought to achieve unity in the church by strict enforcement of existing canons. He was determined to eliminate slackness and inefficiency, to see that churches were kept clean and in good repair, and to ensure that CLERGY not be allowed to neglect their duties. He was willing to use the law courts to secure obedience to the bishops and strict conformity to the services of the BOOK OF COMMON PRAYER. He also proceeded against Puritan pamphleteers, including the notorious William Prynne, Henry Burton, and John Bastwick, who had their ears cut off for writing scurrilous tracts denouncing the established church.

The Growth of Opposition

It is not surprising that these policies were unpopular with both laymen and clergy, many of whom believed them to be popish and superstitious. Some said that Laud was moving in the direction of the Roman Catholic Church, despite his refutation of the views of the Jesuit John Fisher and his statement that he would not accept a cardinal's hat if one were offered to him. The tragedy of Laud's life, indeed a tragedy for the entire church, lay in his inability to appreciate the genuine piety of those who disagreed with his elevated views.

He had few friends and little sympathy for common people.

Although he had no AUTHORITY over the church in SCOTLAND, Laud helped the king formulate the new service book, which so displeased Scots Presbyterians when it was introduced in Scotland in 1637 that a riot at St. Giles Cathedral in Edinburgh led to the outbreak of the Bishops' Wars and the English CIVIL WAR. These hostilities necessitated the summoning of the Short Parliament (1640) and Long Parliament (1640–1660), both of which were dominated by Puritan opponents of the religious policies of Charles and Laud.

In 1640 the Long Parliament impeached the archbishop on a charge of treason. He was sent to prison in the Tower of London in 1641 but was not brought to trial until 1644. After he presented a dignified defense of his actions before the House of Lords it proved impossible to obtain a guilty verdict, so in the end he was condemned by a bill of attainder, which like any other piece of legislation required only a simple majority vote in both houses of Parliament. He was beheaded on Tower Hill on January 10, 1645. Four years later, on January 30, 1649, the king himself would be executed.

William Laud's unmarked coffin was originally interred at the church of All Hallows, Barking, not far from the Tower, but after the Restoration of the monarchy and state church in 1660 it was moved to Oxford. The archbishop's remains now lie, appropriately, before the altar in the chapel of St. John's College.

See also Architecture, Church; Calvinism; Nonconformity; Puritanism

References and Further Reading

Primary Source:

Laud, William. *The Works of the Most Reverend Father in God, William Laud*. Edited by W. Scot and James Bliss. 7 vols. Oxford: John Henry Parker, 1847–1860.

Secondary Sources:

Carlton, Charles. *Archbishop William Laud*. London: Routledge & Kegan Paul, 1987.
Collinson, Patrick. *The Religion of Protestants*. Oxford: Oxford University Press, 1984.
Davies, Julian. *The Caroline Captivity of the Church*. Oxford, UK: Clarendon Press, 1992.
Hill, Christopher. *Economic Problems of the Church*. Oxford, UK: Clarendon Press, 1956.
Lehmberg, Stanford E. *Cathedrals under Siege: Cathedrals in English Society, 1600–1700*. University Park, PA.: Penn State University Press; Exeter: University of Exeter Press, 1996.
Moorman, J. H. R. *A History of the Church in England*. London: A. & C. Black, 1953.

Trevor-Roper, H. R. *Archbishop Laud, 1573–1645.* 2d edition. Oxford: Oxford University Press, 1940, 1962.

STANFORD LEHMBERG

LAUSANNE COMMITTEE ON WORLD EVANGELIZATION

The Lausanne Committee on World Evangelization (LCWE) defines itself as "an international movement for the purpose of encouraging Christians and churches everywhere to pray, study, plan and work together for the evangelization of the world." It is a global evangelistic movement that grew out of an initiative taken by the American evangelist BILLY GRAHAM. The motivation for its origins can be traced to the ecumenical movement and internal theological tensions that developed within Protestantism during the twentieth century. A series of missionary conferences were held during the twentieth century, starting with the 1910 conference in Edinburgh, Scotland (see WORLD MISSIONARY CONFERENCE). The participants in the missionary conferences consisted of both institutional church representatives and representatives of para-church missionary organizations. The 1910 conference in Edinburgh established the International Missionary Council (IMC). The IMC provided a strong impetus for the formation of the WORLD COUNCIL OF CHURCHES (WCC) in 1948. The IMC was integrated into the WCC as part of its Division of World Mission and Evangelism (DWME) at the New Delhi Assembly in 1961. With the integration of the DWME, many missionary organizations that were not denominationally based lost their representation previously held in the IMC.

There was also a growing theological concern among some of the organizations and denominational representatives that the emphasis of the WCC had moved away from a central focus on EVANGELISM and mission. Some of these concerns were related to the theological split, particularly in North America, between those in the SOCIAL GOSPEL movement and those who held theological views more focused on the importance of personal SALVATION. An organization called the World Evangelical Fellowship (WEF) represented these concerns on a global level with the focus on personal salvation and conservative views of scriptural inspiration. The WEF also traces its roots to the first ecumenical initiatives formed as the EVANGELICAL ALLIANCE in 1861 in London, England, which eventually led to the establishment of the IRM in 1910. Despite the existence and efforts of the WEF to which Billy Graham was sympathetic, he and like-minded people felt that a new global initiative for evangelism was needed to build a broader base of cooperation in evangelism. In 1960, Billy Graham

assembled a group of Christian leaders in Montreux, SWITZERLAND, which led to the World Congress on Evangelism held in Berlin, GERMANY, in 1966. Several regional conferences were held leading up to the International Congress on World Evangelism (ICWE) in Lausanne, Switzerland, in 1974. More than 4,000 delegates from 150 nations attended the ICWE in Lausanne, with more than half of the participants coming from third world countries. During the congress, a steering committee was struck under the leadership of John R. W. Stott to draft a document based on the proceedings of the congress. The draftees also included Hudson Armerding and Samuel Escobar, aided by Leighton Ford and Jim Douglas. This document, which became known as the Lausanne Covenant, was signed by congress leaders and delegates in a ceremony on the last day of the gathering. The Lausanne Covenant became an important document within evangelical circles; many organizations adopted it as an additional statement on evangelism. Even before the congress, arrangements were being made to harness the energy that would arise out of such a gathering. Out of this planning came the LCWE in 1976.

Initially, forty-three people were elected by the congress to continue arranging consultations under the leadership of Leighton Ford as chair and Gottfried Osei-Mensah as secretary. The LCWE focuses on being a motivational source and a clearinghouse for information on evangelization throughout the world. It continues to organize conferences, consultations, and publish newsletters worldwide. After the 1974 Lausanne Congress, the LCWE arranged to develop the ideas of the congress further through the Consultation on World Evangelization, which held a meeting in Pattaya, Thailand in 1980. This consultation resulted in an important series of occasional papers on issues concerning world evangelization. Between 1977 and 1985, many regional study consultations, focused on particular themes, were held. This process culminated in a full plenary conference held in Lausanne, Switzerland, in 1989.

In 2004 the LCWE will be hosting the Forum for World Evangelization in Thailand. The LCWE and the Lausanne Covenant are important phenomena of current Protestantism. The organization has enjoyed strong participation from organizations and churches in the third world, and it represents a movement of evangelicals that is more broad-based than other organizations. Through the Lausanne Covenant, it is linked to a new emphasis on theological reflection within the evangelical movement on the place of social action and social justice in relation to the task of evangelism and mission. It also represents a commitment to unity and cooperation in action. DAVID BOSCH has argued convincingly that there has been an increased influence within the LCWE and its consultations on emphasizing social concern, as well as a growing awareness within the WCC of issues related to evangelism. There has also been a conscious effort by the LCWE and the WCC to coordinate conferences and themes. These are signs of convergence despite clear differences between those represented by the LCWE and those involved in the WCC Committee on World Mission and Evangelism.

See also Ecumenism; Evangelicalism; Evangelicalism, Theology of; Missionary Organizations; Missions to Jews; Missions

References and Further Reading

Bosch, D. J. "Ecumenicals and Evangelicals: A Growing Relationship?" *The Ecumenical Review* 40 (1988): 458–472.
———. "Your Will Be Done: Critical Reflections on San Antonio." *Missionalia* 17 (1989):126–138.
———. *Transforming Mission: Paradigm Shifts in Theology of Mission.* New York: Orbis Books, 1991, pp. 405–407, 412, 418–419, 438, 452, 461, 505.
Howard, D. M. *The Dream that Would not Die: The Birth and Growth of the World Evangelical Fellowship 1846–1986.* Sydney, Australia: Paternoster, 1986.
"The Lausanne Covenant." http://www.gospelcom.net/lcwe/covenant.html.
"Records of the Lausanne Committee for World Evangelization—Collection 46," revised January 23, 2002. http://www.wheaton.edu/bgc/archives/GUIDES/046.htm.
Stott, John R. W. "The Lausanne Covenant: An Exposition and Commentary." http://www.gospelcom.net/lcwe/LOP/lop03.htm

CHARLES J. FENSHAM

LAVATER, JOHANN KASPAR (1741–1801)

Swiss philosopher and writer. Lavater was born in Zürich to a well-respected family on November 15, 1741. After studying THEOLOGY and traveling through GERMANY (1763–1764), which increased his attraction to moderate forms of ENLIGHTENMENT thought, he worked as a writer in his native city.

In 1768 Lavater experienced a complete religious transformation. Christ became central to his thought and works, and Lavater wanted to demonstrate the imminence of Christ's presence on Earth. Thus he sought contact with people who were gifted as mediums and "faith healers." Lavater believed that through Christ, the divine powers inherent in every human being could be given an earthly presence, but that complete likeness to Christ could come only in the afterlife. Because he accepted these notions of manifest transcendental experience, Lavater was especially criticized by Enlightenment thinkers.

In 1769 Lavater became the deacon of the Waisenhauskirche, a church related to the orphanage in Zü-

rich, and in 1775 became a minister there. He became the deacon of Peterskirche in 1778 and its minister in 1786. He explored theology and philosophy, poetry and art, psychology and pedagogy, and politics and societal issues. From his extensive literary output, three works are of special significance: *Aussichten in die Ewigkeit (Prospects for Eternity)* (1768–1778), *Geheimes Tagebuch (Secret Diary)* (1771), and *Physiognomischen Fragmente (Essays on Physiognomy)* (1775/1778, published in numerous English editions). The great breadth of his interests and the aura of his personality, as well as his many travels to Germany, DENMARK, and western SWITZERLAND all provided him personal contacts and correspondence with many of his famous contemporaries, including JOHANN WOLFGANG, VON GOETHE, JOHANN GOTTFRIED HERDER, and JOHANN HEINRICH JUNG-STILLING. Many of these friendships he also destroyed. After the FRENCH REVOLUTION—which he at first heralded and later condemned—Lavater vigorously engaged political and patriotic issues in Switzerland. Because of his criticism of the Swiss Republic, he was deported to Basel. During the French occupation of Zürich (1799), he was wounded by a bullet that eventually took his life on January 2, 1801.

Lavater's ideas about physiognomy were incorporated in works of literature (e.g., Dickens) and art. His emphasis on sensitivity and subjectivity influenced PIETISM, as well as ROMANTICISM and early Idealism.

See also Transcendentalism

References and Further Reading

Guidaudeau, Oliver. *Jean-Gaspard Lavater. Étude sur la vie et sa pensée jusqu'en 1786.* Paris: Alcan, 1924.
Sauer, Klaus Martin. *Die Predigttätigkeit Johann Kaspar Lavater (1741–1801). Darstellung und Quellengrundlage.* Zürich, Switzerland: Theologischer Verlag Zürich, 1994.
Weigelt, Horst. *Johann Kaspar Lavater. Leben, Werk und Wirkung.* Göttingen, Germany: Vandenhoeck und Ruprecht, 1991.
———, ed. *Das Anlitz Gottes im Anlitz des Menschen.* Göttingen, Germany: Vandenhoeck und Ruprecht, 1994.

HORST WEIGELT

LAW, WILLIAM (1686–1761)

English theologian. Born in 1686 in Northamptonshire, ENGLAND, William Law was a graduate of CAMBRIDGE UNIVERSITY in 1708; he subsequently earned an M.A. (1712) and was ordained in the CHURCH OF ENGLAND. By 1727 he had found stable employment as tutor to the Gibbon family, which had strong Tory connections.

Law's theological views became associated with those of the Non-Jurors, and he declined to take the oath of allegiance at the accession of George I. Reflecting a theological position characteristic of the High Church party, he wrote in aggressive defense of the Christian life as an embodiment of virtue. He confronted laxity in the church's leaders, and he attacked such popular amusements of the day as the stage. By the 1720s the distinctiveness of Law's outlook was becoming apparent. His noted work, *A Serious Call to a Devout and Holy Life*, appeared in 1728. Its appearance made plain his increasing interest in mystical writers and brought him to the attention of JOHN and CHARLES WESLEY. As the Methodist movement gained momentum, the Wesleys and Law launched an intense and mutually respectful but ultimately brief conversation. Yet there were parallels between Law's intention and the Wesleys' achievement. In 1739 Law published *The Grounds and Reasons of Christian Regeneration, or the New Birth*, a work that early Methodists found congenial. He also founded a school at which he promoted a religious, disciplined life. Another immensely popular work of his was *The Nature and Design of Christianity,* published in 1748, which saw over fifteen editions.

Law died after a brief illness on April 9, 1761. As a teacher and author on the religious life, he influenced succeeding generations of religious reformers in METHODISM and in the OXFORD MOVEMENT.

References and Further Reading

Primary Source:

Law, William. *Christian Perfection*. Carol Stream, IL: 1975.

Secondary Sources:

Baker, Eric W. *A Herald of the Evangelical Revival*. London: Epworth, 1948.
Clarkson, George E. *The Mysticism of William Law*. New York: Peter Lang, 1992.
Walker, Arthur Keith. *William Law: His Life and Thought*. London: SPCK, 1973.

WILLIAM SACHS

LEADE, JANE WARD (1623–1704)

English writer. Born in 1623 in Norfolk, England, Jane Ward became a well-known Protestant visionary, millenarian, and spiritual autobiographer. When she was fifteen years old, a whispering voice urged her to turn from frivolity at a Christmas celebration to participate in a spiritual dance. This aural religious experience initiated an inner crisis, which ended three years later with a vision of pardon. At the age of twenty-one, financial circumstances necessitated her marriage to William Leade, a distant relative. Widowed at forty-six, she committed herself to a life of spiritual virginity, mysticism, prophecy, and prolific writing.

Introduced to the philosophy of JAKOB BOEHME in English translation, Leade was profoundly influenced by his work with its emphasis on mystic revelation and a feminine divine principle. Her four-volume spiritual autobiography, *A Fountain of Gardens* (1696–1701), records her visions, many focusing on Sophia or Wisdom, a figure central to Boehme's work. Leade published more than a dozen other books, including a spiritual guide, *The Heavenly Cloud* (1681), and a commentary on Apocalypse, *The Revelation of Revelations* (1683). Her following grew with the German and Dutch translations of her writings.

With her adopted son, Dr. Francis Lee (who later married her daughter Barbara), Leade founded the Philadelphian Society, a forerunner of the Theosophists. With Leade as its prophet, the society was active in England, GERMANY, and Holland.

Struggling financially in her old age and blind, Leade continued to write by dictating her material to Lee until shortly before her death in 1704. Her prose, often embedded with poetry, emphasizes the inner light of spiritual intuition that guides the soul to its divine origin. Although her work is generally unavailable in print except for excerpts in anthologies, much is accessible electronically at the websitehttp:/www.sigler.org/shofar/janeleade.

References and Further Reading

Shawcross, John T. "Jane Ward Leade." In *Dictionary of Literary Biography*, vol. 131, *Seventeenth-Century Nondramatic Poets* edited by M. Thomas Hester, 120–122. Detroit, MI: Gale, 1933.
Smith, Catherine F. "Jane Leade: The Feminist Mind and Art of a Seventeenth-Century Protestant Mystic" In *Women of Spirit: Female Leadership in the Jewish and Christian Traditions* edited by Rosemary Ruether and Eleanor McLaughlin, 183–203. New York: Simon and Schuster, 1979.
———. "Jane Leade's Wisdom: Women and Prophecy in Seventeenth-Century England." In *Poetic Prophecy in Western Literature,* edited by Jan Wojick and Raymond-Jean Frontain, 55–63. Rutherford, NJ: Fairleigh Dickinson University Press, 1984.

FRANCES M. MALPEZZI

LEE, ANN (1736–1784)

English church reformer. Founder of the United Society of Believers in Christ's Second Appearing, or SHAKERS, Ann Lee was born in Manchester, England, in 1736. A millworker since her early teens, she came into contact with James and Jane Wardley, former Quakers (see FRIENDS, SOCIETY OF), whose enthusiastic manner of WORSHIP had earned them the nickname

"Shakers" and who prophesied the imminence of Christ's return. Against her will, Lee married Abraham Standerin in 1762 and gave birth to four children, all of whom died in infancy.

Convinced that her children's deaths were punishment for what she perceived as her own carnality, Lee began a life of ASCETICISM and became convinced that sexual relations were the source of all evil. She and the Wardleys began to spread her gospel of chastity and were twice imprisoned for desecrating the Sabbath. While confined in the Manchester Infirmary, Lee experienced a vision of Adam and Eve's original sin. She proclaimed that Christ was dwelling in her—a claim that her followers recognized as the Second Coming.

In 1774, "Mother Ann" or "Ann the Word," as she was now called, migrated to North America to proclaim her revelation in an environment more hospitable than Manchester. She and other Shakers eventually settled near Albany, New York, where a religious revival had produced an audience receptive to her message that the millennium had already begun (see REVIVALS). Though her PACIFISM resulted in imprisonment for aiding the British in 1780, Lee attracted a considerable following and, after her release, she successfully proselytized throughout New York and into New England. Although she died in 1784, her labors laid the foundation for eleven Shaker communities, some of which endured into the twentieth century.

See also: Millenarians and Millennialism

References and Further Reading

Marini, Stephen A. "A New View of Mother Ann Lee and the Rise of American Shakerism." *Shaker Quarterly* 28 (1990): 47–62, 95–111.

Stern, Stephen J. *The Shaker Experience in America: A History of the United Society of Believers.* New Haven, CT: Yale University Press, 1992.

WILLIAM M. CLEMENTS

LEGGE, JAMES (1815–1897)

Scottish dissenter. Born into a Congregationalist merchant family, James Legge was the last of four sons. As did his eldest brother, George, he graduated from King's College in Aberdeen, Scotland, and from the Congregationalist seminary in London, Highbury College. Both James and George became noted Christian leaders. After serving with the London Missionary Society among Chinese people in Malacca (1840–1842) and Hong Kong (1842–1873), Legge retired in SCOTLAND. Yet after he received international honors for his outstanding sinological achievements, supporters urged Anglican academics in Corpus Christi College, Oxford, to take this nonconformist as the university's first professor in Chinese language and literature, a position he held from 1876 until his death in 1897.

Scottish Dissenter Orientation

In Aberdeen, Legge excelled in Latin and philosophy, being deeply impressed by the writings of Dugald Stewart (1753–1828), a second-generation philosopher of SCOTTISH COMMON SENSE REALISM. This Neo-Aristotelian empirical philosophy argued against DAVID HUME (1711–1776) for proofs of the existence of God by means of natural theology, an approach deeply influencing the American theologian, WILLIAM PALEY (1743–1805). In addition, it pressed on readers their duties first to God and then to humans, while also providing a wide-ranging account of various levels of warranted beliefs that common-sense understandings also supported. When added to the rigorous training Legge received as a child from the WESTMINSTER CONFESSIONS and the disciplined spiritual form of Congregational life that bordered on SABBATARIANISM, this Scottish philosophy provided an intellectual framework for a comprehensive view of CULTURE and a flexible theistic worldview. Recognizing that there were other kinds of theism beside Christianity, Legge in 1835 began studying Christian scriptures seriously in his typically thorough manner and was quietly converted, joining a local Congregational church in 1836. One year later he applied for seminary studies, specializing in MISSIONS.

Other significant theological influences came from his elder brother's theological writings and the extensive publications of his future father-in-law, John Morison (d. 1858), a Director of the London Missionary Society and editor of that society's periodical, *The Evangelical Magazine and Missionary Chronicle.* Both of these men supported a "moderating" CALVINISM, supported by a postmillennial view of salvation history. This particular form of millennialism promoted the belief that Christ's Spirit would use the efforts of Christians within the world to create a millennial kingdom; their creative efforts reaching a threshhold, whole nations were expected to become filled with humane virtues and spiritual excellences informed by Protestant Christian values. Although not unaware of many ideological hindrances and intellectual challenges to this particular ESCHATALOGY, George Legge (1802–1861) in particular promoted a harmonious vision linking together a humble rationality, systematic scientific discovery, and Christian THEOLOGY. James Legge adopted all of these theological positions as his own, as manifest in his published sermons and more than four hundred extant sermon manuscripts.

Initial Chinese Cultural Challenges

Following in the trail of two notable Protestant pioneer missionaries to CHINA, Robert Morrison (1782–1834) and William Milne (1785–1822), Legge became the principal of the Anglo-Chinese College in Malacca soon after arriving there. This small school he transferred to the newly established British colony of Hong Kong in 1842, teaching Chinese students there until the college closed in 1856. During this period, Legge built up a friendship with the slightly younger Ho Tsun-Sheen (1817–1871), first his Cantonese teacher and later a career evangelist and copastor under the aegis of the London Missionary Society. Together, these two men faced the immensely important problem of how to translate theological terms for "God," "Holy Spirit," "human spirit," and other terms into Chinese. Initially taking a position promoted by Morrison early in his career, Legge ploddingly pursued related studies and was profoundly influenced by Ho Tsun-Sheen's commitment, coming ultimately in 1848 to adopt an alternative position. Already critically informed through Protestant writings in comparative religious study produced by FREDERICK DENISON MAURICE (1805–1872) and Cambridge's Charles Hardwick (1821–1859), Legge became intensely involved in public debates over this translation problem. Using Scottish Realist philosophy and extensive studies in canonical and popular Chinese writings to argue for adopting terms found in the Ruist ("Confucian") scriptures, Legge's final book-length essay of 1852 manifested an informed awareness of much Chinese literature and a generally accommodating strategy for BIBLE TRANSLATIONS. Although for other historical and institutional reasons, his arguments did not convince the publishers of Chinese Bibles in the BIBLE SOCIETIES in Britain or the UNITED STATES, this study became the intellectual foundation for his future missiological developments.

Other matters of basic cultural importance also had to be addressed among Chinese persons. The Chinese had no religious precedents for a "Sabbath culture" which Legge's Scottish Dissenter background and training especially emphasized, so these concepts had to be addressed in sermons and pamphlets. In this realm, Legge remained a convinced Congregationalist in ecclesiastical POLITY, a Reformed Protestant in supporting the LORD'S SUPPER and BAPTISM as the main ordinances, accepting the BAPTISM of infants, and promoting a soberly reflective Christian experience of WORSHIP. With Ho Tsun-Sheen, Legge willingly adapted all of these elements of Sabbath culture into the Chinese context, filling it with Ruist-style terms and ritual sensitivities, and so together the two men promoted a Ruified form of Chinese Christian life.

Throughout his more than thirty years of missionary work, Legge never felt moved like JAMES HUDSON TAYLOR (1832–1904) to live among Chinese persons by assuming their style of life, even though Chinese students lived in Legge's Hong Kong home and Legge was involved daily with Chinese people in their local settings. Nevertheless, the irony remains that Taylor's missiology was based on confrontational apologetic methods that Legge grew to oppose, preferring instead an accommodationist missiology.

Protestant Literature in Chinese

Both Legge and Ho wrote and published in Chinese, with Legge developing a variety of Protestant LITERATURE in this linguistic media. This included evangelistic and Christian educational literature in several different linguistic ligatures and with different intended audiences: novellas about Joseph and Abraham in a fairly literary Chinese, more popular stories about the Prodigal Son and the Prophet Daniel's companions written in demotic Cantonese, as well as sermon outlines for evangelists and spiritual handbooks filled with advice and guidance for coolies making dangerous trips on ship to work in gold mines. Regularly woven into the stories were moral and spiritual challenges, often highlighting important passages in the Ruist canon that supported Christian values.

Dissenter Challenges to British Imperialism and Victorian Values

British COLONIALISM had its unseemly side, which Legge, as a Dissenter, felt obliged to expose. Already in 1844, Legge and Ho had published their criticisms of the opium trade, a battle Legge continued to fight throughout his long life. In Hong Kong he took a public stand against mercantile greed and its excesses, challenged the legitimacy of the coolie trade as just another form of SLAVERY, and led a temporarily successful public campaign against gambling. Once settled in Hong Kong, he established with other missionaries a Union Chapel that sought to embody a Protestant ECUMENISM, while he remained a committed opponent to Roman Catholic traditions.

All of these prophetic stances were consistent with Legge's understanding of the process of SALVATION: a person must repent from sins, be saved by divine GRACE through an initial act of converting FAITH, and then be sustained through faith in pursuing the KINGDOM OF GOD by means of a regenerating practice of Christian virtues. This he taught in a series of sermons presented in Hong Kong in 1872 under a title borrowed from JOSEPH BUTLER (1692–1752), "The Fourfold State of Man." Believing that the Christian life should be growing in sanctity under regenerating grace, Legge expected that this striving toward excellence in all realms of cultured life would be the human means by which the divinely intended millennium would be realized.

Once resituated in Oxford, Legge continued his association with Dissenter churches and missionary institutions. In addition to supporting anti-opium lobbying of Parliament and participating actively in seeking British responses to famine relief for Chinese victims, Legge also promoted educational developments reflecting Nonconformist values. He served on committees that created the first WOMEN'S higher-education institution at Oxford, Somerville College, and supported the establishment of a distinguished Dissenter institution there called Mansfield College.

Protestant Scholarship Engaging China's Religions

Legge's greatest missiological and scholarly contributions appeared in his extensive publications related to Ruist and Daoist canonical literature. While working extensively in Chinese original sources and their commentarial traditions, Legge not only addressed relevant sources in European sinological traditions, but also wove theistic and Christian evaluations in generally critical and prudential ways into his translations and interpretations. His initial evaluation of Master Kong ("Confucius," 551–479 B.C.) in 1861 in the *Chinese Classics* was decidedly negative and uncharitable. But in the same year he publicly delighted in the philosophical debates on human nature promoted by Master Meng ("Mencius," c. 372 B.C.–289 B.C.), comparing his doctrines favorably with those of JOSEPH BUTLER. Later he carefully weighed differences between "myths," "legends," "traditions," and justifiable "historical facts" to decipher ancient Ruist historical texts and begin a process of relieving Master Kong from many damaging legendary claims against his character. Although textually a critical exegete, Legge could still admire certain heroic Chinese within Ruist scriptures and their commentators, but was only able to resolve his scholarly and religious criticisms of Master Kong after making pilgrimages in 1873 to the altar of Heaven in Beijing and to the sage's home town.

Always a confirmed Christian advocate, Legge afterward formulated new ways to address religious themes in Ruist traditions, and so after 1877 he became a controversial advocate of an accommodationist missionary approach to that tradition. Once adopting this position after careful considerations, Legge maintained it to the end of his days, emphasizing it in his partially revised evaluation of Master Kong in the *Chinese Classics* of 1893.

In this regard, Legge also reflected on Christian Scriptures and their status as revealed and historical texts, particularly as he related comparative religious study to missiology. In an unpublished lecture of 1884 Legge, having been trained in biblical redaction criticism, still considered the BIBLE to be divinely revealed and inspired, comparing its claims about Jesus the Messiah to be historical rather than mythical, especially in comparison to Ruist, Daoist, and Buddhist claims about their founders.

Legge's scholarly corpus of translations and commentaries of the Ruist canonical literature extends through eight volumes of the *Chinese Classics* and the first four volumes of *Sacred Books of China* (published between 1861 and 1885). In addition to these, Legge produced renderings in classical Daoism (1891) and a few minor Buddhist texts (1886–1888), always adding to them his reflective Nonconformist and critical Scottish realist assessments. His scholarly interest in "Nestorian" Christians who lived in China during the Tang dynasty (seneth to ninth centuries) was also addressed in an annotated translation and accompanied by an interpretive commentary.

The sum of Legge's assessment of Chinese religious traditions was summarily expressed in 1880 in the first university textbook that he published on Chinese religions, but some of its most important arguments were summarized and argued more concisely a few years later in a pamphlet dealing with "the whole duty of man" in Confucianism and Christianity. There he claimed that though there was much that was admirable in Ruist accounts of human morality, there were notably no similarly general claims related to humans' duties to the supreme being, and so the quality of even the human relationships was at times weakened by a lack of divine motives for sustaining and renewing these relationships. Ultimately Legge sensed that Ruist traditions would fail to survive the progressive encroachment of international foreign powers. Though disappointed at the end of his life that millennial hopes had not been realized, Legge remained faithful to his Christian calling. Calling the Chinese sage his "master" in the mid-1880s, Legge held Jesus Christ as his "master and Lord," and so his missiologic aim remained essentially what it was in 1872: to lead Chinese persons to "look away from Confucius to another Teacher."

See also Catholicism, Protestant Reactions; Dissent; Kingdom of God Missionary Organizations; Millenarians and Millennialism; Nonconformity;

References and Further Reading

Primary Sources:

Legge, James. *The Notions of the Chinese Concerning God and Spirits, with an Examination of the Defense of an Essay on the Proper Rendering of the Words Elohim and Theos, into the Chinese Language by William Boone, D. D.* Hong Kong: Hong Kong Register Office, 1852.

————. "The Sacred Books of China." In *The Sacred Books of the East,* Vols. 3, 16, 27–28, and 39–40, edited by F. Max Müller. Oxford, UK: Clarendon Press, 1879–1891.

————. *The Religions of China: Confucianism and Tβoism Described and Compared with Christianity.* London: Hodder and Stoughton, 1880.

————. "Christianity and Confucianism Compared in Their Teaching on the Whole Duty of Man" In *Non-Christian, Religions of the World.* Edited by William Muir, New York: Fleming and Revell, 1884, pp. 3–36.

————. *Christianity in China: Nestorianism, Roman Catholicism, Protestantism.* London: Trübner, 1888.

Secondary Sources:

Girardot, Norman J. *The Victorian Translation of China: James Legge's Oriental Pilgrimage.* Berkeley: University of California Press, 2002.

Legge, George. *Lectures on Theology, Science and Revelation.* Edited by James Legge and John Legge. London: Jackson, Walford and Hodder, 1863.

Pfister, Lauren F. *Striving for "The Whole Duty of Man": James Legge and the Scottish Protestant Encounter with China.* Frankfurt am Main, Germany: Peter Lang, 2003.

————. "The Mengzian Matrix for Accommodationist Missionary Apologetics." *Monumenta Serica* 50 (2002): 1–25.

LAUREN F. PFISTER

LEIBNIZ, GOTTFRIED WILHELM (1646–1716)

German writer and theologian. Gottfried Wilhelm Leibniz was a Lutheran philosopher, mathematician, and theological irenic who spent most of his career in the diplomatic service of the Hannoverian royalty. During his life, Leibniz spearheaded numerous efforts, all ultimately unsuccessful, to secure reunion between Protestants and Roman Catholics, and later between Lutheran and Reformed churches. In addition, Leibniz's philosophical views, popularized through the work of CHRISTIAN WOLFF (1679–1754), were a centerpiece of the German ENLIGHTENMENT of the early eighteenth century.

Leibniz was born into a noble academic family on July 1, 1646 in Leipzig, Germany. His father was professor of moral philosophy at the University of Leipzig, where Leibniz went on to study law and philosophy from 1661 to 1666. He completed his education in 1667, receiving his Doctorate of Law from the University of Altdorf.

After receiving his degree, Leibniz was offered a university post in Altdorf, which he refused in favor of a diplomatic position under the elector of Mainz, Philipp von Schönborn, accepted at the urging of the Schönborn's influential minister, Johann Christian von Boineburg. During this period Leibniz began an active intellectual career, publishing treatises in law, philosophy, the natural sciences, and mathematics. His primary diplomatic mission during the period, however, was to seek ways in which to diminish the unsettling military threat to GERMANY by FRANCE and its king, Louis XIV (1638–1715). To that end he was sent to Paris in 1672 to present a plan to the French king proposing a military conquest of Egypt. Leibniz was not able to present the plan and, after the deaths of Schönborn and Boineburg, returned to Hannover in 1676, where he entered into diplomatic service under Duke Johann Friedrich.

The remainder of Leibniz's career was spent in the service of a succession of Hannoverian rulers, concluding with Elector Georg Ludwig (1660–1727), later King George I of England. Initially hired to serve as the Hannoverian librarian, Leibniz was later commissioned as councilor to the duke, thus assuming oversight for a variety of projects. His primary official task during his years in Hannover was to compile a history of the House of Brunswick for his Hannoverian employers. Despite expending a great deal of effort on the project, Leibniz's efforts yielded only a single volume, much to the frustration of his patrons.

Although he published a number of essays in scholarly journals on a variety of topics, Leibniz published only a single book-length monograph during his life, the *Essais de Theodicée sur la bonté de Dieu, la liberté de l'homme et l'origine du mal* of 1710. In this wide-ranging treatise in philosophical theology, Leibniz responds to the problem of evil by defending the thesis, famously satirized in Voltaire's *Candide,* that this world is the "best of all possible worlds." Leibniz's reasoning for the claim was grounded in his belief in the so-called Principle of Sufficient Reason. According to the principle, every event, including God's creation of the world, has a sufficient reason explaining why it occurs rather than not. When considering God's perfect goodness, Leibniz thought it clear that the only reason for God's choosing to create one world over another was its relative perfection, and thus, the world actually created must be the best of all possible worlds.

Leibniz's philosophical and theological ideas became influential in pre-Kantian Germany primarily by way of the popularizing work of Christian Wolff, professor of mathematics and philosophy at HALLE and Marburg.

Beyond Leibniz's philosophical contributions to the German enlightenment of the eighteenth century, he is widely noted for his irenic attempts at reunion, first between Protestants and Roman Catholics and later between Calvinists and Lutherans. Beginning in he early 1680s, the Hannoverian court assembled a panel including Leibniz, GERHARD MOLANUS, and Frederick Calixt, son of GEORGE CALIXT, to frame a proposal for reunion to present to the chief Roman Catholic reunion representative, Cristobal de Rojas y Spinola.

The key to Protestant reunion for Leibniz, as well as for Rojas and the theologians at Hannover, was finding an agreeable way to set aside the canons of Trent and to submit the disputed questions to a future council composed of clergy from both Protestant and Roman flanks. Leibniz argued that Trent was not properly an ecumenical council, and thus its declarations and any affirmations of it based on its status as an ecumenical council could be set aside.

The Hannoverians believed that such a position might be well received, especially among the French Roman Catholic clergy. Leibniz thus undertook to send a proposal for reunion directly to the influential French bishop Jacques-Bénigne Bossuet (1627–1704), Leibniz's hopes were buoyed when Bossuet responded initially in encouraging terms.

By 1691, however, the plans for reunion were failing. Bossuet had since made it clear that he was not to be moved on the matter of the ecumenicity of Trent. Leibniz realized that such a position was tantamount to bidding "adieu la réunion." With the death of Rojas, in March of 1695, any hopes of reunion were effectively dashed.

Shortly afterwards Leibniz took up in earnest the formidable project of reunion among Protestant sects. He contended that reunion would require three steps: civil unity, ecclesiastical toleration, and finally, unity of theological belief. Leibniz expressed some doubts about the prospect for this third step, noting that doctrinal differences on predestination and the Eucharist seemed to be especially recalcitrant.

Between 1700 and 1705 Leibniz and Daniel Jablonski, Brandenburg Court Chaplain, collaborated on a project that outlined a theological compromise based largely on the Thirty-nine Articles of the Church of England. In June of 1706, however, an unrelated political dispute flared between Hannover and Brandenburg, leading Georg Ludwig to order Leibniz to cease all negotiations on Protestant union.

Although no sustained effort was spent on reunion efforts after this point, Leibniz's mature writing shows a sustained interest in irenic theology. Leibniz died on November 14, 1716.

References and Further Reading

Primary Sources:

Leibniz, Gottfried. *Sämtliche Schriften und Briefe.* Darmstadt: O. Reichl, 1923–. Also: Berlin: Akademie, 1950.
Leibniz, Gottfried. *Philosophical Papers and Letters.* Translated by Leroy Loemker. Dordrecht: D. Reidel, 1976.

Secondary Sources:

Aiton, E. J. *Leibniz: A Biography,* Bristol: Adam Hilger Ltd., 1985.
Broad, C. D. *Leibniz: An Introduction.* London: Cambridge University Press, 1975.
Courdert, Alison, Gordon Weiner, and Richard Popkin, eds. *Leibniz, Mysticism, and Religion.* Dordrecht: Kluwer Academic Publishers, 1998.
Jolly, Nicholas, ed. *The Cambridge Companion to Leibniz,* New York: Cambridge University Press, 1995.
Jordan, G. J. *The Reunion of the Churches.* London: Constable & Company, 1927.
Loemker, Leroy. *Struggle for Synthesis.* Cambridge: Harvard University Press, 1972.

MICHAEL J. MURRAY

LESSING, GOTTHOLD EPHRAIM (1729–1781)

German playwright and author. Lessing was born on January 22, 1729, in Kamenz, Saxony, the eldest surviving son of an orthodox Lutheran pastor, one of the first translators of Tillotson. His mother was daughter of a pastor. Kamenz is near HERRNHUT, the estate of Count NIKOLAUS LUDWIG VON ZINZENDORF who settled the Moravian Brethren there in 1722. Lessing's *Thoughts on the Moravians* (1750, posthumously published in 1784) praised the Pietist wish to take religion out of the head and put it into the heart (see PIETISM).

From 1741 to 1746 he attended the St. Afra boarding school founded by the duke of Saxony in Meissen in 1543. In September 1746 he went to the University of Leipzig to study THEOLOGY, which he soon neglected to devote himself to the theatrer. At Leipzig, he published his first poems and stories (1747). In 1748 he transferred to medicine, but abandoned that to go to Berlin, resolved to live by his pen. He completed his Master's degree at Wittenberg in 1752, in preparation for which he worked on his *Rettungen* (1753–1754), vindications of thinkers whose writings had been condemned as heterodox. Subjects included the natural scientist Hieronymus Cardanus (1501–1576), accused of atheism for comparing Christianity with Islam and Judaism; [of an *Ineptus Religiosus* (1652),] whose book contained the famous sentence, "Read the Bible just as you read Livy"; and Johannes Cochlaeus (1479–1552), the strongest and most prolific Roman Catholic critic of MARTIN LUTHER, concerning what

Lessing ironically called the "small matter" of indulgences. Later he published other vindications: Berengar of Tours' lost reply to Lanfranc on the LORD'S SUPPER (1770), which to his amusement was welcomed by orthodox Lutherans; a defense of GOTTFRIED LEIBNIZ on eternal punishment (1773); and a work on Adam Neusner, a Unitarian who fled to Constantinople to escape persecution and became a Muslim (1774). In 1756 Lessing translated *A System of Moral Philosophy* (1755) by Francis Hutcheson (1694–1746), which extolled the moral sense, and *A Serious Call to a Devout and Holy Life* (1728) by William Law (1686–1761).

Lessing wrote four great plays: *Miss Sara Sampson* (1755), the first German domestic tragedy; *Minna von Barnholm* (1767), the first truly modern German comedy; *Emilia Galotti* (1772); and *Nathan the Wise* (1779). He wrote a book on aesthetics, *Laocoon, An Essay on the Limits of Painting and Poetry* (1766), and theater criticism, *Hamburgische Dramaturgie* (1767–1768).

In December 1769 Lessing was appointed librarian of the duke of Brunswick's huge library at Wolfenbüttel, with permission to publish without censorship. In 1771 he became a freemason and was engaged to marry Eva Kšnig, widow of an old friend from his Hamburg days, but he could not afford to marry her until 1776. Thereafter followed a blissfully happy year, but on December 25, 1777 their son was born and died some hours later, and Eva herself died in January 1778.

In 1774 Lessing had published the first *Fragment of an Unknown*, which he pretended to have found in manuscript in the library but which was really part of a large *Apology or Defense for Rational Worshippers of God* by HERMANN SAMUEL REIMARUS (1694–1768), professor of oriental languages in the Hamburg Academic Gymnasium. The manuscript had been entrusted to Lessing by Reimarus's daughter Elise. The first installment from the manuscript, or fragment, "The Toleration of Deists," passed without comment.

In 1777, during the happiest year of his life, he published five further extracts ("On the Decrying of Reason from the Pulpit"; "On the Impossibility of a Revelation which all Men can Believe in a Well-Founded Way"; "The Passage of the Israelites through the Red Sea"; "That the Books of the Old Testament were not written to Reveal a Religion"; "On the Resurrection Narrative"). To these Lessing appended the counter-theses of the editor (including paragraphs 1–53 of *The Education of the Human Race* [1780] as though the work of someone else). Lessing argued that the fragments might embarrass the theologian, by knocking down the arguments with which he thought to buttress Christianity, but not the Christian. For

Christians their religion is simply *there*: the paralytic does not care whose theory about the electric spark that cured him was correct. Objections to literal details and to the BIBLE were not objections to the spirit and to religion. Lessing warned against Bibliolatry (a term he found in English). He claimed to be following Luther's spirit if not Luther's writings. Revealed religion contained all the truths taught by reason, but supported them with different argumentation.

The orthodox reaction to the publication of the fragments was fierce. Lessing answered these attacks with a series of pamphlets: *On the Proof of the Spirit and of Power,* with an appendix *The Testament of John,* a dialogue in which the anonymous author of the main pamphlet asks an objecto, ". . . which of the two is the more difficult? To accept and confess the Christian dogmas, or to practice Christian love?"; *A Rejoinder* to a defense of the resurrection story; and, in reply to Johann Melchior Goeze (1717–1786), a large number of pamphlets beginning with *A Parable,* followed by *Axioms, If There Are Any in Such Matters,* which provoked a reply from Goeze, who challenged Lessing to explain what the Christian religion would be if the Bible were lost. Lessing answered in *G. E. Lessing's Necessary Answer to a very Unnecessary Question of Herr Hauptpastor Goeze in Hamburg,* stating that the Christian religion was contained in the creeds of the first four centuries.

In 1778 Lessing published the longest fragment from Reimarus, "On the Intentions of Jesus and his Disciples," sharply distinguishing between the intentions of Jesus and those of the disciples. In July of that year the duke of Brunswick intervened to rule that Lessing would now have to submit his writings on religion to the censor, and in November 1780 Lessing was arraigned by an ecclesiastical court for publishing this pamphlet. Lessing turned back to the theater. In *Nathan the Wise* (1779) he pleaded for tolerance of all religions, provided they show love to all. He drew on his friend Moses Mendelssohn (1729–1786), whom he first met in 1753, for his portrait of Nathan, the Jew. This play initiated Germans into the world of theater for over a century.

Lessing made a contribution to the study of the Gospels in *New Hypothesis concerning the Evangelists regarded as merely human Historians* (1778, published posthumously). The first Christians, law-observant Jews, collected narratives of Jesus written in Hebrew or Aramaic. Matthew extracted material from this collection and translated it into Greek; Luke made his own arrangement of order and translated it into Greek; and Mark drew on a less complete copy. John had to write his Gospel to prevent Christianity from dying away as a mere Jewish sect; he alone showed the Godhead of Jesus and gave Christianity its true consistency so that it would survive "as long as there are men who think they need a mediator between themselves and the Deity; that is, for ever" (para. 63).

The Education of the Human Race (1777; published in 1780, the year before his death) proved to be immensely popular among educated Germans, enabling the Protestant churches to retain the nominal loyalty of a high proportion of the population. The author (whom Lessing introduces as though he were another than himself) "has set himself upon a high eminence from which he believes it possible to see beyond the allotted path of his present day's journey." God (i.e., Nature, para. 84) has used revelation (as well as reason) to bring humanity from the age of the Old Testament, which taught the unity of God, to the age of the New Testament, in which Christ taught the immortality of the soul, to the age of the new eternal gospel, in which right will be done because it is right, not because of any reward. The doctrines of the Trinity (cf. *The Christianity of Reason* [1752–1753, published 1784]), of Original Sin, and of the Son's satisfaction could be given a rational reading. Finally, why should not every individual have been present more than once in this world? Dubious historical facts of alleged revelation have led to reasonable truth sooner than the necessary truths would otherwise have come to be understood. The ugly broad ditch, not to be leapt over by reason, from accidental truths of history to necessary truths of reason (*On the Proof of the Spirit and of Power,* written the same year), was bridged by the process of history in this best of worlds (Leibniz).

In 1785 F. H. Jacobi claimed that when he showed Lessing JOHANN WOLFGANG VON GOETHE's unpublished fragmentary drama *Prometheus,* less than a year before Lessing's death, Lessing said he concurred with Goethe's view as a result of his own reading of Spinoza: it was not possible to believe in the creator-God, for the Deity is One and All. Humans have no need of free will. Jacobi's book led to a lively argument in which Moses Mendelssohn defended Lessing against the charge of Spinozism.

Lessing died on February 15, 1781 in Brunswick. He influenced SAMUEL TAYLOR COLERIDGE, FERDINAND CHRISTIAN BAUR, DAVID FRIEDRICH STRAUSS, and SØREN KIERKEGAARD.

References and Further Reading

Primary Sources:

Chadwick, Henry. *Lessing's Theological Writings: Selections in Translation with an Introductory Essay.* A Library of Modern Religious Thought. London: Adam & Charles Black, 1956.
Trillhaas, Wolfgang. "Zur Wirkungsgeschichte Lessings in der evangelischen Theologie," Germany In *Das Bild Lessings in der Geschichte,* edited by Herbert G. Göpfert, 57–67. Heidelberg, Germany: Lambert Schneider, 1981.

Secondary Source:

Fick, Monika. *Lessing-Handbuch: Leben–Werk–Wirkung.* Stuttgart/Weimar, Germany: J. B. Metzler, 2000.

J. C. O'NEILL

LEUENBERG

See Ecumenical Agreements

LEVELLERS

In the heat of CIVIL WAR in ENGLAND and the destabilization that accompanied it, the Levellers emerged in the years 1644 to 1649 as one of the most conspicuous and noisy "left-wing" popular movements. (The derogatory label, apparently, was first coined by Charles I.) A great deal of their history is elusive—there are no membership lists of Leveller groups—although much is clear. Not exclusively plebeian—they had supporters higher up the social scale and their rank and file, it seems, was swelled with disgruntled, cast-off younger sons of the gentry—and not the most extreme of the radical wings of the 1640s, the Levellers drew their following primarily from London and the New Model Army. As references in their publications to trades and other occupations make clear, Levellers were chiefly an urban phenomenon. Leveller leaders like John Lilbourne (1614–1657), Richard Overton (1642–1663), and William Walwyn (1600–1680) wrote prolifically about the inequalities of wealth, about the sovereignty of the people, about the reform of Parliament and parliamentary representation, the extension of the franchise, about the need for regular elections that would increase the dependency of members of parliament on the electorate, about reform of the legal system and the CHURCH, about free trade, and about religious TOLERATION. Trenchant Leveller voices were plainly heard in the famous Putney Debates of 1647 when army officers and ordinary soldiers came together to air their views on England's post–Civil War future. Leveller publications like *The Case of the Armie Truly Stated* and *An Agreement of the People* offered popular rallying cries. For a time they had their own "newspaper." Levellers, in short, had a propaganda machine at their disposal.

OLIVER CROMWELL and other army leaders who had led these men into battle and admired their spirit and bravery for a time, found Levellers politically useful as a battering ram against both King Charles I and Parliament. Yet in truth Levellers were never as influential as they seemed. They were easily sidelined in the swiftly changing events of early 1649, when the king was put through a brisk public trial and then speedily brought to execution. Desperate but small-scale Leveller mutinies in London, Wiltshire, and Oxfordshire were, with no great effort, suppressed and the ringleaders put to death. (Burford church in Oxford was the most famous setting of Leveller defeat.) However, there were relatively few martyrs and that fact perhaps in itself is an index of their real weakness: a few executions were enough. Cromwell carried the day. Lilburne, Overton, and Walwyn were arrested and imprisoned but released after taking an oath of loyalty to the republic.

By the end of 1649 Levellers had clearly been overcome and although memories of their brief-lived successes of the previous few years may have provided models for the deployment of mass propaganda and mass movements after the Restoration, they soon went into eclipse. With isolated exceptions, they had to wait until the twentieth century to be rediscovered and widely celebrated by liberals and Marxists, the English and Americans, alike. Hailed as democrats ahead of their time, farsighted progressives, the first real socialists in England, protagonists of universal suffrage, Levellers and their leaders were emphatically rehabilitated, although such plaudits frequently went over the top. Levellers were indeed "democrats" but they believed firmly in a property-owning, not total, democracy in which the rights of small property owners were upheld against the oppressive claims of the rich and powerful. Those who had a *dependent* status—laborers, servants, apprentices, beggars, and all WOMEN (together constituting a numerical majority of the population of the day)—were pointedly excluded from the Leveller franchise. Moreover, Levellers held back from interfering with the rights attached to private property. Diggers, not Levellers, were the proto-communists of mid-seventeenth-century England.

Leveller politics—their manifestos, the tracts of their leaders, their contributions to the Putney Debates—have almost always tended to occupy center stage in discussions of the movement. Yet in a period in which politics and religion were inseparable, Leveller insistence on equity and equality clearly took shape within a Christian/Protestant framework. The historian Christopher Hill indeed has connected the Levellers with a trajectory of underground ideas going back to the Lollards of the fifteenth century (Hill 1979:49–66). Religious liberty and political liberty for them went hand in hand. For Levellers the BIBLE, which spoke freely and directly to all people, provided overarching truths on all things. Leveller religion was a kind of "ARMINIANISM of the left," which rejected the exclusivity of Calvinist DOCTRINE in favor of the encouraging belief in the universalism of God's GRACE,

demonstrated by believers in genuine social concern and good works. It helped underpin their convictions about the "natural rights" of humankind. What good was religion if it meant no more than formal observance, pious utterances, psalm singing, private prayer, listening to sermons, and keeping the Sabbath? "Pure and undefiled religion," declared Walwyn—and he spoke for many Levellers—meant "feeding the hungry, clothing the naked, visiting and comforting the sick, relieving the aged, weak and impotent [and] freeing a commonwealth from all tyrants, oppressors and deceivers" (McMichael and Taft 1989:80, 269, 324). For Levellers, many of the clergy were included among these entrenched "obstacles" to social justice. The very titles of Walwyn's writings are eloquent expressions of his practical Christianity—"The Power of Love" (1643), "The Compassionate Samaritane" (1644), "Toleration Justified and Persecution Condemned" (1645/6), and "A Still and Soft Voice from the Scriptures" (1647). Christopher Chisman or Cheeseman, a Leveller soldier and later Quaker, echoed Walwyn and went even further in his claims for the necessity of "practical Christianity."

> The religion of the great ones of our age is a mere shadow, and all their pulpit-prattling is nothing; they are only wolves in sheep's clothing; they are devils transformed into angels of light. But pure religion and undefiled is to visit the fatherless and widows, and to keep ourselves unspotted in the world, which the great professors of our time will not I am sure; for they add house to house, land to land, nay thousands to thousands, while the poor of the kingdom are ready to starve. (Chisman, *The Lamb Contending with the Lion,* 1649)

Such fundamental convictions underlay all that Levellers said and strove for in politics and for which they have become chiefly famous. For them reformed politics was the natural outcome of true religion. They had fought valiantly in the Civil Wars in the New Model Army—"God's Army," no less—to bring about both. Their experience of defeat after 1649 was thus all the more poignant.

See also Communism; Socialism, Christian

References and Further Reading

Primary Sources:

Aylmer, G. E., ed. *The Levellers in the English Revolution.* London: Thames & Hudson, 1975.

Haller, W., and G. Davies, eds. *The Leveller Tracts 1647–1653.* New York: Columbia University Press, 1944.

McMichael, J. R., and Barbara Taft, eds. *The Writings of William Walwyn.* Athens, GA: University of Georgia Press, 1989.

Wolfe, D. M., ed. *Leveller Manifestos of the Puritan Revolution.* New York: Columbia University Press, 1944.

Woodhouse, A. S. P., ed. *Puritanism and Liberty. Being the Army Debates, 1647–1649.* London: J. M. Dent, 1938.

Secondary Sources:

Brailsford, H. N. *The Levellers in the English Revolution.* London: The Cresset Press, 1961.

Gregg, Pauline. *Freeborn John. A Biography of John Lilburne.* London: Harrap, 1961.

Davis, J. C. "The Levellers and Christianity." In *Politics, Religion and the English Civil War,* edited by B. Manning, 125–160. London: E. Arnold, 1973.

Hill, C. *The World Turned Upside Down. Radical Ideas in the English Revolution.* London: MT Smith, 1972.

———. "From Lollards to Levellers." In *Rebels and Their Causes. Essays in Honour of A. L. Morton,* edited by M. Cornforth. London: Lawrence & W., 1979.

Lindley, K. *Popular Politics and Religion in Civil War London.* Aldershot, UK: Scolar Press, 1997.

Manning, B. "The Levellers and Religion." In *Radical Religion in the English Revolution,* edited by J. F. McGregor and B. Reay, 65–90. Oxford: Oxford University Press, 1984.

Mendle, M., ed. *The Putney Debates of 1647. The Army, The Levellers and the English State.* Cambridge: Cambridge University Press, 2001.

Robertson, D. B. *The Religious Foundations of Leveller Democracy.* New York: King's Crown Press, 1951.

R. C. RICHARDSON

LEWIS, C. S. (1898–1963)

A literary and cultural historian, theorist, and critic, a poet and novelist, a moral philosopher, and a Christian apologist, Clive Staples "Jack" Lewis is widely esteemed, especially among Protestants in the United States, for combining academic stature with an ability both to communicate to a wide and diverse audience and to advocate a Christian worldview in opposition to prevailing secular alternatives.

Lewis promoted continuities between post- and pre-war cultures, unlike many Protestant theologians writing after the First and Second World Wars, and he posited continuities between poets and critics and their social and cultural contexts, unlike many of his literary contemporaries. Lewis's principal achievement lay in bridging the gaps between his own culture and the past, between academic and popular cultures, between scholarly and creative writing, and between intellectual rigor and religious belief. He countered the negative mood of his own culture and of prevailing Protestant theologies by redeploying a Romantic interest in the reenchantment of the world, by advocating childlike attitudes as antidotes to contemporary despair, and by restoring joy, pleasure, and celebration as integral parts of a Christian worldview. His principal philosophical point concerned the relational character of human living, from which he argued for the continuity between subjective and objective aspects of human experience and the formation of cultural and religious identity primarily in and through relationships.

Born in Belfast, IRELAND, Lewis received his early education mostly in ENGLAND. He saw action in FRANCE during WORLD WAR I and then returned to University College, Oxford, to complete his education in philosophy, history, and English. He became a fellow and tutor of English at Magdalen College in 1925 and continued in that position until he moved to Magdelene College, Cambridge, in 1955 as professor of medieval and renaissance literature. He lived from 1930 until his death in Headington Quarry outside Oxford with his older brother Warren (d. 1973) and, first, with Mrs. Janie Moore (d. 1951) and then with Joy Davidman (d. 1960), whom he married in 1956.

Cultural Critique

As a cultural critic, Lewis addressed three dominant characteristics of MODERNITY. He argued that the cultural sense of a break with the past was caused not primarily, as many believed, by urbanization and war but by the increasing dependency of society on machines. Beginning in the early nineteenth century, he maintained, advances in technology, by which earlier machines are superseded, were shaping the culture's general attitude toward the past. He further argued that the disenchantment of the world was caused not so much by rationality, as many of his contemporaries believed, as by a shift in AUTHORITY from the external world to individual consciousness. Moreover, he argued that the pervasive feeling of alienation in modern literature and culture was created not by social and economic conditions but by the assumption of discontinuity between the mind and reality, values and facts, and individuals and society.

Lewis viewed bureaucracy as epitomizing the abstraction, depersonalization, and self-preoccupation that plague modern culture, and he viewed obsession with individuality (see INDIVIDUALISM) in the culture as a reaction to the pervasive force of bureaucracy in modern society. Bureaucracy, for example, provides the power structure of Hell (see HEAVEN AND HELL) in his *The Screwtape Letters* (1942) and shapes the political and academic authority in his dystopic narrative of England's future, *That Hideous Strength* (1945). In contrast to the reduction and homogenization of human relationships characteristic of bureaucracy, Lewis advocated the fulfillment of individual potential within a common culture that relates the present to the past and carries moral directives for the future.

Beginning with his return to Christianity in 1929, which he narrates in his autobiography *Surprised by Joy* (1955), Lewis articulated in poems, essays, novels, books, and radio broadcasts his belief that Christianity offers an account of the world that is more complex, capacious, and humanly satisfying than that offered by its primary secular rivals, materialism and narcissism. In such books as *The Abolition of Man* (1943), *Mere Christianity* (1952), and *The Four Loves* (1960), Lewis argued that religious worldviews in general and Christianity in particular meet the needs and desires of human life and actualize its potentials as secular alternatives do not. In *The Problem of Pain* (1940) and *Miracles* (1947), Lewis addressed the two principal modern objections to Christianity, its inability to answer the problem of human suffering (see EVIL) and its reliance on miracles.

Along with his standing as a religious advocate and Christian apologist, Lewis secured academic stature with work in medieval studies, such as *The Allegory of Love* (1936), in Renaissance studies, such as *English Literature in the Sixteenth Century Excluding Drama* (1954), and in cultural and literary criticism and theory with numerous essays, such as *An Experiment in Criticism* (1961). In addition, Lewis achieved popular acclaim in the early 1940s with the publication of *The Screwtape Letters* and the radio broadcasts that, during the early years of the Second World War, recalled English people to Christian belief. This popular standing was extended during the next decade by the success of his novels for children, the Narnia Chronicles, a set of seven separable but related narratives about an alternative world to which visitors from England, particularly children, are called to help in times of difficulty. The Chronicles narrate Narnia's history from its creation in *The Magician's Nephew* (1955) to its destruction in *The Last Battle* (1956). The novels, especially *The Lion, the Witch and the Wardrobe* (1950), the first in the series, include figures such as Aslon the Lion as well as events that are similar to those basic to the Christian story. Lewis also gained popular recognition by the BBC production in 1985 of *Shadowlands,* a play based primarily on the relationship of Lewis with Joy Davidman and starring Joss Ackland and Claire Bloom. After its successful run as a stage play in New York City, *Shadowlands,* in an altered version, became a major Hollywood production in 1993 starring Debra Winger and Anthony Hopkins.

References and Further Reading

Hooper, Walter. *C. S. Lewis: A Companion and Guide.* London: Harper Collins, 1996.

Kort, Wesley A. *C. S. Lewis Then and Now.* New York: Oxford University Press, 2000.

Sayer, George. *Jack: C. S. Lewis and His Times.* San Francisco, CA: Harper & Row, 1988.

WESLEY A. KORT

LEWIS, SIR SAMUEL (1843–1903)

West African statesman. Sir Samuel Lewis is best known for being the first West African to be knighted by the British Crown (1896). He was born on November 13, 1843, in Freetown, the capital city of the British colony of SIERRA LEONE, and grew up in the second generation under British rule. His upbringing was a successful fusion of native Aku virtues such as loyalty, persistence, and obedience to group hierarchy with Wesleyan METHODISM. Lewis studied law in London, and was the third native Sierra Leonean to become a barrister. He quickly acquired a reputation for fairness and objectivity, successfully arguing for the defense or prosecuting as Queen's advocate, as duty and conscience demanded.

Although reluctant to work for the Colonial Government, Lewis joined the Legislative Council in 1882. He supported the annexation of the interior of Sierra Leone, with the intention of spreading the Wesleyan Mission of civilization, SALVATION, and economic self-sufficiency to the unconverted and often economically exploited tribes. His already impressive reputation was enhanced when ENGLAND established the Protectorate from 1890 to 1896, which accomplished exactly what Lewis had envisioned. Following the dictates of his conscience he fought for the elimination of state subsidies for the Wesleyan and Anglican churches in 1892, on the grounds that it was unfair not only to other denominations, but also to the Protectorate's 26,000 pagans, and 9,000 Muslims.

For his unceasing public service and unquestionable integrity, Sir Samuel Lewis was knighted in 1896, and was the first West African Knight in Her Majesty's Empire. He was elected mayor of Freetown in both 1895 and 1899. By 1900 ventures into coffee and kola farming had failed, forcing Lewis to return to the practice of law, where he took on many unpaid cases for the Wesleyan community. In 1901 he was diagnosed with cancer, but financial concerns kept him working until 1902. He sailed to London for surgery, but died on July 9, 1903.

See also Africa; Wesleyanism

References and Further Reading

Hargreaves, J. D. *A Life of Sir Samuel Lewis.* London: Oxford University Press, 1958.

Kabba, Muctaru R. A., ed. consultant. *Sierra Leonean Heroes: Fifty Men and Women Who Helped to Build Our Nation.* 1988. Commissioned by the Sierra Leone government. http://www.sierra-leone.org/heroes3.html (Accessed April 29, 2003).

MARK C. DONAHUE

LIANG A-FA (LIANG FA, LEANG A-FA) (1789–1855)

Chinese churchman. Liang was born Gao He, in the region of Canton (Guangdong), and died in Canton. He came from a farming family and had four years of Confucian schooling. Poverty forced him to give up his education and move to Canton in 1804, where urban vices overcame him and he became a confirmed gambler. His work was cutting the wooden blocks for printing Chinese characters, and he was employed to cut those for the translation of the New Testament prepared by Robert Morrison. Impressed by his work, Morrison invited Liang to be the Chinese printer for the mission press in Malacca, where Christian literature was produced for distribution in CHINA at a time when missionaries could not normally operate there. Liang began work in Malacca in 1815.

Distressed at his moral impotence and decline from the Confucian moral teaching of his youth, Liang sought a remedy in Pure Land Buddhist practice, but in vain. Further study of the Chinese New Testament gradually convinced him of the truth of the evangelical message he was hearing from William Milne, who headed the Malacca mission. In 1816, Liang was baptized. Three years later, he visited his family in China and prepared a tract to explain Christian faith to them and their neighbors. He was arrested, imprisoned, and beaten, and the copies of his tract and the printing blocks were destroyed. After his release, Liang returned to Malacca eager to prepare himself for PREACHING, leaving for China again after Milne's death.

After further study with Morrison, Liang was ordained in 1823, becoming the first Chinese Protestant pastor. For more than thirty years he served as evangelist and pastor in Canton, Macao, Singapore, and Hong Kong. He was also a prolific writer; more than 20 books and tracts of his are listed, including a commentary on the Epistle to the Hebrews, a paraphrase of the letter to the Romans, and an exposition of the Ten Commandments. His long tract with a title usually translated as "Good Words to Admonish the Age" was particularly influential, not least in introducing the leaders of the Taiping Movement to Christian teaching. The tract demonstrates that Liang never abandoned the Confucian moral teaching he imbibed in youth. For him, Christian faith, with its teaching of one fatherly God, divine Savior, and active Holy Spirit, provided a framework that made Confucian ideals attainable.

See also Asian Theology; Bible Translation; Missions

References and Further Reading

Bohr, P. R. "Liang Fa's Quest for Moral Power." In *Christianity in China: Early Protestant Missionary Writings*, edited by S. W. Barnett and J. K. Fairbank, 35–46. Cambridge, MA: Harvard University Press, 1985.

Lovett, R. *History of the London Missionary Society*, Vol. 2. London: Oxford University Press, 1899.

McNeur, G. H. *China's First Preacher. Liang A-Fa 1989–1855*. Shanghai: Kwang Hsueh Publishing House, 1934.

Milne, William. *Retrospect of the First Ten Years of the Protestant Mission to China*. Malacca: Anglo-Chinese Press, 1820.

Spence, Jonathan. *God's Chinese Son: The Taiping Heavenly Kingdom of Hong Xiuquan*, New York: Norton, 1996.

Wylie, Alexander. *Memorials of Protestant Missionaries to the Chinese, Shanghai 1867*. Taipei: Ch'eng-wen Publishing, 1967 (lists Liang's publications, probably incompletely).

ANDREW F. WALLS

LIBERAL PROTESTANTISM

"Liberal Protestantism" is a notoriously vague and loose designation for a broad range of Protestant Christian thought unified less by specific theological claims or doctrines than by a shared liberal approach to certain common themes that arose within Christian theology during the modern period (see MODERNISM). This shared spirit of liberalism is characterized by (1) an open-mindedness toward and respect for new modes of thought in human and natural science; (2) a confidence in the power of human reason guided by experience; (3) a radical emphasis both on freedom from traditional dogmas and creedal formulations and on toleration of doctrinal differences; (4) an ethical optimism and social idealism grounded in the benevolence of God and the social nature of human existence; and, finally, (5) a search, amid the ever-changing cultural and historical context, for the abiding essence of Christianity based in the life, teachings, and person of Jesus Christ.

Liberal Protestantism had its beginnings in the late eighteenth and early nineteenth century in the thought of IMMANUEL KANT (1724–1804) and FRIEDRICH SCHLEIERMACHER (1768–1834) but reached its fullest expression in the theologies of ALBRECHT RITSCHL (1822–1889), ADOLF VON HARNACK (1851–1930), and ERNST TROELTSCH (1865–1923), and the SOCIAL GOSPEL movement exemplified by WALTER RAUSCHENBUSCH (1861–1918) in the United States. It continued to have significant influence within German, French, English, and American THEOLOGY until it went into decline during the decades immediately preceding the Second World War. Its eclipse was largely attributed to criticisms brought by KARL BARTH (1886–1968) and REINHOLD NIEBUHR (1892–1971) among others that it was too accommodating to modern CULTURE, too optimistic in its view of human nature and social progress, and too reductive in its account of the essence of Christianity. Although its enduring legacy remains a topic of considerable debate, especially in regard to its relationship with the REFORMATION, it continues to influence any contemporary theological movement that is interested in bringing the Christian faith critically into some degree of reconciliation with contemporary thought and culture.

Historical Development

Liberal Protestantism finds its roots in the critical philosophy of Kant and the systematic theological response to Kant by Schleiermacher. Kant's attack on classical metaphysics called into question the validity of much of the natural theology tradition, not only of the premodern period but also of the eighteenth-century ENLIGHTENMENT. Traditional arguments for the existence of God, for knowledge of the nature of God's being or human immortality, and so forth, claimed—according to Kant—a knowledge of reality that was not sustainable under criticism, and thus for theology to have meaning, theologians must look for alternative ways of grounding theological claims than in traditional metaphysics. Kant proposed such a grounding in moral or what he called "practical" reason wherein claims for the existence of God and immortality functioned as the necessary postulates for ethics.

Schleiermacher, generally acknowledged as the father of Liberal Protestantism, took up Kant's theological challenge. Yet while agreeing with Kant's critique of speculative natural theology, Schleiermacher nevertheless sought to ground theological claims elsewhere—in what he called the "religious self-consciousness." The essence of Christian piety, he argued, consists in particular religious affections based on humanity's awareness of its absolute dependency on God, the "Whence" of its original and continuing existence. Theological statements thus are read off these affections and represent their verbal, conceptual, and didactic articulation. This reorientation of theology's ground of meaningfulness from traditional metaphysics to an account of human consciousness allowed Schleiermacher to reinterpret his inherited Reformation faith in ways that both maintained continuity with the theological claims of the Reformation (e.g., an emphasis on the sovereignty of God and redemption in Christ) and yet allowed him to radically transform certain of these claims in light of his modern context (e.g., a social rather than biological conception of original sin and an understanding of the divinity of Christ as constituted not by a divine nature *per se* but by Christ's perfect God-consciousness).

Ritschl, although critical of Schleiermacher at points, maintained Schleiermacher's quest for the essence of Christianity and thereby established the basic outlines of Liberal Protestantism as it flourished from the 1860s to 1918 with the conclusion of World War I. Following Kant, Ritschl argued that Christian theology should be freed from all metaphysical speculation and should rather be understood as an attempt to express judgments of value, especially of the saving significance of Jesus of Nazareth. As the archetypal human, Jesus, although threatened by hostile adversaries, trusted absolutely in God's love and power, and in so doing revealed to humanity through his moral perfection humanity's proper response to God. Through following Jesus' example, modern humans can overcome the threat of social and natural evolution, increased INDUSTRIALIZATION and SECULARIZATION, and impersonal, mechanistic NATURE by recognizing the infinite value or worth imparted to humanity by God through Jesus. Collectively those who follow Jesus constitute the KINGDOM OF GOD whose task is progressively to redeem and transform ethically the culture and society in which they exist.

Post-Ritschlian liberalism was thus characterized by an emphasis on the supreme moral and religious example of Jesus, the essential goodness or worth of humanity, and its seemingly infinite capabilities of growth in reason and freedom. This characterization amounted to what Harnack famously summarized in his *Das Wesendes Christentums (What Is Christianity?)* as the essence of Christianity: "firstly, the Kingdom of God and its coming; secondly, God the Father and the infinite value of the human soul; thirdly, the higher righteousness and the commandment of love." With this essence, moreover, came the duty of doing something to correct those conditions—whether through ignorance or social injustice—that stultified the full actualization of the Kingdom of God, of those capacities in humans that promoted human flourishing. For example, in the UNITED STATES, the religious education movement, strongly influenced by the philosophical liberalism and pragmatism of John Dewey, was an expression of the interaction of Liberal Protestantism with the growing religious ignorance of modern culture. Moreover, the Social Gospel movement became the most characteristic expression of Liberal Protestantism in North American Christianity. Its primary leader, Rauschenbusch, developed concepts of social SIN and social SALVATION, harking back to Schleiermacher, in rejection of the late-nineteenth-century tendencies toward INDIVIDUALISM at the expense of community and quietism in the place of social transformation. Thus a movement that was born out of modern challenges to old ways of thinking theologically reached its zenith in the quest to transform that very modern culture into the Kingdom of God.

Before turning to a discussion of the overarching characteristics of Liberal Protestantism, it is important to note a deep and important irony in its historical development. For although Liberal Protestantism came into its own during the late nineteenth century, few theologians during that time actually claimed to be "liberal." In fact, according to Hans-Joachim Birkner, the term "liberalism" was an ideological construct of the antiliberal theologians of the 1920s, who needed a clear picture of the trends in theology over the last century, so that they could put an end to liberalism's growth and perpetuation (Birkner 1976: 33f.). For example, such leading exponents of Liberal Protestantism as ALBRECHT RITSCHL, along with his students Wilhelm Herrmann (1846–1922) and Julius Kaftan (1848–1926), claimed to be thoroughly orthodox and sought not to reduce Christianity to whatever an increasingly secular age could accept, but to maintain Christian truth in its integrity, as testified to by nearly four centuries of Protestant faith and piety. Thus, for Ritschl and his followers, the Reformation's fundamental assertion of the right of the individual believer to judge religious truth for him- or herself under no external AUTHORITY but the Spirit's guidance was something that could never be wholly expunged by the unfortunate biblicism and dogmatism to which Reformation theology itself had succumbed, or so they argued, during the period of Protestant ORTHODOXY in the sixteenth and seventeenth centuries. In a sense, then, these "liberal" Protestant theologians understood themselves to be attempting both to regain the true spirit of the Reformation that had been muted by subsequent developments and to continue that spirit in a modern world quite different from its original, early-sixteenth-century context. Certainly, as they readily acknowledged, there were many differences between the Reformation and Liberal Protestantism—for example, the original Reformers often disparaged "natural" reason in light of their adherence to "scripture alone" and at times supported religious authoritarianism despite their initial resistance to Roman authority. Nevertheless, for theologians like Ritschl, the principle that the believer's own inward experience is a final criterion of FAITH provided the bridge of continuity (and not discontinuity) between the Reformation and Liberal Protestantism.

General Characteristics

Despite its theologically and culturally diverse historical development, Liberal Protestantism can be accurately described as exhibiting the following general characteristics.

1. Openness to New Modes of Thought

Liberal Protestantism maintained the organic unity of truth and thus pursued it wherever it was found. There could be no discontinuity between the truths of SCIENCE or the humanities, on the one hand, and the truth of Christianity, on the other. For example, as HIGHER CRITICISM emerged within the late eighteenth and early nineteenth centuries, Liberal Protestantism embraced its application to the BIBLE so that biblical narratives might be interpreted within the historical context in which they originated. Thus critics such as Schleiermacher's student DAVID FRIEDRICH STRAUSS (1808–1874) in his famous *Life of Jesus* applied such higher criticism to the gospel narratives to separate out the historical or "natural facts" of the stories of Jesus from the nonhistorical, "mythical" material, which represented for him early church interpretations of Jesus' life and significance (see JESUS, LIVES OF). By the early twentieth century, the History of Religions School (*religionsgeschichtliche Schule*) emerged as yet another example of the way in which Liberal Protestants used the disciplines of history and the emerging social sciences to reconstruct the development of Christianity within the plurality of religions. Various strands of JUDAISM and Christianity were revealed in the biblical narratives and in subsequent religious history, so they claimed, and this pluralism of traditions indicated the radical degree to which Christianity was only one religion among others. Thus Troeltsch, one of the most articulate History of Religions critics, went so far as to entertain the possibility that Christianity might be superseded, as it had done to Judaism, by a higher form of religion.

2. Reason and Experience

Liberal Protestants held that Christianity, to speak to the modern world, must be willing to discard old orthodox forms if they were judged to be irrational in the light of modern knowledge or irrelevant to what was regarded as the central core of religious experience. Following the lead of Kant, Liberal Protestants were generally careful to acknowledge the limits to achieving certain knowledge of ultimate reality, yet this epistemic tentativeness was also accompanied by a strong suspicion of dogmatic theological formulations that did not also acknowledge their own tentative status. Moreover to the minds of most Liberal Protestant theologians, their criticisms of received orthodoxy were not only held to be more responsive to the needs of the present time but also more in keeping with the original spirit of the Reformation. The Reformer's insistence on the experiential roots of theological reflection (e.g., in John Calvin's dictum, "We shall not say that, properly speaking, God is known where there is no religion or piety" or Luther's *sola experientia facit theologum,* which stands alongside and informs his *sola scriptura*) was crucial for making theological claims living convictions, born of experience, rather than dogmas received on the basis of some external authority. In this respect, Liberal Protestantism acknowledged its debt to seventeenth- and eighteenth-century PIETISM.

3. Freedom and Toleration

Perhaps one of the most fundamental characteristics of Liberal Protestantism was its insistence on freedom from all external authority in matters of thought, conscience, and religion. This freedom was grounded in the Reformation's claim to a universal priesthood (see PRIESTHOOD OF ALL BELIEVERS) and to the ever-reforming nature of the church. Thus the Roman Catholic sense of infallible and unchanging dogma was replaced by a more fluid, Protestant sense of DOCTRINE, and this in turn contributed to a general sense of tolerance of doctrinal difference that pervaded Liberal Protestantism throughout its history (see TOLERATION). Moreover this tolerance tended to minimize within Liberal Protestantism the relative importance of denominational difference from what it had been for the sixteenth-century Reformation. For most liberals, denominational differences were important for locating one's perspective in one's history but were no longer grounds for mutual recrimination and lack of cooperation. In fact many Liberal Protestants saw themselves as thinking, speaking, and acting for all of Protestantism, not just their own denominational tradition within Protestantism.

4. Ethical Optimism and Social Idealism

The ethical optimism and social idealism of the late nineteenth century grew with and was nurtured by Liberal Protestantism. From the perspective of the twentieth century, this optimism looks perhaps naïve. Nevertheless, the relative peace in Europe, the rapid industrialization and growth of trade, the rising standard of living, the emerging democratic forms of government, and notions of the progressive evolution of culture fit well in that time with various liberal emphases on the infinite worth of humanity, the goodness of creation, and the benevolence of God for God's creation. Moreover the renewed appreciation within Liberal Protestantism of the social or corporate nature of the Christian life (as found, e.g., in Schleiermacher) combined with an ethical focus to the character of Jesus' teaching concerning the coming Kingdom of God (as, e.g., in Ritschl and Harnack) raised the consciousness of the Protestant church's responsibility for the righting of social wrongs and for bringing the social structure itself in line with the ideal of the Kingdom of God on earth.

5. Essence of Christianity and the Centrality of Jesus

Finally, as a response to the emerging historical consciousness of modernity, Liberal Protestants sought to define the perduring essence of Christianity amid the contingencies of history and culture. LUDWIG FEUERBACH's *Das Wesen des Christentums (The Essence of Christianity)* (1841) and, a half-century later, Harnack's *What Is Christianity?* (1900) both represent such influential attempts at removing the layers of husk to get at the essential kernel, in Harnack's phrase. What emerged from this quest was a focus on the life and teachings of Jesus and his significance as the founder of Christianity as distinct from the layers of interpretation placed on him by subsequent generations of his followers. The goal, consequently, was to recover the kernel of Jesus' life and teachings and then to use that kernel as the standard by which all the doctrines of the church are to be judged. As Harnack put it, the essence of Christianity is nothing else than Jesus Christ and his gospel.

Assessment and Legacy

Soon after World War I, Liberal Protestantism as a movement went into decline as the ethical optimism and social idealism of nineteenth-century Europe collapsed. Theologians such as Barth in Europe and Reinhold Niebuhr in the United States began to challenge the credibility of Liberal Protestantism. Liberalism, they argued, was too accommodating to the modern culture in which it lived, too willing to reduce its account of the essentials of Christianity to the values and ideologies of modern society, and thereby, it sacrificed the prophetic voice that characterized Protestantism during the Reformation. This CULTURAL PROTESTANTISM, as it became known by its detractors, ignored the ways in which the Christian faith, with its doctrines of sin and God's judgment of it, calls into question the values of an age and any moral confidence humans might find in notions of social progress.

Whether these criticisms have merit, Liberal Protestantism has continued to decline as the basic assumptions of modernity have eroded. With the advent of POSTMODERNITY, very few theologians would wish to describe themselves as Liberal Protestants, at least not in the way that Harnack would have done a century earlier. Liberal talk about universal "religious experience," its concern for the rights of critical reason, and its belief in human civilization as itself an expression of the divine purpose have all come under attack as modernity itself has been criticized.

If this is so, then is Liberal Protestantism dead? Perhaps one could suggest that whereas Liberal Protestantism as an identifiable theological movement is dead (or at best on its last breath), its liberal spirit in theology still remains. It points to the fact that theologians must be keenly aware of the difficulties of adhering to the thought forms and language of traditional Christian belief within their particular times, cultures, and conceptualities. What theologians say—liberal or otherwise—will inevitably be influenced by the assumptions of their day. What matters, however, is how they are taken up within theology, whether this is done reflectively and critically, with attention to possible losses as well as gains. The legacy of Liberal Protestantism thus might be its recognition that this difficulty must be faced if Christianity itself is finally to survive.

References and Further Reading

Barth, Karl. *Protestant Theology in the Nineteenth Century.* Valley Forge, PA: Judson Press, 1973.

Birkner, Hans-Joachim. "Liberale Theologie." In *Kirchen und Liberalismus im 19. Jahrhundert*, edited by Martin Schmidt and George Schwaiger, 32–42. Göttingen, Germany: Vandenhoeck & Ruprecht, 1976.

Chapman, Mark. *Ernst Troeltsch and Liberal Theology: Religion and Cultural Synthesis in Wilhelmine Germany.* Oxford: Oxford University Press, 2001.

Dillenberger, John, and Claude Welch. *Protestant Christianity Interpreted Through Its Development.* New York: Charles Scribner's Sons, 1954.

Dorrien, Gary. *The Making of American Liberal Theology: Idealism, Realism, & Modernity 1900–1950.* Louisville, KY: Westminster John Knox Press, 2003.

———. *The Making of American Liberal Theology: Imagining Progressive Religion 1805–1900.* Louisville, KY: Westminster John Knox Press, 2001.

Frei, Hans. "Niebuhr's Theological Background." In *Faith and Ethics: The Theology of H. Richard Niebuhr*, edited by Paul Ramsey, 9–64. New York: Harper & Row, 1957.

Gerrish, Brian A. *The Old Protestantism and the New: Essays on the Reformation Heritage.* Chicago: University of Chicago Press, 1982.

———. *Tradition and the Modern World: Reformed Theology in the Nineteenth Century.* Chicago: University of Chicago Press, 1978.

Hutchison, William. *The Modernist Impulse in American Protestantism.* Cambridge, MA: Harvard University Press, 1976.

Rupp, George. *Culture-Protestantism: German Liberal Theology at the Turn of the Twentieth Century.* Missoula, MT: Scholars Press, 1977.

Van Dusen, Henry. *The Vindication of Liberal Theology: A Tract for the Times.* New York: Charles Scribner's Sons, 1963.

JEFFREY HENSLEY

LIBERATION THEOLOGY

Liberation theology is often seen primarily as a Roman Catholic phenomenon, pioneered by Latin Americans in the late 1960s and early 1970s. This view has popularized two fundamental and pervasive misunderstandings of liberation theology, one historical and the other theological. Viewing liberation theology from a broader perspective that gives attention to Protestant contributions will therefore lead to a more appropriate understanding of the phenomenon.

From a historical perspective various liberation theologies emerged at the same time and independently of each other. Even the term *liberation* was used initially without direct connection. One of the very first articles that made use of the term "liberation theology" in the UNITED STATES was authored in 1970 by Frederick Herzog, a white Protestant North American theologian whose work took shape initially in the context of the social tensions of the CIVIL RIGHTS MOVEMENT, focusing on political and economic forms of oppression. African American liberation theology, resisting oppression along the lines of race, was in the making at the same time. JAMES HAL CONE, an African American Protestant theologian in the United States, hit upon the notion of liberation in his own context and began to use the term in his publications. A book on liberation theology by Rosemary Radford Ruether, written in the United States from a feminist Roman Catholic perspective and adding more sustained attention to resisting oppression along the lines of GENDER in addition to matters of race and class, followed only a short time later. The work of these theologians runs parallel to the work of the Latin American priest and Roman Catholic theologian Gustavo Gutiérrez, commonly acknowledged as the "father of liberation theology." The different strands encountered each other only later, not without serious challenges and questions.

From a theological perspective it is important to realize that liberation theology did not develop out of one center, as a great idea or a unified theological school that made its way from the top down. Liberation theology developed in specific settings, independently but simultaneously, from the bottom up where theologians began to reflect on the suffering and hope of people in poverty, of ethnic minorities, of WOMEN, and others, in relation to traditional and newly developing images of God. Even though specific dates can be given, from a theological point of view there is not much use discussing who was "really first." These theologies are not written as accomplishments of individual scholars but in close relation with severe suffering and pressure in many shapes and forms.

The View from the Underside

Modern theology since the ENLIGHTENMENT has generated a new openness for the context of theological reflection. Rather than thinking about God in Godself, modern THEOLOGY explores God in relation to humanity, to the world, and to history and the major events of the time. Liberation theologies differ from this approach in that they pay attention not only to the context as such but also to its underside, its dark side. How does God relate to the large part of humanity that is never noticed by those in power? How does God relate to the world that is exploited and subdued? How does God relate to the histories of the excluded, the histories of minorities, of women, and of people living in poverty? Rather than searching for the correspondences between God and the often rehearsed achievements of MODERNISM, an approach that has usually led to the sanctification of the status quo in one way or another, liberation theologies are concerned about the ruptures and breaks and the forms of SIN manifested in them. Without addressing how God differs from the powers that be and without addressing the reality of sin no real change will take place.

In LATIN AMERICA close encounters with the reality of widespread poverty and economic oppression have set the tone of the debate. Together with their Roman Catholic colleagues, Protestant liberation theologians like José Míguez Bonino came to realize already in the late 1960s and early 1970s that large systemic structures of injustice cannot be corrected by well-meaning efforts of either CHARITY or economic development. Those larger structures that maintain and even enlarge the gap between rich and poor are part of a theological crisis because they separate us not only from our neighbors but also from God. More recently Latin American liberation theologians have developed these concerns further, going beyond the dependency between North and South and pointing out that much of humanity is simply excluded from the gains that the global markets have created for the rich.

In a completely different setting, African American theologians realized that, long after SLAVERY was abolished, their people were still not free. Even well-meaning efforts to become color-blind were no longer an option in a situation where oppression is tied to the color line. The renewed struggle against racism continues in different forms all the way into the present, involving increasingly closer attention to resources from African American culture, as for instance in the work of Dwight N. Hopkins. The various forms of racism are also perceived as a theological problem because, as Cone has pointed out, "Christianity is essentially a religion of liberation," and "any message

that is not related to the liberation of the poor in a society is not Christ's message" (Cone 1986:vii).

Feminist theologians, understanding themselves as partners in liberation theology, have reminded us of the ongoing discrepancy between the place of men and women in church and society. Theology is in crisis, they found, because it has not paid attention to God's walk with half of humanity. Well-meaning efforts of integrating women into the world created by men will not change this situation. One of the pioneers in the Protestant camp, Letty M. Russell, points out that for this reason feminist theologians take "the *via negativa* and describe the contradictions of our past and present social, political, economic, and ecclesial experiences." Out of this awareness of contradiction, women "live out of a vision of God's intention for a mended creation" (Russell 1987:18). Womanist and *mujerista* theologians—women writing from the perspective of African American and Hispanic communities—have subsequently refined the feminist analysis, adding the unsettling experience of close encounters with issues of race and class because minority women often suffer from various forms of oppression. Mirroring the demographic profile of those communities, Womanist theologians such as Delores Williams are generally Protestant and most *mujerista* theologians, such as Ada María Isasi-Díaz and Yolanda Tarango, are Roman Catholic.

More recently Hispanic theologians have zeroed in on issues of identity and CULTURE. In the United States, they point out, Hispanic Americans are often marginalized on grounds of different cultural practices and racial difference. The standard North American image of the melting pot leaves no room for appreciating difference. In response Hispanic Protestant theologians have stressed the validity of a diverse set of Hispanic experiences and cultures and have shown how these perspectives from the margins contribute to a broader understanding of Christianity, God, and the world, promoting community in diversity. "Reading the Bible in Spanish," a phrase coined by Justo González, leads to a specific Protestant way of engaging life and transforming the powers that be.

African and Asian theologians, going beyond typically Western perspectives, have broadened the spectrum of liberation theologies further. Choan-Seng Song, for example, a Protestant theologian born in Taiwan who is writing and teaching both in the United States and in Asia, has argued that theology is not complete unless it includes an account of God's Spirit at work in the long suppressed stories of darkness, suffering, and hope told by the people of Asia. Merely translating traditional concepts into new situations without paying attention to God's presence with the people will no longer do. The liberating power of God will become manifest when the barriers between the sacred and the profane are transcended from the underside of Asian life.

God and the Option for the Excluded

Liberation theologies maintain a deliberate option for people at the margins. Latin American liberation theologians, for instance, have made famous the idea of a "preferential option for the poor," an option that needs to be made not only by those who are not poor but also by the poor themselves. Yet this and other preferential options have frequently been misunderstood. First of all, what is their basis? What motivates theologians to go against the grain of church and society and opt for those that are commonly overlooked by the powers that be? Second, does a preferential option for people at the margins comply with our commonsense understanding of fairness? Does an option for people at the margins mean that liberation theologies have nothing to say for those who are not marginalized?

In response to the first set of questions it must be pointed out that all liberation theologians agree in their own ways that opting for the poor and excluded is closely related to the nature and work of God. Such options are not primarily based on political or ideological assumptions but on theological reflection. Here we are at the very heart of the various theologies of liberation. The point of departure of liberation theology is not primarily social ETHICS—a moral appeal not to forget those who are neglected—or general political or economic assumptions of the common good, but a new vision of God.

Few liberation theologians have made this clearer than Frederick Herzog. Emphasizing that liberation theology starts with God's own walk with humanity, Herzog prefers to talk about "theopraxis," "Christopraxis," and "Spiritpraxis," rather than "orthopraxis," a term frequently used by others to express the practical concern of liberation theology. In this way Herzog addresses a specific problem with North American Protestantism where—on grounds of modern notions of agency and the self—it is often assumed that people can and should pull themselves up by their own bootstraps. God's work with the marginalized everywhere provides a different model: walking with God and with each other, people are enabled to overcome self-centeredness, to build new relationships, and to develop resistance to the oppressive structures of empire.

From the Latin American perspective Gustavo Gutiérrez has emphasized over and over again that liberation theology starts with the specific forms of God's love and God's GRACE manifest throughout the BIBLE. The preferential option for the poor is a theo-

centric option, centered on the theological conviction that God is at work in the liberation of the "least of these." Jose Míguez Bonino and other Protestant Latin Americans, although putting more emphasis on human commitment and responsibility for liberation, would agree.

James Cone's statements are equally strong. He maintains that the "sole reason" for the existence of black theology is "to put into ordered speech the meaning of God's activity in the world, so that the community of the oppressed will recognize that its inner thrust for liberation is not only *consistent with* the gospel but *is* the gospel of Jesus Christ" (Cone 1986:3). This close relation between God's work and the lives of the oppressed is supported by the biblical paradigm of the Exodus where God becomes known as the God of the oppressed, a pattern that is broadened in the New Testament by the resurrection of Jesus Christ, which is taken to indicate God's commitment to all oppressed people.

Letty Russell points feminists to God's future action, which is already present in the action of God through the people of Israel and through Jesus Christ. In this vision the marginalized have a special place. Mary McClintock Fulkerson, a Protestant feminist theologian of the second generation, has argued for what she calls the "theo/acentric character" of feminist theology. Unlike modern theology, this theo/acentric emphasis is not interested in defending the existence of God. From a liberation perspective the question of the existence of God has always been of lesser interest than the question of who God is and what God is doing. The feminist experience of God, not unlike the experience of God in most liberation theologies, grows out of encounters with God in the tensions of life and in new encounters with God that include those who have been marginalized in society and church.

Womanist theologian Delores Williams describes the encounter with God in terms of the situation of black women who are facing "near-destruction situations." God is not an abstract category or ultimate principle but the one who is with the people. God is simply the one who helps them "make a way out of what [they] thought was no way" (Williams 1993: 108). The focus of womanist liberation theology is on God: unlike modern middle-class people, the persons who face "near-destruction situations" point away from themselves.

In agreement with other approaches to the theology of liberation, Hispanic theology maintains that the fundamental theological question is what God we affirm. Protestant Hispanic theology, strongly based on biblical images, affirms God's concern for those in need in its own ways. Justo González points out that "Scripture does not say that God can be found equally wherever we please to look." Hispanic theologians agree with other theologies of liberation that "ours is a God who, having known oppression, shares with the oppressed in their suffering" (González 1990:93, 95).

From the Asian perspective Choan-Seng Song levels the charge that mainline theology has virtually forgotten that "God is a God full of surprises." All liberation theologies would agree on this point. Immersed in the Asian context Song and others have become aware that God is present in the midst of the struggles of the people, and that "theology begins with God's heartache on account of the world." Theology is distorted, therefore, when it tries to think about God in a vacuum or only in regard to God's glory. God needs to be seen first of all in confrontation with "the darkness that poses as a real threat to the birth, growth, and fruition of life" (Song 1991:10, 56). The biblical image that is at the core of this vision is God's creation of the world as victory over darkness.

One more perspective merits to be added here. Vine Deloria, writing from the perspective of Native American religions and thus from beyond the Protestant–Roman Catholic divide, worries that "religion has become a comfortable ethic and comforting aesthetic for Westerners." On the basis of the Native American traditions Deloria argues that God is different: "God is red." This God is in touch with the realities that mainline America has repressed—nature, trees, animals, and birds, and the "voices and places of the land" (Deloria 1994:284, 292). Deloria's vision adds an important impulse to the spectrum of liberation theologies because its focus extends beyond oppressed people to the land and the cosmos as a whole.

In light of this common focus on God in liberation theology, the problem with the second set of questions becomes clearer and thus the response can be brief. In the encounter with God and those who suffer, abstract notions of fairness will no longer do. God is not a machine that distributes goods and services according to predetermined input but establishes relationships with humanity. Even where humans hurt each other and push large groups of people into oblivion, God does not forget about those who get hurt.

God's option for the poor, the marginalized, the hurt—the fact that God does not overlook those rendered invisible by the powers that be—does not mean that God does not care about the wealthy and the powerful—those who inflict pain often without being aware of it, although the relationship takes on different forms. God's care—not unlike parental care—also includes a challenge to those who destroy others and therefore also themselves. Jesus's own ways of acting as portrayed in all four Gospels mirror such challenges in many ways. In addition, because the powerful defy relationships with people who are different, their own

relationship with God is easily distorted. In this situation a call to restore relationship with nonpersons might help to find a way back into a more productive communion with God as well. Liberation theology is thus a challenge for all of theology to examine whether it opens up the worth of other persons. Respect for God and respect for others are closely connected.

Context Is What Hurts

On the cover of one of his books, Choan-Seng Song is characterized as "the master of contextual theologies." In similar fashion liberation theologies in general are often classified as "contextual theologies." From here it is only a small step to collate liberation theologies with modern liberal theology and the attempt to adapt theological reflection to one's own personal setting, centering theological reflection around the personal interests of various groups. In this perspective liberation theologies are seen as nothing more than an ever-expanding set of special interest theologies, at best relevant to specific groups of people, at worst just another outgrowth of postmodern pluralism and relativism. The language of "advocacy scholarship" has at times contributed to the confusion. Liberation theologies thus are seen as catering primarily to the interest of specific groups of different ethnic, gender, or class origins. This view gives permission for the rest of theology to go on with business as usual.

Yet this has not much to do with the dynamic that created the theologies of liberation. Their themes were developed not in relation to the special and private interests of self-contained groups but in relation to deep suffering and pain that, although most strongly felt at the margins and the peripheries, also affects the centers. The point is to understand the deep roots of the common predicament in which both the marginalized and those in power share, without neglecting the obvious differences. Liberation theologies in their own ways embody Paul's well-known insight in I Corinthians 12:26 that if one member suffers, all suffer together. Unlike the various perspectives of privilege that feel they can afford to tend to their own context, the view from the underside of suffering always reflects the whole body. Suffering can ultimately not be limited to one member only. Liberation theologies thus search for the best interest of all, seeking the liberation of both oppressors and oppressed by paying attention to where the pain is greatest. If this is seen, the rest of theology can no longer continue with business as usual. All of theology needs to join in listening to the common pain.

Liberation theologies are therefore not special interest theologies but address the common good from new angles, which now include the underside of history and a new vision of God. In this perspective the context of theology is not what is immediately obvious or closest to home: Context is that which hurts (Rieger 1998b:129–130). In taking another look at the underside of history, liberation theologies start to notice certain aspects of reality that modern liberal theologies will never see. This does not mean that modern liberal theologies are completely unaware of suffering, pain, and structures of oppression, although they tend to see those structures as exceptions, anomalies, merely deviations from the normal course of things. Liberation theologies, on the other hand, understand that suffering, pain, and oppression are not merely accidental but point to a deeper truth about the dominant context itself. Conflicts and tensions do not appear out of nowhere but are produced by the powers that be, and as such point to their unconscious truth that must be constantly repressed to preserve the way things are (Rieger 1998a:75–88).

The true nature of the contextual reality of the underside is not immediately self-evident, surprisingly not even to those who live there. It takes some effort to cut through the covers and to understand. Gutiérrez has insisted with good reason that even the poor must make the option for the poor—many make the option to be rich. At the beginning of the twenty-first century liberation theologies need to add more layers to their current understanding of context in terms of the underside of history. What are the concerns of people on the underside now? What progress has been made in the last thirty years? What are the setbacks? What difference do globalization processes make? There is a certain degree of consensus among liberation theologians that economic challenges will have to be analyzed more closely in relation to all forms of oppression (see the essays in Rieger 1998b).

Here a curious reversal takes place that has not yet reached the level of consciousness of mainline theology. Despite claims to universality, the approaches developed in the centers of theology shape up as special interest theologies if they pay no attention to the deeper malaise that affects us all, oppressors and oppressed alike. We need to realize that, rather than addressing the special interests of one group only, the suffering of people at the margins points to an important part of reality in which, even though often repressed and made invisible, we all participate. Liberation theology is therefore not special interest theology but poses a challenge to all of theology.

Implications

At this point the process of theological reflection changes profoundly. Theology as a whole benefits from listening more closely to voices on the under-side. Theology is freed from its long-term captivity to the context of the modern middle class and from traditionalist appeals to the biblical and traditional texts of the church that forget precisely about the suffering and pain of people on the underside. Liberation theologies serve as a reminder that theology cannot escape the pervasive narcissism of the modern and postmodern worlds without developing genuine respect for God, a project inextricably tied up with developing genuine respect for other persons as well.

Theology indeed begins with the relationship of God, humanity, and the world, as modern theology knows so well, although this relationship needs to be broadened so as to include those who are left out, those who fall through the cracks in a world that prides itself on moving closer together in global connectedness. Liberation theologies thus serve as an invitation to search for new encounters with God in places where theologians and church people hardly bother to look. At a time when theology is becoming more and more a matter of life and death—the poor become poorer, the rich become richer, and over 30,000 children are dying every day from preventable causes—new relationships with God and with humanity need to be built, from the bottom up. Where is God? This question will make a difference only if it no longer avoids the reality of dying children.

See also African Theology; Asian Theology; Black Theology; Ethnicity; Feminist Theology; Liberal Protestantism; Modernism; Native Americans; Political Theology; Postmodernity; Slavery, Abolition of; Womanist Theology

References and Further Reading

Cone, James. *A Black Theology of Liberation*. Second edition. Maryknoll, NY: Orbis Books, 1986 (first published 1970).

Deloria, Vine. *God Is Red: A Native View of Religion. The Classic Work Updated*. Golden, CO: Fulcrum Publishing, 1994 (first published 1973).

Fulkerson, Mary McClintock. *Changing the Subject: Women's Discourses and Feminist Theology*. Minneapolis, MN: Fortress Press, 1994.

González, Justo. *Mañana: Christian Theology in Hispanic Perspective*. Nashville, TN: Abingdon Press, 1990.

Gutiérrez, Gustavo. *A Theology of Liberation: History, Politics, and Salvation*. Revised 15th anniversary edition. Translated by Sister Caridad Inda and John Eagleson. Maryknoll, NY: Orbis, 1988 (first Spanish edition 1971).

Herzog, Frederick. *God Walk: Liberation Shaping Dogmatics*. Maryknoll, NY: Orbis Books, 1988. [Herzog's first essay using the term liberation is "Theology of Liberation." *Continuum* 7 no. 4 (Winter 1970).]

Hopkins, Dwight N. *Down, Up, and Over: Slave Religion and Black Theology*. Minneapolis, MN: Fortress Press, 2000.

Isasi-Díaz, Ada María, and Yolanda Tarango. *Hispanic Women: Prophetic Voice in the Church. Toward a Hispanic Women's*

Liberation Theology. San Francisco, CA: Harper & Row, 1988.

Míguez Bonino, José. *Doing Theology in a Revolutionary Situation.* Philadelphia, PA: Fortress Press, 1975.

Rieger, Joerg. *Remember the Poor: The Challenge to Theology in the Twenty-First Century.* Harrisburg, PA.: Trinity Press International, 1998a.

———, ed. *Liberating the Future: God, Mammon, and Theology.* Minneapolis, MN: Fortress Press, 1998b.

Ruether, Rosemary Radford. *Liberation Theology: Human Hope Confronts Christian History and American Power.* New York: Paulist Press, 1972.

Russell, Letty. *Household of Freedom: Authority in Feminist Theology.* Philadelphia, PA: Westminster Press, 1987. [Russell's first book on feminist liberation theology is *Human Liberation in a Feminist Perspective: A Theology.* Philadelphia, PA: Westminster Press, 1974.]

Song, Choan-Seng. *Third Eye Theology: Theology in Formation in Asian Settings.* Revised edition. Maryknoll, NY: Orbis Books, 1991 (first edition 1979).

Williams, Delores. *Sisters in the Wilderness: The Challenge of Womanist God-Talk.* Maryknoll, NY: Orbis Books, 1993.

JOERG RIEGER

LIBERIA

The predominance of Protestant denominations and the influence of the United States are characteristics of Christianity in Liberia. In the early nineteenth century, white Americans, concerned about the presence of free African Americans, formed a society to encourage African Americans to emigrate from the United States to a colony in West Africa. The American Society for Colonizing the Free People of Color in the United States (later known as the AMERICAN COLONIZATION SOCIETY or ACS) was founded in 1816. The ACS was controversial because its members included both abolitionists and supporters of slavery who wished to rid the United States of free blacks (see SLAVERY; SLAVERY, ABOLITION OF).

Many African Americans opposed the ACS because of its conservative stance on slavery and civil rights for freed people. However, some immigrants were motivated by a desire to return to AFRICA and escape racial oppression in the United States. Others believed that they were enacting God's plan for converting Africans to Christianity. According to a providential reading of history, God had allowed Africans to be enslaved and taken to the United States so that they could be converted to Christianity. The descendants of these Africans had the responsibility of bringing Christianity and Western civilization to their African brothers and sisters.

The first group of settlers arrived in Liberia in 1822. The settlers formed the independent republic of Liberia in 1847. From 1822 to 1866 approximately 12,000 people emigrated from the United States to Liberia. These immigrants included freeborn people, former slaves, and people who were freed by their masters only for the purpose of emigration. A steady stream of African Americans continued to immigrate to Liberia throughout the nineteenth and into the twentieth century. These settlers formed the core of the ruling Americo-Liberian society.

Africans freed from slave ships also contributed to Liberia's population. In 1819 the United States Congress passed a law to resettle in Liberia Africans who were recaptured by the U.S. Navy from slave ships. Many of the recaptives, popularly known in Liberia as "Congoes," eventually assimilated into Americo-Liberian society.

The settlers brought with them their Protestant denominations, including the AFRICAN METHODIST EPISCOPAL (AME), the Baptist (see BAPTISTS), and Presbyterian (see PRESBYTERIANISM) Churches. Organizations associated with these churches, such as mutual aid societies, fraternal organizations, and charities, became important parts of the Americo-Liberian culture. Many Americo-Liberians used Christianity and "civilization" as markers to distinguish themselves from the majority of indigenous Liberians.

Several of the prominent black clergy and intellectuals of the nineteenth century became associated with Liberia and considered the state an important symbol of black NATIONALISM. Reverends Daniel Coker of the AME Church and LOTT CAREY of the Baptist Church were among the first group of settlers. Both ALEXANDER CRUMMELL and Edward Wilmot Blyden worked in Liberia for several years.

Missions in Liberia

Despite the importance of Christianity in their lives, few Americo-Liberians worked as missionaries among indigenous Liberians. United States–based missionaries took up this task. Liberia was overwhelmingly a field for Protestant missionary work; the Roman Catholic Church did not establish a permanent mission until 1906 (see MISSIONS; MISSIONARY ORGANIZATIONS). By the end of the nineteenth century, missionaries from the Methodist, Baptist, Presbyterian, Episcopal, and Lutheran churches worked in Liberia. Many African American denominations, such as the AME Church, the AFRICAN METHODIST EPISCOPAL Zion Church, and the NATIONAL BAPTIST CONVENTION, also sent missionaries to Liberia. Missions provided schools and hospitals for indigenous Africans and promulgated new forms of economic, gender, and social relations among the converts.

Relations between the Americo-Liberians and the indigenous Africans were often uneasy. The Americo-Liberian government assumed the relationship of a colonizer to the indigenous Africans. Despite the significant division between Americo-Liberian society and the indigenous people, the groups interacted and shaped each other. Americo-Liberian families took in indigenous foster children as apprentices, and some Americo-Liberian men had indigenous wives and children in "the country." As Mary Moran has demonstrated, many indigenous Liberians adopted the idea of being "civilized," that is, being Western-educated and Christian.

Many Liberians became involved in the independent church movements of the late nineteenth and early twentieth centuries. WILLIAM WADÉ HARRIS, an indigenous, mission-educated Liberian, was an important evangelist in West Africa. While Harris was imprisoned for opposing Americo-Liberian rule, he received a vision that compelled him to preach the word of God. He encouraged his listeners to abandon their traditional religions, be baptized, and become active Christians. Harris was active in Côte d'Ivoire and the Gold Coast. After French officials expelled him from Côte d'Ivoire in 1915, he continued to preach in Liberia and SIERRA LEONE.

Throughout the period of Americo-Liberian political dominance, which lasted until 1980, the Protestant churches' ministers and institutions largely supported the social order. Many of the ruling elite were leaders within their churches. For example, President William R. Tolbert Jr., who ruled from 1971 to 1980, was also the president of the Liberia Baptist Missionary and Educational Convention.

By the twentieth century, many of Liberia's churches were self-supporting. However, a steady flow of missionaries, largely from the United States, continued to flow into Liberia. In addition to missionaries from mainline churches, missionaries from evangelical churches also worked in Liberia. The missions established radio stations, schools, hospitals, and other social services in the country.

The military coup, which brought Samuel Doe to power in 1980, broke the close relationship between the Protestant churches and the ruling institutions. Paul Gifford has noted that many of Liberia's Protestant churches, unlike churches in other parts of Africa, criticized neither the unequal social order before the coup nor the wide-scale abuse of human rights during Doe's regime. During the 1980s the number of Liberians espousing Christianity and the number of missionaries increased dramatically. Many of the missionaries preached a form of FUNDAMENTALISM and used technology such as video broadcasts to spread their teachings (see PUBLISHING MEDIA).

From 1989 to 1997 a brutal civil war engulfed Liberia. Charles Taylor, a guerilla fighter during the war, became president in 1997. Some preachers interpreted the chaos of the war as a sign that Liberians had to choose between the forces of God and Satan. Other Liberians turned to Christianity as a source of healing and rebirth after the ravages of warfare.

See also African American Protestantism

References and Further Reading

Ellis, Stephen. *The Mask of Anarchy: The Destruction of Liberia and the Religious Dimension of an African Civil War.* New York: New York University Press, 1999.

Gifford, Paul. *Christianity and Politics in Doe's Liberia.* Cambridge: Cambridge University Press, 1993.

Jacobs, Sylvia M., ed. *Black Americans and the Missionary Movement in Africa.* Westport, CT: Greenwood Press, 1982.

Moran, Mary H. *Civilized Women: Gender and Prestige in Southeastern Liberia.* Ithaca, NY: Cornell University Press, 1990.

Sanneh, Lamin. *Abolitionists Abroad: American Blacks and the Making of Modern West Africa.* Cambridge, MA: Harvard University Press, 1999.

Shick, Tom W. *Behold the Promised Land: A History of Afro-American Settler Society in Nineteenth-Century Liberia.* Baltimore, MD: Johns Hopkins University Press, 1977.

MODUPE G. LABODE

LIDDON, HENRY PARRY (1829–1890)

English theologian. Born in Hampshire on August 20, 1829, Liddon greatly influenced nineteenth-century Protestant life and thought. At seventeen, he attended Christ Church, Oxford, returning there in 1859 as vice-president of St. Edmund Hall after having been forced by the bishop of Oxford, SAMUEL WILBERFORCE, to resign as vice-principal of Cuddesdon because of his Romish practices. Anglican ordinands at Cuddesdon were being trained to confront theological Liberalism, so-called Germanism or NEOLOGY. Liddon influenced undergraduate religious life at Oxford with his New Testament lectures, Sunday evenings "tea-and-toast-and-testament" soirées that attracted devotees, including the Victorian Jesuit poet, Gerard Manley Hopkins. Liddon challenged the growing liberalism centered at Balliol under BENJAMIN JOWETT. His Anglo-Catholic influence—"Liddonism"—was unrivaled. Students crowded St. Mary's to hear Liddon's Bampton lectures, along with his inspiring sermons published in *Sermons Preached before the University of Oxford* (1864) and *Some Elements of Religion* (1872).

Neglecting a literary career, Liddon devoted himself to teaching, pastoral care, and church life. His notable publication is *The Divinity of Our Lord and Saviour Jesus Christ* (1867), eight Bampton lectures defending the divinity of Christ under assault from Renan, DAVID FRIEDRICH STRAUSS, and Seeley. A distinguished theologian he assailed *Essays and Reviews* (1860) and *Lux Mundi* (1889), which questioned the CHRISTOLOGY and historicity of the Old Testament. Liddon's abiding interest in the Anglican priesthood occasioned *The Priest in His Inner Life* (1856), and his Assize Sermon of 1869 refuted Disraeli's move to legislate ritualism. An EDWARD PUSEY protégé, Liddon chronicled the *Life of Edward Bouverie Pusey* (1893–1894), celebrated leader of the OXFORD MOVEMENT, canon of Christ Church, and Regius Professor of Hebrew at Oxford. Liddon helped to found Keble College, named for JOHN KEBLE, in 1870 and Pusey House in 1884, institutions he saw as fundamental to maintaining Oxford's historical ties to ANGLICANISM. He was elected three times to the hebdomadal board, Oxford's governing body.

Liddon was appointed canon of St. Paul's (1870–1890), where he reformed the role of the minor canon, supervised the construction of the largest crucifix in an Anglican church, rejected modern settings of old HYMNS, and excluded female choir members (he also opposed WOMEN matriculating to Oxford). Under Liddon's leadership, St. Paul's became synonymous with high churchmanship. He was also named Dean Ireland Professor of Exegesis at Oxford (1870–1882). In "The Place of the Senses in Religion," a sermon preached at St. Paul's in April 1882, three days after the death of Charles Darwin and published as "The Recovery of St. Thomas, with a Prefatory Note on the Late Mr. Darwin," Liddon wanted to accommodate SCIENCE to Anglicanism, an accommodation manifesting a deep anxiety with rather than an acceptance of DARWINISM. An inveterate traveler, Liddon vacationed in SCOTLAND, ITALY, and the Continent; RUSSIA (accompanied in the latter by the mathematician turned novelist C. L. Dodgson, known as Lewis Carroll); Egypt and the Holy Land, copiously recording geography, architecture, and impressions of people and religious practice. Near the end of his career Liddon was denied a bishopric because his supporter and Tractarian sympathizer, prime minister W. E. Gladstone, presumed that he would not have received the support of the Queen. Liddon became ill in July, died on September 9, 1890, and was buried at St. Paul's.

See also Germany; Liberal Protestantism; Theology

References and Further Reading

Primary Sources:

Liddon, Henry Parry. *The Divinity of Our Lord and Saviour Jesus Christ: Eight Lectures Preached before the University of Oxford in the Year 1866,* 14th ed. London: Longmans, 1890.
Liddon Papers. Oxford: Pusey House.
Whitley, W. M., ed. *Henry Parry Liddon 1829–1929: A Centenary Memoir.* London: A. R. Mowbray, 1929.

Secondary Sources:

Chadwick, Owen. *The Victorian Church.* 2 vols. New York: Oxford University Press, 1970.
Chandler, Michael. *The Life and Work of Henry Parry Liddon.* Herefordshire: Gracewing, 2000.
Johnston, John O. *Life and Letters of Henry Parry Liddon.* New York: Longmans, 1904.
Nixon, Jude V. *Gerard Manley Hopkins and His Contemporaries: Liddon, Newman, Darwin, and Pater.* New York: Garland, 1994.

JUDE V. NIXON

LIGHTFOOT, JOSEPH BARBER (1828–1889)

New testament scholar and bishop of Durham. Lightfoot was born at 84 Duke Street, Liverpool to an accountant father. The family moved to Birmingham where he was educated at King Edward's School with E. W. Benson, later archbishop of Canterbury, under the headmastership of James Prince Lee who taught the Greek New Testament. BROOKE FRANCIS WESTCOTT, another product of this school, became Lightfoot's tutor as an undergraduate at Trinity College, Cambridge, from 1847.

Lightfoot taught at the UNIVERSITY OF CAMBRIDGE for many years as fellow, tutor, and professor. He became Hulsean professor of divinity in 1861 and Lady Margaret professor in 1875. His lectures on the Pauline epistles were so widely attended that the hall of Trinity College had to be used. He published commentaries on *Galatians* (1865), *Philippians* (1868), and *Colossians* and *Philemon* (1875). The first of these contained a celebrated essay on "The Christian Ministry" and its development in the early CHURCH. In company with Westcott and F. J. A. Hort he gave English New Testament scholarship a high international standing. His work on the postapostolic writings in *Clement of Rome* (1869, 1890) and *Ignatius* (1885, 1889) caused the prevailing theories of the Tübingen school of New Testament scholarship to be revised, and he also established the authenticity of all of the Ignatian letters previously questioned. In 1879 he was appointed bishop of Durham.

Lightfoot showed himself to be practically effective as a bishop, securing the division of his very large diocese in 1882 to make it more manageable, and raising large sums of money for church building and the development of parsonages and church halls. He encouraged the use of lay ministries and evangelists of the Church Army. He strengthened the ordained ministry in the diocese by using Auckland Castle, the bishop's residence, to train a number of men for ordination at his own charge. He was a supporter of the entry of WOMEN into HIGHER EDUCATION and into the church's ministry. A portrait by Richmond hangs in Auckland Castle where he is buried in the chapel.

References and Further Reading

Primary Sources:

Lightfoot, Joseph B. "Eusebius of Caesarea." In *The Dictionary of Christian Biography.* 1880.
———. *The Apostolic Fathers.* London: MacMillan, 1890.
———. *Leaders of the Northern Church.* London: MacMillan, 1890.
———. *Ordination Addresses.* London: MacMillan, 1890.

Secondary Sources:

Eden, G. R., and F. C. Macdonald, eds. *Lightfoot of Durham.* Cambridge: Cambridge University Press, 1932.
Edwards, D. L. *Leaders of the Church of England 1828–1944.* Cambridge: Cambridge University Press, 1971.
Hort, F. J. A. "Lightfoot, Joseph Barber." In *Dictionary of National Biography.* vol. 33. Oxford, UK: Oxford University Press, 1893.
Robinson, J. A. T. *Joseph Barber Lightfoot.* Durham, UK: Durham Cathedral, 1981.

TIMOTHY E. YATES

LINCOLN, ABRAHAM (1809–1865)

United States president. Lincoln was born near Hodgenville, Kentucky, the son of Thomas and Nancy Hanks Lincoln, who were farmers. Lincoln's parents were members of the ultrapredestinarian Separate Baptist Churches. From them the young Lincoln picked up a strong sense of the absolute divine control of all human events, as well as a suspicion of formal religious institutions. His increasingly distant relations with his father helped alienate him even from the Separates, and when Lincoln settled in New Salem, Illinois, in 1832 as a clerk and farm laborer, his reading of Thomas Paine, Volney, and other ENLIGHTENMENT critics of Christianity gave him a reputation as an "infidel." In 1837, after a period of self-study, he began practicing law in Springfield, Illinois, where his friends recalled that he "was Enthusiastic in his infidelity." He married Mary Todd in 1842, but neither of them developed a strong religious identity.

After the death of his second son, Edward, in 1850, and his father in 1851, Lincoln showed a noticeable softening in his criticism of Christianity. Partly because of political calculation and partly because of being genuinely "perplexed and unsettled on the fundamentals of religion," Lincoln became willing to acknowledge "a simple faith in God," and the Lincoln family rented a pew in Springfield's First Presbyterian Church (although Lincoln himself was infrequent in attendance). He remained, however, convinced of "the doctrine of necessity" and described himself as a "fatalist" who believed more in the mechanistic necessity of all events rather than divine ordination of them.

His election as the sixteenth president of the United States in 1860 and the outbreak of the American CIVIL WAR in 1861 at first brought little change in this. By 1862, however, the frustrating course of the war forced Lincoln to deeper speculation on the personality of God and God's intervention in human affairs. Lincoln's decision to issue the Emancipation Proclamation in September 1862 was prompted in part by a conviction that God had deliberately prevented the war from coming to a quick conclusion so that Lincoln, as president, would have to confront the need for abolishing SLAVERY. Lincoln's last great speech, delivered at his inauguration to a second term as president in March 1865, stressed in eloquent terms the inscrutability of God's purposes and the need for personal humility and mutual charity on the part of humankind in discerning those purposes at the close of the war. He was assassinated in Washington, D.C., by John Wilkes Booth, one week after the surrender of the major rebel army, on April 15, 1865.

Lincoln represents a blending of the skepticism of the late Enlightenment, the predestinarian sensibility of radical sectarian Protestantism, and an ethical uprightness that survived the washing away of its Protestant theological substance. Like many other Protestant Victorian doubters, he could not believe, but could not be comfortable in his unbelief. Although never a member of a church, his public utterances are informed by greater depths of religious speculation than any other American president. As a Republican, he broke with the refusal of Democratic presidents to give public sanction to religious practices by issuing calls for public PRAYER and thanksgiving and dramatically expanding the United States military CHAPLAINCY during the Civil War.

See also Baptists; Slavery, Abolition of

References and Further Reading

Primary Source:

The Collected Works of Abraham Lincoln. 9 vols. Edited by Roy P. Basler. New Brunswick, NJ: Rutgers University Press, 1953.

Secondary Sources:

Barton, William E. *The Soul of Abraham Lincoln.* New York: George Doran, 1920.
Guelzo, Allen C. *Abraham Lincoln: Redeemer President.* Grand Rapids, MI: Eerdmans, 1999.
Temple, Wayne C. *Abraham Lincoln: From Skeptic to Prophet.* Mahomet, IL: Mayhaven Publishing, 1995.

ALLEN C. GUELZO

LITERATURE

In several ways Protestantism is responsible for the rise of vernacular literature. First, Protestants are people of the book in ways that Catholics are not. That is, the BIBLE is the centerpiece of the Protestant faith, and Protestantism encourages both individual and communal readings of biblical stories. Second, the REFORMATION was accompanied by a rise in literacy in Europe. As indicated by its very etymological roots, literature is possible only when people are literate. Although numerous oral tales, legends, and poems circulated before the Middle Ages, individuals depended on poets and storytellers to tell these stories in various gatherings. In addition, the number of extant texts of these stories, such as *Beowulf* (eighth century) and the "Dream of the Rood" (date unknown), was small so that access to the written texts would have been limited. Third, the invention of the printing press in the fifteenth century made it possible for a greater number of texts to be disseminated to the population at large. Simply put, the printing press gave rise to a reading public. Fourth, by the time of the Protestant Reformation, literary texts—foremost among them the Bible—began to be translated in vernacular language. Now, for the first time in history, individuals in GERMANY or FRANCE could read their own copies of the Bible in a language they could understand rather than having the Bible read to them in a language they no longer understood. Thus, not only did the Protestant Reformation revolutionize the religious landscape of Europe but it also gave birth to literature.

To be sure, many of the poems, plays, and tales that circulated before the late sixteenth century had religious themes and some even arose explicitly out of a church setting. Poems such as the "Dream of the Rood" represent the early Middle Ages' fascination with the heroes of pagan religions. At the same time, the poem places Christ and Moses in the guise of these heroes. In Caedmon's "Hymn" (657–680) the poet, most likely a lay worker in a monastery, depicts God as his prince whom he obeys. In the "Hymn" Caedmon also depicts a pilgrim, St. Helena, who journeys to the Holy Land in search of the true cross. The motif of the search for Christ's true cross will also dominate Middle English literature and will find its most famous expression in Sir Thomas Malory's *Morte D'Arthur* (1405–1471), the retelling of the King Arthur legend of the search for the Holy Grail, or the cup of Christ. In addition the poet who wrote *Sir Gawain and the Green Knight* (1375–1400) also produced one of the finest early religious poems in *Pearl,* an eloquent elegy for a child that probes the differences between HEAVEN and earth. "The Vision of Piers Plowman" by William Langland (1330–1387) introduces the method of allegory in dealing with the themes of sinfulness—"The Confession of Envy," "The Confession of Gluttony"—and pilgrimage, "Piers Plowman Shows the Way to Saint Truth."

As the dominance of the church began to be challenged in the late Middle Ages, a religious literature flourished that enabled the populace to interpret the mysteries of their religion in their own way. Whereas the church retold the death and resurrection of Christ in its annual Passion Plays, the LAITY developed cycles of mystery plays that they would perform every year around the times of the festivals of Whitsuntide or Corpus Christi, both of which came seven to eight Sundays after Easter. These plays—the most famous of which are the Wakefield Cycle and the Chester Cycle—emphasized the mystery of Christ's redemption of humankind. Because this redemption had been prophesied in the events of the Old Testament, the action of such plays moved in a cycle from the Creation and the Fall of Humankind to the Flood and to New Testament events such as the Nativity, the Crucifixion, and the Last Judgment. Rather than being performed in churches, these play cycles were performed in streets, and various trade unions or religious guilds often performed one of the plays in the cycle as the cycle moved from one town to the other. The mystery play cycles indicate the desire of the laity to move away from the dominance of the church and to begin to interpret these religious mysteries in their own way.

The most famous collection of religious tales of the fourteenth century is Geoffrey Chaucer's *The Canterbury Tales* (1386–1400). The setting for the telling of the tales is a pilgrimage to CANTERBURY. Although Chaucer completed only twenty-two of the projected 120 tales, the tellers represent a wide spectrum of society from the elite to the poor. The pilgrimage seems merely an excuse to tell these tales, and the trip turns into a carnival in which these pilgrims' world is turned upside down. During this trip they have the opportunity to be their own religious authorities and to question the ways of the church. *The Canterbury Tales* was one of the most popular poems of its time, and more extant manuscripts of Chaucer's poem exist than of any other poem of the time. Chaucer's creation of a vernacular poem that questions much of the church's teachings indicated how deeply the church's AUTHORITY was eroding and how strongly the laity wanted to have their own authority for reading and understanding religious ideas.

Dante Alighieri (1265–1321) had already paved the way for Chaucer, however, in the early fourteenth century in ITALY. The Italian poet's *Divine Comedy* (1308) followed the pilgrimage of Dante the pilgrim from the depths of Hell to the pinnacles of Paradise.

He wrote his poem in Italian in rhyming couplets so that his audience would have access to his religious and political message. Although Dante himself was exiled for his work, the *Divine Comedy* received an enormous popular response. The poem was recited in taverns and public rooms by ordinary Italians, who were no doubt eager to learn the fate of various members of the church and certain political parties whom Dante had placed in various circles of Hell. Although Dante's poem takes its structure from the theology of Thomas Aquinas, his *commedia* functions essentially as a political commentary on his society and the church.

The Sixteenth Century

In 1517 MARTIN LUTHER drafted his ninety-five theses in Wittenberg. Seventeen years later in England HENRY VIII had established himself as the head of the CHURCH OF ENGLAND and as the primary religious authority in that country. By 1603 King James I had commissioned a new translation of the Bible to replace the standard Catholic translation of the Bible. In the sixteenth century the religious tide had begun to turn, and the monolithic authority of the Catholic Church began to crumble as Protestantism slowly made its way through Europe. In addition the sixteenth century continued the era of great exploration that had begun with Columbus in the late fifteenth century. By the time of Shakespeare's late plays in 1611, Spain, FRANCE, and ENGLAND had begun to colonize the New World. The sixteenth century also witnessed the flowering of Renaissance, a rebirth of letters and arts focusing primarily on the recovery of ancient Greek and Latin texts. Renaissance values focused on the dignity of human life and the value of earthly society. The art of Botticelli, Michelangelo, and da Vinci emphasized the beauty of the human body, as Greek art had done, as well as the potential of humankind to discover the secrets of the universe and God. SCIENCE and philosophy flourished in the Renaissance, and the literature of the age, influenced by the Reformation, focused on topics ranging from politics to education.

Christian humanists of the sixteenth century focused on EDUCATION and classical learning. Whereas they emphasized writing in Latin and translation into English, these writers and teachers also used Terence's plays, Virgil's and Horace's poems, and Cicero's rhetoric to teach philosophical and moral truth. Some of these teachers—chief among them Roger Ascham (1515–1568), who was PRINCESS Elizabeth's tutor, and Sir John Cheke (1514–1557)—taught at Cambridge and influenced writers from Edmund Spenser to JOHN MILTON. The emphasis on vernacular languages that arose with the Reformation and the reverence for Latin and Greek classics gave rise to eloquent translations during this period. The most famous are George Chapman's translations of Homer's *Iliad* and *Odyssey,* which John Keats would later immortalize in his sonnet, "On First Looking into Chapman's Homer." In addition to producing these distinguished translations, these humanists also produced the first treatises of literary criticism since Aristotle, Horace, and Longinus. Philip Sidney's (1554–1586) "The Defence of Poesie" offers a powerful apologia for the beauty and utility of poetry.

Trained at Cambridge, Edmund Spenser (1552–1599) produced the greatest poem of the sixteenth century, *The Faerie Queene.* Like much other poetry of the time, Spenser's poem celebrates the sensuous beauty of NATURE and the glorious splendor of the physical world. Yet, the poem is also virulently anti-Catholic, and depicts the Roman Catholic Church as a villain in the poem (see CATHOLICISM, PROTESTANT REACTIONS). *The Faerie Queene* functions as a moral guidebook for its readers. An allegorical tale of quest and discovery, each of the poem's six books teaches the reader the way to learn a particular Christian virtue: holiness, temperance, chastity, friendship, justice, and courtesy.

Drama also takes center stage in the sixteenth century. Christopher Marlowe (1564–1593) retells the well-known story of a doctor who sells his soul to the devil to possess more knowledge in "The Tragical History of Doctor Faustus." Marlowe's tale of good and evil offered theatergoers a dramatic portrait that transcended the mystery play cycles of an earlier era. Faustus told a cautionary tale about the consequences of pride in everyday life, and although his play drew on the church's teachings, it did not have to reenact them explicitly to teach its message.

The greatest poet and playwright of the sixteenth century was William Shakespeare (1564–1616). He was a master of the English language, and his plays, along with the King James Version of the Bible, introduced more new words into the English vocabulary than had ever been present in the language before or since. His plays have been divided into the categories of histories, comedies, and tragedies. Shakespeare was primarily concerned in many of his plays not with religion but with politics. In the histories he offers a dramatic retelling of British history by focusing on the lives of the kings. The comedies, such as a *Midsummer Night's Dream,* provide a sly retelling of ancient stories in a modern setting. Like Spenser, Shakespeare glorifies nature in many of his comedies, and in both his comedies and his sonnets he is a poet of love. In the tragedies Shakespeare turns his attention to the shortcomings of human nature and the consequences of human pride, ambition, and hatred. Although not a religious play, Shakespeare's *King Lear* (1604–1605) offers one of the greatest in-depth examinations of the power of redemptive love as it overcomes hatred born of pride and overweening ambition.

The other great literary achievement of the sixteenth century was the King James Bible (see BIBLE, KING JAMES VERSION). This version of the Bible used the original Greek and Hebrew of the Old and New Testaments to produce a more reliable and accessible translation than previous English translations. The Bible's stylistic and linguistic influence can be traced from Milton to twentieth-century poets such as Randall Jarrell and James Dickey. The historical and literary achievements of the sixteenth century opened the way for the enormous flowering of literature that occurred in later centuries in the Protestant era.

The Seventeenth Century

If England changed rapidly during the sixteenth century, the pace of change increased from the ascension of James I in 1603 to the CIVIL WAR of 1642 to the Restoration of political order in 1660. During these years, increasing religious conflict between Anglicans and Puritans drove many Puritans to seek refuge in the New World. John Winthrop and others had visions of the New World as a new Jerusalem, a "city set upon a hill," which would enable them to begin a new life in a new holy place. Two issues dominated the world during the seventeenth century. One focused on how far the reformation of the church should extend. For most people the extent to which this reform was carried out was almost limitless. Another issue focused on the limits and authority of government. As the monarchy and the Parliament debated about their respective realms of authority, more and more of the populace supported the version of representative government that Parliament offered. In their eyes the monarchy should have no authority independent of the Parliament. Just as the seventeenth century stressed diversity and TOLERATION in religious matters, a tremendous diversity of literature appeared during this century.

Ben Jonson (1572–1637) continued the dramatic tradition begun by Marlowe and Shakespeare. Many scholars still contend that Jonson had a hand in writing some of Shakespeare's plays. Chiefly Jonson's plays, or masques, are political satires and have little to do with religion. Jonson was also a poet who is commonly associated with a group of poets—known as the Cavalier Poets—that included Robert Herrick (1591–1674) and Richard Crashaw (1613–1649). The theme of these poets' works is often expressed in a line taken from Herrick's "To the Virgins, to Make Much of Time": *Carpe diem!* "Seize the day!"

Another group of poets commonly called the Metaphysical Poets examined religion and religious themes in their works. JOHN DONNE (1572–1631) and GEORGE HERBERT (1593–1633) are the most famous of this group. In his early career Donne wrote satirical poems on topics ranging from MARRIAGE to sex. In 1615 Donne became an Anglican priest and the subjects of his poetry changed dramatically. He produced a series of Holy Sonnets in which he announces his total devotion to God and declares his repentance. However, even in his religious poems Donne retains some of his sensuous imagery. In the holy sonnet 14, Donne uses the sexual imagery of ravishing to describe his request to God to take over his heart and soul completely. George Herbert's poetry, unlike Donne's, captures the mystery of the church's LITURGY and DOCTRINE in the form of the poetry as well as in its content. In his book of poetry, *The Temple* (1633), Herbert conducts the reader on a tour of a church in poems like "The Altar" and "The Windows." The physical temple becomes the body as the temple of the Holy Spirit in poems such as "Discipline" and "Denial." Herbert emphasizes the topic of his poems by structuring the poem itself in the shape of the object of study. Thus in "The Altar" the poem's words are shaped like a church ALTAR. Herbert's poetry had its greatest influence on the American Puritan poet Edward Taylor (1642–1729), whose poems are his preparations for taking Holy Communion.

The Metaphysical Poets' concern with religion and religious themes culminates in the magisterial combination of classical and Christian learning found in the poetry of John Milton (1608–1674). Milton found himself embroiled in the politics of the Civil War in the mid-seventeenth century, and his many poems and pamphlets offer a glimpse of the tremendous diversity of his writing. He produced a treatise on the relationship of CHURCH AND STATE, *Areopagitica*, that took its name from the hill in Rome where Paul of Tarsus argued for the virtues of Christianity against the power of the state. His sonnets, at least one of which was addressed to OLIVER CROMWELL, range over political topics and meditations on his blindness. His tract on DIVORCE illustrated his struggles with his own marriage, and the poems on sadness ("Il Penseroso") and happiness ("L'Allegro") offer his ruminations on human nature. Out of his great range of writing, Milton wrote the greatest Christian epic poem of all time, *Paradise Lost* (1674). In the poem Milton retells the biblical story of the Fall of Humankind. Adam and Eve struggle with God's command not to eat from the tree of knowledge. In Milton's poem Satan is depicted as one of God's angels who is ousted from Heaven in a great battle. Satan realizes that God loves Adam more than Satan, so Satan forms a plan to invade Eden and trick the first humans. *Paradise Lost* presents Satan as an attractive creature whom humans cannot help but follow in their misguided state. Milton's epic poem introduced the idea into THEOLOGY that Satan fell from heaven, a view that many Protestants attribute to a mistranslation of Isaiah 14:12 in the King James Bible.

JOHN BUNYAN'S (1628–1688) THE PILGRIM'S PROGRESS combines the pilgrimage theme of Dante's *The Divine Comedy* and the allegory of Spenser's *Faerie Queene* to depict the journey of a soul (Pilgrim) struggling to reach the Celestial City (Heaven). As with any quest narrative, Pilgrim must overcome great obstacles on his journey. The difference between a standard quest narrative and Bunyan's work is that the obstacles arise out of Pilgrim's own sinfulness and that God providentially directs Pilgrim's journey. Bunyan's work expresses the Protestant notion of the responsibility of every human for sinfulness and the inability of our works to save us from despair. Only God's providence and our faith in God, in Bunyan's little morality tale, can lead us to the Celestial City.

In the New World, literature was beginning to take shape in the seventeenth century. Although much of the colonists' reading came from England, new voices rose in the colonies that expressed the religious sentiments of the colonists as well as the frustrations and challenges of this new geographical setting. The poets ANNE BRADSTREET (1612–1672) and Edward Taylor carried forth much of the work of the Metaphysical Poets in their own work, although Taylor's work was not discovered and published until the twentieth century and Bradstreet was reluctant to have her work published in her own lifetime. Bradstreet's poems offer glimpses of a Puritan woman struggling to live her faith in a new setting and to express her faith through poems devoted to everyday events in her life. Taylor's poems reflect the life of a minister striving to incorporate his faith into his professional life. Michael Wigglesworth's (1631–1705) poem "The Day of Doom" casts an apocalyptic glance at the souls of New England who refuse to accept Christ (see APOCALYPTICISM). Perhaps the most effective ways of transmitting faith in seventeenth-century New England were the *Bay Psalm Book* (1640) and *The New-England Primer* (1683). The Book of Psalms provided solace and comfort to colonists confronting the dangers and challenges of the New World. The *Primer,* on the other hand, offered a way of inculcating religion and morality in children as they learned the alphabet through various didactic tales about people who failed to follow the virtues of the Christian religion. The primer teaches religious lessons as the child learns each letter of the alphabet: "In *Adam's* fall, We Sinned All."

A literary genre peculiar to colonial America first appeared in 1682. The Indian captivity narrative presented stories of men and women who had been captured by local tribes of NATIVE AMERICANS but who had eventually been saved by God's gracious providence. The most famous of these narratives is Mary Rowlandson's "A Narrative of the Captivity and Restoration of Mrs. Mary Rowlandson." She tells the story of her captivity as a series of removes from her town. These removes are not only physical moves away from her family and friends but also signify her being removed from God. As she retells the story, the Indians are mostly vicious irreligious savages who have no hope of redemption. By the end of the tale God providentially restores her to her husband and her town, and she has a new view of God in light of her experience.

Another American writer, COTTON MATHER (1663–1728), a theologian and preacher, produced a theological history of New England, *Magnalia Christi Americana; or, The Ecclesiastical History of New England.* Mather's primary purpose was to indicate the ways in which God had delivered the Puritans to this new Christian kingdom and how this new experiment had worked.

Literature of all kinds flourished in the seventeenth century. By the eighteenth century literature produced by Protestants was much less visible than it had been in the previous centuries.

The Eighteenth Century

Very little literature in the Protestant tradition remains from the eighteenth century. The eighteenth century in Europe and America was dominated by political and philosophical revolution. As in the Renaissance, the ENLIGHTENMENT emphasized classical learning and the poetry, drama, and fiction of this century modeled itself on the writings of the Greeks and Romans of antiquity. Because of the various political revolutions occurring in Europe and America, the pamphlet and the newspaper became major literary forms. The eighteenth century also witnessed the rise of the novel in English, and many still argue whether Daniel Defoe's *Robinson Crusoe* or Henry Fielding's *Tom Jones* was the first English novel. Apart from Defoe's novel, though, the fiction of the eighteenth century transmitted genteel ideals and secular virtues in their pages. Although Samuel Richardson's *Clarissa* involves the education of a young woman, her education is conducted not according to religious ideals but according to philosophical truths. In general the eighteenth century witnessed the rise of philosophy as a way of thinking about the world that did not include religion. Philosophy challenged religion on all fronts, and Protestant Christianity was especially challenged with some of the early lives of Jesus that questioned the historicity of Jesus (see JESUS, LIVES OF). In the eighteenth century the world was changing for Protestant Christians, given that no longer was their impetus to reformation the most important idea on the Continent. The rights of persons, equality, liberty, and reason became paramount concerns in the eighteenth century. Reason, not revelation, became the primary way of talking about the human capacity to think about the world. Religion took a back seat to philosophy, a circumstance that would change literature for centuries to come.

The English literary scene was dominated by SAMUEL JOHNSON (1709–1784), the periodicalists Joseph Addison (1672–1719) and Richard Steele (1672–1729), the poet and critic Alexander Pope (1688–1744)—who remarked that the "proper study of mankind is man"—and novelist and social satirist JONATHAN SWIFT (1667–1745). The focus of these writers' works was strictly literary and social; if religion ever came into the discussion, it was because someone wished to make fun of it.

In America, literature reflected much of what was happening in England. DEISM had taken hold both in America and in England, so the view that God's providence ruled the world God created was being challenged by a view of God as a watchmaker who started the world going and was letting it wind down on its own. Benjamin Franklin (1706–1790) was the most vocal American proponent of this position, and Franklin wrote about his position in various works, including his *Autobiography*. There he developed a chart of virtues that he told himself he must follow every day. His dictum, "Imitate Socrates and Jesus," indicated the influence of both rational and religious thought on his life.

Perhaps the most famous American Protestant writer of the eighteenth century was JONATHAN EDWARDS (1703–1758). A pastor in Connecticut, Edwards participated in a number of AWAKENINGS around the Connecticut Valley in which he urged those who had fallen away from PURITANISM to return to their faith. His most famous sermon, "Sinners in the Hands of an Angry God," depicts sinful humankind dangling like a spider over the flames of hell. No human works can save us, Edwards writes, only God's GRACE. Apart from Edwards's sermons and his account of the Great Awakenings, little in the way of literature from a religious perspective exists in America in the eighteenth century.

The focus on rationalism of the eighteenth century gives way by the nineteenth century to a renewal of a focus on the workings of the supernatural in the natural world.

The Nineteenth Century

If the eighteenth century seemed devoid of any focus on religion, the nineteenth century brought religion back into cultural discussions. ROMANTICISM led the way in reintroducing the supernatural to the natural world. FRIEDRICH SCHLEIERMACHER (1768–1834) contended that religion imbued all of CULTURE, and SAMUEL TAYLOR COLERIDGE (1772–1834) argued that the human imagination replicated the act of God's creation in this world. Moreover the natural world was imbued with God's supernatural power, and God was revealed through the book of nature just as strongly as God was revealed through the Bible. By the end of the nineteenth century—in the period known as the Victorian Age—religion still functioned as a guide to human life and as an animating force in the natural world. However, the late nineteenth century witnessed more conflicts between religion and culture than in the Romantic Age, with poet Matthew Arnold (1822–1888) declaring the end of religion and the replacement of religion with poetry. In fact, according to Arnold and others, the close of the nineteenth century will mean the end of Christianity, a prophecy that literature and religion in the twentieth century did not fulfill.

Foremost among the major writers of the early nineteenth century are Coleridge and WILLIAM WORDSWORTH (1770–1850). Each in his own way rejected the artificial poetic style of the eighteenth century and tried to demonstrate that poetry reflected the organic whole that the natural world showed forth. The two poets agreed to work together to establish some principles for poetry, and Wordsworth announced his in his "Preface" to his *Lyrical Ballads*. Coleridge announced his principles in his critical work, *Biographia Literaria*. Wordsworth believed that the subject and language of poetry should be simple; thus he writes about rustic settings and simple people. For Wordsworth "poetry is the powerful overflow of spontaneous emotions." Coleridge argued that the poet is like God, and that the imagination is the primary human faculty. Many of Coleridge's poems deal with the supernatural. Each of these poets believed that nature was infused with the supernatural and poetry provided a way of gaining access to the supernatural. Coleridge more than Wordsworth participated in the work of organized religion and wrote a series of lay sermons on theological topics.

By the later part of the nineteenth century England had begun a series of changes once again. The Industrial Revolution had altered the economic landscape of the country and the gap between rich and poor had widened (see INDUSTRIALIZATION). The pastoral rural settings that the Romantics could talk about so freely were changing with the advent of the railroad and the cities were becoming choked with immigrants from the countryside. In 1859 Darwin's theory of evolution challenged the religious view of creation and offered a new way for humans to think about themselves.

Into this setting came GEORGE ELIOT (1819–1880), an educated woman who had translated DAVID FRIEDRICH STRAUSS's biography of Jesus, *The Life of Jesus Critically Examined,* and LUDWIG FEUERBACH's *The Essence of Christianity,* both of which challenged traditional Protestant notions of biblical history and theology. Eliot's novels captured an England that was changing and the effects of those changes on various classes of people. In *Scenes of Clerical Life* (1858), Eliot's first novel, she struggles to preserve what she views is the best of Christian religion even as she searches for a religion that overcomes the Christian religion. In her finest novel, *Middlemarch* (1871–1872), Eliot presents a woman whose idealism finds no outlet in marriage to an idealistic man. As Dorothea Brooke searches to fulfill her own ideals in Mr. Causabon's plan to gather all the world's myths into one book, she realizes that she lacks the emotional fervor to sustain the marriage. When he dies she marries his cousin, Will Ladislaw, and is able to fulfill her ideals only through his work. At best, Eliot's work offers an important critique of the role of Protestantism in the late nineteenth century.

The Twentieth Century and Beyond

What role has literature played in the development of Protestantism in the twentieth century and beyond? The century has witnessed some of the world's greatest poets and novelists—James Joyce, Marcel Proust, Thomas Mann, William Faulkner, Ernest Hemingway, F. Scott Fitzgerald, John Updike. The literature of the twentieth century has been developed against a backdrop of wars and suffering, political upheavals, religious uncertainty, and unprecedented scientific advances. Some of these novelists have used religion mainly as a target for their criticism. Others, like Updike, have depicted Protestant ministers and laypeople trying to come to terms with the inadequacies and the strengths of their religion.

One of the most interesting developments in the Protestant use of literature in the twentieth century has been the emergence of Christian fiction. Beginning in mid-century, a number of books by romance writer Grace Livingstone Hill were published. These genre novels contained simple situations involving people of the Protestant faith who were called on to make deci-

sions about their faith. Generally, they were intended to be uplifting books that could inspire women, primarily, in their daily walks with God. By the latter part of the century, around 1980, some evangelical Protestant religious publishers began to publish fiction modeled after the novels of Hill. The novels were successful, and the publishers had found a new literary product to sell to their readers. The most famous of these Christian novelists is Janette Oke, a Canadian author who sold well over two million books between 1995 and 2003. For the most part, these Christian novels are didactic and depict situations in which one sinful character must find God. However, various genres of this fiction have been developed so that readers can choose from Christian romances, biblical fiction, apocalyptic fiction, mysteries, and thrillers. The evolution of this popular writing represents the most significant development in the Protestant use of literature in the twentieth century and beyond. The authors writing these novels are attempting to be faithful to the visions of Protestants of the Reformation who desired to present the message of the faith in a form accessible and understandable to individuals and communities.

See also Bible Translation; Literature, German; Publishing, Media;

References and Further Reading

Abrams, M. H. *Natural Supernaturalism: Tradition and Revolution in Romantic Literature.* New York: W.W. Norton, 1971.
———, ed. *The Norton Anthology of English Literature.* 6th edition. 2 vols. New York: W.W. Norton, 1993.
Altick, Richard. *Victorian People and Ideas.* New York: W.W. Norton, 1973.
Aue, Pamela Willwerth, and Henry L. Carrigan Jr. *What Inspirational Literature Do I Read Next?* Detroit, MI: Gale, 2000.
Baugh, Albert C. *A Literary History of England.* New York: Appleton-Century-Crofts, 1948.
Bredvold, Louis I., ed. *Eighteenth Century Poetry and Prose.* New York: The Ronald Press Company, 1973.
Eliot, George. *Middlemarch.* New York: Oxford University Press, 1988.
Lamson, Roy, and Hallett Smith, eds. *Renaissance England: Poetry and Prose from the Reformation to the Restoration.* New York: W.W. Norton, 1956.
Lauter, Paul, ed. *The Heath Anthology of American Literature.* vol. 1. Lexington, MA: D.C. Heath and Company, 1990.
Milton, John. *Paradise Lost.* Norton Critical Editions. New York: W.W. Norton, 1975.
Parrott, Thomas Marc, ed. *Shakespeare: Twenty-Three Plays and the Sonnets.* New York: Scribner's, 1966.
Perkins, David, ed. *English Romantic Writers.* New York: Harcourt, Brace & World, Inc., 1967.
Trilling, Lionel, and Harold Bloom, eds. *Victorian Prose and Poetry.* New York: Oxford University Press, 1973.

Watt, Ian. *The Rise of the Novel: Studies in Defoe, Richardson, and Fielding.* Berkeley: University of California Press, 1957.

HENRY L. CARRIGAN JR.

LITERATURE, GERMAN

The relationship of German literature to the Reformation begins with the spread of humanism, an influence found throughout Protestant literature from the beginning of the modern era to the present day.

Fourteenth-century Humanism was a fundamental precondition for the German REFORMATION. Humanism opposed the dogmatic views of church scholasticism and embraced ancient literature and philosophy (Plato, Cicero). Originating in Italy this movement is closely associated with such figures as Dante Alighieri (1265–1321), Petrarch (1304–1374), and Coluccio Salutati (1331–1406). Humanism braced itself against the political disintegration of the northern Italian city-states and through its profound engagement with the literary achievements of ancient Rome fought the church's rigid scholasticism. With the decline and fall of the eastern Byzantine Empire in the first half of the fifteenth century, Byzantine scholars fled the newly established Ottoman state and turned to the West. They influenced the development of humanism and expanded its study of Greek literature. In GERMANY, where there existed a close relationship to ITALY during the Middle Ages, Humanist circles were more explicitly Christian in orientation than their Italian counterparts but also tended to be more anti-clerical. A number of authors contributed significantly to the growth of sixteenth-century humanism. Erasmus of Rotterdam (known after 1496 as Desiderius Erasmus; 1466–1536) wrote *Encomium moriae* (*In Praise of Folly*), a satire directed against the scholasticism and worldly materialism of the church. He also published the first Greek edition of the New Testament (1516), which was the basis for MARTIN LUTHER's translation of the BIBLE into German. Ulrich von Hutten (1488–1523), an opponent of the papacy after his stay in Rome between 1515 and 1517, wrote *Gespraech Buechlin Herr Ulrichs von Hutten* (Dialogue of Master Ulrich von Hutten, 1521), which denounced the CLERGY and outlined an anti-Roman reform program. Hutten also played an important role in the publication of *Epistolae obscurorum virorum* (Letters of Obscure Men), an anonymous polemic that defended the humanist Johannes Reuchlin (1455–1522) against the Dominicans of Cologne.

The movement of Renaissance humanism brought a surge of popular forms of literature, aided—as was the polemical literature of the Reformation—by the invention of movable type printing. Among these were books such as *Ein kurtzweilig Lesen von Dyl Ulenspiegel geboren uss dem Land zu Brunswick* (The Interesting Story of Till Eulenspiegel, from the Regiae of Brunswick, 1515) by Hermann Bote (ca. 1465–1520), "a mirror of human stupidity" that depicted the lives of "ordinary people," and the anonymous *Historia von D. Johann Fausten: Dem weltbeschreyten Zauberer und Schwartzkünstler* (History of Dr. Johann Faust, the World-Famous Magician and Master of Black Art, 1587), a work that inspired JOHANN WOLFGANG VON GOETHE's *Faust*.

Beginnings

The Reformation initiated by Luther in 1517 contributed two decisive factors toward the development of German literature. The translation of the Bible (New Testament, also called the September Testament, September 1522, the complete translation—*Biblia, das ist, die gantze Heilige Schrift, Deudsch. D. Mart. Luth.*—1534) gradually spread the official language of the early High German-speaking area of Saxony and made it the standard for written and spoken German. Luther enriched the German language with new word constructions and phrases drawn from common speech. Moreover his German-language sermons and biblical exegesis were essential in overcoming long-standing regional language barriers. In addition to translating the Bible, Luther contributed to the first hymnbook of the Reformation, *Geystliches gesangk Büchlein* (Spiritual Song Book) by Johann Walter (1496–1570). This invigorated hymnody, derived its tunes often from folk music, and was also one of the century's most important achievements in poetry.

These achievements in language and literature had an indirect influence on Protestantism in that they facilitated the development of CULTURE in the homes of the Protestant clergy. No less than half of the great German cultural figures—that is, those included in the *Allgemeine Deutsche Biographie* (published by the historical commission of the Royal Academy of Sciences, Leipzig, from 1875 to 1912)—were sons or daughters of Protestant ministers. Among them are important poets like Andreas Gryphius, Jakob Michael Reinhold Lenz, Jeremias Gotthelf, Gottfried August Bürger, and Gottfried Benn. The clerical profession afforded individuals the opportunity to rise socially and so had a way of attracting talented youth, and the atmosphere of learning and meditation fostered their talents. By the middle of the sixteenth century Protestantism had already had a decisive influence on German literature. Representative of this trend are Nikolaus Manuel (c.1484–1530), who performed comic Shrovetide plays during the Swiss Reformation; Hans Sachs (1494–1576), the *Meistersinger* and dramatist from Nuremberg; and Jörg Wickram (ca. 1595–before 1562), a Protestant forced to leave his birthplace in the Catholic city of Colmar who published collections of farcical tales and anecdotes in addition to Swiss Shrovetide plays. The flourishing of such plays demonstrates that they were well received by the common people.

Gradually the Shrovetide plays turned into pedagogical theater. Sixtus Birck (1501–1554) wrote the first German-language plays in this literary genre. Paul Rebhuhn (c.1505–1546), a school principal, performed pieces in classical verse form. The content eventually expanded, and historical elements were added to religious and moral themes. In 1579 Philipp Nicodemus Frischlin (1547–1590) performed *Frau Wendelgard: Ein new Comedi oder Spil, ausz glaubwürdigen Historien gezogen* (Lady Wendelgard: A New Comedy or Play, Drawn from Credible Historical Chronicles), a play that presented characters from the lower social classes. The development of social realism on the stage was furthered by Johannes Stricker (1540–1598) with the everyman drama *Die deutsche Schlömer* (1584) and by Georg Rollenhagen (1542–1609) with the didactic epic *Froschmeuseler*, featuring animal characters, a play that was heavily indebted to the ancient *Betrachomyomachia* (c.500 B.C.E.). At the time of the COUNTER-REFORMATION in the mid-sixteenth century, pre-Baroque literature first appeared in court theaters, influenced by the Italian commedia dell'arte and the English theater troupes. The most celebrated author was Herzog Heinrich Julius von Braunschweig-Wolfenbüttel (1564–1613).

Narrative also shed the traditional style of the Middle Ages. *Das Narrenschiff* (Ship of Fools) (1494) was a satire of contemporary life and customs written in rhyming couplets by Sebastian Brant (1458–1521). Prose emerged as a narrative art form in the early sixteenth century. Johann Fischart (1546–1590) filled his novels, verse satires, and treatises with a Calvinist ethos, and his powerful prose made him the most popular writer of his day. His novel *Affenteurliche und ungeheurliche Geschichtschrift . . .* (1533) marks a further development in pre-Baroque literature.

Baroque

Associated with the image of literature that is disordered, free from style, and contrary to rules, the term "Baroque" has become the standard description of seventeenth-century literature. The attributes of the Baroque were first defined in the nineteenth and twentieth centuries, and they reflected the tripartite division of Germany, where Lutherans, Calvinists, and Catholics were the three established forms of religion. A series of tensions characterize the Baroque style: the conflict between order and chaos, between lust for life and fear of DEATH, between affirmation of the world and nostalgia for the passing of time, and between a divine plan for human SALVATION and human sinfulness. The trauma of the Thirty Years' War (1618–1648), a religious and political war fought on German soil, thoroughly scarred seventeenth-century cultural life and contributed to the tension.

During the Reformation the hymn changed significantly. Luther had emphasized in his compositions the communal world of Christians, and so the Jesuit Friedrich Spee von Langenfeld (1591–1635) adopted in the hymn both the form of popular song and the emotionally intense natural spirit it contained. In the 1994 edition of the *Evangelische Gesangbuch,* the hymnal of the Lutheran and Reformed churches in Germany, one can still find many of the hymns from his collection of songs *Trutznachtigal* (posthumously published in 1649), including the well-known *O Heiland, reiss die Himmel auf.* The most important composer of Protestant hymns in the seventeenth century was the Lutheran PAUL GERHARDT (1607–1676). He wrote hymns of devotion and prayer intended to be sung by the individual. His Passion *O Haupt voll Blut und Wunden* (Oh, Sacred Head, Now Wounded) can be found in both Catholic and Protestant hymnals. In other hymns, such as *Geh aus mein Herz und suche Freud,* NATURE is portrayed as the creator's picture book in which one can find the soul of Christ. The hymns and brilliantly formulated epigrams of the *Cherubinischer Wandersmann* (Cherubic Pilgrim) (1657/1674), written by the mystic Angelus Silesius (actual name, Johannes Scheffler, 1624–1677), who converted in 1635 to Catholicism, emphasized the relationship of the individual to God. Similarly the hymns of Christian Knorr von Rosenroth (1636–1689), a minister's son who popularized Jewish mysticism in his Latin translation *Kabbala denudata* (*The Cabala Unveiled,* 1677/1678 and 1684), were also heavily influenced by the mystical literature of the age.

During this century lyricists concentrated on refining popular German language. Martin Opitz (after 1627 known as Opitz von Boberfeld, 1597–1639), who came from the Protestant middle class, introduced a poetic innovation with his *Buch von der deutschen Poeterey* (The Manual of German Poetry, 1624). It enabled poets to apply ancient verse forms to the German language. Instead of measuring meter by long and short stresses, he called for the counting of accented and unaccented syllables. The majority of poets were also scholars, and in the wake of Opitz's book many of them also published books on poetics. Among these were Philipp von Zesen (1619–1689), a son of a Lutheran minister, who published *Hochdeutscher Helikon oder Grund richtige Anleitung zur hochdeutschen Dicht- und Reimkunst* (1640); Johann

Klaj (1616–1656), who published *Lobrede der Teut-schen Poeterey* (1645); and Georg Philipp Harsdörfer (1607–1658), who published *Poetischer Trichter* (three volumes, 1647–1653). The impact of Opitz's poetics was also felt in the scholarly societies that set out to cultivate the German language by purifying it of foreign words and by establishing a standard orthography. In 1617 Ludwig Fürst von Anhalt-Köthen founded the first of these organizations, *Die Frucht-bringende Gesellschaft* (The Fruitful Society), also known as the *Palmenorden.* The most famous was *Löbliche Hirten- und Blumenorden an der Pegnitz,* founded by Harsdörfer and Klaj. They emphasized the cultivation of poetry in society over the standardization of the German language. The richness and diversity of lyric poetry from the Baroque period—by writers such as Friedrich von Logau (1604–1655), Simon Dach (1605–1659), Andreas Gryphius (1616–1664), and Christian Hofmann von Hofmannswaldau (1617–1679)—usually confuse the reader of today, but closer examination reveals a lyric that follows strict poetic rules. The sonnet was refined, Alexandrine verse was modeled from Roman verse, and rhetorical forms of argument and ornamental phrasing were used. The epigram also achieved its first flourishing moment in German literature. The epigram had a deliberate and formal structure and usually pronounced at its climax a thoughtful, antithetically formulated conclusion. This poetic form stood in contrast to the period's inclination for contradictory formulations, found, for example, in the sonnet. A typical element in Baroque literature is the emblem, an art form constructed of both image and text that contains an (allegorical) image or icon, a title (lemma, motto, or inscription), and a caption (usually an epigram). It reveals a hidden meaning that often concerns a moral, religious, or erotic theme. Without an understanding of the emblem, one can hardly make sense of Baroque dramas and novels.

The most broad-ranging dramatist of the Baroque period was Andreas Gryphius, the son of a Protestant archdeacon. He wrote martyr plays such as *Catharina von Georgien* (1657), historical tragedies such as *Ermordete Majestät oder Carolus Stuardus König von Gross Brittannien* (1657 and 1663) and *Grossmütiger Rechts—Gelehrter/Oder Sterbender Aemilius Paulus Papinianus* (1659), and comedies such as *Absurda Comica: Oder Herr Peter Squentz* (1658) and *Horribilicribifax: Teutsch* (1663). In Germany at the beginning of the seventeenth century there were no permanently established theaters or theater ensembles as we know them today, and amateurs performed plays only on special occasions. English theater troupes came to Germany for the first time in the 1680s and began to popularize Shakespeare. They also brought the notion of the profes-sional theater. This development was useful to Gryphius, as were his studies and the experiences he gained from his numerous travels throughout Europe.

In the seventeenth century the novel underwent a distinct development. The history of the novel in Germany begins with the reception of foreign-language novels translated by Opitz, von Zesen, Harsdörfer, and Johann Michael Moscherosch (1601–1669). Among these works were *Amadisroman* (probably of Portuguese origin), *Daphnis und Chloë* by Longos (third century B.C.), *Satyricon* by Petronius (first century B.C.), and *Aithiopika* by Heliodorus (third century B.C.). In contrast to these earlier romantic novels, the courtly historical novel arose in Germany in the seventeenth century. The plots in these novels usually involve the protagonist in many entanglements and temptations in the imperial court, which he in the end influences to the benefit of all its subjects. The most formally well-knit novel of this type is *Grossmütiger Feldherr Arminius* (two volumes, 1689) by Daniel Casper von Lohenstein (1635–1683), and the last great expression of its kind is *Die Asiatische Banise oder das blutig—doch mutige Pegu* (1689) by Heinrich Anshelm von Zigler und Kliphausen (1663–1696), one of the most famous works of the age, which by 1766 had gone through nine printings and countless serial editions, reworkings, and dramatizations. It plays a role in Goethe's novel *Wilhelm Meister.* Hans Jakob Christoph von Grimmelshausen (1622–1676) had an even more powerful impact with his *Der abentheuerliche Simplicissimus teutsch* (1668–1669), the first important picaresque novel in German literature. It was based in large part on the author's life and describes the world of the Thirty Years' War with rich observations, knowledge, and fantasy. Heroic, political novels of court affairs and picaresque novels continued to be published from the turn of the seventeenth century to the eighteenth century. A late form of the courtly novel was refined by Eberhard Werner Happel (1647–1690), also a minister's son; with this came the so-called gallant poetry, a transition from the Baroque to ENLIGHTENMENT literature. In addition to the short form of the lyric, this new poetic expression gave rise to the gallant novel that emphasized a love story over the political and heroic plot; the creator of this new genre was August Bohse (pseudonym Talander, 1661–1730), and its premier example was the novel *Amor am Hofe* of 1689.

The Eighteenth Century and the Enlightenment

In 1719, when *The Life and Strange Surprizing Adventures of Robinson Crusoe, of York, Mariner* was published (in Germany as *Das Leben und die gantz ungemeinen Begebenheiten des berühmten Engelländ-*

ers *Mr. Robinson Crusoe*, 1720), the literary genre of Robinson stories spread throughout Europe, the most important of which was *Wunderliche Fata einiger See-Fahrer*, published in four parts from 1731 to 1743 by Johann Gottfried Schnabel (1692–1760), also a minister's son. Ludwig Tieck (1773–1853) published a new form of this kind of novel with the title *Die Insel Felsenburg* (1828), which expanded the utopian theme. Johann Christian Günther (1695–1723), who had attended a newly founded Protestant high school in the city of Schweidnitz, was in his day the only true poetic genius, a forebear of the Sturm und Drang literary movement, although he tends to be treated in literary histories as a wastrel student of poetry. His poems combine biography with poetry and were influenced by the formal structure of the Protestant hymn. The Old Testament here replaced Mount Olympus as poetic inspiration.

In the eighteenth century court culture lost its importance as the center of literary activity. Protestant states in Germany assumed leadership of literary culture, just as a cultural rift began to appear between the progressive Protestant north and the Catholic south. Central to this development were the universities in Leipzig, HALLE, and Heidelberg as well as intellectual social circles in Hamburg, Bremen, Zurich, and Berlin. In Hamburg, Barthold Hinrich Brockes (1680–1747) composed his *Irdisches Vergnügen in Gott* (nine volumes, 1721–1748), a collection of poems inspired by the Christian spirit of the Enlightenment that praised the perfection, beauty, and purposeful design of God's creation, and Friedrich von Hagedorn (1708–1754) wrote fables and Anacreontic lyrics in the ranging and worldly spirit of Horace. After 1770 Friedrich Gottlieb Klopstock (1724–1803) also lived in Hamburg. Inspired by JOHN MILTON'S *Paradise Lost,* he composed the verse epic *Der Messias* (1748–1773) in an attempt to create a German national epic. In Leipzig, Christian Fürchtegott Gellert (1715–1769) wrote fables, comedies, and hymns (which are still sung to this day) that combined Pietistic religiosity with didacticism (see PIETISM). Also in Leipzig was the literary reformer Johann Christoph Gottsched (1700–1760), who in the spirit of the early ENLIGHTENMENT attempted to transpose onto German literature the aesthetic principles of French classicism. In Bremen his followers were associated with the newspaper *Neue Beyträge zum Vergnügen des Verstandes und des Witzes* (1744–1748). In Zürich, the city of HULDRYCH ZWINGLI, Johann Jakob Bodmer (1698–1783) and Johann Jakob Breitinger (1701–1776) formulated a literary theory heavily influenced by *Paradise Lost* that placed primary importance not on the imitation of the real but on the representation of the possible. In Berlin the writer and bookseller Friedrich Nicolai

(1733–1811) developed an antireligious form of Enlightenment thought, a tendency traceable to his upbringing in an orphanage at Halle that estranged him from religion. In his novel *Das Leben und die Meinungen des Herrn Magister Sebaldus Nothanker* (1773–1776) he discusses the question of eternal damnation. Karl Philipp Moritz (1756–1793) also suffered through a pietistic-quietist upbringing, which he describes in *Anton Reiser: Ein psychologischer Roman* (published in four parts from 1785 to 1790).

One of the most important writers of the eighteenth century was Christoph Martin Wieland (1733–1813), a minister's son. His novel *Die Abderiten* (1774) is a satire of the simpleminded narrowness and righteousness of SECTARIANISM. Sophie von La Roche (1731–1807), a close friend of Wieland's, chose a different path and became well known as the writer of sensitive epistolary novels, the most famous of which is *Geschichte des Fräuleins von Sternheim* (1771). Counted among these authors of the preclassical era is the art theorist Johann Joachim Winckelmann (1717–1768) from the Protestant city Altmark, who converted to Roman Catholicism in 1754; he saw in Greek art the perfect imitation of nature's beauty. The greatest achievements in German literature of the Enlightenment era are found in works by GOTTHOLD EPHRAIM LESSING.

From the Sturm und Drang Period to the Romantic Era

The literary revolution initiated in 1770 is called Sturm und Drang. The theories of JOHANN GEORG HAMANN and JOHANN GOTTFRIED VON HERDER had a formative influence, and the works of the young Johann Wolfgang von Goethe stand as the central poetic achievements of the movement. The era is characterized by increasing secularization as well as greater personal sensitivity and secular pietistic devotion. The most important representatives of the Sturm und Drang movement were Heinrich Wilhelm von Gerstenberg (1737–1823), a dramatist and Anacreontic poet of occasional poems, and the writer JOHANN HEINRICH JUNG-STILLING (1740–1817)—both influenced by Pietism. Also significant were the dramatist Heinrich Leopold Wagner (1747–1779), the poet Gottfried August Bürger (1747–1794), and the poet Ludwig Heinrich Christoph Hölty (1748–1776), the son of a minister, whose sensitive lyrics were set to music by composers such as Johannes Brahms. Friedrich Müller, also called Maler Müller (1749–1825), wrote poetic idylls, and Johann Heinrich Voss (1751–1826), whose Protestant cast of mind in old age took on a pugnacious demeanor, translated Homer. Also counted among the important figures of the period are the dramatist Jakob Michael Reinhold Lenz (1751–1792), the son of a Baltic general superintendent; Johann Anton Leisewitz (1752–1806); Friedrich Maximilian Klinger (1752–1831); and JOHANN CHRISTOPH FRIEDRICH VON SCHILLER. Nearly all came from Protestant families. During the Sturm und Drang period German literature underwent a decisive transformation in which the poet's subjectivity, not knowledge drawn from outside of literature, determined the truth of a poetic creation. Poetry thus shed its 2,000-year-old ties to philosophy and THEOLOGY. The years between 1779 and 1787 (the year Goethe's *Iphigenie auf Tauris* was published) on through to 1805 (the year of Schiller's death) show this very clearly. Because of its orientation toward ancient Greece, it is also called the classical period under the dominant influence of Herder, Goethe, and Schiller. Today this epoch is generally considered the high point in German literary history.

At the same time, in 1793–1795, ROMANTICISM emerged as a protest against the rigid rationalism of the Enlightenment. Its philosophical roots lie in the idealism of philosophers such as IMMANUEL KANT, Johann Gottlieb Fichte (1762–1814), FRIEDRICH ERNST DANIEL SCHLEIERMACHER, FRIEDRICH WILHELM JOSEPH VON SCHELLING, and GEORG W. F. HEGEL, whose thought is Protestant in origin. The movement began in Jena among the circle of friends surrounding the sons of a minister—August Wilhelm von Schlegel (1767–1845) and Friedrich von Schlegel (1772–1829)—that included Schelling, Fichte, Schleiermacher, and Novalis (actual name, Georg Philipp Friedrich von Hardenberg [1772–1801]), who was deeply influenced by Pietism. The Romantics' point of departure is the central experience of disunity between the self and the world. The individual seeks identity with himself or herself, often at night, while sleeping and dreaming, and ultimately finds it in death. The Romantic movement spread quickly. During this time two friends born in the Protestant city of Berlin, Wilhelm Heinrich Wackenroder (1773–1798) and Ludwig Tieck, who had studied theology, brought to light the art of the German lyric in the Middle Ages (*Herzensergiessungen eines kunstliebenden Klosterbruders*, 1797), which would come to influence the emerging literary culture. The mixing of literary genres is typical of the poetic and theoretical identity of the movement. For example, Friedrich von Schlegel called for "a progressive, universal poetry," and the poetic genius of Ernst Theodor Amadeus Hoffmann (1776–1822) brought together the musical and the painterly; among Hoffmann's notable works are the collection of fairy tales *Undine* (1812–1814) as well as the novel *Lebensansichten des Katers Murr* (two volumes, 1820–1822) and the narrative cycle *Die Serapionsbrüder* (1819–1821). Hoffmann also had an interest in medical questions and in the doctor Justinus Andreas Christian Kerner (1786–1862), whose research on SPIRITUALISM and occultism surfaces in Hoffmann's fiction (for example, in *Die Seherin von Prevorst*, 1829).

At the beginning of the nineteenth century the fascination with folk poetry—a genre that first attracted Herder and Goethe—greatly increased. Achim von Arnim (1781–1831) and Clemens Brentano (1778–1842) published the collection of folk songs *Des Knaben Wunderhorn* (1806–1808); the brothers Jacob Ludwig Karl Grimm (1785–1863) and Wilhelm Karl Grimm (1786–1859) published their *Kinder- und Hausmärchen* (1812–1815). The Romantics—in painting as well as in literature—cultivated a yearning for the infinite in both a temporal and a spatial sense. They discovered the dream and the power of intuition. The novel *Ahnung und Gegenwart* (1815) and the novella *Aus dem Leben eines Taugenichts* (1826) by Joseph Freiherr von Eichendorff (1788–1857) have these typical characteristics. Romanticism valued the Middle Ages, and this led in late Romanticism to the so-called romantic CONVERSION: Friedrich von Schlegel became Roman Catholic in 1808 and Clemens Brentano in 1817; Brentano's close friend Luise Hensel (1798–1876), daughter of a minister and author of the famous *Müde bin ich, geh zur Ruh*, converted in 1818. Counted among the Romantics is the Jewish lyricist, satirist, and essayist Heinrich Heine (1797–1856), who converted in 1825 to Protestantism and as an exile in Paris (after 1831) worked to mediate hostilities between Germany and FRANCE.

Three of the most important poets from the turn of the nineteenth century are difficult to describe as either classical or Romantic. The minister's son Jean Paul (actually Johann Paul Friedrich) Richter (1763–1825), a writer rooted in German idealism, combined in his novels influences from Laurence Sterne and Henry Fielding with elements of sentimentalism and the rococo. Johann Christian Friedrich Hölderlin (1770–1843), who befriended Hegel and Schelling while studying theology, is considered the originator of a new understanding of ancient Greece and was one of the most important poets of German idealism. Heinrich von Kleist (1777–1811), second only to Schiller, is seen as one of the most important dramatists of his age. In his story *Michael Kohlhaas* (1810), Kleist created one of the few convincing characters modeled on Martin Luther in the literature of the Napoleonic era and also stylized the reformer as a forerunner of German nationalism. The Catholic convert Zacharias Werner (1768–1823) wrote the drama *Martin Luther oder die Weihe der Kraft* (1807), a work now fallen into oblivion.

The Restoration and the Biedermeier Period

With the end of the Napoleonic age in 1815 and the Vienna conference of 1814–1815, the era of restoration began and signaled the transition from the Romantic to the Biedermeier period in German culture. The Karlsbad resolutions of 1819 attempted to turn back nationalizing and liberalizing efforts with strict censorship measures. For historians this period is significant because of the importance of Romanticism and the emerging NATIONALISM of the time. The poet Ludwig Uhland (1787–1862) from Protestant Swabia, himself a politically engaged liberal, describes these changes in his ballads. In literature the Protestant theologian Wilhelm Hauff (1802–1827), inspired by Sir Walter Scott, wrote *Lichtenstein* (1826), the first German historical novel. Also at this time the Swiss minister Jeremias Gotthelf (actually Albert Bitzius, 1797–1854) gave moral and didactic depictions of peasant life (for example, *Die schwarze Spinne,* 1842; and *Uli der Knecht,* 1846). The Protestant minister Eduard Mörike (1804–1875) is important as a poet of musical and pictorially vivid lyrics and as a writer of such works as *Maler Nolten* (1832) and *Mozart auf der Reise nach Prag* (1856). Other writers, such as Heinrich Heine and the dramatist Georg Büchner (1813–1837), were inspired to provide penetrating social and political criticism of the restoration before the Revolution of 1848. Büchner's play *Dantons Tod* (1835) presents a historically pessimistic interpretation of the FRENCH REVOLUTION, and his fragmentary tragedy *Woyzeck* (posthumously published in 1878) combines the social and pathological perspectives of naturalism. In this period of transition from idealism to realism appeared the work of the dramatists Christian Dietrich Grabbe (1801–1836) and Christian Friedrich Hebbel (1813–1863). In his theory of *Pantragismus* Hebbel develops a secularized form of original SIN, and he enriched the historicism of the nineteenth century with biblical and historical-mythological plays. Making keen observations in works critical of society and of the period (for example, *Die Epigonen,* 1836; and *Münchhausen,* 1838–1839), the writer Karl Leberecht Immermann (1796–1840) also pointed new directions for the novel.

The hymn of the eighteenth century—most famously represented in the poetry of Gellert and Klopstock—was considered a form of moral instruction, although these songs were never as popular as hymns from the sixteenth and seventeenth centuries (see HYMNS AND HYMNALS). The decline of the hymn continued through the nineteenth century, and only a few Romantic poets, such as Novalis, created spiritual poetry in the form of traditional folk songs, but no hymns by any standard definition. The Biedermeier period often had a tendency toward sentimentality, exemplified by such works as *Psalter und Harfe* (1833) by Philipp Spitta (1801–1859), a minister from a Huguenot family (see HUGUENOTS). Interest in history during the nineteenth century did inspire a number of hymn collections that even now are considered important sourcebooks; exemplary of these is the work of the hymnologist Philipp Karl Eduard Wackernagel (1800–1877) *Das deutsche Kirchenlied von der ältesten Zeit bis zu Anfang des 17. Jahrhunderts* (*The German hymn from ancient times to the beginning of the seventeenth century*; five volumes, Leipzig, 1864–1877).

Realism and Naturalism

At mid-century, with the failure of the Revolution of 1848, there arose in Germany a poetic, bourgeois realism already dominant in other European countries. The most important representatives of realism are Theodor Storm (1817–1888); Gottfried Keller (1819–1890); Theodor Fontane (1819–1898); and Wilhelm Raabe (1831–1910), who was born a Protestant but became a self-described convert to philosophical materialism, measured agnosticism, and human skepticism. An exception to this trend is the Calvinist poet and novelist Conrad Ferdinand Meyer (1825–1898), whose ballads and stories are set in the Renaissance and in the period of religious warfare during the Thirty Years' War. In the decades between 1850 and 1900 the novella (for example, Keller's *Die Leute von Seldwyla,* 1856, and *Das Sinngedicht,* 1882; and Storm's *Der Schimmelreiter,* 1888) and the novel (for example, Keller's *Der grüne Heinrich,* four volumes, 1854 edition/1879 edition; Fontane's *Effi Briest,* 1895, and *Der Stechlin,* 1899; and Raabe's *Der Schüdderump,* three volumes, 1870, and *Das Odfeld,* 1889) achieved a high point. In literary history, epic works of poetic realism found in lyrics by Keller, Storm, and Fontane are too often overlooked. This was also a rich period for the ballad, a genre initiated by Gottfried August Bürger and Ludwig Heinrich Christoph Hölty in 1770, one that reaches its zenith with Goethe and Schiller and is continued by Ludwig Uhland and Heinrich Heine. Fontane created ballads in the realistic mode.

Reacting to the triumph of scientific positivism, INDUSTRIALIZATION, and the creation of an industrial proletariat, Dichter Heinrich (1855–1906), Julius Hart (1859–1930), Gerhart Hauptmann (1862–1946), Johannes Schlaf (1862–1941), Arno Holz (1863–1929), and Max Halbe (1865–1944) embraced the epic and dramatic naturalism of the French writer Emile Zola (1840–1902) and the Norwegian playwright Henrik Ibsen (1828–1906). Naturalism created a style that called for social analysis written in the language of the lower classes; it is based in precise description of sensually experienced reality and the economic and moral suffering of people, which is combined with a criticism of bourgeois society. The literature of naturalism was inspired no longer by theological problems but by scientific theories, physiology, the theory of evolution (see DARWINISM), philosophical positivism, and theories of environmental determinism. However, in many works from this period one can recognize impulses associated with Protestantism, especially in the ethical sincerity of criticism that targets the moral decline of the bourgeoisie and in early works by Hauptmann (*Der Apostel*, 1892; *Hannele*, 1894), which were influenced by the MORAVIAN CHURCH.

Modernism

In 1890, with the prime of naturalism over, literary modernism begins. Its characteristic features are the reception of the literary and philosophical works of FRIEDRICH NIETZSCHE and a pluralism of various and competing styles. Among these are symbolism, *Jugendstil*, decadence, regional art, neo-Romanticism, impressionism, and, after 1910, expressionism. Many of the important authors in the years from 1890 to 1914 came from Protestant backgrounds, including Richard Dehmel (1863–1920), Frank Wedekind (1864–1918), Stefan George (1868–1933), Heinrich Mann (1871–1950), Thomas Mann (1875–1955), and Hermann Hesse (1877–1962); others from assimilated Jewish families converted to Christianity, such as Arthur Schnitzler (1862–1931) and Stefan Zweig (1881–1942). The SECULARIZATION of religious questions was typical in works published in the years around 1900. Authors no longer sought religious confession and theological interpretation to answer the problem posed by death; they considered mortality within concrete, isolated instances of dying. Many novels deal with problems of schooling and family upbringing as well as suicide, such as *Buddenbrooks* (1901) by Thomas Mann, *Unterm Rad* (1906) by Hermann Hesse, and *Die Verwirrungen des Zöglings Törless* (1906) by Robert Musil (1880–1942). If clergymen appear in novels from this decade, they are usually treated very critically. This stems from the conviction that religious forms of devotion have had their day and are no longer believable. Many works of the early twentieth century often contain secularized mysticism, especially those written by Hugo von Hofmannsthal (1874–1929), Rainer Maria Rilke (1875–1926), and Musil (*Der Mann ohne Eigenschaften*, 1930–1942), a mysticism that provides an alternative form of life and consciousness within the anonymity and mechanization of the modern world. With the advance of industrialization and the alienation of urban populations from religion, the culturally formative power of the Protestant minister's house recedes, and literature completely renounces religious themes. Individual fate and the dialectic of life and death step into the foreground. An example of this trend is Gottfried Benn (1886–1956), one of the most important poets of the twentieth century, in whose work religious and metaphysical questions abound but remain unanswered.

In the novels of Max Frisch (1911–1991) the insistent question of self-identity can be seen as a late form of the Protestant questioning of conscience, for example, in *Mein Name sei Gantenbein* (1964). Friedrich Dürrenmatt (1921–1990), the son of a Swiss clergyman, takes this one step further in his dramas (most famously, *Der Besuch der alten Dame,* 1955) by using a radical but logical style to represent the moral destruction caused by two world wars. An exception to this is Mann, the most significant novelist of the twentieth century, who in his later work presented Lutheran religious convictions behind a mask of irony and humor (for example, in *Joseph und seine Brüder*, 1926–1942; *Doktor Faustus,* 1947; and *Der Erwählte*, 1951). The World War and the Nazi dictatorship inspired a few authors to write Christian poetry, for example, Jochen Klepper (1903–1942) and Johannes Bobrowski (1917–1965), an author greatly influenced by Hamann. Nevertheless, the Bible in Luther's translation remained a source of linguistic and poetic power, as shown in the work of the Marxist author Bertolt Brecht (1898–1956) and in younger poets like Günter Eich (1907–1972), Eva Zeller (born in 1923), and Reiner Kunze (born in 1933). After poetry reached a high point in the works of Rilke and Stefan George, it gained renewed importance after 1945. At the same time the second half of the twentieth century witnessed a renaissance of the Protestant hymn, the full appreciation of which is still to come.

See also Calvinism; Literature; Lutheranism

References and Further Reading

Bartel, Klaus J. *German Literary History, 1777–1835*. New York: P. Lang, 1976.

Batts, Michael S. *A History of the Histories of German Literature, 1835–1914*. Montreal, Canada: McGill–Queen's University Press, 1993.

Beutin, Wolfgang, et al. *A History of German Literature*. New York and London: Routledge, 1993.

Emmel, Hildegard. *History of the German Novel*. Detroit, MI: Wayne State University Press, 1994.

Vivian, Kim, ed. *A Concise History of German Literature to 1900*. New York: Camden House, 1992.

Watanabe-O'Kelly, Helen, ed. *The Cambridge History of German Literature*. Cambridge and London: Cambridge University Press, 2000.

ULRICH KARTHAUS

LITURGY

The term "liturgy," derived from the Greek *leitourgia* (*laós,* people, and *érgon,* work), referred originally to public services performed on behalf of the people. By New Testament times, however, the word was used to describe acts of Christian WORSHIP. In contemporary parlance, it is used most commonly by Roman Catholic, Orthodox, Anglican, and Lutheran churches to refer to the words and acts of worship. Other mainline Protestant denominations sometimes employ the term as well, but FREE CHURCH traditions do not usually speak of their worship practices as liturgy. Among Roman Catholic and Orthodox Christians, the term may be used to describe a particular order of worship, a collection of worship services or rites, or the eucharistic (or communion) service alone. Protestant usage of the term refers to the words and acts that constitute the public worship of God, as well as to written services that are provided in officially sanctioned books of worship. Liturgy, then, may refer to the whole pattern of a service of worship, including the specific words said and the acts performed, or it may refer to the printed texts used in those services.

Ranges of Meaning and Use

All assemblies gathered for worship have a liturgy, or a pattern that they follow, but not all churches use the term liturgy to describe what they do in worship. Although Quakers adhere to a set of expectations about what happens when they gather, they would not describe what they do as a liturgy; nor would Baptists, Pentecostals, historically African American churches, or other free church traditions usually use the term. Likewise, those churches are less likely to use liturgical books, placing high value instead on extemporaneous PRAYER and holding to a particular understanding of the movement of the Holy Spirit in worship. In some cases, however, ministers may consult manuals in conducting services of BAPTISM, communion, MARRIAGE, and funerals.

On the other hand, Protestant denominations with traditions of using written texts in their services of worship often describe their worship patterns as liturgies. Churches in the Anglican Communion around the world follow the order for worship set forth in the BOOK OF COMMON PRAYER or similar prayerbooks that have been adapted in content and/or language for other cultural contexts. Fairly strict adherence to the texts and rubrics (directions) provided is expected. Similarly, congregations in the various Lutheran churches throughout the world make use of liturgical books such as the North American *Lutheran Book of Worship.*

Churches with Reformed and Methodist roots are provided with books of worship services that are officially sanctioned by their denominations and recommended, but not required, for use. These churches exercise a balance between form and freedom, following a pattern for weekly worship that incorporates both written texts from service books as well as locally written and spontaneous prayers. In the UNITED STATES, for example, the *United Methodist Book of Worship* and the Presbyterian *Book of Common Worship* provide liturgies for congregations to use or adapt. Denominations that are the result of mergers between denominations, such as the UNITING CHURCH IN AUSTRALIA and the CHURCH OF SOUTH INDIA, also provide service books that may be used as local congregations see fit. In some churches it is considered appropriate to use experimental liturgies or prayers produced by individuals or groups other than denominational officials. Other churches depend most heavily on hymnals, which may include brief orders of worship, ecumenical creeds, and/or services for communion, baptism, and ordination, to provide some measure of liturgical uniformity.

Elements of Liturgy

Generally speaking, Christian liturgy is understood to include prayers spoken by a presider (worship leader) as well as those said by the people, the reading of scripture, the PREACHING of a sermon or homily, congregational singing, baptism, and the LORD'S SUPPER. Liturgical texts provide an outline of a worship service and include the prayers, blessings, and other elements such as calls to worship and declarations of forgiveness. In some cases guidelines are given for extemporaneous prayer, instructions regarding gestures, movements, and the performance of ritual acts. The use of symbols (such as candles or crosses, for example), visual art, processionals, dance, and other forms of MUSIC are also understood to be part of liturgical celebration.

Many Protestant churches provide resources for daily prayer as well as for the weekly assembly. These liturgies center around the reading of scripture, common prayer, and the singing or reading of psalms and canticles. Orders of worship may also be provided for services of healing.

Development of Protestant Liturgies

Although the last five centuries have seen a broad emergence of liturgical practice among Protestants, many contemporary denominations can trace their roots to one of the major reformers, most of whom held to the use of some sort of printed form of worship. In his *Deutsche Messe* (German Mass) of 1526 MARTIN LUTHER adapted the Roman mass by putting it into the vernacular and including German hymns along with other sung parts of the liturgy. The basic word-table structure of the mass was retained, although he did make significant changes to the eucharistic prayer to reflect his rejection of the doctrine of TRANSUBSTANTIATION.

JOHN CALVIN sought to retain the basic pattern of the Roman mass in the liturgy he created for the Reformed churches in Strassburg and Geneva, the *Form of Prayers* (1540 and 1542). His order offered a selection of prayers from which the presider could choose and also made provisions for extemporaneous prayer. Calvin, too, championed congregational song in the form of metrical psalmody.

THOMAS CRANMER's liturgy for the CHURCH OF ENGLAND, *The Book of Common Prayer* (1549 and 1552), most closely followed the form and content of the Roman mass, although the eucharistic theology expressed in the liturgy showed the influence of other Reformation thought. Nearly two centuries later, JOHN WESLEY would commend THE BOOK OF COMMON PRAYER to the emerging Methodist church, although American Methodists would soon adopt a less formal liturgical program, relying instead on a brief outline of worship and extemporaneous prayer. The eighteenth and nineteenth centuries saw Reformed churches follow the same trend, in spite of the intentions of Calvin. The heirs of the Anabaptist traditions perpetuated their Reformation ancestors' aversion to ceremony, sacramental objects, and the liturgical year, shunning formal liturgies in most cases.

In the twentieth century the liturgical renewal movement inspired a broad range of Protestant denominations to rediscover worship practices of the early church and to study anew the liturgical instincts of the reformers, resulting in the production of new liturgical resources. Consequently, a number of Protestant traditions have adopted liturgies that reflect the word-table pattern of the historic CHURCH, and many have returned to using denominationally sanctioned service books. At the same time, a broad approach to the use of liturgical resources prevails across Protestant denominations, and even traditions that historically have adhered strictly to prescribed liturgies have expanded the sources from which material can be drawn. This approach to worship stresses a high level of participation among worshipers through word, ritual, and song, thus recapturing the sense of liturgy as the "work of the people."

See also Anabaptism; Anglicanism; Baptists; Friends, Society of; Hymns and Hymnals; Lutheranism; Methodism; Orthodoxy, Eastern; Pentecostalism; Presbyterianism

References and Further Reading

Bradshaw, Paul, ed. *The New Westminster Dictionary of Liturgy and Worship*. Louisville, KY: Westminster John Knox Press, 2002. [First published in Great Britain in 2002 under the title *The New SCM Dictionary of Liturgy and Worship*.]

Fink, Peter E., S.J., ed. *The New Dictionary of Sacramental Worship*. Collegeville, MN: The Liturgical Press, 1990.

Jones, Cheslyn, Geoffrey Wainwright, Edward Yarnold S.J., and Paul Bradshaw, eds. *The Study of Liturgy*. Rev. edition. New York: Oxford University Press, 1992. [First published in Great Britain in 1992.]

Senn, Frank. *Christian Liturgy*. Minneapolis, MN: Augsburg Fortress, 1997.

Thompson, Bard. *Liturgies of the Western Church*. Philadelphia, PA: Fortress Press, 1980.

White, James F. *Protestant Worship: Traditions In Transition*. Louisville, KY: Westminster John Knox Press, 1989.

———. *The Sacraments in Protestant Practice and Faith*. Nashville, TN: Abingdon Press, 1999.

KIMBERLY BRACKEN LONG

LIVINGSTONE, DAVID (1813–1873)

Missionary-explorer, scientist, abolitionist, and geographer. Livingstone was born in Blantyre, SCOTLAND to a deeply religious but impoverished family. About age eighteen he experienced personal CONVERSION and embraced the novel idea of becoming a medical missionary. Studious and resourceful, he funded his own medical education at Anderson College (Glasgow) and gained acceptance for missionary service with the nondenominational London Missionary Society. He sensed a call to go to AFRICA, and arrived there in 1841.

A few years after his arrival, he rejected a sedentary missionary life and embarked on extensive explorations of the unevangelized African interior. His "discoveries" and exploits—notably the epic transcontinental journey from Luanda to Quelimane (1853–1856)—earned him fame and a brief consulship. Then followed an exploration of the Zambezi-Shire region (1858–1864) and the search for the source of the Nile (1866–1873). Livingstone was impelled by an all-consuming vision of missionary expansion and a passionate conviction that opening up Africa to the twin benefits of legitimate commerce and Christianity was the most effective solution to the pernicious slave trade and key to the continent's material development. His celebrity served as a useful platform for his unflagging antislavery campaign, and his lofty idealism galvanized a new phase of Protestant missionary effort in central and east Africa. An indomitable personality and a remarkable capacity for physical endurance fostered a myth of indestructibility, and his famed meeting with H. M. Stanley in 1871, having been presumed dead, did nothing to reduce it.

At his death Livingstone was extolled as "the greatest man of his generation" and for long his life and legacy were enshrouded in legend. With access to new material, recent scholarship has focused sharply on his failures (as a missionary, explorer, geographer, husband, and father), his personality flaws, and his contribution to British imperial expansion. However, few did more to advance the cause of Protestantism in Africa. By the time of his death, in the village of Chitambo (in present day Zambia), he had preached the gospel to more African tribes than any previous missionary and transformed European views of Africa and Africans. Still, he remains a complex figure, perhaps best thought of as a giant with feet of clay.

See also Slavery; Slavery, Abolition of

References and Further Reading

Primary Sources:

Livingstone, David. *Missionary Travels and Researches in South Africa*. London: John Murray, 1857.
———, and Charles Livingston. *Narrative of an Expedition to the Zambesi and Its Tributaries*. London: John Murray, 1865.

Secondary Sources:

Jeal, Tim. *Livingstone*. London: Heinemann, 1973.
Mackenzie, John M., ed. *David Livingstone and the Victorian Encounter with Africa*. London: National Portrait Gallery, 1996.
Makenzie, Rob. *David Livingstone: The Truth Behind the Legend*. Eastbourne, UK: Kingsway Publications Ltd., 1993.
Ransford, Oliver. *David Livingstone: The Dark Interior*. London: John Murray, 1978.

JEHU J. HANCILES

LOCKE, JOHN (1632–1704)

English philosopher. Locke was born at Wrington, a village in Somerset, to an Anglican family with Puritan sympathies. Though his father fought in the parliamentary army during the CIVIL WAR, Locke himself welcomed the restoration of the monarchy in 1660. Much of Locke's work can be read as a reaction to the religious and civil strife that gripped ENGLAND in the late seventeenth century.

Career

Three years after graduating from Christ Church, Oxford, in 1656, Locke was appointed tutor there, later receiving a dispensation that would allow him to keep that position without being ordained. Locke's chief interests at this time were experimental science and medicine. Although lacking a degree in medicine, Locke became the personal physician of Lord Ashley (later the first earl of Shaftesbury) in 1666, and soon became Shaftesbury's advisor on political, personal, and business affairs. The two shared interests in a Protestant succession, TOLERATION in religion, and economic expansion. When Shaftesbury became involved in trade with the American colonies, Locke helped to draft a constitution for Carolina that included freedom of worship for all except atheists.

Locke's personal fortunes ebbed and flowed with those of Shaftesbury. After Shaftesbury's fall from the position of Lord High Chancellor in 1675, Locke spent four years in FRANCE, coming under the influence of Gassendi's empiricism and hedonism. Upon return to England Locke became associated with Shaftesbury's attempt to exclude the Roman Catholic James II from the succession to the throne. In 1683 Locke followed Shaftesbury into exile in Holland where he formed friendships with many of those preparing the GLORIOUS REVOLUTION. When the Protestant William of Orange seized the English throne from the Catholic James II in 1688, Locke himself crossed back to England in the party of the new Queen Mary II. Locke spent the last fifteen years of his life publishing the works that would give him a significant place in the development of Western thought.

Thought

The breakdown of consensus on government and religion in the seventeenth century compelled Locke to focus on epistemology. Locke believed that establishing the limits of human knowledge would make claimants to truth more modest and therefore more tolerant. His *Essay Concerning Human Understanding* (1689) can be read as an attempt to secure agreement and tolerance against what he considered the excesses of Puritan SECTARIANISM and enthusiasm. Locke held that limited human reason must be supplemented by belief in propositions revealed by God, but reason must determine the probability that a given proposition really is a revelation of God. Locke's *The Reasonableness of Christianity* (1695) is thus dedicated to showing that God's revelation in Scripture is consonant with what human reason can know immediately, although revelation is still necessary to deliver what could not be reached by reason alone. As a good empiricist Locke gathered bits of evidence to support, for example, belief in Jesus's miracles, based on the credibility of the apostles, whose chief function was to gather data to support Jesus's claim to messiahship. If Locke thus sought to counter the fanaticism of unsubstantiated belief, he also stressed the limits of human faculties and our failure to apply them, thus making toleration of others' views imperative. In his famous *Letter Concerning Toleration* (1689), Locke defined the CHURCH as a voluntary association and advocated the toleration of religious practice that does not impinge on the duty of the state. Excluded from this toleration, however, were atheists and those who owed obedience to a foreign power, by which Locke meant Roman Catholics. Locke's epistemology and views on toleration were one with his political vision of a united nation-state whose chief purpose was the defense of individual property rights and not the enforcement of theological truth.

Locke believed in an established church that allowed for a broad range of practices and beliefs. Like the LATITUDINARIANS, with whom he was acquainted, Locke sought to achieve peace by reducing the requirements for being a Christian to the simple and reasonable propositions that God exists and Jesus is Messiah. Locke was accused of SOCINIANISM, although he published a defense of himself against this charge. Nevertheless, Locke steadfastly refused either to affirm or deny the DOCTRINE of the Trinity. In his day Locke was also accused of DEISM, a charge he also denied. He claimed that his *The Reasonableness of Christianity* was written to refute Deists who believed either that revelation was unnecessary or that the fundamental doctrines of Christianity were contrary to reason. However, many historians consider Locke a forerunner to Deism.

Influence

Locke was not an orthodox Christian by the standards of his day, and he found his theological views shared by very few of his contemporaries. He explicitly denied the doctrine of original SIN, and was at the opposite pole from MARTIN LUTHER's and JOHN CALVIN's emphasis on the need for God's GRACE to overcome the depravity of the human person. Locke used the Scriptures extensively but opposed those Protestants who relied on the unexamined AUTHORITY of the BIBLE. Nevertheless, Locke has exerted an enduring influence on Protestant thought and practice in several indirect ways. Locke's insistence that religious belief should answer to standards of evidence external to religion itself appears both in liberal Protestant efforts to demythologize religious belief and correlate it with findings of the natural and social sciences, and in conservative Protestant efforts to find scientific proof of the historicity of the biblical narratives. Locke has also influenced the general Protestant acceptance of religious toleration, and the definition of the church as a voluntary association essentially distinct from the interests of the state and commerce.

See also Anglicanism; Church and State, Overview; Puritanism

References and Further Reading

Primary Sources:

Locke, John. *An Essay Concerning Human Understanding* [1689]. Edited by Peter H. Nidditch. Oxford, UK: Clarendon Press, 1975.
———. *A Letter Concerning Toleration* [1689]. Edited by Patrick Romanell. Indianapolis, IN: Bobbs-Merrill, 1950.
———. *The Reasonableness of Christianity, as Delivered in the Scriptures* [1695]. Edited by John C. Higgins-Biddle. Oxford, UK: Clarendon Press, 1999.

Secondary Source:

Chappell, Vere, ed. *The Cambridge Companion to Locke*. Cambridge: Cambridge University Press, 1994.

WILLIAM CAVANAUGH

LÖHE, WILHELM (1808–1872)

German lutheran pastor. Born on February 21, 1808, in Fürth near Nuremberg, Löhe took his theological training at the University of Erlangen and was appointed to the Neuendettelsau parish near Nuremberg in 1837. While serving this village parish, he supported a mission to German immigrants in North America, founded a DEACONESS community, and led many efforts to renew the church. He served there until his death on January 2, 1872.

Löhe's theological and pastoral work focused on the CHURCH, its life and mission. Influenced in his early years by a Pietist movement (see PIETISM), Löhe became a leader in the struggle to establish a confessional Lutheran church in Bavaria. He called his developed perspective "sacramental Lutheranism," a theology and practice characterized by the centrality of the LORD'S SUPPER. Based on his study of Lutheran and early church sources, Löhe worked to restore historic forms of WORSHIP. His work parallels that of other churchly movements in the nineteenth century such as the MERCERSBURG THEOLOGY and the OXFORD MOVEMENT.

Beginning in the early 1840s Löhe organized the preparation of pastors and schoolteachers to serve German immigrant communities in the American Midwest (see LUTHERANISM, UNITED STATES) and encouraged a mission to NATIVE AMERICANS. This work expanded after Löhe's lifetime to include similar efforts in BRAZIL and AUSTRALIA as well as a mission to New Guinea (see MISSIONS, GERMAN). In 1854 Löhe founded a deaconess house that, in its common life, its worship, and its service of those in need, was to model the apostolic community the whole church was called to be.

Löhe's extensive writings include an ecclesiological treatise, *Drei Bücher von der Kirche* (1845), a manual on pastoral life and practice, *Der evangelische*

Geistliche (1852–1858/1866), orders for worship in his *Agende* (1844/1853–1859), and numerous devotional works.

References and Further Reading

Primary Sources:

Löhe, Wilhelm. *Gesammelte Werke.* 7 vols. Edited by Klaus Ganzert. Neuendettelsau, Germany: Neuendettelsau Freimund-Verlag, 1951–1986.
———. *Three Books about the Church.* Translated and edited by James L. Schaaf. Philadelphia, PA: Fortress Press, 1969.

Secondary Sources:

Ratke, David C. *Confession and Mission, Word and Sacrament: The Ecclesial Theology of Wilhelm Löhe.* St. Louis, MO: Concordia Publishing House, 2001.
Weber, Christian. *Missionstheologie bei Wilhelm Löhe: Aufbruch zur Kirche der Zukunft.* Gütersloh, Germany: Gütersloher Verlagshaus, 1996.

THOMAS H. SCHATTAUER

LORD'S SUPPER

During the Reformation era, the second of the two "evangelical" SACRAMENTS instituted (it was supposed) by Christ became the subject of endless controversy. The various names by which the sacrament was called, most of which could claim biblical warrant, reflected the diversity of interpretation, or at least of emphasis, in the rival doctrines; besides "Holy Communion," it was "the Mass," "the sacrament of the altar," "the Eucharist," "the Lord's Supper," or "the breaking of bread." The Protestant reformers were agreed in their rejection of the medieval mass but were divided over the true meaning of the rite. MARTIN LUTHER and HULDRYCH ZWINGLI defended sharply opposed views of the sacrament as, respectively, an oral reception of the body and blood of Christ, or a remembrance of his DEATH on the cross. A mediating view championed by JOHN CALVIN and others represented the sacrament as an efficacious sign of communion with the ascended Lord: that is, a sign by which the Holy Spirit actually brings about the communion, or increases it. The inner-Protestant divisions and the Protestant critique of the Roman Catholic mass have remained controversial to this day. The history of the sacrament in the Protestant churches has been marked in particular by both a drift toward a simple memorialism and repeated attempts to retrieve the more cryptic meanings discovered in the holy communion by the critics of memorialism. Despite the legacy of acrimonious polemics, recent ecumenical pronouncements and new or revised service books have shown a measure of convergence between what were once supposed to be mutually exclusive views of the sacrament.

Holy Communion in Luther and Zwingli

In LUTHER's first extended treatment of the sacrament, *A Treatise Concerning the Blessed Sacrament of the Holy and True Body of Christ* (1519), Luther took it to be a sign of incorporation, by which believers are made one body with Christ and the SAINTS. He understood the conversion of the elements of bread and wine into Christ's natural body and blood (TRANSUBSTANTIATION) as an analogue of the conversion of believers into his spiritual body, the CHURCH. Although he wanted the cup as well as the bread to be given to the LAITY and stressed the need to receive the sacrament in faith, there was nothing here to suggest that at this time, two years after the outbreak of the indulgences controversy, Luther considered the medieval mass to be an abuse. But in his next thoughts on the sacrament, in *A Treatise on the New Testament: That is, the Holy Mass*, published soon afterward (1520), a remarkable change called for a frontal assault on the Roman Catholic mass. "Testament" replaced "incorporation" as the cardinal term, and to say that the mass is a testament means, Luther concluded, that it is *not* a priestly sacrifice. By "testament" he understood a promise made by someone who is about to die (cf. Hebrews 9:16-17). At the Last Supper, Christ declared his last will and testament to his disciples; he promised them forgiveness of sins and added to the promise, as a sign and seal of his testament, his own true body and blood under the elements of bread and wine.

Luther's *Prelude on the Babylonian Captivity of the Church*, which appeared the same year (1520), repeated and broadened his case against the medieval mass. The Church of Rome, he now said, had subjected the sacrament to three captivities: the withholding of the cup from the laity, the theory of transubstantiation, and the interpretation of the mass as a good work and a sacrifice. For Christ's body and blood to be included in the bread and wine, it is not necessary to imagine that the elements undergo a change of substance. But a much worse error is the misrepresentation of the sacrament as a priestly sacrifice; for a sacrifice is something we offer, a promise, something we receive—by faith. Luther's critique of what he took to be Roman Catholic errors did not lead him to abandon descriptions of the sacrament, when rightly understood, as "the mass" or "the sacrament of the altar." But his rejection of the sacrificial mass was complete, and it had far-reaching consequences for the WORSHIP and ministry of the church.

Other reformers who were in agreement with his critique found Luther's own view of Christ's bodily presence in the elements no improvement over the dogma of transubstantiation. Some of them saw the best clue to the sacrament's true meaning, not in Christ's words, "This is my body," but rather in his directive, "Do this in remembrance of me." Luther's colleague ANDREAS RUDOLF BODENSTEIN VON KARLSTADT argued that the Lord's supper is an occasion for recollection or remembrance, in which the worshiper meditates on Christ's death. In Luther's eyes, this was another variety of the Roman Catholic error: turning the Lord's gift into a human work, this time not a priestly sacrifice, but rather a devotional exercise. Zwingli, too, in his *Commentary on True and False Religion* (1525), understood the sacrament as an activity of remembering. For him, however, it was more than an occasion for private devotion: it was a public celebration, in which the church returned thanks for the one and only redeeming sacrifice of Christ on the cross. To eat Christ's flesh (John 6:51–59) is to believe in his saving death, and his words "This *is* my body" must mean "This *signifies* my body." The very term "eucharist" shows what the Lord's supper is: "the thanksgiving and common rejoicing of those who declare the death of Christ" (*Latin Works*, 3:200). In the last year of his life, in his *Exposition of the Faith* (published in 1536), Zwingli did suggest that the outward eating of the elements parallels an inward "feeding" on Christ by faith. But he could not speak of God as *giving* the inward *through* the outward without jeopardizing his fundamental principle that the Holy Spirit works directly, not through means. Sacramental signs, for Zwingli, were not instrumental but indicative or declaratory; and their proper subject—the subject that does the signifying—was not God or Christ, but rather the Christian or the congregation. Zwingli liked to point out that a *sacramentum* in ancient Roman military usage was an oath of allegiance to the commander-in-chief. Just as in BAPTISM the Christian takes his or her stand with the church and pledges to be a soldier of Christ, so in the Eucharist the entire congregation declares its commitment to Christ and the SALVATION he won on the cross. In a series of impassioned treatises (1526–1528), Luther denied that he meant a crude, local presence of Christ's body and blood in the elements of bread and wine. As God, Christ is present everywhere, and his divine nature imparts its supernatural presence to his humanity; but in the sacrament he is there—by his word—*for me*. Zwingli, Luther thought, missed the point of the sacrament, which is, by offering the communicant Christ's body and blood, to apply to the individual the promise of forgiveness proclaimed generally and to all in the preached word. Indeed, Zwingli reduced the sacrament to a sign of something absent—Christ's body on the cross. But Luther did not attempt to counter Zwingli's mistake with a sounder view of signs. In Luther's view, the bread does not strictly signify Christ's body; rather, the words of Christ bring a single new entity into being out of the bread and the body—"fleshbread"—and to speak of either one separately is to speak improperly. Hence even the wicked receive the body and blood of the Lord into their mouths, although they do it to their own destruction.

Calvin and the Mediating Position

The MARBURG COLLOQUY (1529) seemed to demonstrate that the Lutherans and the Zwinglians had arrived at a final impasse. But a different, more Augustinian conception of signs opened up the possibility of a mediating position, which, in essentials, came to be held in common by MARTIN BUCER, Peter Martyr Vermigli, Calvin, and others. Zwingli thought of a sacramental sign as a pointer to a GRACE that lies in the past; Luther, accordingly, was suspicious of any attempt to distinguish sign from reality in the sacrament of the ALTAR. But a third alternative was to argue that although the signs are not the reality, they are bearers of the reality, which is communion with Christ or participation in his life-giving flesh. The broken bread and the poured wine are not empty signs (*nuda signa*), but efficacious (*signa exhibitiva*). The consecrating words bring about a change in the elements—not of substance, but of use. And Calvin could ask: "Why should the Lord put in your hand the symbol of his body, except to assure you of a true participation in it?" (*Institutes*, 4.17.10). The sacrament is an actual means or instrument by which the Holy Spirit imparts or nurtures union with Christ, raising us up and overcoming the distance between the ascended Lord in HEAVEN and ourselves below, so that we receive the power or virtue of his life-giving flesh. Calvin did not profess to understand how this elevation of the believer works but was content to leave it as a mystery. "In his Sacred Supper Christ bids me take, eat, and drink his body and blood under the symbols of bread and wine. I do not doubt that he himself truly presents them, and that I receive them" (ibid., 4.17.32).

The mediating view differed sharply from the main lines of Zwingli's sacramental THEOLOGY. Holy Communion, in this view, is the actual giving of a gift, not recollection of a gift. The "reality" (*res*) of the sacrament, for Calvin, was not a past event to which believers have access through memory, as they call to mind the benefits Christ's death won for their salvation. He certainly agreed that the LITURGY as a whole includes the thankful response of the congregation for the gift of Christ's benefits. This is the true eucharistic sacrifice, which defines the entire life of Christians—also outside of the liturgy. But the first movement is from the living Christ to the congregation; *he* is the primary subject of the sacramental action, offering them his crucified and risen body. Moreover, what was at stake for Calvin was not just the correct interpretation of the sacrament, but a total conception of how believers are related to Christ. Zwingli explained that "eating" is simply "believing." But Calvin felt, and argued forcefully, that there is more than that to feeding on the bread of life: being a Christian is a matter not solely of beliefs about Christ, but also of a mystical (that is, mysterious) union with Christ by which we become "flesh of his flesh and bone of his bones."

Obviously, the mediating view, as Calvin represents it, was not free from difficulties of its own. HEINRICH BULLINGER, Zwingli's successor in Zurich, told Calvin bluntly that he could not see how Calvin's doctrine differed from that of the papists, who taught that the sacraments actually confer grace. But patience and determination led eventually to the Zurich Consensus (1549), which brought harmony between the French- and German-speaking reformed churches of SWITZERLAND. Sadly, the consensus lost Calvin much of his support among the Lutherans, who had previously believed him to be on their side. No doubt, very few of the evangelicals in GERMANY or Switzerland were able to grasp the intricate polemics that followed between Calvin and his Lutheran critics. But it must not be overlooked that at the practical level of congregational worship the Lutherans and the Calvinists had between them brought about radical changes that were evident to the eye and the ear. The medieval mass was from beginning to end a priestly action conducted in Latin. The people were urged to "communicate" (receive the wafer) once a year, at Easter. But their presence at the mass was not essential; if present, they were left to their private devotions, save when the host was elevated and the bell sounded to indicate that the miracle of transubstantiation had been effected. In contrast, for Luther, Zwingli, and Calvin, despite their differences, reception of the elements by the people was essential to the meaning of the sacrament. Calvin in particular insisted that the sacrament is a *banquet*, and he faulted the medieval mass for robbing the holy banquet not only of its character as a gift, but also of its essentially corporate nature: "[The Lord has] given us a Table at which to feast, not an altar upon which to offer a victim; he has not consecrated priests to offer sacrifice, but ministers [i.e., servants] to distribute the sacred banquet" (*Inst.*, 4.18.12). It followed for Calvin that no gathering of the church should take place without partaking of the Lord's Supper, and he called for communion once a week at the very least.

Holy Communion in the Protestant Churches

Alongside the types of eucharistic doctrine represented by Luther, Zwingli, and Calvin were others that relativized, diminished, or rejected the place of the Holy Communion in Christian worship. Zwingli had already discarded the idea of a means of grace and retained the word "sacrament" only in an unconventional sense. The Anabaptists (see ANABAPTISM), who shared his memorialist interpretation of the Lord's Supper, spoke of the sacrament as one of Christ's "ordinances." Belief in the inwardness of the Spirit's working led others to abandon the outward ceremony altogether, as the Quakers did in ENGLAND (see FRIENDS, SOCIETY OF). The Socinians, though they believed Christ intended the rite to be a perpetual memorial of his death, so denuded it of the old meanings that it lost importance for them, and the English Socinians, too, were chided for not observing it at all (see SOCINIANISM). But the Quakers and the Socinians stood outside the mainstream of the English churches.

In sixteenth-century England, the influence of the mediating eucharistic theology prevailed: THOMAS CRANMER and RICHARD HOOKER both described the holy communion in language that has clear affinities with Calvin's. In the following century, echoes of Calvin can still be heard not only in Puritan writings on the sacrament (see PURITANISM), but also in the writings of Anglican divines who had no taste for Calvin's predestinarianism (see PREDESTINATION). Across the English Channel, in the heyday of Protestant ORTHODOXY, Lutherans and Reformed continued to define themselves in conscious differentiation from each other. But in the eighteenth century sacramental theology throughout Protestantism had to contend with the Enlightenment mentality, which saw in the very concepts of a "means of grace" and a "real presence" idle, if not dangerous, superstitions. In such a world of thought, a simple memorialism had an obvious advantage over CALVINISM and LUTHERANISM alike. The "high church" movements in the Lutheran, Reformed, and Anglican communions during the nineteenth century took the form of protests against apostasy, not least in the DOCTRINE of the holy communion. When the Mercersburg theologian John Williamson Nevin (see MERCERSBURG THEOLOGY) picked up the fallen banner of the Calvinist doctrine of the real presence, not only the Presbyterians, but Episcopalians and Lutherans, too, decried his efforts to revive old "superstitions." Nonetheless, continuing efforts at liturgical renewal in the twentieth century have combined with greater openness between the churches to maintain an interest in the classical types of eucharistic THEOLOGY, to supplement them where they seem lacking, and to stress agreements between old adversaries. The revised service books of the main-line Protestant denominations and such ecumenical statements as the much-discussed document *Baptism, Eucharist & Ministry* are among the fruits of recent reflection on liturgy and the holy communion.

See also: Presbyterianism; Anglicanism

References and Further Reading

Baptism, Eucharist & Ministry. Faith and Order Paper No. 111. Geneva, Switzerland: World Council of Churches, 1982.

Brooks, Peter. *Thomas Cranmer's Doctrine of the Eucharist: An Essay in Historical Development.* New York: Seabury Press, 1965.

Calvin, John. *Calvin: Institutes of the Christian Religion.* Edited by John T. McNeill; translated by Ford Lewis Battles. Library of Christian Classics, vols. 20 and 21. Philadelphia, PA: Westminster Press, 1960.

Clark, Francis. *Eucharistic Sacrifice and the Reformation.* Westminster, MD: Newman Press, 1960.

Gerrish, Brian A. *Grace and Gratitude: The Eucharistic Theology of John Calvin.* Minneapolis, MN: Fortress Press; Edinburgh, U.K.: T. & T. Clark, 1993.

Luther, Martin. *Luther's Works* (American Edition). Edited by Jaroslav Pelikan and Helmut T. Lehmann. 55 vols. St. Louis, MO: Concordia Publishing House; Philadelphia, PA: Fortress Press, 1955–1986.

McLelland, Joseph C. *The Visible Words of God: An Exposition of the Sacramental Theology of Peter Martyr Vermigli, A.D. 1500–1562.* Edinburgh: Oliver & Boyd, 1957.

Rempel, John D. *The Lord's Supper in Anabaptism: A Study in the Christology of Balthasar Hubmaier, Pilgram Marpeck, and Dirk Philips.* Studies in Anabaptist and Mennonite History, no. 33. Scottdale, PA: Herald Press, 1993.

Sasse, Hermann. *This Is My Body: Luther's Contention for the Real Presence in the Sacrament of the Altar.* Minneapolis, MN: Augsburg Publishing House, 1959.

Stephens, W. P. *The Theology of Huldrych Zwingli.* New York: Oxford University Press, 1986.

White, James F. *The Sacraments in Protestant Practice and Faith.* Nashville, TN: Abingdon Press, 1999.

Wisløff, Carl F. *The Gift of Communion: Luther's Controversy with Rome on Eucharistic Sacrifice.* Translated by Joseph M. Shaw. Minneapolis, MN: Augsburg Publishing House, 1964.

Zwingli, Ulrich. *The Latin Works of Huldreich Zwingli.* Edited by Samuel Macauley Jackson et al., 3 vols. New York: G. P. Putnam's Sons, 1912; Philadelphia, PA: Heidelberg Press, 1922–1929.

B. A. GERRISH

LUTHER, MARTIN (1483–1546)

German reformer, professor of Bible at the University of Wittenberg, regarded as the initiator of the Protestant Reformation.

Luther as Student and Professor

Luther was born November 10, 1483, in Eisleben, the son of a copper processor on the rise out of the peasantry, Hans Luder, and his wife, Margarete, nee Lindemann, who was from an Eisenach bourgeois family. Luther began his schooling in Mansfeld, the family residence since 1484. In 1497 his secondary school commenced in Magdeburg, in circles related to the Brethren of the Common Life, and continued in Eisenach. At the University of Erfurt he earned a B.A. in 1502, an M.A. in 1505, and in accord with his father's aspirations, began the study of law. His sensitive conscience drove him into a spiritual crisis, however, after lightning terrified him as he returned to Erfurt in June 1505. He entered the Observant Augustinian monastery there despite parental objections. He dedicated himself totally to the strict regimen of monastic life, from which he hoped to gain merit in God's sight and thus SALVATION. Against his own wishes, his superiors promoted his monastic career, requiring further study in theology, which led to his doctorate in Bible (1512) and his ordination as a priest (1507). The terror of God's presence in his first celebration of the mass was but one sign of his continuing spiritual crisis. His professors taught "in the modern way"—the "via moderna" or nominalism, as represented by Gabriel Biel (c. 1413–1495). Although he rejected Biel's teaching that good works must merit grace, Luther never abandoned certain fundamental presuppositions of his nominalist teachers. His order's vicar for Germany, Johann von Staupitz, recognized his abilities and moved him to the infant university of Wittenberg (founded 1502) to teach (1508–1509, 1511–1546).

His doctoral oath pledged Luther to search the Scriptures and defend their truth at all costs. He began his biblical lecturing with the Psalms (1513–1515), developing his theology through lectures on Romans (1515–1516), Galatians (1516–1517), Hebrews (1517–1518), and Psalms (1519–1521). Later lectures treated Deuteronomy (1523–1524), the Minor Prophets (1524–1526), Ecclesiastes (1526), I John, Titus, Philemon, and I Timothy (1527–1528), Isaiah (1528–1530, 1543–1544), Song of Solomon (1530–1531), Galatians (1531), Psalms (1532–1535), and Genesis (1535–1545). His students also used his postils and several published sermon series as commentaries (e.g., Genesis, 1523–1524; John, 1528–1529, 1530–1532, 1537–1538; I Peter, 1522). Scholars disagree on his precise relationship to biblical humanism, but from his first lectures on he employed linguistic aids and commentaries of humanist scholars such as Johannes Reuchlin and Jean Lefevre d'Etaples. PHILIPP MELANCHTHON, a leading representative of humanist scholarship, became his Wittenberg colleague in 1518 and profoundly influenced Luther's interpretation of the biblical text.

Although his PREACHING always employed "allegorical" illustrations, Luther led a hermeneutical and exegetical revolution in biblical studies as he laid aside the fourfold analysis of Scripture practiced throughout the Middle Ages and sought always to determine the "literal-prophetic" sense of the text. For him that meant that prophecies concerning Christ formed the heart of the Old Testament. His interpretative principles centered on the distinction between the condemning law and the life-restoring gospel, centered on salvation in Christ.

The Beginnings of Luther's Reformation

A variety of duties fell to the able young monk. He represented his monastery on a mission to Rome (1510–1511), served as preacher in the Wittenberg town church (from 1514) and vicar of the Saxon Observant Augustinians (1515–1518). His reading of Augustine and the mysticism of Heinrich Tauler and the *Theologia Deutsch* shaped his developing thought, although he soon abandoned the spiritualizing aspects of their theologies. As professor he composed disputations for academic promotions or supervised students' preparing their own theses for such debates; those of Bartholomew Bernhardi (1516) and Franz Günther (1517) advanced Luther's new ideas regarding sin and grace and the use of Aristotle in theology. In October 1517 abuses connected with the sale of indulgences to raise funds for Archbishop Albrecht of Mainz provoked Luther's protest. Unaware of the intricate financial context of the indulgence sale, he was moved by pastoral concern for those who believed they could purchase release from purgatory for themselves and others and thus failed to take seriously the remorse and trust in Christ that Luther defined as the heart of penance. Therefore he called for public disputation on the practice through his "Ninety-five Theses." Although the first thesis, that the whole life of the Christian is a life of repentance, summarizes an enduring element of his thought, these theses are theologically insignificant. Written for public disputation, they did not necessarily reveal the author's convictions but rather posed critical questions for debate. However, their printing and distribution to large audiences in Germany and beyond constitute the first modern media event and propelled Luther to center stage in European Christendom.

Albrecht and his indulgence preacher, Johann Tetzel, reported Luther's remonstration to Rome. Tetzel's fellow Dominican, Sylvester Prierias, an important advisor of Pope Leo X, pursued charges of heresy against Luther. A fierce polemic against him erupted from the papal court. In April 1518 Staupitz had him present his views to fellow Augustinians at the regular meeting of the order's Saxon province in Heidelberg. The theses of Luther's "Heidelberg Disputation" sketched his "theology of the cross." Although he abandoned use of this term, the concepts of the Hidden and Revealed God, the bondage of the sinful will, and the centrality of Christ's cross (I Corinthians 1:18–2:16) mark his teaching throughout his career. The distinction between *Deus absconditus,* God in his glory, beyond human grasp, whose wrath is perceived as sinners seek to define God, and *Deus revelatus,* God revealed in Scripture and especially in Christ, emphasizes total human dependency on God's self-disclosure and Christ's self-sacrifice to atone for sin.

In October 1518 papal legate Thomas de Vio (Cardinal Cajetan) met Luther at the imperial diet in Augsburg and attempted to elicit Luther's recantation of his views without a real exchange of ideas. Luther fled after unfruitful meetings with Cajetan, fearing a repetition of the imperial-papal execution of another reformer, John Hus, a century earlier. Subsequent political maneuvering between Luther's prince, Elector Frederick the Wise of Saxony, and papal diplomats also produced no settlement.

The leading German Roman Catholic theologian of Luther's generation, John Eck of Ingolstadt, challenged Luther's doctoral supervisor and colleague, ANDREAS BODENSTEIN VON KARLSTADT, dean of Wittenberg's theological faculty, to debate the critical issues raised by Luther's call to reform (Leipzig, June–July 1519). Luther also came to the podium, and Eck led him to confess his conviction that popes and councils could err, that both stand under the authority of Scripture. Controversy over these ideas swirled around the reformer, who in 1520–1521 issued five treatises detailing his proposal for reform of the church: (1) *On Good Works* introduced his faith-based ethic: good works flow from trust in Christ; (2) *To the Christian Nobility of the German Nation concerning the Reform of the Christian Estate* called for the nobility (and implicitly city councils) to institute many specific reforms in church and society; (3) *On the Babylonian Captivity of the Church* assessed the church's sacramental teaching and life, proposing a return to biblical teaching regarding Word and sacrament; (4) *On the Freedom of the Christian* sketched Luther's understanding of salvation through faith in Christ and its implications for daily living under two theses: God's pronouncement of righteousness in the forgiveness of sins frees believers from all enemies (Satan, sin, the law, death, hell) and binds them to love their neighbors; (5) *On Monastic Vows,* an affirmation of the Christian life as the fruit of faith apart from monastic religious exercises (considered to be a preferable way of life in medieval theology) performed to merit salvation on the basis of vows.

By 1519 Luther had developed the core of his thinking in his concept of the justification of sinners before God through faith in Christ. Nominalist presuppositions regarding the power of God's Word and the complete dependency of sinners on God's revelation shaped this doctrine. It presupposed the distinction between passive righteousness in God's sight (the righteousness given without condition by God, consisting solely in God's favor, which regards his chosen people as beloved children) and active righteousness toward other creatures (the performance of love in obedience to God's commands). Key elements of this view of salvation included:

1. Justification as an action of God's Word, whereby the Creator creates a new child of God out of a sinner through the promise of the forgiveness of sins, which bestows Christ's righteousness on believers.
2. Faith as trust in Christ and his death and resurrection as the source of forgiveness.
3. Assurance for believers of their salvation on the basis of the promise contained in the means of grace (God's Word in oral, written, and sacramental forms).
4. Recognition that God's Word makes believers completely righteous in God's sight even though they experience their sinfulness throughout their lives (*simul justus et peccator*).
5. Application of this Gospel only to the repentant (with corresponding application of the crushing, condemning law to the unrepentant).
6. A life lived according to God's commands in the fruits of faith.

Throughout the twentieth century scholars debated the precise time and nature of his "evangelical breakthrough" and formulated various explanations of his "tower experience," a reference to the tower in the cloister where his study was located. In 1545 (preface to volume 1 of his Latin works) Luther dated his breakthrough 1518. By that time he had come to understand faith as *fiducia* (trust), the distinction of the two kinds of righteousness, and the proper distinction of law and gospel as a hermeneutical and pastoral tool.

Emperor Charles V summoned Luther before the imperial diet in Worms in April 1521. Already excommunicated by Pope Leo in January, he was outlawed by a rump session of the diet after his appearance, in which, according to reports a generation later, he said, "Here I stand. I can do no other." Reports from 1521 recorded his words, "I am bound by the Scriptures . . . and my conscience has been taken captive by the Word of God, and I am neither able nor willing to recant since it is neither safe nor right to act against conscience." After he left Worms, knights in the employ of Elector Frederick seized and brought him to the Elector's castle, the Wartburg, where he remained for ten months. In his absence his Wittenberg colleagues proceeded with reforms, thereby arousing popular unrest. Luther returned in March 1522 to preach his "Invocavit" sermons, urging pastoral sensitivity in dealing with the consciences of adherents of the old faith.

Guiding reform demanded a variety of competences, and Luther rose to the challenge, assisted by able co-workers and by the rapidly developing printing industry. At the Wartburg he had prepared his translation of the New Testament, the first German version based on Greek manuscripts, from Erasmus's new edition, which he used along with the Latin text. Over the following twelve years he completed translation of the Old Testament. Recognizing the need for pastors to have model sermons for proclaiming the Gospel, Luther also began the first of a series of sermon collections on the pericopes for the church year at the Wartburg. These "postils" provided a program of continuing education for priests wanting to incorporate Luther's reform into parish life; most people came to Luther's way of thinking through oral proclamation of the message. In treatises over the following years Luther treated various doctrinal and practical topics—justification by faith, the sacraments, marriage and family, schooling, obedience to governmental authority and rulers' responsibilities, trade and usury—and also prepared popular devotional literature. In 1523 his revision of the Latin liturgy, the *Formula Missae,* appeared; in 1526 he completed the *Deutsche Messe,* a service that replaced traditional Latin chants with German hymns while retaining the Catholic form of worship.

The Maturing of Luther's Reformation

Four critical episodes between 1524 and 1525 determined vital features of Luther's Reformation. Younger biblical humanists provided the "shock troops" for his cause, but in 1524 the leading northern European humanist, Desiderius Erasmus, acceded to Rome's pressure and attacked Luther, choosing the issue of the freedom or bondage of human choice in relation to God as the crucial difference between them. In 1525 Luther replied to Erasmus's *De libero arbitrio* with *De servo arbitrio* (On Bound Choice). Written largely on Erasmus's philosophical turf, and thus not completely clear on his own pastoral, law/gospel approach to the disputed questions, this work, counted by Luther among his best, defended his belief that human salvation rests alone on God's gracious decision to choose his own and that sinners cannot trust and obey God apart from the Holy Spirit's turning and re-creating the human will.

Luther also clearly distinguished his program from a tradition of old-style reform, embodied in different ways by his colleague Karlstadt and a former student, THOMAS MÜNTZER. Karlstadt embraced Luther's call for reform enthusiastically but could place it only within the framework of a conceptualization of protest against the ecclesiastical establishment a half millennium old. This approach to reform was biblicistic, moralistic, anticlerical, antisacramental, and millennialistic. Luther and Karlstadt differed in each of these areas, particularly on the literal interpretation of Christ's Words of Institution of the LORD'S SUPPER.

Luther's objections to the mystic spirituality of Müntzer focused on the student's denial of God's working his saving will through the external means of the Word in written, oral, and sacramental forms. The revolt of peasants in many German regions (1524–1525) afforded Müntzer opportunity to pursue his aspirations as an apocalyptic prophet but ended with his execution by victorious princely forces. He remained a symbol for Luther of theological and civil disorder.

Luther's role in the Peasants Revolt was determined by the horror of civil disorder he shared with most Germans with societal responsibilities. His *Admonition to Peace, a Reply to the Twelve Articles of the Swabian Peasants* (May 1525) sharply criticized princely tyranny as well as the peasant appeal to Scripture on behalf of temporal goals. Throughout his career his call to government officials to repent of various abuses belie his reputation as a "toady of princes." As he heard accounts of peasant atrocities and experienced himself the rowdy mob while touring his native Thuringia to calm troubled waters, he also attacked the peasant leadership and its use of Scripture. Convinced that Satan was using peasant violence to discredit and damage the Reformation in what he believed to be the final days before Judgment Day, he called on the inactive Saxon government to take action against the peasants in *Against the Robbing and Murdering Hordes of Peasants*. His harsh words earned him much criticism, although evidence seems to support the minority of scholars who appraise the loss to his Reformation from peasant resentment because of this stand as relatively minor.

In October 1524 Luther laid aside his monastic garb, probably not anticipating that a step taken by many of his monastic followers would also take place in his own life. The next June, Luther married a former nun, Katherine von Bora. This marriage provided a lasting model for Christian marriage and life in the parsonage. Käthe and Martin came to love and exercise spiritual care for each other. She managed their household efficiently and offered theological insight and counsel to her husband and the students who lived with them in the Augustinian cloister given to them by the elector. Of their six children (Johannes, Elizabeth, Magdalena, Martin, Paul, Margareta) two died young. Particularly poignant are Luther's expressions of sorrow at the death of Magdalena at age 13 in 1542.

In May 1525 Duke John assumed the electorate of Saxony at the death of his brother, Frederick the Wise. Admiration and friendship bound Luther with John and his son John Frederick, who succeeded to the throne in 1532. Under John's direction Luther and Melanchthon assumed leadership of a visitation of Saxon parishes in 1527; with Luther's suggestions at hand, Melanchthon issued *Instructions for the Visitors of Parish Pastors,* a handbook of pastoral care, in 1528.

Encountering the disorder of peasant life on the visitation, Luther and Melanchthon reacted theologically with an increased emphasis on preaching repentance through the crushing force of the law. This aroused protests from their former student, Johann Agricola, school rector in Eisleben. He attacked Melanchthon for views both Wittenbergers held; Luther negotiated a settlement, but Agricola's refusal to take seriously Luther's distinction of law and gospel led him a decade later to reassert his view that the law has no place in the Christian life and that the gospel works repentance for believers. That dispute (1538–1540) led to a final breach between teachers and student.

Agricola's publication of his views in catechetical works (1527) moved Luther to assume a task he had long urged colleagues to undertake, composition of a children's CATECHISM. Since 1518 he had followed the medieval practice of preaching on the fundamental elements of the church's ancient program of instruction, the Ten Commandments, the Creed, and the Lord's Prayer; in 1528 and 1529 he held three series of catechetical sermons. From them he published in 1529 a wall-chart catechism, his *Small Catechism* for parents' use in instructing children, and his *German* or *Large Catechism,* an instructors manual for pastors and parents. The *Small Catechism* placed the traditional catechetical elements in a new order, introducing children to the law (Ten Commandments) before the gospel (Creed) so that they could understand why they needed Christ as Savior. After the response of faith (the Lord's Prayer) came brief treatments of BAPTISM and the Lord's Supper (supplemented by instruction on the conduct of CONFESSION and absolution), followed by biblical direction for daily meditation and PRAYER and for the conduct of the godly life within the social structures of the time, the household (family and economic activities), the political community, and the church. As a handbook for Christian living, this primer shaped the lives of Luther's followers to the present.

Luther's piety called for the practice of biblical virtues within the responsibilities to which God calls his people in the household, the state, and the church on the basis of God's gift of new life through God's Word. Inherited in part from his nominalist instructors and formed by his study of the Old Testament, Luther's concept of God's Word led him into conflict with fellow reformers as well as with theologians of the old faith. Against the latter he argued that God's Word does not function *ex opere operato* (automatically, as a magical incantation), but that it operates as a Word of promise that is valid as God's pledge but effective only through faith. Against biblical humanists such as the Swiss reformers HULDRYCH ZWINGLI and JOHANNES OECOLAMPADIUS, whose views of reality had been shaped by platonic presuppositions, Luther argued that God's Word in Scripture, preaching, absolution, and the sacraments creates the reality of which it speaks. God actually changes sinners into his faithful children through his Word.

Luther's teaching on the sacraments (baptism and the Lord's Supper, occasionally also absolution) reflects this ontology of God's Word. His nominalist presupposition that God could form reality in any way God pleases according to God's absolute power led him to believe that God had endowed human words that convey the Gospel of Christ with the power to save (Romans 1:16), that God's baptismal promise creates a new child of God (Romans 6:3–11), and that the bread and wine of the Lord's Supper convey Christ's body and blood for forgiveness of sins (Matthew 26:26–29). He insisted that this body and blood are received through the mouth by all who receive, whether believers or unbelievers, because the presence of Christ's body depends on the Word of God, not on the faith of the recipient; thus, unbelievers also receive, to their judgment (I Corinthians 11:29). (See especially *That These Words of Christ, "This Is My Body" etc. Still Stand Firm* [1527] and *Confession concerning Christ's Supper* [1528].) In 1529 one of Luther's princely patrons, Philip of Hesse, brought him and some of his supporters together with Zwingli, Oecolampadius, and others who shared their position in a colloquy at Marburg. The two sides agreed on fourteen of fifteen doctrinal articles but remained in disagreement over the Lord's Supper. MARTIN BUCER of Strasbourg led attempts to reconcile the two in the 1530s. In 1536 Melanchthon composed the "Wittenberg Concord," to which both Bucer with other me-

diating southern German reformers and Luther and his Wittenberg colleagues agreed. It taught that "with the bread and wine the body and blood of Christ are truly and essentially present, distributed, and received." In 1544 Luther reasserted his teaching against Zwingli's successor Heinrich Bullinger and others in his *Brief Confession concerning the Holy Sacrament*.

The teaching of Luther and his Wittenberg colleagues was brought together in a public statement of faith in 1530 when Melanchthon composed the AUGSBURG CONFESSION as an explanation of the Lutherans' catholic teaching and the reform measures they had undertaken. Melanchthon's work reflected Luther's influence, and he used several items to which Luther had contributed. These included the third section of his 1528 *Confession concerning Christ's Supper*, the "Marburg Articles," the "Schwabach Articles" (a confession issued by several Evangelical governments in 1529), and memoranda regarding reform of ecclesiastical practices (dubbed since the eighteenth century the "Torgau Articles"). From 1536 to 1537 Luther prepared his own confession regarding issues separating him from Roman Catholicism, his SCHMALKALDIC ARTICLES. Composed for use in presenting Evangelical teaching to the papally called council, which finally met in Trent 1545 at the behest of Elector John Frederick who wanted the reformer's doctrinal last will and testament in print, this summary of Luther's thought served to guide his followers' public teaching, along with the Augsburg Confession, its *Apology,* and his catechisms.

Illness, increasing irritability, but also productive work marked Luther's last fifteen years. His second lectures on Galatians (1531; printed 1535) presented in clear, dramatic fashion his doctrine of justification by the forgiving Word of God, which creates and elicits the believer's faith in Christ. His lectures on Genesis (1535–1545) are filled with discourses treating the whole range of biblical teaching. In polemics against Roman Catholic theologians and princes he delineated his doctrine of the church as a creation and agent of God's Word (*On the Councils and the Church,* 1539; *Against Hans Wurst,* 1541).

His writings against the Jews in this period reflect an ugly aspect of medieval culture. Although he had hoped to win Jews to the gospel, a goal outlined in *That Jesus Christ Was Born a Jew* (1523), the absence of Jewish conversions led him to give credibility to anti-Jewish slanders and join in the common critique of Jewish religion and the call for their exile from Christian society in his last years.

As counselor of princes he offered advice and criticism to many governing officials. His grudging approval of the bigamy of Philip of Hesse (1540) rested on pastoral as well as political concerns. An invitation to mediate a dispute among the counts of his native county of Mansfeld in early 1546 drew him back to his birthplace, where he fell ill and died February 18.

At the beginning of Luther's career none other than Zwingli had heralded him as a prophet sent by God to restore the gospel. His students and adherents used his opinions as a secondary authority, replacing popes and councils as the authoritative interpreter of Scripture. After his death his writings proved to be too extensive and varied to continue exercising such authority, but Luther remained, along with the BOOK OF CONCORD, a source for teaching and also a symbol for Lutheran doctrine and the Reformation itself. Succeeding epochs made different uses of his person and thought. The initiation of a model modern edition of his works, the *Weimar Ausgabe,* in 1883 set the scene for intensive research into his life and work throughout the subsequent century, much of it focused in the "Luther Renaissance" of Karl Holl and others in the first half of the century. Luther's theology continues to provide inspiration and provocation to further theological exposition by theologians in all churches.

References and Further Reading

Primary Sources:

Luther, Martin. *Dr. Martin Luthers Werke.* Weimar: Böhlau, 1883.
———. *Luther's Works.* Saint Louis, MO, and Philadelphia, PA: Concordia and Fortress, 1958–1986.

Secondary Sources:

Aland, Kurt. *Hilfsbuch zum Lutherstudium.* Fourth revised edition. Witten: Luther Verlag, 1996.
Althaus, Paul. *The Ethics of Martin Luther.* Translated by Robert C. Schultz. Philadelphia, PA: Fortress, 1972.
———. *The Theology of Martin Luther.* Translated by Robert C. Schultz. Philadelphia, PA: Fortress, 1966.
Bainton, Roland H. *Here I Stand: A Life of Martin Luther.* New York: Abingdon-Cokesbury, 1950.
Bornkamm, Heinrich. *Luther in Mid-Career, 1521–1530.* Translated by E. Theodore Bachmann. Philadelphia, PA: Fortress, 1983.
Brecht, Martin. *Martin Luther.* 3 vols. Translated by James L. Schaaf. Philadelphia, PA: Fortress, 1985–1992.
Ebeling, Gerhard. *Luther: An Introduction to His Thought.* Translated by R. A. Wilson. Philadelphia, PA: Fortress, 1970.
Edwards, Mark U. *Luther and the False Brethren.* Stanford, CA: Stanford University Press, 1975.
———. *Luther's Last Battles: Politics and Polemics, 1531–1546.* Ithaca, NY: Cornell University Press, 1983.
———. *Printing, Propaganda, and Martin Luther.* Berkeley: University of California Press, 1994.
Hendrix, Scott H. *Luther and the Papacy: Stages in a Reformation Conflict.* Philadelphia, PA: Fortress, 1981.
Junghans, Helmar, ed. *Leben und Werk Martin Luthers von 1526–1546.* 2 vols. Göttingen: Vandenhoeck & Ruprecht, 1983, Second edition, 1985.
Kolb, Robert. *Martin Luther As Prophet, Teacher and Hero: Images of the Reformer, 1520–1620.* Grand Rapids, MI: Baker Books, 1999.
Lohse, Bernhard. *Martin Luther: An Introduction to His Life and Work.* Translated by Robert C. Schultz. Philadelphia, PA: Fortress, 1986.
———. *Martin Luther's Theology, Its Historical and Systematic Development.* Translated by Roy A. Harrisville. Minneapolis, MN: Fortress, 1999.
Oberman, Heiko A. *Luther: Man Between God and the Devil.* Translated by Eileen Walliser-Schwarzbart. New Haven, CT: Yale University Press, 1989.
Schwiebert, Ernest G. *Luther and His Times: The Reformation From a New Perspective.* St. Louis, MO: Concordia, 1950.
Siggins, Ian D. Kingston. *Martin Luther's Doctrine of Christ.* New Haven, CT: Yale University Press, 1970.

ROBERT KOLB

LUTHERAN CHURCH–MISSOURI SYNOD, THE

Constituted on April 26, 1847, in Chicago, Illinois, as The German Evangelical Lutheran Synod of Missouri, Ohio, and Other States, the synod was a thoroughly German body. In 1911 The English Evangelical Lutheran Synod of Missouri and Other States joined the synod as a nongeographical district. During World War I the synod omitted the title "German," and in 1947 changed its name to The Lutheran Church–Missouri Synod. From twelve pastors and four lay delegates representing fifteen congregations with approximately 3,000 members at its inception, it grew to number 1,564 pastors and 1,986 congregations with 687,334 members by the end of the nineteenth century. At its sesquicentennial in 1997 it numbered 2.6 million members in 6,145 congregations served by 8,389 pastors. It also has a large system of parochial schools served by 9,951 teachers.

As its name implies, the synod's area of greatest strength in its early history was the American Midwest. The Rev. F. C. D. Wyneken (1810–1876) arrived in northeastern Indiana in 1838 and discovered that many German immigrants were either going without Lutheran pastoral care or were leaving LUTHERANISM for other denominations. He later issued a call for help from GERMANY for more Lutheran pastors and missionaries, which captured the attention of the Rev. WILHELM LÖHE of Neuendettlesau, Bavaria, Germany. Löhe supplied pastors for the American field and, with the aid of Wyneken and Dr. Wilhelm Sihler, established Concordia Theological Seminary in Fort Wayne, Indiana, in 1846. In 1844 Wyneken became aware of a group of Saxon Lutheran immigrants who had settled in the St. Louis and Perry County areas of Missouri. In 1838–1839 this group had followed their bishop, the Rev. Martin Stephan of Dresden, Saxony, Germany, out of the Saxon state church, which they viewed as irredeemably corrupt because of rationalism, to the UNITED STATES to form a pure Lutheran Church. They established a log cabin college in Altenburg, Missouri, in 1839, which later grew into Concordia Seminary, St. Louis, Missouri. In the spring of 1839 Stephan was deposed and the colony struggled with the question of identity, eventually adopting a DOCTRINE of church and ministry formulated by the Rev. CARL FERDINAND WILHELM WALTHER (1811–1887) that affirmed both the divinity of the pastoral office and the priesthood of all believers. Its polity ensured the right of the local congregation to choose its own pastor. Walther vigorously asserted that this doctrine was based on the Scriptures and the Lutheran Confessions. This perspective on Lutheranism, which the Saxons circulated in their paper, *Der Lutheraner* (first published on September 7, 1844), appealed to Wyneken and, when other Löhe colonies in the state of Michigan (Frankenmuth, Frankentrost, Frankenlust, and Frankenhilf) also sought a relationship with Wyneken and the Saxons, things quickly moved toward unity. Meetings in 1845 and 1846 solidified newly formed alliances, and in 1847 the synod was formally constituted.

The new synod devoted itself to "the preservation and furthering of the unity of pure confession," stood against separatism and SECTARIANISM, sought to protect and preserve the rights and duties of pastors and congregations. Its POLITY was democratic in form, and the synod was advisory in nature in matters not touching doctrine. Yet, the synod required unconditional subscription to the BOOK OF CONCORD (1580) of its pastors, teachers, and congregations *quia* ("because"), they believed, the Lutheran Confessions were the faithful exposition of the Holy Scriptures (see CONFESSION). This vigorous confessional subscription, coupled with an insistence on uniformity in doctrine and practice before union, led to tension with other Lutheran bodies throughout its early history, and made it difficult for it to enter into the Lutheran union movements in the twentieth century. At its founding Missouri critiqued what it saw as extremist positions on either side of itself. On the one hand it rejected the "American Lutheranism" of SAMUEL SIMON SCHMUCKER (1799–1873), professor at the Lutheran Seminary at Gettysburg and leader in the Lutheran General Synod, which subscribed only to the AUGSBURG CONFESSION and that insofar as it taught the "fundamental doctrines of Scripture in a manner substantially correct." Missouri rejected this moderate form of confessional subscription as having accommodated itself to American evangelical Protestantism. On the other hand Missouri rejected what it believed were the "romanizing tendencies" of J. A. A. Grabau

and his Buffalo Synod (a synod formed by Prussians in 1845), as well as the Iowa Synod, founded by their former colleague Wilhelm Löhe. Walther and the Missourians feared a return to the "tyranny" of their hierarchical colonial experiment under Stephan.

Later controversies erupted between Missouri and other confessional Lutherans regarding the doctrine and practice, for example, of ELECTION and CONVERSION and pulpit and ALTAR fellowship. In the 1880s divergence of opinion ultimately led to a rupture within the Synodical Conference, which had been formed in 1872 largely under Missouri's lead. Consisting of immigrant midwestern synods that shared a *quia* subscription to the entire Book of Concord, Missouri had hoped that the Synodical Conference would provide the means to achieve Lutheran unity in the United States.

Even in the midst of controversy, however, the synod grew. By 1872 the synod had a membership of 72,120 baptized members, 485 congregations, 428 pastors, and 251 teachers. Between 1887 and 1932 membership grew from 531,357 to 1,163,666. Immigration drove this growth, as the synod worked hard to meet the spiritual needs of the arriving German immigrants.

The twentieth century, with its limited immigration and two world wars, forced the Missouri Synod to grapple with the issue of its German character. World War I forced the synod to anglicize more rapidly than might otherwise have been the case. Yet the transition to English occurred simultaneously with another period of significant growth. By 1962 the synod had 6,192 pastors and 2,456,856 baptized members. Through the radio ministry of Walter A. Maier, the *Lutheran Hour* reached thousands (see MASS MEDIA; PUBLISHING, MEDIA) and the lay-oriented organizations devoted to EVANGELISM, the Lutheran Laymen's League (1917) and the Lutheran Women's Missionary League (1942), enabled the synod to reach previously unreached populations.

Controversy continued, however, this time both with other Lutherans, as well as within the synod. With the language shift, Missouri was increasingly drawn out of what many perceived to be its overly narrow parochial boundaries. In the 1930s the synod explored fellowship with the newly formed AMERICAN LUTHERAN CHURCH, which consisted of several of Missouri's nineteenth-century adversaries, including the Buffalo, Iowa, and Ohio Synods. A fissure began to emerge within Missouri as it struggled anew with the question of Lutheran identity. One group urged faithfulness to the synod's historic doctrine and practice. A second group called for more openness to Christians within other traditions. In 1945 a group of forty-four leaders in the synod, representing this second perspective, issued *A Statement,* arguing that "fellowship is possible without complete agreement in details of doctrine and practice which have never been considered divisive in the Lutheran Church." Beginning in the 1950s the synod's seminary at St. Louis added to the tensions by introducing certain elements of HIGHER CRITICISM. The combined issues of ecumenical posture, biblical AUTHORITY, and biblical interpretation ultimately brought the controversy to its peak in 1974 when most of the faculty and students "walked out" of Concordia Seminary and formed Christ Seminary in Exile, or Seminex. During the next few years the synod suffered a schism as slightly more than 100,000 of its members withdrew to form the Association of Evangelical Lutheran Churches (AELC), which soon became the catalyst in the formation of the EVANGELICAL LUTHERAN CHURCH in America (1988), the largest Lutheran denomination in the United States.

Nevertheless, membership in the synod has remained relatively stable since the 1970s. The synod continues to support its two SEMINARIES, along with a university system that features schools in Ann Arbor, Michigan; Austin, Texas; Bronxville, New York; Irvine, California; Mequon, Wisconsin; Portland, Oregon; River Forest, Illinois; St. Paul, Minnesota; Selma, Alabama; and Seward, Nebraska. CLERGY and lay delegates representing the synod's congregations meet together triennially in convention to conduct the church's business. Its current president, the Rev. A. L. Barry, has served since 1992.

References and Further Reading

Baepler, Walter A. *A Century of Grace: A History of the Missouri Synod 1847–1947.* St. Louis, MO: Concordia Publishing House, 1947.

Dau, W. H. T., ed. *Ebenezer: Reviews of the Work of the Missouri Synod during Three Quarters of a Century.* St. Louis, MO: Concordia Publishing House, 1922.

Forster, Walter O. *Zion on the Mississippi: The Settlement of the Saxon Lutherans in Missouri, 1839–1841.* St. Louis, MO: Concordia Publishing House, 1953.

Hochstetter, Christian. *Geschichte der Evangelische-lutherische Missouri Synode in Nord-Amerika, und ihrer Lehrkämpfe von der sächsichen Auswanderung in Jahre 1838 an bis zum Jahre 1884.* Dresden, Germany: Verlag von Heinrich J. Naumann, 1885.

Marquart, Kurt E. *Anatomy of an Explosion: A Theological Analysis of the Missouri Synod Conflict.* Fort Wayne, IN: Concordia Theological Seminary Press, 1977.

Mundinger, Carl S. *Government in the Missouri Synod: The Genesis of Decentralized Government in the Missouri Synod.* St. Louis, MO: Concordia Publishing House, 1947.

Rudnick, Milton L. *Fundamentalism and the Missouri Synod: A Historical Study of Their Interaction and Mutual Influence.* St. Louis, MO: Concordia Publishing House, 1966.

LAWRENCE RAST

LUTHERAN CHURCH IN AMERICA

The Lutheran Church in America (LCA) was formed in 1962 by a merger of the United Lutheran Church in America (ULCA), the AUGUSTANA EVANGELICAL LUTHERAN CHURCH (Augusta Synod), the Finnish Evangelical Lutheran Church (Suomi Synod), and a Danish body, the American Evangelical Lutheran Church. From its offices in Philadelphia and New York, the LCA's membership extended from the East Coast and the CARIBBEAN to CANADA, Alaska, and Hawaii, combining Lutherans of German, Swedish, Finnish, Norwegian, Icelandic, Slovak, and African descent. Twenty-five years later, in 1988, the LCA merged with the AMERICAN LUTHERAN CHURCH (ALC) and the Association of Evangelical Lutheran Churches (AELC) to form the EVANGELICAL LUTHERAN CHURCH IN AMERICA (ELCA). At its height in 1967, the LCA contained 3.2 million baptized members. By 1988, when it became part of the ELCA, membership had declined to 2.9 million.

Institutional Life

In its POLITY, the LCA balanced the more centralized experience of its Swedish, Danish, and Finnish founders with the more regional expression characteristic of the predominantly German ULCA. In its theology, standard generalizations describing the LCA as the more liberal branch of American Lutheranism, as opposed to the orthodox LUTHERAN CHURCH–MISSOURI SYNOD (LCMS) and the more moderate American Lutheran Church are only partially accurate, although as a body the LCA did stand committed to ECUMENISM, further Lutheran unity, and the findings of modern biblical scholarship.

Early in its history, the LCA became a member of the LUTHERAN WORLD FEDERATION, the Lutheran Council in the USA (LCUSA), and the WORLD COUNCIL OF CHURCHES, and stood as the only American Lutheran member of the NATIONAL COUNCIL OF CHURCHES. The LCA's choice of former ULCA president Franklin Clark Fry (who provided significant active leadership in many of these organizations) as its first president from 1963 to 1968 both reflected and encouraged these wider commitments. Under Fry and his successors, the Rev. Robert J. Marshall (president from 1968 to 1978), and the Rev. James R. Crumley (1978 to 1988), the LCA continued long-standing dialogues with the Reformed tradition and Roman Catholics, developed guidelines for interim sharing of the Eucharist with Episcopalians, and reached out to the leaders of the Orthodox communion. In 1980, the LCA Convention changed the title of its President to "Presiding Bishop."

A "Comprehensive Study of the Doctrine of the Ministry" in 1970 recommended after careful study that LCA bylaws be amended to substitute the word "person" for the word "man" in its description of the qualifications for an ordained minister. Unlike the bitter experience of some churches, the LCA Convention that year approved the ordination of WOMEN by a simple voice vote (see WOMEN CLERGY). Elizabeth Platz became the first woman ordained in the LCA on November 22, 1970.

The LCA responded to the tumultuous events of its time with both theological reflection through its many "social statements" and direct action through its many agencies. Outreach in the area of mission eventually moved from the traditional home and foreign fields to newer fields among the poor and marginalized in society. Two particularly significant efforts included the World Hunger Appeal, which raised nearly 65 million dollars by 1987, and the work of the Lutheran Immigration and Refugee Service. Both of these efforts continued into the ELCA.

As part of the long-standing commitment of Lutherans to an educated CLERGY and LAITY, the LCA supported a number of denominational colleges and SEMINARIES (see HIGHER EDUCATION; CHRISTIAN COLLEGES). While the LCA actually warned of an oversupply of clergy as late as 1980, by the late 1980s seminary enrollments illustrated the clear trends of other mainline denominations: a decline in the overall number of candidates and a student population including more women and second-career candidates (see EDUCATION, THEOLOGY: UNITED STATES).

The Lutheran served as the official magazine of the LCA, and during most of the life of the LCA, it reportedly stood as the most widely circulated denominational periodical in North America. Circulation peaked at 601,000 and dropped slowly to just over 536,000 by 1987.

Congregational Life

In 1964, the LCA Parish Education Curriculum created a coordinated curriculum for use across all ages and programs of the church. This ambitious curriculum also introduced an entire generation of congregational teachers to the findings and contributions of contemporary biblical scholarship, perhaps helping the LCA avoid the schisms experienced in other denominations over issues of biblical literalism. At one time, over 90 percent of all LCA congregations used the program. The *Word and Witness* curriculum, introduced in 1977, combined in-depth adult BIBLE study with EVANGELISM and provided new energy in many congregations.

In 1970, the report of the Joint Commission on the Theology and Practice of Confirmation recommended a fundamental shift in long-standing Lutheran practice, urging that reception of first communion be lowered to approximately grade five and that this reception no longer be tied to the rite of CONFIRMATION, a rite renamed the "Affirmation of Baptism."

The LCA began its congregational life using the *Service Book and Hymnal*, a worship resource developed in the 1950s by several Lutheran bodies, including the ALC and the four churches that ultimately formed the LCA. The 1978 introduction of the *Lutheran Book of Worship* (LBW), also used in the ALC, led to an increased emphasis on the role of BAPTISM in the life of the believer, the increased use of lay men and women in positions of worship leadership, and a gradual increase in the frequency of communion, or LORD'S SUPPER. By 1981, 85 percent of LCA churches used the LBW.

Of the three traditional auxiliaries for men, youth, and women, the church-wide women's group proved most active and enduring. At the church-wide level, Lutheran Church Women (LCW) increasingly redefined its traditional mission to encompass the realm of social justice. The church ended its church-wide auxiliaries for men in 1966, and, in a controversial decision in 1968, also eliminated its youth auxiliary in an effort to emphasize a more holistic approach to youth ministry. A number of significant "youth gatherings," including inter-synodical Lutheran gatherings in 1973 and 1976, drew thousands of Lutheran young people together for Bible study, WORSHIP, and fellowship.

The Evangelical Lutheran Church in America

The Canadian synods of the LCA completed long-standing plans to merge with the Evangelical Lutheran Church of Canada in 1986. Responding to the invitation of the AELC, a group that split off from the LCMS in 1976, the LCA (2.9 million members), ALC (2.3 million members), and the AELC (109,000 members) came together in 1988 as the ELCA. The new church officially began its life on January 1, 1988, with 5.3 million members, 11,000 congregations. and 16,600 pastors.

See also Catholicism, Protestant Reactions; Dialogue, Interconfessional; Episcopal Church, USA; Lutheranism; Lutheranism, United States; Orthodoxy, Eastern

References and Further Reading

Gilbert, W. Kent. *Commitment to Unity: A History of the Lutheran Church in America*. Philadelphia, PA: Fortress Press, 1988.

Lagerquist, L. DeAne. *The Lutherans*. Westport, CT: Greenwood Press, 1999.

Nelson, E. Clifford. "The New Shape of Lutheranism, 1930–." In *The Lutherans in North America*, edited by E. Clifford Nelson. Philadelphia, PA: Fortress Press, 1974.

SUSAN WILDS MCARVER

LUTHERAN SYNODICAL CONFERENCE

Called the Lutheran Synodical Conference when it disbanded in 1967, this federation of American-based synods began in 1872, changing name and membership along the way. As Lutherans, especially Germans, came to America, some confessional-minded sought to gather to maintain THEOLOGY and deal with practical issues held in common, especially MISSIONS and EDUCATION. To sort through theological variations transplanted from Europe and developed in America and to be sure of a common theological position, various Lutherans held free conferences from 1856 to 1859.

Free conferences presumed no official representation, only open discussion using Scripture and the Lutheran Confessions as a benchmark. The General Council took in some groups in 1866, but others considered it lax on altar-pulpit fellowship, lodge membership, and millennialism. The Missouri, Ohio, and Norwegian synods declined participation, whereas the Wisconsin, Minnesota, Illinois, and Michigan synods joined but then withdrew. Subsequent discussions by these synods brought some bilateral fellowship agreements, and in 1871 talks began for multilateral cooperation. In 1872 these resulted in the Lutheran Synodical Conference, officially the Evangelisch-lutherische Synodal-Conferenz. Members pledged themselves to the Scriptures and confessions in the BOOK OF CONCORD to promote FAITH and true DOCTRINE and to avoid error as they worked together. Only an advisory body, this federation proposed a common seminary and a common teachers college but abandoned those plans.

Other efforts included work among African Americans in American and Nigerian missions and through colleges. PUBLISHING was sometimes done jointly, as with hymnals, for example. Over the years members left: the Ohio Synod (1881–1882) over PREDESTINATION, and the Norwegian Synod (1883) with internal dissent. The Evangelical Lutheran Synod (Norwegians) and the Wisconsin Synod broke with the Missouri Synod over fellowship and worship issues in 1955 and 1961 and withdrew from the Conference in 1963. The Conference dissolved in 1967.

See also Christian College; Hymns and Hymnals; Lutheranism, United States; Millenarians and Millennialism

References and Further Reading

Braun, Mark E. "Changes within the Evangelical Lutheran Synodical Conference of North America That Led to the Exit of the Wisconsin Evangelical Lutheran Synod." Ph.D. dissertation, Concordia Seminary, St. Louis, 2000.

Schuetze, Armin W. *The Synodical Conference: Ecumenical Endeavor*. Milwaukee, WI: Northwestern Publishing House, 2000.

ROBERT ROSIN

LUTHERAN WORLD FEDERATION

The Lutheran World Federation (LWF) was founded in Lund, SWEDEN in 1947 by forty-nine churches, all but two of which were in Europe and North America. It is the result of earlier efforts, at first national—the General Council of the Evangelical Lutheran Church in North America (1867) and the General Evangelical Lutheran Conference in GERMANY (1867)—and then international to bring together churches that have a common confessional allegiance. These efforts led to establishing the Lutheran World Convention (LWC) by an assembly of Lutheran personages in Eisenach in 1923. At its third session, 1935 in Paris, the LWC laid the groundwork for a more permanent confederation of churches. World War II did not stop continuing efforts to realize the Paris plan; indeed efforts toward fellowship intensified in caring for orphaned missions and aiding European Lutherans to overcome the war's devastation. That effective relief program for Europe shaped the work of Lutheran World Service that involves a major portion of LWF staff and financial resources.

Member churches subscribe to Lutheranism's confessional basis as stated in the LWF constitution (revised in 1990): "The Lutheran World Federation confesses the Holy Scriptures of the Old and New Testaments to be the only source and norm of its doctrine, life and service. It sees in the three Ecumenical Creeds and in the Confessions of the Lutheran Church, especially in the unaltered Augsburg Confession and the Small Catechism of Martin Luther, a pure exposition of the Word of God" (Art II).

The constitution also states the functions of the LWF: "The Lutheran World Federation:

- Furthers the united witness to the Gospel of Jesus Christ and strengthens the member churches in carrying out the missionary command and in their efforts towards Christian unity worldwide;

- Furthers worldwide among the member churches diaconic action, alleviation of human need, promotion of peace and human rights, social and economic justice, care for God's creation and sharing of resources;
- Furthers through cooperative study the self-understanding and the communion of member churches and helps them to act jointly in common tasks" (Art III).

By 2000 membership in the LWF had increased to 131 churches (including three associate members) and twelve recognized congregations in seventy-three countries, with churches in AFRICA accounting for the greatest growth. Approximately 60 million of the 64 million Lutherans across the globe are included. It is the Lutheran Church–Missouri Synod in the UNITED STATES and some of its associated churches that remain outside the LWF.

Periodic international assemblies are the highest authority of the LWF, and their official reports archive the Federation's history: 1947 Lund, 1952 Hannover, 1957 Minneapolis, 1963 Helsinki, 1970 Evian, 1977 Dar es Salaam, 1984 Budapest, 1990 Curitiba, 1997 Hong Kong, and the tenth assembly 2003 Winnipeg.

Although the ecclesial nature of world LUTHERANISM was already being debated, the LWF in Lund followed the lead of the LWC and described itself as "a free association of Lutheran churches." As the debate intensified, churches increasingly found themselves in pulpit and altar fellowship. This heightened sense of church manifested itself at Dar es Salaam when the LWF took the step of declaring *status confessionis* regarding the effects of apartheid at the LORD'S SUPPER. Then at Budapest two African white churches were suspended because of their attitude toward apartheid, a suspension lifted at Curitiba, BRAZIL. Increasing ecumenical involvement repeatedly put the ecclesial question to world Lutheranism, adding to the pressure to go beyond the "free association." This led, in Budapest, to two precedent-setting assembly actions: (1) amending the constitution by adding "The member churches of the LWF understand themselves to be in pulpit and altar fellowship with each other," and (2) adopting statements on self-understanding and unity, both of which used the terminology "Lutheran Communion."

In Curitiba the assembly adopted a new constitution that embodied a more ecclesial self-understanding of the LWF. It defines the LWF as "a communion of churches which confess the triune God, agree in the proclamation of the Word of God and are united in pulpit and altar fellowship." A council of forty-eight persons was established to carry responsibility for the Federation between assemblies. Reflecting the concept of communion, membership on the council is divided equally between representatives of member churches from the northern and southern hemispheres, and at least 40 percent of its members are WOMEN.

Communion language is also consonant with the fundamental ecumenical commitment of the LWF. It is engaged bilaterally with other Christian World Communions (CWCs) but is also fully committed to multilateral ECUMENISM as exemplified in the WORLD COUNCIL OF CHURCHES (WCC). This ecumenical priority finds typical expression in the Institute for Ecumenical Research, established in Strasbourg in 1963. Strasbourg research professors have been key participants in both multilateral and bilateral dialogues. The LWF has or has had bilateral dialogues with the Anglican Communion, the BAPTIST WORLD ALLIANCE, the WORLD METHODIST COUNCIL, the Orthodox churches (see ORTHODOXY, EASTERN), the WORLD ALLIANCE OF REFORMED CHURCHES, and the SEVENTH-DAY ADVENTIST CHURCH. In many cases these bilateral relationships extend also to joint efforts in witness and service.

The oldest LWF bilateral relationship, begun in 1957, has been with the Roman Catholic Church. In view of REFORMATION history, this dialogue has enjoyed a high priority, and at the turn of the century it had all but completed four phases, producing many joint study papers. At a 1999 ceremony in Augsburg the *Joint Declaration on the Doctrine of Justification,* one of the most significant documents of consensus Ecumenism, was signed by official representatives of the Roman Catholic Church and the LWF. In addition to affirming a basic consensus on JUSTIFICATION, the document declares the mutual condemnations of the sixteenth century to be no longer applicable and thus not church-dividing. Subsequently the two bodies are in conversations with various Christian World Communions in the hope that the effect of the Joint Declaration can be broadened.

The LWF staff is divided among three programmatic departments: World Service, Mission and Evangelism, and Theology and Studies. The secretariat includes offices dealing with ecumenical relations, political affairs and human rights, and communication services. In 1995 the LWF and the WCC together formed Action of Churches Together (ACT) to enable them to respond more immediately and effectively to major global emergencies. The LWF shares the Geneva headquarters of the WCC and other CWCs, and presently has regional offices in AFRICA, Asia, Europe, and North America. The Geneva staff numbers approximately one hundred persons and there are approximately 4,000 field staff in service, relief, and development projects.

References and Further Reading

Brand, Eugene L. "Toward a Lutheran Communion: Pulpit and Altar Fellowship." *LWF Report 26* (1988).

Grundmann, Siegfried. *Der Lutherische Weltbund: Gründung, Herkunft, Aufbau.* Cologne, Germany: Böhlav, 1957.

Nelson, E. Clifford. *The Rise of World Lutheranism. An American Perspective.* Philadelphia, PA: Fortress Press, 1982.

Schjørring, Jens Holger, Prasanna Kumari, and Norman A. Hjelm, eds. *From Federation to Communion. The History of the Lutheran World Federation.* Minneapolis, MN: Fortress Press, 1997.

Schmidt-Clausen, Kurt. "Vom Lutherischen Weltkonvent zum Lutherischen Weltbund." *Die Lutherische Kirche, Geschichte und Gestalten, 2.* Gütersloh, Germany: Gütersloh Verlagshaus, 1976.

Vajta, Vilmos. "From Generation to Generation: The LWF 1947–1982." *LWF Report 16* (1983).

Wadensjö, Bengt. "Toward a Lutheran World Communion: Developments in Lutheran Cooperation up to 1929." *Acta Universitatis Upsaliensis, Studia Historic-Ecclesiastica Upsaliensia 18.* Uppsala, Sweden. 1970.

EUGENE L. BRAND

LUTHERANISM

The term refers to the churches that stem from MARTIN LUTHER's reform efforts. His study of Scripture and struggle with guilt focused Lutheran thought and life on concern for proper, clear biblical teaching; effective pastoral comfort and care; disciplined intellectual work across the spectrum of learned disciplines; and appreciation and use of MUSIC and LITERATURE.

The Reformation

With his colleague PHILIPP MELANCHTHON, Luther guided a REFORMATION centered on doctrinal reform, in contrast to earlier medieval renewal efforts that sought moral and institutional change. These Wittenberg theologians created a paradigm change for Western THEOLOGY in the Religious Peace of Augsburg (1555) by defining the question of the sinner's identity in God's sight as the center of a biblical teaching (although inferior) church within the German Empire.

Their prince, Elector John of Saxony, enlisted Luther and Melanchthon in a princely led equivalent of a medieval episcopal parish visitation in 1527–1528. Their Visitation Articles cultivated pastoral care through the distinction of law (God's commands for human life, which condemn SIN) and gospel (the restoration of life through forgiveness in Christ) and guided the organization of parish life in line with Luther's reform. Luther was willing to permit Christian princes to take a leadership role in church life as "emergency bishops" in the absence of bishops committed to reform. The organizational principles of the Wittenberg Reformation spread to other cities and principalities as those won to Luther's cause composed constitutions or church orders (*Kirchenordnungen*) for WORSHIP, EDUCATION, social welfare, and other areas of church life. Especially influential were those drafted by the Wittenbergers' colleague JOHANNES BUGENHAGEN.

Luther's Reformation preserved the structure of the medieval LITURGY, removing the canon of the Mass, which Luther regarded as a perversion of the LORD'S SUPPER. He retained the pericopal system. Postils on the traditional Sunday and festival texts, modeled after Luther's own, became important tools for continuing education of CLERGY and family devotion. Followers, beginning with Johann Spangenberg (1484–1550) in 1541, took Luther's advice to develop further tools to supplement his CATECHISMS. Among the most popular pattern was that created by student Joachim Mörlin (1514–1571), who copied Luther's outline of law, gospel, and godly living to provide fundamental instruction in the faith. Family use of devotional literature supplemented PREACHING and catechesis for LAITY. Ethical instruction occurred in homiletical and other forms, including imaginative *Teufelbücher* (devil books), which used personification to promote Christian virtue through calls for repentance of specific sins.

Luther and Melanchthon skillfully employed the printing press; however, their students and others disseminated their message by preaching, in GERMANY, Scandinavia, central Europe, ENGLAND, and FRANCE. In the latter two countries, independent reform movements developed, but Danish and Swedish monarchs were won for Lutheranism by pastors from their lands, some of whom were former Wittenberg students. Christian III employed HANS TAUSEN and Bugenhagen to introduce the Reformation in DENMARK in 1536. Opposition remained strong in Danish-ruled NORWAY for more than a generation before preaching and catechesis cultivated a strong Lutheran popular piety. In SWEDEN the independence movement led by the nobleman Gustav Vasa and Lutheran reform led by former Wittenberg student OLAVS PETRI, his brother LAURENTIUS, and Laurentius Andreae, found mutual support. In Swedish-ruled FINLAND, MICHAEL AGRICOLA, also a Wittenberg student, established Lutheran reform as publicist, school rector, and bishop. Beginning in the 1520s, German students from central European domains as well as Poles, Slovaks, Hungarians, and others also brought the Wittenberg message back from the university to their own lands, where printed works had kindled commitment to Luther's ideas. In Latvia and Estonia, Lutheran preachers were using Luther's *Small Catechism* in the native languages by 1550. After 1550 some in HUNGARY and POLAND became Calvinists and some of them in turn Anti-Trinitarians, but strong Lutheran churches remained in Siebenburgen, Hungary, Slovakia, and Poland into the triumph of the COUNTER-REFORMATION in the seventeenth century and beyond.

Confessionalization and Orthodoxy

The process by which the Reformation was consolidated and adapted to political, social, and ecclesiastical structures has been called CONFESSIONALIZATION by scholars since about 1980. For Lutheranism this process began soon after Luther's death (1546) when controversy arose among his and Melanchthon's students over the proper interpretation of their legacy in an atmosphere embittered by the imperial defeat of Lutheran princes in the War of Schmalkald (1546–1547) and Emperor Charles V's attempt to force their people back to Roman Catholic obedience. Melanchthon's efforts to save Saxon pulpits for Lutheran preachers were regarded as betrayal of the gospel by some of his best students; his feeling that they were betraying him in turn led to bitter recriminations. A quarter century of contention ended with the Formula of Concord (1577) and BOOK OF CONCORD (1580), which brought two-thirds of the German Lutheran churches together in doctrinal agreement.

This period witnessed fruitful intellectual activity in the Wittenberg circle. Italo-Croatian student and colleague MATTHIAS FLACIUS (Illyricus), who broke with Melanchthon over a series of doctrinal issues, synthesized Protestant hermeneutics in his groundbreaking *Clavis Scripturae sacrae* (*Key to the Sacred Scriptures,* 1567) and planned the first Protestant church history, the eight-volume *Magdeburg Centuries* (1559–1574), actually written by Johannes Wigand (1523–1587) and Matthaeus Judex (1528–1564). Braunschweig pastor Martin Chemnitz (1522–1586) issued a four-volume *Examination of the Council of Trent,* a sharp critique of Tridentine theology and clear presentation of Lutheran thought. It is important for its emphasis on (1) the AUTHORITY and reliability of Scripture as the sole source of teaching and the proper use of the Christian TRADITION, especially patristic writings; (2) the "excluding expressions," such as "by grace alone," "by faith alone," and "apart from the works of the law," in defining the JUSTIFICATION of sinners; (3) Luther's understanding of original sin as "a turning away from God and hostility toward him"; (4) the SACRAMENTS as forms of God's Word that convey God's favor; and (5) the necessity of the good works that faith produces. These accents are also found in Chemnitz's commentary on Melanchthon's master work on biblical teaching, *Loci communes theologici* (editions 1521, 1535, 1543), one of many such formulations of DOCTRINE by Melanchthon's students. Chemnitz's *Loci* provided a bridge to

and model for later Lutheran dogmatic textbooks. Rich devotional literature arose in the period as well, from Frankfurt/Oder professor Andreas Musculus (1514–1581), Silesian pastor Martin Moller (1547–1606), and many others. Nikolaus Herman (c.1500–1561) and Philip Nicolai (1556–1608), among others, continued the hymnodic tradition begun by Luther (see HYMNS AND HYMNALS).

After the publication of the Book of Concord the established churches of Lutheran Germany and Scandinavia experienced a long period of societal dominance. "Orthodox" theologians set the tone for church life from 1580 to 1700, synthesizing the thought of Luther, Melanchthon, JOHANNES BRENZ, Chemnitz, and other Lutheran predecessors with patristic theology and elements of medieval scholasticism as they addressed the issues of their day in massive dogmatic works. Jakob Heerbrand (1521–1600) and Matthias Haffenreffer (1561–1619) at Tübingen and Leonhard Hutter (1563–1616, Wittenberg) composed doctrinal textbooks that led to the work of Johann Gerhard (Jena), the master of Lutheran dogmaticians, with his *Loci theologici* (nine volumes, 1610–1622) and *Confessio catholica* (1634–1637). His contemporaries Cornelius (1568–1621) and Jakob (1570–1649) Martini had introduced Aristotelian metaphysics into Lutheran theology at Helmstedt and Wittenberg. Thus, Gerhard constructed his dogmatics on an analytic basis, abandoning Melanchthon's philological-rhetorical synthesis of biblical materials, presented with the help of patristic insights and Aristotelian logic; Gerhard adopted the Aristotelian metaphysical approach of J. Zabrella. Gerhard defended biblical authority on the basis of Scripture's divine verbal inspiration. He made fruitful use of the ancient church fathers. The doctrine of justification by GRACE through FAITH in Christ alone remained the center of his teaching, along with God's working his saving will through the "means of grace." Gerhard directed his tightly argued analyses of doctrinal topics toward their "practical use" in parish life. His devotional handbook, *Sacred Meditations* (1606), demonstrates that these dogmaticians preached and taught a warm piety at the same time they constructed their Aristotelian–biblical theology. Like Melanchthon, Gerhard and other Orthodox theologians incorporated ethical instruction into their dogmatic works (see ETHICS).

Gerhard's provided the framework for the systems of Johann Conrad Dannhauer (1603–1666, Strasbourg); Abraham Calov (1612–1686, Wittenberg), whose opus embraced biblical exegesis as well as dogmatics; Johann Andreas Quenstedt (1617–1688, Wittenberg), whose *Didactic-Polemical Theology, or System of Theology* (1685) served as a comprehensive summary of his predecessors' insights and his own biblical study; and Johann Wilhelm Baier (1647–1695, Jena and HALLE). Johann Musaeus (1613–1681, Jena) initiated the Lutheran critique of Enlightened thinkers such as HERBERT OF CHERBURY and Bernard Spinoza. Sebastian Schmidt (1617–1696, Strasbourg) contributed to Talmudic studies and wrote massive biblical commentaries. At Copenhagen, Hans Poulsen Resen (1561–1638), Cort Aslakssen (1564–1624), and Jesper Rasmus Brochmand (1585–1652) represented Lutheran ORTHODOXY effectively. With the work of Pomeranian pastor David Hollaz (1648–1713) and Ernst Valentin Loescher (1673–1749, Wittenberg), a fierce critic of PIETISM, the age of Orthodoxy came to an end.

Although widespread agreement in teaching marked this era, controversies did arise. Wittenberg colleagues Samuel Huber (1547–1624) and Aegidius Hunnius (1550–1603) contended over Huber's view of universal ELECTION; Hunnius nudged Orthodoxy in a "synergistic" direction with his view that election takes place "on the basis of foreseen faith." Danzig pastor Hermann Rahtmann's (1585–1628) spiritualizing views of the Holy Spirit's work provoked new treatment of God's Word as the means of grace that effects God's saving will from outside the believer. Theologians from Tübingen and Giessen disputed over Christ's *kenosis,* "emptying himself" (Philippians 2:7), in the 1620s. Helmstedt professor Georg Calixt aroused criticism from Calov and others with his call for Protestant reconciliation on the basis of the "consensus antiquitatis" of the first five centuries (Vincent of Lerin) in the "syncretistic controversy." His opponents believed his proposal abandoned the integrity of the Lutheran CONFESSION.

The Orthodox era also witnessed further development of Lutheran catechetics, in the theory and actual catechetical texts of Giessen professor and pastor in Ulm, Conrad Dietrich (1575–1639), who incorporated elements of Aristotelian analysis into his questions and answers that interpreted Luther's catechisms. Gerhard's *Sacred Meditationes* and JOHANN ARNDT'S (1555–1621) *Four Books on True Christianity* (1605–1610) and *Garden of Paradise* (1612), among others, enriched popular devotional life. Lutheran hymnwriters, including Paul Gerhardt, enlivened parish life. Württemberg court preacher Johann Valentin Andreae (1586–1654) cultivated social concern and piety.

General Baroque developments shaped modest Lutheran contributions in ART and ARCHITECTURE in this era. Lutheran composers, including MICHAEL PRAETORIUS, Heinrich Schütz, Johann Hermann Schein (1586–1630), Samuel Scheidt (1587–1654), DIETRICH BUXTEHUDE, and JOHANN SEBASTIAN BACH, appropriated Italian developments to create new standards for organ and chorale, cantatas, and the like.

Like their Roman Catholic and Calvinist counterparts, early modern Lutheran secular rulers pursued absolutist ideals in attempting to extend their powers over the CHURCH, usually with success, although the often-ignored Lutheran tradition of defiance of and resistance to governments bent on undermining the church's integrity continued into the seventeenth century (e.g., in the resistance to Calvinist princes in Anhalt, Lippe, and Brandenburg where Paul Gerhardt opposed Elector Frederick William's anti-Lutheran program in the 1660s). More typical of the attitudes of theologians and governmental officials is the defense of ABSOLUTISM by the ducal Saxon counselor Veit Ludwig von Seckendorf (1626–1692), author of a skillful defense of Lutheranism, *Historical and Apologetical Commentary on Lutheranism* (1688–1692), who affirmed that princes held power as God's stewards for society in *The German Princely State* (1656) and *The Christian State* (1685).

SAMUEL FREIHERR VON PUFENDORF, professor of law and princely counselor, defended Lutheran positions against CALVINISM and forged a theory of NATURAL LAW that defined it as rational, agreeing with Christian revelation because it stems from God's design, but not dependent on revelation. With Christian commitment declining at European courts, he formulated a view of church POLITY that challenged the "Episcopal" theory (that God had given princes the responsibility to care for the religion of their people), which had supported princely administration of churches, largely through consistories (see CONSISTORY), since the Reformation. Pufendorf and Christian Thomasius (1655–1728), professor of law in Leipzig and Halle, advanced the increasingly predominant view, "territorialism," holding that by natural law princes bear responsibility for all institutions that support the welfare of the state, including the church (see CHURCH AND STATE, OVERVIEW). Christoph Matthaeus Pfaff (1686–1760, Tübingen and Giessen) and JOHANN LORENZ VON MOSHEIM (1694–1755, Helmstedt and Göttingen) advanced a third definition of church polity, "collegialism," that characterized the church as a community formed by the free association of individuals with the same rights as other institutions within society; princely administration of the church is conducted in behalf of this community.

In the seventeenth century, Roman Catholic authorities harshly persecuted Lutheran and other Protestant communities in central European lands, attempting to exterminate them as churches. Pastors were sentenced to life imprisonment in the galleys, churches confiscated, Lutheran worship and literature forbidden. In Slovakia and other areas the Lutheran percentage of the population was reduced from 85 to 15 percent during the century of suppression. In Hapsburg territories the Patent of Toleration (1781) restored minimal rights to the congregations of those who had preserved their faith with the BIBLE, catechism, and hymnbook.

Pietism

The need for renewal, particularly within established Lutheran churches charged with religious care and supervision of the entire population of a country, became ever clearer in spite of strong programs for cultivating piety in the preaching and devotional literature of Orthodoxy. Several programs for improving church life have borne the label "pietist" since the late seventeenth century. They reflected concerns of sixteenth-century Lutheran theology as well as Arndt's and Gerhard's, and English Puritan and Dutch Reformed devotional literature, with variations introduced in focus and formulation. PHILIPP JAKOB SPENER launched an influential renewal movement. As pastor in Frankfurt/Main he composed a preface for Arndt's sermons on gospel pericopes that became a separate publication, *Pia Desideria,* an effective call for active lay and clerical discipleship. He organized small groups, the *collegia pietatis,* to foster pious living in the midst of the established congregations, with their indifferent majorities, through emphasis on Bible study, the PRIESTHOOD OF ALL BELIEVERS, the practice of obedience to God, and improved preaching and theological education. From the Saxon court (Dresden) and later in cooperation with Brandenburg's government, as pastor in Berlin, Spener encouraged the growth of PIETISM.

Its chief organizer was AUGUST HERMANN FRANCKE, whose *Stiftung* in HALLE, centered around an orphanage, modeled provision of social services, influenced theological students at Halle's university, distributed Bibles and devotional literature, and supported the first serious Protestant attempts at mission outside Europe, among non-Christians in INDIA (Bartholomaeus Ziegenbalg [1682–1719] and Heinrich Plütschau [1677–1746], 1706, Tranquebar) and German emigrants (HENRY MELCHIOR MUHLENBERG, Pennsylvania). NIKOLAUS LUDWIG VON ZINZENDORF founded the ecumenical Herrnhuter Community (see HERRNHUT) with the aid of persecuted Moravian refugees and influenced Lutheran preaching and piety in central Europe and many foreign lands. Württemberg pietism, focused on biblical study, the practice of discipleship in daily life, and eschatological speculation, is aptly reflected in the work of biblical scholar JOHANN ALBRECHT BENGEL (1687–1752), particularly his New Testament commentary, *Gnomen Novi Testamenti* (1742).

German Pietist influences combined with native traditions of piety to create a series of Bible-centered movements for godly living in Scandinavia and central Europe. In Sweden, Henrik Schartau (1757–1825), pastor in Lund, combined a strong commitment to the Lutheran confessions with concern for pious life and a rejection of SECTARIANISM. His use of confession and absolution and his printed sermons shaped popular Swedish piety for generations. Among the important nineteenth-century Swedish revival preachers were lay preacher Carl Olof Rosenius (1816–1868) and pastor Lars Levi Laestadius (1800–1861), whose followers in Sweden and Finland, sometimes given to ecstatic experiences, rely largely on lay leadership and therefore use Absolution as their chief sacrament (see REVIVALS). Other Swedish pietists with spiritualizing tendencies separated from the established church. In Denmark and Norway they remained largely within the established churches. Danish court preacher, bishop, and professor Erik Pontoppidan (1698–1764) directed pietistic renewal, composed an explanation to Luther's *Small Catechism* that remained in use for two hundred years in Scandinavia and North America, and issued a new hymnal. Lay preacher HANS NIELSEN HAUGE traveled across Norway organizing CONVENTICLES and cultivated both a pious life, on the basis of a certain CONVERSION, and economic growth through his preaching. His criticism of rationalistic and immoral church leaders, as well as their fear of separatism, earned him imprisonment. His influence spread far beyond the groups he formed.

His reading of Luther and SØREN KIERKEGAARD moved Johan Vilhlem Beck (1829–1901) to found an Inner Mission society that brought a biblically based proclamation of Christ and encouragement for pious living to the Danish population.

Lutheranism in the Enlightenment

Pietists and Orthodox alike resisted Enlightened thought, which grew out of Orthodox metaphysics in part but increasingly set aside fundamental elements of Lutheran theology, including original sin, Christ's vicarious ATONEMENT, and sacramental teaching. Some early ENLIGHTENMENT thinkers regarded themselves as Lutherans; for example, GOTTFRIED WILHELM LEIBNIZ worked for reconciliation of the Lutheran churches with others, particularly the Reformed, but abandoned central concerns of Lutheran theology. The transitional thought of post-Orthodox theologians, Pfaff, Mosheim, and Johann Franz Buddeus (1667–1729), physicotheology (Johann Albert Fabricius [1668–1736]), Wolffian theology (SIGMUND JAKOB BAUMGARTEN), and NEOLOGY (JOHANN SALOMO SEMLER), represented differing approaches to reconciling reason with Scripture, setting aside specific aspects of Luther's thought while heralding him as an apostle of freedom and enlightened thinking. In Sweden, Orthodox theologians, such as Petrus Munck (1732–1803), worked to counter those influenced by German Enlightenment thinkers (e.g., Nils Vallerius [1706–1764], Uppsala).

The Confessional Revival

Reaction grew to "Enlightened" thinkers' shallow approaches and critical attacks on biblical authority and traditional Christian teaching. In 1817 Claus Harms (1778–1855), pastor in Kiel, posted a new "Ninety-five Theses," calling for renewed commitment to biblical authority and the theology of the Lutheran confessions, with emphasis on the use of the Lord's Supper and Confession and Absolution. From his work and other factors grew a Confessional Revival and "Neo-Lutheranism."

Prussian King Friedrich Wilhelm III's imposition of a union of Reformed and Lutheran churches in 1817, reinforced in 1830, aroused a strong Lutheran consciousness that resulted in fresh expressions of traditional Lutheran emphases within the United Church (e.g., by Ernst Wilhelm Hengstenberg [1802–1869]), and in the organization of the Evangelical Lutheran Church of Prussia (1841) by followers of Breslau professor Johann Gottfried Scheibel (1783–1843).

Within other Lutheran churches the Confessional Revival grew. When Bavarian King Ludwig I commanded that all soldiers kneel before the sacramental elements, the opposition of Erlangen professor Gottlieb Christoph Adolf Harless (1806–1879), a leader of renewal of confessional theology, cost him his position. After teaching in Leipzig and serving as Saxon court preacher he returned to Bavaria as president of the Lutheran Consistory. His program for theological renewal included certainty of personal rebirth through the power of the gospel and commitment to Scripture and the Lutheran confessions. The school that followed him and his colleague Johann Friedrich Wilhelm Höfling (1802–1853) strove to adapt the theology of the Lutheran confessions to nineteenth-century thought and refute the liberal theology of ALBRECHT RITSCHL and others (see LIBERAL PROTESTANTISM AND LIBERALISM). It included Luther scholar Theodosius Harnack (1817–1889), exegete (*Heilsgeschichte*) Johann Christen Konrad von Hofmann (1810–1877), and dogmaticians Gottfried Thomasius (1802–1875) and Franz Hermann Reinhold Frank (1827–1894). The confessional tradition at Erlangen continued in the twentieth century with Ludwig Ihmels (1858–1933), Werner Elert (1885–1954), Paul Althaus (1888–1966), and Hermann Sasse (1895–1976), the latter moving to Australia in the early 1950s.

Close connections and parallels existed between the Erlangen faculty and that in Leipzig under the leadership of Karl Friedrich August Kahnis (1814–1888) and Franz Delitsch (1813–1890), who also encouraged a strong commitment to the Lutheran confessions within their disciplines and the life of the church. Delitsch's engagement for Jewish mission was shared by his fellow Old Testament scholar, the Jewish convert and Orientalist Carl Paul Caspari (1814–1892), who propagated Lutheran confessional theology alongside his colleague Gisle Johnson (1822–1894) at the University of Christiana/Oslo.

In Hesse, Marburg professor August Friedrich Christian Vilmar (1800–1868), influenced by Romantic Roman Catholic views, especially of JOHANN ADAM MÖHLER, minimized the priesthood of all believers and saw the gospel guaranteed through the pastoral office, instituted by God for the church, "Christ's body in its glory." He countered Enlightenment thought with a clear proclamation of Christ's atoning work as "objective fact," which gives life. His clear distinction of Lutheran teaching from that of the Reformed church caused conflict with Heinrich Heppe. Some other leaders of the Confessional Revival shared his strong advocacy of monarchical government.

The Confessional Revival was also promoted in principalities (Theodor Kliefoth [1810–1895], Mecklenburg) and parishes (Ludwig Adolf Petri [1803–1873], Hannover). In Denmark, Kierkegaard and Nicolaj F. Grundtvig sharply criticized the Enlightened church of their time, Grundtvig through an educational and sacramental-liturgical movement that reshaped Danish society and church. In Finland, Fredrik Gabriel Hedberg's (1811–1893) strong emphasis on preaching Christ called Lutherans back to the doctrine of justification.

Hedberg's efforts bore fruit in the forming of a society dedicated to overseas mission. Parallels are found throughout Scandinavia and Germany. In the Bavarian village Neuendettelsau, pastor Wilhelm Löhe provided a model for pastoral care through the use of the Lord's Supper, Confession and Absolution, and small-group Bible study, created a social welfare institution around a home for the elderly and a DEACONESS motherhouse, and founded a mission that first sent pastors to German emigrants in North America (later AUSTRALIA and BRAZIL) and in the 1890s began work in Papua New Guinea. The Christ-centered preaching of Ludwig Harms (1808–1865) in Hermannsburg created a popular revival in the Lüneburger Heide and led to the organization of a mission that, under the direction of Ludwig's brother Theodor (1819–1885), used settlements of German settlers in SOUTH AFRICA as missionary base communities for converting non-Christian native populations like

Löhe's initial work among NATIVE AMERICANS in Michigan (see MISSIONS, GERMAN).

Lutheranism Outside Europe

Lutheran churches exist today in one hundred lands because of European emigration and active mission work. In the seventeenth and eighteenth centuries, Germans left lands plagued by French invasions for North America; Muhlenberg's organizational efforts, above all the formation of the Pennsylvania Ministerium (1748), formed an institutional basis for the church. In the nineteenth century the Muhlenberg synods and newly established churches met the greatest wave of German emigration (1850s–1880s). Löhe's efforts produced the Iowa Synod; his *"Sendlinge"* also helped organize the Missouri Synod, which under the leadership of CARL FERDINAND WALTHER became the largest German Protestant church in America. From his position as pastor and professor/president at Concordia Seminary in St. Louis, Walther organized an ecclesiastical subculture around parishes with an emphasis on preaching, education in parochial schools, publications for laity and CLERGY, and social welfare agencies, such as orphanages. The Ohio and Buffalo Synods and others reproduced this model to some extent. Walther led in the organization of a "Synodical Conference" in 1872 that divided in 1881–1883 because of a dispute over PREDESTINATION.

One member of the Synodical Conference, the Norwegian Synod, represented the wing of Norwegian emigrants strongly committed to the Lutheran confessions, the Lutheran liturgical tradition, and Walther's strong doctrine of PREDESTINATION. Followers of Hauge were grouped together in at least two other synods; three other Norwegian synods held mediating positions. Nearly all these churches united in 1917 in the Norwegian Lutheran Church of America. Swedish immigrants who remained Lutheran formed the Augustana Synod (1860); others founded the Mission Covenant Church (1885). Danish emigrants, divided among followers of Beck and Grundtvig, established two churches, as did Slovaks and Finns, along lines of their understanding of commitment to the Lutheran confessions.

Merger efforts led to the formation of the United Lutheran Church of America from churches of the Muhlenberg tradition (1918), the German-American American Lutheran Church (1930), and, after intensive negotiations, to the AMERICAN LUTHERAN CHURCH (German, Norwegian, Danish churches, 1960) and the United Lutheran Church (German, Swedish, Finnish, Danish churches, 1962). These two bodies, with dissident members of the Missouri Synod, the Associa-

tion of Evangelical Lutheran churches, formed the EVANGELICAL LUTHERAN CHURCH IN AMERICA (1987).

German emigrants to southern BRAZIL began organizing congregations soon after their arrival in the 1820s. Wilhelm Rotermund (1843–1925) formed the first lasting synod in 1886. Four synods united in 1954 as the Evangelical Church of the Lutheran Confession in Brazil; the Evangelical Lutheran Church in Brazil (founded 1900) has held a more confessional position. German settlers and North American Lutheran missions have also organized congregations and church bodies elsewhere in South America.

A. L. C. Kavel (1798–1860) led Lutherans protesting the Prussian Union to Australia in 1838. Mergers in 1921 and 1966 brought together most Australian Lutherans in the Lutheran Church of Australia.

Until the Revolution of 1917, eighteenth- and nineteenth-century German emigrants to RUSSIA and Finns in lands occupied by the Czarist government around 1700 had active congregations across the empire.

Lutheran missions, beginning with Ziegenbalg, have established churches in more than seventy nations. Lutheran missionaries worked with British missions in the early nineteenth century (see MISSIONS, BRITISH), but increasingly Lutherans organized their own training centers at home and new churches abroad. North American denominations have traditionally conducted their own extraterritorial mission work; European churches have relied on mission societies to bring the gospel to unchurched peoples. Among the numerically most fruitful of these mission efforts are the several Batak churches on Sumatra, which composed their own confession of faith (1951) modeled on the AUGSBURG CONFESSION and Reformed confessions, and churches in India, Tanzania, Ethiopia, Namibia, and Madagascar.

Ecumenical Lutheranism

Pressures of nineteenth-century society fostered desires for contact among German Lutheran churches; Harless, Kliefoth, and others organized the General Evangelical-Lutheran Conference in 1868. Under leadership of that conference and the American National Lutheran Council, Lutheran churches from around the world came together in the Lutheran World Convention (1923), reorganized in 1947 as the LUTHERAN WORLD FEDERATION.

Historic differences between Reformed and Lutheran definitions of the Lord's Supper were declared insufficient to prevent church fellowship in the *Leuenberg Concord* (1973) between those churches in Germany. The *Porvoo Agreement* established ALTAR and pulpit fellowship between the Anglican Church and most Nordic and Baltic Lutheran churches in 1993. In 1999, against widespread protest from theological faculties, the Lutheran World Federation reached agreement with the Roman Catholic Church that the historic condemnations of the other's doctrine of justification are no longer valid in the *Joint Declaration on the Doctrine of Justification* and its "Annex."

Lutherans have made important contributions to the wider ecumenical movement (see ECUMENISM). Swedish bishop NATHAN SODERBLOM helped organize Life and Work in 1925. Initial commitment to the Movement for Faith and Order (1927) from Elert and Sasse turned to disappointment when deeper interest in serious doctrinal discussion seemed lacking. William Lazareth (1928–) and Günther Gassmann provided leadership to Faith and Order in the critical period of the "Lima Document," *Baptism, Eucharist, and Ministry* (1982).

Twentieth-Century Lutheranism

Twentieth-century Lutheran theologians have represented a wide spectrum of theological viewpoints (see THEOLOGY, TWENTIETH-CENTURY). Specifically Lutheran accents were brought into theological exchange by Werner Elert, Paul Althaus, and Hermann Sasse at Erlangen and by Peter Brunner (1900–1981) and Edmund Schlink (1903–1984) at Heidelberg as well as by a group of Swedish theologians, including Gustaf Aulén (1879–1977), ANDERS NYGREN (1890–1978), Gustaf Wingren (1910–2000), Bo Giertz (1905–1998), and Bengt Hägglund (1920–).

Twentieth-century Lutherans have confronted hostile governments and societies repeatedly, suffering much at their hands. Lutherans reacted in various ways to the rise of National Socialism. Initial support by some for Adolf Hitler turned to opposition by the mid-1930s in some cases, such as Elert and Althaus. Sasse's early criticism of Nazi racism was reinforced by the activities of German CONFESSING CHURCH leaders, including DIETRICH BONHOEFFER. The martyred Danish pastor Kaj Munk (1898–1944) and Norwegian archbishop EVIND BERGGRAV (1884–1959) led resistance to the Nazi occupiers.

Siberian imprisonment or execution removed all the pastors of German and Finnish Lutheran churches in the Soviet Union by 1940. Lay leadership maintained small groups of believers against sometimes intense persecution. Emigration weakened these churches further after perestroika, but they have begun to gather those seeking religious faith into old and new congregations. In Soviet-dominated central Europe lands, the degree of the oppression of the church varied. Estonian and Latvian churches suffered severe restrictions and pressures; Communist authorities there conducted periodic active campaigns against the Christian faith (see COMMUNISM). Some leaders tried to preserve church life through accommodation and compromise; others met the Communist despotism with confrontation. In Hungary, for example, Bishop Lajos Ordass (1901–1978) was abandoned by many clergymen and jailed by the Communist government in his battle for the integrity of the church. Members of some West African Lutheran churches have suffered death and destruction of churches at the hands of Muslim countrymen in civil wars in the 1980s and 1990s.

At the beginning of the twenty-first century Lutheran churches in northern and western Europe are in crisis because the indifference of earlier generations is producing significant demissions from church membership. Central and eastern European churches are struggling to reestablish their place in their societies. In AFRICA, above all, and in Asia and LATIN AMERICA mission churches are growing, some rapidly, and seem destined to exercise leadership in world Lutheranism.

References and Further Reading

Primary Sources:

Die Bekenntnisschriften der evangelischen-lutherischen Kirche, 11th edition. Göttingen, Germany: Vandenhoeck & Ruprecht, 1992. Translated in *The Book of Concord,* edited by Robert Kolb and Timothy J. Wengert. Minneapolis, MN: Fortress, 2000.

D. Martin Luthers Werke. Weimar, Germany: Böhlau, 1883–1993, partially translated in *Luther's Works.* St. Louis, MO/Philadelphia, PA: Concordia/Fortress, 1958–1986.

Secondary Sources:

Arand, Charles P. *Testing the Boundaries: Windows to Lutheran Identity.* St. Louis, MO: Concordia, 1995.

Bachmann, E. Theodore, and Mercia Brenne Bachmann eds. *Lutheran Churches in the World, A Handbook.* Minneapolis, MN: Augsburg, 1989.

Bergendoff, Conrad. *The Church of the Lutheran Reformation: A Historical Survey.* St. Louis, MO: Concordia, 1967.

Beyschlag, Karlmann. *Die Erlanger Theologie.* Erlangen, Germany: Martin-Luther Verlag, 1993.

Bodensieck, Julius, ed. *Encyclopedia of the Lutheran Church.* Minneapolis, MN: Augsburg, 1965.

Burgess, Andrew S., ed. *Lutheran Churches in the Third World.* Minneapolis, MN: Augsburg, 1970.

Elert, Werner. *Die Morphologie des Luthertums* (Translated as *The Structure of Lutheranism*). Translated by Walter A. Hansen. St. Louis, MO: Concordia, 1962.

Gustafson, David A. *Lutherans in Crisis: The Question of Identity in the American Republic.* Minneapolis, MN: Fortress, 1993.

Lehmann, Arno. *It Began at Tranquebar: The Story of the Tranquebar Mission and the Beginnings of Protestant Christianity in India.* Translated by M. J. Lutz. Madras, India: Christian Literature Society, 1956.

Leske, Everard. *For Faith and Freedom: The Story of Lutherans and Lutheranism in Australia, 1838–1996.* Adelaide, Australia: Open Books, 1996.

Nambala, Shekutaamba V. *History of the Church in Namibia.* Milwaukee, WI: Lutheran Quarterly, 1994.

Nelson, E. Clifford, ed. *The Lutherans in North America.* Philadelphia, PA: Fortress, 1975.

Preus, Robert D. *The Theology of Post-Reformation Lutheranism.* 2 vols. St. Louis, MO: Concordia, 1970, 1972.

Prien, Hans-Jürgen. *Evangelical Kirchenwerdung in Brasilien. Von der deutsch-evangelischen Einwaranerergemeinden zur Evangelischen Kirche Lutherischen Bekenntnisses in Brasilien.* Gütersloh, Germany: Gütersloher Verlagshaus, 1989.

Sasse, Hermann. *Was heisst lutherisch?* Munich, Germany: Kaiser, 1934. Translated as *Here We Stand. The Nature and Character of the Lutheran Faith.* Translated by Theodore G. Tappert. New York: Harper, 1938.

Schjørring, Jens Holger, et al. *From Federation to Communion. The History of the Lutheran World Federation.* Minneapolis, MN: Fortress, 1997.

Stefano, Jesse A. *Missionary Work in the Church of Tanzania in the Past and in the Present.* Erlangen, Germany: Verlag der Evangelisch Lutherischen Mission, 1990.

Vajta, Vilmos, ed. *The Church and the Confessions: The Role of the Confessions in the Life and Doctrine of the Lutheran Churches.* Philadelphia, PA: Fortress, 1960.

ROBERT KOLB

LUTHERANISM, GERMANY

LUTHERANISM originated in sixteenth-century GERMANY in the aftermath of MARTIN LUTHER's excommunication from the Roman Catholic Church and the REFORMATION. Several princes, mostly in northern and central Germany, as well as magistrates of various free imperial cities, supported Luther's reform proposals and established "Evangelical" or "Lutheran" churches in their territories. At first an outlawed movement, Lutheranism came to be a legally recognized form of Christianity in the Holy Roman Empire by the middle of the sixteenth century. Lutheranism often benefited from the support of secular rulers as it was becoming established in Germany, but later faced a continuous struggle to avoid being manipulated by the state.

The Reformation

The initial controversy that led to the establishment of Lutheranism concerned the Catholic practice of issuing indulgences. In 1517 Luther, a priest and Augustinian friar teaching at the University of Wittenberg in Electoral Saxony, raised theological and moral questions about indulgences in his Ninety-five Theses. This ordinary call for an academic debate surprisingly escalated into a major controversy between 1518 and 1520. When Luther was subjected to interrogations by his monastic order and theological representatives of the papacy, his dissatisfaction with church teachings broadened to include issues regarding papal AUTHORITY and the role of good works in the process of JUSTIFICATION. In 1520 he wrote three major treatises calling for extensive reforms of the church's hierarchical POLITY, sacramental piety, and synergistic THEOLOGY. The emperor, Charles V, gave Luther one last opportunity to defend his views at the DIET OF WORMS in 1521. When he refused to recant, he was declared an outlaw as well as a heretic (see HERESY).

Luther's prince, Frederick the Wise, rescued him and hid him away for ten months. In 1522 he returned to Wittenberg to reclaim leadership of a reform movement that, in his absence, had fallen under the influence of ANDREAS BODENSTEIN VON KARLSTADT and other impatient iconoclasts (see ICONOCLISM). Luther proposed to implement changes in church practices more slowly and cautiously than his radical rivals and urged his coworkers to persuade rather than force people to accept the new teachings he derived from the BIBLE alone. Luther published a German translation of the Bible (see BIBLE TRANSLATION) so that the laity could more easily read it for themselves and gradually introduced changes in WORSHIP. He stressed PREACHING as well as the celebration of the SACRAMENTS and made German the language of the LITURGY. Both bread and wine were once again offered to the LAITY when the LORD'S SUPPER was celebrated. Luther retained private CONFESSION as a preparation for participation in holy communion, but stopped assigning penance. He also abolished MONASTICISM and the requirement of clerical CELIBACY (see CLERGY, MARRIAGE OF).

In 1529, after a systematic visitation of all the parishes in Electoral Saxony had revealed widespread ignorance of basic doctrines and disturbingly low levels of morality, Luther prepared the Small and Large CATECHISMS (1529) to instruct both CLERGY and laity. To promote further improvement in communal life he expanded public EDUCATION for both boys and girls and established a common chest to provide stable funding for churches, schools, and poor relief.

Beyond Saxony, Lutheran territorial churches were established in Mansfeld (1525), Anhalt (1526), the four Braunschweig principalities (1526–1542), Hesse (1526), Holstein (1528), Pomerania (1534), Württemberg (1534), and Brandenburg (1536). Nuremberg (1525), Hamburg (1531), Lübeck (1531), and Strassburg (1536) were the most important imperial cities that became Lutheran. In the church orders prepared for these territories by Luther's coworkers, most notably JOHANNES BUGENHAGEN, the princes assumed the jurisdictional power formerly held by bishops but delegated the details of church administration to a CONSISTORY and to pastoral officers known as superintendents.

Luther did not pay much attention to matters of church organization, but expressed his general thoughts about church–state relations in a 1523 treatise, *On Temporal Authority* (see CHURCH AND STATE, OVERVIEW). Although he clearly differentiated between spiritual and worldly governance, Luther urged princes to rule in a Christian manner and protect the CHURCH. He also told citizens they were obligated to obey secular rulers as long as there were no infringements of the practice of true religion. The Peasant's Revolt of 1525 put this theoretical stance to the test. Luther acknowledged that the peasants had legitimate grievances against their rulers but rejected their use of violence to rectify social injustice. In the end he authorized the princes to suppress the rebellion to maintain essential law and order.

At the DIET OF SPEYER in 1526, the emperor, Charles V, agreed to let each German ruler temporarily handle religious affairs for his own territories. Luther's princely sympathizers in Germany created the League of Torgau to protect their interests but were unwilling to ally themselves with other Protestant reformers in SWITZERLAND because Luther, at the MARBURG COLLOQUY, had rejected HULDRYCH ZWINGLI's view of the Lord's Supper. When the second Diet of Speyer in 1529 curtailed the freedom of the Evangelical rulers, they filed an official protestation, which earned them an enduring designation as "Protestants." The emperor agreed to address disputed religious issues again at the Diet of Augsburg in 1530, but when he was presented with the AUGSBURG CONFESSION as a conciliatory summary of Lutheran theology, he rejected it. After Charles V ordered the Protestants to conform to the theology and practice of the Catholic church, they formed a broader military alliance known as the SCHMALKALDIC LEAGUE. With some reluctance Luther now condoned armed self-defense against the emperor.

The Interim Crisis and Subsequent Controversies

In 1546, within a few months of Luther's death, the emperor moved to suppress Protestantism in the Schmalkaldic War. After capturing the elector of Saxony and PHILIP OF HESSE, the key Lutheran leaders, he attempted to restore some elements of Catholicism in their territories through a temporary settlement known as the AUGSBURG INTERIM. MATTHIAS FLACIUS and some other church leaders responded with a campaign of uncompromising resistance, but more conciliatory Lutherans led by PHILIPP MELANCHTHON drafted the Leipzig Interim as a counterproposal. Melanchthon was willing to accept the reintroduction of some Catholic practices to keep the emperor from completely eradicating Lutheranism. In 1552 the princes of the Schmalkaldic League managed to regroup and force the emperor to retreat. In the Peace of Augsburg of 1555 Charles V ratified a new policy according to which each prince would determine the religion of his own territories. With this recognition of Lutheranism as a legal option, religious pluralism now became a permanent feature of German social life (see TOLERATION).

For several decades after the Interim Crisis, strife continued within the territorial churches between the supporters of Philipp Melanchthon, called Philippists, and their critics, known as GNESIO-LUTHERANS. These two parties differed not only in their judgments about which strategy would ensure the survival of Lutheranism but also about issues of belief such as the place of good works in the Christian life, the role played by the human will in the process of SALVATION, and the nature of Christ's presence in the Lord's Supper. Doctrinal disputes proliferated until a mediating party led by Martin Chemnitz and Jakob Andreae restored unity in 1577 by convincing most of the Lutheran churches to accept a more detailed confessional statement known as the Formula of Concord (see BOOK OF CONCORD).

Orthodoxy and Pietism

In the seventeenth century the Lutheran churches of Germany concentrated on the conservative tasks of defending their doctrinal consensus and enforcing conformity to established norms of belief and practice. University professors such as JOHANN GERHARD and Johann Quenstedt combined the use of philosophical argumentation and scriptural exegesis in their comprehensive systematic theologies to demonstrate continuity between the Bible, the creeds of the early church, the writings of Luther, and the official confessional documents of Lutheranism. Their inclination to accent how Lutheranism differed from Roman Catholicism and other forms of Protestantism was reinforced by the religious distrust that ongoing political conflicts provoked. Lutheranism was on the defensive in several regions of Germany, most notably Hesse, the Palatinate, and Brandenburg, because rulers there had converted to CALVINISM. The devastating effect of the Thirty Years' War (1618–1648) especially perpetuated bitter feelings toward Catholics.

There were, however, other important developments during this Age of Orthodoxy besides the refinement of polemical theology. Writers of devotional literature provided practical instruction in Christian living for lay people. Some of them, such as JOHANN ARNDT and his disciple, Christian Scriver, were more inclined to focus on defects within the Lutheran churches than on the errors of other religious groups. They perceived a widespread lack of commitment to spiritual growth among the laity and often blamed church theologians for failing to show how the beliefs they argued about were significant for the fostering of holy living.

Themes introduced by the seventeenth-century devotional writers provided the foundation for the reform movement known as PIETISM, which is most closely associated with the work of PHILIPP JAKOB SPENER. In his 1675 manifesto, *Pia Desideria,* Spener proposed a greater role for the laity in the church, in keeping with the Lutheran notion of the PRIESTHOOD OF ALL BELIEVERS. He also advocated the use of small group meetings to promote spiritual CONVERSION through practical study of the Bible. During the early eighteenth century, AUGUST HERMANN FRANCKE expanded the influence of Pietism in northern Germany through numerous institutions he established in the city of HALLE. Pietism also gained much popular support in southwest Germany, in Württemberg, especially through the leadership provided by JOHANN ALBRECHT BENGEL, a noted biblical scholar.

Supporters of the Orthodox dogmaticians were generally critical of the Pietists, charging them with indifference to DOCTRINE, excessive emotionalism, improper emphasis on good works, and the promotion of separatism. Some radical Pietists did willingly sever their ties with the Lutheran churches. Other groups who wished to retain a connection to Lutheranism, such as the Moravians led by Count NIKOLAUS VON ZINZENDORF, were eventually forced by their critics to reconstitute themselves as separate churches (see MORAVIAN CHURCH).

Post-Enlightenment Theologies

By the middle of the eighteenth century, the critical questioning of traditional Christianity associated with the ENLIGHTENMENT became more widespread in Germany. The way had been prepared by the philosopher GOTTFRIED LEIBNIZ, who, in contrast to the strict confessionalism of Lutheran ORTHODOXY, worked for the reunion of Catholicism and Protestantism. Advocating an even broader toleration, GOTTHOLD LESSING circulated the skeptical biblical criticism of HERMANN REIMARUS. Interest in theological rationalism spread among the Lutheran clergy, but, at the end of the century, the philosopher IMMANUEL KANT posed a new challenge by arguing that pure reason could not establish even the most basic religious truth, such as claims as to the existence of God. Although Kant and the idealist philosopher GEORG W. F. HEGEL rejected key elements of Lutheran theology, they were more interested in constructing a new basis for religion than in discarding it altogether.

This intellectual revolution, combined with hostility toward organized religion stimulated by the social revolutions of the early nineteenth century, eroded the influence of Lutheranism in the lives of many Germans. The traditional theological identity of Lutheranism in Germany also seemed threatened when the king of Prussia decided to merge the Lutheran and Reformed churches in his territories in 1817, the tercentenary of the Reformation. Claus Harms inspired a resurgence of conservative Lutheranism by publishing a new set of ninety-five theses against this PRUSSIAN UNION and Enlightenment religion in general. Efforts to retain a confessionally precise Lutheranism developed elsewhere in Germany, especially in Bavaria through the work of WILHELM LÖHE and theologians at the University of Erlangen. Additional, more pietistic, efforts to reassert Lutheran influence in German society were carried out through theologians such as AUGUST THOLUCK and the founder of the Inner Mission movement, J. H. Wichern.

Other Lutheran theologians were more deeply influenced by Kant's moralistic philosophy and the new liberal theology of FRIEDRICH SCHLEIERMACHER. By the 1870s ALBRECHT RITSCHL had established a school of thought that focused on Jesus as preacher of the KINGDOM OF GOD and on the role of the church as an ethical influence in society. ERNST TROELTSCH and ADOLF HARNACK, the most influential liberal Lutherans of the early twentieth century, supported the application of modern historical-critical methods to the analysis of the Bible and characterized the significance of Jesus in new ways to sustain the relevance of Christianity in the modern world (see LIBERAL PROTESTANTISM AND LIBERALISM. The dialectical theology, or NEO-ORTHODOXY, of KARL BARTH inspired a widespread critical reaction to Liberal Protestantism after World War I, but questions about how the Jesus of history relates to the Christ of faith continued to be a predominant theological concern in subsequent decades in the diverse theologies of Lutherans such as RUDOLF BULTMANN, PAUL TILLICH, FRIEDRICH GOGARTEN, and WOLFHART PANNENBERG.

Church–State Relations

Conquest by FRANCE at the beginning of the nineteenth century had stimulated German national consciousness. After the defeat of Napoleon, Prussia orchestrated the consolidation of the multitudinous states of the former Holy Roman Empire until a unified Germany was finally formed in 1871. Conservative Lutherans generally favored the new authoritarian government because of its commitment to blocking the influence of Catholics, Marxists, and anticlerical socialists in society. Even the leading theological liberals supported the German emperor's military assertiveness in World War I. After Germany's defeat and the formation of the Weimar Republic, the Protestant churches were partially disestablished. For the most part, church leaders did not welcome this new development. When the Nazis came to power in 1933 the churches were invited once again to work more closely with the state. Adolf Hitler pushed the previously autonomous territorial churches (fifteen Lutheran, twelve Prussian Union, one Reformed) into uniting as one Protestant folk church, and the GERMAN CHRISTIANS, a movement sympathetic to the Nazi political agenda, managed to get their candidate elected as its first bishop. Various countermovements quickly emerged. MARTIN NIEMÖLLER created the Pastor's Emergency League in 1933. The CONFESSING CHURCH formed in 1934 and pointedly asserted the incompatibility of Christianity and Nazi ideology in the BARMEN DECLARATION, written by a Reformed theologian, Karl Barth, and two Lutherans, Hans Asmussen and Thomas Breit. Many Lutheran church leaders continued to have reservations about engaging in united resistance to an established government, but there were some notable exceptions. The Nazis executed DIETRICH BONHOEFFER for his involvement in a plot to assassinate Hitler.

After World War II, the various Protestant churches attempted to make a fresh start by working together in a new federation known as the Evangelical Church of Germany (EKD). In 1948 most Lutheran churches also began to coordinate their efforts through the United Evangelical Lutheran Church of Germany (VELKD). After the section of Germany under Russian occupation became the German Democratic Republic (DDR) in 1949, the Lutherans in the East faced a new struggle with a government that proposed to replace Christianity with COMMUNISM. OTTO DIBELIUS and other bishops continuously protested against efforts to limit the independence and influence of the churches. After 1968 it was no longer possible for these church leaders to maintain contact with Lutherans in West Germany, so they reluctantly created their own church federation. Some Lutherans attempted to cooperate with the government as a "church within socialism," without surrendering uncritically to all of its dictates. In the 1980s, however, the churches began to shift away from a strategy of coexistence toward support for the growing protest movement that eventually caused the demise of the DDR. In 1990, the year of national reunification, the churches of East and West Germany were also reunited in the EKD.

References and Further Reading

Barnett, Victoria. *For the Soul of the People: Protestant Protest Against Hitler.* Oxford: Oxford University Press, 1992.
Bigler, Robert M. *The Politics of German Protestantism: The Rise of the Protestant Church Elite in Prussia, 1815–1848.* Berkeley: University of California Press, 1972.
Drummond, Andrew. *German Protestantism Since Luther.* London: The Epworth Press, 1951.
Goeckel, Robert. *The Lutheran Church and the East German State.* Ithaca, NY: Cornell University Press, 1990.
Groh, John. *Nineteenth Century German Protestantism.* Washington, D.C.: University Press of America, 1982.
Helmreich, Ernst Christian. *The German Churches under Hitler: Background, Struggle and Epilogue.* Detroit, MI: Wayne State University Press, 1979.
Lindberg, Carter. *The European Reformations.* Oxford: Blackwell, 1996.
Lund, Eric, ed. *Documents from the History of Lutheranism 1517–1750.* Minneapolis, MN: Fortress Press, 2002.
McGrath, Alister. *The Making of Modern German Christology.* Oxford: Basil Blackwell Ltd., 1986.
Preus, Robert D. *The Theology of Post-Reformation Lutheranism.* vols. 1 and 2. St. Louis, MO: Concordia Publishing House, 1970–1972.
Stoeffler, F. Ernest. *The Rise of Evangelical Pietism.* Leiden, Netherlands: E.J. Brill, 1965.
———. *German Pietism during the Eighteenth Century.* Leiden, Netherlands: E.J. Brill, 1973.

ERIC LUND

LUTHERANISM, GLOBAL

Lutheran churches have their roots in the sixteenth-century REFORMATION centered in Wittenberg, a movement that spread quickly from Germany to central Europe and Scandinavia. During the eighteenth and nineteenth centuries emigrants from these countries established Lutheran churches in North America. This article deals with the 18.5 million Lutherans in the churches of AFRICA, Asia, LATIN AMERICA, and the Pacific who account for more than 30 percent of the 63 million Lutherans worldwide. These churches have their origins in both immigrant communities and the missionary movements of the nineteenth and twentieth centuries. They are part of the global Lutheran Communion served by the LUTHERAN WORLD FEDERATION (LWF) whose members include all but about four million of the world's Lutherans, almost all of whom have close ties to the LUTHERAN CHURCH–MISSOURI SYNOD (LCMS).

Africa

Cape Town was the site of the first immigrant Lutheran congregation in Africa (1780) but whereas other immigrant Lutheran churches came to dot the continent, the real establishment of Lutheranism in Africa is the result of missionary movements. Because of their dependency on foreign churches and MISSION-

ARY SOCIETIES and, as they became autonomous, their partnership with those groups, churches in Africa have been strong advocates of the movement in world Lutheranism from federation to communion. Africa is the most rapidly growing part of the Lutheran communion.

Southern Africa

Lutheranism in southern Africa is the result of efforts to bring together churches rooted in the work of various missionary societies and groups of immigrants. The Federation of Evangelical Lutheran Churches in Southern Africa (FELCSA, 1966) was founded to realize the policy proposed by the LWF of one Lutheran church in the region that would include the MORAVIAN CHURCH. However, the effort was undercut by the United Evangelical Lutheran Church in Southern Africa (UELCSA, 1965), formed by three white German churches in Namibia and SOUTH AFRICA that were equivocal about apartheid. The majority black churches countered by constituting the Evangelical Lutheran Church in Southern Africa (ELCSA, 1975) while leaving FELCSA operational. After an unheeded admonition at its Dar es Salaam Assembly (1977) and at the recommendation of ELSCA, the Budapest Assembly of the LWF (1984) suspended membership of the UELCSA churches, declaring their attitude toward apartheid a *status confessionis*. Upon evidence of a changed attitude toward their black counterparts, the UELCSA churches were restored to LWF membership at its Curitiba Assembly in 1990, clearing the way for the formation in 1991 of the Lutheran Communion in Southern Africa (LUCSA).

Namibia was also affected by the internal apartheid struggle because its German Evangelical Lutheran Church in Namibia (GELC) belongs to UELCSA. Even more important was the participation of the Evangelical Lutheran Church in Namibia (ELCIN) and the Evangelical Lutheran Church in the Republic of Namibia (ELCRN), heirs of Finnish and German missions, respectively, in the struggle for Namibian independence. The churches were assisted in their struggle by an advocacy and leadership training program begun jointly in 1986 by antecedent bodies of the EVANGELICAL LUTHERAN CHURCH IN AMERICA (ELCA). Since Namibia gained independence in 1989 the black and white churches have striven for a united Lutheran church in Namibia. The Namibian population is 95 percent Christian, with Lutherans claiming about 58 percent.

In addition to the churches noted above, LUCSA (near 1.8 million), the legal successor of FELCSA, includes the black Evangelical Lutheran churches in Angola, Botswana, Malawi, Mozambique, Zambia, and Zimbabwe together with the UELCSA churches and the Moravian Church in South Africa.

Central and Eastern Africa

The Evangelical Church of Eritrea (1923), whose roots go back to nineteenth-century Swedish missionary efforts, is the oldest autonomous Lutheran church on the African continent. Early missionaries to Eritrea and Ethiopia endeavored to work within the ancient orthodox Church (see ORTHODOXY, EASTERN), but the evangelical movement triggered initially by the distribution of bibles in Amharic could not be contained. In 1959 the Ethiopian Evangelical Church Mekane Yesus (EECMY) was founded at the Mekane Yesus (Jesus' dwelling place) Church in Addis Ababa and became the first church after the Orthodox Church to be recognized by the government. That recognition survived the 1974 revolution whose socialist government turned its back on Ethiopian Christians, and it enabled EECMY to shelter other Christian groups in its churches. In 1974 the Bethel Synod, supported by the then United Presbyterian Church in North America (see PRESBYTERIAN CHURCH U.S.A.) merged with EECMY, making it a united church. From the beginning EECMY depended heavily on lay leadership in its evangelization efforts and, at the turn of the century, was the fastest growing Lutheran church in the world: 3.35 million members.

This region also contains the Evangelical Lutheran Church in Tanzania (ELCT), the second largest African Lutheran church: 2.5 million members. The terminology of its inner organization—twelve dioceses and five synods with a presiding bishop—reflects its background in missions from GERMANY (see MISSIONS, GERMAN), the Nordic countries, and the UNITED STATES that promoted both episcopal and synodal forms of government. Makumira Lutheran Theological College (1954) has developed into a theological center for the region. The evangelistic zeal of ELCT is evidenced by a "reverse evangelism" project that brings Tanzanian pastors and teachers to Europe and North America where they have become missionaries to their secularized fellow Christians.

The Malagasy Lutheran Church (MLC, 1950) also numbers more than a million members. Half of the island's Christians are Roman Catholics, and other Protestants came together in the union of 1968 that became the Church of Jesus Christ in Madagascar.

In 1993 these and the evangelical Lutheran churches in Congo, Kenya, and Rwanda formed the Lutheran Communion in Central and Eastern Africa (LUCCEA) that has 7.6 million members.

Western Africa

Lutheran churches in this vast part of Africa are mostly small and have their roots in missionary work of the twentieth century. The largest is The Lutheran Church of Christ in Nigeria (1954) with roots both in DENMARK and among Danish Lutherans in the United States. Its sister church, The Lutheran Church of Nigeria, has close ties with the LCMS. The churches of the Cameroon constitute the second largest group of Lutherans, having their roots in the missionary work of the Church of the Lutheran Brethren in the United States. The church in Chad stems from the same mission as does the church in the Central African Republic. The church in Angola has close ties with the Lutherans in northern Namibia, having become independent when the border with Namibia was closed in 1979. Lutherans in Zaire are part of the government-initiated Church of Christ in Zaire, a federation formed in 1972. The roots of the Lutheran Church in Liberia (LCL, 1965) reach back into the nineteenth century when missionaries from the United States began work. LCL has encouraged the small church in SIERRA LEONE, a country that shares LIBERIA's history as a haven for freed slaves.

In 1993 twelve Lutheran churches from the above-mentioned countries founded the Lutheran Communion in Western Africa (LUCWA) with 1.2 million members.

African churches have made good use of radio as an evangelism tool (see MASS MEDIA). Two examples from many are the *Radio Voice of the Gospel,* established in 1963 in Addis Ababa, but shut down by the socialist government in 1977. Christians in Shaba, Zaire, sought Lutheran affiliation because of its broadcasts. Another example is Eternal Love Winning Africa, a transmitter of the SUDAN INTERIOR MISSION used by LCL to broadcast worship services and evangelistic programs to the jungle-bound peoples of the country.

Asia/Pacific

The 6.7 million Lutherans in Asia are to be found in most parts of this vast area with its ancient and highly developed cultures. Most churches are quite small, although with assistance from the LWF they often carry on works of education, development, and welfare far beyond what size may suggest. All but 100,000 of Asian Lutherans are in churches belonging to the LWF including some, such as the Lutheran Church in the Philippines, that maintain close ties with LCMS. The BASEL MISSION and Rhenish Mission were especially instrumental in planting Lutheranism in Asia, although in the twentieth century their work was supplemented and sometimes supplanted by missionaries from Scandinavia and the United States.

India

Lutheranism in INDIA reaches back to 1706 and the arrival of Bartholomew Ziegenbalg who founded what has become the Tamil Evangelical Lutheran Church. It is now one of twelve Lutheran churches, ten of which constitute the United Evangelical Church in India (UELCI, 1975) with 1.6 million members. Member churches have developed from mission work carried on by German, Danish, Norwegian, Swedish, American, and Latvian societies and boards. Conversations with the united Protestant CHURCH OF SOUTH INDIA (1947) led to doctrinal agreement, but the UELCI has not joined. By contrast the small Lutheran church in Pakistan helped form a united Church of Pakistan. After a period of supporting ecumenical theological education, especially in Bangalore, UELCI has concentrated on expanding its own training center, Gurukul Theological College and Research Institute in Madras.

Indonesia

By far the largest Lutheran presence in Asia/Pacific is the Lutheran community in INDONESIA, whose ten churches account for 3.9 million members. The BATAK PROTESTANT CHRISTIAN CHURCH (HKPB) with its 3 million members mostly in Sumatra is the mother church with its own confession developed in 1951. The LWF judged that the Batak confession agrees in substance with the AUGSBURG CONFESSION (its confessional basis) and granted HKBP membership. That judgment remains unique in the Lutheran communion. Six of the other Lutheran churches are outgrowths of the HKPB, which also has congregations in Malaysia and Singapore. Under Indonesian philosophy based on the five principles—belief in a unitary deity, nationalism, democracy, humanitarianism, and social justice—Lutherans have learned to coexist with other Christians and with the large Islamic population. Lutherans are founding members of the Communion of Churches in Indonesia (1950).

Papua New Guinea

The late nineteenth century saw the arrival of missionaries from Neuendettelsau and the Rhenish Mission on this island. When German missionaries were excluded during World War I, missionaries from AUSTRALIA and the United States took over the work. Presently two Lutheran churches constitute the largest Protestant presence in PNG with close to a million members. The Evangelical Lutheran Church of Papua New Guinea (815,000) has been autonomous since 1956. Although the smaller Gutnius Lutheran Church–Papua New Guinea has ties with LCMS, both churches are members of the LWF.

Australia/New Zealand

As immigrant churches, the Australian churches are unique in this part of the world. Although a small Lutheran mission to the aborigines began in 1838, later that year the first contingent of German Lutheran dissenters from the Prussian Union gathered in Adelaide for worship. Another group arrived in 1841 and formed its own church. These were the roots of two parallel church bodies, the United Evangelical Lutheran Church in Australia (UELCA, 1921) and the Evangelical Lutheran Church of Australia (ELCA, 1944). The former was a founding member of the LWF and the latter maintained close ties with the LCMS. A precondition of their 1966 union to form the Lutheran Church in Australia (LCA) was giving up these external relationships, although in 1994 the LCA became an associate member of the LWF. The LCA numbers 94,000 members. Another 1,300 form the Lutheran Church of New Zealand, a district of the LCA.

Hong Kong, China, Taiwan

Lutherans began mission work in CHINA in the mid-nineteenth century, and the former Lutheran Church of China was formed in 1920. Since the founding of the People's Republic of China and the closing of existing churches, an interdenominational Protestantism has arisen on the mainland. The focus of Chinese Lutheranism has shifted to the five churches of Hong Kong (42,800) and the six on Taiwan (16,500). Seven of these are members of the LWF. Until 1985 the LWF maintained a Hong Kong office to coordinate Lutheran approaches to China. Since then contacts have been made directly to the China Christian Council.

Other Lutheran churches in Asia are found in Bangladesh (11,400), JAPAN (32,500), Jordan/Israel (3,000), South KOREA (3,000), Malaysia (88,600), Myanmar (1,500), Singapore (3,000), Sri Lanka (1,200), and Thailand (1,700).

Latin America and the Caribbean

Well into the twentieth century, because of the overwhelming Roman Catholic presence, mission boards did not regard Latin America as a mission land. As in North America and Australia, it was German immigrants who formed the first Lutheran congregations. Not until after World War II, stimulated by the arrival of displaced persons from Europe, did they break out of their linguistic and cultural isolation and reach out not only to them but also to indigenous populations, gradually adopting the Spanish and Portuguese tongues. Even so they have maintained cordial relations with the Roman Catholic churches, not least because of the post-Vatican II Lutheran–Roman Catholic ecumenical dialogues. Lutheran churches of the CARIBBEAN, by contrast, are largely the result of missions of predecessor bodies of the ELCA and the LCMS.

Church leaders have joined in the popular struggle for liberation from poverty and exploitation and the establishment of a just social order, and Latin America is the birthplace of LIBERATION THEOLOGY. Among Protestants these concerns led in 1982 to the formation of the Latin American Council of Churches (CLAI). Sixteen of the Lutheran churches are members.

Together all seven Caribbean churches count 57,200 members and only El Salvador and Honduras are large enough to qualify as members of the LWF. Costa Rica, Ecuador, and Guatemala have "recognized congregation" status. One of the four Mexican churches is also an LWF member (see MEXICO).

The Evangelical Church of the Lutheran Confession in Brazil (ECLCB) with over 700,000 members is the largest Lutheran church on the continent and exemplifies how since World War II the largely German churches are becoming multicultural. ECLCB maintains in Sao Leopoldo the only major Lutheran theological faculty on the continent. ECLCB's sister church, the Evangelical Lutheran Church of Brazil (217,800) was until 1980 a district of the LCMS and maintains close ties with that body. The Evangelical Church of the River Plate (ECRP), based in Argentina but found also in Paraguay and Uruguay, is with 47,000 members the third largest Lutheran church in Latin America. On the same territory is a parallel church that until the mid-1980s was a district of the LCMS. A Spanish-speaking Lutheran seminary founded in 1956 in Buenos Aires merged in 1970 with the older Union Seminary to form the Evangelical Institute of Advanced Theological Study (ISEDET), the premiere Protestant faculty in the area. Unlike Africa and parts of Asia, the LCMS-related churches in Latin America are not members of the LWF.

These churches of BRAZIL and Argentina typify the other emerging multicultural Lutheran churches in Latin America: Bolivia (18,700), Chile (15,000), Colombia (3,300), Guyana (11,000), Nicaragua (3,800), Paraguay (ECRP 3,800+), Peru (2,600), Suriname (4,000), Uruguay (ECRP), and Venezuela (5,100).

References and Further Reading

Bachmann, E. Theodore and Marcia Brenne Bachmann. *Lutheran Churches in the World.* Minneapolis, MN: Augsburg, 1989.

Brand, Eugene L. "Toward a Lutheran Communion: Pulpit and Altar Fellowship." *LWF Report* 26 (1988).

Gaßmann, Günther, Duane H. Larson, and Mark W. Olden-burg. *Historical Directory of Lutheranism*. Lanham, MD and London: The Scarecrow Press, 2001.

Gassmann, Günther. "Lutherische Kirchen," *Theologische Realenzykopädie* 21 (1991): 599–620.

Lutheran World Federation. *Directory—Handbuch*. Geneva, Switzerland: Lutheran World Federation, annually.

"Lutheran World Federation 2000 Membership Figures." *Lutheran World Information* 1 (2001): 4–12.

Nelson, E. Clifford. *The Rise of World Lutheranism, An American Perspective*. Philadelphia, PA: Fortress Press, 1982.

Schjørring, Jens Holger, Prasanna Kumari, and Norman A. Hjelm, eds. *From Federation to Communion, The History of the Lutheran World Federation*. Minneapolis, MN: Fortress Press, 1997.

EUGENE L. BRAND

LUTHERANISM, SCANDINAVIA

Lutheranism has been the dominant form of Christianity in Scandinavia since the sixteenth century. Facing little competition from other religious groups, the Lutheran churches have maintained their vitality primarily through internal reform movements. Most Scandinavians consider themselves Lutherans, but in modern times the forces of secularization have significantly reduced the extent of regular participation in ritual religiosity. As Scandinavian societies have become more pluralistic, the Lutheran churches have needed to reevaluate their roles as folk churches and adjust their relationships with state governments.

The Scandinavian Reformation

In 1397 the Union of Kalmar brought all of the Scandinavian countries together under the rule of DENMARK. The coming of Lutheranism to Scandinavia coincided with the breakup of this union and the creation of modern territorial monarchies. King Christian II of Denmark's failure to suppress a Swedish uprising against his rule in 1520 led to the formation of an independent kingdom of SWEDEN and FINLAND. When Gustavus Vasa, a leader of the rebellion, was elected king in 1523, he took measures to ensure the independence of Sweden by also diminishing the power of the Catholic church in his realm. He chose Laurentius Andreae, a reform-minded archdeacon, as his chancellor, and OLAUS PETRI, who had studied with MARTIN LUTHER in Wittenberg, as preacher to the city of Stockholm. In 1528 the king pressured a Catholic bishop to consecrate several new bishops who were sympathetic to his efforts to create an independent national church. As a result of this event the Swedish church has always claimed to have a historic episcopate in apostolic succession, even though it broke away from Roman Catholicism.

Because of a lack of popular support the Swedish king was cautious about implementing other changes in religious practice, but LAURENTIUS PETRI, who was named archbishop of Uppsala in 1531, and his brother, Olaus Petri, gradually moved the church toward Lutheranism. The reformers briefly lost favor with the king in 1540 for resisting his efforts to control the church completely, but by 1544 the Diet of Västerås was prepared to commit Sweden officially to Protestantism. Nevertheless the confessional character of the church remained vague until a Lutheran Church Order was approved in 1571 and the Uppsala Resolution of 1593 required adherence to the AUGSBURG CONFESSION. As a province of Sweden, Finland concurrently experienced a religious transformation, under the leadership of another Wittenberg-educated bishop, MICHAEL AGRICOLA.

King Christian II was deposed from the Danish throne shortly after he lost control of Sweden and the Danish nobility elected his uncle, Frederick I, as king in 1523. During Frederick's reign, popular support for Protestantism developed in Denmark. HANS TAUSEN, a Wittenberg-educated priest, advanced the movement from the town of Viborg, although Malmö, in Danish-controlled southern Sweden, was also a significant center of reform. In 1526 Frederick made Tausen his chaplain, and the Diet of Odense supported a breaking of ties with Rome. In 1531 the deposed king, Christian II, attempted to reclaim power with the help of Olav Engelbrektsson, a Catholic archbishop in NORWAY, but the insurrection failed. After the death of Frederick I, his strongly Lutheran son, Christian III, completed the establishment of a Lutheran church. In 1536 the Diet of Copenhagen dismissed the Catholic bishops and named Lutheran superintendents to lead the church. Luther's German coworker, JOHANNES BUGENHAGEN, helped draw up a new Church Order for Denmark in 1537. Peder Palladius, another Wittenberg-educated reformer, supplied valuable theological leadership in the following decades and was consecrated as a bishop (superintendent) along with Hans Tausen. In 1536 Norway was reduced to the status of a province under the full control of Denmark and thus became subject to the same religious policies. By 1541 all four of the bishops of Norway were Lutherans. At the same time Denmark established a national Lutheran church in ICELAND.

Orthodoxy and Pietism

After the Reformation era the Scandinavian monarchs continued to consolidate their power and insisted on adherence to Lutheranism to preserve unity in their kingdoms. Denmark and Sweden aspired to be major powers in Europe and, as a result, they become entangled in religious and political controversies that first developed in Lutheran GERMANY.

In the late sixteenth century the kings of both Denmark and Sweden were strictly anti-Catholic but did not require much doctrinal precision in the state churches. King Frederick II of Denmark did not endorse the Formula of Concord, the more elaborate confessional document developed by German Lutherans in 1577. The Swedish church put more stress on correct liturgical forms than on doctrinal details. Sympathy for the theological positions advocated by PHILIPP MELANCHTHON and his Philippist followers was strong, especially in Denmark and Norway.

At the start of the seventeenth century, however, Scandinavia, like Germany, shifted toward strict Lutheran ORTHODOXY. Niels Hemmingsen, the foremost theologian in Denmark, was dismissed from his professorship at the University of Copenhagen in 1579 under suspicion of teaching a Calvinist view of the LORD'S SUPPER (see CALVINISM). New theological leaders such as Hans Poulsen Resen and Jesper Brochmand emerged and had extensive influence throughout the Lutheran world as defenders of orthodoxy. King Charles IX, who ruled Sweden after 1609, also manifested a new zeal for the clarification of correct doctrine.

When the Thirty Years' War broke out on the Continent, the Scandinavian kings came to the defense of their coreligionists in Germany. Christian IV of Denmark mounted a campaign in support of the Protestant Union but was defeated in 1626. GUSTAVUS II ADOLPHUS of Sweden won important victories throughout Germany after entering the war in 1630, but the Protestant forces suffered a major setback when he was killed at the battle of Lützen in 1632.

Near the beginning of the eighteenth century, PIETISM began to spread from Germany to Scandinavia. In 1705 King Frederick IV supported missionaries sent out from HALLE, the north German center of Pietism, to the Danish colony in INDIA. This was the first involvement of Lutherans in overseas mission work. The next king, Christian VI, was called the "Pietist on the throne." He made CONFIRMATION compulsory in 1736 to strengthen religious devotion. His court preacher, Erik Pontoppidan, later a bishop in Norway, published an explanation of Luther's Small Catechism in 1738, which had a long-standing influence on popular religious life (see CATECHISM). The so-called Pleiades, a group of seven pastors in Romsdal led by Thomas von Westen, also nurtured Pietism in Norway and got royal approval to begin missionary work among the Lapps (Sami).

Swedish students who were educated at Halle returned to their homeland as Pietists, as did many thousands of Swedish soldiers who had experienced spiritual renewal while imprisoned in RUSSIA during the Great Northern War of 1713–1721. The growing influence of the MORAVIAN CHURCH, however, and other, more radical Pietists who were critical of Lutheranism prompted the authorities to pass the Conventicles Act of 1726. Henceforth all private religious meetings were prohibited if they were unsupervised by the CLERGY.

Nineteenth-Century Revivals

The critical spirit of the ENLIGHTENMENT began to change religious life in Scandinavia in the late eighteenth century. In 1781 an Edict of Toleration granted religious liberty to all residents of Sweden, although a new constitution in 1809 still obligated native Swedes to adhere to "pure evangelical faith (see TOLERATION)." In Denmark some of the leading cultural figures were openly critical of traditional Christianity. A new constitutional law also granted religious liberty in Denmark in 1849, although the state continued to support the church. Although Lutheranism faced new challenges during these times, one of the most notable features of nineteenth-century Scandinavian religious life was the development of various AWAKENINGS that prolonged the influence of Pietism.

In Norway HANS NIELSEN HAUGE experienced a CONVERSION in 1796 and became an inspirational traveling lay preacher. Despite being a loyal Lutheran he was imprisoned for more than ten years for failing to obey the Danish Conventicle Act of 1741 that prohibited the kind of informal religious meetings he held (see CONVENTICLES). In the long run, however, efforts to suppress Hauge's movement failed. Some Haugeans became forceful representatives of peasant interests after Norway became independent from Denmark in 1814 and succeeded in repealing the Conventicle Act in 1842. The Norwegian awakening movement was renewed in the second half of the nineteenth century and drawn closer to the state church under the guidance of Gisle Johnson, who influenced many clergy through his long career as a lay theological professor in Christiania (Oslo).

In Denmark a strong Pietist movement developed in South Jutland in reaction to rationalism. By the middle of the nineteenth century many Lutherans who were attracted to the stress on penitence, conversion, and SANCTIFICATION found in such groups became associated with the Church Home Mission Society under the leadership of Vilhelm Beck. This organization conducted evangelization and social welfare programs from various inner mission houses that were intended to supplement the official activities led by parish clergy. Some participants eventually split off to form a separate Free Church, but most remained associated with the state Lutheran church.

In Sweden Henrik Schartau, dean of the cathedral in Lund, inspired a revival movement in the early nineteenth century that encouraged catechetical training and strict morality but strongly disapproved of conventicles and other lay activities conducted apart from the clergy (see REVIVALS). Another, more ecstatic, renewal movement developed in northern Sweden, in the 1840s, under the leadership of Lars Laestadius. The Laestadian revival especially influenced the Lapps. Carl Olaf Rosenius, a lay preacher from the north who had also interacted with Methodists (see METHODISM), nurtured another revival movement, based in Stockholm, that became institutionalized in 1856 as the Evangelical National Foundation. As with the Danish and Norwegian inner mission movements, separate meetinghouses developed, although this association remained loyal to the Lutheran church. Later, however, in 1878, some Pietists influenced by Paul Peter Waldenström broke away and formed the Mission Covenant Church. Finland experienced its own revivals, most notably under the leadership of Paavo Ruotsalainen.

Grundtvig and Kierkegaard

Religious life in Scandinavia was also deeply affected in the nineteenth century by two controversial Danes who were fervent Christians but had complicated relations with the state Lutheran churches. NIKOLAJ F. S. GRUNDTVIG, a pastor who was also a noted educational reformer, attempted to revitalize both the church and his country by emphasizing the important role that congregational life should play in developing and sustaining the distinctive CULTURE and national identity of the Danish people. Although he favored the existence of a state Lutheran church, he was also a champion of personal freedom who criticized laws enforcing religious uniformity and compulsory participation. The new constitution of 1849 moved Denmark closer to his ideal of an inclusive church with a freer relationship to the state (see CHURCH AND STATE, OVERVIEW).

SØREN KIERKEGAARD, a theologically trained layman, was a noted critic of Grundtvig and other church leaders whom he thought distorted the true nature of Christianity by offering people a comfortable existence in a nondemanding state church. In 1854 he began an "Attack upon Christendom" that emphasized the difficulty of Christian existence and the contrast between Christianity and worldly culture. Kierkegaard offended many of his contemporaries but became more influential in twentieth-century Protestant theology through his numerous philosophical, psychological, and religious writings.

Social Change and Secularization

Over the course of the nineteenth century, the Scandinavian nations underwent extensive social changes. Finland was conquered by Russia in 1809 and became a separate nation in 1917. Norway passed from the control of Denmark to Sweden in 1814 and attained full independence in 1905. Absolute monarchies evolved into democracies, and governments began to tolerate other expressions of religion besides Lutheranism. Overpopulation and changes in land usage in the countryside forced many to immigrate to North America or move to urban areas. The rate of INDUSTRIALIZATION accelerated in the early twentieth century, drastically disrupting traditional social bonds and patterns of folk piety. In the minds of many, the churches did not adequately respond to the social needs created by these changes and so their attachment to the state churches weakened. Anticlericalism became commonplace in the labor movement and among many intellectuals. SECULARIZATION increased markedly from 1850 onward, although indifference to organized religion was more common than hostility. At the end of the twentieth century, between 90 and 95 percent of the citizens of the Scandinavian countries still identified themselves as Lutheran, but only 3 to 5 percent attended church on a weekly basis.

Continuing Vitality

Although many Scandinavians seemed content with a church involvement limited to major religious holidays and sporadic transitional ritual events such as baptisms, weddings, and funerals, those who were more active in the churches continued to have an impact on their societies and worldwide Lutheranism.

At the start of the century there were deep divisions in the churches of Denmark and Norway between Pietists associated with the inner mission movements, Grundtvigians, and liberal Lutherans. In Norway the tension was so great that the conservatives created their own independent school to train pastors, the *Menighetsfakultet* (Congregational Faculty), in 1908, as an alternative to the theological education offered at the University of Oslo. During World War II, however, Ole Hallesby of the *Menighetsfakultet* and EIVIND BERGGRAF, the bishop of Oslo, brought all factions together to form a Joint Christian Council to work in opposition to the occupying Nazi forces and their collaborators. In 1942 all of the bishops in Norway resigned from the state church in protest. Almost all of the clergy supported them, even though it meant the loss of state salaries, and a self-governing folk church was organized for the duration of the war. In Denmark many pastors and active lay people also gained respect during the war for supporting the resistance movement and helping Jews to escape to neutral Sweden.

Sweden produced a number of internationally influential theologians during the twentieth century. NATHAN SÖDERBLOM, archbishop of Uppsala from 1914 to 1931, made major contributions to ECUMENISM by founding the Life and Work Movement after World War I. It later became a building block in the formation of the WORLD COUNCIL OF CHURCHES. ANDERS NYGREN became the first president of the LUTHERAN WORLD FEDERATION in 1947. Together with other professors at the University of Lund, most notably Gustaf Aulén, he helped stimulate a renaissance in Luther studies in Sweden and pioneered an influential theological methodology known as motif research.

Organizational Changes

During the twentieth century, the administrative structures of the state Lutheran churches in Scandinavia were also changed to allow for more representative decision making and greater self-government. The churches created parish and diocesan councils through which lay people became more involved in the planning of local activities and the selection of clergy. All of the churches introduced the ordination of WOMEN and, in the 1990s, female bishops were elected for the first time in Norway, Denmark, and Sweden (see WOMEN CLERGY). The Norwegian parliament debated the possibility of disestablishing the church in 1981, but ultimately voted to maintain a state church while granting it more autonomy. In Sweden, on the other hand, the church became an independent legal entity in 2000. The clergy are no longer considered civil servants and the government plays no role in the election of bishops.

References and Further Reading

Derry, T. K. *A History of Scandinavia.* Minneapolis, MN: University of Minnesota Press, 1979.

Grell, Ole Peter, ed. *The Scandinavian Reformation.* Cambridge: Cambridge University Press, 1995.

Harmati, Béla, ed. *The Church and Civil Religion in the Nordic Countries of Europe.* Geneva, Switzerland: Department of Studies, The Lutheran World Federation, 1984.

Hartling, Poul, ed. *The Danish Church.* Translated by Sigurd Mammen. Copenhagen, Denmark: Det Danske Selskab, 1964.

Hope, Nicholas. *German and Scandinavian Protestantism 1700–1918.* Oxford, UK: Clarendon Press, 1995.

Molland, Einar. *Church Life in Norway 1800–1950.* Translated by Harris Kaasa. Minneapolis, MN: Augsburg Publishing House, 1957.

Murray, Robert. *A Brief History of the Church of Sweden: Origins and Modern Structure.* Translated by Nils G. Sah-lin. Stockholm, Sweden: Diakonistyrelsens Bokförlag, 1961.

Otteson, Knud. *A Short History of the Churches of Scandinavia.* Århus, Denmark: University of Århus, Department of Church History, 1986.

ERIC LUND

LUTHERANISM, UNITED STATES

Lutheranism is the most widespread and influential form of Protestantism in Germany and Scandinavia, although Lutherans who came from Europe to North America faced a difficult struggle to find their place in a new religious and social environment. Some of their theological commitments, liturgical forms of WORSHIP, and cultural orientations were out of the ordinary compared to the dominant types of Protestantism in early American society. Differences in ethnic origins (see ETHNICITY) expressions of piety, and theological emphases among American Lutherans kept them divided into many different synods for over two centuries. After a long and complex process of adaptation, Lutheranism has come to be one of the major mainstream Protestant traditions in the UNITED STATES. Although unified into fewer church structures than ever before, contemporary American Lutherans are still dispersed in several dissimilar denominations and face the additional challenge of coping with internal diversity within their churches.

The Colonial Period

Lutherans from the NETHERLANDS, GERMANY, Scandinavia, and POLAND came to the Dutch colony of New Amsterdam as early as 1643 but were not allowed to hold their own worship services or call their own clergy until the English took possession of that territory in 1664. Beginning in 1638 Lutherans from SWEDEN and FINLAND also came to the Delaware Valley where they enjoyed greater religious freedom, even after the region passed from the control of the Swedes to the Dutch and eventually the English. In 1708 large numbers of German Lutherans from the region of the Palatinate started to arrive in New York and the Carolinas, but after 1720 Germans increasingly favored settlement in Pennsylvania. Salzburgers, fleeing religious persecution in Austria, established an additional Lutheran presence in Georgia in 1734.

Widely scattered and served by few ministers, the colonial Lutherans continued to depend on support and guidance from Europe. In 1734 a delegation from Pennsylvania, where Lutherans were most densely settled, made a special appeal for help to HALLE, the center of PIETISM in Germany. Hoping to counteract the influence of NIKOLAUS VON ZINZENDORF's MORAVIAN CHURCH among Lutherans in America, Halle sent out a young missionary-pastor, HENRY MELCHIOR MÜHLENBERG, in 1741. He established the first formal governing body for Lutherans in 1748, the Ministerium of North America and, until his death in 1787, also promoted greater cooperation between German and Swedish Lutherans. He helped regularize Lutheran religious life in Pennsylvania, New Jersey, and New York by devising a common LITURGY and the first church constitution. In keeping with Mühlenberg's own inclinations, American Lutheranism in this period was dominated by the spirit of Pietism. Modes of worship, clerical VESTMENTS, and church adornments were all kept simple, and more emphasis was placed on PREACHING and catechizing (see CATECHISMS) than on the celebration of the SACRAMENTS. The LORD'S SUPPER was administered only one to four times a year.

Americanization and Reconfessionalization

During the period when the new American Republic was being formed, Lutherans also reorganized themselves into several associations of congregations within state boundaries. Now, in addition to the Ministerium of Pennsylvania, synods were founded in South Carolina (1787), North Carolina (1791), New York (1792), and Maryland–Virginia (1820). The difficulty of maintaining contact with the expanding population beyond the Appalachian mountains led to the creation of additional synods in Ohio (1818) and Tennessee (1820).

In this rapidly changing world American Lutherans also faced new challenges to the maintenance of their traditional identities. Synods debated whether English should be adopted as the language for worship. Among the educated the influence of rationalistic thought at times eroded interest in the distinctive doctrines of the Lutheran TRADITION. Living as a minority in a world of denominations more diverse than they had ever experienced in Europe, Lutherans also began to consider the possibility of uniting with other religious groups, especially the EPISCOPAL and German Reformed churches (see REFORMED CHURCHES IN AMERICA). Several synods acted independently to resist extensive adaptation of Lutheranism to American CULTURE, but there was also growing interest in the creation of a broader organization that could promote synodical cooperation and foster a common Lutheran consciousness.

In 1820 four synods held a convention to set up the General Synod. Several of the regional synods hesitated to relinquish regulatory power to this new organization, but it functioned for many decades as an important advisory body for Lutherans along the East Coast, primarily because of the strong leadership provided by SAMUEL S. SCHMUCKER. While serving as a professor at the seminary founded by the General Synod at Gettysburg, Pennsylvania, in 1826, Schmucker wrote extensively in defense of Lutheran theology. He was also quite open to making adjustments in thought and practice to help Lutherans fit better into American society. Schmucker favored the formation of SUNDAY SCHOOLS and was not entirely opposed to the use of the "new measures" developed by American revivalists to promote religious conversions (see REVIVALS). He authored a formal appeal for the creation of a union among various denominations, to make sure that America would remain a Protestant nation. This openness to acculturation reached its most controversial expression in 1855 when Schmucker circulated the Definite Synodical Platform, an anonymous pamphlet that proposed a new rescension of the AUGSBURG CONFESSION, omitting what had been taught by European Lutherans about the ceremonies of the mass, private confession, sabbath observance, baptismal regeneration, and the real presence of the body and blood of Christ in the Lord's Supper.

At this time about two-thirds of all American Lutherans were affiliated with the General Synod. There had been some orthodox Lutherans all along who were concerned about the orientation of the synod's "American Lutheranism," but the new proposal to alter the most basic Lutheran confessional consensus created an even greater storm of protest. Several state synods severed their ties with the General Synod. The "Old Lutheran" opposition established a new seminary in Philadelphia in 1864 and created a rival General Council in 1867. Its leading spokesperson was CHARLES PORTERFIELD KRAUTH whose influential book, *The Conservative Reformation and Its Theology*, published in 1871, finalized the trend back to a more traditional and strictly confessional Lutheranism.

Around the same time additional tensions within American Lutheranism developed as a result of the CIVIL WAR. Most Lutherans did not express much concern about the issue of SLAVERY, but there were some notable exceptions such as the strongly abolitionist Franckean Synod, which had been organized in New York in 1837 (see SLAVERY, ABOLITION OF). After the formation of the Confederate States in 1861, five southern synods separated from northern and western Lutherans to form the General Synod, South. This body continued in existence after the war as the United Synod, South (1886).

The Influence of New Immigrants

The movement to maintain traditional Lutheranism in America was enhanced by the arrival of waves of new immigrants from Europe from the 1830s onward. This development also began to shift the center of American Lutheranism away from the East toward the Midwest. In contrast to the Lutherans who came during the colonial era, later immigrants from Scandinavia and Germany generally settled in ethnically homogeneous clusters in frontier areas where they felt little immediate pressure to adopt a new set of cultural patterns. Not all of the Norwegians, Swedes, Danes, Icelanders, and Finns who came to America retained their Lutheran identity, but those who did mostly formed separate synods related to their ethnicity, such as the Norwegian Synod (1853), the Augustana Synod (1860), the Danish Evangelical Lutheran Church in America (1872), and the Suomi Synod (1890). Differences in piety also disunited the Scandinavians. Pietists often lived in tension with the state Lutheran churches in Scandinavia, and when they came to America, they tended to go their own way. Elling Eielson, who emigrated from Norway, produced the earliest of these synods in 1846, and followers of HANS NIELSEN HAUGE, the foremost lay preacher back in NORWAY, formed the Hauge Synod in 1876. Pietists associated with the Inner Mission movement in DENMARK also created their own Lutheran church in America in 1894.

Germans who settled in the Midwest formed new synods in Wisconsin (1850), Texas (1851), and Iowa (1854). A few other groups specifically left Germany to escape trends in religious life there. Some Lutherans opposed to the union of Lutheran and Reformed churches in Prussia (see PRUSSIAN UNION) settled in New York State and founded the Buffalo Synod in 1845. A larger group from Saxony with strong commitments to Lutheran ORTHODOXY settled in the area around St. Louis and organized the Missouri Synod in 1847. C. F. W. Walther (1811–1887), the eventual leader of this latter group, became the most forceful defender of strict confessional Lutheranism in the Midwest.

The LUTHERAN CHURCH–MISSOURI SYNOD took the lead in forming a new federation of synods called the LUTHERAN SYNODICAL CONFERENCE (1872). Through this organization Missouri exercised considerable influence among Midwest Germans and also on the Norwegian Synod. For a while many Norwegian congregations depended on Concordia Seminary in St. Louis for the training of their ministers. A series of controversies, however, blocked any moves toward fuller cooperation among the Midwest synods. Buffalo and Missouri disagreed about the role of ministers and other issues of church POLITY. Estrangement developed between Missouri and Iowa over the AUTHORITY of the Lutheran confessions and the degree to which there must be doctrinal agreement to have

church fellowship (see CONFESSION). The Norwegian and Ohio synods distanced themselves from Missouri in the 1880s when disagreements emerged about the doctrine of PREDESTINATION.

Forms of Church Work

Despite their inability to overcome differences in ethnicity, piety, and THEOLOGY, the various American Lutheran groups were effectively engaged in many forms of church work by the end of the nineteenth century. Most synods still confined their home MISSIONS work to helping immigrants from their own ethnic backgrounds adjust to America and retain their ties to Lutheranism. There was some modest outreach to African American and NATIVE AMERICAN communities. American Lutheran foreign mission work began in INDIA, Madagascar, CHINA, and JAPAN. Most synods maintained their own SEMINARIES, and over fifty Lutheran church colleges were founded before the start of the new century (see CHRISTIAN COLLEGES). The Missouri Synod also created an extensive parochial school system. Some synods were active in establishing charitable institutions, and William Passavant of the Pittsburgh Synod was especially notable among American Lutherans for his work in founding hospitals and orphanages. Following a European model he instituted the DEACONESS movement in American Lutheranism. WOMEN also played increasingly active roles as lay contributors to local church programs and provided important financial support for church work abroad through women's missionary societies. The Walther League (1893) and the Luther League (1895) became national Lutheran youth organizations.

Twentieth-Century Mergers

Lutheran emigration from Europe peaked in 1882. As the twentieth century approached, American Lutherans, with the exception of some churches along the East Coast, were still worshiping predominantly in a language other than English. However, new incentives to merge synods and integrate more fully into America society soon appeared. Patriotic fervor during World War I inspired many Lutherans to put less emphasis on their ethnic backgrounds, particularly if they were of German heritage. The year 1917 marked the four hundredth anniversary of the start of MARTIN LUTHER's Reformation, which also inspired new efforts to promote synodical cooperation. The National Lutheran Council was brought into existence in 1918, linking many synods in the Midwest and the East, with the notable exception of the Missouri Synod. The three largest Norwegian synods came together in 1918 to form the Norwegian Lutheran Church in America. In the same year East Coast Lutherans associated with the General Synod, General Council, and United Synod, South combined as the United Lutheran Church in America (ULCA). In 1930 several German synods in the Midwest merged to form the AMERICAN LUTHERAN CHURCH.

Insistence on the total inerrancy of Scripture (see BIBLICAL INERRANCY) and the necessity of doctrinal agreement as a condition for fellowship or cooperation between churches kept the Missouri and Wisconsin Synods apart from these mergers (see WISCONSIN EVANGELICAL LUTHERAN SYNOD). Some other Midwestern Lutheran groups were more flexible on these issues but were still suspicious in the interwar period of liberal tendencies among East Coast Lutherans (see LIBERAL PROTESTANTISM AND LIBERALISM). In 1930 Norwegian and German Lutherans in the Midwest created a new American Lutheran Conference as a kind of protest against the theological views of the ULCA. After World War II, however, more church leaders across the country began to accept the HIGHER CRITICISM pioneered by Lutheran biblical scholars in Europe and to commit themselves to ECUMENISM. American Lutherans made important contributions to the formation of the LUTHERAN WORLD FEDERATION (LWF) in 1947. Franklin Clark Fry, longtime leader of the ULCA, became president of the LWF in 1957 and also encouraged American Lutheran participation in the WORLD COUNCIL OF CHURCHES.

The next important step toward Lutheran unity took place in 1960 when a new church based in Minneapolis, the American Lutheran Church (ALC), brought together most of the Norwegians, Danes of pietistic background, and the Midwest Germans who had been part of the old ALC. In 1962 the LUTHERAN CHURCH IN AMERICA (LCA), based in New York City, united the East Coast Lutherans of the ULCA with Grundtvigian Danes (see NIKOLAJ F. S. GRUNDTVIG) and most Lutherans of Swedish and Finnish background.

The Missouri Synod's (LCMS) initial willingness to explore relations with the ALC caused the conservative Wisconsin Synod (WELS) to suspend fellowship with it. Then, the decision to ordain women as clergy, approved by both the ALC and the LCA in 1970, and active engagement by the two denominations in ecumenical Dialogue with the Reformed, Episcopal, or Roman Catholic traditions prompted increasingly negative responses from the Missouri Synod (LCMS) (see DIALOGUE, INTERCONFESSIONAL; WOMEN CLERGY). In 1969, after J. A. O. Preus was elected denominational president, the LCMS strongly buttressed its conservative inclinations. It rejected participation in the Lutheran World Federation and began to scrutinize the type of theology being taught at its seminaries. At its 1973 convention the majority of delegates reaffirmed the inerrancy of Scripture, and charged the faculty of Concordia Seminary in St. Louis with failing to teach correct doctrine. Most of the faculty and students left Concordia to form Seminex, a seminary in exile. In 1976 some congregations withdrew from the LCMS to establish the Association of Evangelical Lutheran Churches (AELC).

The AELC sought further collaboration with the ALC and the LCA, which led to the creation in 1982 of a Commission for a New Lutheran Church. In 1988 the three churches united as the EVANGELICAL LUTHERAN CHURCH IN AMERICA (ELCA), which, with more than five million members, became the fourth largest Protestant denomination in the United States at that time.

At the end of the twentieth century the ELCA continued to wrestle with issues such as the appropriate polity of the CHURCH, the direction it should take in its involvement in the ecumenical movement, and its responses to religious and cultural pluralism. Embracing Lutherans of diverse persuasions, it also struggled to articulate a unified stance on controversial social issues such as ABORTION and HOMOSEXUALITY. The LCMS and WELS, with a combined membership of approximately three million, firmly rejected the reshaping of Lutheran identity favored by the ELCA and defended an alternative vision of Lutheranism that emphasized what differentiated it from other forms of Christianity, both Protestant and Catholic.

References and Further Reading

Groh, John E., and Robert H. Smith, eds. *The Lutheran Church in North American Life*. St. Louis, MO: Clayton Publishing House, Inc., 1979.

Gustafson, David A. *Lutherans in Crisis: The Question of Identity in the American Republic*. Minneapolis, MN: Fortress Press, 1993.

Kuenning, Paul P. *The Rise and Fall of American Lutheran Pietism*. Macon, GA: Mercer University Press, 1988.

Lagerquist, L. DeAne. *The Lutherans (Denominations in America, 9)*. Westport, CT: Greenwood Press, 1999.

Nelson, E. Clifford., ed. *The Lutherans in North America*. Philadelphia, PA: Fortress Press, 1975.

Nichol, Todd W. *All These Lutherans: Three Paths toward a New Lutheran Church*. Minneapolis, MN: Augsburg Publishing House, 1986.

Todd, Mary. *Authority Vested: A Story of Identity and Change in the Lutheran Church–Missouri Synod*. Grand Rapids, MI: Eerdmans, 1999.

Trexler, Edgar R. *Anatomy of a Merger: People, Dynamics and Decisions that Shaped the ELCA*. Minneapolis, MN: Augsburg Fortress Publishers, 1991.

ERIC LUND

LUTHULI, ALBERT JOHN (1899–1967)

South African HUMAN RIGHTS leader. Luthuli was born near Bulawayo (now in Zimbabwe) in 1899 to a Zulu chiefly family in the area of Groutville, Natal. His father was a SEVENTH-DAY ADVENTIST evangelist in what was then Southern Rhodesia. Sent back to Groutville as a child, Luthuli attended Adams College, established by the AMERICAN BOARD OF COMMISSIONERS FOR FOREIGN MISSIONS (ABCFM), achieving such distinction that he was appointed to teach there, one of the first Africans to do so in 1921. He emerged as a leader in the community, being elected chief in Groutville in 1934, and in the church, where he became chairman of the Bantu Congregational Church.

In the former capacity he was a modernizing and progressive chief, concerned more with agricultural and social and educational development than with political advance, and supporting institutions, such as the Institute of Race Relations, which were espoused by moderate whites. On the church front he was sufficiently eminent to be chosen as a South African representative at the conference of the International Missionary Council at Tambaram, Madras, in 1938. It was a transforming experience. He traveled to INDIA with Thompson Samkange (1893–1956), a Southern Rhodesian delegate who was to become a close friend and a leading African voice in church and public affairs in his own country. At the conference he encountered Asian Christians whose outlook and engagement sharply contrasted with the social and political passivity characteristic of the churches of Southern Africa, and he came into contact with the ideas of Gandhi and Nehru.

On his return he became increasingly concerned with the rights and dignity of black people in SOUTH AFRICA. He joined the African National Congress (ANC) in 1945, and in 1952 became its president-general. With the election of the Nationalist Government in 1948 and the steady implementation of apartheid, Luthuli became a leading figure in the civil disobedience movement, urging nonviolent resistance to oppression on explicitly Christian grounds. This made him a target for the government. He was deposed from the chieftaincy (although popular sentiment ensured that he was saluted with the title of chief for the rest of his life) and was put under several banning orders and twice imprisoned. In 1957 he was one of the many defendants in a celebrated treason trial. He was acquitted—imputations of violent intent or communist sympathies were patently unsustainable—but banished to Groutville. By now he was a figure of international interest, as the Sharpeville massacre and similar events helped to focus world attention on apartheid South Africa. In 1961 he was awarded the Nobel Peace Prize, the first African to receive it. He died in Stanger, South Africa, on July 21, 1967, after being struck by a railway train.

Throughout his life Luthuli drew the inspiration for his public activity from his understanding of the Christian faith. Some white church leaders who had seen him in his earlier years as the pattern African leader became disturbed as his stance became more radical, and especially lamented his identification with the ANC. However, his racial attitudes remained inclusive ("As an African I worship the God whose children we all are"). He was an enthusiast for Zulu CULTURE, but sought no specifically African form of CHURCH or THEOLOGY. A product of Protestant missions himself, he wanted the widest possible sharing of such institutions as Adams College that the missions had brought. His complaint against white church leaders was their acceptance of domination by the secular state. As for his own people, "The road to freedom," he said "is via the Cross."

See also Church and State, Overview

References and Further Reading

Primary Source:

Luthuli, Albert. *Let My People Go: An Autobiography.* London: Collins, 1962.

Secondary Sources:

Elphick, Richard, and Rodney Davenport, eds. *Christianity in South Africa: A Political, Social and Cultural History.* chapt. 23. Berkeley: University of California Press, 1997.

Ludwig, Frieder. *Zwischen Kolonialismuskritik und Kirchenkampf: Interaktionen afrikanischer, indischer, und europaischer Christen während der Weltmissionskonferenz Tambaram.* Göttingen, Germany: Vandenhoeck und Ruprecht, 2000.

ANDREW F. WALLS

M

MACHEN, JOHN GRESHAM (1881–1937)

American Presbyterian controversialist and New Testament scholar. John Gresham Machen was born July 28, 1881, the son of a prominent Baltimore family. In the 1920s he emerged as the foremost critic of LIBERAL PROTESTANTISM. In popular works such as *Christianity and Liberalism* (1923) and *What Is Faith?* (1925) he argued that liberalism abandoned the central tenets of historic Christianity. What is more, Machen contended that liberal views about Christ, the BIBLE, SIN, and SALVATION reflected the general intellectual decline of American CULTURE and EDUCATION. On this basis he called for a separation of conservative and liberal Protestants.

Although Machen based these arguments on his own Presbyterian convictions, he also marshaled support from his own teaching and study of the New Testament, which extended from his days as an undergraduate at Johns Hopkins University through to his duties at Princeton Seminary from 1906 to 1929, and then at Westminster Seminary until the end of this life. In his two scholarly books, *The Origin of Paul's Religion* (1921) and *The Virgin Birth of Christ* (1930), both of which defended the Bible's truthfulness and traditional Protestant interpretations, Machen earned the reputation as the foremost conservative biblical scholar in the UNITED STATES. Furthermore, his scholarship provided much of the substance for the argument that liberal Protestantism was a severe departure from Christian teaching.

Machen was a popular speaker who many identified as FUNDAMENTALISM's lone scholar. In the northern PRESBYTERIAN CHURCH (PCUSA) his views were the object of much scorn. Over the last decade of his life Machen fought losing battles in trying to preserve older Presbyterian teaching. His combativeness eventually prompted Presbyterian officials in 1935 to bring Machen to trial and suspend him from the ministry. In 1936, only six months before his death on January 1, 1937, he responded by forming the Orthodox Presbyterian Church.

See also Orthodoxy; Presbyterianism

References and Further Reading

Primary Source:

Machen, J. Gresham. *What is Christianity? And Other Addresses.* Edited by Ned. B. Stonehouse. Grand Rapids, MI: Eerdmans, 1951.

Secondary Source:

Hart, D. G. *Defending the Faith: J. Gresham Machen and the Crisis of Conservative Protestantism in Modern America.* Baltimore, MD: Johns Hopkins University Press, 1994.

DARRYL G. HART

MACKAY, JOHN ALEXANDER (1889–1983)

Presbyterian church leader. Mackay was born in Inverness, SCOTLAND on July 5, 1889, of a Scottish Presbyterian family. He studied philosophy and THEOLOGY in Aberdeen and in Princeton, New Jersey, although his philosophical formation was clearly developed in Spain under the mentorship of Miguel de Unamuno, who shaped his mind and soul with the flavor of Iberian existentialism. This study gave him a unique perspective into the Latin American soul and cultural realities. Mackay married his wife, Jane Logan, before his appointment as a missionary educator in Lima, Peru, by the Free Church of Scotland.

Mackay is one of the most important figures in the early years of the Ecumenical Movement and in the Committee for Cooperation in Latin America (CCLA). In the Ecumenical Movement, Mackay was the chairperson for the commission on "The Universal Church and the World Nations" of the Oxford Conference in 1937; a member of the emerging central committee from 1946 to 1948; chairperson of the International Missionary Council from 1947 to 1957; member of the central committee of the WORLD COUNCIL OF CHURCHES, 1948–1954; chairperson of the commission on "The Church's Witness to God's Design" of the Amsterdam Conference of the World Council, 1948; and chairperson of the joint committee of the International Missionary Council and the World Council of Churches from 1948 to 1954.

During this period of ecumenical involvement and contribution Mackay wrote numerous articles in ecumenical journals focusing on ecumenical ECCLESIOLOGY. His work on this area is best articulated in his book *Ecumenics: The Science of the Church Universal*. While involved in the Ecumenical Movement, Mackay was appointed professor of ecumenics at Princeton Theological Seminary (1932–1936) and became president of this institution from 1936 to 1959. His legacy as president of Princeton Theological Seminary is clearly seen in the library collection of this institution, one of the best in the field of Latin American religion in the world, and in the creation of the international journal *Theology Today* (Princeton, New Jersey).

Mackay's theological maturity was nourished and shaped by a rich and challenging experience as a missionary in Peru and as a critical figure in the CCLA. His participation in many important ecumenical and missionary meetings in the continent provided grounding for his missiological contributions. Three important books in the history of Latin American Christianity—*The Other Spanish Christ, That Other America,* and *Christianity in the Frontier*—and his contributions to the CCLA's journal, *La Nueva Democracia* (New York: 1916–1960s), represent Mackay's cross-cultural struggles to understand the place and function of Protestantism in the Latin American continent. His missiological approach, particularly his critical assessment of Christ's images as used by Latin American writers and novelists, has become a rich method to grapple with issues of the gospel and cultures in the Latin American context.

Mackay died in Princeton, New Jersey, on September 6, 1983.

See also Culture; Ecumenism; Latin America; Missiology

References and Further Reading

Primary Sources:

Mackay, J. A. *Ecumenics: The Other Spanish Christ.* New York: Macmillan, 1932.
———. *That Other America.* New York: Friendship Press, 1935.
———. *Christianity in the Frontier.* New York: Macmillan, 1958.
———. *The Science of the Church Universal.* Englewood Cliffs, NJ: Prentice Hall, 1964.

Secondary Sources:

Jurji, E. J., ed. *The Ecumenical Era in Church and Society.* New York: Macmillan, 1959.
Sinclair, John H. *Juan A. Mackay: Un Escosés con Alma Latina.* Mexico City: CUPSA, 1991.

CARLOS F. CARDOZA ORLANDI

MACKENZIE, JOHN (1835–1899)

British missionary. Mackenzie was born August 30, 1835, in Knockando, SCOTLAND. In 1855 he joined the London Missionary Society, which three years later sent him to SOUTH AFRICA, the Cape province. He promptly got into conflict with the Boers of the neighboring Transvaal. Various travels throughout the southern and southeastern part of AFRICA followed. Mackenzie became, by the late 1860s, a determined advocate of further British expansion in Botswana, both to retain a British access to central Africa and to stem the influx of European settlers. In 1878 he became the spokesman for the European settlers and was offered, the following year, the post of British commissioner for Bechuana, although he did not receive the permission of the London Missionary Society to accept the offer.

His vigorous involvement on behalf of British political interests continued all the same. Larger political issues, significantly influenced by the appearance of German interests in Namibia, prompted the London Missionary Society eventually to give its approval for Mackenzie's political involvement in Bechuana. Mackenzie died in Kimberley, South Africa, March 23, 1899.

Mackenzie exerted considerable influence through his prolific pen. He is a classic example of the convergence of missionary impulse and political imperialism, undoubtedly the outgrowth of his experiences in South Africa.

References and Further Reading

Primary Sources:

Mackenzie, John. *Ten Years North of the Orange Rivee. A Story of Everyday Life and Work among the South African Tribes from 1859 to 1869*. Edinburgh: Edmonston and Douglas 1871. Reprinted 1972.

———. *Austral Africa: Losing It or Ruling It*. London: Sampson Low, Marston, Searle, and Rivington 1887. Reprinted 1969.

———. *Papers of John Mackenzie*. Johannesburg: Witwatersrand University Press for African Studies Institute, 1975.

Secondary Sources:

Mackenzie, W. Douglas. *John Mackenzie: South African Missionary and Statesman*. London: Hodder and Stoughton, 1902.

Mueller, John Theodore. *Great Missionaries to Africa*. Grand Rapids, MI: Zondervan, c. 1941.

Sillery, Anthony. *John Mackenzie of Bechuanaland, 1835–1899; A Study in Humanitarian Imperialism*. Cape Town: A. A. Balkema, 1971.

HANS J. HILLERBRAND

MACLEOD, GEORGE FIELDEN (1895–1991)

Scottish church leader and ecumenist. MacLeod was born June 17, 1895, in Glasgow, of a family distinguished in service of the CHURCH OF SCOTLAND. He was educated at Winchester, Oxford, and Edinburgh Universities, interrupted by service in World War I in Salonika and Flanders where he won the Military Cross. He served as minister in parishes in fashionable Edinburgh and depressed Glasgow. His radical pacifist views and his challenges to the establishment led to frequent clashes with the Church of Scotland authorities.

In 1938 he acquired an interest in the ruins of Iona Abbey, which he rebuilt over 27 years with the help of rich benefactors and a group of working theologians and supporters. The community had a particular concern for young people in trouble and the poor of Scottish cities, a work that continued the efforts of THOMAS CHALMERS a century earlier. *Govan Calling* (1934) and *We Shall Rebuild* (1944) were MacLeod's vision of the new social order represented by the IONA COMMUNITY.

MacLeod made intercommunion a passionate concern, which horrified some PRESBYTERIANS, as did his catholicity in worship. He became the first non-Anglican to preach in St. Paul's London, greeted as "a modern prophet." Even in his year as moderator of the General Assembly, he excited opposition with his address "Bombs and Bishops." In 1963, the 1,400th anniversary of the foundation of Iona by Columba was marked ecumenically and its significance in the movement recognized.

MacLeod engaged in the dialogue of religion and politics, as well as the quest for Christian unity, expressed in his book *Only One Way Left,* with his espousal of the causes of peace and justice, hunger, and the environment. On resigning from leadership of the Iona Community in 1967 he became a life peer, created Lord MacLeod of Fuinary. He died June 27, 1991.

See also Ecumenism; Pacifism

References and Further Reading

Primary Sources:

MacLeod, George. *Govan Calling: Sermons and Addresses*. London: Methuen and Co., 1934.

———. *Only One Way Left: Church Prospect*. Glasgow: Iona Community, 1956.

Secondary Source:

Ferguson, Ronald. *George MacLeod, Founder of the Iona Community*. London: Collins, 1990.

TIM MACQUIBAN

MACLEOD, NORMAN (1812–1872)

Scottish theologian. Macleod was born at Campbeltown, Argyllshire, in SCOTLAND and educated at Glasgow College and Edinburgh University. While at Edinburgh he studied under, and was highly influenced by, the renowned theologian THOMAS CHALMERS. After a short career as a tutor and teacher he was ordained in 1838 and gained a reputation as a great orator, preacher, and as one particularly zealous in his parochial duties. Indeed he is remembered as one of the most influential parochial Scottish ministers of the nineteenth century.

In 1851 he was made minister of Barony parish, Glasgow, where he did much to serve the local community, especially the poor, and became keenly interested in foreign MISSIONS. In 1857 he was appointed chaplain to Queen Victoria, whose respect and admiration he had quickly gained. In 1860 his literary career was launched when he became editor of a monthly religious magazine entitled *Good Words*. The magazine was immensely popular, and several of the pieces he wrote for it later appeared in book form. In 1864 he was made convener of the India mission for the CHURCH OF SCOTLAND and in the same year traveled to Egypt and Palestine. Three years later, in 1867, he embarked on his journey to INDIA to visit mission stations throughout the country. On his return to Scotland he did much to encourage further effort in foreign missions. In 1869 he was elected moderator of the General Assembly of the Church of Scotland.

Macleod never fully recovered his health after traveling to India and, after a steady decline, died in 1872. He was the author of many books, the best known of which is his *Reminiscences of a Highland Parish* (1867).

References and Further Reading

Primary Source:

Macleod, Donald. *Memoir of Norman Macleod*. London: 1882.

Secondary Source:

Wellwood, John. *Norman Macleod*. Edinburgh: Oliphant Anderson and Ferrier 1897.

ALEC JARVIS

MADISON, JAMES (1751–1836)

American statesman. James Madison was the fourth president of the United States and a major architect of American constitutional government and advocate for religious liberty. He was a leading figure in the Constitutional Convention of 1787, which produced the U.S. Constitution, and in the First Federal Congress, which drafted the U.S. BILL OF RIGHTS.

Born in Virginia, the eldest of twelve children, Madison was baptized in the Anglican Church. He received his early education from Presbyterian ministers at home and at a boarding school. He traveled north to the evangelical Calvinist College of New Jersey (Princeton), where he was mentored by the College president and Presbyterian clergyman, Dr. John Witherspoon. This education produced one of the most theologically informed of all American statesmen.

When he returned home, he was discomforted by the persecution of dissenting clergy in central Virginia and moved to the cause of religious liberty. Elected to the state legislature in 1776, his first important public act was to propose replacing the language of "toleration" in George Mason's draft of the Virginia Declaration of Rights with the concept of absolute equality in religious belief and exercise. Religious liberty was thus enshrined in the fundamental law of Virginia. In the mid-1780s Madison led the opposition to Patrick Henry's proposal for a "general assessment" or tax to support "teachers of the Christian religion." He orchestrated the defeat of Henry's bill by delaying legislative action on the measure and mobilizing popular opposition to the tax with his trenchant "Memorial and Remonstrance against Religious Assessments." He also reintroduced in the Virginia legislature THOMAS JEFFERSON's "Bill for Establishing Religious Freedom" and shepherded it to passage in 1786. Drawing on the innovative church–state arrangements worked out in revolutionary Virginia, Madison proposed in the First Federal Congress the tentative "first draft" of a measure eventually shaped into the First Amendment to the U.S. Constitution.

Madison championed the idea that all citizens are equally entitled to the natural right to exercise religion according to the dictates of conscience. He rejected the popular notion that religion's survival required the sustaining aid of civil government and that civil government was dependent on an established church to promote social order and stability. Throughout his public career in both Virginia and the nation, he pursued the policies that civil government must not favor one religious sect over others or take cognizance of religion in state actions.

See also Bill of Rights; Jefferson, Thomas

References and Further Reading

Alley, Robert S., ed. *James Madison on Religious Liberty*. Buffalo, NY: Prometheus, 1985.
Ketcham, Ralph. *James Madison: A Biography*. New York: Macmillan, 1971.
Sheldon, Garrett Ward. *The Political Philosophy of James Madison*. Baltimore, MD: Johns Hopkins University Press, 2001.
Weber, Paul J. "James Madison and Religious Equality: The Perfect Separation." *Review of Politics* 44 (1982): 163–186.

DANIEL DRIESBACH

MALAWI

A land-locked country of 45,747 square miles in southeast AFRICA, the former British Protectorate of Nyasaland, Malawi became a republic within the Commonwealth on July 6, 1966. Hastings Kamuzu Banda served as life president from its beginning until 1994 when multiparty elections were forced on the country by world opinion. Malawi boasts fifteen identifiable languages with English and Chichewa as the official ones.

DAVID LIVINGSTONE is credited with opening Malawi to "Christianity, civilization, and commerce" in 1859. Accepting his appeal for missionaries to come and fight the slave trade, the Universities Mission to Central Africa (UMCA) arrived in 1861. The Free CHURCH OF SCOTLAND established the first permanent mission station at Cape Maclear in 1875 and the Blantyre Mission was founded a year later.

Anglican and Presbyterian missionaries from SCOTLAND and SOUTH AFRICA dominated early Protestant mission work. When Catholics and other Protestants appeared, they were deemed as intruders. Three Presbyterian mission groups merged in 1926 to form the Church of Central Africa Presbyterian (CCAP). With the life president being an ordained elder in the Church of Scotland, the CCAP became both the largest and de facto "official" church. Much of the early population growth in both the Protestant and Catholic churches was the result of establishing primary schools.

An extensive health-care ministry is maintained by the SEVENTH-DAY ADVENTIST CHURCH. The ASSEMBLIES OF GOD has recently mushroomed to more than 400,000 members. Although there are the usual varieties of evangelical, charismatic, and Pentecostal groups, AFRICAN INSTITUTED CHURCHES are increasing. Religious statistics greatly vary according to the publication, but the population is approximately 50 to 55 percent Protestants, 20 percent Catholics, and 20 percent Muslims and others.

See also Slavery; Slavery, Abolition of

References and Further Reading

"History of Malawi." Official Website for Ministry of Information. 1999. http://www.maform.malawi.net (February 21, 2003).

Tattersall, David. *The Land of the Lake: A Guide to Malawi.* Blantyre, Malaw: Blantyre Periodicals Ltd., 1982.

WARREN B. NEWBERRY

MARANKE, JOHN (1912–1963)

African church leader. Born Muchabaya Momberume in the Bondwe Mountain region of the Maranke Tribal Trustland of Zimbabwe, John (or Johane) Maranke received a spiritual injunction to establish a church after a near-death experience in 1932. He started the church with the help of his elder brothers and his uncle. The first official ceremony took place on July 20, 1932, near the Murozi River in the Maranke Tribal Trustland. Maranke documented his spiritual awakening and vision in the *Humbowo Hutswa we Vapostori* ("New Witness of the Apostles"). Other practices established by Maranke included a Saturday Sabbath ceremony (*Kerek*), healing sessions, a Eucharist or Passover ceremony, and mountain prayer retreats.

The Apostolic Church of John Maranke consists of a leadership structure of twelve members located in ZIMBABWE and more than 500,000 members, called Apostles (*Vapostori* or *Bapostolo*), in several African countries. The most dominant congregations are located in the Shona areas of eastern Zimbabwe and in Botswana, MALAWI, Zambia, Angola, and Mozambique. Apostles usually possess the spiritual gifts of prophecy and healing. WOMEN also occupy the venerable positions of prophetesses, healers, and ceremonial song composers and leaders. Apostolic congregations observe Saturday Sabbath ceremonies in local languages and dialects. The emphasis on FAITH HEALING is very strong within these congregations. Apostolic beliefs incorporate indigenous customs, especially MARRIAGE and healing models derived from the Shona, with Christian practices.

Maranke was able to create a movement that was able to adapt to changing conditions in many African nations. In the 1980s, some members of this church movement were actively involved in the *chimurenga* (Zimbabwean liberation struggle). There is no gainsaying the fact that the Apostolic Church is a compelling case of doctrinal and ritual revitalization in African Christianity.

The religious movement established by John Maranke also underscores the importance of indigenous creativity in African Christianity. Any serious study of Christianity in AFRICA must recognize the spiritual initiatives and genius of African church founders. It is from this vantage point that one can credibly capture the astonishing range of expressions and modes of Christianity in Africa.

See also Africa; African Instituted Churches; African Theology

References and Further Reading

Daneel, M. L. *Old and New in Southern Shona Independent Churches,* Vol. 1: *Background and Rise of the Major Movements.* The Hague: Mouton, 1971.

Isichei, Elizabeth. *A History of Christianity in Africa: From Antiquity to the Present.* Grand Rapids, MI: Eerdmans, 1995.

Jules-Rosette, Bennetta. *African Apostles: Ritual and Conversion in the Church of John Maranke.* Ithaca: NY: Cornell University Press, 1975.

AKINTUNDE E. AKINADE

MARBURG, COLLOQUY OF

One of the most important religious issues about which MARTIN LUTHER (1483–1546) and HULDRYCH ZWINGLI (1484–1531) presented differing convictions was the bodily presence of Christ in the Eucharist (*praesentia realis*). In 1525 this theological controversy erupted into outright hostilities. In order to resolve them, reformers, primarily from Suebia and the Upper Rhine regions, advanced the idea of a theological conference. Instrumental in bringing it about was Philip, Landgrave of Hesse (1504–1567), who wished to unite the Protestant estates of the empire in a political alliance; this project appeared endangered by conflicting theological views. His first attempts to arrange a meeting in 1528 and 1529 were unsuccessful. After the Second Imperial Diet held at SPEYER in March and April of 1529 he tried again. On April 22, the very day the Diet was closed, he urged the elector of Saxony and the imperial cities of Strassburg, Nürnberg, and Ulm to intensify their combined efforts to reach an agreement. He was afraid that those estates that upheld the old faith might succeed in undermining the mutual understanding of the Protestants by means of theological quarrels over the nature of Christ's presence in the Eucharist. The obstacles were great: Luther disclaimed any common interest between religion and politics; PHILIPP MELANCHTHON (1497–1560) warned that Zwingli's followers, who constituted a powerful pressure group, might open an even greater rift in the church and threaten peace within the empire. It was the elector of Saxony who urged Luther and Melanchthon to attend the meeting and, having secured their agreement, commissioned theologians of the University of Wittenberg to draft the so-called Articles of Schwabach to serve as a basis for the talks.

The foremost advocate of the conference continued to be Landgrave Philip. On July 1, 1529, he signed the letter of invitation, which was to be sent to Luther, Zwingli, JOHANNAS OECOLAMPADIUS (1482–1531), Johannes Sturm, ANDREAS OSIANDER (1498–1552), JOHANNES BRENZ (1499–1570) and—apparently at some later date, Urbanus Rhegius (1489–1591). The conference was scheduled at Marburg on September 29, 1529, and would begin the following day. To secure a positive outcome, these discussions were to abandon the usual rules of academic disputation in favor of a "friendly dialogue without formal arguments"; neither a chairman nor a mediator was appointed. Landgrave Philip, eager to achieve visible success, offered his best services to avoid conflict.

The representatives from the Helvetic Confederation and the city of Strassburg arrived two days early. The theologians Zwingli, Oecolampadius, MARTIN BUCER (1491–1551), and Hedio were joined by Rudolf Collin and Ulrich Funk, magistrates from Zürich, and Felix Frei from Basel. Luther and Melanchthon did not arrive until September 30. Even later, arriving October 2, were Osiander, Brenz, and MICHAEL AGRICOLA (1509–1557), who represented towns of Southern Germany, with Agricola substituting for Urbanus Rhegius, who had fallen ill. They all took up quarters in the landgrave's castle at Marburg.

On October 1, the discussions began. Zwingli was paired with Melanchthon and Luther with Oecolampadius for initial talks. Some progress was made concerning peripheral questions. The core of the dissent, the nature of Christ's presence in the Eucharist, became the topic of the main discussions of October 2 and 3, which took place in the landgrave's private chambers with the prince himself and some distinguished guests attending. Johann Feige, the landgrave's chancellor, gave the welcome address at 6:00 A.M. on October 2, thus formally opening the conference. Luther, Melanchthon, Zwingli, and Oecolampadius, to whom above all the success was entrusted, sat at the table facing each other. Luther pointed out a number of errors of belief that he had observed in the teachings of the others and advanced his own conviction concerning the topical issue of the Eucharist. His

opponents responded, denying vigorously the presence of Christ's body in the sacrament. Luther again quoted the decisive passages from the Bible, which he had written with chalk on the table: "*Hoc est corpus meum*" (this is my body). There followed a lively debate, rather quickly leading to stalemate. Well-known arguments taken from relevant literature were exchanged, but no new aspects put forward.

There were three main questions that dominated the discussion. First of all, there was the correct understanding of Jesus's words spoken at the Last Supper, which Luther considered of paramount importance. Then there was the question of whether it seemed possible that Christ's body should be present in heaven as well as in the sacrament. Finally, relevant patristic writings were examined. In the end there evolved a somewhat better understanding in several aspects, but no common ground was achieved concerning the basic issue. When the landgrave insisted that a middle road should be found, the Lutherans presented the draft of an article of consensus, and Melanchthon pointed to the writings of the fathers as a possible source of unanimity. There were Swiss delegates, however, who steadfastly refused to compromise on the question of the *praesentia realis* (real presence).

Due mostly to the landgrave, a complete failure was avoided. He prompted Luther to formulate fifteen articles, which stated, based on the Articles of Schwabach, what agreements had been reached. The controversial points of view of the Swiss and Strassburg delegates were referred to the future. Luther avoided antagonizing his opponents in any way, and finally his text was signed by all. Articles 1 through 14 contain the essence of common belief. In article 15 Luther summarizes the common basis of Protestant teaching concerning the question of the *praesentia realis*, and states, in a brief and concise manner, the remaining points of dissent only in the end. Thus Luther succeeded in formulating a document of basic understanding between the different groups on reformatory creed at a rather low level, but still clearly defining the border with the dogma of the old church.

Modern literature offers no unanimous answer to the question of whether this is the *concordia* attempted at the time. There can be no doubt that in a practical way a consensus was reached (H. Bornkamm). Landgrave Philip of Hesse, the foster father of the conference, reaped from it the chance of once more presenting, on October 4, his project of a political alliance. It was thwarted by the outbreak of an epidemic on October 5, which demanded a hasty departure from Marburg.

In the end, the outcome of the Marburg talks seems to have satisfied everyone. Each theological persuasion believed itself to have carried the day, and somehow this is correct. Much of the previous religious excitement was diminished in importance, and the personal contacts established allowed a more pragmatic approach and reduced strife and stress. A foundation for further endeavors was laid; Bucer, above all, took advantage of it, working toward greater consensus on the questions of how to understand and celebrate the Lord's Supper. The Concordia Wirtembergensis of 1534 and the Concordia Wittenbergensis of 1536 proved attainable. Landgrave Philip did not hesitate to implement it in his primary goal of a political alliance. The elector of Saxony, nevertheless, found reason to criticize the Articles of Marburg, demanding instead universal adherence to the Articles of Schwabach. With the Margrave of Brandenburg-Ansbach joining forces, his attitude doomed further discussions that took place at Schwabach and Schmalkalden. Therefore, it would not appear justified to overestimate the historic import of the Articles of Marburg. The evolution of Protestant theology, however, undoubtedly owes much to them. The *Confessio Marpurgiana* stands as a first attempt at unifying the different Protestant factions and is to be considered a notable landmark on the road toward the *Confessio Augustana*.

See also Helvetic Confession; Lord's Supper

References and Further Reading

Bezzenberger, Guenter. *Was zu Marpurgh geschah, Eine Einführung in die Geschichte des Marburger Religionsgesprächs im Jahr 1529.* Kassel: Fvang. Pressverband, 1979.

Köhler, Walther. *Das Marburger Religionsgespräch 1529: Versuch einer Rekonstruktion.* Leipzig: Eger & Sievers, 1929.

———. *Das Religionsgespräch zu Marburg 1529.* Tübingen: Mohr, 1929.

May, Gerhard. "Marburger Religionsgespräch." In *Theologische Realenzyklopädie XXII.* Berlin, New York: Walter de Coruyter, 1992. 75–79.

May, Gerhard, ed. *Das Marburger Religionsgespräch 1529.* Gütersloh: 2d ed., Mohr, 1999.

Schirrmacher, Friedrich Wilhelm, ed. *Briefe und Acten zur Geschichte des Religionsgespräches zu Marburg 1529.* Gotha: 1876.

Schmid, Alois. "Marburg, Colloquy of." In *The Oxford Encyclopedia of the Reformation III*, edited by Hans H. Hillerbrand. New York, Oxford: Oxford University Press, 1996. 2–4.

ALOIS SCHMID

MARHEINEKE (MARHEINECKE), PHILIPP KONRAD (1780–1846)

German Lutheran theologian. Marheineke stood in the tradition of mediating and speculative THEOLOGY and was professor of theology at the University of Berlin from 1811 until his death, May 31, 1846. He was a colleague of FRIEDRICH SCHLEIERMACHER at Berlin and preacher at Trinity Church in Berlin, representative of the Protestant clergy as member of the Supreme Consistory. Marheineke was born in Hildesheim, GERMANY, May 1, 1780, the son of a merchant and city council member. He attended the Gymnasium Andreanum and began his university studies in Göttingen in 1789 with G. J. Planck, C. F. von Ammon, C. F. Staudlin, and J. G. Eichorn before going on to study at Erlangen. In 1805 he published a book on the influence of IMMANUEL KANT on Christian ETHICS. After briefly returning to Göttingen he accepted a professorship at Heidelberg where he worked with C. Daub, W. De Wette, and G. F. Creuzer.

Marheineke was influenced by Schleiermacher, Johann Gottlieb Fichte, and FRIEDRICH VON SCHELLING and moved naturally among the circle of Romantic thinkers at Heidelberg. He published his *Christian Symbolic Theology* (1811–1813), which challenged aspects of the work of I. A. Dorner, and was called to the newly founded University of Berlin. There he began a cordial relationship with GEORG W. F. HEGEL and found himself trying to provide a more conceptually oriented understanding of the meaning of Christianity as a form of the Absolute Ideal, organized on the basis of a history of thought encompassing Catholic, Lutheran, Reformed, and Socinian dogmatic topics rather than Schleiermacher's emphasis on the expression of consciousness based on the feeling of dependency. When the split between Schleiermacher and Hegel widened, Marheineke found himself in the Hegelian camp, interpreting Hegel's philosophy and its influence on Christian theology. He succeeded Hegel as rector of the university after Hegel's death. Less materialistic than the left-wing Hegelians, he continued his efforts toward a rationalistic understanding of meaning in the Christian life, accepting orthodox doctrinal structures like the Trinity while offering a Hegelian interpretation of their meaning.

His view of the importance of reason and history as forces in theology would not endear him to the Barthian movement (see KARL BARTH; NEO-ORTHODOXY), limiting his acknowledged influence for much of the twentieth century. His prominence as a Prussian theologian and churchman did not translate easily to the English-speaking world.

References and Further Reading

Primary Sources:

Marheineke, P. K. *The Meaning of Hegelian Philosophy for Christian Theology.* 1842.

———. *A Critique of Schelling's Philosophy of Revelation.* 1843.

———. *The Reform of the Church through the State.* 1844.

———. *The Rise and Development of the Reformation in Germany.* 1846.

———. *Outline of Christian Dogmatic Theology as Science,* Third edition. 1847.

[Marheineke's students, S. Matthies and W. Vatke, published his lectures in 1847–1849; in addition there are collections of his sermons.]

Secondary Sources:

Dreher, L. *Metaphors of Light: P. K. Marheineke's Method and On-going Program of Mediating Theology.* Berlin: Walter de Gruyter, 1998.

Drehsen, V. "Theologische Realenzykopädie." *TRE* 22: 109–115 [with an excellent bibliography of German and French materials].

Pannenberg, W., ed. *Revelation as History.* 1982.

Rupprecht, Eva-Maria. *Kritikvergessene Spekulation: Das Religions und Theologie Verstandnis der spekulativen Theologie P. K. Marheinekes.* 1993.

G. W. MCCULLOH

MARPECK, PILGRAM (c. 1495–1556)

Anabaptist theologian. Marpeck was a lay German burgher and civil magistrate who became a social radical and Anabaptist leader. Born into a politically prominent family in Tirolean Rattenberg on the Inn, he resigned his mining magistrate's office a few days after the execution of the Anabaptist preacher Leonhart Schiemer (see ANABAPTISM). Forfeiting a substantial estate, he and his wife, Anna, traveled to Bohemia, where he was commissioned an Anabaptist elder.

In 1530 Marpeck, employed as Strasbourg's wood and mining administrator, led a group of Anabaptist refugees, and wrote and sponsored the publication of Anabaptist pamphlets. In his *A Clear Response . . . , A Clear and Useful Instruction . . . ,* and "Confession of Faith," he articulated a theological position between the spiritualist positions of Hans Bänderlin, Christian Entfelder, and MELCHIOR HOFMANN and the magisterial position of reformer MARTIN BUCER.

Expelled from Strasbourg in 1532, Marpeck resided in southwest GERMANY and SWITZERLAND before settling in Augsburg in 1543/44. There he served as city engineer, supervising lumbering and the city's water works. While living on municipal property, he corresponded with Anabaptist groups in Alsace, Switzerland, South Germany, and Moravia, and subsidized a number of Anabaptist publications, including his own *Response . . .* to CASPAR SCHWENCKFELD, with whom he had a protracted disagreement.

Although he influenced the Mennonite, Hutterite, and Amish Traditions, Marpeck held a somewhat less sectarian theological position. He supported the civil oath and the payment of taxes, while criticizing the exploitation of the poor and the use of deadly force.

See also Amish; Hutterites; Mennonites

References and Further Reading

Blough, Neal. *Christologie Anabaptiste: Pilgram Marpeck et l'humanité de Christ.* Geneva: Labor et Fides, 1984.

Boyd, Stephen. *Pilgram Marpeck: His Life and Social Theology.* Durham, NC: Duke University Press; Mainz: Philipp von Zabern, 1992.

Klassen, William. *Covenant and Community.* Grand Rapids, MI: Eerdmanns, 1968.

Klassen, William and Walter Klaassen. *The Writings of Pilgram Marpeck.* Scottdale, PA: Herald Press, 1978.

STEPHEN B. BOYD

MARRANT, JOHN (1755–1791)

African-American clergy. Born free in New York in 1755, John Marrant grew up in South Carolina, where he was converted by GEORGE WHITEFIELD and taught a clandestine SUNDAY SCHOOL for slaves, and organized black churches. After fighting with the British during the American War of Independence, Marrant resumed a charismatic PREACHING career in London. On May 15, 1785, he was ordained into the Huntingdon Connexion, a network of Calvinist evangelists founded by LADY SELINA HASTINGS. Marrant subsequently traveled to Nova Scotia to minister and organize churches among exiled black Loyalists; at Birchtown, a settlement of 2,000 blacks, he established a congregation and organized a school.

Marrant developed a Calvinist COVENANT THEOLOGY declaring blacks to be a chosen people. He announced himself a prophet sent to gather blacks into COVENANT communities and prepare them for exodus to Zion, and he contended against the ARMINIANISM of rival Black Methodists. In 1789 Marrant left Nova Scotia for Boston, where he chaplained and delivered a *Sermon* to the African Lodge of Freemasons. He returned to London in 1790, published his missionary *Journal*, and died in 1791.

In 1792, Marrant's Birchtown congregation immigrated to Sierra Leone, where a Huntingdonian chapel operates to this day.

See also African-American Protestantism; Black Methodism

References and Further Reading

Primary Sources:

Marrant, John. "A Journal of the Rev. John Marrant." In *Face Zion Forward: First Writers of the Black Atlantic, 1785–1798,* edited by Joanna Brooks and John Saillant. Boston, MA: Northeastern University Press, 2002.

———. "A Narrative of the Lord's Wonderful Dealings with John Marrant, a Black, (Now going to Preach the Gospel in Nova-Scotia)." In *Face Zion Forward: First Writers of the Black Atlantic, 1785–1798,* edited by Joanna Brooks and John Saillant. Boston, MA: Northeastern University Press, 2002.

———. *Works of John Marrant.* New York: International Microfilm Press (3M Co.), 1969.

Secondary Source:

Potkay, Adam, and Sandra Burr. *Black Atlantic Writers in England and the Americas.* Basingstoke, UK: Macmillan, 1995.

JOANNA BROOKS

MARRIAGE

What Is Marriage?

The CHURCH OF ENGLAND's Common Worship Marriage Service (2000) describes marriage as "a gift of God in creation through which husband and wife may know the grace of God. It is given that as man and woman grow together in love and trust, they shall be united with one another in heart, body and mind, as Christ is united with his bride, the Church." It is also said to bring "husband and wife together in the delight and tenderness of sexual union and joyful commitment to the end of their lives," and to be "the foundation of family life in which children are [born and] nurtured and in which each member of the family, in good times and in bad, may find strength, companionship and comfort, and grow to maturity in love." Very similar descriptions are found in the liturgies of other Protestant churches.

A comparison between this contemporary LITURGY and the BOOK OF COMMON PRAYER of the Church of England (1662) reveals the extent of the change to marital THEOLOGY in the Anglican Church, replicated throughout Protestantism. There is no mention of love, human or divine, in the prefaces of the earlier work. The threefold purposes of marriage are "the procreation of children"; "a remedy against sin, and to avoid fornication; that such persons as have not the gift of continency might marry . . ."; and "the mutual society, help, and comfort, that the one ought to have of the other. . . ." In the new liturgy the connection between marriage and children is considerably attenuated. Marriage supports something else, "family life," and the liturgy is consistent with the intention of a growing number of marrying couples to remain childless. St. Paul's estimation of marriage as a reluctant concession to passion (I Corinthians 7) disappears. The positive acceptance of sexual intercourse within the couple's experience may be compared, in theology and in linguistic tone, with the warning of the earlier liturgy that marriage is not to be undertaken "to satisfy men's carnal lusts and appetites, like brute beasts that have no understanding." The newer work also states that marriage "enriches society and strengthens community." Protestants have integrated romantic love into their doctrine of marriage, and, well in advance of Catholicism, come to regard loving sexual experience as analogous with, or a finite expression of, the love that is God's own being. That marriage enriches society is a reflection of a generation that has seen the ravaging social and economic effects of DIVORCE, particularly on children.

Protestant Emphases

The Protestant reformers all denied that marriage was a SACRAMENT. It is more commonly called an "ordinance." Nonetheless, it is "a gift of God" that mediates God's GRACE. Erasmus pointed out in 1516 that the "great mystery" of Ephesians 5:32, where the author compares the union of man and wife in "one flesh" with the unity of Christ and the church, had wrongly been translated as *sacramentum* in the Latin Vulgate. All the reformers agreed that the original Greek term *mustèrion* offered no biblical warrant for treating marriage as a sacrament. The reformers disliked the requirement of priestly CELIBACY on several grounds. It made marriage look inferior to celibacy. Celibacy, unless God bestowed it as a rare gift, was thought to be a vow that was almost impossible to keep, and which led to immorality and frustration among the CLERGY, and scandal in the CHURCH. Erasmus also pointed out a theological inconsistency. If marriage really is a sacrament, equal to all the others, as the Catholic Church had taught since the Council of Verona in 1184, why deny this sacrament to priests? To Protestant eyes, canon law encouraged promiscuity. A marriage was recognized as valid if consent was exchanged in the present tense by persons of marriageable age (14 for men, 12 for women) before at least two witnesses. Parental consent was not required, and betrothal vows, which were revocable, were thought to encourage premarital sexual experience. Protestants also challenged the jurisdiction of the church over marriage. Marriage was a matter for civil, not just ecclesiastical, law.

Historical "Models of Marriage"

John Witte (1997) has helpfully depicted dominant "models" of marriage in Western Christendom. He identifies LUTHERANISM with the model of social estate; CALVINISM with the model of COVENANT; and ANGLICANISM with the model of commonwealth. MARTIN LUTHER, following St. Paul, thought marriage was God's remedy for sexual SIN, but was positive about its social goods. A family would be ordered by the husband or *paterfamilias* whose AUTHORITY over his household was divinely appointed and exercised. The family would be the place where Christian FAITH and love would be taught, and discipline and hospitality exercised. God ordains marriage to be the bringer of community and social cohesion, and Luther found no contradiction between denying that marriage was a sacrament, and affirming its many divinely appointed goods. His doctrine of the Two Kingdoms led him to regard marriage as both divinely ordained and *worldly*. It was to be subject to civil, not ecclesiastical law, but because God is the author of civil authority, the divine institution of marriage is still upheld.

The "covenant model" of marriage, developed in JOHN CALVIN's later theology, anticipates contemporary Protestant and Catholic teaching (since the Second Vatican Council). The idea of covenant or testament is basic to biblical theology. Just as God enters into a holy covenant with God's own people, so husband and wife enter a holy covenant with each other, with God as guarantor and witness. Calvin based his covenant model of marriage on Malachi 2:14. In his *Commentaries* Calvin teaches that God has three purposes for marriage: the mutual love and support of husband and wife, the mutual procreation and nurture of children (see CHILDHOOD), and the mutual protection of both parties from sexual sin. These purposes are echoed in the Anglican theologian Thomas Becon, a contemporary of Calvin. Although the covenant model is popular in contemporary Protestantism, the same cannot be said for the "commonwealth model." A "commonwealth" is a political body, having a legal basis, which claims to promote the "common weal" or "common good." Anglican theologians were swift to associate marriage with the common weal, given that the health of the institution of marriage had obvious implications for the health of the wider society. State, church, and family were regarded as separate commonwealths, or as a single interlocking commonwealth, all instituted by God for the common good. It is easy to envisage how the commonwealth model also engendered a hierarchical understanding, with God, the king, the archbishop and the *paterfamilias,* heads respectively of their divinely appointed spheres (Witte 1997:76, 96, 243). The statement that marriage "enriches society and strengthens community" is characteristic of the commonwealth model.

Social Change

Because marriage is a civil and social as well as a religious institution it is particularly susceptible to social change. Because social change generally occurs quicker than religious change, enormous tensions arose in the second half of the twentieth century, a period in which social changes were particularly rapid. Most Christians were divided among themselves about how to understand and respond to these changes, and the tension was perhaps most keenly felt in the area of SEXUALITY and marriage. The changes are too numerous to list, but they might include (in so-called developed countries) the rise in affluence, the increase in personal freedom, the cultural elevation of romantic love, lack of respect for traditional authorities, growing INDIVIDUALISM, moral relativism, SECULARIZATION, the dominance of economic values, the availability of contraception (especially the pill), the rise of modern feminism and its onslaught on patriarchy, and the liberalization of divorce laws. There can be little doubt that the liberalization of divorce laws was made easier in Protestant countries because of the removal of the sacramental status of marriage, thereby also removing one of the grounds for assuming its indissolubility. The acceptance, with conditions, of contraception by the LAMBETH CONFERENCE of the Anglican Communion in 1930, and followed generally by Protestant churches, led to a further Catholic–Protestant clash.

In Europe and formerly colonial countries mainstream Protestantism is generally much weaker at the start of the twenty-first century. It is also badly divided across its denominations between Christians who identify themselves as conservative, evangelical, or even fundamentalist, and Christians who identify themselves as liberal, progressive, or inclusive. This divide is at its most obvious in sexual ETHICS. Conservatives generally insist on heterosexual marriage as the only and divinely given institution within which sexual relations are permissible, whereas progressives would extend marriage to lesbian and gay people or else abandon the marital framework altogether in the search for a contemporary sexual ethic. The topic of marriage therefore generates intense controversies, and it is with some of these that the rest of this article is concerned.

Marriage and Sexual Experience

Particular strain is currently placed on the traditional expectation that young persons should not have sexual intercourse before they are married. The very framing of the problem in these terms indicates the long historical centrality of marriage in legitimizing sexual experience in Christianity. Protestants and Catholics alike moved against widespread promiscuity in the sixteenth century by controlling the entry into marriage more strictly. One consequence of reform, in both parts of Western Christendom, was the assumption, quickly becoming normative, that marriage begins with the ceremony within which consent in the present tense is expressed. The distinction between marriage and nonmarriage, which had earlier been blurred by the practice of betrothal, became reinforced, and has remained so until this day, giving rise to precise senses of "before" and "after." This strain is expressed in popular movements such as Promise Keepers and sex education organizations operating under the umbrella term "Abstinence Education."

However, the average age at which men and women first marry continues to rise, and in 2000 in Britain, it was 30 and 28.9 years, respectively, whereas the numbers of people saving sexual experience until marriage was less than 1 percent. There are educational, social, and economic reasons for the rise in the average age of marriage, which are unlikely to be reversed, and the availability of cheap, reliable contraceptives reduces (but by no means eliminates) the likelihood of pregnancy. Although abstinence until marriage may remain an honorable and achievable goal for some Christians, there are reasons for thinking the emphasis on abstinence is insufficient. The Protestant tradition is suspicious of involuntary celibacy, believing it is impossible, except for those few who receive it as a gift, to achieve. Yet many Protestant organizations are in danger of insisting on it for a new generation that not only does not have a vocation to celibacy, but finds most of the old restraints that aided the practice of chastity (social stigma against premarital sex and single-parent families, supervised dating, the separation of the sexes in schools and universities, fear of pregnancy, etc.) have been dismantled. The desire for sexual experience is also likely to be at its height during this period.

There is presently no concerted campaign by the churches in favor of reducing the age of first marriage. Luther's commendation of marriage was based in part on his realism about the near inevitability of sexual experience. Perhaps the way forward here is the recovery of the virtue of chastity. Chastity is not the same thing as virginity, celibacy, or abstinence, but appropriate restraint. Perhaps the bottom line here is the love of children. Because all Christians agree that it is wrong to conceive unwanted children, the appropriate moral rule might be "Never have sex, whether or not with contraceptives, unless you are committed both to your partner and any child you might conceive." In this respect sexual practice might borrow the insight of Aquinas who taught that "Simple fornication is contrary to the love we should bear our neighbor, for . . . it is an act of generation performed in a setting disadvantageous to the good of the child to be born" (*Summa Theologiae*, 2a.154.2).

Some Protestant denominations in the 1980s and 1990s were in danger of abandoning marriage altogether as the norm for sexual experience. The best-known example is probably the document of the PRESBYTERIAN CHURCH (USA), *Keeping Body and Soul Together,* which was presented to the 1991 General Assembly of that denomination but not passed. Perhaps there has never been a more positive church sexuality report for advancing a self-critical understanding of the GENDER inequalities, sexual violence, homophobia, and other malign influences that can be found within Christianity, but it scarcely mentioned marriage. Marriage was not found in the table of contents, and only three and a half pages out of nearly 200 were devoted to it. Browning et al. in their aptly titled *From Culture Wars to Common Ground,* detect in the 1990s how in the UNITED STATES "the family" has become a liberal as well as a conservative issue because of the evidence of declining well-being of children, the impoverishment of women, and the rise of male detachment from families (1997:31). The weakening or even virtual collapse of the concept of marriage in liberal theology from the 1970s onward can now be seen, at the start of the new century, to have been a serious mistake.

Because almost all forms of Protestantism have valued marriage it is difficult to see how a sexual ethic that discounted marriage could ever take hold. Does this mean that ever larger numbers of Protestants will simply disregard their churches' teaching about sexuality, rather as large numbers of Catholics have disregarded their church's teaching about contraception? Not necessarily. Monti (1995) carefully argues the distinction between treating marriage as a norm for Christian sexual teaching, and treating it as a rule. Although the marital norm remains deeply embedded in the TRADITION, if it is imposed as a literal rule for all sexual experience, it is misunderstood. To recover marriage as a norm, he argues, would be to come to regard marriage not simply as a venerable and historical institution, but to appreciate it for the values it embodies, such as steadfast love, commitment, trust, and so on. Furthermore these marital values are to be appreciated even beyond the real marriages where they are found.

Same-Sex Marriages?

This issue will divide Protestants for some time to come. Whereas the major obstacle to the full recognition of HOMOSEXUALITY in Catholicism is the place of the human body within NATURAL LAW, Protestants are more focused on particular biblical passages. In each case the issue is one of both authority (of papal teaching, or Scripture) and interpretation (e.g., whether either Scripture or tradition deals with the precedent of committed same-sex couples who wish to live together until death parts them). It is argued (Thatcher 1999:299–302) that if the covenant model of marriage is selected as normative, life-long covenants between same sex couples are marriages. This solution avoids the awkward dilemmas posed by legal recognition or "blessing" of same-sex relationships. If they are not marriages, then what are they, and what degrees of commitment do they presuppose? The "covenant solution" is undoubtedly a Protestant one, although it would hardly please Calvin. Again, Luther's warning against the dangers of involuntary celibacy would seem appropriate in a different context. If lesbian and gay people are to refrain from sexual experience, then celibacy, contrary to the deepest instincts of Protestant traditions, is being imposed on them. This is not only theologically dubious, it is a failure of neighbor-love and is increasingly attacked as a crass case of unequal treatment. If heterosexual men and women are given marriage, which has the function of legitimizing sexual experience, while homosexual men and women are denied the relief that that institution brings, discrimination on grounds of orientation clearly arises.

Cohabitation

A further area of controversy is the increasingly common practice of people living together before, after, or instead of marriage. Because about seven in every ten couples in Britain and the United States who marry, live together first (and in some countries the proportion is higher still), tension exists (often in the same families) between those who condemn and those who condone (to varying degrees) the practice. It is argued that the churches are able to extend marriage not simply to lesbian and gay couples, but to some couples living together before marriage (Thatcher 2002). There are two crucial steps in this suggestion. First, two kinds of cohabitors need to be distinguished, best expressed by the terms "prenuptial" and "nonnuptial." Prenuptial cohabitors intend to marry (proceed to the nuptials) at some time in the future, whereas nonnuptial cohabitors live together without reference to marriage. Second, biblical and premodern practice, East and West, expected couples to enter marriage by betrothal. Mary and Joseph are the most obvious example. The name of the marriage service in some Episcopalian churches, "the solemnization of matrimony" is reminiscent of earlier times when the marriage was believed already to have begun. What we now think of as the marriage service is in fact the final phase of a process when vows in the present tense become irrevocable. Protestants inherited the practice of betrothal but regarded it suspiciously, not least because it led in some cases to false promises of marriage that in turn produced promiscuity and unwanted pregnancies.

Relics of ancient betrothal liturgies are found, generally unrecognized, in many Protestant marriage services. The future tense question "Will you take . . .?" and the answer "I will," belong originally to the spousals rather than the nuptials, and these two events were once separated in time. "Engagement" is a modern, informal, and inadequate replacement of betrothal. Because there is now widespread sexual experience before marriage, the argument that betrothal would further encourage it lacks conviction. Its reintroduction would allow the passing from singleness to marriage to be negotiated as a process, with liturgical "markers" on the way, and its availability would provoke due pastoral reflection among people informally living together. Whereas betrothal has never been strong in Protestant traditions, Protestant attentiveness to Scripture may yet revive it. St. Paul compares the Corinthian church to a bride betrothed but not yet presented to Christ her "true and only husband" (II Corinthians 11:2–3). Moreover it is likely that the story of Jesus at the well with the Samaritan women (John 4:1–42) is to be understood as a betrothal story because it relies on the conventions found in the betrothals of Rebecca (Genesis 24), Rachel (Genesis 29), and Zipporah (Exodus 2).

Marriage and Power

All parts of Christendom now assert the human love of the partners for one another to be fundamental to marriage. Within Protestantism there has always been tension between men and women being equal partners in mutual love, and being unequal partners in the sharing of power. This tension became acute with the rise of feminism, and the increasing realization that women in the Scriptures are almost uniformly subordinate to men. In particular the "household codes" of the New Testament (Ephesians 5:21–6:9; Colossians 3:18–22; I Peter 2:18–3:7; I Timothy 2:8–15; Titus 2:1–10) all enjoin the submission of wives to husbands and the authority of husbands over wives. Fundamentalist and conservative evangelical Christians understand these texts to teach "male headship," whereas more liberal Protestants either identify the GENDER hierarchy as a contingent historical matter, no longer relevant, or set these texts against others (chiefly Galatians 3:28 and Ephesians 5:21), which seem to express gender equality. A standard way of neutralizing the sexism of these texts is to assume a radical equality of the sexes in the earliest Christianity, which, in the absence of the parousia and as the political implications of the revolutionary ethic became known, was soon overlaid by more familiar and worldly conventions (Ruether 1998). FUNDAMENTALISM in all the world's religions is an extreme, dogmatic phenomenon. In its Protestant versions it manifests itself in male headship and homophobia that are increasingly seen in the secular community as evidence of the failure of Christianity to come of age.

Domestic violence against WOMEN is sufficiently shocking and prevalent for some women to argue that marriage is an unsafe institution. The extent of violence against women and children is only slowly becoming known, and it is a fair assumption that a majority of it always was, and probably still is, unreported. Alongside the practical questions about how to reduce male violence toward women universally are uncomfortable research questions: whether Christianity among the religions has a poorer record in the treatment of women; and whether the negative attitudes toward women that were an undoubted feature of historical theology remain influential, even if they live on in secular forms. Although some marriages are violent, the incidence of violence in heterosexual relationships that are not marriages is considerably greater. Because fundamentalism is based on submission to authority, and authority is associated in Protestant fundamentalism with maleness, the possibility exists that the belief system into which marriages are set predisposes to male–female conflict (Cooper-White 1995).

"Critical Familism" and the "Critical Culture of Marriage"

Don Browning and his coauthors influentially advocate "critical familism" and a "critical culture of marriage." These, they say, "entail a full equality between husband and wife and a commitment to the reflection, communication, and openness needed to implement it" (Browning et al. 1997:2). They examine "power relations" within the family and advocate a "restructuring of the ecology of supports for families so that extended family, church, civil society, government, and market can be helpful to the conjugal couple and their children." The equality of the sexes will require theological explication, given that the assumption of gender equality in early secular liberal humanism lacks theological weight. A theological case for the equality of the sexes might constitute several strands. One is the conviction that women and men alike bear the image of God. Another, derived from renewed Christian Trinitarian thought, sees God as a Communion of Persons-in-Relation, so that human personal relations potentially reflect in a finite way the divine relations between the Persons of God. These analogies are more developed in Catholic and Orthodox thought, largely because they deploy a language that is not obviously biblical. However, Protestantism may have much to learn here, and an implication for the area of marriage is that the *divine* Persons really are fully equal (subordinationism is a clear HERESY). Another

strand is the realization that God in Christ became *human,* not merely male flesh.

Christians commending marriage will be critical also of the CULTURE surrounding it. Linda Waite (2001) has shown convincingly that married people generally enjoy happier, healthier lives than unmarried people, and research on children of broken marriages, although contested, indicates significant problems that, in many cases, are preventable by married couples staying together. Given that marriage may be favorably contrasted with its alternatives, and divorce is not a panacea for the resolution of marital difficulties, Christians do not need to rely solely on theological arguments in their support for marriage. There is, however, a powerful and positive convergence of theological and social thought toward the view that marriages are good for couples, children, and the wider society. In this respect the purposes of marriage stated in countless marriage liturgies stand completely vindicated.

"Rereading" Marriage?

Whatever happens to Protestantism, the emphasis on the BIBLE will remain central to it. Article 12 of the thirty-nine ARTICLES OF RELIGION of the Anglican Church might stand prototypically of the Protestant tradition: "Holy Scripture containeth all things necessary to salvation: so that whatsoever is not read therein, nor may be proved thereby, is not to be required of any man . . . ." Because loyalty to Scripture exceeds loyalty to the Protestant reformers it is possible that Protestants will reread Scripture, taking to it a different agenda from that of the reformers. It may become increasingly clear that the New Testament does not endorse marriage with the enthusiasm, say, of Luther. For example, Jesus in Luke's gospel (20:34–36) warns that "The men and women of this world marry; but those who have been judged worthy of a place in the other world, and of the resurrection from the dead do not marry, for they are no longer subject to death." More familiar are the warnings of St. Paul that marriage is a "worldly affair," and that spouses would be "pulled in two directions" (I Corinthians 7:34), finding it impossible to please each other and please the Lord. Marriage in the thought of Augustine and Chrysostom replicates the suspicion of marriage that Paul himself confides to the Corinthians. Marriage is just not normative in the way the early Protestants, anxious to disassociate themselves from priestly celibacy and marital sacramentality, may have supposed. Of course, a recovery of the strangeness (i.e., to us) of biblical marital teaching may not have predictable consequences for a growing theological understanding. It may, however, lead to a more honest recognition of the dissatisfactions of marriage, and a more effective way of dealing with these pastorally. Further, because in many Western societies only half of adults are married, it may lead to an increasing recognition of holiness amid the unmarried complexity of much personal and social life.

A cursory reading of the Gospels also yields a vision of the family that is spiritually, not biologically, constituted. The family of the church is almost always placed above the biological family in spiritual importance; Jesus identifies everyone who "does the will of God" as his mother and brothers (Mark 3:31–35). The happiness of "those who hear the word of God and keep it" exceeds the happiness of Jesus's mother in bearing and suckling him (Luke 11:27–28). The poor and disabled are invited to dinner in preference to family and friends (Luke 14:12–14). The birth of the "children of God," through trusting God's Word become flesh, are said to be "born not of human stock, by the physical desire of a human father, but of God" (John 1:13). Although these sayings must be read alongside "the elegant and powerful affirmation of marriage and family that is to be found in the words of Jesus" (Post 2000:45), they have hardly been influential in Protestant history, and are capable of challenging conventional assumptions about the content of biblical teaching about families. Christians are having to devote as much attention to their reception of the biblical text as they are to uncovering its "meaning." Perhaps the first step in receiving the teaching of the gospels (and the Fathers) on the ambivalence of marriage and family is to recognize that the church's appreciation of it is partial, and the recovery of its strangeness may prompt new insights from God's Spirit in a postmodern world.

Doctrinal and moral issues cannot be separated from basic questions about how the Bible is read, and about how, and indeed whether, reformed traditions of Christianity continue to reform themselves. If the reign of God in the teaching of Jesus overthrows worldly assumptions in the name of self-giving love, there is warrant here for regarding one's spouse and children as first among "neighbors." This is the priority that the hallowing of marriage in all Christian traditions seeks to protect, although if "agapic" relations are learned and practiced there, they do not end there, because the circle extends outward, even to our enemies (Matthew 5:44).

See also Anglicanism; Catholicism, Protestant Reactions; Clergy, Marriage of; Covenant Theology; Evangelicalism; Lutheranism; Orthodoxy, Eastern; Secularization

References and Further Reading

Browning, Don, Bonnie J. Miller-McLemore, Pamela D. Couture, K. Brynoll Lyon, and Robert M. Franklin. *From Culture Wars to Common Ground: Religion and the American Family Debate.* Louisville, KY: Westminster John Knox Press, 1997.

Common Worship. http://www.cofe.anglican.org.commonworship/books (Accessed April 11, 2002).

Cooper-White, Pamela. *The Cry of Tamar: Violence against Women and the Church's Response.* Minneapolis, MN: Fortress Press, 1995.

General Assembly Special Committee on Human Sexuality, Presbyterian Church (USA). *Keeping Body and Soul Together: Sexuality, Spirituality, and Social Justice.* 1991.

Monti, Joseph. *Arguing About Sex: The Rhetoric of Christian Sexual Morality.* Albany, NY: State University of New York, 1995.

Post, Stephen G. *More Lasting Unions: Christianity, the Family, and Society.* Grand Rapids, MI/Cambridge, UK: Eerdmans, 2000.

Ruether, Rosemary Radford. *Women and Redemption: A Theological History.* London: SCM Press, 1998.

Thatcher, Adrian, ed. *Celebrating Christian Marriage.* Edinburgh and New York: T&T Clark. 2002.

———. *Living Together and Christian Ethics.* Cambridge: Cambridge University Press, 2002.

———. *Marriage after Modernity: Christian Marriage in Postmodern Times.* Sheffield, UK/New York: Sheffield Academic Press/New York University Press, 1999.

Waite, Linda J. *The Case for Marriage: Why Married People Are Happier, Healthier and Better Off Financially.* New York: Broadway Books, 2001.

Witte, John, Jr. *From Sacrament to Contract: Marriage, Religion, and Law in the Western Tradition.* Louisville, KY: Westminster John Knox Press, 1997.

ADRIAN THATCHER

MARTINEAU, JAMES (1805–1900)

English Unitarian, philosopher, and theologian. Born in Norwich, ENGLAND, in 1805, James Martineau was educated at the Norwich Grammar School and at the Lant Carpenter school in Bristol. Following this, he spent some time as an apprentice under the civil engineer Samuel Fox, but, having had a CONVERSION experience, abandoned his pursuit of engineering at the age of 16 to pursue what he felt was his calling to the ministry.

Martineau enrolled in Manchester College, York, in 1822 to begin his ministerial studies. After completing his studies, he took up a pastoral position at the Eustace Street Chapel, Dublin, and later, in 1832, a position as pastor at the Paradise Street Chapel, Liverpool. In Liverpool, Martineau's academic interests came to fruition with the publication of his first book, *Rationale of Religious Enquiry* (1836), in which he advocated the AUTHORITY of reason over Scripture. His reputation as a scholar persisted, and in 1840 he became Professor of Moral Philosophy at Manchester New College. During this time he maintained his pastoral position in Liverpool, but in 1857, when the college moved to London, he left his Liverpool congregation to dedicate himself fully to academic life.

Martineau was highly influenced by German Idealism and spent a year studying in GERMANY from 1848 to 1849. In 1869 he was made principal of Manchester New College, a position he held until his retirement in 1885, and gained the respect of many prominent intellectuals. He is perhaps best known for his arguments in support of theism on the grounds of an ostensible moral law intuited from, and built into, the structure of the universe, and for his support of the authority of human conscience. His published works include *A Study of Spinoza* (1882), *Types of Ethical Theory* (1885), *A Study of Religion* (1888), and *The Seat of Authority in Religion* (1890).

See also Unitarian Universalist Association

References and Further Reading

Carpenter, J. Estlin. *James Martineau*. London: Philip Green, 1905.

Drummond, James, and C. B. Upton. *The Life and Letters of James Martineau*. 2 vols. London: James Nisbet, 1902.

ALEC JARVIS

MARTYRS AND MARTYROLOGIES

Derived from the Greek *martyria*, "testimony, witness, confession [of faith]," the designation of human beings as "martyrs" quickly became limited in the early Christian church to those who gave witness to their faith in Jesus Christ by sacrificing their lives in the face of persecution. Modern Western scholars have expanded this usage, applying the term to all who die for any belief system. Some Hebrew prophets were killed for their proclamation (Matthew 23:30–37), and the period of the Maccabeans produced martyrs as Jews resisted the attempts of the Greek-Syrian monarch Antiochus Epiphanes to impose Hellenistic CULTURE on them and eradicate their religion (168 B.C.). From its inception Christianity has encountered opposition in cultures into which it moved and even in which it had an established history, and it has produced adherents in these situations who were willing to die for their faith. Reports on the deaths of martyrs have been used as devotional literature throughout much of the Christian CHURCH.

Martyrs in Ancient and Medieval Christianity

The Christian claim that Jesus was "Son of Man" elicited almost immediate persecution because this claim, referring to the vision of Daniel (7:13–14), where "One like a Son of Man" had the characteristics of God, was interpreted as blasphemy by Jewish leaders (Matthew 26:64–65: cf. the case of Stephen, Acts 6–7). Christian claims that the church had exclusive knowledge of the true God, the public perception that as outsiders Christians threatened the public good, and Christian resistance to the required religious sacrifices of imperial Rome created widespread persecution and many martyrs between the 60s of the first century A.D. and the legalization of Christianity within the Roman Empire in the early fourth century. Roman officials used a variety of methods of execution in efforts to stamp out those whom they regarded as atheists and traitors because they refused to sacrifice to the emperor for the benefit of the society. Although persecutions generally reduced the number of adherents of the Christian faith temporarily, Tertullian's observation that "the blood of the martyrs is the seed of the church" is true because the willingness to sacrifice oneself for the faith impressed and attracted those outside the church into its midst. The heroic deaths of these witnesses became one basis for the veneration of the SAINTS and their relics in early Christendom because the merit of their sacrifice was regarded as having earned special effectiveness for their prayers and powers.

Christian missionaries have often suffered martyrdom as they sought to preach their message to non-Christian peoples. Earliest examples outside the Roman Empire include executions in Persia, Armenia, and Georgia in the third and fourth centuries. Arian persecution of orthodox Christians produced martyrs especially in North Africa in the fourth and fifth centuries. Resistance of northern and eastern European peoples to the Christian mission led to the killing of many, especially monks, for example, Boniface and fifty-two companions in Frisia (754), or Adalbert of Prague in Prussia (997). Although Islam provided for limited toleration of "people of the Book," that is, Jews and Christians, its advance across North Africa into Spain and into the Byzantine Empire in the seventh and eighth centuries produced Christian martyrs.

Martyrdom declined in Europe in the Middle Ages as Christianity had become the established religion in most parts of Europe, but the advance of Christianity into pagan areas in central and eastern Europe met resistance to Christian CONVERSION, often in the generation after the initial large-scale conversions, in pagan reactions. Defiance of colonization by neighboring Christian powers also resulted in death for monks and other missionaries. The medieval church believed it only right and proper that heretics be executed to protect the faithful from their false ideas, and throughout the Middle Ages some were. Particularly Waldensians in ITALY and followers of John Wycliffe in ENGLAND and Jan Hus in Bohemia who had been slain for their deviant teaching were later heralded as martyrs in Protestant martyrology.

Martyrs in the Reformation

Suppression of calls for reform from humanists and others had begun before MARTIN LUTHER's appearance on the European stage, particularly in Spain in the fifteenth century. When the Protestant reformers began introducing proposals for change in the church's teaching and moral life, Roman Catholic officials used laws against heretics to try to restore the old order. The execution by burning of two of Luther's followers, the Augustinian monks Johann van Esch and Heinrich Voes, in Brussels on July 1, 1523, elicited Luther's comment in a tract, the first attempt at Protestant martyrology, and a hymn (the first he composed) dedicated to their memory. He rejected the medieval view that dying for the faith was a heroic human effort that won merit in God's sight. Instead he viewed martyrdom as a gift from God, the opportunity to give witness to Christ, even though it was at the same time an assault by the devil against God's people. Although his specific definition of martyrdom as God's gift did not prevail among his followers and other Protestants, they did not return to the medieval interpretation of dying for the faith as meritorious in God's sight. Instead they viewed martyrs as casualties in Satan's war against God's truth and as instruments for spreading Christ's gospel. Thus Protestant reports generally viewed martyrdom less as an occasion to relate gory details of human suffering, and more to highlight confession of the biblical message.

Because adherents of the Lutheran REFORMATION often lived in lands controlled by sympathetic princes and municipal governments, Lutherans suffered relatively less persecution in the sixteenth century than did Calvinists under the French establishment and the Dutch under the Habsburg government's Inquisition. Nonetheless Luther himself used accounts of executions and assassinations of Protestants, in German lands (e.g., Heinrich von Zutphen, Leonard Kayser, Georg Winkler) and elsewhere (the English ROBERT BARNES), to proclaim his message in print. Others did the same, including his colleagues PHILIPP MELANCHTHON and JOHANNES BUGENHAGEN, and MARTIN BUCER's associate in Strasbourg, the humanist Spaniard Francisco de Enzinas (ca. 1520–ca. 1552), who chronicled the martyr's deaths of Spanish confessors of Protestant THEOLOGY in GERMANY and other lands.

Persecution of humanist and Protestant reformers began in the 1520s and 1530s in FRANCE. King Henry II revived the prosecution of heretics through the reinstitution of a HERESY court, the *chambre ardente,* in 1548. With the massacre of a group of HUGUENOTS at WORSHIP in Wassy in 1562 by the zealous Roman Catholic duke of Lorraine, François de Guise, religious war broke out in France. The murder of Calvinist believers climaxed with the Saint Bartholomew's Day massacre of August 1572, in which the leadership of the Huguenots, including GASPARD DE COLIGNY (1519–1572), the admiral of France, and many adherents throughout France (estimates vary from five to ten thousand) were killed by Roman Catholic officials and partisans. More Huguenots died for their faith in the quarter century thereafter, until TOLERATION was secured by the EDICT OF NANTES (1598). With its revocation in 1685, persecution broke out again, and more than one hundred Reformed pastors were executed by Roman Catholic authorities as King Louis XIV sought to enforce religious conformity. Under Habsburg rule in the NETHERLANDS, Protestant movements, above all the Calvinist, also produced an estimated 1,300 martyrs between 1523 and 1566, and in the wars that followed during the subsequent half century the government continued to pursue the eradication of Calvinist and Anabaptist churches through violence.

The regime of HENRY VIII had executed Protestant dissidents in England before and after the king's break with Rome (1534). Sir Thomas More, who had as Henry's lord chancellor sent Protestants to the stake, was himself executed for treason because of his refusal to acknowledge Henry as head of the English church (1535); the Roman Catholic Church canonized him as a martyr in 1935. Henry's daughter Mary Tudor, alienated from Henry by his treatment of her mother, Queen Catherine, and herself, was eager to reverse the Reformation instituted by her father and particularly her brother Edward's government (1547–1553) and restore England to papal obedience. Under the guidance of her counselors, including bishop Stephen Gardiner (c. 1497–1555) and archbishop Reginald Pole (1500–1558) as well as priests in the company of her husband, Philip of Spain, she launched a persecution of Protestants that took a toll of more than three hundred men and women between late 1555 and her death in 1558. Among those burned for their faith on charges of heresy were the Protestant bishops John Hooper, HUGH LATIMER, Nicholas Ridley, and archbishop THOMAS CRANMER. The government of Mary's half-sister ELIZABETH I (ruled 1558–1603) executed approximately the same number of Roman Catholics for sedition, especially after Pope Pius V pronounced the queen's deposition. The Roman Catholic church regards many of them, for example, Edmund Campion (canonized 1970), as martyrs.

Anabaptists in the sixteenth century inherited the "outsider" status of their spiritual ancestors, the antisacramental, anticlerical, millenarian protest groups of the Middle Ages (see ANABAPTISM). Their contempt for infant BAPTISM earned them death by drowning instead of the burning normally used to execute heretics. Because they refused to take part in certain aspects of society, they were often persecuted as seditious rather than strictly speaking as heretics, particularly by Lutheran and Calvinist governments that normally rejected the execution of those whom they regarded as false teachers because of their belief that only God's Word and not the temporal sword could correct error and heresy. Beginning with the drowning of the Anabaptist Felix Manz in HULDRYCH ZWINGLI's Zurich (1527) and the executions of most of the sixty who took part in the meetings called "the martyrs synod" in Augsburg (1527), repression of Anabaptists continued throughout the early modern period, with as many as three thousand martyrs' deaths in the sixteenth and seventeenth centuries, most in Roman Catholic jurisdictions.

Martyrdom in the Seventeenth through Nineteenth Centuries

Continued efforts in Roman Catholic lands to repress Protestant movements brought about some martyrdoms in seventeenth-century central Europe. The eradication of Hussite and other Protestant churches in Bohemia and Moravia during the Thirty Years' War involved executions of committed members of these groups as well as extensive exiling of their clerical and lay leadership. As the Habsburg government forcibly returned Lutheran and Reformed congregations in Silesia, Slovakia, and HUNGARY to papal obedience in crackdowns between 1610 and 1670, many of their pastors were condemned to life sentences in the galleys.

Throughout the early modern period Christian missionaries and their converts were laying down their lives for their faith in Asia and AFRICA. In some cases martyrdom resulted from religious and cultural reaction to missionary activity as a foreign and thus threatening element being introduced into society, sometimes in connection with colonializing efforts. In other cases local political forces used Christians as scapegoats to advance their own power. In yet others the church's leadership involved itself in tribal and territorial politics with the result that believers suffered persecution as members of the church but within a larger social context.

Widespread conversion by Franciscans and Jesuits in the second half of the sixteenth century aroused opposition from the traditional culture of JAPAN; beginning in 1587 a half century of persecution brought the martyr's death to several dozen European missionaries and thousands of Japanese believers, many by crucifixion. Similar persecutions produced thousands of martyrs in CHINA in the eighteenth and nineteenth centuries, in KOREA during the nineteenth century.

In East Africa around 1885 bloody persecution of Anglican and Roman Catholic converts broke out as local political forces within the kingdom of Buganda and produced missionary and native martyrs. Such persecution has been often repeated in the confusion of postcolonial Africa. In Uganda in the 1970s dictator Idi Amin put thousands of Christians to death for their faith. Thousands also testified to their faith with their lives in other parts of Asia and Africa, including both missionaries and native believers. Mission Covenant missionary doctor Paul Carlson (1928–1964) and ASSEMBLIES OF GOD missionary J. W. Tucker (1915–1964) were shot in the midst of civil war while working to bring healing and the gospel to the Congo. Presbyterian W. Don McClure (1906–1977) perished at the hands of rebels in Ethiopia, where he had worked for a half century.

Martyrdom in Modern Repressive Societies

Secularizing forces in Europe first turned to violence against Christians during the FRENCH REVOLUTION, as successive ruling factions in Paris sought to establish the religion of reason and eradicate the church. Roman Catholic priests and lay people were executed for their defense of the faith. These events foreshadowed the massive persecutions of Christians in the twentieth century, which produced more Christian martyrs than those of the nineteen previous centuries.

Karl Marx's conviction that religion, above all Christianity, had led to the suppression of the masses stands behind the anti-Christian stance of Marxist parties (see COMMUNISM). The brutal suppression of the Christian church in RUSSIA begun soon after the Bolshevik Revolution included crucifixion of Orthodox clergy (see ORTHODOXY, EASTERN). In addition to an estimated seven hundred thousand Orthodox Christians who became victims of persecution under the Soviet regime, thousands more Protestant and Roman Catholic martyrs laid down testimony to Christ through their deaths when Communist officials in the Soviet Union and, to a lesser extent in satellite states, killed believers by direct sentences to death or through fatal conditions in labor camps, the gulags, to which they were sentenced. The entire ministeria of German and Finnish Lutheran churches in Russia were eliminated by immediate capital punishment or sentences to labor camps, and after Soviet occupation of Estonia and Latvia (1940, 1944/45) Lutheran (see LUTHERANISM), Baptist, and Roman Catholic pastors and other church leaders from those countries were also eliminated by Communist authorities. Police action and officially condoned vigilante violence continued to be directed against BAPTISTS and Pentecostals in the Soviet Union throughout the Communist period, from 1918 into the 1990s (see PENTECOSTALISM). Chinese, Indochinese, and North Korean Communists also employed brutal tactics in the suppression of Christian churches after 1949. The deaths of thousands of martyrs in China did not bring about the end of the church but instead generated the phenomenal growth of underground congregations.

Under the National Socialist regime in Germany and the areas it conquered, Christians gave their lives for their faith from the early 1930s to 1945. Nazi policy planned ultimately to eliminate the Christian churches, but in the twelve years of the Thousand Year Reich it aimed at the submission of the church to its governance and the subversion of the churches through the GERMAN CHRISTIANS movement, with imprisonment and execution used when deemed appropriate. Roman Catholic and Protestant leaders were arrested, and some were put to death by Nazi officials in concentration camps. Many of those who led the resistance to Hitler did so on the basis of Christian convictions and, although executed for treason, earned death in carrying out the dictates of their faith. The German DIETRICH BONHOEFFER (1906–1945), the Danish Kaj Munck (1898–1944), and the Polish Maximilian Kolbe, O.F.M. (1894–1941) typify the roles and spectrum of resistance to the antichristian ideology and practice of National Socialism found among Christians.

Muslim groups have increased significantly the number of Christian martyrs at the end of the twentieth century. The government of Turkey slaughtered Armenian Christians (1894–1896 and 1914–1915) in attempts to cleanse their state of non-Muslim elements; Greek and Syrian Christians within the Ottoman Empire also felt the brunt of this policy. In INDONESIA, Pakistan, NIGERIA, Sudan, and other Asian and African nations, large-scale official or unofficial persecution of local Christian groups was tolerated or implemented by Muslim governments in the postcolonial period, especially after 1970. Tribal warfare and civil violence in west African states, including Nigeria, LIBERIA, and neighboring lands, in the 1980s and 1990s frequently involved attempts by Muslims to eliminate Christian forces in their nations by massacre and assassination. Victims of the violence of Hindu fundamentalists begun in INDIA in the 1990s must also be counted among the most recent Christian martyrs.

The nature of the Christian message, which creates criticism of all cultures and demands public testimony regarding Jesus Christ, invites persecution from those who do not share its understanding of human life and society, and thus, martyrdom is a constitutive element of the history of the Christian church.

Martyrologies

Accounts of the deaths of martyrs circulated in Christian churches by the second century in epistolary form (e.g., on Polycarp [executed c. 167] and on the martyrs of Vienne and Lyon [c. 177]) and became a part of early Christian devotional literature and historical writing, for example, by Eusebius (c. 265–c. 340). Such reports were integrated into the legends of the saints and often elaborated with descriptions of miracles effected by the martyrs or their relics by the early Middle Ages.

With the Protestant Reformation the recounting of the deaths of martyrs took on importance as an instrument of polemic against Roman Catholic persecutors and of the cultivation of Protestant piety. The Protestant stories of dying for the faith focused more on the content of the martyrs' testimony than on their sufferings, and thus served as means of propagating the call for reform and the fresh interpretation of the Christian tradition issued by the reformers. In the mouths of the martyrs were recorded both harsh criticism of the false teaching and superstitious practices of the medieval church and simple presentation of the evangelical message of SALVATION by God's mercy in Christ's DEATH and resurrection. Calls for steadfastness of faith against the devil's forces in the apocalyptic battle of the Last Days accompanied these CONFESSIONS of faith. Luther's published comments on the burning of his Augustinian brothers van Esch and Voes (1523) initiated the use of such accounts as part of the propagation of his views. A number of other such published reports appeared over the next quarter century throughout western Europe.

In late 1549, Luther's former student Ludwig Rabus (1524–1592) lost his position as pastor of the cathedral in Strasbourg as the recatholicizing religious policy of Emperor Charles V associated with the so-called AUGSBURG INTERIM of 1548 was imposed on the city. Only partially employed in the years immediately thereafter, Rabus turned his energies to the creation of a collection of martyr stories, beginning with a Latin volume on biblical martyrs that appeared in early 1552. In 1554 he issued the first of eight volumes of such stories in German, the last of which appeared in 1558; he recast the entire collection in two folio volumes in 1571/1572. Apart from short introductions Rabus did nothing but reprint accounts he had found in other published sources. He intended to place contemporary martyrs in the long context of the struggle of God's people against Satanic attack (see DEVIL). God's providence guided all of world history, particularly the history of his church, Rabus was convinced, and therefore he viewed the martyrdoms he presented as elements of God's combat against the false belief that deprived people of salvation. Because he defined his subject in this eschatological encounter of truth with deception and error (see ESCHATOLOGY), he did not restrict his definition of "martyr" to those executed for their faith and included some who gave dramatic testimony of the Christian message in his compilation. Chief among them was Luther himself. Rabus began with biblical and patristic martyrs, included a few Wycliffites (although not Wycliffe), Hus, and Jerome of Prague, and placed the major emphasis on reports of German, English, French, Dutch, Italian, and Spanish witnesses of Protestant expressions of biblical teaching, most of whom died at the hands of ecclesiastical officials. In fact, in the absence of intense persecution in most Lutheran lands, other forms of pursuing polemic against Roman Catholic attempts at suppressing Lutheran teaching and of recounting the history of the church overshadowed Rabus's preferred genre, and the martyrology did not occupy an important place in LUTHERANISM.

That was not the case among French, Dutch, and English Protestants. Both in Anglican, especially Puritan, circles and among Calvinists in France and other lands, these works inspired resistance to Roman Catholic threats and provided inspiration for personal piety for generations.

The Genevan publisher Jean Crespin (c. 1520–1572) released the first edition of his book of martyrs in 1554. He had become an adherent of JOHN CALVIN after legal studies in Louvain. He established a large printing operation after fleeing to Geneva in 1548 to avoid prosecution, having witnessed the public burning of another Calvinist in Paris, and he produced a variety of academic and religious books, many of them Calvinist, in several languages. His own *History of Martyrs,* issued in ever-expanding editions through 1619, grew as he and his successors added more accounts to their narrative. He used published sources, including Rabus (whose later volumes copied material from Crespin), and also unpublished reports that he gathered as more and more Huguenots were killed for their profession of faith. He provided readers more narrative and interpretation than did Rabus. Crespin began his unfolding of the history of martyrdom in the late Middle Ages, referring to the suffering of Christ and the execution of Stephen but not developing the biblical and patristic roots of the phenomenon in detail. He, too, found the stories of the martyrs to be examples of God's providence and rule over his church because he was confident that their deaths contributed to the defeat of Satan and his forces of deception. The Genevan church leader Simon Goulart (1543–1628) continued Crespin's work after his death. German editions appeared from the pens of Christoph Rab (1590) and Paul Crocius (1608); ex-

cerpted and edited versions were printed in French, German, Dutch, Polish, and Romansh into the early eighteenth century.

Depending on the previously published works of JOHN FOXE (1517–1587), Crespin, and Rabus for his source material, the Calvinist pastor from Antwerp Adriaan Corneliszoon van Haemstede (1520–1562) incorporated many of their accounts with his own reporting of martyrs for the faith from the NETHERLANDS into his *History of the Martyrs Who Shed Their Blood as Witnesses of Evangelical Truth,* published in 1559. He composed the work while living under the threat of arrest in the Netherlands; only after its publication did controversy within the Antwerp Reformed circle drive him to England. His more polished narrative presented details of heresy trials and executions along with the confessions of faith they elicited. He thus provided a book of devotion and instruction that shaped Dutch Calvinist piety. Anonymous editors expanded his volume, which was officially commended to the church by the Synod of Dordrecht of 1578.

Foxe's massive *Book of Martyrs* (as it was popularly designated), first published in 1563 under the title *Acts and Monuments of These Latter and Perilous Days* on the basis of an earlier Latin work, his *Commentary on Events in the Church* (1554), exercised an inestimably strong influence on English Protestant piety. Building on Foxe's desire to demonstrate the catholic roots and nature of Protestant theology he focused on the persecution of Mary Tudor that drove him from England to Rabus's Strasbourg in 1554. His *Commentary* supplemented his early research with other sources, including Crespin, John Bale, and MATTHIAS FLACIUS's *Catalog of Witnesses of the Truth* (1556). Sharp scholarly debate in the nineteenth and twentieth centuries over his historical method and the accuracy of his reporting of cases has largely substantiated his careful and conscientious practice of research in archival and printed sources and of recording his narratives. His literary skill, along with the popular reaction against the Marian persecution, and the threat against England from the papacy and Spain in the later sixteenth century contributed to making his work a major factor in determining the texture of English piety.

Annals of individual Anabaptists' sufferings or of the persecution of their congregations were published throughout the sixteenth century, but the first attempt to gather several into a single work came with *The Sacrifice of the Lord,* edited by Hendricks van Schoonrewoerd, printed in Emden in 1562. This work strove to provide comfort and encouragement for its readers, using hymnody or poetry to present accounts of suffering and confessions of its largely Dutch martyrs. They had served as God's instruments in the battle against Satan. Dutch Anabaptists divided over which representatives of their position were truly worthy martyrs and which was the proper edition of the *History of Martyrs* produced under the leadership of the Haarlem pastor Jakob Outerman and his associates Joost Govertsz and Hans de Ries in 1615. The Anabaptist martyrological tradition came to its climax in the work of Dordrecht preacher Tileman Janszoon van Bragt (1625–1664), the *The Bloody Theater* of 1560, reissued under its popular title, *The Martyrs' Mirror,* in 1685. It contained a rehearsal of earlier martyrs who had rejected infant baptism and then told the stories of over eight hundred such martyrs, largely Dutch, from the sixteenth and seventeenth centuries. It appeared in Dutch, German, and English into the nineteenth century.

Accounts of sacrifice of life for the sake of Christ have continued to appear in print throughout the nineteenth and twentieth centuries. The classics, particularly Foxe's, as well as new popular collections, treating also twentieth-century martyrs, continue to serve as devotional and inspirational literature in some Christian circles.

References and Further Reading

Bourdeaux, Michael. *Faith on Trial in Russia*. London: Hodder, 1971.

———. *Patriarch and Prophets. Persecution of the Russian Orthodox Church Today*. New York: Praeger, 1970.

Boxer, Charles Ralph. *The Christian Century in Japan 1549–1650*. Berkeley: University of California Press, 1951.

Delehaye, Hippolyte. *Les origines du culte des martyrs*. Brussels, Belgium: Société des Bollandistes, 1933.

Frend, W. H. C. *Martyrdom and Persecution in the Early Church*. New York: New York University Press, 1967.

Gilmont, Jean François. *Jean Crespin, un éditeur réformé du SVIe siècle*. Geneva, Switzerland: Droz, 1981.

Gregory, Brad S. *Salvation at the Stake, Christian Martyrdom in Early Modern Europe*. Cambridge, MA: Harvard University Press, 1999.

Kingdon, Robert M. *Myths about the St. Bartholomew's Day Massacres 1572–1576*. Cambridge, MA: Harvard University Press, 1988.

Kolb, Robert. *For All the Saints: Changing Perceptions of Martyrdom and Sainthood in the Lutheran Reformation*. Macon, GA: Mercer University Press, 1987.

Marshall, Paul. *Their Blood Cries Out: The Untold Stories of Persecution of Christians in the Modern World*. Dallas, TX: Word, 1997.

Meier, Kurt. *Der evangelische Kirchenkampf*. 3 vols. Göttingen: Vandenhoeck & Ruprecht, 1976.

Shea, Nina. *In the Lion's Den*. Nashville, TN: Broadman and Holman, 1997.

Talonen, Jouko. *Church under the Pressure of Stalinism: The Development of the Status and Activities of the Soviet Latvian Evangelical-Lutheran Church in 1944–1950*. Jyväskylä, Finland: PSHY, 1997.

Wood, Diana, ed. *Martyrs and Martyrologies*. Oxford, UK: Blackwell, 1993.

ROBERT KOLB

MARY, VIRGIN

The role of the Virgin Mary in theology and religious life has been a contested point between Catholics and Protestants from the early days of the REFORMATION. The primary theological issues of JUSTIFICATION by faith alone and SALVATION through Christ alone, as well as the reformers' insistence on the normative AUTHORITY of scripture, necessarily touched issues concerning the veneration of Mary and the SAINTS, and the role of the saints in the economy of salvation. Although the early reformers rejected many aspects of the medieval Marian cult, in general they retained a devotional attitude toward Mary and accepted the statements of the early creeds and councils concerning her titles and significance: Mary remained the *Theotokos,* the God-bearer or Mother of God, and her status as "ever-virgin" was also reaffirmed. Within several generations, however, a number of factors led to the almost complete disappearance of Mary from Protestant THEOLOGY and a marked decrease in pious devotion to Mary and the saints. Interest in Mary among Protestants was revived with the papal proclamation of the dogmas of the Immaculate Conception (1854) and the Assumption (1950), and Mary again became a topic of debate in ecumenical dialogues. There have been small movements toward a renewal of Marian piety among Protestants (e.g., the Ecumenical Society of the Blessed Virgin Mary), but in general apart from those with high-church interests, Mary has remained a foreigner to Protestant theology and piety.

Martin Luther and the Early Lutheran Tradition

MARTIN LUTHER was raised in a culture steeped in the tradition of veneration of Mary and the saints. He recounted later in life how he was taught to fear Christ, the angry judge, and to rely on Mary as a merciful mother. Luther's initial problems with indulgences led him eventually to reject a role for human merit in salvation, relying instead on Christ as the one mediator before God who provides all the GRACE required for justification. His insights had strong consequences for Marian devotion: Luther rejected any aspect of devotion or piety that in any way led people away from a focus on Christ as loving, sufficient savior. In this light he rejected Mary's roles as intercessor, mediatrix, and co-redemptrix. He criticized certain Marian devotions, such as the *Salve Regina* ("Hail, Queen"), which addresses Mary as "mother of mercy" and calls her "our life, our sweetness, and our hope." He also condemned excessive speculation about Mary, preferring to rely on scriptural witness and the pronouncements of the early CHURCH. Thus he accepted Mary's perpetual virginity, and her title of

Theotokos, adopted at the Council of Ephesus (431) both as a christological statement and to honor her. He was less clear about whether Mary's conception was maculate or immaculate, although he did agree that Mary was purified of SIN at some point before Christ's conception. Of the Marian festivals, Luther suggested that only those directly pertaining to Christ and with a scriptural basis be retained—that is, the festivals for Mary's conception and assumption should be discontinued.

Despite his concerns about the abuses associated with the Marian piety of his day, Luther felt affection for Mary and insisted that she receive due attention and respect. In his treatise on the Magnificat (521) Luther views Mary as a great exemplar of the faith. She reveals the true relationship between grace and merit: rather than counting her "humility" as a meritorious virtue, Luther instead reads the term as "low estate" because her lowliness only highlights God's gracious action in her. Mary herself gives all the praise to God, and her blessedness ("all generations will call me blessed") consists in God's regard of her. She becomes the Mother of God by bearing God's Son, not because she has some special virtues that merit the role. She does not serve as the "mother of mercy" who intercedes with Christ and God for humankind, but rather for Luther her most important role is as a prime example of the faithful Christian.

PHILIPP MELANCHTHON, author of the AUGSBURG CONFESSION and the *Apology* to it, spelled out the Lutheran position toward the saints and Mary: the saints are to be remembered to strengthen one's faith; their good works should serve as examples, but although they (following Scripture) pray for Christians, they are not to be invoked. Invocation of the saints exists neither in the BIBLE nor in the early TRADITION. This view of the proper place of Mary and the saints in the lives of the faithful is codified for Lutherans in the BOOK OF CONCORD (1580); these confessions also include the reaffirmation of Mary's perpetual virginity (in Luther's SCHMALKALDIC ARTICLES of 1537) and her title of *Theotokos,* and praise her as "the most blessed virgin" (Formula of Concord, 1577).

Huldrych Zwingli

Despite his differences with Luther, HULDRYCH ZWINGLI held similar views on Mary. His theology, however, was far more influenced by Erasmus than by Luther. Zwingli's humanism led him to intense study of the BIBLE, as well as Greek and Hebrew, and he was influenced by Erasmus's new biblical translations, his christological focus, and his disgust with the excesses and abuses in the Marian cult. Unlike Erasmus, however, Zwingli's christological focus led him to reject

any invocation of Mary and likewise any intercession or mediation on her part. The proper attitude of Christians toward Mary is one of praise and meditation; in this context, in a 1522 sermon on Mary, Zwingli approved the use of the *Ave Maria* because, he insisted, it is not a prayer, but a greeting and praise. Like Luther, Zwingli affirmed her title of *Theotokos*—her role as Christ's mother is the basis of her praise—and her perpetual virginity. Although Zwingli did not explicitly state a belief in Mary's immaculate conception, he did emphasize her sinlessness and her role in the stainlessness of Christ's conception. Mary remained a model for imitation in her holy life despite her poverty and suffering, particularly because she often meditated on divine mysteries.

HEINRICH BULLINGER, Zwingli's successor in Zurich, also preached sermons in praise of Mary. He not only accepted Mary's title of *Theotokos,* but held to her virginity *ante, in,* and *post partum.* He seems also to have held to her bodily assumption, relating it to the biblical story of the prophet Elijah.

Calvin and Calvinism

JOHN CALVIN, already a second-generation reformer, expressed far less Marian devotion than either Luther or Zwingli. His strong concern that idolatry must be avoided led him to be very cautious when discussing Mary. In particular his concern was to protect the sovereignty of God against any encroachment: veneration of the saints and calling on them for intercession was tantamount to idolatry for Calvin, and revealed the dangers in following another authority outside of Scripture. Much of Calvin's writings concerning Mary and the saints is in fact in the context of anti-Roman polemic. He rejected what he considered to be excesses and superstitions, but—like Luther and Zwingli—he retained the notion of Mary's perpetual virginity, although he did not believe that she had taken a vow. Calvin was readier to believe that Mary was subject to the ordinary forms of human sin, and seemed uncomfortable with the title *Theotokos,* preferring to call her the "Mother of the Son of God." Calvin, like Luther, felt Mary to be a great example of faith who confessed her lowliness before God. Her "blessedness" does not in fact belong to her, but is rather the grace of God. Calvin stressed that Mary's greatest blessing was not to be mother to Jesus Christ, but rather that she was a member of the body of Christ. He calls Mary both a "mirror of faith" and a good teacher.

To help Christians avoid idolatry, Calvin and his fellow pastors recommended removal of images from churches and discontinued the festivals for Mary and the saints. His sober, minimalist approach to Mary is reflected in the later Calvinist tradition: she appears only briefly in the HEIDELBERG CATECHISM (1563) in the context of the creed; in the Second HELVETIC Confession (1566) she is called "ever-virgin," and again mentioned in the context of Christ's birth.

Orthodoxy, Pietism, and the Enlightenment

In its final days the Council of Trent decreed that invocation and veneration of saints (including their relics and images) were both profitable and fitting, while denouncing abuses against legitimate piety. Mary began to be a special focus for Catholic piety and theology in the period after Trent (e.g., the mariological works of Suarez and Canisius, the spread of marian sodalities, the use of the rosary). Protestant interest in Mary decreased, especially as the cult of Mary became associated with "Catholic superstition." Protestant ORTHODOXY, primarily interested in dogma, touched only incidentally on Mary, reiterating the dogmatic formulations of the sixteenth century and rejecting the veneration and invocation of the saints. Pietists (see PIETISM) also paid little attention to Mary in their writings, although they were more interested in the practice of religion and had more knowledge of Catholicism. Many scholars have suggested that rationalism and the ENLIGHTENMENT eliminated any residual interest in the cult of Mary among Protestants, even affecting Catholic theology. Devotion to the Virgin remained more common in the CHURCH OF ENGLAND, and Anglicans continue to be closer to Roman Catholics on this issue than Protestants of other groups.

From the Nineteenth Century to the Present

The Confessional movement and a liturgical revival contributed to a greater interest in Mary and marian devotion among Protestants, particularly under the leadership of August Vilmar (1800–1868) and WILHELM LÖHE (1808–1872). Löhe published a liturgical calendar that contained three Marian festivals, affirmed Mary's perpetual virginity, and emphasized the role of saints as examples. Even greater interest in Mary was renewed with the affirmation of the Immaculate Conception in 1854; Protestants in general opposed the dogma (Karl von Hase and Eduard Preuss), although a few expressed reserved support (W. O. Dietlein).

In the early twentieth century the German "High-Church Movement" (under Friedrich Heiler) focused on liturgical renewal and ECUMENISM, taking a positive stance toward Marian devotion and celebrating Marian feasts. In 1931 the "Brotherhood of Saint Michael" was founded in Marburg, which recognized Mary as

the foremost of all the saints, and promoted the three biblical Marian feasts (which became part of official Lutheran liturgy in GERMANY in 1956). The French ecumenical community of Taizé, with roots in the Reformed tradition, also practices devotion toward Mary. Much of the twentieth-century Protestant thought concerning Mary was, understandably, negative, and those theologians influenced by the search for the historical Jesus in particular began to question long-held assumptions about Mary, including her perpetual virginity, and the virgin birth (e.g., PAUL TILLICH, EMIL BRUNNER).

With the proclamation of the dogma of the Assumption (1950), Protestants again reacted in strong opposition. They especially took issue with the dogma's unbiblical nature, and stressed that it was a blow to ecumenism. The conservative approach of Vatican II toward mariology helped to heal the ecumenical breach, and from the 1950s Protestants again gave new—and more positive—attention to Mary. Several ecumenical dialogues have focused on Mary and the saints, including the U.S. Lutheran–Catholic dialogue, whereas the *Groupe des Dombes* in FRANCE published a two-part study on the issue in 1997 and 1998. These dialogues and study groups have relied on the flowering of biblical scholarship with respect to Mary. Mary has also been the focus of some attention from feminist theologians (e.g., Mary Daly, Rosemary Ruether). Despite the increase in interest in Marian devotion and ecumenical discussions concerning Mariology, the majority of Protestants pay scant attention to Mary and often equate attention to Mary with Roman Catholic "superstition" or as challenging the authority of Scripture.

See also Catholicism, Protestant Reactions; Dialogue, Interconfessional; Jesus, Lives of

References and Further Reading

Anderson, H. George, J. Francis Stafford, and Joseph A. Burgess, eds. *The One Mediator, the Saints, and Mary.* Minneapolis, MN: Augsburg Fortress, 1992.
Kreitzer, Beth. "Reforming Mary: Images of the Virgin Mary in Lutheran Sermons of the Sixteenth Century." Ph.D. dissertation, Duke University, 2000.
Küng, Hans, and Jürgen Moltmann, eds. *Mary in the Churches.* Consilium 168. Edinburgh: T. & T. Clark; New York: The Seabury Press, 1983.
O'Meara, Thomas A. *Mary in Protestant and Catholic Theology.* New York: Sheed and Ward, 1966.
Tavard, George H. *The Thousand Faces of the Virgin Mary.* Collegeville, MN: The Liturgical Press, 1996.
Wicks, Jared. "The Virgin Mary in Recent Ecumenical Dialogues." *Gregorianum* 81 (2000): 25–57.
Wright, David F., ed. *Chosen by God: Mary in Evangelical Perspective.* London: Marshall Pickering, 1989.

BETH KREITZER

MASCULINITY

As used in the humanities and social sciences, the term "masculinity" highlights the ways in which societies define roles, behaviors, and character traits deemed appropriate for men. From this perspective masculinity is not seen as simply the result of an unchanging biologically determined male nature, but rather as the changing product of historical conditions and belief systems. Not only has Protestantism played a significant part in the generation of ideas about masculinity, it has itself been influenced by attitudes to GENDER derived from other sources. This interaction can be illustrated by examining a number of key periods of transition. The first was the era of the REFORMATION, which resulted in a reconfiguration of existing Catholic beliefs about the role of men in society. Then in the eighteenth and early nineteenth centuries, under the impact of PIETISM, EVANGELICAL-ISM, and economic change, a more domesticated and in some ways less stern Protestant ideal of masculinity evolved. By contrast, the second half of the nineteenth century saw a preoccupation with male military and sporting toughness and competitiveness. Finally in the late twentieth century, rapid economic and social change and the growth of feminism resulted in widely divergent Protestant understandings of what constitutes a desirable model of masculinity.

The Reformation

The rejection by all the reformers of celibacy and of the monastic life as the highest calling for men, led to a new emphasis on their God-given role as husbands and fathers. In the commonly named "house father literature" written by German Protestant clergy and in American and English PURITAN MARRIAGE guides, we find a common ideal of the Christian man as the head of the household responsible for both the spiritual and the temporal welfare of his family. Men were regarded as God's representatives within the family to whom servants, children, and wives owed a duty of obedience.

It should not be forgotten, however, that Protestant writers also attached great importance to the fatherly nature and responsibilities of Christian manhood. Men were not to be domestic tyrants but were to love their wives and children. However, we need to be wary of supposing that conduct books and sermons neatly mirrored the realities of family life. Such evidence as survives suggests that in the past, as now, men's relations with their wives and children encompassed a wide range of emotional registers.

In Reformation thought, men had public as well as domestic duties and powers. The divine ordering of the family, with its pattern of male headship, was considered equally applicable to the wider social and political order including the church. The Protestant erasure of both the Virgin Mary and of female saints from religious discourse and symbolism further emphasized the masculine nature of the new Protestant faith. Protestant writers also underlined a man's responsibility for providing for his family as part of the duty of care that men owed to their dependents. Work was to be regarded as a part of a man's religious calling. In this way Protestantism contributed powerfully to a pronounced feature of all Western societies: the definition of masculine selfhood in terms of a man's occupation.

Revivalism and the Domestication of Masculinity

Seventeenth- and eighteenth-century Protestant revivalist movements such as Pietism, METHODISM, and the GREAT AWAKENING redrew traditional definitions of masculinity and femininity. With the decline of CALVINISM, less stress was placed on God as a stern masculine judge and more on his tender loving qualities. At the same time women were no longer regarded as potentially more sinful than men. Increasingly it was men who came to be seen as less naturally religious than women. Economic and social changes also contributed to the sense that masculinity was problematic in religious terms. Industrialization and capitalism led to a separation of home and workplace, and wealth creation and competition were felt to expose men to moral dangers to which women in the home were not subject. As a result, women rather than men came to be regarded as the primary providers of religious instruction for their children, a trend that was reinforced by men's increasingly long absences at their place of work.

Muscular Christianity

If the early nineteenth century witnessed what has been called the feminization of Protestantism, then the second half of the period saw a reaction in favor of what the English clergyman CHARLES KINGSLEY labeled "muscular Christianity." Theologically this involved an emphasis on what were deemed to be Christ's manly qualities of heroism and toughness. It also led to a growing cult of athleticism and sport in which male physical and moral strength were increasingly conflated.

Masculinity in Question in the Late Twentieth Century

In the course of the twentieth century both the feminist movement and the decline of industries requiring male physical strength undermined traditional definitions of men as sole breadwinners and dominant partners within marriage. Gay liberation movements further challenged traditional understandings of theologically acceptable forms of masculinity. In some respects Protestantism has proved more responsive to these changes than some other forms of Christianity, for example, in the willingness of many denominations to relinquish exclusively male patterns of ministry. However, in the second half of the twentieth century deep anxieties and divisions emerged over the extent to which Christian theology should resist or participate in the process of reshaping masculine identities and behaviors. History would suggest that none of the participants in this debate can realistically hope to establish his or her own ideal as the one unchanging definition of masculinity within Protestant thought.

See also Calvinism; Evangelicalism; Feminist Theology; Gender; Great Awakening; Kingsley, Charles; Methodism; Pietism; Puritan Marriage; Reformation

References and Further Reading

Boyd, Stephen B., W. Merle Longwood, and Mark W. Muesse, eds. *Redeeming Men: Religion and Masculinities.* Louisville, KY: Westminster John Knox Press, 1996.

Ozment, Stephen. *When Fathers Ruled: Family Life in Reformation Europe.* Cambridge, MA: Harvard University Press. 1983.

Swanson, R. N. ed. *Gender and Christian Religion.* Woodbridge, Suffolk, UK: Boydell & Brewer, 1998.

Wiesner-Hanks, Merry E. *Christianity and Sexuality in the Early Modern World: Regulating Desire, Reforming Practice.* London and New York: Routledge, 2000.

SEAN GILL

MASS MEDIA

Early Protestantism and Mass Media

It can be argued that a major factor in the development of the Protestant movement was the rise of the first mass medium of the Western world in the form of print. The first printing press in the Western world was developed by Johannes Guttenberg in 1440. By means of print the middle class in Europe gained access to books that in turn led to the proliferation of new ideas and challenges to traditional views. The Protestant Reformer MARTIN LUTHER translated the BIBLE into vernacular German and the printed version of these Bibles reached 100,000 copies in his lifetime. Protestantism spread by means of printed tracts and books and became a phenomenon of the literate middle class.

Marshall McLuhan (1911–1980) was one of the most important media critics of the twentieth century. He developed a theory about the radical impact of new technological media on human CULTURE. "The Guttenberg Galaxy" was his term for the era of print as the new mass medium of the fifteenth century. This is followed by the "electronic age." The focus in this article is on the electronic age and the electronic mass media and their relationship to Protestantism in the twentieth and twenty-first centuries. The electronic and digital technologies of the twentieth and twenty-first centuries are making a radical impact on the development of all religion including Protestantism. McLuhan coined the phrase "the medium is the message," which described the inextricable link between the medium used to communicate and its influence on the message itself. Electronic mass media present Protestantism with unique challenges in the areas of integrity of communication, ETHICS, and, values.

Radio

The Christian religion and the rise of electronic media were from the very beginning closely linked. In one of the earliest trials of wireless telephony, the inventor Reginald Fessenden read passages from the Bible on Christmas Eve 1909.

One of the earliest religious broadcasts in the UNITED STATES was in 1921 when an Episcopal church service was broadcast over the first commercial radio station, KDKA, in Pittsburgh, Pennsylvania. The first Christian Broadcasting Station, WJBT (Where Jesus Blesses Thousands), was established in Chicago in 1922. Christian broadcasting kept pace with the growth of radio stations throughout the United States with a tendency for more conservative and fundamentalist groups to form the vanguard of this movement (see EVANGELICALISM; FUNDAMENTALISM). With the development of the broadcasting networks, the National Broadcasting Company (NBC) and the Columbia Broadcasting System (CBS), there was a move to make special time available to Protestant, Roman Catholic, and Jewish groups. Other religious groups had to make special local arrangements or buy time on local stations to enable them to broadcast. In 1934 the Federal Communications Act mandated noncommercial public affairs programming on all broadcasters, which led to the flourishing of religious radio broadcasts in the United States in the 1930s. The Federal Communications Commission (FCC) was established in 1934. By 1941 the FCC issued the Mayflower Decision, which established that a broadcaster cannot be an advocate. After World War II the Mayflower Decision was relaxed, which led to further growth in religious broadcasting. The proliferation of religious radio broadcasts in the United States made it a leader in the early development of religious broadcasting in the electronic media.

With the inception of the British Broadcasting Corporation (BBC) in the United Kingdom, various Christian denominations were invited to participate in a committee to coordinate religious broadcasts. John Reith, the first director general of the BBC, was an active Protestant Christian. He believed that religion should play an important role in public broadcasting and encouraged ecumenical cooperation. At first Reith encountered resistance from church leaders who were concerned that faith would be trivialized by the new mass medium. Soon the church service broadcasts from St.-Martin-in-the-Fields Anglican Church, London, became popular, which led to a music recording tradition that lasts to the present.

The use of radio broadcasting as a mass medium for Protestant communication was limited by the number of receivers in different countries and populations. By the 1930s the leading countries in radio broadcasting were the United States, GERMANY, and the United Kingdom, with other countries such as FRANCE, ITALY, Holland, DENMARK, CANADA, and SOUTH AFRICA following closely behind.

Television

With the rise of television in the United Kingdom the BBC at first attempted the same approach as with radio. It appeared that with this new mass medium some kinds of religious services were more aesthetically pleasing than others. The first television broadcast of a church service was a Roman Catholic Mass from the Abbey of St. Denis in Paris, France, in 1952. This event raised the ire of Protestants in the United Kingdom and caused much debate about religion and public broadcasting. In the mid-1950s, after some controversy, the American evangelist BILLY GRAHAM's service was broadcast from Glasgow and this event enjoyed an unusually wide audience. The BBC also tried particular religious productions in the early stages of television, like the film *Jesus of Nazareth*, produced in 1956.

In the United States the policy of noncommercial public affairs programming was not successfully transferred to network television because of the high cost of air time and production. Early attempts at religious television broadcasting include the Lutheran Church–sponsored television series of short morality plays featuring animated clay figures with the title *Davey and Goliath*. The show, which started in 1961, enjoyed more than sixty-five episodes. Another classic religious animated show, *A Charley Brown Christmas,* was created by Charles Schulz in 1965. This show is still rebroadcast every Christmas. The National Religious Broadcasters (NRB) association was formed in 1944 to further Christian broadcasting. In 1960 the FCC gave television networks permission to fill their public service slots with paid programming. However, religious broadcasts were also made exempt from the FCC "fairness doctrine," which required equal time for opposing views on television. The television industry and commercial interests started to shape religious broadcasting and the kind of religious values presented in public broadcasting. The result was that the liberal Protestant DENOMINATIONS, which relied on access to networks in radio, became marginalized in the television medium.

It was particularly evangelical and fundamentalist preachers who successfully used the television medium in communication. Billy Graham emerged as an early leader in Protestant television broadcasting when he switched from radio to television with the commencement of the broadcasts of *The Hour of Decision* in 1951. His broadcasts are based on edited versions of public appearances.

In his landmark work on television and religion, William F. Fore (1987) identifies the rise of a new religious phenomenon in television that he describes as the "electronic church," which has since become known as TELEVANGELISM. Such programs are characterized by individual charismatic leadership, expensive production, the use of computers and telephones to personalize contact with audiences, and solicitation of donations from the audience. Seminal in this development has been the influence of religious broadcaster PAT ROBERTSON, who purchased a UHF television station in Portsmouth, Virginia, in 1961 and started the program featuring the "700 Club," which moved to syndication in the 1970s. An important court case, based on an attack by the televangelist Billy James Hargis on journalist Fred Cook, went to the U.S. Supreme Court with a decision in 1969, which found that religious broadcasts were subject to the same rules as political speeches and network commentaries.

During the 1970s televangelism became one of the main features of Protestant broadcasting in the United States. This led to the proliferation of successful televangelist networks such as the Trinity Broadcasting Network (TBN) of Paul Crouch, and Praise the Lord (PTL) of Jim Bakker. During the 1980s the development of cable networks led to an increase in Protestant religious programming on television. The activities of televangelists came under public scrutiny during the late 1980s with several scandals and controversies that affected such prominent figures as the faith healer Peter Popoff, Jim and Tammy Faye Bakker, and Jimmy Swaggart. The result of the scandals was a radical drop in income for many televangelist and Christian Broadcasting channels. In response the NRB launched its Ethics and Financial Responsibility Commission in 1988. In the same year Vision Interfaith Satellite Network (VISN) was launched in the United States. In 1992 this organization changed its name to the Faith and Values Channel (F&V) and claims twenty-six million viewers by satellite. Broadcast networks such as TBN and PTL have responded to their financial decline in the United States by expanding globally on satellite.

Religious broadcasting on television in many countries is regulated by government and functions with particular restrictions and rules imposed by a particular jurisdiction. Thus, for example, in Canada, religious channels have to provide a certain amount of time for religions other than the one that operates the channel. These kinds of developments have been increasingly hard to enforce by governmental jurisdictions because of the proliferation of global satellite television delivery.

Photocopy, Computer, and Internet Media

In 1937 Chester F. Carlson obtained the patent for photocopy technology. The first automated photocopier was produced by the Rochester U.S. company Haloid (later Xerox) in 1959. As photocopy technology became more affordable many church denominations and local congregations were able to purchase the technology and to produce locally their own newsletters, sermons, and papers.

Between 1975 and 1981 the personal computer became available to the public through the work of Apple Computer and the International Business Machine (IBM). The introduction of the personal computer and increasingly powerful software packages made it possible to digitalize texts, to construct databases, and to produce searchable documents. For theological inquiry this caused a revolution in research and production of studies. Thus, in the field of biblical study, as the biblical text became available in the original languages on computer, word search studies and comparisons became possible at a much higher speed than before. Bibles, commentaries, and book collections were published on disk and allowed quick and effective digital access to resources. Within Protestantism the influence of the personal computer became apparent within church offices where local publications proliferated in conjunction with photocopy technology and desktop publication software.

Parallel to these developments was the birth of the Internet. Internet technology originated as a military research project in the United States that sought to create a network of computers, thus decentralizing and safeguarding information by means of multiple storage and access points. In 1968 the Defense Advanced Research Projects Agency was created and by 1970

the first network of five university computers was established. As personal computers and computer workstations multiplied and became more powerful during the 1980s, software developed and became compatible, and federal and governmental agencies provided funding and infrastructure access, it became possible to connect more personal computers to a network of computer technology that spread around the globe. Through new open and compatible technologies, connected to phone lines, cable, and satellite, it became possible to communicate by text (known as E-mail), graphics, voice, music, and live video images. This global interconnection of computers became known as the World Wide Web (WWW). On this web it became possible to post text, pictures, music, movies, and virtually unlimited amounts of information accessible from personal computers. Live text-based communication between individuals and among groups also became possible. Search tools, which allowed one to enter a phrase or subject and search for information, became increasingly powerful and became known as search engines.

These developments were not lost on religious organizations, and Protestant groups became active in posting information and making research and E-mail interaction possible. Most Protestant denominations and institutions presently have information Web sites nationally and internationally. Classic and new religious texts have become readily and freely available on the Internet. The volume of Protestant and other religious material, music, and images on the World Wide Web is staggering. Some Protestant organizations have also started to use E-mail as a form of mass communication. Unsolicited mass mailing over the Internet is known as spam, and is usually not well received. Not all religious sites and not all the information provided are of equal integrity, which raises the issue of Protestantism, mass media, and ETHICS.

Electronic Mass Media, Protestantism, and Ethics

From the time of the inception of electronic mass media, religious leaders have posed questions about these media, and their compatibility with religious values. The scandals of televangelists raised particular questions of temptation and financial ethics in the use of electronic media. Conflicting and controversial material on the Internet raises questions of integrity. A more fundamental question deals with the very nature of the electronic media and their impact on the perception of reality. Marshall McLuhan's conclusion that the medium is the message underlines the inescapable link between the mass medium used and the kind of message that people receive when they are impacted by the medium. William F. Fore points out that it is particularly the hidden assumptions of media and communication that might lead to inadvertent expressions of unintended values. His research points out that mass media tend to select and distort what they mediate. Every subject and image selection represents a judgment with ethical dimensions. By using myth, symbol, image, and fantasy, media create a commonality of perception in society. Other theorists such as the French philosopher Jean Baudrillard argue that perception mediated by the mass media screen can be described as a form of hyperreality. This means that the presence of the camera and the observer changes that which is being observed or filmed, creating a new sense of reality. Such theories challenge Protestant Christians to consider the ethical implications of their attempts to use electronic mass media. The growing interest in examining inter-connections between popular culture, media, and religion should contribute to a more profound understanding of these issues. One of the central questions becomes: "Is what is filmed and broadcast enacted in a way that challenges the authenticity of its message and experience?" As technologies develop and multiply, such fundamental questions will require reflection and response.

References and Further Reading

Eisenstein, E. L. *The Printing Press as an Agent of Change: Communication and Transformation in Early Modern Europe.* New York: Cambridge University Press, 1979.

Erickson, H. *Religious Radio and Television in the United States, 1921–1991: The Programs and Personalities.* Jefferson, NC: McFarland and Company, 1992.

Fishwick, Marshall, and Ray B. Browne, eds. *The God Pumpers: Religion in the Electronic Age.* Bowling Green, OH: Bowling Green State University Popular Press, 1987.

Fore, William F. *Television and Religion: The Shaping of Faith, Values and Culture.* Minneapolis, MN: Augsburg, 1987.

———. *Mythmakers: Gospel Culture and the Media.* New York: Friendship Press, 1990.

Habermass, J. *The Structural Transformation of the Public Sphere.* Translated by T. Burger. Cambridge, MA: MIT Press, 1992.

Hoover, S. M., and K. Lundby, eds. *Rethinking Media, Religion, and Culture.* Thousand Oaks, CA: Sage Publication, 1997.

Hoover, S. M., and L. Schofield Clark, eds. *Practicing Religion in the Age of the Media: Explorations in Media, Religion and Culture.* New York: Columbia University Press, 2002.

Horsfield, P. *Religious Television in America: Its Influence and Future.* New York: Longman, 1981.

McLuhan, Marshall. *The Gutenberg Galaxy.* Toronto: University of Toronto Press, 1967.

McLuhan, Marshall, Quentin Fiore, and Jerome Agel (coordinator). *The Medium Is the Massage: An Inventory of Effects.* Toronto: Bantam, 1967.

Moore, L. *Selling God: American Religion in the Marketplace of Culture.* New York: Oxford University Press, 1994.

Zaleski, J. *The Soul of Cyberspace: How New Technology Is Changing Our Spiritual Lives.* San Francisco, CA: HarperEdge, 1997.

CHARLES J. FENSHAM

MASS MOVEMENTS (INDIA)

Mass movements in India refer to localized processes, usually involving people from lower social strata, in which groups, not individuals, adopted another religion. Since the sixteenth century, mass movements to Islam occurred among peasant classes in rural Bengal and to Sikhism in the Punjab. Into the nineteenth and twentieth centuries, however, "mass movements" most often designated CONVERSION to Christianity among Dalits (formerly called "untouchables") and among other low-ranking groups of the Indian caste system. The advent of Protestant MISSIONS to INDIA during the early nineteenth century served as a catalyst for some of these movements, although mass conversion to Catholicism predated the arrival of Protestant missions. Much of the literature on mass movements addresses socioeconomic, religious, and political motives for conversion along with reactions by local elites and national leadership.

Some have described the Syrian Christians as the first instance of a mass movement in India. These Christians trace their origins to the Apostle Thomas, who allegedly came to India and converted a number of Brahmins along the Coromandel Coast near Mylapore. Unlike participants in most mass movements, however, the Syrian Christians professed high caste (Brahmin) status and avoided efforts to propagate their religion for fear of compromising their status.

In 1540 the first Jesuit missionaries arrived in India. Francis Xavier oversaw what many regard as the first mass movement of conversion in South India. More than 15,000 low-caste fishermen, coming from the Mukkuva and Parava castes, converted to Catholicism and were drawn, as groups, under the authority of the Portuguese crown. Xavier was said to have founded forty-five churches in Travancore state, primarily among these two caste groups.

In contrast to Xavier, the Jesuit Robert de Nobili targeted the upper castes and attempted to keep his missionary efforts outside the dominion of the crown. De Nobili identified himself in dress and lifestyle with various ascetic and ritual practices of Brahmin priests of Madurai. After his death the Madurai mission adopted his models for missionary work and established mission stations in Ramnad, Padukottai, Mysore, Trichinopoly, and Tanjore, as well as in areas within the Arcot district. When John de Britto (d. 1693) arrived in Ramnad he adopted de Nobili's strategy of dressing like a *sannyasi* (or world renouncer), but included in his missionary labors the warrior elite castes of the Maravas and Agamudaiyans of Tinnevelly.

Several notable Protestant mass movements occurred in North India toward the end of the nineteenth century. During the 1870s the Chuhras, a Dalit community of sweepers, leather workers, and agricultural laborers, began converting en masse to Christianity. As a result of their conversion, the Indian Christian population in the Punjab rose from 3,912 in 1881 to 395,629 in 1931 (Webster 1996:39). Other mass movements in North India include the conversion of the Mazhabi Sikhs and of the Bhangis and Chamars in Uttar Pradesh. Although indigenous agents most often were the ones who led mass movements, Methodist, Anglican, and Presbyterian missions were involved in these North Indian movements.

The first large-scale conversion movement in South India occurred among the Nadars (who were previously known as Shanars, and had worked as toddy drawers) of Tirunelveli. As a result of their conversion the Nadars enhanced their social and economic status dramatically. From the middle of the nineteenth century the London Mission Society (LMS) conducted its work within the so-called Tamil Field of South India. Under the influence of the LMS, large numbers of persons from Dalit castes, such as the so-called conch shell and green bangle pariahs and Chuklas of Erode, and from Criminal Tribes such as the Kuruvars of Salem became Christian. Under the auspices of the Church Mission Society (CMS) and the Society for the Propagation of the Gospel (SPG) Dalit groups such as the Chakkiliyans, Pallans, and Shanars of Tinnevelly and Tajore also converted.

Converts within Telugu districts also came predominantly from Dalit castes. Within the Krishna Godavari delta, these included Malas, who worked the land, and Madigas, who were leather workers. In addition to Roman Catholic missions, the Church Mission Society (CMS), American Baptists, Lutherans, and Anglicans all witnessed mass movements of conversion among the Telugu-speaking Malas and Madigas (see Lutheranism; Anglicanism). V. S. Azariah, the first Indian bishop of an Anglican diocese, oversaw the conversion of low-caste Telugus within his Dornakal Diocese. Azariah defended the legitimacy of mass movements in the face of rising criticism from Hindu nationalists.

Debates over mass movements were centered on the issue of motives. Defenders of mass movements within the church interpreted them as an outpouring of the Holy Spirit, which would lead to the eventual conversion of India. They also viewed group conversion as a way for Indians to become Christian without breaking from their families or cultural heritage. Critics, however, described mass converts as nothing more than "rice Christians," implying that they converted for material incentives linked to services provided by foreign missionaries. Other critics have pointed to the coincidence of famine, sociocultural changes created by colonial rule, and caste oppression as causes of mass movements.

During the 1930s debates over the legitimacy of mass movements in India prompted the National Christian Council to commission J. Waskom Pickett, a Methodist minister and social activist, to conduct a nationwide sociological study of mass movements. His published findings in 1933 compiled the results of 3,947 interviews with Christians from mass movement regions. On the basis of these interviews, he concluded that 8.1 percent had converted for nonreligious reasons (education, social status, medical and other assistance from missionaries, legal protection), 34.8 percent for "spiritual" reasons, and 22.4 percent for familial reasons (i.e., because family and friends had converted). The remaining 34.7 percent said they became Christians because they were born into Christian families (Pickett 1933:160–168).

Although heads of mission societies and ecumenical bodies hailed Pickett's study as a vindication of mass movements, criticism from Indian nationalists remained trenchant. Mohandas K. Gandhi, leader of the Indian National Congress, viewed Pickett's findings as grossly exaggerated. Gandhi insisted that Christian conversion occurred primarily for material reasons and denationalized Indians by causing them to despise their own traditions. Other more radical Hindu voices sounded alarms of "Hinduism in danger." This awareness resulted in more aggressive relief efforts by Hindus among the depressed classes. The Arya Samaj, Theosophical Society, Ramakrishna Mission, and other reformist organizations worked among the lower castes, in part, to stem the tide of conversions to Christianity and Islam.

Similar concerns have led Hindu organizations in postcolonial India to call for stricter measures against conversions. These include anticonversion laws in Arunachal Pradesh, Madhya Pradesh, Orissa, and, more recently, Tamil Nadu. These laws prohibit conversion by "force or allurement or by fraudulent means" (Tamil Nadu Ordinance, No. 9, p. 223). Such measures show how the history of mass movements continues to shape the rhetoric surrounding conversion and national identity in India.

See also Colonialism; Missionary Organizations; Post-Colonialism

References and Further Reading

Clough, John E. *Social Christianity in the Orient: The Story of a Man, a Mission and a Movement.* New York: Macmillan, 1914.

Fishman, A. T. *Culture Change and the Underprivileged.* Madras, India: Christian Literature Society, 1941.

Forrester, Duncan. *Caste and Christianity: Attitudes and Policies on Caste of Anglo-Saxon Protestant Missions.* London: Curzon Press, 1980.

Frykenberg, Robert. "The Impact of Conversion and Social Reform upon Society in South India during the Late Company Period: Questions Concerning Hindu-Christian Encounters, with Special Reference to Tinnevelly." In *Indian Society and the Beginnings of Modernization, 1830–1850,* edited by C. H. Philips and Mary Doreen Wainwright. London: School of Oriental and African Studies, 1976.

Harper, Susan Billington. "The Politics of Conversion: The Azariah-Gandhi Controversy over Christian Mission to the Depressed Classes in the 1930's." *Indo-British Review* 15 (1988): 147–175.

———. *In the Shadow of the Mahatma: Bishop V.S. Azariah and the Travails of Christianity in British India.* Grand Rapids, MI: Eerdmans/Richmond, Surrey, UK: Curzon Press, 2000.

Hudson, Dennis. "The First Protestant Mission to India: Its Social and Religious Developments." *Sociological Bulletin* 42 (1993): 37–63.

Oddie, Geoffrey A. "Christian Conversion in the Telugu Country, 1860–1900: A Case Study of One Protestant Movement in the Godavery-Krishna Delta." *Indian Economic and Social History Review* 12 (1975): 61–79.

———. *Religious Conversion Movements in South Asia: Continuities and Change, 1800–1900.* Richmond, Surrey, UK: Curzon Press, 1997.

Pickett, J. Waskom. *Christian Mass Movements in India.* New York: Abingdon Press, 1933.

Webster, John C. B. *The Dalit Christians: A History.* New Delhi: ISPCK, 1996.

CHANDRA MALLAMPALLI

MATHER, COTTON (1663–1728)

New England clergyman. Mather, the best-known New England clergyman of his generation, was born in Boston, Massachusetts, on February 12, 1663. He entered the world with the burden of expectations that came with being the descendant on his father's side of Richard Mather and on his mother's side of John Cotton, for whom he was named. Both of those men were revered as being among the architects of the Puritan way of belief and church POLITY in New England. Cotton's father was no less prominent. The Reverend INCREASE MATHER was pastor of Boston's North Church and president of Harvard College. Increase had spent the 1650s in IRELAND and ENGLAND during the time of Puritan control there, and had made strong and lasting contacts with the men who became the leaders of English NONCONFORMITY after the Restoration of 1660 led to the collapse of the Puritan regime (see PURITANISM) and the exclusion of Puritans from the restored CHURCH OF ENGLAND. These connec-

tions would later be of assistance to his son as Cotton sought to engage in the religious life of the broader Atlantic community. Two of Increase's brothers, Samuel and Nathaniel Mather, were prominent dissenting CLERGY in the British Isles during the decades after the Restoration (see DISSENT).

Cotton entered Harvard in 1674, shortly before his twelfth birthday. His youth, combined with a stammer that afflicted him throughout his childhood, led to his being hazed by fellow students. Despite this he excelled in his studies, demonstrating a love of learning that would be one of the central features of his life. He graduated in 1678 and received his M.A. three years later. He was determined to enter the ministry and preached in various Boston area churches. In 1686 he was chosen by his father's North Church to assume a ministerial position. He shared that pulpit with Increase until the latter's death in 1723. In the early years of the new century the congregation numbered around 1,500, with over a third of that number in full communion.

In 1686 Cotton also entered the first of three marriages, which would see the birth of fifteen children. Shortly thereafter he was thrust into public affairs. His father departed on a mission to England to seek redress from the Dominion of New England, a centralized supercolony that had been imposed on the region by King James II. The GLORIOUS REVOLUTION in England ousted James from his throne. Informed of the rebellion by Increase Mather, the colonists saw opportunity, which they quickly seized. Cotton was one of the key figures behind the April 1689 uprising against the Dominion and its governor general, Sir Edmund Andros. Cotton aided in the interim reestablishment of the old Massachusetts charter government, and he wrote the *Declaration of the Inhabitants,* which justified the rebellion. Meanwhile, Increase successfully lobbied the new monarchs, William and Mary, to restore the separate identities of the New England colonies.

This political turmoil had subsided when the Mathers found themselves immersed in the Salem witchcraft episode (see WITCHCRAZE). In the summer of 1688 Cotton had been much acclaimed for his cure of the afflicted thirteen-year-old Martha Goodwin through months of quiet, nurturing pastoral care. This successful approach was disdained by the authorities in the Salem case. Instead the accusers were given a public legal forum to make their claims, and questionable rules of evidence were adopted by the court. Mather was privately critical of the proceedings, but felt compelled to publicly support the magistrates. The unwillingness of this young man who was not yet thirty to challenge the colony's leadership is understandable, but publishing a justification of the proceedings, *Wonders of the Invisible World* (1692), tarnished his reputation then and for future generations.

Mather devoted much time to private religious devotions. His faith had a strong mystical element in it, and on a number of occasions he claimed to have been visited by angels. This spiritual orientation made him appreciative of the writings of German Pietists (see PIETISM). He encouraged members of his congregation to engage in pietistic exercises. He preached often on the need for personal piety and its expression in good works. *Bonifacius: Essays to Do Good* (1710) was a call to a new piety as well as a manual of good conduct. Benjamin Franklin, the colonial statesman who grew up in Mather's Boston, later recognized the influence that work had on his own beliefs.

Cotton hoped to become, as his father had, a major figure in the transatlantic Puritan community, but his knowledge of England was derived from correspondence alone and not from personal experience. He frequently led with his wrong foot in offering advice to and seeking favors from English dissenters. He came to accuse them of refusing to take colonists seriously and in the process did much to implant a truly provincial outlook in eighteenth-century New England. This should not, however, obscure his incredible learning and prolific output of over four hundred published works.

His most important work was his monumental history of New England, *Magnalia Christia Americana* (1702), which was designed to commemorate the Puritan errand into the wilderness and rekindle a devotion to the ideals of the founding generation. However, he also wrote extensively in other areas, including a scriptural commentary, the massive and never published "Biblia Americana"; natural theology, *The Christian Philosopher* (1721); medicine, *The Angel of Bethseda* (not published until 1972); and scores of sermons and religious tracts. He communicated observations of natural phenomena to the Royal Society, leading to his election as a Fellow in 1713. His controversial propagation of inoculation (based on reading a contribution in the *Transactions of the Royal Society*) during a smallpox epidemic in 1721 represented a turning point in medical practice.

Mather died on February 13, 1728. A man of intense personal piety, he was also one of the best read and most inquisitive men of colonial America. Although his personality prevented him from exercising the leadership in New England for which his intelligence qualified him, he came to be the epitome of the New England Puritan of the early eighteenth century for contemporary religious leaders in Europe and for Americans of later generations.

References and Further Reading

Primary Source:

Mather Papers. Collections of the Massachusetts Historical Society, 4th ser., vol. 8. 1866.

Secondary Sources:

Beall, Otho, and Richard Shryock. *Cotton Mather: First Significant Figure in American Medicine.* Baltimore, MD: John's Hopkins Press, 1954.

Levin, David. *Cotton Mather: The Young Life of the Lord's Remembrancer.* Cambridge, MA: Harvard University Press, 1978.

Lovelace, Richard. *The American Pietism of Cotton Mather.* Grand Rapids, MI: Christian University Press, 1979.

Middlekauff, Robert. *The Mathers: Three Generations of Puritan Intellectuals.* Oxford: Oxford University Press, 1971.

Silverman, Kenneth. *The Life and Times of Cotton Mather.* New York: Harper and Row, 1984.

FRANCIS J. BREMER

MATHER, INCREASE (1630–1723)

American theologian. Born on June 21, 1630, in Dorchester, Massachusetts Bay Colony, Increase Mather became an influential CONGREGATIONALIST minister in Boston, a president of Harvard College, and a colonial ambassador to the English royal court. A prolific author of more than 100 diverse writings, Mather combined Puritan religious tradition and progressive thought as he engaged the theological, historical, political, and scientific issues of his day.

Mather's career began with *The Mystery of Israel's Salvation* (1669), intended to reaffirm the Puritan mission during the English Restoration. His *Life and Death of That Reverend Man of God, Mr. Richard Mather* (1670) was the first colonial biography. Writing these two works quelled Mather's youthful discontent and established his voice. During the 1670s he wrote defenses of the controversial Halfway Covenant and penned several model JEREMIADS, all designed to preserve PURITANISM.

In *A Narrative of the Miseries of New-England* (1688) and *New-England Vindicated* (1689), Mather vigorously defended the compromised rights of his Protestant colony. Politics and history coalesced in both his 1676 account of providential deliverances during settler conflicts with Indians and his 1692 examination of the Salem WITCHCRAZE. Science was added to this mix in *Essay for the Recording of Illustrious Providences* (1684), designed to reveal God's majesty in NATURE. Scientific information, in relation to God's direct intervention in history, informs both *Kometographia* (1683) and *A Discourse Concerning Earthquakes* (1706). In 1721 Mather published a progressive defense of inoculation against smallpox. When Mather died on August 23, 1723, his manuscript autobiography served as a source for his son COTTON MATHER's biographical *Parentator* (1724).

References and Further Reading

Hall, Michael G. *The Last American Puritan: The Life of Increase Mather, 1639–1723.* Middletown, CT: Wesleyan University Press, 1988.
Middlekauf, Robert. *The Mathers: Three Generations of Puritan Intellectuals.* New York: Oxford University Press, 1971.
WILLIAM J. SCHEICK

MATHEWS, SHAILER (1863–1941)

American theologian. Mathews was born in Maine in 1863 to a middle-class Baptist family with an evangelical and pietistic heritage. He graduated from Colby College in 1884 and Newton Theological Institution in 1887. He then taught at Colby from 1887 to 1890 before studying at the University of Berlin from 1890 to 1893, where he encountered ADOLF VON HARNACK and became committed to liberalism. Mathews was appointed to the faculty of the University of Chicago in 1894, became dean of the Divinity School in 1908, and remained there until retiring in 1933. During his career, Mathews wrote more than thirty books and served as editor of several periodicals and reference works.

Mathews was Baptist (licensed, but never ordained, as a Southern Baptist and a president of the Northern Baptist Convention), but his theological work was ecumenical. His influence dominated the Federal Council of Churches of Christ. Because Mathews sought to incorporate critical biblical scholarship and SCIENCE into theological education, he became a leader of LIBERAL PROTESTANTISM and a modernist in the early twentieth century's fundamentalist controversies. Thus, he was on the witness list for the defense at the Scopes "Monkey Trial." The study of sociology convinced Mathews that Christianity was a social movement distinguished by its practices but not its doctrines. He rejected the DOCTRINE of the second coming of Christ because he believed that this doctrine undermined the social mission of the church. Although he was committed to the SOCIAL GOSPEL and was labeled a social activist, he rejected Socialism and advocated altruistic capitalism.

See also Darwinism; Ecumenism; Fundamentalism; Higher Education; Modernism; Socialism, Christian; Sociology of Protestantism; Theology, Twentieth Century

References and Further Reading

Primary Sources:

Mathews, Shailer. *The Social Teachings of Jesus: An Essay in Christian Sociology.* New York: Macmillan, 1897.
————. *Faith of Modernism.* New York: Macmillan, 1924.
————. *New Faith for Old: An Autobiography of Shailer Mathews.* New York: Macmillan, 1936.

Secondary Source:

Lindsey, William D. *Shailer Mathews's Lives of Jesus: The Search for a Theological Foundation for the Social Gospel.* Albany: State University of New York Press, 1997.
THOMAS E. PHILLIPS

MATHIJS, JAN (c.1500–1534)

Dutch Anabaptist. Mathijs, a millenarian Anabaptist who seized temporary control of the city of Münster in northwest GERMANY, was a baker from Haarlem and a disciple of the Anabaptist preacher MELCHIOR HOFMANN. Like Hofmann, Mathijs held strong eschatological beliefs but was willing to express them violently. After Hofmann's arrest in Strasbourg, Mathijs announced that he was the prophet Enoch and began preaching that the millennium was dawning. In January 1534 Mathijs sent emissaries to Münster and they found a warm reception in BERNARD ROTHMANN and Bernard Knipperdolling, the leading clergy and civic leader, respectively. Consequently Mathijs believed that Münster was the site of the New Jerusalem. In February 1534, elections to the city council brought an Anabaptist majority. Mathijs arrived in Münster and during February to April of 1534 Münster turned Anabaptist. Those who were not baptized upon CONFESSION of faith had to leave the city. Mathijs appealed to Anabaptists everywhere to come to Münster, the New Jerusalem, in anticipation of the imminent return of Christ.

On April 4, 1534, in response to a revelation, Mathijs led an assault against the Catholic bishop's troops who besieged the city. Mathijs was killed in the attack. Leadership in the city passed to Jan of Leiden who was captured and executed when Münster fell to the bishop's forces in June 1535.

Mathijs represented arguably the most radical protest of early Protestantism, one that formed an intense eschatological anticipation.

See also Apocalypticism; Eschatology; Millenarians and Millennialism

References and Further Reading

Jürgen-Goertz, Hans. *The Anabaptists.* Translated by Trevor Johnson. London: Routledge, 1996.

Stayer, James M. "Christianity in One City: Anabaptist Münster." In *Radical Tendencies in the Reformation: Divergent Perspectives*, edited by Hans J. Hillerbrand. Kirksville, MO: Sixteenth Century Journal Publications, 1988.

MICHAEL BIRD

MATTHEWS, ZACHARIAH KEODIRELANG (1901–1968)

South African churchman. Matthews was born in Barkely West District, near Kimberley, Cape Colony, SOUTH AFRICA on October 20, 1901, and died in Washington, DC, in 1968. A South African academic, HUMAN RIGHTS leader, and ecumenical churchman, Z.K. (as he was commonly known) was the son of a former migrant miner from Bechuanaland (now Botswana) who had opened a café and under the franchise laws of Cape Colony was entitled to vote. The distinguished writer Sol Plaatje was a cousin. Matthews attended the Scottish Mission's Lovedale Institution and the Fort Hare University College, becoming in 1923 the first black South African to gain a B.A. in South Africa. In 1925 he became the first African principal of Adams College, where the young ALBERT LUTHULI was teaching. In 1928 Matthews married Frieda Bokwe, daughter of the prominent minister John Knox Bokwe. After taking a law degree by private study, he became an attorney in Johannesburg, but in 1933 broke off to study at Yale (M.A. 1934) and the London School of Economics (where he worked in anthropology with Bronislaw Malinowski). For the next few years Matthews was essentially an academic and educator, one of the black elite concerned with the "uplift" of their people.

In 1936 Matthews became lecturer in social anthropology and native law at Fort Hare, eventually succeeding JOHN TNEGO JABAVU as head of African studies there. He served on various public bodies including a Royal Commission on Higher Education in British East Africa and the Anglo-Egyptian Sudan, and from 1942 the Native Representation Council (NRC). Although always a forceful exponent of African rights on the Council, Matthews realized, particularly as the policy of the Nationalist Government unfolded, that his political home lay in the African National Congress (ANC). He resigned in 1950 from the now useless NRC. He proposed, and did much to draft, the Freedom Charter of 1955 "to instill political consciousness in the people and encourage their political activities." He was not, like Luthuli, arrested in the ensuing government action against the promoters of the Charter and of the Defiance campaigns of civil disobedience; perhaps his prominent academic position protected him. At the mass treason trial of 1957, however, he became a target. Although released the next year, he was again arrested in 1960 after calling, with Luthuli, for a national day of mourning for the Sharpeville massacre. He resigned from Fort Hare in protest against new restrictions. He was involved in the Cottesloe Conference that helped to crystallize the official policy of most of the South African churches against apartheid.

Matthews had combined his political and public activity with open identification as a Christian, and had attracted attention within the ecumenical movement associated with the WORLD COUNCIL OF CHURCHES. Already in 1952–1953 he had held a visiting professorship at Union Theological Seminary in New York. In 1961 he became Africa Secretary of the Department of Inter-Church Aid, Refugees and World Service, based in Geneva. He took up the position of refugees in AFRICA (then a little-noticed issue), and succeeded in drawing the attention of the United Nations to it. He was also much involved with the war in Sudan (which he had first visited as a member of the Royal Commission in the 1930s) and the population displacement it caused. He participated in the formation of the All-Africa Conference of Churches. In 1966, with just a short time to live, he identified with his father's country, and became Botswana's ambassador in Washington, DC, and its permanent representative at the United Nations.

The three phases of Matthews's life reflect a transformation in black Southern African Protestantism in the middle decades of the twentieth century, as the extent of white oppression in the region made it a touchstone for the genuineness of Christian, and especially white Christian, professions. In his early days Matthews embodied the aspiration for African development and progress and harmonious race relations with a model based on Western ideas of "civilization." His growing involvement in politics—forced on him rather than self-chosen—represented a new Christian vision in which justice, rather than harmony, was paramount. In his lifetime and since, there were those who thought him too cautious and willing to compromise; but he can now be seen as one of the architects of the new multiracial South Africa. The early decades of the World Council of Churches strengthened the consciousness among Protestants of belonging to a world Christian community. Z. K. Matthews was recognizable as a powerful voice for Africa within that community, socially engaged, challenging racial and political assumptions on Christian ethical grounds, with a THEOLOGY and ECCLESIOLOGY not yet distinctively African, but belonging to the mainstream of Western Protestantism.

See also African Theology; Ecumenism

References and Further Reading

Primary Sources:

Matthews, Z. K. *Freedom for My People: The Autobiography of Professor Z. K. Matthews.* London: Collings, 1981.
———, ed. *Responsible Government in a Revolutionary Age.* New York: Association Press, 1966.

Secondary Sources:

Juckes, T. J. *Opposition in South Africa: The Leadership of Z. K. Matthews, Nelson Mandela and Steve Biko.* Westport, CTN: Praeger, 1993.
Saayman, W. A. *A Man with a Shadow: The Life and Times of Professor Z. K. Matthews.* Pretoria, South Africa: UNISA, 1986.

ANDREW F. WALLS

MAURICE, FREDERICK DENISON (1805–1872)

Anglican theologian. Born in 1805 in Normanstone, ENGLAND, Maurice was an Anglican cleric and theologian. His prolific writing, which included many essays, letters, sermons, and commentaries, was marked by the balancing of theological oppositions, a strong interest in social concerns, and a critical receptivity to secular philosophies. He contributed to the short-lived but important movement of Christian SOCIALISM. Over the course of his life, he held academic posts in London and Cambridge, where he died in 1872.

Early History

Maurice's father was a Unitarian minister, although his mother ultimately embraced CALVINISM, a family split that troubled Maurice until, in 1823, he went as an agnostic to CAMBRIDGE UNIVERSITY to study law. Ineligible for a degree because he refused to subscribe to the THIRTY-NINE ARTICLES of the CHURCH OF ENGLAND, he moved to London and wrote tracts in favor of social reform, a concern to which he would later return. He eventually embraced the faith of the Church of England and in 1830, went to Exeter College, Oxford. After ordination and a brief curacy, he returned to London in 1836 to become chaplain of Guy's College.

Early Writing and Christian Socialism

It was in London that Maurice wrote *The Kingdom of Christ* (1838). In it, Maurice claimed that all forms of Christianity express accurate, if partial truths, because all arise from the basic structure of human nature: the longing for a universal society to which they all give broken witness. Conscious, however dimly, that to be members of family, church, and nation they must also be members of something greater, the KINGDOM OF GOD is manifested when these entities work together to inculcate self-giving relationships to others. Tracing this longing for relation through the Scriptures, Maurice saw in Christ the ultimate revelation that we are already in relation with God, in whom this universal society is joined. The second edition of *The Kingdom of Christ* (1842) highlighted six marks of the spiritual society that manifests this relation that is both nature and destiny, marks that Maurice found in the Church of England, although haunted there, too, by a partisan spirit. His resistance to "partyism" steered between the OXFORD MOVEMENT members who vigorously defended the Church of England and Protestants who called for more official tolerance of religious dissent (see TOLERATION). Along with Quakerism, LUTHERANISM, Calvinism, and Unitarianism, Maurice included secular philosophies in *The Kingdom of Christ* because he believed they, too, could display the impulse toward universal society. His affirmation both of the capacity of secular philosophy to manifest human relatedness and of the mission of the church to manifest the divine source in which that relatedness comes fully to ground made him appear to H. RICHARD NIEBUHR as an example of "church transforming culture."

In 1848 Maurice became professor of theology at King's College, London. With CHARLES KINGSLEY and others, he produced a series of tracts articulating Christian Socialism. Maurice was not a political activist, however; he believed that the members and classes of industrial Victorian society would live together more cooperatively if only their proper nature as relational beings were revealed to them. Although this may seem naïve from the perspective of the catastrophic evil of subsequent centuries, he felt this was the appropriate avenue to social reform for a theologian. Although Christian Socialism did not survive as a movement, the concerns Maurice expressed during its brief activity influenced later figures including BROOKE FOSS WESTCOTT, STEWART HEADLAM, WALTER RAUSCHENBUSCH, and WILLIAM TEMPLE.

From London to Cambridge

King's College, uneasy with Maurice's Christian Socialism, ultimately dismissed him because of his *Theological Essays.* Published in 1853, they displayed a mind seeking honest congruence between human experience and Christian DOCTRINE. Several of the essays deepened Maurice's earlier orientation to the Incarnation as the key to our nature and reflect his resistance to beginning theology from the Fall. His controversial essay "On the Atonement" was an attempt to widen soteriology beyond penal substitution, locating Christ's significance for humanity in the whole of his life. His position was criticized as Abelardian, whose soteriology was out of favor in Maurice's time, although the charge is probably not fair to the essay. His rhetorical query in this essay—"How can God have removed a separation unless there is some One in whom we are bound more closely to Him than our evils have put us asunder?"—anticipates KARL BARTH'S CHRISTOLOGY of a century later, although their motivations were rather different. Most troubling for King's College, however, was Maurice's "Concluding Essay on Eternal Life and Eternal Death," in which he suggested that the biblical term "eternal" referred not so much to an interminable state after death as to the fullness of life in God. This claim was taken by Maurice's detractors to amount to his denial of divine judgment. Despite his attempt to clarify his meaning, he was dismissed by King's College over the issue.

After his dismissal Maurice established the Working Men's College in London, which was congruent with his sense of the theologian's contribution to social reform. There he delivered his lectures on *The Epistles of St. John* (1857), which signaled the turn of his attention primarily to moral theology. This he continued as Knightbridge professor of moral theology at Cambridge from 1866 on. In dialogue with JOSEPH BUTLER and JEREMY BENTHAM he explored *The Conscience* (1868) as a faculty neither immutable nor merely utilitarian, but as a flexible internal expression of moral AUTHORITY developed in relation with others; in *Social Morality* (1869) he returned to the theme of family, empire, and society as developments of the divinely given human propensity for relations and, in the second lecture on universal morality, linked that propensity for relation to the enactment of Christian worship.

References and Further Reading

Primary Sources:

Maurice, F. D. *The Life of Frederick Denison Maurice, Chiefly Told In His Own Letters.* 2 vols. London: Macmillan, 1884.
———. *Theological Essays.* London: James Clark, 1957.
———. *The Kingdom of Christ.* 2 vols. London: James Clark, 1959.
———. *Reconstructing Christian Ethics: Selected Writings.* Edited by Ellen K. Wondra. Louisville, KY: Westminster John Knox, 1995.

Secondary Sources:

Brose, Olive J. *Frederick Denison Maurice: Rebellious Conformist.* Athens: Ohio University Press, 1971.
McClain, Frank, et al. *F.D. Maurice: A Study.* Cowley, MA: Cowley, 1982.
Ramsey, Arthur Michael. *F. D. Maurice and the Conflicts of Modern Theology.* Cambridge: Cambridge University Press, 1951.
Vidler, A. R. *F. D. Maurice and Company: Nineteenth Century Studies.* London: S.C.M., 1966.

JAMES FARWELL

MAYHEW, JONATHAN (1720–1766)

American theologian and preacher. Mayhew was born in the village of Chilmark on the island of Martha's Vineyard in the colony of Massachusetts on October 8, 1720. The original English grantee of Martha's Vineyard and adjacent islands was Thomas Mayhew, whose presence in colonial affairs dates from 1641. His son inaugurated some of the earliest evangelical efforts among Native Americans who resided there, and after his death at sea in 1657, the elder Thomas adopted the cause of Indian missions as his own. Jonathan's birth represented the fifth generation of Mayhews associated with colonial proprietorship and religious activities, beginning with that first Thomas, then Thomas Jr., John, and Experience, Jonathan's father, who was also a clergyman and missionary. Moving from the isolation of an insular home, Jonathan entered Harvard College with its more cosmopolitan atmosphere and exciting swirl of ideas. In 1744 he graduated with honors, and for the next three years studied theology at his alma mater, occasionally teaching school to meet expenses. In 1747 he was ordained and became minister of the West Congregational Church in Boston, a position that he occupied for the rest of a rather short life. During that nineteen-year career his eloquence and zeal drew a great deal of attention, both favorable and unfavorable.

In the controversies of his day Mayhew was decidedly on the liberal side of every issue, approaching debates with an attitude that never accepted orthodox positions for their own sake and that insisted on pursuing questions with a dogged insistence on reasonableness. Arguing chiefly against staple Calvinist doctrines, his intellectual independence was so pronounced that several ministers in Boston feared that he would preach unsound beliefs and replace orthodoxy with questionable tenets. From their perspective, which relied on routine ideas and comfortable habits, he did go too far. Possessed of zeal and an ardor that sometimes bordered on harshness, Mayhew did not shrink from threats of ostracism, but rather set the tone in his day for rational religion. Along with his colleague Charles Chauncy, Mayhew acknowledged the Bible as infallible, but insisted too that human reason must coincide with and validate the essentials of revealed truth. Assuming that scriptural teachings were clear and easily understandable, he argued that people could realize which truths had intrinsic value and which claims were muddleheaded. There was no need to browbeat modern thinkers with references to theological traditions in an attempt to lend ideas greater authority. Christianity without mystery, ethical standards with practical benefit, preaching from common sense, these were notable characteristics of rational religion that became increasingly common among those who represented the Age of ENLIGHTENMENT.

In his effort to free minds from the despotism of old dogmas, Mayhew challenged several traditional beliefs. One had to do with the godhead, and in this regard the young Boston clergyman stands as a prototype of what later came to be called Unitarianism. He rejected Trinitarian thinking as unreasonable and superstitious. God was, he declared, a single, sovereign unit. Jesus could not be equated with God because that would threaten both supremacy and monotheism. However, Jesus was nevertheless to be regarded as higher than all other creatures and still revered as savior of those who sought divine aid in their efforts to be virtuous. In true Arian fashion, Mayhew extolled Jesus as a preexistent mediator between heaven and earth, a moral exemplar whose teachings engendered moral improvement and vindicated the inherent dignity of God's law. His sermons on such matters were widely read on both sides of the Atlantic, some of them prosaically entitled *Seven Sermons* (1749), *Sermons* (1755), *Christian Sobriety* (1763), and *Sermons to Young Men* (1767).

Another traditional viewpoint that Mayhew could not accept concerned the issue of free will, or rather the Calvinist denial of it. He blasted the doctrine of reprobation because it was both unscriptural and blasphemy against a God whom he viewed as eternally benevolent. He decried all notions that painted humanity as depraved and helpless, in need of some all-powerful grace to effect salvation. He deplored references to God as arbitrarily saving only a chosen few, damning all the rest because human nature was utterly devoid of goodness. Mayhew's defense of human agency in spiritual affairs paralleled his reliance on free inquiry and private judgment in pursuit of truth. In Arminian terms, he never tired of championing each person's reliance on free will and personal initiative in their search for salvation. Moreover, this redemption was achieved not through a dramatic sense of rescue but rather through good works and virtuous habits. Whether debating traditionalists of the New Divinity such as SAMUEL HOPKINS or GREAT AWAKENING preachers such as GEORGE WHITEFIELD, Mayhew held his own in debates about human ability, and his eloquence persuaded a growing number of followers in the city. His gospel was one in which free will was part of God's created order, and true religion one of sober effort, preferable to anything that portrayed divine power as vengeful and paralyzed efforts at moral reform.

Representative as he was of liberal tendencies in Christian thought, Mayhew was also fiercely attached to the freedom found in Congregationalist churches, which permitted him to develop such ideas. He identified with congregational polity and strongly criticized the Society for the Propagation of the Gospel in Foreign Parts (SPG) for sending missionaries into New England. The SPG had been created in 1701 by the Church of England to conduct evangelical work among African Americans and Native Americans. Within a few decades, however, most British missionaries relinquished those objectives, focusing on white colonists instead of slaves and Indians. These Anglican agents usually supported the combined interests of monarchical government and episcopal polity, and so when they sent missionaries into territory already settled with Congregationalist churches, Mayhew and others protested quite vigorously. He attacked the presumption that Congregationalists were not proper Christians already and that they still needed evangelizing. In a notable pamphlet of 1763, entitled "Observations on the Character and Conduct of the [SPG]," he charged that the real purpose of Anglican activists in Boston was to introduce bishops into the American colonies. English bishops in colonial America would, he warned, pave the way to further political subservience to royal power. Freedom from interference in church management was as important as open inquiry in theology, and he wanted no outside meddling with ulterior motives hidden behind pious cant.

Consistent with his support for the causes of intellectual and ecclesiastical independence, Mayhew was also an outspoken advocate of political freedom. His 1750 sermon, "Discourse Concerning Unlimited Submission and Non-Resistance to the Higher Powers," attracted a great deal of attention because it articulated convictions held by a broad segment of the population. Men were, he acknowledged, bound to show allegiance to a legitimate monarch who ruled justly, but political obedience had its limits. Civil authority could become tyrannical, and in those aberrant circumstances it was a citizen's duty to disobey those in office, preferring to follow God's law rather than wrongful human oppression. This sermon, preached when Charles I was executed by parliamentarians during the English CIVIL WAR, nurtured incipient patriotism in the American colonies. Many declare Mayhew to be one of the champions of liberty who laid the theoretical groundwork for the later movement for independence. As a more immediate result of this short treatise, in 1751 the University of Aberdeen bestowed the Doctor of Divinity degree on this earnest clergyman who pursued virtue in the secular realm as well as the sacred.

Mayhew's political theories, which justified taking over the reins of government in the face of unjust laws, coincided with his religious affirmations. Both of these elements displayed a personality devoted to freedom of action and inquiry, chief principles of the Enlightenment. Although no one knew it at the time, one of his last sermons was "The Snare Broken," which celebrated the repeal of the Stamp Act and yet again emphasized moral integrity in civil conduct. A cerebral hemorrhage unexpectedly felled the spirited controversialist, and he died from its attendant complications on July 9, 1766. Most of the city mourned the loss of this young liberal, one whose theology pointed to the eventual rise of a new denomination and whose political philosophy came to fruition a decade later.

See also Civil War; Congregationalism; Enlightenment; Great Awakening; Hopkins, Samuel; Unitarian-Universalist Association; Whitefield, George

References and Further Reading

Akers, Charles W. *Called Unto Liberty: A Life of Jonathan Mayhew.* Cambridge, MA: Harvard University Press, 1964.

Bradford, Alan. *Memoir of the Life and Writings of Rev. Jonathan Mayhew.* Boston: C. C. Little & Co., 1838.

Corrigan, John. *The Hidden Balance: Religion and Social Theories of Charles Chauncy and Jonathan Mayhew.* New York: Cambridge University Press, 1987.

HENRY W. BOWDEN

MCFAGUE, SALLIE (1933–)

American theologian. For more than thirty years Sallie McFague taught at Vanderbilt Divinity School in Nashville, Tennessee. She completed her career there as the Carpenter Professor of Theology where she had been dean and was named distinguished theologian in residence at the Vancouver School of Theology in Vancouver, British Columbia. She earned her B.A. from Smith College and her B.D. and Ph.D. from Yale University.

The author of seven books, McFague has spent her career developing a groundbreaking ecological THEOLOGY that asks Christians to take seriously their relationship to the environment. To do this McFague has revamped traditional religious language and models of God.

Her first book, *Literature and the Christian Life* (Yale 1966), published under the name Sallie McFague Teselle, focused on the ways that Christian theology could profitably converse with literature. She tends to keep literature and religion in separate realms, examining the integrity of novels and plays in themselves while at the same time asking in what ways those works of art are relevant to the Christian. Both literature and Christianity celebrate the dignity and beauty of human life even as they confront its profundities and intricacies.

Almost a decade later McFague built on these initial studies in literature and theology to establish what was to become her lifelong work in religious language, models of God, and ecological theology. In *Speaking in Parables: A Study in Metaphor and Theology* (Fortress 1975) she argued that the task of theology is to proclaim the themes of the gospel and that Jesus' parables provide the best model for theology in undertaking this task. The parables are extended metaphors that hold together belief and language and address their hearers in their context. Parables invite open-ended theological reflection and demonstrate the ways that God is in the midst of our temporal and all too human world. McFague later uses her study of parables as the foundation for her metaphorical theology.

According to McFague the Protestant tradition and sensibility are metaphorical, whereas the Catholic tradition is symbolical. The latter, she argues, tends to see similarities and connections between God and creation. The Protestant tradition, however, recognizes the differences and dissimilarities between God and nature and thus emphasizes God's transcendence and the finite nature of creation. Metaphors help us to experience that God is in NATURE but God is not more than nature; thus metaphor shows us what is and is not.

McFague uses her metaphorical theology to construct models of God for an "ecological, nuclear age." In the final pages of her *Metaphorical Theology* (Fortress 1982) she challenged the irrelevance of the traditional model of God the Father. Besides the patriarchal character of that model, it also depended for its vitality on a medieval view of the world of vassal and liege. McFague proposed that we now think of God as Mother, Lover, and Friend, for such models acknowledge the relational character of our world. Her models of God challenge the traditional orthodox Protestant notion of God, espoused most clearly by KARL BARTH, that emphasizes the otherness, or transcendence, of God. Instead McFague constructs models of God that emphasize God's immanence and that stress the social and ecological nature of human existence.

McFague expands these models of God in her later work to construct a planetary theology that offers both a rethinking of Christians' relationship to the environment and the economy, and a revision of classical theological topics such as Christ and SALVATION and life in the Spirit.

See also Ecology; Literature; Theology, Twentieth Century

References and Further Reading

Primary Sources:

McFague, Sallie. *Metaphorical Theology: Models of God in Religious Language*. Minneapolis, MN: Fortress Press, 1982.
———. *Models of God: Theology for an Ecological, Nuclear Age*. Minneapolis, MN: Fortress Press, 1987.
———. *Life Abundant: Rethinking Theology and Economy for a Planet in Peril*. Minneapolis, MN: Fortress Press, 2001.

HENRY L. CARRIGAN JR.

MCGUFFEY READERS

William Holmes McGuffey's series of graduated reading textbooks, originally called the *Peerless Pioneer Readers* and later *McGuffey's Eclectic Readers*, began to appear in 1836. Their compiler wrote the first four in the series while serving on the faculty of Miami University in Ohio. The volumes, which ultimately included six readers and a speller, went through several copyrights and were issued by seven publishing houses by the end of the nineteenth century. Sales of the McGuffey Readers has been estimated at well over a million copies during the 1800s, making them among the best-selling textbooks in American history.

Born in 1800, McGuffey spent his life in HIGHER EDUCATION: as professor at Miami University; then as president successively of Cincinnati College, Ohio University, and Woodward College; and finally as Professor of Moral Philosophy at the University of Virginia, where he served from 1845 until his death in 1873. McGuffey was also an ordained Presbyterian minister, and his religious vocation informed the passages chosen for the Readers, which represented mainstream Protestant values. McGuffey drew from established literary figures such as Shakespeare and JOHN MILTON, contemporary writers whose ethos reflected his own Protestantism, and occasional Scripture passages. He also employed phonics as the basis for early reading instruction, and many of the passages in the textbooks were brief enough to allow memorization, which McGuffey believed to be important mental discipline.

Although the Readers disappeared from most public school curricula during the early 1900s because their selections did not represent American pluralism and were insufficiently topical to engage students' attention, home-schoolers later in the century showed renewed interest in McGuffey's textbooks. They admire the series' clearly demarcated age and reading levels, the brevity of the passages, and those passages' clear reinforcement of conservative Protestant values.

See also Education, Overview

References and Further Reading

Sullivan, Dolores P. *William Holmes McGuffey: Schoolmaster to the Nation*. Rutherford, NJ: Fairleigh Dickinson University Press, 1994.
Westerhof, John H. *McGuffey and His Readers: Piety, Morality, and Education in 19ᵗʰ Century America*. Nashville, TN: Abingdon, 1978.

WILLIAM M. CLEMENTS

MCINTIRE, CARL (1906–2002)

American theologian. McIntire has been called the "P. T. Barnum of American Fundamentalism" because of his colorful theatrics and larger-than-life presence. McIntire, however, was no mere entertainer. One of the twentieth century's most outspoken fundamentalists, McIntire remained steadfastly serious in his mission to rid North American Protestantism of MODERNISM in all its forms.

Shortly after McIntire's birth in Ypsilanti, Michigan, on May 17, 1906, his family moved to Oklahoma where he eventually received his teaching certificate from Southeastern State Teachers College. Later, after earning his B.A. from Park College in Missouri, he enrolled at Princeton Theological Seminary in 1927, which was in the throes of the fundamentalist versus modernist controversy. He fell under the influence of biblical scholar J. GRESHAM MACHEN, a Presbyterian fundamentalist who taught McIntire the principle of separatism—the demand for purity within a DENOMINATION and the refusal to compromise with theological liberalism. McIntire's refusal to associate with liberals went beyond Machen's, fueled by dispensational premillennialism and the accompanying belief that the church had to remain absolutely pure awaiting the imminent return of Jesus Christ. Machen left Princeton in 1929 to start Westminster Theological Seminary, and McIntire went with him. They both eventually took their battle from Princeton to the DENOMINATION as a whole and were eventually ousted from the PRESBYTERIAN CHURCH. McIntire joined with Machen in forming the fundamentalist Presbyterian Church in America and eventually separated further to form his own Bible Presbyterian Church with its flagship communion in Collingswood, New Jersey, which McIntire used as his base of operation for his fundamentalist activities.

In the early 1930s McIntire began building his fundamentalist empire that eventually came to include Faith Theological Seminary, two small Christian colleges, a radio program called *The Twentieth-Century Reformation Hour*, a newspaper called *The Christian Beacon*, the Christian Beacon Press, and a retreat center in Florida. All these institutions were defunct by the end of the twentieth century, except his Bible Presbyterian Church and Faith Theological Seminary, which survived in a church basement in Philadelphia.

In 1941 McIntire formed the American Council of Christian Churches (ACCC) in direct opposition to the NATIONAL COUNCIL OF CHURCHES, the ecumenical organization formed by mainline Protestant churches. Through the ACCC he opposed the ecumenical movement and liberal theology, as well as a host of liberal political causes like COMMUNISM (he supported McCarthy in his anticommunist crusade), socialism, feminism, Vietnam War protests, and the CIVIL RIGHTS MOVEMENT. For McIntire, RUSSIA was the symbol of atheism, communism, and evil, and the UNITED STATES was the symbol of all that is good, its key values being unregulated free enterprise, private property, liberty, and INDIVIDUALISM. In 1948 he made his mission international and formed the International Council of Christian Churches in direct opposition to the WORLD COUNCIL OF CHURCHES, founded that same year.

McIntire is a tragic figure in American religious history who took separatism to the extreme, eventually becoming a "second degree separationist," removing himself not only from liberals but from those evangelicals who refused to separate entirely from liberals. He eventually added to his list of enemies not only modernists, but the NATIONAL ASSOCIATION OF EVANGELICALS, BILLY GRAHAM, ORAL ROBERTS, and even his most famous student, Francis A. Schaeffer. Slowly but surely his empire fell apart. In 1999 McIntire was asked by his board of elders to leave the pulpit of his Collingswood Bible Presbyterian Church.

Statistically McIntire's impact was minimal. His organizations never developed a significant formal following. However, many looked to McIntire as the twentieth century's foremost "fighting fundie." He was key in the development of American Protestantism because he made the link between FUNDAMENTALISM and right-wing politics explicit. His active participation in Barry Goldwater's failed 1964 presidential campaign presaged the rise of the new CHRISTIAN RIGHT and activist fundamentalism in the 1970s and 1980s. McIntire died March 19, 2002.

See also Dispensationalism; Liberal Protestantism and Liberalism; Millenarians & Millennialism; Socialism, Christian

References and Further Reading

Balmer, Randall. "Fundamentalist with Flair." *Christianity Today* (May 21, 2002):50–52.
Baranowski, Shelley. "Carl McIntire." In *Twentieth-Century Shapers of American Popular Religion,* edited by Charles H. Lippy. New York: Greenwood Press, 1989.
Clabaugh, Gary K. *Thunder on the Right: The Protestant Fundamentalists.* Chicago, IL: Nelson-Hall, 1974.
Jorstad, Erling. *The Politics of Doomsday: Fundamentalists of the Far Right.* Nashville, TN: Abingdon Press, 1970.
Longfield, Bradley J. *The Presbyterian Controversy: Fundamentalists, Modernists, and Moderates.* New York: Oxford University Press, 1991.
Reich, Jutta. *Amerikanischer Fundamentalismus: Geschichte und Erscheinung der Bewegung um Carl McIntire,* 2d edition. Hildesheim, Germany: Verlag Dr. H. A. Gerstenberg, 1972.

KURT W. PETERSON

MCPHERSON, AIMEE SEMPLE (1890–1944)

American evangelist. McPherson was born near Salford, Ontario, Canada, on October 9, 1890, and died September 27, 1944 in Oakland, California. The daughter of James and Minnie Kennedy, she was reared in the SALVATION ARMY. In 1908 she embraced PENTECOSTALISM and married an Irish immigrant evangelist, Robert Semple. In 1910 Aimee and Robert Semple left CANADA and sailed for Hong Kong to serve as Pentecostal missionaries. Ten weeks after their arrival, Robert died of dysentery and Aimee lay desperately ill of the same disease in a mission hospital. That fall, recovered and accompanied by her newborn daughter, Aimee sailed for the UNITED STATES.

In 1912 she married Harold McPherson. They settled in Providence, Rhode Island, had a son, and seemed on the road to a typical middle-class life. Then Aimee rediscovered her call to preach, took her children, and hit the sawdust trail. Before long Harold joined her. She began evangelizing in 1915 and first gained public notice during her barnstorming up and down the east coast from 1916 to 1918. Although Aimee proved a resilient preacher, Harold decided against devoting his life to itinerant EVANGELISM, and the couple parted amicably in 1918.

She edited a monthly periodical, *The Bridal Call,* to galvanize support and interest, and late in 1918 she moved with her mother and her children to Los Angeles. The city became Aimee's hub for the rest of her life and the site of Angelus Temple, a 5,300-seat Pentecostal church that opened January 1, 1923. The same year she opened a Bible school to train evangelists (see BIBLE COLLEGE AND INSTITUTES). She began broadcasting on her own radio station KFSG in 1924 (see MASS MEDIA). McPherson called her message the Foursquare Gospel. It focused on Christ, the savior, healer, baptizer in the Holy Spirit, and coming king.

McPherson's citywide evangelistic crusades routinely overflowed the largest auditoriums across America. Dubbed "the female BILLY SUNDAY" by the press, she was the first Pentecostal to enjoy a wide following beyond that movement's boundaries. Her crusades resembled the revival meetings to which Americans were accustomed, manifesting her Pentecostalism primarily when she yielded to public pressure to pray for the sick. Her maternal style and narrative preaching endeared her to her audiences. Noted especially for her elaborately illustrated sermons, McPherson made Angelus Temple rival nearby Hollywood in attracting audiences.

McPherson's mysterious disappearance for six weeks in the spring of 1926 inaugurated six months of highly charged national publicity. Several died searching for her, and thousands of tearful followers participated in memorial services. When she surfaced in southern Arizona, some challenged her claim that she had been kidnapped. A grand jury convened to investigate but was unable to prove wrongdoing. Her following remained loyal, but some reporters now questioned the naïveté many had previously found engaging.

McPherson's 1931 decision to remarry caused a deeper rift among her supporters. Divorced from Harold McPherson in 1921, she married David Hutton, an aspiring musician eleven years her junior. They divorced in 1934 after months of separation, but by then her remaining supporters from the evangelical world beyond Pentecostalism had turned from McPherson. McPherson had two children, Roberta Semple and Rolf McPherson.

The institutions McPherson created became the INTERNATIONAL CHURCH OF THE FOURSQUARE GOSPEL, a Pentecostal DENOMINATION with headquarters in Los Angeles and a missionary outreach around the world.

References and Further Reading

Primary Source:

McPherson, Aimee Semple. *This Is That*. Los Angeles: The Bridal Call, 1921.

Secondary Sources:

Blumhofer, Edith L. *Aimee Semple McPherson: Everybody's Sister*. Grand Rapids, MI: Eerdmans, 1994.
Epstein, Daniel M. *Sister Aimee*. New York: Harcourt Brace Javonovich, 1993.

EDITH L. BLUMHOFER

MEGA-CHURCHES

Protestant "mega-churches" (churches with 2,000 or more attendees per week), have multiplied across North America in recent history. Although there were only about a dozen such churches in 1970, there were over 300 by 1990, and 500 to 700 by 2000. Churches with 2,000+ attendance are not without precedent in Protestant history; CHARLES SPURGEON in London and HENRY WARD BEECHER in Brooklyn, for instance, preached to several thousand people per weekend in the nineteenth century; but the spreading use of electronic microphones and automobiles in the 1930s supported the proliferation of mega-churches, and the 1970s move to larger "full service" schools, supermarkets, and malls, for instance, conditioned many people to expect a range of ministries within a church. North American Protestant Christianity has no monopoly on such churches; AFRICA, Asia, and LATIN AMERICA (combined) have far more Protestant mega-churches than North America. Furthermore the Roman Catholic Church has far more "mega-parishes" in North America than all the mega-churches of the Protestant traditions combined.

John Vaughan, of www.megachurches.net and the quarterly *Church Growth Today,* frequently publishes updated lists of the one hundred largest churches in North America and the fifty largest churches in the world. About 70 percent of America's mega-churches are in the West or the South. About one-third are "independent" churches; the other two-thirds are (quietly) denominational.

There are essentially two types of mega-churches, with very contrasting agendas. Because the mission of many European Protestant churches was once to make Catholics into Protestants, so some mega-churches attract many transfers from other churches. The other mega-churches regard their community as a secular mission field, their "apostolic" mission targets pre-Christian people, and most of the people who join have no church from which to transfer. The mission statement of the Chicago area's Willow Creek Community Church dramatizes this apostolic agenda: "Our mission is to help irreligious people become fully devoted followers of Jesus Christ."

The latter ("apostolic") mega-churches, which are driven to reach and disciple populations with no Christian memory, realized that they would have to reinvent the way they "do church" to achieve their mission. The most influential innovations emerged, historically, in the JESUS MOVEMENT, and in several mega-churches—like Willow Creek and Southern California's Saddleback Church. These bellwether churches influence many other churches through their teaching conferences, publications, and networks—such as the Willow Creek Association (www.willowcreek.com).

Mega-churches, however, are widely misunderstood. Most observers view them through old paradigms, and therefore fail to perceive what they observe.

For instance, when people notice the absence of pipe organs and the presence of "praise bands," they see "opposition to tradition" or "trendy" Christianity; actually, the church is probably attempting culturally "indigenous" ministry, as effective churches do on any mission field. Again, people typically see a mega-church on a Sunday morning, without understanding that such churches are "seven-day-a-week churches" (Schaller). Still again, people often identify a mega-church with a specific community, and are later astonished at the range of its global involvement; or often they identify the church with the social class they see attending a service, and are later astonished by the church's diversity, often including several ethnic-language congregations (see ETHNICTY).

Or, when people see a congregation of several thousand, they attribute the crowd to "great PREACHING." Actually, most mega-churches put fewer of their eggs in the "preaching" basket than traditional churches. The preaching is only part of a planned experience. The WORSHIP service, whether "SEEKER-sensitive" or "seeker-driven," begins where people are, engaging their questions, issues, and hopes. The service introduces Christianity's truth claims and lifestyle. The service's music, or a drama, or a video clip, or a testimony, or a prayer time may be as prominently featured as the "message." The message engages an issue in people's lives, from Scripture, in the people's language in a conversational style. The whole service reflects a more casual, contemporary, culturally relevant, celebrative style than one would likely experience in the smaller traditional church.

When people casually observe a church of thousands, they have no idea that most mega-churches "grow larger by growing smaller." The most important feature of many apostolic mega-churches today is the small group, sometimes called the cell group. Most mega-churches involve thousands of people each week in group life—such as neighborhood groups, BIBLE study groups, nurture groups, support groups, prayer groups, recovery groups, groups for seekers, sports teams, and many groups with some ministry beyond the group. Many mega-churches are no longer churches "with" small groups; they are "meta-churches" (George, 1994) of small groups. In meta-churches, most people first join a group, and then the church; most people learn, in their small group, to be in ministry with other people, and to converse meaningfully about their faith. Ralph Neighbor claims that nineteen of the twenty largest churches on earth are "cell churches."

When people learn about a mega-church's large staff, they have no idea that, actually, the church shepherds and grows its people, and attracts seekers and new members through the ministries of LAITY. A typical apostolic mega-church features a hundred or more lay ministries; most of the members are involved in a ministry for which they are gifted, and many of the lay-led ministries are "outreach ministries" to non-Christian people. The strongest and most reproductive mega-churches are essentially local lay movements.

Although most churches will not, and should not, become mega-churches, the mega-church is a relatively new, important, and multiplying type of church on North America's religious landscape. They now include more within a church's domain—such as Christian schools, sports leagues, fitness centers, food courts, and much else—than ever before. With this trend, however, many mega-churches may be unwittingly planting the seeds of decline. More Christian kids in church schools means fewer Christian kids in the public schools; more Christians pumping iron at church fitness centers means fewer Christians meeting non-Christians at public gyms. The very churches originally reinvented to reach non-Christian people, by preparing and sending the laity into the world as salt and light, could, over time, become evangelical ghettos within the secular city.

References and Further Reading

George, Carl. *The Coming Church Revolution.* Grand Rapids, MI: Fleming H. Revell, 1994.

Gibbs, Eddie. *ChurchNext: Quantum Changes in How We Do Ministry.* Downers Grove, IL: InterVarsity Press, 2000.

Hunter, George G., III. *How to Reach Secular People.* Nashville, TN: Abingdon, 1992.

———. *Church for the Unchurched.* Nashville, TN: Abingdon, 1996.

———. *Radical Outreach: Recovering Apostolic Ministry and Evangelism.* Nashville, TN: Abingdon, 2003.

Hybels, Lynne, and Bill Hybels. *Rediscovering Church: The Story and Vision of Willow Creek Community Church.* Grand Rapids, MI: Zondervan, 1995.

Miller, Donald E. *Reinventing American Protestantism.* Berkeley: University of California Press, 1997.

Neighbor, Ralph W. *Where Do We Go from Here?: A Guidebook for the Cell Group Church,* rev. edition. Houston, TX: Touch Outreach Ministries, 2000.

Schaller, Lyle. *The Seven-Day-a-Week-Church.* Nashville, TN: Abingdon, 1992.

———. *The Very Large Church.* Nashville, TN: Abingdon, 2000.

GEORGE G. HUNTER III

MELANCHTHON, PHILIP (1497–1560)

German reformer. Melanchthon was author of several highly influential Lutheran texts, among them the *Loci communes* (1521, 1535, 1555), the AUGSBURG CONFESSION (1530) and its *Apology* (1531) (see AUGSBURG CONFESSION, APOLOGY OF), as well as the "altered" or *Variata* version of the *Augsburg Confession* (1540). Philip Schwartzerd (who took the Hellenized name

Melanchthon as a boy; in both forms the name means "black earth") brought a rare combination of strengths to the reform movement centered in Wittenberg: linguistic facility, mental and expository clarity, and prodigious energy. A prolific author of textbooks and commentaries, Melanchthon helped extend the intellectual scope of Protestant learning beyond scriptural dogmatics. In so doing he drew suspicion for betraying the more closely focused biblical teaching of Luther.

Humanism

A humanist with interests in the natural sciences and classical literature, Melanchthon was called to teach Greek at the University of Wittenberg. Arriving a year after MARTIN LUTHER posted his Ninety-five Theses, Melanchthon quickly joined the new program, bringing philological and theological acumen to bear in explicating biblical texts. Early on he added the bachelor of Bible degree to the B.A. and M.A. he had earned at Heidelberg and Tübingen, respectively, but to the end of his days he remained a member of the Wittenberg arts faculty. He was an indefatigable proponent of humanistic studies, issuing textbooks and editions of ancient texts and helping to organize both the German humanistic Gymnasium and the Protestant university system. For these efforts he became known as the "Preceptor of Germany."

Drawn to the classics by early immersion in Greek and Latin, Melanchthon promoted the study of classical literature in various ways, among which his virtually single-handed stewardship of the classical canon is possibly the most important. By means of editions and commentaries, Melanchthon brought such authors as Demosthenes, Aeschines, Lucian, Cicero, and Virgil within reach of a readership for whom they might otherwise have been barely more than names. Convinced, like most humanists of the era, that refinement in languages was necessary for any refinement in manners, Melanchthon was a forceful advocate of imitating the foremost models of Greek and Latin prose. He reinforced his efforts with manuals of grammar, logic, and rhetoric that sought, by precept and example, to train the young in the best mental habits. Learning and eloquence being especially valuable for pastors, Melanchthon insisted that evangelical clergy have some humanistic training.

Active as Melanchthon was in promoting humanist learning, the canon of ancient authors he helped shape was clearly determined by religious concerns. Notable by their absence from the pedagogical curriculum are works that might have been taken as glorifying pagan religion. Hence Hesiod's *Works and Days* is a poem Melanchthon promoted, with editions and commentaries, whereas the mythological epic *Theogony* is hardly even mentioned. The more moralistic Euripides is Melanchthon's favorite Greek tragic poet, judging from translations (into Latin verse) of all surviving plays; but Sophocles appears seldom and Aeschylus almost never. Among philosophers, Aristotle's *Ethics* and *Politics* receive attention, whereas the *Metaphysics* is ignored. Plato is mentioned only as the teacher whom the superior Aristotle surpassed. Notwithstanding such selectivity Melanchthon energetically promoted the study of history (which he saw as "philosophy taught by example"), the natural sciences (as evidence of divine majesty and order), and medicine, as a way to fulfill God's command to care for creation.

Theology

Melanchthon was an early and powerful supporter of the REFORMATION cause in its early years, offering lectures on biblical books as part of his Wittenberg teaching repertoire. Academic lectures on the Epistle to the Romans, begun in 1519, became a commentary and the basis for the first edition (1521) of *Loci communes,* a modest but influential manual of evangelical DOCTRINE. In its simplicity and clarity the *Loci* set out in schematic form what Luther had developed in exegetical and polemical writings. In Melanchthon's own terms the categories of Christian experience are reducible to law (which serves to make one aware of sinfulness), SIN (and the corresponding despair at being able to fulfill the law), and GRACE (or the divine reconciliation between a righteous God and a sinful humanity). The ordering of experience in the *Loci* accurately depicts the Reformers' adaptation of the Pauline message of freedom from bondage: the bondage to Jewish Law in the first century is recreated as the penitential-sacramental "Law" of late-medieval Catholicism, and the Pauline gospel of Christian freedom is reinstantiated in the Lutheran doctrine of the ATONEMENT as liberation.

Such liberation, the necessary condition for a truly pious life—that is, one of gratitude for the Atonement—does not entail disobedience to the laws of civil government. On the contrary the believer fully aware of divine goodness in creating and ordering human society will see the civil order as a manifestation of that goodness, and will accordingly be more loyal and obedient than the impious individual who may need the restraint yet balks at its demands. In so doing, the Christian obedient to the law acts as an instructor to neighbors, and thus serves as a model of conduct within the well-ordered society. In Melanchthon's view, God's will is perfectly expressed in the Decalogue, of which each precept contains both a pious and a moral dimension. The pious aspect of the moral laws is fairly obvious: one refrains from adultery, theft, murder, and the like out of obedience to the divine intention. The moral aspect of the First Table is more subtle, but it implies that acts of piety, being just as "external" as acts of the Second Table, instruct and inspire similar behavior in others.

Reverence toward civil institutions as a form of divine governance, although not incompatible with Luther's doctrine of two kingdoms, may have reflected greater optimism than Luther expressed about the possibility of godly rulers. For Melanchthon a Christian monarch was as much obligated to create a society supportive of true DOCTRINE as the lowliest subject was to obey the ruler. Moreover Melanchthon— who considered the classical literature of statecraft, especially Aristotle's *Politics,* instructive for rulers in his own time— was prepared to support these sovereigns' work with visitation protocols, ordination examinations, and renewed emphasis on the study of law, at Wittenberg and elsewhere. Melanchthon's diplomatic work was penetrating and wide-ranging, and thousands of surviving documents attest to his efforts to cooperate with rulers of territories large and small.

Some of this cooperation brought suspicions of being too much of a conciliator, willing to make concessions in faith in the interest of the unity of the CHURCH. His participation in most of the major colloquies and Diets of the time indicates that he was considered, both home and abroad, a skillful theological dialogue partner. Although Melanchthon was generally a more effective negotiator than some of his contemporaries, the image of an irenicist is pushed too far if it suggests that he was willing to compromise on essentials to avoid conflict between the confessions. Research into the interconfessional meetings of the 1530s and later has shown that Melanchthon remained resolute on the doctrines of JUSTIFICATION by FAITH, the AUTHORITY of Scripture over church TRADITION, and the relation of law to gospel.

Melanchthon's doctrine of ADIAPHORA became the point at which he was thought to deviate farthest from original Lutheran teaching. After Luther's death the Schmalkald War of 1547, and the attempted imposition of a Catholic-dominated "Interim" in Protestant churches, Melanchthon found himself torn between acknowledging the permissibility of restoring Catholic practices and denying the authority of the ruler behind the Interim, Elector Maurice of Saxony. He resolved this dilemma by granting that the practices could be returned, but only as *adiaphora,* or "indifferent things," not in themselves detrimental to faith. In this Melanchthon was echoing statements by Luther in his eight Wittenberg sermons of 1522, in which Luther considered many practices of the Catholic tradition valid so long as they were free of idolatry or works-righteousness. Melanchthon's critics of the late 1540s and 1550s, however, saw this concession as nothing but the return of idolatry and works-righteousness, and denied the possibility of any nonscriptural practice being at all "indifferent." Controversy over this issue would continue for decades.

Similar controversies surrounded the later Melanchthon's view of the law in the life of the Christian. Holding from early in his work that the law was not wholly transcended in the embrace of the gospel, Melanchthon held that the pious believer would turn to the law as the expression of the divine will for humanity, not relying solely on love of neighbor as the controlling norm of human action. Such a position was shared by Luther and Melanchthon equally, especially in the wake of the Peasants' War and other forms of radical ANTINOMIANISM, but the directness with which Melanchthon defended the Third Use of the Law—revelation for regulating the Christian life—drew comparisons with JOHN CALVIN and contrasts with Luther. If the doctrine of the Third Use is implicit in Luther, then Melanchthon has not departed from Lutheran teaching; if it is absent from Luther, Melanchthon may certainly be seen as a bridge between Wittenberg and Calvinist Geneva. Like Luther, Melanchthon asserts that a life of works necessarily follows from justification; but the clarity of his assertion, and the question of whether these works are dictated by love or law, make him appear to contradict Luther's insistence that the justified Christian lives a life of spontaneous loving deeds.

Influence

The controversies of Melanchthon's final decades cast a shadow over his reputation in the following centuries. Struggles within LUTHERANISM, and skepticism toward Melanchthon's attraction to pagan thought, led to his being labeled a rationalist and the inspiration of the Lutheran Scholasticism of Johann Gerhard (1582–1637) and GEORGE CALIXT (1586–1656) in the seventeenth century, the Pietist reaction to that being a self-conscious recovery of "true" Lutheranism. Likewise Melanchthon's concessions to secular authority, exemplified by his supposed capitulation to Maurice of Saxony, were thought to lead to the ABSOLUTISM of the seventeenth century. His engagement in the religious dialogues of the period, especially his apparent affinities with "moderates" like Erasmus, Georg Witzel, and MARTIN BUCER, brought him an enduring reputation of a conciliator, long before that term acquired the positive attributes it gained in the second half of the twentieth century.

Melanchthon's posthumous reputation, if not based on caricature, has at least been sufficiently shaped by simplifications and polemical distortions to obscure his relation to Luther and the originality and coherence of his own thought. Ecumenically minded scholars in the 1960s and 1970s approaching Melanchthon as a forerunner of their own work began to recognize the limits of "ECUMENISM" as a rubric for interpreting his work; and somewhat later work on the relation of his humanism (including his support of scientific learning) to THEOLOGY uncovered a complex coherence rather than the dual-career model of earlier views. In addition recent research on the development of confessional communities has uncovered dynamics far too intricate to allow any single thinker to be held responsible for the rise of absolutism.

References and Further Reading

Primary Sources:

Melanchthon, Philip. "*Loci communes* (1521)." In *Melanchthon and Bucer*. Edited and translated by Wilhelm Pauck. Philadelphia, PA: Westminster Press, 1969.
———. *Melanchthon on Christian Doctrine: Loci communes 1555*. Translated by Clyde L. Manschreck. New York: Oxford University Press, 1965.
———. *Orations on Philosophy and Education*. Edited and traslated by Sachiko Kusukawa and Christine F. Salazar. Cambridge/New York: Cambridge University Press, 1999.

Secondary Sources:

Fraenkel, Pierre. *Testimonia Patrum: The Function of the Patristic Argument in the Theology of Philip Melanchthon*. Geneva, Switzerland: E. Droz, 1961.
Kusukawa, Sachiko. *The Transformation of Natural Philosophy: The Case of Philip Melanchthon*. Cambridge/New York: Cambridge University Press, 1995.
Meijering, E. P. *Melanchthon and Patristic Thought: The Doctrines of Christ and Grace, the Trinity and the Creation*. Leiden, The Netherlands: E. J. Brill, 1983.
Wengert, Timothy J. *Law and Gospel: Philip Melanchthon's Debate with John Agricola of Eisleben over Poenitentia*. Grand Rapids, MI: Baker Books, 1997.
———. *Human Freedom, Christian Righteousness: Philip Melanchthon's Exegetical Dispute with Erasmus of Rotterdam*. New York: Oxford University Press, 1998.

RALPH KEEN

MELVILLE, ANDREW (1545–1622)

Scottish academic. Andrew Melville introduced major university reforms and helped establish PRESBYTERIAN-ISM in Scotland. Melville was born at Baldovy and was an exemplary student, demonstrating excellent facility with languages. He graduated from St. Andrews at age nineteen and proceeded to gain a wide-ranging education at Paris, Poitiers, and Geneva with THEODORE BEZA. Melville returned to SCOTLAND in 1574 to become principal of the languishing Glasgow University, which he revived through fundamental changes in the curriculum that he patterned after the educational methods of French humanist Petrus Ramus. Melville later extended similar reforms to Aberdeen and St. Andrews, where he became principal of St. Mary's College in 1580. He also worked to eliminate the remainder of the Episcopal system and helped draft the Genevan-styled *Second Book of Discipline* (1578), which passed the General Assembly under his leadership.

Melville firmly rejected the ecclesiastical supremacy of the monarch and frequently clashed with James VI, whom he famously dubbed "God's silly vassal," on account of the king's hindrance of PRESBYTERIAN-ISM. In 1584, Melville was charged with treason and left for ENGLAND. He eventually resumed teaching at St. Andrews in 1586, but experienced continued conflicts with the king, who worked to curb Melville's influence by removing him as rector of St. Andrews (1597) and excluding him from the General Assembly. In 1606, Melville was summoned before the English Privy Council and confined to the Tower from 1607 to 1611. He spent the remaining years of his life in exile in the University of Sedan, FRANCE. His writings include a commentary on Romans and much well-received Latin poetry.

References and Further Reading

Durkan, John, and James Kirk. *The University of Glasgow, 1451–1577*. Glasgow UK: University of Glasgow Press, 1977.
McCrie, Thomas. *The Life of Andrew Melville*. Edinburgh, 1819.
Wright, Ronald, ed. *Fathers of the Kirk*. London: Oxford University Press, 1960.

SCOTT MCGINNIS

MENNO SIMONS (1496–1561)

Anabaptist leader and theologian. Menno Simons, a former Catholic priest of Friesland, became, after the late 1530s, the most prominent leader of the peaceful Anabaptists in the NETHERLANDS and Northwestern GERMANY. Gradually his influence came to predominate many Anabaptist groups elsewhere in Europe, who then called themselves MENNONITES.

Menno, son of Frisian farmers, was ordained a priest in 1524, but was quickly influenced by the Reformation to doubt the traditional Catholic teaching of the mass, and embarked on his own study of the Bible. Even so, he remained the vicar of Pingjum, and then of Witmarsum, Friesland, throughout the most tumultuous period of the early REFORMATION in the Netherlands (1524–1535). He read the works of the church fathers, the Dutch humanist Erasmus of Rotterdam, and Protestant leaders such as MARTIN LUTHER (1483–1546), MARTIN BUCER (1491–1551), and HEINRICH BULLINGER (1504–1575), and his sermons become increasingly evangelical. By 1533, however, the Reformation in the Netherlands followed the Anabaptist teachings of MELCHIOR HOFMANN (1500–1543), who preached purification of believers and the church for the imminent return of Christ. At the height of this popular reform movement Menno watched as the apocalyptical crusade spun wildly out of control; in the spring of 1535 his younger brother, Peter, who had joined the Anabaptist kingdom in Münster, Westphalia, was killed in the authorities' crushing of the Anabaptist occupation of the Frisian monastery Oldeklooster. In response, Menno wrote a tract against the Münsterite kingdom and its king, Jan van Leyden, but with its capture on June 25 he decided against publication.

Despite his growing unease with his own Catholic office and his conviction that the Anabaptists were right about the sacraments, Menno did not quit his position and side with them until January 1536. For the rest of his life, he lived a peripatetic existence, hounded by the authorities, protected by followers or noble friends, moving first to East Frisia, then to the archbishopric of Cologne, and finally to Schleswig-Holstein. No haven was entirely safe, and many of his supporters died hiding his whereabouts from the authorities. Finally, on January 13, 1561, at his last refuge on a noble estate near Oldesloe, Holstein, Menno breathed his last. However, the church he reformulated from the Anabaptist movement endures today in the Mennonite churches around the world.

Throughout his reform career, Menno not only fled the persecution of the Catholic authorities, but also was forced to defend his ideas against the attacks of Lutheran and Reformed theologians, who condemned Anabaptists and Mennonites as inextricably linked to the notorious Münsterites. Menno's case was not helped by his continued adherence to Hofmann's unusual incarnation doctrine, which stipulated that Christ had not received his humanity from Mary but had brought it with him from heaven. In early 1545 Menno and Johannes a Lasco (1499–1560), the Polish superintendent of the Reformed church in Emden, debated this and the other doctrines that divided Mennonites from the Reformed: Menno's depreciation of original sin, his emphasis on salvation as a life-changing act, his rejection of infant baptism and adherence to believer's baptism, and his insistence that ministers be called by God rather than be hierarchically appointed on the basis of formal theological training. In his numerous writings Menno defended the Mennonite position on these issues, striking a middle position between Catholic penitential practice and the Protestant's justification by faith.

Menno also had to fight against some Anabaptist leaders, such as David Joris (1501–1556), who depreciated the external elements of religious practice and allowed infant baptism to avoid detection by the persecuting authorities. Menno insisted on a visible church, distinct from the world and from what he saw as the apostasy of the mainstream churches. In this believers' community, Christians were to live in love and obedience to the gospel, and the ban, or shunning, was used to ensure that all members lived accordingly. The practice proved controversial, for some of Menno's associates wished to apply it within families, and while Menno generally opposed such rigor, in the end his reputation as a hard-liner was established.

Following the Anabaptist approach to salvation, Menno stressed a third path to reform, one that combined identification with the suffering of Christ, Christian discipline, and the communal and personal ethics of late medieval Catholicism with the pacifistic piety of Erasmus and the Reformation's emphasis on *sola scriptura* and justification by faith. The result was a process of discipleship leading to the "new person in Christ." The most notable distinction between Mennonites and Protestants was the former's absolute insistence on believers' baptism. Menno also defended the Anabaptist/Mennonite insistence on nonviolence for the Christian and refusal to swear an oath of allegiance to the state or in any way participate in civic government.

Menno's central work was *The Fundament of the Christian Life*, published first in 1539. In its importance for the Mennonite community, it compares to JOHN CALVIN's (1509–1564) *Institutes* for the Reformed Church. Baptism was administered only to adults who had already repented from their hearts, experienced the rebirth, and who had committed themselves to inner spiritual renewal and identification with the true people of God. After baptism, believers were to assist each other in the difficult process of discipleship, for Menno conceived of the Christian faith as a public commitment to Christ and his people. Hence, his church was a visible one, where together the people of God sought to follow the apostolic church and renounce the world.

See also Anabaptism; Hofmann, Melchior; Mennonites.

References and Further Reading

Augustijn, C. "Erasmus and Menno." *Mennonite Quarterly Review* 69 (1986): 497–508.

Brunk, Gerald R., ed. *Menno Simons: A Reappraisal.* Harrisonburg, VA: Eastern Mennonite College, 1992.

Friesen, Abraham. *Erasmus, the Anabaptists, and the Great Commission.* Grand Rapids, MI: Eerdman, 1998.

Hamilton, Alastair, Sjouke Voolstra, and Piet Visser, eds. *From Martyr to Muppy: A Historical Introduction to Cultural Assimilation Processes of a Religious Minority in the Netherlands: The Mennonites.* Amsterdam: University of Amsterdam Press, 1994.

Visser, Piet, and Mary Sprunger, eds. *Menno Simons: Places, Portraits and Progeny.* Altona, Manitoba: Friesens, 1996.

Voolstra, S. *Menno Simons: His Image and Message.* North Newton, KS: Bethel College, 1997.

Wenger, J. C., ed. *The Complete Writings of Menno Simons.* Scottdale, PA: Herald Press, 1956.

GARY K. WAITE

MENNONITES

This term is presently used to designate most of the churches descending from sixteenth-century ANABAPTISM. Because the rise of Anabaptism predates MENNO SIMONS's association with the movement by some ten years, not all groups have adopted the term. Communal Anabaptists, or HUTTERITES, are named after their most important leader, JAKOB HUTTER (1500–1536). The AMISH are named after their most important leader, Jacob Ammann (c.1644–c.1730). Since 1796 Menno's Dutch followers have called themselves *Doopsgezinde*; Swiss Anabaptists still prefer the term *Taufgesinnte*. Under the influence of Ludwig Keller (1849–1915) and his writings, German Mennonites in the late 1800s toyed with the idea of calling themselves *altevangelische Taufgesinnte*. The term *Menist* was first used in an edict of 1545 issued at Emden by Countess Anna of Oldenbourg, which recommended TOLERATION for the followers of Menno. Based on a theological judgment by John a'Lasco, it distinguished the peaceful followers of Menno from the Spiritualist followers of David Joris, and the revolutionary followers of Jan van Batenburg. To divorce themselves from the Münsterite stigma and get out from under the condemnation of an edict promulgated by the Second DIET OF SPEYER in 1529 that declared rebaptism a capital offense and referred to all persons baptized upon their confession of faith as *Wiedertäufer*, other Anabaptists also adopted the term. These factors, together with the overriding similarities between Menno's theology and that of the Swiss Brethren (or Anabaptists), and the translation and dissemination of his 1539 *Fundamentboek* into German in the 1580s made Menno known far and wide and so his name gradually came to be adopted for most of the movement.

Origins of Anabaptism

Anabaptism emerged in Zurich, SWITZERLAND, on January 21, 1525, when a number of HULDRYCH ZWINGLI's (1484–1531) radical followers, led by CONRAD GREBEL (1498–1526) and Felix Mantz (1498–1527), baptized one another upon their confession of faith in the Zurich home of Mantz's mother, forming the first "believers' church" of Early Modern Europe. Based not so much on Zwingli's teachings as on those of Desiderius Erasmus (1469–1536), whose writings influenced both groups, these radicals took as their theological point of departure Erasmus's interpretation of Matthew 28:16–20—Christ's "Great Commission." Beginning with the Council of Nicea (325) and its quarrel with Arianism, Church Fathers, seeking a Trinitarian baptismal formula (which they found in Matthew 28:18–20), had begun to associate this passage with the baptismal passages in the Acts of the Apostles (2, 8, 10, and 19) because the apostles, in every one of the passages that narrated a baptismal event, had always baptized only in the name of Jesus. To explain this apparent discrepancy became the concern of virtually all scholars.

The Matthew and Acts passages had therefore come together long before Erasmus dealt with them in his paraphrases of the Gospel of Matthew (1522) and Acts (1523). Erasmus, however, broke with church TRADITION in this instance and interpreted the Matthew passage very differently. Ignoring the baptismal issue and concentrating instead on the interpretation of the entire passage, Erasmus argued that the apostles had themselves interpreted the Great Commission in these baptismal passages, especially in St. Peter's "Pentecost Sermon" contained in Acts 2. That interpretation focused on two kinds of teaching, one before and another after the CONVERSION of the listener. It began, said Erasmus, with the proclamation of the Gospel—and here the Acts 8 passage featuring Philip and the Ethiopian eunuch with its central emphasis on Christ, was especially exemplary—proceeded to the response of the hearers in repentance and conversion, and culminated in the BAPTISM of the converted where the baptizand took an oath of obedience to Christ. This was then followed by a second kind of teaching—"teaching them to obey everything I [Christ] have commanded you." It was under this second kind of teaching that Christian discipleship was taught. This interpretation of Christ's Great Commission was adopted by the Swiss Brethren—and by Menno Simons some ten years later—and can be seen explicitly in Mantz's *Protestation* of December 1524, BALTHASAR HUBMAIER's (c.1480–1528) *Old and New Believers on Baptism* (1526), BERNARD ROTHMANN's *Concerning the Two Confessions* (1533), Menno Simons's *Meditations on the 25th Psalm* (1537) and *Fundamentboek* (1539), Thomas van Imbroik's *Confession* (1559), Peter Walpot's *Artikelbuch* (1577), and the Swiss Brethren's 1585 *Einfaltiges Bekanntnus*. Other documents, too numerous to mention, contain an implicit replication of the Erasmian interpretation. Indeed a group of Moravian Hutterites under the leadership of Joseph Hauser informed the Elbing (Prussia) city council as late as 1603 that they read the biblical interpretations of only one writer—those of Desiderius Erasmus.

The discovery of this connection between Erasmus's paraphrases of the Great Commission and the Anabaptist/Menno core theological perspective is important for a number of reasons, not least of all because it establishes a separate intellectual origin for the Swiss Brethren but also because it explains the similarities between their position and that of Menno Simons. Furthermore it distinguishes these two branches very clearly from the revolutionary and mystical branches of the Radical Reformation, as well as from MELCHIOR HOFMANN (1495–1543) who was so influential in the beginning of the Dutch Anabaptist movement. The beginning of Dutch Anabaptism has therefore to be seen as a conflict between the Hofmann heritage and the teachings of Menno Simons, with the latter emerging victorious after the Münster revolution (1534–1535).

Influence of Melchior Hofmann

Hofmann is regarded as largely responsible for introducing a version of Anabaptism in the northern regions of the Holy Roman Empire. He began his reformation work as a Lutheran lay minister in Livonia in 1523, but his tendency to cater to the masses quickly alienated the ruling elites. In 1525 he was forced to have his ministry validated by MARTIN LUTHER himself, but his certificate of ORTHODOXY did him little good. City after city continued to expel him until he finally found temporary sanctuary in Stockholm. There, in 1527, he published his commentary on Daniel, demonstrating his predilection for apocalyptic thinking. Later in Lübeck and Kiel he, for a time, enjoyed the goodwill of the king of DENMARK. As DEACON of the Nikolai Church in Kiel, he acquired a printing press that he used mostly to attack Luther's surrogates in the region. This brought him the opposition of Luther as well as that of the local authorities. When ANDREAS RUDOLF BODENSTEIN VON KARLSTADT—alienated from Luther ever since the latter's return from the Wartburg in March of 1522—himself came into the region, Hofmann joined him. Together they attacked Luther's doctrine of the real presence. Little wonder that Hofmann's teaching was condemned at the 1529 Flensburg Disputation.

Forced to flee the region, Hofmann made his way to Strasbourg where Luther's eucharistic enemies lived. When his reception there was no friendlier, he made contact with outsiders like Hans Denck and the "Strasbourg Prophets." From them he absorbed his later emphasis on the "inner Word" and other herterodox positions. His views on the incarnation he took from CASPAR VON SCHWECKFELD (1489–1561). Referring to Christ's physical body as "heavenly flesh," it argued that Christ had passed through Mary like water through a sieve, thus avoiding being contaminated with original SIN. His apocalyptic thinking also took a more radical turn here. No longer satisfied, along with so many other sixteenth-century thinkers, with merely proclaiming the imminence of the end of the age, Hofmann now began to argue that Christ's return had to be prepared for by a great cleansing of the godless in the world. Once that had happened, the new Elijah promised, Christ would return in 1533 in the city of Strasbourg.

In the meantime, in 1530, Hofmann returned to Emden. There, in soil prepared by the Sacramentarians and the Brothers of the Common Life, he quickly baptized some 300 persons. As elsewhere, such a public and dramatic break with the past brought persecution in its wake. Leaving a disciple, Jan Volkerszoon, in charge, Hofmann once again took to the road. However, he could not stay away from the scene of such success for long and so, a year later, he returned, baptizing another group of persons. However, when on December 5, 1531, Volkerszoon and ten others were executed at the Hague for rebaptism, Hofmann—perhaps on the advice of Schwenckfeld and SEBASTIAN FRANCK—ordered a halt to all baptizing. PREACHING and admonition, however, were to continue.

Like a magnet, Hofmann was drawn back to Strasbourg again. The authorities were not pleased when they discovered his presence, and so he was expelled. Restless and unsettled, he turned his steps to the north again, this time to Hesse and eventually to Leeuwarden where his follower, Obbe Philips, was located. The approach of 1533, however, drew him back to Strasbourg to witness the prophesied return of Christ. The authorities, fearing that his prediction of the cleansing of the godless would lead to revolution, thought it best for him to witness his predicted events from behind prison walls, so they had him incarcerated. There he died ten years later, declared by his own Dutch followers to have been a false prophet.

Bernard Rothmann's Reform

While the Hofmann saga was running its course, Rothmann, another erstwhile follower of Luther, began a reformation movement in the Westphalian city of Münster. Having studied at the universities of Cologne and Wittenberg, Rothmann nevertheless soon came to be attracted to Zwingli's teachings and then to even more radical positions. In 1531 he, too, made the pilgrimage to Strasbourg where he met with MARTIN BUCER and WOLFGANG CAPITO, Strasbourg's two magisterial reformers, but also with Martin Cellarius and Schwenckfeld. Like Hofmann, he may also have encountered Cellarius's apocalyptic thinking here, although it does not appear to have had any immediately apparent impact on him. Within the year he returned to Münster and began to reform the city in earnest. The arrival of Hendrick Roll in August 1533—one of the so-called Wassenburger Predikanten—accelerated the radical direction of the movement.

The Münster Colloquy of August 1533 between Rothmann, his followers, and some Lutheran and Catholic clerics, was a watershed event in the reformation of the city. Nor did it find Rothmann unprepared: his thoughts on the two major topics of debate—baptism and the Eucharist—had already been laid out in his *Bekenntnisse van beyden Sacramenten, Doepe vnd Nachtmaele* (Confession Concerning the Two Sacraments). In the tract he categorically rejected the concept of objective grace in the SACRAMENTS. Unable to defeat Rothmann on the basis of *scriptura sola*—a principle laid down as the foundation for theological debate within the empire by the 1523 Nuremberg Imperial Edict—his opponents were forced to fall back on tradition and the development of church history.

Whereas Hofmann's theology contained elements of apocalyptic violence, Karl-Heinz Kirchhoff has confirmed Rothmann's own argument that the reformation movement in Münster was initially of a peaceful nature. Unlike the Swiss Brethren, however, Rothmann posited a greater parity and parallelism between the Old and New Testaments that left the door open for a later emphasis on Old Testament violence. He argued that the Old Testament consisted of types of the reality that had appeared in the New. These types, although superseded by the reality contained in the New Testament, nevertheless constituted a kind of archetypal foundation of what had come.

Rothmann's emphasis on the importance of the Old Testament increased with the arrival of Jan van Leiden and Gerard Boekbinder in the city on January 13, 1534. On February 24, JAN MATHIJS—the new prophet who had superseded Hofmann the false prophet—himself appeared in the city, declaring Münster to be the New Jerusalem and the site of Christ's imminent return. The appearance of a new prophet meant that Hofmann's ban on baptism could be rescinded. Consequently Rothmann, his followers, and even Gerhard Westerberg—Karlstadt's brother-in-law—were quickly baptized. Rothmann's emphasis on the restitution of a suffering apostolic church could also be sacrificed because the "time of harvest" had arrived

and the KINGDOM OF GOD on Earth was about to be inaugurated. This was justified by a new emphasis on the Old Testament clearly present in Rothmann's 1534 *Restitution* where the author argued that the Old Testament was not as irrelevant to the Christian as some had earlier thought, especially because this had been the only Scriptures known to Christ and the apostles.

Rothmann's attitude toward the use of violence changed with the transition of his emphasis from a suffering church to that of the kingdom of God and the arrival of the "time of harvest." Already before the kingdom's inauguration the elect were permitted to defend themselves; after its arrival they would go on the offensive until the entire world would be conquered. They set out on the road to this kingdom by gaining control of the city in early 1534 through the support of the guilds, but it was not until after Mathijs's death in the summer of 1534 that Jan van Leiden began to transform Münster into the New Jerusalem. By August he had had himself proclaimed a second King David. Rothmann became his royal orator, and Berndt Knipperdolling—a former city mayor—his chief minister. Community of goods was introduced along with a severe form of Old Testament justice, to be followed shortly by polygamy itself.

Under siege from summer 1534 to June 24, 1535 by the combined forces of the Protestant duke of Hesse and Franz von Waldeck, Catholic bishop of Münster, food gradually became scarce and rumors of cannibalism surfaced. Inhabitants sought to escape, only to be cut down by the besieging forces. In early June 1535 enemy soldiers were informed how entrance to the city might be obtained. They entered at night, and when dawn broke a great slaughter ensued. Jan van Leiden, Berndt Knipperdolling, and Bernard Krechting were taken alive. Bernard Rothmann, however, was never found—dead or alive. The captured leaders were interrogated, tortured, and finally executed. Their bodies were placed into three separate cages and raised up the spire of Lamberti Lambert's church. There they remained until the nineteenth century as a warning to all who would revolt against church and state. In January 1536, some six months after Muenster's collapse, Menno Simons left the Catholic Church and cast his lot with the erstwhile followers of the discredited movement.

Early Development of Menno Simons

Menno Simons (c.1496–1561) was born near Witmarsum, in the small Frisian village of Pingjum. Little is known of his early life. Ordained into the priesthood by the bishop of Utrecht in 1524 at the age of twenty-eight, he appears to have been fairly well educated, knowing Latin and some Greek and possessing some knowledge of the Church Fathers. Appointed priest at Pingjum in 1524, Menno soon came to doubt the Catholic doctrine of the Eucharist (1525) and then infant baptism (1531), but nevertheless remained in the church. In 1532 he was transferred to Witmarsum where, in 1534, he encountered emissaries from Münster. His brother Pieter's involvement with the revolutionaries in their aborted attempt to take over the Old Cloister near Bolsward in early 1525, leading to his execution, occasioned Menno's attack on Jan van Leiden (1536) in his unpublished (until 1627) *Een gantz duidlijcke end klaer bewijs . . . Tegens de grouwelijcke end grootste blasphemie van Jan van Leyden* (Against the Blasphemy of Jan of Leyden). Menno experienced a profound conversion of his own while writing the piece, a conversion that eventually led to his leaving the Roman Catholic Church. He wrote about his conversion in two subsequent semiautobiographical tracts: the "Spiritual Resurrection" of 1536 and "The New Birth" of 1537.

Menno followed up his two tracts on conversion in 1538 with his "Meditations on the 25th Psalm," which clearly reflects the Erasmian "Great Commission" influence. Then, in 1539, he wrote his most important book, *Een Fundament vnd klare Anwisinge, van de heylsame vnd Godtsellyghe Leere Jesu Christi . . .* (The Foundation of Christian Teaching). Known as the *Fundamentboek,* it became the book around which Menno built his church. As a motto he chose I Corinthians 3:11: "For no man can lay any foundation other than the one already laid, which is Jesus Christ." He repeated the motto in all his other works. It was a motto that pointed to the Christ-centeredness of his theology. A person "converted" from a Münsterite—or even a Melchiorite—position could not have written such a book only three years after the cataclysmic demise of the revolutionary movement. It took a man who had been studying the BIBLE for some fourteen years to do so. Menno, therefore, cannot ever have belonged to that movement—revolutionary or pacific. It was precisely because he had remained untainted by it that he could become the leader of a new movement, one that stood in conflict with it.

Emergence of "Menno's Church"

Through his writings and itinerant preaching Menno now began to build a new movement on the ashes of the old, ashes that clearly demonstrated the bankruptcy of the Melchiorite/Münsterite ideology. Based on conversion and peaceful suffering, Menno established congregations that his followers clearly labeled as "Menno's church" in contradistinction to the earlier movement. If former revolutionaries wished to join that church, they had to be reformed. If they entered without being reformed, they had to be excluded through the application of the ban. So successful was he that already in 1542 an imperial edict singled him out and placed a price on his head. The edict forced Menno to move first to Frisia, then up the Baltic coast at least as far as Lübeck, if not Danzig itself. Upon the recommendation of John a'Lasco to Duchess Anna of Oldenbourg only two years later, as we have seen, Menno's followers were distinguished from those of David Joris and Jan van Batenburg—that is, from the Spiritualists and the revolutionaries. This is remarkable, coming only seven years after Münster. It points to the fact that others besides Menno and his followers—indeed outsiders—recognized the nascent "Mennonite" church to be different from the previous movement.

Along the way, Menno spent some time in Cologne until it also became too dangerous. Eventually he was allowed to settle in Oldesloe, near Lübeck, under the protection of the count of Ahlefeld. Here he was permitted to have his own printing press and to publish his writings in relative peace.

Menno appears not to have known much—if anything—about the Swiss Brethren, and never mentions such names as Felix Mantz or Conrad Grebel. Yet his theology—because of the two groups' common dependency on the Erasmian interpretation of the Great Commission—bears striking similarities to that of the Swiss Brethren. He did differ from them on the Incarnation and on the strict use of the ban, but the essentials were strikingly similar, although these were differences that crept into his theology after his conversion.

Establishing the Church

After Münster, Menno was forced to work on two fronts: to build a church cleansed from the Münsterite influence and to defend that church against attacks from without. The latter were severe because, with few exceptions, opponents chose to associate the movement with revolution and excesses such as polygamy to discredit it. Menno himself came repeatedly to be called a "Münsterite" simply because of his brother's execution. He was called on to justify himself and his movement in debates with John a'Lasco in 1544 and Martin Micron in 1554. Yet as an accused Münsterite, Menno was forced, internally, to move against those very remaining Münsterite sympathizers in the person of Jan Batenburg and his followers. He was also forced to take issue with and reject the Spiritualist David Joris and his followers. In 1547 Adam Pastor, ordained by Menno and Dirk Philips in 1542, had to be excommunicated for denying the preexistent divinity of Christ. As early as 1540, Obbe

Philips—overcome by doubts about his own "calling," which had come through the Münsterites—left the movement.

It is important, in assessing the relationship of the Dutch "Mennonites" to the Swiss movement, to note that Rothmann's *Confession Concerning the Two Sacraments* plays an important role in Menno's thinking as well as the thinking of South German Anabaptists such as PILGRAM MARPECK. For Menno the document demonstrated the extent of Rothmann's apostasy as manifested in his later tracts. Such apostasy, combined with the fact that the Münsterite movement before the arrival in Münster of Jan van Leiden and Jan Mathijs in January/February 1534 had been peaceful in nature, convinced Menno that the movment had been derailed by men like Jan van Leiden. Hence his attack on the latter rather than on Rothmann in his *Blasphemy*. The fact that the Anabaptist leader Marpeck could incorporate Rothmann's *Confession* nearly verbatim in his own 1542 *Vermannung; auch gantz klarer gruendlicher vnd unwider sprechlicher bericht zu warer Christlicher puntsvereynigung* (Admonition and Clear, Fundamental and Incontestable Account), makes it clear that, even though there were differences between the various parties involved, the similarities between Swiss/South German Anabaptism, Menno Simons, and the pre-Melchiorite Rothmann were great.

Seeds of Division

It was alien ideas—such as the Melchiorite doctrine of the incarnation and the strict application of the ban in the Dutch churches resulting from the Münsterite past—that gave rise to future conflict. These differences became contentious issues when the Dutch and Swiss/South German movements made contact and began to talk to one another. One of these was the "question of the origin of Christ's flesh." It was discussed at a conference held August 24, 1555, in Strasbourg only some six years before Menno's death. That conference rejected the Dutch position, deciding that it was more important to observe Christ's commands than to speculate about the mystery of how Christ had become flesh. In 1557 a second conference took place in Strasbourg; this time the issues were the doctrine of original sin and the severe application of the ban, the latter having become a problem in the NETHERLANDS. The first, an internal Swiss and South German problem, was resolved amicably, but the second, which was directed at the Dutch, remained divisive. Menno, who had sought to win the High Germans to his views in the spring of 1557, was rejected, although the conference expressed the hope that an outright rupture between the two groups might be avoided. This was not to be, however, because Menno and his partner,

Leenaert Bouwens, rejected the proffered hand, and in 1559 the Dutch elders pronounced a ban on the High Germans.

Menno, who died in 1561, regretted having agreed with Bouwens in favor of a severe application of the ban in their congregations. Already in 1555–1556 the "Waterlanders" separated from Menno, Bouwens, and Dirk Philips over precisely this issue. They took their name from the lakes and river region north of Amsterdam in which they lived. By 1568 they began to hold their own church conferences and call themselves "Doopsgezinde." Another separation from Menno's group took place in 1567 when Flemish Anabaptists who had fled persecution in what was to become Belgium and settled among the Frisians decided to go their own way. Cultural and other differences exacerbated attempts to resolve the disputes, and even Dirk Philips's intervention could not heal the rupture. These internal divisions had a ripple effect and spread over northern Europe, creating conservative and more moderate groups. Even among the Flemish themselves a division occurred between conservatives and moderates in 1594, with the conservative group calling itself "Old Flemish." Only four years later a similar split divided the Frisians.

Yet in spite of these internal divisions more and more of the groups outside of the Netherlands adopted the name "Menist" for themselves. They did so because—even in Danzig in the late fifteenth century—the name came to denote a legally tolerated religious group different from the *Wiedertäufer,* which were regarded to be revolutionary. In other words, Anna of Oldenbourg's 1544 recognition of the "Menists" as a peaceful and productive, nonrevolutionary religious movement became a kind of legal precedent by which "Anabaptists" could be granted toleration. One scholar has called the "Menist" name a *Schutzname*—a name that protected the Anabaptists, and so wherever possible it was adopted. When religious toleration became established, however, many of these same groups reverted back to their original names, except in North America where the term "Mennonite" encompasses most of the groups deriving from the Radical Reformation.

Not everyone accepted the increasing divisions within the Dutch Mennonite church, however. Some members left the churches; others sought ways of healing the ruptures, sometimes through the creation of new Mennonite confessions of faith that were to be adopted by the rival factions. Especially the more moderate groups—in spite of the opposition of the "Old Flemish" and "Old Frisians"—insisted on reunion. In 1591 the so-called Young Frisians and High Germans united on the basis of the "Concept of Cologne," an agreement reached before the attempt at merger. Soon a number of Waterlanders, under the leadership of Hans de Ries, joined the union, although an invitation to the Old Flemish and Old Frisians in 1603 was not accepted. Nevertheless the attempts at reuniting the various groups of Dutch Anabaptists did have some success in the early years of the seventeenth century.

Long-term Changes

It was another development within the seventeenth century, however, that fundamentally changed the nature of the movement for many years to come. In the process of being granted toleration under what is known as *Schutzbriefe* (letters of protection), Menists were generally forced to promise to lead unobtrusive lives, hold their religious services in private homes so as not to attract attention, and to avoid all proselytizing. The first of such *Schutzbriefe* appears to have been issued in East Friesland in 1626. It was soon followed by one issued for the German territories of the Danish king and another by the Count Palatine of the Rhine. All of these documents contained a proselytizing prohibition. Many of them also demanded sizable sums of "protection" money from the "heretics." Combined with the merciless persecution during the sixteenth century, such *Schutzbriefe* of the seventeenth century completed the transformation of an originally aggressive missionary movement that so irritated sixteenth-century rulers and establishment churchmen. Mennonites, more and more, now became "the quiet in the land."

In the following centuries other influences reconfigured the internal relationships in the Anabaptist/ Mennonite movement. South German Mennonites came increasingly under strong Pietist influences (see PIETISM), whereas Dutch and north German Mennonites came under the influence of rationalism. This led, in the nineteenth century, to three major regional Mennonite centers in Europe: the *Verband* of Mennonite churches in the south; the *Vereinigung,* representing most Mennonite churches in northern GERMANY and Prussia; and the *Doopsgezinde* of the Netherlands. Furthermore, the creation of nation states gradually, and the Napoleonic Wars suddenly, eroded the Mennonites' ability to retain their exemptions from military service. Thus their time-honored principle of nonresistance came under attack. When their ability to purchase land in Prussia came to be tied to military service in the 1780s, large numbers of Prussian Mennonites decided, in 1789, to migrate to New Russia at the invitation of Empress Catherine II. Other groups followed in 1803 and 1835. Still others departed for the UNITED STATES.

Because of a revival in the Russian Mennonite churches in the late 1850s, another split occurred when the Mennonite Brethren Church was created. This was followed by the Russian government's attempt, in 1873–1874, to remove the Russian Mennonites' military exemption granted them on their entrance to the country. The exodus that followed cut across any internal divisions, with the more conservative migrating to CANADA's prairie provinces—especially Manitoba—and the more progressive moving to the plains states of the United States. Here they joined Swiss Mennonites, who had arrived from the Palatinate much earlier, to form the three largest groups of Mennonites: the so-called Old Mennonites (Swiss and German origin); the General Conference of Mennonites (largely made up of Dutch/Russian Mennonites); and the Mennonite Brethren. The post–World War I period brought another great exodus of Mennonites from RUSSIA. These settled primarily in Canada. Aside from these larger groups are the Amish, the Hutterites (sixteenth-century communal Anabaptists), the Holdemann people, and a number of other groups scattered across Canada and the United States. Since the 1920s some of the conservative Old Colony Mennonites of Manitoba have settled in MEXICO; others, like the Bergthalers, moved to Paraguay where they were joined by Mennonites fleeing Russia in 1929/1930. A later exodus of Mennonites from Russia during World War II brought another wave of settlers to Paraguay and BRAZIL, whereas about 100,000 more have come from Russia to Germany since the late 1970s.

Global Identity

Beginning in 1925 with the first Mennonite World Conference held in Basel, Switzerland, to commemorate the 400th anniversary of the birth of Anabaptism in Zurich, Mennonites from around the world have gathered periodically to celebrate a common faith but a growing racial and ethnic diversity. MISSIONS programs, beginning with that of the Dutch *Doopsgezinde* in the nineteenth century in Dutch colonies, have, during the twentieth century, led to the establishment of indigenous Mennonite churches in INDONESIA, INDIA, AFRICA, LATIN AMERICA, JAPAN, and other countries so that today Mennonites of non-European origin outnumber those of European origin. Institutions of higher learning, especially in Canada and the United States—but increasingly elsewhere as well—have, and are continuing to be, established. Often beginning as BIBLE INSTITUTES designed to foster the faith, they have gradually been transformed—like similar institutions of other denominations earlier—into liberal arts colleges and eventually into universities with theological seminaries as their counterparts (see

CHRISTIAN COLLEGES; HIGHER EDUCATION). At the same time, aside from the more conservative groups, Mennonites have become increasingly active politically, become business entrepreneurs, and moved into the professions in ever-greater numbers, with many holding down prestigious university positions especially in Canada and the United States, but not only there. Through the North American relief agency, Mennonite Central Committee, established to assist suffering Russian Mennonites after World War I, they have established a worldwide presence to aid—irrespective of political or religious affiliation—all peoples suffering under conditions of war or natural disasters. At the same time, as a positive extension of their pacifist principles of nonresistance (see PACIFISM), they are actively involved in conflict resolution and offender reconciliation programs in the United States and Canada that are finding ever-expanding application. Like the Dutch Mennonite *Heeren* depicted in some of Rembrandt van Rijn's paintings, Mennonites are no longer "the quiet in the land" they once were presumed to be.

References and Further Reading

Brunk, Gerald R., ed. *Menno Simons: A Reappraisal.* Harrisonburg, VA: Eastern Mennonite College, 1992.

Clasen, Claus-Peter. *Anabaptism: A Social History.* Ithaca, NY: Cornell University Press, 1972.

Deppermann, Claus. *Melchior Hoffman.* Edinburgh: T. & T. Clark, 1987.

Doornkaat Koolman, J. ten. *Dirk Philips, vriend en medewerker van Menno Simons, 1504–1568.* 2d edition. Scottdale, PA: Herald Press, 1981.

Dyck, C. J. *An Introduction to Mennonite History.* 3d edition. Scottdale, PA: Herald Press, 1993.

Estep, William R. *The Anabaptist Story.* Reprint, Grand Rapids, MI: Eerdmans, 1989.

Friesen, Abraham. *Erasmus, the Anabaptist, and the Great Commission.* Grand Rapids, MI: Eerdmans, 1998.

Goertz, Hans-Juergen. *Die Täufer.* Munich, Germany: Beck, 1980.

Horsch, John. *Menno Simons: His Life, Labors, and Teachings.* Scottdale, PA: Mennonite Publishing House, 1916.

Keller, Ludwig. *Geschichte der Wiedertäfer und ihres Reiches zu Muenster.* Muenster, Germany: 1880.

Krahn, Cornelius. *Dutch Anabaptism.* 2d edition. Scottdale, PA: Herald Press, 1981.

Kühler, W. J. *Geschiedenis der Nederlandsche Doopsgezinde in de zestiende eeuw.* Reprint, Haarlem: 1961.

Meihuizen, H. W. *Menno Simons: Ijveraar voor hut herstel van de Nieuw-testamentlische gemeente, 1496–1561.* Haarlem, The Netherlands: 1961.

Stuuperich, Robert, ed. *Die Schriften Bernard Rothmanns.* Münster, Germany: Kühler and Meiheizen, 1970.

Vos, Karel. *Menno Simons, 1496–1561: Zijn leven en werken en zijne reformatorische denkbeelden.* Leiden, The Netherlands: Brill, 1914.

Williams, George H. *The Radical Reformation.* 3d edition. Kirksville, MO: Sixteenth Century Journal Publishers, 1992.

ABRAHAM FRIESEN

MENNONITES, GENERAL CONFERENCE OF

The General Conference (officially General Conference Mennonite Church) was founded in 1860 and is composed of Mennonite congregations in the UNITED STATES and CANADA.

Mennonites from Europe began immigration to Pennsylvania in the late seventeenth century. The churches were isolated and all used some form of the German language, although the inroads of English soon began. John H. Oberholtzer (1809–1895), a young minister from the Swamp Mennonite congregation in Bucks County, led a progressive group that wanted to bring Mennonites into the mainstream of American religious life. In 1847 he and ten other ministers and deacons were expelled from the larger church group. They formed the East Pennsylvania Conference of Mennonites and introduced the new practices of SUNDAY SCHOOLS, written constitution, and mission work. To reach out to similar-minded Mennonites he set up a print shop and began publication of a Mennonite periodical, *Religiöser Botschafter.*

The General Conference organizational meeting was May 28–29, 1860, at West Point, Iowa with Oberholtzer as chairman. The conference Plan of Union invited all American Mennonites to unite for fellowship and common church work but did not prescribe any creed or practices other than fellowship based on the BIBLE and the teachings of MENNO SIMONS (especially believers BAPTISM and nonswearing of oaths). Orthodox Christian DOCTRINE was no doubt assumed. Later statements of belief called for salvation through faith, nonresistance and PACIFISM, nonconformity to the world, CHURCH DISCIPLINE, and avoidance of secret societies. The Plan of Union permitted freedom and autonomy for all congregations (and by implication, for individual Christians) to follow their own consciences and practices, within this loose framework. According to H. P. Krehbiel, the first historian of the conference, dogmatism and "nonessentials" were to have no place. They believed: "In essentials unity, in nonessentials liberty, in all things love."

Growth and Conference Work

The General Conference grew modestly through the years. In the late nineteenth century a large immigration of Prussian and German-Russian Mennonites, settling in the Great Plains, joined. By 1896 there were seventy-six churches with 8,886 members. In 2000 there were 397 North American churches with 59,915 members (United States 35,333 and Canada 24,582), with additional churches in South America. It was the second largest Mennonite conference in North America, ranking behind the Mennonite Church (MC). The main areas of General Conference membership are eastern Pennsylvania, Indiana, Ohio, Illinois, and Iowa (of Swiss and German descent); and Kansas, Oklahoma, Nebraska, South Dakota, North Dakota, California, and the provinces of Canada (of Prussian and German-Russian descent). In 1946 a group of Illinois churches, the Central Conference of Mennonites, joined as a group. The area churches are organized into six district conferences (Eastern, Central, Western, Northern, Pacific, and the Canadian Conference of Mennonites). The U.S. headquarters is at Newton, Kansas, and the Canadian at Winnipeg.

The conference has focused on three areas of conjoint work: (1) home and foreign MISSIONS; (2) publication; and (3) EDUCATION. In 1880 Samuel S. and Susie K. Haury began missionary work among Cheyenne and Arapaho Indians in Oklahoma. Overseas work began in INDIA by Peter A. and Elizabeth Penner and John F. and Susanna Kroeker in 1900. Other early conference work concentrated in CHINA and the Belgian Congo. The longest-running periodicals were *The Mennonite* and *Der Bote,* in English and German. The conference publishing house for books is Faith and Life Press of Newton (see PUBLISHING, MEDIA).

The conference desired an educated leadership and encouraged schools, sponsoring the Wadsworth Institute of Wadsworth, Ohio (1868–1878); Witmarsum Seminary of Bluffton, Ohio (1921–1931); and Mennonite Biblical Seminary at Chicago, founded in 1945, which later moved to Elkhart, Indiana, where it collaborated with Goshen Biblical Seminary to form the Associated Mennonite Biblical Seminary. The General Conference relates to (but does not own) the following colleges: Bethel College, North Newton, Kansas; Bluffton College; Freeman Junior College (1903–1985); Conrad Grebel College; Rosthern Junior College; Canadian Mennonite Bible College; and Columbia Bible College (see BIBLE COLLEGES AND INSTITUTES; CHRISTIAN COLLEGE).

During World War II the conference cooperated with other Mennonites to sponsor a program of civilian public service. Worldwide relief activities are coordinated by the Mennonite Central Committee, which the conference helps to sponsor. After World War II the church began efforts of social justice, disarmament, and broadening the membership to become a multicultural, multiethnic church.

The General Conference Tradition and Identity

Rooted in the Mennonite tradition, General Conference people tend to see their church as the voice and vanguard of progressive Mennonitism. H. P. Krehbiel referred to them as the "progressive part" of Mennonitism (1898). C. Henry Smith called them tolerant, liberal Mennonites with the spirit of progress (1941). S. F. Pannabecker said they are characterized by cooperation, congregational independence, and tolerance of wide diversity (1975). General Conference historians developed an approach to history and identity (somewhat different from the Goshen school) that actively engaged the world and CULTURE. A portion of General Conference Mennonites, however, eschew the label of progressivism and identify with FUNDAMENTALISM. Moreover, some Mennonites from other groups question the General Conference tradition as being too open and individualistic.

Merger and Cooperative Future

In the 1980s the General Conference began exploring cooperative steps and merger with the larger Mennonite Church (MC), and in 1995 the two conferences voted to merge, not without opposition. The merger was completed in 2002. The name of the united denomination is Mennonite Church USA. The joint periodical is *The Mennonite*. Both groups adopted a united statement of doctrine, "Confession of Faith in a Mennonite Perspective" (1995). Concurrent with the U.S. merger, the sizable Canadian Mennonite component formed an independent entity called Mennonite Church Canada.

References and Further Reading

Barrett, Lois. *The Vision and the Reality*. Newton, KS: Faith and Life, 1983.

Juhnke, James C. *A People of Mission: A History of General Conference Mennonite Overseas Missions*. Newton, KS: Faith and Life, 1979.

Kaufman, E. G. *General Conference Mennonite Pioneers*. North Newton, KS: Bethel College, 1973.

Krehbiel, H. P. *The History of the General Conference of the Mennonites of North America*. 2 vols. Newton, KS: Herald Publishing, 1899, 1938.

Pannabecker, Samuel F. *Open Doors: The History of the General Conference Mennonite Church*. Newton, KS: Faith and Life, 1975.

Smith, C. Henry. *The Story of the Mennonites*. Berne, IN: Mennonite Book Concern, 1941.

KEITH L. SPRUNGER

MERCERSBURG THEOLOGY

In his classic work, *America. A Sketch of Its Political, Social, and Religious Character* (published by Scribners in 1855), PHILIP SCHAFF wrote:

In the United States German philosophy and theology come into living contact with the whole Anglo-American form of Christianity, and thus become essentially modified. While they act upon the latter, they undergo themselves a process of transformation. From the collision, the mutual attraction and repulsion, of these two elements there has arisen . . . a theological movement, which . . . has kept the whole German Reformed communion . . . for the last ten or twelve years, in an almost constant agitation, the end of which cannot yet possibly be seen (p. 163)

The "theological movement" of which Schaff wrote has been called "the Mercersburg Theology" because it was centered in the small south-central town of Mercersburg, Pennsylvania. There it is still possible to see the beautiful grounds and Gothic chapel of the Mercersburg Academy, successor on the site of the college and theological seminary of the German Reformed Church that served as host to this theological movement in the nineteenth century.

Origins

Schaff did not see fit to note that the two most prominent figures enlisted in the cause of the Mercersburg Theology were JOHN WILLIAMSON NEVIN and Schaff himself. As Schaff already suggested in 1855, the development of this theological movement was aided, at least in part, by the "German philosophy and theology" of the time. The thought of GEORG W. F. HEGEL, FRIEDRICH SCHLEIERMACHER, and IMMANUEL KANT was implemented and supplemented by the historical perspectives of Isaac Dorner and JOHANN AUGUST NEANDER. However, it is necessary to understand the formation of this movement as a reaction to the increasing subjectivization of American religion in the nineteenth century. The work of the Mercersburg thinkers has not substantially arrested that process; that is, because the process has gone hand in hand with the democratization of American life, the creation of a mass society in which knowledge is one-dimensional.

It was, of course, natural that Mercersburg should have been hospitable to the influence of German thought. It was after all the educational center for many German-speaking Americans who had resided in Eastern Pennsylvania and the Cumberland and Shenandoah Valleys for perhaps a hundred years. The German Reformed Church, like its sister Lutheran and Moravian denominations, was to fashion a folk culture known as Pennsylvania Dutch (more accurately, Pennsylvania German). Along with their Anabaptist Mennonite and Amish cousins they provided a cultural refuge in an English-speaking world (see MENNONITES; ANABAPTISM; AMISH). This sense of ethnic separation, however modest it may have become, was certainly a nurturing factor in the response of the Mercersburg thinkers to the American penchant for revivalistic and pietistic religion (see ETHNICITY).

John Nevin's Development

John Nevin was born on February 20, 1803 (see ETHNICITY) in the Cumberland Valley of Pennsylvania and spent his early years on the farm of his parents in Franklin County. Nevin later recognized with great favor the influence of his family, the common school, and the Presbyterian Church of Middle Spring. He was brought up in Old School PRESBYTERIANISM, which represented an orderly catechetical system that entailed the use of biblical questions, a work called the *Mother's Catechism,* and the *Shorter Catechism* of the Westminster Assembly (see CATECHISM).

When Nevin entered Union College in Schenectady, New York, in 1817 he encountered a religious life in contrast to his Old School Presbyterianism. His sense of living in the orderly life of the church, from birth to DEATH, was challenged by the revivalistic emphasis on subjective CONVERSION experience recited by narrative testimony (see REVIVALS). When he completed studies at Union College in 1821 he was uncertain about his future and plagued by the anxieties that had been generated by the revivalistic threat to his sense of well-being and religious harmony. After two years spent at home on the farm Nevin enrolled at Princeton Theological Seminary, the institution very much at the heart of the Reformed tradition in America.

Charles Hodge took leave of his position at Princeton to study in Europe just at the time of Nevin's graduation and the latter spent the following two years assuming Hodge's teaching responsibilities. By 1828 Nevin was licensed as a minister by the Carlisle Presbytery and selected as a professor of biblical literature for the new theological seminary being established near Pittsburgh. While at Western Theological Seminary he began the study of German scholarship in church history and THEOLOGY, discovering there a source of healing for the intellectual distress caused by his earlier encounter with the pietistic subjectivism of revivalistic EVANGELICALISM. His work came to the attention of those responsible for the oversight of Marshall College and the German Reformed theological seminary located at Mercersburg, not too far from Nevin's ancestral home. In 1840 he joined Friedrich Rauch at Mercersburg and began a theological career that was to create an American movement very much at odds with what to Nevin and Schaff was a "new religion"—an American Christianity out of continuity with the historic church.

Rauch was a native of Hesse Darmstadt and educated at Marburg, Giessen, and Heidelberg before coming to America in 1831. He became ill and died on March 2, 1841, but not before he had assisted Nevin in his study of German philosophy and theology. Rauch certainly deserves attention in any serious encounter with the formative stage of the Mercersburg movement. The influence of Hegel found its way into Rauch's book *Psychology,* which was probably the American introduction of the Hegelian philosophy of mind in the English language. That philosophy also enabled Nevin to develop a doctrine of the CHURCH that rejected the Puritan distinction between visible and invisible churches in favor of a full-bodied historical church as the manifestation of the Incarnation, the Body of Christ.

The Anxious Bench was published in 1843 (revised and enlarged in 1844) as a polemic in opposition to "new measures" revivalism. In it Nevin established the position that was to occupy most of his scholarship for the rest of his life and set up the themes of "Bible and private judgment" as characteristic of Nevin's critique of the American religion in the making. The contours of an Evangelical Catholicism were taking shape as he published his lectures on *The Genius of the Heidelberg Catechism.* Some scholars suggest that this direction in Nevin's work places him among the neoconfessional thinkers of the nineteenth century. This is to disregard the manner in which Nevin interprets the *Catechism* as an irenic and reconciling work, transcending Lutheran, Calvinistic, and Tridentine confessionalism.

Partnership with Philip Schaff

Nevin's status as an important American religious thinker and controversial scholar was enhanced by the appointment of Schaff as a Mercersburg colleague in 1844. Schaff's skills as a church historian were to complement Nevin's work as a historical theologian. The young Swiss-German Reformed historian had been educated at Tübingen, HALLE, and Berlin. Influenced by F. C. Baur, Dorner, Neander, FRIEDRICH THOLUCK, and Julius Muller, he had just begun his career as a lecturer at the University of Berlin. A month after Schaff arrived in America, he heard Nevin preach a sermon on "Catholic Unity" at Salem Church in Harrisburg, Pennsylvania at a joint convention of the German and Dutch Reformed denominations. Schaff was delighted to hear the church portrayed not as a collection of believing individuals, but as a new creation manifesting the gift of the incarnate Christ. He and Nevin had obviously posted similar scholarly agendas.

Schaff's inaugural address was published in 1845 under the title *The Principle of Protestantism.* The address itself immediately plunged the Mercersburg schools further into the controversy generated by Nevin's *Anxious Bench.* The two professors were going against the grain of the individualistic and pietistic moralism that was becoming generally characteristic of American Christianity. Influenced by a not uncritical deference to Hegel's theology of development, Schaff anticipated the advent of an age in which the concrete reality of the Church Catholic would rise above the subjectivism of post-Reformation Protestantism. The revolutionary nature of Schaff's view of church history was that the REFORMATION did not represent a radical disjunction with medieval Christianity, as many Protestants claimed, but was rather "the legitimate offspring" and "greatest act" of the Catholic Church—the revealing of "the Evangelical dimension inherent in the true catholic nature of the one, Holy, Catholic and Apostolic Church." Neither the Roman Catholic Church nor the REFORMATION heritage could be dismissed. Later in his life, after becoming America's leading church historian and a member of the faculty of Union Theological Seminary in New York City, Schaff seemed to translate his view of organic historical development into a kind of eclecticism that anticipated the ecumenical age. Perhaps he should have been less sanguine of what the future synthesis of Roman and Protestant elements would be like. It may have been sufficient for Schaff and Nevin to espouse their advocacy of a Reformation Catholicism while waiting to observe what form would emerge in the future. They were realistic in their mission to return the Reformed Church to its Germanic context as a response to the revivalistic and pietistic spirit of American denominationalism. Schaff at any rate was not willing to translate that same sense of tradition into his later encounter with romantic ecumenicity.

In 1845 Schaff and Nevin were in essential agreement. Their historical and theological views formed the justification for Schaff's HERESY trial in the same year and a gradual schism in the German Reformed Church. The controversy was advanced by the publication in 1846 of Nevin's *The Mystical Presence. A Vindication of the Reformed or Calvinistic Doctrine of the Holy Eucharist.* Although the title may seem to imply a confessional posture, the book readily attempts to place Calvin's understanding of mystical real presence in a reconciling position between Lutheran and Tridentine theologies on the one hand, and HULDRYCH ZWINGLI's notion of memorial and sign, on the other. Again, Nevin's interpretation of the Eucharist engages the whole of church history rather than a one-sided evangelical or Roman history. Christian WORSHIP is centered in the Eucharist, said Nevin, because it is not mere subjective or memorial action. Christian worship is incarnational; it is the objective presentation of the Incarnation combined with the communal response of the faithful. Just as the Incarnation presents the divine as God-man, in contrast to an abstract notion of an absolutely transcendent divine, so the central act of human response reflects the divine-human encounter. We have to do therefore with *presence* that is not static location or substantiation, but dynamic and inexhaustible (mystical). What is communicated is the presence of the Incarnation, not the localized presence of a singular other preconceived being. Nevin's *Mystical Presence* is probably one of the most important, although largely ignored, works in American theology, ignored because it was not compatible with the rationalizing inclinations characteristic of nineteenth-century thinkers like WILLIAM ELLERY CHANNING, Hodge, and HORACE BUSHNELL. It is a work deserving the attention of American intellectual historians.

Liturgical Influence

Nevin's theology of the Eucharist and Schaff's *Principle of Protestantism* led the two professors to become involved in the effort to find liturgical foundations for the German Reformed Church in the United States. In 1849 Nevin was appointed chair of a committee assigned to evaluate historical liturgical forms that might serve as guidelines for use in American congregations. Nevin turned over the chairmanship of the liturgical committee to Schaff in 1851, at the same time that he resigned his position at Mercersburg and moved to Lancaster. For Nevin the necessity of an altar liturgy, with a text of common prayer and action, making possible the mystical presence of the Incarnation, was in contrast to the expectations of many of the Americanized leaders of the church, who simply wanted an anthology of prayers with a pattern of WORSHIP for optional use.

Schaff remained at Mercersburg after Nevin's resignation until 1863. By 1866 Nevin had again become active in the Reformed Church and had become president of the successor to Marshall College of Mercersburg, Franklin and Marshall College. American Protestantism continued its advance away from the Evangelical Catholicism envisioned by Schaff and Nevin. To Nevin's despair of the Protestant failure to embrace the wholeness of Christianity was added the failure of Roman Catholicism to recognize its Evangelical dimension when it permitted the promulgation of papal infallibility in 1870. By the time of Nevin's death in 1886 the Mercersburg theology had lost its vigor. Its rigorous theological and historical critique of American religion had become somewhat domesticated, its ideas left for research into the early writing of Nevin and Schaff, the work of a provisional LITURGY, and the pages of *The Mercersburg Review,* a quarterly journal begun under Nevin's editorship in 1849. Many of the ideas of the Mercersburg theologians left their mark on subsequent church history and in the liturgical life of many clergy and congregations of the Reformed tradition in America.

Assessment

It remains for us to summarize several basic themes at work in the Mercersburg movement. Nevin and Schaff both maintained that the "church question" was the most profound and essential issue facing American Christianity. They resisted the unchurchly spirit that reduced the Christian tradition to mere idea, to subjective experience, or to a moral and ethical platform. The church is the visible means whereby the divine-human encounter is a dynamic presence in the world.

This meant, second, that the church is an article of faith, not a mere organizational and utilitarian project conducive to private conversion. The ancient verbal symbols of the church, the creeds, recognized this by affirming: "we believe in the Holy Catholic Church" (Apostles) or "we believe in one Holy Catholic and Apostolic church" (Nicene).

Further, the individual exists as individual-in-community, one whose existence is never individualistic, but part of the Body of Christ in the world. The priesthood of believers is an organic reality; one is part of the priesthood, not a priest unto himself or herself. The individual exists both as part of the priesthood of Christ and is nourished in and by that priesthood. The mystical presence of the Incarnation is celebrated and received in the holy Eucharist. The church is the priesthood of Christ and is present in history. It exists not merely as an assembly of believers in this moment, but throughout time. This means that the church lives in communion with the "living and the dead," and the prayers of the church are those of the members of the Body of Christ, past and present. One lives in and by the church not by subjective experience, even when that experience is motivated by private use of the Bible.

The Incarnation is the presentation and representation of what St. Paul called "a new creation." To be human is to live in this new creation, just as one is born into the old creation. Again, as a new creation the Incarnation is the fulfillment of our humanity *in this* world. This makes the Mercersburg theology a public theology. The events of history find their meaning by Eucharistic reflection on what is happening. Without the general confession of our failure to be receptive to the divine-human encounter and our gratitude (Eucharist) for that encounter we are left with the narcissistic vision of human judgment by itself.

It is not difficult to see the manner in which this theology resists the mainstream of American religious and cultural life. The Mercersburg theology is at once churchly and political. Although its fundamental affirmations may seem to constitute a complicated pattern of thought, they only seem so if they are not understood from within their own frame of reference, and instead are judged by criteria derived from the presuppositions of modernity and experiential religion. Neither fundamentalist nor secularist can take comfort from Mercersburg.

References and Further Reading

Binkley, Luther John. *The Mercersburg Theology*. Lancaster, PA, 1953

Bricker, George H. *A Brief History of the Mercersburg Movement*. Lancaster, PA: Lancaster Theological Seminary, 1982.

De Bie, Lindin J. *German Idealism in Protestant Orthodoxy: The Mercersburg Movement, 1840–1860*. 1990.

Goetz, Ronald G., et al. *Faithful Witness: A Festschrift Honoring Ronald Goetz*. Elmhurst, IL: Elmhurst College, 2002.

Kloeden, Gesine von. *Evangelische Katholizität: Philip Schaffs Beitrag zur Ökumene—eine reformierte Perspektive*. Münster, Germany: Lit, 1998.

Maxwell, Jack Martin. *Worship and Reformed Theology: The Liturgical Lessons of Mercersburg*. Pittsburgh, PA: Pickwick Press, 1976.

Nevin, John Williamson, et al. *Catholic and Reformed: Selected Theological Writings of John Williamson Nevin*. Pittsburgh, PA: Pickwick Press, 1978.

Schenck, B.S. *Mercersburg Theology Inconsistent with Protestant and Reformed Doctrine*. Philadelphia: Lippencott, 1874.

Swander, John I. *The Mercersburg Theology: A Course of Lectures*. Philadelphia: Reformed Church Publication Board, 1909.

Wentz, Richard E. *John Williamson Nevin: American Theologian*. New York: Oxford University Press, 1997.

RICHARD E. WENTZ

MERLE D'AUBIGNÉ, JEAN HENRI (1794–1872)

Swiss historian. Merle D'Aubigné was a leader of the Swiss *réveil* and a popular church historian. Born of Huguenot ancestry in Geneva (see HUGUENOTS), Merle D'Aubigné was converted to Calvinist ORTHODOXY through Robert Haldane. After ordination in 1817, he studied under FRIEDRICH SCHLEIERMACHER and JOHANN A. W. NEANDER in Berlin, before becoming pastor to the French Reformed Church in Hamburg (1818–1823) and then court preacher to the king of the NETHERLANDS in Brussels. In 1831, back in Geneva, he became a leading figure, with Leon Gaussen, in the establishment of the *Société Évangélique*, which claimed to be part of the National Church. However, the authorities treated Merle D'Aubigné as a schismatic, suspending him from his position as a minister in November. In 1832, he became the first president of the Society's new *École de Théologie*, serving as Professor of Historical Theology until his death. Only with the constitutional changes of 1848 did Merle D'Aubigné accept his separation from the National Church, and join the Free Evangelical Church of Geneva.

Dissatisfied with the nationalist interpretation of the REFORMATION expressed by the Germans with whom he had celebrated the tercentenary of 1517, Merle D'Aubigné was unashamedly committed, in his writing, to JOHN CALVIN's theology. His main work was a massive history of the REFORMATION. Although his work was originally written for French readers, it had a rapidly growing appeal for English Protestants, especially after 1838, when Princeton awarded him a doctorate. He was an active supporter of the EVANGELICAL ALLIANCE, YMCA, and Red Cross.

See also Calvinism; YMCA/YWCA

References and Further Reading

Primary Sources:

Merle d'Aubigné, J. H. *History of the Reformation in the Sixteenth Century*. 5 vols. Edinburgh, UK: Oliver and Boyd, 1846–1853.
———. *History of the Reformation in Europe in the Time of Calvin*. 8 vols. London: Longman, 1863–1978.

Secondary Sources:

Biéler, B. *Un Fils du Refuge*. Paris: Je Sers, 1934.
Roney, J. B. *The Inside of History: J. H. Merle d'Aubigné and Romantic Historiography*. Westport, CT: Greenwood Press, 1996.

C. F. STUNT

METHODISM

Methodism originated as a renewal movement within the eighteenth-century CHURCH OF ENGLAND. It developed a distinctive ethos and distinctive practices that were in tension with the traditions of the Church of England. By the end of the century Methodism had separated from the parent church and become a distinct DENOMINATION. In the nineteenth century it spread rapidly in the English-speaking world. Through missionary work it also became strong in some parts of AFRICA and Asia. Today there are over seventy million Methodists and nearly a hundred separate churches in the Methodist tradition.

Origins and Early Development

Methodism developed from the evangelistic initiative of the Anglican clergyman, JOHN WESLEY (1703–1791).

Always deeply serious and utterly methodical (hence the name of the movement, originally a derisive nickname), Wesley underwent a deeply moving spiritual experience on May 24, 1738, after which he felt called to preach in the open air in areas where there was little pastoral provision afforded by the contemporary church and where the people were effectively unchurched. This "field preaching" began at Kingswood, near Bristol in 1739.

In 1740 some of Wesley's converts requested his help in developing a disciplined Christian life. As a result he formed the first Methodist societies whose members agreed to abide by the rules he gave them. These rules specified a very high level of commitment both to the official worship of the Church of England and to the devotional exercises of the societies. Central to Wesley's work was the belief that the movement had been raised up "to spread scriptural holiness throughout the land" and to restore belief in the call to Christian holiness as a vocation for all. The members of the societies were pledged to "do no harm, by avoiding evil in every kind," "to do good of every possible sort and, as far as is possible, to all men," and "to attend upon all the ordinances of God."

In 1742 Wesley began the innovation of recruiting lay preachers to assist him in his work. They were sent out into various circuits (patterns of travel) to preach. The societies multiplied rapidly and by 1791 there were over 70,000 Methodist members in Britain (see METHODISM, ENGLAND).

Wesley maintained a strict, even autocratic, control of the movement until his death. After 1791 the annual Conference of Traveling Preachers, which he had instituted in 1744, exercised corporate control over the movement, now already almost a separate denomination.

Spirituality and Ethos

Wesley was insistent that the Methodists use all the means of GRACE, both the *instituted means,* those specified in Scripture, such as PRAYER and reception of holy communion (see LORD'S SUPPER), and the *prudential means,* that is those that had developed later in the church but had been found fruitful in promoting spiritual growth. Among the latter were the practices that developed within Methodism, such as the meeting in class and the annual Covenant and Watchnight services.

Wesley was particularly insistent that all the members meet weekly in classes, small fellowship groups where they prayed together, confessed their faults to each other, and shared their spiritual experience and trials, all under the direction of the class leader appointed by the traveling preacher. This system of mutually accountable discipleship has continued within parts of Methodism to the present, although class meetings are no longer compulsory. They are now usually less frequent and less concerned with discipline and correction, although the principle is still treasured (see CHURCH DISCIPLINE).

Wesley wanted all Methodists to attend both the regular services of the parish church and the preaching and other services in the society. His brother CHARLES (1707–1788) set the Methodist doctrines and experience to verse and became the most prolific hymn writer in Christian history, producing about 9,000 HYMNS in all, of which about 200 are still in the British Methodist hymnal and over fifty in the U.S. hymnal. About thirty to forty are more widely used in other denominations. It was largely through the Wesleys that hymn singing became established more widely in the British Protestant churches.

The ethos of Methodism was, and has continued to be, one of warm fellowship. The Methodists, in their societies, took the injunction to "bear one another's burdens" seriously, and the interdependent "connectional" nature of the movement reinforced a strong sense of identity.

The Split from the Church of England

The joyful and intimate ethos of Methodism contrasted with the very formal worship of the Church of England. Many of the clergy distrusted what they saw as the Methodists' emotionalism and subjectivity, even accusing them of teaching "justification by feeling." In some cases they repelled Methodists from their churches. In return many Methodists increasingly felt that the ANGLICANISM they encountered was not true religion and, despite Wesley's wishes, they much preferred their own distinctive style of WORSHIP to that of the official church. Wesley had hoped to "provoke the ordinary ministers to jealousy," that is, to emulate his activity, but he increasingly found that they resented his breaking of the rules by PREACHING in their parishes. He continued to believe that the Methodists should remain within the Church of England and both he and, even more, his brother Charles warned against any separation. However, circumstances eventually forced him to take a course that led directly to a breach in America and, indirectly, in Britain.

In 1771 Methodist work began in America. At the time there were very few Anglican clergy there and thus no possibility of the Methodists receiving the SACRAMENTS from them as they could in ENGLAND. Wesley failed to persuade the Church of England bishops to ordain CLERGY for America. In 1784, believing there was no alternative and that, as a presbyter, he had the AUTHORITY to do so, he set aside THOMAS COKE as "superintendent" for America and he gave the new American church a service book and a threefold order of ministry based on the Anglican model. This was a clear breach of Anglican discipline. Immediately the Americans at the BALTIMORE CONFERENCE organized themselves as the METHODIST EPISCOPAL CHURCH. Coke and his successors took the title of "bishop." In Britain the turning point came when, after Wesley's death, the societies demanded that those preachers who had not been ordained as Anglican clergy be given the right to administer the sacraments to them. In 1795 the Conference acceded to this request under the Plan of Pacification.

Ecclesiology and Organization

The organization of Methodism developed piecemeal and in reaction to practical needs, leaving a legacy of missionary pragmatism for Methodism alongside a deep sense of its providential ordering. Wesley always insisted on the interdependence of all societies in his movement. He opposed any idea that each congregation should be independent; rather, they should all share resources as determined by the global needs of mission. The societies, and the preachers, were in connection with him. When he died the authority he had exercised personally in British Methodism passed to the annual CONFERENCE of the preachers, which was responsible for stationing the ministers, that is, assigning them to their areas of work and for the rules and discipline of the Connexion. In America the bishops did the stationing, but the conference retained the overall control of the rules, called *The Discipline,* and policy.

To this day the *Connexional Principle* remains fundamental to Methodist ECCLESIOLOGY. The Conference is still the final authority and exercises episcope or oversight over each Connexion.

An important difference between U.S. and British practice has been that, from the nineteenth century onward, British Methodism has granted complete autonomy to its original overseas missionary districts, whereas the UNITED METHODIST CHURCH has given control of local affairs over to regional conferences (e.g., in Southern Europe), but has kept the regional churches concerned linked to the quadrennial General Conference of the United Methodist Church, in which they are represented. For churches in the British tradition, connexionalism is national. For the United Methodist Church it is a global principle.

The WORLD METHODIST COUNCIL, dating back to the first Methodist Ecumenical Council of 1881, represents nearly a hundred churches in the Methodist tradition. It meets every five years for fellowship and mutual consultation but only has moral authority and it cannot bind its member churches.

Developments and Divisions

The flexibility of the Methodist system and the energy of the CIRCUIT RIDERS and traveling preachers meant that Methodism spread very rapidly on the frontier in America (see FRONTIER RELIGION), and by the mid-nineteenth century became the largest of the denominations—a position it held until the 1920s. In Britain Methodist membership increased fivefold until the 1840s. The energy of the local preachers, lay preachers who were unpaid, staying in their everyday jobs and evangelizing near home, helped spread Methodism into most small towns and many villages.

All later Methodist churches stem—whether by imitation, missionary endeavor, or schism—from either the Methodist Episcopal Church, founded in 1784, or the British Wesleyan Methodist Connexion. In Britain the PRIMITIVE METHODISTS, starting in 1812, and the Bible Christians (1815) aimed to revive the original field preaching of the Wesleys and to reach out to the poor at a time when they felt the Wesleyans were becoming too settled and respectable. The Primitives were more successful than any other nineteenth-century British Protestant church in attracting the support of the rural poor and miners.

All branches of British and American Methodism were vigorous in overseas missionary work and between them worked especially intensively in sub-Saharan Africa, in southern Asia, and in CHINA. Partly through returning migrants, partly through MISSIONS, small Methodist churches were established in most continental European countries (see METHODISM, EUROPE).

Methodism suffered many splits from the 1790s onward. Some of these, for instance the Protestant Methodists in the UNITED STATES and the Methodist New Connexion in Britain, were occasioned by resentment at the exclusive representation of the ministers in the conferences and thus in key decision making. These and other churches gave lay people a key role in decision making at every level. Discrimination against black people led to the setting up of the AFRICAN METHODIST EPISCOPAL CHURCH and the AFRICAN METHODIST EPISCOPAL CHURCH ZION in the United States (see also BLACK METHODISTS). In both the Methodist Episcopal Church (1872) and the British Wesleyan Connexion (1878) laymen were eventually admitted to the Conference. In America some new churches in the Wesleyan tradition, such as the WESLEYAN HOLINESS CHURCH and the CHURCH OF THE NAZARENE, represented a conservative reaction on the part of those who felt the main Connexion was diluting the strength of original Wesleyan teaching and becoming too "liberal." In Britain most of the smaller connexions reunited with the Wesleyan Methodist Church in 1932 to form the Methodist Church of Great Britain. In America a split in the Methodist Episcopal Church occasioned by the CIVIL WAR was ended in 1939. In 1968 that church united with the EVANGELICAL UNITED BRETHREN, a church of German immigrant origin that was thoroughly Wesleyan in ethos and THEOLOGY, as the United Methodist Church.

Sociology/Social Involvement

Wesley's aim was to go "not to those who need you but to those who need you most" and he made many converts among the poor, particularly in the rural industrial areas of Britain. A consequence of the Methodist emphasis on self-discipline and thrift was a degree of upward social mobility in the nineteenth and early twentieth centuries, although Methodism continued to appeal to many among the poor, especially in rural and urban industrial areas. By the mid-twentieth century the average Methodist both in Britain and the United States tended to come from the lower middle classes, with few adherents among the very poor or the highest social classes.

Wesley placed great emphasis on social holiness and was active in campaigning against many social evils, including the slave trade (see SLAVERY; SLAVERY, ABOLITION OF). Methodists played a prominent role in most places in the TEMPERANCE Movement. Some later enthusiastically endorsed the SOCIAL GOSPEL. In Britain in the early and mid-twentieth century, under the leadership of people like Henry Carter and Edward Rogers, the Conference produced a series of impressive statements outlining the Christian attitude to many social problems. In the 1960s and 1970s most branches of Methodism opened all levels of ministry and office to both sexes (see WOMEN CLERGY).

The Theology of Methodism

Wesley claimed that Methodism was "the old religion, the religion of the BIBLE." He placed great emphasis on the Trinity and orthodox CHRISTOLOGY. He argued that his teaching was in strict conformity with that of the Anglican reformers, although not all contemporary Anglicans agreed with him. He regarded the doctrines of JUSTIFICATION by grace through FAITH and of Christian holiness as central to Christian experience and living. He was above all concerned with what he called practical divinity.

Wesley was frequently locked in controversy with CALVINISM because his theology was Arminian (see ARMINIANISM). He believed the offer of SALVATION was open to all. He opposed any idea of limited ATONE-MENT for the elect only, citing Psalm 145, "His mercy is over all his works."

Within the general framework of trinitarian Protestant ORTHODOXY, Wesley emphasized what have been called the four "alls," that all people *need* to be saved, that they all *may* be saved, that they may be saved to the *uttermost* (the doctrine of perfect love), that they may *know* they are saved (the doctrine of "assurance," regarded as the privilege of the believer and based on the "witness of the spirit," Romans 8:15).

Wesley's doctrine of Christian perfection (see SANCTIFICATION) was the most controversial. Calvinists, who believed that sin would always remain in the believer, contested it sharply. Wesley had to hedge it around with limitations. He believed that Christians could be saved from conscious sin, but accepted that sin through ignorance could still occur and that what he called "sinful tempers," unrecognized as such, could remain in believers.

Wesley accepted the primacy of Scripture as the ultimate authority in practice and DOCTRINE, but also took TRADITION, reason, and experience as secondary authorities. Today the four are sometimes called the Wesleyan Quadrilateral. His "Forty-four sermons" (a selection from a larger corpus) became acknowledged as setting a standard for Methodist preaching. His "Twenty-five articles" (based on the original Anglican THIRTY-NINE ARTICLES) and his "Notes on the New Testament" were also seen as setting standards. Throughout the nineteenth century Methodism remained within the Arminian evangelical tradition. In the early twentieth century, large numbers of Methodists on both sides of the Atlantic came under Liberal Protestant influence to the extent that LIBERAL PROTESTANTISM is, arguably, now dominant in the main British and American Connexions. In recent years there has been an impressive revival of Wesley scholarship in the United States and Wesleyan insights have been fruitfully applied to many contemporary problems.

Liturgy

Methodism has a dual heritage in both liturgical and extempore worship stemming from Wesley's commending of the traditional Anglican offices and his use of the "preaching service" and extempore prayer. In recent years both U.S. and British Methodism have been deeply influenced by the Liturgical Movement and have produced new and enriched eucharistic rites. Many Methodists, however, greatly prefer the extempore prayer services that prevailed in the nineteenth and early twentieth centuries. Others, recovering Wesley's strong emphasis on "constant communion" and perceiving the heritage of the Revival to be eucharistic as well as evangelical, want to restore the Eucharist to a central position in Methodist worship.

Ecumenism

Wesley was deeply appreciative of a wide range of spiritual traditions within Christendom, and, in his sermon, *The Catholic Spirit,* he commended good relationships with all, but without any theological indifference. The British Conference in 1820 called on the Methodist people to "ever maintain the kind and catholic spirit of primitive Methodism," and Methodists such as William Shrewsbury, JOHN R. MOTT, Albert Outler, Pauline Webb, and Geoffrey Wainwright have contributed to the ECUMENISM. In CANADA (1925) and AUSTRALIA (1977) Methodists have entered into united churches with others in the "reformed" tradition, and in the Indian subcontinent into unions involving Reformed and Anglicans (1947, 1970) (see UNITED CHURCH OF CANADA and UNITING CHURCH IN AUSTRALIA). The British Methodist, Rex Kissack, maintained that the search for unity was an "ecclesial consequence of the doctrine of Christian Perfection."

References and Further Reading

Carter, D. *Love Bade Me Welcome, A British Methodist Statement on the Church.* London: Epworth, 2002.

Davies, R. E. *Methodism.* London: Penguin, 1963.

Franks, Thomas E. *The Polity, Practice and Mission of the United Methodist Church.* Nashville, TN: Abingdon, 1997.

Heitzenrater, R. *Wesley and the People Called Methodists.* Nashville, TN: Abingdon, 1995.

Maddox, R. *Responsible Grace—John Wesley's Practical Theology.* Nashville, TN: Kingswood, 1994.

Rack, H. *Reasonable Enthusiast, John Wesley and the Rise of Methodism,* 3d edition. London: Epworth, 2002.

Rattenbury, J. E. *The Eucharistic Hymns of John and Charles Wesley.* London: Epworth, 1948.

———. *The Evangelical Doctrines Hymns of Charles Wesley's Hymns.* London: Epworth, 1941.

Robbins, B., and D. Carter. "Connexionalism and Koinonia." *One in Christ* 34 no. 4 (1998).

Runyon, T. *The New Creation, John Wesley's Theology Today.* Nashville, TN: Abingdon, 1998.

Turner, J. M. *Conflict and Reconciliation, Studies in Methodism and Ecumenicalism in England, 1740–1982.* London: Epworth, 1985.

———. *John Wesley, The Evangelical Revival and the Rise of Methodism in England.* London: Epworth, 2002.

Vickers, John A., ed. *A Dictionary of Methodism in Britain and Ireland.* London: Epworth, 2000.

Wainwright, G. *Methodists in Dialog.* Nashville, TN: Kingswood, 1995.

Watson, D. Lowes. *The Early Methodist Class Meeting.* Nashville, TN: Discipleship Resources, 1992.

Westerfield Tucker, Karen B. *The Sunday Service of the Methodists, Twentieth Century Worship in Worldwide Methodism.* Nashville, TN: Kingswood, 1995.

DAVID CARTER

METHODISM, ENGLAND

The Methodist movement arose out of the evangelical revival started in America and experienced in continental Europe in the 1720s (see REVIVALS; EVANGELICALISM). It became centered in ENGLAND on the itinerant preaching ministry of JOHN and CHARLES WESLEY, Anglican clergymen ordained in Oxford. The Holy Club they founded while at the University attracted GEORGE WHITEFIELD and other sympathetic supporters of the revival. The group received the nickname "Methodists" as a derisory description of the methodical approach they adopted to holy living, including regularity of PRAYER and BIBLE study and celebration of the SACRAMENTS, as well as regular visiting of prisons and workhouses in the city.

In WALES the movement was Calvinistic, under the influence of Howell Harris (see CALVINISM). John and Charles quarreled with Whitefield and distanced themselves from the Moravians, despite earlier cooperation. A Moravian group who journeyed with them to Georgia greatly influenced the spirituality and POLITY of the movement. On their return from the Americas where their missionary efforts were unsuccessful, the Wesleys found in their spiritual confusion comfort from Peter Bohler and the fellowship of the group at Aldersgate in London. These conditions, and the reading of MARTIN LUTHER's *Commentary on Galatians* by Charles and the *Preface to the Romans* by John, led to their CONVERSION experiences in May 1738 with an assurance of the forgiveness of sins and the experience of the New Birth. These led to a decision in 1739 to take up an itinerant preaching ministry after Whitefield's departure for Georgia (see ITINERACY). This was primarily among those untouched by the church, either in pulpits opened to them by sympathetic and enlightened clergymen like William Grimshaw (1708–1763) of Haworth or in the open air, among the miners of Kingswood and other common people. Societies were formed in London, Bristol, and Newcastle as the major urban centers from which the Methodist mission spread. Through open air PREACHING and in meeting the societies the experience and practice of justifying and sanctifying GRACE at the heart of Wesleyan THEOLOGY was shared.

The 1740s witnessed the distancing of the Methodist movement from the Moravians to whom they owed much of their inspiration (see MORAVIAN CHURCH). John Wesley quarreled with the Fetter Lane Society over the question of quietism or stillness. The followers of the Wesleys experienced persecution from the hands of hostile mobs stirred up often by unfriendly Anglican clergymen or local gentry, such as those in Wednesbury in 1743. Many of the upland industrial parishes of northern England proved to be fertile ground for the growth of the Methodist groups. Local societies were divided into bands and classes for prayer and Bible study (the principal means of grace) for whom rules were devised. The *Character of a Methodist* (1741) set out guidance for followers of the Wesleys' doctrine of Christian Perfection. Such societies were grouped under circuits established after the first quarterly meeting held at Todmorden, Yorkshire, in 1748 to which preachers were assigned by Wesley for EVANGELISM and mission by annual stationing.

From 1744 John Wesley gathered the ordained Anglican clergymen and his lay helpers or assistants together for an annual CONFERENCE. They and the societies and circuits they served were "in connexion" with Wesley, the basis for all subsequent Methodist church polity, made distinct by its connexionalism. The consolidation of preaching rounds and circuits served by a growing number of itinerant preachers and an army of self-taught local lay persons (using Wesley's fifty-four–volume *Christian Library* and numerous pamphlets) ensured the rapid spread of Methodism in areas where ANGLICANISM and Old Dissent were weakest (see DISSENT), particularly the North, Wales, and the West (especially Cornwall) and in the growing industrial towns. From the 1760s chapels began to supplant the earlier domestic location of worship in barns and rooms. To secure the continuance of the movement, John Wesley prepared the *Deed of Declaration* (1784) establishing the annual conference as the constitutional and legal entity holding all Methodist property secured on a model deed and passing all legislation binding on all members and congregations in connexion. In this same year Wesley reluctantly ordained two men to a ministry of word and sacrament for the American work in defiance of the CHURCH OF ENGLAND, which was unable to do so. This and further ordinations for SCOTLAND and then ENGLAND, Wales, and IRELAND, ensured that the growing breach with the Church of England was widened, although the Wesleys always protested their allegiance to the church and denied they were dissenters. The provision of a *Sunday Service* for the use of Methodists in America (1784) underlined the breach, although it was based on the Anglican BOOK OF COMMON PRAYER, which Wesley prized highly. Wesley's hymnal of 1780 and the extraliturgical services for covenants, love feasts, watchnights, and vigils, established a different mode of worship far freer and more varied than that of the Established Church.

Solidification and Division

By 1791, the year of John Wesley's death, Methodism was established throughout the British Isles, including a dependent connexion in Ireland where a separate conference was held, and elsewhere in the English-speaking world. There were 72,476 members and 470 meeting houses, governed by a connexional organization headed by the annual conference, adhering to a body of doctrine based on Wesley's selected sermons and *Notes on the New Testament*. Methodism's development as a DENOMINATION gained pace despite the disruptions after Wesley's death as different personalities struggled for control. Bureaucratic structures emerged to replace his personal leadership. Connexional officers (secretary, book steward, editor) were selected from among the ministers. An annual president was elected from the Legal Hundred to preside over the Conference. Chairmen of newly formed districts acted as dispensers of discipline and administration in between (see CHURCH DISCIPLINE). Such centralization proved the strength and weakness of Methodism. It could not prevent schisms that were caused more on issues of church polity and where power lay than on any doctrinal grounds.

With Alexander Kilham, a radical in an age of revolution, challenging clerical domination of the Conference, the Methodist New Connexion was created, after his expulsion, in 1797. Wesleyan Methodism set its face against radicalism and revivalism at a time of social and political unrest, fearing the loss of privileges for its preachers. The Primitive Methodist Connexion (see PRIMITIVE METHODIST CHURCH) was created in 1811 from one such division, through the influence of Lorenzo Dow and CAMP MEETINGS at Mow Cop (1807) and elsewhere. Bourne and Clowes were its leaders after their expulsion from the Wesleyan Connexion. Independents Methodists, Tent Methodists, Bible Christians, and Protestant Methodists were among the many splinter groups divided from the mainstream of Methodism in the early nineteenth century. Nevertheless Methodism continued to grow apace with spectacular increases in membership up to the 1840s. Under the strong leadership of Jabez Bunting, who dominated the expanding work in MISSIONS and educational affairs, and the theological expertise of Adam Clarke and Richard Watson, whose books influenced generations of ministers, a more professional and educated ministry emerged around a concept of the pastoral office, to teach and discipline the Methodist people. From 1835 theological colleges sprang up to meet the needs of training for a more upwardly mobile membership, requiring preaching informed by more formal education.

This contributed, in reaction to the OXFORD MOVEMENT of Catholic revival, a more hostile attitude to the Church of England, with a vigorous chapel and school building program to rival the Established Church in the towns and cities. Two teacher-training colleges were established in London, at Westminster and

Southlands. Nineteenth-century Methodism tended to emphasize the latent nonsacramental and anti-Catholic sentiments of many of Wesley's followers. The need for proselytism through Sunday schools and MISSIONS work at home and overseas (the Wesleyan Methodist Missionary Society was formed in 1814) highlighted denominational rivalry, as did the building of grander chapels, first in the classical style and later in the Gothic aping Anglicanism. The Victorian era was the age of the great pulpit orators and public lectures, with men like Morley Punshon drawing vast crowds to popular chapels and Exeter Hall in London.

The 1851 Census revealed that the Anglican monopoly of religion in England and Wales had been broken. There were as many Methodists and Roman Catholics in a nation divided between a growing number of denominations. The Wesleyans represented the most socially advanced of the Methodists, a privileged shopocracy and labor aristocracy of the increasingly wealthy, who fled town centers for villas in the suburbs where new chapels were built, leaving the ministry to the poor to the few. The Primitive Methodists in contrast consisted of many coal miners in the North East and agricultural laborers in Eastern Britain. Wesleyan Methodism was torn apart by internal dissent in the 1840s in revolt against a perceived centralized clerical autocracy, leading to the creation of the United Methodist Free Churches (UMFC) in 1857. Only gradually over the next seventy-five years was Methodism reunited, with the union of the UMFC, Bible Christians, and Methodist New Connexion (MNC) in 1907 to create the UNITED METHODIST CHURCH, and its union with the Primitive and Wesleyan Methodists to create the Methodist Church of 1932. The Independent Methodists and the Wesleyan Reform Union stayed out.

Return to Roots

The late nineteenth century saw an attempt by Methodism to connect with its original mission alongside the poor, stung by the defection from the MNC of one of its ablest evangelists, WILLIAM BOOTH, who created the SALVATION ARMY. Through the establishment of central halls as preaching places and social action in a new initiative spearheaded by Hugh Price Hughes in London in the 1880s, and other new work such as the establishment of the National Childrens' Homes by T. B. Stephenson, towns and cities found Methodism at their heart once more from the 1890s. The Bermondsey settlement of John Scott Lidgett was indicative of the way in which late nineteenth-century Methodists abandoned the earlier no-politics rule and became involved in local and national politics. Social Christianity became a byword for mission and EVAN-GELISM. The number of Methodist MPs and local councilors, particularly in the Liberal and nascent Labor parties was very significant before the Second World War, contributing to the development of the Welfare State.

At the time of union in 1932, the Methodist Church had nearly one million members and over 4,000 ministers. By 2002 this was fewer than 350,000 with half the number of ministers, many retired and nonstipendiary. The heavy reliance on local preachers to serve Methodist pulpits and Sunday schools has not reduced, even though numbers have declined from over 34,000 to fewer than 10,000. This still represents nearly three times the number of ordained ministers.

The demographic changes of the twentieth century meant that decline was felt more in the industrial heartlands of the north and rural areas where many chapels were closed in a process of rationalization (see INDUSTRIALIZATION). New growth in the coalfields lasted only fifty years but growth in new housing areas, particularly in the South, shifted the emphasis on ministries from inner city work to thriving suburbia and new towns. Methodism's survival in the face of a general decline in churchgoing has been secured by its vigorous youth work, its commitment to change in worship and preaching styles, and its place in the ecumenical movement. Its stance on social responsibility issues has ensured its continuing place in the social and political framework of the nations.

Although traditional SUNDAY SCHOOLS have declined in numbers and importance, Methodism's commitment to youth work, particularly through uniformed organizations such as Boys' and Girls' Brigades, the Methodist Association of Youth Clubs, and Methsocs' work among college and university students is reflected in the strength of lay leadership within the church.

The worship and preaching of twentieth-century Methodism has reflected the impact of the Liturgical Movement. A mixture of formal and free worship is now general with the use of two books authorized by the Conference, the *Methodist Service Book* (1975) and the *Methodist Worship Book* (1999), reflecting changes in the use of more inclusive language and the adoption of patterns of worship more in common with Anglicanism, with formal prayers and music used freely in more frequent services of holy communion, or LORD'S SUPPER. All-age WORSHIP is regularly experienced in many larger churches where services focused on the sermon are less common. More participatory worship has supplanted the hegemony of preacher and organ. The *Methodist Hymn Book* (1933) gave way to *Hymns and Psalms* (1983), which included much twentieth-century hymnody, notably by

Fred Pratt Green, while retaining a significant number of Wesley hymns (see HYMNS AND HYMNALS).

Mission and Ecumenism

The ecumenical century brought unions of churches overseas but none involving the Methodist Church in Britain. Talks with the Church of England (which failed in the 1970s) and the United Reformed Church are moving toward a possible covenant. On the ground many ecumenical partnerships have been formed with shared churches and worship. Missionary agencies are working more cooperatively than in the previous fierce denominational competition. A joint Anglican–Methodist United College of the Ascension in Birmingham prepares people for mission and works with mission partners over the world. In ministerial training, too, the ecumenical imperative and financial pressures have created a number of joint colleges, courses, and federations, particularly in Manchester, Birmingham, Cambridge, and Salisbury. The trend toward more nonresidential training has led to the closure of all the nineteenth-century colleges. Methodist scholarship, once strong there and in university theology departments, is now more thinly spread. Nevertheless the contribution of Methodists to biblical scholarship in the past century has been considerable, particularly the work of A. S. Peake, Vincent Taylor, Kenneth Grayston, and Morna Hooker in Manchester, Leeds, Bristol, and Cambridge (see HIGHER EDUCATION; EDUCATION, THEOLOGY; EUROPE).

The nineteenth-century preoccupation with moral welfare, drinking, and gambling issues has developed through the Christian Citizenship department and its successor the Division of Social Responsibility, to include more concern for international issues, of poverty, peace, and justice. Work at home in the health, EDUCATION, prison, and industrial sectors through CHAPLAINCY and political awareness has continued these emphases in Methodist outreach.

Although the Conference has reduced its size and slimmed its structures to reflect changes in a more collaborative mode of working within a connexional team, the Methodist emphases underlined in the recent *Our Calling* statements remain: in worship, to increase awareness of God's presence; in learning and caring, to help people grow as Christians through mutual support and care; in service, to be good neighbors to all in need and challenge injustice in God's world; in evangelism, to make more disciples of Jesus Christ. In these, British Methodism seeks to be alert to the challenges of the twenty-first century, offering the wider church the benefits of its Wesleyan legacy of free worship and the pursuit of social holiness in a spirit of personal and corporate renewal.

See also Methodism, Europe; Methodism, Global; Methodism, North America;

References and Further Reading

Baker, Frank. *John Wesley and the Church of England.* Nashville, TN: Abingdon Press, 1967.
Cooney, Dudley Livingstone. *The Methodists in Ireland: A Short History.* Dublin, Ireland: Columba Press, 2001.
Davies, Rupert, and Gordon Rupp, eds. *A History of the Methodist Church in Great Britain.* 4 vols. London: Epworth Press, 1965–1988.
Heitzenrater, Richard. *Wesley and the People called Methodists.* Nashville, TN: Abingdon Press, 1998.
Hempton, David. *Methodism and Politics in British Society 1750–1850.* London: Hutchinson, 1984.
Kent, John. *Wesley and the Wesleyans: Religion in Eighteenth-Century Britain.* Cambridge: Cambridge University Press, 2002.
Langford, Thomas A. *Methodist Theology.* London: Epworth Press, 1998.
Milburn, Geoffrey. *Primitive Methodism.* London: Epworth Press, 2002.
Milburn, Geoffrey, and Margaret Batty, eds. *Workaday Preachers: The Story of Methodist Local Preaching.* London: Methodist Publishing House, 1995.
Tabraham, Barrie. *The Making of Methodism.* London: Epworth Press, 1995.
Turner, John Munsey. *John Wesley: The Evangelical Revival and the Rise of Methodism in England.* London: Epworth Press, 2002.
———. *Modern Methodism in England 1932–1998.* London: Epworth Press, 1998.
Vickers. John A. *A Dictionary of Methodism in Britain and Ireland.* London: Epworth Press, 2000.
Wakefield, Gordon S. *Methodist Spirituality.* London: Epworth Press, 1999.

TIM MACQUIBAN

METHODISM, EUROPE

Methodism has spread all over the European continent. Beginnings came more often by laypersons than by missionaries and reached from the eighteenth to the twentieth century. Everywhere on the Continent, Methodist presence has developed in a context of long-standing established churches, including Protestant, Roman Catholic, and Eastern Orthodox (see ORTHODOXY EASTERN). The initial aim was sometimes to renew the established church, sometimes to deliberately build up an independent, or free church. Methodism has remained a minority church in all countries.

Early Missionaries

The first who brought Methodism to various places on the Continent came from Great Britain. In Gibraltar a Methodist society was established by laypeople as early as 1769. In 1804 a missionary was sent. The work focused on soldiers and English-speaking inhabitants. In the 1820s attempts were made to work in

Spanish, leading to the establishment of a school a decade later. Hampered by the political situation, missionaries tried to distribute Bibles in Spain. Regular visits to several Spanish cities were possible only after the revolution of 1868. Work developed particularly well in Barcelona and from there to the Balearic Islands. In 1871 a first missionary was stationed in Porto, Portugal. As in Gibraltar and later in Spain, schools were the most important enterprises of the Methodist mission in Porto.

Gibraltar was a bridgehead for the Methodist presence on the Iberian Peninsula, as were the Channel Islands for FRANCE. METHODISM came to the Channel Islands in 1775 and developed in English and French. In 1790 a Methodist tradesman from Guernsey made a trip to France and realized the need to help French Protestantism. A year later THOMAS COKE made a prospect visit to Paris and designated a missionary for Normandy. The mission in France came on a more prosperous footing thanks to a new missionary sent in 1818. The mission aimed at bringing revival to the Reformed Church while maintaining Wesleyan ARMINIANISM. It had its strongholds around Nîmes in the southeast, but spread to many French cities with Protestant minorities. It also reached out to French-speaking SWITZERLAND (1840–1900), struggling with the presence of Darbyism, named after JOHN NELSON DARBY. French Methodism was among the first British mission fields that gained a large autonomy (1852). Its self-understanding remained ambiguous between a society for the renewal of the Reformed Church and an independent free church.

In SWEDEN a British Methodist engineer asked the Swedish Missionary Society to send a preacher for his workmen. A first missionary arrived in 1826. His successor became instrumental in the conversion of later leaders of free churches and in the establishment of societies for welfare and revival within the Lutheran State Church. On a fund-raising campaign in the UNITED STATES, he urged U.S. Methodists to send missionaries to Sweden, but criticized also the spiritual life in the State Church within which he developed his Methodist societies. Back in Sweden he came under violent attack for his criticism and was forced to leave the country in 1842. He was not replaced. More than a decade later, U.S. Methodists would begin a mission.

In GERMANY a Methodist layperson from Britain went to see his sick father in Württemberg in the South in 1830. He shared his Christian experience and returned to ENGLAND. The new converts requested the Missionary Society to send him as a missionary. He went to his homeland and established Methodist societies within the Lutheran State Church. In 1870 the mission reached out to Vienna,

Austria, where no public worship was allowed. Since 1848 a U.S. branch of Methodism had also taken up a mission in Germany. Talks about a union of the two branches soon developed, but it lasted until 1897 when the British Methodists in Germany and Austria merged into the Methodist Episcopal Church (MEC).

During the nineteenth century, there was much poverty in most parts of Europe. Toward the end of the century thousands of people left Europe each day to seek a better life in the United States. The MEC began to develop foreign-language missions within the United States. Norwegian/Danish, Swedish, and German-speaking domestic missions grew particularly fast. Up to the 1920s more Methodists spoke these languages in the United States than in Europe. They supported the mission initiatives in continental Europe and received new members by migration.

Mission initiatives from the MEC to Scandinavia were strongly linked to the seamen's mission (Bethel Ship) in New York, which had been led by a Swede since 1845. Converts of the Bethel Ship mission went back to NORWAY (1849), Sweden (early 1850s), DENMARK (1857), and FINLAND (1859). Methodist societies were being established. First missionaries were officially sent to Norway in 1853, to Denmark in 1858, to Sweden in 1866/67, and to Finland in 1883. On both sides of the Atlantic, Scandinavian Methodists opposed the mission of MORMONISM and were in a competition with followers of HANS NIELSEN HAUGE or NICOLAJ FREDERICK GRUNDTVIG. All converts of the Bethel Ship mission stressed a Holiness message shaped by PHOEBE WORRALL PALMER and implemented it also in its social consequences (see HOLINESS MOVEMENT). Methodism expanded particularly quickly in Sweden where it reached its peak of growth around 1910 with about 16,000 adult members. However, Sweden has suffered by far the greatest decline to 4,000 adult members in 2000.

Mission initiatives from the United States to German-speaking Europe in the nineteenth century covered a territory much larger than what today constitutes Germany, Austria, and Switzerland. The MEC took up its mission directly after the revolutions of 1848. It wanted to take profit from the new religious tolerance and hoped to work independently of the state churches, but it was still not possible in all German territories. The first missionary sent to Germany had been born a German Jew. He started in Bremen, the seaport for emigrants to the United States. He planted the Methodist presence in major cities and from there on to the surrounding regions. In Saxony Methodism spread by a private initiative of a layperson in 1850 and was soon united with the rest of the German mission. In 1856 the MEC mission started in Protestant regions of Switzerland where it grew rapidly.

Among German immigrants in the United States, two other branches of Methodism came into being around 1800: the United Brethren in Christ (UBC) and the Evangelical Association (EA). In the United States the two churches merged in 1946 to form the EVAN-GELICAL UNITED BRETHREN CHURCH (EUBC). The larger one, the UBC, was the smaller one on the European continent. The UBC came to Germany in 1869, never developed very strongly, and merged with the MEC in 1905. The EA sent its first missionary to Germany in 1850. Ministry began in Württemberg close to where the British Methodists were established. The mission had to remain within the state church and the possibility to organize as a dissenting church was given only in the 1870s. In 1866 the EA expanded to Switzerland and in 1868 to the Alsace, which was still part of France at that time. Up until World War I, the EA spread to most parts of the German empire. Whereas the EA and the MEC had started their missions in different parts of Germany and with different ecclesial identities, they came to work side by side in many regions by the end of the nineteenth century. In some regions of Germany and Switzerland the EA became numerically almost equal to the MEC. In 1914 it had 16,600 adult members in Germany and 7,000 in Switzerland (including the Alsace). The MEC had 29,000 in Germany and 10,000 in Switzerland.

Expansion Up to the 1920s

The strong growth of Methodism in Scandinavia and in German-speaking countries in the 1870s and 1880s was favored by the discontent with liberalism among people in the state churches and by the Holiness revival movement, which swept from the United States to segments of European Protestantism (see REVIVALS). Methodists had always focused on SANC-TIFICATION and now felt strengthened. In Scandinavia the holiness message had stronger social implications and around 1900 Methodists in Denmark were particularly involved in building up Central Missions in the big cities. In the German Empire and in Switzerland the holiness movement was more individualistic and conservative, influenced by Robert P. and HANNA W. SMITH. The major diaconal thrift in German Methodism was linked to a strong DEACONESS movement. It became a major European contribution to U.S. Methodists at the end of the nineteenth century.

Beside these major regions of Methodist presence in Europe, mission was also taken up in other countries. Toward the end of the nineteenth century European Methodists, particularly within the MEC,

dreamed of conquering Catholic, even sometimes Orthodox, countries in Europe. The euphoria of expansion remained until the mid-1920s when it was shattered first by shrinking funds and finally by the worldwide economic crisis. The vision of expansion to the Catholic West and South of Europe and to the Orthodox East grew out of earlier experiences in such countries and of the growth in Scandinavia and German-speaking Central Europe.

Quite astonishingly, Orthodox Bulgaria was among one of the older Methodist mission fields. The AMER-ICAN BOARD OF COMMISSIONERS FOR FOREIGN MISSIONS was already present in the Ottoman Empire when requests came to work in its Bulgarian part because of the first Bulgarian translation of the BIBLE. The American Board asked the MEC for cooperation. The former began in the southern part in 1858, the latter in the northern part in 1857. At first they aimed at bringing a spiritual renewal to the Orthodox Church. In the 1860s they realized the difficulties and began to build up congregations. Progress was slow. "Bible women" played an important role in bringing biblical knowledge and basic educational skills to women in villages. Schools were established. In between the Balkan wars before World War I, the MEC organized aid for the suffering people and gained recognition.

Around 1900 Austrian Methodists (MEC) were asked to send a preacher to the Voyvodina (today Serbia) where Germans had settled. From there, the Methodist presence spread to other parts of HUNGARY and of what later became Yugoslavia. After World War I the American Board handed over its work in Macedonia to the MEC. The government of Albania, a Muslim country, asked the MEC to build up HIGHER EDUCATION in the country. For a short period the MEC thought that Bulgaria could become the base for a strong development of Methodism in the whole Balkan region and to the southern parts of the Russian Empire. However, with the economic crisis even the established mission hardly survived.

In the northern parts of the Russian Empire, Methodism entered the field toward the end of the nineteenth century. From the Grand Duchy of Finland, which belonged to the Russian Empire, a preacher was sent in 1889 to St. Petersburg for a ministry among the Finnish and Swedish people. In 1907 a superintendent was appointed to St. Petersburg and the mission expanded to the surroundings and to five different language groups including Russians. In the Baltic States, which also belonged to the Russian Empire, the MEC had been involved in mission partly coming from the German Empire to the west and partly coming from St. Petersburg to the east. Preachers were sent to Lithuania in 1905, to Estonia in 1907, and to Latvia in 1911. When the EA had reached the eastern part of the

German Empire, it also planned to cross the border to the Russian Empire. Visits to Latvia since 1908 led to the sending of a preacher in 1911. During World War I the Baltic States were in the midst of the battle lines; after the war they became independent. The MEC (Latvia, Lithuania, and Estonia) and the EA (Latvia) continued their ministry and experienced a steady growth up to World War II and the Russian occupation.

After the October Revolution in Russia in 1917 only a deaconess remained in St. Petersburg. She bravely ministered to people in need. In the early 1920s the Central European bishop of the MEC planned a large program of support to RUSSIA with diaconal, educational, agricultural, and theological implications. He aimed not only at building up a Methodist presence but also at supporting the suffering Russian Orthodox Church. American fear of working together with "Bolsheviks" and the economic crisis prevented the implementation of the plan with the exception of some support for reconstructing Orthodox theological schools. The Methodist work in St. Petersburg was extinguished in the 1930s.

The expansion to Catholic countries in western and southern Europe was promoted by the history of Italian Methodism. With the establishment of the new kingdom of ITALY in 1861, the British sent their first missionaries to Italy. Many well-trained, liberally minded Catholic clergy left the Roman Catholic Church. Some were influenced by Protestants in the country, specifically Waldensians and PLYMOUTH BRETHREN, and joined them or the British Methodists. The same happened in the MEC when it began its Italy mission in 1871. Many leading Methodists, especially in the MEC, misinterpreted the rejection of anti-modernist Catholicism by the intelligentsia as the beginning of the collapse of Catholicism. The Italian mission received abundant financial support and built chapels, central missions, and schools, but the membership was never particularly high. In the 1920s under the Fascist government, which favored the Catholic Church, and under the economic crisis the dream of a powerful Italian Methodism was shattered.

When the Italian mission began with good prospect, the MEC leaders pushed a strong mission to Catholic countries. In 1905 the MEC opened a new field in France. It chose to work in a region where the British Methodists had no churches and that was close to Switzerland and Italy. The work made good progress, albeit not as strong as in German-speaking areas. A large reconstruction project began after World War I north of Paris, but could not be completed because of the economic crisis. On the Iberian Peninsula, the MEC was offered the opportunity to take over the churches and schools of the American

Board. In 1909 the MEC was forced to decline because of lack of money. A decade later it took over two independent schools in Spain.

Another expansion occurred after World War I. The Methodist Episcopal Church South wanted to bring help to a devastated Europe. It chose war-torn countries without any Methodist presence: Belgium, POLAND, and Czechoslovakia. With strong support of the Women's Foreign Missionary Society, relief work was taken up in each capital and in major cities in 1920. Together with social and diaconal work, a religious component was proposed with distribution of Bibles, Bible studies, and evangelistic preaching. The latter was particularly successful in Czechoslovakia where hundreds of thousands of Catholics were leaving the Roman Church, some of them joining Protestant churches. Among the lasting achievements in Poland were the English-language schools in Warsaw and other cities.

Crises and Difficulties

Crises and difficulties came from outside and inside Methodism. Problems from within were heavily linked to personal issues and church policy whereas theological, economic, and political challenges were linked to the context. The largest Methodist body in continental Europe, the MEC, also had to face the heaviest internal difficulties. In the late 1880s a new leadership in Italian Methodism criticized the pioneers for their adaptations of Methodist rules and reinforced total abstinence from alcohol. In the beginning of the twentieth century one of the superintendents in Norwegian Methodism was among the strongest advocates of the Pentecostal revival and a split occurred within the church (see PENTECOSTALISM). In the 1920s the former leader of the Central Mission in Copenhagen and then bishop for Northern Europe was taken to court for misuse of funds at the Central Mission and finally had to resign.

Economically all Methodist missions needed financial support from their mother churches. They managed to survive the crises in the late nineteenth century. In the early twentieth century the larger Methodist churches in Scandinavia, Germany, and Switzerland were close to being self-supporting with the exception of debts on property. They also contributed in money and personnel to the mission overseas. The smaller Methodist churches to the west, south, and east, whether from the British or the U.S. tradition, remained heavily dependent on subsidies. The MEC and the MEC South had launched a Centenary campaign in 1919 and wanted to expand their worldwide mission. After a tremendous start the income dropped and the first cuts in programs had to be made even before the severe global economic crisis of 1929.

Financial pressure hastened structural changes. British Methodism, on the forefront of ECUMENISM, urged its missions on the Continent to unite with other Protestant churches. In France there was such a union in 1935, in Spain in the mid-1950s, and in Italy a union of the two Methodist branches, or what was left of them, in 1946, and a federation with the Waldensian Church in the 1970s. The EA had limited its mission essentially to German-speaking Europe and had developed a strong enough basis to survive. The MEC South wanted to retreat in the 1930s, but the Methodists in all three countries were determined to continue—even against their mother church—and won. Under different circumstances Belgian Methodists entered a union with other Protestants in the late 1960s. Between the two world wars, the MEC pushed the larger Methodist churches in Scandinavia, Germany, and Switzerland to become self-supporting. These larger churches eventually helped smaller missions that were threatened to be closed down. Finally the retreat hit the missions in western and southern Europe. The schools in Spain had to be closed because of the civil war and in France the Reformed Church was offered the opportunity to take over what they could and would after the total abandonment by the MEC.

The political changes led to additional difficulties. Fascism with its support of the Catholic Church made survival difficult for the small minority of Protestants in Portugal, Spain, Italy, and Albania. Hitler's regime in Germany wanted to control social and youth work. Methodist churches had to give up their own organizations or adapt. Church activities were restricted. The German Methodists were not prepared to relinquish control and did not realize the totalitarian character of the National-Socialist government. With limited success, they tried to safeguard their activities, but did not speak out against injustice or the treatment of Jews. Stronger prophetic words and acts are known among Methodists from the MEC South in Belgium, Poland, and Czechoslovakia or from personal initiatives of Methodists like the Swiss consul in Budapest.

The rise of COMMUNISM smashed the Methodist presence in Russia in the 1930s and in the Baltics during World War II, with the notable exception of Estonia where Methodism experienced revival in the midst of persecution. After World War II several central European countries came under Communist governments. In almost all countries a Methodist presence continued, but the situation was different in each country and often changed from open persecution to hidden surveillance. In Bulgaria the leadership of all Protestant churches was taken to public trial for treason and espionage and condemned. The Methodists were no longer allowed to organize the church according to its own rules.

Recent Developments

After the breakdown of communism a Methodist presence returned to all countries where it had been destroyed with the exception of Albania, Bulgaria (1989), Russia (1990), Latvia (1991), and Lithuania (1995). From Russia, new initiatives have developed in Ukraine (1994) and Moldova (2000). At present the European Methodist Council unites the British and the Irish Methodists; the autonomous or united churches in Italy, Portugal, and Spain; and the United Methodist Church. The latter is divided into four episcopal areas: Northern Europe (Denmark, Estonia, Finland, Latvia, Lithuania, Norway, Sweden), Eurasia (Moldova, Russia, Ukraine), Germany, and Central and Southern Europe (Austria, Bulgaria, Croatia, Czech Republic, France, Hungary, Macedonia, Poland, Serbia, Slovakia, Switzerland). In central and eastern Europe Methodist churches have experienced a decade of growth after the fall of communism. In many parts of western Europe the churches have declined, mostly since the 1960s.

Methodist bodies have come to Europe and developed small churches. Some of their missions have reached countries without a previous Methodist presence: the Korean Methodist Church in Kazakhstan, Kirghizia, ROMANIA, and Tajikistan, and among Methodist Holiness churches, the CHURCH OF THE NAZARENE in the NETHERLANDS and the Free Methodists in Greece.

References and Further Reading

Barclay, Wade Crawford. *History of Methodist Missions.* vol. III, *The Methodist Episcopal Church 1845–1939: Widening Horizons 1845–95.* New York: The Board of Missions of The Methodist Church, 1957.

Copplestone, J. Tremayne. *History of Methodist Missions.* vol. IV, *Twentieth-Century Perspectives (The Methodist Episcopal Church 1896–1939).* New York: The Board of Global Ministries, The United Methodist Church, 1973.

Eller, Paul Himmel. *History of Evangelical Missions.* Harrisburg, PA: Evangelical Press, 1942.

Findlay, G. G., and W. W. Holdsworth. *The History of the Wesleyan Methodist Missionary Society.* vol. IV. London: Epworth, 1922.

Short, Roy H. *History of Methodism in Europe.* [Based on an unfinished manuscript of Bishop Paul N. Garber.] Office of the Secretary of the Council of Bishops of the UMC, 1980.

Sommer, C. Ernst, and Karl Steckel, eds. *Geschichte der Evangelisch-methodistischen Kirche: Weg, Wesen und Auftrag des Methodismus unter besonderer Berücksichtigung der deutschsprachigen Länder Europas.* Stuttgart, Germany: Christliches Verlagshaus GmbH, 1982.

Streiff, Patrick Ph. *Der Methodismus in Europa im 19. und 20. Jahrhundert.* EmK Geschichte—Monographien 50. Stuttgart, Germany: Medienwerk der Evangelisch-methodistischen Kirche, 2003.

PATRICK STEIFF

METHODISM, GLOBAL

Methodism began in the 1730s as a spiritual revival and renewal movement—termed a "society"—within the CHURCH OF ENGLAND under the leadership of JOHN and CHARLES WESLEY, both Anglican clergy. Originally based in Oxford and London, METHODISM soon extended beyond those cities to the far reaches of the realm and across the English border to IRELAND, SCOTLAND, and WALES through the efforts of itinerant lay preachers, enthusiastic society members, and sympathetic Anglican and Dissenting clergymen. Parish boundaries were disregarded in the compulsion to "spread scriptural holiness," although normally the regular hours for worship in parish churches were not to be infringed upon. "I look upon all the world as my parish," wrote John Wesley in 1739. Always mission-oriented, Methodism grew in the British Isles and beyond through the organized efforts of administrative "conferences" and by more spontaneous EVANGELISM. By the twenty-first century, Methodism could boast a "world parish" consisting of numerous Methodist, Wesleyan, and united church denominations in over one hundred countries, with most of those denominations linked informally through the WORLD METHODIST COUNCIL.

Methodism of the "First Generation"

Methodists in Britain and in Ireland were organized as a "connexion" or an affiliation of Methodist societies bound by common regulations and governance, with John Wesley as their head. As such they supported the expansion of Methodism at home and abroad: to SWITZERLAND (native land of preacher John Fletcher); to "His Majesty's Dominions" in the West Indies, Bermuda, the Maritime Provinces, and parts of Upper CANADA; and to the American colonies that became the UNITED STATES. After Wesley's death in 1791 the connexion continued under the direction of an annually elected president (British and Irish Methodism have no bishops) along with, in Britain, the "Legal Hundred" that had been established in 1784 as the supreme legislative body. Debates soon arose regarding governance, relations between the LAITY and the preachers, and Methodism's legal and ecclesiastical ties with ANGLICANISM—in particular, Methodist ordinations and the desire of Methodists to receive the SACRAMENTS at the hands of their own ministers. Over the next century the connexion fragmented as groups claiming to be Wesley's true successors formed their own alliances. The predominant Methodist body in Britain was the Wesleyan Methodist Connexion, later named the Wesleyan Methodist Church. Others included the PRIMITIVE METHODIST Connexion (1811); and the Methodist New Connexion (1797), the Bible Christians (1815), and the United Methodist Free Churches (1857) that in 1907 merged to constitute the UNITED METHODIST CHURCH. All of these bodies united in 1932 as the Methodist Church. Methodism in Ireland was not nearly so fissiparous, with only the Primitive Wesleyan Methodist Connexion separating from the Wesleyan Methodist Connexion in 1818; reunion was achieved in 1878 with the creation of the Methodist Church in Ireland. All of these bodies were committed to the proclamation of the heart-warming gospel overseas, sometimes even establishing mission outposts before the arrival of commerce or representatives of the expanding British Empire, both of which usually had the effect of easing missionary access.

Methodism first crossed the Atlantic in the 1760s: to Antigua, where planter and lawyer Nathaniel Gilbert preached to slave and colonist in his own home; and to the American colonies and Newfoundland when immigrants and "traveling" preachers formed Methodist societies (see ITINERACY). In 1784 the Methodist Episcopal Church was founded in the United States at the so-called Christmas Conference in Baltimore (see BALTIMORE CONFERENCE), and to the ongoing work of lay preachers and leaders was added a ministry ordered as deacon, elder (presbyter), and superintendent (renamed "bishop"). All men, lay or ordained, who were entrusted with the task of PREACHING were expected to itinerate, thus enabling the gospel to be carried to new settlements and to established communities that either had not yet heard the Christian story or had become lukewarm in their commitment to it. Evangelistic outreach and mission (domestic and foreign) by CLERGY and laity, men and (in a more circumscribed sense) WOMEN, was a priority for the Methodist Episcopal Church (1784–1939) and for the other Methodist bodies that emerged in the United States through separation or merger. These denominations, some of which took an episcopal form of government whereas others opted to elect presidents of conference rather than bishops, had a significant role in planting Methodism around the globe. Among them should be noted: the AFRICAN METHODIST EPISCOPAL CHURCH (1816); the AFRICAN METHODIST EPISCOPAL ZION CHURCH (1821); the Methodist Protestant Church (1830); the Wesleyan Methodist Connection (1843), later named the Wesleyan Methodist Church; the Methodist Episcopal Church, South (1844); the Free Methodist Church (1860); and the Colored (later changed to Christian) Methodist Episcopal Church

(1870). The Methodist Church came into being in 1939 through the union of the Methodist Episcopal Church, the Methodist Protestant Church, and the Methodist Episcopal Church, South. The Methodist Church joined with the EVANGELICAL UNITED BRETHREN CHURCH in 1968 as the United Methodist Church.

In 1801, 196,502 white and "colored" Methodists were accounted for in Europe (almost exclusively Britain and Ireland, a venture into FRANCE being unsuccessful), Nova Scotia, Newfoundland, Canada, the United States, and the West Indies (see CARIBBEAN). During the next fifteen years Wesleyan Methodists in Britain looked to other areas, notably SIERRA LEONE (first visited in 1795), SOUTH AFRICA, Ceylon (Sri Lanka), Java (INDONESIA), INDIA, and AUSTRALIA, largely under the leadership of THOMAS COKE, who died on shipboard while crossing the Indian Ocean. By 1816 over one hundred missionaries were listed by the Wesleyan Methodist Connexion; two years later, the Connexion officially constituted the General Wesleyan Methodist Missionary Society (see MISSIONARY SOCIETIES). During this same period, attention in the United States focused on Methodist expansion with the nation, and for the Methodist Episcopal Church, the establishment of societies in Upper and Lower Canada. Relations between British and American Methodists soured because of conflicts regarding the Canadian missions, and the War of 1812 exacerbated the situation. The Methodist Episcopal Church in 1828 granted independence to the Methodist Episcopal Church in Canada that existed alongside Wesleyan Methodists organized according to the British plan, although friction continued. The influx of British immigrants who brought with them the practices and politics of the smaller British denominations also added to the mix. Eventually most of the groups that originated in Britain, along with the Methodist Episcopal Church in Canada, united in 1884 to establish the Methodist Church that in 1925 merged with Presbyterians and Congregationalists to constitute the UNITED CHURCH OF CANADA.

Factors in the Spread of Methodism

The circumstances that gave rise to Canadian Methodism, or aspects of it, have been repeated in other places throughout the world. First of all, Methodist missionary efforts in a single country, especially work before the twentieth century, may be traced to denominations in the United States or in Britain and Ireland, or both. Over time, often after a period of tension, some of these groups merge, whereas others choose to remain separate. Thus some Methodist denominations of the second generation may follow the POLITY and practices of the parent DENOMINATION, they may choose or adapt one style of governance among those offered by the founding denominations, or they may blend different styles together. For this reason some second-generation Methodist denominations have presidents of conference, some have bishops, and some have both.

Second, the spread of Methodism may come from organized missionary efforts, it may result directly or indirectly from patterns of immigration, and it may be a consequence of the establishment of military bases abroad. Emigration by British Methodists and the posting of British forces exerted an impact on the development of Methodism in Canada as well as in South Africa, Australia, and India. In a reversal of these patterns, non-Methodist immigrants or visitors who embrace Methodism may, on return to their native land, take Methodism with them; in such a manner Methodism was introduced to parts of continental Europe and Scandinavia from the United States.

Third, history has shown that disputes within Methodist denominations sometimes lead to divisions, a tendency perhaps attributable to Methodism's weak ECCLESIOLOGY. Such fissiparousness has given birth to new ecclesiastical families with their own mission identities, such as the SALVATION ARMY and the Pentecostal movement (see PENTECOSTALISM). In spite of this unfortunate attribute Methodists have also shown a willingness to unite with others of the Methodist family and to enter into broader church unions. Like the United Church of Canada, the CHURCH OF SOUTH INDIA, the CHURCH OF NORTH INDIA, and the UNITING CHURCH IN AUSTRALIA each include a Wesleyan component.

Finally Methodist denominations launched by missionary work soon adopt the priority of evangelism and mission and begin their work alongside groups from the first generation. Methodism in CHINA can be traced, for example, to work by Methodists from the United States, Britain, and Canada. Korean Methodists (see KOREA), whose origins are in Methodism from the United States, are in the twenty-first century sending missionaries to the United States where Methodism, along with much of mainline Protestantism, is in decline. Singaporean and Malaysian Methodists, with spiritual roots both in Britain and in the United States, have helped to open new mission fields in Cambodia and elsewhere in Southeast Asia.

The histories of European, African, Asian, and South Pacific Methodism are therefore integrally tied, but often not exclusively so, to the stories of Methodism in Britain, Ireland, and the United States. The introduction of Methodism into Central and South America came, not surprisingly, principally from the United States. Methodism in the Caribbean and the South Pacific is of the British type. Methodist outreach at first was predominantly to those nations where the gospel had not yet been heard. Only later, because of what was perceived as ineffectual "gospel" ministry by other Protestants, the Roman Catholics, and the Orthodox (see ORTHODOXY, EASTERN), did Methodists move into countries where those churches were already present. The establishment of places for preaching and the building of churches have not been the only tasks of Methodist missionaries. In most countries great attention has been given to the development of institutions for EDUCATION and for social services.

Representatives of "Second-Generation" Methodism

Although it is not the "state" church, the Free Wesleyan Church of Tonga claims the membership of the royal family, several of whom have served as local preachers and avid supporters of church work. Methodism arrived in the "Friendly Islands" in 1822 through the labors of British Methodist Walter Lawry, who departed after fourteen difficult months. John Thomas and John Hutchinson were sent from Sydney in 1826 to resume the mission, joining two Tahitians whose work had been fruitful in Nuku'alofa. Other missionaries soon arrived. By the 1850s most of the islands were nominally Christian and Methodist, a result aided by the CONVERSION of the ruling chief who would become King George Topou I and by the work of native Tongans who themselves would also participate in missions to Fiji, Samoa, and Papua New Guinea. Dissension over the connectional relation between Tongan Methodism and Methodism in Australia that fractured the church in 1885 was only partially healed in 1924. The Free Wesleyan Church became truly autonomous in 1977, although it maintains missiological links with the Uniting Church in Australia. The denomination is responsible for much of the secondary education in the kingdom and through its mission board oversees the work of Tongan congregations in other countries.

Methodism was introduced into BRAZIL in 1835 when Rev. Fountain E. Pitts of the Methodist Episcopal Church arrived in Rio de Janeiro and soon formed there a society for English-speaking persons. Although Pitts returned to the United States, others continued and expanded his ministry until 1841 when the South American missions were suspended. Work resumed in 1867 when Junius E. Newman of the Methodist Episcopal Church, South, was authorized to establish a Methodist presence in Rio and in the state of São Paulo where hundreds of Confederate sympathizers had immigrated after the CIVIL WAR in the United States. Under Newman's direction the first Methodist church in Brazil opened in 1871, and by the 1880s native Brazilians were actively forming congregations. Although the Methodist Episcopal Church sent representatives in the 1870s, it was the work and financial support of the Methodist Episcopal Church, South that dominated and from which, in 1930, the independent Methodist Church in Brazil was born. The Methodist Church was the first church in LATIN AMERICA to become a member of the WORLD COUNCIL OF CHURCHES. Since the late 1920s the Free Methodist Church has also been at work in Brazil, its first missionaries coming from JAPAN.

The first Methodists in NIGERIA were Africans: a group from Sierra Leone who in the late 1830s settled in Abeokuta; and an ex-slave living in Badagry. With requests for assistance from both these areas, British Wesleyan Methodist THOMAS BIRCH FREEMAN and two helpers came to Nigeria in 1842. Wesleyan Methodism spread west and north; eastern Nigeria was the focus of the Primitive Methodists beginning in 1893. The churches of each British denomination existed as separate districts until 1962 when they formed the Methodist Church Nigeria. In a variation on the usual patterns of Methodist organization, a prelate oversees the six archdioceses that constitute the Methodist Church Nigeria. There are other Methodist denominations in Nigeria, among them the African Methodist Episcopal Zion Church; the Christian Methodist Episcopal Church; the Zion Methodist Church in Nigeria; and the Nigeria Annual Conference of the United Methodist Church, created in 1992, that owes its origin to the missionary enterprises of the Evangelical United Brethren and its ecclesiastical predecessors whose work began in 1905.

Whereas in Nigeria the denominations that arose from British and American roots have remained separate, in GERMANY, to which had come a Wesleyan Methodist lay evangelist in the 1830s (to Württemberg) and a Methodist Episcopal clergyman in 1849 (to Bremen), there was a merger of the two groups (1897). Additional unions with United Brethren (1905) and the Evangelische Gemeinschaft (1968) created the Evangelisch-methodistische Kirche, which is a part of the United Methodist Church. German Methodists were instrumental in spreading Methodism to other German-speaking countries, to German-speaking communities in Eastern Europe, and to the Baltic region.

Missionaries to Korea were affiliated with the Methodist Episcopal Church (from 1884) and the Methodist Episcopal Church, South (from 1895) and principally engaged in education and medical work. Evangelism occurred, at first secretly and subtly, and later, as Korean worries about foreigners dissipated, more openly. Translation and publication of the BIBLE (see BIBLE TRANSLATION) and of Christian literature was given priority. A Korean Conference of the Methodist Episcopal Church was formed in 1908; one for the Methodist Episcopal Church, South was organized in 1918. These merged in 1930 (nine years before their parents in the United States did so) to form the autonomous Korean Methodist Church. Political tensions inside and outside of Korea have troubled the denomination, yet its membership has steadily increased, and it has been intentional in evangelistic outreach, such as in RUSSIA and in Central Asia.

See also Methodism, England; Methodism, Europe; Methodism, North America

References and Further Reading

Davey, Cyril J. *The March of Methodism: The Story of Methodist Missionary Work Overseas.* New York: Philosophical Library, 1951.

Garrett, John. *Footsteps in the Sea: Christianity in Oceania to World War II.* Suva, Fiji: Institute of Pacific Studies, University of the South Pacific; and Geneva, Switzerland: WCC Publications, 1992.

Harmon, Nolan B., ed. *The Encyclopedia of World Methodism.* 2 vols. Nashville, TN: The United Methodist Publishing House, 1974.

Oduyoye, Mercy Amba. *The Wesleyan Presence in Nigeria, 1842–1962.* Ibadan, Nigeria: Sefer, 1992.

Westerfield Tucker, Karen B., ed. *The Sunday Service of the Methodists: Twentieth-Century Worship in Worldwide Methodism.* Nashville, TN: Kingswood, 1996.

KAREN B. WESTERFIELD TUCKER

METHODISM, NORTH AMERICA

Methodism has been one of the most influential religious movements in North America, both in CANADA and especially in the UNITED STATES. Some historians of American religion believe that METHODISM has not received the attention it deserves for its shaping of American CULTURE. Two of them have commented, ". . . Methodism rivals PURITANISM in its force and intensity, its ability to mobilize followers, to generate new modes of communication and organization, and to instill habits of industry, sobriety, and mutual accountability" (Hatch and Wigger 2001:11). Methodists have effected the minds and behavior of the nation's people not only by their sheer numerical strength, but by their conviction that divine SALVATION is available to all and that personal Christian commitment must be demonstrated socially.

Beginnings in North America

Methodism began as a lay PREACHING movement in North America about 1760 under the leadership of Robert Strawbridge (c.1732–1781), an Irish immigrant farmer in Maryland. Philip Embury (1728–1773) and his cousin Barbara Heck (1734–1804), also Irish immigrants, were responsible for the early founding of Methodist work in New York City in 1766. As the movement took root in the colonies, Methodist founder JOHN WESLEY (1703–1791) dispatched a few of his British preachers to America to nurture and direct its societies and their component small groups called classes. One of these lay missionary preachers was FRANCIS ASBURY (1745–1816), who arrived in Philadelphia in 1771 and became the foremost leader of early American Methodism.

In the years after the American Revolution, it was increasingly apparent to Wesley that his followers in the New World required a formal ecclesiastical organization that would solidify their identity, stabilize their ministry, and provide for the administration of the SACRAMENTS of BAPTISM and the LORD'S SUPPER. In December 1784 at its "Christmas Conference" in Baltimore, Maryland (see BALTIMORE CONFERENCE), the American Methodist preachers under Wesley's instructions formed a new church, which they named the Methodist Episcopal Church (MEC). They chose an episcopal form of church government with Asbury and THOMAS COKE (1747–1814) as their first superintendents (bishops). Some of their lay preachers, including Asbury, were ordained, and a worship book called *The Sunday Service of the Methodists in North America . . . ,* which included Articles of Religion, was adopted. The new church had approximately 110 preachers and 20,000 members, one-tenth of whom were African American.

The MEC experienced rapid growth. The Wesleyan conviction that all people are loved by God and may be forgiven of their sin attracted many despite Methodism's rigorous spiritual and moral discipline (see ARMINIANISM; CHURCH DISCIPLINE). Circuit-riding preachers, appointed by the bishops, fanned out across the country proclaiming the message of salvation and organizing new congregations (see CIRCUIT RIDING; ITINERACY). By 1825 MEC membership reached 340,000.

Struggles with Division

The DENOMINATION experienced severe difficulties during the earlier decades of its life. Perhaps the first major problem was caused by James O'Kelly (1735–1826), one of those ordained in 1784. At the church's first General Conference in 1792, O'Kelly challenged the final AUTHORITY of the bishops to appoint the preachers to their circuits and congregations (see BISHOP AND EPISCOPACY). He proposed that any preacher unhappy with a proposed appointment be able to appeal it and, if sustained by his fellow preachers, the bishop must give him a different appointment.

When his proposal failed, O'Kelly and his followers walked out of the MEC and formed the Republican Methodist Church. The Republican Methodists later joined the Congregationalists.

Two other serious schisms in the MEC were tied to the issue of race. Although African Americans were part of the MEC from its beginning, they experienced the harsh reality of racial discrimination. When an MEC African American preacher, RICHARD ALLEN (1760–1831), and some of his Methodist friends encountered problems because of their race at the predominantly white St. George's MEC in Philadelphia, he led them out and eventually in 1816 founded the AFRICAN METHODIST EPISCOPAL CHURCH (AME). Allen was its first bishop. Similar mistreatment of African Americans, initially at the John Street MEC, New York City, prompted James Varick (1750–1827), Christopher Rush (1777–1873), and others to leave the MEC to form the AFRICAN METHODIST EPISCOPAL ZION CHURCH (AMEZ) in 1820. Varick and Rush were its first bishops. Both the AME and the AMEZ were Wesleyan in THEOLOGY and comparable to the MEC in organizational structure.

A fourth division in the MEC occurred in 1830. In the early years of the nineteenth century there was growing sympathy to give local preachers, who did not possess full CLERGY rights, and lay people broader participation in the life of the church. A reform party emerged in the 1820s that agitated for change. After a few years of intense negotiation, which created severe animosity, the reformers' cause was brought to the 1828 MEC General Conference, its governing body. When their position was rejected, the reformers met in Baltimore in November 1830 and organized the Methodist Protestant Church (MP). Their initial membership numbered approximately 5,000. The new church did not have bishops and gave lay people representation in its policymaking bodies.

Although the membership of the MEC was diminished by the departure of those who became members of the AME, AMEZ, and the MP, overall growth in church membership continued to soar. By 1843 the MEC numbered 1,069,000 members. This growth was concurrent with the Second Great Awakening (see AWAKENINGS), a wave of evangelical revivalistic religion that engulfed much of the nation in the years preceding the CIVIL WAR. During this era popular revival techniques were developed and CAMP MEETINGS were widely and effectively employed by many American Protestants, including Methodists.

Slavery and War

The issue of SLAVERY was divisive among Methodists as it was among the BAPTISTS and Presbyterians (see PRESBYTERIANISM). Wesley vehemently condemned slavery in his 1774 tract *Thoughts Upon Slavery* and considered it "the sum of all villainies." At its organizing Christmas Conference, the MEC adopted legislation to eliminate slave holding and trading among its members (see SLAVERY, ABOLITION OF). However, the antislavery rule was short-lived because of regional pressures, and by the early nineteenth century antislavery sentiment had grown considerably. In 1843, after it became clear that the MEC was not yet ready to deal fully with the issue, abolitionist leaders Orange Scott (1800–1847), Luther Lee (1800–1889), and Lucius C. Matlack (1816–1883) led a group of lay and clergy dissidents to form the Wesleyan Methodist Church (now WESLEYAN CHURCH).

No longer able to avoid the issue that many suspected would further split the church, the MEC's 1844 General Conference directly confronted the slavery question. Much of the debate centered on Bishop James O. Andrew (1794–1871), one of the church's five episcopal leaders, who was a slaveowner by marriage. When the delegates voted to suspend Andrew from exercising his episcopal duties, the southern delegates drafted a Plan of Separation that resulted in the formation in 1845 in Louisville, Kentucky, of the Methodist Episcopal Church, South (MECS). The new denomination had a membership of approximately 450,000.

Just before the Civil War, another group in the MEC expressed dissatisfaction over the church's adoption of more formalized WORSHIP, the decline of camp meetings as evangelistic gatherings, and Methodism's accommodation to middle-class worldly values. Led by John Wesley Redfield (1810–1863) and Benjamin T. Roberts (1823–1893), these reformers formed the FREE METHODIST CHURCH in 1860.

The Civil War was especially difficult for the MECS. Between 1860 and 1865 its membership fell from 750,00 to 500,000. Many of its churches were destroyed or badly damaged. Its future was in question. However, the 1865 Palmyra Manifesto, which originated in the Missouri Annual Conference of the MECS, affirmed an intention that the denomination retain its identity and continue its ministry. A few years later the MECS settled the issue of the future of its black membership by encouraging the formation of the Colored Methodist Episcopal Church (CME), a new denomination formed in 1870. In 1956 the CME changed its name to the Christian Methodist Episcopal Church.

Growth and Mission

During the period of Reconstruction through the early decades of the twentieth century, the MEC and MECS enjoyed spectacular growth. By 1920 MEC membership was approximately 4,000,000, the MECS membership 2,000,000. The denominations strengthened their national and overseas mission work, which had begun before the Civil War. They continued their commitment to education through SUNDAY SCHOOLS and the founding of many more institutions of HIGHER EDUCATION such as Rust College (1866), Syracuse University (1870), and West Virginia Wesleyan College (1890).

The Wesleyan emphasis on holy living (SANCTIFICATION) gave birth to an important movement in the nineteenth century. PHOEBE WORRALL PALMER (1807–1874), an MEC laywoman, was an early advocate for this HOLINESS MOVEMENT. Toward the end of the century there was intense theological debate concerning how Wesleyan sanctification led to Christian perfection, the believer's being made perfect in love, a prominent idea developed in Wesley's theology. Was Christian perfection something gradually attained by divine GRACE, or was it instantaneously granted as a "second blessing," the "first blessing" being the sinner's JUSTIFICATION or forgiveness? Those who stressed the latter approach promoted their views through REVIVALS, camp meetings, and publications. When it became obvious that the mainstream of Methodism preferred the gradualist approach, the instantaneous "second blessing" advocates separated from Methodism and eventually formed "holiness churches," such as the CHURCH OF THE NAZARENE (1907) and the Pilgrim Holiness Church (1913). From these holiness roots came the modern Pentecostal movement, one of the most significant Protestant developments in North America in the twentieth century (see PENTECOSTALISM). Among the larger Pentecostal churches are the CHURCH OF GOD IN CHRIST (1907) and the ASSEMBLIES OF GOD (1914).

Nineteenth-century Methodists promoted mission work in their cities and countryside as well as overseas. Although Methodist WOMEN were not granted full clergy rights until the next century (see WOMEN CLERGY), they were at the forefront of denominational mission work forming organizations, collecting funds, recruiting workers, and serving on the mission field. Methodist women were also prominent in the TEMPERANCE movement, which advocated abstinence from alcoholic beverages. FRANCES E. WILLARD (1839–1898), MEC laywoman, was one of the movement's outstanding leaders. By the end of the nineteenth century women could also participate in some of the Methodist denominations as DEACONESSES who provided educational and health care ministries as well as services to immigrants.

The churches of Methodism provided support to their nation during both World Wars I and II. They also survived the Great Depression that began in 1929. Through the first half of the twentieth century church memberships continued to grow.

The twentieth-century ecumenical movement had a profound effect on much of North American Methodism. After several decades of negotiation the MEC, MECS, and MP decided to reunite in 1939 to become The Methodist Church (MC) with 6,560,000 members. In 1968 the MC entered into a union with the EVANGELICAL UNITED BRETHREN (EUB), a church with historic ties to Methodism, to form the UNITED METHODIST CHURCH (UMC). At union the UMC had 10,220,000 members making it not only the largest Methodist denomination in North America but also its largest Protestant denomination. The UMC also had regional groups, called Annual Conferences, in North America as well as AFRICA, Asia, Europe, and LATIN AMERICA.

Methodist preaching in Canada began as early as 1765 in Newfoundland with Lawrence Coughlan (?–1785), one of Wesley's Irish itinerant preachers. Work expanded in Nova Scotia as well as Upper and Lower Canada in the late eighteenth and early nineteenth centuries. Subsequently, a number of Methodist denominations were formed. A union of churches in 1884 brought almost all Canadian Methodists into The Methodist Church of Canada, a church that exerted considerable influence on the nation until in 1925, when it had approximately 400,000 members, it united with Presbyterians and Congregational churches to form the UNITED CHURCH OF CANADA.

Future Issues

There are a number of issues facing North American Methodism, especially the largest of its denominations. Declining membership is one of the most serious problems. By 2000 UMC membership had fallen to 8,400,000 from its high in 1969 of 10,872,000, a loss of 2,472,000 or 23 percent. The AME, AMEZ, and CME denominations also experienced losses in membership although in more modest proportions.

The UMC has also been troubled by theological and social controversy. Although the UMC is a multiracial church, it is predominantly white. It has struggled for decades with the issue of racism and the role of ethnic persons in its pastoral and lay leadership. There are also continuing disputes between the theologically conservative and liberal parties in the denomination concerning the nature and authority of the BIBLE, and the place of EVANGELISM in relationship to social action ministries. Some have been concerned that traditional DOCTRINE and doctrinal standards in the denomination have been ignored. Furthermore, one of the most debated issues has been whether homosexual persons should be ordained and appointed to serve in pastoral ministry. This has been a most contentious issue at the denomination's General Conferences.

Because many of the Methodist denominations have congregations and missions in nations outside North America, each of them has questioned how best it may relate to its people in other lands. The predominantly North American churches have wrestled with the manner in which they should assist their members in other nations to adapt traditional theological, structural, and ministerial work to their own native cultures (see CULTURE).

Many of the Methodist denominations have strongly supported a connectional system of church government in which each local church belongs to a regional, or annual, conference of other churches presided over by a bishop or other official. Within this connectional relationship clergy are appointed to their congregations, denominational programs are promoted, and funds are collected for the support of the denomination's ministries and institutions beyond the local church. There has been some question whether the connectional system is outmoded and should be replaced with a system that gives more power and authority to the local congregation.

North American Methodism remains vital and exerts an important influence on local, regional, and national life.

References and Further Reading

Campbell, James T. *Songs of Zion: The African Methodist Episcopal Church in the United States and South Africa.* New York: Oxford University Press, 1995.

Hatch, Nathan O., and John H. Wigger, eds. *Methodism and the Shaping of American Culture.* Nashville, TN: Kingswood Books, 2001.

Kirby, James E., Russell E. Richey, and Kenneth E. Rowe. *The Methodists.* Westport, CT: Greenwood Press, 1996.

Lakey, Othal H. *The History of the CME Church,* Revised edition. Memphis, TN: The CME Publishing House, 1996.

Lyerly, Cynthia Lynn. *Methodism and the Southern Mind, 1770–1810.* New York: Oxford University Press, 1998.

McEllhenney, John G. *United Methodism in America: A Compact History.* Nashville, TN: Abingdon Press, 1992.

Richey, Russell E., Kenneth E. Rowe, and Jean Miller Schmidt, eds. *The Methodist Experience in America.* Nashville, TN: Abingdon Press, 2000.

———, eds. *Perspectives on American Methodism: Interpretive Essays.* Nashville, TN: Kingswood Books, 1993.

Semple, Neil. *The Lord's Dominion: The History of Canadian Methodism.* Montreal and Kingston, Canada: McGill-Queen's University Press, 1996.

Westerfield Tucker, Karen B. *American Methodist Worship.* New York: Oxford University Press, 2001.

Wigger, John H. *Taking Heaven by Storm: Methodism and the Rise of Popular Christianity in America.* New York: Oxford University Press, 1998.

Yrigoyen, Charles Jr., and Susan E. Warrick, eds. *Historical Dictionary of Methodism.* Lanham, MD: Scarecrow Press, 1996.

CHARLES YRIGOYEN JR.

METHODIST EPISCOPAL CHURCH CONFERENCE

The concept of CONFERENCE is perhaps the central feature of Methodist POLITY and identity. The construct of conference has had many forms as it developed in the Methodist Episcopal Church in America (1784–1939), the Methodist Church (1939–1968), and continuing in the present United Methodist Church (1968–). Yet throughout American METHODISM, the conference has referred to a body of preachers (and later LAITY) who exercise various legislative, judicial, and executive functions of the church. Conference has defined the Methodist movement in political ways resembling the branches and roles of the federal government. It has been shaped by its sociopolitical context, but has often functioned as an embodiment of intensely held theological notions of Methodist mission. Conference seeks to balance creative tensions at the heart of Methodist notions about ministry: that representative ministry has obligations to the local parish and its laity, while also having missional obligations to the entire Methodist church in wider geographic settings for the sake of the world. Toward this end, the conference is an organization that administers and deploys pastors to local parishes. It also seeks to link those local churches administratively to wider geographic, national, and international bodies of Methodism in a chain of regularized interaction: with other conferences on the regional level (in bodies known since 1939 as Jurisdictional Conferences); and on the national and international level as well (through a body known since 1792 as the General Conference).

Methodism has regarded its conference structures historically as the primary body through which ministry and ordination are regulated. Methodist ordination is conferred only through conference membership and Episcopal oversight (see BISHOP AND EPISCOPACY). This is in contrast to some Protestant churches, which authorize ordination in relation to local church boards or national accrediting agencies. Methodist ministry is defined through the processes of debate and organizational AUTHORITY vested in the annual conference. Conferences meet annually in each designated geographic area to decide matters of policy, and to confirm appointments of pastors to respective local churches.

Historical Development of Conference

From the inception of the Wesleyan revival in Britain, JOHN WESLEY found gathering his lay preachers or "helpers" in a regular conference served the missional needs of revival. Wesley described Methodist organizational forms as ad hoc, secondary to the mission of revival. Wesley borrowed the concept of a conference from his history as priest within the connectional Anglican parish system. Yet from 1744, Wesley transformed the Anglican notion of connected geographic parishes to focus on the preachers themselves, creating a covenant body to ensure "the spread of holiness and the reform of the nation, especially the churches." In conference Wesley was able to set policy, engage in supervision and training of his largely uneducated pastors, and deploy ministers to take advantage of local revival AWAKENINGS. Wesley transferred such features to the American scene, when he sent lay preachers to serve the fledgling but spontaneously growing lay movement from 1769 until the Revolutionary War.

Even before there was a Methodist Episcopal Church in America, conference was a key organizing concept for the movement. Methodist preachers traveled far across the colonial American landscape, PREACHING regularly in numerous public settings and chapels (see CIRCUIT RIDERS). As persons were spiritually awakened, they were invited to join small Methodist classes while also directed to partake of the SACRAMENTS through Anglican parishes. Wesley designated his representative superintendents in America to meet quarterly to ensure preachers continued to proclaim a conversionist message of Wesleyan assurance and holistic transformation, as well as stimulating the necessary movement of preachers along their preaching circuits.

FRANCIS ASBURY presided over the first quarterly conference of the Methodist preachers in America in 1772. The first annual conference in America for which we have documentary record was held in 1773, overseen by Thomas Rankin, a Scot who had served under Wesley. As a tool of governance, conference adapted as the fledgling movement grew in numbers and geographic distance: first through quarterly meetings (1769–1773), then through a single annual conference as the limited size of the movement allowed (1773–1779), and then through multiple sessions of a theoretically single conference held across various geographic areas (1779–1792).

In the aftermath of the Revolution and its disruption of the Anglican ministry, Wesley responded to calls from the Methodist societies for a sacramental ministry and consecrated a limited episcopacy to ordain pastors for the American mission field. By this action Wesley effectively recognized the emergence of an independently constituted Methodist Church. The founding of The Methodist Episcopal Church in America subsequently occurred at the so-called Christmas Conference in 1784 (see BALTIMORE CONFERENCE). As the Methodist Episcopal Church launched its early mission to America, ordained pastors ("presiding elders") and their more numerous lay pastors met quarterly, with all coming together annually with their bishops. The first two bishops consecrated for America were Asbury and THOMAS COKE.

For Methodists in America, missional needs, rather than regularities of church order, have been primary in the historical development of the conference concept. Asbury, more than any other figure, decisively shaped the conference to reflect both democratic and missional ideals. His own personal charisma and political ambitions transformed the conference from a mere administrative meeting of preachers for appointments and supervision into the single most important ecclesial form shaping Methodist identity. The conference idea under Asbury's leadership from 1784 to 1816 became a highly integrated network of moving preachers. This system of ITINERACY matched preachers to Methodist communities organized in small classes, arranged in a linked hierarchy of circuits, districts, and—from 1796 onward—in annual conferences dedicated to geographical areas. Conference carefully balanced Asbury's own authority in regulating the pastors, with emerging democratic ideals.

Asbury fought to retain exclusive power to deploy his preachers to ever wider and marginal areas of the American frontier. Yet at the same time conference allowed preachers some measure of democratic participation, adapting policy, structure, and ecclesiastic identity to the growing demands for representation and rights in the early American Republic. While Asbury lived he oversaw almost all of the various annual conferences—some 224 of them. He exercised almost absolute episcopal authority over policy and appointments, based on his experience derived from a lifetime traveling and preaching across America. From his death in 1816, successor bishops could not, or would not, operate in such an authoritative manner. The first native-born bishop, William McKendree, instituted the policy in 1816 that appointments would be made through a more collaborative process with the assistance of presiding elders over districts. The Methodist Episcopal Church conferences after Asbury repeatedly faced the need to adapt to changes in the political and social culture of a rapidly westward growing America.

The Methodist Episcopal Church held competing views within it about the proper relationship of episcopal authority to democratic principles in conferences, which twice erupted in schism in 1792 and 1830. These schisms formed the Republican Methodists and the Methodist Protestant Church, respectively. With these splits many members inclined toward more democratic processes in conference were drained away from the Methodist Episcopal Church. One could read the history of the church and its schisms as a referendum on the conference ideal and its oscillating emphases between centralized authority and democracy. The split of American Methodism into its northern (Methodist Episcopal Church) and southern branches (Methodist Episcopal Church, South) occurred in part over regional apprehension that slave-owning southern bishops might be assigned by General Conference to preside over antislavery conferences in the North (see SLAVERY; SLAVERY, ABOLITION OF). Additionally southern bishops feared interference with their strong authority in southern conferences—particularly on the sensitive subject of slaveholding—by centralized legislation coming out of the national General Conference pressing the historic disciplinary antislavery commitments of Methodism. The split into northern and southern Methodist branches, enacted by the Plan of Separation adopted in Louisville, Kentucky, in 1845, had an immediate effect on the relationship between episcopal authority and conferences. The separation enshrined a regionalism in annual conferences, tying bishops to a particular set of conferences in closely related areas of CULTURE. It only entrenched patterns of regionalism already held before the split, and further isolated each region from the influence of the other. The results were that the Methodist Episcopal Church tended to have a stronger national General Conference and more democratically minded episcopal leadership, whereas the southern branch attempted to protect its regional segregation and culture through authoritarian bishops controlling relatively weaker annual and general conferences.

After the conclusion of the CIVIL WAR, the northern church increasingly followed the culture on a number of fronts: organizing conferences more effectively on the lines of emerging business practices and rules of order; and moving toward more inclusive lay representation at General Conference. It granted General Conference representation to laymen in 1872, but resisted inclusion of laywomen there until 1904. The northern Methodists allowed both men and WOMEN to participate as lay delegates to annual conferences in 1932. (Southern Methodists by contrast promoted earlier lay representation for men in annual conferences, stemming from the necessity to rebuild the church quickly in the post–Civil War era.) In the late nineteenth century, both northern and southern churches resisted initial attempts by women for ordination and membership in the conferences. Only in 1956 did women finally win the right to membership in full connection to the conferences of the Methodist Church, the essential condition for ordination (see WOMEN CLERGY).

Reunion of the two branches into a newly constituted Methodist Church (1939–1968) was predicated on a diplomatic balancing of powers that still shapes the conferences today. A Judicial Council was created as appellate power to moderate the two old antagonists—the northern-dominated General Conference and the strong southern episcopacy. Also six Jurisdictional Conferences were created in five regions, segregating African American Methodists into one separate Central Jurisdiction. These institutions were designed to protect annual conferences as they sought to serve the political and cultural agendas of their constituencies. The ironic results of these actions only entrenched regional and racial division in the church—the status quo ante hellum condition of 1845 that prompted the split. Moreover the effect of this regional and racial segregation was to render the annual conferences themselves increasingly weaker in the face of the Judicial Council.

Power also slowly flowed toward other national agencies such as the Board of Mission and the Board of Church and Society, reflecting mid-twentieth-century cultural commitments to the concept of big business and franchise. Since 1968 and the creation of the UNITED METHODIST CHURCH through union with the EVANGELICAL UNITED BRETHREN CHURCH, conferences have continued to lose power on a number of fronts. First, conference legislation and episcopal actions have been increasingly subject to appeal to the Judicial Council. Also, since the 1960s, the role of caucus groups in Methodism has strengthened. As in larger society, these special-interest advocacy groups have grown in institutional influence and organizational sophistication, using media effectively to lobby annual conferences and General Conference for the passage of policy reforms on select issues.

Finally, annual conferences and their episcopal leadership have found their political and appointive powers weakened in the face of growing local congregational and lay powers. In particular, more decisions are being made by the laity at the local church level with regard to appointments. In the last thirty years, bishops have exercised their greatest power not so much through annual conferences, but through reclaiming their teaching office to the church (in some ways mirroring the caucus trend), and through their leadership on the boards of national and international Methodist church agencies. These appear to be trends that will continue to reshape the role of conference in Methodist mission and ecclesial polity for the foreseeable future.

Interpretative Significance of Conference

The historian Russell Richey has noted that conference is the defining body of Methodist identity and historical narrative. Methodist history unfolds in relation to annual conferences from year to year (with General Conference policy decided every four years). Despite Methodism's distinctive commitment to the conference concept, Richey has argued convincingly that conference has an extremely flexible range of meanings. Conference regulates Methodist pastoral identity, shaping the connection between preachers and their congregation in both space and time. Indeed with every annual conference, the shape of the conference changes geographically with the reading of the new appointments, remaining in effect for one year. The language of conference has developed an ecclesial term—conference—with its focus on the mechanics of church order. There is also a more dynamic and ineffable term: "The Connection." When Methodists speak of "The Connection," they hearken back to the more familial-based usage of John Wesley to his "connexion" of preachers. Frank Baker, the British Methodist scholar, has argued that connectionalism is one of the greatest contributions made by Wesley to Protestant ecclesiastical polity.

The notion of connection is invested in the annual conference, but is not coextensive with it. Connectionalism in the annual conference guards each individual parish from becoming inwardly focused, isolated, or completely dominated by its local culture or concerns. The notion of connection stresses that the missional sum of the Methodist body worldwide is greater than its conference or church parts. At conference, pastors and laity come together in a binding fashion, to "speak freely what is in their hearts." Conference seeks to gather representatives of "The People Called Methodist" to extend Christian witness, service, and sacramental presence for a fixed time to the parishes of the geographically bounded conference—all with a view toward transforming the entire world. When Methodists speak of "being in the connection," this takes the construct of conference polity and invests it with a more spiritual, theological, and sacramental nature. Such usage is rooted in Wesley's idea that conferencing is an ordinary channel of God's presence—a means of GRACE to the world. Thus, the real power of conference remains its capacity to stimulate and sharpen its members through mutual obligations found in connection to one another and to God. Taken at is best the connection found in conference shifts the focus from political and organizational aspects of the Conference body to its missional and sacramental nature in forming Methodist identity and practice. As of the year 2000 there were sixty-four U.S. annual conferences and fifty-five others around the world, according to the official Web site of the United Methodist Church (www.umc.org).

The conferences of the present-day United Methodist Church still find themselves significant bodies for determining Methodist identity and policy, although there are challenges. Conferences are facing issues of globalization that often strain local identity. Moreover, they face acute limits to their authority, in an increasingly litigious, pluralistic, antiauthoritarian, and individualistic culture (see INDIVIDUALISM). Despite its various permutations historically and culturally, conference will most likely remain an essential ecclesial form through which Methodists understand themselves, their encounter with American culture, and the world.

See also Methodism, Europe; Methodism, Global; Methodism, North America

References and Further Reading

Frank, Thomas Edward. *Polity, Practice, and the Mission of the United Methodist Church.* Nashville, TN: Abingdon Press, 1997.
Kirby, James E., Russell E. Richey, and Kenneth E. Rowe. *The Methodists: Student Edition.* Westport, CT: Praeger Press, 1998.
Klaiber, Walter, and Manfred Marquardt. *Gelebte Gnade: Grundrißeiner Theologie der Evangelisch-methodistischen Kirche.* Stuttgart, Germany: Christliches Verlagshaus, 1993.
Norwood, Frederick A. *The Story of American Methodism.* Nashville, TN: Abingdon Press, 1974.
Richey, Russell E. "Conference as a Means of Grace." In *Early American Methodism.* Bloomington and Indianapolis: Indiana University Press, 1991.
———. *The Methodist Conference in America: A History.* Nashville, TN: Abingdon Press, 1996.
Richey, Russell E., Kenneth E. Rowe, and Jean Miller Schmidt. *The Methodist Experience in America: A Sourcebook.* Nashville, TN: Abingdon Press, 2000.
Schneider, A. Gregory. *The Way of the Cross Leads Home: The Domestication of American Methodism.* Bloomington and Indianapolis: Indiana University Press, 1993.
Wigger, John H. *Taking Heaven by Storm: Methodism and the Rise of Popular Christianity in America.* New York and Oxford: Oxford University Press, 1998.

W. HARRISON DANIEL

MEXICO

As a stream of religious DISSENT, Protestantism in Mexico can be said to constitute several tributaries that have followed contours unique to the Mexican landscape, ebbing and flowing in response to internal and external factors and events. In terms of spiritual lineage the works of exiled Spanish priests in the sixteenth and seventeenth centuries served as a long-suppressed cultural and theological fountainhead. These combined with liberal French and Anglo-American thought to provide the headwaters of reform in the fledgling Republic. The subsequent engineering by U.S. missionaries and their sponsor agencies certainly shaped much of the infrastructure of early Mexican Protestantism; however, the later inflow of Pentecostal revivalism carried the stream over and far beyond the limited banks of the mainline project. The charting of that process requires careful historicization; otherwise, our view of the contemporary muddied waters of Mexican dissident religiosity would remain clouded indeed.

Iberian Antecedents

As Spain proved key to the defense of Roman Catholicism in the sixteenth century, so too did it water its own seedbeds of Erasmian humanism, *alumbradismo,* and theological reform. Cardinal Francisco Ximenes's *Complutense Polyglot* Bible (1514–1522) represented the apex of the former movement, whereas Teresa de Avila (d. 1582) and Juan de la Cruz (d. 1591) successfully channeled the mystical tendencies of the second. Twelve Jeromian monks of Seville's St. Isidore monastery, imbibing too freely of smuggled Lutheran and Calvinistic wine, fled the Inquisition's grasp, and found refuge in SWITZERLAND, GERMANY, ENGLAND, and the NETHERLANDS. Of these, Casiodoro de Reina (d. 1594) and Cipriano de Valera (who studied and taught at CAMBRIDGE UNIVERSITY and Oxford University) proved the most prolific in Scripture translation (see BIBLE TRANSLATION) and pamphleteering. Their joint opus, the *Reina y Valera* Bible of 1602 (Valera consummated Reina's earlier work), heralded Spain's literary Golden Age, and endured to foment and nourish later movements of religious dissent in Spain and its former colonies in LATIN AMERICA.

Castille and Aragon's political union and successful military routing of Moorish Grenada (1492) further emboldened a national church bent on expelling the Jewish presence from the Iberian Peninsula. The contemporaneous discovery of new lands in the looming shadow of northern European HERESY beckoned Spain to unprecedented prominence as the "savior of Rome, evangelizer of the globe, and hammer of heretics." The pastoral care of the expanding flock in the new territories required continued vigilance against *converso* and *marrano* subterfuge as well as Lutheran heresies and indigenous "idolatry." A review of Inquisitional records in New Spain and Peru demonstrates the care with which church and crown sought to extirpate religious—and political—dissent.

National Independence

In a sense the story of Protestant origins and growth in Mexico is as much a story of Roman Catholic privilege, dominance, declension, and struggle over against an emergent state. During the young nation's decade-long War of Independence (1810–1821) and later Wars of Reform (1858–1860) and French Intervention (1861–1867), the hierarchy aligned itself perennially with royalist and conservative parties. Rural priests such as Miguel Hidalgo and José Morelos, however, opted to lead the populist revolt for independence. The young Republic's original guarantee of a religious monopoly for the Catholic religion at the price of the secularization of many church-owned missions and properties set in place a template of perennial struggle and accommodation between CHURCH AND STATE. The conflict flared into full-scale civil war under the presidency of Benito Juárez (1858–1872), whose Laws of Reform divested the Catholic Church of its monopoly over religious services, and secularized control of MARRIAGE and cemeteries. The titanic dueling usually found Protestants and other liberals cheering on the latter protagonist. Under the patronage of Mexico's most revered executive, a group of dissident priests known as the "Constitutionalist Fathers" severed ties to Rome and reconstituted themselves in 1861 as the *Iglesia de Jesús,* a proto-Anglican church movement, which soon sought succor from the U.S. Protestant Episcopal Church (see EPISCOPAL CHURCH, USA).

Although British and U.S. BIBLE SOCIETIES took advantage of brief post-Independence interludes to introduce Bibles into the country, broader dissemination of these did not occur until the arrival of missionaries in the latter half and final quarter of the eighteenth century. The Wars of Texas Independence (1835–1836) and American Intervention (1846–1848), justified by ideologues of Manifest Destiny, permitted U.S. Protestant denominations and agencies to establish beachheads deep into former Mexican lands now situated along Mexico's new northern border. With the floodgates of Catholic privilege weakened considerably, Protestant missionary incursion flowed freely up until 1910. Presbyterian Melinda Rankin sponsored BIBLE colporteurs and other outreach into Nuevo Leon state from her Brownsville, Texas base. Baptist James Hickey arrived into that state's capital, Monterrey, in 1862. In 1864 he established the Thomas Westrup family, formerly immigrant English Anglicans, as pioneer converts in the region. Other denominations and movements soon followed: Quakers (see FRIENDS, SOCIETY OF), and Northern BAPTISTS (1871); Congregationalists (see CONGREGATIONALISM) and Northern Presbyterians (1872); Northern and Southern Methodists (1873); Southern Presbyterians (1874); Associate Reform Presbyterians (1878); Southern Baptists (1880); Brethren and SEVENTH-DAY ADVENTISTS (1891); and CHURCH OF THE NAZARENE (1903).

Several patterns soon emerged. With an overwhelming advantage in tactical, financial, and educational resources, missionaries were able to overwhelm the scattered nascent nuclei of Mexican Protestants, and established themselves as the primary interlocutors vis-à-vis state and federal governments. Early Protestantism built on existing networks of Masonic and other liberal political clubs, with whom they shared strong antipathies toward the Catholic Church. Converts represented the middling commercial and artisan classes, and benefited enormously from the educational enterprise of the missions. Their mestizo background reflected Protestantism's inability—in spite of great efforts—to realize substantial inroads into elite Mexican society and its indifference (lamented by Benito Juárez, a Zapoteco from Oaxaca state) toward the country's significant indigenous minorities. A division of labor soon developed, with missionaries remaining in urban areas increasingly tied by railroads, and Mexican ministers fanning out to smaller towns and rural settlements. Generally in the case of splintered U.S. communions, U.S. Southerners flourished in the Mexican North, whereas U.S. Northerners prospered in the Center and West. By 1905 Mexico's *evangélico* (the term more accurately reflects the nomenclature for Latin American Protestantism) community numbered about 22,000, with half of these belonging to Methodist communions.

Revolution

The long rule—initially democratic and then dictatorial—of Porfirio Diaz (1877–1911) saw an increasing rapprochement between his government and the Catholic Church. The great INDUSTRIALIZATION realized under his regime, however, required immense flows of capital from the UNITED STATES and Britain. Thus the restrictions of the 1857 Reform were kept in place, albeit honored more in the breach than otherwise. Diaz's increasingly despotic rule fed a growing opposition that broke out into armed rebellion in 1910 upon the fraudulent denial of the presidency to Francisco Madero, a Liberal landowner from the northern state of Coahuila. The revolt quickly deposed Diaz, as military chieftans throughout the country swore allegiance to Madero. However, palace intrigue resulted in Madero's assassination in 1913 and the implosion of his reformist project. The Mexican Revolution soon engulfed the country in a conflagration that cost one million lives (a tenth of the population) and uprooted another million persons northward or to other points in the Republic. Far from remaining immune to the state of affairs, Mexican Protestants, representing by this time a second generation of leadership, threw in their lot with the insurgents, providing key military and civilian leadership and support at critical junctures. The conflict drove missionaries northward to the United States, from whence they lamented their would-be progeny's engagement with the revolutionary project and their own prior ambivalence toward the Diaz regime. Mexican Protestantism's clear commitment to the emergent revolutionary regime carved out a valuable space in Mexican society, as many took up prominent state and federal government positions in the Venustiano Carranza and subsequent administrations. Key pedagogues such as Moisés Sáenz left an important imprint on the educational system. Protestants generally assented to the harsh anticlerical strictures of the 1917 Constitution, aimed as these were against Catholic CLERGY. As a result Catholic counterrevolutionary *cristero* rebels (1926–1929) in the West targeted *evangélicos* as often as they did agrarian reformers, socialists, soldiers, and government teachers.

The Revolution debilitated several Protestant institutions, draining native talent from evangelization efforts, and further constricting foreign clerical prerogatives. Two other developments, however, proved equally definitive in the future trajectory and growth of Protestantism: missionary intromission and Pentecostal revivalism.

In line with developments elsewhere, U.S. missionary strategists sought to minimize competition and maximize resources. A cooperative conference held in Cincinnati in 1914 carved up Mexico into confessional territories, assigning one or several to each U.S. denomination, and transferring properties and, presumably, Mexican personnel and converts. The absence of Mexican voices at the conclave complicated the Cincinnati Plan's implementation on the ground during the following decade, and heightened nationalistic sentiments among Mexicans, many of whom felt betrayed in their longstanding confessional loyalties. The plan produced mixed results. On the one hand, Congregationalists failed to maximize their new franchise in Guadalajara and Jalisco, contenting themselves with small middle-class cul-de-sacs. On the other hand, Presbyterians (see PRESBYTERIANISM) began substantial incursions into indigenous nations in the South, especially Chiapas. (The South also saw gains for Seventh-day Adventists.) Southern Methodists (see METHODISM; METHODISM, NORTH AMERICA) continued their growth in the northern states of Chihuahua, Coahuila, Nuevo Leon, Sonora, and Tamaulipas, in tandem with great progress in border conferences in Texas and New Mexico, whereas their northern (U.S.) counterparts tended central Mexico (Mexico City, Puebla, and Hidalgo) and southern California. In tandem with the Revolution's nationalism, Mexican Protestants agitated for autonomy, with the biggest communion, the Methodists, achieving this in 1930, when both branches combined into the Mexican Methodist Church. By that year the national census counted a nationwide Protestant population (including foreigners) of 130,322. Soon thereafter, Lázaro Cardenas, arguably Mexico's most leftist president (1934–1940), welcomed missionary linguists affiliated with the WYCLIFFE BIBLE TRANSLATORS and Summer Language Institute (SLI) to points throughout the country to work among indigenous nations and help realize Benito Juárez's long-stymied dream.

Pentecostalism

While mainline Protestants consolidated their place in Mexican society and negotiated the new territorial divisions, revival embers arrived, borne by returned refugees, direct and indirect participants in Los Angeles's AZUSA STREET REVIVAL (1906–1909) and its aftermath. The first of these, Romana Carbajal de Valenzuela, returned to her native Villa Aldama, Chihuahua, in 1914 to usher her Catholic family into the Pentecostal movement. Other evangelists soon followed, sweeping down from Mexican American communities in California, Arizona, New Mexico, and Texas, and taking advantage of the ecclesiastical vacuum created by the Revolution. Valenzuela's conversion of Rubén Ortega, the sole remaining Methodist pastor in Chihuahua City, and her CONVERSION of several Methodist and Baptist families in Torreón, Coahuila, proved emblematic of the upstart movement's penchant for building on older seedbeds of *evangélico* belief. Yet, Pentecostals found the vast majority of their converts among Catholic peasants, laborers, artisans, and small vendors, and realized important initial inroads into northern indigenous peoples like the Ceri of Sonora. The class location of the new believers brightened Protestantism's prospects. As much a movement of labor and migration as of religious belief and practice, PENTECOSTALISM successfully rode the crests of the many back-and-forth tides of human movement precipitated by macro political and economic events of the twentieth century (e.g., Revolution, Repatriation, Bracero Guestworker Program, Operation Wetback, Immigration Reform Acts of 1965 and 1986, etc.). Mobility and scarcity bred solidarity and fecundity. Pentecostal churches provided significant opportunities for the assertion of autochthonous leadership and cross-border collaboration. Among the flagship denominations to emerge by mid-century were the *Iglesia Apóstolica* (tied to a sister Mexican American denomination in the United States, the Apostolic Assembly), the *Asambleas de Dios,* the *Iglesia de Dios en la República Mexicana,* and the *Luz del Mundo.* Ecclesiastical polities run the gamut from congregational to episcopal to prophetic, with a decided preference for the religious equivalent of the military *caudillo* or chieftain, that is, with elements of strong, charismatic, and often autocratic

personalism in leadership. Doctrinal variety and heterodoxy also characterize the movement, especially in those sectors far removed from missionary control. For example, the *Iglesia Apóstolica* and *Luz del Mundo* churches and a wider constellation of smaller groups espouse a Oneness theology; indeed, *apostólicos* may constitute fully one-third of Mexican Pentecostalism.

In spite of their religious dissident status, Pentecostals proved adept in appropriating elements of popular Mexican culture, especially musical idioms. Thus, they recaptured the *fiesta* of Mexican culture, and suffused it with affectivity and corporeal sensation. They created new sonic spheres that resonated in the ears and bodies of would-be converts. The liturgical reform proved infectious. By the last quarter of the century pneumatic Christianity emerged as the majority expression within Mexican Protestantism and a strong minority one within Catholicism (by the post–Vatican II Charismatic revival).

Late Twentieth-Century Growth and Issues

The reconfiguration of late twentieth-century Protestantism also came with a price: the loss of political coherence. The corruption and decrepitude of the governing party (*Partido Revolucionario Institucional* [PRI]) left Protestants increasingly bereft of a traditional ally in the newly competitive universe of Mexican national and state politics. The 1990 diplomatic rapprochement with the Vatican and the 1992 reform of the Constitution's articles on religion "leveled" the field of religious competition in favor of the still-hegemonic Catholic Church. The ascendancy of the Catholic-based party, the *Partido de Acción Nacional* (PAN), augured renewed vindications of long-lost *cristero* wars and a muscular Catholicism's recapture of the public square. A militant leftist splinter from the governing PRI, the *Partido de la Revolución Democrática* (PRD) found great difficulty in shedding its congenital antireligious bias inherited from earlier Marxist progenitors. In the end, Protestants split their votes equally among the presidential options in the 2000 elections. Although Roman Catholic prelates were customarily quoted in the weekly and daily press on a variety of issues, Protestant voices were generally sought out only on matters of religious intolerance. Ideological commitments represent the gamut from traditional to liberationist positions. Opponents from both ends of the political spectrum found ironic common ground in their critiques of Protestantism as a witting and unwitting tool of U.S.-led capitalist expansion. Catholic apologists fretted over the fracturing of a national religious identity (Mexico as Guadalupan and Catholic), and anthropologists decried the splintering of ostensibly previously homogeneous indigenous communities. In 1979 Mexican anthropologists succeeded in having the Education Secretariat sever a nearly four-decades-long working relationship with the SLI.

Growth continued apace, nevertheless. At century's end, the 2000 Census counted a Protestant population of 4,897,104 (including Seventh-day Adventists), or 5.8 percent of the country's total population, ages five years and higher. (JEHOVAH'S WITNESSES were reported at over a million and Mormons at over 200,000.) The religious minorities kept pace with and even superseded national population growth, achieving a notable demographic presence. More telling, though, were the regional and local variations. Protestants were reported to constitute 22 percent of Chiapas's population, 19 percent of Tabasco's, 18 percent of Campeche's, 16 percent of Quintana Roo's, 11 percent of Yucatan's, and 10 percent of Oaxaca's and Morelos's—rates as high as almost quadruple the national figure and matched only by those of Baja California and Chihuahua states. Clearly geographical proximity to the country's Protestant northern neighbor cannot explain the surge in the south. Indeed Mexico's other northern border states ranked closer to the national average. Accordingly scholars of religious change have been compelled to examine more closely regional and historical particularities; among these: globalization, migration, economic vicissitudes, cultural flux, religious remittances, indigenous aperture, and Catholic division and fatigue.

The case of Mexican Protestant history and experience presents several issues for further examination. The relative success and failure of its varied streams—mainline and Pentecostal—among varied social classes prompt a query into the agency of converts and practitioners, into the efficacy of missionary leadership and intromission, and into the "mexicanization" of religious dissent. The expanding religious pluralism in the indigenous South presses the point over tolerance and competing legal regimes (communitarian consensus vs. individual rights of belief), and over compatible cosmovisions and religiosities. Finally the exclusion or retreat of *evangélicos* from the public square in the latter half of the twentieth century suggests that the diverse internal composition of the movement has had profound social and civic implications.

See also Anti-Trinitarianism; Baptist Missions; Calvinism; Evangelism; Liberal Protestantism and Liberalism; Lutheranism; Missionary Organizations; Missions; Missions, North American; Mormonism; Revivals

References and Further Reading

Baez Camargo, G., and Kenneth G. Grubb. *Religion in the Republic of Mexico*. London: World Dominion Press, 1935.

Balderrama, Francisco E., and Raymond Rodríguez. *Decade of Betrayal: Mexican Repatriation in the 1930s*. Albuquerque, NM: University of New Mexico Press, 1995.

Baldwin, Deborah J. *Protestants and the Mexican Revolution: Missionaries, Ministers, and Social Change*. Chicago: University of Illinois Press, 1990.

Bastian, Jean-Pierre. *Los disidentes: sociedades protestantes y revolución en México, 1872–1911*. México, D.F.: El Colegio de México, 1989.

Butler, John Wesley. *History of the Methodist Episcopal Church in Mexico*. New York: The Methodist Book Concern, 1918.

Camp, Roderic A. *Crossing Swords: Politics and Religion in Mexico*. New York: Oxford University Press, 1997.

Gil, Kenneth D. *Toward a Contextualized Theology for the Third World: The Emergence and Development of Jesus' Name Pentecostalism in Mexico*. Frankfurt, Germany: Peter Lang, 1994.

Haven, Gilbert. *Mexico: Our Next-Door Neighbor*. New York: Harper and Bros., 1875.

Hernández Castillo, Rosalva Aída. *Histories and Stories from Chiapas: Border Identities in Southern Mexico*. Translated by Martha Pou. Austin: University of Texas Press, 2001.

Maldonado, David Jr., ed. *Protestantes/Protestants: Hispanic Christianity within Mainline Traditions*. Nashville, TN: Abingdon Press, 1999.

Menéndez y Pelayo, Marcelino. *Historia de los heterodoxos españoles*. Madrid, Spain: Librería General de Victoriano Suárez, 1911–1933.

Rankin, Melinda. *Twenty Years among the Mexicans*. Cincinnati, OH: Chase & Hall, 1875.

DANIEL RAMÍREZ

MIDDLETON, THOMAS FANSHAW (1769–1822)

First Anglican and Protestant bishop in INDIA. Middleton was born in Kedleston, Derbyshire where his father was rector. He was educated at Christ's Hospital, where he was contemporary with Charles Lamb and SAMUEL TAYLOR COLERIDGE, and Pembroke College, University of Cambridge (see CAMBRIDGE UNIVERSITY). He was ordained in 1792 and served as curate of Gainsborough, Lincolnshire. In 1808 he published a scholarly work on the Greek article in the New Testament, which ran to five editions. After two incumbencies he was appointed prebendary of Lincoln Cathedral in 1809. In 1811 he moved to London as vicar of St. Pancras and served as archdeacon of Huntingdon, also joining in the work of the SOCIETY FOR THE PROPAGATION OF CHRISTIAN KNOWLEDGE.

In 1814 he was appointed first Anglican bishop of Calcutta with ecclesiastical jurisdiction over the territories administered by the East India Company and their chaplains. Confronted by missionaries belonging to a voluntary society like the CHURCH MISSIONARY SOCIETY, without formal links to the ecclesiastical legal framework, he wrote "I must either licence them or silence them." He strengthened church life and founded Bishop's College, Calcutta, in 1820, with the aim of creating an educated ministry, aiding missionaries on first arrival, educating Muslims and Hindus, and translating the Scriptures and publishing Christian tracts (see BIBLE TRANSLATION). His friendliness to BAPTISTS like WILLIAM CAREY was appreciated. In 1817 Ceylon (present-day Sri Lanka) was added to his diocese and he ordained a DEACON in Colombo in 1821.

Middleton did his best to lay firm and secure foundations for the church in India, from which his successors might benefit. His anxiety to earn respect for his office caused him to appear remote, and he suffered from contrast with the charm of his immediate successor, the poet and hymn writer Reginald Heber (1823–1826), and the lengthy and masterful episcopate of Daniel Wilson (1832–1858). He was a conscientious and scholarly bishop with impossibly large and ill-defined responsibilities. He died in Calcutta and is buried in Calcutta Cathedral.

References and Further Reading

Primary Source:

Middleton, Thomas F. *The Doctrine of the Greek Article Applied to the Criticism and Interpretation of the New Testament.* New York: Eastburn, Kirk and Co., 1813

Secondary Sources:

Dictionary of National Biography. vol. 37. London: Oxford University Press, 1894.
Gibbs, M. E. *The Anglican Church in India 1600–1970.* London: ISPCK, 1972.
Kaye, J. W. *Christianity in India.* London: Smith, Elder, 1859.
Le Bas, C. W. *Life of Thomas Middleton.* 2 vols. 1831.
Neill, S. C. *A History of Christianity in India 1707–1858.* Cambridge: Cambridge University Press, 1985.

TIMOTHY E. YATES

MILLENARIANS AND MILLENNIALISM

"Millennialism" and "APOCALYPTICISM" are two terms often misued. They are terms many historians use with a clear sense of what they mean but perhaps a less-firm grip on what others hear. As a result, much of the discussion of millennialism has wandered, sometimes wildly, from assertions of its centrality to its dismissal as marginal. The millennial dimension of the REFORMATION and the development of Protestantism should be explored less in the specific identification of any given individual as an apocalyptic or millennial thinker and more in the dynamics of apocalyptic time

and its impact on the thinking of various figures, both in their formal theological reflections and in their polemical and activist pronouncements. Few periods in history reflect more strikingly than the Reformation two of the basic principles of millennial and apocalyptic dynamics: (1) *one person's messiah is another's Antichrist;* and (2) *wrong does not mean inconsequential.* It is therefore necessary to begin this essay with a set of definitions.

Millennialism

"Millennialism" is defined as the belief that at some point in the future, a messianic era of peace, prosperity, justice, and fellowship will commence and last for 1,000 years. "Millenarians" are those who subscribe to this belief. The term "millennialism" derives from the bracketed detail peculiar to Christianity (Revelation 20:1–7), but the crucial issue, something noted by church fathers as well as modern anthropologists, is the notion that God's justice will manifest itself on Earth, in public, in a radical transformation of social and political norms. In its secular forms, we have come to call this idea "revolution." Millennialism's this-worldly orientation makes it politically subversive by nature (Daniels 1992), and accordingly most religious elites prefer to substitute a more apolitical ESCHATOLOGY, in which the advent of cosmic justice puts an end to the physical world entirely, with rewards and punishments meted out in spiritual realms (HEAVEN AND HELL).

Millennialism has two major tensions, between hierarchical and demotic, and between restorative and progressive. Hierarchical millennialism expects a world-conquering or world-ruling emperor to establish the one true way and impose its peace upon the world; it views the cosmic enemy as chaos (Cohn 1993) and seeks the messianic solution in order. In the form of myths about the "last emperor," hierarchical millennialism played a critical role in the politics of the Middle Ages, undergirding the most ambitious political agendas from Constantine onward, including many of the "Holy Roman emperors" who attempted to rule over ITALY and GERMANY.

Demotic millennialism views the messianic kingdom as a kind of holy anarchy in which transformed individuals live just lives without need for a state or other overarching coercive AUTHORITY. Here the empire represents the cosmic enemy, and the messianic solution comes from a world in which aristocracy vanishes and each commoner gets to enjoy the fruits of his honest labor undisturbed. "And each shall sit under his fig and vine, and none shall make him afraid" (Micah 4:3). Most of the more radical forms of millennialism, or those most frequently alluded to as such, reflect this demotic tradition, which, not surprisingly, many ecclesiastical elites consider anarchic and dangerous.

Both of these forms use mixtures of rhetoric from two further orientations: the restorative, in which the messianic kingdom returns the "saved" to an earlier, pristine state that time and man have corrupted, and the progressive, in which mankind will step into a world never before seen, one that will create new forms and (often) new technologies. The former appeals to those with conservative attitudes and tendencies toward magical thinking in which the restoration will arrive as the result of divine intervention. The latter, the progressive, tends to welcome and encourage innovation and to see in social and political change paths to a messianic future.

Apocalypticism

The critical issue, however, concerns the question of timing. Only with great difficulty can one identify or observe the impact of millennial beliefs during "normal time"—that is, during periods when most millennial believers think that this fallen world will long endure. Under such conditions, even the most subversive demotic millennialism tends to have largely conservative effect. Paul could council slaves to "obey your masters" (I Ephesians) and subjects to "obey the powers that be" (Romans 13:1), not because such political structures were just, but because "you know how long the night is gone, how soon the dawn" (Romans 13:11–12). Only when believers become convinced that the advent of the kingdom is imminent do they become active, creating a millennial movement. This apocalyptic sense of urgency transforms quiescent beliefs into a range of passions all the more intense because of the immediacy of these final cosmic transformations. The term "apocalyptic" here designates both the sense of the imminent transformation whereby this world ruled by evil will become the messianic kingdom and the scenario whereby such a transition will occur. (Note that this differs fundamentally from the more common definition of millennial, which is both imminent and this-worldly [Cohn 1957]. One can be apocalyptic without being millennial [e.g., MARTIN LUTHER and probably Paul], and one can be millennial without being apocalyptic [Hippolytus and Ussher].)

In the apocalyptic we find two major tensions, between violent and peaceful transition, and between active or passive human roles. In the first set of tensions, on the one hand we find cataclysmic scenarios in which vast devastation purifies the world to make way for the messianic kingdom. On the other hand, we find transformative scenarios in which,

through a turning of the heart and will, humanity changes its ways and converts the paths of justice. "And they will beat their swords into plowshares and spears into pruning hooks; nation shall not lift up sword against nation, nor study war any more" (Isaiah 2; Micah 4).

The second major tension, between active and passive, opposes on the one hand those who believe that humans have no significant role in the process, that God, the stars, the ineluctable forces of history and the cosmos carry out this work and humans can at best prepare, repent, and hope that they will be among the "saved" and on the other hand those who believe that the believer becomes not the recipient, but rather the tool of the transformative will of these cosmic forces. Almost all secular millennial movements tend toward activism (no God on which to rely), whereas religious institutions most often favor passive scenarios (we must await God).

Apocalyptic scenarios can lead either to millennial outcomes here on Earth or to eschatological resolutions beyond the physical plane. Millennial believers tend to favor active apocalyptic scenarios, whereas eschatological believers tend to favor passive apocalyptic scenarios. Only with the advent of weapons of mass destruction has the possibility of active cataclysmic eschatological scenarios—the destruction of the world by man—become a possibility.

Finally, the apocalyptic represents one of the few religious beliefs subject to disconfirmation. Every apocalyptic believer in history has been mistaken, but not inconsequential. The impact of apocalypticism on history, therefore, is that of the unintended consequences of actions undertaken in mistaken anticipation of events that did not occur. Unlike apocalyptic beliefs, however, millennial beliefs cannot be falsified. The disappointment of expectation may sour believers in a specific apocalyptic timetable or scenario, but the belief in an eventual messianic era proves far more durable. Apocalyptic time comes episodically, bringing millennial beliefs, hidden in normal time, into the public sphere.

One cannot emphasize enough that all of these options—millennial and apocalyptic—remain fluid, that believers, especially during periods of apocalyptic expectation, can run though a kaleidoscope of possibilities. Indeed, disappointment often provokes a dazzling display of apocalyptic "jazz," whereby the believers rewrite the scenario of imminent transformations and millennial goals to keep their faith alive. In cases where the apocalyptic movement has achieved significant power before disappointment, failure can lead to "upping the ante" and still more extravagant displays of apocalyptic commitment (Baumgarten 2000).

Pre-Reformation Apocalyptic Millennialism

Using these definitions, we can make the following general remarks about pre-Reformation Europe. From the thirteenth century at least, once Joachim of Fiore had revivified in ecclesiastical circles the millennial traditions of the early church banished by Augustine, Latin Christians had an intensely varied range of millennial options, from the hierarchical salvation that some thought would come from a last emperor or angelic pope to the demotic ones that moved peasants and townsfolk alike to imagine a world without aristocracy. Moreover, late medieval CULTURE seems especially susceptible to apocalyptic outbreaks, although that may be more the illusion created by an increasingly developed documentation that permits us to identify moments that were no less plentiful in earlier eras.

The emergence of an aggressive form of demotic millennialism constitutes perhaps the most portentous development in the later middle ages. Starting with the Shepherd's Crusades (1250, 1321) and Fra Dolcino's revolutionary Spiritual Franciscanism (1300–1307), we find an active cataclysmic scenario aimed at destroying the powerful—ecclesiastics, the rich, the aristocracy. The impact of the Inquisition in particular, which had proved relatively effective against Catharism, seems to have aggravated the problem of millennialism, inspiring even radically passive groups (Franciscans) to take up violence (Dolcino at the execution of Sigarelli in 1300). In the aftermath of the Black Death, which at once seemed to fulfill the most horrific of passive cataclysmic scenarios (only to disprove it by passing from the scene) and to generate some of the most active forms of passivity (flagellants, pogroms against the Jews), we find a range of commoners' revolts (Jacquerie in 1358, English Peasants War in 1381), inspired by millennial visions denouncing the corruption of lay and ecclesiastical courts (John of Rupescissa), and invoking some of the most demotic biblical exegeses ("When Adam delved and Eve span, who was then the Gentleman?"). These millennial revolts seem closely linked to biblical translation into the vernacular, and commoners' more direct access to the contents of the BIBLE.

Nowhere can one see the full range of these at work better than in the impact of biblical translation and dissemination, including a vernacular Bible, on Czech society (see BIBLE TRANSLATION). Czech millennialism began with a biblically inspired demotic reform of the Czech Church inspired by Jan Hus in the early fifteenth century. It shifted to more radical and millennial expectations after Hus's betrayal and execution at the Council of Constance (1415), producing the Taborites, an active transformative group that, under

the pressure of both external enemies and disappointment at the failure of passive apocalyptic timetables (February 1420), turned into active cataclysmic apocalypticism. The Hussite reform demonstrates a characteristic tendency among Christian renewal movements to split between more conservative "reform" (Utraquists) and more radical, indeed revolutionary, egalitarian movements. The Adamites then split from the Taborites, forming a restorative millennialism that sought to re-create Eden on the antinomian premise that they had become divine and transcended all human and legal restraints. They mixed, according to one chronicler, free love (primarily and typically for men) with a merciless violence against outsiders whom they considered of an inferior race (St. Clair 1992).

It is difficult to guess whether the advent of the printing press in the mid-fifteenth century had a stimulating effect on apocalyptic beliefs (as it would in the early sixteenth century) or again whether it merely increased the historian's documentary base and awareness of a phenomenon that was already at a fever pitch. But certainly the fall of Constantinople to the Turkish Muslims in 1453 stimulated widespread apocalyptic concerns in both the East and the West of Christendom. The end of the fifteenth century again (or still?) represents a period of intense apocalyptic expectation, as well as some extraordinary new millennial developments including:

- The emergence of a new kind of gnostic science (*magus* tradition), which shows a particularly empirical bent (Franciscan postapocalyptic in origin) toward a slow transformational apocalyptic process involving the acquisition of knowledge by which man could transform the earth (postmillennialism)
- The perceived discovery of a new world by Columbus (inspired by prophecies of both Joachim and Pierre d'Ailley), and the expulsion of both Muslims and Jews from Spain in 1492
- The advent of 7000 Annus Mundi according to the Greek *era mundi*, which according to some calculations came in 1492; in the most common, in 1500. This created a "Y7K" Easter Table crisis among Russian Orthodox ecclesiastics and inspired special paintings from both Botticelli and Dürer in 1500.
- The common resort of major rulers of the day, especially Francis I of France and Charles V, to the last emperor.

The combination of apocalyptic speculation and new and rapid sociopolitical change made the advent of the sixteenth century one of intense expectation that moved rapidly from disappointment to new date. In particular, the year 1524 stands out as a date that, designated both for religious and astrological reasons, had wide ranges of people actively concerned. Indeed, the early sixteenth century constitutes one of those rare public apocalyptic moments simultaneously detectable in Mediterranean Islam, Christianity, and JUDAISM.

Luther, Apocalyptic Time, and Thomas Müntzer

Martin Luther, trained as an Augustinian canon and relatively conservative in his social attitudes, never became a millennialist. One might argue that behind his decision to translate the Bible into German and make it, through printing, available to untold masses of readers and listeners lies a kind of technological Joachitism whereby the printed vernacular would serve as the vehicle for the Holy Spirit to enter each individual, thereby transforming the world at the approach of the end. But his introduction to Revelation, whose very canonicity he suspected, makes it clear that he disapproved of explicitly millennial beliefs. But whatever one argues about Luther's millennialism, there is considerably more evidence that he at least entertained apocalyptic notions of the imminence of the end of time (Modalsi 1983). The evidence is at best ambiguous, however, with some clearly apocalyptic statements in the early years when Luther broke decisively with the Roman Church, called the papacy antichrist, and identified openly with Jan Hus (1520). Luther voiced the fear in the early 1520s that he might not complete his translation of the Bible before the end, and in his violent denunciation of the rebels invoked apocalyptic urgency. But in the aftermath, he distanced himself from any such speculation. At the end of his life, his *Supputatio annorum mundi* (1540) placed the present in the year 5500 from the creation, thus (implicitly) giving a 500-year buffer according to a traditional millennial scheme of the ages of the world, at the same time he made less formal and more apocalyptic remarks (Klaassen 1992).

From the standpoint of millennial movements, Luther's importance lies only partially in what he said and did, and far more in how others perceived him and understood him and his writings. Like John Wycliffe and Hus before him, Luther's attacks on the church and embrace of a vernacular Bible set off a dynamic whose consequences went far beyond his intentions (Hillerbrand 1988; Edwards 1975). Indeed, as Luther found himself forced rapidly into the status of heretic, he reconsidered Hus (whom he had assumed, as he was taught, was a madman) and by 1523 wrote that "we are all Hussites." As with Hus, Luther found that others took his teachings still farther. In particular, his

translation of the Bible in the age of printing made available to commoners a text full of millennial hopes and prophecies (previously minimized by an antimillennial CLERGY), triggering a wide range of millennial beliefs and movements. Luther's attack on the church, both because it rapidly devolved into the most apocalyptic name-calling (the church as the "whore of Babylon," the papacy as the "Antichrist"), and because it seemed to contemporaries that this constituted an unprecedented, world-shattering struggle, placed Luther himself at the center of apocalyptic speculation—in particular the notion that Luther was one of the "two witnesses" who marked the end of time (Peterson 1993). Nothing better illustrates the autonomous nature of apocalyptic expectation than whatever actors in such times say or do. These deeds register on a semiotically aroused audience in ways far different from what their authors originally intended. Indeed, once Luther's more conservative views became apparent, more radical figures did not hesitate to accuse *him* of being the antichrist.

The first explicitly millennial movement in the Reformation came from THOMAS MÜNTZER, a parish priest who, inspired initially by Luther, quickly joined more radical Christians, plunging into millennial beliefs with a circle of activist apocalyptic prophets in Zwickau. Müntzer eventually became the leader of a commoner uprising that, like the English Peasants' Revolt of 1381, invoked the Adam and Eve narrative to call for the abolition of the aristocracy. The ensuing war of 1524–1525 illustrates the explosive mixture of apocalyptic prophecy, millennial notions, and access to the biblical text by commoners (Blickle 1981). Luther's role as failed mediator and eventually enthusiastic supporter of the nobles' slaughter of the peasants drew critical lines between politically acceptable reformers (who could count on the support of princes) and radical millennialists who did not spare Luther the title of ANTICHRIST any more than Luther had spared the pope. These events recapitulated the dynamics of the Taborites in their split with Hus, illustrating how easily, especially under conditions of aristocratic exploitation, a passive, transformative apocalyptic movement can become active and violent.

Anabaptists

Luther, therefore, walked a tightrope across apocalyptic falls as he tried to avoid slipping either into the millennial fanaticism of the radicals or into the mystified institutions of the Catholic Church. But others went much farther. The most radical were generally grouped under the rubric "Anabaptists" (see ANABAPTISM) in that they rejected infant BAPTISM (and the ecclesiastical order that insisted on its efficacy) and insisted that the believer undergo baptism as part of a conscious, adult CONVERSION, a turning to the Lord. This produced highly self-conscious salvific communities that were, by definition, voluntary and radical. These imitators of the apostolic life formed classic millennial "cells" and lived in a proleptic perfection that anticipated an imminent apocalypse. Such beliefs, steeped in millennial lore and expectations, found adherents among people of all social standings, but had a particular appeal to commoners. They also had a very high incidence of WOMEN (characteristic of active transformative groups) who played prominent roles in the Anabaptist communities. As with most radical demotic millennialists, the Anabaptists had no central organization, but rather constituted a wide-ranging assortment of acephalous communities and individuals whose religious convictions and affiliations could change with great speed and intensity.

Almost all of these Anabaptists began (as far as we can reconstruct) in extremely pacific forms, refusing to participate in any aspect of state coercion and avoiding among themselves any signs of hierarchy, manifesting all the signs of a zealous active transformative apocalyptic leading to a demotic millennial kingdom. One might imagine that people for whom "love thy enemy as thyself" and "forgive seven times seventy" would remain radical pacifists (see PACIFISM), but under the conditions in which they spread, at least some of them became active cataclysmic apocalyptic zealots and hierarchical millennialists. According to Norman Cohn (1957), they prefigure modern totalitarian fascism.

This turn to the violent derives in part from the deeply hostile reception that Anabaptists got from both Catholics and other Protestants, especially in the late 1520s. Both the Catholics and the reformers who had control of the levers of power attacked these radicals as the worst kind of heretics and, whenever possible, burned them at the stake. True to the pacifist martyrdoms of the early church, they met their fate with great courage and resolute faith. This hostility, however, undermined transformative apocalyptic scenarios and increased the appeal of passive cataclysmic ones. Apocalyptic delirium fed violent imagination, and when God failed to intervene, triggered a shift toward active cataclysmic transitions to the millennial kingdom.

The Heavenly Jerusalem at Münster

Apocalyptic prophecies circulated with increasing intensity among Anabaptists who, fleeing persecution, became increasingly mobile. The Anabaptist MELCHIOR HOFMANN prophesied about the advent of the millennial kingdom in 1533 (Depperman 1983), as did French Protestants in the circle of Marguerite of Navarre (Crouzet 2001). At its approach, German-speaking Anabaptists became increasingly active, first focusing on Strasbourg as the site where the Heavenly Jerusalem would descend to earth, then on Münster, where, in a dramatic election in 1533, they won control of the city council. BERNHARD ROTHMANN, a preacher at least in part inspired by Hofmann's prophecies, provided the key shift from 1533 to 1534 as an apocalyptic date, and upped the ante from passive to active cataclysmism: God will come, he assured his listeners, "but vengeance is a prior task of the servants of God. . . . We have to be his tools and must attack the godless on the days that the Lord will determine" (Vogler 1988:107). The Anabaptist city council expelled all unbelievers, including the bishop; Catholic and Protestant troops, unable to agree on anything else, allied to free the city from such fanatics. With prophecy redated to Easter 1534, Anabaptists from all over North Germany and the NETHERLANDS set out for the city to participate in the advent of the millennial kingdom. After several changes in leadership, from JAN MATHIJS (d. 1534) to "King" Jan van Leiden (d. 1535), the starving inhabitants finally were routed by the enemy. Punishments were swift and thorough.

The drama at Münster displays a wide range of characteristic dynamics of apocalyptic millennialism:

- The gathering represents an apocalyptic activation of a previously radically passive religiosity.
- The high number of women (probably 70 percent or more), illustrates the prominence of women in demotic movements.
- Their claims to universal sovereignty, including the minting of coins intended to be valid throughout the world, reflect a characteristic megalomania.
- The growing aggressiveness with which the Anabaptists, once majoritarian, treated Catholic and Protestant citizens illustrates the ways in which access to power brings on more coercive forms of religiosity.
- The royal, even imperial, forms that the messianic kingdom took illustrate how apocalyptic power-holders can shift from demotic to hierarchical millennialism, prefiguring the emergence of totalitarian movements in the modern world.
- Their use of cannons to shoot propaganda tracts to the soldiers besieging the city (first recorded case of aerial pamphlet bombing) illustrates the ingenuity with which apocalyptic groups use information technology.
- Their reaction to the failure of apocalyptic expectations displays—for the first time in documentary detail—the kinds of "upping the ante"

brought on by the desperate effort to deny prophecy failed: authoritarianism, patriarchal ANTINOMIANISM (polygamy but not polyandry), violence, including public executions of dissenters, and ever more elaborate street theater intended to reignite hope (Midelfort 2001).

- The decision of authorities, once the Anabaptists had fallen to the sword, to keep the bodies of the condemned leaders in iron cages hanging from the Lambertskirche illustrates the profound hatred that the *Schärmerei* (fanaticism) of the millennial enthusiasts can inspire in others.

Along with the Peasants' War, the debacle at Münster became a byword for the excesses of the radical Reformation, giving ammunition to the conservatives who wanted to limit the dynamic of reform and forcing the Anabaptists back into a profound quietism (Melchiorites, HUTTERITES, MENNONITES, Familists, and others). This ability to survive the apocalyptic catastrophe of Münster suggests the underlying commitment of Anabaptism to pacific demotic religiosity.

Calvin and the Puritans

One of the more opaque chapters in the millennial history of the Reformation concerns the fate of CALVINISM, especially in ENGLAND and SCOTLAND. JOHN CALVIN, with his thoroughgoing Augustinianism and double PREDESTINATION, could hardly be accused of engaging in the kind of popular millennialism of the Anabaptists and the peasant revolutionaries. Indeed, one might argue that his THEOLOGY represents a specific repudiation of both their apocalyptic errors and their millennial errors so manifest in 1533 (Crouzet 2001). However scrupulous Calvin's theology, at a more practical level his experiment with a godly city of Geneva based on the "utopian" mosaic blueprint represents a particularly chaste (and therefore more successful) form of millennialism. In any case, his theology produced some of the most vigorous and effective forms of millennialism among Anglo-Christians, the English Puritans (see PURITANISM), and the Scottish followers of JOHN KNOX (Hotson 2000).

Certainly more pragmatic elements mark the culmination of Puritan millennialism both in England and in North America in the seventeenth century, which, one might argue, laid some critical foundations for modern democracies. The Mayflower charter represents a particularly good example of a demotic "millennial" constitution. And the English CIVIL WAR (1640–1660), in which a king was, for the first time in European history, executed by a revolutionary regime that sought to establish a commonwealth, sees a florescence of demotic millennial movements—Diggers,

LEVELERS, Fifth Monarchists, Ranters, Quakers—unmatched since the early Reformation (Hill 1990). The Quakers (see FRIENDS, SOCIETY OF) exhibited the same millennial fervor, the same dynamic that led a follower of GEORGE FOX to break with Calvin and declare himself messiah (Naylor's messianic entrance to Bristol in 1656), and the same ability to return, after the failure of activism, to radical forms of pacifism that characterized the Anabaptists.

Millennial themes continued to appear in many forms of Protestantism, both postmillennial (activist transformational) and premillennial (passive cataclysmic), which seem to alternate periods of ascendancy, apparently as a repeating trip switch that reverses with disappointment. In the eighteenth and nineteenth centuries, great outdoor revival movements (see REVIVALS) swept though whole regions in Anglo-Christian lands (the two Great AWAKENINGS). These movements share much in common with the medieval revivalist "peace movements" like the French Peace of God (990s–1030s) and the Northern Italian Great Allelulia of 1233. According to millennial scholars, postmillennialism plays a central role in the emergence of many modern characteristics—science and technology, radical social reform, democratic institutions, emancipation—while premillennialism became the trademark of the antimodern "fundamentalists" who today play a significant role in American life (O'Leary 1994; Gorenberg 2000). Among the more consequential shifts in millennial thinking wrought by Anglo-Christians, we find a strong philo-Semitic theme (see PHILO-SEMITISM; JUDASIM) that, rather than the dominant medieval scenario whereby Jewish messianic behavior revealed the work of Antichrist, embraced Jewish messianic hopes to return to Zion as a positive contribution to the apocalyptic scenario. This shift not only encouraged and supported the emergence of Jewish Zionism from the nineteenth century onward, but also encouraged extensive periods of positive-sum interactions with Jews.

Conclusions: Historians and Unintended Consequences

In many ways, the history of millennialism in the Reformation, or rather the millennial history of the Reformation, still awaits composition. For so long, theological and scholarly agendas have shared the horror and repulsion toward the excesses of active cataclysmic apocalyptic millennialism. Historians, in synthesizing the Reformation, have characteristically dismissed the pervasive nature of the phenomenon and tried to restrict its discussion to the most flagrant examples (Ozment 1991). Norman Cohn may have contributed to this tendency by associating these fanatical revolutionary movements with twentieth-century totalitarianism. But Cohn also emphasized the radical egalitarianism of these groups, as did Christopher Hill in his study of English millennialism of the seventeenth century. In conclusion, consider four major areas worthy of further investigation: demotic religiosity, religious violence, and philo- and anti-Judaism, and modern capitalism.

Demotic Religiosity

Demotic religiosity emphasizes the following essential themes: equality before the law, the dignity of manual labor, direct access to sacred scripture and to God on the part of all the faithful, and ICONOCLASM. These themes can and do exist outside of millennial and apocalyptic frameworks, but the essential demotic millennial dream—swords into plowshares, all enjoying the fruit of their honest labor—imagines a world where such values rule, the egalitarian messianic kingdom. From the earliest stages of the Protestant Reformation, the link between this demotic religiosity and apocalyptic time played a central role, especially notable in a work by Luther's close friend Lucas Cranach, the *Passional Christi und Antichristi*, an illustrated pamphlet aimed at and very popular among the simplest (and largely illiterate) population. Here Christ appears as a modest and poor man, of the people, while the antichrist appears as the Pope surrounded by ecclesiastical pomp and splendor. Luther's own identification of the papacy (rather than any single pope) with Antichrist produced a more elastic apocalyptic framework at the same time as it identified hierarchy with Antichrist, a central theme among the most radical millennialists from Anabaptists to Quakers. The multiple ways in which this brand of millennialism injected demotic themes into both the religious and social life of Reformation Europe deserves attention.

Religious Violence

The most consistent failure of the Reformation by modern standards was the way in which groups that had all begun with a discourse of religious tolerance (see TOLERATION) and voluntarism consistently turned to religious coercion when they took power. In the words of one historian, "tolerance, in the Protestant Reformation, was a loser's creed" (Grell and Scribner 1996). Having emphasized voluntarism when they were minorities, group after group of reformers took their accession to power as a mandate from God to impose the "true" religion. The behavior of the Münster Anabaptists offers a startling example of what has become a plague of fledgling democracies—the elec-

toral rise of a regime that puts an end to the institutions that allowed it to come to power. The ferocious religious wars that plagued Europe from the early sixteenth to the mid-seventeenth centuries resulted partly from the basic intolerance of long-standing Christian claims to a monopoly on SALVATION, partly from the justified fear of allowing "other" (especially millennial) forms of Christianity to take hold, partly to the warfare between commoners and elites that informed so much of post-plague European society.

And yet the more quietistic forms of demotic religiosity, with their active transformational attitudes, their emphasis on free will in conversion (both among Christians and Jews), and their radical egalitarianism, also produced some of the most tolerant forms of religiosity. The Puritan Commonwealth began with the removal of (almost) all censorship in 1640, a policy change that had an electrifying effect both on English printing and more broadly on the emergence of a "public sphere" that laid one of the central foundations of modern democracies—free speech and public media of communication (see PUBLISHING, MEDIA). JOHN MILTON's notions of tolerance (*Aereopagitica*) found a broad audience among English Christians, attitudes that survived into the Restoration. In an important sense, the American Revolution represents the first time in Christian history that tolerance became a winner's creed, and no small part of that shift occurred by mutual consent among various religious denominations, many of them millennial, that church should not avail itself of state power. With this division of CHURCH AND STATE, the UNITED STATES managed to harness the zeal of demotic millennialism to the demands of democratic culture, allowing its voluntaristic dimensions to flourish while pruning back the temptation to coercion.

Philo- and Anti-Judaism

Luther's relationship with Jews illustrates a pattern that characterizes much of the apocalyptic interaction between Jews and Christians over the last millennium. In the enthusiasm and optimism of early stages of expectation, with a sense of assurance that God is about to intervene on their side, apocalyptic believers tend to approach Jews favorably, at once because their voluntary CONVERSION is a necessary element of all Christian apocalyptic scenarios, and because their demotic religiosity has more in common with Jewish religiosity than with that of the hierarchical church. But with the failure of apocalyptic expectations, Luther, as many disappointed hopefuls before and after him, turned against the Jews, making them the apocalyptic scapegoat whose failure to convert prevented the *Parousia*. This pattern of Philo-Semitism in the early, optimistic stages of apocalyptic hope followed by ANTI-SEMITISM in the aftermath of failure may account for many of the outbursts of anti-Jewish violence in Christian history over the last millennium. Nonetheless, sustained periods of good relations between Jews and Christians have contributed significantly to both economic development and the emergence of a tolerant civil society. The Anglo-Christian rewriting of the apocalyptic scenario to favor Jewish autonomy (at least temporarily) derives from the philo-Judaic tendencies of demotic millennialism.

Modern Capitalism

MAX WEBER's *Protestant Ethic and the Spirit of Capitalism* represents one of the most famous and neglected historical works of the twentieth century. In it Weber argues an important role for the unintended consequences of Protestant theology. His most detailed focus concerns the effects of predestination on subsequent generations of Calvinists, especially of English Puritans. But his broader concerns include the importance of VOCATION with its intense emphasis on the dignity—indeed, the divinely willed nature—of manual labor. All four of the denominations that Weber points to as particularly contributive to the "spirit of capitalism"—Puritans, Quakers, Quietists, and Methodists—represent the most demotic of the forms of Protestantism, all with important millennial aspects, some that periodically surge forward at apocalyptic moments. Weber describes believers whose extraordinary religious discipline and commitment to the dignity of manual labor enabled them to make a great deal of money, but whose demotic values restrained them from "selling out" and joining the aristocracy. The question deserves reconsideration, with attention to the role of demotic millennialist responses to disappointed apocalyptic expectation as a significant factor in the emergence of so powerful an egalitarian discipline. Similar dynamics seem probable in the emergence of both science and technology. It will take several generations of research before scholars can assess the impact of millennialism in all its varieties on the course of the Reformation and Protestantism and its contribution to the emergence of the modern West.

See also Catholicism, Protestant Reactions; Chiliasm; Fundamentalism; Politics; Rapture; Tribulationism

References and Further Reading

Baumgarten, Albert I. *Apocalyptic Time*. Leiden, The Netherlands: Brill, 2000.
Blickle, Peter. *The Revolution of 1525: The German Peasants' War from a New Perspective*. Translated by Thomas A.
Brady, Jr. and H. C. Erik Middlefort. Baltimore, MD: Johns Hopkins University Press, 1981.
Cohn, Norman. *Cosmos, Chaos and the World to Come*. New Haven, CT: Yale University Press, 1993.
———. *The Pursuit of the Millennium*. Fairlawn, NJ: Essential Books, 1957.
Crouzet, Denis. "Circa 1533: Anxieties, Desires and Dreams." *Journal of Early Modern History* 5, no.1 (2001): 24–61.
Daniels, Ted. *Millennialism: An International Bibliography*. New York: Garland Press, 1992.
Deppermann. Klaus. *Melchior Hoffman: Social Unrest and Apocalyptic Visions in the Age of Reformation*. Translated by Maclom Wren; edited by Benjamin Drewery. Edinburgh, U.K.: T. & T. Clark.
Gorenberg, Gershom. *The End of Days: Fundamentalism and the Struggle for the Temple Mount*. New York: Free Press, 2000.
Hill, Christopher. *Antichrist in Seventeenth-Century England*. London: Verso, 1990.
Hillerbrand, Hans. "Radicalism in the Early Reformation." In *Radical Tendencies in the Reformation: Divergent Perspectives*. Edited by Hans Hillerbrand. Kirksville, MO: Sixteenth Century Journal Publishers, 1988.
Hotson, Howard. *Paradise Postponed: Johann Heinrich Alsted and the Birth of Calvinist Millenarianism* (International Archive of the History of Ideas, vol. 172). Dordrecht, The Netherlands: Kluwer Academic Publishers, 2000.
Klaassen, Walter. *Living at the End of the Ages, Apocalyptic Expectation in the Radical Reformation*. Lanham, MD: University Press of America, 1992.
O'Leary, Stephen D. *Arguing the Apocalypse: A Theory of Millennial Rhetoric*. Cambridge, MA: Harvard University Press, 1994.
Ozment, Stephen. *Mysticism and Dissent, Religious Ideology and Social Protest in the Sixteenth Century*. New Haven, CT: Yale University Press, 1991.
Peterson, Rodney. *Preaching in the Last Days: The Theme of the "Two Witnesses" in the Sixteenth and Seventeenth Centuries*. New York: Oxford University Press, 1993.
St. Clair, Michael J. *Millenarian Movements in Historical Context*. New York: Garland Publishing, 1992.
Vogler, Günter. "The Anabaptist Kingdom of Münster in the Tension Between Anabaptism and Imperial Policy." In *Radical Tendencies in the Reformation: Divergent Perspectives*. Edited by Hans Hillerbrand. Kirksville, MO: Sixteenth Century Journal Publishers, 1988.
Weber, Max. *The Protestant Ethic and the Spirit of Capitalism*. Translated by Stephen Kalberg. Los Angeles, CA: Roxbury, 2002.

RICHARD LANDES

MILLER, WILLIAM (1782–1849)

American theologian. Miller founded the Millerite movement on the basis of his prediction that Jesus would return to Earth about the year 1843. Born in Pittsfield, Massachusetts, February 15, 1782, Miller wandered into DEISM briefly in his youth. Later he studied the BIBLE and became persuaded that he was called to preach, and he traveled to share his message in the 1830s and early 1840s. He preached to thousands of people across the northeastern UNITED STATES and, in concert with Joshua V. Himes, created an energetic millennial movement (see MILLENARIANS AND MILLENNIALISM). When the year 1843 passed, Miller and other leaders of the movement reconsidered but did not renounce their predictions. First they looked for Jesus by the end of the Jewish year 1843, which ended in March of 1844 on the common calendar. Finally Miller followed others in his own movement in focusing on the precise date, October 22, 1844. When the clouds did not "burst asunder" on that day it came to be known as the Great Disappointment. Miller himself gave up revisions of his prophecy. He continued to believe in the imminent appearance of Jesus until his death in Low Hampton, New York, in 1849. Some of his followers, on the other hand, took the Millerite message as their foundation for what became the SEVENTH-DAY ADVENTISTS.

Bible Facts

William Miller shared a common Protestant impulse to return to the Bible, and only the Bible, for understanding of past, present, and future. When Miller returned from fighting in the War of 1812 he studied his Bible with the aid of only a concordance to reach his own conclusions about the message of scripture. Like many residents of the United States in his generation, Miller believed that the Bible was open to reading by all Christians. He asserted that it was the duty of believers to reject traditional and hierarchical authorities and to use their own common sense to approach the clear truths of the Bible. What Miller found in the Bible were "facts." The words of the Bible, and the details of Scripture, had the AUTHORITY of scientific data for Miller. Again taking an approach common in his generation, Miller saw his reading of the Bible as a kind of exercise in Baconian induction (see BACON, FRANCIS): the facts were there on the page, the reader could assemble the facts, and out of the accumulation of facts conclusions could be drawn. Most significant for the dating of the end, numbers in the Bible became facts to plug into a holy arithmetic. According to Miller anyone could see that the 2,300 days of Daniel 8:14 pointed to the end in 1843—assuming, of course, that the 2,300 days should count as years and that the count should begin at the fall of the Persian Empire in 457 B.C. Similarly, the reign of the Roman Catholic Church, which Miller dated at 583 A.D., began the count of the 1,260 days—counted as years—of Revelation 11:3 and 12:6. Again, the numbers pointed to 1843. Supernatural wonders constituted the end, but empiricism provided the method for dating the end.

Camp Meeting Revivalism

Miller had only to look around him to find an effective technique for spreading his message in the 1830s. In both the United States and the British Isles, Protestants had developed ITINERACY, outdoor preaching, and mass ceremonies of religious commitment. In the United States, Methodists especially, but also Presbyterians and Miller's own BAPTISTS, had refined these traditions into the CAMP MEETING. Christians and potential converts assembled at a meeting ground, sometimes prepared to stay for days to listen to emotional PREACHING, pray, sing, and hope for profound religious experience. At least since the famous Cane Ridge camp meeting in Kentucky in 1801, American Protestants had the camp meeting available as a means to spread their message and experience.

Although Miller often preached in individual congregations, he and his fellow Millerites had their greatest impact in camp meetings. Camp meetings allowed them to reach larger numbers of people; more important, camp meetings remained available as existing denominations and congregations became more hostile toward Millerites. In the 1840s Millerites even built their own Great Tent to carry from place to place so that they could hold meetings in inclement weather—and perhaps as an attraction in itself, to draw in the curious. Not neglecting urban populations, Miller and his compatriots preached in large halls and tabernacles to inspire REVIVALS in cities, including New York.

Evangelical Conversion

The main goal of camp meetings, and often the first goal of Millerite lecturers, was to bring individuals to the dramatic religious experience of CONVERSION. Millerites, like their evangelical neighbors, understood conversion as a moment of receiving the grace of God in the heart and thus the beginning of a life as a committed Christian.

At the moment of conversion, the convert might experience the "heart strangely warmed" of JOHN WESLEY, exhibit uncontrolled physical manifestations such as convulsive movements, and even lose consciousness. After conversion revivalists hoped that converts would read the Bible, seek to lead a moral life, and join a community of Christians in a congregation.

Miller's message of the hoped-for return of Jesus Christ connected to the conversion experience in two ways. First the nearness of the return of Christ impressed listeners with the seriousness of their religious state. If Christ were to return immediately, all people would be judged. The Millerite message left little room for delay, and thus heightened the pressure for immediate conversion. The effectiveness of Millerite preaching as a means to bring individuals to conversion was a major reason that non-Millerite preachers invited Millerites to speak to congregations and camp meetings.

For Miller and his compatriots, however, the more significant connection between the Millerite message and conversion ran the other way. Miller and Millerite lecturers hoped that they could persuade people to become converted both to a Christian life and to belief in the imminent return of Christ. Conversion was but the first step; adherence to the anticipation of Christ had to follow or Miller's success remained incomplete. For some converts, in fact, the acceptance of the anticipation of Christ's return either gave specific content to the conversion experience or became a second religious experience in itself—the functional equivalent, perhaps, of the experience of holiness in Methodist traditions (see SANCTIFICATION).

Come Out of Babylon?

Miller always believed that his message added to, but did not displace, evangelical Christianity. After all, he shared the conversion orientation, the Bible-centeredness, and the mission impulse of his evangelical contemporaries (see EVANGELICALISM). Much as preachers in existing denominations appreciated the conversions that Miller and his fellows inspired, though, they became increasingly impatient with Millerite insistence on focusing on the end times. Individual congregations and specific camp meetings began to exclude Millerite lecturers and to seek to silence persistent Millerite converts who sought to bring their message to the center. The more they found themselves asked to be silent, the more aggressive Millerites became in their insistence on having their message told; the more aggressive they became, the more they were silenced. As had happened repeatedly from the very origins of Protestantism, those who thought that they would act as reformers became schismatics.

Although he expressed skepticism about existing churches, Miller himself did not lead the call to leave the existing denominations. The leadership of the Millerite movement was no longer exclusively in his hands by the early 1840s. Those who had risen to leadership in the movement began to call all existing denominations Babylon. The next step followed easily: the Bible gave a specific injunction to "come out of her, my people" (Revelation 18:4). Millerites, therefore, began to leave their churches. Millerite leaders insisted that they were not creating a new DENOMINATION. Denominations were, after all, part of Babylon. Instead, Millerites adhered to a loosely or-

ganized movement that had as its purpose watching for the end of the world.

The Return of Christ and the Burning of the Earth

Miller himself sketched the chronology and images of the end of the world to which Millerites adhered. He placed most of the events predicted by the Bible in the past. The central event to come, and the center of all of Miller's thinking, was Christ's breaking through the clouds to return again to earth:

> The clouds have burst asunder. The heavens appear. The great white throne is in sight—Amazement fills the universe with awe—he comes—he comes behold the savior comes, lift up your heads ye saints he comes!—he comes!!—he comes!!! (Miller to Truman Hendryx, March 26, 1822)

Miller adhered to premillennialism—the belief that Christ would return before the millennium—rather than the increasingly popular postmillennialism—the belief that the millennium could be achieved before the return of Christ. The meaning of the return of Christ did not rest in simple chronology for Miller, however. Miller saw the dramatic, personal, imminent return of Christ as the central symbol of—the central promise which made true—the reality of a transcendent, supernatural power that governed the universe. Miller's neighbors may have seen in canals, railroads, the establishment of the American republic, and a host of other changes signs of the improvement of humankind and thus reasons to focus on this world as the locus of Christian promise. Miller viewed his neighbors' hopes as a distraction and a delusion. If Christ came once miraculously, personally, and physically, then Christ would come again and in the same way. If God's word about the first coming was true, then God's word about the second coming—as Miller understood it—had to be true. The image of Christ breaking through the clouds meant to Miller the truth of God's very being.

If Miller sought to turn the attention of his contemporaries from this world to another, he did so dramatically in the further details of his eschatological interpretation (see ESCHATOLOGY). After Christ's return through the clouds, Miller expected the burning of the earth. He imagined in one depiction of the end,

> a flame more pure,—a searching, cleansing, penetrating flame of fire,—that searched every nook and corner of the globe; . . . and thus destroyed all that had life, and all on which the curse of sin was found. . . . The monuments of man . . . The works of art . . . The cities, villages, and towns . . . the vain philosophy of former generations . . . the more modern customs and fashions of

the day . . .—these all did melt away. (Bliss, Memoirs, 406–412)

At the time of the burning of the earth, Miller anticipated that the saved among the dead would rise and that they, along with the faithful living, would be caught up with Christ. Thus spared the terrible purification by fire, the saved could witness the introduction of the millennium: the age of perfect peace at the end of all time. Although Millerism falls under the category of millennial and millenarian movements, it was not the millennium itself on which Miller focused his imagination. His anticipation always centered on the return of Christ, whether or not his hopes were fulfilled in 1843.

References and Further Reading

Primary Sources:

Miller, William. *Evidence from Scripture and History of the Second Coming of Christ, about the Year 1843; Exhibited in a Course of Lectures.* Troy, NY: Kemble and Hooper, 1836.
Millerites and Early Adventists Source Collection. Ann Arbor, MI: University Microfilms International, 1979.

Secondary Sources:

Bliss, Sylvester. *Memoirs of William Miller Generally Known as a Lecturer on the Prophecies, and the Second Coming of Christ.* Boston: Joshua V. Himes, 1853; reprint New York: AMS Press, 1971.
Doan, Ruth Alden. *The Miller Heresy, Millennialism, and American Culture.* Philadelphia, PA: Temple University Press, 1987.
Judd, Wayne R. "William Miller: Disappointed Prophet." In *The Disappointed: Millerism and Millenarianism in the Nineteenth Century,* edited by Ronald L. Numbers and Jonathan M. Butler, 17–35. Bloomington and Indianapolis: Indiana University Press, 1987.

RUTH ALDEN DOAN

MILTON, JOHN (1608–1676)

English writer, poet, and theologian. John Milton was born in London, England, on December 9, 1608. He spent most of his life in the same city, where, sixty-eight years later, he died and was buried. Extraordinarily well-educated, especially in classical and scriptural languages, Milton was destined by his parents for religious service. Far from the stereotypically dour exponent of English PURITANISM, Milton nonetheless steadfastly supported Puritan opposition to the Protestantism of the Anglican establishment. An early ally of the Presbyterians in their polemical attacks on the oppressive and corrupt prelatical hierarchy (1641–1642), he later became sharply critical of the Presbyterians' own attempts to curtail intellectual and religious freedom, for reasons he articulates most

memorably in *Areopagitica* (1645). By the end of the 1640s Milton had further distanced himself from the Presbyterians and indeed the majority of his countrymen by advocating the people's right to remove their monarch, and even put him on trial as subject to law. Appointed Secretary for Foreign Tongues after King Charles's trial and execution, he successfully defended the English regicides against their outraged Continental detractors, Catholic and Protestant. Once OLIVER CROMWELL (1599–1658) died, however, and the government fell into chaos, Milton failed to persuade his countrymen to establish a republic. A target of disdain and derision during the Restoration (1660–1688), the blind outcast nevertheless composed *Paradise Lost* (1667), with its attempt to justify the ways of God to humans, at the same time that he was suffering through the collapse of all that he had fought for. He later published the two other masterpieces for which he is best remembered, *Paradise Regain'd* and *Samson Agonistes* (1671).

Family Life and Education

The poet's parents, Sara and John Milton, resided with their growing family on commercially affluent Bread Street. Their house stood in the busy heart of the city, destined for utter destruction in the great fire of 1666. Cheapside was adjacent, massive old St. Paul's Cathedral and its grammar school (which Milton attended) loomed a short walk away, and the Mermaid tavern—frequented at that time by dramatists Ben Jonson, William Shakespeare, Francis Beaumont, and John Fletcher—served refreshment in the vicinity. The Milton family inhabited rooms above the father's scrivener's shop. Apprentices and servants also occupied the bustling household, and the Miltons prospered through the scrivener's shrewd real estate transactions as well as through the economically indispensable though morally controversial practice of usury.

Frank Kermode, in what has become a commonplace of Milton scholarship, described young Milton as "his father's chief investment," and some have construed the scrivener's scrupulous cultivation of his son's talents as an early instance of MAX WEBER's (1864–1920) Protestant Ethic. While Weberian elaborations of Milton's development have proven ponderous, anachronistic, and undiscriminating, religion was undoubtedly the senior Milton's main motive in lavishly providing for the poet's education. A long-awaited first son, he was set apart by his parents, like the biblical Samson, for service to God. To attain knowledge of God through Scripture seems also to have been a personal spiritual imperative for the father. Early biographers prominently record that Milton's father had, as a boy, been disinherited by his Roman Catholic father after he found an English Bible in his son's chamber. If we may judge by the weight given this patriarchal narrative in early biographies of the poet, the father's disobedience in the pursuit of scriptural knowledge, and consequent alienation from his father, became a foundational family story. Young Milton thus pursued his studies, or was induced to pursue them, as if he were on a mission from God. Tutors instructed him in classical and scriptural tongues, and even as a child he often toiled past midnight, attended by a nurse appointed by his father. So began the long history of eyestrain and headaches that culminated in the total blindness suffered by the poet in his forties.

Despite these studious labors, life in the Milton household ran counter to the stereotypical depiction of Puritans as opposed to music, merriment, and fiction. Milton's father, though primarily a businessman, was also a habitual artist—a musician who when disinherited, supported himself by singing, and whose adult compositions ranged from solemn religious madrigals to rollicking court entertainments. Instructed by his father, the poet played the organ throughout his life and sang skillfully. Heavenly bliss, as depicted in *Paradise Lost,* consists of angelic singing, dancing, and lovemaking. Deviating sharply from received traditions, the monistic-materialist epic poet put bodies, food, and sex in Heaven as on Earth.

Protestant Versus Puritan

Milton is nonetheless better described as a Puritan than as a Protestant. The term "Protestant" in its most general and primitive sense is a negative one, signifying a Christian who does not belong to the Church of Rome. Among the English during the seventeenth century, the term "Protestant" also had a more pointed and roughly opposite meaning, one relevant to local religious and political controversies. At the time, "Protestant" often referred to contented worshippers in the CHURCH OF ENGLAND, as opposed to separatist sects or NONCONFORMISTS like the Puritans. "Puritan" thus indicated a believer disgruntled with the established orthodoxy, while "Protestant" indicated an orthodox believer. In the polemical terms of his specific historical situation, Milton was a Puritan who believed that English Protestants had left the work of REFORMATION unfinished.

Milton's protest against English Protestant orthodoxy depends on a progressive model of truth, memorably set forth in *Areopagitica* (1645), the most revered and influential of Milton's prose works. The first printed work devoted to advocating freedom of the press, it includes or anticipates every major argument that has ever been advanced in support of such freedom, including, prominently, its instrumentality to religious liberty and the pursuit of truth. At the time of its publication, Milton was dissenting from efforts to achieve religious conformity sponsored by the newly dominant PRESBYTERIAN faction, which had itself been deemed unorthodox (not Protestant) by the previous, Episcopal regime. Milton's career as a religious controversialist had in fact begun with tracts that supported Presbyterian attempts to reform or undo Prelatical Episcopacy (1641–1642).

To explain the doctrinal uncertainty with which Christians must cope, Milton in *Areopagitica* claims that the truth expressed by Christ and his apostles became fragmented and scattered in subsequent generations. Christians are duty-bound to seek the pieces and restore truth's original form, a task that will not be completed until doomsday: "we have not found them all, Lords and Commons, nor ever shall doe, till her Masters second coming." The ongoing search for truth requires us "to be still searching what we know not by what we know, still closing up truth to truth as we find it." This conscientious, unceasing labor Milton opposes to Presbyterian complacency: "it is not the unfrocking of a priest, the unmitering of a bishop, and the removing him off the Presbyterian shoulders, that will make us a happy nation" (Wolfe 1953–1982: 2, 549–551). Unlike Milton, the Presbyterians did not see truth as the apocalyptic goal of an incessant, temporal quest and would have been content simply to replace the previous church hierarchy with their own system. Provoked in part by Milton's writings promoting divorce as a remedy for failed marriages (1643–1645) and fearing that tolerance of diverse beliefs would foster social disorder, they looked to prepublication licensing as a way of squelching heretical opinions before they could be heard.

For Milton, however, HERESY could mean "only the choise or following of any opinion good or bad in religion or any other learning" (Wolfe 1953–1982: 7, 246). In this neutral sense, heresy is not a dangerous intellectual contaminant that calls for quarantine, but instead a dynamic moment in an intellectual and spiritual process, a moment that instigates further exploration. As a consequence, new schools of thought and deviations from existing ones will inevitably occur. As the Presbyterians' own recent history illustrated, what was once deemed heresy may become ORTHODOXY, from which new heresies will eventually depart, "ev'n to the reforming of Reformation it self" (Wolfe 1953–1982: 2,553). The believer who knuckles under, following fixed doctrines without confirmation of conscience, "only because his pastor says so, or the Assembly so determines," Milton describes as "a heretick in the truth" (Wolfe 1953–1982: 2,543). The conscientious heretic thus appears in Milton's presentation as the only praiseworthy Christian, while the complacent exponent of customary orthodoxy takes on the aspect of a contemptible timeserver. Milton himself, as his Latin theological treatise, *De doctrina Christiana* (undiscovered until 1823) details, was by the end of his life variously, and by orthodox standards criminally, heretical in his beliefs. Though doctrinally he must be deemed a sect of one, his theology includes heresies that fall under the following rubrics: ANABAPTISM, ANTI-TRINITARIANISM, ANTINOMIANISM, anti-Sabbatarianism, Arminianism, millennalism, vitalist materialism, mortalism, polygamy, and Quaker spiritualism.

Secretary for Foreign Tongues

As exemplified by *Areopagitica,* the prose works Milton published in the 1640s track his increasingly heretical divergence from the Presbyterian orthodoxy with which he had allied himself early in the decade—an orthodoxy itself deemed heterodox under the previous Episcopal system. Although subsequent generations took inspiration from them, these religious and political tracts had little contemporary effect. True, the bishops were undone in the 1640s, but they were restored with the monarchy in 1660. Marriage law long remained unchanged despite Milton's arguments for divorce. *Areopagitica* failed to persuade Parliament to repeal the Licensing Order. Finally, Milton's arguments against monarchical ABSOLUTISM in *The Tenure of Kings and Magistrates* (1649) also went largely unnoticed, but that tract's publication on February 13, 1649, two weeks after King Charles's execution, does seem to have drawn the attention of the new government, for Milton was soon appointed its secretary for foreign tongues.

Cromwell's council charged Milton with defending the English regicides from their outraged detractors at home and abroad. The first opponent was Charles I himself. Charles justified himself and royal prerogative in a posthumous book entitled *Eikon Basilike* (The Image of a King), which elicited public sympathy for the beheaded monarch by portraying him as a Christ-like martyr. In *Eikonoklastes* (The Image Breaker), Milton responded by exposing Charles's treacheries during the civil war, including his willingness to open England to Roman Catholic powers in return for military assistance. The sentimental appeal of Charles's pamphlet met with more success than Milton's matter-of-fact exposure of the monarch's treachery. Milton enjoyed better fortune in the court of European public opinion. Shortly after Charles's trial and execution, the reigning intellectual powerhouse of mid-seventeenth-century Europe, the celebrated Claudius Salmasius, was hired to condemn the English regicides. He produced a weighty, pedantic tome that predicted bloody vengeance would light on the English for killing their king. Charged with replying quickly, Milton, then virtually unknown in Europe, composed a light-footed, point-by-point refutation of Salmasius's attack, replete with devastating satiric abuse. *Pro populo Anglicano defensio* ("Defense of the English People") exalted Milton's continental reputation to almost Cromwellian proportions.

Milton's greatest contemporary celebrity occurred in the same decade as his greatest losses. The strain of rapidly replying to Salmasius cost him the remainder of his already failing eyesight by 1652, a loss his enemies deemed divine punishment for his impious attacks on King Charles. Also in 1652, Mary Powell died after giving birth to a third daughter, Deborah. Their son, John, born less than a year previously, perished only a few months after his mother. Milton's eyesight, wife, and only son—all gone in the same year. He married a second wife, Katherine Woodcock, in 1656, and with her he seems to have found wedded happiness; but she died only two years after their marriage, also because of complications from childbirth. Two of his best-loved sonnets—"When I consider how my light is spent" and "Methought I saw my late espoused saint"—date from this period and seem to reflect the trauma he underwent because of his blindness and his second wife's death. By the end of the 1650s, he was a lonely, blind, twice-widowed father of three, who, after the death of Cromwell in 1658, had to endure the rapid disintegration of the English Commonwealth he had labored so intensely to defend.

In repeated, futile publications that argued in favor of establishing a republic, the once-celebrated defender of the English people pleaded with his countrymen not to restore the monarchy, though he seems to have foreseen his arguments would go unheeded. With the Restoration looming, Milton's fame quickly translated into calumny, and he became an object of scorn and insult among the people he had defended. Derided as a "blind guide," he was mocked for having "scribbled [his] eyes out" to no effect, berated for having "thrown [his] dirty outrage on the memory of a murdered Prince as if the Hangman were but [his] usher" (Masson 1965: 661). Royalist Roger L'Estrange commented that Milton had "resolved one great question, by evidencing that devils may indue human shape" or, allowing that Milton might indeed be human, L'Estrange observed that he gave "every man a horror for mankind when he considers [Milton is] of the race" (Masson 1965: 690).

It would be difficult to overstate the desire for bloody vengeance among some Royalists at the Restoration, or the narrowness of Milton's escape from it. Although they were already dead and buried, the corpses of Cromwell, Ireton, and Bradshaw were disinterred for the anniversary of Charles's execution in 1661 and then subjected to gruesome public abuse and display. Spectacular capital punishment for the still-living Milton was eagerly anticipated by some and was indeed inflicted on those regicides who had not had the sense to flee or die before the Restoration. Though theories abound, no one has been able to explain exactly how he managed to survive unscathed to complete and publish the three great poems for which he is now chiefly remembered. *Paradise Lost* was perhaps half finished in 1660 and remained unpublished until 1667; *Paradise Regained* and *Samson Agonistes* came out in 1671.

In *Paradise Lost,* the epic composed during the period of this devastating defeat and disappointment, Milton declares his intention to tell of humanity's fall and yet "justify the way of God to men" (1, 26). Some modern readers have construed his epic as an exercise in punitive Protestant didacticism, and consider his theodicy to be an entrapping ruse. Considered in its specific historical situation, however, the epic and its declared purpose appear instead to be testimony to the author's resolute religious faith and indomitable spirit.

See also Anabaptism; Anti-Trinitarianism; Antinomianism; Arminianism; Millenarians and Millennialism.

References and Further Reading

Barker, Arthur. *Milton and the Puritan Dilemma, 1641–1660.* Toronto: University of Toronto Press, 1956.

Darbishire, Helen, ed. *Early Lives of Milton.* New York: Barnes and Noble, 1965.

Dobranski, Stephen B., and John Rumrich, eds. *Milton and Heresy.* Cambridge: Cambridge University Press, 1998.

Empson, William. *Milton's God.* Cambridge: Cambridge University Press, 1981.

Fallon, Stephen M. *Milton Among the Philosophers.* Ithaca, NY: Cornell University Press, 1991.

Hill, Christopher. *Milton and the English Revolution.* London: Faber and Faber, 1977.

Kerrigan, William. *The Sacred Complex.* Cambridge, MA: Harvard University Press, 1983.

Masson, David. *Life of John Milton.* 6 vols. Gloucester, MA: Peter Smith, 1965.

Patterson, Frank H., ed. *The Works of John Milton.* 18 vols. New York: Columbia University Press, 1931–1938.

Rumrich, John. *Milton Unbound.* Cambridge: Cambridge University Press, 1996.

Shawcross, John T. *John Milton and His Influence.* Pittsburgh, PA: Duquesne University Press, 1991.

Wolfe, Don M., gen. ed. *The Prose Works of John Milton.* 8 vols. New Haven, CT: Yale University Press, 1953–1982.

JOHN P. RUMRICH

MISSIOLOGY

Missiology is the academic study of all dimensions of the Christian mission: biblical and theological foundations; history of Christian expansion since the founding of the church; and contemporary practice, theory, and strategy. The basis for the scientific study of MISSIONS was laid in the nineteenth century, although mission studies became established only in the twentieth century. The term "missiology" was first introduced in Europe. Although the term appears in English by 1924, in the Anglo-American world the preferred term was "mission studies" or "philosophy of missions." After 1965 "missiology" gained wide acceptance in North America. In contemporary usage missiology and mission studies are more or less interchangeable.

Background

Already in the first phase of the Christian church, leaders reflected on the process by which people were recruited and incorporated into the CHURCH. These reflections and debates constitute important strands of the New Testament. In the seventh century Pope Gregory the Great followed closely the evangelization of the "Angli," the English, and advised on appropriate methods and standards. Occasionally missionaries or theologians wrote treatises on aspects of missionary work, but the notion of a theory of mission was not put forward until the sixteenth and seventeenth centuries—for example, Roman Catholics José de Acosta, Thomas a Jesu, and Cardinal Brancati; Protestants Hadrianus Saravia, Justus Heurnius, Gisbertus Voetius, and Johannes Hoornbeeck—as missionary activity was increasing. Even so, a comprehensive theory was not attempted until late in the nineteenth century. The introduction of the concept of a general theory of mission gave an indispensable impetus to a new stage in mission studies in the twentieth century and contributed to the emergence of missiology.

In 1811 German theologian FRIEDRICH SCHLEIERMACHER broke new ground when he included "missions" in his *Brief Outline of the Study of Theology.* This was apparently the first time any theologian saw fit to introduce missions into the theological syllabus. In Schleiermacher's scheme, missions belonged with practical THEOLOGY. He had family ties to the Moravian missionary movement and was personally sympathetic to missions. Schleiermacher and several of his colleagues had begun offering courses of lectures in the history of missions to their students, although the theological curriculum was resistant to innovation and the attitude toward missions cool. Inadvertently Schleiermacher contributed to the problem by the ambivalent tone of his proposal: "*Conditionally* [sic], the *Theory of Missions* might also find a point of connexion here; a theory which, up to the present time, is as good as altogether wanting." The tentativeness of this proposal provided grounds for setting it aside indefinitely.

Anthropology and linguistics were beginning to develop as academic fields; but as these new disciplines gained academic respectability the antagonism between them and missionaries grew. This was the period when "scientific racism" was on the rise and missionaries initially registered opposition to these new ideas. The scientific community regarded missionaries as intellectual inferiors and adversaries of SCIENCE. On the other hand mission societies wanted candidates to have practical training and it was assumed that the missionary training institutes sponsored by the various missionary societies best understood the kind of preparation required (see MISSIONARY ORGANIZATIONS). Fueling the tension was the fact that missions bore a certain social and intellectual stigma.

The modern mission movement slowly gathered momentum during the nineteenth century. However, mission leaders found themselves preoccupied with the practical issues involved in missionary work rather than theoretical questions. Occasionally a mission leader spoke of the need for critical reflection on the mission process. In 1829 William Orme, a secretary of the London Missionary Society, called for the development of an empirically based understanding of missions: "What we want is, not an increase of reports of yearly proceedings and of arguments derived from Scriptures . . . but a condensed view of the knowledge and experience which have been acquired during the last thirty or forty years." Orme believed this kind of information drawn from experience would lead to improved training of missionary candidates and more efficient and effective deployment of personnel and financial resources.

The call for development of a "science of missions" would be heard regularly in the future. A Congregationalist pastor with direct ties to the AMERICAN BOARD OF COMMISSIONERS FOR FOREIGN MISSIONS, Edward A. Lawrence, wrote in *Modern Missions in the East* (1895): ". . . there is a Science of Missions. By an inductive study of the facts and experiences of the past and present, the near and the remote, it discovers the underlying principles." Similarly, Robert E. Speer, Presbyterian Church Board of Missions secretary and a major missions thinker, argued in his *Missionary Principles and Practice* (1902) that the materials were now available to spell out "a science of missions." For Speer this science would consist of basic principles of missionary action derived from careful research of the experience of missions over the previous century.

Throughout his long tenure Speer himself engaged in research and writing on the history and practice of missions.

Emergence of Missiology

After several abortive attempts in the UNITED STATES (Princeton, 1838), GERMANY (Erlangen, 1864), and SCOTLAND (New College, 1867–1872) to include mission studies in the theological curriculum, the first permanent professorship in missiology was established at the University of HALLE in 1896 with Gustav Warneck (1834–1910), generally regarded as the founder of missiology, the incumbent. Joseph Schmidlin (1876–1944), a protégé of Warneck's, began lecturing in missiology in the Roman Catholic Faculty of Theology at Münster in 1910 and was appointed to a chair in missiology in 1914. The crown of Warneck's pioneering scholarship was the publication of his five-volume *Missionslehre* (1892–1903). Schmidlin produced a Roman Catholic counterpart with his *Katholische Missionslehre im Grundriss* (1919; Eng. trans., *Catholic Mission Theory,* 1931).

Several clusters of developments account for the emergence of missiology at the beginning of the twentieth century. First, as early as 1830, missionary leaders were calling for the scientific study of the missionary process and this conviction grew in intensity over time. To be credible, intellectual inquiry had to conform to the model and standards set by science. Mission leaders believed that scientific knowledge would ensure missionary effectiveness. Second, the founding of the Student Volunteer Movement in 1886 presaged a period of rapid missionary expansion based on recruitment of large numbers of new missionaries educated in colleges and universities. Missions now looked to colleges and universities as allies, and this called for academically acceptable course offerings in missions (see HIGHER EDUCATION).

A third development was the growing emphasis being placed on empirical studies. The large international missionary conferences, including the 1900 Ecumenical Missionary Conference in New York and the WORLD MISSIONARY CONFERENCE held at Edinburgh, Scotland, in 1910 underscored the importance of historical and statistical studies of missions. Stimulated in part by the work of sociologists, mission researchers compiled massive amounts of data on the social impact of Christian missions on the cultures to which missions had gone. The goal was to demonstrate the power of the Christian message to eradicate "social evils"—alcoholism, opium addiction, subjugation of WOMEN and children, footbinding, infanticide, inhuman prison conditions, poverty, blood feuds, unsanitary living conditions, caste, SLAVERY—and improve the quality of life. For example, James S. Dennis's three large volumes, *Christian Missions and Social Progress* (1897, 1899, 1906), cataloged the ameliorative impact of missions in Asia and AFRICA on social problems.

At Edinburgh in 1910 three decisions were taken that contributed directly to the development of missiology. It was agreed to (1) institute research centers such as the Missionary Research Library in New York where comprehensive data would be assembled and made available for research, (2) establish the *International Review of Missions*, and (3) encourage the founding of chairs of mission studies and the introduction of a missions curriculum in SEMINARIES and faculties of theology. From the beginning mission studies have been marked by a high degree of international and ecumenical cooperation (see ECUMENISM). These steps were essential to the progress of the worldwide Christian movement.

Multidisciplinary Character

During the nineteenth century, mission studies were concerned primarily with the history and practice of missionary work. Mission activity was conceptualized in terms of *plantatio ecclesiae,* that is, implanting the church as it was known in the West in other parts of the world where it was not yet established. It was assumed this posed no special theological questions and the theology of the Western Christian tradition was universally applicable. The study of CULTURE from the perspective of the sociological and anthropological disciplines was not yet established and linguistic science lay in the future. It made sense, then, to approach missions in terms of historical experiences.

Not everyone was satisfied with this approach, however. Karl Graul (1814–1864) became director of the Leipzig Mission in 1844. This mission's largest program was among the Tamils in Southeast India. Graul was determined to promote the "scholarly development of missions as a discipline." He set out to do this by going to INDIA in 1849 where for the next four years he immersed himself in the language, literature, and culture of the Tamils. Graul remarked that he made "East India to be my university for studying the discipline of missions." He mastered both classical and colloquial Tamil and wrote several books dealing with the Tamil language and culture. One of his goals was to formulate "a general theory of missions." In 1864 Graul was appointed lecturer in missions at Erlangen University but died shortly after delivering his inaugural lecture. Thus, Graul was not allowed to complete the program he had set for himself. His work, nonetheless, informed as it was by the seminal years he spent in India, contributed directly to defining missiology as a multidisciplinary field.

Starting with Warneck and Schmidlin, missiology has been conceived as a field of study that draws on biblical studies, THEOLOGY, history, the social sciences, and the subfields of each in order to do its work. In this sense missiology is a synthetic discipline that depends on resources developed by other specialists that can be used to illuminate the issues raised by missionary action. However, this has also been a source of continuing criticism from other disciplines as well as self-doubts on the part of missiologists. In 1971 James A. Scherer characterized American missiology as being "generally immature and underdeveloped" so far as scholarship is concerned, although subsequent developments to be noted below have altered this.

Missiological Traditions

Within the field of mission studies, various traditions have developed. Broadly speaking these can be grouped under three heads: Continental, Anglo-American, and Roman Catholic. The Continental tradition has emphasized the importance of missiology as an autonomous academic discipline adhering to the highest scientific standards and theoretical rigor. It answers to the university rather than to the church.

Anglo-American missiology has remained close to the church and mission agencies, and has been marked by a spirit of pragmatism and openness to experimentation. It has been less concerned with academic respectability. The Anglo-American penchant for statistics and strategies has been criticized by Continental missiologists as far back as Warneck, who in 1900 derided the slogan of the Student Volunteer Movement—"The evangelization of the world in this generation"—for its triumphalist activism and naïve optimism.

Roman Catholic missiology reflects the importance of Canon Law in the unfolding witness of the church in the world, the role of the hierarchy in guiding the work of the missionary, and in establishing the church in new places. Vatican Council II modified Catholic missiology in important ways but not in terms of ecclesiastical relations. At the same time there are recognized differences among Roman Catholic missiologists based on national and cultural particularities. German Catholic missiology was influenced by Joseph Schmidlin with his emphasis on the dogmatic foundations of missions. In 1923 the Belgian Jesuit Pierre Charles established an annual seminar, Semaines de Missiologie, the proceedings of which were published, that was widely influential. Charles emphasized the traditional Catholic teaching of *plantatio ecclesiae* as the basis for missionary work. Spanish missiology that focused on the extensive history of the missions has been the hallmark of Spanish Catholicism whereas French missiologists have concentrated on the theological foundations of missions. In addition to these varied national and cultural streams, Rome exerts influence on all Catholic missiology. In 1919 Pope Benedict XV instituted the teaching of missiology at the Pontifical Urban University and in 1932 the Pontifical Institute of Missionary Science was authorized to grant the doctor in missiology degree. The same year the Gregorian University also began granting the doctorate in missiology.

Among Protestants another set of polarities in missiology have developed: conciliar and evangelical. The distinctive theological views of each of these traditions on a range of issues—*inter alia,* the theology of other religions, the nature of SALVATION, the content of evangelization, the relationship between word and deed, the meaning of the KINGDOM OF GOD, ESCHATOLOGY—have been active ingredients in shaping the missiological response.

Major Theoretical Ideas

Notwithstanding the recognition that for mission studies to be carried out effectively a proper theoretical framework is required, mission theory has remained incomplete. The following four themes represent essential elements in the development of mission theory since the mid-nineteenth century.

1. *The goal of mission.* By 1850 certain elements of a theory of mission had begun to be identified. Two of the most influential theoreticians in the nineteenth century were mission secretaries who enjoyed long tenures with their respective mission societies and exerted wide influence on mission thought and practice. Henry Venn (1796–1873) was honorary clerical secretary of the CHURCH MISSIONARY SOCIETY, the largest Anglican missionary society, from 1841 to 1872. RUFUS ANDERSON (1796–1880) was appointed to the administrative staff of the American Board of Commissioners for Foreign Missions in 1826 and from 1832 to 1866 he served as administrative secretary. Founded in 1810 as the first American foreign mission, the ABCFM was the largest American mission agency throughout the nineteenth century.

Working independently of each other Anderson and Venn arrived at remarkably similar ideas concerning the goal of mission and the means of achieving it. Indeed, their contribution lay not in the originality of their thought so much as their ability to formulate comprehensively and clearly ideas that had been present in policy statements and official pronouncements for at least a generation but needed to be brought together in a workable form. Anderson and Venn held that the goal of mission was the establishment of an indigenous church, rather than a church that was permanently dependent on foreign support. A church could be said to have become indigenous when it demonstrated that it was self-governing, self-financing, and self-propagating. The task mission agencies faced was to formulate policies in each of these three areas that would assist the fledgling church to move from dependency on the mission to independence. Anderson and Venn were critical of missionary policy and practice that subverted the achievement of this fundamental goal. Ironically, the strongest opposition to their attempts to translate these ideals into program policies came from their own missionary colleagues.

2. *The foundation of mission.* The modern mission movement long lacked a firm theological foundation. Academic theologians largely ignored missions and missionaries understood their role to be that of reproducing the kind of church they were familiar with in the homeland. Since 1800 missions were understood as attempts to carry out the Great Commission based on the appropriate motivation.

Historical studies have identified at least a dozen motives that have guided Protestant missions since the seventeenth century. When European governments issued charters for trading companies in the seventeenth century, typically a provision was included that required these companies to evangelize the "natives" along with providing CHAPLAINCY services to the European community. A so-called prudential motive was invoked in seventeenth-century New England when the British saw the possibility of using the Puritan missions to the Indians as a protective shield against both Roman Catholic missions and French influence from Canada. The Puritans (see PURITANISM) appealed to *gloria Dei* and Christian compassion for perishing souls as a motive. From within this Calvinist tradition, SAMUEL HOPKINS in the late eighteenth century developed a theology of "disinterested benevolence" and humanitarianism that provided powerful motivation for the first generation of American foreign missions. Obedience to the Great Commission was introduced in the eighteenth century along with an appeal to eschatology. The nationalist motive in various guises—manifest destiny, American benevolence, guardianship of less-fortunate peoples—ebbed and flowed throughout the past three centuries. What is noteworthy is that missionary motivation remained in flux throughout these three centuries. The focus on motivation emphasizes human initiative and responsibility.

Challenged by KARL BARTH's emphasis on *actio Dei* as before all else, the theology of mission began to be developed after 1950 based on the *missio Dei.* The foundation of mission is God's saving initiative. Authentic missionary work is always a response to the *missio Dei* and human motives must be judged in light of God's mission. This way of speaking about the foundation of mission has been widely accepted by missiologists as an important clarification. It has contributed to the development of a vigorous theology of mission.

3. *Church growth.* In 1955 Donald A. McGavran, DISCIPLES OF CHRIST missionary to India, published *The Bridges of God.* McGavran had been studying missionary strategies and methods for more than two decades in India and had become profoundly critical of the results of the classical mission method—what has been called the "mission station" approach—and proposed that mission strategy start from careful observation of the social unit within which people live. McGavran drew on the pioneering studies conducted by J. Waskom Pickett of "mass movements" in India over the previous century (see MASS MOVEMENTS, INDIA). It was observed that wherever large numbers of people had become Christian they did so as groups. This reflected the fact that these people came from group-oriented cultures. If missions were to be effective, McGavran argued, they must respect the cultural dynamics of these people groups. Starting with a theology of individual conversion, missions had insisted on "extracting" individuals from their culture with the result that such people became alienated from their kith and kin. McGavran held that missions must adopt a strategy that worked with the cultural grain to minimize the cultural dislocation people experience when they become Christian. He conducted extensive surveys of existing missions and the resulting churches to demonstrate the actual results of the work being done and taught his students how to do similar studies. McGavran believed that the classical methods inevitably resulted in static mission stations rather than vibrant churches. Although Church Growth theory was criticized both theologically and methodologically, it became the main source for revitalizing American missiology in the 1960s and 1970s.

4. *Contextualization.* By the eve of World War II in 1941, the churches in Asia, Africa, and the South Pacific that had been established through missionary agency were deeply frustrated. Whereas missions professed to be committed to the emergence of *indigenous* churches, missionaries and mission structures showed little evidence of being ready to hand over responsibility and control. By the end of World War II two unrelated developments pointed to imminent and fundamental change. First, it was becoming clear that the nationalist movements among the people colonized by European powers could not be stopped. Missions were subject to the same forces as were colonial powers. It was only a matter of time until all colonies

would gain their political independence. The day of COLONIALISM—political and ecclesiastical—was rapidly ending.

A second development was less evident but of great consequence for missions. During the 1940s a dynamic new influence had entered the world of missions: anthropology and linguistics. Increasingly, the nineteenth-century concept of the "indigenous church" had to be questioned. It was not a matter of challenging the insights of Venn and Anderson; rather the difficulties stemmed from the way their ideals had been consistently violated by their contemporaries and their successors. The Anderson–Venn program had not been given a fair trial. Wherever one turned the story was the same: missionaries did not trust local leadership and successfully maneuvered to maintain their control. After several generations the missions remained in charge. Those few missionaries who did break rank to pursue another course—for example, John Nevius and ROLAND ALLEN—were roundly criticized. Missionary practice had nullified the Anderson–Venn formulation.

Cultural anthropologists laid the foundation for a new theoretical construct. The theory of *contextualization* shifted attention from foreign structures to the discovery of the resources within the culture that were indispensable to a viable Christian faith in that particular culture. Instead of starting with foreign forms and structures, the new church ought to be allowed to strike root in its own cultural context and develop in response to that environment. Theologically, the incarnation provided the basis for contextualization theory. In cultural terms contextualization theory minimized the role of the outside broker and maximized the role of indigenous leadership.

Professional Publications and Associations

Critical study is foundational to any academic discipline. In the modern academic world professional associations assist by carrying out several important functions, including (1) establishing scholarly standards for a field, (2) sponsoring meetings where members meet for scholarly exchange, (3) encouraging publication through sponsorship of scholarly journals and monographs, and (4) certifying those who qualify as members of a scholarly guild. Although the process was long and arduous, by the 1970s missiology could claim to have developed the necessary mechanisms to be recognized as a scholarly guild.

Publications

Study of the Christian mission has been fostered by the convening of periodic gatherings of missionary leaders and scholars to address timely issues and the publication of specialized journals and monographs. The earliest initiatives took the form of the publication of periodicals and monographs. In 1813 Josiah Pratt, secretary of the Church Missionary Society, established *The Missionary Register* as a private venture. This monthly journal provided remarkable comprehensiveness coverage. Pratt compiled and published statistics on all Christian missions, including Roman Catholic, worldwide, thus creating a prototype for future mission publications. As was typical of many of these early periodicals, Pratt's journal had an international circulation. At the time of the first international missionary conference held at Liverpool, United Kingdom, in 1860, a bibliography containing dozens of items was compiled. Although much of this material would not meet twenty-first century standards of scholarship, it indicates something of the publishing industry that had grown up around the missionary movement (see PUBLISHING MEDIA). In 1874 Gustav Warneck established a journal, *Allgemeine Missionszeitschrift,* for the purpose of fostering the scientific research and writing on mission topics. Warneck set a high standard both in terms of the quality and quantity of his own work as well as in stimulating others to develop as scholars. Royal G. Wilder founded the *Missionary Review of the World* in 1878. *MRW* became the leading monthly journal published in the United States. From 1888 to 1911 A. T. Pierson, an energetic interpreter of missions, served as editor (1888–1911).

In 1912 the *International Review of Missions* was launched and quickly established itself as the foremost Protestant scholarly missions journal published in English. During the period 1920–1960, North American contributions to the *IRM* were nurtured by an annual gathering of mission executives and professors in New York. This off-the-record and unofficial gathering was devoted to brainstorming and vigorous discussion of priority concerns. Kenneth Scott Latourette, Yale University missions historian, served as secretary and would report the results of the meeting to the editor of the *IRM* and suggest topics and writers. This proved to be a highly productive process that fulfilled some of the purposes of a professional society.

Schools of Mission and Study Centers

In Europe and in North America long-standing mission study programs were in crisis in the 1960s. Both Roman Catholic missionary orders and Protestant mission agencies that had been at the forefront of the modern mission movement since early in the nineteenth century were experiencing a steady decline in the number of missionaries in service. They could no longer justify maintaining training programs and these were now being curtailed or closed down. In North America, university and seminary administrations were even phasing out long-established programs in mission studies with endowed chairs. The prestigious Kennedy School of Missions of Hartford Seminary Foundation, founded in 1917 and a major training center, closed its doors in 1967. All of these programs had been based on the Anglo-American tradition of mission studies.

This was also a period of change and reorientation for Roman Catholic SEMINARIES and institutes. In the aftermath of reforms set in motion by Vatican Council II the number of vocations dropped precipitously. Catholic seminaries in the United States reorganized and consolidated their mission training at Catholic Theological Union in Chicago in 1969–1970.

However, during this time a countermovement was taking shape. In 1965 Fuller Theological Seminary founded the School of World Mission and Institute of Church Growth. That same year Trinity Evangelical Divinity School organized its School of World Mission and Evangelism. Both schools were committed to offering programs in *applied missiology* and were at the forefront of a new phase in mission studies. These new schools of mission were enrolling far more students than had studied in the former mission studies programs.

The renewal in mission studies in North America can be linked to several facts. First, the Church Growth Movement, stimulated by the initiative and vision of Donald McGavran, provided a clear and fresh focus for missions. McGavran was not interested in mission studies in general. He insisted the study of the Christian mission concentrate on church growth. Although mainstream Protestant missions rejected Church Growth, Evangelicals welcomed McGavran's views, especially his confidence that a challenging new stage in missions lay ahead. Rejecting talk of crisis he argued that this moment was "the sunrise of missions," not the sunset. Convinced that conventional missions had reached the end of their usefulness McGavran was especially interested in assisting mid-career missionaries to get retooled and reoriented for the next phase of ministry. It soon became evident, however, that leaders of the churches of Asia, Africa, and LATIN AMERICA were eager for advanced training and by 1980 their numbers surpassed that of mid-career Western missionaries in the burgeoning schools of world mission in North America.

Missiological Associations

In the nineteenth century Gustav Warneck (1834–1910) organized mission study conferences in GER-

MANY. These laid a foundation for later professional associations dedicated to mission studies. One of the earliest professional missiological societies was the Deutsche Gesellschaft für Missionswissenschaft founded in Germany in 1918. A main purpose was to sponsor publication of the prestigious monograph series, "Missionswissenschaftliche Forschungen."

In the United States, the Fellowship of Professors of Missions of the Atlantic Seaboard was formed in 1917 by professors teaching missions in universities and seminaries in the Northeast. The group met two times each year. In 1952 a new Association of Professors of Missions was founded as a North American organization serving professors teaching in graduate schools accredited by the American Association of Theological Schools. Later the APM amended its rules to allow those teaching missions at the college level to affiliate.

In 1968 and 1970, European missiologists met to lay plans for an International Association for Mission Studies. When the new organization was formally inaugurated in 1972 it included members from North America and immediately set out to make its membership truly global. Over the years IAMS has held several of its assemblies in Latin America and Africa. It publishes the journal *Mission Studies*.

In 1972 a meeting was held in Nashville, Tennessee, to explore the possibility of founding a professional missiological society for North America. The following year the American Society of Missiology was formally organized. The purpose of the ASM is to provide academic and professional support to scholars in the field of mission studies. In contrast to the several antecedent organizations and activities, the ASM has fulfilled all the functions of a professional society. From the beginning the ASM welcomed into membership scholars from all Christian traditions and has incorporated into its procedures mechanisms to ensure that the three main streams—conciliar Protestant, evangelical Protestant, and Roman Catholic—are represented in all boards and committees. In contrast to predecessors' organizations that restricted membership to academics only, ASM has welcomed field missionaries, agency administrators, and students into its ranks.

ASM meets annually in June. The Association of Professors of Mission continues as a separate organization but meets annually in conjunction with ASM. Since 1973, ASM has published *Missiology: An International Review,* a leading scholarly quarterly. In addition, ASM cooperates with Orbis Books to publish a scholarly monograph series that by 2001 numbered thirty titles. ASM also sponsors a dissertation series that is published in association with University Press of America. The ASM was active in several international bibliography projects in the 1990s dedicated to developing both general and specialized bibliographies accessible electronically to scholars throughout the world.

In 1990 the Evangelical Missiological Society was founded. This represented, in part, a reorganization of the Association of Evangelical Professors of Mission. The EMS adopted the theological framework of the Interdenominational Foreign Mission Association, Evangelical Fellowship of Mission Agencies, and Fellowship of Frontier Missions. Membership is limited to those who subscribe to the doctrinal standards of these agencies and is open to professors, missionaries, and administrators. The EMS sponsors an annual meeting, held in conjunction with other evangelical associations, including the Evangelical Theological Society. Regional meetings of the EMS are held each year. EMS regularly publishes monographs and volumes of its proceedings.

Academic Status and Degrees

In Canada and the United States the Association of Theological Schools (ATS) has approved graduate programs in missiology since the 1970s. The following doctoral degrees have been awarded for work in missiology: Doctor of Philosophy (Ph.D.), Doctor of Missiology (D.Miss.), Doctor of Theology (Th.D.), Doctor of Education (Ed.D.), and Doctor of Ministry (D.Min.).

Conclusion

Missiology was established during the period when mission was understood as the extension of Christendom to other parts of the world. The collapse of Christendom and the emergence of new centers of Christian vitality in the non-Western world requires that missiology be rethought in light of this emerging future.

References and Further Reading

Graul, Karl. *Concerning the Position and the Significance of Christian Missions.* 1864.
Müller, K. *Mission Theology: An Introduction.* Nettetal, Germany: Steyler Verlag, 1987.
Myklebust, O. G. *The Study of Missions in Theological Education,* 2 vols. Oslo, Norway: Egede Institute, 1955 and 1957.
Scherer, J. A. "Missions in Theological Education." 1971. [cf. Schmidlin, J. *Katholische Missionslehre im Grundriss.* (1919) English translation, *Catholic Mission Theory,* 1931.]
Shenk, W. R., and G. R. Hunsberger. *The American Society of Missiology.* Maryknoll, NY: Orbis Books, 1998.
Tippett, A. *Introduction to Missiology.* Pasadena, CA: William Carey Library, 1987.

Verkuyl, J. *Contemporary Missiology.* Grand Rapids, MI: Eerdmans, 1978.

Verstraelen, F. J., ed. *Missiology: An Ecumenical Introduction.* Grand Rapids, MI: Eerdmans, 1995.

Walls, Andrew F. "Structural Problems in Mission Studies." In *International Bulletin of Missionary Research,* 15, no. 4 (October 1991): 146–155.

WILBERT R. SHENK

MISSIONARY ORGANIZATIONS

The Christian church may be called missionary by its very nature. Thus, when defining mission, one may well characterize everything that the church does as "missionary." Understood in this manner, the church as such exists as a missionary enterprise. There is much that is valid about this perspective, although the emphasis in this article is *not* on *all* the church's mission activities. The "missionary" emphasis will be on doing mission across specific boundaries. Formal church or voluntary associations (see VOLUNTARY SOCIETIES) that conduct mission and create special structures to carry out those activities across boundaries (e.g., language, geography, culture, race, tribe, etc.) will be our focus. Thus our first distinction involves the functional character of a missionary organization.

The second distinction is theological and points to the difference between mission and mission(s). "Mission" will be used as a theological term to refer to God's activity in the world (the *missio Dei*). MISSIONS, on the other hand, refer to how the church participates in God's activities. In this article "missions" points to particular missionary activities of churches and Christians through their specific structural and legal organizations.

Missionary organizations throughout church history can be divided into five general groups: Catholic, Ecumenical Protestant, Evangelical Protestant, Orthodox, and Pentecostal. Each stream of missionary activity has its own genius, its own history, and its own charism. Some mission organizations have had great prominence in the history of the Christian mission. The Society of Jesus (the Jesuits), for example, founded by the Spaniard Ignatius Loyola in 1534, accepted the old monastic vows of poverty, chastity, and obedience in service to the papacy. This Company of Jesus went forth into the world to spread the orthodox faith and to fight against religious HERESY or revolt. Jesuit missionaries included such famous figures as Francis Xavier, Apostle to the Indies; Robert de Nobili, the Christian Brahmin; Matteo Ricci, who opened the door to CHINA; the founders of the Reduction of Paraguay; and Eusebius Kino, builder of missions in MEXICO and the American Southwest. The Jesuits built on the revival of mission organizations in the thirteenth century with St. Francis of Assisi, the

"Father of the Poor," together with the "brother preachers" of the Dominicans who formed the "Societas Fratrum Peregrinantium propter Christum inter Gentes" (The Company of brethren dwelling in foreign parts among the heathen for the sake of Christ). Most Protestants trace the modern history of mission societies back to WILLIAM CAREY's amazing accomplishments in INDIA and to his creation of the "Particular Baptist Society for Propagating the Gospel among the Heathen" (1792). Carey's principle "Expect great things from God, attempt great things for God" has become an important guiding light for many Protestant mission societies around the world.

Other mission organizations have worked for decades with little notoriety. These organizations are nevertheless a fascinating reminder of the relationship between church and mission. The Women's Missionary Movement of the late nineteenth and early twentieth centuries encompassed millions of WOMEN. Indeed it was probably the largest mass women's movement up to that time. Like other missionary movements, the Women's Missionary Movement was born out of a fervor for missions; however, it was also born out of the desperation of women—especially single women—who felt called to be missionaries but were rejected because of GENDER. The tenacity of these "called" women, however, won the day. Beginning in 1861 with the women's Union Missionary Society, the Women's Missionary Movement began while birthing at least another forty such organizations by the turn of the century. Observing the success of these missionary organizations, denominational churchmen gradually opened their mission societies to single women. Eventually the women's boards merged with the denominational boards, and the once-vibrant Women's Missionary Movement faded from the scene. Gone was the golden era of "female agencies."

As early as 1782 former black slaves in the United States such as David George, Amos Williams, and Joseph Paul sought to transplant their church from South Carolina and Georgia to Nova Scotia, SIERRA LEONE, Jamaica, and the Bahamas. These men became the first unofficial African American missionaries before the American foreign missionary movement had been solidly launched (see AFRICAN AMERICAN PROTESTANTISM). A notable black mission society dating back to the late nineteenth century is the Lott Carey Baptist Foreign Mission Convention founded in 1897. By studying this one particular mission society we can better grasp how the idea of mission played itself out within one segment of the black Baptist American experience over a period of one hundred years.

Thus, whether Catholic or Protestant, large or small, distinguished or stealthy, church or parachurch, black or white, European or non-Western, male or female, the history of Christian mission is well told through the story of missionary organizations.

Roman Catholic

Catholic missions, viewed over the course of history, were performed mostly by monks, religious orders, and congregations. Although Roman Catholic missionary organizations have differed considerably in ideals and methods from Protestant missions, it is possible to discern a certain parallelism both in terminology and ideas among them all. The orders seemed to be predestined for missionary work by their spirituality, organization, TRADITION, and vast experience.

In the Middle Ages it was the religious who were the missionaries: Benedictines, the Celtic missionaries, Cistercians, Trinitarians, and eventually the Dominicans, Franciscans, Carmelites, and Augustinians. Other orders followed including the Jesuits and many recent congregations such as the Picpus Fathers, Oblates of Mary Immaculate, Marists, Pallottines, Holy Ghost Fathers, Salesians, Scheut Fathers, White Fathers, Divine Word Missionaries, Sacred Heart Missionaries, and Holy Family Missionaries. Following the model of the Paris Foreign Missionaries various missionary societies of secular priests were founded: the Milan Foreign Missions Seminary, the African Missionaries (Lyons), the Mill Hill Fathers, and the Maryknoll Fathers. In addition, there have been a large number of women's missionary orders in the course of history, especially since the last century, although it is only recently that they have been recognized within missiological literature.

The organization of Roman Catholic mission across the world appears, at first, to function in ways that are too complicated to outline in any simplistic fashion. Nevertheless Catholic missions proceeds organizationally along two very broad tracks. First, missions are carried out primarily by religious orders and congregations that are usually characterized by specific "charisms." The second track involves church AUTHORITY. The bishop in his diocese has proper authority over missionary activities. All missionaries and missionary orders are subject to this authority in all the various activities that have to do with the exercise of the apostolate. This stipulation means that every religious order and congregation enters into a contract with the local bishop to secure ecclesiastical rights to do missions.

There are, finally, numerous organizations and coordinating agencies besides religious orders in which Roman Catholics cooperate with social, governmental, or religious partners for implicit or explicit missionary purposes. These organizations include trade unions, political movements, social and developmental agencies, and associations of laypersons. All of them contribute to the content and work of Catholic missions.

Ecumenical Protestant

With the increase of missionary awareness in the Protestant world beginning with PIETISM in eighteenth-century Europe, independent missionary organizations came to promote the bulk of the missionary agenda. Missionary societies began to take shape across the emerging Protestant world, even if their origin, relationship to established churches, and theological motivation were quite varied in nature. Thus Protestants, after over 150 years of mission dormancy, came to reflect more and more the organizational genius for missions developed earlier by Roman Catholics. When the REFORMATION rejected monastic societies, one of the best organizational tools for missions was discarded. Scholars claim, nevertheless, that the ancestral roots for the new Protestant mission societies of the eighteenth century were monastic communities, Catholic religious orders, the "religious societies" in ENGLAND, and the revival movement of the Moravians (see MORAVIAN CHURCH). Missionary societies were seen as a direct expression of the dynamism of the community now needing a specific organizational tool to carry out its work.

The dynamism for foreign mission, therefore, took shape outside the established churches and inside the newly formed missionary societies. This development was promoted by the tendency in the eighteenth and nineteenth centuries to form associations. With the founding of the Particular Baptist Missionary Society by William Carey (1761–1834), mission became the responsibility of well-organized groups. In 1795 the London Missionary Society was founded followed in 1796 by two Scottish missionary societies and in 1797 by the Netherlands Missionary Society. In 1799 the CHURCH MISSIONARY SOCIETY was founded by Anglicans who had withdrawn from the London Missionary Society. In the German-speaking world, the German Christianity Fellowship (*Christentumsgesellschaft*) was founded in 1780. The forerunners of all these mission societies, however, were the great mission organizations of the eighteenth century: the Danish-Halle Mission (1705) and the Moravian Mission (1732).

The "great century" of Protestant missions is often associated with the nineteenth century. European churches continued to play the dominant role during this time in regard to mission and church expansion. Nevertheless Protestant churches themselves were unable or unwilling to initiate, administer, or support foreign mission. Within this void, voluntary mission organizations increasingly came into being throughout Europe and the UNITED STATES. Societies that organized early in the nineteenth century included the BRITISH AND FOREIGN BIBLE SOCIETY (1804), the London Society for Promoting Christianity among the Jews (1804), the AMERICAN BOARD OF COMMISSIONERS FOR FOREIGN MISSIONS (1810), the Edinburgh Medical Missionary Society (1814), the American Baptist Missionary Board (1814), the BASEL MISSION (1815), the AMERICAN BIBLE SOCIETY (1816), and the Berlin Society (1824).

Protestant Christianity never developed a global center of missionary administration. The fragmentation of mission has, in fact, been labeled "typically Protestant" from its nineteenth-century beginnings until today. Societies divided at a minimum along national and confessional lines, and generally present a picture of competition. Successful attempts at making Protestant mission more cooperative in recent years has, happily, also marked some of contemporary Protestant missions.

The development of missionary organizations in the nineteenth century developed in three distinct stages. First, missionary societies arose with the express intention of avoiding confessional "wars" so as not to transfer European ecclesiastical battles into new church communities around the world. Nineteenth-century Germany itself is a great example of this trend. Among the newly formed "united" mission societies in Germany were the Basel Mission (1915), the Berlin Missionary Society (1800), the Rhenish Missionary Society (1828), the North German Missionary Society (1836), and the Gossner Mission Society (1836).

A second wave of missionary societies emphasized confessional adherence and ecclesiastical structure. Parochial concerns now took precedence over the lofty idea of Christian unity. Confessional renewal caused doctrinal splits within already existing mission societies. Thus in 1836, for example, the Dresden Mission Association broke away from the Basel Mission, regarding itself as a mission "in the spirit of the Lutheran Church." In 1848 the society transferred to Leipzig, becoming known as the Leipzig Lutheran Missionary Society and, as such, as the continuation of the Danish-Halle Mission.

Finally a third wave of "faith missions," especially under Anglo-Saxon influence, provided further impulses for the creation of independent mission societies and/or faith missions. Inspired by J. H. Taylor and the CHINA INLAND MISSION (1865)—one of the largest missionary societies at that time—there arose a large number of similar foundations all over the world. These faith-based missionary organizations, function-

ing with a minimum of hierarchy and authority, form a significant portion of missionary activity today.

Whereas nineteenth-century mission was dominated by European mission societies, American Protestant missions became the strongest force in the twentieth century. The United States was considered a mission field by the European missions until the middle of the nineteenth century for Protestants, and until 1907 for Catholics, although the United States soon became the major source of mission energies. This trend has continued until the present day. Missionary organizations in the United States became more organically linked with their churches by 1914. A direct connection between mission societies and their respective Baptist, Presbyterian, Episcopalian, Methodist, Brethren, and Lutheran churches, for example, became more apparent than what had existed in Europe.

Although this general trend in North American and European mission will probably continue well into the first part of the twenty-first century, one of the newest and most significant developments is the increase in missionaries sent out by "non-Western" nations. The average growth rate of Third World Protestant missionaries during the 1980s and 1990s was over 13 percent, with India, NIGERIA, Congo, Myanmar, BRAZIL, PHILIPPINES, Ghana, and KOREA leading the way. Over 60,000 Protestant missionaries were sent out from the Two-Thirds World nations in the early 1990s. If this trend continues in the twenty-first century, more Protestant missionaries will be sent from or within Two-Thirds World countries than from the West by 2010.

Evangelical Protestant

Evangelicals are hard to classify. They do not represent an institution but a movement that exists in practically every church tradition worldwide, including some churches labeled Ecumenical Protestant. Their ranks vary from Fundamentalists to Neo-Evangelicals, from Confessional Evangelicals to Charismatics, from Pentecostals to Catholic Evangelicals. In terms of numbers, evangelical mission organizations are formidable and growing. Their numbers in missionary personnel are significantly larger than Ecumenical Protestants. What distinguishes Evangelical Missions is a particular balance of the following theological teachings: the absolute authority of Scripture as the Word of God, the necessity of FAITH in the ATONEMENT of Christ for SALVATION, an existential saving encounter with Christ through the Holy Spirit, a devout regenerate life, social engagement, and the obligation to evangelize non-Christians.

The swift expansion of Christianity in the nineteenth century was attributed in part to the work of many Protestant mission societies representing the Evangelical Awakening (see AWAKENING). It was this awakening that brought fresh missionary enthusiasm to the whole mission endeavor. The resistance to rationalism and MODERNISM was pivotal, as was reaction against moribund ecclesiastical ORTHODOXY.

A strong stimulus to evangelical missionary renewal in North America came at the turn of the twentieth century from the Student Volunteer Movement (SVM, 1888) together with the World's Student Christian Federation (WSCF), founded in 1895. The SVM, with the watchword "the evangelization of the world in this generation," produced pioneers of the twentieth-century ecumenical movement like JOHN R. MOTT, J. H. Oldham, and W. A. VISSER'T HOOFT.

Evangelical mission societies after 1910 organized themselves into various associations. Evangelicals and Ecumenicals worked together within the framework of the International Missionary Council (IMC, 1921) until a "separation of minds" occurred with the "marriage" of the IMC with the WORLD COUNCIL OF CHURCHES in 1961. At that time new umbrella organizations were formed and older ones were strengthened, such as the Evangelical Foreign Missions Association (EFMA) and the Interdenominational Foreign Mission Association (IFMA). The IFMA had been formed in North America (1917) to strengthen the "faith missions" that were independent and largely pro-dispensationalist. In 1945 the EFMA (formerly the Evangelical Foreign Missions Association) was formed to perform a similar service for North American denominational missions affiliated with the NATIONAL ASSOCIATION OF EVANGELICALS (NAE). Separatist fundamentalist groups formed the Fellowship of Missions (FOM) in 1972 as a breakaway movement from the Associated Missions, organized in 1948 by the International Council of Christian Churches. In 1985 the Association of International Mission services (AIMS) was founded by charismatic leaders "to further world evangelization through a consortium of member church, mission agencies and training institutions." These, and other associations of evangelical mission organizations, testify both to the great vibrancy and entrepreneurial nature of evangelical missions, and to their great toleration for division.

Many evangelical missions do not seek to participate in associations. They remain fiercely independent. These include mission societies like the PLYMOUTH BRETHREN's Christian Missions in Many Lands, the LUTHERAN CHURCH–MISSOURI SYNOD, and the SOUTHERN BAPTIST CONVENTION, the largest Protestant mission in North America with over 4,000 missionaries serving in 113 countries.

WYCLIFFE BIBLE TRANSLATORS, Campus Crusade for Christ International, and Youth with a Mission (YWAM) are examples of the evangelical trend for huge parachurch mission organizations with thousands of workers all across the world.

The most effective fellowship in fostering collaboration among Evangelicals is the World Evangelical Fellowship, formed in 1951 and The Lausanne Committee for World Evangelism created by BILLY GRAHAM in 1974. The Lausanne Movement has been instrumental in rallying Evangelicals for missiological discussion and missionary action.

Besides evangelism and church planting, "development cooperation" and diaconal concerns are undertaken by EVANGELICAL mission organizations. On the international level WORLD VISION and the Evangelical Alliance Relief Fund (the TEAR fund) are examples.

Orthodox

Variations in doctrine, national character, and historical events have greatly shaped how missions have been understood, organized, and carried out by individual Orthodox churches (see ORTHODOXY, EASTERN). From an early date we have evidence of how rapidly the church spread throughout the East. Churches existed in Persia, Armenia, India, Georgia, and Ethiopia. Special missionary activities were manifested by the church in Persia as monks from this church pressed forward as far as India and Turkestan.

The missionary zeal that characterized missions in the first millennium can be witnessed only in pockets after 1054. The reasons for this slowing of missions are complex. The fall of Constantinople in 1453 certainly condemned the church to a defensive posture. In the Orthodox churches from the seventeenth through the twentieth century, missionary activity was confined almost exclusively to Russian initiatives. The "great captivity" of the ancient churches of the Middle East under the Islamic rule of the Ottoman Empire made most mission efforts difficult if not impossible. In Russia the tradition of mission expansion by "colonist monks" was stifled from 1682 to 1796 by strict imperial controls. The basis then of most new missionary work, although difficult to compare with Catholic and Protestant trends, was found primarily within the monastic communities. From 1828 until the Russian Revolution in 1917, various Orthodox mission ventures were undertaken not only to reverse the trends of apostasy to Islam among the eastern Russian but also to plant new churches and construct and maintain numerous charitable and educational institutions. The Russian Revolution (1917) brought a sudden close to the missionaries' work.

Today a number of societies in the Orthodox Church have accepted the mandate of missions in foreign places such as Uganda, Tanzania, Kenya, and Sudan, not to mention Western nations like the United States. Participation in the ecumenical movement along with the care of Orthodox living in countries without traditional Orthodox presence are high priorities. Another concern touches "foreign" missionary societies moving into "traditional" territories to do missions among peoples that Orthodox communities have seen for generations as their own.

Pentecostal

Since the beginning of the twentieth century PENTECOSTALISM has come to represent one of the most energetic forces of mission in the history of Christianity. The dizzying array of Pentecostal movements, churches, and organizations makes any attempt at categorization impossible. David Barrett tries to label some of these movements with headings such as: Classical Pentecostals, Black/Non-White Indigenous Pentecostals, Neo-Pentecostals, Isolated Radio Pentecostals, Chinese House-church Pentecostals, Charismatics, Catholic Charismatics, and Crypto-charismatics. However they are labeled, it is obvious that tens of millions of Christians worldwide identify themselves with renewal movements, and these movements are rapidly growing. Without doubt, Pentecostal Christians, since the initial revivals in Topeka, Kansas (1901), and the influential AZUSA STREET REVIVAL in Los Angeles (1906–1909), form one of the largest segments of the Christian church today. The growth of Pentecostalism in LATIN AMERICA, for example, must be termed as nothing less than explosive. Recent statistics suggest that two-thirds to three-fourths of all Protestants are Pentecostals. Of the 66 million "Classical Pentecostals" in the world, fully half are in Latin America. Brazil, which is the largest Roman Catholic country in Latin America, also has the largest population of Classic Pentecostals, Charismatics, and Neo-Pentecostals numbering 79 million, according to the *New Dictionary of Pentecostal and Charismatic Movements*. Pentecostal movements in Latin American countries have strong ties to North America and Europe. Renewal movements in Africa and Asia, in contrast, often claim independent origins apart from their American or European counterparts; however, no matter where their origins may be located, global Pentecostalism reflects a zeal for mission that affirms that every believer is directly responsible for mission.

Pentecostal missionaries have always been more adept at practice than theory. Nevertheless Pentecostal missiologists are starting to articulate more forcefully the theological distinctives that make them Pentecostal. It can be affirmed, however, Pentecostals and Evangelicals share conservative doctrinal views regarding the Bible, humankind without Christ ("lost"), and salvation.

The diversity of global Pentecostalism does not make possible any talk about "a" Pentecostal theology. Six factors are important in grasping the nature of Pentecostal mission.

1. The spiritual foundation for all mission is a relationship with Jesus and "second" experience or baptism in the Spirit.
2. The authority for mission is the Bible.
3. The imminent Second Coming of Christ compels mission activity now.
4. The gospel of God's kingdom should be proclaimed with the expectancy of signs and wonders confirming the truth of the message.
5. EVANGELISM and healing take priority over social and/or political action.
6. Organizational flexibility is the norm.

The primary mission genius of Pentecostals is that each believer being empowered by the Holy Spirit is a missionary. This belief has led to both dynamic and divergent forms of outreach locally and globally. It raises the question, however, about how Pentecostals structure their communal witness, maintain continuity over time, and interact with other Christian churches. Mission efforts usually follow five basic organizational patterns: episcopal, presbyterial/congregational, congregational, individual, and parachurch.

When many mainline churches were struggling or declining in the 1980s and 1990s the Pentecostal movement grew by over 8 percent worldwide. The myriad of ecclesiastical structures and parachurch ministries within the Pentecostal movement underline the vitality and pragmatism of their efforts at contextually relevant ministries. Many scholars maintain that Pentecostal spirituality is the most viable form of Christianity in a postmodern, post-Western, and postcolonial world (see POSTMODERNITY; POST-COLONIALISM).

Conclusion

Because of the great variety and number of mission societies still active today, two pressing questions must be debated as Christians redefine the nature of mission and missions. First, with the ongoing shift in global Christianity to the East and South, do we still need missionary organizations to send missionaries to Third World countries? Are foreign missionaries a theological necessity for a church's obedience to the gospel or, rather, a negotiable historical contingency? Second, with so many competing mission societies and church agendas vying for their niche in the world's religious marketplace, what missiological role does Christian unity play?

Concerning the future role of missionary organizations, responses range from renewed calls for moratoriums against missionaries to calls for more missionaries to carry out the expansion of the church. What is clear in all these debates is that no church can survive by being strictly a "sending" or a "receiving" church. In an age of globalization the church catholic needs to use its gifts wisely to respond to the world's needs. Mission organizations can serve as those places where Christians pose the stewardship question concerning how to best distribute the church's resources, human and otherwise. Mission organizations like the United Evangelical Mission (VEM) in Germany are experimenting with new organizational forms to carry out this mission. They have transformed themselves into the mission arm not only of their traditional German congregations but also of their partner churches worldwide.

Christian unity will remain the greatest mission challenge in a fragmented world, with fragmented Christians promoting fragmented views of missions—but what does "unity" mean? Does it demand organizational unity or merely unity of purpose? At Edinburgh in 1910, mission organizations courageously affirmed their unity of purpose. That unity soon waned, however, under the pressure of modernity and World War I. The integration or organizational marriage of the International Missionary Council into the WCC at New Delhi (1961) has also been hailed as both a great ecumenical leap forward for mission and, likewise, "the funeral of mission." Christian missions should never be reduced to an entrepreneurial enterprise where the strongest organizations win. Competition may reflect present practice but history teaches that it undermines God's mission. Jesus's prayer for unity, "that they may be one," still has force as churches continue to organize themselves to do God's mission in the world.

References and Further Reading

Anderson, Gerald H. "American Protestants in Pursuit of Mission: 1886–1986." In *Missiology: An Ecumenical Introduction,* edited by F. J. Verstraelen. Grand Rapids, MI: Wm. Eerdmans, 1995.

Beaver, R. Pierce. *Pioneers in Mission: A Source Book on the Rise of American Missions to the Heathen.* Grand Rapids, MI: Eerdmans, 1966.

———. *All Loves Excelling: American Protestant Women in World Mission.* Grand Rapids, MI: Eerdmans, 1968.

———. *American Missions in Bicentennial Perspective.* Pasadena, CA: Wm. Carey Library, 1977.

Bosch, David. *Transforming Mission.* Maryknoll, NY: Orbis, 1991.

Jongeneel, J. A. B. "The Protestant Missionary Movement from 1789 to 1962." In *Missiology: An Ecumenical Introduction,* edited by F. J. Verstraelen. Grand Rapids, MI: Eerdmans, 1995.

Neil, Stephen. "Mission Boards and Societies." In *The Concise Dictionary of Christian World Mission,* edited by Stephen Neil, Gerald H. Anderson, and John Goodwin, 389–405. Nashville, TN: Abingdon Press, 1971.

Phillips, James M., and Robert T. Coote. *Toward the 21st Century in Christian Mission,* 9–41. Grand Rapids, MI: Eerdmans, 1993.

Robert, Dana. *Gospel Bearers, Gender Barriers: Missionary Women in the 20th Century.* Maryknoll, NY: Orbis, 2002.

Spindler, M. R. "The Missionary Movement and Missionary Organizations." In *Missiology: An Ecumenical Introduction,* edited by F. J. Verstraelen. Grand Rapids, MI: Eerdmans, 1995.

Wind, A. "The Protestant Missionary Movement from 1789 to 1963." In *Missiology: An Ecumenical Introduction,* edited by F. J. Verstraelen. Grand Rapids, MI: Eerdmans, 1995.

Yates, Timothy. *Christian Mission in the 20th Century.* Cambridge: Cambridge University Press, 1994.

RICHARD H. BLIESE

MISSIONS

Spreading the Christian message across cultural and ethnic boundaries has been one of the primary activities of Protestantism since the late eighteenth century. Small groups of Protestants engaged in missions before then, although it was not until after the ENLIGHTENMENT that evangelical theology, voluntarism, entrepreneurial capitalism, European expansionism, and ideas of human choice converged to propel Protestantism outward. The nineteenth century, called by historian Kenneth Scott Latourette the "Great Century" of Protestant missions, saw the organization of VOLUNTARY SOCIETIES, both denominational and ecumenical, through which Protestants raised money to send cross-cultural missionaries around the world. In witnessing to the gospel missionaries engaged in BIBLE TRANSLATION, PREACHING, teaching, PUBLISHING, healing ministries, charitable works, and movements for social justice. Cooperation among mission organizations gave birth to twentieth-century ecumenical movements. Despite ethical questions about the relationship among missions, Euro-American imperialism, and the globalization of modern capitalist CULTURE, the effectiveness of Protestant missions was demonstrated by the existence of a thriving, non-Western majority church by the end of the twentieth century.

Early Protestant Missions

At the time of the REFORMATION in the sixteenth century, cross-cultural mission was a defining feature of multinational Catholicism. Concerned with building national European churches, Protestant reformers did not place a high priority on missions, especially because they rejected the chief mission agent, the celibate priest. The Reformation nevertheless laid the groundwork for the development of Protestant missions with the principle that each nation deserved the BIBLE in its own language. Consumed by religious wars and the growth of theological systems, the principle of vernacular bible translation had little impact beyond Europe in the 1500s. The idea that loyal subjects should practice the religion of their rulers deterred early Protestants from undertaking cross-cultural missions beyond their national borders.

As the first Protestants engaged in overseas exploration, the Dutch were the first to develop a substantial interest in cross-cultural missions. Hadrian Saravia (1531–1613), of mixed Spanish and Flemish blood, was the first Protestant theologian to argue that Jesus's postresurrection command to teach all nations applied to the present-day church. Chaplains accompanying Dutch trading and military parties were the first Protestant missionaries in Dutch territories of Formosa, BRAZIL, the East Indies, Ceylon, and New Amsterdam (see CHAPLAINCY). They learned the native languages and catechized and baptized indigenous inhabitants. By 1688 Dutch chaplains had translated the New Testament into Malay, the first translation of the Scriptures into any southeast Asian language.

As groups of Protestant colonists began leaving Europe for the New World some of them felt responsible for evangelizing the NATIVE AMERICANS. When the English Puritans (see PURITANISM) entered Massachusetts in 1630 they carried with them a charter giving them the responsibility to evangelize the Indians. Puritan minister JOHN ELIOT (1604–1690) became the most important Protestant missionary in the colonial period. Congregational pastor in Roxbury, Massachusetts, Eliot began preaching to the Indians in 1646. He translated prayers, instructional materials, and ultimately the Bible into Algonquin, publishing the first New Testament in America in 1661, and the Old Testament in 1663. By 1674 he had gathered eleven hundred Christian "praying Indians" into fourteen Puritan-style Indian villages. Despite the persecution of Christian Indians by English colonists during King Philip's War of 1675–1676, they persisted in their faith. In 1698 there were thirty-seven full-time Native American preachers and teachers serving thirty churches in New England. By the time of the American Revolution at least 133 Indian pastors had served in southern New England. The most famous was Samson Occom (1723–1792), a Mohegan Indian who spent twelve years as a missionary among the Montauk Indians of Long Island, New York.

The rise of PIETISM stirred mission interest among Lutherans in the late 1600s. The reformers' emphasis on translating the Scriptures, combined with Pietism's good works and reliance on Bible study for spiritual sustenance, shaped a distinctive Protestant stance that differed from Catholic missions. When King Frederick IV of DENMARK decided to send missionaries to his colony of Tranquebar, INDIA, he found volunteers among the pietistic Germans studying with AUGUST HERMAN FRANCKE (1663–1727) at the University of HALLE. Bartholomaus Ziegenbalg (1682–1719) and Heinrich Plutschau (1677–c.1746) arrived in Tranquebar in 1706. Despite persecution from the Danish soldiers, they learned Tamil and Portuguese and founded schools and churches among mixed-race peoples. They translated the Lutheran CATECHISM, prayers, and hymns into Tamil, and made converts both from Catholicism and low-caste Hinduism. Ziegenbalg translated the New Testament into Tamil. Additional recruits from Halle University continued the mission, and by the end of the century it counted between eighteen and twenty thousand converts.

The most important group of early Protestant missionaries were the Unitas Fratrum, or Moravians (see MORAVIAN CHURCH), who in the 1730s sent missionaries to African slaves in the CARIBBEAN, Indians in North America, and the KhoiKhoi in SOUTH AFRICA. As the persecuted remnants of the followers of Jan Hus, the Moravian Pietists sent out families who established self-supporting communities among oppressed peoples. Embodying peaceful Christian principles through their communitarian lifestyles, the Moravians have supported the highest percentage of missionaries in proportion to their numbers of any Protestant group. They saw themselves as leaven rather than trying to convert whole societies. By their use of family units and unmarried WOMEN as missionaries they introduced the family as the normal agent of Protestant missions.

The Modern Missionary Movement

In 1792 British shoemaker WILLIAM CAREY (1761–1834) gave a paper challenging Calvinistic fatalism and arguing that Jesus's postresurrection command to go into all the world was still binding on his followers. Aware of the work of the Moravians and the Puritan missionaries, Carey saw the mercantile expansion of western Europe as an opportunity for spreading its religion as well. Convinced by his "Enquiry," BAPTISTS organized the Baptist Missionary Society (1792) to send Carey and his family as missionaries in India. Carey and his associates translated parts of the Bible into forty-four languages with the assistance of native language-helpers. Sharing Carey's vision, different denominations began organizing missionary societies to raise money and send missionaries abroad (see MISSIONARY ORGANIZATIONS). The London Missionary

Society (LMS, 1795), intrigued by the voyages of Captain Cook, sent Congregationalist missionaries to the South Pacific. In 1797 the LMS opened a mission in SIERRA LEONE and in 1799 it opened one in Cape Town, SOUTH AFRICA. With a strong evangelical abolitionist base, the CHURCH MISSIONARY SOCIETY (CMS, 1799) sent Anglican missionaries to West Africa in efforts to fight the slave trade (see SLAVERY; SLAVERY, ABOLITION OF). Through the transatlantic evangelical revival mission enthusiasm spread to North America and back to Europe. The first North American missionary society to organize for overseas missions was the AMERICAN BOARD OF COMMISSIONERS FOR FOREIGN MISSIONS (1810), which sent missionaries in 1812 to India. American Baptists founded their mission society in 1814 and started work in Burma. British Methodists organized in 1818 and American Methodists in 1819. On the Continent, the voluntary impulse took form in the founding of the BASEL MISSION (1815) and the Berlin Society (1824). By the end of the century mission societies of all denominations were operating around the world.

Motivated by millennial fervor, concern for the SALVATION of non-Christians, desires to glorify God, hopes of benefiting humanity, and the spirit of progress, Protestant missionaries set out with optimism to convert the non-Western world to Christianity. With Enlightenment ideals of free human agency that challenged the religious fatalism of earlier generations, missionaries believed that educating people about the Gospel would cause them to choose to follow Jesus Christ. Following the precedent of the early Lutheran pietistic missions, the new Protestant mission societies focused on Bible translation as their first priority. To convert individuals and gather them into churches required making the Scriptures available in the vernacular languages. Along with translation and preaching by ordained males, missionary wives assisted their husbands and engaged in teaching and in home visitation. Indigenous helpers were essential partners in the tasks of EVANGELISM and Bible translation from the beginning. Usually the first converts to Christianity worked with the missionaries. In West Africa, for example, SAMUEL AJAYI CROWTHER (1807–1891) helped translate the Bible into Yoruba, and eventually became the first African Anglican bishop and supervisor of missionaries (see ANGLICANISM).

The nationality, denominational affiliation, class, and GENDER of the missionaries influenced their attitudes and policies in the mission fields. Because most Continental missionaries came from the economic ranks of craftsmen and farmers, they carried agrarian ideals to their new contexts. Anglicans and Lutherans (see LUTHERANISM), themselves members of state churches, often saw their missionary goals to include building national churches that mirrored preexisting social structures. Missionaries from SCOTLAND and ENGLAND, products of the industrial revolution (see INDUSTRIALIZATION), saw themselves as agents of EDUCATION and progress. Scottish missionaries, led by Alexander Duff (1806–1878) in India, placed a strong emphasis on schools up to the college level. Promoting the "3 Cs"—"Christianity, commerce, and civilization"—came to characterize the social attitude of British missions in AFRICA. American missionaries often saw themselves as spreading democracy among peoples trampled by oppressive governments. In the mid-nineteenth century the reigning mission policy of Britain and the UNITED STATES was that of "three-self theory," formulated by Henry Venn (1796–1873) of the CMS and RUFUS ANDERSON (1796–1880) of the American Board. The goal of missions was to make converts and gather them into churches characterized by self-government, self-support, and self-propagation. By the late nineteenth century, social services and support for HUMAN RIGHTS had become central aspects of missions. Medical missionaries founded hospitals and clinics, and educational missionaries in Asia were pushing their best schools to collegiate levels. Perhaps the most significant new feature of late nineteenth-century missions was a powerful women's movement, in which voluntary societies run by women sent unmarried women into the field as teachers, doctors, evangelists, and social workers. The influx of unmarried women missionaries meant that female missionaries outnumbered males by two to one, and women's issues became important for missions.

Although missionaries usually saw their work as nonpolitical, their presence often promoted European expansion. With British control of India it became the major nineteenth-century mission field of the British mission societies. After CHINA was forced open to western trade by the mid-century opium wars, missionaries began working in treaty port cities under the infamous "unequal treaties." Fascination with East Asia and concern for the SALVATION of "China's millions" made China the other major mission field of Protestantism by the end of the century. By the late nineteenth century, the United Kingdom and GERMANY were competing for global empire. In 1885 Europe held the Berlin Conference and carved Africa into sections under the control of different European countries—Britain, Germany, FRANCE, Portugal, ITALY, and Belgium. The scramble for Africa disrupted missions, as missionaries of the "wrong" nationality were put under the control of alien powers, or forced out of their traditional areas. By the end of the century, Protestant missions were operating under colonial governments all over the world (see COLONIALISM).

The Twentieth Century

The twentieth century began with approximately 16,700 Protestant foreign missionaries in the field. As partners in the monumental task of world evangelization, yet as scattered minorities in non-Christian contexts, missionaries felt the need to overcome denominational divisions for the sake of their work (see ECUMENISM). The ecumenical WORLD MISSIONARY CONFERENCE in Edinburgh in 1910 stood as a monument to missionary visions of unity that began with William Carey's unrealized hopes for global missionary conferences every ten years. At Edinburgh, missionaries from Europe and North America systematically discussed the emerging issues of world Christianity, such as the rise of nationalism, the persecution of Asian Christians, and the growing non-Western churches. After the conference, American mission statesman JOHN R. MOTT (1865–1955) traveled through Asia organizing regional and national Christian councils consisting of missionaries and local Christian leaders. The various missions and councils of churches created the International Missionary Council (IMC) in 1921 to guide the transition from missions to "younger churches." Church unity movements in different countries resulted in the formation of Protestant union churches such as the Church of Christ in China (1927); the Church of Christ in Thailand (1934), and the CHURCH OF SOUTH INDIA (1947). The peak of the ecumenical movement came with the founding of the WORLD COUNCIL OF CHURCHES in 1948, into which the IMC merged in 1959.

Another major trend in twentieth-century missions was the rise of NATIONALISM among colonized peoples. With European brutality and vulnerability revealed in the two world wars, wholesale rejection of European colonialism grew rapidly during the century. As providers of Western education, missions in many cases trained the nationalist leaders who began challenging Western control. Starting with India in 1948, nationalists succeeded in throwing off the yoke of colonialism, a process that continued into the 1970s (see POST-COLONIALISM). Many of the first presidents of new African countries had been mission-educated. The antimission rhetoric of nationalism was another blow to Western missionaries who had suffered impoverishment, internment by the Japanese, and even death during World War II. Communist victory in China in 1949 resulted in the expulsion or imprisonment of Western missionaries (see COMMUNISM). During the 1950s and 1960s civil wars often took on anti-Western and anti-Christian tones, as in Algeria, the Congo, and Kenya. By 1971 Christian leaders in the PHILIPPINES, Kenya, and Argentina, as well as the All Africa Conference of Churches a few years later,

called for a "moratorium" on Western missionaries. Missionaries should "go home" so that non-Western churches could stand on their own feet. Although some missionaries assisted in nationalist struggles, the mission movement was branded a tool of imperialist forces and was rejected by new governments in Asia, Africa, and LATIN AMERICA. By the early 1970s the numbers of Western missionaries from mainline denominations were steadily dropping in response to antimission currents both at home and abroad.

Yet a new wave of theologically conservative evangelical and Pentecostal missionaries began outnumbering those of older denominations. As Protestantism declined in Europe the United States became the largest provider of missionaries. In 1974 evangelistic missions created the LAUSANNE COMMITTEE FOR WORLD EVANGELIZATION (LCWE), a network of Christian groups attempting to evangelize the world and plant churches among all "unreached peoples." The LCWE and its partners held over thirty international consultations and numerous regional conferences. Freed from the burden of Western paternalism by the end of colonialism, non-Western Christian movements, many of them Pentecostal, entered a period of rapid growth. By the end of the twentieth century an estimated 4,800 mission-sending agencies were sending hundreds of thousands of missionaries from all parts of the world to other cultures, including to "post-Christian" Europe. Although the mission impulse among churches of the European Reformation waned, the youthful vigor of churches in Asia, Africa, and Latin America breathed new life into Protestant missions.

References and Further Reading

Anderson, Gerald H., ed. *Biographical Dictionary of Christian Missions.* New York: Macmillan Reference USA, 1998.

Hutchison, William R. *Errand to the World.* Chicago: University of Chicago Press, 1987.

Latourette, Kenneth Scott. *A History of the Expansion of Christianity.* 7 vols. New York: Harper & Bros., 1938–1946.

Moreau, A. Scott, ed. *Evangelical Dictionary of World Missions.* Grand Rapids, MI: Baker Books, 2000.

Neill, Stephen. *A History of Christian Missions.* New York: Penguin Books, 1964.

Robert, Dana L. *American Women in Mission: A Social History of Their Thought and Practice.* Macon, GA: Mercer University Press, 1997.

———. "Christianity in the Wider World." In *Christianity: A Social and Cultural History,* 2d edition, part VI, edited by H. Kee, et al. Upper Saddle River, NJ: Prentice Hall, 1998.

Walls, Andrew. *The Missionary Movement in Christian History.* Maryknoll, NY: Orbis, 1996.

Yates, Timothy. *Christian Mission in the Twentieth Century.* Cambridge: Cambridge University Press, 1994.

DANA L. ROBERT

MISSIONS, BRITISH

From the late eighteenth century, British foreign MIS-SIONS generated wide-ranging Christian proselytizing and institution building throughout the world, but focused in AFRICA, Asia, and Oceania. Supported in Great Britain by extensive public contribution of funds and drawing significantly on WOMEN's support, British foreign missions, predominantly evangelical in inspiration, grew rapidly from the 1830s, peaking in worldwide reach and domestic social power by the end of the century. Until superseded by American missionary activity in the twentieth century, British missions led the modern Protestant missionary expansion, contributing at the turn of the twentieth century some 10,000 Protestant missionaries, or about 60 percent of the European and North American total, and some £1.5 million annually (US $8 million), or about 50 percent of funding expended to support all Protestant foreign missions (see MISSIONARY ORGANIZATIONS). British missions operated at the forefront of the vigorous nineteenth-century missionary movement that transformed Christianity into a global religion.

Growth in British foreign missions was linked to the eighteenth-century rise of EVANGELICALISM, but was also significantly shaped and driven by Britain's emergence as an industrial and imperial society with power and influence that extended far beyond the bounds of the formal British Empire (see COLONIALISM). The transnational, and particularly transatlantic, nature of Evangelicalism generated an ambitious cooperative vision in British missions that extended EVANGELISM and church building beyond the nation and the empire in a broadly unified cultural vision. Yet by the 1840s growing evangelical missionary success inspired denominational competition between churches both in Britain and the colonies, and emulation in nonevangelical British religious traditions, particularly High Church ANGLICANISM. As a socially diverse set of Nonconformist churches challenged the political and social privileges of the national church—the CHURCH OF ENGLAND—missionary enthusiasm was further stirred by waves of revivalism from the 1840s to the 1890s (see REVIVALS) and the complex dynamics of denominational and theological competition and controversy between Evangelicalism and ANGLO-CATHOLICISM as well as Anglicanism and NONCONFORMITY.

Operating in an emerging age of modern voluntary religious associational life, British missions balanced between the ECUMENISM encouraged by common evangelical reformist assumptions and the competitive SECTARIANISM characteristic of the Anglo-American religious world. Throughout the nineteenth century British foreign missions were consistently associated with largely evangelical humanitarian projects for social reform, most notably the abolition of SLAVERY (see SLAVERY, ABOLITION OF). The commercial and industrial societies of northern Europe and the Atlantic world, where growing national identities emphasized the legal rights of free citizens and free labor, reinforced the evangelical culture of independency and social reform through spiritual regeneration. In this wider culture of religious reformism, British missions were responsible over the nineteenth century for a significant channeling overseas of the British charitable impulse.

From the 1870s British missions experienced a second wave of growth, fueled by the emergence of "the new imperialism," continuing evangelical revivalism, new High Church Anglican missions inspired by the OXFORD MOVEMENT and emerging Anglo-Catholicism, and an increase in missions to women and by female missionaries. By the early twentieth century, however, British missions faced new challenges from emerging colonial NATIONALISMS abroad and changing conceptions of empire and imperial engagement at home. British foreign missions, although arguably at their most influential overseas in the early decades of the twentieth century, began to lose social power and support at home in the face of the SECULARIZATION of British society and emerging crises of war and nation, brought on first by the South African War (1899–1902) and later by World War I (1914–1918). Decolonization in the mission field and the rise of autonomous indigenous churches changed the focus of British missions in the twentieth century from proselytizing and European trusteeship designed to build "Christianity and civilization" abroad to an emphasis on partnership and development in areas of historic British missionary concentration—INDIA, AFRICA, Oceania, and CHINA.

Throughout the nineteenth century, British missionaries and mission theorists debated philosophy and method, including the nature and organization of indigenous churches, the connection between Christianity and Western culture, and questions of race, particularly as they related to indigenous leadership and self-governance. Missionaries also disagreed over whether primacy should be given to proselytizing and itinerancy or to EDUCATION and church and institution building. Generally speaking, British foreign missions shared with most Protestant missions a broad ENLIGHTENMENT outlook that emphasized human rationality, humanitarian action, and faith in the ability of human societies to progressively improve themselves through individual initiative. They were also conditioned, however, by Western imperialism and particularly by their extensive operation within, and varied responses to, the British Empire. Despite often being vehicles for

Western, paternalist, and racial biases, missions also transmitted the fundamentally egalitarian principle of the equality of human souls, which indigenous Christians often generalized to the creation of independent churches and anticolonial initiatives.

The first attempts to construct missionary histories were colored by Victorian biases: beginning in the 1840s and carried through to the 1950s, a celebratory tradition tended to hagiography and exhaustive accounts of British-based missionary agencies that emphasized the heroic efforts of selfless religious men to bring relief and regeneration to "heathen" societies in the grips of degenerate social and belief systems. From the 1960s new studies have redefined our understanding of British missions. Decolonization, economic and social approaches to history, and postmodernism (see POST-MODERNITY) have generated more critical approaches that investigate the "cultural imperialism" of missions and that bring the local experience of missions and indigenous voices to the fore. Study of British missions has increasingly detailed the relationship of imperial power to missionary activity, yet also has sought to explain a worldwide range of individual missions in terms of their unique denominational circumstances, religious motivations, gendered projects, and social, political, and personal alliances. Indigenous responses to what was in effect a highly diverse international proselytizing effort have also drawn attention. Indigenous cultures, languages, and social and ethnic identities differed enormously, generating a wide variety of outcomes in a missionary encounter where European aims toward CONVERSION, education, and institution building—themselves interacting either in concert or opposition to imperial or local governance—were often subverted by local interests, both colonial and indigenous. Thus, despite the frequent complicity of missionaries with imperialism, it becomes difficult to construct any clear and meaningful characterization of a generic "missionary imperialism," for religious dynamics and uses proved fluid and unpredictable across the diversity of denomination and locality in a worldwide "mission field" where rapidly changing cultural and political circumstances meant missionaries and the communities they initiated could not be uniformly co-opted to imperial purposes. Thus, generalizations that hold for one mission field often do not hold, in theory or in practice, in others.

Origins

Before the 1790s British missions were sporadic and limited to areas of direct imperial engagement in North America and India. When compared to extensive Roman Catholic missions associated with the sixteenth-century Spanish and Portuguese Empires, the British came late to missionary activity. Until the eighteenth century, with the extension of the British Empire, the emergence of an evangelical theology emphasizing engagement with the world, and the growth of voluntary religious associations supporting reform and CHARITY, Britain lacked the political, theological, and organizational foundations for vigorous missionary activity. Crown-sponsored colonial expansion movements to revive Anglican piety inspired the earliest organized British attempts to advance Christianity overseas: in 1699 and 1701, respectively, the Anglican SOCIETY FOR PROMOTING CHRISTIAN KNOWL-EDGE (SPCK) and the SOCIETY FOR THE PROPAGATION OF THE GOSPEL (SPG) were created under crown charters, supplemented by the creation of the Scottish SPCK in 1710. Although theoretically committed to propagating Christianity throughout the world, the SPCK and the SPG, until the nineteenth century, devoted their attention almost exclusively to providing Anglican colonial CLERGY in settlements in North America and British garrisons throughout the Empire.

The extensive British missions of the nineteenth century had their origin and impetus in the Evangelical Revival of the eighteenth century. Drawing on German pietistic strains (see PIETISM), such as the community of the Moravian Brethren, emphasizing a theology of personal religion and responsibility, the evangelical revivalism of the Methodist movement led by JOHN and CHARLES WESLEY popularized an ATONE-MENT-based Arminian theology with an emphasis on activism, PREACHING, and conversion (see ARMINIAN-ISM). Over the course of the eighteenth century Evangelicalism shifted many Anglicans away from sacramentalism and many nonconformists away from rationalistic CALVINISM to a vision of social transformation achieved through individual conversion. With its strong military metaphors of fighting idolatry and formalism, emerging evangelicalism had a universalistic social agenda at home of reforming aristocratic immorality and lower-class "depravity" that also fueled a growing movement to abolish slavery from the 1780s.

British evangelical thinking and organization to support foreign missions first emerged in the 1780s and was tied intimately to abolitionism and a growing insistence on the responsibility of the LAITY to actively engage the world. Some historians, in accounting for the emergence of the British missionary movement at this time, emphasize transformations in theology as the single most important causal element. New theological formulations such as the Baptist Andrew Fuller's *The Gospel Worthy of All Acceptation* (1785) argued, following JONATHAN EDWARDS's moderate Calvinism, that human responsibility provided a channel through which God's sovereignty could spread Christianity. This approach was developed by the famous Baptist missionary to India, WILLIAM CAREY, who with the publication of *An Enquiry into the Obligations of Christians to Use Means for the Conversion of the Heathens* (1792), became the most influential theorist of the Anglo-American missionary movement. Here Carey emphasized the necessity of voluntarism to secure mass lay and clerical support and insisted that missions should advance "the spread of civil and religious liberty," reinforcing the calls of other advocates of missions, such as the Wesleyan Dr. THOMAS COKE and Anglicans associated with the East India Company like Charles Grant.

Missionary appeals led to the founding of missionary societies in the 1790s. The Baptists, led by Carey, formed the Baptist Missionary Society (BMS) in 1792; interdenominational evangelicals, led by Congregationalists, formed the London Missionary Society (LMS) in 1795; and Evangelical Anglicans, led by CHARLES SIMEON and John Venn, a leader of the influential CLAPHAM SECT, formed the CHURCH MISSIONARY SOCIETY (CMS) in 1799. The Wesleyan Methodist Missionary Society, formed in 1818, organized Coke's missions of the 1780s under a national organization. Similarly, Scottish societies rapidly sprang up (Glasgow and Scottish Missionary Societies in 1796), whereas many local Scottish associations sent contributions to a Congregationalist LMS, also extensively supported in WALES and Ulster. The parallel founding in the 1790s in North America of local committees to evangelize indigenous populations, followed by their organization under the AMERICAN BOARD OF COMMISSIONERS FOR FOREIGN MISSION (ABCFM) and the establishment of several American denominational societies, demonstrated the interconnectedness of Anglo-American religious culture. The General Assembly of the CHURCH OF SCOTLAND, fearing the possible association of overseas missionary supporters with political radicalism, only organized to support missions in 1824 and saw this effort split with the secession of the Free Church of Scotland (see FREE CHURCH) in 1843. Over the course of the nineteenth century virtually every British denomination, from Presbyterians and Quakers (see FRIENDS, SOCIETY OF) to Primitive Methodists and Strict Baptists, established independent missionary societies that were generally willing to accept state aid, but not state control.

Although religious determinants are central to explaining the origins of the British missionary movement, many historians suggest that other crucial, if not paramount, factors connected to British exploration and imperial expansion underpin the missionary movement. British missionary expansion began at the end of a century in which European knowledge of the world expanded enormously, from the founding of the Indian Empire in Bengal in the 1750s and the rise of "orientalist" scholarship to the exploratory Pacific voyages of Captain James Cook beginning in the 1760s. These developments focused attention on India and the South Seas as two of the earliest British missionary fields. Additionally, Parliamentary debates over the right conduct of the British Empire in the 1770s and 1780s, influenced by the rebellion in the American colonies, featured arguments advancing the moral exercise of imperial power for the benefit of indigenous populations. Debates over slavery emphasized parallel themes, drawing, in particular, evangelical Anglicans led by WILLIAM WILBERFORCE into advocacy for the application of Christian influence to British overseas power. The age that saw the rapid INDUSTRIALIZATION of Britain also experienced an attendant rise in an independent middle class determined to redefine British society at home and abroad. Growth in support of overseas missionary projects was further reinforced by conservative reactions to the FRENCH REVOLUTION in the 1790s, which helped direct evangelical reformism overseas, away from suspect work among potentially radical lower-class domestic populations. Both a general British Christian sense that expanding "atheistical" French influence in the age of Napoleon must be opposed and a growing millennialism in an age of extended warfare fueled the evangelical missionary impulse (see MILLENARIANS AND MILLENNIALISM). Thus, by the early nineteenth century, missionary enterprise became one of several forces to ideologically support and condition imperial power and expansion.

The First Wave: British Missionary Development to 1870

From their foundations until the 1830s, British missions received lackluster support. Evangelical supporters of missions, Nonconformist and Anglican alike, faced opposition from High Church Anglicans and critics like Sydney Smith, whose 1808 *Edinburgh Review* article labeling missionaries "little detachments of maniacs" reflected more general conservative suspicions that mission supporters were tainted by association with radicalism and thus represented a danger to political and social order, both at home and abroad. General evangelical successes of the age, such as the creation of the Crown Colony SIERRA LEONE in 1806 as a settlement of ex-British slaves, the 1807 abolition of the slave trade, and the insertion of pro-missionary clauses in the renewed East India Company charter in 1813, must be balanced against suspicion in government circles where officials, although supporting Anglican ecclesiastical expansion when it supported colonial authority, shrank from the "enthusiasm" of evangelical culture. Nevertheless, the general observation by British officials of neutrality toward religion, at home and abroad, ensured general freedom of development to missions and emerging Christian communities of all denominations.

Early missions were also troubled by difficulty recruiting missionaries. The Anglican CMS, for example, resorted to German missionary recruits, most famously Johann Ludwig Krapf, sent to Ethiopia in 1837. Like nonconformist societies, the CMS relied heavily on artisinal and lower middle-class recruits because the more "gentlemanly" regular CLERGY were unwilling to volunteer for missionary service. Furthermore, early difficulties establishing control over missionaries in the field led to controversies raised by commercial trading or missionary liaisons with local women. From the 1820s increased bureaucratic control over missions addressed these problems, including stricter vetting and training standards for recruits (mirroring training for home ordination) and general acceptance of the principle that missions would support themselves primarily through voluntary contributions, resisting direct involvement in local or colonial commerce.

In the decade of the 1830s foreign missions grew rapidly, boosted by antislavery agitation, particularly controversies surrounding Nonconformist missions to West Indian slaves. The 1834 achievement of the abolition of slavery in the British West Indies was tied to currents of middle-class political reform that had brought democratic extension of the franchise in the Reform Bill of 1832. Progressive humanitarian optimism was further forwarded by the campaigns of Wilberforce's successor, Thomas Fowel Buxton, to create a government-sponsored humanitarian development expedition to the Niger River. Missionaries were central to this plan to regenerate a West Africa despoiled by "illegitimate" slave trading with legitimate commerce in cotton and other agricultural goods produced by independent Africans. As public debate increased over these issues, missionary support grew, buttressed by the return to Britain in the late 1830s of well-known missionaries, notably ROBERT MOFFAT of SOUTH AFRICA and John William of the South Seas, who, martyred in 1839, was subsequently constructed as one of the first great iconic missionary "heroes."

In several spheres missionaries now emerged as participants in debates over "native rights" against planter, settler, and trader interests, as in the West Indies, West and South Africa, and the Pacific Islands. Missionaries offered a range of solutions to the problem of native rights, but all involved advancing legal protections that would, reinforced by free labor and Christian literacy, encourage Westernized, self-sufficient, indigenous settlements. Characteristically the plans of Nonconformists to transform slave communities in the West Indies were strongly gendered, dependent on the creation of Westernized patriarchal families and villages as the necessary basis for economic development, settled residence, and respectable pious community. Crucial to support for projects of this nature were the "domestic" concerns of British female supporters in education, childcare, and domestic economy outside of the home and nation. By the 1840s the dominant "modernization" strategy of British missions had emerged, founded in education and training, relying on the building of churches, schools, hospitals, and printing houses and based in a reflexive assumption of the superiority of Western culture and European economic, social, and political organization taken as standards of "civilization."

Most missionaries accepted the general idea of the British Empire as a providential force for good, although many remained willing to criticize imperial authorities and brave ill will in Britain when larger humanitarian interests were compromised. This is evident in the highly public careers in the 1830s and 1840s of Nonconformists like William Knibb in the West Indies and JOHN PHILIP in South Africa, who championed their particular vision of indigenous interests when white planter, settler, black Christian, and tribal interests clashed. British missionaries took the advancement of the gospel as their principal goal, and collaboration with imperial and colonial governments varied significantly in different mission fields depending on whether cooperation seemed to help or hinder central proselytizing and humanitarian goals. In the 1830s and 1840s public and Christian attention was focused on areas of imperial friction in the CARIBBEAN, Africa, India, and China, particular interest growing in the large populations and sophisticated ancient cultures of Asia. In India the "age of reform" under the influence of evangelical Anglican administrators and missionaries, Hindu reformers like Rammohan Roy, and Utilitarian East India Company officials led to the abolition of Hindu ritual practices like *sati* (ritual self-immolation by widows) and female infanticide, and also ushered in the opening of India to missionaries without license in 1833. In China, although missionary agencies unequivocally opposed the destructive opium trade, they nevertheless welcomed the "providential" opening of China to missions established by the "free trade" imposed after the Anglo-Chinese (opium) Wars (1839–1842; 1856–1860). Whereas in both India and China the major British and American societies rapidly founded mission stations, Christian converts remained a minuscule proportion of large Hindu, Islamic, Buddhist, and ethnoreligious populations. Missionaries instead had their largest impact in catalyzing indigenous religious traditions to renewal and reform movements, such as the Brahmo Samaj and Arya Samaj movements in India.

Translation of the BIBLE into native vernaculars, supported by Bible and tract societies like the BRITISH AND FOREIGN BIBLE SOCIETY (1804), remained a mainstay of missionary practice from the time of "pioneer" missions in Africa, the South Seas, and India (see BIBLE SOCIETIES). Emphasis on literacy and preaching had powerful long-term effects including the foundation of thousands of schools and dozens of colleges and the transformation of previously oral languages, particularly in Africa and the South Seas, into written forms. Missionary schools also provided increasingly coveted educational opportunities for indigenous groups to advance their interests in a rapidly transforming colonial world. Education became a favored strategy from the 1840s as hoped-for mass conversions upon the proclamation of the gospel failed to materialize. English education supported colonial administration, but also provided a *lingua franca* in areas of diverse indigenous cultures, most notably exemplified in India, where higher education designed for upper-caste Indians was pioneered as a settled mission strategy in Scottish missions under the leadership of Alexander Duff. Educational strategies, dovetailing in particular with assumptions underlying Indian imperial governance, forwarded a broader approach of "leavening" foreign cultures with Western and Christian ideas. Yet, in general, missionary theorists did not foresee perpetual British control of missions, rather in the 1850s leaders like Henry Venn at the CMS and RUFUS ANDERSON at the ABCFM argued for the goal of "self-supporting, self-governing, self-extending" indigenous churches. Thus, the strong cultural biases of much missionary practice were tempered by visions of independence for slowly emerging indigenous Christian communities.

Institutional strategies, such as educational work, were expensive and required that missions develop into nationally extensive and powerful charities. By the 1840s evangelical missionary societies, demonstrating the health and vigor of their denominations, innovated new forms of domestic support: national public meetings (most famously held in Exeter Hall, London), local missionary unions and work parties, missionary fairs, pageants, and exhibitions, door-to-door collections (often by children), extended church-to-church deputation lecturing tours by paid fund-raising agents and returned missionaries, and extensive mass publication of periodicals and books disseminated in Britain by the millions through a national network of local parish and chapel associations. High Church Anglicans, shaken by political and church reforms of the 1820s and 1830s, were inevitably drawn into Victorian voluntaristic religion as the SPG, in competition both with Nonconformists and evangelical Anglicans, abandoned state aid in the 1830s to rely entirely on voluntary support. By 1860 the largest of the British missionary societies, the CMS, was collecting approximately £250,000 per year (about a quarter of the British total) and had sent out 423 missionaries in sixty years. Foreign missions had grown to be the third largest Christian charitable cause in Britain, falling only behind church building and education in fund-raising success.

The growing work and its financial needs inevitably shaped the message the societies transmitted in Britain, with audiences responding to tales of savagery and ignorance, reinforced by the widespread missionary representation of non-Europeans as good-hearted but ignorant children in need of education and paternalistic guidance. Domestic presentations of foreign fields often emphasized both the destructive effects of western trade and settlement and the violence, superstition, and ignorance purportedly bred of "heathen" religions. Missionaries invariably argued for the desperate need of non-Christians for European religion and tutelage. In this way missionary societies rapidly became the most widely influential representation of foreign cultures and imperial conditions throughout the British Isles.

The support for missions and recruitment of missionaries crossed class lines, but missionary recruitment was strongest among the "respectable" mechanic classes—artisans, tradesmen, and clerks (often firmly undenominational in outlook)—whereas financial and political support relied on the urban manufacturers and professionals making up the middle classes (often firmly denominational in identity). Educated middle-class men provided the bulk of leadership, especially in Britain, although the societies depended heavily on activist women both as organizers and financial supporters who often marshaled the charity of children, operating through the channels of the SUNDAY SCHOOL movement.

The rapid growth of British missions peaked in the early 1840s but could not be sustained in the face of the economic downturn of the "hungry forties" and a series of setbacks in several mission fields. Among these were the collapse of the Niger Expedition in 1842, the failure to establish successful communities of former slaves in the West Indies, and, despite enthusiastic expectations for success, the intensely antiforeign reaction of the Chinese to missionaries who entered the country under unequal treaties enforced by gunboat diplomacy. Isolated missionary triumphs—such as the return of the explorer and missionary DAVID LIVINGSTONE from Southern Africa in 1856, reemphasizing the message that "Christianity and commerce" could save Africa from the ravages of slavery, or the opening of the interior of China to missions in 1858—were counterbalanced by further troubling events such as the Indian rebellion in 1857 and the Jamaican Morant Bay rebellion in 1865. Colonial rebellions led to negative attitudes in government, literary, and anthropological circles regarding the potential of "subject races" to achieve "civilization." Although missions continued to operate in India, Africa, the South Seas, and elsewhere, missionary enthusiasm, always most vigorously advanced by a minority of British Christians, waned through the 1860s.

The Second Wave: British Missions 1870 to 1914

From the 1870s British missions entered a "new era" of expansion, coinciding with the "new imperialism" of the late century, which peaked in the 1890s. From a modest number of ten denominational societies in 1840, new missionary societies proliferated, numbering over fifty by 1890. The emergence of interdenominational, evangelical "faith missions" and of Anglo-Catholic missions both contributed to the growth of new societies and set a continuing trend toward smaller size and diversity in missionary agencies. New patterns of missionary practice also came to challenge and supplement the prevailing strategy of evangelical missionary modernization of earlier decades. Both Anglo-Catholic and faith missions fed on the rapid rise of lay involvement, most notably that of women and university students. Some new missions also challenged older practices that tied missions clearly to imperialism, Westernization, and assumptions of European cultural and racial superiority.

Late-Victorian missionary expansion was inaugurated by a number of high profile missionary "martyrdoms," including in 1871 the death of Anglican bishop J. C. Patteson in Melanesia and in 1873 the death of Livingstone in the African interior. Livingstone's 1856 visit to England had inspired the founding of the first independent Anglo-Catholic mission, the Universities Mission to Central Africa (UMCA) in 1859. Anglo-Catholic missions, which operated under episcopal leadership, grew in number, to include the Oxford Mission to Calcutta, the Cambridge Mission to Delhi, and missionary efforts in overseas dioceses from South Africa to Melanesia. The murder of the UMCA's first bishop, C. F. Mackenzie, on the Zambesi River in East Africa in 1862, generated a reaction in Anglo-Catholic missions against both commerce

and the transmission of "civilization" as missionary ideals. Developing a strategy that sought to retain only the essentials of the Christian faith while building indigenized mission communities around Christian families and the church, High Church missions of this sort drew on a romantic medievalism, which made them more sympathetic to "primitive" forms of culture.

Evangelical missions saw similar developments. More widely influential than the Anglo-Catholic pattern, faith missions grew with the spread of the revivals of the Second Evangelical Revival, influenced from the late 1850s by American revivalists like D. L. MOODY and IRA SANKEY, who cultivated an impatient desire for large-scale, instantaneous Christian conversion. The CHINA INLAND MISSION (CIM), founded in 1865 by JAMES HUDSON TAYLOR, was the first faith mission, growing by 1899, with over 800 missionaries, to rival the largest denominational societies. Faith missions proliferated in the 1880s by drawing on charismatic evangelicals across denominations and sending out, without assured financial support, all willing missionary candidates, female or male. Emphasizing itinerant preaching and adoption of indigenous dress and language, faith missions flooded missionary fields with enthusiasts, an example followed by other revivalistic agencies, like the SALVATION ARMY, which from the 1880s sent often lower class, lay missionaries overseas in enormous numbers. Anglican circles were drawn into the movement through the annual KESWICK CONFERENCES from 1875, which provided a more "respectable" expression of revivalistic religious enthusiasm. Because the "holiness" theology that characterized these movements emphasized SANCTIFICATION beyond conversion that could elevate the consecrated above the sinful world, this "higher life" culture embraced missionary work as an ultimate act of sanctification (see HOLINESS MOVEMENT; HIGHER LIFE MOVEMENT). This orientation was further reinforced in the movement by premillenialist convictions that impending divine judgment required immediate evangelistic action.

Victorian revivalism invigorated British missions in the 1880s, but also unleashed criticisms that denominational missions had become too worldly and bureaucratic, charges that were reinforced by secular critics who attacked poor records of conversion in many established missions. Notably, holiness-inspired missionaries not only often criticized traditional institutional strategies as dry and unspiritual (in favor of direct proselytizing for immediate conversion) but also criticized Western cultural elements such as European dress and Westernization strategies such as HIGHER EDUCATION), support of trade, and insistence on settled agriculture. Nevertheless, certain denominational societies, particularly the CMS, were able to harness the new enthusiasms, seeing significant growth in recruits and funds. In particular support grew in the British universities, especially Cambridge (see CAMBRIDGE UNIVERSITY). The resulting wave of university-educated, middle- and upper-class missionaries significantly influenced late-Victorian missions through the Student Volunteer Missionary Union (SVMU, a wing of the Student Volunteer Movement) and the YOUNG MEN'S and YOUNG WOMEN'S CHRISTIAN ASSOCIATIONS (YMCA/YWCA).

By the 1890s a growing international Christian student movement, born of charismatic Evangelicalism but increasingly influenced by ECUMENISM, focused on creating a unified and "scientific" missionary project from Anglo-American Protestant foundations. As British missionary enthusiasm peaked, international student leadership emerged in the missionary movement. International missionary conferences dating from the 1860s, and growing through the 1880s, built a sense of momentum in foreign missions. Inspired by American student leaders like JOHN R. MOTT, the SVMU ambition to achieve its famous watchword, "the evangelization of the world in this generation," seemed realistic in the 1890s, given the expansion of missions in the previous decade.

The holiness movement significantly increased lay involvement and influence in missions, giving lay activists new sanction to move beyond traditional clerical leadership. This was most significant in the case of women, who, reacting to expanding female social roles in late-Victorian society were able to draw on religious justifications, both in holiness Evangelicalism and Anglo-Catholicism, to act on the inspiration of faith to embrace missionary careers, both at home, as in the DEACONESS movement, and abroad. From the 1880s single female missionaries, in particular, grew in numbers and influence, representing over one third of the missionaries supported in the field by the major British denominational societies by 1899. Married and unmarried women taken together made up over half of the British missionary force and provided the majority of funds and fund collectors at home. However, despite the emergence of female missionary heroic figures such as MARY SLESSOR, the contribution of women has been largely ignored in traditional accounts of missions.

Missions to women also grew in this era, particularly in India where, in the wake of the Indian rebellion of 1857, missionaries sought new strategies to influence an Indian society largely resistant to Christian proselytizing. The development of zenana (female home) visitations by female missionaries as a strategy designed to change Indian society at the level of the family justified women's public activity.

Throughout the mission fields similar strategies emerged. Social transformation through the evangelization of women and education for girls was bound up with efforts at social amelioration like medical missions, which paralleled developments in the late-Victorian domestic response to urban poverty. British women increasingly developed a sense of international responsibility for non-Western women and children in an age of rising imperialistic fervor, emphasizing a "maternalist" strategy for "civilizing" foreign cultures through the domestic transformation of women, families, manners, and morality. In missions British women often found considerable freedom to teach, preach, and engage in professionalizing social service.

British missions were forced ever more insistently in the late nineteenth century to confront or accommodate the rising tides of political, economic, cultural, and popular imperialism. In part, growing missionary interest among university men can be attributed to growing concepts of "muscular Christianity" advanced in the public schools and ideas of "England's mission" to the "younger races" articulated in university circles. The celebrated departure for the CIM in 1885 of the "Cambridge Seven," university athletes led by upper-class cricketer C. T. STUDD, reinforced growing university recruiting in holiness circles by the CIM and CMS through the 1890s. Missionary responses to the age of high imperialism, however, were neither uniform nor simple. Denominational societies, like the CMS, WMMS, and SPG in particular, showed themselves willing in many circumstances to cooperate with imperial authorities; however, other societies such as the UMCA and CIM found themselves, for varied reasons, in conflict with imperial culture and purposes.

In the age of the "new imperialism" many missionary societies leaned more heavily toward advocating British imperial expansion, such as the annexation of Fiji as a Crown Colony in 1875 at the urging of WMMS missionaries, the declaration of a British protectorate over southern Bechuanaland in 1884 at the urging of LMS missionaries like JOHN MACKENZIE, the creation of a Nyasaland (MALAWI) protectorate in 1889 at the urging of Scottish missionaries, and the declaration of a full protectorate over Uganda in 1894 at the urging of the CMS and its supporters. East and Central African missions in particular grew in the context of the European scramble for territory in Africa, fed on the reports of explorers like Henry Morton Stanley and the example of sacrificial missionary deaths like that of JOHN ALEXANDER MACKAY. Rivalry with the French and Germans as well as with Roman Catholics and Muslims helped to drive missions to vigorously pro-imperial stances. In some cases, such as that of the High Church missions under the direction of the SPG, a vigorous "missionary imperialism" was forwarded in the late 1890s that foresaw a close and direct integration of Church and Empire. Pro-imperial attitudes, however, could still be combined with criticisms of the destructive influence of colonists and settlers, the destructive effects of colonial trade and labor practices, and a questioning of particularly exploitative imperial practices.

Positive attitudes to the empire, or to imperial annexation and subsequent Westernization processes were widespread, but not universal. Whereas in many missions faith continued in commerce, properly directed, as a providential force supporting Christianity, debates over the value of Western commerce and civilization divided missionaries, leading some to question the legitimate goals of missionary cooperation with imperialism. Late in the century the Church of Scotland mission at Blantyre, Nyasaland (Malawi), for example, in contrast to the Free Church of Scotland mission 350 miles north at Livingstonia, resisted the commercial drive of Cecil Rhodes's British East Africa Company in favor of a British protectorate that would maintain the authority of indigenous chiefs. Despite the debates over the nature of imperial governance, however, more than any other missionary sending culture, British missions came to be suffused with pro-imperial attitudes. Enthusiasm tied to Westernization did, however, generate criticism from other national missionary cultures, particularly in German missions, where theorists like Gustav Warneck argued for an "internationalist" approach designed to temper the enthusiasms of eager Anglo-American students in favor of encouraging indigenous churches.

Rejection of Westernization or imperial collaboration as missionary strategies did not necessarily mean rejection, in theory or in practice, of the hardening "scientific" racism that characterized late Victorian Britain. From the beginning of British missions, as well as British antislavery agitation, evangelical insistence on the equality of souls had operated in dynamic tension with broader cultural assumptions of the superiority of Western culture and white Europeans. Racist assumptions and behavior, especially regarding the African "dark continent," remained widespread, and grew in the late-Victorian period. In the Niger mission in the 1880s, for example, holiness influenced CMS missionaries, in the name of doctrinal purity and discipline, undermined the Anglican church's first black bishop, SAMUEL CROWTHER. Western prejudices grew with improved imperial communications as missionaries more frequently traveled the steamship lines between Britain and the mission field. Although the majority of missionaries rejected the scientific racism of Victorian anthropology, thus rejecting the genetic

inferiority of non-Europeans, they still generally assumed indigenous cultures to be evil and inferior, often acting to eliminate indigenous "superstition" to allow the "child races" to attain civilization. As indigenous Christian congregations grew rapidly, especially in Africa and India, British missionaries often found themselves struggling with resentful converts to maintain European control.

The heyday of British missions in the 1890s ended rapidly, however, as the Chinese Boxer Rebellion of 1899, with its violent antiforeign sentiment, the difficult South African (Boer) War of 1899–1902, and increasing colonial nationalisms brought imperial anxiety and a dropping off in the growth of funds, recruits, and confidence. The student movement, with its increasing emphasis on professionalization, grew in influence, advancing the academic study of missions, or MISSIOLOGY, and advocating more sophisticated training of missionaries in the language and culture of receiving societies. Emphasizing the ecumenical potential in transnational evangelistic Christianity, and the social conscience of the emergent SOCIAL GOSPEL, student leaders increasingly embraced a "fulfillment" theology, which saw non-Christian religions as vehicles through which dialogue with Christianity would fulfill divine purposes in the evolution of faiths. Through the student movement, Christian MODERNISM with its questioning of the inerrancy of the Bible (see BIBLICAL INERRANCY), and LIBERAL PROTESTANTISM, both evangelical and otherwise, led some missionaries to question traditional proselytizing strategies. Perhaps most famous among these was CHARLES FEER ANDREWS, who left his educational mission in India to collaborate in the religious, social, and nationalist reforming of Indian leaders like Rabindranath Tagore and Mohandas K. Gandhi.

Missionary ecumenism led to religious amalgamation, such as the union of Congregationalists and Presbyterians in South India in 1908, and the influential WORLD MISSIONARY CONFERENCE in Edinburgh in 1910, which, although still dominated by European concerns, for the first time saw significant addresses from "native" clergy. Twentieth-century ecumenism, championed by JOSEPH H. OLDHAM through the Continuation Committee of the Conference, began as an effort to unify Protestant missions and advance ideals of humanitarian trusteeship in colonial and imperial policy. Through the student movement and the World Missionary Conference the evangelical missionary movement flowed into the foundation of ecumenical institutions in the twentieth century, such as the International Missionary Council in 1921 (chaired by Mott and Oldham) and ultimately the WORLD COUNCIL OF CHURCHES in 1937.

Despite the trends toward unity inherent in missionary ecumenism, neither faith-based missions nor Anglo-Catholicism could be comfortably reconciled to the ecumenical movement. Conservative Evangelicals, both inside and outside of the student movement, increasingly attacked liberal Protestantism as a betrayal of faith in the inerrant Bible and the transformative power of preaching and PRAYER; High Church Anglicans resisted efforts at ecumenical union as a congregational betrayal of apostolic church order. Vigorous conservative evangelical resistance to these trends, which developed into full-fledged FUNDAMENTALISM in the 1920s, rapidly opened persistent cleavages in British missions in the twentieth century.

British Missions since 1914: Indigenous Churches, Decolonization, and Mission

From the late nineteenth century an increasing number of mission stations spawned indigenous churches, raising the challenge both of transferring leadership and confronting colonial nationalisms that understandably interpreted missions as part of a rejected colonial complex. Indigenous Christians persistently faced clerical, cultural, and racial prejudice from missionaries who often insisted converts conform to European standards of behavior and education. One response, as in the West African missions of the CMS, where heavily Africanized missions and pastorates under African Christian leaders like Archdeacon DANDISON CROWTHER and JAMES JOHNSON resisted European missionary racism and control, was the founding of independent churches (see AFRICAN INSTITUTED CHURCHES). In Africa the so-called Ethiopian churches usually emerged as the result of schism with Western missionaries over leadership and the acceptability of African traditional practices such as polygamy, faith healing, and exorcism, producing a great diversity of Christian communities, most numerous in NIGERIA, the Congo, Kenya, and South Africa.

British missions now faced the dilemma of determining the relationship of Christianity to CULTURE—the question of which Western cultural forms were necessary to non-European expressions of Christianity. Although the majority of British missionaries, with notable exceptions, retained belief in the natural and appropriate association of Western cultural forms to the spread of Christianity and the progress of "civilization," indigenized forms of Christianity, especially in Africa rapidly emerged (see AFRICAN THEOLOGY). Similar processes resulted in independent, federated, and amalgamated churches emerging at different rates in different areas: in JAPAN in the 1870s and 1880s, in China in the 1920s and 1930s, and India in the 1940s. In addition, the churches in the so-called

white-settlement colonies, like CANADA and AUSTRALIA, developed their own independent missionary agencies, making the idea of "British missions" appear antiquated as British denominations, Anglicanism in particular, became world communions increasingly distanced from British leadership and control.

The challenge of facing colonial independence movements was exacerbated by World War I, which seriously strained European resources and confidence in the superiority of Western civilization and morality while throwing local churches more fully on their own resources. In the postwar period, the divide between liberal developmental ecumenism and conservative faith-based evangelism also widened. By 1930 previously high levels of evangelical unity had been shattered. Overall, despite continuing loyalty from traditional constituencies, British domestic support for foreign missions in the opening decades of the twentieth century declined, missionary giving as a percentage of consumer spending decreasing after 1914. After 1929 economic depression and the rise of fascism in Europe undermined the foundations of Victorian progressive optimism, leading to absolute declines in income and recruits through the 1930s, despite the continuing resonance of popular imperialism in the interwar period. American leadership in world missions emerged rapidly, displacing British. At the same time indigenous independence movements expanded, reliant on a leadership often trained in mission schools, where Westernizing educational programs inevitably transmitted concepts of liberal, nationalist independency.

Particularly in the Indian fields the interwar era saw conflict between those missionaries who insisted on a conservative imperial vision of continuing "trusteeship" and control, and those who sympathized with progressive transformation to national independence. Missionaries were drawn into and divided by the conflicts of the era of decolonization. The ordination, for example, of V. S. AZARIAH (1874–1945) as the first South Asian Anglican bishop in 1912, a natural outgrowth of initiatives toward indigenous church leadership set by the YMCA, raised opposition from traditionalist missionaries focusing on higher caste conversion, particularly over Azariah's attempts to advance mass conversion from the lowest castes. In China problems arose more intractably, where missionary education and influence advanced rapidly during the era of pro-Western reforms after the Boxer Rebellion of 1899. Churches grew rapidly, Protestant Chinese membership rising to about 250,000 in 1915, whereas by 1925 some 8,000 Protestant missionaries, 50 percent American, flooded the country. Yet missionaries, protected since 1842 by unequal treaties, found themselves strongly implicated in left-leaning

Chinese circles as "cultural imperialists," and all were ultimately expelled by 1952 after Chinese Communist rule. Similar difficulties arose in Africa, with missionaries dividing in the 1920s over the morality of supporting the practice of forced labor, the activities of African nationalist political groups, and the wisdom of proscribing traditional African practices. British missions thus found themselves challenged in complicated ways by the politics of nationalism and decolonization and forced to decisions on issues that could and did set them at odds with nationalists. Notably, whereas many missionaries criticized more brutal forms of exploitational colonialism that betrayed traditional paternalist assumptions of missionary practice, virtually no missionaries—even J. H. Oldham, the most progressive ecumenist defender of humanitarian colonial "trusteeship" and critic of racism—believed Christianity, despite its core impulse to spiritual equality, was incompatible with colonialism.

After the Second World War decolonization resulted by 1970 in widespread national independence in South Asia, Asia, and Africa. The accustomed environment in which British missions had operated shifted irrevocably with the collapse of the British Empire, the growth of nationalist Islam, and the emergence of an anticolonial and antimissionary nationalist communism, especially in Asia. Additionally, British missions were diminished in political, social, monetary, and popular support in a Britain itself declining in adherence to Christianity. Postcolonial realities were perhaps most clearly acknowledged in the speeches and publications of Max Warren, former General Secretary of the CMS, and Anglican bishop STEPHEN CHARLES NEILL, who argued that missions need to shed cultural arrogance and racism and come to terms with their colonial past (see POST-COLONIALISM). The emergence of postcolonial political turbulence, however, particularly in Africa, meant missions, churches, and often authoritarian nationalist governments clashed. Nationalist and Marxist indictments of Christianity as an alien colonial imposition became common in the 1970s, especially in formerly Portuguese Africa and in South Africa where the apartheid regime attracted criticism and resistance.

Nationalist and indigenous Christian responses to the perceived ongoing "cultural imperialism" of Western theology led to calls for a moratorium on Western mission, which in Britain reinforced a postcolonial reorientation of missionary strategy. Although many British missions remain oriented to faith-based gospel proselytizing, traditional denominational societies, themselves retrenching, amalgamating, and renaming since the 1960s, have increasingly embraced a vision of "partnership" with churches traditionally associated with their missions. British and British-influenced missions (such as those based in Canada and Australia) are more strongly characterized by mission "partnership" than are American missions, which, drawing more heavily on conservative evangelical support, retain a greater emphasis on charismatic evangelism. Late twentieth-century British missions have expanded, under the impetus of charismatic renewal movements, from about 7,500 missionaries in the 1970s to almost 19,000 in the year 2000, yet remain dwarfed by American missions, fielding nearly 120,000 missionaries at the turn of the century. As with all modern Protestant missions in the final decades of the twentieth century, British missions have been increasingly drawn into worldwide missionary fellowships and international charitable aid activities, but have also seen the persistence in the number of small, independent missionary agencies under the influence of charismatic evangelical growth.

Since the end of World War II, Britain and Western Europe have seen a significant decline in Christian belief and activity. The diminishing support for British missions in the postwar period is undoubtedly linked to waning religious practice in Britain, the passing of the British Empire, and the adoption of many of the missionary movement's social relief efforts by international nonprofit humanitarian charitable relief agencies, the twentieth-century heirs to many of the currents of nineteenth-century humanitarian missionary interest. This decline, however, is also linked to the growing vitality of the churches that have emerged out of historic British missions, which now exist in communion with British congregations, or as part of the growing stream of late twentieth-century postdenominational Christianity (see THEOLOGY, TWENTIETH-CENTURY, GLOBAL). British missions, then, have played a significant, if at times ambiguous, role in the transformation of Protestant Christianity from a largely European faith to a diverse part of a world Christianity embraced by close to two billion adherents at the turn of the twenty-first century.

References and Further Reading

Bickers, Robert A., and Rosemary Seton. *Missionary Encounters. Sources and Issues.* Richmond, Surrey, UK: Curzon Press, 1996.

Bowie, Fiona, Deborah Kirkwood and Shirley Ardener, eds., *Women and Missions: Past and Present. Anthropological and Historical Perceptions.* Providence, RI and Oxford: Berg, 1993.

Comaroff, Jean, and John Comaroff. *Of Revelation and Revolution. Christianity, Colonialism, and Consciousness.* Vol. 1. Chicago & London: University of Chicago Press, 1991.

Cox, Jeffrey. "The Missionary Movement." In *Nineteenth-Century English Religious Traditions. Retrospect and Prospect,* edited by D.G. Paz. Westport, CT: Greenwood Press, 1995.

Huber, Mary Taylor, and Nancy C. Lutkehaus, eds. *Gendered Missions: Women and Men in Missionary Discourse and Practice*. Ann Arbor: University of Michigan Press, 1999.

Maughan, Steven. "Civic Culture, Women's Foreign Missions, and the British Imperial Imagination, 1860–1914." In *Paradoxes of Civil Society. New Perspectives on Modern German and British History*, edited by Frank Trentmann. New York: Berghahn, 2000.

Neill, Stephen, *A History of Christian Missions*, rev. ed., ed. O. Chadwick. Harmondsworth, Middlesex, UK: Penguin Books, 1986.

O'Connor, Daniel, ed., *Three Centuries of Mission. The United Society for the Propagation of the Gospel, 1701–2000*. London and New York: Continuum, 2000.

Porter, Andrew. "Religion and Empire: British Expansion in the Long Nineteenth Century, 1780–1914," *Journal of Imperial and Commonwealth History* 20, no. 3 (Sept. 1992): 370–390.

Stanley, Brian. *The Bible and the Flag. Protestant Missions and British Imperialism in the Nineteenth and Twentieth Centuries*. Leicester, UK: Apollos, 1990.

———. *The History of the Baptist Missionary Society, 1792–1992*. Edinburgh: T & T Clark, 1992.

Thorne, Susan. *Congregational Missions and the Making of an Imperial Culture in Nineteenth-Century England*. Stanford, CA: Stanford University Press, 1999.

Ward Kevin and Brian Stanley, eds., *The Church Mission Society and World Christianity, 1799–1999*. Grand Rapids, MI: Eerdmans, 2000.

Walls, Andrew F. *The Missionary Movement in Christian History. Studies in the Transmission of Faith*. Edinburgh: T&T Clark, 1996.

Yates, Timothy. *Christian Mission in the Twentieth Century*, Cambridge: Cambridge University Press, 1994.

STEVEN S. MAUGHAN

MISSIONS, GERMANY

History of the German Missionary Societies

Missions were—at the outset—not significant features of the German Protestant churches. In fact, a statement written by the theological faculty of Wittenberg in 1651 can be considered a rejection of efforts of an explicit missionary character by the Lutheran orthodoxy. Nevertheless the congregational dimension had a missionary orientation from the very beginning.

No one personifies the contradiction between determination and objection to missions as evidently as Baron Justinian von Welz (1621–1668). The way that the imperial estates in Regensburg handled his plans to establish a missionary society speaks for itself. Welz, who was devoted to ascetic ideals, was convinced that God could also call laymen—besides the consistorial statutes—into mission. After his proposal encountered violent objections and refutations, Welz left for the Dutch colony of Surinam after he was ordained an apostle of the gentiles by Friedrich Breckling in Holland. His further fate in Surinam remains unknown.

After two hundred years of lack of involvement, interest in participation in mission arose in Germany. AUGUST HERMANN FRANCKE assigned two missionaries to the Danish King Frederick IV for his Indian subjects living in the Danish colony of Tranquebar in INDIA. These two missionaries, ZIEGENBALG (1682–1719) and PLÜTSCHAU (1675–1752), signalled the beginning of a continuous interest in missions in Germany. Ziegenbalg had five principles for his work: Because everybody should be able to read the gospel, EDUCATION was an unalterable requirement for the mission; therefore the BIBLE should be made available in the native language. For the sermon, complete knowledge of the thoughts and the religious and cultural traditions of the people was of fundamental importance. The missionary work aimed at a personal CONVERSION. Last, an Indian church with its own clergy should emerge as soon as possible. Subsequently the first Indian pastor, Aaron, was ordained in 1733. Ziegenbalg was succeeded by missionaries, whose work was of similar significance, for example C. F. Schwartz (1724–1798), whose diplomatic and political activities were supported by a close friendship to Haidar Ali, or Fabrizius (1711–1791), who was distinguished by his great translation work. As a result of rationalism, the mission in Tranquebar disappeared and was eventually continued by the Leipzig Mission Society.

At the same time as the Tranquebar-Mission started out, the Moravian Brethren of HERRNHUT (see MORAVIAN CHURCH), founded by NIKOLAUS LUDWIG VON ZINZENDORF, also began their missionary activities. At first the Moravian mission focused on the Danish West Indies (August 21, 1732, on St. Thomas, later also on St. Croix and St. Jan), then it continued in Greenland (May 20, 1733) and in Surinam (1738). The Moravian missionary Georg Schmidt began working with the Hottentots in SOUTH AFRICA in 1737; Rauch founded the mission to the North American Indian tribe of the Mohicans in 1740; Zeisberger went to the Iroquois in 1749 and after 1770 to the Delawares. Between 1801 and 1838 Moravian missionaries also worked with the Cherokee Indians. Additionally the Brethren missionaries established missions in Egypt, Persia (medical mission by Hocker), on Sri Lanka, the Gold Coast, the Nicobar Islands, and in India ("Brethren's Garden" near Tranquebar and Serampore in Bengal). Attempts to begin missionary activities among the Samojedes in RUSSIA and the Danish Lapps were unsuccessful. In the later years missions started on Jamaica (1754), Antigua (1756), Barbados (1765), St. Kitts (1777), Tobago (1790), and in Labrador (1751 and 1764).

The missionary THEOLOGY of Zinzendorf corresponded with his other theological thinking, which was radically Christocentric. For him the actual missionary was Jesus Christ, the missionaries were only his helpers. The recipients of his work were the despised people, to whom "nobody else would go" (black slaves, Inuit, American Indians, Hottentots) and who were the "predisposed first-born" by the Holy Spirit.

Both important missions of the eighteenth century laid the foundation of a rapidly increasing spectrum of German missionary efforts. On February 1, 1800, Johannes Jänicke (1748–1827) opened up a missionary institute in Berlin, which his son-in-law Rückert continued as Berlin Missionary Society (*Berliner Missionsgesellschaft*). One of the most famous representatives of this missionary society is Karl Gützlaff (1803–1851), missionary to CHINA and founder of the "Christian Union for the Promotion of the Gospel in China through Chinese."

In 1815 the Basel Missionary Society (*Baseler Missionsgesellschaft*), or BASEL MISSION, began its activities by establishing a missionary institute, which was at first directed by C. G. Blumhardt (1779–1838). The new missionary society was supported by many charitable unions throughout GERMANY. In 1821, missionaries of Basel took over its mission territory within the Swiss and German colonies along the Volga-River. The work in RUSSIA had to be suspended in 1835 because of a ukase of the Russian Czar. Nevertheless the Basel Society continued its pastoral presence in the Caucasus with its missions in Georgia up to the twentieth century.

The Basel Society was the first of a group of large missionary societies that deliberately refrained from emphasizing denominational differences and took precautions not to transfer them from Europe into their new congregations. Aside from the Basel Society, the Berlin Society, the Rhenish Mission Society (*Rheinische Missionsgesellschaft*), the North German Missionary Society of Bremen (*Norddeutsche Missionsgesellschaft*), and the Gossner Missionary Society (*Gossnersche Missionsgesellschaft*) belong to this group. In complement to the scientific education in the missionary institution in Basel, the pilgrim's mission of St. Chrischona was founded in 1840. Figures such as Samuel Gobat (1799–1879) and Ludwig Schneller (1820–1896) originated from this missionary society.

The reconsideration of the church and its confessions, which determine the appearance of the church, triggered a second wave of missionary societies. Some of them were founded by secession from a previous society. In 1836 the Dresden Missionary Union dissolved its ties to Basel, regarding itself from this time on as the mission of the Lutheran church (see LUTHERANISM). In 1848 the headquarters were transferred to Leipzig, and the name was changed to Evangelical Lutheran Mission Society of Leipzig (*Evangelisch-lutherische Mission zu Leipzig*). Hereafter the mission society considered itself also as successor of the Danish-Halle Mission in Tranquebar. After the fall of the Iron Curtain in 1989 the Leipzig Society tried to carry on its tradition and reactivated its work in regions, which were in the meantime in the care of the Leipzig Mission West, which eventually had become a part of the Evangelical Lutheran Mission in Lower-Saxony (*Evangelisch-lutherisches Missionswerk in Niedersachsen*).

The Evangelical Lutheran Mission, also known as the Hermannsburg Mission Society, was inaugurated in 1849 by Ludwig Harms (1808–1865). This missionary society was a branch of the Bremen Society. Because of an ecclesiastical schism the Mission of the Evangelical Lutheran Free Churches, also called Bleckmar Mission, separated eventually from the Hermannsburg Mission Society. Today the Hermannsburg Society is mainly connected with the Evangelical Lutheran Church of Hannover, whereas the Bleckmar Mission is tied to the *Selbstständige Evangelisch-lutherische Kirche*. The Neuendettelsau Mission Society regards itself also explicitly as part of the Lutheran church, as does the Evangelical Lutheran Missionary Society of Schleswig-Holstein, which was established by Jensen in Breklum in 1876.

Denominationalism led to the establishment of many missionary societies, but these groups were outnumbered by the missionary societies that were established as a result of the Neo-Pietism. The work of JAMES HUDSON TAYLOR and the CHINA INLAND MISSION of 1865 led to the founding of the Alliance Mission of Barmen in 1889, the Liebenzell Mission in 1892, and the Neukirchen Orphan's and Missionary Institute (*Waisen- und Missionsanstalt Neukirchen*) in 1878. In addition, the number of missionary societies focusing on special assignments increased noticeably.

Even before the colonial age, however, German missionary societies could be found on every continent on Earth. The Basel Society worked in West Africa (between 1827 and 1831 in LIBERIA, between 1828 and 1883 on the Gold Coast), and the Bremen Society (between 1847 and 1884) was active on the Slave Coast. SOUTH AFRICA was the location of the Moravian Mission (Cape Colony, Kaffraria), the Rhenish Society (Cape Colony, Namibia among the Namaquas and the Hereros), the Berlin Society (Cape Colony among the Korannas, Kaffraria, Natal, and Transvaal), and the Hermannsburg Society (Natal, Transvaal, and among the Zulu and the Bechuanas). In India the Basel Society worked on the east coast (between 1834 and 1885), the Leipzig Society in Tamil Nadu, the Hermannsburg Society among the Telugus mainly in Andra Pradesh, the Breklum Society in Jeypur, the Gossner Society along the Ganges and among the

Kols, and the Moravian Mission in Himalaya. Missionaries of the Gossner Society were also active in INDONESIA, the ones of the Rhenish Society also worked on Borneo, on Sumatra among the Batak (Nommensen), and on Nias. After the failure of Gützlaff, the Basel Society, the Rhenish Society, and the Berlin Society remained in China. America was mostly the work of the Brethren missionaries, but the Hermannsburg Society soon started to send missionaries as pastors for the German immigrants to North and South America. In AUSTRALIA the large German missionary societies (Gossner Society, Leipzig Society, Moravian Mission, Hermannsburg Society, Neuendettelsau Society) all established stations. Missionaries were sent out to NEW ZEALAND by the Bremen Society, the Hermannsburg Society, and the Gossner Society, which was additionally operating in New Guinea.

In the second half of the nineteenth century the Near and Middle East also became a domain of the German societies. In 1852 the Berlin preacher Friedrich A. Strauss (1817–1888) and the former mission inspector to the Basel Society Christoph Hoffmann (1815–1885) founded the Jerusalem Union to support Gobat's missionary activities in Jerusalem. Previously, in 1846, Christian Friedrich Spittler (1782–1867) and the St. Chrischona Mission, named after a village near Basel, Switzerland where, since 1840, missionaries were trained, established a "brethren's home," which Gobat took over in 1854 as a preschool of the Abyssinian Mission. In 1854 the Kaiserswerth Institutes started working in Palestine, at first in the German hospital and in the Girl's Institute "Talitha Kumi," after the massacre among the Christians in the Lebanon in 1860, also in Beirut (girl's orphanage), and later in Smyrna. Keffenbrink-Ascheraden founded a leper asylum called "Jesus Aid," which was continued by the Brethren in 1881. The Pilgrim's Mission undertook a mission to Ethiopia by proposing a pilgrim's route called "apostle route," which would connect Jerusalem and Gondar over twelve stations. After 1875 the Hermannsburg Society operated in the Urmia region in the northwest of Persia but limited the efforts to spreading the gospel among the so-called Nestorians (Assyrians).

The beginning of the colonial age led to the establishment of many more missionary societies in Germany. Liberal theologians recognized mission as a Christian duty (see LIBERAL PROTESTANTISM AND LIBERALISM). The society that represented the liberal interests best was the General Protestant Missionary Society (*Allgemeiner Protestantischer Missionsverein*), inaugurated in 1884. All large missionary societies began working in the German colonies. In Togo the Bremen Society was active; in Cameroon the

Basel Society as well as the Baptist Missionary Society had missions, and after 1912 also the Gossner Society. German South-West Africa (later Namibia) was the place for the Rhenish Society. The German African Society, which later changed its name to the Bethel Society worked in German East Africa along with the Bavarian Missionary Society for East Africa (later a part of the Leipzig Society), the Neukirchen Society, the Leipzig Society around Mt. Kilimanjaro, the Moravian Mission, the Berlin Society, and after 1914 also the Hermannsburg Society. In New Guinea, the Rhenish Society and the Neuendettelsau Society were active; the Liebenzell Society worked on the Caroline Islands and the Admiralty Islands; the city of Tsingtao in China was the place for the Berlin Society and the General Protestant Missionary Society. In general, China played an important role for the missionary societies. Besides the three societies already operating in the country and the German Mission to the Blind of Hildesheim, missionary activities were started by the Alliance Mission of Barmen, the St. Chrischona Mission, the Liebenzell Society, the Kiel Mission to China, the Sisters of the Berlin Women's Union in Hong Kong, the Berlin Women's Missionary Society for China, and the Silesian Deaconesses of the motherhouse "Friedenshort." Additionally, the General Protestant Missionary Society worked in JAPAN according to liberal theology.

In the Near East the already established societies were joined by the Auguste-Victoria Foundation on the Mount of Olives in Jerusalem and the Mount Carmel Mission, which is still working in Lebanon today. At that time the Sudan Pioneer Mission, the later *Evangelische Mohammedanermission Wiesbaden,* started its mission. As a reaction to the persecution of the Armenian people, Ernst Lohmann (1860–1936) and Schuchardt founded the *Hilfsbund für christliches Liebeswerk* (Support League for Christian Charity), which continues to operate in Armenia and Lebanon today. Additionally the German Orient Mission, which was set up by Lepsius, started working in east Turkey and the northwestern part of Persia, later also in Syria. Although the efforts of a German mission to the Jews around Lake Urmia came to a wretched end, the branch of the Hermannsburg Society working in this area made itself independent in 1907, calling itself hereafter "Union for Lutheran Mission to Persia." This union started missionary work among the Kurds in Mahabad in 1913, which was brought to a sudden and somewhat violent end in 1940, eventually leading to the dissolution of this union.

The attempts made by Ernst Jakob Christoffel (1876–1955) turned out to be more successful. In 1909, his mission to the blind began in Malatia in

Turkey. After World War I, operating within the Turkish borders became impossible for the mission, but the work of Christoffel could be successfully continued in Tabriz and Isfahan.

World War I resulted in a great breakdown for the German missionary societies. The missionary work in the German colonies, which was pursued during the colonial age and which was desired and supported by Wilhelm II, came to a complete end, despite all efforts to retrieve the colonies that went on even in national-socialistic times. In addition, the development toward independent churches was promoted because the German societies faced difficulties in refilling the vacant positions and because many missions had to be assigned to local personnel due to the war.

Even after the collapse of the colonial empires and after the development of independent churches, the missionary societies stayed in touch with the regions in which they previously worked. Since then, the German missionary societies and the independent churches that emerged as a result of their work have created numerous partnership agreements.

Methods of Missionary Work

The missionary interest of Justinian Ernst Welz (1621–1668) was evidently influenced by his monastic ideals, thus placing him in the tradition of the early church. However, the principles of the mission of Ziegenbalg already focused on the enculturation of the gospel in the Indian civilization. Even though standard missionary methods gained acceptance by all German missionary societies during the nineteenth century, the methods differed considerably between the individual societies. The following standard methods can be distinguished: schools, with a controversy over whether non-Christian students are invited or not; hospitals, especially after the great increase of the medical missions; evangelization of the rural population, starting with short preaching trips to establishing Bible study groups, usually aiming at a personal conversion; work of missionary aid organizations, for example concerning crafts or industry, trade, or art; publications, for the supporters in Germany as well as in the native language. Regarding translation work, German missionaries, such as Hermann Gundert, whose research on Malayalam is still most important for this southern Indian language, made notable progress in many languages.

Besides these standard methods, some missionary societies developed certain peculiarities. The Hermannsburg Society practiced at first an early communism among its missionaries and colonists. The General Protestant Missionary Society, which changed its name to "German East-Asia Mission" in 1929 and which is today a member of the Association of Churches and Missions in South West Germany (*Evangelisches Missionswerk Südwestdeutschland*), not only referred deliberately to the "elements of truth already existing" in the non-Christian religions and civilizations, but also recorded in its statutes as a major goal to promote the general cultural development in the non-Christian civilizations. As a result many representatives of this missionary society became professors of their corresponding subjects after their return to Germany, for example Richard Wilhelm who worked as a sinologist.

Because WOMEN could often not be reached by the missionary societies because of the cultural situation on the site, the large missionary societies developed special branches for the mission to women. Additionally, independent women's missionary societies started their work: The Berlin Woman's Missionary Society for China (*Berliner Frauenmissionsverein für China*) in 1850, the oriental work of the Kaiserswerth Deaconess Motherhouse in 1851, the German Mission to the Blind of Hildesheim in 1890, the Woman's Mission of Malche in 1898, and the German Woman's Missionary Prayer Union in 1900. The most important women's missionary society was the Women's Society for Christian Education of the Female Sex in Eastern Countries (*Frauenverein für Christliche Bildung des Weiblichen Geschlechts im Morgenlande*), also known as "Woman's Oriental Union" which was started in 1842.

The medical mission was a significant component of all missionary effort from the time of the Danish-Halle Mission in Tranquebar, where five missionary physicians were continuously on duty between 1729 and 1791. Although it was not until the beginning of the nineteenth century that special societies for medical mission were founded: Union for Medical Mission of Stuttgart in 1898; the Bern Union for Medical Mission in 1904; the Gossner Aid Union for Nursing in the Mission Stations; and the Rhenish Union for Medical Mission, both in 1906; the Berlin Union for Medical Mission; the Bavarian Union; the Leipzig Main Union; and the Halle Union for Medical Mission, all in 1908; the Hermannsburg-Hannover Union; and the Bremen Union in 1909; the East Frisian Union for Medical Mission in 1910; and in 1911–1912 also the corresponding unions in Kassel, Marburg, and Herrnhut. The last special union established was the Missionary Medical Union of the Brethren and their Friends (*Missionsärztlicher Verein der Brüdergemeine und ihrer Freunde*) in 1912. As early as 1909 the ten unions existing at that time decided to set up an umbrella organization, which was constituted on October 19, 1909 as "Federation of the German Unions for Medical Missions." Of particular significance was the German Institute for Medical Mission (*Deutsches Institut für ärztliche Mission*) in Tübingen that originated from the work of Paul Lechler (1849–1925). This institute began working in 1909 and included a medical school and a hospital for tropical diseases.

Like the medical mission, the diaconal mission was also methodically determined by the humanitarian aid that was to be given. The humanitarian aid enabled the missionary society such as the Christoffel or the Hildesheim Mission to the Blind or the societies working with leprosy patients to combine elements of a medical mission with elements of the diaconical and evangelistic mission.

After World War II the classical methods, which are still employed today, were supplemented by new methodological aspects, such as questions on partnership, enculturation, and contextualization. The methods of missionary work are today mostly contextual. Before 1918 most missionary methods suffered from the assumption developed under the influence of an ideology that equated spreading Western civilization with promoting Christianity. After World War II the missions could free themselves from this ideological captivity. Today they are trying to determine their relationship to globalization.

Federations

The German Evangelical Missionary Council (*Deutscher Evangelischer Missionsrat*) was founded in 1885 as Missionary Committee and later became the executive body of the Conference of German Protestant Missionary Societies (*Deutscher Evangelischer Missionstag*). This organization, at first called *Deutscher Evangelischer Missionsbund,* was established in 1922 with the purpose of improving the coordination between the joined missionary societies. In 1933 the name was changed to Conference of German Protestant Missionary Societies. It was a federation of thirty-four Protestant missionary societies that were regularly sending out missionaries, and eight organizations in Germany keyed to world mission. The general assembly of this Conference met annually. The contact with the German church was maintained through the Protestant Liaison Board for World Mission (*Evangelische Arbeitsgemeinschaft für Weltmission*), which was set up in 1963. In 1964 the Association of Evangelical Missionary Societies in the German Democratic Republic left the listed organizations and stayed independent until 1991, when it became part of the Association of Protestant Churches and Missions in Germany (*Evangelisches Missionswerk in Deutschland*). The Conference of German Protestant Missionary Societies was dissolved in 1976 because the missionary societies were to a large extent integrated into the churches.

However, the dissolution of the Conference of Missionary Societies was preceded by the fiercest controversy in its history which dealt with the question if the focus of mission work should be restricted to outside Europe. The controversial understanding of the mission led in 1974 to the foundation of the Association of Evangelical Missions (*Arbeitsgemeinschaft Evangelikaler Missionen*). This association has its headquarters in Korntal-Münchingen and is joined by thirty-four regular members and twenty-three extraordinary members, whereas only twenty-four regular members belong to the legal successor of the Conference of Missionary Societies, the Association of Protestant Churches and Missions, which additionally maintains special relationships with ten partner organizations. All German missionary societies and their domains are listed in the annually published Yearbook of Mission.

The Association of Protestant Churches and Missions in Germany was founded in 1975 and acts as umbrella organization for all missionary affairs in Germany. The headquarters are located in Hamburg; its work concentrates on missionary theology, research, public relations, support of ecclesiastic activities in matters of mission and evangelization, theological education in the countries traditionally in care of German missionary societies, and cooperation with the WORLD COUNCIL OF CHURCHES and its Commission on World Mission and Evangelism.

Mission Studies

The scientific study of missionary methods started in Germany early in the nineteenth century (Flatt, FRIEDRICH SCHLEIERMACHER, Friedrich Ehrenfeuchter (1814–1878)) and was at first considered as a part of practical theology as well as of church history. Still, it took until 1896 before Gustav Warneck (1834–1910) was appointed to the first professorship especially occupied with mission studies. On the base already laid, Warneck emphasized the increase of knowledge, which was brought to practical theology and church history by mission history. Beginning in 1908 professorial chairs for mission studies were established, the first one in HALLE. Also, mission studies became a regular subject at the theological faculties of the German universities. Sometimes this subject was even taught outside of theological faculties, as was the case with Walter Freytag (1899–1959), who taught at the philosophical faculty of Hamburg, because a theological faculty did not exist, while the colonial institute wanted to study the effects of the missions in the German colonies. In his *Evangelische Missionslehre* of 1892–1903 Warneck emphasized the church-planting function of the mission and underlined the concept of identity between church and people. To him the intention of the mission to completely Christianize the entire world was yet unquestioned.

Today chairs for mission studies have been established at the theological faculties of the universities of Heidelberg, Berlin, Wuppertal, Hamburg, Erlangen, Neuendettelsau, and Munich. Since 2000 the University of Göttingen has had a special institute for oriental church and mission history. In 1957 the Academy of Mission at Hamburg University was founded, which is now jointly sponsored by the Evangelical Church in Germany, the Association of Protestant Churches and Missions, and the faculty of Evangelical Theology of the University of Hamburg. The mission seminary of the Evangelical Lutheran Mission in Hermannsburg remains as the only place for an independent ecclesial missionary education in Germany. Apart from that, training of the missionaries is a supplement to the regular study of theology.

The programs, models, and goals of missions were always controversial issues, but some of the controversies have gained great importance. One of these issues is the idea of Warneck, that the transplantation of the church would simultaneously mean the "planting" of the church into the religion and the civilization of the nation, thus implanting the church into the people's tradition. With his concept, which was later carried on by Bruno Gutmann (1876–1966) and Christian Keysser (1877–1961), Warneck did not only think about integrating pre-Christian values and customs, but also about a reaction that would stimulate and enrich the German congregations. Another concept that originated from the sphere of the German mission studies was the idea of the "Missio dei," which was contributed by Karl Hartenstein (1894–1952). After the missionary conference at Willingen in 1952 the concept of the Missio dei became a crucial issue of mission studies. In Germany a programmatic example of this notion, which reconsiders the understanding of mission as fundamentally new, was Georg F. Vicedom. Unlike the church-centered missionary conceptions, the concept of the Missio dei sees the triune god as the subject of the mission. God is the one who sends out as well as the one who is sent. The church is included in God's universal SALVATION plans; mission therefore becomes the paragon of divine actions. Thereby the church loses the burden of enlightening a godless world. This concept opens up new perspectives for the church in regard to its devotion to the world, its solidarity with the poor, and its coexistence with people of different faiths.

Mission as a venture that especially depends on dialogue was the subject emphasized by Hans-Werner Gensichen, who was preceded by Hendrick Krämer (1888–1965) with his idea of mission as communication. The dialogue has its final reason in the incarnational principle of Christianity. Experiencing the community with Christ simultaneously spins off a dialogue with other experiences of community previously made, such as family, tribe, or caste. It is the solidarity of the Christians that qualifies all previous experiences of community as preliminary to the new experience. The testimony is surrounded by dialogue, and within the dialogue both partners are entitled to bear witness; thus the dialogue is not used for the testimony. The frankness of the dialogue is not to be limited. Thus dialogue in this conception means a living devotion to the other.

JAMES FREDERICK SCHÖN sharpened this conception further with his thesis about Bi-Identität, which deliberately tries to bear the tension between the two religious poles during the missionary process. Another development within this conception is the model of konvivenz (convivence) introduced by Theo Sundermeier, which emphasizes the mutual life as foundation of all reason. This model correlates the impulses that were previously initiated in Germany with the reception of LIBERATION THEOLOGY of LATIN AMERICA, the Minjung theology of KOREA, and the Dalit theology of India. In this process convivence is the fundamental requirement for a change in perspective. Context is decisive. The missionary stays listening and learning all the time. The church as a community explains the biblical texts, unfolding them anew each time in a new context, knowing that the text came into existence under its own contextual circumstances. One of the Christocentric starting points of this theological thinking is that Jesus lived with the people, not for the people. Convivence today is tied to the convivence of Jesus.

A special case within mission studies is represented by the research on mission history, which contains the critical examination and theological reflection of the history of missions as well as the search for new descriptive models. The first Protestant compendium of mission history in Germany was written in 1743 by the theologian Friedrich Samuel Bock (1716–1786) of Königsberg. Bock was especially interested in the effect of missions on his homeland. His book concluded with principles of missionary methods for successful evangelization. Evidently Bock focused not only on historical questions, but also on finding a historical and theological judgment. For the sake of a better practice, the theologian Friedrich Lücke (1791–1855) of Göttingen demanded in 1840 a "more truthful" mission history and a new mission theory based on this knowledge. Since the year 1800 evangelical theologians increasingly occupied themselves with mission history: in 1800/01 Flatt (Tübingen), in 1825/26 Krafft (Erlangen) and Lücke (Bonn), in 1852 Wuttke (Halle). Later representatives are Sack (Bonn), Nitzsch (Berlin), Wiggers and Schliemann (Rostock). Epochal was the book by Blumhardt, *Attempt of a General Mission History of the Church of Christ,* written between 1828 and 1837. The first large studies on mission history followed in the seventies of the nineteenth century: Friedrich Nippold (Bern), Gustav Plitt (Erlangen), Christlieb (Bonn), and Carl H. Plath (Berlin). In Plath's description, *The Choosing of the People in the Light of the Mission History,* presented in 1867, a strong undertone of COLONIALISM was already noticeable. At that time Germany was about to enter the circle of the colonial powers.

After World War II many attempts were made to renew the nature and the appearance of mission history, such as: mission history as profane history, or as church history (Heinz Frohnes), as history of extra-European Christianity instead of the classic approach (Klaus Koschorke), as history of border crossings (Andreas Feldtkeller), or as history in the sign of Bi-Identität Ulrich (Schoen). Much of this work is still in progress.

In recent times growing attention has been drawn to the fact that not only foreign religions but also Christian churches of Africa have started missionary activities in Germany. In view of the circumstance that a considerable percentage of the German population does not have any religious ties, the missionary efforts seem to be justified. The old distinction of Lücke between foreign and inner mission gives way to the perception that mission is an enterprise that is to be undertaken everywhere.

See also Evangelism, Overview; Inculturation; Missionary Organizations; Missions; Protestant Christian Church of Indonesia

References and Further Reading

Fiedler, Klaus. "It is time to write the history of German-speaking evangelical missions." *Direction 28,* no. 1, Spring 1999, pp. 28–45.

Gensichen, Hans-Werner. *Glaube für die Welt.* Gütersloh, Germany: Gütersloher Verlagshaus, 1971.

Grundmann, Christoffer. *Gesandt zu heilen.* Gütersloh, Germany: Gütersloher Verlagshaus, 1992.

Hammer, Karl. *Weltmission und Kolonialismus.* Munich, Germany: Kösel, 1978.

Hanselmann, Siegfried. *Deutsche Evangelische Palästinamission.* Erlangen, Germany: Verlag der Evangelisch-Lutherischen Mission, 1971.

Heyden, Ulrich van der, and Heike Liebau. *Missionsgeschichte, Kirchengeschichte, Weltgeschichte.* Stuttgart, Germany: Franz Steiner Verlag, 1996.

Koschorke, Klaus. *Christen und Gewürze: Konfrontation und Interaktion kolonialer und indigener Christentumsvari-*
anten. Göttingen, Germany: Vandenhoeck & Ruprecht, 1998.

Luedemann, Ernst-August. *Vision: Gemeinde weltweit: 150 Jahre Hermannsburger Mission und Ev.-luth. Missionswerk in Niedersachsen.* Hermannsburg, Germany: Verlag der Missionshandlung, 2000.

Miller, Jon. *Missionary Zeal and Institutional Control: Organizational Contradictions in the Basel Mission on the Gold Coast, 1828–1917.* Grand Rapids, MI and London: Eerdmans Pub. Co and RoutledgeCurzon, 2003.

Müller, Karl, and Werner Ustorf. *Einleitung in die Missionsgeschichte.* Stuttgart, Germany: Kohlhammer, 1995.

Neill, Stephen, Gerald H. Anderson, and John Goodwin. *Concise Dictionary of the Christian World Mission.* Nashville, TN: Abingdon Press, 1971.

Oehler, Wilhelm. *Geschichte der Deutschen Evangelischen Mission.* Baden-Baden, Germany: Wilhelm Fehrholz, 1949–1951.

Oermann, Nils Ole. *Mission, Church and State Relations in South West Africa under German Rule (1884–1915).* Stuttgart, Germany: F. Steiner, 1998.

Railton, Nicholas. *No North Sea: The Anglo-German Evangelical Network in the Middle of the Nineteenth Century.* Leiden, The Netherlands and Boston: Brill, 2000.

Raupp, Werner. *Mission in Quellentexten: Geschichte der Deutschen Evangelischen Mission von der Reformation bis zur Weltmissionskonferenz 1910.* Erlangen, Germany: Verlag der Evangelisch-Lutherischen Mission, 1990.

Sundermeier, Theo. *Konvivenz und Differenz.* Erlangen, Germany: Verlag der Evangelisch-Lutherischen Mission, 1995.

Vicedom, Georg F. *Missio Dei.* Munich, Germany: Christian Kaiser Verlag, 1958.

Wright, Marcia. *German Missions in Tanganyika, 1891–1941: Lutherans and Moravians in the Southern Highlands.* Oxford, UK: Clarendon Press, 1971.

MARTIN TAMCKE

MISSIONS, NORTH AMERICAN

North American Protestantism has typically been missionary at heart, although numbers and effectiveness of missionaries have ebbed and flowed over three centuries. In 2002, North American Protestant foreign missionaries in all categories numbered about 136,000, or 32 percent of the world total.

Birth of North American Missions

Immigrants to North America in the 1600s and 1700s were mostly Protestants from ENGLAND and Europe. Whatever the motivations of the earliest colonists—discovery, conquest, or trade—Christian mission was part of the mix. Puritan settlers in New England saw themselves as part of God's mission to transform the wilderness into a garden paradise. Evangelizing the heathen was written into the charters of Plymouth, Massachusetts Bay, Connecticut, and Virginia colonies.

Earliest Protestant mission efforts among American Indians began in 1642 on Martha's Vineyard, off the Massachusetts coast, by Puritan Congregationalists.

The most prominent early missionary was JOHN ELIOT (1604–1690), "Apostle to the Indians," who from 1646 worked successfully among the Pequots of Massachusetts. By 1674 Eliot had gathered 3,600 Christian Indians into fourteen self-governing villages. Eliot published an Algonkian translation of the Scriptures, the first BIBLE printed in North America. Christians in England organized the Society for the Propagation of the Gospel in New England to support Eliot's work, the first Protestant society organized exclusively for foreign missions. Eliot's pattern was followed elsewhere. By some estimates approximately 20 percent of the Native American population of New England was converted, although the work rapidly disintegrated after 1675 because of warfare between colonists and Indians.

JONATHAN EDWARDS served as missionary to the Housatonic Indians at Stockbridge, Massachusetts, for six years in the 1750s. In the wake of the Great Awakening (see AWAKENINGS) Edwards set forth a thesis that in various forms has been argued by North American Protestants from CHARLES FINNEY to Kenneth Scott Latourette: Missions and revival are intimately linked. God renews the CHURCH through successive waves of revival that, despite setbacks, extend the mission outreach of the church and will lead finally to the full coming of God's Kingdom (see KINGDOM OF GOD).

Edwards' prospective son-in-law, DAVID BRAINERD (1718–1747), who died young after modestly successful mission work among Indians in New York, Pennsylvania, and New Jersey, inspired others to missions by his self-sacrifice. An agent of the Scottish Society for Propagating of Christian Knowledge (SSPCK), Brainerd kept a journal that was published and, together with a heroic biography by Edwards, had wide impact. Henry Martyn and WILLIAM CAREY were among many inspired to missionary service by Brainerd's example.

Some European Protestants came to North America primarily as missionaries to the native population or to work among colonists. Moravian Brethren established communities at Salem, North Carolina, Nazareth and Bethlehem, Pennsylvania, and elsewhere, partly to reach American Indians. The Anglican SOCIETY FOR THE PROPAGATION OF THE GOSPEL (SPG) sent JOHN WESLEY and others to America in the 1730s to minister to colonists and convert the Indians. Although largely ineffective in Indian EVANGELISM, the SPG had considerable success in converting African slaves (see SLAVERY).

After the disruption of the Revolutionary War, the Second Great Awakening, much more widespread than the first, renewed churches in New England and the South and spread revival fires along the frontier in Kentucky and elsewhere (see REVIVALS). This renewal birthed the CAMP MEETING movement and gave fresh impetus to missions and to abolitionist and social reform movements (see SLAVERY, ABOLITION OF).

Missions and North American Expansion

As the frontier shifted westward, so did missionary efforts. Presbyterians and Congregationalists formed the American Home Missionary Society in 1826 to evangelize New England settlers in western New York State. Methodist CIRCUIT RIDERS and Baptist farmer-preachers planted congregations along the shifting frontier. Methodists and other groups sent missionaries to California and Oregon Territory. Missionary work continued among NATIVE AMERICANS but was often undermined by encroachment upon and expropriation of Indian lands. In Idaho Territory, Presbyterian missionary Sue McBeth in the 1870s effectively trained leaders among the Nez Perce Indians, a tribe that in turn evangelized others.

The Rise of Foreign Missions

Even before the frontier reached the Pacific Coast, Protestants set their sights on foreign lands. The first American-born foreign mission societies (see MISSION ORGANIZATIONS) arose in the early 1800s: The AMERICAN BOARD OF COMMISSIONERS FOR FOREIGN MISSIONS (ABCFM, 1810), the American Baptist Missionary Union (1814), the African Baptist Missionary Society (organized by Black Baptists in 1816), and the United Foreign Missionary Society (1817). Foreign mission societies were formed also by the DUTCH REFORMED CHURCH (1832), Methodist Episcopal Church (1833), FREE WILL BAPTISTS (1833), PRESBYTERIAN CHURCH in the U.S.A. (1837), and Southern Baptists (1845) (see SOUTHERN BAPTIST CONVENTION).

The ABCFM arose in part out of the famous student "Haystack Prayer Meeting" at Williams College in 1806. Founded by Congregationalists, the ABCFM soon included Presbyterian and Reformed supporters. In 1812 the ABCFM sent out its first five missionaries, including Adoniram and Ann Judson and Luther Rice, all bound for INDIA (see JUDSON FAMILY). En route Rice and the Judsons changed their views on BAPTISM, leading the Judsons to become the first American Baptist missionaries to Burma and prompting the organization of American Baptist missions in 1814.

"The Great Century"

During what Kenneth Scott Latourette called "The Great Century" (1815–1914), U.S. and Canadian foreign mission societies increased from three to about one hundred. North American Protestantism became the dominant force in world missions, by 1910 contributing about $13 million annually, 43 percent of the world total.

Revival in 1857–1858 gave fresh impetus to foreign missions. New missionary societies were formed. Many were initiated by WOMEN, including the Women's Union Missionary Society (1861), Woman's Board of Missions (1869), and the (Methodist Episcopal) Woman's Foreign Missionary Society (1869). During the 1870s women formed new mission societies or "auxiliaries" at the average rate of one per year, launching a major women's missionary movement.

As sending agencies multiplied, hundreds of missionaries served overseas, particularly in India, Burma, and AFRICA. In 1900 North American missionaries totaled 4,891, including 400 from CANADA, constituting 27 percent of the global Protestant mission force. By the end of the century CHINA emerged as the major North American field; in 1910 some 1,784 North American missionaries were serving there.

Through most of the nineteenth century the majority of North American missionaries served in America, evangelizing the frontier in outreach to Indians, blacks, Hispanic Americans, and new urban immigrants. This changed, however, as the frontier reached the Pacific and as North Americans became increasingly globally conscious. Josiah Strong's books *Our Country* (1886) and *The New Era; or, The Coming Kingdom* (1893) popularized the view that America was key in civilizing and Christianizing the world.

North American missionaries planted growing churches in many lands. In 1853 Presbyterians John and Helen Nevius went to China where they ministered for forty years. In 1885 John Nevius began advocating a "new mission method" of establishing self-propagating, self-supporting, and self-governing indigenous churches, an approach that proved increasingly fruitful. Nevius shared his vision with Presbyterian missionaries in KOREA in 1890, sparking extraordinary growth in the Korean Presbyterian Church, which reported 100,000 members by 1933.

The Student Volunteer Movement

Missionary activity expanded greatly with the formation of the STUDENT VOLUNTEER MOVEMENT for Foreign Missions (SVM) in 1888, sparked by a missionary awakening among college students. A group of women students at Mount Holyoke College in 1878 formed a secret association, pledging their lives to missions. Grace Wilder, a member of this band, helped awaken missionary interest in her brother, Robert. For months Robert and Grace prayed together for a missionary awakening, asking God for 1,000

volunteers. Robert Wilder helped form a student missionary society at Princeton University in 1883.

Robert Wilder carried his missionary passion to DWIGHT L. MOODY's Summer Conference at Northfield, Massachusetts, in 1886 and was instrumental in getting Presbyterian ARTHUR TAPPAN PIERSON (1837–1911) to promote foreign missions there. Pierson's stirring addresses in 1886 and in subsequent years prompted the organization of the SVM in 1888.

The SVM was the fruit of the revivalism of Moody (1837–1899), of student missionary awakening, and of Pierson's missionary vision. Pierson, later editor of *Missionary Review of the World,* had been influenced by British Baptist mission leader Joseph Angus and the ESCHATOLOGY of GEORGE MÜLLER. In 1879 Pierson shifted from a postmillennial to a premillennial understanding of history, convinced that world conditions would worsen until Christ's return, which probably was imminent (see MILLENARIANS AND MILLENNIALISM). The work of proclaiming Christ was urgent. Christian missionaries were to spread the word and "speed the coming" of Jesus Christ.

Pierson promoted the famous SVM watchword: "The evangelization of the world in this generation." At the 1886 Northfield Conference, Pierson urged, "All should go, and go to all." One hundred volunteered; the next year 2,100 (1,600 men; 500 women) enlisted, and thousands more later. Early volunteers included Methodist JOHN MOTT (1865–1955) and Presbyterians Robert Wilder and Robert Speer; all became lifelong missionary leaders. "The missionary enterprise in the UNITED STATES was entering a period of enormous vitality with a crusading spirit . . . fueled by duty, compassion, confidence, optimism, evangelical revivalism, and premillennialist urgency" (Anderson 1988:98). The motive of love for and obedience to Christ merged with a growing sense of America's "Manifest Destiny" to be a civilizing light to the world.

Pierson supported the organization of the interdenominational Africa Inland Mission, one of the earliest so-called faith missions, founded in 1895. Meanwhile Baptist pastor ADONIRAM JUDSON GORDON, "father of faith missions," founded the Boston Missionary Training Institute in 1889 to supplement denominational missions by training "lay" men and especially women missionaries.

Other premillennialist mission leaders were Albert Benjamin Simpson (1843–1919), founder of the CHRISTIAN AND MISSIONARY ALLIANCE, and Cyrus Ingerson Scofield (1843–1921), who founded the Central American Mission in 1890 and whose influential SCOFIELD REFERENCE BIBLE was published as a resource for missionaries.

Simpson was a Canadian Presbyterian. In 1881 he resigned his pastorate in New York City and shortly thereafter formed his independent Gospel Tabernacle to reach the poor and train missionaries. In 1883 Simpson founded The Missionary Union for the Evangelization of the World and a year later a missionary training college in New York City that eventually became Nyack College and Alliance Theological Seminary. Simpson's organization sent its first missionaries to Congo in 1884. Simpson stressed a "Fourfold Gospel" based on Jesus Christ as "Savior, Sanctifier, Healer, and Coming King." Although not Pentecostal, Simpson's theology had much in common with later PENTECOSTALISM, particularly the Foursquare Church. In 1887 Simpson organized the Christian Alliance and the Evangelical Missionary Alliance, later merged as the CHRISTIAN AND MISSIONARY ALLIANCE.

Women played a key, if often underrecognized, role in the rapid increase of missionary personnel in the late 1800s and early 1900s. Magazines such as *Woman's Work for Women* (Presbyterian) and *Woman's Missionary Friend* (Methodist Episcopal) multiplied, feeding a growing network of prayer, study, and financial support. Discrimination against single women as missionaries prompted the formation of many "female agencies" between 1860 and 1900, such as the Woman's Union Missionary Society (1861) and the Women's Board of Missions (1869). By 1900 forty-one American women's agencies were supporting over 1,200 single women missionaries in dozens of countries. Together with married women serving under other boards, women constituted 60 percent of the American Protestant missionary force in the 1890s.

Most women's missionary activity was carried out under the rubric of "Woman's Work for Women"—a recognition that in many lands only women missionaries could evangelize women, but also often a limitation on women's ministries. After 1910 most women's agencies were merged into existing denominational boards, losing their autonomy and dynamism.

Mott effectively promoted missions in his role as intercollegiate secretary for the YOUNG MEN'S CHRISTIAN ASSOCIATION (YMCA) after graduating from Cornell in 1888. In 1900 Mott reaffirmed the SVM watchword but reinterpreted it in less millennialist terms in *The Evangelization of the World in This Generation*. Mott reported in 1892 that through SVM inspiration over 500 volunteers were serving on foreign fields and thousands more were preparing.

U.S. annexation of the PHILIPPINES after the Spanish-American War (1898–1899) awakened Protestant missions interest there. Because the Philippines had long been under Spanish control, American anti-Catholicism combined with a sense of national purpose as added motivations for Protestant missions (see CATHOLICISM, PROTESTANT REACTIONS). "God marked the American people as His chosen nation to finally lead in the regeneration of the world," said Senator Albert Beveridge after visiting the Philippines.

Some Protestants demurred, sensing a coming shift in global missions. Theologian William Newton Clarke said the world was entering a time of "crisis in missions"; it was "quite impossible that within the lifetime of a generation Christ should become intelligently known by all men." Mott disagreed, saying the SVM watchword did not imply the CONVERSION of the world and calling for an increase in Protestant missionaries from some 15,000 in 1900 to 50,000.

The Ecumenical Missionary Conference in New York City (1900) marked a high point in interdenominational missionary cooperation (see ECUMENISM). The gathering attracted 3,100 "delegates and missionaries" from 200 North American, European, and British missions, and crowds totaling 200,000. Participants included mission personnel (predominantly North Americans) from the larger denominations but also from smaller groups like the MENNONITES and Free Methodists (see FREE METHODIST CHURCH OF AMERICA). U.S. President William McKinley opened the conference, speaking of "the missionary effort which has wrought such wonderful triumphs for civilization." The conference recognized the growing contribution of women and held a mass women's missionary rally. The conference published statistics on world missions and was a precursor of the influential WORLD MISSIONARY CONFERENCE in Edinburgh in 1910.

For nearly half a century, Robert E. Speer (1867–1947) gave stellar leadership to the Board of Foreign Missions of the Presbyterian Church in the U.S.A. Influenced by Moody, Pierson, and the SVM, although never ordained, Speer became a prominent interpreter of foreign missions. Under his leadership Presbyterian missionaries increased from 598 in 1891 to a peak of 1,606 in 1927, making the Presbyterian board the largest American missionary agency of the time.

North American Protestant missions seemed to be riding a swelling tide. Foreign missionaries increased from 2,176 in 1890 to 4,159 in 1900, then to over 9,000 by 1915. Mott said in 1910 that a worldwide "rising spiritual tide" meant that "victory is assured if the present campaign be adequately supported and pressed."

The "Great Century" of Protestant missions ended, however, with the crisis of World War I. The broadly ecumenical Edinburgh Missionary Conference of 1910 celebrated the great missionary achievements of the previous half-century and remarkable Protestant consensus about foreign missions, but the North American Protestant missionary enterprise was already in a time of transition.

Nearly 13,000 SVM volunteers reportedly entered foreign missionary service between 1886 and 1936, but by the 1920s the movement was in decline and underwent major theological reorientation that paralleled the shift in mainline Protestantism. At the 1927 SVM convention in Detroit, influential missionary Sherwood Eddy publicly repudiated the watchword, "The evangelization of the world in this generation."

Three Streams after 1900

Early in the twentieth century the apparent North American Protestant missionary consensus began to fragment. Three distinct streams shaped the course of missions in the 1900s: Ecumenical Protestantism, FUNDAMENTALISM, and Pentecostalism.

Ecumenical Protestantism

The Ecumenical Movement grew directly out of the 1910 Edinburgh Conference and the formation of the International Missionary Council (IMC) in 1921. Many theologically conservative mission leaders initially supported the Ecumenical Movement but abandoned it when in their view the growing concern with church unity began to undercut missions and church extension. By 1925 North American Protestant missionaries numbered 13,608, nearly half the worldwide total. Most were serving under mainline Protestant boards, but a growing number—nearly 20 percent—were now serving with newer "faith" missions or other groups.

Wars and the Great Depression disrupted the missionary enterprise to some extent, but the biggest change proved to be theological. In 1932 the Rockefeller-funded Laymen's Foreign Missions Inquiry report, *Re-Thinking Missions,* polarized the missions movement. The report seemed to undermine faith in the uniqueness of Jesus Christ and proposed that missionaries work cooperatively with other major religions toward one uniting world faith. Although most mission leaders rejected the report, the Protestant missions consensus evaporated. The 1938 meeting of the IMC (in effect the first major ecumenical council of churches) shifted attention from traditional mission work to social issues and interchurch relations.

Mainline Protestant missions soon accepted the more liberal view of missions—which in reaction gave added impetus to fundamentalist missions. The

theological shift was soon reflected in the mainline missions force, which dropped from about 10,500 in 1925 to 6,800 in 1970 and 2,600 in 1985. Yet during this period the total number of American Protestant foreign missionaries rose from 13,100 to 37,803.

Mainline missions increasingly focused on interchurch cooperation and ecumenical efforts. Most mainline mission boards endorsed the integration of the IMC with the WORLD COUNCIL OF CHURCHES at New Delhi in 1961. In theory this union signaled that mission was integral to the church's being. Similarly, the Foreign Missions Conference of North America became the Division of Foreign Missions of the NATIONAL COUNCIL OF CHURCHES in 1950.

Debate about the nature of mission continued within ecumenical Protestantism. The role of the church as a missionary agency was questioned, particularly in the 1960s when some theologians argued that God was more at work in secular liberation movements than in Christianity; thus "the world should set the agenda for the church" (see LIBERATION THEOLOGY). Bishop STEPHEN CHARLES NEILL cautioned, however, that "if everything is mission, nothing is mission." Meanwhile the preponderant North American foreign missions thrust shifted to fundamentalist, Pentecostal, and evangelical groups.

Fundamentalism

Tensions latent at Edinburgh 1910 surfaced with the rise of fundamentalism, whose leaders included prominent premillennial missionary statesman Robert Speer. Fundamentalists were increasingly concerned with the impact of theological liberalism on missions (see LIBERAL PROTESTANTISM). The fundamentalist versus modernist controversy raged as fiercely on the mission field as at home. In China BAPTISTS and Presbyterians organized the Bible Union of China to counter theological liberalism.

In 1917 fundamentalists formed the Interdenominational Foreign Mission Association of North America (IFMA), a fellowship of nondenominational faith missions. Member agencies included CHINA INLAND MISSION, Central American Mission, and Africa Inland Mission. Henry Frost of China Inland Mission was the first IFMA president.

As faith missions flourished, new agencies such as the Latin America Mission (1921) and India Mission (1930) were formed. Bible institutes such as MOODY BIBLE INSTITUTE in Chicago and others in Toronto and Los Angeles supplied a steady stream of mission candidates. By 1990 nearly 100 agencies were affiliated with the IFMA, representing over 8,000 North American missionaries.

Pentecostalism

As the twentieth century dawned, a new movement arose that eventually produced the largest Protestant missionary force. Pentecostalism was born with missionary passion. When Agnes Ozman (1870–1937) was baptized with the Holy Spirit and spoke in tongues on January 1, 1901, at Bethel Bible College in Kansas (often seen as the birth of modern Pentecostalism), she viewed the experience as empowerment for witness. So did virtually all early Pentecostals. A former Methodist who in 1894 enrolled in Simpson's training institute in New York, Ozman engaged in city missionary work and later with her husband traveled in Pentecostal evangelistic work. In 1917 she and her husband affiliated with the newly formed ASSEMBLIES OF GOD, soon to become the largest U.S. Pentecostal denomination.

Key to the rise of Pentecostal missions was the 1906–1909 AZUSA STREET REVIVAL in Los Angeles. An interracial movement led initially by African American Holiness preacher William Seymour, Azusa Street became known for the phenomena of speaking in TONGUES, prophecy, and healings (see FAITH HEALING). People baptized in the Spirit felt this was God's latter-day gift for world evangelization. Thousands from around the world made their way to Azusa Street; many returned home as Pentecostal missionaries. Azusa Street's monthly paper, *The Apostolic Faith,* reported prophecies that God would send out missionaries "to preach the full gospel in the power of the Spirit." Speaking in tongues was God's gift for evangelism in all the world's languages. "God is solving the missionary problem," said *The Apostolic Faith,* "sending out new-tongued missionaries." By 1910 over 185 North American Pentecostal missionaries had ventured overseas in the wake of Azusa Street.

Many early Pentecostal leaders had roots in METHODISM or the HOLINESS MOVEMENT. In some cases whole denominations, such as the CHURCH OF GOD (Cleveland, Tennessee), accepted glossolalia as God's latter-day gift and became Pentecostal. Pentecostal denominations soon organized mission boards; the Pentecostal Holiness Church formed its foreign mission board in 1911 and the Church of God (Cleveland, Tennessee) three years later. World evangelization was a major motive for founding the Assemblies of God in 1914.

Earliest Pentecostal missionaries were of three types. The largest and most effective group consisted of those already serving with other boards who after Spirit-baptism became Pentecostals. The second group were untrained, inexperienced folk who in Pentecostal zeal went to foreign lands without financial resources, believing God would provide. Although some proved effective, many returned home when resources failed to materialize. The third group consisted of men and women who received BIBLE COLLEGE or institute training before venturing overseas. More than a dozen Pentecostal Bible institutes were formed in the two decades after the Azusa Revival. As new denominations and missions were formed, the number of Pentecostal missionaries rose dramatically. By 1987 North American Pentecostal denominations had deployed well over 2,600 foreign missionaries and reported nearly 20,000,000 overseas constituents.

From Fundamentalism to Evangelicalism

Three major mid-twentieth-century shifts significantly influenced the course of North American missions, and the first was the growth of EVANGELICALISM. Although fundamentalism continued as a strong current within North American Protestantism, the emergence of evangelicalism out of fundamentalism toward the end of World War II was important for foreign missions. Evangelicals founded many missions agencies, such as Missionary Aviation Fellowship (1944), Far East Broadcasting Company (1945), and Greater Europe Mission (1949). Some of these, notably WORLD VISION (1950), were primarily evangelical relief agencies. The Evangelical Foreign Mission Association (EFMA), organized in 1945, networked evangelical agencies from Reformed, Wesleyan-Holiness, and Pentecostal traditions, although in practice most missions worked fairly independently. Beginning in the 1960s the EFMA and the IFMA worked cooperatively, particularly in publishing.

Renamed the Evangelical Fellowship of Mission Agencies in 1992, the EFMA in 2001 had 90 member agencies representing approximately 15,000 North American missionaries. It included not only denominational boards but also interdenominational ministries and independent groups such as the Mission Society for United Methodists, which were formed as evangelical alternatives to mainline denominational boards. By 1973 evangelical mission agencies accounted for 85 percent of the personnel and two-thirds of the funding of North American Protestant foreign missions.

By the late twentieth century many evangelical missions (with notable exceptions) came to see Roman Catholics as partners in world evangelization, feeling more at home with theologically conservative Catholics than with liberal Protestant agencies. One result was the founding of the American Society of Missiology (ASM) in 1972, which brought together conservative evangelical, "conciliar" Protestant, and Roman Catholic scholars. The ASM quarterly *Missiology* promoted missiological research and facilitated growing recognition of missiology as an academic discipline.

In the evangelical missions resurgence, a key role was played by the BILLY GRAHAM Evangelistic Association (BGEA). The BGEA supported several international missions conferences, including the seminal 1974 International Congress on World Evangelization in Lausanne, SWITZERLAND, that produced the Lausanne Covenant. The Lausanne Conference prompted increased evangelical missions cooperation, greater concern with social justice, and a theological consensus (the Lausanne Covenant) that provided the doctrinal basis for many new missions organizations (see LOUSANNE COMMITTEE FOR WORLD EVANGELIZATION).

From Pentecostalism to Charismatic Christianity

In the 1960s the Charismatic Renewal in both Roman Catholicism and mainline Protestantism emerged through Pentecostal influence. The resultant popularizing of Pentecostal experience sparked increased interest in missions and greater cooperation between Catholics and Protestants. Pentecostal leaders such as DAVID DU PLESSIS and Vinson Synan promoted "charismatic bridges" between Pentecostals and Charismatics and across the Catholic–Protestant divide.

The Charismatic Movement gave fresh impulse to North American missions and led to the formation of new agencies and new groups such as Vineyard Christian Fellowship. Vineyard now supports many missionaries around the world, often through independent charismatic missions agencies.

Missionary-sending Agencies

The third significant twentieth century development was the rise of missionary-sending agencies in many nations where North American and European missionaries evangelized successfully during the nineteenth century. These new missions multiplied rapidly in the late 1900s. By 2000 the number of missionaries sent out by these newer agencies probably had surpassed those deployed by North American missions; many came as missionaries to America. Relatedly, reflecting the globalization of missions, by 2001 many North American agencies such as World Vision, WYCLIFFE BIBLE TRANSLATORS, and Youth With A Mission (YWAM) had internationalized in both structure and personnel.

Increasingly North America came to be recognized as a mission field. In 1984 influential missiologist J. E. LESSLIE NEWBIGIN entitled his Warfield Lectures at Princeton Theological Seminary, "Can the West Be Converted?" Newbigin termed this the "crucial ques-

tion" and called for "an effective missionary encounter" with North American CULTURE. These shifts set the scene for North American Protestant missions at the dawn of the twenty-first century. Over the previous century fundamentalism reluctantly gave birth to evangelicalism and evangelical missions; Pentecostalism joyfully, but with some surprise, birthed the Charismatic Movement; and Protestant missions served as midwife at the birth of multiplying Two-Thirds World mission agencies.

Missions in the Twenty-first Century

In 2000 U.S. Protestantism had approximately 118,700 missionaries working abroad (28 percent of the world total) and Canada had 16,500 (4 percent of the world total). Thus the North American foreign missionary force was approximately 135,200, 32 percent of the total worldwide. In addition to career missionaries, this total included a growing number of short-term and "non-residential missionaries" who, often for political reasons, did not take up official residence in their nation of service. Although the numbers of North American missionaries continued to rise, they were becoming a proportionately smaller segment of the world total.

The North American missionary force changed dramatically during the twentieth century, reflecting trends and dynamics noted above. At the beginning of the century the great majority of North American Protestant missionaries were affiliated with historic mainline denominations. The number of mainline missionaries peaked at about 14,000 in the mid-1920s. Because of rapid increase in fundamentalist, Pentecostal, and evangelical missionaries, by 1968 the combined total of IFMA- and EFMA-affiliated foreign missionaries surpassed that of mainline agencies. Most of the increase since 1968 has come, however, from new evangelical, Pentecostal, and charismatic agencies, many unaffiliated with IFMA or EFMA.

In 2000 the North American Protestant overseas missionary force counted approximately 40,000 U.S. and 3,000 Canadian full-time missionaries (excluding short-termers) working in some 200 countries. These missionaries served under 814 North American mission agencies (693 U.S. and 121 Canadian). By 2000 these agencies were also sponsoring some 3,500 non–North American missionaries, plus some 73,000 national workers.

A major trend evident by 2000 was the peaking of the numbers of full-time "career" missionaries and a dramatic rise in short-term missionaries, "tentmakers," nonresidential workers, and nationals sponsored by North American agencies. By 2000 U.S. mission agencies were annually deploying nearly 100,000 short-term (two weeks to one year) workers, although the total number of short-termers, including those sent by local churches and other organizations, may have been as high as 500,000.

Of the 693 U.S. mission agencies identified in the 2001–2003 *Mission Handbook,* only 56 were founded before 1900. The number of U.S. mission agencies increased steadily from the 1930s on; the forming of new agencies peaked in the 1980s, when a total of 141 were founded. By far the largest growth was in mission agencies not affiliated with any denomination. Thus the twentieth century saw a dramatic shift from denominational to nondenominational, interdenominational, and independent societies. By 2000 agencies not denominationally affiliated outnumbered denominational ones nearly five to one.

As of 1998 the five largest U.S. mission agencies were the Southern Baptist International Mission Board (4,562 U.S. workers deployed outside the United States), Wycliffe Bible Translators USA (2,930), YWAM (1,817), Assemblies of God Foreign Missions (1,543), and New Tribes Mission (1,514). The largest Canadian agencies were Wycliffe Bible Translators of Canada (415 workers serving outside Canada), Christian and Missionary Alliance in Canada (210), Brethren Assemblies (192), New Tribes Mission of Canada (187), and the Pentecostal Assemblies (165).

These data reflect four trends in North American missions at the beginning of the twenty-first century: (1) decreasing denominational and increasing nondenominational agencies and missionaries; (2) decreasing numbers of long-term, full-time missionaries and increasing numbers of short-term, bivocational, and other mission personnel; (3) relative increase in Pentecostal and charismatic missionaries; and (4) growing internationalization and globalization of mission agencies. By 2000, for example, Wycliffe Bible Translators International was the coordinating structure for over thirty national Wycliffe sending agencies and a dozen affiliates around the world.

As the twenty-first century began, some observers warned of a looming financial crisis for North American missions attributed to an aging donor base, retirement of "Baby Boomers," and the increasing debt load and (perhaps) isolationism of the rising generations.

References and Further Reading

Anderson, Gerald H. "American Protestants in Pursuit of Mission: 1886–1986." *International Bulletin of Missionary Research* 12 no. 3 (1988): 98–118.
Austin, Alvyn. "Loved Ones in The Homelands: The Missionary Influence on North America." *Evangelical Studies Bulletin* 14 no. 1 (1997): 1–5.
Barrett, David B. "The Twentieth-Century Pentecostal/Charismatic Renewal in the Holy Spirit, with Its Goal of World Evangelization." *International Bulletin of Missionary Research* 12 no. 3 (1988): 119–129.
Barrett, David B., and Todd M. Johnson. *World Christian Trends, AD 30–AD 2200.* Pasadena, CA: William Carey Library, 2001.
Beaver, R. Pierce, ed. *American Missions in Bicentennial Perspective.* Pasadena, CA: William Carey Library, 1977.
Chaney, Charles L. *The Birth of Missions in America.* Pasadena, CA: William Carey Library, 1976.
Coote, Robert T. "Twentieth-Century Shifts in the North American Protestant Missionary Community." *International Bulletin of Missionary Research* 22 no. 4 (1998): 152–153.
Hoyle, Lydia Huffman. "Nineteenth-Century Single Women and Motivation for Mission." *International Bulletin of Missionary Research* 20 no. 2 (1996): 58–64.
McClung, Grant. "Explosion, Motivation, and Consolidation: The Historical Anatomy of the Pentecostal Missionary Movement." *Missiology* 14 no. 2 (1986): 159–172.
McGee, Gary B. "Missions, Overseas (North American)." In *Dictionary of Pentecostal and Charismatic Movements,* edited by Stanley M. Burgess and Gary B. McGee, 610–625. Grand Rapids, MI: Zondervan, 1988.
Robert, Dana L. "The Origin of the Student Volunteer Watchword: 'The Evangelization of the World in This Generation.'" *International Bulletin of Missionary Research* 10 no. 4 (1986): 146–149.
Russell, Thomas. "Can the Story Be Told Without Them? The Role of Women in the Student Volunteer Movement." *Missiology* 17 no. 2 (1989): 159–175.
Siewert, John A., and Dotsey Welliver, eds. *Mission Handbook: U.S. and Canadian Ministries Overseas 2001–2003.* Wheaton, IL: Evangelism and Missions Information Service, 2000.

HOWARD A. SNYDER

MISSIONS TO JEWS

Protestant interest in evangelizing the Jews started with the REFORMATION. MARTIN LUTHER, during his early career as a reformer, believed that the Jews would join his new brand of Christianity, and made attempts at missionizing Jews. Protestant attempts at evangelizing Jews continued in the sixteenth and seventeenth centuries, and a major Protestant mission to the Jews came about in the eighteenth century in GERMANY in the wake of the Pietist revival (see PIETISM). Pietist thinkers such as AUGUST HERMANN FRANCKE and PHILIPP JAKOB SPENER took special interest in the Jews, considering them to be heirs to biblical Israel. In 1728 Pietists established in HALLE the Institutium Judaicum, a missionary center that trained evangelists and produced literature specifically for Jews. Although Pietist missionaries considered the Jews to be morally and spiritually doomed without the ameliorating gospel, they approached Jews expressing appreciation for their role in history. Evangelizing the Jews, they believed, was a manifestation of love and goodwill toward that people. The Institutium Judaicum closed down in 1791 as Pietist interest in the Jews declined.

19th Century Expansion

A strong impetus for evangelizing the Jews arose in Britain in the early years of the nineteenth century. Inspired by Messianic hopes, which included an expectation for the national restoration of the Jews as part of the End Times events, British Evangelicals saw a special calling in evangelizing the Jews. The largest of the British missionary societies (see MISSIONARY ORGANIZATIONS) was the London Society for Promoting Christianity Among the Jews. Established in 1808 the LSFPCATJ enjoyed the support of the official church, as well as the Nonconformists (see CHURCH OF ENGLAND; NON-CONFORMITY). The London Society operated in dozens of Jewish communities around the world, including in the Ottoman Empire, in czarist RUSSIA, and among the Falasha in Ethiopia. At the peak of its activity in the late nineteenth century it employed more than 200 missionaries.

The London Society served as a model for a number of missionary societies in Britain, Germany, Scandinavia, the UNITED STATES, CANADA, AUSTRALIA, and SOUTH AFRICA. Among them were the American Society for Meliorating the Condition of the Jews (established in 1816), the Berlin Society for the Promotion of Christianity Among the Jews (established 1822), and the London-headquartered Mildmay Mission to the Jews, which subscribed to a dispensationalist messianic outlook and was, like the LSFPCATJ, also active in a number of countries. The missionary movement in America grew considerably in the late nineteenth century and early twentieth century as a result of the influence of the dispensationalist messianic faith of American Protestants, which brought about a growing interest in evangelizing Jews (see DISPENSATIONALISM). From one small society in the 1870s, the number of missions grew by the 1920s to more than forty societies employing hundreds of missionaries. Among the more prominent missionary societies in America in the twentieth century were the Chicago Hebrew Mission (called since 1953 the American Messianic Fellowship) and the American Board of Missions to the Jews, which changed its name in 1983 to the Chosen People Ministries. In addition, a number of Protestant denominations, including the PRESBYTERIAN CHURCH U.S.A. and the SOUTHERN BAPTIST CONVENTION, established special departments for missionary work among the Jews.

New missionary societies appeared constantly on the scene, using new techniques for targeting new groups in the Jewish populations. In 1970 Moishe Rosen established JEWS FOR JESUS in San Francisco to evangelize Jewish members of the counterculture. Noted for its innovative methods, Jews for Jesus, originally an arm of the American Board of Mission to the Jews, soon broke away from its mother organization and became the predominant organization in the field.

Focus on Palestine

Of special importance for Protestant missions has been evangelizing among the Jews in Palestine. Beginning in the early nineteenth century Protestant missions sent evangelists to propagate the gospel among the small Jewish population there. By the mid-nineteenth century, it became evident that there was a surplus of missionary activity among the Jewish population of Palestine and missions began shifting their attention from the Jews to the Arab population. The strong missionary presence in the country made an impact on the educational, medical, and economic infrastructure of Palestine. In the twentieth century the Israeli government chose to tolerate the missionary presence, and Protestant missionary activity persisted after the establishment of the State of Israel in 1948, which many evangelical Christians saw as preparing the ground for the events of the End Times. However, the large missionary presence stirred some hostile reactions, especially among members of the Orthodox Jewish community, including unsuccessful attempts at passing legislation intended to put a stop to the missionary activity in the country.

Jewish Reaction

Not only in Israel, but in other parts of the world as well, the extensive missionary activity aroused negative reaction among Jews. Jewish leaders have seen such attempts as a manifestation of long-term hostile Christian attitudes toward JUDAISM and a refusal to accept the legitimacy of the Jewish existence outside of the church. At the same time many poor Jews took advantage of the medical, educational, and relief services that the missions were offering. Unable to organize an effective Jewish boycott of the missions, Jewish community leaders tried to counter the missionary influence by providing the same services the missions were offering. The Christian missionary efforts have ironically served as an incentive for Jews to enlarge the scope of educational activities and philanthropic work among their disadvantaged brethren.

The geographic focus of missionary work shifted throughout the years. In the 1920s the Soviet authorities closed down all missionary stations in Russia. In the late 1930s and early 1940s the Nazis banned missions in Germany as well as in other countries in

Nazi-occupied Europe. The German missionary societies never reopened. With the opening of the ex-Soviet bloc to Christian missionaries in the late 1980s, missions to the Jews have been active there, as well as among Jewish immigrants from Russia in Israel, the United States, and Germany. In the 1950s–1960s a new movement of interfaith dialogue gained momentum and mainline Protestant churches decided to stop their efforts at missionizing among the Jews. The field of missionary work among the Jews became exclusively the realm of conservative Evangelicals, many of whom view the Jewish people as destined to play an important role in the messianic age (see PHILO-SEMITISM). In addition to evangelizing the Jews, evangelical missions have promoted the idea of the centrality of Israel among evangelical Christians who have become ardent supporters of Israel in the American political arena.

The appreciative attitude Pietists and evangelical missions have shown toward the Jewish people, and their claim that the acceptance of Christianity made Jews fulfill their Jewish destiny rather than betray it, gave rise to a community of Jewish converts to Christianity that continued to view themselves as Jews. In the late nineteenth century and the first decade of the twentieth century, some missions even attempted to establish Hebrew Christian congregations. The Jewish Christian community received a strong boost in the 1970s with the rise of Messianic Judaism, a more assertive movement of Jewish converts that gave expression to the new emphasis on ethnic pride and a search for Jewish roots. Missions to the Jews were first suspicious of the new movement, but soon came to appreciate the effectiveness of the Messianic Jewish centers in attracting new converts. Missions such as the Chosen People Ministries and Jews for Jesus have moved to establish Messianic Jewish congregations themselves, thus turning Messianic Judaism into the central arm of the missionary movement.

Conclusion

In sum, Protestants have seen the propagation of the Gospel among the Jews as an important mission. In relation to the size of the Jewish community, missions to the Jews have been among the largest and best funded among Protestant missions, and their activity the most extensive. The Protestant missionary attempts have brought about a large and vigorous movement of converts to Protestant Christianity, the largest Jewish movement of voluntary converts to Christianity in modern times. They have also left a strong mark on the development of Jewish–Christian relationships and indirectly influenced the charitable and educational infrastructure of the Jewish community.

References and Further Reading

Ariel, Yaakov. *Evangelizing the Chosen People.* Chapel Hill: University of North Carolina Press, 2000.

Clark, Christopher M. *The Politics of Conversion.* Oxford, UK: Clarendon Press, 1995.

Thompson, A. E. *A Century of Jewish Missions.* Chicago, IL: Fleming H. Revell, 1902.

YAAKOV ARIEL

MODERNISM

Modernism is a conceptual term encompassing variously related (but also divergent) cultural movements and trends beginning in the late nineteenth century and evolving through the mid-twentieth century. Although primarily a set of Western phenomena, it also affected events throughout the world because of colonial and other hegemonic relations, and was sometimes influenced in turn by cultures under the sway of the West. As historical data its various components had earlier forms that continued to manifest themselves in diverse pockets and guises even into the twenty-first century. In general they can be assessed as reactions to nineteenth-century developments in bourgeois CULTURE under the nation state, and an attempt to (re)appropriate and (re)situate the Western tradition in novel contexts in continuous as well as disjunct ways. In more philosophical terms one could say that Modernism was a particular crisis of humanism (cf. Edmund Husserl) and an attempt to address that crisis. Chief motifs and forces of this crisis included anxiety and disillusionment; industrialized SECULARIZATION; disorientation and melding of the individual; horror of war and domination; failure of representation; and the emergence of new consciousness and voices. Historiographically Modernism is also tied to Postmodernism or POSTMODERNITY, which succeeds and presupposes it. The relation of Modernism to Protestantism is deep and varied, involving give and take between the two, challenges and oppositions.

As a torrent of events chiefly projected in ART and thought, Modernism intersects with but does not equal "modernity" of the said period. Accordingly this essay focuses on that intersection and relates it to Protestant religion. Rather than a summary history in strict chronological order or a catalog of acts and events, the approach adopted here is thematic and suggestive, with the aim of catching in interlocking themes some salient crosscurrents of Modernism, its times, and Protestant concerns. When possible, treatment is also given to the internal dynamics in different realms.

Death, Malaise, Horror, and Disintegration

The apprehension of DEATH invading the palpitations of life had been a recurrent theme in times past, but its latest return in ROMANTICISM did not go beyond thematization and certain stylistic oddities in artistic expression here and there. This was attributed to the grounding strength of Western metaphysics since Plato and Aristotle, and of teleological thinking that gave human beings a sense of purpose (high or low) in life, history, and the world. Even GEORG W. F. HEGEL's *Phenomenology of the Spirit* did not—any more than the FRENCH REVOLUTION—remove these pillars from Western consciousness. Rather, metaphysics and teleological thinking were given a more dynamic, historical (political) spin, and were thus able to overcome or at least withstand temporarily the latest onslaughts of skeptical and pessimistic thought. The latter, moreover, did not cast doubt on the legitimacy of representation as such, but only its objectivity. Finally the practical force of theistic belief, as opposed to its truth or necessity, was rarely put into question.

As the nineteenth century rolled on, this state of affairs began to unravel. Already in Giacomo Leopardi, Francisco de Goya, and SØREN KIERKEGAARD dislocation of the individual from the divinely sanctioned scheme of things was becoming manifest. As had occurred in the Mannerist poet Ronsard during the crisis of humanism in the sixteenth century, WILLIAM JAMES was able to say in 1868 that he sensed a "horrible fear of [his] own existence"—a horror enlarged in Robert Louis Stevenson's Jekyll and Hyde. It was a sort of malaise symptomatic of what FRIEDRICH NIETZSCHE would characterize as the DEATH OF GOD, the end of a robust role for FAITH in God in human society and thus also the end of coherence of meaning and value. The poet Charles Baudelaire, having caught a sense of the horrific from Edgar Allan Poe, would give striking expression to this in his rebelliously psalmic *Fleurs du mal*. Even the pantheistic sentiments of earlier Romanticism evaporated in the Symbolist verse of Paul Verlaine, Arthur Rimbaud, and Stéphane Mallarmé, despite its inclusion of figures from classical myth. Instead NATURE is depicted without an ulterior spiritual sense, in an opacity reflected in the later Italian painter Giorgio Morandi's works, and what remains is the reflection of an ambiguous self. As Gertrude Stein would later put it: "There is no there there." Ezra Pound and T. S. ELIOT, with their often opaque free verse were both heirs to and innovators on this Symbolist dislodgment of affect, although in it the absence of divinity still allowed for a cryptic symbolic force that led deeper than the words to the veiled abyss of the human psyche perhaps, but not to discursive sense. Claude Debussy, Aleksandr Scriabin, and the early Maurice Ravel provided the musical analog to this Symbolist trend, whereas the lack of narrative immediacy in the paintings of Jean Renoir and Claude Monet led the way in its pictorial sibling called, then pejoratively, impressionism. It may seem odd that this novel style should have arisen at a time when Charles Peirce was working out his theory of signs, which he called semeiotic, but built into his triad of object, sign, and interpretant was an implicit nexus of referentiality consistent with the pragmatist dispensing of any prior metaphysics, and anticipatory of Ferdinand de Saussure's structural linguistics and Albert Einstein's relativity.

If representation was eliminated in painting (and other arts) as much by lack of a metaphysical order as by the establishment of photography as the new pictorial art, form itself was also emancipated as a result. Just as line and color were freed from obeying higher calls, so syntax and sound in the poetic art underwent their autonomous fragmentation in Ezra Pound and Eliot. In the case of James Joyce's *Portrait of an Artist as a Young Man,* in which the casting off of faith in God constituted the moment of freedom, the novelistic structure also assumed the logic of serial photographic moments frozen in time bearing no responsibility to each other. Yet the discrete moments still added up to the impression of a whole. In *The Dubliners* the same effect obtained between the short stories, but in *Finnegans Wake,* Joyce took the (nonsensical) fragmentary freedom to such transgressive lengths that constant microscopic change still added up to a monumental valedictory to sense with neither an external narratival coherence and wholeness nor the fault of incompletion.

Whereas the Anglo-Francophone avant-garde and their followers were coming away from discursive rhetoric and sense, some Austro-Germans, in another face of Modernism, were mourning more openly the passing of an age. What Nietzsche diagnosed as the advancing nihilism of the age became the terminal (sometimes manic but often opulent) melancholy of Gustav Mahler, Gustav Klimt, and Raink Maria Rilke on the Austrian side and the sparer Thomas Mann and Stefan George in GERMANY, whereas in Egon Schiele and Oskar Kokoschka the naturalism of the nineteenth century converged with *verismo* opera of ITALY in their shared social realism. At the same time, however, the abandonment of tonality in French painting and music was pushed further, first by the free atonality (with no key) of Arnold Schoenberg and his pupils as well as the bitonality (two simultaneous keys) of Béla Bartók, and then recodified into the system of dodecaphonic composition, in which all twelve pitches of the chromatic scale are given equal status and priority. Wassily Kandinsky, originally Russian, led the way in pictorial abstraction, using geometry and color as constructive elements in a painting free from representation.

New Voices, Consciousness, and Perspectives

The disintegration of *fin de siècle* bourgeois society triggered, then, not only a dismantling of forms, but also a clearing of space for new paths, forms, and voices. The aesthetic practice of Monet, Debussy, Pound, and F. L. Wright all drew inspiration from the Far East, yet it was within the West itself that deeper transformations occurred. Just as the seventeenth century saw the establishment of the male bourgeoisie, emancipated from the nobility in the nineteenth century not only as an autonomous but also a dominant force in cultural politics, so also the Modernist "period" helped solidify the appearance of other political and cultural subjects hitherto emarginated. Children and youth, who had been featured in the fiction of Charles Dickens, now received broader attention (see CHILDHOOD) in the production of children's books and comics, child labor legislation, the urbanistic thought and actions of a Jane Addams, the fiction of J.R.R. Tolkien, C. S. LEWIS, and the autobiographical voice of a Dylan Thomas.

In Europe and America, WOMEN, with significant Protestant contribution, gained suffrage after persistent struggle, and Henrik Ibsen's explorations notwithstanding, female writers such as Virginia Woolf and Simone de Beauvoir sought to stake out a permanent place for women with their own views of themselves, of men and the world, of human relations, with their own uses of language and form. The bitonality of GENDERS explored in Woolf's *Orlando* and *A Room of One's Own* also resonated with the multiple, interdividual voices of *The Waves,* whereas the difficulty of an "aristocratic" Joyce or Eliot would meet its counterpart in the writing of a Gertrude Stein, inspired as it was by Cubist painting. However, participation in public life for women would not be restricted to mental and artistic pursuits, but would extend to the new frontier of athletics and, eventually, access to public office. By contrast, the hypostasis of the terse, rough, and lone male hero had its narration in Ernest Hemingway and the emerging Westerns of Hollywood cinema (see MOVIES). In the midst of these developments tension between the sexes found explosive venting in the fiction of D. H. Lawrence and in Tennessee Williams's *A Streetcar Named Desire,* extending earlier critique of the bourgeois family by Ibsen and August Strindberg, Americanized by Eugene O'Neill. At the same time, love between men and between women became more visible, already codified in Sigmund Freud's quasimetaphysical "HOMOSEXUALITY" and increasingly a matter of public contention (see FREUDIANISM). Marcel Proust devoted a tome to it, Oscar Wilde suffered for it, Stein enjoyed it, and Woolf and Anaïs Nin, although married, had

their episodes with it. The latter, even more than Vladmir Nabokov and Marguerite Duras, pushed the bounds of "permissible" love in her life and art, erasing—almost—the borders between the two.

In America an enslaved black population gained tentative freedom before being ghettoized by segregation and poverty (see SLAVERY; AFRICAN AMERICAN PROTESTANTISM). Nevertheless the contributions of African Americans to SCIENCE, the arts, and political conscience grew, along with greater mobility, to the blossoming of the Harlem Renaissance of the 1920s. As Langston Hughes took the lead in black letters, instilling in his poetry the earthy dignity, rhyme, and rhythm of the black vernacular, the musicians of ragtime, blues, and jazz would also make their mark on the world map and, moreover, energize the popular and high art traditions not only of the Americas but also of Europe as well. The effects of this are traceable in the rags of Erik Satie and Igor Stravinsky, the jazzy compositions of Leonard Bernstein, and even in the aleatory techniques of high Modernism. Indeed, the trailblazing of Louis Armstrong and Ethel Waters would see its reward in the ensconcement of Thelonius Monk and Charles Mingus, with their searching compositional and improvisational procedures, as exponents of a new high American musical culture. These transformations invite comparison with developments in the burgeoning of Yiddish literature, theater, and music, and their effects on the mainstream of Modernist culture. Between the Jewish and black cultures stood the Gershwin (George and Ira) and Marx brothers as figures of cross-fertilization.

Farther south Modernism was charged with political force from the start. It was in the Nicaraguan poet Rubén Darío that the term had its beginning in 1890: as a manifesto of cultural release from Spain. "Postcolonial" from the outset (see POST-COLONIALISM), then, practitioners of Modernist culture there sought to reappropriate Western traditions in their own context. The poets Pablo Neruda and Ernesto Cardenal mingled their love with politics, whereas Miguel Ángel Asturias and Jorge Luis Borges carved out for themselves a mythopoeic world that harked back to the pre-Columbian past, interpenetrating with the historic one. In French Antilles, on the other hand, the resistance to colonial dominance took the form of direct critique and analysis in Aimé Césaire and Frantz Fanon. In these ways the formerly colonized joined rebels from the West itself in fashioning an alternate world. In this connection the "primitivism" of Stravinsky's "Rite of Spring" and Pablo Picasso's use of African masks added (somewhat disingenuously) to self-critique of the West.

Underlying the emergence of alternate worlds in both Europe and the Americas was the play between consciousness and what Freud called the unconscious. Even as James conceived of consciousness as a stream, Freud was engaged in probing the unconscious and its relation to the former. Dreams became important as playground of the unconscious, where the conscious passed off what it could not openly express. Picking up on the trail of the Romantics, expressionism, then Dada, surrealism (led by André Breton and Giorgio de Chirico)—like jazz at its improvisatory best—all became artistic conduits for that unconscious, not only in the life of the individual but of society and the world as well. Techniques of automatic writing and stream of consciousness flourished, pushing beyond what rational thought and creation were capable of, but also commenting on the strange state of things. Even more explicitly than Woolf's *Mrs. Dalloway,* Joyce's *Finnegans Wake* is perhaps the most ambitious and compendious work on the precarious and multivalent nocturnal side of human culture and life, a guide to the Modernist, nonmetaphysical cosmos straddling between sanity and madness.

Apocalypse, Progress, and Alienation

Although Joyce in his *Portrait,* and Vincent van Gogh in his landscapes were capable of atheological ecstasy, most Modernists were less prone to joyous revelations. The Italian futurists were in the artistic minority in aligning themselves unproblematically with the march of technological progress, and although they did open up a new material universe for art, their sanguine plunge into the future was matched perhaps only by that of the Marxist revolutionaries and their inimical capitalist industrialists. Already Herman Melville's *Moby-Dick* and Hugo von Hofmannsthal's Lord Chandos were signaling their horror of violent domination, and Joseph Conrad's exposé on the Belgian Congo made that horror concrete. Within the industrializing West, concern with suicide as an early subject of Emile Durkheim's sociology was followed by presentiments of societal collapse in Edvard Munch's "Scream" and William Butler Yeats's "Second Coming." Within half a century of the horrifically novel American CIVIL WAR and the Franco-Prussian War, that unthinkable apocalypse burst in World War I.

Whatever illusions remained of *fin de siècle* societal order evaporated, and yet returned under different guise. As Eliot's *The Waste Land* was registering the shattered cultural and spiritual landscape, Schoenberg was constructing his new Serialist system; and the Empire State building and Bauhaus were each exalting in its way the new constructivist AESTHETICS worked out in the collage and montage of a Kurt Schwitters or Sergey Mikhaylovich Einsenstein; Benito Mussolini

was steadily mounting his apparatus of fascism, the newest technology of state and society; and Joseph Stalin, his communist variation (see COMMUNISM). In other words a new totality was being hammered out whose form was also its content. In it the archetypal heroes of Carl Jung (see JUNGIANISM) found their incarnations equally on messianic newsreels, comic strips, and cartoons. In this way politics and art shared in a self-justifying form, a sort of text with its own context, and partly because of this homology, the mighty machinery of TOTALITARIANISM was attractive to not a few artists and thinkers. Whereas a film of Fernand Léger's could still celebrate the dance of machines in the rolling 1920s, Charlie Chaplin's *Modern Times* and *The Great Dictator* together constituted a double critique of the economic and political trends of the ominous 1930s, and called into creative question the Nietzschean foray beyond good and evil, explored in Joyce's *The Exile* and Andre Gide's *L'immoraliste* in a still bourgeois context, and given up by Simone Weil under the industrial regime. The drama of Bertolt Brecht turned the alienation of Marxian analysis into a reverse aesthetic principle that was at once pedagogic: to alienate the consumer of art and thus provoke thought.

Although cultural critics of the Frankfurt School were intent on negating everything, and existentialists such as Jean-Paul Sartre and Albert Camus would radicalize the alienation of the individual, it was Samuel Beckett's postwar theater of the absurd that pushed the problem the furthest. What he offered as the crisis of humanism was the posthuman: a postholocaust, postatomic answer to Nietzsche's superhuman, drained of every vim. In this way the apocalypse of World War II had its postmortem in High Modernism, a vision of posthistory without meaning, but also without end. Yet even against the postconsumerist burial in Beckett's *Happy Days* that coincided with the beginning of the Postmodern, a trace of meaning insisted on being examined. The voice of the victim in HOLOCAUST literature, commencing with Elie Wiesel's *Night* (but already presaged by the uncanny Franz Kafka), was a reminder that whatever else was abandoned, memory could not be erased. The broken, fragmentary nature of that memory relinquishing the privilege of a grand narrative became a condition of Postmodernity, both in art and cultural politics.

Modernism and Protestantism

The relation of Protestantism to Modernism as discussed above is complicated by two historiographic problems: terminological and chronological. First, what Protestants (and Catholics) meant by Modernism had more to do directly with the religious liberalism of the time than with the Modernist cultural vanguard (see LIBERAL PROTESTANTISM AND LIBERALISM). Second, many of the encounters between Protestants and Modernism, although begun around the first half of the twentieth century, would continue or develop more fully later, sometimes with a time lag. Examples of this include questions of SEXUALITY, ordination of women (see WOMEN CLERGY), and use of spirituals in mainstream hymnody (see HYMNS AND HYMNALS). Still, neither of these poses insuperable difficulties in historiography. The first can be solved by examining root concerns underlying both kinds of Modernism, whereas the latter is both a function of secularity and the lingering potential of historic forces.

In his analysis of capitalist society at the turn of the twentieth century, MAX WEBER traced its spiritual inspiration to Protestantism, especially CALVINISM. Rationalist thinking and a pious work ethic were pinpointed as decisive factors, although it may be said that the humanist side of the REFORMATION was also operative in that cultural thrust. The Emersonian version of it was amplified by James (see RALPH WALDO EMERSON; TRANSCENDENTALISM). Notwithstanding the irreducibility of ambiguity to which he held (cf. the French Symbolists), James believed—aptly in the age of robber barons—in the Promethean human subject, the proverbial self-made man later denounced in its grossest instance in Orson Welles's films. Yet it was this sort of protean, autonomous individual that constituted the bourgeois subject of the (earlier) Modernist landscape. Even Nietzsche's and Kierkegaard's radical anthropologies bore an ambiguous relation to it.

Within the ambient political economy, the Promethean bourgeois individual was such by relying on one thing: knowledge, or science, in its latest cultural form. In the Protestant world, as in classics, science had taken the guise of HIGHER CRITICISM in biblical interpretation. The plain sense of Lutheran exegesis, stripped of allegorical elaborations, now yielded to literary, historical, and form criticism, resulting in the construction of metanarratives threatening to replace any integral biblical account. CHRISTOLOGY split, then, into a symbolism of humanity (see DAVID FRIEDERCK STRAUSS) and a quest for the historical Jesus (see ALBERT SCHWEITZER; JESUS, LIVES OF). The liberal theological lineage of FRIEDRICH SCHLEIERMACHER, including ALBRECHT RITSCHL, ERNST TROELTSCH, and ADOLF VON HARNACK, accepted this path, and extended its methodologies into THEOLOGY and church history. Albrecht Ritschl opposed natural theology as bridge to Christian faith, yet rested content with Christianity as a subjective appropriation. His pupil ERNST TROELTSCH proposed a philosophy of religion that would, through its historical study of religious consciousness, place Christianity—as a science—in concourse with other ideologies of the time, like materialism and aestheticism. ADOLF VON HARNACK's search for an essence of Christianity was a dehistoricizing phenomenology anticipating Husserl's "science" of noetic analysis. On the social front, humane and charitable action were a frequent concomitant to the theological enterprise of Liberal Protestantism. In this, even evangelical associations such as the YMCA, YWCA (see YMCA/YWCA), and the SALVATION ARMY joined more liberal reformers in promoting wholesome Christian life and the "progressive" agenda of a SOCIAL GOSPEL. As these societies piggybacked on the force of Western powers, they were able to bring their version(s) of Protestant Christianity and modern culture to countries throughout the globe.

Although much of this Christianity was symptomatic of the same conditions underlying postmetaphysical Modernism in the arts, it had its opponents in the church. The Roman church issued stern admonitions against any erosions of churchly TRADITION, AUTHORITY, and autonomy because the "Modernist" movement had gained followers within her own ranks. In Protestant churches the dissent bore diverse types of critical response. One was in the intense fragmentation of ecclesial form into more denominations and subdenominations in the UNITED STATES. Some of these movements were meant to unify all churches, but fell quickly into their own SECTARIANISM. Some arose out of the historical rift between the North and South and the institution of Jim Crow segregation. Later, however, the opposite occurred in the creation of such larger denominations as the UNITED METHODIST CHURCH or UNITED CHURCH OF CHRIST. Even transchurch cooperation began in the WORLD COUNCIL OF CHURCHES on the model of the United Nations. In CANADA most Protestant churches merged under the aegis of a UNITED CHURCH OF CANADA. In South India all Protestant churches united after Indian independence, ending the colonial existence of those churches (see SOUTH INDIA, CHURCH OF). In ENGLAND even bolder gestures of ECUMENISM took place in the St. Alban's Fellowship, which brought together the Orthodox and Anglicans in dialogue and common study (see ORTHODOXY, EASTERN; ANGLICANISM). As churchly fragmentation had a complex relation to the lack of firm doctrinal unity, it was also that same fragmentary pliancy that allowed for recombinations of fellowship previously unconceived.

Just as in secular Modernism, the lack of a viable spiritual life was a concern to Protestants. The decay of both PIETISM and liberal Christianity meant that other points of spiritual grounding had to be found. Although occultism, theosophy, and anthroposophy were common in the Modernist spiritual landscape, most Protestants other than Unitarians (see UNITARIAN UNIVERSALIST ASSOCIATION) had to refer to the Catholic tradition. Here the CHURCH OF ENGLAND provided much leadership. By the 1920s EVELYN UNDERHILL had distinguished herself by her scholarship on the mystics and her spiritual counsel. Aided by previous decades of Anglican patristic scholarship and a Catholic spiritual director, she was able to reintroduce the wealth of the Catholic tradition to her fellow Anglicans, beginning with the Desert Fathers and through the medieval mystics. Into this study she also blended the insights of psychology, thus setting a trend of strong Anglican interest in that field. Bolstering Underhill's work was the liturgical research of Dom Gregory Dix, an Anglican Benedictine who devoted his life to recovering the grammar and form of Catholic and Orthodox LITURGY, in a Christian search for symbolism that Modernist culture was also groping toward. What began thus as the labor of Anglicans in spirituality and liturgy then became the cornerstone of the wider Liturgical Movement among Protestant churches.

In America, where liberal Protestantism and the SOCIAL GOSPEL often went hand in hand, a revolt occurred. While H. RICHARD NIEBUHR contemplated historic models of relations between Christianity and culture and C. S. Lewis was scrutinizing the contemporary scene, H. R.'s brother REINHOLD took the lead in what came to known as the NEO-ORTHODOXY Movement. Critical of the meliorist attitude of liberalism rejected also by Modernists, Niebuhr reminded his public of the reality of SIN. In this he had the agreement of the Anglican T. S. Eliot and the Presbyterian psychiatrist and analyst Karl Menninger, but to this realization Niebuhr would wed the "combative" praxes of SOCIALISM and PACIFISM, inspiring such activists as those of the Fellowship of Reconciliation and the FELLOWSHIP OF SOUTHERN CHURCHMEN in the 1930s. Less accommodating toward the secular vanguard, however, was FUNDAMENTALISM, born in the early 1910s as an evangelical reaction (see EVANGELICALISM) against the encroachments of science and liberalism in biblical interpretation. Against historical criticism and DARWINISM, BIBLICAL INERRANCY and substitutionary redemption by Jesus' death were proclaimed. In their millenarian outlook, fundamentalists shared in the anxious APOCALYPTICISM of the secular Modernists, although with literalist prospects of triumph (soon secularized by the Hitlerites). As in Modernist aesthetics, the fundamentalists' Bible was its own interpreter, providing its own context and justification. In this ironic way fundamentalism became the most staunchly Modernist Protestant movement.

More sophisticated than both Niebuhr and the fundamentalists was KARL BARTH's own Neo-orthodoxy—European style. With wine in hand and Mozart in the ear, Barth sought the recovery of narrative in Christian theology. Eschewing the conceptual enclosure and artificial unity of systems then still present (even in the more engaged Modernist PAUL TILLICH), Barth espoused a grand biblical narrative at odds with Modernist preferences and claims—lost in the abstract designs of church stained glass. Yet his own narrative strategy was influenced by the spiraling style of some Modernist writing. Even more striking is his advocacy, against the more moderate position of EMIL BRUNNER, for autonomy of the Christian faith and the Word of God—a commonality with the fundamentalists that earned him the label "fideist" from his critics, although he did not go as far as to repudiate historical criticism. It must be noted, in any case, that his entry into the mythopoeic world of the Bible was politically targeted at the violent seduction of Nazism, and stylistically related to the literary procedures in Modernist LATIN AMERICA. On both counts Barth was resisting the mimetic force of a liberal society being subverted into a base narrative, but also trying to recover for the Bible what W. Benjamin would have called the "aura" of the work of art.

If disillusionment with the old metaphysical world was sidestepped both by liberal Protestantism and its critics, it was openly confronted by others. DIETRICH BONHOEFFER, in speaking of "the world come of age," was acknowledging the maturity of humanity in sloughing its reliance on comforting doctrines and knowledge. However, instead of turning from faith and the church and proceeding toward an atheological openness and indeterminacy in aesthetics and ethics, as Modernists and their existentialist associates were wont to do, Bonhoeffer proposed—in a world that had already known both Mrs. Dalloway and Hitler—a Kierkegaardian naïveté in faith and an analogy of the I–Thou relation between God and human being amounting to a radicalization of contingency. PROCESS THEOLOGY tried to convert this into philosophical terms, whereas Death of God theologians have problematized it in various existential and ethical ways, sometimes in concert with FEMINIST THEOLOGY. The deinstitutionalizing ECCLESIOLOGY suggested in such expressions of Christianity had already found an experiment in JAPAN's Mukyokai (Nonchurch) movement, but its fuller philosophical articulation awaited the invention of Postmodern theology. In the interim it was the streams of the spirituals and gospel music of black BAPTISTS—even more than the fine collaborations of W. H. Auden and BENJAMIN BRITTEN—that bathed Protestant Christianity in a childlike eagerness for God.

See also Anti-Semitism; Bultmann, Rudolf; Confessing Church; Coffin, Henry Sloane; Ecology; Economics; Ethics; Feuerbach, Ludwig; Hymns and Hymnals; Nationalism; Political Theology; Rauschenbusch, Walter; Sociology of Protestantism; Sports; Sunday School; Theology, Twentieth-Century

References and Further Reading

Audi, Robert, ed. *The Cambridge Dictionary of Philosophy.* 2d edition. Cambridge: Cambridge University Press, 1999.

Baker, Houston A., Jr. *Modernism and the Harlem Renaissance.* Chicago: University of Chicago Press, 1987.

Diepeveen, Leonard. *The Difficulties of Modernism.* New York: Routledge, 2003.

Faulkner, John Alfred. *Modernism and the Christian Faith.* New York: The Methodist Book Concern, 1921.

Ferrall, Charles. *Modernist Writing and Reactionary Politics.* Cambridge: Cambridge University Press, 2001.

Goodheart, Eugene. *Modernism and the Critical Spirit.* 2d edition. New Brunswick, NJ: Transaction Publishers, 2000.

Juschka, Darlene M. *Feminism in the Study of Religion: A Reader.* London: Continuum, 2001.

Kort, Wesley A. *"Take, Read": Scripture, Textuality and Cultural Practice.* University Park: Pennsylvania State University Press, 1996.

Pippin, Robert. *Modernism as a Philosophical Problem: On the Dissatisfactions of European High Culture.* Cambridge, MA: B. Blackwell, 1991.

Sánchez-Boudy, José. *Modernismo y Americanismo.* Barcelona, Spain: Bosch, 1970.

Tracy, David. "Form & Fragment: The Recovery of the Hidden and Incomprehensible God." In *Reflections.* Princeton, NJ: Center of Theological Inquiry, 2002.

DAVID U. LIU

MODRZEWSKI, ANDRZEJ FRYCZ (ANDREAS FRICIUS MODREVIUS) (c.1503–1572)

Polish theologian. Modrzewski was born in Wolborz (Sieradz), POLAND, to a minor aristocratic family. He studied at the University of Krakow between 1517 and 1519 and in Wittenberg between 1532 and 1553, where he befriended PHILIPP MELANCHTHON. From 1536 to 1550 he traveled to many European countries.

Modrzewski began his writing career in 1543 with the publication of his first work *De poena homicidii* (*About the sentence of homicide*), in which he objected to an unjust and discriminatory law. *De Republica emendanda* (*About the Improvement of the Republic*) gained him international renown. The first edition, incomplete because of clerical censure, appeared in Krakow in 1551, with two later editions published in Basel in 1554 and 1559. In this work he presented a program of regime reforms, which generally sought to abolish the primacy of the aristocracy in society, strengthen the power of the monarchy, and improve the situation of townspeople and peasants. Modrzewski also proposed religious reform measures, such as the abolition of clerical CELIBACY, Holy Com-

munion (see LORD'S SUPPER) under two kinds, and lay involvement in decision making in the CHURCH. Moreover, he proposed that representatives of all social classes were to participate in the elections of bishops (see BISHOP AND EPISCOPACY), whereas the pope should be elected by representatives of all churches for a one-year term.

Modrzewski's notions, not exempt from utopian radicalism, triggered negative reactions within the Catholic hierarchy, for whom Modrzewski was a dangerous heretic (see HERESY). On the other hand, Calvinists appreciated him, even though he never submitted his official membership to the Calvinist Church (see CALVINISM). In the mid-1560s the paths of Modrzewski and the Calvinist Church diverted, Modrzewski having shown support for the radical Italian theologian Francesco Stancaro, who argued that the Christ was mediator according to his human nature, an opinion the church vigorously opposed. At the request of King Sigmund August, Modrzewski tried to mediate the conflict over the Trinitarian dogma and Christ's divinity. He presented his views in the work *Silvae quattuor,* published posthumously in 1590. In this work he took the position of nonconfessional UNIVERSALISM, perceiving religion, defined as a few core truths involving SALVATION, mostly as moral doctrine. Although critical toward the traditional Trinitarian dogma, he also kept Anti-trinitarians at a distance because they did not accept the eternity of Christ and infant baptism (see ANTI-TRINITARIANISM). Modrzewski's exploration of these inextricable "forests" (*silva* means forests, brushwood, or thicket) of the most complicated theological problems confirmed his opinion that chances for an end of religious conflict were small. In this situation he believed the monarch carries a specific responsibility. The monarch should try to bring unity among Christians but also guarantee the same rights in religion and freedom of WORSHIP for all dissenters.

See also Calvin, John; Dissent; Toleration

References and Further Reading

Primary Source:

Modrevius, Andreas Fricius. *Opera omnia.* Edited by Casimirus F. Kumaniecki. vols. 1–5. Varsoviae, Poland: PIW, 1953–1960.

Secondary Sources:

Kot, Stanislaw. *Andrzej Frycz Modrzewski. Studium z dziejow kultury polskiej wieku XVI.* Cracow, Poland: Krakowska Spolka Wydawnicza, 1923.

Seguenny, Andre, and Waclaw Urban. "Andrzej Frycz Modrzewski." In *Bibliotheca dissidentum.* Vol. XVIII. Baden-

Baden, Germany & Bouxwiller, France: Editions Valentin Koerner, 1997.

Williams, George H. "Erasmianism in Poland. An Account and an Interpretation of Major, Ever Diminishing Current in Sixteenth-Century Polish Humanism and Religion 1518–1605." *The Polish Review* 22 (1977): 3–50.

LECH SZCZUCKI

MOFFAT, ROBERT (1795–1883)

British missionary. Born in Ormiston, SCOTLAND, December 1, 1795, Moffat was trained as a gardener. He was recruited by the London Missionary Society and in 1817 was sent to southern AFRICA. After gaining fame for converting the notorious frontier freebooter, Jager Afrikaner, he and his wife, Mary, settled at Kuruman among the Tswana where they created a green oasis in semidesert land.

Robert from the beginning sought to master the Tswana-Sotho language so as to translate the BIBLE. The mutually understandable Tswana-Sotho family of languages are understood widely across southern Africa. In 1840 he was able to publish the complete New Testament, a vital contribution to the spread of Christianity over a vast area. Moffat, by this time the father-in-law of DAVID LIVINGSTONE, completed the translation of the Old Testament in 1857 and the complete Bible in Tswana was published the same year.

Moffat also established a close relationship with Mzilikazi of the Ndebele. Mzilikazi had led his people in a breakaway from Chaka's Zulu empire and, after many adventures, established his Sparta-like kingdom beyond the Limpopo in what is now ZIMBABWE. Moffat made three long treks to visit this military kingdom and established a very close relationship with Mzilikazi. This opened the way for the entry of Christianity into Zimbabwe and also aided Livingstone's work farther north.

In March 1870 the Moffats left Kuruman for the last time and returned to Britain. Moffat's *Missionary Labours and Scenes in Southern Africa,* published in 1842, was a most popular and effective propaganda tool for the missionary cause—a cause for which, although deeply affected by Mary's death in 1871, Moffat maintained until 1878 an exhausting program of speeches and lectures. He died in Leigh, ENGLAND on August 10, 1883.

See also Bible Translation

References and Further Reading

Moffat, J. S. *The Lives of Robert and Mary Moffat.* London: Fisher Unwin, 1885.

Northcott, C. *Robert Moffat: Pioneer in Africa.* Cambridge, UK: Lutterworth, 1961.

ANDREW C. ROSS

MOFFATT, JAMES (1870–1944)

Scottish biblical scholar. James Moffatt was born in Glasgow, SCOTLAND, in 1870 and graduated from the University of Glasgow in 1889 with a degree in classics. He then studied THEOLOGY at the United Free College of Glasgow, where he was introduced to biblical criticism by A. B. Bruce, and graduated in 1894. After ordination in the CHURCH OF SCOTLAND in 1896, he served as pastor at Dundonald, Ayrshire. He married Mary Reith of Aberdeen in 1896. In 1901 he published the erudite encyclopedic work *The Historical New Testament,* for which he received a doctorate from St. Andrews in 1902. In 1911, he became minister of the Broughty Ferry Free Church, and later that year he published *Introduction to the Literature of the New Testament.*

From 1911 to 1915 Moffatt served as Professor of Greek and New Testament at Mansfield College, Oxford. In 1913 he published the first edition of his translation of the New Testament. The translation of the Old Testament followed in 1924. He returned to Glasgow as Professor of Church History, serving there from 1915 to 1927, and continued to be a prolific writer of lectures and scholarly articles. In the process he became a recognized expert on all of the traditions of Scottish PRESBYTERIANISM.

In 1927, Moffatt was invited to the Washburn Chair of Church History at Union Theological Seminary in New York. His primary publication of the period was *The First Five Centuries of the Christian Church* (1938). Moffatt served as editor for a 17-volume biblical commentary published between 1927 and 1949. He retired in 1939 and lived in New York, often in bad health, until his death in 1944. During those last years, he served as secretary to the committee that developed the Revised Standard Version of the Bible.

See also Bible Translation

References and Further Reading

Primary Sources:

James Moffatt. *The Historical New Testament.* Edinburgh: T & T Clark, 1901.

———. *Literary Illustrations of the Bible.* London: Hodder and Stoughton, 1905.

———. *Introduction to the Literature of the New Testament.* New York: Charles Scribner, 1911.

———. *The Theology of the Gospels.* London: Duckworth, 1912.

———. *A Critical and Exegetical Commentary on the Epistle to the Hebrews.* Edinburgh: T. & T. Clark, 1924.

———. *The Holy Bible, Containing the Old and New Testaments. A New Translation.* New York: R. and R. Smith, 1926.

———. *The Presbyterian Churches.* London: Methuen, 1928.

———. *The First Five Centuries of the Christian Church.* London: Univ. of Loudon Press, Ltd., Hodder and Stoughton, Ltd., 1938.

———. *The Thrill of Tradition.* New York: Macmillan, 1944.

DAVID BUNDY

MÖHLER, JOHANN ADAM (1796–1838)

Roman Catholic church historian and theologian. Möhler was born May 6, 1796, in Igersheim in Württemberg. Educated at the seminary at Erlangen and in the Catholic theological faculty at the University of Tübingen, Möhler was then appointed to that faculty after ordination. He was strongly influenced by F. W. Schelling and August Neander, and his first book, *Einheit in der Kirche* (1825), showed a marked debt to FRIEDRICH SCHLEIERMACHER. He later became more critical of Schleiermacher, especially on Trinitarian issues. Between 1832 and 1838 he published five editions of *Symbolik,* his comparison of confessional statements of the Catholic and various Protestant churches. Several Protestant theologians wrote replies, most notably FERDINAND CHRISTIAN BAUR. The debate with Baur (including Baur's *Der Gegensatz des Katholicismus und Protestantismus,* Möhler's *Neue Untersuchungen,* and lengthy articles by both) remains the most important exchange on the theological significance of the Reformation in the first half of the nineteenth century. In 1835 Möhler joined the faculty of the University of Munich, but failing health allowed him to lecture there for only one term. He died April 12, 1838, in Munich.

Möhler's *Symbolik* influenced Catholic ecclesiology and the understanding of tradition into the twentieth century. Starting in the 1920s, a revival of interest in his *Einheit in der Kirche* influenced both Catholic and Orthodox theology. He is especially notable as a nineteenth-century Catholic theologian who gave sometimes appreciative, sometimes critical, but always serious attention to his Protestant contemporaries.

References and Further Reading

Primary Sources:

Fitzer, Joseph. *Moehler and Baur in Controversy, 1832–1838: Romantic—Idealist Assessment of the Reformation and Counter-reformation.* Tallahassee, FL: American Academy of Religion, 1974.

Himes, Michael J. *Ongoing Incarnation: Johann Adam Möhler and the Beginnings of Modern Ecclesiology.* New York: Crossroad Herder, 1997.

Secondary Sources:

Möhler, J. A. *Symbolism.* New York: Crossroad Herder, 1997.

———. *Unity in the Church.* Washington, DC: Catholic University of America Press, 1996.

MICHAEL J. HIMES

MOLANUS, GERHARD WOLTER (1633–1722)

German theologian. Molanus was a German Lutheran theologian and church politician who advocated a Protestant monachism and participated in reunion conferences which sought ecclesiastical unity with Rome. Molanus was born in Hameln, North Germany, on November 11, 1633, and died on September 9, 1722, in Hannover. After studying in Helmstedt (1651–1655), he taught at the University of Rinteln (1659–1674), first as a professor of mathematics and after 1664, as a professor of THEOLOGY as well. In 1671 he became a conventual of the monastery of Loccum, in 1674 consistorial director of the duchy of Calenberg (Hannover), and in 1677 abbot of Loccum. Molanus lived a celibate life. He emphasized that only certain excesses of MONASTICISM were non-Protestant and anti-Christian. The reformers fighting against a degenerated monkhood had emptied out the baby with the bathwater. He rejected any curtailment of the ecclesiastical order that was related to a pious believer.

Molanus's significance as a theologian is based on his participation in the efforts for religious reunification, which were initiated by Cristobal Rojas y Spinola. Beginning in 1676 Rojas regularly visited the Guelphic courts on behalf of Habsburg imperial politics and religious reunion. The decisive conference took place in 1683, the year in which Vienna was freed from Turkish siege.

For Molanus the innovation in his reunion strategy was that reunification between Catholics and Protestants should occur despite the divergent principles of the two sides. Whereas Rojas aimed for an authoritarian uniformity, Molanus insisted on free space for specific Protestant positions. As a first step toward agreement, he proposed that the controversial tenets should be formulated as clearly as possible. Therefore Molanus divided the controversies into two categories: those of first rank (communion theology and practice, JUSTIFICATION, MARRIAGE of the CLERGY, validity of Protestant ordination, responsibility of the Protestant estates according to Imperial Law) and those of lesser importance. The first-rank issues had to be settled in internal Protestant agreements and clarifications, eventually replacing the reformation confessions by a series of indispensable doctrines. The pope should accept the Protestants as true members of the church; the Protestants should agree to submit themselves to the pope. In Molanus's opinion, it was not a question of negotiating between two different churches, but whether disagreements could be settled, or allowed to exist within one church.

Thereafter, the discussion should focus on other controversial issues such as TRANSUBSTANTIATION, cults of SAINTS and relics, purgatory, prayers for the dead, papal AUTHORITY in matters of faith, Mary's immaculate conception (see MARY, VIRGIN), and indulgences. Molanus insisted that this discussion be conducted not on the basis of any condemnation of Protestant affirmation, but exclusively on the basis of Holy Scripture. The reunified church had to provide freedom for the indispensable positions of Protestantism.

See also Clergy, Marriage of

References and Further Reading

Dolle, C. A. *Lebensbeschreibung aller Professorum Theologiae zu Rinteln.* vol. 2, 331–338. Bückeburg, Germany: Althans, 1752.

Otte, H., and R. Schenk. *Die Reunionsgespräche im Niedersachsen des 17. Jahrhunderts.* Göttingen, Germany: Vandenhoeck & Ruprecht, 1999.

Weidemann, Heinz. *Gerhard Wolter Molanus, Abt zu Loccum.* 2 vols. Göttingen, Germany: Vandenhoeck & Ruprecht, 1925–1929.

MARTIN TAMCKE

MOLTMANN, JÜRGEN (1926–)

German theologian. Moltmann is widely considered the most influential Protestant theologian during the last three decades of the twentieth century. He was born in Hamburg, Germany, in 1926 and was professor of theology at Tübingen University from 1967 to 1994.

During his time as a prisoner of war in England (1945–1948), Moltmann was converted through an experience of God's presence in the midst of despair. Upon his return to Germany he studied at Göttingen, where the theology of KARL BARTH was in ascendancy. Convinced that Barth's theology could not be surpassed, he was initially an historical theologian. His first publications were on early modern Reformed theology and DIETRICH BONHOEFFER. But his Göttingen teachers, Otto Weber, Ernst Wolf, and Hans Joachim Iwand, provided him with new perspectives: an eschatological view of the church's mission in the horizon of the kingdom of God (Weber and the Dutch theologian A. A. van Ruler), the church's engagement with the new and urgent questions of the postwar world (Wolf), and a dialectical interpretation of the cross and resurrection (Iwand). At an early stage Moltmann's thought entered a lifetime dialogue with Marxist humanists, particularly Ernst Bloch, whose *Principle of Hope* was instrumental in the origination of Moltmann's theology, and with Jewish philosophers and theologians, such as Franz Rosenzweig and Abraham Heschel. From the beginning Moltmann's thought evidenced an openness to the East (Eastern Orthodoxy and Eastern Europe) and to the ecclesial

and political *oikoumene* (ecumenism). He would later be in significant dialogue with theologies throughout the developing world, often visiting churches and theological centers in the Third World while maintaining a periodic presence in theological and ecclesial communities of the United States and Britain.

Moltmann became known throughout the English-speaking Christian world upon the English publication of his *Theology of Hope* in 1967. This was followed by *The Crucified God* in 1972. These first two major books seem very different from each other, although the difference is the key to his whole theological career. The appearance of *Theology of Hope* was announced on the front page of the *New York Times,* which was struck by Moltmann's ability to open Christian theology to the new sensibility of the time in which people were encouraged by possibilities of shaping a humane future and at the same time frightened by the new realities of nuclear and environmental destruction. *Theology of Hope* interpreted the resurrection of the crucified Christ in terms of promise, hope, and mission within an eschatological horizon. Moltmann's project of rehabilitating a futuristic ESCHATOLOGY went against the grain of twentieth-century liberal theology, which had attempted to remove all eschatological/apocalyptic elements from a "modern" faith. This new eschatology, however, made the biblical God plausible to a future-oriented time.

In *The Crucified God* Moltmann worked against what he thought was a too optimistic interpretation of hope in Europe and North America by focusing on the cross of the risen Christ. Here Moltmann deals with God's relation to sin, death, and evil in terms of the power of suffering love and solidarity. The massive inhumanity of twentieth-century systems of domination and the suffering of their victims comes to the fore. In 1975 *The Church in the Power of the Spirit* completed the trilogy of books that set forth Moltmann's new theological vision. This book focuses on the mission of the Spirit emerging from the event of the cross and resurrection, entering the godforsaken world in sacramental presence, and preparing for the coming kingdom in which the world will be transformed in correspondence to the resurrection.

After these programmatic studies, Moltmann developed his systematic theology, which he preferred to call "systematic contributions to theology," in six volumes: *The Trinity and the Kingdom* (1980), *God in Creation* (1985), *The Way of Jesus Christ* (1989), *The Spirit of Life* (1991), *The Coming God* (1996), and *Experiences in Theology* (2000). As was already clear in *The Crucified God,* the dialectic of cross and resurrection requires a trinitarian mode of thought. The crucifixion and resurrection are not external to the Trinity, rather they constitute the relationships of the

Triune community. Thus Moltmann's mature theology is structured by the theme of the trinitarian history of God with the world. This history in which God both affects and is affected by the world is also the history of the divine persons whose communion includes the world within their love.

Moltmann's praxis-oriented eschatology led to what he and Johannes Metz called "Political Theology," which attempts to undermine the religious idols and ideologies that undergird the humiliation and subjugation of people and the exploitation of the earth. The focus on the resurrection leads to a desire for radical historical change, but the cross as the center of Christian theology insists that such change be rooted in solidarity with the victims of society in a common struggle for freedom through the realization of human rights. These reflections proved crucial for opening the way to various LIBERATION THEOLOGIES.

One of Moltmann's lasting contributions is his reconception of the doctrine of God. He offers a fresh treatment of the relationship of divine sovereignty and human freedom by expanding and making more consistent the tradition's understanding of God as trinitarian love. We know God through the narratives of Jesus and the Spirit, but because God is as God reveals Godself, we may speak of the intersubjective relationships of the divine persons. Thus Moltmann criticized the separation of the immanent Trinity and the economic Trinity. Opposed to monarchical and monotheistic concepts of God, Moltmann conceptualized the unity of the divine persons in relationship by retrieving the ancient doctrine of *perichoresis,* according to which the persons of the Trinity are related to each other by coinherence. They are both three and one in their mutual indwelling. He argued against much of the tradition that, because God is so involved in creation that God can be affected by God's creation, theology must speak of God's receptive suffering as well as action. God is conceived in terms of freedom and mutuality instead of the traditional terms of domination and subjection. The resulting social doctrine of the Trinity provided Moltmann's thought structure for new interpretations of the relation of the individual person and community, God and the world, and the church and the world.

Moltmann's messianic ecclesiology is strongly pneumatological. It seeks to free the church from the civil religion of society toward an open friendship modeled on Jesus's solidarity with the poor. In *God in Creation* Moltmann addressed the ecological crisis with a renewed theological understanding of nature and human beings as God's creation. The nonhuman creation is included in the trinitarian history of God. In the course of developing his doctrine of creation Moltmann created a distinctive doctrine of the Spirit ac-

cording to which the Spirit suffers with the creation's bondage to decay, keeping it open to God's future. While refusing pantheistic conceptions of God, Moltmann stressed a "panentheistic" view of God's immanence in creation through the Spirit. God's relationship to God's creation is one of mutual indwelling. Human beings are not owners and dominators of nature, but belong with nature in a community of intricate reciprocal relationships. Moltmann's doctrine of creation and the Spirit also issued in a new Christian appreciation of bodiliness with important implications for SEXUALITY and communal life.

Moltmann's messianic CHRISTOLOGY led to new perspectives on Christian discipleship in the awareness that all life on this planet stands now literally in an apocalyptic end-time situation. Moltmann's theology, however, typically strikes a more contemplative chord as well. Faith is not just a modality leading toward action, but is also doxology, the praise of God in joy. Similarly, theology is not just a theory of practice but is also the enjoyment of God rooted in God's freely given love in creation and redemption.

See also Barth, Karl; Bonhoeffer, Dietrich; Christology; Eschatology; Liberation Theologies; Sexuality

References and Further Reading

Bauckham, Richard. *The Theology of Jürgen Moltmann.* Edinburgh: T & T Clark, 1995.
———, ed. *God Will Be All in All: The Eschatology of Jürgen Moltmann.* Edinburgh: T & T Clark, 1999.
Conyers, A. J. *God, Hope, and History.* Macon, GA: Mercer University Press, 1988.
Meeks, M. Douglas. *Origins of the Theology of Hope.* Philadelphia: Fortress Press, 1974.
Morse, Christopher. *The Logic of Promise in Moltmann's Theology.* Philadelphia: Fortress Press, 1979.

M. DOUGLAS MEEKS

MONASTICISM

The First 1500 Years

The word "monasticism", "monk," "monastery," and "monachism" derive from the Greek *monos*, alone, referring to someone who lives alone or apart from others. Although somewhat similar practices occur in JUDAISM, Buddhism, Hinduism, and Islam, it was the action and teaching of Christ that inspired women and men to undertake the particular form of life known as Christian monasticism. This was a phenomenon of massive significance in the first one and a half millennia of the Christian era. It was seriously challenged in the Protestant REFORMATION. It continued in the less affected parts of Europe and was revived in some Protestant contexts and spread with missionary expansion, though subsequently further diminished by secularization.

Christian monasticism had an early beginning. Some historians have argued that the Pentecostal experience of a common life (Acts 2:44, 4:32) was so revolutionary that it could be safely contained only in discrete communities at a remove from the normal processes of society and politics. Additionally, the practice of Jesus in "going apart" has to be noted, also his call, "If you wish to be perfect, go, sell your possessions, and give the money to the poor, . . . then come, follow me," and his words about those "who have made themselves eunuchs for the sake of the kingdom of heaven." St Paul, likewise, was influential; see, for example, I Corinthians 7, where he assumes that most men and women will marry but advocates the single life. Each of these elements played a part in the birth of this movement, whereas the phrase "Seven times a day do I praise Thee" in Psalm 119 later determined the monastic pattern of prayer, with its intensive use of the psalter.

The movement as such began in A.D. 271, when a young Egyptian, Antony, heard Jesus' words about being perfect and withdrew to live alone in a desert place, dedicated to PRAYER and manual work. His lifelong commitment inspired a remarkable development as thousands of Christian women and men in Egypt followed his example, living initially as hermits and practicing what became known as "the solitary warfare of the desert," but gradually associating in groups embracing a common life. In the fourth century, the movement added the ideal of surrendering personal choice in obedience to a community leader. Thus, although the eremitic ideal of "solitary warfare" persisted, and has persisted to the twenty-first century, the notion of a praying community united in a common life under the three vows—of poverty, chastity and obedience—came to characterize Christian monasticism in its dominant form.

The movement spread throughout the Mediterranean world from the fourth century. Important for its consolidation was the propagation of the spiritual teaching of the Egyptian monastics by John Cassian (c. 360–435). His writing was influential for the best part of a thousand years and carried the early spirituality of the desert ascetics across much of western Europe, reaching Europe's outermost, Celtic fringes in the sixth century. In its Celtic form in IRELAND and the British Isles, it was marked by extreme penitential austerity, a strong missionary impulse, and great art embodied typically in the Book of Kells and the Lindisfarne Gospels. The powerful abbess Hilda of Whitby exemplifies the role of WOMEN in Celtic monasticism.

An important landmark was the *Rule of St. Benedict*, written in ITALY in the early sixth century. This practical, moderate and flexible distillation of the monastic ideal won its way throughout the monasteries of western Europe.

After the time of Benedict, monasticism evolved from countercultural phenomenon to central social and religious institution of pre-Reformation Europe. From small communities of ten or twenty men or women simply housed, monasteries came to comprise communities often of several hundred, with imposing buildings and large landed estates and fulfilling a range of social functions (medical and legal, for example) and uniquely important for both learning and the arts. Exemplifying the musical aspect of the tradition in the twelfth century was the gifted Hildegard of Bingen in GERMANY, underlining the intense focus of the Benedictine rule on WORSHIP. A community might sing and pray the seven canonical hours of the divine office in their abbey for up to eight hours of the day. The abbots were often powerful territorial leaders in the church, and this ecclesiastical as well as economic and social preeminence, although compromised by a system known as *commendam*, which put many monasteries under the control of secular authorities, was characteristic.

The monasteries tended to develop in distinctive groups. Thus, the great abbey at Cluny in FRANCE was by the eleventh century the center of inspiration and authority to sixty-seven others within the Benedictine tradition in ENGLAND, France, Germany, Italy, and Spain, all marked by sophisticated worship, scholarship in THEOLOGY, biblical study, and spiritual instruction. In medieval Europe, a series of developments and reforms followed, creating other new groups. For example, a movement to recover the eremitical element in the tradition culminated institutionally in the Grande Chartreuse in SWITZERLAND, where the life of a hermit was combined with elements of common life in the Carthusian order. Similarly, the Cistercian order was founded at Citeaux in France at the end of the eleventh century to recover an extreme austerity and simplicity of life, avoiding some of the feudal ties of the Cluniac tradition and practicing pastoral farming with the help of lay-brothers. By the fifteenth century, there were more than 900 Cistercian communities of women and 700 of men throughout Europe. Observing the three vows of monasticism, but replacing the settled, property-owning community with itinerant PREACHING and dependence on alms (hence "mendicant"), were orders of friars, founded in the thirteenth century by St. Francis and St. Dominic, also the Augustinians and the Carmelites, all immensely influential in pre-Reformation Europe.

There is another extensive story of monasticism, continuous from the earliest Christian centuries to the modern period, associated with the Eastern Orthodox and Oriental Churches (see ORTHODOXY, EASTERN). With its strong early consolidation in the Byzantine Empire (so that there were, for example, eighty monasteries in Constantinople by the sixth century), Eastern monasticism developed on lines quite different from those in the west. In its Oriental forms, it carried the Gospel to the easternmost limits of the Eurasian land mass. It attracted large numbers of women and men and developed rich traditions of mystical prayer and theology in, for example, its Greek and Russian forms. This Eastern monasticism was almost entirely untouched by the Protestant Reformation, however.

The Protestant Critique

Reform had been characteristic of the monastic movement almost throughout its history. Thus, St. Bernard called on the Cistercians in the twelfth century to follow their rule "to the last dot," and later St. Francis created an order renouncing even commonly owned property.

By the fourteenth century, although reform was continuing, there was growing internal uncertainty about the value and purpose of monasticism, with increasing criticism of abuses. Among the latter, in England, was Langland's poem *Piers Plowman* (c. 1360–1370), where the self-indulgent ease and luxury of some monks and friars is contrasted with the "pure faith" of "simple ploughmen and shepherds and poor common labourers," a view that anticipated the Reformation theme of the PRIESTHOOD OF ALL BELIEVERS. Also in England over the next two decades, Geoffrey Chaucer's *Canterbury Tales* appeared, with searching comic portraits of a prioress, a monk, and a friar. More systematic if less memorable was the criticism by the priest and theologian John Wycliffe, an acquaintance of Chaucer. His fierce objection to "all orders which hold property" was a developing theme by this time, and his advocacy of the state's seizure of such "haughty possessions" under certain conditions made him something of a forerunner of the Reformation. Wycliffe's ideas influenced Jan Hus (1370–1415) in Bohemia, where his followers forcibly closed numerous monasteries.

As the Reformation was breaking, monasticism had a number of humanist critics, including François Rabelais in France, initially a Franciscan, Ulrich von Hutten in Germany, a Benedictine, and the Dutch scholar, Desiderius Erasmus, an Augustinian. His *In Praise of Folly* (1511) has a section titled "Monks" in which, alongside his specific criticisms, he observes that "all men detest them to the height." This great humanist made this observation just six years before the appearance of the Ninety-five Theses, and it indicates the fate facing monasticism within the ambit of the Reformation.

MARTIN LUTHER was himself a monk, and even continued to wear his Augustinian habit for many years after initiating his protest. In his writings the Protestant critique of monasticism finds its definitive form. He wrote only one long work on the subject, *The Judgement of Martin Luther on Monastic Vows* (1521). In this tract, his fundamental insight of JUSTIFICATION by FAITH alone is applied to the issue of lifelong vows, "Though a monk be chaste, obedient, poor, and full of all virtues, and doing all the works you like to name, yet without faith will he not be condemned in spite of the works?" In five parts, the tract repeats this key test relative to "the Word of God . . . faith . . . evangelical freedom . . . the commandments of God . . . and common sense and reason." Luther's purpose was not polemical, but to help those at that time abandoning monastic life to "return to the road all other Christians take and follow Christ in a confident and good conscience." He honored the great historic figures of the movement (e.g., Anthony, Bernard, Francis) and extolled poverty, chastity, and obedience when they serve the kingdom of heaven. When, however, these virtues are believed to "earn" the kingdom or to elevate their practitioners above ordinary Christians, they are "a terrible mistake." Luther's treatment of the question here is spirited and deeply engaged. In addition to this tract, there are some 1,500 other references to monasticism, some quite substantial, scattered throughout his writings. Strikingly, among them are numerous comments on married life as a "far severer training in faith, hope, love, patience and prayer, than there is in all the monasteries, . . . a place among the highest levels of spiritual life."

Other reformers also developed a theological case against monasticism, including Luther's friend PHILIPP MELANCHTHON, HULDRYCH ZWINGLI in Zurich, and JOHN CALVIN in Geneva, though none as thoroughly as Luther. Thus there developed an agreement in the northern European states where Protestantism was in the ascendant that monasticism was a mistaken form of Christian life.

The vigor with which monasticism was suppressed varied. In Germany, in the prevailing princely anarchy, the suppression of some monasteries was relatively orderly, with pensions provided for monks and nuns and resources redirected to educational and charitable ends. But in other cases, as Luther deplored, "the nobles . . . [the] monasteries." In Switzerland, the process was orderly but severe; in SWEDEN, NORWAY, and DENMARK, it was much more gradual. In England (and Ireland slightly later), the process was shamelessly political. Although pensions were provided, the state carried through a systematic suppression between 1535 and 1540, seizing all monasteries and their assets for its own ends. In SCOTLAND, the process was comprehensive but slower.

The fate of the thousands of monks and nuns in northern Europe varied considerably. At one extreme, some of the terrible violence that marks the Reformation was visited on them, as in the case of those Carthusians in London who refused to take the oath of Royal Supremacy. Others fled to countries where Roman Catholic princes ruled, or, as in the Low Countries, moved from Lutheran to Roman Catholic districts. Some (in England, for example), evicted from the great monasteries, continued discreetly in small communities. Others were "re-educated," as in Zurich. Some communities of women in Germany adopted the Lutheran faith but continued to live together by their vows. Monks in many places became parish CLERGY, observing the reformed faith. Some married, like the nun Catherine von Brora, who married the monk Martin Luther.

Inevitably, the heritage of the continuous round of monastic prayer and worship was largely lost in the churches of the Reformation. Lutherans, however, adapted the old services of Matins and Lauds from the monastic Breviary. Archbishop THOMAS CRANMER followed this example in England, reducing the seven canonical hours to morning and evening offices in a BOOK OF COMMON PRAYER suitable for a literate LAITY.

Continuing Monasticism

Estimates suggest that the number of men and women continuing in the monastic life in Europe in the later sixteenth century was just short of half of the pre-Reformation total. The great majority of these were in continuing Roman Catholic countries, France, Italy, southern Germany, Portugal, and Spain, with others also in eastern Europe.

This continuing monasticism was characterized by further reform and development, partly in response to the challenges of Protestantism. During the COUNTER-REFORMATION, the Council of Trent (1545–1563) called for enhanced discipline. New orders appeared, including the Capuchins, with strong social concerns, a characteristic also of a new women's order, the Ursulines. Brotherhoods and sisterhoods of prayer and pastoral work, eschewing the tradition of withdrawal from the world, and known as "oratories," also appeared at this stage. The most striking sixteenth-century innovation was the formation by Ignatius Loyola of the Society of Jesus, the Jesuits (1540). Ignatius decreed that there should be no common participation in the monastic pattern of prayer, thus dispensing with

one of monasticism's oldest features, and stressing such activities as countering Protestant teaching and ministering to unbelievers and the poor. The Jesuits and numerous other orders were energetically missionary in INDIA and the east and the Americas from this time.

The subsequent story of this continuing monasticism has been one largely of ebb and flow, with secularizing forces and state hostility especially evident in the later eighteenth and early nineteenth centuries, revival in the nineteenth century, and further strong expansion outside of Europe. Decline was marked in the second half of the twentieth century in Europe and North America, but further expansion occurred in Asia and AFRICA. More than one million (four-fifths of them women), were participating in the monastic life among Roman Catholicism's more than one billion members at the beginning of the third millennium.

In a small way and as a distinctly minority VOCATION, monasticism returned to the Protestant churches after the Reformation period. Sometimes, this took a modified form, as in the Anabaptist Jacob Hutter's *bruderhof* communal villages in sixteenth-century Moravia (see ANABAPTISM), responding to the text about having "all things in common," and Nicholas Ferrar's seventeenth-century Anglican family-community at Little Gidding in England, while the Anglo-Catholic revival in the nineteenth century (see ANGLO-CATHOLICISM) saw the founding of numerous Anglican variants on traditional Roman Catholic orders, these expanding with the missionary movement. Some of these took interesting contextualized forms, like the women's community, *Chama cha Mariamu Mtakatifu* in Tanzania, a series of ashrams in India such as the *Christa Seva Sangha,* and the missionary order in the Pacific, the Melanesian Brotherhood, where young men take vows for an agreed limited number of years before turning to married life. To a lesser extent, Lutherans have resumed the monastic life, with ventures in Europe and the UNITED STATES in the later twentieth century, including a version of the Bruderhof movement, starting in Germany. Other communities with a family dimension are the IONA COMMUNITY, starting among Presbyterians in Scotland, and a radical Methodist group, the Ecumenical Institute, Chicago. Others have Marxist elements, such as the Society of the Catholic Commonwealth, and Johan Devananda's Devasarana Collective Farm in Sri Lanka. With over one hundred members, both Roman Catholics and Protestants, the monastery founded at Taize in France in 1940 has attracted many young people by its deep devotion and its counter-cultural orientation, suggesting new, ecumenical possibilities for the future.

References and Further Reading

Johnston, William M., ed. *Encyclopedia of Monasticism.* 2 vols. Chicago, IL: Fitzroy Dearborn, 2000.

Knowles, David. *Christian Monasticism.* London: Weidenfeld and Nicholson, 1969.

Luther, Martin "On Monastic Vows," in *Luther's Works*, vol. 44. Edited by James Atkinson. Philadelphia, PA: Fortress Press, 1966.

The Rule of St Benedict. Translated by Justin McCann. London: Sheed and Ward, 1999.

DANIEL O'CONNOR

MOODY BIBLE INSTITUTE

This school in the heart of Chicago was established in 1886 to implement evangelist DWIGHT L. MOODY's vision to provide practical training for lay EVANGELISM. From modest beginnings it has become a degree-granting institution with a variety of graduate and distance-learning programs. Since the 1890s its graduates have influenced EVANGELICALISM around the world.

In the 1880s Dwight Lyman Moody was at the height of his fame as a transatlantic evangelist. He had begun humbly in Chicago, and despite a schedule that left him little time to focus on that city's needs, he remained deeply committed to the church he had established as well as to the efforts of the Chicago YMCA. Tireless and practical, Moody surveyed American Protestantism and concluded that SEMINARIES could not keep up with the demands of America's bustling cities. Demographic changes and swelling immigrant populations demanded a new approach from the churches. Moody worried that many Americans might never hear the gospel. Although he did not oppose seminary training, Moody thought that seminaries often educated people away from the masses. For Moody (who was uneducated and unordained), facility in Greek mattered far less than familiarity with the King James Version of the BIBLE. He thought the times demanded "gap men"—people who could communicate effectively in the gap he identified between the educated clergy and the teeming unchurched masses. Chicago seemed the ideal laboratory in which to test this idea. Its swelling immigrant population made it America's fastest-growing metropolis, and intersecting railroad lines justified its boast to be a national transportation hub. Moody could work through his existing networks, and students could combine study and outreach in one of the country's principal cities.

Chicago offered another advantage in the person of Emma Dryer, a teacher at the Illinois State Normal University when she first met Moody in 1870. With Moody's encouragement, Dryer soon turned her teaching skills to Christian education. Moody urged her to consider a home and school modeled on deaconess training schools. Its purpose would be to train female lay Christian workers. Dryer countered with a proposal for a training school for men and women, but Moody hesitated. His unexpected successes in Europe in the next few years propelled him to fame, and not until the mid-1880s would he carry forward the plans he had discussed with Emma Dryer a decade earlier. Dryer, meanwhile, supervised a growing array of training classes. She appointed students to city neighborhoods for house-to-house visitation and cooperation with local churches. In 1879 she spent a few weeks at a deaconess home run by some of Moody's friends in England. She saw firsthand an impressive training program for home and foreign missionary work.

At a meeting on city evangelization in 1885 Moody challenged his Chicago friends to raise funds to build a permanent Bible institute in the city, and soon money began to come in. In 1886 Moody outlined his expanded vision. His modest commitment to educating female city missionaries had evolved into a broader plan to train men and women who would study in the mornings and apply their studies in afternoon evangelistic outreaches. On January 23, 1886, the *Chicago Tribune* reported Moody's modest curricular intentions: "Never mind the Greek and Hebrew, give them plain English and good Scripture." On Moody's birthday, February 5, 1887, Moody and a group of prominent Chicagoans adopted a constitution for the Chicago Evangelization Society. A week later, they had a charter. Year-round classes at the Training Institute of the Chicago Evangelization Society began in September 1889.

Because the Institute emerged over many years, people have advanced different dates for its founding. The school (which became Moody Bible Institute after Moody's death) recognizes 1886 (the year in which Moody outlined the vision the Institute ultimately implemented) as its founding date. Its first full-time superintendent, REUBEN ARCHER TORREY, assumed his post in 1889. Within a few years the Institute sponsored evening classes and organized its offerings in three clusters: practical work, music, Bible.

Bible institutes like Moody played an important role in post–CIVIL WAR Protestantism. In Britain and the United States, such schools trained lay people as well as clergy in what Moody liked to call "applied Christianity." Moody Bible Institute was not the first Bible institute planted in the United States, but Moody's energy, reputation, and inspiration gave his school immediate national prominence. The institute owed an enormous debt as well to Emma Dryer whose efforts between 1871 and 1886 cultivated the network and organized forms of outreach that ensured the

Institute's success. The inspirational Moody and detail-oriented Dryer parted ways shortly after the Institute opened.

After Moody's death in 1899, Moody's three children, Will, Paul, and Emma Moody Fitt, carried forward their father's efforts in markedly different ways. As more American Protestants overtly accommodated faith to culture, Moody's sons continued their father's tradition of welcoming to the summer conferences Moody had established in Northfield, Massachusetts, people of varying theological views. Moody Bible Institute (where Moody's son-in-law, A. P. Fitt had influence) laid claim to Moody's most conservative legacy. Moody Bible Institute faced the emergence of theological MODERNISM with a staunch affirmation of Moody's evangelistic message and a renewed commitment to education that assumed the verbal inspiration of Scripture. In the first half of the twentieth century, Moody Bible Institute stood squarely in the fundamentalist camp. It cherished the cluster of beliefs that came to be dubbed "the fundamentals"— among them the virgin birth, the substitutionary atonement, the physical resurrection, the premillennial return of Christ, and the verbal inspiration of Scripture. After 1909, Moody students studied their Bibles through the lens provided by C. I. Scofield in the notes to his famous SCOFIELD REFERENCE BIBLE. This text reinforced a growing tendency to limit women's public ministry roles, and it also supported the inclination to distance Moody Bible Institute from PENTECOSTALISM.

In the early 1890s, Moody Bible Institute began publishing a twice-monthly bulletin that lasted just over a year. It returned in 1900 as the *Institute Tie,* a monthly magazine intended primarily for Moody alumni and supporters. In 1907 it broadened its scope and audience, offering book reviews, religious news, Bible study helps, and inspirational articles. From 1910 a new title, *The Christian Worker's Magazine,* reflected these changes. In 1920 this magazine became *The Moody Bible Institute Monthly.* Since 1938 *The Moody Monthly* has become a major conservative Protestant magazine that effectively extends Moody Bible Institute's international influence.

The radio voice of Moody Bible Institute is known as WMBI. It first went on the air in Chicago in 1926. After World War II the Institute began purchasing additional stations to create the Moody Radio Network. Its programming is broadcast around the world, and the radio studies at the Institute offer state-of-the-art facilities to train students as Christian broadcasters.

In 1946 the Institute expanded its offerings to include a program in missionary aviation. Like much of what was done at Moody Bible Institute over the years, this program became a model for others to emulate.

One of Moody Bible Institute's most influential endeavors, the Moody Institute of Science, began in 1945 with an agreement between the Institute and Irwin Moon, a pastor and amateur scientist who by 1945 had demonstrated an ability to engage crowds with narrated science experiments. Moon joined Moody Bible Institute's Extension Department in 1938. In 1939 he presided over a Sermons from Science pavilion at the San Francisco World's Fair. His experiments met with such success that he took his program on the road. During World War II he produced two films using time-lapse photography. With these achievements in hand, he asked Moody to sponsor a laboratory to enable scientific studies that featured God as creator. The first film, "God of Creation," was released in 1946 and showed that Moon intended to use cutting-edge technology to make his point. More than twenty science films followed, each between 30 and 60 minutes long. By the late 1950s church rentals exceeded 15,000 per year. With the advent of video and CD technology, the audience expanded exponentially. The success of Sermons from Science made it inevitable that other types of films would follow. Videos for children, for family viewing, and for devotion and teaching as well as films designed for home educators took their place in the 1980s beside the popular science films.

Also related to Moody Bible Institute is the Moody Press. A major publisher of popular Christian literature, Moody Press evolved from the Bible Institute Colportage Association. Moody believed in mass production of inexpensive Christian literature, and from the 1890s the Bible Institute (through what became Moody Press) issued an expanding line of Bibles, missionary biographies, helps for Christians, Bible study aids, and Christian education materials. Moody Press reaches around the world, and its revenues help fund the Institute's educational programs. In addition the Institute has produced innumerable tracts, pamphlets, and other literature for free distribution.

Within twenty years of its founding, Moody Bible Institute began extension programs that quickly found their niche and gave the Institute a presence in every state, generally through conferences and special series focused on equipping lay people for practical Christian work. Distance learning and online studies extend educational opportunities ever more widely. In addition to reaching out with cutting-edge technology, the Institute invites people in for events that have gained a place on conservative Evangelicals' calendars. Founder's Week has become an Institute tradition. The Institute sets aside the week that includes

Moody's birthday (February 5) for services featuring prominent conservative Protestant leaders. Thanks to the Moody Broadcasting Network, Founder's Week has a national audience. Other Institute-sponsored annual events that draw enormous registrations include a pastors' conference and a church musicians' conference.

Moody Bible Institute is accredited by the American Association of Bible Colleges. Its tax-exempt land on Chicago's near North Side abuts the city's gold coast, but a few blocks to the west students still find evidence of the desperate human need that first attracted Moody to the site.

See also Bible; Bible Colleges and Institutes; Civil War; Evangelicalism; Evangelism; Modernism; Moody, Dwight Lyman; Pentecostalism; Scofield Reference Bible; Seminaries; Torrey, Reuben Archer; Young Men's Christian Association

References and Further Reading

Brereton, Virginia. *Training God's Army.* Bloomington: Indiana University Press, 1990.
Dorsett, Lyle. *A Passion for Souls.* Chicago: Moody Press, 1997.
Findlay, James. *Dwight L. Moody.* Chicago: University of Chicago Press, 1969.
Gertz, Gene A. *MBI: The Story of Moody Bible Institute.* Chicago: Moody Press, 1986.

EDITH L. BLUMHOFER

MOODY, DWIGHT LYMAN (1837–1899)

American revival preacher. Moody was born on February 5, 1837, in Northfield, Massachusetts, a hamlet on the banks of the Connecticut River in the northwest corner of Massachusetts. Northfield was a very attractive place, which Moody viewed as "home" during much of his adult life. The juxtaposition of this sylvan spot so dear to Moody's heart with his career as America's greatest urban revivalist of the late nineteenth century reflected well the ambiguities of national life in the same period as the country rapidly transformed itself from a largely rural to a largely urban society.

Early Years

In 1854 Moody left home to go to Boston. There he began to be drawn directly into the world of nineteenth-century evangelical Protestantism. He joined the Boston YMCA (see YMCA/YWCA), created by Evangelicals specifically to appeal to young people new to the city like himself. He also began to attend one of the best-known evangelical parishes, Mount Vernon Congregational Church. The historical record suggests young Moody's woeful initial readiness for church membership, but nurtured by parishioners and his own enthusiasm, Moody eventually became a church member in May 1856. At the same time, he was also entering the world of business. He became a salesman in his uncle's retail boot and shoe business, one of the key industries that shaped the economy of Boston. Thus by accident or personal choice, the young man was aligning himself with economic and cultural forces that fundamentally shaped both his life and the nation's history throughout the last half of the nineteenth century.

In 1856 Moody decided to move to Chicago, one of the newest, yet most promising metropolitan centers of the nation. Quickly he established himself as an enterprising young businessman, again as a boot and shoe salesman. However, religious interests steadily drew his attention away from economic concerns. He joined the Chicago YMCA, and within a short time had become its president. This put him in almost daily contact with many of the up-and-coming young businessmen whose personal wealth could be turned to evangelical missionary enterprises, especially among the poor and unchurched within the city. By 1860 Moody had organized a small nondenominational sabbath school for poor children who lived in the rundown areas of the near-North Side of Chicago. The pietistical, individual-conversion orientation so characteristic of EVANGELICALISM was at the center of Moody's work now, and the noticeable nondenominationalism of the YMCA and the little sabbath school were also clear precursors to his work after 1875 as a national revivalist.

In the late 1860s and early 1870s, Moody was readying himself for his new endeavors. He hired a young singer and harmonium player, IRA B. SANKEY, to aid him in his religious services. Sankey's music was to be a binding force in Moody's great REVIVALS of the 1870s and after. In 1867 the evangelist ventured overseas to ENGLAND for the first time, indicative of his widening personal horizons, and of the transatlantic nature of Evangelicalism, which nurtured the new aspects of his work. After a time of personal travail in 1870, a powerful religious experience struck him, perhaps his first deeply felt "conversion experience." This event helped to focus and reenergize his life. Finally, in 1871 the great Chicago Fire destroyed all the physical aspects of his life—his home, his sabbath school, and the YMCA's building. To rebuild would be a daunting task. Characteristically, when faced with such challenges, Moody decided to strike out anew in another place. In June 1873, with Sankey at his side, the evangelist left for England.

Sojourn in England

The two years spent in Great Britain were a crucial time for Moody as an urban revivalist. He was adapting revivalism, formerly a key expression of Evangelicalism in small-town and rural America, into a larger, more formal and institutionalized structure that met the spiritual needs of people moving in massive numbers into the new urban industrial centers of America. Ironically, England was the laboratory in which he developed most of the techniques and practices used later in his urban "campaigns" in the UNITED STATES. This included religious services multiple times a week for extended periods in a large auditorium in the downtown area of a city. These urban "tabernacles" were simply secular buildings seating thousands of people. The service utilized massed choirs as well as Sankey's sweet tenor voice (destroyed after a few years because of the absence of modern sound systems). This was mass urban revivalism, far more like the revival work of BILLY SUNDAY and BILLY GRAHAM in the twentieth century than the smaller, more intimate efforts of CHARLES FINNEY just a few years earlier. Moody's simple message of God's transforming love, his storytelling ability (always helpful when focusing on biblical materials), and his image as a clearly religious person possessing the aura and demeanor of a contemporary businessman were all characteristics and key ingredients in his work. Careful analysis of statistics published at the time regarding CONVERSIONS at the mass revivals suggest that Moody did draw many people into the church's orbit (he always referred people to local churches as they left his "inquiry rooms"), but that in the long run the revivals did not affect church membership to any large degree. Beginning in 1875 and continuing into the early 1880s, Moody conducted mass revivals in most of the principal urban centers of the United States, in Brooklyn, New York, and in Manhattan, Boston, Chicago, and eventually smaller cities such as Indianapolis, Louisville, and places on the West Coast. They seemed to be important and spectacular manifestations of religious interest and enthusiasm, but historical perspective also suggests that these revivals had become highly organized, routinized creations of men, not the unexpected "showers of grace" that appeared suddenly from on high according to earlier accounts extending back to New Testament times.

Shift in Focus

By the mid-1880s there were indications that "fields white for the harvest" made possible by mass revivalism were less and less in evidence. Moody sometimes shifted his own work into a different mode: revivals centered in local churches, lacking the mass appeal of previous efforts but perhaps rooted more firmly in local communities and therefore more closely aligned with, rather than in competition with, local pastors and their congregations. Moody also sought to develop other avenues by which to carry on the work of the churches.

In 1875 he returned to his birthplace in Northfield, Massachusetts, to live permanently. Especially there he developed new approaches to EVANGELISM. Concerned about the commonly named "unchurched masses" of the new urban industrial centers, who seemed largely impervious to the blandishments of his revivals, Moody searched for a way to create a new cadre of religious "gapmen." These were to be young people knowledgeable in urban ways and trained to reach out on a more intimate and personal level to the "unsaved" in the slums of America's cities. In the mid-1880s he established two schools in Northfield, one for women and one for men, a traditional approach to education in New England. The Northfield School for Women and Mt. Hermon School for boys never fully achieved his evangelistic goals, although they eventually evolved into two excellent private secondary academies animated by Moody's spirit and frequent physical presence. Given their location, the schools were less effective in preparing young people as revivalists or dispensers of evangelical tracts among city dwellers.

A seemingly more promising effort in Chicago paralleled the work in the East. In 1886 the Bible Institute arose on the near-North Side with the specific intent of training people for work in the teeming working-class neighborhoods close by. Moody found it difficult to provide constant leadership there, although he raised the money to run all three schools until his death. Gradually the Bible Institute was taken over by other evangelical leaders and became MOODY BIBLE INSTITUTE, a well-known evangelical educational institution today.

Final Years

In the 1890s Moody's life seemed a mixture of pluses and minuses. Conservative theologically all his life (he was a biblical literalist and believed in premillennialism), Moody's irenic temper nevertheless enabled him to maintain good relations with theological liberals from evangelical backgrounds such as William Rainey Harper, the first president of the University of Chicago, and preachers WASHINGTON GLADDEN and Lyman Abbott. Moody might be called a cautious "prefundamentalist" because he died before the major controversies in this arena erupted just before World War I. Clearly, though, he was buffeted by the ideological conflicts that were developing in American Protestantism.

His personal life, centered around his family at his beloved home in Northfield, seemed to blossom in his later years. He became greatly overweight, however, and his demanding schedule of revival campaigns and traveling put constant stress on his body. In November 1899 the evangelist suffered a series of small heart attacks in the midst of a revival in Kansas City, and he was forced to return home suddenly. Slowly his heart gave out, and he died in Northfield, surrounded by his family, on December 22, 1899.

See also Biblical Inerrancy; Fundamentalism; Millinarians and Millennialists

References and Further Reading

Dorsett, Lyle W. *A Passion for Souls: The Life of D. L. Moody.* Chicago: Moody Press, 1997.

Findlay, James F., Jr. *Dwight L. Moody: American Evangelist, 1837–1899.* Chicago: University of Chicago Press, 1969. Reprinted in paperback. Grand Rapids, MI: Baker Book House, 1973.

JAMES FINDLAY

MOON, SUN MYUNG (1920–)

Korean church leader. Born to a Presbyterian family in North Korea on January 6, 1920, Sun Myung Moon is known as the founder of the UNIFICATION CHURCH, whose followers are also known as the "Moonies." Moon began his public ministry in South Korea in 1945, claiming to be God's messenger for a new age. In 1951 Moon began to write his teachings called the *Divine Principle.* Four years later Moon founded the Holy Spirit Association for the Unification of World Christianity in Seoul. In 1972–1973 he moved his headquarters to Tarrytown, New York, where his movement took on a world-evangelizing emphasis. He soon became surrounded by controversies over fundraising, tax evasion, and indoctrinating techniques. Moon was convicted of tax evasion in 1982, fined $25,000, and sentenced to eighteen months in prison. In the 1990s he and his church moved to BRAZIL and purchased large regions of rain forest.

The central tenets of Sun Myung Moon's teaching, found in his *Divine Principle,* announce Moon as the messenger sent by God to bring about the originally intended restoration that Jesus Christ was supposed to bring. God is understood as a duality (much like yin and yang), and creation is seen as an emanation of God. The divinely intended purpose for humanity to reach perfection and form a perfect society oriented around the family was thwarted when Eve was tempted by Lucifer into forbidden love, thus causing the spiritual fall of humanity, and entered prematurely (i.e., before they had attained perfection) into MARRIAGE with Adam, thus causing humanity's physical fall. Although Jesus redeemed humanity spiritually, another Messiah (who was prophesied to come from KOREA) was needed to bring about its physical SALVATION through the example of holy marriage and the procreation of perfect children. Moon proclaimed himself as this second Messiah and with his movement announces the aim of unifying of all religions and God's intended universal salvation.

References and Further Reading

Primary Sources:

Moon, Sun Myung. *God's Will and the Ocean.* New York: HSA-UWC, 1987.
———. *God's Will and the World.* New York: HSA-UWC, 1985.
———. *Science and Absolute Values: 10 Addresses.* New York: ICF Press, 1982.

Secondary Sources:

Chyssides, George D. *The Advent of Sun Myung Moon: The Origins, Beliefs and Practices of the Unification Church.* New York: St. Martin's, 1991.
Sontag, Frederick. *Sun Myung Moon and the Unification Church.* Nashville, TN: Abingdon, 1977.

JIN PAK

MORAL MAJORITY

The conservative political action group Moral Majority burst onto the American political scene during the campaigns and elections of 1980, when it mobilized thousands of conservative voters and augmented the Republican landslide that carried Ronald Reagan to the White House.

A group of five men—Baptist minister JERRY FALWELL foremost among them—founded Moral Majority in June 1979. Cofounder Paul Weyrich, the son of German Catholics, played an instrumental role in giving the group its ecumenical flavor by convincing fundamentalist pastors to cooperate with political conservatives from across the theological spectrum. The new group included Evangelicals, Catholics, Mormons, and even atheists—all of whom subscribed to the notion that they represented a "moral majority" among America's citizenry.

This political cooperation marked a departure for fundamentalists, who for most of the twentieth century had espoused separatism from nonfundamentalists to preserve ORTHODOXY. Whereas previous fundamentalists stressed doctrinal purity, Falwell and his "cobelligerents" temporarily set aside theological disagreements in their pursuit of the broadest possible political constituency. Televangelists like Falwell and Texan James Robison used their airtime to deliver politically charged messages to the millions of Americans who watched them each week. They also utilized their enormous mailing lists to distribute the "Moral Majority Report," the group's newsletter.

Leaders described Moral Majority's political platform as "pro-life, pro-family, pro-moral, and pro-American." The group fought ABORTION, pornography, HOMOSEXUALITY, and feminism. Moral Majority endorsed the traditional two-parent family structure, a strong national defense, and American support for Israel. This final point reflected the dispensational heritage of the group's fundamentalist leaders, who believed Israel would play a critical role in the events of the end times foretold in the Book of Revelation. They supported the Jewish state enthusiastically.

Otherwise, Moral Majority concentrated its agenda on domestic (or, as they put it, "moral") concerns. Leaders decried liberal developments—the elimination of school prayer, the legalization of abortion, and the rise of secular humanism in public schools—that threatened to destroy the United States' "Judeo-Christian heritage." Moral Majority poured its efforts and its money into politically conservative campaigns dedicated to stemming the tide of moral erosion sweeping the country. And the group succeeded to a remarkable extent; even conservative estimates of the Moral Majority's influence in the 1980 elections reveal massive impact at the polls. Moreover, Moral Majority managed to mobilize the vote among conservative Protestants, a group many liberal Protestants and secularists considered politically dormant (see LIBERAL PROTESTANTISM AND LIBERALISM).

The heady optimism that dominated the first years of Moral Majority's existence waned, and Falwell decided to fold the organization in 1986. But subsequent developments suggested that Moral Majority had effects that lasted far longer than its seven-year lifespan. Televangelist PAT ROBERTSON made a credible run at the White House in 1988. Republicans wrested control of Congress away from Democrats in 1994 owing largely to the mobilizing power of groups similar to Moral Majority, such as the Christian Coalition. Moral Majority paved the way for conservative Protestants to embrace ecumenical cooperation in the political arena—cooperation unthinkable to a previous generation of separatists.

See also Christian Right; Dispensationalism; Fundamentalism; Politics; Televangelism

References and Further Reading

Liebman, Robert C., and Robert Wuthnow, eds. *The New Christian Right: Mobilization and Legitimation*. New York: Aldine, 1983.
Lienesch, Michael. *Redeeming America: Piety and Politics in the New Christian Right*. Chapel Hill, NC: University of North Carolina Press, 1993.
Martin, William. *With God on Our Side: The Rise of the Religious Right in America*. New York: Broadway Books, 1996.

SETH DOWLAND

MORAL REARMAMENT

Created in 1938, Moral Rearmament (MRA) is an association of activists committed to improving public life through personal moral change. The primary idea driving this international movement is the belief that complex social problems are the outgrowth of individuals' failure to live up to their full potential as moral-spiritual beings. MRA's founder was Frank Buchman (1878–1961), a Pennsylvania-born Lutheran minister who began his ministry with college students in the UNITED STATES and ENGLAND, but redirected his energies to the reconciliation of sociopolitical conflicts in the 1930s. Buchman stirred controversy almost everywhere he went, warning of sexual perversion on university campuses, attempting to befriend high-ranking Nazi officials, intervening in labor strikes, and denouncing COMMUNISM with vehemence. Controversy aside, Buchman helped resolve a myriad of conflicts around the globe, encouraged the belief that moral perfection is possible (see PIETISM), and played a key role in the growth of the twelve-step groups that have helped millions overcome their personal addictions. A seemingly ordinary man on the surface, Buchman's extraordinary influence grew from his investment in a small circle of individuals who themselves invested in others, spreading his vision like seed.

Buchman's Early Career

Frank Buchman discovered the power of forgiveness at a conference for evangelical Christians in Keswick, England, in the summer of 1908. At the time he was bitter about a falling-out with his Lutheran overseers in Philadelphia, but decided to write letters of apology to each of the individuals involved. The experience gave Buchman a tremendous sense of liberation and, with a newfound enthusiasm, he took a position in 1909 as a campus minister with the YOUNG MEN'S CHRISTIAN ASSOCIATION (see YMCA/YWCA) at the Pennsylvania State College. His time with the YMCA would have a formative influence on him, giving him the resources to build his own ministry in the future. Under the tutelage of YMCA leaders, Buchman became even more committed to the ideal of absolute moral purity, began the practice of morning quiet times, and learned to build his ministry one person at a time through careful listening and dialogue. He also learned how to coordinate large outreach events modeled on the nineteenth-century tent meeting, was exposed to an international network of evangelical Christians, and met many of the people who would work for him for decades to come.

Although culturally American in his penchant for cleanliness, his sociability, and his affinity for big events, Buchman was a committed Anglophile his whole life through. This love of England was mutual to some extent because Buchman had the greatest following in England, and to a lesser extent other English-speaking countries like the United States, CANADA, AUSTRALIA, NEW ZEALAND, and SOUTH AFRICA. For years Buchman was active on the campus of England's Oxford University such that people called his circle of men the Oxford Group, a name they embraced until changing it to Moral Rearmament in 1938. The reason for this change was Buchman's contention, at a time when the world was on the brink of yet another cataclysmic war, that social problems were fundamentally the outgrowth of individuals' unwillingness to compromise. With almost three decades of success showing young people how to make peace with God and with others, Buchman was ready to apply his method of reconciliation to labor strikes, political disputes, and other conflicts needing mediation. To widen its appeal and effectiveness, MRA decided to downplay its Christian roots and presented moral reconciliation between people as its central tenet.

Buchman's Later Career

This new direction was one Buchman had already been moving toward for some time. During the mid-1930s, for example, he repeatedly tried to open a dialogue with the Nazi Party in GERMANY, a fruitless endeavor that unfortunately earned Buchman the reputation of a fascist sympathizer. Although he was willing to engage the Nazis, one group Buchman made no attempt to reach was the Communist Party, anathema to MRA's message of class cooperation and religious freedom. During World War II, MRA supported the Allied war effort through patriotic films, conferences, and plays. After the War's end the MRA invited representatives from dozens of nations to its retreat centers in Michigan and Caux, SWITZERLAND, to heal the wounds caused by war. MRA also helped rebuild industry in Britain and in areas of Western Europe and was particularly active in keeping Communism out of the industrialized region of Germany known as the Ruhr. In the mid-1950s MRA launched a world tour of plays criticizing the extremes of both

Communism and capitalism, one of the last major projects Buchman undertook before his death in 1961.

MRA's Influence

During his life Buchman influenced many people who took his ethos of radical reconciliation in new directions. In 1935 it was an Oxford Group chapter in Akron, Ohio, that helped a man named Bill Wilson overcome his dependency on alcohol. Wilson went on to found Alcoholics Anonymous (AA) and incorporated the Oxford Group's ideas of self-examination, acknowledgment of character defects, and restitution for harm done into his new movement; AA then became the blueprint for all other twelve-step groups to come. MRA also set into motion the traveling youth show Up With People in the mid-1960s before it ventured on its own in 1968. Again in the 1980s MRA held the Caux Round Table, which produced the Caux Principles, a standard of business ethics in many university business programs. Currently MRA has chapters in the United States (also called Initiatives of Change), the United Kingdom, Australia, INDIA, BRAZIL, Kenya, and JAPAN.

See also Evangelicalism; Keswick Movement

References and Further Reading

Buchman, Frank. *Remaking the World: The Speeches of Frank Buchman*. London: Blandford Press, 1961.

Driberg, Tom. *The Mystery of Moral Re-Armament: A Study of Frank Buchman and His Movement*. New York: Alfred A. Knopf, 1965.

Henderson, Michael. *The Forgiveness Factor: Stories of Hope in a World of Conflict*. London: Grosvernor Books, 1996.

Lean, Garth. *On the Tail of a Comet: The Life of Frank Buchman*. Colorado Springs, CO: Helmers & Howard, 1988.

TYLER FLYNN

MORAVIAN CHURCH

The Moravian Church, also known as Unity of Brethren or *Unitas Fratrum* (Czech: *Jednota Bratrská*, German: *Brüdergemeine*), is one of the oldest Protestant denominations. It traces its roots back to the fifteenth-century Czech Reformation, but owes its modern character and organization mostly to its renewal under the leadership of Count NIKOLAUS LUDWIG VON ZINZENDORF (1700–1760) at HERRNHUT in 1727. As a result of its pioneering mission work, the Moravian Church is now an international body, consisting of nineteen provinces, with about 800,000 members in twenty-five countries.

The Ancient Unity

The first period in Moravian history is known as the time of the ancient Unity and stretches from 1457, when the early Brethren first organized themselves as an independent group, to the 1620s, when the re-Catholization of the Czech lands led to the Unity's institutional extinction there.

The formation of the Unity in the wake of the Hussite revolution was directly related to feelings of dissatisfaction with the worldliness of the ecclesiastical *status quo* and the desire to return to the purity of the apostolic era. Prompted by the prophetic preaching of the archbishop of Prague, Jan Rokycana, a group under the leadership of Rokycana's nephew, "brother Rehor" (Gregory, d. 1474), moved to Kunvald, a small village in rural northeastern Bohemia, where they established their first congregation in 1457–1658. Calling themselves "Brethren of the Law of Christ" (*fratres legis Christi*) the community accepted the Sermon on the Mount as their guiding principle, embraced a disciplined and simple life removed from urban centers, and rejected civil obligations such as oaths and military service. The belief that only worthy clerics are able to administer the SACRAMENTS effectively persuaded the Brethren in 1467 to separate completely from the established CHURCH by electing three priests. Desiring to connect their new clerical order to the apostolic tradition, one of the priests obtained consecration from a Waldensian elder (although historians consider it doubtful whether this step really provided the Unity with a valid claim to apostolic succession). Despite persecutions the Unity soon gained a considerable following throughout Bohemia and Moravia, although it always remained a minority, never representing more than 5 percent of the whole population.

With the advent of a new generation of leaders in the 1490s, notably Lukás of Prague (1458–1528), the Unity's original stance of withdrawal from the world softened. Membership now became open to town-dwellers and nobles, the church was organized on the basis of a synodical government, and Lukás provided a sophisticated interpretation of its THEOLOGY. His central theological principle was the distinction between essential, ministrative, and incidental matters. Essential for SALVATION, according to Lukás, is God's saving work in Jesus Christ and the human response in faith, love, and hope. Ministrative matters include scripture, the sacraments, and the church and its discipline. Incidental, finally, are matters such as church government or forms of WORSHIP that can be changed according to circumstance. Although Lukás gave soteriological primacy to GRACE rather than works, he maintained that FAITH must express itself in obedience to God's will. Accordingly, the Unity continued to place great emphasis on strict CHURCH DISCIPLINE, but it did not regard itself in an exclusive sense as the only "true" church.

From 1522 on, the Unity's ecumenical openness showed itself in numerous contacts with other REFORMATION groups. The Brethren sent several delegations to Wittenberg and gained MARTIN LUTHER's friendly approval of their confession *Apologia verae doctrinae* (1538). It also had cordial relations with PHILIPP MELANCHTHON and MARTIN BUCER, who like Luther admired the Brethren's practice of church discipline. After 1540 the Brethren turned increasingly to the Reformed tradition, corresponded with JOHN CALVIN and THEODORE BEZA, and sent many of their theological students to Reformed universities. Still, the Unity maintained in some points its own position, for example, by rejecting the idea of the *jus reformandi* that placed the responsibility for the reform of the church into the hands of the secular government.

Throughout the sixteenth century, the Unity experienced further persecutions but also the growth of a branch in POLAND and a German-speaking branch in Moravia. It produced the first Protestant Hymnals (see HYMNS AND HYMNALS) (1501, 1505, 1519), published numerous confessions and CATECHISMS, and worked on a Czech BIBLE TRANSLATION, the six-volume Kralice Bible (1579–1594), which came to be regarded as a classic of the Czech language. Ecumenical deliberations designed to strengthen the political position of the Protestant side resulted in 1570 in an agreement between the Polish branch of the Unity and the Polish Lutherans and Calvinists, known as *Consensus of Sendomir,* and in 1575 in the presentation to Emperor Maximilian II of a common confession supported by all Protestants in Bohemia, the *Confessio Bohemica.*

The seventeenth century brought the Unity a brief moment of legal recognition (1609), but after the defeat of the Protestants at the Battle of the White Mountain (1620) the Brethren again faced severe persecution, some being exiled, others forcibly converted to Catholicism. Several thousand members left Bohemia and Moravia, including the young priest Jan Amos Komenský (1592–1670), and mostly settled around Lesho (Lissa) in Poland. The Peace of Westphalia (1648), which put the Czech lands under Habsburg control, definitively burst any hopes of restoring the Unity in its homeland. The distinguished career of Komenský as bishop, scholar, and educator marks the end point in the history of the ancient Moravian Unity, although remnants of the Polish branch continued to exist until the 1940s.

The Renewed Moravian Church

The renewed Moravian Church regards itself as standing in continuity with the ancient Unity, although strictly speaking the Moravian tradition has only one formative influence besides German PIETISM and the leadership of Zinzendorf. Moreover, until the 1760s the Moravians are more accurately characterized as an interdenominational renewal movement than as a church. Today its rich history, its liturgical and devotional tradition, and its lively sense of fellowship, rather than a specific confessional stance or ethnic origin, defines Moravian identity.

The formation of the renewed Moravian Church until 1760 is inseparably intertwined with the life and leadership of Count Zinzendorf, who permitted a group of Protestant refugees from Moravia, in part descendants of the ancient Unity, to settle on his estate Berthelsdorf in Upper Lusatia (Saxony) in 1722. The village, named Herrnhut ("under the Lord's watch"), soon attracted numerous Pietists and religious seekers from other places and grew into a colony aspiring to be a true community of awakened believers according to the example of the apostolic church. Inner tensions caused a severe crisis in 1726 that required Zinzendorf's active intervention. In May 1727 he introduced two sets of *Statutes,* which outlined his vision of Herrnhut as a community based on fraternal love, as communal COVENANT. On August 13, 1727, the community was ready to celebrate Holy Communion (see LORD'S SUPPER) at the Lutheran parish church at Berthelsdorf and experienced a profound moment of spiritual renewal and reconciliation. With a new sense of unity and purpose, Herrnhut was now on its way to become the center of an evangelistic renewal movement of international scope.

The community's inner development showed itself in the emergence of a set of distinct practices and customs: the members addressing each other as "brother" and "sister" (hence the name *Brüdergemeine* or Brethren's Unity), the use of the lot to discern God's will for important decisions, small circles ("bands") for devotional conversation, the division of the community into groups according to age, sex, and marital status ("choirs"), a continuous PRAYER watch, and specific liturgical forms such as the Lovefeast (an *agape*-meal), the *Singstunde* (a hymn service), and WASHING OF FEET. In 1728 Zinzendorf began to give out short scripture passages as "watchwords" for every day, a tradition continued from 1731 to the present in printed form as Moravian *Watchwords* or *Daily Texts.* Instrumental for the community's external development was the cultivation of a large network of contacts and friends and the decision to begin MISSIONS in places where no one had yet proclaimed the gospel. The first Moravian missionaries, Leonard Dober and David Nitschmann, were sent in 1732 to the slaves on the island of St. Thomas in the West Indies (see SLAVERY). Other ventures followed rapidly: Greenland (1733), Suriname (1735), SOUTH AFRICA (1737), and Pennsylvania in North America (1740), among others. At the same time, the Moravians organized numerous societies throughout Europe, including the Fetter Lane Society in London, which proved instrumental for JOHN WESLEY's conversion.

Although Zinzendorf had originally envisioned the Moravian community to be part of the Lutheran state church, it gained some measure of ecclesiastical autonomy when the last bishop of the ancient Unity, Daniel Ernst Jablonsky, passed on the Moravian episcopal succession to the Herrnhut Moravians by consecrating David Nitschmann in 1735 and Zinzendorf in 1737. In 1742 Frederick the Great granted the Moravians ecclesiastical privileges for Prussia, and in 1749 the English parliament recognized the Moravians as an "ancient Protestant Episcopal church." From 1738 on additional settlement congregations were established in GERMANY, ENGLAND, the NETHERLANDS, and Pennsylvania. Another important development during the 1740s was the so-called Sifting Time (cf. Luke 22:31), a time of intense religious fervor and liturgical creativity in which Zinzendorf's "blood and wounds theology" was carried to the extreme. The Moravians attracted large numbers of followers but also became the object of public controversy with hundreds of books and pamphlets being published on both sides.

By the 1750s the Moravian Brethren formed a vibrant international community, united by a tight net of contacts, a shared sense of commitment to Christ, and a distinct liturgical culture. Although the Moravians emphasized personal CONVERSION and SANCTIFICATION, they understood the Christian life in terms of Luther's *simul justus et peccator* and believed in "sinners' holiness" rather than Christian perfection as propounded by the Wesleys. The core of Moravian spirituality was the inner experience of Christ's presence and the joyful recognition that his death on the cross had paid for one's sins. The spiritual life of the Moravian communities, marked by a strong emphasis on fellowship and simplicity, involved an elaborate rhythm of liturgies and worship, yet it expressed itself also in specific styles of MUSIC and ARCHITECTURE and even in particular work and business ethics. Laypeople, including WOMEN, shared much of the responsibility for the numerous pastoral and administrative tasks.

Zinzendorf's death in 1760 confronted the Moravian community with the enormous challenge of having to establish new structures of leadership. Three general synods (1764, 1769, and 1775) adopted a constitution and set up a central governing board at Herrnhut, the Unity Elders' Conference (UEC). The Moravians in England and IRELAND, in Germany and neighboring countries, and in the North American colonies were organized as provinces. The responsibility for the mission fields lay in the hands of a central mission board attached to the UEC. August Gottlieb Spangenberg (1704–1792) now emerged as the leading figure, toning down the more radical features of Moravian piety to lessen the tension with the established Protestant churches. His biography of Zinzendorf (1772–1775), his doctrinal compendium *Idea Fidei Fratrum* (1779), and the 1778 hymnal prepared by Christan Gregor effectively shaped Moravian theology and worship for the next hundred years. Discouraging growth at the expense of other denominations, the Moravians maintained a large network of nonproselytizing ministries to members of the confessional churches ("diaspora-work"). New missions were begun in South RUSSIA (1768), Egypt (1768), and Labrador (1772), whereas numerous boarding schools flourished in the congregations at home. FRIEDRICH SCHLEIERMACHER spent five formative years in Moravian schools (1783–1787) and later credited the Moravians with having revealed to him the importance of religious feeling.

The most important development in the nineteenth century was the demand of the North American and British provinces for more autonomy. "Home rule" was gradually implemented between 1818 and 1857 and allowed the American Moravians to expand at the Western frontier and to adapt to the American Protestant mainstream. New mission work commenced in Nicaragua (1849), South Australia (1849), Tibet (1853), British Guyana (1878), Alaska (1885), and East Africa (1891). Evangelistic outreach in Bohemia and Moravia was begun in 1862. The general Synod of 1869 initiated steps to lead the established mission fields gradually toward more independence, a development that gained further momentum when World War I forced many German missionaries to withdraw.

The political events of the twentieth century placed a considerable strain on the Moravian Church, especially in Europe, as nationalistic sentiments threatened to undermine its interprovincial unity, and World War II resulted in the devastation of many Moravian congregations and institutions. Singularly important for the development of the modern Moravian Church was the general Synod of 1957 in Bethlehem, Pennsylvania, which affirmed the church's continuing unity, adopted a new Church Order with the doctrinal basis "The Ground of the Unity," and prepared the way for the transformation of the mission fields into self-governing provinces. Accordingly, fourteen new provinces were recognized between 1960 and 1988: Alaska, Costa Rica, the Eastern West Indies, Guyana, Honduras, Jamaica, Labrador, Nicaragua, South Africa, Suriname, Tanzania Rukwa, Tanzania South, Tanzania South-West, and Tanzania West. Most of these provinces have membership in the WORLD COUNCIL OF CHURCHES and other ecumenical bodies. In addition the Moravian Church maintains congregations in North India, operates a home for handicapped children near Jerusalem, and carries out mission work in Zambia, Siberia, and Albania.

Like many other Protestant denominational families, the contemporary Moravian Church has become very diverse ethnically, culturally, and theologically. More members now live in AFRICA (ca. 510,000) and South and Central America (ca. 194,000) than in Europe (c.30,000) or North America (c.53,000). The common council and highest AUTHORITY in matters of DOCTRINE and church order is the international Unity Synod, which meets every seven years and includes elected delegates from each province. Common to the whole Unity is also the threefold order of deacon, presbyter, and bishop (see CLERGY); the use of the *Daily Texts* (now published in about 45 languages); and its Church Order. Although the Moravian Church does not possess its own confessional statement, the "Ground of the Unity" affirms that faith in the triune God, the confession of Jesus as Lord, and fraternal fellowship between the believers form the basis for the worldwide Unity. The ancient creeds and various Protestant confessions are acknowledged as important testimonies of faith. The musical and liturgical traditions, especially the celebrations of Christmas Eve and Easter Morning, remain at the heart of Moravian piety and have in some cases also enriched the life of other Protestant denominations.

References and Further Reading

Brock, Peter. *The Political and Social Doctrines of the Unity of Czech Brethren in the Fifteenth and Early Sixteenth Centuries.* The Hague, The Netherlands: Mouton, 1957.

Crews, C. Daniel. *Confessing our Unity in Christ: Historical and Theological Background to "The Ground of the Unity."* Winston-Salem, NC: Moravian Archives, 1994.

Hahn, Hans Christoph, and Hellmut Reichel, eds. *Zinzendorf und die Herrnhuter Brüder: Quellen zur Geschichte der Brüder-Unität von 1722 bis 1760.* Hamburg, Germany: Wittig, 1977.

Hamilton, J. Taylor, and Kenneth G. Hamilton. *History of the Moravian Church: The Renewed Unitas Fratrum 1722–1957.* Bethlehem, PA: Moravian Church of America, 1967.

Hutton, Joseph E. *A History of Moravian Missions.* London: Moravian Publications Office, 1922.

Podmore, Colin. *The Moravian Church in England, 1728–1760.* Oxford, UK: Clarendon Press, 1998.

Říčan, Rudolf. *The History of the Unity of Brethren: A Protestant Hussite Church in Bohemia and Moravia.* Translated by C. Daniel Crews. Bethlehem, PA: The Moravian Church in America, 1992.

Stoeffler, F. Ernest. *German Pietism during the Eighteenth Century.* Leiden, Netherlands: Brill, 1973.

Strupl, Milos. "Confessional Theology of the Unitas Fratrum." *Church History* 33 (1964): 279–293.

Unitas Fratrum: Zeitschrift für Moravian und Gegenwartsfragen der Brüdergemeine. 1978ff. [Biannual journal of Moravian studies containing articles in English and German English and regular bibliographical updates.]

Zeman, Jarold K. *The Hussite Movement and the Reformation in Bohemia, Moravia and Slovakia (1350–1650): A Bibliographical Study Guide.* Ann Arbor, MI: Michigan Slavic Publications, 1977.

PETER VOGT

MORE, HENRY (1614–1687)

English theologian. The seventh son of an established family of Lincolnshire gentry, More was born at Grantham in that county in October 1614, and then educated at Eton and Christ's College, CAMBRIDGE UNIVERSITY. After his graduation and ordination, in 1641 More became a Fellow of Christ's College, a position he held until his death, rarely leaving his rooms at Christ's, except to visit London or stay with his friend, the philosopher Anne Conway at her estate in Warwickshire.

More's first publication, the *Psychodia Platonica* of 1642, was an important early manifesto for what was to be later known as Cambridge Platonism. A unique synthesis in Spenserian stanzas of early Protestant mystical illuminism and patristic and classical Platonism, these poems also revealed the poet's preference for the new philosophy of Galileo and Descartes and his decisive rejection of both the CALVINISM of his upbringing and the philosophy of the scholastics. This characteristic blend of rational Platonic THEOLOGY and broadly Cartesian natural philosophy appealed to a generation that had reason to question the dogmatic certainties of an earlier age, and was powerfully influenced by the discoveries and methods of the new experimental philosophy.

The most prolific of the CAMBRIDGE PLATONISTS, with over thirty works published in his lifetime, More is now remembered mainly for his natural theology, notably the tracts against "Enthusiasm" and "Atheism" of the 1650s. However, it was also his many theological writings and millenarian commentaries published after 1660 that helped establish his role as one of the leading voices of a moderate "Latitudinarian" party (see LATITUDINARIANISM) within the Anglican Church. After the publication of his Latin *Opera Omnia* in 1675–1679 his earlier English works were made available to a wider Continental audience.

More's contributions to Protestant theology and its philosophical presentation were considerable, if not always easy to categorize. Greatly influenced by Origen and the Neoplatonists, More was a necessitarian, believing that God's goodness was preeminent among his attributes. A follower of Calvin's humanist opponent, SEBASTIAN CASTELLIO, More was a perfectionist, holding that Christ's sacrifice allowed the faithful to achieve a species of spiritual perfection or illumination in this life. This theological optimism and illuminism was the logical foundation of his rational theology, ETHICS, and Platonic psychology and metaphysics. His more controversial defense of the DOCTRINE of preexistence, and lifelong fascination with "evidences" for the world of spirits, were both corollaries of this rational philosophical theology, as was a skeptical epistemology that led him to emphasize the fundamental necessity of religious tolerance, a view that was not always shared by his more dogmatic contemporaries in the church.

See also Anglicanism; Toleration

References and Further Reading

Primary Sources:

More, Henry. *Psychodia Platonica.* London: 1642.
———. *An Antidote against Atheism.* London: 1653.
———. *Conjectura Cabbalistica.* London: 1653.
———. *Enthusiasmus Triumphatus.* London: 1656.
———. *Immortality of the Soul.* London: 1659.
———. *An Explanation of the Grand Mystery of Godliness.* London: 1660.
———. *A Collection of Several Philosophical Writings.* London: 1662.
———. *A Modest Enquiry into the Mystery of Iniquity.* London: 1664.
———. *Enchiridion Ethicum.* London: 1667.
———. *Divine Dialogues.* London: 2 vols., 1668.
———. *An Exposition of the Seven Epistles to the Seven Churches.* London: 1669.
———. *Enchiridion Metaphysicum.* London: 1671.
———. *Opera Omnia.* London: 3 vols., 1675–1679.

Secondary Sources:

Crocker, Robert. "A Bibliography of Henry More." In *Henry More, 1614–1687: Tercentenary Studies,* edited by Sarah Hutton, 219–247. Dordrecht, The Netherlands: Kluwer Academic Press, 1990.

———. "The Role of Illuminism in the Thought of Henry More." In *The Cambridge Platonists in Philosophical Context,* edited by G. A. J. Rogers, et al. Dordrecht, The Netherlands: Kluwer, 1997.

Nicolson, M. H. *The Conway Letters.* rev. edition by Sarah Hutton. Oxford, UK: Clarendon Press, 1992.

Ward, Richard. *The Life of Henry More, Parts 1 and 2.* Edited by Sarah Hutton, et al. Dordrecht, The Netherlands: Kluwer Academic Press, 2000.

ROBERT CROCKER

MORMONISM

Mormonism was a response to the Second Great Awakening of Protestant revivalism in New York State (United States) in the 1820s. In this "burned-over district," named to describe the converting fire of the Holy Spirit, Mormonism shared that widespread premillennial outlook typified by WILLIAM MILLER and SEVENTH DAY ADVENTISM. It exhibits a form of religious protest against existing churches believed to have departed so far from divine truth that they were no longer vehicles of salvation. Accordingly, the church describes itself in terms of restoration, indicating that the Protestant REFORMATION was radically insufficient to cope with the errors of the ages. Shortly after Christ's resurrection, and because of human sin, God removed crucial rites and teachings from the earth; without these, salvation, in its distinctive Mormon form of exaltation, would no longer have been attainable. These ritual and doctrinal truths were restored, along with the Aaronic and Melchizedek priesthoods, through visions and divine personages to the founding prophet, Joseph Smith, Jr. (1805–1844). In 1830 he published *The Book of Mormon* and inaugurated this new church. Since that time, Mormonism has successfully developed into a distinctive form of Christianity that is difficult to equate with any of the major orthodox traditions, especially not the Protestant world of its origin.

Restoration Churches

Smith's original group was called the Church of Christ; this name changed to The Church of the Latter Day Saints in 1834 before assuming—by divine revelation—its final designation as The Church of Jesus Christ of Latter-day Saints (LDS) in 1838. This is not, however, the only group within the broader realm of Smith's restoration, for after his death in 1844, about half the membership lapsed and a crisis was averted in the 1840s and 1850s only with the addition of many emigrant British and European converts. Several groups emerged, each headed by a prophet-like leader claiming to be Smith's authoritative successor.

James J. Strang (1813–1856), a recent convert, claimed the prophetic role and, followed by perhaps a thousand saints, including one of the twelve Apostles and Joseph Smith's mother, was crowned king at Beaver Island, Michigan. He further developed polygamy, baptism for the dead, and endowment rituals and, although he was killed in 1856, this movement continued throughout the nineteenth and twentieth centuries largely in Wisconsin and New Mexico (Quinn 1994:209–12). Sidney Rigdon (1793–1876), a close associate of Smith, headed a smaller group that collapsed in 1876 after a flurry of prophecies of vengeance and polygamous commitments.

The extant Reorganized Church of Jesus Christ of Latter Day Saints (RLDS) was established in 1853 on the belief that the true restoration movement should be led by a lineal descendant of Smith. After much deliberation Smith's son, Joseph III, was ordained as its prophet on April 6, 1860. As greatly averse to polygamy as his mother, he would not join the Utah Church and hardly even accepted that his father had introduced and practiced plural marriage. Accordingly, the RLDS Church rejected polygamy, temple ritual, baptism for the dead, and the rites of endowment that were already distinguishing the evolving Utah-based church. RLDS commitment to continuous revelation remained deep, with notable revelations in 1985 permitting the ordination of women and in 1968 and 1984 prompting the building of a new temple at Independence, Missouri, near its church headquarters. This was deeply symbolic for all Mormons because Smith's earliest prophecies affirmed that Zion, the New Jerusalem, would be established at Independence. Though Mormons only lived in Independence for about one year (1832 through 1833), before being driven out, they remained committed to that eschatological site. The fact that the RLDS owns the temple site there is paradoxical, for it fulfills LDS as well as RLDS hopes, even though the RLDS use of it is radically different from LDS ideals. The RLDS view temples as public places open for religious services, education, and welfare and do not require any special recommendation for access. As such they are Protestant in emphasis. They practice no baptism for the dead, no endowments, and follow mainline Trinitarian orthodoxy with a stress on grace and salvation in Christ. Baptism of those aged eight or over is, however, followed immediately by confirmation. Their Sacrament Service uses bread and unfermented grape juice (the LDS use water), while marriage is regarded more sacramentally than in the Protestant tradition at large. The Reorganized Church of Jesus Christ of Latter Day Saints also calls itself, less formally, The Saints Church, and happily engages with mainstream denominations, seeing itself as part of the ecumenical world of Christianity, even though many mainstream denominations may find its Mormon roots problematic.

Protestant Leaders

A significant issue for historical theology concerns the relationship between Joseph Smith's textual and interpretative contribution to the RLDS movement and, say, that of Simon Kimbangu to The Church of Jesus Christ through the Prophet Simon Kimbangu, which joined the World Council of Churches in 1969. A slightly similar point could even be raised in connection with MARTIN LUTHER (1483–1546) and LUTHERANISM or WESLEY and METHODISM, highlighting a basic Protestant fact that distinct individuals have been dramatically important parts in formulating Christian thinking and practice under very particular social and historical constraints. The time frame of history not only demonstrates the complexity of interaction among biblical texts, patristic formulation, and the paradoxical debates of diverging traditions, but also demands caution over the precise nature of orthodoxy in light of cultural contexts of faith. In this sense the notions of Reformation and restoration offer themselves for both theological and sociological analysis.

Fundamentalism and Polygamy

If the RLDS Church reflects the ecumenical end of the restoration spectrum and the Utah-based LDS Church its center ground, then its exclusive end is occupied by several small groups often described as Mormon fundamentalists. "Fundamentalist" carries a distinctive connotation in Mormonism when compared with Protestant FUNDAMENTALISM at large. It is not primarily concerned with theories of biblical inspiration and interpretation, but with the authority of authentic prophets, their teaching, and practice. Mormon fundamentalism applies more to the family than to the Scriptures, in particular to the practice of plural marriage that developed in early Mormonism but was formally forbidden by the LDS Church in its manifesto of 1890, under government pressure, and was practically abandoned by the 1920s under church threat of excommunication. Small numbers remained committed to polygamy as a divinely revealed truth that had only been eschewed by LDS authorities for political expediency. One folk tradition described how the traditionalist Prophet John Taylor, who believed in polygamy despite persecution and was president of the church from 1880 to 1887 prior to Wilford Woodruff (1807–1898; whose 1890 manifesto prohibited polygamy), had received a special religious experience in 1886. Jesus Christ and the deceased Joseph Smith appeared and told Taylor to set apart several individuals to perpetuate polygamy, a story that validated several groups claiming authority as true perpetuators of Joseph Smith's original work and intention. One of these, The Fundamentalist Church of Jesus Christ of Latter-day Saints, has branches in both Arizona and Utah. Another, The Apostolic United Brethren, has groups in Utah and elsewhere with perhaps some 10,000 members in the 1990s. Its influential leader Rulon Allred (1906–1977) was assassinated in 1977 by members of another fundamentalist segment claiming priority in prophetic leadership. A degree of accommodation between these relatively small groups of polygamists and the legal arm of several states suggests that fundamentalist Mormonism is likely to continue on a low-profile basis. The major Utah-based LDS Church would prefer a complete absence of polygamy in all restoration-related groups to avoid reinforcing the popular but misinformed notion that Mormons "proper" still practice polygamy.

Prophet and True Church

Mormonism explains its origin in terms of Joseph Smith's youthful confusion over the multiplicity of largely Protestant religious messages, of his desire for certainty over the true church, and of subsequent divine restoration of truth. An angel warned against joining existing churches and promised further divine assistance. These visions began in 1820, and in 1823 Moroni appeared, telling Joseph about metal plates. These he finally obtained in 1827 and rendered into English by mystical means variously described as special spectacles, a seer stone, or the Urim and Thummim. Within Mormon tradition Moroni was the son of Mormon, the final prophet who wrote the history contained on the plates, and who added a postscript prior to burying them in approximately A.D. 421 before he died. His reappearance as a resurrected being was the means of restoring the plates to human history. These accounts have attracted considerable attention among critics scrutinizing the magical folk-world of earliest Mormons, including crystal divination, treasure hunting, and the influence of Hermeticism and alchemy (Brooke 1994). Devout Saints have objected to their religion being reduced to a superstitious origin.

Book of Mormon

If Mormonism is a religious response to Protestant revivalism and interdenominational strife, then the *Book of Mormon* mirrors the book-focused biblicism of that early nineteenth-century religiosity. Its contents present a history of ancient American peoples whose ancestry lay in the Holy Land of the Old Testament. These Jaredites migrated from the region of the Tower of Babel to America, where a series of internecine conflicts led to their destruction between 600 and 300 B.C. Further migration from Jerusalem to America was led by Lehi about 600 B.C. When Lehi died, his two sons, Nephi and Laman, headed opposing factions. The Nephites, largely obedient to God, maintained the tradition of record keeping, while the Lamanites were disobedient. The resurrected Jesus appeared not only to his disciples but also in America:

this united the Nephites and Lamanites for some centuries until disobedience once more bred hostility, with the Nephites being destroyed in about A.D. 231. The remnant Lamanites straggled on becoming the ancestors of Native Americans, thus explaining why Mormons engaged in special missions to Native Americans. These themes of obedience and disobedience parallel the phases of faith and error depicted in the historical books of the Old Testament.

The Mormon Church's interpretation of the origin of the *Book of Mormon* has been disputed from the outset by opponents of Mormonism. One alternative theory argued that Smith imitated Solomon Spaulding's manuscript depicting a fictive migration to America. Others saw no need for any preexisting text because Joseph Smith was, himself, a sufficiently creative author. Certainly the book strongly resembles the Bible and repeats many of its themes and modes of expression including a division of the text into named books of chapter and verse.

Canonical Texts

Despite the foundational nature of the book to Mormonism's initial growth, its current profile is relatively low and it is possible to attend LDS meetings without hearing references to it. Nevertheless it assumes the status of a canonical text, shared with the Bible; indeed, an increasingly popular subtitle of the *Book of Mormon* is "Another Testament of Jesus Christ," which also indicates the continued importance of the Bible, specifically in its King James Version, to the saints. Both books provide proof texts, illustrative stories, and devotional reading, and the relationship between them and personal prayer is a noteworthy aspect of LDS spirituality. Mormons often ask prospective converts to read the *Book of Mormon* prayerfully so that God may move them inwardly and attest to the truthfulness of the text and its message. Here Mormonism reflects its Protestant roots in commitment to sacred texts and their authority demonstrated by the internal witness of the Holy Spirit.

Two further volumes, *The Pearl of Great Price* and the *Doctrine and Covenants*, may be added to Mormonism's canonical texts or standard works, as they are called. The relatively short *Pearl of Great Price* of 1851 expresses many LDS ideas and, despite several revisions, remains one of the best overviews of Mormon textual style and religious concerns. It includes the Books of Moses and Abraham, part of Matthew's Gospel in Joseph Smith's version, and part of the history of Joseph Smith's life. The Book of Moses offers a patchwork of ideas of early Mormonism in which the biblical Moses is depicted as encountering God and Satan before moving into the mundane world

of sin and salvation. Moses is tempted after the fashion of Christ's temptation, and there ensues a Genesis-styled creation story including the realization that the disobedience of the Fall was intrinsically positive. The character of Enoch emerges as a preacher, as does the notion of a special priesthood and of the atoning sacrifice of Jesus Christ long before the incarnation. Some see echoes of Freemasonry in this book in its allusions to Cain, who became Master Mahon under the administration of Satan. Cain, and Lamech after him, became masters of the great secret, and the book ends with Noah and a sense of doom and destruction awaiting a wicked world.

The Book of Abraham is seen as "a translation of some ancient records . . . from the catacombs of Egypt" originally written by Abraham. The Book includes illustrations of Egyptian scenes interpreted as sacrifices associated with Abraham. Its preoccupation is with the inheritance of a special priesthood into which Abraham is ordained, having been saved from the sacrificing priests of Egypt. It includes the basic Mormon plan of salvation with the Gods organizing the earth, in texts strongly reminiscent of Genesis, and ends with the creation of Adam and Eve. The sections from Matthew's Gospel (chaps. 23 and 24) afford examples of the way in which Joseph Smith represented biblical texts with appropriate amendments and additions. The extract from the history of Joseph Smith reflects the religious enthusiasm surrounding Smith's boyhood, his sense of confusion and desire for the truth, and the theophany in the woods that promised him divine guidance. It refers to the translation of the *Book of Mormon* and to ordination into the Aaronic and Melchizedek orders of priesthood.

The *Doctrine and Covenants* is a collection of revelations received by Joseph Smith and his prophetic successors. Divided into sections and verses, it also resembles the biblical format. This volume is significant because the greatest number of these revelations are dated after the publication of the *Book of Mormon* in 1830 and document the various changes that took the church in a unique direction and away from its original and more Protestant matrix. It covers many aspects of church organization and of belief. For example, section 89 presents the Word of Wisdom enshrining the dietary code now involving abstinence from tea, coffee, alcohol, and tobacco. Section 132 outlines the eternity of marriage and the propriety of plural unions. Two concluding declarations deal with the abandonment of polygamy (1890) and the ordination of worthy males regardless of race or color (1978). The RLDS *Doctrine and Covenants* contain many more revelations than its LDS counterpart because its prophets offer regular and frequent directives to their church.

Church Structure and Organization

LDS Church organization follows a pyramidal hierarchy headed by the prophet-president recruited as the senior of the twelve apostles. As with all major office holders, he is supported by two counselors. Beneath him and the twelve are the seventy individuals who bear responsibility for regions of the world. Local organization is by stakes, led by stake presidents, subdivided into wards led by bishops. Stakes are named from the symbolic representation of the posts supporting the overarching tent of the Kingdom of God. Stake presidents and ward bishops are lay workers, unpaid and self-supporting through their secular employment. Mormons speak of "calling" leaders to their office, held for three to five years, before "releasing" them again. All moves are believed to be under the direction of the Holy Spirit and involve a relatively rapid turnover of personnel, with individuals moving up and down within the formal organization rather than following an inevitable, upwardly directed, career path. Senior posts are held by Melchizedek priests actively involved in temple rites. There is a developmental plan within the two priesthoods with boys entering the Aaronic priesthood at age twelve, becoming, in turn, deacons, teachers, and priests; and at about age nineteen they are ordained into the Melchizedek priesthood as elders. They may, subsequently, be ordained High Priests, as are local bishops and other key office holders. The office of Seventy is also a subdivision of the Melchizedek priesthood. There are no offices for women, who are expected to participate in the priesthood of their husbands.

Other functionaries include patriarchs whose office has undergone radical change over the history of the church (Bates and Smith 1996). Joseph Smith ordained his father as first patriarch, an office held by lineal successors of the Smith family until 1979, when the emphasis shifted to numerous regional patriarchs. These confer blessings by the laying on of hands, especially for young people setting out on their mission or their life's work. The patriarchal blessing is believed to come by direct inspiration of the Holy Spirit: it is written down, kept by the individual concerned and by church records, and is not disclosed to people at large. This patriarchal office serves as a mystical complement to the bureaucratically formal duties of the bishop. Still, each father is also said to have a patriarchal role within his family and may give blessings when required.

Missionaries, Protestant and Mormon

Missionary work underlaid Mormonism's early success. While missionaries were often older people, today most are in their early twenties. After brief training, including basic language learning, men serve for twenty-four and women for eighteen months, at their family's expense. This period reinforces missionaries in their own faith as much as it leads to new converts: it also helps prepare future church leaders. If it is true that active missionary work was a relatively new phenomenon in Western Christianity born not in the Reformation but in the late eighteenth and early nineteenth centuries (van Rooden 1996), then Mormonism must be considered as one prime example of this essentially Protestant process.

Temples and Chapels

Mormonism uniquely possesses sacred buildings of two types—temples and chapels. Temples host key rituals ensuring salvation or, in Mormon terms, exaltation. There are very few temples in each country or state compared with the many chapels that serve as local meetinghouses open to all. Temples are open only to members holding a certificate of recommendation granted by local church leaders after a formal interview. This establishes the bearer as living a morally acceptable life, supporting the church and its leaders, paying a tithe, and observing the dietary codes. Chapels are the local meeting places open to all and host numerous events, including the weekly Sacrament Service. This uses bread and water in a strongly memorialist rite conducted by Aaronic priests under overall Melchizedek control. The water is dispensed in individual cups and anyone may participate, including small children. Once a month a Fast and Testimony Meeting frames the Sacrament Service; this emphasis upon testimony also echoes Protestant Evangelicalism and stresses the importance of personal experience in the life of the believing member of the community.

Temple Rites

Temple rites, including baptism for the dead, eternal marriage, and endowments for the living and the dead, distinguish the church from its Protestant origin. The baptismal font, large enough for total immersion, stands on the backs of twelve life-size oxen and occupies the temple basement. Temple marriage is for all eternity and not only for this life and is achieved by a ritual "sealing" of partners that constitutes the basis of parental authority over the eternal family group. Endowment ceremonies of ritual washing and anointing, cleansing from worldly taint, and vows that dedicate members in obedience to God are both educative and salvific. Through a series of rooms, and by film, Mormons are taught the Plan of Salvation involving the preexistent world when all dwelt with God as intelligences, the Fall, the Atonement of Christ, repentance and obedience to the rites of the church, and the promise of eternal destinies in the afterlife. Initiates who enter into solemn covenants with God and vow to live according to divine laws are granted promises safeguarding their resurrection into the higher heavenly realms in a profound conquest of death (Buerger 1994). Special ritual clothing includes footwear, hats, robes, gloves, and an apron, and reflects Joseph Smith's brief period as an initiated Freemason. The Endowment unites husband and wife as a pair progressing together into a divine status according to the LDS ideology that all are "gods in embryo." These rites underpin the hope of family-focused eternal life including dead kinsfolk. The ideal family unit of heaven would be polygamous, a practice introduced in 1833 and only officially abandoned in 1889 and 1990 due to severe governmental opposition.

Smith was a political as well as a religious leader and, following opposition and civil unrest, was killed in 1844 in Carthage, Illinois. This the Saints saw as martyrdom. A brief leadership conflict favored Brigham Young (1801 through 1877), who continued the western trek and established the Salt Lake basin as a Mormon heartland, though it attained statehood as Utah only in 1896. Temple-building, extensive missionary work, and intensive bureaucratic church management yielded one of the most successful of all nineteenth-century groups of Protestant origin.

Doctrinal Emphases

Mormons distinguish between salvation and exaltation. Salvation for Mormonism is grounded in the removal of original sin through the suffering and death of Christ. Thereafter individuals are responsible for keeping their vows, obeying divine laws, and fulfilling their obligations associated with the temple rituals that permit endowed, sealed, and married Saints to attain exaltation, the highest status in the series of the three heavens of the telestial, terrestrial, and celestial kingdoms. LDS theology developed an emphasis up the suffering of Christ in Gethsemane, including the sweated blood of atonement, and holds strong reservations about depicting the cross. Here it diverges from the traditional Protestant theology of the cross. The efforts of Christ in atonement are matched by the efforts of Mormons in attaining exaltation. Having initially drawn away from Protestant evangelical notions of rebirth, Mormonism, at the dawn of the twenty-first century, expresses an inevitable tension between grace and endeavor, reflecting its Protestant ancestry and its own activist ethic of progression into

deity through obedience to the laws and ordinances of the gospel.

Global Presence

The growth of Mormonism from tens in 1830 to some 11,000,000 by 2000 has encouraged the idea that Mormonism is set to become the next world religion after Islam (Stark 1984). While the nineteenth-century church grew in the United States as a result of European migrant converts, most twentieth-century growth was within North America. The late twentieth and early twenty-first centuries, however, witnessed major developments in Latin America and elsewhere, encouraged by the new revelation of 1978 admitting black males to the priesthoods for the first time. Still, the church's ethos and organization remain under strong North American, indeed Utahan, control, and this is likely to continue in a world where global institutions offer a powerful identity transcending indigenous custom.

References and Further Reading

Arrington, Leonard J. *Brigham Young, American Moses.* Urbana and Chicago: University of Illinois Press, 1986.

Bates, Irene M., and E. Gary Smith. *Lost Legacy, The Mormon Office of Presiding Patriarch.* Urbana and Chicago: University of Illinois Press, 1996.

Brooke, John L. *The Refiner's Fire, The Making of Mormon Cosmology, 1644–1844.* Cambridge: Cambridge University Press, 1994.

Buerger, David John. *The Mysteries of Godliness: A History of Mormon Temple Worship.* San Francisco: Smith Research Associates, 1994.

Bushman, Richard L. *Joseph Smith and the Beginnings of Mormonism.* Urbana and Chicago: University of Illinous Press, 1984.

Davies, Douglas J. *The Mormon Culture of Salvation.* Aldershot: Burlington Ashgate, 2000.

Mauss, Armand L. *The Angel and the Beehive, The Mormon Struggle with Assimilation.* Urbana and Chicago: University of Illinois Press, 1994.

McConkie, Bruce R. *Mormon Doctrine.* 2nd ed. Salt Lake City, UT: Bookcraft, 1979.

Quinn, Michael D. *The Mormon Hierarchy Origins of Power.* Salt Lake City, UT: Signature Books and Smith Research Associates, 1994.

Rooden, Peter van. "Nineteenth-Century Representations of Missionary Conversion and the Transformation of Western Christianity." In *Conversion to Modernities: The Globalization of Christianity,* edited by Peter van deer Veer. New York and London: Routledge, 1996.

DOUGLAS J. DAVIES

MORRISON, CHARLES CLAYTON (c.1874–1966)

American publisher. Morrison was a 34-year-old minister in Chicago when he bought the religious periodical *Christian Century.* The *Christian Century,* founded at Des Moines, Iowa, in 1884 was published by and for members of the DISCIPLES OF CHRIST denomination. Acting as its editor and publisher from 1908 to 1947, Morrison used the influential journal to voice his views on a wide range of social and political issues including PACIFISM, prohibition, women's suffrage, racism, and ECUMENISM.

Morrison was an advocate and subsequently a leader of the ecumenical movement. He was a delegate to the WORLD MISSIONARY CONFERENCE in 1910, and was an ardent supporter of several ecumenical bodies including the Federal Council of Churches and the WORLD COUNCIL OF CHURCHES. In support of his ecumenical philosophy, Morrison amended the title of the *Christian Century* to include the subtitle "An Undenominational Journal of Religion" in 1917.

Although Morrison supported U.S. participation in World War I, he did so in the spirit of WOODROW WILSON's statement that it would be the "war to end all wars." Morrison later repudiated armed conflict and was involved firsthand in the Kellogg–Briand Peace Pact of 1928—a treaty designed to outlaw WAR. He was also vocal in his condemnation of CAPITAL PUNISHMENT and racism, and was an ardent supporter of women's suffrage. Conspicuously, Charles Morrison lobbied for prohibition since the time he acquired the *Christian Century.* His campaign mounted as passage of the Volstead Act neared, and continued because of the widespread flouting of the act's provisions.

Charles Morrison campaigned vigorously for the separation of CHURCH AND STATE, believing it to be vital to the spiritual health of the nation. To that end, Morrison was one of a handful of prominent Protestant leaders who designed and founded Protestants and Other AMERICANS UNITED FOR SEPARATION OF CHURCH AND STATE.

Although best known for his involvement with the *Christian Century,* Morrison also founded the ecumenical quarterly *Christendom* and was its editor from 1935 to 1939. To satisfy his own interest in PREACHING, he founded the *Pulpit,* a journal of contemporary preaching in 1929.

Charles Clayton Morrison died on March 2, 1966, in Chicago.

See also Periodicals, Protestant; Publishing, Media; Temperance

References and Further Reading

Delloff, Linda M. "C. C. Morrison: Shaping a Journal's Identity; pt. 1." *Christian Century* 101 (1984): 43–47.
Haseldon, Kyle. "Charles Clayton Morrison at Ninety." *Christian Century* 81 (1964): 1486–1488.

HELEN FARLEY

MOSHEIM, JOHANN LORENZ (1693–1755)

German Lutheran theologian. Shaped by both Lutheran ORTHODOXY and the ENLIGHTENMENT, Mosheim was one of the leading theologians and churchmen of his day. Through his groundbreaking historical works he is often considered the founder of the discipline of modern church history.

Born in 1693 to a family of modest circumstances in Lübeck, Mosheim found distinguished patrons who financed both his schooling in Lübeck and later his studies at the University of Kiel. He received his master's degree in 1718 and was named lecturer at Kiel the following year. Mosheim established himself academically in 1722 with an extended critical response to JOHN TOLAND's *Nazarenus,* in which he criticized the Deist presuppositions of Toland's views of early Christianity as unhistorical (see DEISM). In it Mosheim displayed two traits that characterized much of his later career: rigorous investigation of the historical sources and a commitment to preserving the divine AUTHORITY of the New Testament Scriptures. In 1723 he accepted a position as professor of THEOLOGY at the University of Helmstedt. There, Mosheim developed as an extraordinarily prolific scholar, publishing widely in both German and Latin on ETHICS, homiletics, biblical criticism, rhetoric, and especially church history. He declined a professorship at the newly established University of Göttingen in 1734. However, in 1747 he accepted the call as chancellor and professor of theology in Göttingen, where he remained until his death in 1755.

Mosheim represents a mediating position between Lutheran orthodoxy and the early Enlightenment. Against advocates of natural religion Mosheim consistently maintained the authority of supernatural revelation and the centrality of the church's proclamation and SACRAMENTS. In this sense he extended the Lutheran orthodox tradition into the eighteenth century. Opposing NATURAL LAW advocates such as CHRISTIAN THOMASIUS of territorialism, Mosheim also became a vigorous defender of the independence of the church and CLERGY within the state. At the same time Mosheim was not adverse to a moderate Wolffian rationalism of CHRISTIAN WOLFF, and he differed with earlier Lutheran orthodoxy on a number of points. He rejected the verbal inspiration of Scripture and distanced himself from traditional CHRISTOLOGY. In place of the metaphysical and mystical assumptions of Lutheran orthodoxy he emphasized an enlightened moralism.

Mosheim's greatest contribution to Protestantism lies in his church historical works. He broke with older confessional models and severed theological judgments from the work of the historian. The historian's task was to evaluate the sources even-handedly and identify the coherent themes throughout the centuries. Consequently, Mosheim's work exhibited an openness to other traditions, and he developed a tolerant understanding of HERESY that reflected his Enlightenment commitments. His most original work concentrated on the early church (*De rebus Christianorum ante Constantinum Magnum commentarii* [1753]) and the problem of heresy (*Anderweitiger Versuch einer vollständigen und unpartheyischen Ketzergeschichte* [1748]). The oft-revised *Institutiones historiæ christianæ antiquioris et recentioris* (final edition 1755) was translated into English, German, Dutch, and French and reprinted frequently in Europe and America. It became the dominant church historical textbook of nineteenth-century Protestantism.

See also Church and State, Overview

References and Further Reading

Primary Source:

Mosheim, Johann Lorenz. *Institutes of Ecclesiastical History, Ancient and Modern.* Translated by James Murdock. New Haven, CT: A. H. Maltby, 1832.

Secondary Sources:

Mulsow, Martin, et al., eds. *Johann Lorenz Mosheim (1693–1755): Theologie im Spannungsfeld von Philosophie, Philologie und Geschichte.* Wiesbaden, Germany: Harrasowitz, 1997.

Stroup, John. *The Struggle for Identity in the Clerical Estate.* Leiden, Netherlands: Brill, 1984.

JONATHAN N. STROM

MOTT, JOHN RALEIGH (1865–1955)

American missionary statesman and ecumenical architect. Mott was born at Livingston Manor, New York, and grew up in Postville, Iowa, in a devout Methodist home. His parental home, friendship with the evangelist Dwight L. Moody, and wide reading in the history of the evangelical movement shaped Mott's ecumenical EVANGELICALISM. He was educated at Upper Iowa University (1885) and Cornell University (1888). In 1891 he married Leila White.

At Cornell, Mott became leader of the Cornell University Christian Association, developing it into the largest student Young Men's Christian Association (YMCA) in the United States. In 1886 Mott participated in DWIGHT L. MOODY'S (1837–1899) summer conference for students at Northfield, Massachusetts, and was among the one hundred students who signed what became the Student Volunteer Movement

(SVM) pledge: "It is my purpose, if God permits, to become a foreign missionary." Although Mott would never serve as a missionary, he became one of the primary leaders of the movement that would send more than 20,000 students into foreign missions over the next five decades. Adopting the slogan "The evangelization of the world in this generation," Mott and the SVM caught the rising tide of student interest in foreign missions. He organized the SVM around the quadrennial missionary conventions that attracted thousands of students from all over North America. Mott soon took steps to organize SVMs throughout the world.

Upon graduation from Cornell, Mott accepted a one-year assignment with the Inter-Collegiate YMCA as traveling secretary. His gifts for friendship and communication with students, abilities as a visionary leader and astute judge of character, and astonishing capacity for work quickly became known. Mott served the YMCA as student secretary from 1889 to 1915, and as general secretary from 1915 to 1931. Evangelical in character and evangelistic in thrust, the YMCA was closely identified with the foreign missions movement. Its nondenominational character and worldwide network furnished Mott the ideal base from which to conduct his multifarious activities. From the beginning he fostered openness toward all Christian traditions, including Roman Catholics. As YMCA leader in 1897 he began actively working to include the Orthodox Churches.

With a vision of uniting Christian students throughout the world, Mott organized the World's Student Christian Federation (WSCF) in 1895. He served as the WSCF secretary between 1895 and 1920 and as chairman from 1920 to 1928. An inveterate traveler, Mott canvassed the universities of Europe, the Middle East, and Asia to draw students into the WSCF. He emphasized the equality of all nationalities and the inclusion of women. He organized international conventions of the WSCF in Tokyo (1907) and Constantinople (1911). By 1900 he was widely known and could count as personal friends many Christian leaders from all continents.

In 1893 Mott took the lead in founding the Foreign Mission Conference of North America (FMCNA). This brought together many of the Protestant mission agencies in Canada and the United States. When the idea of a WORLD MISSIONARY CONFERENCE (WMC) was conceived in 1907, Mott used the FMCNA to mobilize North American participation. He insisted that the conference foster cooperation. The WMC held at Edinburgh, Scotland, in June 1910 with Mott as moderator, was attended by 1,200 delegates sent by missionary societies. It marked the high point of Mott's leadership as missionary statesman. It was decided at Edinburgh to set up a continuation committee with

Mott as chair. In 1912 and 1913 Mott spent twenty months traveling throughout the world to encourage the organization of national Christian councils. Some thirty councils resulted from this work. These became the foundation for subsequent ecumenical relations and work. Although World War I interrupted the momentum of these initiatives, the work of the continuation committee resulted in the founding of three organizations: International Missionary Council (IMC, 1921), Life and Work Movement (1925), and Faith and Order (1927). J. H. Oldham, coordinator of EDINBURGH 1910, became secretary of the IMC. Mott chaired the IMC from 1928 to 1946.

By 1910 Mott was an eminent world Christian leader. His friendship with President WOODROW WILSON (1856–1924) started when the latter was on the faculty of Connecticut Wesleyan University and Mott was active in campus ministry. In 1914 President Wilson invited Mott to accept appointment as U.S. ambassador to China, an offer he declined; but he did agree to serve on peace commissions to Russia in 1916 and Mexico in 1917.

An incurable ecumenist, Mott thought in the broadest possible terms and bent every effort to bring peoples and groups together. At Edinburgh in 1910, Bishop Charles Brent, a friend of Mott, caught the vision for what would become the ecumenical movement. From his position in the IMC after 1921, Mott worked closely with longtime colleagues in the Faith and Order and Life and Work movements to bring about a unified organization. This was finally achieved in 1948 with the creation of the WORLD COUNCIL OF CHURCHES (WCC) in Amsterdam, a fitting climax to his lifelong quest for unity. At age 83 Mott was named honorary president of the WCC.

John R. Mott remained a layman throughout his life. It was observed that he used his status as a layman to advantage in relating to church leaders of many traditions. By nature self-assured and with no ecclesiastical dignity to protect, he met leaders of all ranks freely and did not hesitate to bring together representatives of various traditions for consultation and cooperation.

See also Moody, Dwight Lyman; World Council of Churches; World Missionary Conference; YMCA/YWCA.

References

Primary Sources

Mott, John R. *Strategic Points in the World's Conquest,* New York: F.H. Revell. 1897.
———. *The Evangelization of the World in This Generation.* New York: Student Volunteer Movement. 1900.
———. *The Pastor and Modern Missions.* New York: Student Volunteer Movement. 1904.
———. *The Decisive Hour of Christian Missions.* New York: Laymen's Missionary Movement. 1912.
———. *The Present World Situation.* New York: Student Volunteer Movement. 1914.
———. *The Present-Day Summons to the World Mission of Christianity.* Nashville, TN: 1931.
———. *Addresses and Papers.* 6 vols. New York: Association. 1946–1947.

Secondary Sources

Fisher, Galen M. *John R. Mott: Architect of Cooperation and Unity.* 1952.
Hopkins, C. Howard. *John R. Mott, 1865–1955, A Biography.* 1980.
Mackie, Robert C. *Layman Extraordinary: John R. Mott.* 1965.
Matthews, Basil. *John R. Mott: World Citizen.* 1934.

WILBERT R. SHENK

MOTT, LUCRETIA COFFIN (1793–1880)

American abolitionist and women's rights leader. Born on Nantucket Island, Massachusetts, to a Quaker family, Lucretia Coffin married James Mott in 1811 and moved to Philadelphia, Pennsylvania, where she became a minister in the SOCIETY OF FRIENDS in 1821. Starting in the 1820s, Mott began lecturing on TEMPERANCE, PACIFISM, and the abolition of SLAVERY.

In 1833 she and her husband attended the inaugural convention of the American Anti-Slavery Society. She then cofounded two women's abolitionist organizations. Many opposed her activism; attempts were made to ransack her home and revoke her ministerial credentials. In 1840 she and her husband were delegates to the World's Anti-Slavery Convention in London. There she and other women, including ELIZABETH CADY STANTON (1815–1902), were infuriated when prohibited from being seated due to their sex.

This event galvanized Mott's commitment to women's rights and sealed her friendship with Stanton. In 1848 the two organized the first U.S. women's rights convention in Seneca Falls, New York. This convention produced the Declaration of Sentiments modeled on the DECLARATION OF INDEPENDENCE. In 1866 Mott established the American Equal Rights Association with Stanton and was elected its first president.

For the remainder of her life, Mott served as elder stateswoman to the women's rights movement. She also supported freedom of religion; in 1867 she was a founding member of the Free Religious Association with Isaac Mayer Wise, RALPH WALDO EMERSON (1803–1882), and Robert Dale Owen. She died in 1880 in Philadelphia. Her legacy is a passion for liberation motivated by the Friends' faith in the Inner Light.

References and Further Reading

Bacon, Margaret Hope. *Valiant Friend: The Life of Lucretia Mott.* New York: Walker, 1980.

———. *Mothers of Feminism: The Story of Quaker Women in America.* San Francisco: Harper & Row, 1986.

Greene, Dana, ed. *Lucretia Mott: Her Complete Speeches and Sermons.* New York: Edwin Mellen, 1980.

EVELYN A. KIRKLEY

MOVIES

In assessing the relevance of cinema to the study of Protestantism, one concludes that popular movies have limited value as a source for understanding the Protestant tradition because much of the portrayal of religion in the movies is superficial or stereotypical. However, contemporary movies provide an important medium through which many of society's perceptions of religion in general are communicated. In this sense, knowledge of how movies tend to portray Protestantism can provide helpful insight into cultural attitudes and prejudices about elements of Protestant traditions or doctrine. In addition, Protestant churches might express interest in contemporary movies because of increasing concern over films that appear excessively violent or that transgress certain moral and ethical considerations. The student of Protestantism should approach contemporary movies knowing there will be little that will pass as documentary and much that will reveal contemporary cultural perceptions of religion.

Contemporary Films and Religion

Popular movies have not been kind to organized religion, particularly Christianity. Generally, when popular movies treat religion or religious subjects, they do so in superficial and stereotypical fashion. Roman Catholicism has been a favored target in movies such as *Dogma* and *The Exorcist.* In such films, even if religion is not the primary subject, it is often portrayed as corrupt or strangely out of touch with contemporary and secular society. Protestantism has fared little better in films such as *Inherit the Wind, Elmer Gantry,* or *Leap of Faith* where Protestant piety is portrayed as corrupt, simple minded, or superfluous. Non-Christian religions get less attention in contemporary films, although Judaism has provided the on-screen milieu for films like *A Price Above Rubies,* Islam occasionally appears in popular films but usually in less than flattering terms, and Hinduism and Buddhism rarely appear in films (*Gandhi* and *Little Buddha*). Yet for all the avoidance of religion as a topic and the negative stereotyping of religion in contemporary movie productions, there are still those films that treat religion positively, or at least honestly, allowing the humanity of religious characters and the frailty of religious

institutions to be portrayed with substance and integrity. We see this in *Places in the Heart*, where southern racism goes hand in hand with the local church, but where the church also becomes the setting for a vision of God's radically egalitarian Kingdom. We see this in the all-too-human sinner/saint evangelist portrayed by Robert Duvall in *The Apostle,* and in the struggle of faith versus society presented in *Dead Man Walking.*

Films that treat religion come in many varieties. Although those that treat Protestantism as a subject are rare, there are many that rely upon Protestantism to set the stage or the parameters of the film. Protestantism often becomes the backdrop for some presentation of secular values or ideology presented either through a critique of religion or through a simplistic presentation of faith. In such films, religious traditions are often portrayed in stark contrast to secular culture and appear out of step with the modern world. An example would be the treatment of Amish traditions in the film, *Witness.* Although the Amish tradition itself maintains its boundaries apart from secular culture, one must be careful in watching a film like *Witness* and ask if the tradition is being portrayed in accordance with Amish belief or as a plot device. While one can learn about Amish belief and culture in this film, one certainly gains an incomplete picture of Amish faith. Thus, in many cases, popular movies depicting religion are poor sources for learning about Protestantism or Protestant principles. One might learn more about society's prejudices about religion than about religion itself.

Some films rely almost solely on sentimental stereotype, while others seem overtly antagonistic to some forms of Protestantism. We see both the stereotypical element and the antagonistic tendency in a film like Steve Martin's *Leap of Faith,* where evangelistic Protestantism is highlighted for its corruption and sleaziness. Even films that are not about religion but use religious characters tend to fall into this pattern. An example would be the psychotic religious fanatic portrayed by Robert De Niro in Martin Scorsese's *Cape Fear.* If movies routinely distort religion as many scholars claim, is there any chance of learning anything about Protestantism from watching popular films that use Protestant traditions as subjects? There is a chance if viewers watch critically with an informed background of the religious tradition. Otherwise, uninformed and uncritical viewers will leave the cinema house believing most Protestants are at best out of touch with modern culture and at worst suffering from psychotic delusion.

Positive Portrayals of Protestantism

A couple of examples will illustrate how movies can present Protestantism with integrity without sensationalizing the religious impulse. One can rarely count on popular movies approaching documentary status; however, some do present the viewer with a credible and honest portrayal concerning elements of Protestant traditions or Protestant beliefs. For example, *Witness* offers many viewers an introduction to a tradition from the radical Protestant movements as they are transplanted to America. In all likelihood, some viewers had little or no knowledge of Amish and radical Protestant traditions when they began to watch *Witness.* In such a case, the movie provides an introduction of sorts to this tradition. In a similar vein, *The Apostle* introduces and treats another movement that exists largely outside of the Protestant mainstream yet is more familiar on the popular religious landscape, Southern charismatic and evangelical Protestantism. However, some viewers and even critics erred in viewing the film as a portrayal of PENTECOSTALISM, which it is not. Rather, the film portrays a more general type of Southern folk religion that might be characterized as holiness or even charismatic, but in order to appreciate the way the film portrays, critiques, and showcases this Holiness-type of religion, one needs to have some working understanding of the tremendous variety of worship practice and faith within the broad Protestant tradition referred to as Holiness religion.

Some films, such as *Witness* and *The Apostle,* can serve as introductions or popular portrayals of Protestant traditions provided one watches them with a critical and informed mind. Other films, like *Places in the Heart,* might be successfully used to illustrate a Protestant characteristic or teaching. For example, the plot, character development, and surprise ending of *Places in the Heart* hinges on the central Protestant tenet of grace. Whereas human effort and will are flawed in this movie and characterized by greed, racism, infidelity, and disaster, the movie ends on a note of hope—a note punctuated by a vision of the Kingdom of God, where grace overcomes human failure. That this vision of heavenly grace occurs in the context of Protestant communion opens the movie to fruitful interpretations of understandings of grace, sin, and redemption within the Protestant tradition.

Finally, movies might be a fruitful area of study for students interested in Protestantism because popular films are increasingly coming under attack by religious bodies, politicians, and other cultural critics for what many perceive to be excessive violence, gratuitous sexuality, and the general presentation, if not glorification, of values hostile to traditional religious teachings. Those interested in the Protestant critique of society and popular culture would be interested in what some critics perceive to be a hostile approach to traditional values in popular films in general.

Conclusion

Although some popular films, like *The Apostle* and *Places in the Heart,* demonstrate how movies can present Protestant traditions and beliefs with integrity, even if incompletely, students of Protestantism should turn to movies as a study source with caution. Movies that reflect upon or employ Protestantism often tell us more about society's conceptions of religion or cultural attitudes concerning religiosity than about the religious tradition itself. In addition, adherents to traditional Protestant beliefs might be interested in studying what some critics perceive to be hostility in popular films toward traditional Christian value structures. That said, however, movies can enrich one's study of the place of Protestantism in society and of secular culture's relationship with dominant religious traditions and values.

References and Further Reading

Martin, Joel W., and Conrad E. Ostwalt, Jr., eds. *Screening the Sacred: Religion, Myth, and Ideology in Popular American Film.* Boulder, CO: Westview Press, 1995.

May, John R., ed. *Image and Likeness: Religious Visions in American Film Classics.* New York: Paulist Press, 1992.

Medved, Michael. *Hollywood vs. America: Popular Culture and the War on Traditional Values.* New York: Harper Collins, 1992.

Miles, Margaret. *Seeing and Believing: Religion and Values in the Movies.* Boston: Beacon Press, 1996.

Wall, James M. *Church and Cinema: A Way of Viewing Film.* Grand Rapids, MI: Eerdmans, 1971.

CONRAD OSTWALT

MUHLENBERG, HENRY MELCHIOR (1711–1787)

German theologian. Henry Melchior Muhlenberg was born on September 6, 1711, in Einbeck, a village in the Duchy of Hannover that was the site of an eleventh-century pilgrimage shrine purportedly containing a drop of Christ's blood. The town suffered from the ecclesiastical and political controversies of the REFORMATION and fell victim to the ravages of the Thirty Years' War. The son of a burgher, brewer, and cobbler, the young Muhlenberg was confirmed according to Lutheran custom in the Neustadter Church in Einbeck. In this church he came under the influence of Valentin Benkhard, whose theology had led him to LUTHERANISM from a Roman Catholic background.

Muhlenberg was educated in the local Latin and German schools and received a scholarship to the new University at Göttingen in 1735. Although he entered the theological department of Göttingen in 1737, he was sent to the University of HALLE in 1738 to obtain a degree under the direction of Gothilf August Francke, son of AUGUST HERMANN FRANCKE, who was

PHILIPP JACOB SPENER's protégé in the development of German PIETISM. Muhlenberg was ordained in Leipzig in 1739 and assumed pastoral duties in Grosshannersdorf, only to face financial constraints that sent him back to Halle in 1741, where Francke persuaded him to accept a call to serve several congregations in Philadelphia, New Hanover, and New Providence, Pennsylvania, in America.

Pietist Influence

Muhlenberg is usually called a "Pietist," meaning that he was influenced by the Pietist movement that had emerged in the seventeenth century, which had its counterparts in Jewish Hasidism and Roman Catholic Quietism. The movement is difficult to define or narrowly conceptualize. The term itself refers to the emphasis on the demonstration of intensive practice of FAITH and godliness. In a sense, Pietism may be understood as the pursuit of the SANCTIFICATION of life that, in the judgment of MARTIN LUTHER, had been linked to faithful response to God's justifying GRACE. Luther knew that although works did not justify, they were a natural outgrowth of JUSTIFICATION. Succeeding generations struggled with the problem of works—evidence of God's holiness working in the lives of those who lived by grace through faith. Human beings are always impatient with their own imperfections, those of others and of society. They seek to define and imitate holiness. They seek pious dedication and behavior; hence the term "pietism." A century after the Reformation, much of church life seemed to be characterized by commitment to doctrinal matters, often assuming that assent to the propositions contained in such statements as the AUGSBURG CONFESSION was sufficient evidence of Christian faith. Along with proper standards of PREACHING and dedication to certain forms of WORSHIP, confessionalism appeared to be satisfied with dogmatic determinants. The Pietistic mind found this unacceptable and sought to complete the Reformation by emphasis on a renewal experience accompanied by a piety that set Christian life in contrast to the ways of the world.

Pietism took many forms. It had no single manifestation or set of criteria for membership. Muhlenberg was undeniably and inevitably influenced by Pietism. His personal life had strong moralistic and holiness assumptions in opposition to card playing, dancing, and most forms of sensual pleasure. His aim as a pastor in America was to guide his parishioners toward a subjective experience that would be henceforth nurtured by the ministrations of the CHURCH and its leadership into a life of sanctification. Muhlenberg's pastoral theology has been called one of liturgical revivalism, although ecclesiological revivalism might be more accurate, because Muhlenberg was much too free and unstructured in his understanding of worship to make the concept of LITURGY meaningful.

Muhlenberg in America

When Muhlenberg came to southeastern Pennsylvania in 1743, he observed a religious life that was all too typical of an immigrant people in a colonial setting. The effects of the Reformation had not yet become rigidly and denominationally coded. Many of the people were Germans, Dutch, or Swedes whose religious life reflected the circumstances of their national and ethnic history. The Germans, for whom Muhlenberg was to have primary responsibility, were mostly artisans and farmers from the Rhineland, Saxony, and Bavaria. They had come from a culturally and religiously diverse land not yet politically unified. The ideas and practices of Anabaptists (see ANABAPTISM) mingled with those of the early reformers Luther, JOHN CALVIN, HULDRYCH ZWINGLI, and the Catholic Tridentine Reformation. They were to establish themselves among the English and Scotch-Irish. These German people were generally devoid of pastoral leadership and were accustomed to providing for their own religious life by means of hymns remembered, Bibles read, and the available devotional theology like that of JOHANN ARNDT's *True Christianity*. It was difficult to maintain ecclesiastical or theological discipline among a people accustomed to managing their own lives and identifying themselves in ethnic fashion (see ETHNICITY).

Muhlenberg's task was to organize these people and their autonomous and free-spirited congregations into effective Lutheran constituencies. Because he was successful at this task, he is often regarded as the "patriarch" of American Lutheranism and credited with the founding of the American Lutheran Church. Having been called to serve three congregations and reconcile differences among Lutherans and other German Protestants, Muhlenberg reported eighty-one congregations in Pennsylvania and adjacent areas by 1771. He guided the preparation of an American hymnal in 1782 and assisted in the establishment of synodical order and the formation of a Lutheran order of worship. This last was more of a directory of worship than a liturgy. It regarded the sermon as the center of the service, with the pietistic goal of enhancing the CONVERSION experience and encouraging dedication to practical holiness.

Assessment

Although Muhlenberg was a successful organizer and reconciler, his Pietism enabled him to accept the independence of the people and shape American Lutheranism in a way that was congenial to anticolonialism and a church life independent of European ecclesiasticism and hierarchical habits. American Lutheranism at this stage of its development would reflect the theology of Luther, Arndt, Spener, and Francke without the confessional and institutional formations usually essential to the transmission of ideas, beliefs, and practices. Muhlenberg was perhaps unique in his commitment to traditional Lutheranism while softening it with his pietistic inclinations. This approach enabled him to be the person for his time and place among Americans in process of shaping a democratic spirit both politically and religiously. Muhlenberg died in 1787 in the course of America's movement from confederation to federal republic. He had prevented Count NICHOLAS VON ZINZENDORF from convincing all Germans in eastern Pennsylvania that their confessional backgrounds were of no consequence whatever. He had been called out of his immediate pastoral jurisdiction many times, visiting New York, New Jersey, Maryland, Virginia, and Georgia as a kind of "bishop," reconciling conflicts and providing encouragement.

See also Lutheranism, Germany; Lutheranism, United States

References and Further Reading

Glatfelter, Charles H. *Pastors and People: German Lutheran and Reformed Churches in the Pennsylvania Field, 1717–1793. Vol. II: The History.* Breinigsville, PA: The Pennsylvania German Society, 1981.

Nelson, E. Clifford, ed. *The Lutherans in North America.* Philadelphia, PA: Fortress Press, 1975.

Roeber, A. G. *Palatines, Liberty, and Property: German Lutherans in Colonial British America.* Baltimore, MD: Johns Hopkins University Press, 1993.

Stoeffler, Ernest F. *German Pietism During the Eighteenth Century.* Leiden, The Netherlands: Brill Publications, 1973.

Tappert, T. G., and John. W. Doberstein, trans. *The Journals of Henry Melchoir Muhlenberg.* 3 vols. Philadelphia, PA: Evangelical Lutheran Church Ministerium of Pennsylvania, 1942.

Wallace, Paul A. W. *The Muhlenbergs of Pennsylvania.* Philadelphia, PA: University of Pennsylvania Press, 1950.

RICHARD E. WENTZ

MÜLLER, GEORGE (1805–1898)

German pietist, pastor, and philanthropist. Müller was born near Halberstadt, GERMANY on September 27, 1805, the son of a Prussian businessman. He studied at the University of HALLE in preparation for ordination. While at the university he sensed a call to foreign MISSIONS. When the Berlin Missionary Society rejected his application, he applied and was accepted by the London Society for Promoting Christianity Among the Jews. Shortly after arriving in London for training in 1829, however, he became ill and was sent to Devon to recuperate. While there he became friends with several leaders of the emerging PLYMOUTH BRETHREN movement. This proved to be a turning point in his life. He broke with the Society, accepted appointment to a small chapel in Devon, and joined the Brethren cause. While there he implemented the practice for which he became renowned. He vowed never to accept a salary, raise funds, or incur any indebtedness. Rather he would trust God to supply his needs.

In 1832 he moved to Bristol where he served a church, taught school, and worked with orphans. He patterned the Bristol orphanages after those he had seen in Halle that had been operated by the Pietists. Starting with of a handful of children, his orphanage grew to care for over 2,000. The five buildings cost £115,000 to build and £26,000 annually to run. During the course of his life he received over £1,500,000 in donations with which he educated 123,000 children, circulated 275,00 Bibles, housed 10,000 orphans, and supported 189 missionaries. In his last years Müller traveled to the various missions he sponsored. His support came from the sale of his autobiography, which he first published in 1837, and from the donations of readers. He died alone in his room at age 92 on March 10, 1898, without a penny to his name.

See also Pietism

References and Further Reading

Primary Source:

Müller, George. *A Life of Trust: Being A Narrative of the Lord's Dealings with George Müller.* London: James Nisbet, 1837.

Secondary Sources:

Pierson, Arthur Tappen. *George Müller of Bristol.* London: Pickering & Inglis, 1899.

Steer, Roger. *George Müller: Delighted in God.* Wheaton, IL: H. Shaw, 1975.

D. WILLIAM FAUPEL

MÜNTZER, THOMAS (1491–1525)

Protestant reformer. A radical Spiritualist Protestant reformer, Müntzer was an early follower of MARTIN LUTHER. Luther recommended Müntzer as a substitute pastor for the city of Zwickau in 1520. His theological intemperance caused his dismissal in 1521. Müntzer then went to Prague and predicted a coming judgment on the "godless." Finding no support in Prague, Müntzer returned to Saxony as pastor of Allstedt

(1523–1524), where he introduced the first Protestant vernacular LITURGY. He also called for opposition to the Wittenberg program of reform and the imposition of "true" religion. As a Spiritualist, Müntzer credited faith to the direct inspiration of the Holy Spirit, not to PREACHING or the Scriptures. Because Luther rejected force and emphasized God's use of Scripture and the preached Word to give FAITH, he and Müntzer became implacable enemies. Thinking the Peasants War (1524–1525) to be the beginning of God's judgment, Müntzer joined with a peasant band that was defeated at Frankenhausen (May 15, 1525). Müntzer was captured, tortured, and executed. The writings of Luther, PHILIPP MELANCHTHON, and other Lutheran leaders made Müntzer a Satanic figure for generations of Germans.

Little is known of Müntzer's early life, but he was probably born before 1491 at Stolberg. His family background is uncertain, although he may have come from the urban artisan class. Müntzer studied at the University in Wittenberg (1517–1519), but not with Luther. Nonetheless, Luther recommended him to the city of Zwickau as a temporary replacement for the permanent pastor, Johannes Egranus. Müntzer's inflammatory sermons against the local Franciscans proved his credentials as an adherent of the new teaching, although he also attacked Egranus's moderation. Dismissed from his post in 1521 he went to Prague. At first welcomed by local Hussites (followers of Jan Hus), a HERESY that had successfully revolted against the Roman Church in the fifteenth century, his *Prague Manifesto* predicted a coming judgment beginning in the city and spreading to the rest of the world. He succeeded only in making himself unwanted in Prague. Returning to Saxony, Müntzer became pastor of Allstedt (1523–1524), a small city that belonged to the Protestant elector of Saxony, but was almost surrounded by hostile Catholic territory. At Allstedt he introduced the first Protestant liturgy in the vernacular. Müntzer also began to criticize Luther's theology in "Protest or Offering about True Christian Faith and Baptism" and "On Contrived Faith." His preaching drew audiences from the surrounding villages. Catholic nobles, especially Count Ernst of Mansfeld, forbade their subjects to attend and complained to the elector of Saxony. In response Müntzer engaged in personal attacks on the count and other "godless" rulers who hindered the Word of God. In a sermon before the Saxon princes (July 13, 1524) on the second chapter of Daniel, Müntzer sought to persuade the Saxon princes to employ force to defend and impose the REFORMATION.

Thoroughly alarmed by these developments, Luther wrote "A Letter to the Princes of Saxony Concerning the Rebellious Spirit" denouncing Müntzer as a false prophet and urging the princes to silence him. Under pressure the city council of Allstedt dismissed Müntzer. Müntzer's whereabouts for the next few months are uncertain, although it is clear that he was at Nuremberg and spent time among the peasant insurrectionists in South Germany. During this time he published the "Highly Provoked Defense and Reply to the Soft-living Flesh at Wittenberg" and the "Printed Exposé of the False Faith of the Unfaithful World" attacking Luther and Luther's theology. Returning to Saxony in August 1524 and February 1525, he appeared in Muhlhausen, an imperial city wracked by social and religious tensions. Müntzer helped lead a revolution (March 16) that replaced a conservative city council with one favoring the Reformation. During the Thuringian Peasants War, Muhlhausen and Müntzer joined in the revolt. Müntzer believed that it marked the beginning of the judgment of the godless and the establishment of God's Kingdom on earth, (see KINGDOM OF GOD). The peasant army was routed and slaughtered at Frankenhausen (May 15), and Müntzer was captured, tortured, and executed. Luther, Melanchthon, and other Lutherans initiated a vilification of Müntzer that lasted well into the twentieth century. Beginning in the late nineteenth century, however, Marxists lionized him as a proletarian revolutionary.

Müntzer's theological differences with Luther extended far beyond the political sphere. Drawing to some extent on late medieval mysticism, Müntzer was convinced that saving faith required a painful CONVERSION followed by exclusive obedience to the will of God evidenced in a godly life. According to Müntzer, Luther taught Christians that suffering was not necessary and that a truly godly life was impossible. Müntzer traced Luther's error to a reliance on the dead letter of Scripture rather than the living Spirit of God. Appealing to the New Testament, especially Acts and the letters of Paul, Müntzer argued that the Holy Spirit effected faith in the believer directly through the Inner Word and not through the medium of the Outer Word of Scripture. He condemned the learned Clergy's monopoly of the Outer Word and its use to justify the tyranny of the common people by secular rulers. Müntzer's appeal to the spirit was an attempt both to enfranchise the LAITY and to enable them to replace a godless regime with one in which Christ ruled through the faithful. Only then could the mass of the population be freed from the crushing burdens that made adherence to the will of God impossible. Müntzer's disciples (e.g., Hans Denck and Hans Hut) made his theology part of the radical tradition in the sixteenth and seventeenth centuries.

References and Further Reading

Primary Source:

Matheson, Peter, ed. and trans. *Collected Works of Thomas Müntzer*. Edinburgh: T&T Clark, 1988.

Secondary Sources:

Friesen, Abraham. *Thomas Müntzer, a Destroyer of the Godless: The Making of a Sixteenth-Century Religious Revolutionary*. Berkeley: University of California Press, 1990.
Goetz, Hans-Juergen. *Thomas Müntzer: Mystic-Apocalyptic-Revolutionary*. Edinburgh: T&T Clark, 1993.
Gritisch, Eric W. *Reformer without a Church: The Life and Thought of Thomas Muentzer, 1488(?)–1525*. Philadelphia, PA: Fortress Press, 1967.
Scott, Tom. *Thomas Müntzer: Theology and Revolution in the German Reformation*. New York: St. Martin's Press, 1989.

R. EMMET McLAUGHLIN

MUSIC

The music of the Protestant churches established following the REFORMATION differed in significant ways from that of the Catholic church of the Middle Ages. All of the major reformers had reservations about the use of elaborate music in religious services. MARTIN LUTHER, whose own love of music was well known, thought that it could be as important as PREACHING in spreading the word of the Scriptures and encouraged lay participation through his development of hymns. JOHN CALVIN came to regard the unaccompanied singing of congregational Psalms as the only acceptable form of music in the LITURGY, and his Genevan church banned the use of organs and trained choirs. Like Luther, HULDRYCH ZWINGLI was fond of music and was himself an accomplished performer, but he concluded that music had no place whatever in true WORSHIP and could in fact be a detriment; it was eliminated from the services of his church at Zurich in 1525 until the end of the century. The Anabaptists (see ANABAPTISM) likewise eschewed organs.

In ENGLAND, many Puritans (see PURITANISM) followed the lead of the Continental reformers, especially Calvin, in arguing for simpler congregational music, preferably metrical Psalms sung without accompaniment. The CHURCH OF ENGLAND, however, managed to remain a *via media* between the extremes of radical Protestantism on the one hand and Roman Catholicism on the other. Despite the urging of the Puritans, organs were not silenced, except during the period of the Interregnum following the English CIVIL WAR of the seventeenth century, and trained choirs continued to provide elaborate music in the cathedrals, if not in ordinary parish churches.

Equally important was the introduction of vernacular liturgies in all of the Protestant churches. This meant that all settings of Latin texts used earlier were now proscribed; not only were new texts using the language of the people demanded, but also new musical settings of these texts had to be provided. This led to a burst of new composition, perhaps most clearly manifested in Luther's hymnody, the Genevan Psalter, and the anthems and canticles written for the English church by such masters as Thomas Tallis, William Byrd, Orlando Gibbons, and HENRY PURCELL. ANGLICAN CHANT became popular as a peculiarly English form of Psalm singing. This was paralleled in Germany by the work of such composers as Praetorios or Gebhardt.

The Baroque era witnessed the creation of much fine church music. Of paramount importance were the cantatas and Passions by JOHANN SEBASTIAN BACH and the oratorios of GEORGE FRIDERIC HANDEL, including especially *Messiah*.

Among later developments of major significance was the widespread development of hymn singing in England and America, manifest in the publication of such hymnals as *Hymns Ancient and Modern* in 1861. Twentieth-century composers, especially English writers like RALPH VAUGHAN WILLIAMS, Sir Charles Villiers Stanford, Herbert Howells, BENJAMIN BRITTEN, and Gerald Finzi, left great examples of liturgical music as well as religious works on a larger scale suitable for concert performance. In GERMANY, HUGO DISTLER sought to combine the Baroque tradition with the contemporary idiom. Popular music, including African American spirituals, found its way into many Protestant churches, especially in America, during the nineteenth century, while the late twentieth century brought the realization that a majority of Protestant Christians lived outside the Western tradition and that the "globalization" of music might broaden the Protestant tradition by bringing in new forms of expression from AFRICA and other third-world countries. In addition, especially among evangelical Protestants there was a commitment to contemporary forms of popular music, such as rock, giving rise to the genre of "Contemporary Christian" music. All of these topics, reflecting the variety of musical expression and importance of it in Protestant worship, are addressed in greater detail in other articles in this volume.

See also Hymns and Hymnals; Music, American; Music, English Church; Music, Global; Music, Northern European; Music, Popular

STANFORD LEHMBERG

MUSIC, AMERICAN

Protestant MUSIC in America in some respects followed the patterns, styles, and forms developed in Europe, but in other respects evolved a synthesis that often exceeded and extended the European models to create new manifestations. Thus every national immigrant group—English, German, Scandinavian, Dutch, French, Swiss, Polish, Hungarian, etc.—and every Protestant denomination—Lutheran, Reformed, Anglican, Baptist, Methodist, Congregational, Presbyterian, Moravian, Mennonite, etc.—brought with them their European tradition of ecclesiastical and domestic devotional music-making. Whereas the early settlers simply repeated the traditions they inherited, their successors modified them in distinctive ways, and eventually created entirely new forms of sacred music influenced by jazz (e.g., the African-American spiritual, the revivalist hymn), which spread to Europe and throughout the world.

Early Psalmody

The English Protestant colonists along the East Coast—whether they regarded themselves as Anglican, Puritan, Separatist, Congregational, Presbyterian, or Baptist—were singers of metrical psalms in their places of WORSHIP and in their homes. The Puritan/ Separatists brought with them Ainsworth's Psalter (Amsterdam, 1612), which made use of many Genevan psalm tunes. Problems with singing these tunes led to the creation of the *Bay Psalm Book* (1640), which required just a handful of the simpler English psalm tunes, as found in Ravenscroft's psalter. In later revisions, now generally called the *New England Psalm Book*, it was used by Congregationalists and some Presbyterians (see CONGREGATIONALISM; PRESBYTERIANISM), and its ninth edition (1698) included a small supplement of tunes, the first music printing of Colonial North America. Anglicans (see ANGLICANISM) and some BAPTISTS (see BAPTISTS, UNITED STATES) sang the Psalms of Sternhold and Hopkins to the same simple English psalm tunes. As in ENGLAND, these Psalms were sung unaccompanied and "lined-out" in public worship; that is, each line was first sung by a single voice (the Clerk), then repeated by the congregation. Thus the Psalm was sung line by line twice, once by the solo voice of the Clerk and once by the congregation. Tempos were extremely slow, and the psalm tunes were frequently modified by the oral transmission.

Musical Reforms

A reform in congregational singing, which led to other musical reforms, began around 1700. This was the change from "usual singing" (lining-out) to regular singing (stanza by stanza). At least one church in Boston had already made the change before the end of the seventeenth century, but this did not become a significant movement until the 1720s (although the practice of lining-out continued in the Southern States well into the nineteenth century and was still being practiced in some African-American congregations in the twentieth century). Some of the influence for change came from England, where the *New Version of the Psalms* of Nahum Tate (1652–1715) and Nicholas Brady (1659–1726) was introduced at the same time as organs were coming into use as accompanying instruments in English urban churches. The Tate and Brady Psalms became extremely popular in America and were sung by more than Anglicans. Similarly, the hymns and psalms of ISAAC WATTS (1707/1719), which also became widely sung in eighteenth-century America, especially among Presbyterians and Congregationalists, were intended to supplant the practice of lining-out when they were introduced in England. But in the American colonies there was also the influence of other language groups that had always sung their congregational songs stanza by stanza, such as the Dutch Reformed congregations in the Hudson Valley (see DUTCH REFORMED CHURCH), the Swedish Lutherans in Delaware, and German Lutherans in Pennsylvania (see LUTHERANISM, UNITED STATES). (Lutherans at Gloria Dei Church, Philadelphia had the use of an organ, the earliest recorded instrument in the American colonies.) The impetus for the change to "regular singing" in the 1720s came from New England CLERGY, notably Thomas Symmes (1677–1725) and Walter, who argued that the unskilled noise of "usual singing" undermined the spirit of worship and therefore should be abandoned in favor of singing by "rule," that is, from notation rather than by ear. The change was fiercely resisted by some but soon became the norm in New England. To effect the change, singing schools were created, led by singing masters who would teach the rudiments of music, as well as psalm tunes and simple anthems, from tune books either imported from England or, the increasing practice, edited by the local singing masters who were largely self-taught composers.

Singing schools, with their singing masters, had begun in England but were never the important phenomenon that they became in North America, spanning the eighteenth to twentieth centuries. The most important of the American singing masters was William Billings (1746–1800). The most prolific and the most distinctive of the composers of the early national period, Billings wrote rugged, energetic psalm tunes, small-scale anthems, and fuguing tunes that gave the impression of counterpoint but were in reality modified homophony. Among Billings's many contemporary composers in New England were Supply Belcher (1751–1836), Daniel Belknap (1771–1815), Lewis Edson (1748–1820), and Daniel Read (1757–1836).

The Great Evangelical Awakening (see AWAKENINGS) of the mid-eighteenth century did much to break down the monolithic tradition of psalmody by the promotion of the freer hymns of Watts and JOHN and CHARLES WESLEY, which brought in their wake livelier musical forms for both hymnody and other forms of vocal/choral church music. Other forms of church music were being developed in Pennsylvania. In Philadelphia, James Lyons published a number of collections of psalm-tunes and modest anthems that were used by Anglicans/Episcopalians and Lutherans; in Lancaster, Conrad Beissell and other members of the Ephrata Cloister composed simple four-part settings of hymns and prayers; and in Bethlehem, a whole range of composers created a rich variety of congregational, vocal, and choral music accompanied by string and wind instruments and organ for congregations of the MORAVIAN CHURCH. Beginning in New England but then expanding as far as Ohio, as the country expanded westward, Shaker communities (see SHAKERS) developed their unaccompanied hymnody with folk-like melodies, to which they danced, jumped, and shook in their worship.

Northern and Southern Traditions

Protestant church music in America began to move in new directions from around the second decade of the nineteenth century. In the North, European ideals were cultivated and in the South folk-song models were explored, and both were strongly influenced by the Second Great Awakening, the consolidation of EVANGELICALISM with its enthusiastic and emotionally charged singing. In the northern states, Lowell Mason (1792–1872), Thomas Hastings (1784–1872), and William Bradbury (1816–1868) wanted to displace the home-grown and rustic music-making of their predecessors in favor of "better" (meaning European) music composed according to refined taste and sensibilities. Lowell Mason published many collections of hymns, chants, and anthems, issued in long print-runs, and established a music academy in Boston. He encouraged strong and effective congregational singing, supported by choirs and organs. Hastings pursued a similar program and published what amounts to the manifesto of these reformers: *A Dissertation on Musical Taste* (1820). Bradbury was the author of the ubiquitous "Jesus loves me, this I know" that epitomizes the SUNDAY SCHOOL hymnody tradition that he virtually created by the constant stream of small, square booklets of such songs and hymns that he published. Bradbury's hymnody fostered the development of the revivalist or gospel hymn associated with IRA SANKEY (the evangelist DWIGHT L. MOODY's mu-

sical partner), PHILIP P. BLISS, FANNY CROSBY, and others.

By the end of the nineteenth century, urban churches had cultivated a musical professionalism that replaced choirs with a paid quartet, and congregational singing was much reduced. A concert style of music predominated for both vocal and organ music, being promoted by such composers as Dudley Buck, one of the founders of the American Guild of Organists. Large-scale religious works were composed the "Boston Classicists," such as Horatio Parker's *Hora Novissima*.

In the southern states, where most people lived in rural communities, a different style predominated in the churches, one derived from folk song. To make it easier for people to read music, systems of shape-notes (basic geometric-shaped note heads that designated relative pitches) were devised, and many tune books incorporating such systems were published. Among the most important of these were *Kentucky Harmony* (1816), *Southern Harmony* (1835), and *Sacred Harp* (1844). Many of these tune books had the music arranged in three rather than four parts, following the example of many eighteenth-century English tune-books, a tradition that appears to have been introduced by Playford's 1677 psalter. Shape-note singing in rural America was in strong contrast with the professionalism of the music of the churches in cities and major towns. Indeed, the "fasola" singing of the music of the *Sacred Harp* (now in four parts) continues to this day.

Southern CULTURE depended on SLAVERY for its prosperity. African-American slaves were frequently excluded from the churches or were confined to high galleries, supplied with external stairways, where they were neither to be seen nor heard. At revivalist CAMP MEETINGS, attendees were racially segregated both in the arena of the meeting and in the tented dormitory areas. The African Americans would sing among themselves late into the night, and the white folk would stay up to listen to this different way of singing. Thus evolved the distinctive genre of religious song, in which biblical images (such as Moses, and the children of Israel entering the Promised Land) were used to express heart-felt desires for emancipation and freedom. The spiritual, with its integrity, sincerity, and power, is now known throughout the world.

Renewals and Reforms

By the end of the nineteenth century, the effect of the English OXFORD MOVEMENT, which began as an Anglican phenomenon, was visible and audible in the Protestant churches of America. Church buildings were neo-gothic in style; organs, previously in a gallery at the rear of churches, were now visible at the front of the sanctuary. Choir members, now also visible, faced each other in divided chancels, and were often vested, if not in the customary Anglican cassock and surplice, at least in a suitable colored robe. The primary music that they sang was anthems, a form borrowed from Anglican tradition, though most likely composed by an American even if in an "English" style. But there were exceptions. One was the composer Charles Ives, who created a distinctive American sound by combining the melodies of folk hymns within formal structures with a distinctively non-European approach to tonality. The connections between text and tone in his Psalm settings are remarkable examples of musical hermeneutics. Others who created a distinctive American sound for Protestant church music included Aaron Copland and Roger Sessions.

The second decade of the twentieth century saw various attempts to reform Protestant church music. A principal concern was to make it more relevant and connected to the order of worship within which it was heard. Another was to draw choir members from the congregation and rely less on paid performers. Yet another was to either raise or keep musical standards high. A number of societies and institutions were founded to further such aims, including The Hymn Society of America (1922), Westminster Choir College (1926), and the School of Sacred Music at Union Theological Seminary, New York (1928). There were also the Episcopal Evergreen church music conferences (from 1923), overseen by Winfred Douglas and others, at which new compositions by Leo Sowerby (1895–1968), Healcy Willan (1880–1968), and Randall Thompson (1899–1984) were prominent.

There were other strands of Protestant church music as well. The music of revivalism and the gospel song continued into the twentieth century, fostered by such composer-publishers as Alexander and Rodeheaver. Later, such music was ued by BILLY GRAHAM Crusades and thus achieved worldwide recognition. In black churches, another form of revivalism developed, the "black gospel" music of Charles Tindley and Thomas A. Dorsey, which later gave birth to gospel choirs and embraced a concert style closely related to that promoted by the stage and recording industries. But whatever its "secular" associations, black gospel music is firmly earthed in the worship and experience of African-American congregations. Jazz idioms were explored by both black and white musicians to convey religious faith and feeling; examples include Duke Ellington's "In the Beginning God" and Dave Brubeck's "Jazz Mass."

Since the 1960s, American Protestant church music has diversified and now embraces an astonishingly broad range of musical style and genre. Particularly pervasive is contemporary Christian music, which is promoted not simply as an alternative to traditional forms, but as the only valid form of Christian musical expression in the twenty-first century. Its characteristic praise choruses—a development of the earlier Sunday School hymnody and children's mission choruses—are projected on screens, rather than printed in songbooks, and accompanied by keyboards and rhythm instruments commonly used in the secular world of popular music. Although lines are commonly drawn between "contemporary" and "traditional" worship music, some churches attempt to combine both in what is referred to as "blended" music. It is debatable whether one can continue to speak of patterns of Protestant church music any more, because the clearly defined musical traditions of "Episcopalians," "Lutheran," "Methodist" (see METHODISM, NORTH AMERICA) and so forth have all but disappeared from many of the congregations of those denominations.

A new phenomenon is the growth of immigrant congregations from Pacific Rim countries, principally KOREA and Taiwan. Whereas much of the worship music they usc was developed from the late nineteenth-century revivalist styles that the missionaries brought with them when they founded churches in their countries of origin, they are beginning to create worship music that reflects more of their cultural origins. Thus, at the beginning of the twenty-first century, new immigrants are importing music forms as did the immigrants at the beginning of the colonial period, except that they now come from an entirely different continent.

See also Hymns and Hymnals; Music, English Church; Music, Northern European; Music, Popular; Revivals

References and Further Reading

Abbington, James. *Readings in African American Church Music and Worship.* Chicago, IL: GIA. 2001.
Chase, Gilbert. *America's Music: From the Pilgrims to the Present,* 3rd rev. ed. Urbana, IL: University of Illinois Press, 1987.
Davison, Archibald T. *Protestant Church Music in America.* Boston: Schirmer, 1933.
Ellinwood, Leonard. *The History of American Church Music.* New York: Morehouse-Goreham, 1953.
Gould, Nathaniel D. *Church Music in America, Comprising Its History and Its Peculiarities at Different Periods.* Boston: Gould and Lincoln, 1853; reprint, New York: AMS, 1972.
Scholes, Percy A. *The Puritans and Music in England and New England.* Oxford, UK: Clarendon, 1969.

Stevenson, Robert Murrell. *Protestant Church Music in America: A Short Survey of Men and Movements from 1564 to the Present.* New York: Norton, 1966.

ROBIN A. LEAVER

MUSIC, ENGLISH CHURCH

The great tradition of church music in England was altered significantly as a result of the introduction of Protestant doctrines in the sixteenth century. After the Reformation, English texts supplanted medieval Latin and there was a demand for simpler singing. A compromise was reached during the reign of ELIZABETH I, in which elaborate anthems and canticles could still be performed in the cathedrals and Chapel Royal, whereas simple congregational Psalms were characteristic of parish churches. The civil war of the seventeenth century disrupted the life of the Anglican Church, but traditional liturgies and music were reinstated after the Restoration of the monarchy in 1660. The cathedral choral tradition declined in the eighteenth and early nineteenth centuries, but revived during the Victorian era and the twentieth century, with many fine examples of church music being written and choirs maintaining high musical standards. Despite early Puritan objections, organs remained important in Anglican churches. Other Protestant denominations, especially Congregationalists, Presbyterians, and Methodists, generally favored simpler music but often borrowed from the repertoire of the established church.

The Reformation

Church music flourished in the English church during the years before the break with Rome in 1533. There were nineteen cathedrals, each of which had a choir of men and boys who sang daily services. Ten of the cathedrals were monastic in organization. They offered several daily masses, of which the most elaborate was generally the Lady Mass sung in honor of the Virgin. It frequently included polyphonic music with boys from a monastic song school supplying treble lines. The other daily offices were generally sung by the monks alone in plainsong or Gregorian chant. The nine secular cathedrals were served by priests who were not in monastic orders. Their choirs of men and boys also offered daily masses and services with Latin texts, generally according to the Use of Sarum codified at Salisbury cathedral. Small organs had been used for centuries.

As is well known, HENRY VIII (1509–1547) broke the ties between England and Rome in 1533 to obtain his divorce from Catherine of Aragon and validate his marriage to Anne Boleyn. Protestant teachings, especially the doctrines of MARTIN LUTHER and JOHN CALVIN, were influential in reshaping the state church of

which he was named Supreme Head. The monasteries were dissolved between 1536 and 1540, and the monastic cathedrals were converted into secular establishments, called cathedrals of the new foundation because they were given new statutes and revenues. More important was the introduction of the BOOK OF COMMON PRAYER during the reign of Henry's son Edward VI (1547–1553). Compiled by THOMAS CRANMER, the archbishop of Canterbury, the first Prayer Book published in 1549 was a compromise between traditional liturgies and Protestant services influenced by the German reformers. It provided a Communion service, which was basically a translation of the Mass and services of Matins and Evensong or Morning and Evening Prayer based on the monastic hours. Throughout, use of the English language was required: this was a matter of great importance to the choirs because, virtually overnight, it became illegal to use any of the existing settings of Latin texts. A revised Prayer Book issued in 1552 was still more Protestant in character, and rejected additional doctrines and liturgies of the medieval church. After the Reformation cathedral choirs were made up of about twelve men, known as vicars choral or (if they were not in holy orders) lay clerks, and about ten boys, who were generally educated in choir schools.

Calvin's arguments for unaccompanied congregational singing of Psalm texts were adopted in many places, especially in parish churches that had never had trained choirs. A simple unison setting of the Communion service and other liturgies was provided by John Merbecke, whose *Book of Common Prayer Noted* was first published in 1550.

After Edward VI's early death in 1553, the throne passed to his half-sister Mary Tudor, the daughter of Henry VIII and his first wife, Catherine of Aragon. She had been raised as a Catholic and had never deviated from that faith. She did everything she could to restore Catholic worship with Latin Masses and traditional music, but it was obvious that the Reformation could not be undone. Westminster Abbey might be turned into a monastery again (it had become one of several new cathedrals under Henry VIII), but it was generally impossible to reestablish the other religious houses and to eradicate Protestant teachings.

The Elizabethan Church

Mary—who came to be known as "Bloody Mary" because about three hundred Protestants, including Archbishop Cranmer, were executed during her reign by being burned at the stake—died in 1558 after ruling for only five years. She was followed by Elizabeth I, the daughter of Henry VIII and Anne Boleyn. Brought up as a Protestant and in any case not recognized by the papacy as a legitimate ruler, she restored the Book of Common Prayer with its English liturgies and music.

During the reign of Elizabeth (1558–1603), English Puritans continued to demand further reform in the state church. Some Puritan leaders had been among the Marian exiles who fled to Frankfurt and Geneva to escape persecution and possible death in England. Heavily influenced by Calvinistic teachings, they deplored elaborate church music and sought to silence organs and trained choirs. They favored metrical Psalms, sung in unison by the entire congregation to simple music with one note for each syllable of the text, and they came very close to persuading the Convocation of 1563 to outlaw the use of organs in church services. Were it not for the Queen herself they might have succeeded, but Elizabeth loved fine church music and supported some of England's greatest composers, especially Thomas Tallis (c. 1505–1585) and William Byrd (1543–1623), who composed works of great beauty for use in her Chapel Royal and in the cathedrals. The revised Prayer Book of 1559 did continue to mandate the use of English texts and generally favored musical settings that were easily understood by lay men and women, although (for the benefit of "those who delight in music," such as the Queen) it permitted the singing of polyphonic anthems only once in each service. Cathedral choirs were reconstituted and organs remained in use.

William Byrd himself remained a Catholic, but Elizabeth made no attempt to interfere with his private beliefs (indeed, she generally avoided making "windows into men's souls"), and it may be that some of Byrd's Latin masses and motets were sung at the Chapel Royal. Byrd's masses for three, four, and five voices rank among the greatest compositions of the age. Some of the realm's finest musicians, including instrumentalists, performed at court. Elizabeth made it clear that she enjoyed the music more than the preaching. Although Communion came to be celebrated infrequently, only weekly or monthly in the cathedrals and several times a year in parish churches, the Elizabethan composers provided a number of settings of its sung sections (the Kyrie, Creed, Sanctus, Agnus Dei, and Gloria in excelsis, which was transferred to the end of the service) as well as simple motets and elaborate anthems. The principal Anglican services were Morning and Evening Prayer. Daily Evensongs and Sunday Matins were the chief glories of the cathedrals, and some of the finest compositions were settings of the canticles, the Magnificat and Nunc dimittis at Evensong, Te Deum and Jubilate at Matins. The composers active under Elizabeth, in addition to Tallis and Byrd, were Christopher Tye (c. 1500–1573), Robert Parsons (d. 1570), and Richard Farrant (d. 1581).

The Early Seventeenth Century

The death of Elizabeth and the succession of her Scottish cousin James I (1603–1625), the first ruler of the Stuart line, did not mark a significant change in church music. Verse anthems became more common in the Chapel Royal and cathedrals; these involved the use of soloists alternating with sections for the full choir, often accompanied by string instruments rather than organ. Notable composers of verse anthems, as well as services and full anthems, included Thomas Tomkins (1572–1656), Thomas Weelkes (c. 1575–1623), and Orlando Gibbons (1583–1625). The greatest of these, whose works remain glories of the Anglican tradition, was Gibbons. The son of a professional musician, Gibbons was a chorister at King's College, Cambridge, and was named organist of the Chapel Royal while still a young man. He later served as organist of Westminster Abbey as well. He died of a seizure in 1625 at Canterbury, where he had gone to lead the royal musicians in welcoming Henrietta Maria, the French bride of Charles I to England. His most famous works are the Short Service in F, the full anthem "Hosanna to the Son of David," for use on Palm Sunday, and the Advent verse anthem "This is the record of John."

Puritan opposition to the established church intensified under Charles I (1625–1649). Unlike his father, who maintained the Elizabethan *via media* by appointing both traditionalists and reformers to bishoprics and other positions of authority, Charles favored the high-church party led by WILLIAM LAUD, an Oxford scholar whom he named archbishop of Canterbury in 1633. Often known as ARMINIANS because they were influenced by the Dutch theologian Jacobus Arminius, they introduced elaborate liturgies, vestments, and altars, bringing back a number of practices that had been rejected at the time of the Reformation. The Puritans regarded these as popish and superstitious. Their views, voiced in the Long Parliament that met in 1640, led to polarization between parliamentarians and royalists and finally to the outbreak of the English Civil War in 1642. A number of cathedrals and other churches were damaged in the fighting, and many organs and altars were destroyed. Anglican worship according to the Book of Common Prayer was banned and cathedral choirs were disbanded. Laud was executed at the order of Parliament in 1645 and Charles I himself was publicly beheaded at Whitehall on January 30, 1649.

During the Interregnum—the years without a monarchy, 1649–1660, during most of which time OLIVER CROMWELL ruled as Lord Protector—both Presbyterians and Congregationalists held services in England. The Presbyterians, like the Anglicans, believed in a state church but opposed episcopacy and popish practices, whereas the Congregationalists, better known during the period itself as Independents, rejected an established church and government regulation of religion altogether. Liturgical practice in parish churches and cathedrals varied. At Exeter, for instance, a wall was erected in the middle of the cathedral so that the Independents might worship in the nave and the Presbyterians in the choir. In accordance with Puritan belief music was limited to congregational singing of metrical Psalms, generally to the texts that had been published by Sternhold and Hopkins in 1562.

The Restoration

Both the monarchy and the Anglican church were restored in 1660, two years after the death of Oliver Cromwell. Charles II, the older son of Charles I, ruled from 1660 to 1685. There had been talk of accommodating the Presbyterians, if not the Independents, by having a broader state church than before, but narrower interests prevailed and the Restoration church was similar to that of Elizabeth or James I. A slightly revised Prayer Book was brought into use in 1662 and was destined to remain the official liturgy until the twentieth century. Cathedral musical establishments were restored as rapidly as possible, but in most places it was years before new or rebuilt organs were in place. It was also difficult to reestablish the choirs. Some men who had sung before the war came back, although there were no boys with unchanged voices who were familiar with the old services. This is one of the reasons that many Restoration anthems make little use of treble lines, emphasizing men's singing instead.

The best-known composer of the era was HENRY PURCELL (1659–1695). Indeed, he is generally regarded as England's greatest musician to live during the years between Byrd and Elgar. The son of a Chapel Royal tenor, he joined that choir as a chorister in 1669. When only twenty he was appointed organist at Westminster Abbey, and two years later he was named one of the Chapel Royal organists. In addition to church music he wrote several Odes for state occasions and a number of fantasias for orchestra as well as England's first opera, *Dido and Aeneas.* His church music includes three services, of which the finest is the Evening Service in G Minor, full anthems such as the simple "Remember not, Lord, our offences" and the more elaborate "Hear my prayer, O Lord," and verse anthems, including "Thy Word is a lantern" and "My beloved spake," a worldly ode to spring. He also wrote a few anthems to Latin texts—it is perhaps a sign of a more tolerant age that they were accepted—including the impressive "Jehova quam multi sunt hostes." Purcell (like Mozart) was only thirty-six

when he died, and one can only imagine what he might have accomplished had he lived longer. The other well-known composer of the period was John Blow (1649–1708), who was one of Purcell's teachers and survived him by more than a decade. Also organist at both Westminster Abbey and the Chapel Royal, Blow left a larger number of anthems than Purcell, including three works sung at the coronation of James II in 1685.

James, Charles II's younger brother, succeeded him because Charles left no legitimate children. An avowed Roman Catholic, James was content for several years to leave the church as it was, but by 1688 he was interfering with the establishment. The birth of his son in 1689 was a signal to many political leaders that he needed to be removed from the throne so that there would not be an unending line of Catholic monarchs. As a result of the so-called Glorious Revolution, James and his heirs were excluded from the succession and the throne passed to William III, the Protestant ruler of the Netherlands, and his wife Mary, James's daughter, who was also a Protestant. Anglican liturgy and music changed little under them or their successor, Queen Anne (1702–1714).

The Eighteenth Century

The eighteenth century is often regarded as being a low point in the history of the Church of England and its music. Religious life was dominated by rationalism rather than zeal, and services were often maintained as a matter of routine rather than enthusiasm. Choirs declined because men often continued to sing long after their voices had decayed, boys were poorly trained, and rehearsals were infrequent. Amateur instrumentalists played more often in parish churches than organists. The most important composers were Jeremiah Clarke (c. 1673–1707), William Croft (1678–1727), Maurice Greene (1696–1755), William Boyce (1711–1779), and Thomas Attwood (1765–1838).

The greatest musical achievement of the century was the establishment of music festivals in cathedral cities. The famous Three Choirs Festival, bringing together the choirs from Gloucester, Worcester, and Hereford cathedrals, is usually said to have begun in 1715, but in fact there were earlier, less formal, gatherings. Works by Purcell and Croft were performed at the first festivals, but by 1736 the music of George Freidiric Handel began to dominate. Born in Saxony in 1685, Handel had come to England in 1710 and lived there continuously from 1712 until his death in 1759. His Te Deums and anthems, including those composed for the Duke of Chandos and for the coronation of George II, were sung in cathedrals, but works like the oratorio *Samson* and the "Ode on St.

Cecilia's Day" were banned because they were not settings of liturgical texts and had no place in traditional services. Even the famous *Messiah,* first performed at Dublin in 1741 and at Covent Garden in London in 1743, was at first thought unsuitable for performance in churches. It was regarded as a secular entertainment when it was first sung by the Three Choirs in 1757, and was relegated to a public hall at Gloucester instead of the cathedral. It was only in the year of Handel's death that performance in Hereford cathedral was permitted, and then only because no other hall could accommodate the expected audience. By the end of the century *Messiah* was regularly sung by large massed choirs in several of the cathedrals as well as in Westminster Abbey. Choir festivals spread to a number of cities, including Birmingham, Leeds, Liverpool, and Norwich, and attracted large crowds.

The Nineteenth and Twentieth Centuries

The apathy and neglect that characterized the church during the eighteenth century continued well into the nineteenth. Musical standards in the cathedrals remained low. Choral services were simply abandoned for a time at Bristol. In London the number of singing men at St. Paul's fell from forty-two to six, whereas the men at Westminster Abbey were allowed to send deputies who, according to a contemporary report, performed without skill or enthusiasm. The situation in parish churches was no better.

Those who fought for reform included the organist Samuel Sebastian Wesley, who published an outspoken plea for change in 1854, and Maria Hackett, who spent much of her life fighting for better conditions for choirboys. More important was the influence of the OXFORD MOVEMENT, which sought to restore the dignity and beauty of high-church liturgy and ceremonial. This affected some parish churches earlier than cathedrals; the movement for musical reform can be traced to the parish of All Saints Margaret Street, London, in 1839, and Leeds parish church in 1841. Some parish churches sought to emulate cathedrals, and their choirs sang some of the simpler works from the cathedral repertoires.

The great development of hymnody also dates from the early Victorian era, and owes much to the high-church Tractarians of the Oxford Movement. Earlier, hymn singing was not characteristic of either cathedral or parish worship. The first modern English hymn book was compiled by Bishop Reginald Heber and published in 1827. It included only words, not music. The earliest hymnal with music was *Hymns Ancient and Modern.* Published in 1861, it had sold more than five million copies by the end of the decade. One of the most prolific writers of hymn texts was CHARLES

WESLEY (1707–1788), younger brother of the founder of Methodism, JOHN WESLEY.

The nineteenth century also witnessed the introduction of modern organs with pedals. The first known pedal-board in England, only an octave in length, was installed at the parish church of St. Mary Redcliffe in Bristol in 1726, but as late as 1810 only two cathedrals had organs with pedals. This situation says something about the organ music played in England, since the works of Bach and his contemporaries could not be performed without pedals. A number of large organs were displayed at the Crystal Palace for the Exhibition of 1851. In particular a large three-manual organ with pedals made by Henry Willis attracted attention, and some of it was later installed in Winchester cathedral. Willis also built what is often regarded as the first typical modern English organ, an instrument with more than one hundred stops built for St. George's Hall, Liverpool, in 1855. Organs conceived in this style—romantic in approach, with a number of voices imitating orchestral instruments—dominated until about 1954, when the organ designed for the Royal Festival Hall in London followed a more baroque scheme with reed stops in the French style.

Samuel Sebastian Wesley was the consultant for the Willis organ in Liverpool. Named organist of Hereford cathedral at the age of twenty-two, he later served at Exeter, Winchester, and Gloucester and was a prolific composer of church music. Some of his anthems rank among the finest of the Victorian cathedral works. They are often lengthy and include sections for a solo singer; perhaps the best example is "The Wilderness," published as part of a collection of twelve anthems in 1853. Among the other popular Victorian composers of church music were John Goss (1800–1880); T. A. Walmisley (1814–1856), who amazingly served as organist of three Cambridge colleges (King's, St. John's, and Trinity) as well as the University church of Great St. Mary's simultaneously; and Sir John Stainer (1840–1901), composer of the famous oratorio *The Crucifixion.* In addition to writing the music for the Gilbert and Sullivan operettas, Sir Arthur Seymour Sullivan (1842–1900) left a number of popular works for the church.

Twentieth-century composers continued this tradition, but enhanced it by providing works of greater spirituality and musical interest. Much of the repertoire of English cathedral and parish church choirs still consists of the anthems and services of Sir Hubert Parry (1848–1914), Sir Charles Villiers Stanford (1852–1924), and Charles Wood (1866–1926). Church music may not have been the chief interest of Ralph Vaughan Williams (1872–1958) or Benjamin Britten (1913–1976), but both have left masterpieces. Herbert Howells (1892–1983) did concentrate his talents on the church; his finest religious compositions, including the "Collegium Regale" services written for King's College, Cambridge, and the movingly simple Christmas carol "A Spotless Rose," are unsurpassed.

At the end of the twentieth century the tradition of English church music remained strong. Changes had taken place; in particular girls had joined boys at many cathedrals, either in separate choirs or as part of a mixed ensemble, and women's voices often dominated choirs in parish churches. Although many traditional musicians disapproved, there were experiments with new musical and liturgical styles. Services in Methodist and Congregational churches were less formal than those in the Church of England, but the choice of anthems was much the same. Hymns had gained greater importance in most services; new hymns continued to be composed and new hymnals to be published. There was distress because of the decline of church attendance in England and worry about the future of musical establishments, but so far as music was concerned the century ended in good form.

See also Arminianism; Book of Common Prayer; Calvin, John; Cranmer, Thomas; Cromwell, Oliver; Elizabeth I; Henry VIII; Laud, William; Luther, Martin; Oxford Movement; Purcell, Henry; Wesley, Charles; Wesley, John

References and Further Reading

Barrett, Philip. *Barchester: English Cathedral Life in the Nineteenth Century*. London: S.P.C.K., 1993.
Clutton, Cecil, and Austin Niland. *The British Organ*. London: B. T. Batsford, 1963.
Dearnley, Christopher. *English Church Music, 1650–1750*. London: Barrie & Jenkins, 1970.
Hutchings, Arthur. *Church Music in the Nineteenth Century*. London: Herbert Jenkins, 1967.
Lehmberg, Stanford E. *Cathedrals under Siege: Cathedrals in English Society, 1600–1700*. University Park: Penn State Press, and Exeter: University of Exeter Press, 1996.
———. *The Reformation of Cathedrals: Cathedrals in English Society, 1485–1603*. Princeton, NJ: Princeton University Press, 1988.
Le Huray, Peter. *Music and the Reformation in England, 1549–1660*. London: Herbert Jenkins, 1967.
Long, Kenneth R. *The Music of the English Church*. London: Hodder and Stoughton, 1971.
Routley, Erik. *Twentieth Century Church Music*. London: Herbert Jenkins, 1964.
Stevens, Denis. *Tudor Church Music*. London: Faber and Faber, 1961.
Temperley, Nicholas. *The Music of the English Parish Church*. 2 vols. Cambridge: Cambridge University Press, 1979.

STANFORD LEHMBERG

MUSIC, GLOBAL

This term is often used interchangeably with world, ethnic, international, or multicultural music. "Third-World music" may be found occasionally, but is inaccurate and carries vestiges of COLONIALISM. "Global music," however, also presents some difficulties. The first relates to perspective: What music is global and what music is not? Although Christian song has been transmitted across language groups and cultures since the apostolic era, Carlton Young notes a first wave of global song during the missionary movement of the nineteenth and twentieth centuries as European and North American church music became the global musical currency. Late in the twentieth century, Euro–North American churches have become aware of musics produced by Christians from non-Western cultures. Interest in global music today reflects a demographic shift between 1950 and the turn of the twenty-first century. Where once 70 percent of baptized Christians lived in the northern hemisphere now only 30 to 35 percent of Christians do, with 65 to 70 percent living in the southern. This second wave of global music from the two-thirds world is the subject of this article.

The second difficulty with "global music" is the political nature of "globalization." As an economic strategy, globalization is often associated with the spread of Western economic approaches and cultural values around the world, especially those from the UNITED STATES. This connection of globalization—and by association, global—with cultural assimilation is unfortunate. For the most part those who promote the use of global music within Euro–North American WORSHIP have the opposite intent; they strive to bring the authentic musical voice of Christians from the far reaches of the globe into Western LITURGY as a reminder that the CHURCH, although gathered locally, is a part of the universal body of Christ.

For the purpose of this article, global music will signify Christian songs originating beyond Euro–North American cultural contexts. Protestant Hymnals (see HYMS AND HYMNALS) produced in the UNITED STATES, CANADA, and some countries in Europe included Christian songs primarily from sub-Saharan AFRICA, Asia (especially eastern Asia), LATIN AMERICA (including Spanish- and Portuguese-speaking countries), and the CARIBBEAN. Christian music from the Middle East, Eastern Europe, the former Soviet Republics, and the Polynesian islands have been less widely disseminated. Christian music created by NATIVE AMERICANS and African Americans is beyond the scope of this article. Although global music often includes instrumental and dance forms, the focus here is on congregational songs.

This article considers ecumenical and denominational strands of activity since the mid-1960s that have led to the general inclusion of global song in hymnals and hymnal supplements published in the United

States, Canada, and western Europe since the late 1980s. Whereas this article is organized by confessional tradition, those who compile collections and use global song do so with an ecumenical spirit (see ECUMENISM). Specific issues are addressed in the brief bibliography.

Influences of Vatican II

Before the liturgical reforms of the Second Vatican Council (1962–1965), Christians beyond the Euro–North American context primarily sang Western hymns in translation. Although folk tunes from "native" cultures appeared occasionally in Western collections, these tunes were often domesticated by eliminating intervals difficult for Western singers and by adding keyboard harmonizations. Even original compositions by non-Western composers were regularly composed in Western musical styles. Colonial missionaries and their converts often assumed that indigenous cultural forms were technically and aesthetically inadequate or even inherently evil, incapable of conveying sound Christian THEOLOGY. Admittedly, specific melodies, musical instruments, and rhythmic patterns are often associated with non-Christian cultural practices. In many cultures, however, indigenous musical resources have been wedded with the gospel to produce musical expressions that are liturgically faithful and culturally relevant.

The *Constitution on the Sacred Liturgy* (1963) produced by Vatican II promoted liturgy inculturated in the linguistic patterns, metaphors, dance, and music of individual cultures while sharing a common historical liturgical shape throughout the world. Mass settings based on specific musical/cultural idioms began to appear in the 1960s. These included *Missa Luba*, a Congolese mass, and *Missa Qamata*, a Xhosa mass setting from SOUTH AFRICA by Benjamin Peter John Tyamzashe. Spanish-language masses included *Misa Criolla* (Ariel Ramírez), an Argentine mass based on indigenous folk rhythms, and several Central American masses, represented by *Misa Campesina Nicaragüense* (Carlos Mejia Godoy) and *La nueva misa mesoamericana* (Guillermo Cuéllar). Because they were composed in vernacular styles, these masses paved the way for establishing cultural identity through congregational music. The *Ten-year Report of The Milwaukee Symposia for Church Composers* (1992), an unofficial Roman Catholic document that included participation by Protestants, elaborated on the proposals of Vatican II in the section entitled, "Cross-Cultural Music Making." Liturgical inculturation also caught the attention of many Protestants.

World Council of Churches Contributions

The WORLD COUNCIL OF CHURCHES (WCC) publications, international assemblies, and church music symposia are important sources for global song. Initial efforts centered on *Cantate Domino* (melody edition, 1974; full-harmony edition, 1980), published by the WCC and edited by hymnologist Erik Routley (1917–1982). Appearing in three earlier editions (1924, 1930, 1951) published by the World Student Christian Federation, the WCC version was a radical departure from these, containing 202 selections in thirteen languages with participation by Roman Catholics and Orthodox Christians for the first time. Texts appear in the original language and, usually, in English, French, and German. In spite of the broader global perspective of the fourth edition, the collection retained the feel of a European hymnal and many of the songs were harmonized without regard to the CULTURE of origin. Later culturally focused publications such as *African Songs of Worship* (1986), edited by Taiwanese ethnomusicologist I-to Loh, and *Brazilian Songs of Worship* (1989), edited by Brazilian composer Jaci Maraschin, avoid some of the pitfalls of *Cantate Domino*.

The Sixth General Assembly in Vancouver (1983) was a turning point for integrating global song into WCC liturgies. Liturgical/musical *animateurs* (animators) from around the world provided leadership for assembly worship. Publications of songs from this assembly and succeeding events in Canberra (1991) and Harare (1998) have been important sources for transmitting global song throughout the world. Some of the primary animateurs include I-to Loh (Presbyterian, Taiwan), Patrick Matsikenyiri (United Methodist, ZIMBABWE), Simei Monteiro (Methodist, BRAZIL), George Mxadana (South Africa), Pablo Sosa (Methodist, Argentina), Per Harling (Lutheran, SWEDEN), Dinah Riendorf (Ghana), and Terry MacArthur (United Methodist, USA). MacArthur served as the worship consultant for the WCC during both the Canberra and Harare Assemblies. Although not a WCC publication, *Thuma Mina: Internationales Ökumenishches Liederbuch* (1995), edited by Dieter Trautwein and endorsed by the Association of Protestant Churches and Mission in GERMANY, reflects the spirit of the WCC gatherings. Trautwein coordinated worship for the Vancouver Assembly.

Lutheran Contributions

The focus on culture and worship by the LUTHERAN WORLD FEDERATION (LWF) and its assemblies (ten through 2003) have set the stage for incorporating global song into liturgy. *Laudamus*, with six editions from 1952 to 1990, is a collection used in these gatherings. The 1990 Supplement was the first to focus on global song with another edition planned for 2003. Gerhard Cartford and Mark P. Bangert, participants in LWF consultations on worship, have been among the foremost proponents of global song for the Lutheran church (see EVANGELICAL LUTHERAN CHURCH IN AMERICA) in the United States.

Other Lutheran representatives include Howard S. Olsen (b. 1922), who collected songs from eastern Africa and edited several editions of *Tumshangilie Mungu: Nyimbo za Kikristo za Kaifrika* published by the Lutheran Theological College in Tanzania. Selected songs appear in the United States in *Lead Us, Lord* (1977) and *Set Free* (1993). Swedish Lutherans deserve special mention in the dissemination of global song. Anders Nyberg collected three volumes of South African Freedom Songs during apartheid, selections that were published in the United States as *Freedom Is Coming* (1984). Upon return to Sweden he taught Swedish young people how to sing in the South African style. The publication and recording of these songs have been significant in antiapartheid awareness in Europe. Per Harling has promoted global song and liturgy both for the WCC (*Worshipping Ecumenically*, 1995) and through a series of ten documentaries entitled "The Whole World Sings" for Swedish television. His folk mass *Träd in i dansen* (1993) provides a Swedish contextualiztion of the liturgy.

In the United States a Lutheran-based ensemble, Bread for the Journey, has published two collections of global songs, *Global Songs: Local Voices* (1995) and *Global Songs 2* (1997) along with recordings. *With One Voice* (1995), a hymnal supplement for the *Lutheran Book of Worship* (1978), and the Spanish-language hymnal, *Libro de Liturgia y Cántico* (1998), edited by Pedro Suarez, reflect significant global diversity. The African American Hymnal, *This Far by Faith* (1999), is also an excellent source for African songs.

Methodist Contributions

Methodists have been leaders in collecting, composing, publishing, and incorporating global song into worship. Pablo Sosa (b. 1933) spearheaded this movement in South America with successive editions of *Cancionero Abierto* (Open Songbook) begun in 1974 and continuing through the 1990s. Sosa's earlier hymnal, *Cantico Nuevo* (1962), reflected virtually only Euro–North American musical traditions. *Cancionero Abierto,* however, encouraged indigenous compositions by South Americans. Its informal format with cassette recordings brought new authors and composers to light. This collection has influenced Spanish-language songbooks and hymnals published in the

United States by United Methodists such as *Celebremos* (1979) and *Celebremos II* (1983), edited by Roberto Escamilla and Elsie Shoemaker Eslinger, and *Mil Voces Para Celebrar* (1996), edited by Raquel Martínez, as well as hymnals published by other Protestant denominations.

The Global Praise Project (GPP) of United Methodists has made significant contributions to the dissemination of global song. Begun in 1992 through the General Board of Global Ministry, the GPP has been led by S. T. Kimbrough Jr., general editor, and Carlton R. Young, musical editor. The GPP brings together leading church musicians and composers from around the world to share songs, plan publications, and design conferences that encourage the singing of global songs by local congregations. In addition to WCC animateurs Harling, Loh, Matsikenyiri, Monteiro, and Sosa, other GPP leaders include Raquel Guitierrez-Achón (Cuban-American), Tom Colvin (SCOTLAND/Africa), Melva Costen (African American), Ludmilla Garbouzova (RUSSIA), Hartmut Handt (Germany), Ivor Jones (ENGLAND), Jorge Lockward (Dominican Republic), George Mulrain (Trinidad and Tobago), and Lim Swee Hong (Singapore).

Global Praise I (1996, rev. 1997) and *Global Praise II* (2000) are two general collections with a broad diversity of world song. Focused collections include *Africa Praise Songbook* (1998) compiled by Matsikenyiri, *Russian Praise* (1999) compiled by Garbuzova, *Caribbean Praise* (2000) compiled by Mulrain, and *Tenemos Esperanza/Temos Esperança/We Have Hope* (2002) edited by Lockward. *Songs for the World: Hymns by Charles Wesley* (2001) provides fresh settings of Wesley's hymns by composers around the world.

Celebremos I and II and *Hymns from the Four Winds* (1983), a collection of Asian American hymns edited by I-to Loh, foreshadowed the GPP. These collections have had a significant impact on hymnals used by the United Methodist Church, including the *United Methodist Hymnal* (1989), edited by Carlton Young, *The Faith We Sing* (2000), a hymnal supplement edited by Gary Alan Smith, and *Come, Let Us Worship* (2001), a Korean-English United Methodist Hymnal published jointly with the PRESBYTERIAN CHURCH (PCUSA).

Reformed Contributions

Reformed traditions have also contributed to the collection and dissemination of global song. Most notable are the work of the IONA COMMUNITY (Scotland) and I-to Loh (Taiwan). Tom Colvin (1925–2000), a member of the Iona Community, served in several countries including Malawi and Ghana as a missionary from the CHURCH OF SCOTLAND. He encouraged the development of indigenous song, often pairing Christian texts with traditional melodies. His publications, *Fill Us with Your Love* (1969) and *Come, Let Us Walk This Road Together* (1997), have provided materials for several hymnals in the United States, especially the hymn "Jesu, Jesu, Fill Us with Your Love." The Iona Community was also at the forefront of promoting global song from South Africa during apartheid. John Bell and the members of the Wild Goose Resource Group (WGRG) edited two global collections, *Many and Great: Songs of the World Church* (1990) and *Sent by the Lord* (1991). Subsequent publications by the WGRG usually include global songs among their varied contents, providing a sung complement to the prophetic message of justice and peace for which the Community is known.

I-to Loh (b. 1936), Presbyterian Church of Taiwan (PCT), has been the leader in collecting, promoting, and publishing Asian Christian songs. Following in the footsteps of D. T. Niles (1908–1970), Sri Lankan ecumenist with the WCC, cofounder of the East Asian Christian Conference, and editor of the *E.A.C.C. Hymnal* (1963), Loh encourages compositions from diverse Asian musical idioms, thus fostering an Asian Christian liturgical identity. He conducted his research through extensive travel under the auspices of the UNITED METHODIST CHURCH and while teaching at the Asian Institute for Liturgy and Music in Manila, culminating in *Sound the Bamboo* (1990, rev. 2000), an English-language song collection from more than twenty countries and over thirty-five languages in transliteration. A project for the Christian Conference of Asia, *Sound the Bamboo* has prepared the way for several PCT publications such as *Ban-bîn Siong-chàn* (Let All Nations Praise, 1994) and *Seng-si* (Holy poems/hymns, 2005) that bring global song to Taiwan.

The *Presbyterian Hymnal* (PCUSA, 1990), Canadian *Book of Praise* (1996), *Sing! A New Creation* (2001), a supplement for the CHRISTIAN REFORMED CHURCH IN NORTH AMERICA) and REFORMED CHURCH OF AMERICA, and the Spanish-language *El Himario Presbiteriano* (1999) are North American Reformed hymnals containing global song.

Mennonite Contributions

Mennonite congregations have been exposed to global song through Mennonite World Assemblies, song collections produced for these events, and their primary hymnal, *Hymnal: A Worship Book* (1992), a joint publication for congregations in the Believers Church Tradition. Mary Oyer (b. 1923), a primary proponent for global song among MENNONITES, studied music extensively in Africa and taught with I-to Loh in

Taiwan. A tradition with a strong sense of world missions, Mennonites use global song as a symbol of partnership in mission with Christians around the world.

Evangelical Contributions

Evangelicals have begun to give attention to global song. SIL International (formerly the Summer Institute of Linguistics) works "with language communities worldwide to facilitate language-based development through research, translation, and literacy" (www.sil.org). SIL has translated portions of the BIBLE into over 450 languages. The SIL Web site contains nearly 150 ethnomusicological monographs on specific cultural groups.

Global song collections for specific events include *Aleluya: Let the Whole World Sing*, edited by Corean Bakke and Tony Payne, for the Lausanne II Congress on World Evangelization (Manila, 1989), and *World Praise* and *World Praise 2*, edited by David Peacock and Geoff Weaver, for the Baptist World Alliance Congresses (Buenos Aires, 1995; Melbourne, 2000). The latter volume contains 117 songs from approximately fifty countries. Although these collections offer a broad global repertoire, hymnals used by most evangelical congregations incorporate few world songs.

Other Protestant hymnals with a significant global repertoire include the *New Century Hymnal* (UNITED CHURCH OF CHRIST, 1995), *The Chalice Hymnal* (DISCIPLES OF CHRIST, 1995), and *Voices United* (UNITED CHURCH OF CANADA, 1996).

Issues and Recommendations

Although Western publications include more global music, the musical traffic from the Euro–North American church to the two-thirds world continues. Songs from the ecumenical Taizé Community in FRANCE and the Iona Community have spread throughout the world. Praise choruses from the publishers of Contemporary Christian Music (CCM) are another source of song sung globally. Because of their brevity and textual repetition, these songs are relatively easy to translate into other languages and transmit without printed music. The song staples for Pentecostals and, increasingly, for other denominational bodies, CCM threatens, on the one hand, to engulf the myriad global voices from the world church. On the other hand, the practice of claiming Western copyright "ownership" of communally created global song by publishers inhibits its dissemination.

The following recommendations are suggested in conclusion: (1) Offer training for Western-educated church musicians in leading non-Western musical styles including short-term immersion experiences in other cultural settings; (2) Encourage ethnohymnological research that provides information on cultural context, biographies, and faithful presentations of indigenous musical styles; (3) Produce authentic recordings (audio and video) that help Western musicians learn musical styles through the ear and see the movements that may accompany these songs; (4) Develop creative leadership that encourages appropriate and sustained use of global music as sung prayer within worship; (5) Promote musical gatherings in which Christians from various cultural backgrounds may share their song with each other. As the mosaic of twenty-first century Christian music unfolds, global song represents the global face of the incarnate Christ.

References and Further Reading

Bangert, Mark P. "Dynamics of Liturgy and World Musics: A Methodology for Evaluation." In *Worship and Culture in Dialogue,* edited by S. Anita Stauffer, 183–203. Geneva, Switzerland: The Lutheran World Federation, 1994.

———. "Liturgical Music, Culturally Tuned." In *Liturgy and Music: Lifetime Learning,* edited by Robin A. Leaver and Joyce Ann Zimmerman, 360–383. Collegeville, MN: The Liturgical Press, 1998.

Corbitt, J. Nathan. *The Sound of the Harvest: Music's Mission in Church and Culture.* Grand Rapids, MI: Baker Books, 1998.

Farlee, Robert Buckley, et al. *Leading the Church's Song.* Minneapolis: Augsburg Fortress, 1998.

Hawn, C. Michael. *Gather into One: Praying and Singing Globally.* Grand Rapids, MI: Wm. B. Eerdmans, 2003.

Kimbrough, S. T. Jr. "Practical Considerations for Promoting Global Song." *The Hymn* 51 no. 4 (October 2000): 22–29.

Maynard-Reid, Pedrito U. *Diverse Worship: African-American, Caribbean and Hispanic Perspectives.* Downers Grove, IL: InterVarsity Press, 2000.

Young, Carlton R. "Ethnic and Minority Hymns in United States Mainline Protestant Hymnals 1940–1995: Some Qualifying Considerations." *The Hymn* 49 no. 3 (July 1998): 17–27.

C. MICHAEL HAWN

MUSIC, NORTHERN EUROPEAN

Protestant MUSIC constitutes more than church music. Certainly Protestantism gave rise to specific worship music, but the influence of Protestantism on music affected more than the compositions intended for WORSHIP. From its beginnings in the sixteenth century, Protestantism gave rise to "secular" religious ballads—that is, songs of specific religious content, often polemic in nature, that were sung outside the context of worship. However, even the hymns and psalms of congregational worship were also sung in secular contexts. Similarly, domestic devotional music developed in parallel with the music of the church, music that

often introduced new styles and forms that eventually made their way into the public worship of the churches. Protestant music in all its forms—public and private, ecclesiastical and nonecclesiastical—is a direct product of its primary theological concerns.

Reformation Principles of Music

The foundation of Protestant theology is the *solo Scriptura* principle—that the foundation for Christian faith and life is to be found in the BIBLE rather than in the decrees of the CHURCH. Thus Scripture provided the primary texts that were set musically in all REFORMATION traditions—such as Lutheran chorales, whose texts were frequently mosaics of biblical concepts and phrases; Genevan Psalms, which rendered the biblical Psalms in metrical form; or Anglican anthems that were almost exclusively settings of biblical texts, most frequently from the Psalms, although the different traditions variously interpreted the biblical material with regard to the function of music in public and in private.

For MARTIN LUTHER music was a gift of God that should be employed to praise God and proclaim God's Word in a variety of forms and styles by voices and instruments. Thus the Lutheran tradition of music, ecclesiastical and domestic, is rich in choral, vocal, and instrumental forms. JOHN CALVIN also regarded music as a gift of God but was more restrictive than Luther with regard to its use in public worship. Such music had to be majestic without secular association and sung without accompaniment—instrumental music for Calvin was part of the ceremonial of the Temple that had been rendered obsolete by the sacrifice of Christ—and consist almost exclusively of metrical Psalms, a distinctive feature of Reformed/Calvinist worship. For HULDRYCH ZWINGLI, music itself, rather than instrumental accompaniment, was rendered invalid for public worship by the New Covenant; therefore, for him, no music was permitted in the Christian assembly. Thus the churches of Zurich, and those under its influence, banished music from public worship and congregational Psalmody was resisted until the very end of the sixteenth century. However, Zwingli was not the musical Philistine that he is often portrayed. Although he banished music from public worship he nevertheless commended its use in private worship. He composed both texts and music for such devotional use and effectively led the way for others, notably the later Puritans (see PURITANISM), who although protesting about the use of music in public worship nevertheless practiced it in their homes.

The question "How Protestant is Protestant music?" is not easy to define in terms of musical styles and forms, given that music composed for the Catholic LITURGY continued in use among many Protestants. Gregorian hymn melodies were sung by Lutherans and Anglicans alike (see LUTHERANISM; ANGLICANISM), and some of the melodies of the Genevan Psalter were adaptations of Gregorian chant. Music by Catholic composers were reworked by Michael Praetorius in the early seventeenth century for use in Lutheran churches, and, similarly, Catholic-composed motets continued to be sung in Lutheran liturgies well into the eighteenth century, from the anthologies of Erhard Bodenschatz (1576–1636) and Melchior Vulpius (1570–1615) issued in the early seventeenth century. The Motets of Orlando di Lassus (1532–1594) were reissued in London, Geneva, and La Rochelle in the 1570s with new French texts so that they could be sung as domestic devotional music among French-speaking Calvinists. In the nineteenth and twentieth centuries much Catholic church music was incorporated into Protestant worship.

Reformation Patterns of Music

Lutheran

Luther's reformation of the music of worship was a synthesis of continuity and discontinuity. On the one hand, he retained the use of Gregorian chant, emending or exchanging the associated texts with biblical material (in both Latin and German), and on the other, introduced vernacular congregational singing. The Latin schools, which customarily had provided much of the music of the churches, were reformed and the school choirs continued to sing traditional chants (published in anthologies edited by Kasper Friedrich Lossius, Johannes Spangenberg, Johann Keuchenthal, and Franciscus Eler) in the evangelical Mass, Matins, and Vespers. The same choirs also sang polyphonic settings of the Ordinary as well as chorale motets based on the melodies of the new congregational hymns, settings that were sung in alternation with the congregation singing in unison. Such singing was introduced by organ chorale preludes based on the melodies that were sung. Other motets were composed on the prose texts taken from the weekly Gospel lections, the *Evangelien-motetten*. The long list of composers of these Lutheran genres include Walter, Dietrich, Calvisius, Hassler, Lechner, Franck, among others. As the Lutheran Reformation spread into Scandinavia, much of German church music was supplied with Danish and Swedish texts; chant forms continued in use, as in Jesperssøn's *Gradual* (1573); and newly written hymns began to appear, as in Thomissøn's *Den danske Psalmerbog* (1569).

Calvinist/Reformed

Calvin, following the example of the practice of German congregations in Strassburg, developed the metrical Psalm in French as the primary music of worship. Working with poets Clément Marot and Theodore Beza and composers Lois Bourgeois and Claude Goudimel, the Genevan Psalter was created (completed in 1562). These sturdy Psalms were sung in unaccompanied unison in the churches, although when they were sung domestically they were performed in harmonized versions, voices doubled by instruments if they were available. Composers such as Bourgeois, Goudimel, Le Jeune, and Jean Pieterszoom Sweelinck created various homophonic and polyphonic settings of the melodies of the Genevan Psalter, which in the sixteenth century were never sung in the churches. However, in later times, when organs and choirs had come into use in Reformed churches, these settings of the Genevan Psalm tunes were sung in public worship. As CALVINISM spread throughout Europe so did the Genevan Psalm tunes, which were sung in the respective vernacular to the same melodies, such as the German versions by Lobwasser, the Dutch by Datheen, as well as others in many different European languages.

Anglican

The English Reformation was first influenced by Lutheran reforms and then moved in a more pronounced Calvinist direction. Thus the metrical Psalms constituted congregational song for much of emerging ANGLICANISM. The Psalter of Sternhold and Hopkins (1562) became the basis of Anglican parish church music, sung unaccompanied and "lined-out," that is, sung by the congregation line by line after the parish clerk. Beginning in 1563 a succession of four-part settings of the English psalm tunes were published for domestic vocal and instrumental use, such as the tune books edited by Este, Daman, Ravenscroft, and Playford. In the cathedrals of England, however, a more developed church music was established, with choirs made up of men and boys, accompanied by organs. Through-composed settings of Prayer Book canticles and anthems on Biblical texts were provided by many composers, such as Tallis, Byrd, Gibbons, Tomkins, among others.

Other Traditions

In addition to the above-mentioned traditions, there were others. The Bohemian Brethren, the followers of Jan Hus, were both precursors and inheritors of the reforming movement. Already in the fifteenth century they had developed vernacular Czech hymnody, largely based on Latin models. By 1500 these had been translated into German and proved to be a specific influence on the development of the Lutheran chorale—Luther and his colleagues were particularly influenced by the German Bohemian Brethren hymnal of 1531. Later Bohemian Brethren hymnals exhibit both Lutheran and Calvinist influence, especially new tunes that were clearly modeled on Genevan Psalm tunes. The Bohemian Brethren, or *Unitas Fratrum,* later evolved into the MORAVIAN CHURCH, which had a distinctive music tradition.

The Anabaptist (see ANABAPTISM) tradition, the disparate groups of pacifist and nonpacifist believers who were united in their common rejection of organized ministry and acceptance of adult BAPTISM, although differing on many other aspects of belief and practice, cultivated their own music in the form of hymnlike songs. These were often martyr-songs celebrating their co-religionists who had been executed because of their faith. Some were sung to folklike melodies; others were sung to Lutheran and other melodies. Representative collections of these songs include the Dutch *Een Geestelijck Liedt-Boecxken* of Joris (c.1576/82) and the Swiss-German *Ausbund* (1564).

Post-Reformation Musical Developments

Italian musical styles became influential in the seventeenth century, especially the polychoralism and figured bass of the Gabrielis and Monteverdi in Venice. Schütz (who studied in Venice), Schein, Michael Praetorius, and others in GERMANY were especially influenced by Italianate forms. During the century the genre of spiritual "Concert" was developed, an extended musical composition that alternated solo and choral passages on biblical texts with interspersed chorales. Ultimately this would develop into the distinctive Lutheran church cantata. Among the composers of the developing form were Hammerschmidt, Briegel, Buxtehude, Pachelbel, Bruhns, and others, eventually culminating in the fully developed form exhibited supremely in the cantatas by JOHANN SEBASTIAN BACH, but also including those of GEORG PHILIPP TELEMANN and Graupner in the eighteenth century. German church music was used extensively in Scandinavia but there were some notable indigenous composers such as the Swedish J. H. Roman.

During the seventeenth century Lutheran composers developed concerted settings of "Historia," that is, musical settings of the Nativity, Passion, Resurrection, and Ascension of Christ, with a particular emphasis on Passion compositions, notable composers of which were Schütz and J. S. Bach. Most of these were intended for liturgical use but before the end of the century they began to be performed independently, and, through Italian influence, the Protestant tradition

of biblical oratorios, that would flourish in the following century, was begun. In North Germany organ music was particularly developed, much of it chorale-based but included freely composed forms by such composers as Böhm, Buxtehude, and Pachelbel, culminating in the organ works of J. S. Bach.

For much of the first half of the seventeenth century in ENGLAND, church music was reduced to congregational psalmody or eliminated altogether during the Presbyterian Commonwealth period. With the restoration of the monarchy and Anglicanism in 1660 a new beginning was made with church music. Because what few organs there were had been destroyed and church music foundations dismantled during the Commonwealth period, composers connected with the Chapel Royal—principally Humphrey and HENRY PURCELL—developed the verse anthem (a genre that made predominant use of solo voices with shorter choral sections) with string accompaniment. Although the use of strings followed the style of the French court—where the new king, Charles II, had spent his exile years—these verse anthems are, in terms of length and content, the Anglican equivalent of the seventeenth-century Lutheran cantata. Some of Purcell's occasional pieces, such as his "Odes to St. Cecelia" (1683 and 1692) presage Handelian oratorio (GEORGE FRIDERIC HANDEL). For domestic devotion composers such as Henry Lawes, Blow, and Purcell, among others, composed strophic songs and Psalms.

Pietism and Rationalism in the Eighteenth Century

PIETISM in a variety of forms significantly influenced the music of Protestantism in the seventeenth and eighteenth centuries. A number of factors contributed to its rise, including the widespread popularity of Lewis Bayly's *Practice of Piety*—translated into various European languages—and the impact of the Thirty Years' War, which led to an internalized and intensely personalized spirituality. Even those who opposed Pietism as such were nevertheless influenced by it to some degree. Thus Lutheran orthodox hymn writers PAUL GERHARDT and Martin Rinckart wrote texts of such personal spirituality, and composers such as Crüger and Ebeling set them to lighter and more intimate melodies that contrasted with the ruggedness of the earlier chorale melodies. Lutheran Pietists objected to concerted and complex musical forms and advocated instead the primary use of simplified hymnody, with easy and accessible tunes. Freylinghausen's *Geistreiches Gesangbuch* (1704–1714) contained such tunes and exercised considerable influence within and outside of Germany in the eighteenth century, being used not only by Lutherans but also Moravians and early Methodists. The small-scale, aria-like melodies, with strophic texts, were first introduced into domestic devotions but in time began to be introduced into the worship of the churches. The influence of such music can be found in various collections, such as Bach's *Musikalisches Gesangbuch* (1736) in Germany, Bachhofen's *Musicalisches Hallelujah* (1727) in SWITZERLAND, Schutte's *Zangwijzen van Stichtelijke Gezangen* (1760) in the NETHERLANDS, and the many music books published in England after the rise of EVANGELICALISM in general and METHODISM in particular, such as Madan's Lock Hospital *Collection* (1760).

In Europe generally the twin influences of Pietism and Rationalism led to a decline of elaborate church music, reducing the role of music to little more than simple hymns with organ accompaniment, and an occasional homophonic anthem, if there was a choir available. Thus vocal music accompanied by instruments was rarely heard within liturgical worship but was used extensively in independent performances of oratorios, especially in the second half of the eighteenth century, such as the programs of the Berlin *Singverein.*

In the earlier eighteenth century in England composers such as Greene, Croft, and others composed many new anthems for cathedral use, issued in engraved editions available by subscription, whereas the older anthems and services were accessible in the anthologies of Boyce and Arnold. In addition to music for public worship, cathedrals offered occasional musical festivals. Such occasions gave rise to the oratorios of Handel that were regularly performed in London and elsewhere from the 1730s, notably *Messiah,* which was not only sung in complete performances in churches and concert halls but its individual choruses and arias were widely included in church services as anthems around the turn of the century.

The Moravian Church, an offshoot of German Lutheran Pietism, owed much to eighteenth-century Lutheran musical traditions, which through its missionary endeavors were transplanted in various countries throughout the world, especially in North America. It has continued its own tradition of musical worship with instruments to the present day, a rich amalgam of congregational, vocal, choral, and instrumental (strings, winds, and organ) music.

Restoration and Romanticism

Around the beginning of the second quarter of the nineteenth century there were various moves in Germany to counteract the limiting effects of Pietism and Rationalism with regard to Protestant worship music. An important center of reform was Berlin, where was introduced a new liturgical *Agenda,* with appropriate liturgical music, a new hymnal that eliminated the alterations of the previous generations. A. W. Bach, Felix Mendelssohn's organ teacher, also issued a new anthology of organ settings of the chorale melodies. Felix Mendelssohn composed various Psalm settings and other church music for use in the Berlin cathedral in a somewhat restrained style. Mendelssohn, Brahms, and others wrote unaccompanied motets and organ music for church use, but also composed religious music for performance in "secular" concert halls, such as Mendelssohn's oratorios *Elijah* and *St. Paul,* together with his "Reformation" Symphony that makes use of Luther's *Ein feste Burg,* and Brahms's *Ein deutsches Requiem,* a work that was also performed in churches, although not liturgically.

In England church music was influenced both by the Tractarian movement and ROMANTICISM: daily choral services were restored in the cathedrals, and the cathedral musical tradition expanded into parish churches, including the building and use of organs. On the one hand, music was inspired by Catholic tradition, such as the hymns found in *Hymns Ancient and Modern* and the musical supplements of the journal, *The Parish Choir* (1846–1851), issued by the Society for Promoting Church Music. On the other hand, much music was inspired by Victorian sentimentalism, as represented by Sullivan's long-forgotten oratorio, *The Light of the World,* and Stainer's ever-popular *Crucifixion.* Novello and other publishing companies supplied the increasing demand for anthems in "octavo" editions of a few pages, mostly in the secular musical style of the day rather than the long-standing cathedral music tradition. Composers such as Barnby and Simper supplied much of this more popular music, whereas S. S. Wesley and later Stanford, Parry, and Wood, among others, made their distinctive contributions to the tradition of cathedral music.

The Broadening of Styles, Forms, and Content

At the beginning of the twentieth century Protestant church music in Germany was marked by two parallel developments: the restoration of the earlier music of seventeenth and eighteenth centuries and the composition of new liturgical music. Collected editions of the music of Bach, Handel, and Schütz had appeared in the second half of the nineteenth century. To these were now added editions of the music of DIETRICH BUXTEHUDE, Lübeck, Michael Praetorius, Scheidt, and Johann Walter. Among the vigorous school of new composers of church music were David, Distler, Marx, Arnold, Mendelssohn, Raphäel, Pepping, Petzold, Stern, and Kurt Thomas, whose music explores twentieth-century tonality while at the same time reflecting the forms and genres of earlier Lutheran church music. Many church music schools were founded and there was a blossoming of choirs and choral music in the churches and the influential tradition of trumpet and trombone ensembles. The new hymnal, *Deutsches evangelisches Gesangbuch,* for use in the regional churches was issued in 1915. Many of these new developments, however, were interrupted by the rise of Nazism, the Third Reich, and the Second World War. They were later reestablished in the postwar years, with the founding of more church music schools; the lay *Kirchen-Tag* movement, which developed its own music forms; and the issuing of a new hymnal, *Das Evangelischen Kirchengesangbuch,* which, although it did include examples of contemporary hymnody, was almost exclusively committed to the older hymnic forms. Among the new composers were Bender, Fortner, Ramin, Reda, Ruppel, and Zimmermann, and inspiration was drawn from non-German traditions such as jazz and African American spirituals.

Church music in England was similarly affected by the Second World War. Among the prewar composers who continued to write for the cathedrals tradition of anthems and services include Baistow, Harris, Holst, Howells, Ireland, and RALPH VAUGHAN WILLIAMS. Some of these continued to be active in the postwar period, where they were joined by BENJAMIN BRITTEN, Davies, Joubert, Tippett, among others. In addition to composing music for worship they also wrote larger-scaled religious pieces, such as Vaughan Williams's *Job,* Tippett's *A Child of Our Time* (which uses African American spirituals), and Britten's varied works, such as *Rejoice in the Lamb, Saint Nicolas,* and the massive and moving *War Requiem.*

The iconoclastic 1960s led to an explosion of popular musical styles and forms being introduced into Protestant worship. In Germany the influence of jazz and various popular styles has been prominent. In England the door to less traditional worship was opened by Geoffrey Beaumont's extraordinary popular *Folk Mass,* written toward the end of the 1950s, although in a 1930s Broadway style. In its wake come a plethora of musical styles and forms performed mostly with the instruments of popular culture rather than traditional instruments, with a widespread abandonment of the organ, although traditional forms of worship music, with newly composed music alongside earlier examples, continues in cathedrals, collegiate chapels, and notable parish churches. New hymnals have been introduced in most European countries, which, like other music heard in the churches, is no longer closely identified with one language group, denomination, or country. Protestant church music has become for many an eclectic fusion of different styles, forms, and traditions, from every continent of the globe, with music promoted by modern commercialism predominating.

See also Hymns and Hymnals; Music, English Church; Music, American; Music, Popular

References and Further Reading

Blume, Friedrich. *Protestant Church Music: A History.* New York: Norton, 1974.
Etherington, Charles L. *Protestant Worship Music: Its History and Practice.* New York: Holt, Rinehart & Winston, 1962.
Fellowes, Edmund. *English Cathedral Music.* Edited by Jack A. Westrup. London: Methuen, 1969.
Hutchings, Arthur. *Church Music in the Nineteenth Century.* New York: Oxford University Press, 1967.
Liemohn, Edwin. *The Organ and Choir in Protestant Worship.* Philadelphia, PA: Fortress, 1968.
Routley, Erik. *Twentieth Century Church Music.* Carol Stream, IL: Agape, 1984.
Spink, Ian. *Restoration Cathedral Music 1660–1714.* Oxford, UK: Clarendon Press, 1995.
Temperley, Nicholas. *The Music of the English Parish Church.* 2 vols. Cambridge: Cambridge University Press, 1979.
Webber, Geoffrey. *North German Church Music in the Age of Buxtehude.* Oxford: Oxford University Press, 1996.
Westermeyer, Paul. *Te Deum: The Church and Music.* Minneapolis, MN: Fortress Press, 1998.

ROBIN LEAVER

MUSIC, POPULAR

A major consequence of the emergence of protestant church in the wake of the REFORMATION movement in the sixteenth century was the integration of popular music with religious lyrics. MARTIN LUTHER believed in the congregation being an integral part of the service, and this meant singing. Luther wrote a number of hymns for his congregation to sing; the most popular is "A Mighty Fortress."

The Beginnings

The second colony established by ENGLAND in America, the Plymouth Bay Colony, published the first book of songs, *The Bay Psalm Book,* in what would become the United States. Through the U.S. CIVIL WAR, however, the most popular religious music was composed by ISAAC WATTS (1674–1748) and JOHN (1703–1791) and CHARLES (1707–1788) WESLEY.

After the Civil War there was a revival in the United States in urban areas led by evangelists DWIGHT MOODY (1837–1899) and IRA SANKEY (1840–1908). The two joined forces in Chicago in 1871 and held revivals where Sankey would usually begin with singing to prepare the crowd for Moody's sermon. Sankey was responsible for developing the American hymn during this period, although this type of song goes back to England and Isaac Watts. These songs, sometimes called "hymns of human composure," differed from previous religious music because they were not songs directly from the Bible (e.g., the Psalms set to music), but rather a song inspired by the Bible.

Ira Sankey was a somber, serious man whose most famous number was "The Ninety and Nine," a song about a lost soul coming back to the Christian fold. Sankey sang his songs before Moody spoke, gathering a crowd and "warming up" the audience for the sermon. Moody was a salesman before he became a preacher, so he looked at his crusades in terms of a sales pitch; the music was the bait, the sermon was the pitch, and the altar call where sinners came forward to commit or recommit their lives to Christ was "lowering the net" or the closing for the sale.

Sankey wrote a number of the songs he sang and also used songs by other composers. He collected many of these songs into a series of songbooks that sold over six million copies. This was in the latter part of the nineteenth century, when publishing and sheet music dominated the music industry. Sankey's success paralleled the success of The Tin Pan Alley publishers, with one important exception: Sankey proved there was an incredible market for white gospel songs outside the normal music outlets. This would continue to be the story of white gospel music. As with secular music, there was a large market and musically it would be similar to Tin Pan Alley's songs, but people bought gospel music in different places and for an entirely different reason. They bought gospel music for *religious* reasons (to inspire a religious experience or to help worship services in churches), while people bought secular music for entertainment and social prestige.

The next major revival was led by evangelist BILLY SUNDAY (c. 1862–1935) and his song leader, Homer Rodeheaver (1880–1955). Rodeheaver was an energetic, likeable man who played the trombone and brought entertainment into gospel music. Unlike the somber and serious Sankey, Rodeheaver clowned on stage, did humorous skits with his trombone, and presented a more lively view of Christianity. The number he was best known for was "Brighten the Corner Where You Are."

Rodeheaver began the first record label that recorded only white gospel music. Rainbow Records, founded in Winona Lake, Indiana, was an extension of Rodeheaver's publishing company. Although the major secular record labels all recorded gospel music during their early years, Rainbow Records set the precedent for the future of gospel recording.

Black Gospel Music

Black gospel has its own separate and distinct culture, although there are some similarities with white gospel.

In the early 1870s the Fisk Jubilee Singers were on tour singing Negro Spirituals, religious songs that came from the slave culture. The spirituals became the first music from African Americans to be nationally known. The Fisk Jubilee Singers excited audiences all over the world with these numbers, performed originally by a group of seven men and three women.

The next major event in black gospel occurred in the first part of the twentieth century when Thomas A. Dorsey (1899–1993), the music minister for the Pilgrim Baptist Church in Chicago, began writing and publishing songs. Dorsey came out of blues music (as a blues singer he was known as Georgia Tom, and played piano for Ma Rainey), but soon renounced the blues for gospel. In 1930 at the National Baptist Convention (Negro) in Chicago, two songs written by Thomas Dorsey were performed. The songs, "How About You" and "Did You See My Savior," were the first gospel songs done at that convention. For black gospel, the term "gospel" meant a song whose composer was known. Traditionally, hymns (most written by the Wesleys, Isaac Watts, and other hymn writers) or Psalms were sung. Dorsey's song created a great deal of excitement at the convention; when the convention goers went home, they took Dorsey's songs with them.

Back in Chicago, Dorsey worked with a number of singers, including Sallie Martin (1896–1988) and Mahalia Jackson (1911–1972), and toured nationally between 1932 and 1944. He became the "father of gospel music" and established an annual convention for gospel singers. Dorsey's two most famous songs, "Precious Lord, Take My Hand" and "Peace in the Valley," have become standards and have been recorded by numerous artists, white and black.

The Holiness and Pentecostal Movements

Two movements within the church have proven instrumental in both gospel music as well as secular music. The holiness movement occurred in the black church in the 1890s; in 1900 the Pentecostal movement occurred in white churches. These movements, characterized by emotional services, speaking in tongues, passionate preaching, and innovative music, were not widely accepted by mainstream Christianity in either culture, but a number of early rock 'n' roll pioneers, including Little Richard, Elvis Presley, Jerry Lee Lewis, Sam Cooke, and others came out of these movements. This first generation of rock 'n' rollers captured the spirit and frenzy of the Holiness or Pentecostal movements in their secular music. This is the essential link between gospel music and early rock 'n' roll. However, later generations of rock artists, especially those from Great Britain, did not have this connection with gospel music.

Gospel and Popular Music

Gospel music's influence on secular music is through individual performers, not on the music as a whole. However, secular music has had a great impact on gospel music, particularly contemporary Christian music beginning in the late 1960s. Contemporary Christian music evolved from the Jesus Movement, where socially active youth who confronted Vietnam and the civil rights struggle increasingly found the answer to their questions to lie in an intense, personal relationship with Jesus Christ.

This led to a number of singers and songwriters using the basic pop song format—and recording industry practices—to write and sing about Jesus for recordings. As contemporary Christian music evolved, it tended to mimac the dominant trends in popular music, providing a Christian alternative to secular music. Although the lyrics were different, the music was similar.

As Christianity became a subculture in the United States, gospel music became a subgenre of pop music. It has its own market and outlets (Christian bookstores), its own media (radio stations, periodicals, and TV shows), its own educational system (religious schools), and its own music industry with its own stars.

Gospel music is unique because the performers view themselves primarily as ministers rather than entertainers. The performers are different than their secular counterparts because they demand that audiences agree with their religious beliefs. Gospel music audiences, in turn, demand that artists agree with them; the audience wants a music that supports, confirms, and encourages their faith.

Although gospel music is an important, vital music in America, by the beginning of the twenty-first century it became a music separate from non-gospel or secular music with few artists able to succeed in both fields.

References and Further Reading

Baker, Paul. *Why Should the Devil Have All the Good Music?* Waco, TX: Word, 1979.

Boyer, Horace, text; photography by Lloyd Yearwood. *How Sweet the Sound: The Golden Age of Gospel.* Washington, DC: Elliott & Clark Publishing, 1995.

Cusic, Don. *The Sound of Light: A History of Gospel Music.* Bowling Green, OH: Bowling Green State University Proplar Press, 1990.

Harris, Michael W. *The Rise of Gospel Blues: The Music of Thomas Andrew Dorsey in the Urban Church.* New York: Oxford University Press, 1992.

Heilbut, Anthony. *The Gospel Sound.* New York: Simon and Schuster, 1971.

Howard, Jay R., and John M. Streck. *Apostles of Rock: The Splintered World of Contemporary Christian Music.* Lexington: University Press of Kentuky, 1999.

Johnson, James Weldon, and J. Rosamond Johnson. *American Negro Spirituals.* New York: Viking, 1925.

Nettl, Paul. *Luther and Music.* New York: Russell and Russell, 1948.

Sankey, Ira D. *My Life and The Story of the Gospel Hymns.* Philadelphia, PA: The Sunday School Times, 1907.

DON CUSIC

N

NANTES, EDICT OF

The Edict of Nantes, proclaimed by King Henry IV of France on April 30, 1598 and registered by the parliaments of Paris on February 25, 1599, ended the series of eight wars of religion that tore the kingdom of FRANCE for thirty-six years (from 1562 to 1598). The Edict was the product of two years of negotiations between Henry IV's commissioners and Protestant representatives. As the first sentence in Article I shows, the Edict intended above all to be an edict of pacification looking to stop the cycle of violence. "First, that the recollection of everything done by one party or the other (. . .) remain obliterated and forgotten as if no such things had ever happened." Indeed, first the recollection of the preceding troubles had to be erased. Thus Article II states, "forbidding all our subjects, of whatsoever estate or quality, to revive its recollection, to attack, resent, insult or provoke one another by reproach of what took place for whatsoever cause, to dispute, contest, quarrel, nor to become outraged or offended from act or word; but to refrain and live peacefully, together as brothers, friends, and co-citizens, lest the contravenants be punished as breakers of peace and disturbers of public tranquillity."

After the first national synod of the Reformed Churches of France, held in Paris in 1559, and with a Protestant Church that was organizing in a kingdom concerned about maintaining its unity of faith, followed a period marred by civil wars ("troubles by way of religion" as was said at the time) interrupted by truces and edicts of pacification. The failure of the COLLOQUY OF POISSY (September 1561), which attempted to end the theological discord that threatened the unity of France, opened the way to civil war.

The first three wars of religion started with the massacre of the Protestants in Vassy in 1562 and opposed the Protestant armies to the royal armies from 1562 to 1570. The Edict of Amboise (1563) ended the first war of religion thanks for the most part to Michel de L'Hospital, a precursor who was already claiming, "even the heretic does not cease to be a citizen." The pacification gained from the Peace of Saint-Germain, which was signed in 1570, set an important precedent for the Edict of Nantes because it granted some freedom to the Protestants: freedom of conscience, a limited freedom of worship, and four safe places (La Rochelle, Cognac, Montauban, and La Charité sur Loire). The peace of Saint-Germain was challenged, however, by the terrible massacres of the Saint-Barthélémy that caused the death of thousands of Protestants in Paris on August 24, 1572 and in other towns a few days or weeks later (Bourges, Saumur, Angers, Lyons, Bordeaux, Toulouse, etc.). More wars of religion ensued. The eighth—and last—war (1585–1589) saw a shift in alliances.

At first Henry III had deposed his heir presumptive, the Protestant Henry of Navarre and future Henry IV, of all his rights. Overwhelmed by the Ligue (the Catholic party), however, Henry III reconciled with his cousin before being assassinated while Paris was under siege (August 1589) and France risked falling under Spanish hegemony. Henry of Navarre agreed in 1593 to convert to Catholicism (whence the expression "Paris is well worth a mass"). He was crowned king of France in 1594 and signed peace with Spain in May 1598, at a time when he was trying through the Edict of Nantes to have Catholicism, "the Kingdom's religion," coexist with the "so-called Reformed religion." Henry of Navarre had been excommunicated and had his rights to the crown abrogated by Pope Sixtus V with the Bull of September 29, 1585, even though the archbishop of Bourges had already absolved him in Saint Denis as he had received his abjuration on July 25, 1593. It would take more than two years of tense negotiations with the papacy for Pope Clement VIII to absolve and lift all sanctions against Henry IV on September 17, 1595. This episode shows how great the papacy's ambitions still were in the sixteenth century, even though the States and their CLERGY were starting to enjoy greater autonomy from Rome's power.

Assessing the Text

The text of the Edict is made up of a solemn edict in a preamble and ninety-three articles: fifty-six "secret and particular" articles dealing mostly with places of worship; a warrant stipulating the royal subsidy to be used for the pastors' wages, the running of academies and colleges (in compensation for the tithe paid to the clergy); and a warrant specifying the geographic location of safe places. It is significant that after the first two Articles that tend to the pacification of minds, Article III is devoted to the full reestablishment of Catholic WORSHIP: "We ordain that the Catholic, Apostolic and Roman Religion shall be restored and reestablished in all places and localities of our Kingdom and under our obedience, where the exercise of it has been interrupted, to be peacefully and freely exercised, without any trouble or hindrance." While confirming that Catholicism was the religion of the kingdom and by restoring this religion where it had been abolished (in some regions of the South), the Edict of Nantes granted the king's subjects who belonged to the "so-called reformed religion" (according to the phrasing of the time), some rights and important dispensations. The Edict of Nantes remains within the frame of the Ancient Regime, which granted not so much individual rights, but rather rights to members of a given community, in this case, the group of people belonging to the "so-called reformed religion." The Edict awarded—which is no small matter—full freedom of conscience to Protestants, with Article VI specifying that they could not be compelled to participate in Catholic worship and that each head of a family was free to perform with his kin a "private devotion." Exempt from contributing to the costs of fixing up churches and buying sacerdotal VESTMENTS, Protestants were no longer forced to decorate the front of their houses on Catholic holy days, but simply had to "suffer" that their houses be decorated by royal officers (on days of Catholic processions, for example). Although they could not be the object of forced proselytism and their children could not be removed to be integrated to the Catholic church (Article XX), Protestants still had to respect Catholic days of rest and pay the ecclesiastical tithe (Article XXV).

A broad freedom of conscience did not mean freedom of worship. In the Edict of Nantes the latter is sparsely allotted to Protestants, being even more restricted than what had been temporarily granted by the Edict of Saint-Germain in 1562, which had instituted freedom of worship across the kingdom. In the Edict of Nantes, on the other hand, public Protestant worship is subject to a list of authorized locales: places where Protestant service had been celebrated in 1596 and during the first months of 1597. Furthermore, in Paris and in many cities, Protestant worship was relegated within the confines of the suburbs (Article XI) or their vicinity (Article XIV). Thus the temple used by Parisian Protestants would be transferred in 1606 to Charenton in the near suburbs, after having been in two other places around Paris.

So as "justice be rendered and administered to our subjects without suspicion, hate, or favor," the "Chambres mi-parties," composed of Catholic and Protestant officers sitting side by side, would be instituted (Articles XXX to LXII). This disposition would be quite randomly applied. In Paris, for example, the "Chambre de l'Edit" included only one Protestant counsel for sixteen Catholic counsels. As for the safe places promised to the Protestants "for the freedom of their conscience" and "for the guarantee of their persons, wealth, and belongings," it was "all the places, towns, and castles they held to the end of last August" (that is, August 1597), or about one hundred and fifty places of garrison and safety that were mostly found in Guyenne, Languedoc, and in the Rhone valley. The king promised to contribute to the cost of worship through warrants, in particular the subsidy of pastors, but some of these warrants would never be applied, especially the first one that provided to pay Protestants a sum of forty-five thousand ecus to manage their businesses and support their pastors. The Edict of Nantes saw its application slowed down by the reluctance of the parliaments to register it. The parliament of Paris registered it in February 1599 and the one in Grenoble in April 1599, but the parliament of Rouen would register it only in 1609 and after the request of Henry IV. The members of Parliament feared in part that Protestants would invest local authorities as a consequence of Article XXVII that opened to them "all Estates, Dignities, Offices, and public charges whatsoever, Royal, Seigniorial, or of Cities of our Kingdom, countries, lands, and lordships under our obedience."

The Edict of Nantes opened a new era by acknowledging that the Catholics and Protestants of France were both subjects of the same king. In that the Edict went farther than the *cujus regio ejus religio* principle of the Peace of Augsburg (1555) that declared the religious homogeneity of the territories ("to each region its religion") and granted the *jus emigrandi* to the subjects who wished to move to a state true to their faith. The Edict of Nantes goes farther inasmuch as it recognizes as subjects of the same king people of different faiths, thus starting to shake the idea that the political unity of society has to be obtained through unity of faith. Still, nothing in the edict leads to belief that it is "a foundational text for religious tolerance" (Grandjean, in Grandjean and Roussel, 1998:7), nor a text that completely gives up the idea of the religious unity for the political collectivity. The word "tolerance" itself does not appear in the text of the Edict and at the time, the word "tolerance" did not have the positive connotation it would later acquire. In the seventeenth century, "to tolerate" still had the negative connotation of "to bear" as in "to suffer" (see TOLERATION). In this context, the point is only to organize the coexistence and therefore civil peace between peoples of different faiths in spite of the prevailing intolerance. Because at the time restoring the religious unity of the kingdom could not be achieved, one made do with a division of faith, while hoping to see one day this unity of faith reestablished in the kingdom. Because it does not give up on the idea of religious unity of the kingdom, the Edict of Nantes, in some regards and even though it pretends to be "perpetual and irrevocable," carries in itself the seed of its own revocation, which would indeed occur in 1685 (FONTAINEBLEAU, EDICT OF). The historian Janine Garrisson thought it a "bastardized *cujus regio, ejus religio . . .* taking into account opposing forces, and conceding to a pressure group (the Protestant political assemblies)" (Garrisson 1985:17–18).

Importance of the Edict

Even though the Edict of Nantes should not be made into a declaration of religious tolerance, its reach should not be underestimated. By spelling out pragmatic rules allowing the control of religious intolerance, this Edict shows the first signs of the emergence of an autonomous political reason against religious matters. If not tolerance, it institutes peace by law, while confirming the privileges of the royal power on the many factions and setting up for an absolute monarchy. Another misinterpretation would be to consider that the text is de facto in favor of Protestants because it finally grants them rights. It may indeed grant some rights to the Protestants, but it reminds in Article III that the goal is to "reestablish in all places and localities" of the kingdom the Catholic Apostolic and Roman religion, which is even in the hearts of the Reformed fiefs. Agrippa d'Aubigné (1552–1630), the Protestant writer who was an ardent defender of his co-Calvinists, was not fooled as he noted in his 1610–

1620 *Histoire Universelle* (ed. by André Thierry, t.9., Genève, Droz 1995:225), that according to the wisest, the "peace of Nantes" "was advantageous for Catholics and ruinous for Protestants."

The Edict of Nantes was enforced until about 1629 when the Edict of Grâce d'Alès, published after the fall of La Rochelle, confirmed the civil and religious clauses of the Edict of Nantes, but eliminated the "safe places." Protestants, who then lost their military and political privileges, found themselves completely at the mercy of the royal will as to whether the clauses of the Edict of Nantes would be applied. From the reign of King Louis XIV, the Edict, reduced to its religious privileges, was applied "rigourously": the "Chambres mi-parties," consisting of Catholic and Protestant judges and created to enforce it, were simply used to forbid Protestants anything to which they were not formally entitled. Numerous professional, cultural, familial, and political interdictions, accompanied by persecution in the South of France, curbed religious freedom and prepared the revocation of 1685.

Revocation

The revocation of the Edict of Nantes was made official by the Edict of Fontainebleau that gave Pastors the strict injunction either to convert or to leave the kingdom of France within two weeks. The faithful, on the opposite, were forbidden to emigrate. As subjects of the "R.P.R.—*Religion Prétendue Réformée*" (so-called Reformed Religion), they would more often be persecuted, even though they were supposedly tolerated, until their renunciation. The revocation of the Edict of Nantes led to a vast movement of emigration of pastors and believers (who left in secret) to the Protestant states of Europe (SWITZERLAND, Brandenburg, United Provinces, ENGLAND). In France, the "Desert" period started, referring to the secret organization of Reformed communities punctuated by the war of the Camisards. In November 1787 French Protestants would regain their civil status thanks to the Edict of Tolerance signed by Louis XVI, which announced their reintegration within the national community and which would be favored by the FRENCH REVOLUTION.

Along with the historian Bernard Cottret (in Grandjean and Roussel 1998:447), one can admit, and with a touch of irony, that "the Edict of Nantes fully succeeded. It succeeded twice: by confirming the civil peace, in a France bled dry after half a century of fratricide wars; and by programming, in due time, the eradication of the Reformed minority and its integration within a State Catholicism." Bernard Cottret is nevertheless prompt to add, "the success is only partial with regard to the latter since Protestants survived their proscription and even drew a new evangelical legitimacy from their interdiction."

See also Bayle, Pierre; Church and State, Overview; Fontainebleau, Edict of; France; French Revolution; Huguenots; Poissy, Colloquy of

References and Further Reading:

Christin, Olivier. *La paix de religion. L'autonomisation de la raison politique au XVIe siècle.* Paris: Seuil, 1997.

Garrisson, Janine. *L'Edit de Nantes et sa révocation. Histoire d'une intolérance.* Paris: Seuil, 1985.

Grandjean, Michel, and Bernard Roussel, eds. *Coexister dans l'intolérance. L'édit de Nantes (1598).* Geneva, Switzerland: Labor et Fides, 1998.

Joxe, Pierre. *L'édit de Nantes. Une histoire pour aujourd'hui.* Paris: Hachette Littératures, 1998.

JEAN-PAUL WILLAIME

NATIONAL ASSOCIATION OF EVANGELICALS

A conservative Protestant organization in the United States, the National Association of Evangelicals that was begun in the 1940s and continued into the twenty-first century has sought to reach a broader audience by moderating the earlier image of FUNDAMENTALISM while maintaining the fundamentalist doctrinal teachings. The origins of the National Association of Evangelicals (NAE) are associated with the early ministry of J. Elwin Wright. Wright's father led an itinerant ministry based in New England. In 1924 the younger Wright took over his father's ministry and through the 1930s expanded it, traveling coast to coast as well as inviting a wide range of Holiness and Pentecostal, Baptist and Methodist, independent and ethnic churches to join his cadre of fundamentalist Protestants.

Wright's desire to reach a broader constituency seemed opportune; however, his efforts were pre-empted by the formation of the American Council of Christian Churches (ACCC) in October 1941 by the radio-preacher CARL MCINTIRE. McIntire formed the ACCC in opposition to the Federal Council of Churches. With its emphasis on fundamentalist teachings and separatist purity, the ACCC provided McIntire with a platform into the 1970s for his advocacy of right-wing politics and apocalyptic religion.

With the challenge of the ACCC before him, Wright convened a planning meeting in St. Louis in April 1942. In May 1943 in Chicago the NAE was formally begun. From its inception, issues and leaders shaped the ethos of the NAE. For example, the NAE denounced liberalism and the Federal Council of Churches and the specific interpretation by the NAE of various Christian doctrines (the nature of the BIBLE, the birth of Christ, the sinfulness of humanity, the ATONEMENT, and the resurrection and return of Christ) hearkened back to earlier fundamentalist creeds. In response to criticism by the ACCC that they wavered in their adherence to fundamentalism, in 1944 the NAE forbade any denomination from holding dual membership in the NAE and the Federal Council of Churches (or its successor the NATIONAL COUNCIL OF CHURCHES). Thus, although the leaders of the NAE sought to rise above sectarian conflict, the very identity of the organization was anchored in a politics and theology of separatism.

Another issue that shaped the identity of the NAE was the network of organizations associated with it. The National Religious Broadcasters were established in 1944 with a close connection to the NAE. During the late 1920s, with the emergence of federal regulations and commercial radio networks, broadcast time was often made available for religious programs as a public service. In many cases commercial networks turned to recognizable denominational members of the Federal Council of Churches. The National Religious Broadcasters was established to set ethical and technical standards for religious broadcasters and to lobby on behalf of the members of the NAE for their right to receive free time or to purchase time for religious radio programming. Similarly, the NAE supported organizations such as the Evangelical Theology Society, the Evangelical Press Association, and the Evangelical Foreign Missions Association. Another organization within this same theological orbit and begun shortly after the founding of the NAE was the YOUTH FOR CHRIST movement, an association that accepted the doctrinal standards of the NAE and whose first field representative was BILLY GRAHAM, a long-time supporter of the NAE.

Although Graham always remained sympathetic to the work of the NAE, the early years of the organization more clearly show the stamp of Harold John Ockenga. Born in Chicago in 1905, Ockenga entered Princeton Theological Seminary in 1927, although he chose to follow JOHN GRESHAM MACHEN and finished his ministerial studies at Westminster Theological Seminary in 1930. Ockenga officiated as president of the NAE from 1942 to 1944, and his combination of organizational abilities and fundamentalist beliefs gave a face to the NAE in its early years. Thus, by the 1950s the NAE contained fifteen small denominations in addition to a mixture of parachurch organizations, independent congregations, and individuals. Its membership had opened up to Pentecostal and Holiness groups, although the SOUTHERN BAPTIST CONVENTION, the LUTHERAN CHURCH–MISSOURI SYNOD, the REFORMED CHURCH IN AMERICA, and the Southern Presbyterian Church had all remained outside the NAE.

In the 1960s and 1970s issues of political and scriptural authority, never far below the surface, emerged once again. The NAE opposed John F. Kennedy in the presidential election not only for his liberal social views but above all for his Roman Catholicism. Ockenga doubted Kennedy's dedication to the separation of CHURCH AND STATE, and the NAE challenged its members to stand up and be counted as Protestants. The Washington D.C. office of the NAE, first opened in 1943, maintained close contacts with the trio of Republican presidents, Dwight Eisenhower, Richard Nixon, and especially Ronald Reagan.

In addition to seeking political clout, the NAE also sought to exercise influence in biblical studies. Dissatisfied with the Revised Standard Version of the Bible that first appeared in 1952, the NAE, together with the CHRISTIAN REFORMED CHURCH and the New York Bible Society, undertook a new translation of the Bible. The result was the New International Version that finally appeared in 1978. Although popular among many elements of conservative Protestantism, scholars have pointed out how closely it resembles in textual, exegetical, and stylistic matters the Revised Standard Version that it was supposed to supplant.

By the end of the twentieth century the NAE faced challenges as blacks formed a separate National Black Evangelical Association, the National Religious Broadcasters severed their relationship with the NAE, and new organizations vied for the leadership of conservative Protestants in America. Nevertheless, the NAE in 2000 claimed a membership of over 42,000 congregations from fifty member denominations and 250 parachurch ministries and educational institutions.

See also Evangelicalism

References and Further Reading

Carpenter, Joel A. *Revive Us Again: The Reawakening of American Fundamentalism.* New York: Oxford University Press, 1997.

Marsden, George, ed. *Evangelicalism and Modern America.* Grand Rapids, MI: Wm. B. Eerdmans, 1984.

McLoughlin, William G. *Modern Revivalism: Charles Grandison Finney to Billy Graham.* New York: Ronald Press, 1959.

WALTER H. CONSER JR.

NATIONAL BAPTIST CONVENTION OF AMERICA

The National Baptist Convention of America (NBCA) was formed after a dispute between Richard Henry Boyd, publisher of the National Baptist Publishing Board and the NATIONAL BAPTIST CONVENTION, U.S.A. over the ownership of the publishing board. The history of the convention is tied inextricably to R. H. Boyd and his legacy of racial self-determination coupled with a pragmatic sense of interracial cooperation.

Formation of the National Baptist Publishing Board

Formation of the NBCA is tied to the formation of the National Baptist Publishing Board (NBPB), founded in 1896 by R. H. Boyd. Boyd, born into slavery, received an education at Bishop College in Texas and was an active participant in the Texas Black Baptist conventions before the formation of the National Baptist Convention (NBC) U.S.A. After a dispute over the withdrawal of an invitation to Black Baptist writers to publish in the *Baptist Teacher,* a northern white Baptist publication, the NBPB was founded by Boyd with the support of other leaders in the convention such as Emmanuel K. Love. The publishing house, chartered yet unincorporated, was placed under the control of a board consisting of nine men, with Boyd at the head. The arrangement, in theory, would help to shield the publishing board from denominational interference. Interference, however, would come with Boyd's successful management. Boyd's entrepreneurial spirit helped him to establish a relationship in Nashville, Tennessee with the publisher of the Southern Baptist Publishing board at the time, James Frost. The relationship with Frost in terms of sales and support helped Boyd to quickly establish the primacy of the NBPB in supplying SUNDAY SCHOOL and other materials such as pulpit robes and church pews to black churches. Boyd even created the Negro doll company, selling black dolls through the publishing house as well.

As a result of Boyd's business acumen the publishing board was incorporated as a separate entity in 1898. Incorporating the board allowed it to affiliate with whatever convention it would choose, and this would have future ramifications for the National Baptist Convention U.S.A. claims to the publishing house. Like the other convention boards, Boyd's suggestion that the publishing board should be separate in the constitution from other boards was enacted, and the publishing board worked together with the home missions board. The convention president E. C. Morris issued a directive in 1905 requiring that the two boards separate their activities. The publishing board defied his directive, and this would prove to be one of the sources of contention that would exacerbate the growing dissension between the convention and the publishing board. Boyd's successful combination of beliefs in racial self-determination, racial uplift, and interracial cooperation increased the boards' revenue to over two million dollars by 1915. The financial gains were such that Morris and others in the National Baptist Convention U.S.A. wanted to obtain greater control of the publishing board.

Boyd's entrepreneurial spirit as a publisher was fraught with dissension. Management concerns over the publishing board led to accusations of Boyd's using the board's funds to finance mortgages for other business ventures within the city of Nashville, where the publishing board was located. Boyd also held the copyrights for all the Sunday school commentaries for twenty-eight years, meaning that Boyd and his family profited personally from the sale of the board's published materials. The move rankled convention president Morris, and for ten years, from 1905 to 1915, battles were waged to attempt to wrest control of the board away from Boyd. Boyd's contention, however, was that the publishing board had been created separately from the convention in 1896, and that the constitution of the convention did not contain instructions for the creation of the publishing board. Boyd also believed that the movement to place the publishing board underneath the convention's purview would ruin profitability. The accusations against Boyd grew, and the dissension as well.

The Publishing Board Splits from the NBC U.S.A.

The ownership issue finally came to a head at the 1915 meeting of the NBC U.S.A. The disputes surrounding the ownership of the publishing board were challenged at the convention meeting in Chicago when a suit was bought to court there against Boyd, the publishing board, and the home Mission Board that continued to work with the publishing board against the NBC U.S.A. president's wishes. What was ultimately at question was whether the publishing board would be under the purview of the convention or Boyd. The ruling in the case was that the publishing board should come under the purview of the convention. Boyd had previously filed an injunction to prevent this from happening. The judge also ruled that the publishing board and its supporters were an illegal convention. Rather than acquiescing to the ruling, Boyd and his supporters left the convention, taking the publishing board records with them.

On September 9, 1915 the group met at Salem Baptist Church in Chicago to form a new convention, called the National Baptist Convention unincorporated, or the Boyd convention. The conflict surrounding the ownership of the publishing board was that, insofar as the National Baptist Convention U.S.A had never legally incorporated, it was thus unable to take ownership of the publishing board in its name. A 1916 statement entitled the "The Rightful and Lawful Ownership of the National Baptist Publishing house" served to vindicate Boyd and his supporters from their detractors.

The newly formed National Baptist Convention, unincorporated, was initially termed the "Boyd Convention," but changed its name to the National Baptist Convention of America (NBCA). The NBCA formed additional boards to work with the convention, and aligned itself with the Lott Cary Convention, a group that had been affiliated with the NBC U.S.A. The association with the Lott Cary Convention, however, would dissipate by the 1940s, when the NBCA began to sponsor foreign MISSIONS.

Boyd's death in the early 1920s did not displace the Boyd family's interest in the NBCA publishing concern. Since his death, the center of the NBCA convention has been the publishing board affiliation, with a succession of Boyd family members at the helm. The close arrangement would once again cause a split within the NBCA in 1988. The issue arose over provision of convention materials and the relationship of the publishing board in its provision of materials and speakers to the convention. The split resulted in the formation of the National Missionary Baptist Convention of America, which is affiliated with the National Baptist Publishing board, but not the NBCA. The current president of the NBCA is Dr. Edward E. Jones, Sr.

See also Baptist Family of Churches; Baptists; Baptists, United States; Publishing, Media

References and Further Reading

Fitts, Leroy. *A History of Black Baptists.* Nashville, TN: Broadman Press, 1985.

Harvey, Paul. *Redeeming the South: Religious Cultures and Racial Identities Among Southern Baptists 1865–1925,* Chapel Hill: University of North Carolina Press, 1997.

Lincoln, C. Eric, and Lawrence H. Mamiya. *The Black Church in the African American Experience.* Durham, NC: Duke University Press, 1990.

Washington, James Melvin. *Frustrated Fellowship: The Black Baptist Quest for Social Power.* Macon, GA: Mercer University Press, 1986.

ANTHEA D. BUTLER

NATIONAL BAPTIST CONVENTION U.S.A.

Beginnings

The National Baptist Convention U.S.A. (NBCUSA) was founded on September 24, 1895 as an organization of black Baptist conventions that had attempted several times to organize and reorganize within their constitutive ranks. The history of the NBCUSA is a history centered on uniting black Baptists on the one hand, and a history of dissensions and splits since the Convention's inception.

Black Baptists, depending on geographic location, shared different tracks historically. Baptists in the northern states formed a few state conventions, including the Providence Baptist Association, formed in 1834 by black Baptists in Ohio. Other Baptist organizations formed in the North, such as the Woods River Association in Illinois and the Amherstberg Association in Canada and Michigan, were early attempts at formation of black Baptists conventions. Initially black Baptists in the South were affiliated with state biracial organizations because of the issue of SLAVERY. In the reconstruction period several associations were formed in conjunction with white American Baptists who had divided from their white southern counterparts over the issue of slavery. State black Baptist conventions began to be formed in addition to these organizations as well, and the push for a national black Baptist convention began to materialize. Members of smaller black Baptists groups formed the Consolidated American Baptist Missionary Convention, which existed from 1866 to 1870, although controversy festered within this organization and others attempting to combine regional black associations because of the amounts of funds donated by white Baptist groups like the American Baptist Home Missions Society. Disputes over the degree of autonomy these contributions bought (or the lack thereof) caused the Consolidated Convention to break up. Debates over the degree of assistance that should be received and acknowledged from white Baptists organizations divided black Baptists. Those who desired assistance, integrationists, were pitted against those who wanted autonomous organizations, called separationists. The rift between these two groups played a major role in the formation of the NBCUSA in 1895.

Formation of the Convention

The formation of the NBCUSA was the combination of three separate groups: The Foreign Mission Convention of the United States (1880), which was to administer MISSIONS abroad; the American National Baptist Convention chartered in 1886; and the National Baptist Education Convention formed in 1893 for fundraising for Baptist educational institutions. The formation of the NBCUSA centered on the invitation for three black Baptist ministers, William J. Simmonds, Emmanuel K. Love, and William H. Brooks, to publish in the quarterly publication *Baptist Teacher*. White Southern Baptist separatists, however, criticized the invitation, and the director of the American Baptist Publishing Society, Benjamin Griffith, withdrew the invitation, suggesting that the articles be written as tracts for black Baptist churches. Yet ministers like Love were convinced there was a need for a separate publication society for black Baptists, and convened a group for a national convention. At a meeting in Atlanta, Georgia on September 28, 1895 the convention was formed with a combination of black Baptist members from the southern, northern, and western sections of the UNITED STATES.

The first president was Reverend Edmund Morris. The new organization began, structured along the lines of ministries that previous smaller conventions functioned in: education, foreign missions, home missions, and educational board. In 1896 the board added the National Baptist Publishing Board, with Richard Henry Boyd, an activist in the Texas Baptist convention, as secretary. The convention's major purpose was to foster self-determination for black Baptists; however, contentions arose soon after the convention's formation between integrationists and separationists. In 1897 a group of convention members broke away from the convention, forming the Lott Carey Foreign Mission Convention. This group wanted to have greater cooperation with white Baptists and disagreed with the administration of the NBCUSA foreign missions operation. Women's issues and concerns were addressed by the convention in 1900 when Nannie Helen Burroughs, educator, challenged the convention with a speech to its constituency, entitled "How the Sisters are Hindered from Helping." Despite considerable resistance from the male members of the convention, her quest to establish a forum for women's issues within the convention prevailed and the Women's Convention was formed. Within the convention its duties were largely to collect missionary funds, and to educate young WOMEN as homemakers and wage earners with a message of racial uplift.

Divisions within the Convention

The convention's first split was over the issue of the publication board and money. R. H. Boyd, publisher of the National Baptist Convention publishing board, established the publishing board as an alternative to the white Baptist boards that did not publish literature for black Baptists. Under Boyd's leadership the publishing board became a very successful venture. The board, incorporated before the NBCUSA, ran its affairs independently of the convention, and the board's success prompted President E. C. Morris to attempt to bring the publishing board under the auspices of the convention. Boyd's view was that the publishing board belonged to him and his family, not the denomination. In 1915, at the convention in Chicago, a lawsuit was filed by the convention to determine who had the rights to run the publishing board. The ruling went against Boyd, but Boyd and his supporters rallied to form the National Baptist Convention Unincorporated—later changed to the NATIONAL BAPTIST CONVENTION OF AMERICA—allowing Boyd to keep possession of the publishing board.

Despite the split, the specialized boards Morris designed to run the convention worked well until his death in 1922. Succeeding him in office was Lacey Kirk Williams, who held the office of president until 1940. During this time period, Williams's openness to cooperation resulted in a partnership with the Southern Baptists to open American Baptist Theological Seminary in Nashville, Tennessee in 1924 for the training of black Baptist ministers. Other alliances formed during his tenure included a working relationship between the American Baptist Home Missions board and The American Baptist Publication Society. After Williams's presidency, the Rev. D. V. Jemison came to the presidency of the convention during the war years, and was succeeded in 1953 by one of the more controversial presidents of the Convention, Rev. Joseph H. Jackson.

Jackson, a moderate in terms of race relations, felt that the appropriate manner in which to advocate for African Americans' civil rights was through the court system, and believed that the NAACP would change the racial climate of America. His position of "gradualism" was not accepted throughout the denomination, however, most notably by MARTIN LUTHER KING JR., civil rights leader, and at this time a member of the convention. Growing tension between Jackson and King, who publicly disagreed with Jackson's policy of gradualism at the Convention in 1956, led to strained relations within the denomination. The 1961 convention, however, would bring the issue of gradualism and tenure of the president of the convention to a head. A resolution at the 1961 convention requesting that Jackson be renominated as the president of the Convention was adopted, despite a large number of opponents to the measure. A group opposed to Jackson wanted Gardner C. Taylor, noted preacher and pastor of Concord Baptist Church of Christ in Brooklyn, New York to stand for the presidency.

Fighting broke out among the factions, and the group wanting Gardner C. Taylor to stand for the presidency was unable to prevail against the convention. A vote was taken that Jackson won. The results sealed the opponents' resolve; the following day, September 11, 1961, the group announced a committee meeting of its own. After a period of organization the splinter group subsequently elected Taylor president of their new convention, the PROGRESSIVE NATIONAL BAPTIST CONVENTION, at a meeting in May of 1962. Jackson, who would lead the con-

vention until 1982, continued to lead in a more conservative fashion, and despite his political conservatism, was a well-respected religious leader in African American circles. After his presidency, Theodore Judson Jemison took leadership of the convention from 1982 until 1994, and then Henry C. Lyons—perhaps the most infamous president of the National Baptist Convention—took office.

The beginnings of Lyons's tenure as president looked promising. Lyons, who had worked with Jemison to replace Joseph Jackson as president in the 1960s, seemed primed to take the convention in a new direction. Arranging business deals on behalf of the conventions, Lyons was able to secure contracts and funds for the convention on the strength of inflated membership numbers of the denomination. These deals, however, were not consummated, and Lyons accepted funds for services such as mailing lists that included members of the KU KLUX KLAN as forged members of the convention. The scandal was revealed when Lyons's second wife set fire to a home in Tampa, Florida that Lyons shared with a mistress. Investigators began to uncover the details of Lyons's other life, and racketeering charges were brought against Lyons. Despite these charges, convention members and leaders endeavored to keep Lyons in office as long as possible; however, Lyons was forced to resign from the presidency in 1998. Several prominent members of the denomination ran for president, including Rev. E. V. Hill of Los Angeles. The Rev. William Shaw of Philadelphia was elected as Lyons's successor at the 1998 convention meeting. Lyons was subsequently convicted on racketeering charges in 1999, and he began serving a 5½-year prison sentence in June of 1999.

The Lyons debacle was the most serious blow to the history and reputation of the National Baptist Convention, and subsequent leadership has attempted to redeem the image of the convention. The number of members that the Convention president can elect has been trimmed from twenty-nine to four. Additionally the convention's actual stated membership attributed to inflated figures by Lyons remains in question; however, the current president, William J. Shaw, estimates the membership in the conventions as of 2002 to be 7.5 million.

See also African American Protestantism; Baptists; Baptists, United States

References and Further Reading

Fitts, Leroy. *A History of Black Baptists.* Nashville, TN: Broadman Press, 1985.

Harvey, Paul. *Redeeming the South: Religious Cultures and Racial Identities Among Southern Baptists 1865–1925*, Chapel Hill: University of North Carolina Press, 1997.

Higginbotham, Eveyln Brooks. *Righteous Discontent: The Women's Movement in the Black Baptist Church, 1880–1920*. Cambridge, MA: Harvard University Press, 1993.

Washington, James Melvin. *Frustrated Fellowship: The Black Baptist Quest for Social Power*. Macon, GA: Mercer University Press, 1986.

ANTHEA D. BUTLER

NATIONAL COUNCIL OF CHURCHES

Officially titled the National Council of Churches of Christ in America, the National Council of Churches (NCC) was founded in November 1950, in Cleveland, Ohio. It was probably the most significant expression of the ECUMENISM that flourished in American Protestantism during the first two-thirds of the twentieth century. In its heyday in the 1950s and 1960s the NCC was the umbrella organization for more than thirty Protestant denominations and churches in the United States, representing approximately thirty-two million church-goers.

The ecumenical movement emerged in the early twentieth century as a formal institutional expression marking efforts toward cooperation and unity to counteract the powerful centripetal forces inherent in Protestantism everywhere and especially in the UNITED STATES. Its roots lay among national evangelical "benevolent societies" of social and moral uplift that flourished in antebellum America. These included the AMERICAN BIBLE SOCIETY, the American Tract Society, and agencies to reform excessive drinking, the prison system, and ultimately, SLAVERY (see also SLAVERY, ABOLITION OF). Revivalism, a fundamental expression of evangelical Protestantism (see EVANGELICALISM, REVIVALS), had always possessed a considerable tinge of the ecumenical spirit, as seen in the careers of the greatest American revivalists such as GEORGE WHITEFIELD, CHARLES GRANDISON FINNEY, DWIGHT LYMAN MOODY, and their successors. Ecumenical agencies expressed much of the social conscience of the mainstream churches even after the CIVIL WAR, as revealed in the churches' cooperative work with education among recently freed slaves in the South, and in the rapidly developing international peace movement of the late nineteenth and early twentieth centuries.

By the beginning of the twentieth century, it was clear to church leaders that the patchwork of ecumenical efforts needed to be consolidated at the national level. Thus in 1908 mainstream Protestants created the Federal Council of Churches, the immediate forerunner of the NCC. This organization functioned until 1950, when it became necessary to further extend the ecumenical umbrella (chiefly in areas of international mission work and education), and the National Council of Churches came into being.

The time of the National Council's creation and its early years represented the apogee of interest in and commitment to the ecumenical movement generally in the churches. This was especially symbolized by efforts toward new combinations of denominations, within the families of Methodist and Lutheran churches, and within more disparate groups, such as the UNITED CHURCH OF CHRIST, formed in 1957 by the merger of Congregational Christian and EVANGELICAL AND REFORMED Churches (see METHODISM, NORTH AMERICA; LUTHERANISM, UNITED STATES). These attempts at large institutional arrangements in the churches were also occurring in an age of increasing bureaucracy and institutional size in the business world, in government, in the military, and in private nonprofit agencies generally.

In many ways the National Council of Churches simply extended and expanded the functions of the Federal Council. At the outset many of the key national officers of the NCC maintained similar positions to those they held in the earlier organization, and the earliest programmatic emphases of the NCC scarcely varied from its predecessor. The Federal Council had shown an interest in international affairs, especially after World War I, and even more so in the aftermath of World War II, as America expanded its influence throughout the world and the United Nations took shape. Interest in foreign affairs thus was always a part of the National Council's agenda. Speakers from the State Department and from governments overseas were often present at the great triennial assemblies of the National Council. John Foster Dulles, the well-known Secretary of State under President Dwight Eisenhower, was a leading lay member of the NCC before he entered government service. The NCC always embraced a moderate to liberal position on foreign policy issues, endorsing anti-Communist but not McCarthyite views of the outside world (see LIBERAL PROTESTANTISM AND LIBERALISM). This made it generally sympathetic to the outlook of official Washington in the 1950s and early 1960s. Efforts to provide physical and medical aid to poor and war-disrupted areas worldwide, especially through CHURCH WORLD SERVICE, a major subsidiary of the NCC, was another way the ecumenical organization involved itself in affairs outside the United States. The National Council was also deeply involved in the worldwide ecumenical movement, centered especially in the work of the WORLD COUNCIL OF CHURCHES with headquarters in Geneva, SWITZERLAND. Officials of the NCC often became American Protestantism's representatives on the boards and agencies of the World Council, and eventually among the top executives of the World

Council. EUGENE CARSON BLAKE, a leading Presbyterian and official in the NCC, became the executive director of the World Council in the mid-1960s. Inevitably such commitments ensured the ongoing international focus of the NCC.

Even more important than its international concerns were the activist social concerns of the National Council at home. This had also been a central emphasis of the Federal Council of Churches, strongly influenced by the "SOCIAL GOSPEL" movement within the churches in the early twentieth century. Although somewhat hesitant in its early days, the NCC eventually became deeply involved in the great movement toward racial justice that swept across the country in the late 1950s and throughout the 1960s (see CIVIL RIGHTS MOVEMENT). New national leadership in the organization and the rising tempo of events unfolding in the South eventually caused the NCC to create a special agency in June 1963 called the Commission on Religion and Race. This agency was to direct all efforts in support of groups pressing for change in race relations throughout the country. This small group of church people, well-financed and effectively working with similar groups in the individual churches tied to the National Council, directly involved the mainstream Protestant churches in a number of ways in the racial struggles of the 1960s. The Commission successfully coordinated efforts to include significant numbers of whites (40,000) in the March on Washington in August 1963, and it became an important member of the Leadership Conference on Civil Rights, the chief private lobbying group that aided in the eventual passage of the Civil Rights Act of 1964. Under the Commission's direction within the Leadership Conference, the churches played an important role in stirring grassroots support for the bill in predominantly rural and Republican areas of the Midwest that greatly helped pass the bill in Congress. The Commission also deeply involved the churches directly in the civil rights conflicts in the South, especially in Mississippi. The NCC quietly sponsored and helped to plan with the young activists of the Student Nonviolent Coordinating Committee (SNCC) the training sessions held in Ohio before 800 college students went to Mississippi in the famous "Summer of '64." In addition, over 300 ministers were recruited that same summer to spend time in the Magnolia State (Mississippi) serving as adult but sympathetic "advisors" to the Freedom Centers created as the nerve centers of the "movement" in that deep South state. In September 1964 the Commission on Religion and Race and the National Council established the Delta Ministry, a small and ongoing voice of the liberal Protestant churches in Mississippi supporting racial justice in the midst of great strife and tension. The National Council supported this special ministry of twenty to thirty ministers and lay people for over a decade. It remains a little known yet important part of the overall struggle for racial justice in the United States, and one of the best examples of the NCC's long commitment to activism and social justice.

By the late 1960s a national backlash was developing, chiefly among whites, against the constant public attention paid to racial issues. Because of their deep involvement, the principal mainline churches also felt the sting of this backlash. For this and other reasons, declines in membership and giving set in that have not yet been reversed. These developments affected the National Council because its finances are determined by annual appropriations made to it by the member churches. The Black Power movement also created crises of identity in many of the mainline churches, especially those with significant groups of minority members. These disputes further weakened the churches and the NCC. Finally, after 1965 the National Council and many of its member denominations became increasingly critical of the Johnson Administration's escalation of the war in Vietnam. The close alliance between mainstream churches and federal officials that had flourished because of a common front on civil rights and the Great Society now began to unravel. When President Richard Nixon and the Republicans came into office in 1968 and again in 1972, they turned to a new political force emerging among American Protestants—people from evangelical backgrounds in churches that were gaining massive numbers of new adherents and increasing public respect (see EVANGELICALISM).

All these developments contributed further to the loss of national prestige and influence by the NCC. Since the early 1970s the National Council of Churches has experienced painful retrenchment in budgets and programs, but continues to express the public concerns of a large segment of the American public and of American Protestantism. The future of the NCC and of mainline Protestantism remains to be seen.

References and Further Reading

Cavert, Samuel M. *The American Churches in the Ecumenical Movement, 1900–1968.* New York: Association Press, 1968.

Findlay, James F., Jr. *Church People in the Struggle: The National Council of Churches and the Black Freedom Movement, 1950–1970.* New York: Oxford University Press, 1993.

JAMES FINDLAY

NATIONAL PRIMITIVE BAPTIST CONVENTION

The National Primitive Baptist Convention is the name for a group of black Primitive Baptist churches that came together in a national organization in 1907. Unlike the majority of white Primitive Baptists, churches in this convention allow denominational organizations, including SUNDAY SCHOOLS and aid societies. In the late twentieth century, the convention claimed some 250,000 members (although the real number of members was probably far less), concentrated largely in the southeastern portion of the UNITED STATES, with Huntsville, Alabama as its denominational headquarters.

Primitive Baptist Theology, Structure, and Practice

Before the CIVIL WAR, most black Primitive Baptists were slaves who worshipped with their masters in Primitive Baptist congregations (see PRIMITIVE BAPTIST CHURCHES). The Primitive brethren were staunchly opposed to tract societies, Sunday schools, BIBLE SOCIETIES, MISSIONARY ORGANIZATIONS, SEMINARIES, and REVIVALS. All were contrary to God's sovereign will; all encouraged the expansion of man's wisdom and the diminution of God's sovereignty. Theologically the Primitives upheld the total depravity of natural man; personal and unconditional ELECTION; special ATONEMENT; irresistible GRACE; and preservation of the SAINTS. Most white Primitive Baptists historically eschewed larger denominational structures above the level of associations, that is, groupings of churches in local areas that meet annually for fellowship. Denominational organizations have been seen as human contrivances that are not of New Testament origin and thus illegitimate. In the twentieth century, however, groups such as the National Primitive Baptist Convention accepted Sunday schools, denominational organizations, and a paid CLERGY into the organization.

Historically most Primitive Baptist churches have been pastored by lay elders, men (never WOMEN) who feel called to preach and have no expectation of making a living doing it (see WOMEN CLERGY). Most Primitive Baptists oppose instrumental church MUSIC, believing that nowhere in the New Testament are believers commanded to play instruments in sacred WORSHIP, and that instrumentalists call attention to themselves and thus draw attention away from the sovereignty of God. Primitive Baptists also typically practice footwashing (see FEET, WASHING OF) as an ordinance. Whereas the Primitives see it as an ancient "landmark," in fact the practice seems to have arisen mostly in the early twentieth century, as the Primitives sought to distinguish themselves more from mainline missionary Baptist practice. Footwashing often climaxes services as the brethren and sisters tearfully bond over the powerfully affecting ritual.

Origins of the National Primitive Baptist Convention

After the CIVIL WAR, African Americans of nearly every denomination separated themselves from whites and formed independent churches and denominational organizations. Black Primitive Baptists formed numerous churches throughout the South. It was not as clear whether they would form denominational organizations, given the historic opposition of the Primitive Baptists to human contrivances. However, in the summer of 1907 participants gathered at the National Meeting of Colored Primitive Baptists of America in Huntsville, Alabama, and formed the National Primitive Baptist Convention. Importantly, the opening convention set up a fairly conventional Baptist denominational structure, including a National Women's Auxiliary Convention as well as a National Superintendent for the Young People and a Sunday School Congress. They also supported a variety of educational institutions and later a National Primitive Baptist publishing house in Huntsville.

Primitive Baptists historically had expressed opposition to specific schools of THEOLOGY, and were often distrustful of secular education altogether. Black Primitive Baptists, however, valued education, as might be expected given the avid desire for education evinced by so many illiterate ex-slaves after the Civil War. The clear need for black religious organizations to band together an embattled people in a hostile Jim Crow South, moreover, meant that the normal Primitive Baptist opposition to nearly any kind of organization did not have the same impact among black Primitive Baptists. By the late twentieth century the National Primitive Baptists operated a publishing house, a National Memorial Center, a youth camp and nursing home (both in Florida), several academies and Bible institutions (see BIBLE COLLEGES AND INSTITUTES), and a variety of other enterprises. State conventions are centered mostly in the South, including Florida, Georgia, North Carolina, Virginia, Tennessee, and Texas. Alabama remains the convention's center of strength because of the denominational headquarters in Huntsville. The National Primitive Baptist Convention is therefore mostly a southern regional group.

The National Primitive Baptist leadership proclaims a set of beliefs in accord with the Baptist mainstream together with Primitive Baptist additions: the BIBLE as the only rule of faith and practice; congregationalism in POLITY; SALVATION and BAPTISM by immersion as a necessary requisite for church membership; church ordinances of baptism, the LORD'S SUPPER, and the washing of the saints' feet; the pastor and deacon as the scriptural officers of the church;

freewill tithes and offerings for support of the CHURCH; separation of church and state (see CHURCH AND STATE, OVERVIEW); and the great commission to spread the Gospel of Christ. In 2002 the National Primitive Baptist Convention's website featured a convention leader holding a Ph.D., certainly a rarity in other Primitive Baptist circles and indicative of the more mainstream attitudes the National Primitive Baptists hold toward education or an ordained pulpit, in comparison to their more "primitivist" white brethren.

See also African American Protestantism; Slavery; Slavery, Abolition of

References and Further Reading

Lambert, Cecil Byron. *The Rise of the Antimission Baptists: Sources and Leaders, 1800–1840.* New York: Arno Press, 1980 (reprint).
"National Primitive Baptist Convention." http://www.natlprimbaptconv.org (Accessed May 20, 2002).
"Primitive Baptist Web Station." http://www.pb.org (Accessed May 20, 2002).

PAUL HARVEY

NATIONALISM

Within modern historiography, research on nationalism has become one of the main scholarly activities and one of the main scientific branches. Many different theories are applied to this subject. An older school of scholars, led by Friedrich Meinecke, Carlton J. Hayes, and Hans Kohn, distinguished between a Western and an Eastern type of nationalism. For them, the Western type of nationalism was characterized by the subjective political decision of citizens who wanted to become members of a certain nation. By contrast, they argued, the Eastern type of nationalism was based on objective cultural criteria such as language, customs, and history. Although FRANCE was the prototype of the former form of nationalism for them, they considered countries like GERMANY and POLAND as prototypes of the latter. The political implications of this distinction were far-reaching and should not be overlooked. The Western type of nationalism was associated with progressive political developments such as liberalism and democracy (see LIBERAL PROTESTANTISM AND LIBERALISM). The Eastern type, by contrast, seemed to have been dominated by reactionary and irrational forces and even, at a later stage, by a synthesis of nationalism and racism.

New Approaches to Nationalism

Newer studies take a different approach. They recognize that "objective" factors play a role also in French nationalism, for example, as do "subjective" elements in German or Polish nationalism. For Ernest Gellner and Karl W. Deutsch, the genesis of modern nations, and the genesis of modern nationalism, is to a large degree shaped by processes of modernization in the field of politics and mass communication. As individual citizens of a certain territory become involved in these processes, they become carriers of a specific form of nationalism. Some historians and political scientists also apply insights of social psychology as they attempt to explain the phenomenon of nationalism. As the policy of formation of an in-group is successful, out-groups are singled out. The success of nationalism, therefore, not only depends a great deal on the mobilization of feelings of loyalty, of belonging, and of solidarity, but also on the intensification of feelings of hostility, of prejudice, and on resentments. For the growth of French nationalism, for example, anti-British feelings were essential, with Joan of Arc as an anti-British national symbol, whereas for German nationalism, antagonism against France fulfilled the same function. This list of mutual expressions of hostility could be prolonged so that it would include most European countries and many countries beyond. In this sense one could write a history of nationalism by looking at the various conflicts in European history since the Middle Ages, at the wounds inflicted by one nation on other nations, and vice versa, and at the way these wounds were heroicized and in this way kept from healing, at least for a long time.

In the course of the nineteenth century, not all levels of the various societies were affected by nationalism at the same time and to the same degree. First and foremost nationalism seems to have been an attitude for the upper middle classes. The Industrial Revolution and urbanization (see INDUSTRIALIZATION) provided a chance for the bourgeoisie to participate in the movement of nationalism and even to claim a leading role in national politics. The members both of the old nobility and of the new working class were much slower in this matter. By 1914, however, there was no group or social class in any European country whose political attitude was not strongly influenced by national feelings. As the war of 1914 began, people from all walks of life in all European countries raced to arms and believed in the national slogans with which the bloodshed was justified.

In recent years studies on the origin and political meaning of nationalism by Benedict Anderson, Ernest Gellner, and Eric Hobsbawm have stressed other aspects. These authors understand nationalism not only as a daily subjective decision but also as a mental construct, that is, as a powerful product of collective human imagination. They argue that the nation was invented in the minds of the people in a period of rapid social change so that they were able to conceive a certain kind of order with regard to the different languages, cultural codes, and also to the different views of the past and the future. They acknowledge that there exists a close relationship between national imagination and propaganda on national issues in which, as they also argue, the image of enemies is just as important as the image of the collective national self.

Symbols of Nationalism

Nationalism is characterized by several highly distinctive features. In the area of cultural and political representation, nationalism makes frequent use of such symbols as the national flag, the national anthem, and national holidays. In the era of decolonization such flags, anthems, and holidays were explicitly invented for some of the new nations. Furthermore, national heroes are remembered in statues, battles in which national independence was achieved in national monuments. The architecture of the national capital is understood to possess special significance, just as national customs are seen as the embodiment of the national character. A special effort is made to preserve the national language. In all European countries the national language has been recorded in the course of the nineteenth century. In some cases a national language, including a grammar and parts of the vocabulary, have been invented. Today it is often forgotten that some of the languages in Europe, but also in AFRICA and Asia, are rather artificial products of nineteenth-century linguistic and semantic efforts serving the aim of national politics. Equally important was the writing of national history. In almost all countries, historians writing national history followed the same scheme: They described a golden age of national unity long past, and very often located in early medieval times; they then pointed out the downfall of the nation, which often occurred in later medieval or early modern history; and they concluded their accounts by telling their readers of the new age of national glory that has just begun or that would soon begin and on which all political efforts should concentrate. In this sequence, national heroes have their part just as battles for national independence. In some cases even battles that had been lost gained a special significance in national memory as they were praised as heroic, although unsuccessful efforts in the struggle against the nation's enemies. For nationalism, therefore, the idea of the nation at war possesses a special meaning. Allegiance to a special nation demanded the ultimate sacrifice of the members of a nation, including the sacrifice of their lives. Wars thus were seen and still are seen as the ultimate test for a person's or a social group's national loyalty.

Christianity and Nationalism

Over the years the relationship of nationalism and Christianity, and in particular the relationship of nationalism and Protestantism, has changed a great deal. In the years between 1789 and 1815, that is, in the decades of the FRENCH REVOLUTION, of Napoleon's rise to power, and the subsequent downfall of Napoleon, Protestants in many parts of Europe were confronted for the first time with new political emotions that were expressed by members of the educated upper class: The central idea behind these feelings was the belief in the defense of one's own country, and one's own CULTURE and religion, against hegemonial French claims and French domination. Perhaps the modern term "nationalism" is not quite suited if one wants to characterize these beliefs, and "patriotism" would be a better term. As the coalition of several European powers defeated Napoleon in 1813, emotions ran high and patriotism was, at least among some members of the younger generation, transformed into nationalism. When the three hundredth anniversary of the beginning of the REFORMATION was celebrated in Germany in 1817, for example, many of the speakers combined their praise of the tradition of Protestantism with strong anti-French notions of national liberation and German national progress. Even though these ideas were suppressed in many parts of Europe in the following years in which the Austrian chancellor Metternich attempted to restore the Ancien Régime, by 1817 the modern idea of nationalism had been born.

In the decades before and after the Revolution of 1848, many members of Christian churches in Europe were hesitant to join movements of national liberation. Much rather were they prepared to take the side of political conservatism. As they were afraid of any kind of revolution, and as they witnessed the atheistic propaganda of many leaders of socialism, modern nationalism appeared to them more like a danger than a promise or an attractive political option. By the second half of the nineteenth century these reserved opinions on nationalism had changed. In countries like ITALY and Germany, at long last political unification had been achieved. For all who believed in nationalism this success was accompanied by a huge effort of political mobilization, and by a huge wave of national sentiments, although even in countries that had been united for a long time, political feelings of nationalism triumphed and assumed a new kind of political quality. By 1880 the Europe of states and great powers had been transformed into the Europe of nations, of nations large and small, of nations that enjoyed full political sovereignty, and of others who still struggled to become independent.

In some cases national emotions were particularly strong and led to new forms of religious legitimacy for the nation. As a result of the Franco-Prussian war and of German unification, for example, leading German churchmen believed in the national awakening, or revival, of the whole German nation. For them, through the victory over France that they considered as a special divine blessing, the Germans had become a "chosen people" and Germany a "chosen nation." For some of these churchmen, God's people of the first covenant served as the example that they wanted to follow. For them, consequently, the Germans had become God's children of a new COVENANT. They exhorted the German people to obey God's commands, just as they warned them of God's severe punishments if they strayed from the right godly path. Such feelings and such attitudes can also be found in other Protestant nations during the era of imperialism, as for example in Great Britain and in the UNITED STATES. In retrospect it is obvious that this kind of interpretation of national politics as a manifest destiny had severe consequences. In domestic politics non-Christian groups and parties were excluded from national politics, as for example socialists; in foreign policy matters, non-Western countries were seen as the logical objects for Western domination and colonization.

In the decades from 1880 to 1914 for many members of the Western world, nationalism had replaced religion as the most important norm in political ethics and in political practice. Furthermore, it is in these very decades that ideas derived from social DARWINISM, and in particular ideas rooted in racial myths, began to transform traditional nationalism. In Great Britain, the United States, and Germany, leading politicians perceived their countries as "teutonic" nations, that is as nations of a superior race and as nations that consequently carried the heavy burden of civilizing the rest of the world, although this new type of nationalism was not influenced solely by social Darwinism and racism. As part of worldwide power politics, this new nationalism was also shaped by considerations of national egoism, of political expansionism, and of militarism. For traditional Christianity the rapid growth of Germanic myths was a particular challenge. By 1914, therefore, nationalism had become a power that no longer supplemented Christian teachings, but a veritable rival of Christianity that propagated a set of norms and practices that were opposed to the Ten Commandments and other Christian beliefs.

Anti-Semitism and Nationalism

Within this new brand of militaristic, expansionist, and racist nationalism, modern ANTI-SEMITISM posed a special danger. By the 1920s, for some proponents of this variety of nationalism, the Hebrew BIBLE was no longer part of the Western heritage they were ready to honor. It appeared to them as part of the traditional cultural baggage they were prepared to discard. They were no longer ready to invest any effort in converting Jews to Christianity; rather, they argued, Jews were a separate nation rooted in a separate and inferior race. All attempts for CONVERSION and assimilation were in vain and should be stopped immediately. These arguments were supported not only by Protestants but also by many Catholics. Modern anti-Semitism was a matter not only of predominantly Protestant countries like Germany, therefore, but also of Catholic countries like Poland. Germany was the first European country, however, in which a variety of nationalism shaped by racism and anti-Semitism became the guideline of national politics, as was the case in 1933 after Hitler's rise to power. Churches in Germany were not prepared to deal with this challenge. At first both Catholics and Protestants praised Hitler as they saw in the new *Reich* a kind of national revival. By the summer and fall of 1933, German Catholics were divided. Many continued to support the National Socialists; others began to withdraw into the traditional Catholic milieu. Among German Protestants opinions were also split. One part joined the anti-Semitic and nationalistic movement of the GERMAN CHRISTIANS. For them, the Hebrew Bible was a Jewish book that contained no truth or any meaningful message for a German Christian. Another part began to assemble in the CONFESSING CHURCH. These pastors and laypersons resolved to defend the whole Christian heritage. As long as Hitler did not interfere in church matters, many members of the Confessing Church wholeheartedly supported Hitler's foreign and domestic policies. Although they refused to accept racist nationalism as a new kind of political religion, they continued to honor the older tradition of a coalition between secular nationalism and self-confident Protestantism. Only few members of the Confessing Church actively joined political resistance against Hitler, thus distancing themselves also from Hitler's perverted notion of nationalism.

Post-War Nationalism

After the Second World War the relationship between nationalism and the Christian churches changed once again. Although National Socialism had been defeated, COMMUNISM now seemed to pose a new threat.

For many members of Christian churches, Stalin's expansionist foreign policy seemed like a return of the aggressive atheism of the radical wing of the French Revolution. Just as churches had supported patriotism in defense of religion against Napoleon, in post-1945 Europe, churches strengthened nationalism as a defense against Stalin. As Western Europe began to move toward unification, the Christian churches were, once more, in search of a new political orientation. Traditional nationalism, even in the French version of Gaullism, no longer sufficed as the feeling of European pride and unity began to grow. By the 1990s, as a result of mass migration, many countries of Europe had de facto been transformed into multireligious and multicultural societies. By the end of the twentieth century the impact of SECULARIZATION and dechristianization had created a completely new scenario, although there were also indications of a revival of religion and partial rechristianization. For these developments, nationalism no longer played a significant role. Rather, a lively debate had begun about the place of the Christian churches in a uniting Europe.

Outside of Europe, in Africa, Asia, the Americas, and AUSTRALIA, the relationship of Christianity and nationalism has developed in many different ways. In the course of the nineteenth and twentieth centuries, nationalism has become a worldwide movement. In each country that achieved independence, nationalism has been and in many cases has remained the main force in POLITICS. In each case the role of the relationship of religion and nationalism would deserve a careful analysis. In some countries, like INDIA, Christians are but a small minority and are confronted by the vehement strength of Hindu nationalism. In other cases—for example, in most countries in LATIN AMERICA—Christians form the majority as in Europe, although tensions have arisen between traditional Catholicism and new Protestant revival movements. Nationalism is invoked by both sides as a means of preserving the conservative order and as a means of social liberation. The position of Christians in Islamic countries in the Near East is again different. Secular as well as fundamentalist regimes consider nationalism as a guideline in political life. Whether nationalism will also dominate political thinking in the twenty-first century has yet to be seen as in an era of globalization new forms of international cooperation begin to emerge.

References and Further Reading

Alter, Peter. *Nationalism.* London: Arnold, 1995.
Anderson, Benedict. *Imagined Communities: Reflections on the Origin and Spread of Nationalism.* Rev. ed. London: Verso, 1999.
Breuilly, John. *Nationalism and the State.* Manchester: Manchester University Press, 1993.
Chickering, Roger. *We Men who Feel Most German. A Cultural Study of the Pan-German League 1886–1914.* Boston: Allen & Unwin, 1984.
Colley, Linda. *Britons: Forging the Nation 1707–1837.* London: Vintage, 1996.
Deutsch, Karl W. *Nationalism and Social Communication.* Cambridge, MA: M.I.T. Press, 1996.
Gellner, Ernest. *Nations and Nationalism.* Oxford, UK: Blackwell, 1998.
Hobsbawm, Eric. *Nations and Nationalism since 1780: Programme, Myth, Reality.* Cambridge: Cambridge University Press 1999.
Hutchison, William R., and Hartmut Lehmann, eds. *Many are Chosen: Divine Election and Western Nationalism.* Minneapolis, MN: Fortress Press, 1994.
Kohn, Hans. *The Age of Nationalism.* Westport, CT: Greenwood, 1976 (reprint).
Lehmann, Hartmut, and Hermann Wellenreuther, eds. *German and American Nationalism. A Comparative Perspective.* Oxford, UK: Berg, 1999.
Winkler, Heinrich August, and Hartmut Kaelble, eds. *Nationalismus, Nationalitäten, Supranationalität.* Stuttgart, Germany: Klett-Cotta, 1993.

HARTMUT LEHMANN

NATIVE AMERICANS

Protestant Christianity was introduced among Native peoples of North America in the seventeenth century with the arrival of Anglo-Europeans fresh from the Protestant REFORMATION. Pilgrims and Puritans (see PURITANISM; PILGRIM FATHERS) were intent on establishing lives free of economic, political, or religious restraints imposed in their homelands by unsympathetic governing bodies. They were just as intent on extending the "Christian fayth" to Native residents throughout New England. The history of Protestantism among the indigenous peoples of North America is rife with cruelties, ironies, and inconsistencies. The messengers of the gospel often confused Christianity and Euro-American CULTURE, requiring Native converts to submit to the dictates of both. Strong ties between civil and ecclesiastical authorities frequently made the policies, and often the personnel, of the two indistinguishable and equally harmful to Native peoples. Colonization devastated Indian communities and often continued to undermine the work of Native leaders in the church (see COLONIALISM). Despite this painful history, Protestant churches among Native Americans also were marked by courageous Native leadership, inspiring witness, and faithful congregations. Although church attendance waned over the last century and the numbers of Native CLERGY are much lower entering the twenty-first century than the national average, it is estimated that today 10 to 25 percent of the Native American community claim Protestant affiliation of some kind.

Early Missions

Although initially fewer than two dozen colonial clergymen undertook any amount of missionary activity, all thirteen colonies engaged in MISSIONS to Indians. Puritan ministers were among the first to make a point of learning the local Native tongue, and began preaching to the local tribes by mid–seventeenth century despite rigorous parish demands. Notable among them was Thomas Mayhew Jr. (1621–1657), the first of five generations of Mayhews who worked among the Wampanoags of Martha's Vineyard. JOHN ELIOT (1604–1690) of Roxbury, near Boston, was noted for devoting forty years to preaching among the Massachusets. The missionaries gathered Native believers into "praying towns" that were governed and shepherded largely by Native converts. Training Native leadership for these towns was a major goal of both Eliot and the Mayhews. To that end Eliot translated and published the BIBLE (the first Bible of any kind printed in North America), grammars, and tracts into Algonkian, the language of both the Wampanoags and the Massachusets (see BIBLE TRANSLATION), and began to teach the converted to read and write, as well as to evangelize their own.

At its height in 1674, just before the outbreak of King Philip's War, about 1,100 American Indians lived in Eliot's praying towns (only 119 of those baptized). Along with another 500 converts in the Plymouth Colony and about 600 families on Martha's Vineyard, Christian Indians made up about 10 percent of New England's Native population. The war, which pitted Indian nations against the settlers and each other, resulted in the incarceration of the Christian Indians by the colonial government, many of whom had refused to fight. The praying towns never fully recovered. Nevertheless the colonial era produced a total of ninety-one praying towns and 133 Native preachers and teachers in New England alone.

One of the most capable and well known of the "Puritan Indians" was Samson Occom (1723–1792), a Mohegan. Occom was schooled by Eleazar Wheelock, a Congregational minister and the founder of Dartmouth College. Occom became a Presbyterian minister, missionary, teacher, hymn writer, fundraiser for Indian education, and a leader of his people's westward emigration. He not only exhorted his people to Christian faith, but Occom also led them in challenging legal and political authorities for just treatment under colonial laws. Concern for both body and soul of his people caused Occom to eventually break with Wheelock's incessant paternalism, challenging Wheelock's commitment to serve the best interests of Indian people. Occom became a respected preacher offering religious leadership. He also provided political leadership during years of conflict with settlers and governments. By all appearances Occom was an Indian Puritan. His ability to translate the Christian message into both inspirational and practical expressions of faith encouraged the growth of Native Christian communities.

Protestant Christianity among Native Americans did not make great headway in the eighteenth century, as settlers moved onto Indian lands. The Moravians (see MORAVIAN CHURCH), under the guidance of NIKOLAUS LUDWIG VON ZINZENDORF of Saxony (1700–1760) and missionary David Zeisberger (1721–1808), had one of the few missions to succeed in establishing Indian churches and communities. Unfortunately, as the republican era gained military strength, even Christian Indian communities suffered atrocities and unrelenting pressure to move out of the way of advancing Euro-American settlers. At the end of sixty years of living among and interceding for Native peoples, Zeisberger's work left only pockets of Native Christians in the Ohio valley and CANADA.

Nineteenth Century Upheaval

The nineteenth century was ushered in by "cataclysmic outbreaks of religious enthusiasm" known as the Second Great Awakening (see AWAKENINGS). The REVIVALS fueled a new missionary wave and the advent of voluntary organizations spawned just for mission work (see VOLUNTARY SOCIETIES). Renewed interest in Native Americans focused on the "civilizing" effects of educating the young. In cooperation with the federal government and assisted by the $10,000 Civilization Fund voted by Congress for Indian education in 1819, Protestant and Catholic churches opened both boarding and day schools across the country. Christian reformers in the church and government believed that forced separation from Indian homes would help the next generation better assimilate to the dominant culture regardless of their interest in doing so.

The AMERICAN BOARD OF COMMISSIONERS FOR FOREIGN MISSIONS (ABCFM) was one of the earliest mission organizations. It began in 1810 as a joint effort of the Congregational, Presbyterian, and several smaller Reformed churches, and half of its funding went to Indian missions. The ABCFM began its work among the southeastern tribes, where members of the Five Civilized Tribes (Cherokees, Choctaws, Chickasaws, Creeks, and Seminoles) sent out a call for teachers and schools. Along with Moravians, Baptists, and Methodists (see METHODISM, NORTH AMERICA), the ABCFM established mission schools and compounds throughout the Southeast to help their students become acculturated and Christian. Despite the high level of Euro-American cultural practices already in place in these tribes (tribal governments patterned after the federal government, schools and churches, tribal newspapers, large farms that even used slave labor), ultimately even more schooling failed. Native acceptance into American society was denied.

The federal government's forced removal of Native Americans to Indian Territory in the early 1830s cut short the work of the ABCFM and other mission stations. Although the missionary effort was damaged, the Five Civilized Tribes nearly destroyed, and fully a quarter of Cherokee lives alone lost in the Anglo greed and avarice that prompted the "Trail of Tears," many Protestant Natives carried their faith with them to the new land. The few ordained Native clergy, and a few missionaries, continued to proclaim the gospel. One of the most prominent was Jesse Bushyhead (1804–1844), a Baptist minister and Cherokee mixed-blood. He was the first Cherokee pastor of his own church in the Cherokee nation. Bushyhead was, at the same time, a justice on the Cherokee Supreme Court (and eventually Chief Justice). He also lobbied Washington for Cherokee political rights and against removal. Failing to prevent it, Bushyhead then led one of the bands of Cherokees in their forced march to Indian Territory. Largely because of the work of a small core of Native preachers who ministered to the spiritual, political, and social needs of the people, Protestant Christianity survived the tragedy of removal. Although association with the government weakened the church's influence, Christianity continued to give hope to many within the disheartened and dispossessed nation.

As Euro-Americans moved west, pushing Indian peoples ahead of them, mission work continued to and within Native American communities. Methodist missionary John Stewart (1786–1823) went out among the Wyandotte in the Ohio valley. A man of Native American and African American parentage whose brief life was marked by his devotion to preaching to and living with the Wyandottes, Stewart is credited with beginning Methodist interest in Indian missions. He was also responsible for raising up the first Native preachers. By the time the 700 Wyandottes were forced to move west in 1843, 200 were Methodists, including preachers, exhorters, and class leaders. Methodist CIRCUIT RIDERS provided many preaching stations among Native Americans, although church establishments were rare.

Methodist reliance on local American Indian preachers assisted in the strengthening of Native Christianity. Perhaps best known of the Native Methodist preachers during the early nineteenth century was William Apess (1798–1838?). A Pequot, Apess became an itinerant Methodist preacher, leader, and instigator of the Mashpee Revolt of 1833, and writer of several books, including his autobiography. These writings are perhaps his greatest legacy because they illustrate not only the heart of a man given to Christian ministry, but an astute insight into the inequities both Christian and non-Christian Indians faced at the hands of "Christian America." His "Eulogy on King Philip," given to a Boston audience on the 160th anniversary of Wampanoag sachem King Philip's death, is an eloquent indictment against his Anglo brothers and sisters for perpetuating crimes against Indians that started with their Puritan progenitors. Apess epitomized Indian preachers who believed their place in the Kingdom equal to that of their Anglo peers, and who found hope for both body and soul of their people in Protestant Christianity, despite the flaws of the messengers.

By the end of the nineteenth century, Native Americans were segregated on reservations across North America, and Christian mission churches dotted the landscape. Comity agreements and President Grant's Peace Policy (1869–1882) divided the reservations among Christian churches to continue the work of "Christianizing and civilizing" Native Americans. Rather than eliminating corrupt Indian agents and providing greater Christian influence on the reservations as hoped, the policy intensified interdenominational conflict and gave way to the 1887 Dawes Severalty Act. This legislation, with the approval and urging of the churches, broke up the reservations into individual plots of land to encourage the "civilized" art of farming. It merely impoverished American Indians by allowing nearly 90 million acres of "excess" reservation lands to end up in non-Indian hands. Despite these government policies, backed by the Protestant reformers, Protestantism on the reservations, if it did not flourish, at least held ground.

Native Leadership

As had been the case from the beginning of the Christian church among Native Americans, indigenous pastors provided an effective means of propagating the faith. They spoke the language, knew the people and the culture, and could provide trusted leadership. James Hayes, a Nez Perce, was one of eighteen men schooled at the McBeth Mission in Idaho and ordained as a Presbyterian minister in 1884. Sisters Sue McBeth (1830–1893) and Kate McBeth (1832–1915) and their niece Mary Crawford (1863–1946) were responsible for running the school from 1874 to 1932. They prepared the students to fill pulpits throughout the northwest. Hayes, who was awarded an honorary doctorate from Whitworth College in 1929, was such a gifted evangelist that he preached to tribes from the border of Canada to the desert southwest. The Shivwits of Utah named their church the James Hayes Presbyterian Church because of his ministry among them. He served as the pastor to the Tutuilla Presbyterian Church on the Umatilla reservation in eastern Oregon for seven years before serving one of the six Presbyterian churches of the Nez Perces for thirty years. Hayes was a respected leader of the Christian Nez Perces who, as a pastor, sought to meet the spiritual and material needs of his people in an era that allowed few opportunities for giving leadership of any kind to one's people.

By the early twentieth century the needs of the Indian population were out of all proportion to the rest of the UNITED STATES. Publication of the Meriam Report in 1928, a privately funded though federally supported study entitled "The Problem of Indian Administration," revealed that the health, education, and welfare of reservation Indians was far inferior to that of the cultural mainstream. Christian reformers who had long endorsed the government position that assimilation was the most desirable Indian policy were forced to reconsider. Assisted by the devastating statistics of the Meriam Report, Indian Commissioner John Collier challenged the prevailing opinion and encouraged an Indian New Deal that sought to restore to the tribes their self-determination and means for becoming self-reliant. Strong opposition to the Indian Reorganization Act of 1934 came primarily from the reformers who believed that the act reopened the door to the practice of Native cultural and religious practices the church had been trying to eradicate for centuries.

The fears of the reformers were not ungrounded. By mid–twentieth century, Native Christian leadership was largely in the hands of the LAITY, with hardly more than two hundred Native ministers serving the entire Protestant Indian population. The Depression dried up many funds for Indian churches, the Indian New Deal opened up new avenues other than the church to Native leadership, and, indeed, the Collier years encouraged a resurgence of Indian religions or syncretistic movements, such as the peyotists of the Native American Church. Furthermore, the federal government's attempt to terminate reservations and encourage Native settlement in urban areas in the 1970s caused nearly half of the Native population to leave their reservations. Indian churches struggled to remain open.

In the latter part of the twentieth century, mainline Protestant churches recognized that even after centuries of missionary work among Native Americans, few Indian churches were self-sustaining and only a handful had their own ministers. Concerned with dwindling numbers of Native clergy and empty churches, Protestant church boards began to follow the lead of the federal government and to consult Indian Christians about their future in the church. The result was an effort to bring Native Americans into the church leadership and to provide training specifically geared toward raising up a new cadre of Native pastors to lead Indian churches. By appointing Native American clergy and laity to positions on general boards, consulting committees, and task forces, Native Americans began to have a voice in determining their place in the church and in assessing their needs and roles.

Future Prospects

Today American Indian communities of faith continue to struggle with the injustices and inequities of reservation life and with remnants of a pervasive paternalism in the church. Protestant Indian churches must grapple with extremes of poverty, unemployment, illness, and teen suicide, the continuing legacies of reservation life. Years of missionization have left many churches unable to sustain themselves and in conflict over what are acceptable cultural elements in the church. Despite the greater accessibility of church boards and committees within the larger church, Native Americans still remain on the periphery of church decision making.

Despite a history that has tried to subjugate American Indians to the dominant society and often relegated Christian Indians to second-class citizenship within the church, capable and gifted Native women and men, clergy and lay, continue to emerge. In most mainline denominations, Native American theologians are also emerging to participate in the interpretation of the gospel and the evangelization of Native peoples. A long history of inspiring Native leadership gives hope that Indian churches will again flourish and provide influential leaders not only for American Indian churches and communities, but for the Protestant church and society at large.

References and Further Reading

Axtell, James. *After Columbus: Essays in the Ethnohistory of Colonial North America.* New York: Oxford University Press, 1988.

Bowden, Henry Warner, and James P. Ronda, eds. *John Eliot's Indian Dialogues: A Study in Cultural Interaction.* Westport, CT: Greenwood Press, 1980.

Kidwell, Clara Sue, Homer Noley, and George "Tink" Tinker. *A Native American Theology.* New York: Orbis Press, 2001.

Martin, Joel W. *The Land Looks After Us: A History of Native American Religion.* New York: Oxford University Press, 2001.

McBeth, Kate. *The Nez Perces Since Lewis and Clark.* New York: Fleming H. Revell Co., 1908. Reprint, Moscow: University of Idaho Press, 1993.

McLoughlin, William G. *Cherokees and Missionaries, 1789–1839*. New Haven, CT: Yale University Press, 1984.

McNally, Michael D. *Ojibwe Singers: Hymns, Grief, and a Native Culture in Motion*. New York: Oxford University Press, 2000.

O'Connell, Barry, ed. *On Our Own Ground: The Complete Writings of William Apess, a Pequot*. Amherst: University of Massachusetts Press, 1992.

Treat, James, ed. *Native and Christian: Indigenous Voices on Religious Identity in the United States and Canada*. New York: Routledge, 1996.

BONNIE SUE LEWIS

NATIVISM

"Nativism" is a preference for persons from one's native land and antagonism toward outsiders. Historically, nativists have expressed their views by promulgating negative views of aliens, advocating immigration restriction and limitations on immigrants' civil rights, and occasionally even rioting and violence. Although nativist biases may arise from many sources, they have often been associated with religious prejudice. From the beginnings of European settlement, nativism looms large in the history of American Protestantism.

Colonial Era to the Civil War

The New England Puritans were intensely anti-Catholic, viewing the papacy as a perversion of true Christianity and the pope as the ANTICHRIST. Further south, the province of Maryland, granted by James I to the Roman-Catholic Calvert family in 1632, saw continual conflicts between Protestants and Catholics. After the accession of William and Mary to the English throne in 1689, the CHURCH OF ENGLAND was established in Maryland and the capital transferred from Catholic St. Mary's to Protestant Annapolis.

The American colonists reacted fiercely to the 1774 Quebec Act (passed by Parliament after ENGLAND won Quebec from the French in the Seven Years' War), both for granting religious freedom to the province's Roman Catholics and for extending Quebec's boundaries to the Ohio River. As the Revolutionary War approached, patriot pamphlets sometimes portrayed British ministers as colluding with Rome to enslave the American colonists.

Although antebellum America remained overwhelmingly Protestant, a growing Catholic presence—from 30,000 in 1790 to 600,000 in 1830—exacerbated latent nativist impulses. Combining religious and political fears, nativist ministers and pamphleteers cautioned that Catholicism threatened both religious freedom and American liberty. Some nativists took to the streets. In August 1834 a mob burned down the Ursuline Convent School in Charlestown, Massachu-

setts, after months of incendiary anti-Catholic sermons by some of Boston's leading ministers, including the evangelical leader LYMAN BEECHER, pastor of the city's Park Street Church. In *A Plea for the West* (1835), Beecher warned of a Catholic plot to control the vast American interior. Infidelity and popery, agreed the Protestant journal *Home Missionary,* represented the twin threats facing the West.

In New York City, a group of Protestant leaders including businessman and reformer Arthur Tappan, writer Theodore Dwight, and Presbyterian minister William C. Brownlee spearheaded the nativist cause. The *American Protestant Vindicator,* a biweekly edited by Brownlee, appeared in 1834. "Jesuits are prowling around all parts of the UNITED STATES . . . to disseminate popery," Brownlee warned. The painter and inventor Samuel F. B. Morse promoted the nativist cause as well. Denouncing Catholic immigration in pamphlets of the 1830s, Morse proclaimed: "We must . . . stop this leak in the ship, through which the muddy waters from without threaten to sink us." Morse, too, combined patriotic and religious themes, declaring: "Our religion, the Protestant religion, and Liberty are identical, and liberty keeps no terms with despotism."

The Brownlee group also promulgated the scurrilous anti-Catholic tract *Awful Disclosures of Maria Monk,* first published in the *Vindicator* in 1835, and then in book form. This work described the alleged debaucheries of nuns and priests at Montreal's Hotel Dieu Hospital and Convent, including the strangling of infants born from these illicit unions and their burial in the convent basement. Maria Monk, the putative author, claimed to have been a nun in the convent; in fact, she had been briefly confined in a nearby Catholic institution for prostitutes. Monk was soon exposed as a fraud and her "awful disclosures" discredited as a fabrication. A New York Protestant opposed to the nativist excesses, the editor William L. Stone, investigated the Montreal convent and repudiated the accusations. Despite its sordid origins, *Maria Monk's Awful Disclosures* enjoyed a long life. Over 300,000 copies were printed down to 1860, and new editions continued to appear in the twentieth century.

As the 1840s and 1850s brought a surge of Catholic immigration from GERMANY and especially famine-ridden IRELAND, nativist agitation persisted, with Protestant ministers still in the forefront. The interdenominational American Protestant Association (1842) mobilized Protestants against the Catholic menace. Protestant-dominated public-school committees prescribed readings from the King James BIBLE, even in Catholic neighborhoods. In 1840, New York's Roman Catholic bishop, John Hughes, charging that the Public School Society, a private charity, was inculcating

Protestantism through the King James Bible and other reading material, demanded public aid to Catholic schools. The Protestant CLERGY denounced Hughes's proposal, and the Common Council rejected it overwhelmingly. Similar controversies erupted in Philadelphia and other cities.

Once again the conflict turned violent. The "Bible riots" that erupted in Philadelphia in 1844 left sixteen dead and thirty buildings in ruins. In New York City only the militant Bishop Hughes, who posted armed guards in Catholic churches and institutions, prevented similar violence by Protestant mobs. Such outbursts of nativist violence were often fueled by native-born workingmen facing job competition from immigrant Catholic laborers.

The nativist American Party—also called the Know Nothing Party because members were sworn to secrecy—flourished in the mid-1850s. Advocating immigration restriction, the exclusion of Catholics from public office, and a long waiting period for naturalization, the American Party elected six governors in 1855, and in 1856 garnered 21 percent of the vote for its presidential candidate, Millard Fillmore. It faded thereafter, as many of its members joined the new Republican party.

Civil War through the 1920s

Nativism remained central in American Protestantism after the CIVIL WAR, as thirteen million immigrants, mostly from southern and eastern Europe, poured in between 1865 and 1900. An estimated five million Catholic newcomers arrived between 1870 and 1910, together with many eastern European Jews. The strengthening of papal AUTHORITY during the long pontificate of Pius IX, including his *Syllabus of Errors* (1864), the 1869–1870 Vatican Council (attended by forty-five U.S. bishops), and the proclamation of papal infallibility in 1870–1871, along with the naming of the first U.S. cardinal in 1875, intensified nativist, anti-Catholic sentiment among U.S. Protestants. The proliferation of Catholic parochial schools stirred controversies in many states as Protestant legislators sought by various means to thwart the parochial-school movement. The nativist American Protective Association, founded in Clinton, Iowa in 1887, soon spread across the midwest.

The nativist movement became embroiled in party politics because the immigrants voted mostly Democratic, whereas northern, native-born Protestants were predominantly Republican. Republican candidates in the 1870s and 1880s frequently advocated policies directed at Catholics and other immigrants, such as prohibition and sabbatarian laws, opposition to parochial schools, and requirements for English-language instruction in the schools. In New York City, Protestant ministers and reformers carried on a running battle with the city's Democratic organization, Tammany Hall, with its teeming ranks of immigrant (and largely Catholic) voters. Thomas Nast, the political cartoonist who witheringly attacked the corrupt Tammany leader William Marcy "Boss" Tweed, also targeted the alleged Catholic conspiracy to take over America. In one notorious Nast cartoon published in *Harper's Weekly* in 1871, foreign Catholic priests caricatured as crocodiles swarm ashore and prepared to devour American schoolchildren while a smirking Tweed and his henchmen look on.

Nativism played a direct role in the 1880 presidential contest. A few days before the election, when a delegation of New York City Protestant ministers visited the Republican candidate James G. Blaine, one of them, Samuel D. Burchard, publicly denounced the Democrats as the party of "Rum, Romanism, and Rebellion." When Blaine failed to repudiate Burchard's slur, the city's Catholic voters turned out en masse to cast ballots for Democrat Grover Cleveland, who narrowly carried New York State and thereby won the presidency.

The EVANGELICAL ALLIANCE, a Protestant ecumenical organization founded in 1867 with branches in some forty American cities, espoused nativist positions, particularly after the Congregationalist minister Josiah Strong became general secretary in 1886. In his influential work *Our Country* (1885), Strong listed "Immigration" and "Romanism" among the seven deadly perils facing America. Addressing the Evangelical Alliance in 1887, the writer and Columbia University professor H. H. Boyesen described his repugnance toward the immigrants pouring into New York and marveled at native-born Americans' willingness "to mingle this coarse and brutal strain in their own fresh and vigorous blood." At the same conference Episcopal bishop Samuel Harris of Michigan articulated the blend of THEOLOGY, racism, and nativism prevalent in Gilded Age American Protestantism: "[T]he consistency of the divine purpose in establishing our evangelical civilization here," Harris asserted, "is signally illustrated in the fact that it was primarily confided to the keeping of the Anglo-Saxon race."

On another front, the Immigration Restriction League was founded in 1894 by a group of Boston patricians, including Senator Henry Cabot Lodge, Protestants all. For years the League campaigned for a literacy test for immigrants, a strategy calculated to exclude unschooled newcomers of the kind arriving in large numbers from southern and eastern Europe.

Whereas some Progressive-era reformers urged aid and support for immigrants and celebrated the diversity they brought to American life, others embraced nativism, blaming immigrants for municipal corruption and denouncing the conservative, hierarchical Catholic church as a barrier to reform. The virulently anti-Catholic periodical *The Menace,* founded in 1911 by Missouri editor Wilbur Franklin Phelps, won a circulation of one million by 1914. In addition to printing and distributing nativist and anti-Catholic publications, Phelps also ran a lecture bureau of nativist speakers. Phelps accused the Knights of Columbus, a Catholic fraternal organization, of planning a war of annihilation against non-Catholics. Some sixty other nativist and anti-Catholic publications circulated in these pre–World War I decades.

Nativism surfaced again strongly in the 1920s, a decade sometimes described as the last stand of American Protestant hegemony. The Immigration Act of 1924 restricted immigration to 164,000 annually, imposed a national-origins quota system that discriminated against immigrants from southern and eastern Europe, and excluded Asians entirely. The revived KU KLUX KLAN, which attracted throngs of working-class and lower-middle-class Protestants in the early 1920s, was rabidly nativist. The Klan's central principles, wrote Imperial Wizard Hiram W. Evans in 1926, were "loyalty to the white race, to the traditions of America, and to the spirit of Protestantism." The Masonic Order, to which many Protestants belonged, was also strongly nativist and anti-Catholic at this time. Proclaimed one Masonic publication: "The Protestant has been practically ousted from political life, . . . and schools as well as municipal departments reflect the influence of the Church of Rome."

Nativism shaped the presidential politics of the 1920s. The 1924 Democratic convention rejected a platform plank criticizing the Ku Klux Klan, and refused to nominate New York governor Alfred E. Smith for president, primarily because of his Catholicism. Smith won the Democratic nomination in 1928, but lost to Protestant Herbert Hoover, amid nativist charges that the Vatican would surely control any Catholic president. (Hoover himself did not exploit the religious issue, however.)

1930 to the Close of the Twentieth Century

In the Depression decade of the 1930s nativism found some virulent defenders, especially in the ranks of the fundamentalist movement. Gerald Winrod of Kansas, publisher of *The Defender* magazine, regularly engaged in anti-Semitic (see ANTI-SEMITISM) and anti-Catholic diatribes, as did the Rev. William Bell Riley, the fundamentalist Baptist minister and Bible-school head in Minneapolis. Riley opposed Al Smith in 1928 out of an unwillingness "to have Rome rule at Washington." Citing the notorious anti-Semitic forgery *The Protocols of the Elders of Zion,* Riley warned darkly of a Jewish–Bolshevik anti-American conspiracy.

In general, however, nativism diminished as a force in American life, and in American Protestantism, after 1930. President Franklin D. Roosevelt, an Episcopalian, brought many Catholics and Jews into his administration, and called for national unity in the struggle against the Depression. As a war leader in 1941–1945 Roosevelt urged the nation to set domestic divisions aside and unite in the battle to defeat fascism. The celebrated "Four Chaplains"—two Protestant ministers, a Catholic priest, and a Jewish rabbi—who gave up their life jackets to sailors and went down together on the *U.S.S. Dorchester* when it was struck by a torpedo off Newfoundland in January 1943 offered a compelling image of wartime national unity transcending longstanding sectarian divisions.

The reaction against nativism and religious prejudice intensified as the horrors of the Nazi holocaust became known and as the nation mobilized for the Cold War struggle with the Soviet Union. The Cold War era's celebration of a somewhat generic religious faith, as a counterweight to godless COMMUNISM, muted traditional nativist hostilities. Reconciliation among Protestants, Catholics, and Jews, symbolized by such events as National Brotherhood Week, figured prominently in the public CULTURE of the 1950s. Some Protestant leaders, including the Rev. NORMAN VINCENT PEALE, opposed John F. Kennedy's 1960 presidential candidacy on religious grounds, but they were few in number and widely criticized. Kennedy addressed the issue convincingly and won election as the first Catholic president.

In the cultural wars of the late twentieth century, entrenched Protestant–Catholic divisions gave way to new conservative–liberal alignments that crossed sectarian boundaries. Surging immigration from LATIN AMERICA and various Asian countries in the late twentieth century swelled the ranks of Catholics, Hindus, and Buddhists on the American religious scene, but in contrast to past periods of heavy immigration, this did not produce a nativist reaction. Although some called for stricter immigration laws, they did so on economic rather than religious grounds, and generally avoided the denigratory language of past anti-immigrant crusades.

Concluding Reflections

Any assessment of the links between American Protestantism and nativism must be hedged with caveats. Not all Protestants were nativists. Even in periods when nativism reached high levels, some Protestant leaders—often from the liberal end of the spectrum—deplored the demonization of Catholic newcomers and other aliens (see LIBERAL PROTESTANTISM AND LIBERALISM). The Quaker settlement-house leader Jane Addams, for example, consistently opposed nativist bigotry, as did most SOCIAL GOSPEL ministers. In the nativist 1920s, some Protestant leaders, mostly liberal "Modernists" but including some Evangelicals and fundamentalists, appealed to Jesus's teachings and the democratic ideology of equality to deplore nativist prejudice against alien and minority groups. Further, those Protestants who did espouse nativism at various periods in American history were far from alone. Labor unions fearing job competition, conservatives worried about an influx of immigrant radicals, rural folk troubled by the explosive growth of cities, and "Anglo-Saxon" racists with no particular religious orientation all helped fuel nativist movements.

When the caveats have been noted, however, an unassailable fact remains: from the seventeenth to the twentieth centuries, vast numbers of American Protestant leaders and laypersons embraced nativist ideologies, and helped swell the ranks of nativist movements.

References and Further Reading

Billington, Ray Allen. *The Protestant Crusade, 1800–1860.* Chicago: Quandrangle Books, 1964.

Dolan, Jay P. *The Immigrant Church: New York's Irish and German Catholics, 1815–1860.* Baltimore, MD: Johns Hopkins University Press, 1975.

Dumenil, Lynn. *The Modern Temper: American Culture and Society in the 1920s.* New York: Hill and Wang, 1995.

Handy, Robert T. *A Christian America: Protestant Hopes and Historical Realities.* New York: Oxford University Press, 1984.

Higham, John. *Strangers in the Land: Patterns of American Nativism, 1860–1925.* New Brunswick, NJ: Rutgers University Press, 1955.

Hunter, James Davison. *Culture Wars: The Struggle to Define America.* New York: Basic Books, 1991.

Marsden, George. *Fundamentalism and American Culture: The Shaping of Twentieth-Century Evangelicalism, 1870–1925.* New York: Oxford University Press, 1980.

Marty, Martin E. *Righteous Empire: The Protestant Experience in America.* New York: The Dial Press, 1970.

Noll, Mark A., ed. *Religion and American Politics: From the Colonial Period to the 1980s.* New York: Oxford University Press, 1990.

Trollinger, William Vance Jr. *God's Empire: William Bell Riley and Midwestern Fundamentalism.* Madison: University of Wisconsin Press, 1990.

PAUL BOYER

NATURAL LAW

The term *natural law* refers to moral law that is rooted in human nature. It therefore precedes human choices and it transcends positive law, cultural difference, and historical change. Such a concept is explicit in classical Greek and Roman thought (e.g., Plato [c. 428– c. 348 B.C.], Aristotle [384–322 B.C.], the Stoics, and Cicero [106–43 B.C.]) and implicit in the biblical tradition. Examples are seen in the Wisdom literature's acknowledgment of moral wisdom drawn from natural experience and present in foreign cultures, the prophet Amos's assertion that pagan nations are subject to the same moral law as Judah and Israel (Amos 1), and the Apostle Paul's affirmation that the Gentiles have the law of Moses effectively "written on their hearts" (Romans 2:15).

Through John Chrysostom (c. 347–407) and Augustine (354–430), in particular, classical notions of natural law were incorporated into Christian tradition and modified by it, so that its genesis is ascribed to the God of the Christian Scriptures, whose own revealed moral law explicates what is already present in created nature. Although other figures such as Isidore of Seville (c. 560–636) and Gratian (twelfth century) contributed to the development of Christian thinking on these matters, it was Thomas Aquinas (1225–1274) who, aided by Aristotle as well as Augustine, constructed in his *Summa Theologiae* (Ia IIae, Qq.90–108, "De Legibus") a fully fledged theory in a systematic theological framework, and thereby provided the standard reference point for subsequent generations.

Early Reformers

As mediated by late Scholasticism, however, Aquinas's natural law legacy found a mixed reception among the early reformers. Although MARTIN LUTHER (1483–1546) acknowledged that there is a (natural) law written on the human heart, he regarded the corruption of reason by SIN—in particular, by the sinful will to self-justification—to be such as to render that law almost entirely obscure to human view. Besides, Luther's confidence in the ability of FAITH to generate loving, moral conduct freely and spontaneously inclined him to deny the need for Christians to be instructed by law of any kind (that is, the need for a "third use" of the law). Luther's younger colleague, PHILIPP MELANCHTHON (1497–1560), however, was less sanguine. Although he agreed that obedience to the law is not the route to JUSTIFICATION, he reckoned that those who have been justified need the moral guidance that law can provide; and in true Scholastic fashion he believed that the content of that law, although present in the Old and New Testaments, is best discovered through the natural reasoning of Aristotle (*Epitome philosophiae moralis*, 1541). JOHN CALVIN (1509–1564) followed Melanchthon in affirming the "third [morally instructive] use" of law, but, approximating Luther's pessimistic estimation of the capacity of sinful reason, looked for that instruction in the Decalogue. Whatever their differences, John T. McNeill has demonstrated that all three continental reformers recognized the natural politicoethical wisdom of the pagan Greeks and Romans, and appealed to natural law when treating civil or political matters. This was also true of the English reformer, RICHARD HOOKER (c. 1554–1600), whose *Laws of Ecclesiastical Polity* closely follows Aquinas's "De Legibus," not least in treating natural law and Scripture as complementary authorities, and in rating highly the power of natural reason to perceive our moral duties, if not the requirements of SALVATION.

The Protestant tendency to acknowledge natural law in political matters was intensified by the intermittent religious wars that ravaged Europe from 1562 to 1648. Given the demise of the international AUTHORITY of the papacy and the Holy Roman emperor, Hugo Grotius (1583–1645), the heterodox Dutch Calvinist, sought in natural law a ground for the basic principle of an international order of sovereign states—*pacta sunt servanda* (*De iuri belli ac pacis*, 1625). Grotius has long been viewed as a pioneer of the secularization of natural law theory because of his famous admission that its principles would stand *etiamsi daremus non esse Deum* ("even if we granted that God does not exist"). This conventional reading has not gone unchallenged, however. Oliver and Joan O'Donovan, for example, have argued that Grotius's intention was precisely to deny that there is an autonomous rational politics; and to assert that all human relations, including those beyond the jurisdiction of human law (for example, in a state of WAR) are subject to the claim of divine law—a law that finds its supreme expression in the Old and New Testaments.

John Locke

Like Grotius, the Puritan JOHN LOCKE (1632–1704) was moved by religious strife to search out a natural basis for political order (see PURITANISM). This he found in the law that derives from the creaturely and social nature of human beings, and which consists fundamentally in the duty to make and keep promises and commitments. Although Locke was epistemologically rationalist—the law of nature is known by the rational interpretation of sense-experience, and not by revelation—he was ontologically theistic: the ultimate origin and authority of the law of nature lies in the will of God, not reason (*Essays on the Law of Nature*, 1664; *Two Treatises of Civil Government*, 1690). Here Locke reflects the voluntarism characteristic of Protestant natural law theory.

Immanuel Kant

IMMANUEL KANT (1724–1804) is commonly understood to be an ethical rationalist in a fuller sense than Locke. He insisted not only that reason rather than revelation is the ultimate arbiter of the content of morality, but also that moral law issues from practical reason *as distinct from* natural (for example, social) inclinations (*The Foundations of the Metaphysics of Morals*, 1785). Furthermore, he had no truck with the claim that the moral law needs the divine will as the ultimate source of its authority. Nevertheless, Kant may be considered a kind of natural law theorist, given that he conceived of moral law as grounded in the nature of human reason; and his theory cannot be classified as secularist because he held that belief in the existence of a benevolent God is necessary for the intelligibility of the concept of moral duty.

Friedrich Schleiermacher

In reaction against the abstract rationalism of Kant's ETHICS and its lack of a soteriological context, and under the lingering influence of Moravian PIETISM, FRIEDRICH SCHLEIERMACHER (1768–1834) developed what might be considered a dynamic concept of natural law. Here law is not a heteronomy, but rather a "life-process" in which nature is progressively organized by the active and immanent power of reason, so as to promote community and liberty simultaneously. Accordingly moral life is less a matter of dutiful obedience than of participation in a divine power (note the echo of Luther); and ethics is less normative moral doctrine than phenomenology of the "redeeming," moralizing activity of reason in history. Although Schleiermacher did not think recourse to the Christian TRADITION necessary for the discernment of this activity, he may have held the traditional view that Christian ethics presents the observations of natural or philosophical ethics more sharply.

Georg W. F. Hegel

On this point GEORG W. F. HEGEL (1770–1831) was less equivocal and more radical, being in no doubt that Christian THEOLOGY and ethics have been sublimated into philosophy. Nevertheless, Hegel shared Schleiermacher's predilection for a dynamic concept of natural law, which he conceived as the perfective process in which absolute Spirit or Mind *(Geist)* progressively realizes itself in the world through the development of the consciousness of human freedom—a development in which he considered the REFORMATION to have played a decisive part by advocating the freedom of the individual conscience from ecclesiastical and dogmatic heteronomy (*Phenomenology of Spirit*, 1807).

Twentieth Century

The moral complacency of the cultural optimism implied by the immanentist concept of natural law espoused by Hegel and Schleiermacher was laid bare when the progressive self-realization of Reason or Mind manifested itself in the barbarities of the First and Second World Wars. This is certainly how the signs of the times were read by KARL BARTH (1886–1968), who rejected natural law as an arbitrary concept, capable of being filled with any—even Nazi—moral content. "All arguments based on natural law are Janus-headed," he once wrote. "They lead to Munich" (*A Letter to Great Britain from Switzerland,* 1941). In spite of his unrelenting repudiation of natural law (or, to be more precise, the conclusions of natural reason unilluminated by the Word of God), Barth was happy to affirm on theological grounds certain normatively structured relationships that are "natural" in the sense that God has created them constitutive of human beings (*Church Dogmatics,* III/4). These were deliberately less specific than the "divine mandates" (labor, MARRIAGE, government, CHURCH) of DIETRICH BONHOEFFER (1906–1945), which lent themselves, Barth feared, to the divinization of particular historical forms.

Arguably even more thorough than Barth in his dismissal of natural law is Stanley Hauerwas (1940–). Disposed to read Christian ethics in Anabaptist, pacifist terms (see ANABAPTISM; PACIFISM), Hauerwas accuses the natural law ethic of being "accommodationist" because of its association with just war theory (*The Peaceable Kingdom: a Primer in Christian Ethics,* 1983). Moreover, Hauerwas provides no place in his thought for anything equivalent to Barth's created relational structures.

Considerably less skeptical than Hauerwas, and slightly less so than Barth, is REINHOLD NIEBUHR (1893–1971). While sharing Barth's view of natural reason as corrupted by sinful interests, and criticizing Catholic natural law theory for endowing moral norms with a pretentious precision and universality and for asserting them with a rationalistic self-confidence, Niebuhr nevertheless acknowledged that a sufficient awareness of the moral claims of "essential human nature" remains to disturb the human conscience (*The Nature and Destiny of Man,* vol. I).

Of Barth's contemporaries, EMIL BRUNNER (1889–1966) was the most affirmative of natural law (*Justice and the Social Order,* 1943). Attributing the evils of twentieth-century totalitarianism to the tradition of legal positivism and its relativization of the idea of justice, Brunner urgently felt the need to recover the idea of transcendent, natural law. The particular notion he advocates is voluntarist and theologically qualified: it is the sacred will of God, standing behind a mere fact of human nature, that commands our respect for it; and although natural man is capable of a certain unaided awareness of the orders of creation, sin's epistemic distortion makes enlightenment by special divine revelation indispensable.

Current Consideration

At the end of the twentieth century and the beginning of the twenty-first, there are signs that natural law is meeting with increasing approval in diverse Protestant circles. In Scandinavia, for example, a strong tradition of interest in the ethics of creation and natural law has developed among Lutheran theologians, the best known of whom are Gustaf Wingren (1910–2000; *Creation and Law,* 1958) and K. E. Løgstrup (1905–1981; *The Ethical Demand,* 1956). In ENGLAND the evangelical Anglican, Oliver O'Donovan (1945–), gives prominent place in his Christian ethic to the idea of a created order of which all humans have a certain, albeit limited, natural knowledge (*Resurrection and Moral Order: An Outline for Evangelical Ethics,* 1986).

References and Further Reading

Bexell, Göran. "Is Grisez's Moral Theology Rationalistic? Free Choice, the Human Condition, and Christian Ethics." In *The Revival of Natural Law: Philosophical, Theological, and Ethical Responses to the Finnis-Grisez School,* edited by Nigel Biggar and Rufus Black. Aldershot, UK, and Burlington, VT: Ashgate, 2000.

Biggar, Nigel. *The Hastening that Waits: Karl Barth's Ethics.* Oxford: Oxford University Press, 1993, 1995.

Braaten, Carl. "Protestants and Natural Law." *First Things* 19 (1992): 23.

Chroust, A. H. "Hugo Grotius and the Scholastic Natural Law Tradition." *New Scholasticism* 17/4 (1943): 101–133.

Dunn, John. *Locke.* Oxford: Oxford University Press, 1984.

Frey, Christofer. *Die Ethik der Protestantismus von der Reformation bis zur Gegenwart.* Gütersloh, Germany: Gütersloher Verlagshaus Gerd Mohn, 1989.

Helm, Paul. "Calvin and Natural Law." *The Scottish Bulletin of Evangelical Theology* 2 (1984): 5–22.

Little, David. "Calvin and the Prospects for a Christian Theory of Natural Law." In *Norm and Context in Christian Ethics,* edited by Gene Outka and Paul Ramsey, 175–197. New York: Charles Scribner's Sons, 1968.

McNeill, John T. "Natural Law in the Teaching of the Reformers." *Journal of Religion* 26 (1946): 168–182.

O'Donovan, Oliver, and Joan Lockwood. *From Irenaeus to Grotius: A Sourcebook in Christian Political Thought.* Grand Rapids, MI: Wm. B. Eerdmans, 1999.

Troeltsch, Ernst. *The Social Teaching of the Christian Churches.* 2 vols. Midway Reprint ed. Chicago and London: University of Chicago, 1976.

NIGEL BIGGAR

NATURE

The study of "nature" has been a preoccupation of humanity since records began, frequently with a religious motivation. However, the birth of what might be called "modern science" in the seventeenth century led to transformed attitudes to nature of such magnitude that the phrase "Scientific Revolution" is often applied to the climactic upheavals in human thought and achievement. Although it would be extremely foolish to identify one simple cause of this phenomenon, there can be no doubt that the Protestant REFORMATION played an immense part. This is not for one moment to deny the roles of Catholicism or even non-Christian religions like Islam, but simply to emphasize the unique importance of Protestant thought of the emergence of modern science.

The "Scientific Revolution"

For the first fifteen centuries of the Christian era, authority on matters of dispute lay in church TRADITION and scripture, generally taken together. At the hands of MARTIN LUTHER and other reformers scripture was given a higher authority than the edicts of the Fathers, and newer more accurate texts were to supplant the Latin Vulgate. With the increased circulation of the scriptures it became possible for individuals to contemplate nature without recourse to a body of received teaching that would inhibit any serious progress in new understanding. The great doctrine of the priesthood of all believers would liberate thinking about both God and nature.

In more specific ways reflections on nature were profoundly altered by the rise of Protestantism. Perhaps the most important of these was what may be called the *deanimation of nature*. Up to this time nature had generally been conceived as a living entity, if not a divine one. Often represented with a capital N, such a Nature could be a subject rather than an object, and statements like "Nature abhors a vacuum" merely reflect this conception of an animate being. It possessed a life of its own and, like all living beings, possessed a certain unpredictability. Scientific study would therefore have a built-in element of imprecision, and notions like the "laws of nature" would be less likely to emerge.

The idea of Nature as intrinsically divine went far beyond the ideas of the medieval church, and was widespread in primitive animistic religion. For this to be true, the practice of manipulating part of God was readily seen as irreverent if not actually blasphemous. Its elimination from the stock-in-trade of popular thinking began with the rediscovery of the createdness of all things, promoted by a fresh look at Genesis and

Psalms, for example. Nature had to be deified as well as deanimated.

What emerged from this double process of demythologization of nature was a metaphor of immense strength and plausibility. The world of nature was neither divine nor living: it was essentially mechanical. ROBERT BOYLE compared it to the great clock in Strasbourg Cathedral whose working can be completely explained in terms of wheel, levers, springs, and so forth. This *mechanization of the universe* was perhaps the most distinctive feature of the new science, and its origins lay deep in Protestant thought. It denies personality and purpose to nature itself. The functional teleology within nature was, according to Boyle, impressed upon it by the Creator. The notion of "nature" exerting its own will was not only absurd, it was also impious, locating purpose and intention within inanimate matter instead of in the will of a personal God. Boyle saw, as did many of his contemporaries, that if "nature" is evacuated of all divinity, if it is not to be identified with God but seen as a creation by him, then it can become quite properly an object of study, manipulation, and experiment. Such views were entirely consonant with the teaching of both Old and New Testaments.

But how was such a new nature to be studied? In a word, by observation and experiment. When the navigator William Watts observed, "The thoughts of the philosophers have been contradicted by the unexpected observations" of himself and others, he was signaling the priority of experience over tradition. Similarly FRANCIS BACON urged "men to sell their books and build furnaces" and promoted his inductive method of approaching nature, a method that involved countless experiments and observations. That this dedication to experiment flourished especially in Calvinist countries like Holland (see CALVINISM) has been observed by many commentators as evidence of the Protestant ethos of testing as well as of hard work.

Experimentation, however, must mean manipulating and to some extent controlling the earth. Indeed, Bacon used the metaphor of a male dominating a female and imposing his will upon her. Justification for the subjugation of nature in the interest of human welfare came abundantly from biblical references to technology and their exposition by Protestant theologians. Thus also came yet another element of Reformed thinking that at the very least cannot have hindered science. This was its clear rejection of Manichean views that nature is somehow intrinsically evil, and therefore to be as much avoided as its opposite error of the divine universe. Bacon spoke of nature as "the work of His [God's] hands" and JOHN CALVIN of "this most delightful theater" in which we should take "pious delight."

Finally, the notion that nature could be studied as an act of worship and to the glory of God was prominent in the writing of many Protestant men of science in those early days. God had given men two books, of nature and of scripture. Both deserved the closest attention.

It remains to add a word about issues of sociology rather than belief.

A theory advanced in 1938 by Robert Merton connected the emergence of science in the seventeenth century with the rise of Protestantism in general. In particular, that specific form of Protestant religion known as PURITANISM was identified as being especially favorable to the science then emerging. Thus a high proportion of Puritans (not merely Protestants) in the membership of the early Royal Society, England's academy of science, enabled Merton to argue that Puritan attitudes "did much to encourage" its growth.

Criticism has mainly come on two grounds. First, the almost exclusive claims for Protestantism have had to be modified in the light of significant scientific work by Roman Catholics, such as Copernicus, Galileo, and many later figures, especially in FRANCE. They cannot be ignored. Nevertheless, there does seem to be a correlation between prominence in science and religious allegiance.

The other main objection to Merton's thesis resides in the difficulty of defining a "Puritan." On one hand a person with that title is sometimes regarded as a kind of ascetic fundamentalist, whereas on the other he may be considered rather as a dangerous political radical. Many difficulties disappear if Puritanism is considered theologically rather than politically. From this point of view a Puritan will hold strongly to the teaching of the BIBLE as opposed to that of church or tradition, but may not necessarily support the Parliamentary cause in the English revolution. He might even be a "moderate Anglican."

If modern-day skeptics are right, and there is no unequivocal proof that science was actively encouraged by Puritan theology, it may still be true that both may have been the outcome of a common cause or causes, including new movements of social and economic change and of a libertarian philosophy. However this may be, a general correlation seems inescapable in the 1600s between the promotion of science and a strongly Biblical and therefore Protestant theology.

Some would suggest an explicit causal relationship between science and Puritanism, arguing that the latter "caused" the former. Whereas it was once customary to see science as a product of our Greek inheritance, liberated from its bondage to religion at the Renaissance, R. Hooykaas now proposes a view that is its polar opposite. Science may be understood far better as an offspring of that Biblical theology that was rediscovered at the Reformation. On this view Greek philosophy may be seen as an inhibiting force for 1,500 years, and its displacement by a Biblical theology of both nature and work at last permitted the rise of experimental science.

Some Further Interactions between Protestantism and Nature

The Copernican Revolution

The first major step to modern science was as early as 1543, when Copernicus proposed that the earth rotated about the sun rather than the age-old belief that the sun went around the earth. Much has been made of the fact that Copernicus was a canon of the Roman Catholic Church, thus minimizing the role of Protestantism even in early modern science. However, this overlooks several facts. First, the Polish astronomer belonged to a group that had strong links with Erasmus, the reformer who remained within his Catholic Church and emphasized the importance of scripture. Several Lutheran (see LUTHERANISM) scholars became close friends and advisers, such as his assistant Rheticus and the clergyman Osiander, who wrote (anonymously) a Preface for Copernicus's great book, *De Revolutionibus*. The reaction against Protestantism known as the COUNTER-REFORMATION was still in the future.

The subsequent reaction to Copernicanism was at first muted, although opposition came from both wings of the church. PHILIPP MELANCHTHON had serious difficulties, although basically these stemmed from his Aristotelianism rather than his Protestant theology. Galileo, a Catholic, was more famously punished by his church for Copernican views. Underlying the favorable reception of Copernican thought within Catholic and Protestant circles was a realization that the Bible could be interpreted in many ways, and that to insist on a literal interpretation of many of its statements about nature was to ignore the doctrine of "accommodation" articulated (but not invented) by Calvin and other reformers who said that the Holy Spirit accommodated Himself to common usage to bring understanding to all who read scripture. Thus references to the sun traveling through the heavens were not intended as exact scientific descriptions but rather as assertions of beauty, regularity, and so forth. This principle of "accommodation" became a prominent feature of Reformation thinking about nature.

Newtonianism, Deism, and Natural Theology

After the eventual triumph of the Copernican system, and JOHANNES KEPLER's replacement of its circles by ellipses, ISAAC NEWTON incorporated the newly discovered laws of celestial motion in a much larger synthesis that embraced physical phenomena throughout the entire universe. His universal system (Newtonianism) magnificently vindicated the mechanization of science. God would now be seen as a Clockmaker who started the universe and then left it to run according to its own laws. This is a classic case of DEISM, and appealed particularly to those Protestants of Unitarian tendencies. Newton was secretly one of these, whereas some of his contemporaries, such as WILLIAM WHISTON, were more open about their Unitarianism. The latter denomination included many sympathetic to natural science, one of whom, JOSEPH PRIESTLEY, became a well-known minister. In eighteenth-century England the chief institutions for promoting a study of nature were the Dissenting Academies (see NONCONFORMITY, DISSENT), and prominent among these were several run by those with Unitarian sympathies.

However, a failure of Newton's predictions to square exactly with a few reported observations led him to invoke direct if occasional interventions of the Deity. This retreat from a strict deism has been aptly called "semi-deism," and became a favored position for many Protestants for the next two or three centuries. Despite being dismissed as a mere "God-in-the-gaps" strategy in the twentieth century (by D. M. Mackay and many others), it has persisted as an expression of popular faith.

One other consequence of a mechanical, clocklike universe was the revival in Protestant churches of natural theology. In the seventeenth century Newton hoped that his system would help "considering men" to a belief in a divine Creator, whereas Boyle established his "Boyle lectures" to be a demonstration of the value of the new science as a pointer to God. Natural theology was embedded in the writing of the great naturalist John Ray, as in his *The wisdom of God manifested in the works of creation* (1691). It became a popular genre in the eighteenth century as men looked "from nature up to nature's God," with books like *Physico-theology* (William Derham) and even more unlikely titles such as *Insect Theology* and *Water Theology*. The movement reached its climax in the dawn of the nineteenth century with the magisterial *Natural Theology* of the Anglican minister WILLIAM PALEY. Although receiving some hard knocks during the Darwinian controversies (see DARWINISM), it had a minority following among Protestants and Catholics until the twentieth century. It survived its famous rejection by KARL BARTH and has even reappeared as a by-product of research in the physical sciences.

Darwinism and the Protestant Response

In 1859 Charles Darwin published his *Origin of Species*. Creating a considerable stir at the time, it was more than "a storm in a Victorian tea-cup" as some would have it. Vocal opposition came for a variety of reasons, most of which were not theological (it demeaned humanity, it could lead to social unrest, it was scientifically unproven, etc.). Some members of Protestant sects were indeed affronted by its apparent assault of Genesis (they had forgotten Galileo), and so were a number of leading Roman Catholics. However, many Protestant churchmen felt that evolution might be the way in which God chose to work, and eloquent spokesmen for this view included HENRY DRUMMOND (Presbyterian) and CHARLES KINGSLEY (Anglican). In America evangelicals such as Asa Gray and Charles Hodge were energetic in their defense of Darwinism and sought to include it within their wider theological framework.

With hindsight it might appear that a firm Trinitarian rejection of deism helped these men and many others to appreciate more clearly the multifaceted interactions of God with God's creation. Moreover, from the Incarnation came light on the huge problems of suffering and evil thrown up by a "nature red in tooth and claw." Such questions of theodicy engaged many Protestant theologians from WILLIAM TEMPLE onward and made Paleyan natural theology look curiously old-fashioned.

A much more strident opposition to Darwinism did not appear until the twentieth century, with the rise of the "creationist" movement among American evangelicals (see EVANGELICALISM). It received much publicity in the notorious Scopes trial when issues of teaching evolution in schools came to a head. Since then the movement has found favor in some fundamentalist groups of Protestants in Europe, Asia, and Australia (see FUNDAMENTALISM).

One further trend associated with Darwinism was the creation and promulgation of the myth that the Christian church was always in conflict with natural science. The arguments over Genesis were seen as paradigmatic of the whole science–religion relationship. The myth was promoted in books by two American Protestants, Andrew White (Episcopalian president of America's nonsectarian Cornell University) and J. W. Draper (Methodist and strongly anti-Catholic chemist). Each had his own axe to grind. Then a group in England, led by T. H. Huxley, sought by all means to undermine the church by this conflict mythology. There were a few nominal Anglicans and several self-professed agnostics in their ranks. Their great achievement was the establishment of a conflict paradigm that, although historically discredited, remains a constituent of popular folklore whose very existence helps to explain some of the later overreactions of Protestants to the claims of science.

Questions of Ecology

As the twentieth century drew to a close, questions relating to global warming, increasing pollution, and loss of biodiversity became matters of urgent public concern. They had been matters of concern to scientists for over a hundred years and to some theologians long before that. However, by the 1960s "the environment" entered popular English vocabulary. At this time a provocative essay suggested that Christian theology is to blame for our environmental crisis by encouraging ideas of human "dominion" over the earth and its contents (L. White, 1966/7). Although the Protestant church is not specifically attacked, it is distinctively Protestant doctrines that are blamed, and the alternative proposed is the naturalistic theology of St. Francis of Assisi. Generally regarded as historically flawed, this thesis is inconsistent with the many pronouncements by early Protestants such as Calvin, William Derham, and others urging stewardship of the earth, not pillage of its resources. In the twenty-first century several Christian groups have been formed with the express purpose of addressing environmental issues in a biblical way. Although not sectarian in constitution, their present membership is predominantly in an evangelical Protestant tradition. They include the John Ray Initiative in the United Kingdom and the Au Sable Institute in the United States.

References and Further Reading

Brooke, J. H. *Science and Religion: Some Historical Perspectives.* Cambridge: Cambridge University Press, 1991.

Deason, G. B. "Reformation Theology and the Mechanistic Conception of Nature." In *God and Nature: Historical Essays in the Encounter between Christianity and Science,* edited by D. C. Lindberg and R. L. Numbers, 167–191. Berkeley and Los Angeles: University of California Press, 1986.

Dillenberger, J. *Protestant Thought and Natural Science: A Historical Interpretation.* London: Collins, 1961.

Harrison, P. *The Bible, Protestantism and the Rise of Natural Science.* Cambridge: Cambridge University Press, 1998.

Hooykaas, R. *Religion and the Rise of Modern Science.* Edinburgh: Scottish Academic Press, 1972.

Livingstone, D. N., D. G. Hart, and M. A. Noll, eds. *Evangelicals and Science in Historical Perspective.* New York: Oxford University Press, 1999.

Russell, C. A. *Cross-currents: Interactions between Science and Faith.* Leicester: IVP, 1983; reprint London: Christian Impact, 1995.

Webster, C. *The Great Instauration: Science, Medicine and Reform 1626–1660.* 2nd ed. London: Peter Lang, 2002.

COLIN A. RUSSELL

NAUDÉ, CHRISTIAAN FREDERICK BEYERS (1915–)

South African churchman. Naudé was born in SOUTH AFRICA in 1915, with roots deep in Afrikaner tradition and CULTURE and the piety of evangelical CALVINISM. Naudé was one of eight children, the son of a Dutch Reformed minister and a deeply religious and quietly dominant mother. Both parents were fervently anti-British and unquestioning in their allegiance to the Afrikaner cause. In 1940 Naudé joined the elitist Afrikaner Broederbond. Given the strong connection between Afrikaner identity and theology, it is not surprising that he should graduate from the theological school of the patriotic Stellenbosch University to be ordained as a minister of the DUTCH REFORMED CHURCH (DRC), of which he later would act as moderator in the Southern Transvaal.

Naudé's disillusionment with the DRC and Afrikaner politics was gradual. Paradoxically it was norms instilled into him by his family in the context of Afrikaner piety—notably a sense of social and political justice—that, translated into a different situation, would in time see him bearing prophetic witness against that very tradition. This move was precipitated by the Sharpeville massacre and the DRC's rejection of the antidiscriminatory resolutions of the Cottesloe Consultation, sponsored by the WORLD COUNCIL OF CHURCHES (1960).

In 1962 Naudé started *Pro Veritate,* an ecumenical journal inspired by the CONFESSING CHURCH struggle in Germany, followed in 1963 by the founding of the Christian Institute of Southern Africa (CI), aimed at serving the church in working for justice and reconciliation. Stripped of ministerial status in the DRC, Naudé directed the CI until its banning in 1977. At this time Naudé was served a personal banning order that was to last seven years. In 1980 he resigned from the DRC after its refusal to unite with black DR churches. Naudé's banning was lifted in 1984, and the following year he became general secretary of the South African Council of Churches.

The role played by Naudé in the struggle against apartheid and the transition to democracy is acknowledged in South Africa and internationally as one of great significance.

References and Further Reading

Charles Villa-Vicencio, and John W. de Gruchy. *Resistance and Hope: South African Essays in Honour of Beyers Naudé.* Cape Town, South Africa: David Philip, 1985.

JOHN W. DE GRUCHY

NAUMANN, FRIEDRICH (1860–1919)

German social reformer. Naumann was born at Störmthal March 25, 1860 and died at Travemünde August 24, 1919. He came from a Lutheran parsonage in Saxony, and after studying Theology in Leipzig and Erlangen he became an *Oberhelfer* assistant at the *Rauhen Haus* in Hamburg. From 1885 to 1890 he was a minister in Langenberg/Erzgebirge, and from 1890 he was *Vereinsgeistlicher* (chaplain) of the Inner Mission in Frankfurt/Main. Early in his career Naumann concerned himself with social issues. He supported the Protestant worker's association (*Evangelische Arbeitervereinsbewegung*), and beginning in 1890 he took part in the *Evangelisch-sozialen Kongreß*. In 1895 he founded the magazine *Die Hilfe,* which was an important organ of the social liberal movement until the end of his life.

Naumann first of all admired the court chaplain (*Hofprediger*) Adolf Stoecker. However, under the influence of Max Weber and Rudolf Sohm, he separated from Stoecker and his conservative Christian-socialist ideas. Naumann connected the social issue and the problem of nationalism, and he combined the demands for democratic and social reform with a call for a strong German nation. Consistently Naumann was involved in politics and eventually founded a party (*Nationalsozialer Verein*). In 1897 Naumann left his parish and moved to Berlin to live there as a publicist and politician. After a few unsuccessful attempts, Naumann was elected as a member of the *Reichstag* in 1907.

Through his numerous lectures, his books and articles, as well as his books of travels and his aesthetics, he became an influential representative of the German *Bildungsbürgertum* (bourgeoisie). In his book *Mitteleuropa* (1915) Naumann called for a European confederation of states. By 1919 Naumann was chairman of the liberal *Deutsche Demokratische Partei* and was influential in the formulation of the new constitution.

Naumann's work for a democratization of society and his demand for the broad participation of all social groups was a result of both his political and his Christian beliefs.

References and Further Reading

Primary Sources:

Milatz, Alfred. *Friedrich-Naumann-Bibliographie.* Düsseldorf, Germany: Droste, 1957.
Naumann, Friedrich. *Werke.* Edited by Walter Uhsadel, et al., 6 vols. Cologne and Opladen, Germany: Westdeutscher Verlag, 1964ff.

Secondary Sources:

Heuss, Theodor. *Friedrich Naumann. Der Mann. Das Werk. Die Zeit.* Munich, Germany: Siebenstern Taschenbuch Verlag, 1968.
vom Bruch, Ruediger, ed. *Friedrich Naumann in seiner Zeit.* Berlin, Germany: de Gruyter, 2000.

Norbert Friedrich

NEANDER, JOHANN AUGUST WILHELM (1789–1850)

German theologian. Neander was one of the founders of modern Protestant church historiography who understood church history as the history of piety. Like others before him he viewed history biographically, even though initially he published thematic monographs.

Neander was born David Mendel in a Jewish family in Göttingen, Germany, but converted to Christianity through his experiences with classmates in the Gymnasium (high school) and after reading Friedrich Schleiermacher's *Reden über die Religion (Speeches on Religion).* He was baptized in Hamburg in 1806 and took a symbolic new name. That same year he decided to study Theology and moved to Halle, where Schleiermacher was teaching. Because of the Napoleonic wars he moved to Göttingen, where he decided on an academic career devoting himself to early Christianity and New Testament topics. In 1811 he became a lecturer at the University of Heidelberg, and two years later, when he was twenty-four, Schleiermacher facilitated his appointment as professor of church history at the recently founded University of Berlin. There he taught, with enormous knowledge of the original source materials and attention to detail, until his death in 1850. In 1839 he was elected to membership in the Berlin Academy of Sciences.

August Neander was the originator and most important representative of what was called *Pektoraltheologie*—theology of the heart (from the phrase *"Pectus est, quod theologum facit"*—the heart makes the theologian). Instead of a rationalistic pragmatic understanding of history, he saw the subject of church history as the dialectical tension between the spirit of Christ and the spirit of the world. Friend of students, of deep personal piety, involved in the revival movement of his time, he may be seen as one of the fathers of modern Evangelicalism. Unlike Ferdinand Christian Baur, he did not offer a clear language and system in his scholarship.

References and Further Reading

Primary Sources:

Monographs on Clement Alexandrinus (1811), Julian (1812), Bernhard of Clairvaux (1813), Chrysostomos (1822), Tertullian (1824).

Allgemeine Geschichte der christlichen Religion und Kirche. 11 vols. 1826–1851 (transl. New York 1882); *Geschichte der Pflanzung und Leitung der christlichen Kirche durch die Apostel* [*Petrinismus, Paulinismus, Johanneismus*]. 2 vols. 1832/33 (transl. New York 1847); *Das Leben Jesu.* 1837 [in response to David Friedrich Strauß] (transl. New York 1848); *Gesamtausgabe der Werke.* 14 vols. 1862–1875.

Secondary Sources:

Harnack, Adolf von. *Rede auf August Neander.* Berlin: G. Reimer, 1889.

Kaufmann, Frank. "August Neander and Ferdinand Christian Baur." In *Foundations of Modern Church History.* New York: Peter Lang, 1992.

Schaff, Philip. *August Neander. Erinnerungen.* Gotha: Perthes, 1886.

Schneider, Karl Theodor. *August Neander, Beiträge zu seinem Leben und Wirken,* 1894.

GERHARD SCHWINGE

NEE, WATCHMAN (NI TUOSHENG) (1903–1972)

Chinese church leader. An internationally recognized Chinese Protestant church leader who in the 1920s created a new Chinese vocabulary for the Christian Holiness movement in his major work, *The Spiritual Man,* Watchman Nee also set standards for independent "local churches" that profoundly affected developments in mainline and separatist church work within twentieth-century CHINA. Nee was born in Swatow (Guangdong province), China on November 4, 1903. He was a third-generation Chinese Congregationalist and was deeply influenced by PLYMOUTH BRETHREN theology and KESWICK MOVEMENT spirituality. Consequently he promoted an antidenominational vision of church life that promoted Chinese Christian leadership in churches and a sectarian exclusivism. More significantly, *The Spiritual Man* presented the first systematic attempt at explaining a trichotomist view of spirituality in Chinese, and so influenced many more Chinese and foreign Christians than those actually participating in "Little Flock" congregations. By 1949 more than 500 assemblies in China were directly associated with Nee's movement.

Although he was imprisoned in 1952 by the Communist government, and died while still a prisoner on June 1, 1972, his influence spread by other means. English translations of many of his writings were first produced in the 1950s and later translated into more than twenty other languages, making him a well-known and sometimes controversial theological influence. In seeking for holiness, Nee placed the spirit in principled opposition to the soul and body, producing a form of SANCTIFICATION that tended toward anti-intellectual and ascetic patterns of life. Its extremities met needs of those under the duress of China's tumultuous modernity, and so has also received attention in some international circles of EVANGELICALISM, PENTECOSTALISM, and FUNDAMENTALISM.

See also Congregationalism; Holiness Movement; House Churches, Asia

References and Further Reading

Primary Source:

Nee, Tousheng. *Ni Tousheng zhushu quanji (A Comprehensive Collection of the Works of Watchman Nee).* 30 vols. Hong Kong: Heavenly Manna Press, 1991–1995.

Secondary Sources:

Kinnear, Angus I. *Against the Tide: The Story of Watchman Nee.* Eastbourne, Sussex, UK: Victory Press, 1973.

Lam, Wing-hung. *Shuling shenxue: Ni Tousheng sixiang de yanjiu (Spiritual Theology: A Study of the Thought of Watchman Nee).* Hong Kong: Chinese Graduate School of Theology, 1985.

Leung, Ka-lun. "Shuling ren yu Ni Tousheng de sanyuan renlun—jian lun Bin Luyi shimu dui ta de yingxiang" ("Trichotomistic Anthropology of Watchman Nee in *The Spiritual Man*—Also Discussing the Influence of Jessie Penn-Lewis on Nee"). *Alliance Bible Seminary Centenary* 13 (December 1999): 183–232.

LAUREN F. PFISTER

NEILL, STEPHEN CHARLES (1900–1984)

Anglican missionary scholar. Neill was born on December 31, 1900 in Edinburgh, SCOTLAND, and became one of the twentieth century's most notable leaders of Christian mission, and scholars of mission and its sources in Christian history. A graduate of Trinity College, CAMBRIDGE UNIVERSITY, Neill became an Anglican missionary in INDIA in 1924 and was consecrated bishop of Tinnevelly in 1938. Forced to return to ENGLAND for health reasons in 1944, he taught at Cambridge until 1947 when he became active in international ecumenical affairs (see ECUMENISM). Neill became a major figure in the organization of the CHURCH OF SOUTH INDIA in the late 1940s, an ecumenical union DENOMINATION formed from Protestant groups that had developed missionary presences during the colonial era. At the same time Neill was also active in the formation of the WORLD COUNCIL OF CHURCHES and became a noted lecturer on ecumenical matters.

A prolific writer, Neill gained large audiences for his books, several of which continue to be cited frequently. His most notable works, all of which have gone through multiple editions and several of which remain in print, include: *A History of the Ecumenical Movement* (first published in 1953), *Anglicanism* (1958), *Christian Faith and Other Faiths* (1961), and *History of Christian Missions* (1964). Neill's influence rested on his recognition that the era of MISSIONS based on colonial empire was ending, and that the churches faced the challenge of grounding mission in indigenous forms. As a result he became an avid proponent of Christian dialogue with other religions. Late in life he remained active as a theological lecturer and served faculties in disparate locations including GERMANY and Kenya.

Neill died on July 20, 1984 in Oxford, England. His autobiography, *God's Apprentice* (which appeared in an edited form in 1991, after his death), offers the most substantive assessment of his legacy to date.

See also Colonialism; Dialogue, Interconfessional; Missions

References and Further Reading

Primary Sources:

Neill, Stephen, ed., *A History of the Ecumenical Movement.* 2 vols. Philadelphia, PA: Westminster, 1967–1970.

———. *Anglicanism.* New York: Penguin, 1958, 1965; subsequent editions, London: Mowbrays, 1977.

———. *Christian Faith and Other Faiths.* Oxford: Oxford University Press, 1961; Downers Grove, IL: InterVarsity Press, 1984.

———. *History of Christian Missions.* New York: Penguin, 1964, 1973, 1986.

———. *History of Christianity in India: Beginnings to 1707.* Cambridge: Cambridge University Press, 1984.

———. *History of Christianity in India, 1707–1858.* Cambridge: Cambridge University Press, 1985.

———. *God's Apprentice: The Autobiography of Stephen Neill.* London: Hodder & Stoughton, 1991.

Secondary Source:

Cragg, Kenneth and Chadwick, Owens, eds. *Stephen Charles Neill, 1900–1984.* London: British Academy, 1986.

WILLIAM SACHS

NEOLOGY

The term *neology,* roughly meaning "new word," denotes German Protestant (mainly Lutheran) THEOLOGY that was prominent in the middle decades of the 1700s. Neologian theologians embraced the ideas of the ENLIGHTENMENT while remaining within the church and seeking to purify theology and defend Christianity. Leading representatives include Johann Friedrich Wilhelm Jerusalem (1709–1789), Friedrich Samuel Gottfried Sack (1738–1817), and JOHANN JOACHIM SPALDING (1714–1804). JOHANN SALOMO SEMLER (1725–1791) is also sometimes classed with the Neologians. The term "neology" signified that this movement was a *new* teaching, presumably in contrast to the systems of orthodox theology prevalent at that time. However, this term is something of a misnomer, given that Neologians were attempting to restore what they understood to be the original and pure form of Christianity, not to introduce a new teaching.

Neology and Deism

Influences on Neologians were many because they tended to be philosophically eclectic. They were not system-builders but administrators and reformers. Their main concern was religious and pastoral, not philosophical. As a result they borrowed selectively from GOTTFRIED WILHELM LEIBNIZ, CHRISTIAN WOLFF, and English deists, in spite of the fact that Leibniz and Wolff were, in most respects, far more theologically conservative than were the English deists, and in spite of their anxiety about the tendencies of radical deists.

For this reason, it is important not to simply classify the Neologians as German deists, at least if DEISM means the philosophical agenda advanced by the radical French and even English critics of Christianity or by biblical critics such as HERMANN SAMUEL REIMARUS. Although the Neologians seemed radical and destructive enough to orthodox Protestant theologians, unlike the radical deists they were not anticlerical and did not seek the elimination of the CHURCH. On the contrary, leading Neologians were ordained ministers and filled important roles in the church. For example, Jerusalem served, in 1771, as vice president of the CONSISTORY (the regional church council) of Wolfenbüttel. He also served for some years as court preacher and several times was offered the position of general superintendent of the state church in Magdeburg. Neologians, then, did not desire the end of the church. In fact, Neology may be regarded as an apologetic effort directed against the attacks of rationalist critics of Christianity. An example of their apologetic efforts was Spalding's 1756 translation of Bishop JOSEPH BUTLER's defense of revealed religion and critique of rationalism, *The Analogy of Religion.* At the same time, although loyal supporters of the church, they were sharply critical of some of its doctrines and practices. It is this criticism for which they are best known. However, even their critical program arose, not solely from rationalistic impulses but instead from their conviction that they were continuing the task of purifying religion that had been begun but, in their opinion, left incomplete by the sixteenth-century reformers. Accordingly, their critical and reforming agenda must be seen in the light of their ecclesiastical commitments and their theological temperament, which was, in comparison with the radical deists, quite conservative.

Neology and Natural Religion

Like the deists, Neologians affirmed the concept of natural religion. Natural religion was regarded as the original and universal religion of the human race at its beginning. However, in calling this original religion natural, Neologians did not intend to distinguish it from revealed religion. Natural religion was not, in their conception, a religion derived strictly from human reasoning; instead it rested on an original revelation to humankind. Further, subsequent revelations (the religion of Moses and, later, Christianity) were necessary to restore this original religion. Neologians disagreed as to the historical function of Christianity in this scheme, some holding it to be merely a confirmation of the original religion, others regarding it as a further development of that religion. Nonetheless Neology stood for the belief that Christianity does not in any way contradict natural religion and is in fact another revelation of natural religion. Of course, what they understood by Christianity differed somewhat from the orthodox conception. In their view natural religion and Christianity are essentially a matter of moral duties toward God and neighbor, the promise of future blessedness, plus ancillary doctrines about God. However, they argued, to this simple, moral religion had been attached a great many doctrines, rites, and practices that do not correspond to natural religion and that in fact obscure it. The sixteenth-century reformers, they held, had made a good beginning in the return to natural religion; however, the return had been interrupted by the rise of Protestant ORTHODOXY. The task at hand, as they saw it, was to pick up where the reformers had left off.

Continuing Reform

It is important to keep this point in mind because it shows that Neology was part of a broader eighteenth-century movement of reform and change in the Protestant churches, a movement whose other prominent member was PIETISM. Although the specific aims of Pietists differed significantly from those of the Neologians, the overall goal of the two was ostensibly the same, that is to continue the reforming work of MARTIN LUTHER and the other reformers. Neology and Pietism were thus jointly opposed to the assumption of orthodox theologians that the church's main task was maintaining purity of DOCTRINE. For the Neologians

and the Pietists, on the contrary, the main concern was the Christian life and the need to promote sound practice. Although neither entirely discounted the importance of doctrine, both tended to judge its role and the validity of particular doctrines by their relation to the Christian life. Both were concerned to overcome what they saw as a deleterious separation between doctrine and practice at work in orthodox Protestant theology. Of course Pietists and Neologians had dramatically different conceptions of the Christianity that would result from their reforming work. They also had correspondingly different interpretations of Luther and the REFORMATION. Pietists took orthodox theology for granted and wished to emphasize practice as a necessary complement to pure doctrine. Neologians, on the contrary, were interested in a wholesale renovation of doctrines, some of which they regarded as obstacles to sound practice. As a result, Neologians generally proved to be more critical of specific doctrines than did Pietists. As the century progressed, Pietists increasingly came to see the danger of Neology's questioning and rejecting doctrines. Accordingly they began moving in a more conservative direction and warmed to the interests of the orthodox theologians. However, in spite of these significant differences between the two movements, we understand Neology rightly only if we recognized its intention to do for its own generation what Luther did for his and only if we see the vital similarity between Neology and Pietism and their common struggle against the orthodox theological establishment. The lesson to be drawn is that the central theological issue in GERMANY in the 1700s was not, as it was in other countries, whether Christianity is the true religion. The Neologians affirmed the validity of Christianity as heartily as did the Pietists and orthodox theologians. The issue was instead about how best to understand Christianity and the role of doctrine in relation to practice.

Revelation and Reason

The Neologians' critique of traditional doctrine rested on their view of natural religion and revelation. In orthodox theology of all confessions in this period, revelation was understood to be a supernatural communication of truths that are beyond human comprehension. The doctrine of the Trinity, for example, was generally regarded as a doctrine that human reason could neither discover nor understand. It rests, it was held, on biblical passages that reveal truths about God. Because the biblical truths surpass human understanding, they must, it was argued, have been supernaturally communicated to the human authors of the BIBLE through an act of inspiration. Neologians rejected every aspect of this theory. They did not accept the premise that revelation is the impartation of incomprehensible truths because in their view true religion is simple and moral. The doctrines of natural religion, they held, constituted a few tenets such as belief in God, in God's providential care, in the immortality of the soul, and future blessedness. Consequently, revelation contains only the doctrines required for obedience to God's moral commands. The revelatory importance of Jesus Christ, then, was not that he disclosed hitherto unknown and intrinsically incomprehensible doctrines, but that he demonstrated true religion in his own day and thus showed the way back to it. They also rejected the orthodox view of the Bible's inspiration. Because the Bible's truths are not supernatural, there was no need to believe in a supernatural mechanism for their transmission. This conviction was buttressed by the Neologians' involvement in the budding biblical criticism of their day. Analysis of the various sources behind Genesis and other biblical books tended to convince them that the Bible's composition was a completely natural process and not superintended by supernatural providence.

With such a view, Neologians were committed to the agreement between reason and revelation and to overcoming the opposition between the natural and the supernatural. This placed them in opposition both to orthodox theology and to extreme rationalists. In disagreement with orthodox theologians, Neologians did not hold that revelation is above human reason; instead, they asserted, it is fully reasonable. At the same time, unlike the more extreme rationalists, they did not suggest that reason is autonomous and can replace revelation. Although the content of revelation is fully reasonable, revelation is not thereby rendered unnecessary. On the contrary it was the means by which humankind had originally received the truths of natural religion and was subsequently needed to help humankind return to natural religion.

View of the Bible

Their critical attitude toward revelation and inspiration did not induce the Neologians to reject the Bible's validity. Unlike Reimarus, for example, they did not question the truthfulness and honesty of the apostles. On the contrary, they saw in the Bible the perfect antidote to orthodox theology's proliferation of complex doctrines through the construction of creeds. The Bible, they held, although the product of human thought, bears witness to the simplicity of natural religion in contrast to the speculative and incomprehensible doctrinal edifice of orthodox theology, with its authoritarian and supernatural overtones. It is evident, then, that one of the underlying disagreements between Neology and orthodox theology was a her-

meneutical issue, that is, how the Bible is to be interpreted. Orthodox theologians insisted that the ecclesiastical creeds express the sense of Scripture and are therefore the only sure guide to its meaning. The Neologians contrasted the Bible and the creeds and argued that the creeds distort the meaning of the Bible. In place of the creeds they employed the notion of natural religion and its relation to the practical life as their hermeneutical guide. As a result various Neologians began giving up such doctrines as original SIN, ATONEMENT by penal satisfaction, and the Trinity, not only because of their reputed lack of significance for the practical Christian life but also because of their poor attestation in the Bible. In addition to this hermeneutical issue, the Neologians had ecumenical concerns. Like later theological liberals, they were convinced that creeds were inherently divisive, unnecessarily separating Christians on the basis of nonessential beliefs (see LIBERAL PROTESTANTISM AND LIBERALISM).

Critical Christology

Not surprisingly, Neologians did not adhere to the orthodox understanding of Jesus Christ. In particular, the doctrine of the Trinity came in for special criticism. Jerusalem, for example, attacked the supposed continuity between the Bible and the tradition of Trinitarian thought (see ANTI-TRINITARIANISM). He drew attention to the diversity of opinion among early church leaders. Further, he argued that the statements of the early church fathers were so indefinite and vague that both proponents and opponents of the doctrine of the Trinity could appeal to them for support. Certain of them, notably Justin Martyr, were demonstrably not orthodox, at least by later standards. Finally, Jerusalem noted that, whereas the fathers most influenced by Plato are usually the ones called on to support the doctrine of the Trinity, it was non-Platonic writings such as Clement, Barnabas, and Polycarp, writings that are reticent to attribute divinity to Christ, whose teaching most resembles that of the New Testament. Here Jerusalem was introducing the ideas of doctrinal development and diversity. They represented a potentially serious blow to the Trinity and other doctrines because they suggested discontinuity between the Bible and the creeds, with unfavorable results for the creedal tradition.

With respect to interpreting the New Testament, Jerusalem was impressed by Jesus's statement that "The Father is greater than I." This functioned for him as a hermeneutical benchmark by which all other christological statements were judged because it clearly asserts the subordination of Jesus to God the Father. He also put great emphasis on the fact that

Jesus did not expressly claim to be the Logos spoken of in the prologue to John's Gospel. Our understanding of the Logos, he argued, must be taken from the ancient Jewish way of thinking and not from Philo's Platonizing theology. If we understand it so, then the Logos of John's Gospel is seen to be not a preexistent being but instead simply the message of Jesus about God the Father. Consequently, the orthodox view of the incarnation, involving the union of the second person of the Trinity with human nature, is judged to be without Scriptural warrant. Jesus is not the incarnate God but rather the supreme proclaimer of God. This example reveals the Neologians' strategy—profess allegiance to the Bible's true teaching, argue on historical and philological bases that the Bible often does not mean what orthodox theologians have proposed that it means, and then offer a revised interpretation that diminishes the supernatural dimension of the Christian faith and represents the Bible as agreeing with their conception of natural religion.

Neology's Decline

Neology's eventual demise was signaled by GOTTHOLD EPHRAIM LESSING's critique. Although there are similarities between Lessing's theology and that of some Neologians, he opposed their understanding of reason and revelation. Discerning Lessing's own theology poses challenges to the scholar but it can at least be said that he objected to the Neologians' attempt at identifying the content of revelation with a core of simple moral truths and with their subsequent rejection of doctrines like the Trinity. Lessing's attitude toward such doctrines is somewhat complex; however, his overall approach is clear. Like the Neologians, he could not accept these doctrines at face value, although unlike the Neologians, he believed that the doctrines contain important truths that can be rescued through proper philosophical thought and rational comprehension. So, for example, he subjected the doctrine of the Trinity to an analysis that anticipates that of later idealists such as GEORG W. F. HEGEL. The doctrine of the Trinity emerges from this analysis as a completely rational truth about the eternal being of God derived in an utterly speculative manner. In short, Lessing agreed with the Neologians about the impossibility of simply accepting orthodox doctrines in their customary sense. He disagreed with them in his unwillingness to simply reject them wholesale and to reduce revelation to a minimal rational and moral content. Reinterpretation, not rejection, was Lessing's strategy. In this way it was Lessing and not Neology that pointed toward the main developments in Protestant theology in the nineteenth century.

References and Further Reading

Primary Source:

Jerusalem, Johann Friedrich Wilhelm. *Betrachtungen über die vornehmsten Wahrheiten der Religion.* Edited by Wolfgang Erich Müller. Niedersächsische Bibliothek Geistlicher Texte, vol. 2. Hannover, Germany: Lutherisches Verlagshaus, 1991.

Secondary Sources:

Allison, Henry E. *Lessing and the Enlightenment: His Philosophy of Religion and Its Relation to Eighteenth-Century Thought.* Ann Arbor: The University of Michigan Press, 1966.

Aner, Karl. *Die Theologie der Lessingzeit.* Hildesheim, Germany: G. Olms, 1964.

Barth, Karl. *Protestant Theology in the Nineteenth Century: Its Background and History.* London: S.C.M. Press, 1972.

Hirsch, Emanuel. *Geschichte der neueren evangelischen Theologie.* Vol. 4. Gütersloh, Germany: Bertelsmann, 1949–1954.

Lütcke, Karl-Heinrich. "Glaubwürdigkeit durch Bildung. Zum Pfarrerbild und zur Sicht der Theologienausbildung in der Neologie (besonders bei Spaulding und Lüdke)." In *450 Jahre evangelische Theologie in Berlin.* Edited by Gerhard Beiser and Christof Gestrich. Göttingen, Germany: Verlag Vandenhoeck & Ruprecht, 1989.

Müller, Wolfgang Erich. "Von der Eigenständigkeit der Neologie Jerusalems." *Neue Zeitschrift für systematische Theologie* 26 (1984): 289–309.

SAMUEL M. POWELL

NEO-ORTHODOXY

The labeling of theological movements is usually a haphazard, sometimes a misleading, undertaking, especially when it occurs before it is quite clear what is transpiring within such movements. No appelative, however, is more ambiguous than the term "Neo-Orthodoxy," the nomenclature applied to a twentieth-century movement of a number of theologians in Europe, North America, and (to a lesser extent) Great Britain during the approximately fifty-year period ending around 1960 to 1965. The label was probably concocted by critics of the phenomenon so named; it was consistently rejected by almost all of those to whom it was applied; and, although the THEOLOGY in question was perhaps "new" (Neo-), it was certainly not a conscious return to any particular ORTHODOXY except, as we shall argue here, in the most general sense of the term.

Perhaps significantly, the term was used chiefly in the English-speaking world where, for complex reasons, a tendency to generalize and categorize frequently obscures important distinctions. Thus Neo-Orthodoxy came to designate Christian thinkers as distinctive as KARL BARTH, EMIL BRUNNER, RUDOLF BULTMANN, FRIEDRICH GOGARTEN, Gustav Aulen,

ANDERS NYGREN, W. A. VISSER'T HOOFT, Suzanne de Dietrich, REINHOLD and H. RICHARD NIEBUHR, JOHN and DONALD BAILLIE, PAUL TILLICH, DIETRICH BONHOEFFER, and others, despite the often significant differences among them. Tillich, for example, regularly distinguished his own approach, which was governed by an intentional "apologetic" interest, from the "kerygmatic" theology of the Barthian school; and Barth on occasion seemed to consider Tillich only marginally Christian. Whereas H. Richard Niebuhr was close in important ways to both Tillich and Brunner, his more famous brother, Reinhold, was suspicious of the tendency in most explicitly "systematic" theology to ignore the ambiguity of historical judgments in its quest for integration and finality. Thus, although alliances may certainly be discerned among various of these thinkers, it remains an open question whether they have enough in common to be thought a distinctive movement, and whether there is any legitimate reason for calling such a movement Neo-Orthodox.

Opinions on both questions vary still today. The interpretation offered here will elaborate on the following thesis: What the theologians usually associated with this term share is a common confrontation by profound questions arising from the end of an era (Modernity), and the belief, variously applied, that these questions can be addressed meaningfully only by Christians who are prepared to go back *behind* Modernity in their search for a way into the future. Thus Neo-Orthodoxy, despite its severe limitations as a descriptive label, may be said to apply to this movement as a search for roots *(radix)* that go deeper than the contemporary; it should not, however, suggest the reinstatement of any particular or alleged orthodoxy, after the manner, for instance, of the so-called radical orthodoxy of current interest.

Christianity and the End of Modernity

Much to the puzzlement of many of his North American students, Paul Tillich frequently announced to his classes in the UNITED STATES that the nineteenth century ended on August 1, 1914. There can be no doubt that "The Great War," as it was called before World War II, constituted for most of these thinkers a decisive watershed. As Tillich would later say, the war "absolutely transformed" him:

> A night attack came, and all night long I moved among the wounded and dying men, and much of my German classical philosophy broke down that night—the belief that man could master cognitively the essence of his being . . . , the belief in the identity of essence and existence. [TIME Magazine, vol. LXXIII no. 11 (March 16, 1959): 47]

Although the war punctuated the demise of the Modern vision, however, for sensitive Europeans it only made obvious what was already brewing in the social upheavals created by the late phase of the Industrial Revolution (see INDUSTRIALIZATION), that is, the recognition that scientific and technological ingenuity did not translate automatically into Progress. Liberal Christianity had so naively endorsed Modernity, abandoning in the process the "negative" dimensions of historic Christianity (SIN, evil, the demonic, etc.) to accommodate the faith to the great expectations of the ENLIGHTENMENT, that Liberalism had nothing to say in the face of Modernity's humiliation (see LIBERAL PROTESTANTISM AND LIBERALISM). Barth in Europe and Reinhold Niebuhr in America found themselves, with others of their generation, cast back on scripture and TRADITION in their attempt to comprehend the *Zeitgeist* and to address, as Christians, their contemporaries.

Barth, whose earliest writings predate World War I, and whose electrifying *Romerbrief* (commentary on Paul's *Romans*) is widely regarded as the first call to arms of the new theology, had already experienced the limitations of theological Liberalism before the black day on which he discovered the signatures of many of his revered Liberal teachers in a newspaper statement endorsing the war policies of Kaiser Wilhelm II. Like Reinhold Niebuhr a little later on in his pastorate in Henry Ford's Detroit, Barth in his small Swiss parish of Safenwil, a mill town, soon realized the inadequacy of Liberal Christianity for addressing the growing rift between unchecked capitalism and unorganized labor. Both men, moreover, grasped intuitively the manner in which Christianity, by the very fact of its (legal or cultural) establishment, lent its support to the economic and political status quo. Reclaiming the legacy of SØREN KIERKEGAARD, their critique targeted not only Liberalism but Christendom as such, that is, the identification of the Christian faith with the regnant values and pursuits of Western (and notably Middle Class) societies. To exercise a prophetic ministry in the world, the Christian church, they realized, would have to speak and act from a vantage point transcendent of its immediate historical context. Barth found this vantage point in a christological-existential ("pneumatic") reading of the scriptures; Niebuhr in the Hebraic prophetic tradition, informed by Augustinian and Lutheran perspectives.

Of neither of these men, however (and in this they are representative of most of the theologians under discussion), could it be said that they acted out of "conservative" Christian concern against the reigning Protestant Liberalism of the period. Not only had they themselves been thoroughly formed by nineteenth- and the early twentieth-century Liberal schools, including the SOCIAL GOSPEL, neither of them ever relinquished certain rudimentary assumptions of Liberalism—notably, as W. Pauck has observed, the assumption that all theology is historically conditioned. Barth has often been accused of biblicism—or, alternately, taken up by biblicists as one of their own! However, Barth's approach to the BIBLE has nothing in common with biblical literalism. He reads the scriptures as one conspicuously informed by the specificities of twentieth-century existence; and what he finds in the Bible is a "strange new world" that is at least as foreign to biblicism and FUNDAMENTALISM as it is to theological MODERNISM. Although he mistrusted the attempt of Bultmann to "demythologize" the New Testament, he was well aware of the pitfalls of reading ancient texts as though they were immediately accessible to the scientific mind. Similarly, Reinhold Niebuhr, whose Germanic background made him sensitive to both the positive and the negative legacies of LUTHERANISM, had no interest in conserving Lutheran doctrine. He used MARTIN LUTHER, as he used Augustine, to counter the PIETISM, sentimentality, and moralism of American religion and life, and as an alternative to the doctrinaire CALVINISM so prominent in U.S. history. Comparable observations could be made of Brunner, Tillich, Aulen, and other participants in this renewal.

In short, "Neo-Orthodoxy" was driven primarily by a concern for the present and impending future, not for the preservation of the past. These theologians visited the past—whether through a fresh encounter with scripture, the history of doctrine, philosophic traditions, or literature and the arts—for the light that it could shed on the present. Western civilization was in crisis (the earliest designation of the new theology, and still perhaps the best, was "theology of crisis"). The question was whether, beyond the impasse of Modernity, the West could recover hope for the future, and whether the religion that had aligned itself too uncritically with modern Western presuppositions and ideals could contribute to such a project.

If one may generalize, the answer given by these thinkers was that such a hope could be fashioned only if (1) the rationalism of Modernity was seriously displaced or supplemented by ways of knowing that could do greater justice to the human spirit; (2) the utopianism of Modernity were challenged by biblical and pragmatic realism; (3) the anthropological optimism of Modernity were countered by an honest recognition of the human capacity for evil, its collective pathos, and the tragic dimension of existence.

1. The critique of rationalism meant, for all concerned, the rediscovery of the Pauline and Reformation emphasis on divine revelation. Barth was the great champion of revelation—to the point, in Bonhoeffer's well-known criticism, of presenting the world with a new "positivism of revelation." There can be no doubt, however, that it was the very one-sidedness of Barth's "fideistic" conception of the knowledge of God that shocked a complacent European church into a new realization of its actual distance from its CULTURE. In his famous confrontation with Emil Brunner over the question of "natural theology" (or "general revelation"), Barth set the tone for a revitalized appreciation of the potentiality of Reformed faith for prophetic vigilance—an appreciation much needed in the face of the current Nazi ideology. It was this same sense of "the infinite qualitative distinction between time and eternity" that informed the famous BARMEN DECLARATION, which was chiefly the work of Karl Barth. Brunner, H. Richard Niebuhr, and Tillich, all of whom also pursued the theme of revelation, nevertheless understood more poignantly than Barth that a Christianity relevant to the post-Christendom world could not afford to abandon so totally its historic dialogue with human reason. Tillich's "method of correlation" gives revelation priority in terms of the Christian message, although it assumes that in human thought and experience there is and must be, nonetheless, a preparation for gospel *(praeparatio evangelica.)*

2. The challenge to Modern utopianism, whether in its capitalist or its Marxist expression, was particularly addressed by Reinhold Niebuhr, whose *Moral Man and Immoral Society* many consider a classic of this movement. In the midst of a nation more devoted to utopian fantasy than any other (what has been called *The American Dream*), Niebuhr in his books and almost daily journalistic commentary attacked the pretensions of the Modern project. In his *Faith and History* Niebuhr argued that both of the founding traditions of Western civilization embrace a realism wholly ignored by Modernity. The KINGDOM OF GOD, contrary to popular Liberalism, could only be approximated, not realized, in history. This did not imply for Niebuhr an ethic of passivity, however. Despite the ambiguity of history and the duplicity of human motivation, proximate goals must be sought, and can be achieved.

3. Perhaps the greatest challenge to the Modern world view, however, was the nearly unanimous decision of these theologians that the anthropological optimism of the Modern experiment was without foundations. In Europe, where Existentialism presented a secular critique with which Christianity could often make common cause, and where events made unavoidable the reality of human sin and suffering, the recurrence of neglected hamartiological themes in Christian theology was not surprising: Paul Tillich could even revive the discussion of "the demonic" in

the GERMANY of the 1930s. In America, however, the anthropological realism of the Niebuhrs, JOHN COLEMAN BENNETT, GEORGIA HARKNESS, and others was received with shock and disdain. Reinhold Niebuhr's picture appeared on the cover of TIME magazine's twenty-fifth anniversary issue above the heading "Man's story is not a success story." Throughout his life this most renowned of American theologians, who, arguably, inspired more concrete activity in the area of social ethics than any Christian thinker in history, was accused of "pessimism." His magnum opus, *The Nature and Destiny of Man,* delivered as the Gifford Lectures as German bombs were falling on Edinburgh, contained two whole chapters on sin. In a society that seemed to its policy-making classes to surpass forever the dark predictions of the pre-Modern world, such an emphasis could only appear retrograde. Yet, Niebuhr argues, with most other spokespersons of this movement, that unless contemporary society could find the courage to acknowledge the stark reality of such evils as racism, poverty, violence, crime, WAR, and genocide (Auschwitz), civilization would flounder on the rocks of a repressive and illusionary idealism.

A Quest for Wholeness

The effective demise of Modernity evoked in thoughtful Christians and others the suspicion that something had been lost in the transition from the Medieval and Reformation ages to the Modern epoch. Silently, one felt, a certain insidious reductionism had occurred. The high anthropology contained in the traditions both of Athens and Jerusalem had been extricated from the pathos and sense of the tragic equally important to those foundational traditions. The result was a techno-culture documented, somewhat later, by Jacques Ellul and others—a civilization fixated on the naive yet dangerous concept of human mastery over nature and history, undergirded by a religion deprived of mystery, depth, and the dialectical tensions between faith and doubt, hope and history, love and suffering. Such a religion could hardly withstand the scrutiny of the great nineteenth-century "mis-evangelists" (Rosenstock-Huessy's designation of LUDWIG FEUERBACH, Sigmund Freud, FRIEDRICH NIETZSCHE, and Karl Marx), let alone the world-shattering events that ushered in the century that was supposed to have become "The Christian Century."

What had been lost, and what might be recovered through a reexamination of the biblical, medieval, Reformation, and other dimensions of the pre-Modern tradition? Such a retrospective interest was bound to seem regressive to a society and church indoctrinated in "the Religion of Progress" (George P. Grant.) It is said that his fellow-students at Union Theological Seminary in New York City registered astonishment when the young Dietrich Bonhoeffer made reference, as he regularly did, to the sixteenth-century reformers. Undoubtedly it was this "novel" respect for tradition that suggested to critics of the movement the nomenclature, Neo-Orthodox.

Certainly the Reformation was of particular interest to the majority of these thinkers—to the extent, indeed, that some have proposed that the movement is more accurately designated Neo-Reformation Theology. Submerged aspects of the Reformation began to dominate theological-ecumenical discourse: its christological-soteriological core; the "material principle" of JUSTIFICATION by GRACE through FAITH; the "formal principle" of the primacy of scripture (*sola scriptura*); the alternative to Christendom's triumphalism named by Luther *theologia cruces,* and so forth. Yet the reworking of classical Protestantism was only part of the "research" characteristic of the period. Eventually, Barth's grand enterprise impelled him to review the entire evolution of Christian thought. Such an observation can be made of Brunner, Aulen, and Tillich as well, and Tillich's work represents a quite unprecedented Protestant interest in both the history of philosophy and medieval theology. Above all, biblical exegesis and the origins of Christianity necessarily acquired a new prominence in theological discourse, and indeed Neo-Orthodoxy inspired and was inspired by a whole new era of biblical scholarship.

As intimated, however, none of this implies an antiquarian interest. As with all profound revolutions, what was occurring here was a search for foundations—for "a usable past." Furthermore, what particularly informs this search is an obvious and even a deliberate attempt to overcome the simplism and one-sidedness of theological Liberalism through a greater grasp of the whole tradition. For that reason the most influential among these theologians were led to enucleate whole new "systems" of theology—and this in an age when systematic theology or Christian dogmatics were considered passé. Barth, Brunner, and Tillich all produced magnificent multivolumed works that compare in scope and imagination only with those of Thomas and JOHN CALVIN. The smaller but highly influential publications of both Niebuhrs, Bultmann, HENDRIK KRAEMER, Nygren, Bonhoeffer, and others all manifest a quest for wholeness that, with a few exceptions, was lost to subsequent theological movements. Barth's *Kirchliche Dogmatik* of course constitutes the most remarkable testimony to this twentieth-century search for wholeness; nevertheless, what the old Barth said of his labors could be thought representative of the movement generally:

I said to myself, "If I am a theologian, I must try to work out broadly what I think I have perceived as God's revelation. What I think *I* have perceived. Yet not I as an individual but I as a member of the Christian Church." This is why I call my book *Church Dogmatics*. (Erler and Marquadt 1986:113)

This deceptively simple statement contains yet another dimension of the quest for wholeness—its orientation toward the CHURCH. In marked contrast to the "academic" bent of much subsequent Christian scholarship, all of the leading thinkers of this movement understood their *raison d'être* as theologians to be bound up with the community of Christ's discipleship. Most of them in fact began their professional careers as parish clergy; and, although they were all critical of empirical Christianity, they did not manifest anything approaching the detachment from or cynicism concerning the churches that has often typified more recent theological reflection. It is indeed probable that the ecumenical movement itself could not have come to be apart from their witness and work because most of them were personally active in the WORLD COUNCIL OF CHURCHES and other ecumenical agencies throughout their careers (see ECUMENISM).

Given both the depth and scope of this movement and the association of its leading lights with the actual life of ecumenical Christianity, it is perhaps strange that the movement has exercised so little lasting influence within the churches; yet, although the great theologians of Neo-Orthodoxy continue to inform academic theology in most present-day Christian SEMINARIES and elsewhere, their impact on ecclesiastical life seems deplorably minimal. Despite the fact that Neo-Orthodoxy represents a clear alternative to both theological Liberalism and ultraconservative religion, the struggles of the churches today still reflect the conventional polarization of Right and Left; indeed, the theologians of this movement are all too often co-opted, *in absentia,* for membership in one or other of these camps. No doubt this presages a cultural incapacity for nuance that is especially conspicuous in the North American context, as well as preoccupation with the allegedly "practical" and with sheer survival. Yet it is surely unfortunate that this great revitalization of Protestantism did not translate itself more concretely into the life of the churches—and precisely at a time when the humiliation and depletion of mainstream Protestantism requires of these churches exactly such a theological renewal.

In part, the failure can be explained by the emergence, just at the conclusion of the period under discussion (1960–1970), of social concerns that were not sufficiently anticipated by the leading figures of this movement: questions of race, GENDER, sexual orientation, the environment, multiculturalism, religious plurality, the demise of Marxism and the subsequent hegemony of U.S.-dominated economic globalism, and so forth. Although important background for all such questions may (and should be!) gleaned from the writings of these theologians, response to the instabilities and crises concerned had of course to come from Christian spokespersons for the issues and identities directly involved in them. This has necessitated a specificity of concern, the negative consequence of which has been a loss both of the wholeness sought in Neo-Orthodoxy and of its orientation toward the ecumenical church. One suspects that such identity- and cause-specific theologies were obliged by the very character of their agendas to set aside the quest for wholeness; but it is equally necessary for the future of the Christian movement generally that it should recover that quest as it seeks to conduct its mission of hope in a post-Christendom, post-Modern civilization. Perhaps something of that nature is already occurring in the attempts, here and there, to listen again to the remembered voices of our near past.

References and Further Reading

Primary Sources:

Aulen, Gustaf. *The Faith of the Christian Church.* Philadelphia: Muhlenberg Press, 1948.
———. *Christus Victor: An Historical Study of the Three Main Types of the Idea of the Atonement.* London: Society for Promoting Christian Knowledge, 1953.
Barth, Karl. *The Knowledge of God and the Service of God.* Gifford Lectures 1937–1938. London: Lodder and Stoughton, 1938.
———. *Evangelical Theology: An Introduction.* New York: 1963.
———. *Dogmatics in Outline.* London: Philosophical Library, 1949.
———. *The Humanity of God.* Richmond, VA: John Knox Press, 1960.
———. *The Word of God and the Word of Man.* New York: Harper & Row, 1957.
Baillie, Donald. *God Was in Christ: An Essay on Incarnation and Atonement.* London: Faber & Faber, 1947.
Baillie, John. *Our Knowledge of God.* New York: Charles Scribner's Sons, 1939.
Bonhoeffer, Dietrich. *The Cost of Discipleship.* London: SCM Press, 1948.
———. *Ethics.* London: SCM Press, 1955.
———. *Letters and Papers from Prison.* London: SCM Press, 1953.
Brunner, Emil. *The Theology of Crisis.* New York: Charles Scribner's Sons, 1929.
———. *The Divine–Human Encounter.* London: SCM Press, 1944.
———. *Dogmatics.* 3 vols. Philadelphia, PA: Westminster Press, 1950–1992.
Bultmann, Rudolf. *Theology of the New Testament.* 2 vols. New York: Charles Scribner's Sons, 1951.
———. *Primitive Christianity in its Contemporary Setting.* New York: Meridian Books, 1956.

———. *Essays*. New York, 1955.

Niebuhr, H. Richard. *The Meaning of Revelation*. New York: MacMillian, 1941.

———. *Christ and Culture*. New York: Harper & Row, 1951.

Niebuhr, Reinhold. *Interpretation of Christian Ethics*. New York: Harper & Brothers, 1935.

———. *Beyond Tragedy*. New York: Charles Scribner's Sons, 1937.

———. *The Essential Reinhold Niebuhr*. Edited by R. M. Brown. New Haven: Yale University Press, 1986.

Nygren, Anders. *Agape and Eros: A Study of the Christian Idea of Love*. Philadelphia, PA: Westminster, 1953.

Tillich, Paul. *Systematic Theology*. Chicago: University of Chicago Press, 1951–1963.

———. *The Protestant Era*. Chicago: University of Chicago Press, 1948.

———. *The Shaking of the Foundations*. New York: Charles Scribner's Sons, 1948.

———. *The Courage to Be*. New Haven, CT: Yale University Press, 1952.

Secondary Sources:

Baum, Gregory. *Twentieth Century Theology: An Overview*. Maryknoll, NY: Orbis, 1999.

Erler, Rolf Joachim, and Reiner Marquard, eds. *A Karl Barth Reader*. Translated by Geoffrey W. Bromiley. Grand Rapids, MI: Wm. B. Eerdmans, 1986.

Hall, Douglas John. *Remembered Voices: Reclaiming the Legacy of "Neo-Orthodoxy."* Louisville, KY: Westminster John Knox Press, 1998.

Gaudin, Gary, and Douglas John Hall. *Reinhold Niebuhr (1892–1971): A Centenary Appraisal*. Atlanta, GA: Scholars Press, 1994.

Heron, Alasdair. *A Century of Protestant Theology*. Philadelphia, PA: Westminster, 1980.

Hordern, William. *A Layman's Guide to Protestant Theology*. New York: Macmillan, 1955.

Kegley, Charles. *The Theology of Emil Brunner*. New York: Macmillan, 1962.

———, and Robert W. Bretall, eds. *The Theology of Paul Tillich*. New York: Macmillan, 1952.

———, eds. *Reinhold Niebuhr: His Religious, Social and Political Thought*. New York: Macmillan, 1956.

Pauck, Wilhelm. *From Luther to Tillich: The Reformers and Their Heirs*. San Francisco: Harper & Row, 1984.

Peerman, Dean, and Martin E. Marty. *A Handbook of Christian Theologians*. Cleveland, OH: World Publishing Company, 1965.

Robinson, John A. T. *Honest to God*. 40th Anniversary edition. Louisville, KY: Westminster John Knox Press, 2003.

Smart, James D. *Revolutionary Theology in the Making*. Richmond, VA: John Knox Press, 1964.

DOUGLAS JOHN HALL

THE NETHERLANDS

Origins of the Dutch Reformation (Sixteenth Century)

The Dutch Republic came into being in the sixteenth century during the revolt against the Spanish power. In the first decades of that century, the many territories at the estuaries of the Rhine, Meuse, and Scheldt Rivers had been successively included under the rule of the Emperor Charles V in a process of centralization that had already been started by the Burgundian Dukes. Around 1550, the Netherlands consisted roughly of the present Kingdom of the Netherlands, the Kingdom of Belgium, and the Grand Duchy of Luxemburg. Because King of Spain Charles V usually resided in Madrid, he was represented in the Low Countries by a governor in Brussels. At the head of the provinces, stadholders were his representatives. The total population of the Netherlands was about 2,000,000; the density was greatest in Flanders and Brabant.

As in other European countries, in the Netherlands the Roman Catholic Church was seriously affected by many abuses. At least the burden of tradition hindered the effects of the biblical message. At Antwerp, the biggest mercantile center of Western Europe, signs of the REFORMATION movement first came to light. Nearly immediately, the church and state authorities deemed it necessary to respond. HERESY was considered a deadly danger for society. In 1519, the University of Louvain had already condemned MARTIN LUTHER's books. The first MARTYRS of European Protestantism were two Antwerp monks, Hendrik Vos and Johannes van Essen, who were executed in the marketplace at Brussels on July 1, 1523.

Nevertheless, everywhere evidence of growing Protestantism could be noted, including in the northern provinces, partly as a consequence of the criticism of former ages and partly due to the direct influence of Luther himself. From the very beginning, Protestantism promoted the vernacular translation, printing, and distribution of the BIBLE (see BIBLE TRANSLATION). This was true in the Netherlands by the early 1520s. Besides the direct impact of the Lutheran Reformation, the Swiss reformers HULDRYCH ZWINGLI and HEINRICH BULLINGER had a certain influence in these regions. In many towns, Erasmus's humanistic criticism of the Catholic Church and theology created a certain susceptibility to Reformation ideas. The first martyr in Holland was a married priest, Jan Pistorius of Woerden, burned in The Hague in 1525.

Luther was reluctant to instruct his followers to organize an underground church if the prince did not accept a Protestant CONFESSION, as was the case in the Low Countries. Therefore, his influence remained restricted. Anabaptists were the first to appeal to the broad masses in the Netherlands and to create a separate church organization secretly outside the Catholic Church. In 1530, Jan Volkertsz Trypmaker, a disciple of MELCHIOR HOFMANN, traveled throughout the northern provinces to bring BAPTISM on confession of faith.

He was executed in 1531. Persecution of ANABAPTISM was extremely severe.

Great commotion in the Netherlands was caused by the revolutionary apocalyptic preaching of those Anabaptists who believed the New Jerusalem had arrived in the city of Münster (Westphalia) under the leadership of Jan van Leiden, who proclaimed himself King of Sion (1534). Community of goods and polygamy were proclaimed, while every opposition was suppressed. Order was restored in Münster in 1535, and the Anabaptist leaders were punished severely. After this revolutionary period, Anabaptism entered a new phase in which nonviolence became its main characteristic along with believers' baptism. Nevertheless, tales of the Münster excesses haunted the quiet Anabaptists for generations.

It was MENNO SIMONS who was able to acquire the leadership in the Dutch Anabaptist movement in opposition to Georg David and other, more radical preachers. Menno constantly traveled through Dutch and German regions to assemble the scattered flock. The so-called "MENNONITES" remained a strong minority in the Netherlands. In the 1540s, CALVINISM entered the provinces bordering FRANCE. JOHN CALVIN sent Pierre Bruly to Valenciennes in 1544, but Bruly was arrested and executed early in 1545, becoming the first martyr of the Reformed Church in the Netherlands. Despite the increasing persecution, Reformed congregations were founded, at first in the southern provinces. Calvinism became rather popular among the West Flemish workers. In the 1560s, demonstrations for religious freedom arose in Tournai and other cities. The first Calvinistic (or Reformed) preachers arrived in the northern provinces in the 1550s. Many Reformed people escaped the severe oppression and fled to the surrounding territories, such as Emden (eastern Frisia). Refugee communities were founded in London and other English ports, as well as in some German cities. Synods have been held since 1562.

The first generation of Dutch Calvinists gave accounts of their creed and their expectations in the wordings of the BELGIC CONFESSION in 1561, composed by the Walloon preacher Guy de Brès (c. 1522–1567). In 1563, the Dutch translation of the HEIDELBERG CATECHISM was published. Both texts soon received official AUTHORITY as confessional documents of the DUTCH REFORMED CHURCH. The church's aggressive attitude in POLITICS provided Calvinism with an entrance to certain classes of the nobility, who were concerned about preserving their rights.

Besides the Anabaptist and Calvinistic churches, various smaller groups came into existence. The House of Love (also called Familists) was a secret sect founded by Hendrick Niclaes (c. 1501–1580), with branches in GERMANY and ENGLAND. It attracted members in the world of merchants, printers, and artists. Dirck Volckertz Coornhert (1522–1590), one of the leading supporters of William of Orange, developed into the most fervent champion of tolerance and rejected the idea of a visible church.

The Dutch Revolt

The year 1566, known as the "Miracle Year," was a turning point in the development of Dutch reformation. An alliance of nobles requested mitigation of King Philip's policy against the Protestants and more political freedom. Calvinistic open-air sermons were delivered everywhere. A nationwide storm of ICONOCLASM followed from the extreme south far into the north. In many places the local authorities now granted the use of church buildings to the Reformed, who took advantage of the confusion to extend their organization. King Philip reacted furiously, keeping a firm hand on the execution of the antiheresy edicts as well as on the rights of the crown. The Duke of Alba, Philip's best strategist, put down the insurrection with a huge army, and budding possibilities were stopped. Disappointed in their action of protest, the opposition leaders were forced to submit to the King's measures or flee en masse, among them Prince William of Orange, one of the stadholders, who had shown himself as Alba's great adversary. Many Protestants who could not flee were put to death.

But it was Alba's ruthless application of legal measure that drove the large group of waverers into the arms of the Calvinistic party. Resistance grew little by little. In the end, the King had to call back Alba and to proceed more cautiously. But all of his attempts to win over his adversaries failed. The war intensified. Political and economic interests coincided with the people's desire for religious freedom. William of Orange, who had returned from his exile, went over to Calvinism in 1573 and succeeded in bringing together a massive resistance movement. He had a very keen perception of the national interest, as well as a firm belief in civil tolerance. Under completely new circumstances, William became the leader of the oppositional forces.

The problem was how to hold together the two confessions. All sorts of solutions were tried. In 1579, the rebellious northern provinces promulgated the Union of Utrecht, by which the absolute freedom of each province to regulate its own religious status was guaranteed. However, the great federal state that William had in mind broke up under the pressure of separatist and religious tendencies. Holland and Zeeland, the bulwark of resistance to Spain, became the scene of Calvinistic intolerance at its most extreme (Lecler 1960). Catholics were granted freedom of conscience, but were forbidden to assemble in churches or private houses.

The States General (i.e., practically the entire northern provinces) abjured Philip II as their sovereign in 1581. The Spanish troops could preserve the southern provinces only; in 1585 they conquered Antwerp. Everyone who did not want to embrace the Catholic religion had to go into exile. The North took advantage of the stream of emigrants, most of whom were Calvinists. The dominating presence of Protestantism in the North and of Catholicism in the South was clearly influenced by military and political factors. It cannot be proved, however, that Protestantism prevailed by force.

The Dutch revolt became a heroic struggle that did not end until 1648 (Peace of Munster). From that time onward, the United Provinces were an independent republic under the leadership of the States General. The stadholder—always a Prince of Orange in most of the provinces—naturally participated in federal policies. He was a member of the Reformed Church and felt obliged to defend its position. However, the Reformed Church can by no means be considered the established church of the republic.

The Golden Age (Seventeenth Century)

The provinces kept their sovereign rights, including in ecclesiastical matters, and were concerned with the education of the Reformed ministers. Gradually universities were founded, one in nearly each province; the Reformed ministers got their education at theological faculties.

Toward 1600, tensions in the Reformed Church came to light that can be characterized as "moderate" versus "strictly orthodox," soon personified in two Leyden professors, JACOBUS ARMINIUS (1560–1609) and FRANZ GOMAR (1563–1641). The theological controversy was over the doctrine of PREDESTINATION, but in a short time it widened to encompass the political scene. ARMINIANISM, in a way a theological revival of humanism tending to Erastianism (THOMAS ERASTUS), was supported by influential magistrates, especially in Holland and Zeeland, whereas the Gomarists relied on stadholder Prince Maurice, son of William. To end the debate, Maurice called the National Synod of the Reformed Church in the city of Dort in 1618. The Arminian party (REMONSTRANTS) was condemned, and the Remonstrant ministers were banished. In 1619, they founded their own church organization, the Remonstrant Brotherhood, in Antwerp. Only after the death of Maurice (1625), under the stadholdership of his brother, Prince Frederick Henry, were Remonstrants allowed to have their own church buildings and even a theological seminary at Amsterdam.

Although several edicts forbade nonreformed services, in actual practice TOLERATION was generally great. It is difficult, if not impossible, to give sound statistics about the number of church members in this period. On the whole, in the republic the Catholic Church constituted about 40 percent of the population. Catholics were strongest in those parts of Brabant, Flanders, and the valley of the Meuse that were conquered by the republic in the last decades of the war against Spain.

In the realm of the Dutch East and West Indian Companies, in Asia, SOUTH AFRICA, and North and South America, several Reformed congregations were founded during the seventeenth and eighteenth centuries. These were mostly administered by the ecclesiastical boards in patria. In addition to the Dutch members, these churches had always a great number of natives who had been catechized and baptized as Reformed. Without developing missionary activities in the modern sense, Dutch ministers were working on religious and educational programs, often in the vernacular.

Dutch CULTURE has been marked by Protestantism, as is shown by, for example, the important place which the authorized version ("Statenvertaling") of the Bible, made by order of the States General (1637), was given in LITERATURE, fine arts, and even everyday life. Ministers and consistories (see CONSISTORY) tried to shape society according to their ideal of godliness and felt obliged to combat age-old papal customs. Influenced partly by English PURITANISM and partly by the broad European pietistic movement of that age (see PIETISM), the so-called "Further Reformation" (*Nadere reformatie*) reacted against dead ORTHODOXY, poor PREACHING, lax discipline (see CHURCH DISCIPLINE), and worldliness. Sometimes local administration supported the pietists' program. But in contrast to Reformed principles, appointing a new minister was a matter not for the ecclesiastical authority, but for the magistrates, who also tried to maintain order in the many theological and ecclesiastical quarrels.

In the course of the seventeenth century, different scholastic systems developed within Reformed THEOLOGY. Most important was the dispute between G. Voetius (1589–1676) and JOHANNES COCCEJUS (1603–1669). Voetius and his school were strongly opposed to the philosophy of Rene Descartes, whereas the Coccejanists were open to new philosophical concepts. Voetius was one of the champions of the Puritan "Further Reformation," but he warned against forms of piety outside the church in the CONVENTICLES of godly people. Hence he condemned the reformation program of the Walloon minister J. de Labadie (1610–1674). De Labadie founded a pietistic sect that after his death settled in Wieuwerd (Frisia), led by Anna

Maria van Schurman, who before her CONVERSION was celebrated as Europe's most erudite woman.

The Enlightenment (Eighteenth Century)

Ideas of the ENLIGHTENMENT were widely accepted in the tolerant atmosphere of the republic, provided that the value of religion was not disputed. Although dismissed from his service as Reformed minister in Amsterdam, B. Bekker (1634–1698) was famous for his struggle against superstition and witch trials (see WITCHCRAZE). Among the many refugees who fled to the republic and furthered the progression of modern ideas was PIERRE BAYLE (1647–1706), the editor of the widely read *Dictionaire Historique et Critique*. The radical ideas of Benedict de Spinoza (1632–1677) caused a nearly universal opposition from the side of the Reformed theologians; only some of the Collegiants, a loose, interdenominational group of Protestants on the extreme left wing, were in sympathy with him. Among the Remonstrants, biblical criticism was accepted to a certain extent, as was shown by, among others, H. Grotius (1583–1645). Grotius was not only a famous jurist, but also a prolific theological writer who argued in favor of a Christian-humanistic ecumenicity. In Grotius's footsteps, J. Lecler (1657–1736) and his successor J. J. Wettstein (1693–1754) lectured on critical theology at the Remonstrant seminar.

When Count NICKOLAUS LUDWIG VON ZINZENDORF, visited Amsterdam in 1736 and following years, to promote his mission work in the Dutch colonies, he met with great sympathy among Mennonites as well as among Collegiants. Since that time, a small MORAVIAN CHURCH has existed in the Netherlands with its center in Zeist near Utrecht. Since the eighteenth century, the Moravian Missionary Society has directed its activities mainly toward Surinam. The Moravians stimulated Dutch Protestants to the missionary task, as was later done by the pioneers of the British missionary societies (see MISSIONARY ORGANIZATIONS). In 1797, J. M. van der Kemp (1747–1811) and others founded the Dutch Missionary Society, which sent its missionaries to INDONESIA.

The Years of Revolution

The "ancien régime" in the Netherlands came to an end in 1795, when the Seven Provinces were conquered by French troops and the principles of the French Revolution were introduced, resulting in the founding of the (only theoretically independent) Batavian Republic. The stadholdership was abolished, a centralized democratic administration was inaugurated with presidency and parliament in The Hague. The Orange party was silenced, and the so-called "Patriots," who formed the revolutionary party, now held the seats of government.

Scarcely any hostility was shown by Dutch revolutionaries toward religion or churches as social phenomena. Indeed, they themselves regarded the Batavian Revolution as a sign of Divine Providence (Bornewasser 1981). But the National Assembly decided that no ruling church should exist in the free Netherlands (August 5, 1796); henceforth, CHURCH AND STATE would remain separate. Whereas Catholics and the dissenting Protestants welcomed the end of discrimination toward their churches wholeheartedly, the Reformed Protestants accepted the new situation only reluctantly and feared great financial problems once the announced ending of the age-old subsidy from the public funds was effectuated. But after a few years, restorative forces mitigated the revolutionary achievements. In 1806, Holland became a kingdom under Napoleon's brother Louis. From 1810 to 1813, the country was incorporated in the French Empire under Napoleon Bonaparte, a period of pauperization and national humiliation.

The first census was taken in 1809. The territory of Louis's kingdom was smaller than the present borders of the Netherlands. Corrected according to the present situation, of the total population (c. 2,200,000), approximately 38.3 percent were Catholic, 55.5 percent were Reformed, 2.8 percent were Lutheran, 1.8 percent were Jewish, 1.4 percent were Mennonite, and 0.2 percent were Remonstrant.

The Nineteenth Century

After the fall of Napoleon's hated empire, the European states restored the prerevolutionary status as much as possible. In the Low Countries, the Orange regime returned as monarchy. It was decided to unite the so-called "Spanish Netherlands" in the South with the territory of the Northern Netherlands. Under the reign of King William I (son of the last stadholder), the Low Countries were again one state as they were under Charles V, but not for long. In 1830, the South revolted against the North because of the so-called "repressive regime" of the king. Out of the Belgian Revolution arose the Kingdom of Belgium in 1831, under King Leopold of Saxony-Coburg. The western part of Luxembourg was added to Belgium, and the city of Luxembourg and its region became the Grand Duchy of Luxembourg under William of Orange-Nassau.

In 1814, after many years of uncertainty, financial support for the churches from the side of the government of the new kingdom could be granted, even to the non-Reformed churches. Nevertheless, the principle of division between church and state was maintained. However, in conformity with the restorative tendencies of that period, the king acted as patron of the churches and succeeded in giving the Reformed as well as the Lutheran churches regulations controlled by the state. The old Reformed confessional statements dating from the sixteenth and seventeenth centuries were no longer obligatory, notwithstanding many protests from the orthodox wing. Increasingly, church life became divided by theological and ecclesiastical parties that differed on the maintainance of the Reformed confession, varying from advocating total freedom via a broad moderate party to proponents of strict consistency.

During the nineteenth century, Dutch society evolved (albeit slowly) toward modernity. Later than in the surrounding countries, INDUSTRIALIZATION really set in after the 1840s. For national consciousness, the social question became urgent toward the end of the century. In 1848, the Constitution was revised according to the principles of democracy, but in terms of parliamentary elections, the system of proportional representation and universal suffrage was not introduced until 1919. In accordance with this slow process, the Netherlands Reformed Church of the nineteenth century continued to act like the national church (*Volkskerk*) of past times. The House of Orange belonged to the church, as did most of the leading personalities in the world of politics and learning. They voted as conservatives or liberals, and the practice of infant baptism was unchallenged.

In the three state universities at Leyden, Groningen, and Utrecht, the theological faculties were theoretically neutral, but in reality Protestant. On the whole, the academic theology was moderately liberal (in the sense of FRIEDRICH SCHLEIERMACHER and his German adepts) or modern (under the influence of the modern sciences and positivistic or empirical thinking). Biblical criticism was flourishing under the leadership of men like A. Kuenen (1828–1891), professor of the Old Testament at Leyden. Also at Leyden, C. P. Tiele (1830–1902) had a great influence on the study of comparative religion. Orthodox theologians were inspired by the Swiss-French-German *reveil* of, for example, A. Vinet (1797–1847). Inspired by the latter, J. H. Gunning Jr. (1829–1905), Reformed minister and professor in Amsterdam and Leyden, related orthodoxy and modern culture. Gunning is considered one of the fathers of so-called "ethical" theology, which emphasizes the existential and personalistic elements of faith.

In the course of the nineteenth century, the strictly orthodox Reformed theologians and laymen were increasingly reacting against the mainstream theology. Two secessions occurred, in 1834 and 1886, leading to the foundation of separated Reformed Churches, the greatest part of which decided to unite as Reformed Churches in the Netherlands (*Gereformeerde Kerken in Nederland*) in 1892. A small group kept aloof from that union as the Christian Reformed Churches (*Christelijke Gereformeerde Kerken*). The Calvinistic Church in the Netherlands originally called itself *Gereformeerd,* which was transformed to *Hervormd* in the beginning of the nineteenth century; the Calvinistically inspired secession churches restored for themselves the old name, *Gereformeerd.* Both names are translated as "Reformed."

The revival of orthodox Calvinism led to the founding of independent theological schools. After the first secession, a school was started at Kampen, today called the Theological University of the Reformed (*Gereformeerde*) Churches. The Free University in Amsterdam, founded in 1880, has its roots in the neo-Calvinistic movement in the Netherlands; its theological faculty provided the education for the ministers coming from the 1886 secession. Therefore, the Reformed Churches had at their disposal two theological faculties after 1892. Its leading theologians of this first generation of scholars were ABRAHAM KUYPER (1837–1920) and H. Bavinck (1854–1921).

The orthodox-reformed secessions were religious phenomena as well as emancipatory movements. At the same time Catholics, after having been discriminated against for centuries, were now juridically emancipated and tried to improve their position in society.

Inspired by the international *reveil* as well as by the rebirth of Calvinism, the orthodox Protestants started elementary schools on a confessional basis alongside the state schools, in which religious education could evidently be not more than a common denominator of Christian belief in its broadest sense. Like the Catholics, orthodox Protestant leaders subsequently organized their own political parties in the second half of the century, in order to realize their school system and, in general, to safeguard their interests in society that Guillaume Groen van Prinsterer (1801–1987) was pioneering.

The Twentieth Century

As was already the case in politics and education, Protestants and Catholics built up their own organizations in the press, the trade unions, broadcasting, sports, and other areas etc. Alongside them, the socialists had their own organizations. In the first half of the twentieth century, Dutch society became thus compartmentalized (*verzuild,* or "pillarized"). This system promoted citizens' involvement in public life. By the end of the century, the "pillarization" had lost its strength.

Between the two World Wars, dialectical theology (see NEO-ORTHODOXY) gained support in the Reformed (*Hervormde*) Church; the *Gereformeerden* mostly were against it. The younger "ethical" theologians also were not charmed by KARL BARTH and his friends (with the exception of EMIL BRUNNER). Their leading theologians were, for example, G. van der Leeuw (1890–1950), professor of the history of religions and liturgiologist at Groningen, and Oepke Noordmans (1871–956), minister of the Reformed Church. At the theological left, H. Bergson and ALBERT SCHWEITZER, among others, were influential.

The Netherlands were neutral during World War I, but became involved in World War II. During the German occupation (1940–1945), Nazi ideology showed its barbaric consequences in the oppression of spiritual freedom and human values, and in the extermination of about 100,000 Jews (see HOLOCAUST). The churches called for resistance, and many people, including from the ranks of priests and ministers, sacrificed their lives.

The mutual solidarity in wartime cut across traditional party loyalties within the *Hervormde* Church. The "New Course" (*Nieuwe Koers*) tended toward the clear confession of Jesus Christ as the Lord and inspired deadlocked reorganization proposals. A new Church Order (1951) introduced a confessionally bound synod instead of the former neutral officialdom, and stimulated evangelizing activities, even taking up certain positions on political problems.

Ecumenical cooperation, as shaped by the WORLD COUNCIL OF CHURCHES, was warmly welcomed (see ECUMENISM). The first secretary-general was the Dutch theologian WILLEM ADOLPH VISSER'T HOOFT (1900–1985), and the first Assembly was held in Amsterdam in 1948. HENDRIK KRAEMER (1888–1965) was the first director of the Ecumenical Institute at Bossey near Geneva.

As earlier, in the second half of the twentieth century Dutch Protestantism was susceptible to various types of foreign theology. RUDOLF BULTMANN's *Entmythologisierung* received remarkably little attention among the liberals, who were open to a christological orientation but also to PAUL TILLICH's modernity. Most influential were Barth and his school; K. H. Miskotte (1894–1976), *Hervormd* professor at Leyden, was an original representative of this theology. Leading dogmaticians in the 1950s and after—more or less independant from Barth—were G. C. Berkouwer (1903–1996), *Gereformeerd* professor at Amsterdam (Free University), and A. A. van Ruler (1908–1970), *Hervormd* professor at Utrecht University.

The theological position of the *Gereformeerd* professor K. Schilder (1890–1952) at Kampen caused fierce debates about the doctrine of baptism and certain questions of canon law, leading to a secession in 1944, known as the "Liberation" (*Vrijmaking*). The "Liberated" (*Vrijgemaakt*) Reformed Churches are maintaining an isolated position within Dutch Protestantism because of their strict Calvinistic orthodoxy. In contrast, in the Reformed Churches "synodal" (*"Gereformeerd synodaal"*) there is a striking ecumenicity.

After more than two centuries without any missionary project, several missionary societies became active during the nineteenth century. Nearly all these societies are now united and are cooperating with the International Missionary Council of the World Council of Churches. The missionary school, which was formerly in Rotterdam and Oegstgeest, is now in Utrecht.

During the twentieth century, Dutch churches were faced with a fast-growing process of secularization, notwithstanding a considerable increase of Evangelicals. By the year 2000, about 40 percent of the total population of the Netherlands (16,000,000) were considered unchurched. About 31 percent were Catholics and 14 percent were Dutch Reformed (*Hervormd*). The other Reformed churches together (mostly, besides the *Gereformeerde Kerken*, of a more strictly Calvinistic character) composed about 7 percent of the population, whereas Muslims (mainly immigrants from Surinam, Morocco, and Turkey) made up about 6 percent. The remaining churches and religious groups (including, among others, the Remonstrant, Lutheran, and Mennonite Churches) accounted for about 2 percent of the population. After many preparatory talks. the *Hervormde* Church (with about 1,918,000 members) and the Gereformeerde Church (667,000 members), together with the Lutheran Church (20,000 members) planned to unite in 2004 in a new church entity, the Protestant Church in the Netherlands.

Despite the overall declining number of church members, contemporary Dutch Protestantism is characterized by a high degree of lay participation and openness for the world, its tasks, and needs.

References and Further Reading

Augustijn, Cornelis. "Niederlande." In *Theologische Realenzyklopädie*, edited by Gerhard Müller, vol. 24. 477–502. Berlin, Germany: De Gruyter & Co, 1990.

Augustijn, Cornelis, Frits Gerrit, Murk Broeyer, et al., eds. *Reformatorica: Teksten uit de Geschiedenis van het Nederlandse Protestantisme*. Zoetermeer, The Netherlands: Meinema, 1996.

Berkhof, Hendrikus. *200 Jahre Theologie: Ein Reisebericht*. Neukirchen-Vluyn, Germany: Neukirchener Verlag, 1985. 106–122.

Blok, D. P., W. Prevenier, et al., eds. *Algemene Geschiedenis der Nederlanden.* 15 vols. Haarlem/Bussum, Netherlands: Fibula-Van Dishoeck, 1977–1982.

Bornewasser, Johannes. "The Authority of the Dutch State Over the Churches, 1795–1853." In *Britain and The Netherlands*, edited by A. C. Duke and C. A. Tamse, vol. VII, 154–175. The Hague, Netherlands: Nijhoff, 1981.

Duke, Alastair. *Reformation and Revolt in the Low Countries.* London: Ronceverte, 1990.

Israel, Jonathan. *The Dutch Republic: Its Rise, Greatness, and Fall 1477–1806.* Oxford, UK: Clarendon Press, 1995.

Jong, Otto Jan de. "Niederländische Kirchengeschichte seit dem 16. Jahrhundert." In *Die Kirche in ihrer Geschichte*, edited by Bernd Moeller, vol.3/M2. 193–233. Göttingen, Germany: Vandenhoeck und Ruprecht, 1975.

Knippenberg, Hans. *De Religieuze Kaart van Nederland.* Assen/Maastricht, Netherlands: Van Gorcum, 1992.

Lecler, Joseph. *Toleration and the Reformation*, vol. 2. 191–323. London: Longmans, 1960.

Nauta, Doede, Aart de Groot, et al., eds. *Biografisch Lexicon voor de Geschiedenis van het Nederlandse Protestantisme.* 5 vols. Kampen, Netherlands: Kok, 1978–2001.

Schöffer, Ivo. *A Short History of the Netherlands.* 2nd ed. Amsterdam, The Netherlands: Allert de Lange.

van den Berg, Johannes. "Die Frömmigkeitsbestrebungen in den Niederlanden." In *Geschichte des Pietismus,* edited by Martin Brecht, vol. 1. 57–112; vol. 2, 542–597. Göttingen, Germany: Vandenhoeck und Ruprecht, 1993, 1995.

van der Zijpp, Nanne. "Netherlands." In *The Mennonite Encyclopedia,* edited by Harold S. Bender, C. Henry Smith, et. al., vol. 3. 824–843. Scottdale, PA: Mennonite Publishing House, 1957.

AART DE GROOT

NEVIN, JOHN WILLIAMSON (1803–1886)

American theologian. Nevin was the author of the MERCERSBURG THEOLOGY and critic of "new measures" revivalism, SECTARIANISM, and American INDIVIDUALISM, Nevin advocated a catholic and incarnational Christianity.

Born February 20, 1803 in Cumberland Valley, Pennsylvania and raised into "old school" PRESBYTERIANISM by Scotch-Irish parents, Nevin graduated from Union College (Schenectady, New York) and Princeton Seminary (Princeton, New Jersey), and was ordained by the Carlisle Presbytery. He joined the faculty of Western Theological Seminary in 1829 where he delved into German theology, ROMANTICISM, and the church histories of JOHANN AUGUST NEANDER. In 1840 Nevin was called to the German Reformed Church seminary and Marshall College in Mercersburg, Pennsylvania, where Friedrich A. Rauch exposed him to German idealism and Hegelian philosophy.

Nevin and his colleague PHILIP SCHAFF articulated the main points of the Mercersburg Theology over the next decade in books and articles in *The Mercersburg Review.* They envisioned the church as an organic, catholic unity, developing through history as the continuing presence of Christ's incarnation. In *The Anxious Bench* (1843), Nevin railed against revivalism, praising instead traditional catechetical systems. In *The Mystical Presence* (1846), Nevin addressed the significance of the SACRAMENTS, especially the Eucharist (LORD'S SUPPER), claiming that through them the faithful come into mystical union with the reality of Christ's life. Titles of his later books, *History and Genius of the Heidelberg Catechism* (1847) and *Antichrist: the Spirit of Sect and Schism* (1848), speak to their contents. After leaving Mercersburg in 1853, Nevin continued to write and teach, and contributed to liturgical revisions within the German Reformed Church.

Nevin died June 6, 1886 in Lancaster, Pennsylvania.

See also Revivals; Theology

References and Further Reading

DiPuccio, William. *The Interior Sense of Scripture: the Sacred Hermeneutics of John Williamson Nevin.* Macon, GA: Mercer University Press, 1998.

Wentz, Richard E. *John Williamson Nevin: American Theologian.* New York: Oxford University Press, 1997.

ERIKA W. DYSON

NEW AGE MOVEMENTS

The term *New Age Movements* usually refers to a specific stream of spiritual beliefs and practices that began to rise above the banks of esotericism about 1965 and flowed out into the wider occidental and oriental cultures. The mouth of the stream begins in the nineteenth century with what WILLIAM JAMES called the "mind-cure movement"; and its doctrinal beliefs were most fully articulated by Theosophy's founder, Helena Petrovna Blavatsky (1831–1891) in the 1880s. It was a disciple of Mme. Blavatsky, English theosophist Alice Bailey (1880–1949), who coined the term "new age" as it is currently used. New immigration legislation in the UNITED STATES in 1965 opened flood gates for Asian religious traditions to pour into North America, and these irrigated and fertilized the nearly dormant metaphysical beliefs of America's previous century.

The final third of the twentieth century experienced widespread revolt against religion understood as institutional or organized practice; and this revolt was incited in large part by New Age Spirituality seeking to make room for itself in the Western establishment. The term *spirituality* entered and transformed the secularized vocabulary by which the West, dominated by a scientific culture, was struggling to understand itself. Spirituality eschews DOCTRINE and dogma, preferring to foster a nonauthoritarian atmosphere of believing. Nevertheless, New Age Spirituality incorporates an identifiable set of tenets or beliefs that make it recognizable as a confluence of Asian metaphysics, classic esotericism, and Western psychology.

The key conceptual tenets of New Age metaphysics, epistemology, and psychology begin with a commitment to:

1. *Holism,* which is the principle that the whole is greater than the sum of the parts. Holism is identified with emergence in evolutionary theory; and in the New Age it is the metaphysical principle undergirding healing as witnessed in the holistic health movement.

2. *Monism,* or belief in the unity of all being, is a New Age metaphysical tenet that is articulated with reference to Brahmanism in ancient INDIA and ascribed to other Asian symbols, such as the Chinese yin-yang, said to depict complementary unity or harmony. The monistic unity is occasionally referred to as "God"; and many New Age adherents are pantheists.

3. The doctrine of the *higher self* incorporates Western psychology, such as Abraham Maslow's aspirations toward "peak experience," into monistic and holistic metaphysics. The spiritual quest becomes one of rising from our lower self to the higher self, and thereby realizing the oneness our self shares with the unity of all being, with God.

4. The classic Aristotelian notion of *potentiality* is ascribed to the psychological task of actualizing the metaphysical potential that is said to lie within each of us, the potential to realize cosmic oneness, a realization that leads to personal healing and global harmony.

5. *Reincarnation* in its Hindu and Buddhist forms provides the backdrop for New Age psychoanalysis, wherein retrieval of past lives and reversal of karma become a means for healing in the present incarnation.

6. The New Age sees itself as taking a scientific rather than a religious approach to spirituality; and *evolution* provides a screen on which we can project change, dynamism, and most important, transformation. Evolution is seen here as progressive and transformatory, as orienting us toward a future "Age of Aquarius."

7. *Gnosis* understood as profound inner knowledge gained through consciousness raising becomes the means by which self-transformation and even planetary transformation are pursued.

8. *Jesus* sometimes plays a role in New Age Spirituality; but this Jesus is frequently divorced from the Christ of the Christian churches. According to the New Age vision, Jesus is a spiritual person who has actualized his own potential for transformation and has actualized his higher self; so Jesus becomes a model for us with his same potential.

New Age ideas permeate what scholars call *New Religious Movements,* even when those religious movements are not necessarily new. These ideas are borne by the media and promoted by spiritual entrepreneurs through movements such as acupuncture, astrology, channeling, crystals, ecofeminism, gnosticism, health foods, hypnotherapy, psychics, metaphysical bookstores, neo-shamanism, tarot, traditional medicines, transpersonal psychology, UFO belief, and yoga. Because such spiritual practices appear to be noninstitutionalized, practitioners can maintain normal institutional affiliations. Thus New Age beliefs and meditative practices influence many mainline Protestant and Roman Catholic congregations. In instances where practitioners are adherents to tight cultlike New Religious Movements, New Age beliefs are pitted against orthodox Christianity.

The metaphysical commitments and spiritual practices of New Age belief are incompatible with many theological and ethical commitments made by REFORMATION Protestants. The Reformed tradition especially emphasizes the transcendence and holiness and personalness of God the creator. Here God is *other,* sharply distinguishable from the creation. New Age monism and pantheism, in contrast, conflate creator with creature, God with the human self. New Age attempts to elevate the self into the sphere of the divine; and the spiritual task becomes one of realizing the divinity that lies within. Protestants, in sharp contrast, see the spiritual task in terms of realistically recognizing that God alone is holy; and this includes viewing ourselves as creatures, of celebrating ourselves as truly human.

When it comes to the ETHICS of love, we can distinguish between love of self and love of the other. The New Age spiritual task of pursuing one's higher self to climb up to the divine contrasts sharply with the Lutheran emphasis on love of neighbor. Instead of loving God because God is in reality one's own self, the Lutheran lets both God and neighbor remain other and defines love in terms of loving someone who is other.

On the other hand, many Protestants appreciate the wholesomeness of much that New Age Spirituality sponsors. Its celebratory mood accompanied by an optimistic affirmation of human unity with NATURE and with God yields an empowering set of spiritual practices that positively edify the lives of many adherents. Even though some right-wing Protestants have accused New Age practitioners of serving Satan and practicing satanic rituals (see DEVIL), no indisputable evidence has confirmed this accusation. New Age Spirituality overlaps with Protestant and Roman Catholic spirituality in many healthy ways, even though from time to time it needs theologically critical assessment.

References and Further Reading

Blavatsky, Mme. H. P. *The Secret Doctrine*. Madras, India: Theosophical Publishing House, 1890.

Huxley, Aldous. *The Perennial Philosophy*. New York: Harper, 1944, 1970.

James, William. *The Varieties of Religious Experience*. London: Longmans, Green, and Co., 1928.

Peters, Ted. *The Cosmic Self*. San Francisco: Harper Collins, 1991.

TED PETERS

NEW ZEALAND

Christianity has been a very self-conscious tradition in New Zealand. It has been seen either as a whole, particularly in accounts of Christianity on the Maori, or in denominational forms. More recently scholars have sought to investigate Christian links with CULTURE and society. Although the literature has been extensive, it has studiedly avoided using the Protestant category, except where it intruded unavoidably on national politics. Ian Breward did indeed explore the Bible in Schools movement, and Peter O'Connor the militant Protestant tradition, but the present author is unusual in using the Protestant category in research of patterns of spirituality.

Nevertheless it is altogether clear that the Protestant label is a natural category. Until the Second Vatican Council, mutual differences with Catholicism were fundamental, and despite levels of intermarriage, and some embarrassment about public sectarianism (in striking contrast to AUSTRALIA), few Protestants would enter Catholic churches or vice versa. Protestantism in New Zealand, however, should not be viewed simply as a polemical tradition. It was a form of Christianity, a form represented by a notion of AUTHORITY shaped around the BIBLE and an ECUMENISM within which denominational differences flourished comfortably. It is this tradition that this article analyzes.

Protestant Missions

The earliest Christian activity in New Zealand was a product of the evangelical missionary movement. Lay missionaries of the CHURCH MISSIONARY SOCIETY (CMS) preached and catechized from 1814, but their Anglican identity was evident only in the 1820s when ordained priests joined them. These priests were, however, mostly of the Simeon tradition, wore black Genevan gowns, and had friendly relations with Wesleyan missionaries who arrived in 1823 (see WESLEYANISM). All the missionaries emphasized the translation and circulation of the Bible (see BIBLE TRANSLATION), and catechetical work, searching for evidence of CONVERSION before they would administer BAPTISM. They worked within existing tribal structures, respecting the mana (moral authority, prestige) of chiefs. The arrival of Catholic missionaries in 1838 challenged their approach to MISSIONS.

Planting of Protestant Churches

European settlers began to arrive from the 1830s and systematic colonization began in 1840, helped by the annexation of the country and agreement with the Maori people in 1840. There never was much doubt of the predominantly Protestant tone to the community. Unlike Australia, all immigrants were voluntary and a better class of settlers was dominant, many with some church connections, whereas the impoverished Irish Catholic proportion was a modest 14 percent or so. On the other hand, in a voluntarist environment the resources to establish formal church structures were not easily found. In the little settlements founded by Edward Gibbon Wakefield's New Zealand Company, members of each DENOMINATION sought to raise pledges to build churches and hire ministers, but colonists had little by way of spare capital, and were perhaps lacking many keen members. A CHURCH OF SCOTLAND minister, John Macfarlane, was sent out with the settlers to the Port Nicholson (Wellington) settlement in 1840, but in an uneasily postestablishment age, neither the British government nor the home denominations made provision for the financial needs of churches. The settlement of Otago in 1848 was made in collaboration with the new Free Church of Scotland (see FREE CHURCH), and the settlement of Christchurch in Canterbury in 1851 was organized on supposedly Anglican lines, and even provided a bishop, but these were exceptions, ensuring only that the South Island was rather less secular than the North Island. In most places settlers from different denominations combined to raise money for a church and the salary and housing of a minister. Often people of all denominations would support each denominational enterprise because the pattern of religion was effectively a community activity. This was the strength of Protestant ecumenism. Meanwhile denominational structures established in Australia at first had sway in New Zealand as well, until being gradually replaced by indigenous authority.

Establishment and Nonestablishment

Anglicans were from the first a kind of para-establishment in the colony. The British government contributed to the salary of the first bishop, George Augustus Selwyn, who was drawn from an Oxford–Eton tradition. Selwyn had hoped to preserve a state church, and objected to government assistance for denominations other than the CHURCH OF ENGLAND. Subsequently the government officials reduced or declined state support of religious bodies. State aid was gradually recommenced from the 1950s with programs of chaplains in hospitals and prisons and support for church-based education, because by then support for all traditions including Catholicism and non-Christian traditions did not awaken sectarian tension. Meanwhile ANGLICANISM maintained a role in most parts of New Zealand as an informal establishment, the church of the respectable and the social leaders. This form of Anglicanism was very different from the Protestantism of the CMS missionaries, however. Although full-blown ritualism was unacceptable in the nineteenth century and rare in the twentieth century, most Anglicans used the term Protestant to refer to churches other than their own and the Roman Catholic Church. They declined opportunities of cooperation with other Protestants until the campaign by the Bible in Schools League in 1914.

English Dissent

In contrast, the Presbyterian Church of New Zealand, which was itself composed of former members of the Church of Scotland and of the Free Church, identified with English Dissenters of orthodox theology—Methodists, Congregationalists, and BAPTISTS—and together were called the Protestants. They cooperated together, largely ignoring Calvinist–Arminian debates, and in the early twentieth century shared a common magazine and talked for many years of combining into the Evangelical Protestant Church of New Zealand. These schemes came close to fruition in the 1950s when a more ecumenical Anglican Church decided to join the discussions, but it was the Anglicans who in 1976 vetoed the proposed merger. By this time Protestant had ceased to be a meaningful label for anything.

Political Protestantism

Nevertheless, in its heyday in the century before 1975 the Protestant rallying cry was not only religiously but also socially and politically significant. Protestant voices often voiced an identification with truly democratic and "British" traditions. Protestant leaders who disagreed in theological matters demonstrated their fundamental unity in their united campaigns to purify society and POLITICS. Their greatest campaign was the attempt to prohibit the consumption of alcohol (see TEMPERANCE). The prohibition movement was a pan-Protestant movement. It was led by a combination of Methodists, Presbyterians, Baptists, Congregationalists, early feminists (who formed the women's Christian Temperance Union), and even some middle-class Freethinkers. There was an extraordinary concentration of ministers in the movement, which came within an ace of success in 1919. Other movements also emerged, to control gambling and to reintroduce Bible knowledge to the primary school curriculum—it had been excluded when state education was introduced in 1877 in the hopes of Catholic participation.

The uglier side of pan-Protestantism was seen in the tradition of touring Protestant lecturers, although the New Zealand public was never as attentive as were Australians in their more divided society. In general Catholics were well integrated into society and were active in politics in a nonsectarian manner, so it was considered bad form to criticize their involvement. In general, New Zealand politicians were horrified at the thought of sectarian violence and preferred not to conduct politics on the basis of a "sectarian position." Consequently those who attempted to impose moral standards on the rough-and-ready colonial society were generally pushed to the outer fringes. However, in the tense atmosphere of World War I, the Protestant Political Association was founded and gained extensive public support. It alleged that Catholics were shirking the war effort and claiming an undue influence in government jobs. The Reform Government of 1911–1925 was led by a prominent Orangeman, William F. Massey, and it listened carefully to Protestant and moralist pressure groups. Although the Prohibition and Bible in Schools campaigns failed to succeed in national referendums, the Reform government passed the Marriage Amendment Act of 1920, which made Catholic criticisms of Protestant MARRIAGE illegal. Later in the 1920s the level of secularity increased and the Protestant voice quickly faded.

Protestant Piety

The active Protestant community in nineteenth-century New Zealand formed a consciously respectable grouping, seeking to emulate traditional practices and patterns of life. Piety had two foci: the church and the home. In the home the "family altar" was common with devotions of PRAYER and Bible reading led by the paterfamilias. In the church a congregational pattern was assumed; the congregation was a caring group, and although the pastor or minister had the key spiritual responsibility, in most cases the lay leaders of the congregation were a more stable force, sensitive to the vicissitudes of colonial existence. SUNDAY SCHOOLS were also important because many of the Protestant traditions of a previous era had given way to evangelical patterns (see EVANGELICALISM). The sermon was of great importance, and in New Zealand CHARLES SPURGEON's many printed sermons were very influential. HYMNS were popular and they left a profound legacy on collective consciousness, but the most popular of them were the revivalist hymns of IRA DAVID SANKEY and his colleagues (see REVIVALS). The Protestant culture was reflected in the disregard for the SACRAMENTS, although in the early years of the Otago Province, where Presbyterians predominated, there were public holidays for the quarterly communion (see LORD'S SUPPER) season.

New Forms

The institutional Protestant churches represented some 35 percent of the New Zealand population, and with Anglicans were about three-quarters of the population, although levels of nominality were fairly high, particularly for Presbyterians and Anglicans. The smaller churches were active far beyond what their nominal adherence might have suggested. The highest levels of activity were seen in churches planted in New Zealand after the birth of the colony, notably the PLYMOUTH BRETHREN, the SALVATION ARMY, and the [Campbellite] CHURCHES OF CHRIST. Each of these at their height attracted adherence from about one percent of the population. New Zealand was often seen as a hothouse for sectarian Protestantism, given the colonial tendency to discount tradition, and to respond to vigorous EVANGELISM, high levels of lay involvement, and less formal approaches to ministry and church services. Although New Zealand fell short of the color and freedom of American religiosity—religion was always allied to propriety in this very British colony—the planting of Pentecostal churches in the 1920s increased the range of Protestantism. In the early 1960s there was a flourishing of new and highly informal patterns of PENTECOSTALISM in the so-called Charismatic Movement, which made a deeper impression in New Zealand than in any other first-world society.

Protestantism's Decline

This flourishing of new forms, which has persisted under constantly changing labels and forms, seemed to be an inverse image of the parallel decline of the institutional Protestant churches. The BILLY GRAHAM Crusade of 1959 marked the high point of Protestantism, but within five years levels of membership in the Presbyterian, Methodist, and Anglican churches slumped dramatically. There was a rapid decline in ministerial recruits. By 2000 the large institutional Protestant churches were a shadow of their former selves, gravely reduced in their potential to operate as national institutions. Secular society had discounted the value of religion, and the lack of distinctiveness in the predominantly liberal tone of church leadership had reduced the power to respond to alien forces. Much was expected of the ecumenical movement, but the failure of church union left the church leaders bereft of directions. The Catholic Church seemed to have stronger forces of resistance, although by the 1990s, these influences were powerful in this church as well. Older style Evangelicalism slowly declined from the 1970s, but much of its life flowed toward the Pentecostal movement. The issue of ordination of homosexual ministers split institutional Protestantism, and the Methodist church cemented its liberal leadership, whereas the Presbyterian Church wavered uncertainly, and evangelical forces became more dominant among new ordinands.

Signs of New Life

By the 1980s the Presbyterian and Methodist churches were being rejuvenated in surprising ways by the immigration of large numbers of Pacific islanders, whose cultures had been transformed by the London Missionary Society (LMS) and the Wesleyan Methodist Missionary Society (see MISSIONARY ORGANIZATIONS). The LMS was largely Congregationalist, but this church was so small in New Zealand that it merged with the Presbyterians in 1969. So in urban areas, particularly in the largest city of Auckland, the majority of mainline Protestants by 2000 were Polynesian, although leadership remained largely in the hands of Europeans. Other signs of new life were apparent in a new lay interest in THEOLOGY, the decline in the old secular exclusion of religion from society, and interest in different forms of spirituality. Some Protestant churches sought to take advantage of these trends, although it was a very different pattern from the Protestantism of old.

See also Congregationalism; Methodism; Presbyterianism

References and Further Reading

Breward, Ian. *A History of the Churches in Australasia.* Oxford: Oxford University Press, 2001.

Darroch, Murray. *Everything You Ever Wanted to Know About Protestants: but Never Knew Who to Ask.* Wellington, NZ: Catholic Supplies, 1984.

Davidson, Allan. *Christianity in Aotearoa.* Wellington, NZ: Education for Ministry, 1991.

Davidson, Allan, and Peter J. Lineham, eds. *Transplanted Christianity: Documents Illustrating Aspects of New Zealand Church History.* 4th ed. Palmerston North, NZ: Massey University, 1997.

Lineham, Peter J. "How Institutionalised Was Protestant Piety in Nineteenth-Century New Zealand?" *Journal of Religious History* 13 no. 4 (1985): 370–382.

———. "The Nature and Meaning of Protestantism in New Zealand Culture." *Turnbull Library Record* 26 (1993): 59–76.

O'Connor, Peter S. "Protestants, Catholics, and the New Zealand Government, 1916–1918." In *W. P. Morrell: A Tribute: Essays in Modern and Early Modern History Presented to William Parker Morrell Professor Emeritus, University of Otago,* edited by G. A. Wood and P. S. O'Connor, 185–202. Dunedin, NZ: University of Otago Press, 1973.

PETER J. LINEHAM

NEWBIGIN, J. E. LESSLIE (1909–1998)

British missionary statesman. Lesslie Newbigin was an outstanding figure in the twentieth-century ecumenical movement. Raised an English Presbyterian, he was ordained by the CHURCH OF SCOTLAND in 1936 for missionary service in INDIA. In 1947 he became one of the first bishops in the newly united CHURCH OF SOUTH INDIA (CSI, diocese of Madurai and Ramnad). After a period as general secretary of the International Missionary Council at the time of its integration with the WORLD COUNCIL OF CHURCHES (1959–1965), Newbigin returned to serve as bishop in Madras until retirement in 1974. Five years of teaching mission and ECUMENISM at the Selly Oak Colleges in Birmingham, ENGLAND, were then followed by eight years as pastor of a local congregation of the United Reformed Church in the racially and religiously mixed inner suburb of Winson Green. For the last quarter-century of his life Newbigin was active as a Christian apologist amid what he saw as the intellectual and spiritual apostasy of the West.

Described by an Indian colleague as "a bishop on the run," Newbigin was also an energetic speaker and writer. In *The Reunion of the Church* (1948) he defended the terms and form of the "organic union" of Anglicans, Presbyterians, Congregationalists, and Methodists in the CSI. His thinking blossomed into a full-blown ECCLESIOLOGY in *The Household of God* (1953), which sought to integrate the Protestant, Catholic, and Pentecostal dimensions of the church. This classic book lay behind his drafting of the famous description of "the unity we seek" adopted at the New Delhi Assembly of the World Council of Churches in 1961. Newbigin's MISSIOLOGY, with its strong local and pneumatological emphases, was set out in *The Open Secret* (1978). His program for the "encounter with modernity" occupied *Foolishness to the Greeks* (1986) and *The Gospel in a Pluralist Society* (1989).

Whether in the face of Hinduism, Islam, Marxism, secularism, or neopaganism, Newbigin preached a Gospel based on the cross and resurrection of Christ that would fit into no other worldview than that of which it was the cornerstone.

See also Anglicanism; Congregationalism; Methodism; Presbyterianism

References and Further Reading

Primary Source:

Lesslie Newbigin. *Unfinished Agenda: An Autobiography.* London: SPCK, 1985; updated edition, Edinburgh: St. Andrew Press, 1993.

Secondary Source:

Geoffrey Wainwright. *Lesslie Newbigin: A Theological Life.* New York and Oxford: Oxford University Press, 2000.

GEOFFREY WAINWRIGHT

NEWMAN, JOHN HENRY (1801–1890)

English churchman and cardinal. Long before his death on August 11, 1890 at Edgbaston, ENGLAND, John Henry Newman was recognized as one of nineteenth-century England's premier religious figures. At a certain level, his significance is readily understood. The central figure in the Tractarian, or OXFORD MOVEMENT that began in the CHURCH OF ENGLAND at Oxford in 1833, Newman effectively dispersed the movement's key figures and their influence by his conversion to Roman Catholicism in 1845. As ANGLO-CATHOLICISM, the movement entered a new Anglican phase while Newman turned his prolific pen and powerful mind toward a spiritual and intellectual defense of the Catholic Church. Newman also has been acknowledged as an unusually influential scholar of early Christian thought, and especially as one who sought to explain the nature and influence of Christian belief and TRADITION for the modern world. Although he was eventually elevated to the office of cardinal in the Catholic Church, he seemed to continue on the sort of intensely personal spiritual journey that marked every stage of his life and, in turn, has become emblematic of modern religious experience.

From his formative years, Newman seemed marked for an idiosyncratic path. Born in London on February 21, 1801, Newman first had to overcome family struggles. His father, at first a banker, suffered a job loss during English bank failures in 1816 and turned to brewing. The family's relocation and lowered status seem to have impelled Newman's quest. He began his spiritual journey under the influence of EVANGELICALISM, proving himself devout, and even vowing to live a celibate life, at a young age (see CELIBACY). He received the B.A. from Trinity College, Oxford, in 1820, became a Fellow of Oriel College in 1822, and was ordained in the Church of England in 1824. By 1831, Newman had become one of the select university preachers, but by that time he had also become associated with the small group of Oxford divines who would form the Tractarian nucleus. The group gained its name from the series of tracts they published that challenged the influence of Evangelicalism in the Church of England and called for renewed forms of ancient Catholic practice and belief by contemporary Anglicans.

In part Newman's religious journey proceeded as academic investigation. His early, major works included *The Arians of the Fourth Century* (1833) and *Lectures on the Prophetical Office of the Church, viewed relatively to Romanism and popular Protestantism* (1837). Throughout his life Newman issued such scholarly works in a steady stream. They were never removed from his spiritual quest and the public polemics it encouraged. Tract 90, the final of the series, in which Newman challenged the Church of England's THIRTY-NINE ARTICLES, proved the most controversial. There he challenged the church's prerogative in demanding that its CLERGY subscribe to tenets that might infringe Anglo-Catholic convictions. Rightly, ecclesiastical authorities viewed this publication as a challenge to their AUTHORITY from one whose loyalty had become suspect.

More notable then and now was Newman's *An Essay on the Development of Doctrine* (1845), which served as the fulcrum for his shift from ANGLICANISM to Roman Catholicism. In this work Newman introduced the novel idea that Christian belief, and the church, can change over time yet in doing so remain faithful to Christian origins. Earlier, Newman had joined Tractarian colleagues in arguing that Anglican authenticity lay in forms of continuity with ancient precedent in belief and WORSHIP. Accepting the idea of doctrinal development gave Newman a way to accept the papacy as an office that was not present in early Christian experience, but could represent a faithful form of adaptation to changed circumstances. By this conclusion, Newman not only made his religious transition, but also marked CONVERSION as a central fact of modern life and ensured that development would remain a key category for Christian thought.

In a sense, Newman's writing as a Roman Catholic continued the polemical tone that he had begun in his Tractarian years. His *Lectures on certain Difficulties felt by Anglicans in submitting to the Catholic Church* (1850) and *Lectures on the Present Position of Catholics* (1851), the latter of which resulted in a libel action in which Newman was fined, were followed by

his most noted book, *Apologia pro Vita Sua* (1864), an autobiographical advocacy of the Roman Catholic Church. But there were always other themes in his writing. Throughout his Anglican and Roman Catholic years, Newman continually published sermons and pastoral works designed to guide the spiritual life. Often the reader finds Newman reading Scripture in light of contemporary experience, an approach that has become central to the modern apologetic task. *The Idea of a University* (1852) originally appeared to modest notice but became a milestone in modern efforts to integrate modern education with Christian belief.

Less noticed among the changes that marked Newman's life were profound instances of religious continuity. As both an Anglican and a Roman Catholic, Newman viewed Christianity as a call to live an ascetic life within the community. While still an Anglican, he formed a rather monastic group of men at Littlemore and continued that initiative with papal endorsement as a Catholic with the founding of an English Oratory. Late in life he became embroiled in the controversy over Vatican Council I, in 1870, in which papal infallibility was asserted. In response to William Gladstone, Newman argued that Catholics could be both loyal to their nation and faithful to their church. Elevated to the office of cardinal in 1879 by Pope Leo XIII, Newman died in August 1890.

References and Further Reading

Chadwick, Owen. *Newman*. Oxford, UK: Oxford University Press, 1983.

Culler, A. Dwight. *Imperial Intellect*. New Haven, CT: Yale University Press, 1955.

Faber, Geoffrey. *Oxford Apostles*. New York: Scribner, 1934.

Griffin, John R. *A Historical Commentary on the Major Catholic Works of Cardinal Newman*. London: Peter Lang, 1993.

Ker, I. T. *Newman and the Fullness of Christianity*. London: T. & T. Clark, 1993.

Martin, Brian. *John Henry Newman*. Oxford, UK: Oxford University Press, 1982.

Rowell, Geoffrey, ed. *Tradition Renewed: The Oxford Movement Conference Papers*. Allison Park, PA: Pickwick Publications, 1986.

Turner, Frank M. *John Henry Newman: The Challenge to Evangelical Religion*. New Haven, CT: Yale University Press, 2002.

WILLIAM SACHS

NEWTON, ISAAC (1642–1727)

English physicist. Issac Newton was born in 1642 to a yeoman family in Woolsthorpe, Lincolnshire. At age ten he was sent to the King's School at Grantham, where he began tinkering with mechanical devices, and in 1661 he enrolled in Trinity College, CAMBRIDGE UNIVERSITY, receiving a Bachelor of Arts in 1665.

The curriculum at Trinity College, focused on Aristotelian philosophy, seemed untouched by the intellectual and religious upheavals of the time, particularly Protestantism and the CIVIL WAR. On his own, Newton pursued mathematics and began to develop calculus. He also began to study the new physics. He spent eighteen months primarily at Woolsthorpe starting in June 1665, when Cambridge was closed because of plague. During that time, he consolidated his work on calculus and pursued his studies in physics and optics. In Protestant ENGLAND there was no need to equivocate about his support of the Copernican system. His work in physics led to his discovery of our modern concept of universal gravitation; it was published in his *Mathematical Principles of Natural Philosophy* in 1687. His work on optics involving a prism showed that white light is composed of a spectrum of colors; it was published in his *Opticks* in 1704.

Two areas of interest to Newton were largely unknown to scholars until the twentieth century: alchemy and THEOLOGY. Newton thought alchemy might be the key to understanding his mechanical concept of NATURE. Although he wrote much on the subject, it was never published; perhaps he thought his findings too tentative. In theology Newton studied the BIBLE and the early fathers and concluded that the DOCTRINE of the Trinity was false. He also attempted to establish a correlation between biblical prophecy and historical events.

Newton became a fellow of Trinity College in 1667, and by 1669 was Lucasian professor. He remained at Cambridge until 1696, when he moved to London, first as warden, then as master of the mint. Had his anti-Trinitarian ideas been known, he would have been dismissed from Cambridge. He had been a fellow of the Royal Society since 1672, and in 1703 he was elected president. Both positions at the mint and the Royal Society lasted until his death in 1727.

See also Anti-Trinitarianism; Science

References and Further Reading

Primary Sources:

Newton, Isaac. *The Principia: Mathematical Principles of Natural Philosophy.* Translated by Anne Whitman and I. Bernard Cohen. Berkeley, CA: University of California Press, 1999.
———. *Opticks.* 2nd ed. New York: Dover Publications, 1979.

Secondary Sources:

Cohen, I. Bernard. *The Newtonian Revolution.* Cambridge: Cambridge University Press, 1980.
Dobbs, B. J. T. *The Janus Faces of Genius: The Role of Alchemy in Newton's Thought.* Cambridge: Cambridge University Press, 1991.
Westfall, Richard S. *Never at Rest: A Biography of Isaac Newton.* Cambridge: Cambridge University Press, 1980.

SHEILA J. RABIN

NIEBUHR, H. RICHARD (1894–1962)

American theologian. Although less well known than his older brother, REINHOLD NIEBUHR, Helmut Richard Niebuhr exercised great influence over Christian thought in the twentieth century. Both brothers are regarded for their contributions to Christian ETHICS, yet H. Richard recognized in himself a particular calling to renew the church.

Niebuhr was born on September 3, 1894 in Wright City, Missouri, son of Pastor Gustav and his wife Lydia Niebuhr. Raised in the parsonage of the Evangelical Synod of North America, where his father was minister, Niebuhr grew up in a German-speaking immigrant community. After graduating from Elmhurst College in 1912 and Eden Theological Seminary in 1915, he was ordained in 1916. He held a pastorate in St. Louis while pursuing graduate studies at Washington University (M.A., 1918). He undertook doctoral work at Yale University, earning a B.D. (1923) and a Ph.D. (1924). He taught at Eden (1919–1922, 1927–1931) and served as president of Elmhurst (1924–1927). Appointed to the faculty of Yale Divinity School (1931), Niebuhr was named Sterling Professor of Theology and Christian Ethics (1954), where he served until his death in 1962.

Niebuhr stands at a crossroads in twentieth-century Protestant thought, at the nexus of liberalism and NEO-ORTHODOXY. His first book, *The Social Sources of Denominationalism* (1929), argued that denominational divisions are attributable to sociological differences, disclosing that neither human beings nor their communities escape from certain historical conditions and limited understanding. His doctoral dissertation on ERNST TROELTSCH (1865–1923) and the work of MAX WEBER (1864–1920) both contributed to this sociological analysis. Niebuhr asserted that denominational strife testifies to the failure of the CHURCH to transcend social conditions, indicating a fundamental hypocrisy and moral inauthenticity within ecclesial life. However, renewal within the church will occur when Christians renounce worldly attachments, seeking only the fellowship of love for God and neighbor.

Sovereignty of God

The Kingdom of God in America (1937), a continuation of Niebuhr's sociological contributions, typologically examines American churches in light of the REFORMATION emphasis on the reign of God. He examines the tension between the sovereignty of God over the Christian and the corruption of the world within American religious history and CULTURE. He criticizes institutionalized liberalism within the church, which ultimately attempts to establish the KINGDOM OF GOD without dependence on God's initiative. Niebuhr concludes that theological liberalism is impotent to transfigure the present realities precisely because it jettisons the dynamism of radical faith in God.

If Niebuhr's earlier works exhibited a certain religious and historical relativism, *The Meaning of Revelation* (1941) extended that "relativism" to the discussion of revelation itself. However, his relativism did not devolve into skepticism: God is sovereign over the realm of history in which revelation occurs. In a synthesis of the insights of Troeltsch and KARL BARTH (1886–1968), Niebuhr unites the "critical thought" of the former and the "constructive work" of the latter. For Niebuhr, the human self is fundamentally social, existing within a network of relationships and continually reshaped through those relationships. Thus the self is constituted in a particular historical community. Similarly, because revelation is the communal and personal appropriation of God's word mediated through memory, revelation is limited to the contingencies of each community. Yet God's word, as such, is objective and authoritative, transcending the limits of human society. As Barth argued, Niebuhr contends that FAITH provides its own evidence, because God's word makes intelligible our history.

Faith, for Niebuhr, is confidence in God as the "source of good" while reason informs and directs this faith. *Radical Monotheism and Western Culture* (1960) seeks to overcome idolatrous finite conceptualizations about God and to supersede worldly centers of value with a dynamic radical faith in the "principle of being," the power of SALVATION in the world. While confessional theology and ethics never transcend their finite gods, "radical monotheism," as absolute fidelity to God, recognizes all events as transparent to "the one." Thus radical faith becomes incarnate through an undivided ethical response in every realm in which a person acts.

Ethics of Relation

Because human concepts about God are limited and finite, Niebuhr explains, Christian ethics is not subordinate to dogmatic theology. The relational character of the human self is such that theology occurs within a context of moral reflection and concerns itself primarily with the relationship between the self and others, including God. Thus, in *Christ and Culture* (1951), a sociohistorical typology, ethical reflection saturates Niebuhr's inquiry into how particular cul-

tures have related to Christ. Between the extremes, "Christ against culture" and "the Christ of culture," three cultural types emerge. Although Niebuhr was unwilling to choose definitively a single typology, he prefers "Christ the transformer of culture" as most harmonious with personal CONVERSION.

The dialectical nature of moral reflection motivated Niebuhr's moral philosophy. *The Responsible Self* (1963), published posthumously, explores a mediating position between subjectivist ethics and traditional moral philosophies. Ethical action is the personal response to others and to God, grounded in human dependence on God as the source of goodness. When human beings relate to God through friendship rather than fear, authentic ethical transformation appears concretely within the world.

Niebuhr's significance as a theologian is manifested in his critical appropriation of sociohistorical methods in the service of neo-orthodox theology. His Christian ethics and reflection on the DOCTRINE of God influenced a generation of thinkers, contributing to developments within narrative theology and Christian social thought.

See also Denomination; Ethics; Liberal Protestantism and Liberalism; Theology; Theology, Twentieth Century; Theology, Twentieth Century, North American

References and Further Reading

Primary Sources:

Niebuhr, H. Richard. *Theology, History and Culture: Major Unpublished Writings.* Edited by William Stacy Johnson. New Haven, CT: Yale University Press, 1996.

Secondary Sources:

Diefentaler, Jon. *H. Richard Niebuhr: A Lifetime of Reflections on the Church and the World.* Macon, GA: Mercer University Press, 1986.
Keiser, R. Melvin. *Roots of Relational Ethics: Responsibility in Origin and Maturity in H. Richard Niebuhr.* Atlanta, GA: Scholars Press, 1996.
Sherry, Terrence Owen. *The Christo-Morphic, Hermeneutical Theology of H. Richard Niebuhr: Shaped by Christ.* Lewiston, NY: Edwin Mellen Press, 2003.
Thieman, Ronald F., ed. *The Legacy of H. Richard Niebuhr.* Minneapolis, MN: Fortress Press, 1991.
Werpehowski, William. *American Protestant Ethics and the Legacy of H. Richard Niebuhr.* Washington, DC: Georgetown University Press, 2002.

J. S. FLIPPER

NIEBUHR, REINHOLD (1892–1971)

American theologian. Reinhold Niebuhr was born in Wright City, Missouri, on June 21, 1892, and died June 1, 1971. He and his brother, H. RICHARD

NIEBUHR, became the twentieth century's most influential American-born theologians and ethicists, with the possible exception of WALTER RAUSCHENBUSCH. Their sister, Hulda, taught Christian education at McCormick Theological Seminary. This remarkable family confluence of brilliance and theological leadership has led some to confuse the Niebuhr brothers with each other. Reinhold taught at Union Theological Seminary in New York City. He emphasized a realistic understanding of human nature, a Lutheran/Augustinian understanding of GRACE as undeserved forgiveness, and a public and political ETHICS of love and justice. His brother, H. Richard, taught at Yale and emphasized an ethics of response to the dynamic sovereignty of the living God in and over all life, and a trinitarian understanding of the CHURCH. One could contend that the brothers' early decision to avoid each other's turf left their theological ethics somewhat incomplete without supplementation by the themes of the other.

As pastor of Bethel Evangelical Church in Detroit (1915–1928), Niebuhr saw idealistic forms of Christianity functioning to cover up automobile companies' injustice to workers. Henry Ford agreed with admonitions to love one another while he laid off workers two or three days per week, not providing for health care, retirement, or even continuation in the job past age fifty-five, rationalizing that he was paying more per day than the workers could get elsewhere. Church members heard admonitions to love as encouragement to avoid conflict, and thus to avoid supporting workers' demands for justice. Influenced by the power realities of Detroit, and by the tragedies of two world wars and the Great Depression, Niebuhr rejected his early liberal idealism and optimism about human nature, and found theological depth in St. Augustine's penetrating analysis of human self-seeking and self-deception. He advocated Christian realism, "the disposition to take all factors in a social and political situation, which offer resistance to established norms, into account, particularly the factors of self-interest and power."

A Realist Understanding of Human Nature

Niebuhr's classic two-volume work, *The Nature and Destiny of Man,* showed the inadequacy of rationalistic, romantic, and complacent modern understandings of human nature; they are one-dimensional, whereas our human reality is dialectical and paradoxical. Only a religion of revelation can do justice to both our freedom and our finiteness and understand the character of our evil. The eternal God is made known not by negating temporal limitations, but rather by self-disclosure within the finite and historical world.

Therefore, human nature is understood as being related to the eternal God, free and self-transcendent; yet created finite, so that creaturely limitations and historicity are essentially good and not evil. Furthermore, the mercy that makes judgment on our SIN sufferable is affirmed.

In our sin, we *distrust* the source of our dialectical freedom and finitude, our self-transcendence and our limitation, and so cannot accept the tension. Sin as *pride* and *will to power* seeks to deny our finitude, covering it up with the drive to political, economic, religious, moral, or intellectual power and self-righteousness. Sin as *abandonment of responsibility* (which Niebuhr called *sensuality*) seeks to deny our self-transcendence, burying it in addiction to drugs, sex, fatalism, authoritarianism, or conformism. Yet we know better: both forms of sin are denials of the reality of our dialectical nature. So we cover up our sin with *self-deception* and *rationalization*. When this distrustful drivenness and self-deception occur in the context of *concentration of power,* the inevitable result is injustice by the powerful over the powerless. The most destructive sin is the pride of powerful nations and powerful concentrations of economic wealth, which can more plausibly pretend to transcend finitude, more persuasively justify self-interest, and more powerfully suppress and destroy rivals.

The first step in remedying sin must be *faith,* the gift of trust in the source of our freedom and finitude. But this does not suffice to remedy the vicious cycles of sin, because even if forgiven, we are still sinful. Christian ethics as admonition to love is ineffective; it enables self-righteousness, self-adulation, and blindness to the injustices that we perpetrate. More effective are analyses of the human situation that disclose the limits of human possibilities and the propensities of sin. Niebuhr's is not an ethics of "oughts" so much as an ethics of *realistic diagnosis*. His writings are full of penetrating diagnoses of the ironies of self-pretense, self-deception, rationalization, nationalism, self-congratulation, ideological pretense that justifies special economic privilege, idolatrous claims to absolute truth or wisdom, and cynical claims to be above it all while in fact wallowing in powerless and disengaged complacency. His students recall this irony also subtly directed, with a wry smile, at his own pride. He invariably took the side of the subjugated, the underdog, the less powerful. His realism knew that the powerful often dominate the powerless and rationalize special greed and privilege. Therefore, the remedy must include *checks and balances against concentration of power*. Workers need unions to check the concentrated power of corporations, nations need democracy and separation of powers to check and balance the power of rulers, and the world needs international engagement to check the rise of authoritarian dictators like Hitler and Stalin. Niebuhr advocated early U.S. entry into World War II, and he diagnosed and opposed the illusions of military power in the Vietnam War.

Criticisms

Niebuhr has been criticized for defining love as self-sacrifice and self-abasement and for emphasizing the preponderantly male sin of pride, while underdiagnosing the more female sin of abandonment of responsibility and the need of the powerless for self-assertion. Hence his defenders now place greater emphasis on the self-deprecation pole of his dialectic of sin, and on mutual love and webs of relationship. He has been criticized for promoting a perfectionistic and individualistic understanding of the way of Jesus; hence his followers highlight Jesus's confrontation of the powers over their injustice. They also place greater emphasis than he did on God's empowering grace and dynamic reign within the drama of history and on the church as experience of regeneration and hope as well as forgiveness.

See also Niebuhr, H. Richard; Rauschenbusch, Walter

References and Further Reading

Primary Sources:

Niebuhr, Reinhold. *Moral Man and Immoral Society.* New York: Scribner's, 1932.
——. *Nature and Destiny of Man.* 2 vols. New York: Scribner's, 1941 and 1964.
——. *The Children of Light and the Children of Darkness: A Vindication of Democracy and a Critique of Its Traditional Defense.* New York: Scribner's, 1944.
——. *Man's Nature and His Communities.* New York: Scribner's, 1965.
——. *Faith and Politics: A Commentary on Religious, Social and Political Thought in a Technological Age.* Edited by Ronald Stone. New York: George Braziller, 1968.
Robertson, D. B. *Reinhold Niebuhr's Works: A Bibliography.* Lanham, MD: University Press of America, 1983.

Secondary Sources:

Gaudin, Gary A., and Douglas John Hall, eds. *Reinhold Niebuhr: A Centenary Appraisal.* Atlanta, GA: Scholars Press, 1994.
Stone, Ronald. *Professor Reinhold Niebuhr: A Mentor to the Twentieth Century.* Louisville, KY: Westminster John Knox, 1992.

GLEN H. STASSEN

NIEMÖLLER, MARTIN (1892–1984)

German churchman and theologian. Niemöller was born in Lippstadt (Westphalia), son of Pastor Heinrich and Paula Niemöller. His chosen career was service in the German Imperial Navy, and during World War I he rose to the rank of a highly decorated U-Boat Commander. He experienced GERMANY's defeat and the revolution following it as an utter collapse of all traditional German values. Refusing to serve the new republic, he left the navy and began to study THEOLOGY to teach Christianity as the power needed to reestablish law and order. Ordained in 1924, he became a pastor. He became a supporter of the emerging Nazi movement, convinced that it would rebuild German identity on a Christian basis.

In 1931 Niemöller was called to serve a prestigious parish in Berlin. After Adolf Hitler's ascendancy to power in 1933, the "GERMAN CHRISTIAN" movement's advocacy of a Christianity based on race and Aryan principles (and in support of the Nazi government) called forth Niemöller's resistance in the formation of the "Young Reformers Movement" and the "Pastors' Emergency League." It was the 1934 "Barmen Theological Declaration" (see BARMEN DECLARATION) with its decisive christological focus, that provided Niemöller with the theology with which to disown his erstwhile nationalistic conservatism and affirm the ground of resistance. Although not free of ANTISEMITISM, he experienced the Nazi's "Aryan Legislation" as a *status confessionis*: the gospel was at stake. Calling Germany's development an injustice and neopaganism, Niemöller was arrested and spent the last years of the Nazi regime in a concentration camp.

After Germany's defeat in 1945, and deeply affected by its burden of guilt, Niemöller worked for the renewal of the church and reconciliation with Germany's former enemies. However, his radical opposition in the late 1940s to Germany's remilitarization, nuclear weapons, and anticommunism minimized his role. The WORLD COUNCIL OF CHURCHES elected him as one of its six presidents in 1961.

See also: Confessing Church

References and Further Reading

Bentley, James. *Martin Niemöller 1982–1984.* New York: The Free Press, 1984.
Schmidt, Dietmar. *Pastor Niemöller.* Translated by Lawrence Wilson. Garden City, NJ: Doubleday & Company, 1959.

MARTIN RUMSCHEIDT

NIETZSCHE, FRIEDRICH (1844–1900)

German philosopher. Best known as the philosopher of nihilism who proclaimed the death of God and the advent of the superman, Nietzsche was born in Röcken, Prussia, October 15, 1844 and grew up in nearby Naumberg. His father and maternal grandfather were Protestant pastors and his paternal grandfather was a Protestant superintendent and defender of the faith. He received his secondary education at Schulpforta, Germany's foremost Protestant boarding school, and then enrolled in the University of Bonn to study THEOLOGY. He soon transferred to classical philology, completing his Ph.D. at Leipzig, where he met and befriended the composer Richard Wagner and the classicist Edwin Rohde.

In 1869 he became professor of classical philology at the University of Basel but grew increasingly more interested in philosophy than philology. During this time he published his *Birth of Tragedy Out of the Spirit of Music,* in which he laid out his famous analysis of art in terms of the Apollinian/Dionysian duality, as well as his *Untimely Meditations,* including a critique of DAVID FRIEDRICH STRAUSS's *Life of Jesus* and *Human, All-Too-Human.* He retired from teaching in 1879 because of ill health and lived for the next ten years in SWITZERLAND, the French Riviera, and ITALY. During this period, he completed the *Dawn, Joyful Wisdom,* his magnum opus *Thus Spoke Zarathustra, Beyond Good and Evil,* the *Genealogy of Morals, Twilight of the Idols,* the *Antichrist, Nietzsche contra Wagner,* and his autobiography *Ecce Homo.* In 1889 he suffered a mental breakdown from which he never recovered, living the remaining years of his life first in an asylum in Basel, then with his mother in Naumberg, and after her death with his sister in Weimar. During this period his sister, the widow of one of Germany's leading anti-Semites, refashioned Nietzsche in her husband's image, altering his existing works and fabricating a new work, the *Will to Power,* out of his discarded notes to bring this about. These distortions facilitated the appropriation of Nietzsche's thought by the fascists and Nazis and delayed an adequate appraisal of his work for many years. Nietzsche died in Weimar, August 25, 1900.

Nietzsche and Christianity

Nietzsche remarked late in life that "the Protestant pastor is the grandfather of German philosophy." He was referring to the German idealists, but the observation is equally true in his own case. Devout as a child, he increasingly opposed Christianity as he grew older and sought to replace it with a philosophical vision that drew heavily on pagan sources and especially the Greek notion of the Dionysian. He proclaimed that "God is dead," and saw this fact as the source of a spiritual malaise he called nihilism. He believed that modern science with its demand for evidence was undermining belief in the Christian God and all of the values predicated on this belief. He believed that this devaluation of the highest values would result in the collapse of European civilization and wars "the like of which the world has never seen."

Life, as Nietzsche understood it, is nothing other than the will to power, a struggle of all beings with one another for dominance. The suffering that this struggle engenders leads the weak to imagine a pacific transcendent reality free of strife where they can find peace. This move, according to Nietzsche, began with Plato and came to fruition in Christianity, which he calls "Platonism for the people." Christianity is thus the product of human weakness, a form of slave morality. It fosters an ascetic ideal that enthrones weakness and undermines nobility. For Nietzsche the death of God makes it possible to overcome these unhealthy Christian values and attain a new nobility that he portrays in his famous image of the superman.

The superman, according to Nietzsche, does not seek a transcendent world free from suffering but mastery in this one. He accepts this world as it is, rejecting all pity and efforts to ameliorate suffering. This is the meaning of Nietzsche's doctrine of the eternal recurrence of all things, which mandates the affirmation of all things that have ever been or will be, thus a love of fate or what he calls *amor fati.* Nietzsche contrasts this Dionysian fatalism in his later thought with Paul's image of Christ on the Cross. Christianity, he argues, is antilife. The last Christian died on the Cross, and historical Christianity is only the product of Paul's resentment and desire for revenge. The true struggle for our time in his view is thus "Dionysus versus the Crucified."

Although the anti-Christian elements of Nietzsche's project are clear, there is considerable evidence that Nietzsche's thought owes a great deal to Christianity. Indeed, although the pagan sources of his central conception of the Dionysian are undeniable, the concept is also deeply indebted to the Christian notion of God as it is received and transfigured by German idealism.

Nietzsche's Influence

Nietzsche's work had an important influence on philosophers such as Karl Jaspers, Martin Heidegger, Albert Camus, Theodor Adorno, Herbert Marcuse, Georges Bataille, Michel Foucault, and Jacques Derrida; social theorists such as Oswald Spengler and MAX WEBER; writers such as Thomas Mann, Hermann Hesse, André Malraux, George Bernard Shaw, Rainer Maria Rilke, Stefan Georg, William Butler Yeats, and D. H. Lawrence; composers Gustav Mahler and Richard Strauss; the architect Le Corbusier; psychologists Sigmund Freud, Alfred Adler, and Carl Jung; and theologians such as PAUL TILLICH, Lev Shestov, Martin Buber, and Thomas J. J. Altizer.

References and Further Reading

Primary Source:

Colli, Giorgio, and Mazzino Montinari, eds. *Werke: Kritische Gesamtausgabe.* Berlin, Germany: de Gruyter, 1967–.

Secondary Sources:

Biser, Eugen. *Gott ist tot, Nietzsches Destruktion des christlichen Bewusstseins.* Munich, Germany: Kösel-Verlag, 1962.
Deleuze, Giles. *Nietzsche and Philosophy.* Translated by Hugh Tomlinson. New York: Columbia University Press, 1983.
Jaspers, Karl. *Nietzsche und das Christentum.* Munich, Germany: Piper, 1952.
Kaufmann, Walter. *Nietzsche: Philosopher, Poet, Antichrist.* 3rd ed. New York: Random House, 1968.
Müller-Lauter, Wolfgang. *Nietzsche: His Philosophy of Contradictions and the Contradictions of his Philosophy.* Urbana: University of Illinois Press, 1999.
Pfeil, Hans. *Von Christus zu Dionysos: Nietzsches religiöse Entwicklung.* Meisenheim am Glan, Germany: Hain, 1975.
Valadier, Paul. *Jésus-Christ ou Dionysos: la foi chrétienne en confrontation avec Nietzsche.* Paris: Desclée, 1979.

MICHAEL ALLEN GILLESPIE

NIGERIA

Protestantism in Nigeria was born from the project of British evangelicals to revive Africa from the effects of the slave trade by introducing "Christianity, civilization, and commerce." The missions began from Freetown in SIERRA LEONE, where they had made converts among liberated African slaves, notably the Yoruba from southwestern and the Igbo from southeastern Nigeria. By the mid-1840s Anglicans of the Church Missionary Society (CMS) and Wesleyan Methodists had established missions back in Yorubaland around a core of African returnees. They were soon followed by American Southern Baptists. Scottish Presbyterians opened a mission at Calabar on the Cross River to the far southeast in 1846. The key figure of the CMS Yoruba Mission was SAMUEL AJAYI CROWTHER, the ex-slave who translated the Bible into Yoruba and in 1864 became the first African to be consecrated an Anglican bishop. In 1857 he initiated a further CMS operation, the Niger Mission, with its main bases along the Lower Niger river.

Up to the end of the nineteenth century, the Protestant missions had probably gained no more than 20,000 converts, a tiny proportion of the population, heavily skewed toward the coastal towns, particularly Lagos. In the 1890s the blockage of earlier moves toward church autonomy under African leadership and strains between missionary teaching and some African customs (especially polygamy) led to some secessions and the foundation of what were known as the "African" churches. They retained most of the liturgy and doctrine of the parent Protestant missions with a degree of cultural Africanization.

The imposition of colonial rule—substantially complete by 1905—enabled missions to push rapidly into the interior, and many new Protestant societies entered the field (in addition to a large Roman Catholic expansion, especially in Igboland). Thus the Qua Iboe Mission from northern Ireland occupied Ibibio country in the southeast; Dutch Reformed missionaries set up among the Tiv of central Nigeria; and other evangelicals such as the Danish Lutherans, the SUDAN INTERIOR MISSION, and the Sudan United Mission, both interdenominational, operated in Nigeria's vast "Middle Belt." With their schools and medical facilities, and diffuse association with the culture of the colonial order, missions were by the 1920s attracting mass support in the more developed southern parts of the country. Protestant missionaries were particularly active in language work and Bible translation, which often had a powerful role in shaping the ethnic consciousness of local elites. The leaders of the nationalist movement were disproportionately the products of their schools.

Yet amid all this success, many Nigerians came to feel that the mainline mission churches did not meet their religious needs. Between 1915 and the mid-1930s, against a background of epidemics and social upheaval, a new wave of Christian independency emerged in the south, led by prophets such as Garrick Braide in the Niger Delta during World War I and the leaders of the Aladura ("praying") movement among the Yoruba, who were often teachers or active members of Protestant missions. Although their concerns for healing, visionary guidance, and protection from witches and evil spirits had traditional roots, their evangelical core was further inflected by Pentecostal influences from Britain or America, now felt in Nigeria for the first time. Bodies like the Christ Army Church, the Cherubim and Seraphim, and the Christ Apostolic Church emerged; others would follow over the years, whether through secession or the emergence of new prophets.

As nationalism got under way from the late 1940s, the mission-linked churches came under pressure both to Africanize their top leadership and to achieve a fuller cultural adaptation or "contextualization" of their teaching and liturgy. The study of "African traditional religion" was pioneered in the religious studies departments of the new universities, notably by two Methodists, the ex-missionary Geoffrey Parrinder and the Nigerian minister E. B. Idowu. AFRICAN THEOLOGY searched for points of consensus between the core values of traditional religion and Christianity, where the earlier emphasis had been on the difference. Ecumenism was also in the air, although a scheme for church union between the Anglicans, Methodists, and Presbyterians foundered in 1965, perhaps because it was too much driven by external models. The years around Nigeria's independence in 1960 were marked by vigorous church growth in the hitherto less Christian areas of the Middle Belt and the north. As ethnic and regional conflict intensified in the 1960s it became colored by religious difference, especially as more and more Nigerians converted to the world religions. In the civil war of 1967–1970, there was a tendency to stereotype the breakaway southeastern region, Biafra, as "Catholic," whereas Biafra saw itself as the victim of a "Muslim" Nigeria. Protestantism did not fit this religious coding of political difference, and symbolically it was fitting that the Nigerian military ruler, Yakubu Gowon, was himself an Anglican from a minority northern group.

Since the 1970s a wave of neo-Pentecostal or "Born-again" Christianity has seemed to sweep all before it. Its origins lay in the growing influence of diverse, mostly American, Pentecostal evangelists who had conducted REVIVALS in Nigeria since the 1950s and attracted Nigerians to their BIBLE COLLEGES in the United States, and in the wider expansion of what began as campus religious fellowships. Although the religious concerns of the born-agains show much continuity with those of earlier churches like Aladura, their idiom is very different: they are oriented toward the modern and the universal, rather than to the uniquely African, and highly effective in the use of electronic mass media. The mainline Protestant churches, having lost many of their young people to them, are themselves increasingly penetrated by born-again influences.

Nigeria's population of perhaps 120,000,000 people is divided fairly equally between Muslims and Christians (Christian growth having been much greater in recent decades). Although Roman Catholics easily constitute the largest single church and predominate in some parts of the country, Protestants (of all kinds) probably constitute over two thirds of the Christian total. In its strongly voluntaristic character, and in its dominance by the evangelical tradition whose most recent fruit is the born-again movement, Nigerian Christianity overall continues to bear the stamp of its Protestant origins.

See also Dutch Reformed Church in Africa; Pentecostalism

References and Further Reading

Ajayi, J. F. A. *Christian Missions in Nigeria*. London: Longmans, 1965.
Crampton, E. P. T. *Christianity in Northern Nigeria*. London: Chapman, 1979.
Kalu, O. U. *The Embattled Gods: The Christianization of Igboland*. Lagos: Minaj, 1996.
Omoyajowo, A. J. *Cherubim and Seraphim*. New York: Nok, 1982.
Peel, J. D. Y. *Religious Encounter and the Making of the Yoruba*. Bloomington: Indiana University Press, 2000.

J. D. Y. PEEL

NONCONFORMITY

The word *Nonconformity* is applied in Britain, particularly ENGLAND and WALES, to churches that do not conform to the Established Church. Although that logically includes Roman Catholics and, in SCOTLAND, Episcopalians, it is generally taken to describe non-Episcopalian Protestants, particularly BAPTISTS, Congregationalists Methodists, Presbyterians (outside the CHURCH OF SCOTLAND), Quakers, and Unitarians. It also embraces a wide sectarian spectrum from PLYMOUTH BRETHREN to Peculiar People. Sometimes the phrase "Evangelical Nonconformity" is used, reflecting the dominant temper and excluding Unitarians (see UNITARIAN UNIVERSALIST ASSOCIATION).

Precision is therefore difficult. The concept varies subtly but significantly in different parts of the British Isles. In IRELAND there has been no Established Church since 1869 and in Wales since 1912. Yet Nonconformity was a force in Welsh life at least until the last quarter of the twentieth century: to what did it not conform? In Ireland, except perhaps the North, the Anglican Church was never a popular, although it was certainly a social, force; Irish Protestantism of all shades was determined by its reaction to Roman Catholicism. If English Nonconformity was shaped by its reaction to ANGLICANISM, so Scottish Nonconformity was shaped by PRESBYTERIANISM. Indeed most Scottish Nonconformists were dissident Presbyterians. Even so, denominational interaction within Britain was significant. It was fueled, especially in England, by immigration, and in Ireland, Scotland, and Wales by anglicization, although Nonconformists, especially in Wales, were notable linguistic and cultural nationalists. English Nonconformist leadership and scholarship was heavily accented by Irish, Scottish, and Welsh ministers, for example, the Scottish PETER TAYLOR FORSYTH and the Welsh C. H. Dodd.

Early History

Although the word is primarily of nineteenth-century origin, overtaking the earlier DISSENT and in turn overtaken by a preference for "Free Churches," the concept has been a feature of British life since the seventeenth century, with discernible sixteenth-century origins and a suggestive fourteenth-century prehistory. Thus Nonconformity's historians have been fascinated by congruences with John Wycliffe's Lollards. It was, however, the REFORMATION that liberated the concept, the Elizabethan Settlement that confirmed it, and the so-called Puritan Revolution that turned it into a certainty. The distinctive groupings of "Old Dissent"—Baptists, Independents (or Congregationalists), Presbyterians, and Quakers (see FRIENDS, SOCIETY OF)—were in existence by 1660. The first two had evolved chiefly in England since the reign of ELIZABETH I; the third had also evolved in the rest of Britain, most notably in Scotland, as well. They had their martyrs (the Separatist Barrow and Greenwood, executed in 1593), their lost leaders (ROBERT BROWNE), their heroes (the Mayflower PILGRIM FATHERS of 1620), their spiritual and cultural leaders (JOHN MILTON), and their political aspirations (OLIVER CROMWELL).

The determinative dates for Nonconformity's institutional existence are 1660 (the restoration of the monarchy), 1662 (the ejection of ministers unable to accept the BOOK OF COMMON PRAYER and THIRTY-NINE ARTICLES and the restored church's failure in England, Ireland, and Wales to comprehend that major portion of reluctant Nonconformists who objected to the nature rather than the principle of establishment), and 1689 (when Trinitarian Protestant Dissenters were legally tolerated). There were parallel developments in Scotland, where the nature of the Presbyterian establishment took longer to clarify. Thereafter Britain was an ecclesiastically divided yet also increasingly plural society. Nonconformists were citizens, albeit second-class ones. They were largely, but never wholly, excluded from political leadership and from the English universities. They were subject to the threat more often than the reality of discrimination when it came to their births, their marriages (especially between 1753 and 1836), and their burials, or when it came to the payment of tithes and church rate.

Nonconformity developed a distinctive culture. The realities and opportunities of TOLERATION largely preserved it from a ghetto mentality. Nonetheless ECCLESIOLOGY and the contemporary social climate encouraged a complex of cousinhoods, at once pervasive and localized, of which the Quakers furnish the best-known examples. This fostered commercial strengths, especially as the Industrial Revolution developed (see INDUSTRIALIZATION), and was accompanied by a theological and literary culture that was both popular and classical. JOHN BUNYAN, RICHARD BAXTER, ISAAC WATTS, Philip Doddridge, and also Daniel Defoe and Thomas and Humphrey Gainsborough exemplify this.

The Evangelical Revival profoundly affected eighteenth-century Nonconformity. It galvanized Baptists and Congregationalists (see CONGREGATIONALISM), it changed the direction of Quakers, and, by reaction, it shaped the development of many, especially English Presbyterians, into Unitarianism. It also provided in METHODISM a clutch of denominations whose totality made them the largest non-Anglican Protestant body outside Scotland. Methodists, especially Wesleyans (see WESLEYANISM), disliked the Nonconformist label. Legally that is what they were and culturally that is what they became.

Nineteenth Century

The story of nineteenth-century Nonconformity is one of numerical growth, spiritual assurance, ecclesiastical experiment, and political discovery. Nonconformists were determined to secure civic and ecclesiastical parity. The former was steadily achieved by legislation beginning symbolically in 1828 with the repeal of those seventeenth-century relics, the Test and Corporation Acts. The latter inspired a carefully organized movement to disestablish the Anglican Church. This succeeded in Ireland (1869) and Wales (1912). It has yet to happen in England. Scotland, as always in ecclesiastical matters, took its own path. Nonconformity's constitutional concern with rights, symbolized in the career of Edward Miall, was superseded by a concern with Right: the belief that legislation could moralize a nation, symbolized by the phrase, "Nonconformist Conscience," coined in 1891.

Nonconformists felt a special affinity for the UNITED STATES. Their knowledge of the world was developed by influential foreign missionary societies (see MISSIONARY ORGANIZATIONS). Their ministers—the Wesleyan Hugh Price Hughes, the Baptist CHARLES HADDON SPURGEON, the Congregational Joseph Parker, the Unitarian JAMES MARTINEAU—were men of national, indeed transatlantic, note. So were Nonconformist politicians—the Quaker John Bright, the Unitarian Joseph Chamberlain. Nonconformist products were household names: Colman's Mustard, Fry's cocoa, Lever's soap, Crossley's Carpets, Wills' Tobacco, Hartley's Jams. They built theological colleges in Oxford and Cambridge as well as in the industrial cities. There was a distinctive Nonconformist ARCHITECTURE, and an infectious Nonconformist hymnody (see HYMNS AND HYMNALS). The poet ROBERT BROWNING was one of them. William Gladstone, of course, was not, but it was a paradox of Victorian Britain that the Liberal party, its prime political success story, was popularly regarded as the Nonconformists' party.

Their numerical strength was revealed by the Religious Census of 1851. Numerical parity with Anglicans was surely imminent in England. It had already been achieved in Wales. That, however, was never to happen, although growth continued into the early twentieth century.

Twentieth Century

The scent of success and the experience of social assimilation had their effect. Nonconformity was negative. Why not conform? Nonconformity's distinctives had permeated society, coloring its fabric and determining its temper. This process was quite as insistent as its reverse. Nonconformists turned to reexamine their churchmanship. Ever since the Scottish disruption of 1843, which issued in the Free Church of Scotland, the phrase and concept of a "FREE CHURCH" had proved attractive. From the 1890s Free Church cooperation heralded the twentieth century's characteristic ecclesiastical motif: ECUMENISM. The Free Church Council movement fed into the BRITISH COUNCIL OF CHURCHES of the century's second half. From the Baptist J. H. Shakespeare to the Baptist Ernest Payne, culminating in the Congregational/United Reformed John Huxtable and the Methodist Harry Morton, Nonconformity's leaders, only half-jokingly termed "Dissenting Primates," were ecumenical leaders. Church reunion (for Methodists in 1907 and 1932) and union (between English and English-speaking Welsh Congregationalists and English Presbyterians to form the United Reformed Church in 1972 and then with Churches of Christ in 1981 and Scottish Congregationalists in 2002) punctuated the century. The political momentum was dissipated much sooner. Although eight twentieth-century prime ministers (H. H. Asquith, David Lloyd George, Stanley Baldwin, Ramsay MacDonald, Neville Chamberlain, Harold Wilson, James Callaghan, and Margaret Thatcher) had demonstrably close Nonconformist connections, the Nonconformist Conscience had effectively vanished even before Lloyd George tried desperately to exploit it between the Wars. In the century's last quarter, despite a still lively social and confessional witness, Nonconformity's numbers slumped. In the redefinition of the nation's ecclesiastical life, the new non-Anglican churches, frequently of immigrant origin, were seldom associated with traditional Nonconformity. Yet its values of personal faith, representative churchmanship, biblical scholarship, and a keen sense of the Christian citizen's due place in the body politic, remain foundational values for British society.

References and Further Reading

Bebbington, D. W. *The Nonconformist Conscience: Chapel and Politics 1870–1914.* London: George Allen and Unwin, 1982.

Binfield, C. *So Down to Prayers: Studies in English Nonconformity, 1780–1920.* London: J. M. Dent & Sons Ltd., 1977.

Davies, Rupert, ed. *The Testing of the Churches 1932–1982: A Symposium.* London: Epworth Press, 1982.

Hastings, Adrian. *A History of English Christianity 1920–1988.* London: Collins, 1986.

Mills, W. Haslam. *Grey Pastures.* London: Chapels Society, 2003.

Munson, James. *The Nonconformists: In Search of a Lost Culture.* London: SPCK, 1991.

Sellers, Ian. *Nineteenth-Century Nonconformity.* London: Edmund Arnold, 1977.

Watts, Michael R. *The Dissenters: From the Reformation to the French Revolution.* Oxford, UK: The Clarendon Press, 1978.

———. *The Dissenters: The Expansion of Evangelist Nonconformity 1791–1859.* Oxford, UK: The Clarendon Press, 1995.

CLYDE BINFIELD

NORTH INDIA, CHURCH OF

The Church of North India (CNI) was established at Nagpur in 1970 following several decades of conversation and negotiations involving Anglicans, BAPTISTS, CHURCH OF THE BRETHREN, Congregationalists, DISCIPLES OF CHRIST, Methodists, and Presbyterians. Formal negotiations leading to the union of churches were preceded by cooperation and consultation among missionaries during the nineteenth and twentieth centuries. Local conferences involving the various mission boards, convened at Bombay, Calcutta, and Madras, were followed by broader regional conferences in North and South India. The first North Indian Conference comprised six mission societies meeting at Calcutta in 1855. This body met again in 1857 at Benares and in 1862 at Lahore. The LORD'S SUPPER was celebrated together at Lahore by missionaries of differing Christian traditions. Territorial comity (dividing the land to avoid overlap) was a further expression of unity and a first step toward a united church in North India. The WORLD MISSIONARY CONFERENCE at Edinburgh in 1910 furthered the concern for unity and cooperation for world evangelization through a united Church of Christ in every country.

In INDIA the nationalist movement provided impetus toward a merger. NATIONALISM was an outcome of the Western education provided by missionary schools and colleges. Indian Christians who contributed positively to the nationalist movement included Susil Kumar Rudra (1861–1925), Surendra Kumar Dutta (1878–1942), K. T. Paul (1876–1931), and VEDANAYAKAM SAMUEL AZARIAH (1874–1945). The national struggle for freedom from colonial rule involved the church shedding its Western accretions.

History

The earliest Protestant missionaries, Bartholomäus Ziegenbalg at Tranquebar and WILLIAM CAREY at Seramapore, envisioned an indigenous Indian Church rather than a replica of European Christianity, an ideal not always achieved. One of the earliest attempts to create an independent Indian Church was by Lal Behari Dey at Calcutta, who proposed a United Church of Bengal free of missionary control and encompassing all denominations. The attempt failed, but Dey influenced S. Pulney Andy at Madras, who worked to realize a National Church in India, which was inaugurated in 1886 and which aimed at uniting all denominations. The Calcutta Christo Samaj was formed in 1887 by Kali Charan Banerjee and J. G. Shome as an independent and self-supporting congregation, but this dissolved in 1894. A similar movement of dissent in Bombay, known as the Bombay Native Christian Church or the Western India Native Christian Alliance, appeared in 1871 but came to an end in 1895. These attempts, all less than successful, were manifestations of the growing nationalist movement and a desire for the self-identity of Indian Christians. Formation in 1905 of the National Missionary Society was a successful expression of Christian nationalism and example of interdenominational cooperation.

Discussions on the possibility of church union in North India began in 1929. A Basis of Negotiation was prepared in 1937. Meanwhile, in 1924, a Congregational–Presbyterian merger had formed the United Church of Northern India, which then entered into official discussions with Anglicans, Baptists, and Methodists. These churches claimed about a million members in all. A Scheme of Union was drafted that made provisions both for believer's BAPTISM and infant (sponsored) baptism, and for unification of the ordained ministries of the uniting churches to take place at the inauguration of union. The negotiators thus anticipated the complicated question of the relationship of the new church with the CHURCH OF ENGLAND.

Negotiations were carried out through a series of Round Table Conferences in 1930 in Delhi, 1931 in Nagpur, 1937 and 1939 in Lucknow, and 1941, 1947, and 1948 in Allahabad. The Negotiating Committee met in 1955, 1957, 1959, 1965, and 1970. The CNI was formally inaugurated on November 29, 1970 in a splendid celebration at the All Saint's Cathedral in Nagpur through a unification rite validating the ordination of the participating traditions. Uniting members included the Church of India, Pakistan, Burma and Ceylon (Anglican); the United Church of Northern India; the Council of Baptist Churches of Northern India; the Church of the Brethren; the Methodist Church (British and Australian); and the DISCIPLES OF CHRIST, but not the Methodist Church in Southern Asia (later reconstituted as the Methodist Church in India), which rejected the Plan of Union.

Characteristics

The CNI is an Episcopal church in communion with the Church of England. The negotiators from the beginning sought to preserve the important distinctive features of the divergent Western traditions represented. The confession of Jesus Christ as Lord is the primary basis of union. The CNI Statement of Faith is a precise affirmation of the historic Christian faith. "The Holy Scripture is accepted as containing all things necessary to SALVATION and as the standard of faith, and the Apostles' Creed and Nicene Creed as witnessing to and safeguarding the faith" (Sahu 1994:159).

Formation of the CNI was seen by some as an innovative ecumenical event that broke the rigidities of denominationalism and led to new expressions of the historic episcopacy, LITURGY, and church structure (Perumalil and Hambye c. 1972:296). In 1972 a Joint Council was created for intercommunion of the CNI together with the CHURCH OF SOUTH INDIA and the Mar Thoma Church as an ecumenical instrument "working towards a visible manifestation of unity of the three autonomous churches (not yet structurally or constitutionally one), yet living and acting like one Church of Christ in India" (Dharmaraj 1980:51). Negotiations continued with the Methodist Church in India as well as conversations with the Lutherans and other churches.

Today, the CNI is a territorial hierarchy of about twenty-five dioceses with more than 3,000 congregations and a membership of more than 900,000 representing twenty or more languages and cultures stretching across most of India (excluding the southern states of India) united in Christian witness and worship.

See also Colonialism; Congregationalism; Dialogue, Interconfessional; Ecumenism; Methodism; Post-Colonalism; Presbyterianism

References and Further Reading

Dharmaraj, A. C. "The Indian Response to Ecumenism: A Protestant View." In *Ecumenism in India: Essays in Honour of the Rev. M.A. Thomas*, edited by Mathai Zachariah. Delhi, India: ISPCK, 1980.

Hedlund, Roger E. *Roots of the Great Debate in Mission: Mission in Historical and Theological Perspective*. Revised and enlarged. Bangalore, India: Theological Book Trust, 1993, 1997.

Perumalil, H. C., and E. R. Hambye, eds. *Christianity in India: A History in Ecumenical Perspective*. Alleppey, India: Prakasam Publications, c. 1972.

Rouse, Ruth, and Stephen C. Neill, eds. *A History of the Ecumenical Movement 1517–1948*. Philadelphia, PA: Westminster Press, 1954.

Sahu, Dhirendra Kumar. *The Church of North India: A Historical and Systematic Theological Inquiry Into an Ecumenical Ecclesiology*. Frankfurt, Germany: Peter Lang, 1994.

ROGER E. HEDLUND

NORWAY

Introduction

Norway constitutes an area of approximately 387,000 square kilometers occupying the western part of the Scandinavian Peninsula and the islands of Svalbard and Jan Mayen. It is one of the five Nordic nations, and for this reason its history and relations are closely related to the rest of the Nordic countries. After more than 400 years in union with DENMARK, Norway became a constitutional monarchy May 17, 1814. Later the same year a looser union with SWEDEN was established. The parliament is called Storting; the parliamentarian system was introduced in 1884. Universal suffrage for men was given in 1898 and in 1913 extended to include WOMEN. Since the breakup of the union with Sweden in 1905, Norway has been an independent nation state, but was occupied by GERMANY from April 9, 1940 to May 8, 1945.

The population is about 4.3 million, mainly of Nordic heritage. Because of immigration, however, multiculturalism and multireligiousness is increasing. The indigenous people are the Sami (about 30,000). Since the end of the nineteenth century Norway has had two official languages, Norwegian (heavily influenced by Danish) and New Norwegian (based on Norse and dialects). Recently also the Sami language has become the official language in parts of northern Norway.

The majority of the population lives in urban areas. The capital is Oslo (about 500,000 inhabitants), which is also the seat of government, parliament, and king. For historical reasons the ecclesiastical center, however, is Trondheim with its cathedral, dedicated to St. Olav.

Although oil and gas constitute a cornerstone of the economy, traditional industry—fishery, forestry, manufacturing, and shipping—still is important.

Norway is a member of NATO and an associate member of the West European Union, but not of the European Union. Twice (1972, 1994) a majority has voted against joining this union.

Eighty-seven percent of the population belong to the Church of Norway, which consists of eleven bishoprics. The church is organized as a Lutheran state church with the king as the constitutional head. He exercises his AUTHORITY through the government, whereas the parliament deals with legislation concerning the church. During the last decades the church has obtained a certain degree of autonomy and its own bodies.

The Church of Norway is a member of the LUTHERAN WORLD FEDERATION and the WORLD COUNCIL OF CHURCHES.

History

Norway has been populated for thousands of years. It was ruled by clans, each of which dominated a certain area, but became a united land during the eleventh and twelfth centuries. During the Viking Age (800–1050) the Viking chiefs plundered the coasts of Europe and brought new cultural and religious impulses back to Norway. Previously the Norse religion with its myths about gods and heroes had been the indigenous religion.

Christianization

The start of unification of Norway is often linked to the victory of King Harald Fair-Haired in the battle of Hafrsfiord in 872, although he controlled only the coastal areas. One of his sons, King Haakon the Good, returned to Norway about 950 after a Christian upbringing in ENGLAND and became the first missionary king. However, he did not succeed in introducing the new religion. More important to the Christianization of Norway was King Olav Haraldson, who died in the battle of Stiklestad in 1030. After his death he became the patron saint of Norway and his grave the center of a cult that brought pilgrims from all over Europe to the cathedral that was erected to his memory in Trondheim (Nidaros).

One may say that Norway was Christianized by Viking kings who had met Christianity abroad. Although the Norse religion had a local basis, linked with clans and local aristocracy, the new religion transcended such boundaries and was more apt to unify the country and to be basis of a "modern" European monarchy. Thus Christianization and unification of a land became two sides of the same coin. Organized mission, however, first of all from the British Isles, but also from the south (from Germany over Denmark), had prepared the soil.

During the eleventh century the former pagan cult was replaced by Christian WORSHIP, churches were built, and Christian laws were established. A change of cult took place, followed by a new ethos. To what degree and when the Norwegians really became Christians, however, has been a matter of disagreement among historians.

The Medieval Church

The Norwegian bishops belonged to the archdiocese of Bremen (Germany). In 1104 a Nordic archdiocese was established in Lund, and in 1152–1153 a papal legate, Cardinal Nicholas Breakspear (later Pope Adrian IV), visited Norway and founded the archdiocese of Trondheim.

The strengthening of power of the church led to conflicts with the monarchy. By tradition any royal son could claim the throne if the ting (the old regional assembly) accepted him, although the church claimed primogeniture and priority of legitimate sons. This involved the church in a civil war that lasted until 1217. Then followed a glorious cultural and political era until the Black Death in 1349–1350. The plague killed more than half of the population, with disastrous consequences for both state and church. Only one of the bishops survived, and the power of the aristocracy declined. Danes and Swedes filled the gaps in the civil and ecclesiastical administration. Before the plague a personal union with Sweden had been established in 1319. Under Margaret I of Denmark all three Scandinavian states were united under one king (Union of Kalmar 1397). This meant the beginning to the end of the Norwegian medieval state. The council of state did not manage to promote either their own or Norway's interests, and political power and decisions were transferred to Copenhagen and the Danish kings and nobility. One crucial consequence was the Lutheran REFORMATION, which came as a royal decree in 1536–1537.

The Reformation of Norway

From the beginning of the sixteenth century to the breakup of the union in 1814, Norwegian history and church history are closely linked to Denmark, and decisions were made in Copenhagen. National historians have seen this as a time of Danish colonization and exploitation. For this reason the Reformation has been seen as a historical break and as a strengthening of Danish rule. Others have stressed that this also was a time of growth, and that the union gave access to European CULTURE.

The reformation of Norway has been characterized as a reformation without a reformer. The Norwegian council of state tried in the turbulent 1520s and 1530s to promote Norwegian independence during the battle of the Danish–Norwegian throne, although the members were split. As Archbishop Olav Engelbrektsson led the council of state he tried to maintain the Catholic Church, but ended on the losing side of the conflict between Christian II and Christian III. For that reason he chose to flee the country in the spring of 1537.

There was no popular movement to back a reformation, although most of the population and CLERGY seem to have been indifferent. In that way Norway became no "Scandinavian Ireland," although reduced to a Danish province. The former mighty Catholic bishops were removed from their seats, and some churches were plundered and the treasures shipped to Copenhagen. The king confiscated the properties of the church, and used the wealth to improve administration and create an integrated state; otherwise, the king chose a careful and peaceful way to introduce LUTHERANISM. Most of the clergy remained in their offices, thus prompting no drastic changes. The main innovations were the appointment of superintendents to replace the bishops and a new, Lutheran Church Order (1537–1539, Latin/Danish). To implement the ideas of Lutheranism and to standardize LITURGY and organization, the superintendents were to make regular visitations and also gather the clergy in synods. However, long distances, difficult travels, and a passive vicarage made this difficult. Thus it took a long time to change religious views and habits of ordinary people, and in isolated parts reminiscences of Catholicism survived to the beginning of the nineteenth century. In 1550 the BIBLE was published in Danish (see BIBLE TRANSLATION), and a few years later came a service book and a hymnbook (see HYMNS AND HYMNALS). Thus a Lutheran service with hymns in a more understandable language took on a firmer form.

The most important consequence of the reformation was a close link between church and state/king. The king was head of the church, and the superintendents and ministers were servants of both God and king. The negative consequence was a decline of the school system run by the church and financed by incomes that now were lost.

The Age of Lutheran Orthodoxy and Absolutism

The second part of the sixteenth and most of the seventeenth century marked an era of teaching the people the evangelical faith and defending the right Lutheran faith against heresies (see HERESY). King Fredrik II sympathized with the followers of PHILIP MELANCHTHON and in 1580 banned the BOOK OF CONCORD, the main symbol of Lutheran ORTHODOXY. In time he had to yield to orthodoxy, but the confession of the Church of Norway (in addition to the three creeds from the old church) still consists of MARTIN LUTHER's Little Catechism and the AUGSBURG CONFESSION.

Because of fear of Sweden and the growing importance of Norway's natural resources, the Danish kings took a stronger interest in Norway. The most outstanding was King Christian IV. He made several long journeys through the country, founded towns, and promoted sawmills, mining, and salt-works. He also gave Norway its own Church Order (1607).

In 1629 the king took measures to strengthen CHURCH DISCIPLINE and morals. Stricter laws against immoral behavior were introduced, and lay "helpers" were appointed to assist in supervising parish members. Furthermore, the knowledge of the clergy was improved by the requirement of a degree in theology from the University of Copenhagen before entering ministry. This requirement for theological qualifications remained until it was abandoned for certain groups by the General Synod in the 1990s.

As in the rest of Europe, the seventeenth century was the age of charges against people accused of being witches and wizards allied with the DEVIL. Probably 1,000–2,000 such processes took place in Norway during the seventeenth century, and several hundred ended with a death sentence (see WITCHCRAZE).

Under King Christian IV the nobility lost some of its influence, although an increasing number of civil servants and professional officers got important roles in the administration of the dual monarchy. At the same time an increasing bourgeoisie claimed their part of the political power. This resulted in the introduction of ABSOLUTISM in 1660. The Danish council of state lost its power, the kingdom became hereditary, and the king had the absolute power. The kingdom became a sacral monarchy and the clergy the king's employees.

An important goal of the absolutist policy was standardization of laws and official practices, including church and services. King Christian V gave a new codex of laws for Norway (Norwegian Laws of 1687) in which laws concerning church and religious life were a part of the general laws of the state. A part of these church laws regulated the life of the church until the end of the twentieth century. Furthermore, a Danish–Norwegian Church Ritual had been introduced in 1685, regulating the different services in detail. This Church Ritual dominated the Norwegian tradition for the next 200 years and turned Sunday service into a psalm mass. The singing of psalms became an important part of the Lutheran worship.

The Age of Pietism and Enlightenment

The greatest change in church life during the eighteenth century came with the pietistic reform movement, which spread from Germany to Norway through Denmark.

PIETISM in Denmark–Norway was a revival "from above," promoted by the king and nobility, and spread through the clergy to the parishes. It reintroduced CONFIRMATION (1736), which was abandoned by the Reformation, established a public church school system (1739) with confirmation as final examination, reformed the system dealing with pauperism, and introduced MISSIONS (to the Eskimos and the Sami people) as a Christian duty.

The compulsory confirmation was based on learning by heart an explanation of the CATECHISM (consisting of 759 questions and answers) written by the pietistic theologian and later bishop Erik Pontoppidan. For almost 200 years this explanation became the main source of Norwegians' knowledge of what was true Christianity, and how a pious Christian should live. During the second part of the nineteenth century the public church school was secularized and modernized, partly by Norwegian followers of the Danish theologian and poet NICOLAJ F. S. GRUNDTVIG.

Radical Pietism also made its way to Denmark–Norway. For this reason the authorities introduced an act (1741) to control CONVENTICLES. It put the vicars in charge of supervising such lay activity. The aim was to secure religious unity and social order. It could not, however, prevent the CHURCH OF THE BRETHREN from gaining influence among the bourgeoisie and clergy, and during the following century this type of Christianity made a strong impact on the Norwegian church and theology. Today the Brethren's distinction between an organized church of all baptized and a kernel of true believers has become standard Norwegian ecclesiology.

In many ways Pietism was a movement of ENLIGHTENMENT, although a Christian Enlightenment, with a basis in the bourgeoisie and the court. Later in the eighteenth and in the first part of the nineteenth century, the same social groups became the basis of a more secularized Enlightenment. It was first of all an elite phenomenon and therefore of less influence in Norway than in Denmark.

The Age of Revivalism and Democratization

During the era from the French Revolution to World War I, Norway went through dramatic changes. It went from ABSOLUTISM to DEMOCRACY, from a society of estates to a society of equals, from an agrarian society to urbanization and early INDUSTRIALIZATION, from being a part of a multinational state to become a nation state. These changes also made a great impact on the church.

In 1811 the king founded the University of Christiania (Oslo) as the first national institution in Norway. The lectures started two years later, and the purpose was to supply the state with civil servants, not just a clergy. The first teachers of theology, Peter Hersleb and Stenerus Johannes Stenersen, represented a mild biblical orthodoxy. This was also the time of the Napoleonic Wars, in which Denmark–Norway tried to remain neutral, but got involved on the French side stemming from hostile actions from England. The consequence was a disaster to Norway attributed to a sea blockade, which caused starvation and illness. The clergy, inspired by ideas of the Enlightenment, made a great effort to help their parishioners. At the end of the wars Denmark had to give up all rights to Norway in the Treaty of Kiel (January 1814). With support of the Great Powers, Sweden intended to establish a new union, although this plan was delayed and an important interlude took place in the spring of 1814.

The Danish crown prince, Christian Fredrik, was governor of Norway, and together with the nobility and civil servants he organized a rebellion against the Treaty of Kiel. A constituent assembly, gathered at Eidvoll, declared a new, democratic constitution and elected Christian Fredrik as king. After a short war with Sweden, however, he had to resign, and a new personal union was established.

Although the constitution at the time was most radical, it continued the policy of religious unity. Paragraph 2 stated that the Evangelical-Lutheran religion remained the official religion of the state, which it still is. During the assembly freedom of religion had been mentioned as one of the principles, but in the final version it had vanished. There is disagreement concerning the reason. Some have called it a slip of the pen, but more likely freedom of religion was not an actual problem. Norway was a religiously homogeneous society, and religion was still considered "the glue" that kept society together and gave reasons for morality and loyalty. Later this function was replaced by NATIONALISM and freedom of religion was no longer a threat. Thus the religious legislation was gradually liberalized from the 1840s.

First of all, the Act of Conventicles, which was an obstacle to groups of religious revivalism, was abandoned (1842), and a new act permitting dissenters to remain Norwegian citizens and practice their faith was introduced (1845). Religious revivalism had occurred in most of nineteenth-century Protestant Europe, but it made a greater impact on the Norwegian society (see REVIVALS). For a long time this revivalism has been interpreted as a popular reaction to the Enlightenment and theological rationalism. For that reason the continuity between the Pietism of the early eighteenth century and religious revivalism has been stressed. However, during the last decades such revivalism has been seen as a part of the modernization of society. For this reason the novelty of these movements has been underlined, that is, how they broke the unity of a premodern agrarian society, created new social forms, and represented an early MODERNISM.

A common feature of these early religious revivalist groups was the time when they occurred (about 1800), and their charismatic leadership. In Norway the well-known HANS NIELSEN HAUGE (1771–1824) had his mystical experience in 1796, which aroused a vocation to preach and to begin a nationwide awakening combined with merchant enterprises (see AWAKENINGS). Contrary to previous Pietism, this new religious revivalism was led by the LAITY and expressed its new self-conceit. Furthermore, it represented a challenge to traditional society with its subordination. For that reason the political authorities treated such awakening movements severely and arrested the leaders. They were seen as rebellions, which becomes quite clear in the case against Hauge, who was treated as a threat against the state.

Hauge was arrested in 1804, accused of serious crimes, and was kept in prison for almost ten years, which broke his health and made him more cooperative with the official church. His fate made him the martyr of the laity and the patron saint of what has been called a Norwegian counterculture, although in his last will the "rebel" admonished his followers to remain in the church and to respect the clergy. In a longer perspective his followers were totally integrated in the church, and some of the second generation (among them Hauge's own son) studied theology and became ministers. A new awakening in the 1850s under the leadership of the confessional orthodox Gisle Johnson (1822–1894), professor of theology at University of Christiania, led radical Pietism of the early revivalism into Lutheran orthodoxy, and even political conservatism. Thus "awakening" Christianity became the Christianity of the official church. It also implicated an end of the religious unity of the state, and opened society to modern, religious pluralism. In this way religious revivalism gave an important contribution to the SECULARIZATION of society.

Another distinctive mark of religious revivalism was the emphasis on morality. Daily work was seen as a service to God and the new life after CONVERSION was expected to be a sober and simple life. This led to an active and productive ethos and then to an improvement of living conditions. Some revivalists became rather wealthy, and revivalism was important in establishing a middle class as well as a farmers' opposition in the parliament. This illustrates how religious revivalism created an early social mobility, which inaugurated a breaking up of traditional and stable agrarian society, although revivalism could also turn into open rebellion. In the north of Scandinavia, a religious awakening around the Swedish minister LARS LEVI LÆSTADIUS (1800–1861), beginning in the 1840s, made its way into the Sami population and established an ethnic religiosity throughout the region. This was one of the elements in a rebellion that took place in Kautokeino in northeast Norway in November 1852. Some from the Sami population killed the local merchantman and the constable and harassed the minister, the main local agents for the authorities. Later on, Laestadinism became the most influent religious awakening in the north with a great impact on church and society, *but* the rebellious attitude was replaced by a sectarian antimodernism and Lutheran confessionalism.

From the middle of the nineteenth century religious revivalism developed into organized societies promoting missions both abroad and inside Norway (see MISSIONARY ORGANIZATIONS), and at the same time establishing sorts of free churches within the boundaries of the state church. Moreover, revivalism and a new freedom of religion also paved the way for establishing traditional free churches. In 1814 some Norwegians had returned from English prisons as Quakers (see FRIENDS, SOCIETY OF) and were persecuted by the authorities. Some immigrated to America, but after 1845 they could remain and practice their belief. Already in 1843 a Roman Catholic parish was started in Christiania, and in 1851 a constitutional ban against Jews (see JUDAISM) living in the country was abandoned. In the 1850s came Mormons (see MORMONISM), Methodists (see METHODISM), and BAPTISTS and in the following decades minor groups broke away from the established church and founded their own congregations such as Lutheran Presbyterians (see PRESBYTERIANISM). In the beginning of the twentieth century came Pentecostals (see PENTECOSTALISM), later secularized humanism, and in the last decades charismatic CHRISTIAN RIGHT groups, NEW AGE MOVEMENTS, and, because of immigration, other world religions such as Islam.

The Age of Conflicts and Reforms

Although religious revivalism actualized the question of individual identity, modernization of the society challenged the traditional identity of the church centered on the clergy. From the middle of the nineteenth century new concepts such as "state church" and "folk church" expressed new relations between state, people, and church. A democratization of the church became a part of a general political democratization.

Professor Johnson was the most influential person in the church during the second half of the nineteenth century. He represented both orthodoxy and pietism and suppressed the Norwegian followers of Grundtvig because of their religious and political liberalism. His own political conservatism was based on traditional Lutheran loyalty to the authorities according to Paul's commandment in Romans 13. During a constitutional battle in the 1870s and 1880s, where the issue was establishment of a parliamentarian system, the king engaged himself on the conservative side and made plans for a coup d'état. The conflict ended in 1884 with a conservative government being impeached, and a parliamentary system was gradually introduced.

In the beginning of 1883, when the situation was very tense, Johnson published an appeal to friends of Christianity in Norway. It attacked the Liberal Left Party and its democratic politics. Four hundred fifty prominent men in church and society, among them all the bishops, signed it. This appeal scandalized the church for decades and made the gap between the church and the democratic and national movement obvious. The church was considered an enemy to democratic and national issues such as rights and needs of an increasing urban working class and the demand for a separate Norwegian Consular Service to promote Norwegian interests within the Union.

It was first at the turn of the century that religious revivalism approached national revivalism, and during the conflict with Sweden in 1905 religious nationalism occurred, seeing the national history as an expression of the will of God. The prime minister, Christian Michelsen, used the church to give legitimacy to his rebellion government after the breakup of the Union (June 7). The unilateral break was backed during the service the following Sunday, and the clergy supported the government in two plebiscites: upon the breakup of the Union (August 13) and upon accepting a new monarchy (November 12–13).

Democratization of society in the second part of the nineteenth century changed the concept of the church into a "folk church," which describes an inclusive and democratic church. The result was not a separation of CHURCH AND STATE like in other European nations during the nineteenth century, but a combination of state church and freedom of religion. Furthermore, the integration of religious revivalism into the official church and the modernization of the state church into a "folk church" show how the process of modernization mostly took part as a peaceful transformation. For this reason it makes good sense to interpret the long tradition of having an integrated Lutheran State Church as an important prerequisite for the building of a Norwegian social democratic, welfare state.

The most important change in Norwegian church life during the nineteenth century was, however, reforms of hymnbook and liturgies. A Norwegianized hymnbook by Magnus B. Landstad, minister and poet, was authorized in 1869, and parts of it are still present in the latest hymnbook from 1985. Toward the end of the nineteenth century, Gustav Jensen, practical theologian and church leader, started a process of reforming liturgies, restoring them according to both pre-Reformation traditions and revivalism, a concept that characterizes even today's liturgies.

Since the middle of the nineteenth century a movement within the church sought to establish democratic church bodies and even separate church and state. During the twentieth century it led to reforms like the establishment of parish councils (1920), bishopric councils (1933), a national council (1969), and a general synod (1984). Furthermore, a bishops' conference became an official body in 1934. The main problem is that few members of the church (2 to 3 percent) take part in the elections. Thus the bodies are not representative to the majority of the members of the church. Recently this has become obvious in dealing with ethical challenges from the modern society like abortion and gay partnerships, which threaten to split the church.

In the beginning of the twentieth century, however, it was the traditional teaching of the church and the relationship between Christianity and modern CULTURE and science that represented the main challenges. It resulted in a major conflict between church and theology and led to the establishing of a private theological faculty (1908), which claimed to represent orthodoxy against modern, liberal theology (see LIBERAL PROTESTANTISM AND LIBERALISM). This conflict reached a peak in 1920 when an assembly of members of various Christian organizations met in Oslo under the leadership of Ole Hallesby, a teacher at the private theological faculty. They proclaimed there would be no cooperation with liberal theologians and ministers. Around 1930 the conflict subsided as the result of a new consciousness of the church and its role in the history of the nation. In July of that same year, 900 years of Norwegian Christianity were commemorated in Trondheim in the presence of all the bishops, the king, the government, and members of parliament and representatives from other Protestant churches. In the 1930s the influence from KARL BARTH and dialectical theology (see NEO-ORTHODOXY) also contributed to change the agenda of Norwegian theology.

At the beginning of the 1930s an international economic crisis had driven tens of thousands of people into unemployment and pauperism, while the political tensions increased. The church was hostile to socialism and a growing Labor Party, but the party abolished its former critical attitude to church and religion and came to power in 1935, forming a government and managing to unify a split nation. This became important regarding the German occupation on April 9, 1940 and the later resistance against a collaborative Norwegian Nazi government.

Although former conflicts within the church decreased in the 1930s, new awakenings occurred: a middle-class awakening around the Finnish–Swedish preacher Frank Mangs and the Oxford Group Movement (1934). Furthermore, the main challenges came from a radical and secularized cultural elite who criticized both Christian doctrine and sexual morality and sought emancipation through psychoanalysis. However, during the German occupation it turned out that the church and the people still constituted an integrated unit. Eivind Berggrav, bishop of Oslo, managed during autumn 1940 to unite different fractions of the church in a joint resistance against the Nazi regime. In February 1942 the bishops, as an act of protest against Nazification of the youth, resigned from the civil part of their offices, but remained in service of the church. On Easter Day (April 4, 1942) most of the clergy followed the bishops in reading a declaration, called "Foundation of the Church," from the pulpits. This declaration stated that the Christian loyalty to the authorities depended on the authorities' upholding of law and justice, although the Nazi authorities had violated this, and for that reason the clergy laid down the civil part of their offices. These actions led to the arrests of leaders within the church and Christian organizations and to a bitter conflict between the church and the Nazi state that lasted to the liberation in May 1945.

Postwar and Old Conflicts

In 1945 the leaders of the church had made plans for a rechristianiazation of society and hoped for more autonomy, although they were soon disappointed. Some of the same controversies with secular radicalism from the 1930s reoccurred, and a proposition of a national council was turned down in parliament by the Labor Party (1953). The party's vision for postwar Norway was to build a welfare state, whereas church leaders wished to renew society on the basis of Christian morality and creed.

In 1953–1954 even the theological tensions from the first decades of the twentieth century rose to surface. In a sermon transmitted by radio, Ole Kristian Hallesby warned nonconverts of damnation to Hell. This resulted in a major dispute. The bishop of Hamar, Kristian S. Schjelderup, responded stating that such threats were not compatible with the Gospel of Love. Hallesby and other conservatives accused the bishop of heresy. The government settled the matter after a round of theological hearings, and Schjelderup continued as bishop. The conflict was sharpened when Schjelderup in 1961 ordained the first female minister in spite of fierce protests from other bishops, conservatives, teachers of the private theological faculty, and leaders of Christian organizations. In May 1993 the first female bishop, Rosemarie Køhn, was installed precisely in the bishopric of Hamar, and female ministers have since become a normal part of church order.

In the 1960s the theological conflicts were fueled by the influence from existential theology and the question of the historical Jesus, at the same time as the Cold War with nuclear rearmament and the inhuman consequences of capitalism faced the church with new challenges. The call for Christian social ethics and the influence from the theology of hope led to a new social-ethical consciousness, and within the frame of ecumenism this was followed up in the 1980s and 1990s through impulses from both liberation theology and contextual theology.

At the beginning of the new millennium the church is split between pietistic-inspired traditionalism and modernizing liberalism, but united in social-ethical engagement within an ecumenical and international context.

References and Further Reading

Brohed, Ingmar, ed. *Church and People in Britain and Scandinavia.* Lund, Sweden: Lund University Press, 1996.

Hope, Nicholas. *German and Scandinavian Protestantism 1700–1918.* Oxford: Oxford University Press, 1995.

Hunter, Leslie S., ed. *Scandinavian Churches.* London: Faber and Faber, 1965.

Molland, Einar. *Church Life in Norway, 1800–1950.* Minneapolis, MN: Augsburg Publishing House, 1947.

Orning, Hans J., and Therese Tjeldflaat, eds. *Literature in English on Norwegian history ca. 800–1800: Bibliography.* Oslo, Norway: Historisk institutt, 1995.

Österlin, Lars. *Churches of Northern Europe in Profile.* Norwich, UK: The Canterbury Press, 1995.

DAG THORKILDSEN

NYGREN, ANDERS (1890–1978)

Swedish church leader. Nygren was born November 15, 1890 in Göteborg, SWEDEN and died October 20, 1978 in Lund, Sweden.

Known primarily for his work as a professor of theological ethics and the philosophy of religion at the University of Lund (1921–1949), Nygren addressed fundamental topics of philosophy, THEOLOGY, and ETHICS. As a theologian he used "motif research," grounded in historical analysis, to identify *Agape* (divine, self-giving love) as the essential theological concept or category (i.e., "motif") of Christianity. Nygren distinguished this motif, restored to a central place in the church's soteriological formulations by the Lutheran REFORMATION, from *Eros* (self-oriented love), with its Platonic roots. The "Lundensian School," represented by Nygren, used motif research to analyze important theological issues such as revelation, ATONEMENT, and ethics.

As a philosopher Nygren applied motif analysis to religions beyond Christianity. Theoretically philosophers and theologians alike could search for the basic motif in each respective religion, through the application of this scientific methodology.

As a clergyman, Nygren, ordained in 1912, served as bishop of Lund (1949–1958) and was elected the first president of the LUTHERAN WORLD FEDERATION (1947–1952). Nygren helped oversee the rebuilding of Lutheran churches in post–World War II Europe, while encouraging the scholarship of others.

As an ecumenist, Nygren was active before World War II in the Conferences on Faith and Order (Lausanne, 1927; Oxford, 1937) and instrumental after the war in establishing the WORLD COUNCIL OF CHURCHES.

See also Ecumenism; Lutheranism, Scandinavia; Theology, Twentieth Century

References and Further Reading

Primary Sources:

Nygren, Anders. *Agape and Eros.* Translated by Philip Watson. London: Society for the Propagation of Christian Knowledge, 1953.

———. *Meaning and Method.* London: Epworth Press, 1972.

Secondary Sources:

Badcock, Gary. "The Concept of Love: Divine and Human." In *Nothing Greater, Nothing Better,* edited by Kevin Vanhoozer, 30–46. Grand Rapids, MI: Wm. B. Eerdmanns, 2001.

Kegley, Charles, ed. *The Philosophy and Theology of Anders Nygren.* London and Amsterdam: Feffer and Simons, 1970.

WILLIAM R. RUSSELL

O

OBERLIN, JOHANN FRIEDRICH (1740–1826)

Lutheran Pietist educator. Oberlin was Lutheran pastor in a remote parish in the Vosges Mountains near the French–German frontier. Although Oberlin spent his entire career in this isolated locale, he became well known for exemplary PIETISM and for his innovative educational methods.

Born on August 31, 1740, in Strassburg (now Strasbourg, FRANCE), Oberlin's childhood years were in a home steeped in education and Lutheran Pietism. His father was a teacher, and his mother descended from a long line of Lutheran ministers who married daughters of other Lutheran ministers. After earning a doctor of philosophy degree, Oberlin was a private tutor for three years before accepting a call to a pulpit in the *Ban de la Roche* (*Steintal,* Valley of Rocks), a poverty-stricken pocket of LUTHERANISM.

Oberlin typified Pietist efforts to combine intense FAITH with concern for the worldly needs of the poor and downtrodden. He supported the charitable institutions maintained by Pietists at HALLE. He lived a simple ascetic lifestyle. For years he abstained from coffee and sugar because slaves produced them. Deeply concerned about the poverty and isolation of his adopted home, Oberlin became a tireless local booster and reformer. He promoted agricultural innovation, such as fertilization of crops, and he spearheaded bridge and road construction, at times single-handedly beginning a project until individual peasants joined him, gradually creating a community effort.

Educational Reform

Oberlin's educational reforms were consistent with his interest in assisting the destitute. Determined to improve the general conditions in his long-suffering par-ish and appalled at the stifling environment in peasant households, Oberlin's system began with children at age three or four, much earlier than was customary. He organized these young children in small groups for instruction that lasted only a few hours, several times per week, thus avoiding a lengthy separation from parents. For teachers he hired young, unmarried women from the community. On public occasions he referred to these teachers as "leaders of tender youth," thereby presenting a warm, gentle image. Students acquired useful skills, particularly knitting, but also carding and combing of flax, and they took walks to collect and identify local insects, plants, and rocks. They received religious instruction and learned to read maps, especially to locate their homes and significant local geographic features but also the countries of the world. Oberlin's school also taught cleanliness, habits of hygiene, and manners, which Oberlin hoped that children would carry back into their homes. Lessons were in proper French only, not the local dialect, which was a mixture of French, German, local idioms, and Italian borrowed from workers imported by the local lord. When student's interest lagged, Oberlin and his teachers used magic tricks to keep their attention. Aside from educational achievements Oberlin believed that in the long run skills students acquired would benefit the community by making it less isolated.

Oberlin was also involved in the public school, which took students at age six or seven. Here only men taught, but otherwise Oberlin's program was also creative. For example, teachers taught demonstration lessons, which colleagues observed and evaluated. He gave credit vouchers to reward parents whose children attended regularly, and he provided free books and materials to parents unable to pay but who made an effort to educate their children. In return Oberlin expected recipients of aid to live what he considered a pious life, including avoidance of taverns and not keeping dogs, which he determined was a luxury. He also refused to confirm (admit to church membership) children who did not attend school regularly, thereby punishing parents who neglected their children's schooling. He stipulated compulsory education until the age of sixteen. Thus, whether spearheading projects to improve the local economy or immersing himself in the local educational system, Oberlin demonstrated uncommon activism in charitable endeavors.

An International Figure

Although Oberlin lived almost all of his professional life in the secluded *Ban de la Roche,* he nevertheless became well known among intellectuals and theologians, primarily for his dynamic combination of faith with works. Word of Oberlin spread largely through networks of correspondence, and his exchange of letters with JOHANN HEINRICH JUNG-STILLING, a well-connected Radical Pietist who in turn informed his correspondents of Oberlin's work, was particularly instrumental. Jung-Stilling and other Radical Pietists cherished wilderness or desert experiences, citing those of Moses and Jesus, and they thought that Oberlin's ministry in the *Ban de la Roche* fit this model. Oberlin's correspondence with the BRITISH AND FOREIGN BIBLE SOCIETY brought English visitors to his community. Some English visitors kept detailed journals of Oberlin's activities, which were published and read widely within mission circles. Tsar Alexander I of Russia became an admirer of Oberlin after learning of the isolated Lutheran from a baroness who was attracted to Oberlin's interest in ESCHATOLOGY. When in 1813 Alexander invaded France through Alsace, he sent a messenger to Oberlin bearing a letter of safe conduct and instructed his troops to avoid the *Ban de la Roche* as much as possible.

One event was especially instrumental in Oberlin's fame. In 1778 he took in a wandering stranger, who turned out to be Jacob Lenz, a popular playwright. Lenz was not only physically in need—hungry, dirty, cold, with a festering sore on one foot—but he was also psychologically devastated. After an incident in which Lenz seized scissors from Oberlin's wife and threatened suicide, Oberlin sent Lenz away, and soon thereafter the dissipated playwright died. Although intellectuals hotly debated Oberlin's treatment of Lenz, the incident also spread Oberlin's renown.

In fact, Oberlin's fame extended even to the North American frontier. When in 1832 American evangelical reformers sought to establish a community of enlightened values and Christian simplicity in Ohio, they immediately drew upon Oberlin for inspiration.

As Oberlin in his valley battled Satan, they determined to fight evil in the Mississippi Valley. Consequently, they imitated Oberlin's educational system for their children, and they named their college after him.

Oberlin died on June 1, 1826. He was buried in the church graveyard at Fouday, a village in the *Ban de la Rouche.*

References and Further Reading

Kurtz, John W. *John Frederic Oberlin.* Boulder, CO: Westview Press, 1976.
Oberlin, Johann Friedrich. *Memoirs of John Frederic Oberlin, Pastor of Waldbach, in the Ban de la Roche.* London: Holdsworth and Ball, 1829.
———. *Berichte eines Visionärs über den Zustand der Seelen nach dem Tode.* Leipzig, Germany: F. A. Brockhaus, 1837.
Oberlin, Johann Friedrich and Wilhelm Steinhilber. *Nichts ohne Gott.* Stuttgart, Germany: J. F. Steinkopf, 1961.

STEPHEN LONGENECKER

OBSERVANCES

Observances are acts and customs of devotion or discipline, individual or corporate, especially those repeated at specified times and according to prescriptions as to frequency, intention, or performance. In the anthropological study of any community, including Protestant churches and groups, observances are examined and interpreted as being indicative of the community's beliefs, relationships, social roles and trends in development, and ambivalent views.

Protestant Ambivalence with Regard to Observances

In classical Protestant thought, observances may be acts of obedience to God's revealed will, or acts of human initiative; in the latter case, they may be judged to be permitted by God's law, or questionable, or wrong. On the Protestant understanding of redemption, observances, even when acts of obedience to God's revealed will, may be obligatory, and may be acts of faith, but do not secure God's favor through any intrinsic merit. When they are acts of conformity with the rules of the faith community, they may be commendable, but may not infringe on the freedom and responsibility of the individual or particular church. Observances that are understood as divine acts in the church through obedient human instrumentality are obligatory, and are means of GRACE, but interpretation of their sacramental efficacy differs among Protestant theologies. As to what is required or permissible in observances in general: Reformed doctrine has tended to restrict observances strictly to acts mandated in Scripture, whereas Lutheran, Anglican, and Methodist traditions incline to encourage observances compatible with Scripture. The Quakers (see FRIENDS, SOCIETY OF) and others have concluded that no external observances have any divine sanction, and that, although Christians may gather for meeting, all that is required is a waiting on God, preferably in silence, for the gift of the Inward Light, which may prompt a sharing of reflection, testimony, exhortation, confession, or prayer.

From the beginning, Protestantism has warned against the abuse of observances, not least those divinely mandated. Medieval customs had, in the reforming view, added unworthy human accretions to divine institution and primitive simplicity, reduced divine things to triviality, encouraged superstition, misdirected to creatures adoration attributable only to God, and tempted the user to rely on human deserving or bargaining rather than on God and God's grace. These dangers, to which all religious life is vulnerable, all go back, so the Reformers agreed, to a separation of observances from the Word of God.

The Word: Proclaimed, Heard, Obeyed

Protestantism agrees that the Word of God is encountered in Scripture, and has often identified the Word directly with Scripture. This has meant that Protestant churches have felt the immediate impact of HIGHER CRITICISM of the BIBLE (historicity, ethical consistency, source-criticism, comparative religion). Some Protestants simply ignore these challenges, whereas others respond to them as liberating, in that God is understood as leading all creation, all humanity, by the Eternal Word, most fully and definitively uttered as the Incarnate Word, among people who recorded and interpreted the events. This was done with divine help, which nonetheless worked with them within their personal and cultural limitations. This approach has been summed up: "The Bible is the word of those to whom the Word of the Lord came."

The Protestant apprehension of the Word as the gracious self-impartation of the all-merciful Trinity has often been lost in popular Protestantism, when the Bible has been viewed as a book of rules. However, especially since the work of C. H. Dodd, the essential narrative character of both Testaments has aided Protestants and others to present the Bible as the story of progressive divine–human covenant friendship, a story so told that successive generations of believers become incorporated into it.

The canon, or recognized list, of biblical books presented Protestantism with a decision. The first Reformers accepted the Septuagint Canon of the Old Testament, as it had been transmitted by the Eastern and Latin Churches. Soon, however, Protestant churches reduced at least to secondary status the "Apocryphal" or "Deutero-canonical" books and retained only those Hebrew or Aramaic books that had been canonized by the Rabbis at Jamnia in 70 A.D.

The Word, in or as Scripture, is to be read in the WORSHIP of the congregation. There, and in oral or written spiritual counsel, it is to be expounded and applied. In classical Protestantism a preacher may insist only on principles provable from Scripture as being indispensable for saving belief. The Word is not solely information, nor is the reading and exposition of the Word solely didactic in purpose: the individual Christian is summoned to hear, read, mark, learn, and inwardly digest.

Sacraments

Classical Protestantism insists on the dominical SACRAMENTS, for which Scripture attests institution and AUTHORITY from Jesus. This represents a DISSENT from the Roman assertion of seven sacraments, of which the Anglican Article 35 says that five (CONFIRMATION, Penance, Orders, Matrimony, and Extreme Unction) are not divinely mandated ceremonies but "have grown partly [out] of corrupt following of the Apostles, partly are states of life allowed in the Scriptures." The remainder are BAPTISM and the "Holy Communion," or "LORD'S SUPPER." We must note that MARTIN LUTHER himself included Confession and Absolution as a sacrament, but most later Lutheran thought does not follow him. Some extremist wings of the Reformation, together with the Society of Friends and the Quaker-influenced SALVATION ARMY, deny to these or any sacraments any degree of authority, and recommend instead an inward dedication of the spirit, and communion by PRAYER and fellowship. The Salvation Army has found it necessary to create a substitute for baptism (or confirmation) in the form of Recruitment Under the Flag.

Baptism in classical Protestantism has assumed as normative administration to the children of Christianity-professing families, baptismal promises being made either by godparents or families, the implied obligations being taken on by the baptized at an age of responsible choice. This is usually called "paedobaptism" or "infant baptism," but a more reasonable title might be "heritage-baptism." Such a pattern originally assumed the conversion to Protestantism of whole communities (kingdoms, principalities, city-states). Other Protestant traditions (Anabaptist, MENNONITE, Baptist, Old German Baptist, CHURCH OF THE BRETHREN) baptize only on the candidate's personal profession of faith, on the ground that discipleship cannot be inherited, but can only be an individual choice. This is usually called "believer-baptism" (again, a more apt title might be "profession-baptism"). Independency (CONGREGATIONALISM), although confessing the voluntaristic principle for church membership, has retained heritage-baptism, as has METHODISM. By the later twentieth century, even in paedobaptist churches, where once parents had been told unambiguously that it was their Christian duty to present their children for baptism, a dual practice had grown up, some parents presenting their infant children and others declining to do so, expecting the children to make the choice themselves.

The matter and form of baptism (to use the medieval categories, which ecumenical interaction has brought back into Protestant use) are usually water, poured with the words, "[Name], I baptize you in the name of the Father and of the Son, and of the Holy Spirit," with sometimes interpretative additions, as for instance in some Presbyterian use, "[Name], child of the covenant, I baptize you. . . ." Most Protestants baptize by pouring (albeit often in a reduced form of sprinkling from the fingers). Anabaptists traditionally baptize by pouring, but English BAPTISTS in the early seventeenth century introduced baptism by immersion, appealing to Paul's image in Romans 6 of baptism as a funeral. Similar reasoning influenced Alexander Campbell and the Christian Church (DISCIPLES OF CHRIST). Those who baptize by pouring point out that in Paul's Hellenistic world the essential act of a funeral was in fact a pouring, whether of soil or dust or pebbles or, if need be, water. The doctrine of intention is little discussed except in ecumenical contexts: as in Roman Catholic THEOLOGY, the intention is generally to be inferred from the "form," or words of administration. The Roman Catholic revision of catechesis and initiation, principally the "Rite of Christian Initiation of Adults," has provoked much heart-searching and rethinking in some older Protestant denominations, as has Faith and Order Paper 111, *Baptism, Eucharist, and Ministry,* although resultant liturgical revision in those churches has not met with settled or always positive response.

Confirmation among Protestants differs widely in usage and interpretation. Anglicans require confirmation by bishops as the usual gateway to communicant status; Lutherans and Reformed concentrate on a protracted period of catechetical instruction before admission to communion. Anglicans (and Methodists, since the 1960s) lay on hands in confirmation.

Absolution may be considered as an appendix to baptism because in principle it restores the penitent to the communicant status belonging to the baptized; even this restoration is felt only on an emotional level to be necessary. Lutherans and Anglicans have always administered absolution (see ANGLICANISM; LUTHERAN-

ISM); the Reformed declare forgiveness, and have traditionally exercised an office of readmission and restoration; the UNITING CHURCH IN AUSTRALIA and the British Methodist Church have included orders for reconciliation in the late twentieth-century service books. Whether any Protestant church would include this ministry within the category of sacraments, a sacramental affinity is obvious.

Holy Communion, or Lord's Supper, is variously celebrated among Protestants, and no less variously interpreted. Where it is kept at all, it is observed as an act of obedience to the traditionally recorded command of Jesus at his Last Supper. Because of this basis, some Protestant traditions include within it the washing of feet (see FEET, WASHING OF). Biblical criticism has obliged Protestants, even more directly than other Christians, to respond to doubts about the historicity of the New Testament accounts of the Last Supper and the commands there incorporated. Even when the New Testament language is interpreted entirely figuratively, some Protestants flinch at the imagery of eating flesh and drinking blood. The rite differs among the Protestant churches, although many of the denominations have followed the arguments of Dom Gregory Dix and restored the putative ancient "four-fold shape" of taking + thanking + breaking + sharing, which includes a reintroduction of the Eucharistic Prayer. Many denominations, since the close of the nineteenth century, have abandoned the use of wine for the unfermented juice of the grape, so as to provide an alcohol-free environment. Admission to communion is in some Protestant churches, especially of the "gathered church" tradition, strictly guarded. Among older Protestant churches, conservative Lutherans are alone in limiting communion to those who believe in the real presence of Christ (although Lutheran doctrine refuses to admit the concept of transubstantiation because that language submits divine grace to presumptuous human reason). In pastoral ministry Protestants meet problems about the right frequency for individual communion, and emotional difficulties about the imagery.

Sacraments as a generic concept are not uniformly conceived among Protestants. Because "sacrament" does not occur in the New Testament (unless the term "mystery" in I Corinthians 2:7 has such a sense), many Protestants, especially in the Americas, dislike it and prefer "ordinances," as expressive of the divine mandate. Yet others prefer, especially in pastoral theology, to use the generic concept of "means of grace," under which are subsumed not only the sacraments but also prayer, reading of Scripture, and religious conference, as appointed ways in which to wait on God, and as means by which God confers prevenient, justifying, and sanctifying grace. The efficacy of sacraments is much disputed: in classical Protestantism, a real gift (according to the specific sacrament) is really offered, and how it is received makes that gift either beneficial, meaningless, or actually spiritually perilous. To take up the scholastic categories in discussion of sacraments, categories that Protestant theology has tended to decry but has found it necessary often to reinstate, sacramental causality is a major concern. All Protestants who retain sacramental worship agree that without faith, through which gifts of grace are received and made effective, sacramental acts are, for some meaningless, but certainly unfruitful. Also, the church's internal relations and witness in society make sacramental worship blasphemous if they do not reflect the gracious, forgiving, sacrificially generous character of God asserted in sacramental customs, words, symbols, and acts. (This principle, stated by Paul in I Corinthians 10–11, is as emphatically stated by Roman Catholics and Eastern Churches as by Protestants.)

On another level, there seems to be a deep division among Protestants over sacramentology, which is not along denominational lines. At least since the eighteenth century, there has been a tendency to describe sacraments as "purely" (or even "merely") "symbolic." Tillich has argued that this is less negative than it sounds, given that symbols participate in the reality of that which they represent; but at least in popular terms, this sort of expression means that the only effect of sacraments, or other symbolic acts, is solely psychological—that the Eucharist, for example, is simply a subjective remembering of past events, even of an absent Christ. Lutheran tradition asserts that an objective gift is given absolutely; Reformed and Anglican traditions seem to assert that an objective gift is given conditionally; Methodism has been ambivalent as to what to assert, but sings in an almost Lutheran key. To resolve this dilemma, Protestant sacramentology turns to the "occasionalism" of Duns Scotus: even if there is no inevitable causal link between liturgical performance and divine act, the divine faithfulness to the covenant promises that, when the sacramental rite is performed obediently, and with an obedient intent, then, however unworthy the minister as a person, the divine presence is granted and the gift is given. This COVENANT theology has sometimes been matched in Protestant worship and spiritual guidance with a covenanting approach to personal CONVERSION, baptism and affirmation of baptism, and covenanting as self-dedication for SANCTIFICATION.

Ordination

In classical Protestantism, presidency at sacramental worship has required ordination, so that the act may be seen as representative of the whole church and endorsed by its authority and thereby Christ's authority, and as the act for which the whole church accepts responsibility. In Lutheran and Reformed traditions ordination is linked with a specific call, and in Anglican tradition ordination must be linked with a specific "title" parish or other ministry. The setting of ordinations reflects the respective ecclesiologies: the Reformed ordain preaching elders in the specific parish, but as an act of the presbytery; FREE CHURCHES ordain in the local congregation, neighboring clergy gathering for the event; Anglicans ordain by bishops, usually in the respective cathedral church. Methodists ordain at their Annual Conferences (but consecrate bishops in American Methodism at Jurisdictional Conferences). From the "radical reformation" onward, there has been a strain of Protestant inclination that argues that the PRIESTHOOD OF ALL BELIEVERS makes ordination unnecessary, even wrong.

Protestant churches have not yet come to a common mind about the relative elements in an ordination rite. All agree that prayer is essential, usually with the imposition of hands associated, but not all see a need for a settled form for such a prayer. Often, more attention is given to the wording of the Examination, or "Vows," which precede that prayer. The Examination is thus often treated as the core of the rite, as binding promises, and as a reassurance to the congregation that this candidate is rightly admitted to ordination, instead of the promises being introductory to the prayer, and setting out some of the needs that God will be asked to supply.

Many, but not all, Protestant churches have, since the close of the nineteenth century, but more in the closing decades of the twentieth, begun to admit WOMEN to ordained ministry (see WOMEN CLERGY).

Prayer and Fasting

With all other Christians, Protestants esteem prayer as the privilege and duty of all God's children, and all Protestant churches offer counsel in the manner of praying. In both private devotion and public worship, free prayer is valued as faith-prompted and faith-guided response to the Holy Spirit; this does not prevent Protestant spiritual guides from offering written prayers as models or instruments of devotion. Since the period after the First World War, the Roman, Lutheran, and especially Anglican forms and principles of the Daily Office, or Hours, have won appreciation and even imitation in the less-formal denominations—but it is important to note that the tradition of urging and aiding daily devotion, individual and domestic, has never entirely failed in Lutheran, Reformed, and Free Church communities.

Regularity in daily prayer is commended by Protestant guides as ordering the personal life of faith according to God's gift of temporal existence, and as a graciously offered means for the inward ordering of will and emotions.

Fasting, a biblically sanctioned discipline, has a place in some Protestant traditions, although in the nineteenth century it fell into disfavor, whether through diminished devotion or through a loosening of the link between spirituality and the sense of the body. Classical Protestantism associated fasting with the penitential seasons and special times of public repentance; in more evangelical and "fundamentalist" circles, it has been a constant feature of personal intercession at all seasons.

Singing

Protestantism has encouraged Christian song from the beginning, and sought to open singing to all Christians, both in corporate worship and in private devotion (see HYMNS AND HYMNALS). The style and repertoire have varied by traditions and through time. Reformed traditions have tended to concentrate on the Psalms (at least one Reformed denomination will sing nothing else but the Psalter). Metrical Psalms or paraphrases have supplied at least part of nearly all Protestant hymnic resources. Luther's and later Lutheran hymns ranged more freely; Anabaptist hymnody began as the defiant songs of imprisoned martyrs. ISAAC WATTS led English-language hymnody into a wide range of doxology and meditation, and JOHN and CHARLES WESLEY developed a hymnody of faith experience, in quest of Christian perfection. In the later twentieth century mega-churches and other centers of evangelical worship began to develop different styles of worship music. The "Praise and Worship" movement works to engage the gathered people in upbeat song compatible with popular entertainment song; the "SEEKER-driven" service style expects fewer and fewer people to be comfortable with corporate singing (see SEEKER CHURCHES), and makes generous use of songs sung *to* rather than *by* the gathered assembly on a Sunday, whereas the more committed core congregation sings together on Wednesday or whatever is the usual day for committed disciples.

Life-Cycle Rites: Marriage and Funeral

"Occasional Offices," or "Pastoral Offices," which mark the life cycle, are indispensable in any society, whatever the professed faith. Protestantism has usually denied MARRIAGE the status of a sacrament, not to ignore its divine origin or its significance for God's will and human obedience, but because the civil society has been seen as the divinely appointed judicatory for this aspect of life. Nonetheless nearly all Protestant churches have provided marriage rites, often before they established any other liturgical norms. Reformed traditions long omitted the ring, as being a custom of pagan origin and an object of superstition: the nineteenth century saw a reversion to older customs, largely because of social pressures. By the end of the twentieth century, in English-speaking Protestantism, considerable demands were being made for couples to write their own vows, and (in the UNITED STATES) for the insertion into the service of a "Unity Candle." In this matter the older Protestant caution with regard to symbols has apparently ceased to function. Protestant churches have historically provided no standard rites for marking adolescence; in North America, the Latin American observance of a young woman's fifteenth birthday, adopted in Latin American churches, began by the start of the twenty-first century to appear in Anglo-American practice.

Distinctive among Protestant traditions was the early Reformed mineralizing trend in the funeral rite, prompted by distrust of the medieval obsession with prayer for the dead, and by disgust at the way in which that obsession had been exploited by some church practices such as stipends for requiem masses. More typical of Protestantism, especially as it developed, was the Lutheran funeral chant, "In the midst of life we are in death. . . . Suffer us not, at our last hour, by any pains of death to fall from thee." Protestant distrust of prayer for the dead seems to have been altered by the First World War, after which many Protestant funeral liturgies and other services allow for such petitions (see DEATH AND DYING).

The Calendar

The concept of "observances" is most used of the observance of times and seasons—Advent, Christmas, Lent, Easter, Pentecost, Trinity, Saints' Days. Lutherans and Anglicans preserved much of the medieval calendar, while omitting much of the overgrown sanctoral cycle; Reformed and more radical Protestants kept only the Lord's Day. Some churches (Seventh Day Baptists, SEVENTH-DAY ADVENTISTS) reverted to the Sabbath, on biblical grounds.

Reformed and Methodist churches, and numerous evangelical churches, have come to value the fuller Christian Calendar, as a means of displaying the Gospel story through the circle of the year, of ordering the corporate reading of Scripture to range over the full treasury of the Bible with balance, and of helping preachers escape the tyranny of their own interests. This is similar to the Protestant rediscovery of the structured Divine Office, which has helped individuals and groups to establish a new stability in their devotional and emotional lives. The celebration of the SAINTS has also spread in Protestant circles (the German Evangelical Brotherhood of St. Michael, the United Methodist Order of St. Luke, for example); and both Protestants and Roman Catholics celebrate one another's saints, including those who died as Protestant or Roman Catholic MARTYRS, at Christian hands.

References and Further Reading

Baillie, Donald M. *The Theology of the Sacraments and Other Papers.* London: Faber and Faber, 1957.

Bianchi, Enzo. "Introduction." In *Comunità di Bose: Il libro dei Testimoni: Martirologio ecumenico (The Bose Community: The Book of Witnesses: An Ecumenical Martyrology).* Edited by Cinisello Balsamo. Milan, Italy: Edizioni Paolini, 2002.

Boers, Arthur Paul. *The Rhythm of God's Grace. Uncovering Morning and Evening Hours of Prayer.* Brewster, MA: Paraclete Press, 2003.

Brilioth, Yngve. *Eucharistic Practice, Evangelical and Catholic.* Translated by Gabriel Hebert. London: SPCK, 1930.

Jennings, Theodore W. Jr. *Loyalty to God: The Apostles' Creed in Life and Liturgy.* Nashville, TN: Abingdon Press, 1992.

Klassen, William. *The Forgiving Community.* Philadelphia, PA: Westminster Press, 1966.

Lovegrove, Deryck W., ed. *The Rise of the Laity in Evangelical Protestantism.* London: Routledge, 2002.

Marshall, I. Howard. *Last Supper & Lord's Supper.* Exeter, UK: Paternoster Press, 1980.

Micklem, Nathaniel, ed. *Christian Worship: Studies in its History and Meaning by Members of Mansfield College.* Oxford: Oxford University Press, 1936.

———. *Prayers and Praises* [1941]. London: Independent Press, 1954.

Riggs, John W. *Baptism in the Reformed Tradition: An Historical and Practical Theology.* Columbia Series in Reformed Theology. Louisville, KY and London: Westminster/John Knox Press, 2002.

Spens, Will. *Belief and Practice.* 2d edition. London: Longmans, Green & Co., 1917.

Taylor, Peter Forsyth. *The Church and the Sacraments* [1917]. 3d edition. London: Independent Press, 1949, reprinted 1964.

Thompson, Bard. *Liturgies of the Western Church.* Cleveland, OH, and New York: Meridian Books, 1961.

Tillich, Paul. *Systematic Theology.* 1-vol. edition. London: James Nisbet & Co., 1968.

Tripp, David H. *The Renewal of the Covenant in the Methodist Tradition.* London: Epworth Press, 1969.

Turner, Henry W. *Profile through Preaching: A Study of the Sermon Texts Used in a West African Independent Church.* [World Council of Churches Commission on World Mission and Evangelism Research Pamphlets, no. 13]. London: Edinburgh House Press, 1965.

Webber, Robert E. *Common Roots: A Call to Evangelical Maturity.* Grand Rapids, MI: Zondervan Publishing House, 1979.

White, James F. *Protestant Worship: Traditions in Transition.* Louisville, KY: Westminster/John Knox Press, 1989.

———. *Protestant Worship and Church Architecture* (1964). Reprinted Eugene, OR: Wipf and Stock, 2003.

Winter, Harry F. "Presbyterians Pioneer the Vatican II Sunday Lectionary. Three Worship Models Converge." *Journal of Ecumenical Studies* 38 no. 2–3 (Spring–Summer 2000): 127–150.

Wolfe, Howard H. *Mothers Day and the Mothers Day Church.* Kingsport, TN: Kingsport Press, 1962.

DAVID H. TRIPP

OCHINO, BERNARDINO (1487–1564)

Italian anti-Trinitarian. Bernardino Ochino began his career as a reformist Franciscan in his native ITALY, and ended it as a controversial Protestant theologian in exile. Born in Siena, Ochino joined the observant Franciscans around 1504, but moved in 1534 to the even more austere Capuchin order, where he was vicar general (1538–1542) and a popular preacher. A 1536 meeting with the Catholic reformer Juan de Valdés is credited with pushing Ochino further toward Protestant ideas of reform. Ochino's works from this period, such as the *Seven Dialogues,* show that his interest in themes such as JUSTIFICATION by FAITH preceded his self-identification as Protestant. Ochino's association with the Italian evangelical movement made him an object of inquisitorial suspicion, leading him to flee Italy along with Peter Martyr Vermigli in 1542.

Now identifying as Protestant, Ochino became a popular but controversial preacher to the Italian community, first in Geneva, where he married, and then in Augsburg in GERMANY, ENGLAND, and finally Zurich in 1553. His works from this period included a satire of the papacy, tracts in support of the English Reformation, and a series of dialogues on issues ranging from the Eucharist (see LORD'S SUPPER) to polygamy. Accused of ANTI-TRINITARIANISM and other heterodox ideas, Ochino was banished from Zurich in 1563, and moved to POLAND and then to Moravia, where he died in 1564. Ochino was both a popular and influential Protestant theologian and a more searching thinker on the religious issues of his time than most of his contemporaries could countenance.

References and Further Reading

Primary Sources:

Ochino, Bernardino. *Seven Dialogues.* Translated by Rita Belladonna. Ottawa, Canada: Dovehouse Editions, 1988.

———. *Tragedy or Dialogue of the Unjust Usurped Primacy of the Bishop of Rome. 1549.* London: G. Richards, 1899.

———. *Dialogue de m. Bernardin Ochin, touchant le Purgatoire.* Paris: Librairie Générale, 1878.

Ochino, Bernardino, et al. *The Tragedy.* London: Grant Richards, 1899.

McNair, Philip, ed. *Patterns of Perfection.* Cambridge, UK: Anastasia Press, 1999.

Secondary Sources:

Bainton, Roland. *The Travail of Religious Liberty*. Philadelphia, PA: Westminster Press, 1951.
Benrath, Karl. *Bernardino Ochino of Siena*. Translated by Helen Zimmern. London: James Nizbet & Co., 1876.

DEBORAH K. MARCUSE

OECOLAMPADIUS, JOHANNES (1482–1531)

Swiss reformer. Oecolampadius was born Johannes Hausschein (variant spellings: Huszgen, Hussgen, Heussgen) at Weinsberg, GERMANY in 1482. Following Humanist custom, he took a Greco-Latin form of his name in 1510.

Oecolampadius's well-traveled career connected him to the most important people, events, and ideas of sixteenth-century Europe. As a student he earned B.A. and M.A. degrees at Heidelberg (1503), studied law at Bologna, THEOLOGY at Tübingen, and completed a doctorate at Basel (1518). As a teacher he tutored the sons of Palatinate Landgrave Philip at Mainz (1506–1510), taught Greek at Heidelberg (1512–1513), and lectured on the BIBLE at Basel (1522–1531). As a pastor he served at Weinsberg (1510–1512, 1516–1518), Augsburg (1518–1521), Basel (1515–1516, 1522–1531), and as chaplain to Franz von Sickingen at Ebernburg (1522). He was even a monk in the Birgittine monastery at Altomünster near Augsburg (1521–1522).

These experiences prepared him to make enduring academic and ecclesiastical contributions. Academically, Oecolampadius traveled in learned Humanist circles, working and exchanging ideas with leading Roman Catholic and Protestant scholars and activists. His interest in the sources of Christianity largely stems from scholarly relationships with men such as Johannes Reuchlin, Jakob Wimpfeling, Erasmus, MARTIN BUCER, MARTIN LUTHER, PHILIPP MELANCHTHON, ANDREAS RUDOLF BODENSTEIN KARLSTADT, and HULDRYCH ZWINGLI.

As an academic, he mastered the "three sacred languages" (Greek, Hebrew, and Latin), which he used to edit, translate, and publish ancient texts, particularly the church fathers and the Bible (he assisted Erasmus with the Greek New Testament). This body of work, together with a usable Greek grammar, made historical and linguistic resources accessible to his contemporaries. Furthermore Oecolampadius's academic teaching career (at Heidelberg, Mainz, and Basel) influenced hundreds of students, a number of whom (e.g., Theobald Billicanus, JOHANNES BRENZ, and Hans Denck) went on to provide notable leadership in church and society.

Roman Catholic and Protestant Debate

Ecclesiastically, Oecolampadius actively participated in major meetings between Roman Catholics and Protestants. At the Baden Disputation in 1526 he distinguished himself with his respectful demeanor and eloquent knowledge of the issues (the Mass, purgatory, prayers to SAINTS, etc.). Even though Baden remained Roman Catholic, Oecolampadius emerged as a leading voice for reform in SWITZERLAND.

The recess of Baden stipulated a follow-up disputation, scheduled for Bern in early 1528. The Reformed party, represented by Zwingli, Oecolampadius, Bucer, WOLFGANG CAPITO, and others, won an impressive victory. The establishment of the Reformed church in both city and canton soon followed and, given the status of Bern, this event proved decisive for the course of reform in Switzerland.

A third important meeting in which Oecolampadius participated was the MARBURG COLLOQUY of 1529. Lutheran prince PHILIP OF HESSE called the meeting, hoping the theologians could agree as a step toward building a coalition of German-speaking Protestants. The key issue, differing notions of the presence of Christ in the LORD'S SUPPER, proved immovable. Oecolampadius was an able and loyal lieutenant to Zwingli and his view that Christ is present "spiritually" in the Lord's Supper. However, neither doctrinal agreement nor political alliance was obtained.

Oecolampadius's ecclesiastical activities also focused on Basel. Calls for religious reform in the city were heard throughout the 1520s. These calls, occasionally expressing themselves violently, increased toward the end of the decade, as they eventuated into unrestrained iconoclastic riots in early 1529 (see ICONOCLASM). The Roman Catholic city council's policy complicated matters—tolerating differences in faith without declaring itself for or against reform. In addition the publishing industry and the university in Basel provided havens and outlets for reform thinkers and activists. Moreover Basel's guilds, with their control of the city's economy, made them necessary players on the religious/political/economic stage. Finally, because Switzerland shared borders with FRANCE and Germany, it was convenient for refugees, with their innovative ideas and practices. At various times influential representatives of various Reform movements, including Erasmus, Karlstadt, THOMAS MÜNTZER, and BALTHASAR HÜBMAIER, lived in Basel.

As pastor at St. Martin's church and lecturer in Bible at the university, Oecolampadius engaged this situation—particularly after he initiated contact with Zwingli at Zurich in December 1522. This produced a fruitful collaboration on theological and practical levels. Oecolampadius's biblical lectures at the university became increasingly popular, particularly after he began lecturing in German in 1523. At times several hundred auditors from the city would attend his classes, giving him a platform on which to address eager listeners. Further he skillfully approached the city council and influenced the guilds to promote reform. In April 1529 the city fathers enfranchised the Reformed faith in Basel by adopting Oecolampadius's "Reformation Act."

Theological Influences

Oecolampadius was also an able representative of Swiss Reformed theology. His view of Holy Communion, although akin to Zwingli's, also had its distinguishing character. He delineated his view in the influential "*Genuina expositio verborum Domini interpretatione: Hoc est corpus meum*" (1525). He maintained a "symbolic" understanding of the sacrament by arguing that the elements signified the body and blood of Christ, which were spiritually eaten by the faithful. Using church fathers as references, Oecolampadius connected Tertullian's phrase that the Lord's Supper is a "*figura corporis*" (representation of [Christ's] body) with Augustine's notion that faith accomplished the sacrament. Oecolampadius's interpretation of Jesus' words, "This is my Body," places the metaphor in the predicate, in contradistinction to Zwingli, who understood the verb metaphorically.

Furthermore his theology of CHURCH DISCIPLINE, an important mark of Reformed Protestantism, anticipated JOHN CALVIN's Geneva. Oecolampadius sought to use excommunication as a means to restore sinners to SALVATION rather than as punishment, by instituting a CONSISTORY of lay presbyters—thinking that the civil realm ought to be administered by the church. This proposal failed in Basel, where the ban remained a civil concern.

References and Further Reading

Primary Source:

Staehelin, Ernst. *Briefe und Akten zum Leben Oekolampads.* 2 vols. Leipzig, Germany: M. Heinsius, 1927.

Secondary Sources:

Fudge, Thomas. "Icarus of Basel? Oecolampadius and the Early Swiss Reformation." *The Journal of Religious History* 21, no. 3 (October 1997): 268–284.

Rupp, E. Gordon. *Patterns of Reformation.* 1–46. London: Epworth Press, 1969.

Staehelin, Ernst. *Das theologische Lebenswerk Johannes Oekolampads.* Leipzig, Germany: M. Heinsius, 1939. Repr. New York: Johnson Reprint, 1971.

Walton, Robert. "Oecolampadius, Johannes." In *Encyclopedia of the Reformation.* Edited by Hans Hillerbrand. 4 vols, vol III, 169–171. Oxford: 1997.

WILLIAM R. RUSSELL

OLDHAM, JOSEPH H. (1874–1969)

Protestant missionary statesman. Oldham was born in Girgaum, INDIA, in 1874 of Scottish parents. He was educated at Edinburgh Academy and Trinity College, Oxford. He was a member of the evangelical Oxford Inter-Collegiate Christian Union with his friends and contemporaries Temple Gairdner, Paget Wilkes, and Alek Fraser, all future missionaries. Wilkes introduced him to JOHN R. MOTT in 1894. Oldham became first general secretary of the Student Volunteer Missionary Union in 1896 and YMCA secretary in Lahore (1897–1901). Here he married Alek Fraser's sister, Mary. They returned to Edinburgh on health grounds, where Oldham studied THEOLOGY at New College and in HALLE, Germany under Gustav Warneck (1901–1905).

As secretary of the WORLD MISSIONARY CONFERENCE at Edinburgh in 1910 his role was influential in making the conference immensely significant for both mission and ECUMENISM. He became secretary of the Continuation Committee and of the International Missionary Council (1921–1938) and first editor of the *International Review of Missions* in 1912. He was active on behalf of German Protestant missions in fund-raising and preventing the expropriation of mission property after 1918 and GERMANY's defeat in World War I. He became deeply involved in AFRICA and wrote *Christianity and the Race Problem* (1924) and *What is at stake in East Africa* (1929), as well as serving on a royal commission. He worked with Bishop GEORGE BELL to coordinate protests against Nazi policy on church affairs after 1934. He was active in the "Life and Work" and "Faith and Order" conferences, which contributed to the provisional formation of the WORLD COUNCIL OF CHURCHES in 1938. He attended the WCC in 1948 and was made an honorary president.

Although Oldham was handicapped by profound deafness for most of his life, he remained influential in later life through his coeditorship of *The Christian Newsletter* (1939–1945). He died on May 16, 1969 at St. Leonard's-on-Sea in Sussex, ENGLAND.

References and Further Reading

Primary Sources:

Oldham, J. H. *A Devotional Diary.* London: SCM, 1923.
———. *White and Black in Africa.* London: Longman, 1930.
———. *Life is Commitment.* New York: Harper & Row, 1953.

Oldham, Joseph Houldsworth. *Christianity and the Race Problem.* New York: George H. Doran Company, 1924.
———. *The Resurrection of Christendom.* London: Sheldon Press and New York: Macmillan, 1940.
———. *The Church Looks Ahead.* London: Faber and Faber, 1941.
———. *New Hope in Africa.* London: Longmans, Green, 1955.

Secondary Sources:

Bliss, Kathleen. Articles in *Dictionary of National Biography.* Oxford: Oxford University Press, 1981.
———. Articles in *Mission Legacies.* Edited by G. H. Anderson, et al. New York: Orbis, 1994.
Clements, Keith. *Faith on the Frontiers: A Life of J. H. Oldham.* Edinburgh: T. & T. Clark, 1999.

TIMOTHY YATES

OPPONG (OPPON, OPON), KWAME SAMPSON (c. 1884–1965)

African clergy. Oppong was born about 1884 in Brong Ahafo in Ghana to a slave family originating from Burkina Faso. He was an itinerant laborer and an accomplished magician/herbalist, and had served several prison terms for petty crimes before his CONVERSION. In 1917 he had a vision in which God called him to proclaim God's Word, but with a peculiarly African nuance—accompanied by the destruction of fetishes and the rejection of witchcraft. He was aided in his ministry by a "stone" from which he could read the Scriptures. In his lifetime he earned the two opposing sobriquets, Sebewie meaning "one who ends life" and Sebetutu meaning "one who takes away amulets."

The workers at the BASEL MISSION disapproved of his PREACHING, especially his use of threats to coerce conversion, but the Methodist mission co-opted his evangelistic ministry and at least 20,000 people responded to his ministry and joined the Methodist Church. As a result the Methodists were able to build a sanctuary in the center of Kumasi, capital of the Asante kingdom, and Wesley College, a teacher-training college. Several Asante men entered the Methodist ministry. The Methodist missionary W. G. Waterworth accompanied Oppong on his journeys.

Oppong's ministry was similar to that of his contemporary WILLIAM WADÉ HARRIS. Like Harris, Oppong transformed mission Christianity, contextualizing it to meet the needs of Africans. By so doing he succeeded where several expatriate missionaries had failed to convert local people for almost a hundred years.

See also Methodism, Global; Missions

References and Further Reading

Debrunner, Hans W. *The Story of Sampson Oppong.* Accra, Ghana: Waterville, 1967.
———. *History of Christianity in Ghana.* Accra, Ghana: Waterville, 1965.
Haliburton, G. M. "The Calling of a Prophet: Sampson Oppong." *Bulletin of the Society for African Church History* 2 (1965): 84–86.
Southon, A. E. *Gold Coast Methodism.* London: Cargate Press, 1934.

CASELY B. ESSAMUAH

ORDINATION

See Clergy; Laity

ORTHODOXY

Derived from the Greek *orthodoxia* (*orthos* meaning "right" and *doxa* meaning "belief or opinion"), orthodoxy means right belief, as contrasted with HERESY or heterodoxy. The term is not biblical and became important in the developing Christian church of the second century through its conflict with Gnosticism and with the Trinitarian and Christological controversies of the fourth and fifth centuries. Orthodoxy functions as the way of distinguishing and safeguarding authentic doctrines of the CHURCH. For a particular DOCTRINE to qualify as part of orthodoxy, usually it must either be explicitly included in the BIBLE or be a belief proposed by the faithful (*sensus fidelium*) as implicit within the Bible.

Within the context of Protestantism, the term orthodoxy has an even more specific meaning than right belief. Protestant orthodoxy represents a period extending from the second half of the sixteenth century to the end of the eighteenth century when Lutheran and Reformed theologians developed highly sophisticated theological systems that became the standard theological understandings of the Lutheran and Reformed churches. It is often called Protestant Scholasticism for its resemblance to medieval scholasticism, the technical precision and rigor of much of late medieval theology. This essay briefly charts Protestant orthodoxy's development out of the REFORMATION of the sixteenth century, charts its history through three periods of its development, and then discusses the factors that contributed to its decline before the dawn of the nineteenth century.

Development

At one time, historians of theology viewed Protestant orthodoxy with some suspicion for being a theological movement that fixed the creative insights of the first generations of the Reformation and thereby turned them into arid scholastic systems of doctrine devoid of piety. By the end of the sixteenth century, so they argued, the dynamic, personal, and perhaps unpredictable faith of MARTIN LUTHER (1483–1546), for example, with his emphasis on a theology grounded in revelation and not reason, had been turned by his followers into a dry legalism based more on Aristotelian metaphysics than Paul's notion of JUSTIFICATION by FAITH. More recently, historians of this post-Reformation period have carefully corrected this misperception by noting the deep continuities between the thought of the initial reformers and its subsequent development into systems of doctrine by orthodox Lutheran and Reformed theologians. These continuities can best be seen when one understands the inevitable change that took place institutionally and theologically between the first decades of the Reformation and its subsequent development into what became the church traditions of Protestantism.

The generation of pastors and theologians who immediately followed the first generation of reformers faced a number of challenges in establishing and guiding the faith of the Lutheran and Reformed churches. First, those who followed the reformers necessarily needed organization and structure to their new Christian existence outside of Roman Catholicism. Thus ecclesiastical regulations, confessional texts, and CATECHISMS had to be generated to provide definition and instruction in these new faith traditions. Second, a new generation of CLERGY needed to be educated to continue the PREACHING and teaching of the Reformation. Consequently, centers of theological learning emerged as the places where the systematic reflection on Reformation faith and piety could take place. Third, this systematic reflection allowed the subsequent generation of Protestant orthodox theologians to extend and further nuance the theologies of the sixteenth-century reformers through both developing more fully their own internal differences (e.g., what distinguished Lutherans from Reformed, etc.) and struggling through issues and/or problems that the first generation of reformers had not or could not have anticipated. Fourth, and finally, Protestant thinkers continued to defend the Reformation theologically against its Roman Catholic critics, and through this process used and developed for themselves the logic and subtlety characteristic of medieval scholasticism that their Catholic opponents had used against them. Thus each of these challenges—the needs for confessions and order, schools, further theological refinement and defense—contributed to the development of Protestant orthodoxy out of the Reformation.

History

As a way of understanding the history of this movement, scholars have suggested a three-part division to Protestant orthodoxy: (1) early orthodoxy (c. 1560–

1620); (2) high orthodoxy (c. 1620–1700); and (3) late orthodoxy (c. 1700–1790). Such a division is artificial but nevertheless helpful in noting the progression of thought within the movement as well as the diversity of issues it faced over the course of the first two centuries of Protestantism.

Early orthodoxy (c. 1560–1620) focused on the initial two challenges of developing ecclesiastical polities and confessions, and the academies of learning in which to teach them. If the Reformation churches were to survive and ultimately flourish, then a confessional basis had to be established (see CONFESSIONS), ecclesial organizations had to be constructed, and sound theological training had to be provided for its clergy. During this period Lutheran orthodoxy produced the Formula of Concord (1577) and BOOK OF CONCORD (1580), which helped both to unify LUTHERANISM and to set out its distinctives from the Calvinists. Major Lutheran theologians during this early period of Protestant orthodoxy included Jakob Andreae (1528–1590), one of the authors of the Formula of Concord, and Johann Gerhard (1582–1637), whose nine-volume *Loci theologici* (1610–1621) set the stage for the flourishing of Lutheran orthodoxy during the seventeenth century.

Although the Book of Concord established a doctrinally definitive canon for much of Lutheranism, Reformed Protestants did not provide themselves with creedal books but rather through a multiplicity of confessions of faith referred their followers to scripture, as Calvin's INSTITUTES OF THE CHRISTIAN RELIGION (1559–1560) had done. Reformed theologies published during this first phase of Protestant orthodoxy took the form of commentaries on the HEIDELBERG CATECHISM (1563) and the BELGIC CONFESSION of 1561. THEODORE BEZA (1519–1605), perhaps the most important Reformed theologian of this early period, was the successor to JOHN CALVIN (1509–1564) as head of the church and theological academy of Geneva. The establishment of this theological academy in 1559 was crucial for the development of Reformed orthodoxy, not only because it educated many of the theologians who would define the future of Reformed theology during this period, but also because it served as a model for the establishment of other centers of Reformed theology throughout Europe.

The transition to the high period of orthodoxy (c. 1620–1700) can be linked to the controversies over the doctrine of PREDESTINATION raised by the teachings of the Dutch Reformed theologian JACOBUS ARMINIUS (1559–1609) and dealt with at the Synod of Dort (1618–1619). Arminius held that Christ died for all and that the grace offered to all is accepted by virtue of a decision by the will of each person. The Synod gathered representatives from all parts of the Reformed church (except FRANCE) to form a council wherein they condemned Arminius's theology as Pelagian. It argued that God chooses the elect not on account of the faith God foresees in them, but on account of God's predilection alone. Over against ARMINIANISM, as the movement came to be called, it maintained that GRACE is irresistible and cannot be lost. The controversy persisted beyond Dort, thus necessitating a further creedal formula (the *Consensus helveticus*), drafted in 1675 by influential Reformed theologians including François Turrettini (1629–1687), which both reaffirmed the teachings of Dort (e.g., limiting SALVATION to the elect alone) and argued for the immediate imputation of Adam's sin to all his descendants.

During this period of orthodoxy, moreover, comprehensive dogmatic works, Protestant *summas,* were published. The Lutheran theologian Abraham Calov (1612–1685) wrote a twelve-volume *Systema locorum theologicorum* (1655–1677), but perhaps more influential was his father-in-law Johann Andreas Quenstedt (1617–1688) and his *Theologica didactico-polemica sive Systema theologicorum,* which functioned as a compendium for Lutheran orthodoxy. This high period, therefore, was characterized by the increasing sophistication of Protestant dogmatics and yet, especially in light of the Arminian controversy within Reformed Protestantism, it also reflected an increased prominence of internal polemics.

There are several causes for the decline of Protestant orthodoxy that took place during its eighteenth-century late period (c. 1700–1790). First, the revolutions in natural and human SCIENCE that characterized the late seventeenth and early eighteenth century and the onset of the ENLIGHTENMENT raised serious challenges to the scholastic method of Protestant orthodoxy. Biblical criticism, for example, became increasingly prevalent, thereby forcing the Protestant theologians of the eighteenth century to focus on issues of the historicity of biblical events rather than on the subtleties of dogmatics. Second, various forms of DEISM, skepticism, and even atheism arose during this time, which forced theologians away from primarily focusing on the systematic articulation of the faith for the faithful to engaging in apologetics with thinkers critical of Christianity in general. Third, and finally, PIETISM arose as a Protestant alternative to orthodoxy. PHILIPP JAKOB SPENER (1635–1705) argued in his pietist manifest *Pia desideria* (1675) that orthodoxy had become too exclusively polemical and thus ended up undermining the faith and piety of the very Christians that it sought to defend. Orthodoxy for Spener had lost sight of the fact that theology is not an end in itself but a means to deep faith, a faith that is lived and visible in its piety.

Conclusion

Protestant orthodoxy was a continuous development of the Reformation as Protestantism became more institutionalized and codified in its faith and practice. It expounded many themes that were implicit and underdeveloped in the Reformation and thereby contributed to the articulation of Protestant theology. Thus along with Pietism, Protestant orthodoxy mediated in important ways the Reformation to the modern world.

References and Further Reading

Armstrong, Brian G. *Calvinism and the Amyraut Heresy: Protestant Scholasticism and Humanism in Seventeenth-Century France.* Madison: University of Wisconsin Press, 1969.

Barth, Karl. *The Theology of the Reformed Confessions.* Louisville, KY: Westminster John Knox Press, 2002.

Gerrish, B. A., ed. *The Faith of Christendom: A Source Book of Creeds and Confessions.* Cleveland, OH: World Publishing Company, 1963.

Heppe, Heinrich. *Reformed Dogmatics Set Out and Illustrated from the Sources.* London: George Allen & Unwin, 1950.

McNeil, J. T. *The History and Character of Calvinism.* New York: Oxford University Press, 1954.

Muller, Richard A. *After Calvin: Studies in the Development of a Theological Tradition.* Oxford: Oxford University Press, 2003.

———. *Post-Reformation Reformed Dogmatics: The Rise and Development of Reformed Orthodoxy, ca. 1520 to ca. 1720.* 4 vols. Grand Rapids, MI: Baker Book House, 1987–2003.

———. *Christ and the Decree: Christology and Predestination in Reformed Theology from Calvin to Perkins.* Grand Rapids, MI: Baker Book House, 1988.

Preus, Robert D. *The Theology of Post-Reformation Lutheranism.* 2 vols. St. Louis, MO: Concordia, 1970–1972.

Schmid, Heinrich. *The Doctrinal Theology of the Evangelical Lutheran Church.* Minneapolis, MN: Augsburg Press, 1961.

Trueman, Carl R., and R. Scott Clark, eds. *Protestant Scholasticism: Essays in Reassessment.* Carlisle, UK: Paternoster Publishing, 1999.

van Asselt, Willem J., and Eef Dekker, eds. *Reformation and Scholasticism.* Grand Rapids, MI: Baker Book House, 2001.

JEFFREY HENSLEY

ORTHODOXY, EASTERN

The Eastern Orthodox Church, or simply the Orthodox Church, is a family of autocephalous (self-governing) churches that understands itself to be in an unbroken continuity with the church established by Christ and his apostles. The Orthodox are historically based in Asia Minor and Greece (erstwhile Byzantium), Syria, and the wider Middle East; since the tenth century, in the Balkans and Rus', and subsequently in RUSSIA. Within the past two centuries, particularly with the increase in the movement of peoples, the Orthodox presence is experienced in significant communities and thriving missions worldwide.

The local autocephalous churches that together constitute the Eastern Orthodox Church today are generally reckoned as: the Church of Constantinople (since the sixth century known as the Ecumenical Patriarchate), and the churches of Alexandria, Antioch, Jerusalem, Russia, Georgia, Serbia, Romania, Bulgaria, Cyprus, Greece, Albania, POLAND, the Czech Lands, and Slovakia, as well as the Orthodox Church in America (whose autocephaly is not yet universally recognized). Other autonomous churches are those of Sinai, FINLAND, JAPAN, and Ukraine.

The theological underpinnings of the Orthodox Church are expressed in the seven Ecumenical Councils (from Nicea 325 to Nicea II 787). These and other universally received councils, together with patristic writings, canons, and liturgical texts and rites, are conceived as based on the Scriptures and as the context for the right understanding and application of Scripture. Put another way, Scripture is understood as the normative revelation concerning God and his saving acts, yet Scripture is read within the totality of the church's TRADITION according to its canon of truth.

Many of the sources of Orthodox THEOLOGY are shared by the different Christian traditions. Part of what makes the Orthodox synthesis particular is a close adherence to the combined AUTHORITY of patristic and conciliar witness. Yet the etymology of "Orthodox"—right praise, right glorification—is also expressive of Orthodox tradition, such that theology is integrated into, and receives life and expression in, the church's worship of God—in both the experience and the textual content of that WORSHIP.

A History of Division

In the most basic Orthodox understanding, the history of divided Christendom is a history of division from the Orthodox Church. The first significant split occurred in the aftermath of the Council of Chalcedon (451). The "Oriental Orthodox" or "non-Chalcedonian" churches (Coptic, Ethiopian, Syrian, Armenian, and Malankara-Syrian), although closely related to the Chalcedonian Eastern Orthodox and involved in a promising dialogue since the 1960s, remain divided from them to this day (see DIALOGUE INTER-CONFESSIONAL).

The split of the Latin West from the Greek East is difficult to pinpoint to a single date, although a formal excommunication did take place between Rome and Constantinople in 1054. Relations between Greek and Latin Christendom underwent vicissitudes for centuries before and after that date, but a regularized full communion between the two has not existed during the second millennium.

The main theological reasons for the split are commonly understood as concerning the nature of papal primacy, and the addition by the West of the *filioque* clause to the Nicene-Constantinopolitan Creed—according to which the Holy Spirit proceeds from the Father *and the son*. Other factors of varying degrees of theological significance that are cited include the DOCTRINE of purgatory and of material hell-fire, the use of unleavened bread in the eucharist (see LORD'S SUPPER), and later dogmas concerning the Virgin Mary (notably her immaculate conception). All of these are rejected by the Orthodox Church. Entirely nontheological factors also contributed greatly to the gradual estrangement between the churches.

The Orthodox Church and Protestantism

Historically the REFORMATION, the formation of the CHURCH OF ENGLAND, and the genesis of the FREE CHURCHES and Pentecostal bodies (see PENTECOSTALISM) tend to be seen by Orthodox as further splits from an already estranged West. During the Middle Ages the Orthodox Church was for the most part removed, geographically and ecclesiastically, from Western Christendom. This meant that the factors leading to the Reformation, as well as the Reformation itself (together with the COUNTER-REFORMATION) had but a tangential bearing on the Orthodox Church.

For its own part the Orthodox Church in the mediaeval period was experiencing different extents of oppression stemming from Muslim, Ottoman, and Mongol rule in the former Byzantine empire and the North. Orthodox detachment from the drama of the Reformation is therefore partly geographical, partly theological, and also partly sociopolitical, in that the Orthodox of this period were for the most part not in a position to flourish theologically or ecclesiastically in a way that could be seen as a response to the West.

Yet the centuries-long siege of Orthodoxy did not prevent interaction of one kind or another with the Christian West. Before the Reformation there was not only the unfortunate interaction precipitating from the Crusades (of which the Orthodox East was one of the victims), but also two notable attempts at reunion—at Lyons (1274) and Ferrara-Florence (1438–1439)—which failed when they were rejected by Orthodox, either at the councils themselves or shortly thereafter.

From the point of view of the reformers, the Greek East was in some ways a compelling body, particularly insofar as the reformers studied and admired the Greek church fathers of the early centuries. On the other hand, the Byzantine church, with its vibrant love of iconography and its strong piety for Mary (the *Theotokos,* or Mother of God), appeared to many Protestants to be as decadent and idolatrous as Rome.

The Orthodox, for their part, either distanced themselves from the phenomenon of Protestantism, or, on several notable occasions, sought to engage in a kind of theological dialogue, particularly as instigated by Protestant confessions of faith. In 1573–1574 the Lutheran theologians at Tübingen sent a copy of the AUGSBURG CONFESSION to the ecumenical patriarch Jeremias II, in Greek translation, soliciting a response. The reply was a friendly, theologically rich, but honest and critical text, responding to each article. It represents a useful insight into Orthodox theology of the period, as well as an index of theological convergences and divergences with early LUTHERANISM.

Some fifty years later, a less helpful exchange took place at the hands of ecumenical patriarch Cyril Loukaris, an educated Greek who knew Latin and was in close association with Calvinists. His Confession, published in Latin in Geneva in 1629 (and subsequently in numerous translations), attempted to show Orthodoxy in contrast to Roman Catholicism, but was in virtually every respect Calvinist in its doctrine and thus highly misleading and unrepresentative. It was condemned at no fewer than six Orthodox councils in the ensuing decades.

Subsequent attempts at codifying confessions of faith were also problematic, such as that of Peter Moghila, metropolitan of Kiev, which sought to counterbalance the CALVINISM of Loukaris with a CONFESSION that was laced with uncredited references to Roman CATECHISMS. It was approved, after the introduction of numerous corrections, yet from the perspective of future centuries it is viewed as an unfortunate and distorting influence on Orthodoxy. The period of "confessionalism" thus represented a mixed legacy of contact between Protestants and Orthodox.

Modern Ecumenical Relations

Since the late nineteenth to the early twentieth century, with the spontaneous and nearly universal rise of the modern ecumenical movement, Orthodox theologians have been striving to explore anew the schisms that produced multiple Christian confessions, and also to respond to the trends of thought identified with the Renaissance and the ENLIGHTENMENT.

Some of the most important and creative twentieth-century voices were those of the Russian emigration who were either in contact with Europe or found themselves exiled there in the decades surrounding World War II. Figures such as Sergius Bulgakov, Nicolas Afanasiev, Vladimir Lossky, Georges Florovsky, and later, John Meyendorff and Alexander Schmemann were thinkers who reacted to their encounter with the West with a simultaneous welcome of familiarity—an experience of the enduring spiritual and theological nearness of Christians despite centuries of estrangement—and a zeal for expressing what lay at the heart of Orthodoxy. These authors sought to return to patristic and liturgical sources, accompanied by the critical methodology that is usually associated with the West.

A particular theological and spiritual contact was nourished between Orthodox and Anglicans (see ANGLICANISM) by the Fellowship of Sts. Alban and Sergius. Spurred on the Anglican side in part by the spirit of the nineteenth-century OXFORD MOVEMENT, and on the Orthodox side by a living ecumenical spirit, the Fellowship (founded in 1927) was a vehicle for the encounter of some of the best theological and spiritual minds either side had to offer.

Through the WORLD MISSIONARY CONFERENCE in Edinburgh in 1910, and more especially through the Faith and Order meetings from the 1920s onward, the Orthodox have participated—with a combination of enthusiasm and misgiving—in multilateral and bilateral theological dialogues. Some of the Orthodox churches were founding members of the WORLD COUNCIL OF CHURCHES in 1948, and after the 1961 assembly in New Delhi, all the canonical churches eventually took membership. Particularly with respect to membership in large, multilateral ecumenical "councils of churches," the Orthodox have expressed serious theological concerns that their membership not be misconstrued as an acceptance of others as "churches" in the full sense of that word, or that the Universal Church consists in a combination of all the existing Christian confessions. Such theological concerns, as well as sociopolitical tensions resulting from the fall of COMMUNISM, have resulted in the withdrawal of some of the Orthodox churches from all formal ecumenical contacts (see ECUMENISM).

The Orthodox Church currently enjoys bilateral relations with the Roman Catholic Church as well as with a wide range of Protestant churches. These include formal dialogues at the world level, as well as national and regional dialogues of varying degrees of formality. Bilateral dialogues have engendered in many cases closer relations, as well as honest documentations of convergences and disagreements in the faith and life of the churches.

References and Further Reading

Gros, Jeffrey, Harding Meyer, and William G. Rusch, eds. *Growth in Agreement II*. Grand Rapids, MI: Wm. B. Eerdmans and Geneva: WCC, 2000.

Louth, Andrew. *Discerning the Mystery*. Oxford: Oxford University Press, 1983.

Meyer, Harding, and Lukas Vischer, eds. *Growth in Agreement*. Geneva, Switzerland: WCC, 1984.

Runciman, Steven. *The Great Church in Captivity*. Cambridge: Cambridge University Press, 1968.

Valliere, Paul. *Modern Russian Theology: Bukharev, Soloviev, Bulgakov*. Grand Rapids, MI: Wm. B. Eerdmans, 2000.

Ware, Kallistos. *The Orthodox Church*. 2d edition. New York/London: Penguin, 1993.

PETER C. BOUTENEFF

OSHITELU, JOSIAH OLUNOWO (1902–1962)

African church leader. Beginning his career in the Anglican Church, Josiah Olunowo Oshitelu founded the Church of the Lord, one of the major branches of the Aladura religious movement, in NIGERIA in 1930.

Oshitelu was born in the town of Ogere, in the Ijebu area near the African coast. An Anglican catechist and teacher, Oshitelu was dismissed in 1926 because he claimed to have visions, which were brought on by extensive fasting and devotions. The visions revealed a script with holy words and names that had miraculous power. He was assisted in interpreting his dreams and visions by Shomoye, a Christian elder who later became his apostle to West Africa. Oshitelu emerged in 1929 to begin a healing and preaching ministry in the Aladura tradition. He attacked idolatry, traditional medicine, and fetishes, and healed by using PRAYER, fasting, and holy water. He condoned polygamy and had seven wives himself (see PLURAL MARRIAGE).

In 1930, considering the culture, CUSTOMS, and manners of the land in which he lived, Oshitelu founded the Church of the Lord. Christianity's requirements of monogamous marriage, male dominance, and the emphasis on belonging exclusively to one DENOMINATION were in contrast with the indigenous practice of multiple cult membership, polygamy, and the acceptance of some WOMEN as religious leaders (see WOMEN CLERGY). Further, the local popularity of the tenets of Rosicrucianism, FREEMASONRY, esoteric Islam, qabalah, and traditional Yoruba religion gave rise to a syncretistic atmosphere that influenced Oshitelu's visions. The use of occult literature remains popular in the Church of the Lord.

The Church of the Lord was successful, and it soon spread into all regions of Nigeria, including the Islamic north, where its use of Islamic dietary rules and prayer forms ensured its acceptance. Subsequently the church found acceptance in both ENGLAND and the UNITED STATES.

Josiah Oshitelu died in 1962.

See also Africa; African Instituted Churches, Nigeria; African Theology

References and Further Reading

Probst, Peter. "The Letter and the Spirit: Literacy and Religious Authority in the History of the Aladura Movement in Western Nigeria." *Africa* 59 no. 4 (1989): 478–495.

Turner, Harold. W. *History of an African Independent Church*. Oxford: Clarendon Press, 1967.

HELEN FARLEY

OSIANDER, ANDREAS (c. 1498–1552)

German Lutheran. Osiander was born December 19, 1498 (or 1496) at Gunzenhausen, southwest of Nürnberg, and he died October 17, 1552 at Königsberg. After some study in Leipzig, Altenburg, and Ingolstadt, Osiander was ordained a priest in 1520. Around the time he became a preacher for St. Lorenz in Nürnberg, Osiander publicly supported MARTIN LUTHER, helping bring the REFORMATION to Nürnberg. He backed Luther at Marburg in the 1529 exchange with HULDRYCH ZWINGLI over Christ's presence in the LORD'S SUPPER. Osiander also attended the 1530 presentation of the AUGSBURG CONFESSION and signed Luther's 1537 SCHMALKALDIC ARTICLES with their strong position against Rome.

His broader humanist-influenced interests served religion with his 1537 publication of a harmony of the Gospels, and advanced SCIENCE with his 1543 publication of Copernicus's *On the Revolutions of the Heavenly Spheres,* for which he provided a preface. Opposition to the AUGSBURG INTERIM forced him to move to Königsberg where, despite lacking a theological degree, he became head of the university's theological faculty.

Although most often in the Lutheran camp, Osiander's ideas on the indwelling presence of Christ and a growing belief in saving righteousness sparked sharp controversy in later life because most Lutherans saw Osiander as differing with Luther on the issue of JUSTIFICATION. Never one to skirt confrontation and known for an often intemperate tongue and pen, Osiander became embroiled in controversy over how Luther and his supporters understood justification. To avoid any role for human works, Osiander taught that SALVATION was by GRACE grasped by FAITH in Christ as Christ dwells within the individual, in a near mystical sense, and the believer becomes righteous. Critics charged that this view destroyed confidence in the objective work of Christ for all humankind. Instead of being declared righteous, justification became an internal process of becoming acceptable to God. The dispute was unresolved when Osiander died. Article III of the Lutheran 1577 Formula of Concord rejected his position.

References and Further Reading

Hirsch, Emanuel. *Die Theologie des Andreas Osiander und ihre geschichtlichen Voraussetzungen.* Göttingen, Germany: Vandenhoeck und Ruprecht, 1919.

Seebass, Gottfried. "Andreas Osiander." In *The Oxford Encyclopedia of the Reformation,* edited by Hans J. Hillerbrand, vol. 3, 183–185. New York: Oxford University Press, 1996.

———. *Das reformatorische Werk des Andreas Osiander. Einzelarbeiten aus der Kirchengeschichte Bayerns.* vol. 44. Nurnberg: Verein für Bayerische Kirchengeschichte, 1967.

Stupperich, Martin. *Osiander in Preussen 1549–1552. Arbeiten zur Kirchengeschichte.* vol. 44. Berlin: Walter de Gruyter, 1973.

ROBERT ROSIN

OVERBECK, FRANZ CAMILLE (1837–1905)

Swiss theologian. Born into an irreligious family among expatriate merchants in St. Petersburg in November 1837, Overbeck's father was a German Lutheran who had been brought up in ENGLAND and his mother was a Catholic, daughter of French parents. The children were brought up Lutheran at Overbeck's grandmother's insistence. Overbeck witnessed the February 1848 revolution in FRANCE during one year's schooling at St. Germain near Paris. His family moved to Dresden and there the twelve-year-old Overbeck, who spoke fluent French, English, and Russian, first began to master German. He formed a friendship at school with Heinrich von Treitschke who educated him in irreligion, although they later parted because of Treitschke's fanatical patriotism. "Nothing would sooner extinguish the last sparks of patriotism in me than the demand to convert back to Christianity for the sake of this Empire."

He studied THEOLOGY at Leipzig 1856–1857 (when he gave up saying his prayers at night) and at Göttingen 1857–1859. Returning to Leipzig he gained the right to teach at a university in 1864, having abandoned the thought of being a pastor in the resolve to study church history "without illusion." In 1869 he was called to Basel to a chair of "Critical Theology" newly created by a reform party. In Basel, he and FRIEDRICH NIETZSCHE had rooms in the same boarding house and ate their evening meals together until Overbeck's marriage in 1876. Overbeck's *How Christian Is Our Present-day Theology?* and Nietzsche's *David Strauss the Confessor and Writer* appeared in the same year (1873). Both books ridiculed the apologetic and liberal attempts to restate Christianity for the modern age.

Overbeck argued that when Christianity abandoned its belief in the imminent end of the world and sought to construct a theology or write literature it was doomed. He taught New Testament by giving the barest philological interpretation of the text, strictly avoiding any HIGHER CRITICISM of form or content of the books of the New Testament that might shake their religious aspect in the eyes of his students. Overbeck despised ADOLF VON HARNACK's scholarship and called him "the spoiled favourite of public opinion."

In 1920 KARL BARTH cited Overbeck: "Only a heroic Christianity, opposed to every age, completely basing itself on itself can avoid the fate of Jesuitry," that is, "the crypto-ascetic representation of Christianity in the world; modern theology, indeed the theology of Protestantism, is an ideal and sublime Jesuitry." Barth thought he had constructed a theology that would escape Overbeck's strictures.

Overbeck brought out a second edition of his *Christianity* in 1903. His scholarly reflections were written on more than 20,000 loose octavo sheets, some on both sides, and stored alphabetically in over fifty cartons and boxes now in the Basel University Library. Selections were published by Overbeck's pupil and friend, C. A. Bernoulli. A modern edition of *Werke und Nachlass* in nine volumes began to appear in 1995.

Overbeck died on June 27, 1905.

References and Further Reading

Primary Sources:

Overbeck, Franz. *Über die Christlichkeit unserer heutigen Theologie: Eine Friedensschrift.* Leipzig: Fritsch, 1873. 2d edition without *Eine Friedensschrift* in the title, with Introduction and Supplement on the reception of the 1st edition, 1903. *How Christian Is Our Present-day Theology?* Translated by Martin Henry. Edinburgh: T. & T. Clark/Continuum, 2003.

———. *Werke und Nachlass in neun Bänden.* Stuttgart/Weimar, Germany: J. B. Metzler, 1995–.

Secondary Sources:

Brändle, R, and E. W. Stegemann, eds. *Franz Overbecks unerledigte Anfragen an das Christentum.* Munich, Germany: Chr. Kaiser, 1988.

Henry, Martin. *Franz Overbeck: Theologian?: Religion and History in the Thought of Franz Overbeck.* Frankfurt am Main, Germany: Peter Lang, 1995.

J. C. O'NEILL

OXFORD MOVEMENT

Originating among a small group of academic clergy within the university of Oxford in the late 1820s and early 1830s as a response to what they perceived as a series of fundamental challenges to the privileged status of the CHURCH OF ENGLAND, the Oxford Movement became one of the most significant forces in nineteenth-century ANGLICANISM, and the precursor of the modern Anglo-Catholic party (see ANGLO-CATHOLICISM). It represented a departure from the traditional Protestantism of the Church of England and, at the same time, introduced a rival theological perspective to the growing liberal tendencies among many Victorian Churchmen. The Oxford Movement thus initiated a lengthy period of fierce and sometimes bitter controversy not only within Anglicanism itself but also with other denominations, at both an academic and parochial level.

Origins and Early History

It was generally accepted by the mid-nineteenth century that the starting date of the Movement was Sunday, July 14, 1833, when JOHN KEBLE, a professor of poetry, preached the sermon in the university church at the service marking the opening of the legal assizes. The subject of this Assize Sermon was "National Apostasy," a response to the recent action of the Whig-led government in abolishing ten Anglican bishoprics in Ireland. This traditional date went largely unchallenged until scholars in the later twentieth century argued that the Movement's origins were in fact more complex and protracted, reaching back into the 1820s, and involving an understanding not only of the ecclesiastical but also of the political, social, and economic conditions in early nineteenth-century England.

The combined impact of INDUSTRIALIZATION and urbanization was rapidly changing the appearance of the country, with ramifications for many aspects of its life. Shifts in population, and rising wealth among the middle classes, had already resulted in a radical campaign for the reform of Parliament, culminating in the First Reform Act of 1832. However, alongside this campaign for political reform ran others for the elimination of what growing numbers of radicals saw as the corruption of the whole traditional system of privilege and patronage in both state and Church. Among these was the Anglican stranglehold over the educational system. Entry to Oxford and Cambridge universities was reserved to those willing to subscribe to the THIRTY-NINE ARTICLES, effectively excluding non-Anglicans. The universities in their turn supplied the Established Church with the bulk of her clergy, about half of all graduates proceeding to take holy orders. Similarly membership of both Houses of Parliament was in theory exclusively Anglican.

The problem for the ecclesiastical element of this Establishment was that the growth of towns had been matched by a corresponding expansion of Protestant DISSENT, especially among the urban middle classes, partly accounted for by the recent arrival of new forms of Dissent, notably METHODISM. Thus political and religious radicalism often went hand in hand. The vast, but unequally distributed, wealth of the Established Church, along with what radicals saw as its undeserved privileges, both originating in the preindustrial past, were offensive to increasingly powerful minorities in England. The initial resistance of the traditional governing classes to change, however, had gradually given way to a policy of reforming the most glaring abuses. In 1828 the repeal of the Test and Corporation Acts, dating from the seventeenth century, had formally allowed Dissenters to sit in Parliament, a largely symbolic gesture because in reality some already did so through the passing of annual indemnities. In the following year Emancipation had done the same for Roman Catholics, although this now opened the Established Church to the possibility of legislation affecting it being passed by a body no longer exclusively Anglican. In 1830 the half century of near-monopoly of government by the Tories gave way to a Whig-led ministry, theoretically less well disposed to the Church. During the subsequent battle for Parliamentary reform Tory-appointed bishops in the House of Lords largely opposed change, compounding their unpopularity in the country. This process of constitutional upheaval extended to the Church itself in 1833 with the abolition of the ten Irish bishoprics, given that Anglicanism was then the Established faith not only of England and Wales but also of Ireland, despite its minority appeal in the latter country. Thus the five years leading up to Keble's Assize Sermon appeared to undermine the mutual support of Church and state dating back to the REFORMATION.

They were also the years in which a group of increasingly like-minded academic clergy at Oxford university had come together to fight a series of campaigns to attempt to halt this erosion of Anglican privilege. Oldest among them was Keble himself, a traditional High Churchman who had already achieved fame when his collection of poems celebrating the Anglican liturgical calendar, *The Christian Year,* had been published in 1827. What characterized most of the other members of this group, however, was their comparative youth. JOHN HENRY NEWMAN had been born in 1801, Richard Hurrell Froude in 1803, and EDWARD BOUVERIE PUSEY in 1800, although the latter was not formally part of this group until 1834. These men had not only their youth in common but also the fact that they were all at one time or another Fellows of Oriel College, the intellectual powerhouse of early nineteenth-century Oxford. These four are generally acknowledged, each in his own particular way, to be the originators of the Oxford Movement. In addition there were also a number of other individuals who contributed significantly to its early history, among them the minor poet Isaac Williams, Robert Wilberforce, the son of the great emancipator WILLIAM WILBERFORCE, and Henry Manning the future Cardinal archbishop of Westminster. In was in the mid to late 1820s, as Newman moved away from his original EVANGELICALISM, and Froude became increasingly attracted to the Fathers and medieval Catholicism, that these individuals joined forces to oppose the growing attacks on the privileged position of the Established Church.

In 1828 the Member of Parliament (MP) for Oxford university, Robert Peel, who was also the leader of the Tories in the House of Commons and Home Secretary, announced his conversion from champion of the Anglican Establishment to supporter of Catholic Emancipation. As such he felt morally obliged to resign and seek reelection as MP for the university. Keble, Newman, and Froude now joined forces as leaders of the campaign that led to Peel's defeat, ironically as defenders of an Establishment that a few years later they themselves were to vehemently criticize. However, within weeks of this success Newman, Froude, and Robert Wilberforce were engaged in a new battle to impose their conception of the role of a tutor within their college, one that they saw as moral and spiritual as well as academic. This led to a rift with the provost of Oriel, Edward Hawkins, who in 1830 finally cut off the supply of new pupils to his three brilliant, but insubordinate, tutors. Newman, Keble, Froude and their circle were also staunch in defense of the beleaguered bishops, some of whom found themselves the objects of physical intimidation by pro-reform mobs. Political opposition to the new Whig-led government culminated in 1833 with the abolition of the ten bishoprics and Keble's Assize Sermon. This was then swiftly followed by a meeting between Froude, representing the rising generation from Oxford, and a group of older and more traditional High Churchmen, which resulted in petitions from 7,000 clergy and 230,000 laity in defense of the Church. In September 1833 Newman launched the first of the *Tracts for the Times*, initially short pamphlets of a few pages each, from which the Movement derived its most familiar nickname, that of "Tractarian." Altogether by 1841 some ninety *Tracts* had been published, the later ones much more substantial works of theology, the complete set eventually running to about 3,500 pages in six volumes.

Initially these new Tractarians, aware of their weaknesses in terms of both numbers and influence, were at pains to enlist the support of other larger and more powerful forces within Anglicanism. At this stage their concept did not envisage the creation of a new "party" within the Church of England, but rather a revivification of the Church as a whole. Thus using his contacts among his former friends in the Evangelical party, Newman began to write letters to, and articles for, its newspaper, the *Record*. Assaults on the Anglican exclusiveness of Oxford university also enabled the Tractarians to form alliances with High Churchmen, Evangelicals, and others in its defense. In 1834, for instance, a bill was introduced into Parliament seeking to abolish subscription to the Thirty-nine Articles upon matriculation, and the Tractarians were but one of a number of groups that successfully opposed it. In 1836 this was followed by the appointment by the Whigs of R. D. Hampden as Regius professor of divinity at Oxford, considered by many apart from the Tractarians as a dangerous liberal in his teaching, which enabled a fresh alliance with other Churchmen from a variety of parties to protest against this further imposition.

Theological Concepts and Controversies

By the mid-1830s, however, it was becoming clear that this group of young men from Oxford represented something novel in the history of Anglicanism. Increasingly they did not conform to the traditional internal groupings that had evolved since the Reformation. Superficially similar to High Churchmen, they also displayed some of the zeal and enthusiasm of the early Evangelicals. In some ways they appeared deeply conservative in their defense of Anglicanism; in others they seemed dangerously radical in their attitude to the Establishment. This led many Churchmen at the time, and has led some of their subsequent historians, into a sense of confusion and bewilderment when attempting to categorize the Oxford Movement. In reality Tractarianism was the ecclesiastical counterpart of a number of secular movements in 1830s England, in that they were both conservative and radical at the same time. Most prominent of these secular movements was the so-called Tory Radical alliance in politics and economics that brought traditional Tories and working-class radicals together to promote the first legislation to control the hours of work in the new textile factories, and which then bitterly opposed the introduction of the new Poor Law of 1834. Unlike these short-lived campaigns, however, the Tractarians initiated an ecclesiastical force that was to become a permanent feature of Anglicanism.

What then were the leading ideas of the Oxford Movement, how did these set their proponents apart from other Churchmen, and why did they prove to be so controversial? One way of approaching these questions is to compare the Tractarians to other churchmen of the period. For instance, one theological concept that the Tractarians appeared to share with more traditional High Churchmen was an emphasis on the apostolic succession of the episcopate (see BISHOP AND EPISCOPACY). Yet where the Tractarians differed was in the degree of emphasis that they put on it, seeing it as an absolutely essential component of a Church. Here they sought to compare themselves to the Caroline Divines of the seventeenth century, and in this, as in other ways, claimed they were recovering concepts subsequently "lost" to Anglicanism. To emphasize this they edited a collection of works by the great Anglican apologists, which they called the *Library of Anglo-Catholic Theology.* Yet High Churchmen also saw themselves as equally the inheritors of the Caroline Divines, and responded by pointing out that Tractarians often quoted in a very selective way from the latter. In addition no previous Anglican theologians had interpreted the apostolic succession in the uncompromising Tractarian sense, which seemed to effectively "unchurch" Christians of nonepiscopal denominations. However, for Tractarians, episcopacy was central to AUTHORITY in Christianity, and was the theme of the first of the *Tracts,* where Newman argued that the apostolic succession was the true source of Anglican authority, and—crucially for the constitutional context of the time—was beyond the power of government legislation. The real source of the Church of England's authority over the people of England, argued Newman, lay not in its wealth, the superior education of its clergy, nor in its links to the state, but rather in the spiritual descent of its bishops from the Apostles.

This led on to a further difference with High Churchmen. In the years from 1760 they had emerged as a powerful force within the Establishment, and by 1830 had more of their party on the episcopal bench than at any time since the so-called GLORIOUS REVOLUTION of 1688. This was in large part as a result of the influence of their pressure group, the Hackney Phalanx, in some ways similar to the Evangelical CLAPHAM SECT, and its links with the Tory prime minister, Lord Liverpool. With Liverpool's death in 1827, however, followed rapidly by years of constitutional upheaval, High Churchmen were thrown into disarray as an organized force within Anglicanism. This left a vacuum that the Tractarians now filled, although increasingly the latter group developed a very different view of the concept of Establishment. Decades of working within and through the traditional linkages between Church and state had left High Churchmen with a profound respect for the Establish-

ment. For the Tractarians the constitutional disputes of 1828–1833 had transformed everything. The Church's remaining links to the state had changed from being an advantage to a potential danger, a view made explicit by Froude in his *Tract* number 59, "Church and State" of 1835. Tensions between the two groups were obvious from the early 1830s with clear High Church disapproval of the *Tracts* themselves as too individualistic and speculative; High Churchmen preferred to work through the more traditional means of editorial committees, enforcing consensus and constraint.

For the Evangelicals early cooperation with the Tractarians in the battles to defend Oxford university in its Anglican exclusiveness subsequently turned first to suspicion, and then to outright hostility. One major issue of concern for the Evangelicals was the attitude of the Oxford Movement to the Reformation. Differences between the two groups became explicit with the publication of the first part of Froude's *Remains* in 1838. Froude had died of consumption in 1836. Newman and Keble assembled and edited his journals, letters, and other unpublished writings into two memorial volumes. Appearing in 1838 and 1839, respectively, they revealed the hidden life of an Anglican clergyman who loved medieval saints, used the Roman Breviary, practiced austere penances, and above all reviled the Reformation. "I hate the Reformation and the Reformers more and more"; "The Reformation was a limb badly set—it must be broken again in order to be righted"; "I am every day becoming a less and less loyal son of the Reformation" (Froude ed. Newman and Keble vol. I 1838:389, 433, 336). These were sentiments that, in the religious world of the 1830s, were almost unimaginable as coming from the pen of a cleric in what was thought to be the orders of an unambiguously Protestant Church. If they were shocking to most Anglicans, they were particularly outrageous to the Evangelicals with their reverence for the Reformers. Many sympathetic to the Oxford Movement, both at the time and subsequently, have thus seen the publication of the *Remains* as a fatal error on the part of its editors. However, by the later twentieth century many scholars considered it to have been a deliberate act of provocation on the part of Newman in particular, intended to filter out the less enthusiastic followers of the Movement, to appeal directly to the romantic imaginations of the rising generation both at Oxford and in the wider Church. Be that as it may, the appearance of the *Remains* marked the point of final and open breach between the Tractarians and the Evangelicals. This was symbolized by the proposition, originating in Evangelical circles, to reaffirm Oxford's loyalty to the Reformation by erecting a memorial to the three Protestant martyrs burnt in

Oxford during the reign of the Catholic Queen Mary, THOMAS CRANMER, HUGH LATIMER, and Ridley. If the Tractarians agreed to contribute to the costs they would effectively disown Froude; if they did not, then their collective loyalty to the English Reformation would be called into question. When they duly refused to subscribe, other Anglicans were free to draw their own conclusions.

In a variety of other ways the theological views of the Tractarians put them at variance with both contemporary and historical Anglicanism. One of these was the Tractarian approach to the Fathers and the early Church. Traditionally High Churchmen had appealed to the Fathers in justification of the Reformed English Church, but in such a way that used the Fathers to corroborate Anglicanism as the normative model of the true Church. Newman and his friends shifted the emphasis and tended to see the Church of England as true only insofar as she was in agreement with antiquity. Once again the focus of authority was shifted by the Tractarians, and once again they claimed a historical group of theologians for their own by publishing many works by the Fathers in an English translation in the *Library of the Fathers*. In a broader sense too the Oxford writers used history itself to combat what they saw as the greatest theological peril facing nineteenth-century Christianity—what Newman in his *Apologia* called "Liberalism." He defined this as "the anti-dogmatic principle and its development"; "the mistake of subjecting to human judgement those revealed doctrines which are in their nature beyond and independent of it" (Newman ed. Svaglic: 54, 256). English liberal theologians like Hampden or THOMAS ARNOLD reduced everything in Christianity to the human level; Newman, in contrast, saw Christianity as a record of divinely inspired events and statements beyond human reason. From his extensive reading of early Church history Newman conceived liberalism as the contemporary version of the classic heresies (see HERESY) to be resisted as firmly in his day as his hero, Athanasius, had resisted Arianism in the fourth century. However, this placed the Tractarians in opposition to yet another, and growing, school of thought within the Church of England.

Tractarian Developments

What was becoming clear as the years passed, therefore, was that there were growing divergences between Tractarians and other parties within the Established Church. The reason for such fractures was that the Oxford Movement was traveling in a progressively more Catholic direction. One measure of this was the *Tracts* themselves. Most of them passed through several editions, each tending to revise the text in a particular way: downgrading or eliminating references to, or agreements with, the Reformers, and emphasizing instead the doctrines and writings of the Catholic past. This exemplified one problem all observers of the progress of the Movement were faced with—that its theological ideas were never static, but rather dynamic, evolving over time. This made it all the harder to define its nature, and compounded the bewilderment of some contemporaries.

One doctrinal area where this was particularly the case was sacramental theology, and especially the Eucharist. There is surprisingly little in the *Tracts* themselves on this subject, partly because the Tractarians were only just beginning to address these issues in the early years of the Movement. As the 1830s progressed, however, the Tractarian leaders began to reject many of the concepts originating with the Reformation. Behind their developing sacramental concept of Christianity was also the influence of ROMANTICISM. Keble's *Christian Year* had been the first manifestation of the connection between the English Romantic poets and Tractarianism, and many of the early pioneers of the Movement were also minor poets themselves, their works collected into the volume called *Lyra Apostolica* in 1836. The concept of the natural leading into the supernatural that was found in much Romantic poetry, especially that of WILLIAM WORDSWORTH and SAMUEL TAYLOR COLERIDGE, was also one of the bases of Tractarian sacramental theology, of bread and wine transformed into the body and blood of Christ, for instance. However, the most systematic and developed Tractarian theology of the Eucharist was the work of Robert Wilberforce. His discovery of the medieval Scholastics and sixteenth-century Jesuits gave him a framework of Latin terminology in which to work, and his book *The Doctrine of the Holy Eucharist* presented Tractarian theology as a complete system, the Eucharist interpreted as the earthly counterpart of the eternal pleading of the Son before the Father through the merits of his own earthly sacrifice on the cross, a real participation in the heavenly liturgy. However, this was not published until 1853. Thus the Tractarian search for a Eucharistic theology had moved through a number of stages lasting over twenty years before finally evolving into a coherent system.

Another evolution was also under way within the Oxford Movement from the late 1830s, that of the growing disillusionment of Newman with Anglicanism, and the rival attraction of Rome. The precise details of his first doubts in the summer of 1839, recorded in his *Apologia* of 1864, came under close scrutiny by a number of scholars in the late twentieth century, and as a result can no longer be accepted uncritically. What remains uncontested, however, is that it was his reading of the history of the early Church, and especially his study of the classic heresies, that began to raise in his mind the possibility that Anglicanism was in a similar relationship to contemporary Rome as the Donatists or Monophysites had been in the past. To test the true Catholicity of Anglicanism, Newman took fourteen of the Thirty-nine Articles and subjected them to close theological, historical, and linguistic analysis in what was to be the last of the *Tracts*, number 90. In effect an attempt to reconcile the central statement of Anglican belief with modern Roman Catholicism, it resulted in another storm breaking over the heads of the Tractarians, if anything more severe than that caused by the *Remains*. Many bishops now condemned the new *Tract* in their Charges, placing the Oxford Movement in the paradoxical position of exalting episcopal authority to a degree previously unseen in Anglican history, but having to endure the profound disfavor of actual bishops. Newman's response was to retreat into semimonastic retirement at Littlemore, a village a few miles outside Oxford, where he approached his personal struggle from a different viewpoint. Is it possible, among all the competing and mutually exclusive contemporary forms of Christianity, to find the true one? Returning again to the early Church and the Fathers as his inspiration and models, Newman argued that, like all ideas, Christianity itself is not static but dynamic, and follows a path of development over time. He devised seven tests for determining between legitimate and illegitimate developments, the latter being the origins of heresy. His conclusion was that, although some Churches satisfied some of the tests, only Rome displayed them all. Thus in October 1845, shortly before the fruits of his researches his *Essay on the Development of Christian Doctrine* was published, he was received into the Roman Catholic Church.

Later History and Evaluation

For Newman's closest friends in the Movement his loss was a bitter blow, although it would be a mistake to extend the feelings of a few intimates to what was becoming by 1845 a churchwide movement. For several generations of historians largely sympathetic to Tractarianism, the events of 1845 were a catastrophe. However, by the beginning of the twenty-first century, detailed research was painting a different picture. By 1845 most supporters of the Movement had not been brought into it by personal contact with Newman, but by reading its extensive literature. Indeed, there is some evidence that suggests many Tractarians were, in fact, relieved that he had finally left the Anglican fold. He had become a figure of controversy and, as such, an increasing liability to those who remained

convinced of the catholicity of the Church of England. His removal was a liberation that would allow the Movement to return to its original aim of revitalizing Anglicanism, and from 1845 the main focus of this would no longer be Oxford university but rather the parishes.

Here the story was one of steady expansion. In 1840 parishes with Tractarian incumbents numbered a few dozen; by 1870 they were counted in their hundreds, representing perhaps five percent of the parishes of the Church of England, concentrated mainly in the rural south where Anglicanism was generally at its strongest. Here Tractarians revived the Daily Service of choral morning and evening prayer, increased the frequency with which the Eucharist was celebrated, began to wear surplices and stoles, lit candles on newly restored ALTARS, and removed the privately rented pews to replace them with free seating. In many of these things Tractarians of this generation were often little more than in the vanguard of what was becoming a larger Anglican movement of liturgical and pastoral renewal. Local opposition to Tractarians did manifest itself, but by the late 1850s most of this had been successfully contained by a policy of patience, caution, and flexibility, which tended to distinguish these years from the earlier ones at Oxford.

Then starting about 1860 a younger generation began to advocate a more developed ceremonial. Arguing that works such as Wilberforce's on the Eucharist, combined with a number of favorable legal judgments, had established a more Catholic interpretation of the service of Holy Communion, Eucharistic VESTMENTS, incense, and other pre-Reformation practices began to creep back into Anglican worship. Initially hesitant, and sometimes divided among themselves on this issue, the older generation of Tractarians eventually came to adopt these so-called Ritualist practices. Despite attempts to restrict them legally, mainly through the Public Worship Regulation Act of 1874, by the 1890s it was clear that Tractarian theology and Ritualist practices now went together. By 1904 the number of churches with Anglo-Catholic incumbents, as they now called themselves, had risen to over 2,000, and it was clear that the inheritors of the Oxford Movement had become a large and permanent feature of Anglicanism.

As the twentieth century opened there was a strong feeling of optimism among Anglo-Catholics. It seemed that their party was the growing one, and only a matter of time before it became the dominant voice within Anglicanism, both in its mother Church and the overseas provinces. As the century moved into its second half, however, optimism diminished and Anglo-Catholics once again began to look like a beleaguered minority. The liberalism that Newman had so feared seemed to have become the creed of most Anglican theologians and many bishops. Evangelicalism was experiencing a revival based on the charismatic movement, and Rome was revising its liturgical practices in the wake of the Second Vatican Council, which appeared to leave Anglo-Catholics looking like nineteenth-century relics. By the 1970s the growing pressure for the ordination of women assaulted the three interconnected Tractarian concepts of authority, ministry, and sacraments. In 1992 the General Synod of the Church of England finally followed a number of other Anglican provinces and approved the ordination of women. In the following decade some four bishops and several hundred other clergy left the Church of England, mainly following Newman into the Roman Catholic Church.

Yet despite these reverses it is clear that the Oxford Movement represented both one of the most significant forces that have shaped modern Anglicanism, and at the same time perhaps the greatest discontinuity in its history. It reasserted the spiritual and sacramental foundations of the Church of England at the moment of its greatest peril since the English CIVIL WAR, if in ways previously unfamiliar to its theologians and at the cost of internal conflict. It was a major influence in reshaping the liturgical, pastoral, and theological life of Victorian England. It has had a profound affect on ECUMENISM, especially in relations between the Anglican, Roman Catholic, and Orthodox Churches (see ORTHODOXY, EASTERN). In the person of Newman it nurtured one of the most original theologians of the modern era. Its greatest failure, perhaps, was in not realizing the intentions of its originators in becoming a vehicle for a Churchwide revitalization of Anglicanism. They never intended to create a new party within Anglicanism, but rather to represent Anglicanism as a whole. However, the historical circumstances of their times, combined with their own disinclination to compromise, made that an impossible task.

See also Altars; Anglicanism; Anglo-Catholicism; Arnold, Thomas; Asceticism; Authority; Bishop and Episcopacy; Broad Church; Catholic Reactions to Protestantism; Catholicism, Protestant Reactions; Church and State, Overview; Church of England; Civil War, England; Clapham Sect; Coleridge, Samuel Taylor; Cranmer, Thomas; Denomination; Dissent; Ecclesiology; Ecumenism; England; Episcopal Church, United States; Evangelicalism; Glorious Revolution; Heresy; Industrialization; Keble, John; Latimer, Hugh; Liberal Protestantism and Liberalism; Liddon, Henry Parry; Methodism; Newman, John Henry; Orthodoxy, Eastern; Pusey, Edward Bouverie; Reformation; Romanticism; Thirty-nine Articles; Vestments; Wilberforce, William; Women Clergy; Wordsworth, William

References and Further Reading

Bentley, James. *Ritualism and Politics in Victorian Britain: The Attempt to Legislate for Belief.* Oxford: Oxford University Press, 1978.

Brendon, Piers. *Hurrell Froude and the Oxford Movement.* London: Paul Elek, 1974.

Hardelin, Alf. *The Tractarian Understanding of the Eucharist.* Uppsala: Uppsala University Press, 1965.

Herring, George. *What Was the Oxford Movement?* London and New York: Continuum, 2002.

Imberg, Rune. *In Quest of Authority: The 'Tracts for the Times' and the Development of the Tractarian Leaders 1833–1841.* Lund: Lund University Press, 1987.

Newsome, David. *The Parting of Friends: A Study of the Wilberforces and Henry Manning.* London: John Murray, 1966.

Nockles, Peter. *The Oxford Movement in Context: Anglican High Churchmanship 1760–1857.* Cambridge: Cambridge University Press, 1994.

O'Connell, Marvin R. *The Oxford Conspirators: A History of the Oxford Movement 1833–1845.* London: University of America Press, 1969.

Rowell, Geoffrey. *The Vision Glorious: Themes and Personalities of the Catholic Revival in Anglicanism.* Oxford: Oxford University Press, 1983.

———, ed. *Tradition Renewed: The Oxford Movement Conference Papers.* London: Darton, Longman and Todd, 1986.

Toon, Peter. *Evangelical Theology 1833–1856: A Response to Tractarianism.* London: Marshall, Morgan and Scott, 1979.

Viass, Paul, ed. *From Oxford to the People: Reconsidering Newman and the Oxford Movement.* London: Gracewing, 1996.

Yates, Nigel. *Anglican Ritualism in Victorian Britain 1830–1910.* Oxford: Oxford University Press, 1999.

GEORGE HERRING

P

PACIFIC ISLANDS

Protestant missionary interest in the Pacific arose from the voyages of European explorers, notably James Cook (1728–1779), and the rise of the evangelical missionary movement. The London Missionary Society (LMS) made the Pacific its first missionary field. Missions begun at Tonga and the Marquesas in 1797 faced local opposition and were aborted. The Tahitian mission initially struggled, but by 1815 the impact of literacy, people movements, and the alliance between missionaries and leading chiefs laid significant Christian foundations. The traditional rituals, gods, and places of worship were rejected and replaced by large church buildings, Christian worship, and the introduction of codes of laws regulating moral and civil behavior.

Polynesia

Tahiti set the pattern for missionary expansion throughout Polynesia as Christianity spread to other islands, often through indigenous agency. From his base at Raiatea, John Williams, who arrived in Tahiti in 1817, trained and took these indigenous evangelists to new places. Papeiha's pioneering work at Aitutaki (1821) and Rarotonga (1823) led to the rapid CONVERSION of the Cook Islands. This success and LMS expansion under Williams to Samoa (1830) was retold in Williams's missionary classic, *A Narrative of Missionary Enterprises in the South Sea Islands* (1837). Williams was killed in the New Hebrides (Vanuatu) in 1839. The LMS work expanded to Niue, Tuvalu, and Tokelau. The AMERICAN BOARD OF COMMISSIONERS FOR FOREIGN MISSION (ABCFM) worked in Hawaii (1820) and Kiribati. Methodists began in Tonga (1822), and spread to Samoa (1829) and Fiji (1835).

The LMS, ABCFM, and Methodists aligned themselves with notable chiefs, such as Pomare II in Tahiti, Kamehamaha in Hawaii, Malietoa in Samoa, Tafa'ahau in Tonga, and Cakobau in Fiji. This gave the missions status and aided the process of conversion. Missionary ECCLESIOLOGY was changed dramatically by these alliances. The arrival of British and French colonial influences undermined this chiefly authority except in Tonga, where an independent kingdom was established. The Protestant monopoly was challenged by the arrival of French Catholic missionaries, particularly in the Society Islands, and the emergence of French Polynesia. The LMS work there was taken over by the Société des Missions Évangéliques (Paris Mission).

Melanesia

The Protestant expansion from Polynesia to Melanesia presented considerable challenges to the hundreds of Pacific island teachers and evangelists who undertook this mission along with European missionaries. In contrast to the relative homogeneity of Polynesia in language, culture, and customs, Melanesia presented a bewildering variety of some 1,200 languages, much more fragmentation in social patterns, and hostility toward outsiders. Endemic diseases such as malaria resulted in considerable sickness and death among the missionaries and their families. The LMS pioneered work in Vanuatu, New Caledonia, and Papua (1871). Presbyterians from Nova Scotia, SCOTLAND, AUSTRALIA, and NEW ZEALAND worked in the middle and southern islands of Vanuatu (1848). G. A. Selwyn, Anglican Bishop of New Zealand, founded the Melanesian mission (1849), recruiting young men and women from the islands to train for work among their own people. Initially based in Auckland, the mission moved its headquarters to Norfolk Island (1867), with the northern islands in Vanuatu and Solomon Islands the focus of their work. Fijian and Samoan Methodists, under the leadership of George Brown, inaugurated work in New Britain (1875), the Papuan islands (1891), and western Solomon Islands (1902). Lutherans from the Neuendettelsau mission (1886) and Rhenish mission (1887) followed German colonization in New Guinea. Australian Anglicans began working in Papua (1891). The Queensland Kanaka mission, later renamed the South Sea Evangelical mission, founded by Florence Young, originated in Queensland among Melanesian laborers and moved to the Solomon Islands in 1904.

Cooperation and Challenges

With the exception of the LMS and Methodists in Samoa, Protestant missions in the nineteenth century practiced comity among themselves to avoid duplicating efforts. Comity did not extend to Mormons (see MORMONISM), SEVENTH-DAY ADVENTISTS, and Catholics, resulting in some religious rivalry and clashes. Missions made significant contributions to health, and education. World War II had a devastating impact on parts of Melanesia. After the war, most missions were slow in encouraging indigenous control of the church, but from the 1960s, both political and ecclesiastical independence were gained. The influx of new missions, particularly into the highlands of Papua New Guinea, resulted in an overconcentration of missions in some areas and to reintroduction of some old-fashioned patterns of missionary dependence.

Since the 1970s, the indigenous churches throughout the Pacific have had to compete with vigorous charismatic and Pentecostal groups who often cut across what have become established ways of being Christian, producing divisions in some small communities. The impact of migration to New Zealand, Australia, and North America resulted in a significant Pacific Islander diaspora in which Pacific island churches figure prominently. Political and economic challenges in the last two decades of the twentieth century led to civil war in Bougainville and coups in Fiji and the Solomon Islands. Roles of the churches in these situations have ranged from the significant peace-making work of the Melanesian Brotherhood, to involvement in reconciliation and pastoral care, to the alignment of some church leaders with political extremes.

Influences

Protestant Christianity won considerable acceptance among many Pacific Islanders in a variety of forms and has become an essential part of many island cultures. The distinctive features brought by Protestant missionaries, such as the centrality of the BIBLE and PREACHING, hymn singing (see HYMNS AND HYMNALS), Sunday observance, and strict attitudes toward morality, are still identifiable. Protestant THEOLOGY has been expressed pragmatically through action rather than deep reflection. Since the Second Vatican Council, Roman Catholics have worked with the Melanesian Council of Churches (1965) and Pacific Council of Churches (1966), and cooperation in areas such as theological education has fostered ecumenical relations, even though distance and expense make these relations difficult to sustain (see ECUMENISM). The traditional Protestant churches and Catholics have worked together, notably in the Melanesian Institute and national and regional organizations. Dimensions of traditional CULTURE still flourish alongside and within churches. The smallness of many Pacific communities and the vastness of Pacific geography make island states vulnerable to global forces. The legacy of Protestant missionary activity in the Pacific Islands is now in the hands of Pacific Islanders.

See also Catholic Reactions to Protestantism; Catholicism, Protestant Reactions; Missionary Organizations; Missions; Pentecostalism

References and Further Reading

Forman, C. W. *The Island Churches of the South Pacific: Emergence in the Twentieth Century.* Maryknoll, NY: Orbis, 1982.

Garrett, John. *To Live Among the Stars: Christian Origins in Oceania.* Suva, Fiji: University of the South Pacific/Geneva, Switzerland: WCC Publications, 1982.

———. *Footsteps in the Sea: Christianity in Oceania to World War II.* Geneva, Switzerland: WCC Publications/New York: Friendship Press, 1992.

———. *Where Nets Were Cast: Christianity in Oceania Since World War II.* Suva, Fiji: University of the South Pacific/Geneva, Switzerland: WCC Publications, 1997.

ALLAN K. DAVIDSON

PACIFISM

The Pacifist Impulse

The word "pacifism" was coined in 1901 by the Frenchman Emile Arnaud. In its original meaning it included both those who rejected WAR of every kind and advocated refusal of military service in the case of conscription, and those who strove to create a warless world but conceded the legitimacy of warfare as a last resort. In English-speaking countries, however, the term has usually been used to refer exclusively to absolute pacifists, whereas peace advocates who accept the possibility of just wars are referred to as internationalists or *pacificists* (the English historian A. J. P. Taylor's definition). In this entry, the term is used in the narrower sense of those rejecting all war.

Christian pacifists derive their inspiration from Jesus's love commandment in the New Testament and what they believe to have been the antimilitarism of the early church until Emperor Constantine's conversion in 313 brought about "the fall of Christianity" (G. J. Heering's phrase). Thereafter, until the end of the eighteenth century pacifism has been almost exclusively sectarian and until the end of the nineteenth century almost exclusively Protestant. In the twentieth century absolute pacifism has drawn adherents also from Catholics and Orthodox (see ORTHODOXY, EASTERN) as well as from Hindus, Buddhists, and humanists.

This entry begins by surveying first the pacifist impulse among medieval precursors of the Protestant REFORMATION, and then the idea and practice of nonresistance in the Anabaptist–Mennonite tradition with its rejection of participation in the state. The peace testimony of the Quaker SOCIETY OF FRIENDS, which crystallized around 1660, accepted participation in government provided it did not entail personally bearing arms. Those Quakers who broke this rule were expelled from the sect unless they expressed regret at their action—until the Society's discipline was relaxed toward the end of the nineteenth century. The entry's last section deals briefly with the changing relationship between pacifism and Protestantism in the course of the twentieth century.

Nonresistance: From Anabaptism to Mennonitism

Among the forerunners of the Protestant Reformation pacifism was espoused by several late medieval sects, including the Waldenses in continental Europe, the Lollards in England, and the Czech Brethren in the kingdom of Bohemia. In the Bohemian Reformation of the fifteenth century, initiated by Jan Hus (d. 1415), pacifism emerged in the teachings of the rural self-taught theologian, Piotr Chelčický. After his death his ideas were taken over by the Czech Brethren, the *Unitas Fratrum,* which was formally established in 1467. Chelčický and his disciples put special emphasis on Jesus's love commandment that extended to enemies as well as to family and friends. In Chelčický's view there was no such thing as a just war—despite the successive crusades undertaken to crush the heretical Hussite movement. However, the Czech Brethren, like the Waldenses and the English Lollards, had abandoned pacifism by the beginning of the sixteenth century. Attempts have been made to connect the Czech Brethren with the rebirth of pacifism in the

early 1520s at the outset of the Anabaptist movement. However, despite analogies in doctrine, no evidence has so far been discovered to support this theory.

The Zürich patrician CONRAD GREBEL was responsible for the first assertion of pacifism in the Protestant Reformation of the sixteenth century. It formed part of a nonviolent "Anabaptist vision" that rejected the state as "outside the perfection of Christ," even though the magistrate's sword was set up by God to curb the wicked and defend the good (see ANABAPTISM). Grebel died in 1526; the next year his Swiss Brethren incorporated nonresistance *(Wehrlosigkeit)* in their SCHLEITHEIM CONFESSION, although it was many decades before the doctrine was accepted by all Anabaptists. In 1535, for instance, Anabaptists, under the leadership of a Dutchman, Jan of Leiden, had seized control of the north German city of Münster, where they proceeded to establish a New Jerusalem by force of arms until the city was recaptured by its bishop.

The most consistent of the Anabaptist nonresistants were found in the Hutterite communitarian settlements established in Moravia from the early 1530s on. HUTTERITES demonstrated their pacifist radicalism by refusing to pay war taxes or to manufacture weapons or undertake *corvées* (labor service) useful to the military.

Apart from the German-speaking areas of central Europe, Anabaptism spread to Poland-Lithuania in the 1550s, where nonresistance was adopted for a time by some Polish ANTI-TRINITARIANS, and a lively controversy arose in that church between nonresistants and anti-nonresistants. More important for future developments was the spread of Anabaptism to the NETHERLANDS, where the ex-Catholic priest MENNO SIMONS reshaped its ideology; apart from the Hutterites, Anabaptists eventually became known everywhere as MENNONITES.

Simons's attitude to war was somewhat ambiguous; at any rate, it has become the subject of debate among modern scholars. After his death in 1561, however, his followers adopted nonresistance as an article of faith. Henceforward disfellowshiping became the usual fate of any Mennonite who bore arms or trained for war. The Dutch authorities from 1575 on recognized the sect's pacifism and exempted members liable for the militia in exchange either for a money commutation or noncombatant labor service. In areas of GERMANY—as well as in POLAND and in RUSSIA, too—wherever Mennonites were settled under the *ancien régime* a similar arrangement was worked out with the ruler, with minor variations in each case.

During the late eighteenth century and on into the nineteenth century, first the Dutch Mennonites (known now as *Doopsgezinden,* i.e., BAPTISTS) and then their brethren in Germany, under the combined influence of nationalism and theological MODERNISM, abandoned nonresistance. Their young men henceforward served as combatants when conscripted, and the objection was lifted to undertaking public office even of a military character. Apart from Mennonites who had emigrated around 1800 to the Russian Empire, where the government had allowed the sect's conscripts to undertake civilian forestry service after the introduction of universal military service in 1874, only in North America did the still predominantly rural Mennonites continue to adhere to pacifism—along with the closely linked CHURCH OF THE BRETHREN, which had emigrated to the New World at the same time as the Mennonites. With few exceptions, Mennonites in both the American Revolution and the CIVIL WAR were (as in peacetime) able to purchase exemption from the draft by paying a small fine. They did not object to doing this; indeed they regarded it as Caesar's prerogative to make such demands. After 1865, neither in the UNITED STATES nor in CANADA, where Mennonites had also settled, was conscription any longer enforced before World War I.

Sources of Quaker Pacifism

Today pacifism and Quakerism are often identified; however, in fact the Quaker peace testimony rejecting all war either "for the Kingdom of Christ" or for "the kingdoms of this world" became the accepted doctrine of the Society of Friends only in 1661, shortly after the restoration of the monarchy under Charles II. GEORGE FOX, founder of Quakerism, seems to have adopted a personal pacifism as early as 1650, although during the 1650s many Quakers served under OLIVER CROMWELL in England's Commonwealth army. There were pacifists in the new sect but they remained a minority until near the end of that decade; and for at least several decades thereafter there were still nonpacifists among the membership.

At first, for many Quakers pacifism remained an individual faith restricted to renouncing personally the use of weapons. This stance can be seen most clearly in the case of the Quakers who accepted office in Rhode Island; in that capacity they organized military defense alongside their non-Quaker colleagues. Quakers in Pennsylvania ruled that colony alone from its foundation by WILLIAM PENN in 1682 until their formal withdrawal from government in 1756 near the outset of the French and Indian War. For this withdrawal the Quaker "saint," JOHN WOOLMAN, had been largely responsible. Penn had envisaged Pennsylvania as a "holy experiment," a Quaker commonwealth in which his coreligionists could practice Christian pacifism and human brotherhood. Although Quakers, unlike Mennonites, did not indeed reject participation in the

state in principle, they were forced to make a number of compromises to remain in power—in a colony, moreover, in which Quakers had eventually become a minority. Woolman objected chiefly to the war tax levied by the Quaker-dominated assembly, veiled though it was as money voted "for the king's use."

At home in ENGLAND a pattern had soon emerged to deal with the militia draft. The Society did not merely expect members to refuse to serve personally; Friends required them also to refuse either to hire a substitute or even pay the small fine levied on defaulters. Failure to suffer distraint of goods, often to a value much in excess of the original militia fine, or imprisonment if the objector did not possess sufficient property to cover the amount of the fine, entailed disownment of the recalcitrant Quaker. Although of course there was no militia draft in Quaker Pennsylvania, the English pattern was adopted by Quakers in the other American colonies—and subsequently during the Revolutionary War and in the New Republic. The draft faded out in the antebellum era, but military conscription was reimposed by both sides for the duration of the Civil War. Although the Lincoln administration was quite sympathetic to Quaker conscientious objectors (COs), some suffered severe hardships, especially under Confederate rule. Torn between their Society's testimony against SLAVERY and its peace testimony, many young Quakers in the North joined the Unionist army; their Meetings were often lenient in dealing with them, even though they had infringed the Society's discipline (see CHURCH DISCIPLINE).

Quakerism had emerged in the mid-seventeenth century as part of the left wing of English PURITANISM. Mennonite–Anabaptist nonresistance seems to have exercised little, if any, influence on the shape taken by the Quakers' peace testimony. According to Quakers, the Inner Light within each individual was central; no priesthood nor pastorate was needed to gain understanding of God's will. Even the BIBLE, although worthy of reverence, was not an essential instrument of salvation. For Quakers, therefore, pacifism was not based on any specific New Testament texts; it was not based, either, on the Law of Love, as it was in the Anabaptist–Mennonite tradition. For them it was the spirit of Jesus' teaching that undergirded their devotion to peace. Although the impact of EVANGELICALISM from the end of the eighteenth century changed the emphasis in some sections of the Society on both sides of the Atlantic, this was to some extent offset in the twentieth century by the decline of a Christ-centered faith among liberal Quakers. Both orientations continued to produce pacifists and nonpacifists. Although formally pacifism remained a Quaker tenet throughout most sections of the Society, the practice of disownment was discarded.

Besides founding Pennsylvania, Penn was *inter alia* the author of a tract he entitled an *Essay towards the Present and Future Peace of Europe* (1693). In it he proposed the establishment of a European parliament. True, his peace plan exerted little influence at the time. From the end of the eighteenth century on, however, Quakers took a lead in the new international peace movement, which grouped pacifists and nonpacifist peace advocates in the struggle to establish world peace. Quakers like William Allen were active, along with non-Quaker pacifists, in establishing the London Peace Society in 1816. For the rest of the century Quakers formed the backbone of the British peace movement. They produced in Jonathan Dymond, who died prematurely in 1828, the movement's most widely known publicist. "Dymond on peace" was read—on both sides of the Atlantic—by thousands who had no other contact with Quakerism. Pacifism had now gained some support among other British Protestant churches such as the Congregationalists, Methodists, and Presbyterians (see Congregationalism; Methodism; Presbyterianism).

In the United States, with a few exceptions like Lucretia Coffin Mott, Quakers stood aloof from the nonsectarian peace movement for most of the century. During the antebellum era pacifism acquired vigorous proponents in such nonsectarian Protestants as William Ladd and his American Peace Society, William Lloyd Garrison and his radical New England Nonresistance Society, and Elihu Burritt and his League of Universal Brotherhood. The American peace movement went into recession with the outbreak of the Civil War, although the twentieth century eventually brought it renewed vigor.

Pacifism and Protestantism in the Twentieth Century

The majority of COs during the two world wars and in Vietnam War America—and in peace-time continental Europe, too—still came from a Protestant background, often "from unexpected quarters." Jehovah's Witnesses produced the largest number of jailed objectors. In the twentieth century, however, it has been less easy than in previous centuries to distinguish the Protestant input to the pacifist movement. Take, for instance, the case of that dedicated Quaker, Edward Grubb. In World War I he became treasurer of the British No-Conscription Fellowship, the bulk of whose members were nonreligious socialists. Again, the Peace Pledge Union, founded by the Anglican canon H. R. L. "Dick" Sheppard in the mid-1930s, included a large number of nonreligious pacifists. On the other hand, the American War Resisters' League, which became a haven for nonreligious pacifists, included Protestants among its membership. The Fellowships of Reconciliation, organized internationally after 1918, although at first predominantly Protestant, eventually recruited Catholics, Jews, and humanists. The influence of Gandhian nonviolence was felt not only by Protestants like Martin Luther King Jr., in the 1960s, but by the Albanian Ibrahim Rugova from Kosova, in the 1990s. Protestants also worked alongside other antimilitarists in the post-1945 antinuclear movement.

Pacifism, of course, remained a minority position in the mainstream Protestant churches, even if in English-speaking countries its support had increased considerably since 1918. In discussion of war, leading Protestant theologians, like Reinhold Niebuhr with his incisive polemic *Why the Christian Church is not Pacifist* (1940), led the attack on pacifism.

In conclusion, two related developments of significance deserve brief mention. One is the large-scale pacifist movement that emerged in the Soviet Union after the Revolution. Its adherents included Tolstoyans, who followed the Master's teachings on nonviolence, and a number of Russian dissenters, who had espoused pacifism, as well as sects of Western origin like the Baptists, evangelical Christians, and Seventh-Day Adventists. At first the Soviet government provided generously for conscientious objection, although under Stalin the pacifist movement was ruthlessly suppressed, including the hitherto privileged Mennonites. In North America in the second half of the century, Mennonites, more fortunate than their Soviet coreligionists, mostly abandoned their former political quietism, replacing it by a more active form of peacemaking akin to the Quaker position and that of others who strive for a warless world.

See also Peace Organizations

References and Further Readings

Ballou, Adin. *Christian Non-Resistance in All Its Important Bearings Illustrated and Defended.* Edited by Larry Gara. New York and London: The Garland Library of War and Peace/Garland Publishing, 1972.

Brock, Peter. *The Quaker Peace Testimony 1660 to 1914.* York, UK: Sessions Book Trust, 1990.

———. *Freedom from Violence: Sectarian Nonresistance from the Middle Ages to the Great War.* Toronto: University of Toronto Press, 1991.

———. *Freedom from War: Nonsectarian Pacifism 1814–1914.* Toronto: University of Toronto Press, 1991.

———. *Soviet Conscientious Objectors 1917–1939: A Chapter in the History of Twentieth-Century Pacifism.* Toronto: privately printed, 1999.

———, and Nigel Young. *Pacifism in the Twentieth Century.* Syracuse, NY: Syracuse University Press, 1999.

Bush, Perry. *Two Kingdoms, Two Loyalties: Mennonite Pacifism in Modern America.* Baltimore and London: The Johns Hopkins University Press, 1998.

Niebuhr, Reinhold. "Why the Christian Church Is Not Pacifist." In *The Essential Reinhold Niebuhr: Selected Essays and Addresses*, edited by Robert McAfee Brown, 102–119. New Haven and London: Yale University Press, 1986.

Schlabach, Theron F., and Richard T. Hughes, eds. *Proclaim Peace: Christian Pacifism from Unexpected Quarters*. Urbana and Chicago: University of Illinois Press, 1997.

Stayer, James J. *Anabaptists and the Sword*. Lawrence, KS: Coronado Press, 1976.

PETER BROCK

PALEY, WILLIAM (1743–1805)

English theologian. Paley was born at Peterborough, ENGLAND, of Yorkshire stock, in July 1743, and educated at Giggleswick School, of which his father was master. He matriculated at Christ's College, CAMBRIDGE UNIVERSITY in 1758, graduated BA as Senior Wrangler in 1763, was elected Fellow of Christ's in 1766, and ordained priest in 1767. He served as College tutor until 1776, after which he was preferred to a living in the diocese of Carlisle where he eventually became archdeacon and chancellor. He there revised and wrote up his Cambridge lectures in a series of books that made him famous. Paley died May 15, 1805 and is buried in Carlisle cathedral.

William Paley was the last English Protestant theologian to exert a worldwide influence. From 1785 to the mid-1860s his books were standard in Britain, America, and the British Empire, although the irruption of Darwinian ideas in the 1860s seemed to destroy the "Argument from Design" on which Paley's system was based (see DARWINISM). There was a drastic slump in his reputation, and a sudden falling away from Christianity among the educated classes. Religion ceased to be a public concern in the Protestant, Anglophone world; and THEOLOGY became an option rather than a necessity for scientists and philosophers. Hence no subsequent theologian, however cogent, has attracted much attention outside a dwindling enclave of believers.

Moral and Political Philosophy (1785) was the most popular textbook in that field in America from the 1790s to the CIVIL WAR. *Horae Paulina* (1790) was an original defense of the authenticity of St. Paul's epistles. The first edition of *Evidences of Christianity* (1794) sold out within a day; the work was required for all undergraduates at Cambridge down to 1920. *Natural Theology* (1802) has again become a matter of dispute among biologists and physicists. In reverse order, as Paley intended them to be read, the books present a systematic account of the reasons for Christian belief, and of the moral and political consequences entailed by it. They gave perfect expression to (and therefore helped both to define and to reinforce) the leading scientific, theological, and ethical ideas of his time and place. What Leslie Stephen called Paley's "utter inability to be obscure" has commended his work to generations of Anglophones, but repels all who believe that profundity must be enigmatic.

See also Ethics; Nature; Science

References and Further Reading

Primary Source:

Paley, Edmund, ed. *The Works of William Paley, D.D., with Additional Sermons, etc.* London: Rivington et al., 1825. [Reprint of 1830 printing of this edition, edited by V. Nuovo. Bristol: Thoemmes, 1998.]

Secondary Sources:

Clarke, M. L. *Paley: Evidences for the Man*. London: S.P.C.K., 1974.

Le Mahieu, D. L. *The Mind of William Paley: A Philosopher of His Age*. Lincoln: University of Nebraska Press, 1976.

Waterman, A. M. C. "A Cambridge 'Via Media' in Late Georgian Anglicanism." *Journal of Ecclesiastical History* 42 no. 3 (1991): 419–436.

A. M. C. WATERMAN

PALMER, PHOEBE WORRALL (1807–1874)

American methodist lay theologian, author, revivalist, and humanitarian. Palmer was the dominant personality in the nineteenth-century HOLINESS MOVEMENT, an interdenominational Protestant effort to preserve and promote the doctrine of Christian perfection as taught by JOHN WESLEY (1703–1791).

As a revivalist Palmer traveled widely throughout North America and the British Isles, beginning in 1840. She participated in over three hundred REVIVALS and CAMP MEETINGS. She also hosted a popular weekly religious gathering, the "Tuesday Meeting for the Promotion of Holiness," in her home in the city of New York for over thirty years.

As a lay theologian and author, as well as popular preacher, Phoebe Palmer largely defined how the Holiness Movement interpreted and appropriated John Wesley's doctrine of Christian perfection, or "entire sanctification." She published nearly a score of books, the best known being *The Way of Holiness* (1843). She also edited an internationally circulated magazine, *The Guide to Holiness,* from 1864 to 1874.

In her writings, as well as her preaching, Palmer taught a modified version of Wesley's doctrine, a "shorter way" to Christian perfection. This "way" emphasized that sanctification occurs in an instant, stressed the necessity of complete surrender of oneself to God to be "perfected," and (at least in Palmer's later years) encouraged believers to expect a supernatural in-filling with divine power, a "baptism with the Holy Spirit," as "evidence" of their SANCTIFICATION by God.

For many years Phoebe Palmer also carried on a ministry of prison visitation and led organizations to help the homeless poor, orphans, and those unable to afford needed medical care. Palmer was also a "feminist" of sorts, authoring a highly influential book, *The Promise of the Father* (1859), that argued for the right of women to exercise their gifts and abilities in various forms of ministry in Christian churches.

References and Further Reading

Oden, Thomas C. *Phoebe Palmer: Selected Writings.* New York: Paulist Press, 1988.
Raser, Harold E. *Phoebe Palmer, Her Life and Thought.* Lewiston, NY: The Edwin Mellen Press, 1987.
Wheatley, Richard. *The Life and Letters of Mrs. Phoebe Palmer.* New York: Palmer and Hughes, 1876.
White, Charles E. *The Beauty of Holiness: Phoebe Palmer as Theologian, Revivalist, Feminist, and Humanitarian.* Grand Rapids, MI: Francis Asbury Press, 1986.

HAROLD E. RASER

PANNENBERG, WOLFHART (1928–)

German theologian. The writings of Wolfhart Pannenberg had a major impact on the shape of Protestant philosophical and systematic theology in the last four decades of the twentieth century. His interest in ecumenical dialogue, his passion for relating theology to philosophy and the sciences, and his desire to offer a rational presentation of Christian doctrine were all fueled by his ambiguous response to the dominant Protestant theological methods that he encountered as he studied theology in Germany in the years after World War II.

Biography

Born in 1928 in Stettin, GERMANY (now in POLAND), Pannenberg was baptized as a Lutheran, but had little contact with the church in early childhood. His family moved to Berlin in 1942, and in the last year of World War II, at the age of sixteen, Pannenberg was trained in the German army but avoided combat because of illness. After the war he returned to school, where he was encouraged by a teacher to examine the plausibility of Christianity. Pannenberg became convinced that the Christian worldview was philosophically compelling. He undertook theological studies at the universities of Berlin, Göttingen, and Basel (where he studied under KARL BARTH). Pannenberg completed his academic training at the University of Heidelberg, where in 1954 he published his dissertation on Duns Scotus's doctrine of PREDESTINATION. He taught for a few years at Heidelberg and Wuppertal, and in 1961

was appointed to the chair in systematic theology at the University of Mainz. In 1967 he accepted the chair in systematic theology at the University of Munich, where he was also the director of the Ecumenical Institute until his retirement in 1993.

Ecumenical Scope

Although Pannenberg affirmed the Lutheran and German Protestant roots of his thought, he always rebelled against developing a merely confessional theology (see CONFESSION). Instead he insisted that theology must keep in mind the global Christian community, both geographically and historically. Pannenberg's involvement in the WORLD COUNCIL OF CHURCHES and his frequent trips to America and other countries provided significant opportunities for ecumenical dialogue (see ECUMENISM). More so than most Protestant theologians, Pannenberg's writings carefully engage a broad spectrum of Roman Catholic and Eastern Orthodox thinkers. On the other hand, his writings do not interact as deeply with other world religions, nor with FEMINIST and LIBERATION THEOLOGY. Nevertheless, his theology has had a broad appeal both to liberal theologians, who appreciate his willingness to engage the atheistic and historical critiques of modernity, and to conservative theologians, who appreciate his defense of orthodox doctrines like the resurrection of Jesus Christ.

Theology and Philosophy

Pannenberg was concerned that both Barth's appeal to revelation and RUDOLF BULTMANN's appeal to existence represented a theological retreat into fideism, an attempt to escape the need to present cogent arguments for the truth claims of Christianity. Convinced of the importance of philosophical rigor for the task of theology, Pannenberg immersed himself deeply in the classical Greek philosophers as well as IMMANUEL KANT, GEORG W. F. HEGEL, and others. His interest in medieval philosophy was already evident in his dissertation. In *Theology and the Philosophy of Science* (1976) Pannenberg engaged the hermeneutical proposals of his contemporaries (e.g., Hans-Georg Gadamer) as well as earlier contributors (e.g., Wilhelm Dilthey) and attempted to locate theology among the sciences. He proposed a comprehensive task for the theologian: providing a provisional understanding and explanation of all things under the aspect of their relation to God. This task involves two interrelated movements, one "philosophical" and the other "systematic" (or dogmatic). The philosophical movement ("from below") is methodologically prior, but the systematic movement, which presents the coherence of the Trinitarian idea of God as the all-determining reality, has material primacy.

Theology and Science

In addition to treating the broad philosophical issues of epistemology and metaphysics, Pannenberg also engaged contemporary SCIENCE throughout his career. For him cosmology and anthropology are particularly relevant for theology. Because theology is about God as creator of all things, it must show how the biblical idea of God relates to scientific explanations of the cosmos. One of his more controversial proposals was the linking of field theory in physics to the Christian doctrine of the divine Spirit through a broader philosophical concept of "field." Noting that human self-understanding shapes our understanding of God, Pannenberg also explored the anthropological sciences. In *Anthropology in Theological Perspective* (1985), he engaged sciences such as biology, psychology, sociology, and history, arguing that the natural openness of human beings to the infinite cannot be explained by scientific proposals that ignore the intrinsic "religious thematic" of human existence. The latter requires systematic theological analysis.

Systematic Theology

The fruit of Pannenberg's lifelong engagement in ecumenical, philosophical, and scientific dialogue are brought together in his magnum opus, the three-volume *Systematic Theology* (1991–1998). Here the figure/ground relation between philosophical and systematic theology is reversed; both remain in the picture but the focus is now on a comprehensive presentation of Christian DOCTRINE. In volume I he describes this as a sublation of his earlier philosophical work into systematics; volume II provides an integrated presentation of his understanding of the doctrines of creation, anthropology, and Christology; and volume III treats the relation between the Holy Spirit, the church, ELECTION, and the consummation of the world. All three volumes are linked by Pannenberg's ongoing concern with material themes that had interested him early in his career. For example, in the 1960s Pannenberg had contributed to the growing interest in a "theology of hope" with his idea of God as the "power of the Future," and this continues to shape his eschatological reflection in all three volumes (see ESCHATOLOGY). Similarly, his commitment to the centrality of the doctrine of Trinity is evident not only in the early chapter devoted to it, but as the organizing theme of the whole work, which concludes with this sentence: "The distinction and unity of the immanent and economic Trinity constitute the heartbeat of the divine love, and with a single such heartbeat this love encompasses the whole world of creatures" (1998: 646).

See also Catholicism, Protestant Reactions; Orthodoxy, Eastern; Theology, Twentieth Century

References and Further Reading

Primary Sources:

Pannenberg, Wolfhart. *Anthropology in Theological Perspective*. Translated by M. J. O'Connell. Philadelphia, PA: Westminster Press, 1985.
———. *Jesus—God and Man*. Translated by Lewis L. Wilkins and Duane A. Priebe. Philadelphia, PA: Westminster, 1968; 2nd edition, 1977.
———. *Systematic Theology*. Vols. I–III. Translated by G. Bromiley. Grand Rapids, MI: Wm. B. Eerdmans, 1991–1998 (German: 1988–1993).
———. *Theology and the Philosophy of Science*. Translated by F. McDonagh. Philadelphia, PA: Westminster Press, 1976.

Secondary Sources:

Albright, Carol Rausch, and Joel Haugen, eds. *Beginning with the End: God, Science, and Wolfhart Pannenberg*. Chicago, IL: Open Court, 1997.
Braaten, Carl E., and Philip Clayton, eds. *The Theology of Wolfhart Pannenberg*. Minneapolis, MN: Augsburg, 1988.
Grenz, Stanley. *Reason for Hope: The Systematic Theology of Wolfhart Pannenberg*. Oxford: Oxford University Press, 1990.
Shults, F. LeRon. *The Postfoundationalist Task of Theology: Wolfhart Pannenberg and the New Theological Rationality*. Grand Rapids, MI: Wm. B. Eerdmans, 1999.

F. LeRON SHULTS

PARACELSUS (PHILIPPUS AUREOLUS THEOPHRASTUS BOMBASTUS VON HOHENHEIM) (1493–1541)

German doctor, philosopher, and theologian. Paracelsus was born in Einsiedeln in the canton of Schwyz, and trained in medicine with his father. Little is known about his education, but he practiced medicine in numerous cities of southern GERMANY and SWITZERLAND in the 1520s and 1530s. Although he never officially left the Catholic church, he was linked with several of the reformers of his day, including JOHANNES OECOLAMPADIUS, who supported him in Basel. He published few works in his lifetime, the most successful being his surgical treatise, *Grosse Wundarznei* (Great Miracle Medicine 1536). The majority of his medical and alchemical works were published shortly after his death, but his theological writings (considered by many to be heretical) were not published until the twentieth century (see HERESY).

Paracelsus was a name he self-consciously adopted around 1527, indicating that he surpassed the famous

Celsus, who in the first century A.D. had written a comprehensive medical encyclopedia. He rejected much of the medical establishment of his day, challenging the ancient authorities and insisting that the knowledge of NATURE must be based on a Christian cosmology and then on experience. He used chemical remedies, and he wrote most of his works in German, frequently inventing new terms and earning comparisons with reformer MARTIN LUTHER. He is considered a forerunner both of the scientific method and of modern chemistry.

His theological and ethical writings, although less well known, did exert an influence, particularly on marginalized groups with apocalyptic and millenarian expectations such as the followers of SEBASTIAN CASTELLIO and CASPAR SCHWENKFELD. Their most direct influence on Protestantism was through theologians with a mystical bent, especially VALENTIN WEIGEL (1533–1588), the Lutheran pastor who provided much of the impetus behind the Pietist movement (see PIETISM), and the mystic and Pietist JAKOB BOEHME (1575–1620), who synthesized many Paracelsian elements in his writings. Even further afield, a new religion of the "two lights" (nature and grace), was founded based on Paracelsus's writings, called "Theophrastia Sancta." One of its early promoters, the Tyrolean schoolteacher Adam Haslmayr, linked it closely with the emerging Rosicrucianism in the early seventeenth century.

References and Further Reading

Grell, Ole Peter, ed. "Paracelsus: The Man and His Reputation, His Ideas and Their Transformation." In *Studies in the History of Christian Thought*, vol. LXXXV, edited by H. A. Oberman. Leiden, The Netherlands: Brill, 1998. [See this text for listing of primary sources and bibliography.]

BETH KREITZER

PARKER SOCIETY

Founded in 1840 for "the publication of the Fathers and Early Writers of the Reformed English Church," the Parker Society issued its first Annual Report in 1841. Very much a Cambridge production (see CAMBRIDGE UNIVERSITY) intended to counter Oxford's concentration on *The Library of Anglo-Catholic Theology* (1841f.), the Society sought the support of "*everyone* who duly estimates the value of faithful and devoted followers of our blessed Redeemer who are revered as the Fathers of the Reformed English Church—men who counted not their lives dear . . . when placed in the balance against the blessings which, by laborious . . . efforts, they sought to secure to this Protestant land."

When Lord Ashley chaired a general meeting at the Free Masons Tavern, Lincoln's Inn Fields (May 1842), a vote of thanks was passed to George Stokes, the Society's founder, for "his entire devotion." Stokes was the author of a work entitled *British Reformers,* published by the Religious Tract Society in 1827. In February 1841 a very different kind of tract appeared from the pen of JOHN HENRY NEWMAN (the celebrated "Tract XC") to prompt much establishment debate in mid-Victorian England. Aware that MATTHEW PARKER (first archbishop of Canterbury to ELIZABETH I) "was a great collector of ancient and modern writing," Stokes was clear that recourse "to such originals and precedents" would result in "true knowledge" of past theological conflict. His success in recruiting scholars of caliber to edit, and subscribers to support, a venture sponsored by the Pitt Press of Cambridge University proved a considerable achievement; and historians of the nineteenth century ought to pay more attention to the ideals that prompted Stokes to enlist innumerable clerical dons to the "good old cause" when "evangelicals," and England's Protestants in particular, seemed to be under threat from the OXFORD MOVEMENT. By the end of 1842 more than six thousand subscribers were receiving, for the modest annual outlay of one pound, "several valuable volumes" a year. Heading the subscription list were the Dowager Queen Adelaide and Albert, prince consort to Queen Victoria herself; and if neither primate supported a venture encouraged by numerous diocesan bishops, the High Churchman W. E. Gladstone (at that time vice-president of the Board of Trade and master of the Mint) was a fully paid-up member.

By 1843 seven thousand subscriptions had been received; and with James Scholefield (Regius professor of Greek in the University of Cambridge) at the helm as editorial secretary, regular primary-source publications circulated to disseminate "a general knowledge of the principles and doctrines held and taught by Cranmer, Ridley, Parker, Whitgift, and their learned and venerable coadjutors" (see THOMAS CRANMER and JOHN WHITGIFT).

In short here was an attempt to rally "every member of the Church of England" opposed to the work of those—such as JOHN KEBLE, Newman, and EDWARD PUSEY—working hard to revive Catholic traditions. The council urged the faithful to ponder the Tractarian challenge; and entirely convinced that a "NATIONAL effort" [*sic*] was underway, its Annual Report claimed that the Parker Society had done much "to benefit this Protestant land." A fourth Report (May 1845) noted that the membership had remained constant at seven thousand. Furthermore, it duly stressed the Society's *raison d'être* to make widely known "the works by which the Fathers of the Reformed English Church sought to diffuse scriptural truth." However, if the suspicions of John Charles Ryle (a leading Protestant who was consecrated bishop of Liverpool in 1880) were correct, "the many goodly volumes published by the Parker Society" slept "quietly on library shelves, unopened and uncut."

PETER NEWMAN BROOKS

PARKER, MATTHEW (1504–1575)

Archbishop of Canterbury. Parker was born in Norwich, ENGLAND in 1504 and died in 1575 at Lambeth Palace. Parker, who guided the CHURCH OF ENGLAND during the determinative years of the reign of ELIZABETH I, was consecrated to the archbishopric of Canterbury, on December 17, 1559 (by bishops Barlow, Scory, Coverdale, and Hodgkins in the chapel of Lambeth Palace). This event was long the issue of bitter controversy between Roman Catholic and Anglican apologists. It proved to be the pivotal moment for the self-definition of the reformed Church of England, finally removed from the Roman obedience by the accession of Queen Elizabeth I, as a church ministerially continuous with the apostolic succession of bishops.

Parker had been most unwilling to accept the office, but Elizabeth had finally overruled his misgivings. In the reign of HENRY VIII, Parker had been attached to both Queen Anne Boleyn and Queen Katherine Parr, and had received various church promotions, including a fellowship of his Cambridge College, Corpus Christi (1527) and the deanery of a small educational center for CLERGY, at Stoke-by-Clare, in Suffolk, in 1535. He was becoming interested in MARTIN LUTHER's reforming ideas, but modified them by his equal interest in the early patristic Christian writers. Although he had been suspected of heretical attitudes to Catholic ceremonies (1539), he was appointed master of his college (1544), and then made dean of Lincoln Cathedral in 1552. The new queen, Mary I, dismissed him in 1554, partly because of his Protestant beliefs, partly because in 1547 he had married, partly because he had espoused the cause of Lady Jane Grey. Unlike many leading Protestants he did not flee the realm during Mary's reign, but lived in secrecy and frequent flight until Elizabeth succeeded. He later looked back on this time of obscurity and danger as a time of quiet opportunity for study, reflection, and prayer.

One of the first tasks of the new regime was to bring back a Protestant LITURGY. The Prayer Book of 1559 was the result: the Second Prayer Book of Edward VI (1552), which was THOMAS CRANMER's second liturgical program, more markedly Protestant than that of 1549, was in essence restored, but with delicate—yet significant—changes. The "Black Rubric," which insisted that kneeling for Communion (see LORD'S SUPPER) did not imply belief in transubstanti-

ation, was removed; at Communion, the 1549 and 1552 words of administration were combined. Thus, for the bread: "The Body of our Lord Jesus Christ, which was given for thee, keep thy body and soul unto everlasting life" (1549) and "Take and eat this in remembrance that Christ died for thee, and feed on him in thy heart by faith with thanksgiving" (1552). The 1550 Ordinal (book of services for ordinations) was reintroduced, and was used for Parker's own consecration. Elizabeth had wished that Parker should take part in these liturgical measures, but his health prevented this. Nonetheless the reinstated and revised reformed liturgical pattern was and is determinative of the character of the Church of England as Parker inherited and was to maintain, protect, and defend it.

Parker's Influences

As Primate of All England, Parker attempted to steer the Church of England on a course independent of Rome but not by the stars of Geneva. His disciplinary restraints on Puritans (see PURITANISM) and his rules about liturgical garments (the Injunctions of 1565 for his Province of Canterbury) were unpopular. Trivial as this issue may seem to later times, these details focused wider and more urgent disputes of belief and allegiance. The VESTMENTS of the pre-Reformation liturgy—alb, amice, girdle, stole, and chasuble (for a priest)—carried for reformers of Calvinist or Zwinglian persuasion the overtones of the "sacrifices of masses" and the sacerdotal system that the REFORMATION had abjured. The black gown favored by the Reformed churches of SCOTLAND or the Continent, although satisfactory for PREACHING, otherwise spoke not only of a systematic theology such as JOHN CALVIN's but also of a disciplinary rigor that the majority of the English found as unwelcome as the medieval church's ways. Parker's choice of cassock, surplice, tippet (black scarf indicative of literacy), and academic hood was a mediating program: as "choir habit," it set the clergy apart, but with modesty, and the academic elements stressed the reforming insistence on the clergy as servants of the Word. In another area of mediation, Parker contributed largely to the "Bishops' Bible" (1568), which he kept clear of polemical marginal notes, and hoped that it would supplant the Calvinistic GENEVA BIBLE.

Parker's "Table of Kindred and Affinity" (1563), applying a rigorous version of the Levitical code to MARRIAGE, affected English church and state law until the end of the twentieth century. Under Parker's presidency the THIRTY-NINE ARTICLES of Religion came to their final form, and were imposed on clergy and educators for their subscription in 1571. Parker's most lasting bequest is often judged to be his care to rescue manuscripts from the chaos of the Reformation period to provide foundations for future historical research.

References and Further Reading

Primary Source:

Bruce, John, and Thomas Thomason Browne, eds. *Correspondence of Matthew Parker, D.D. Archbishop of Canterbury. Compromising letters written by and to him, from A.D. 1535, to his death, A.D. 1575.* Parker Society, vol. 33. Cambridge: Cambridge University Press, 1853.

Secondary Sources:

Gee, Henry. *The Elizabethan Prayer Book and Ornaments, With an Appendix of Documents.* London: Macmillan, 1902.
Jenkins, Claude. *Bishop Barlow's Consecration and Archbishop Parker's Register: with some new documents.* [London: reprinted from *The Journal of Theological Studies*, October 1922]. London: SPCK for the Church Historical Society, 1935.
Lacey, T. A. *Marriage in Church and State*, revised by R. C. Mortimer. London: SPCK, 1959.
Mozley, J. B. "Parker, Matthew." In *Dictionary of National Biography.* vol. XV, 254–264. Reprinted, Oxford: Oxford University Press, 1921–1922.
Neill, Stephen. *Anglicanism.* Revised edition. Harmondsworth, UK: Penguin Books, 1960.
Ramsey, Ian, et al. *Subscription and Assent to the Thirty-Nine Articles: A Report of the Archbishops' Commission on Christian Doctrine.* London: SPCK, 1968.

DAVID TRIPP

PARKER, THEODORE (1810–1860)

American preacher. Parker was born in Lexington, Massachusetts, August 24, 1810 and died in Florence, ITALY, about three months shy of his fiftieth birthday on May 10, 1860. He had traveled to Europe in a vain attempt to recover from tuberculosis.

Parker may well be the greatest intellect the American pulpit has produced. For fifteen years he was the pastor of the Twenty-eighth Congregational Society in Boston, where 3,000 people crowded the Music Hall every Sunday to hear a sermon from this eloquent, brilliant, and controversial preacher. Greatly influenced by TRANSCENDENTALISM, Parker developed a theology based on intuition, which he called the voice of God. Religious AUTHORITY was not based on the BIBLE, the church, or even Jesus, but in conscience or higher law. Although his congregation was Unitarian, most Unitarians in his era considered Parker heretical and would not associate with him. However, Unitarians eventually became what Parker proclaimed, and he is generally credited with marking the emancipation of Unitarianism from all semblance of Christian ORTHODOXY.

It was not just ecclesiastical reform that came under Parker's scrutiny, but social reform as well. His critical judgments addressed political and judicial corruption, the plight of WOMEN, slum owners, low wages, and dishonest business practices. It was for SLAVERY that he reserved his harshest words, labeling it the "sum of all villainies." Parker's involvement in the antislavery movement was far ahead of most clergymen of his time.

See also American Unitarian Association; Slavery, Abolition of; Social Gospel

References and Further Reading

Primary Source:

Parker, Theodore. *Centenary Edition of the Works of Theodore Parker.* 15 vols. Boston: American Unitarian Association, 1907–1910.

Secondary Sources:

Chesebrough, David B. *Theodore Parker: Orator of Superior Ideas.* Westport, CT: Greenwood Press, 1999.
Dirks, John Edward. *The Critical Theology of Theodore Parker.* New York: Columbia University Press, 1948.

DAVID B. CHESEBROUGH

PEACE ORGANIZATIONS

As followers of Jesus Christ, who is known as the Prince of Peace, Christian churches are themselves "peace organizations." The series of consultation meetings in 1990–1995 between representatives of various church traditions, mostly Protestant, sponsored by the Faith and Order Commission of the NATIONAL COUNCIL OF CHURCHES of Christ in the United States, focusing on the apostolic character of the church's peace witness, agreed:

> that Christians, following our Lord and Savior Jesus Christ, are called to be peacemakers. We consider this a common confession of the faith once delivered to the apostles, basic to our Christian unity. In a world of violence, be it in the streets or in warfare, churches affirm that peace is the will of God, and that peace has been shown to us most clearly in the life, teachings, death, and resurrection of Jesus Christ. Peacemaking is most deeply rooted in Christ and the unity of the church, and such unity is a gift of the Holy Spirit linked to repentance and forgiveness. Through the power of the Holy Spirit, we are enabled to practice peacemaking as a way of participation in the life and death of Christ. . . . Our peace with God impels us toward peace with neighbor and love of enemies.

Different churches have understood that call differently or have evaded it almost entirely. In the first two centuries Christians were almost all pacifists, understanding that following the teachings of Jesus meant being committed to nonviolence. By the middle ages, however, this was a very compromised ideal. Of the REFORMATION groups, only those related to the Anabaptists attempted consistently to recover this peacemaking command (see ANABAPTISM). Over the centuries Protestant peacemaking has grown, with the increased destructiveness of weapons, with the increased knowledge of practices that are effective in making peace, with the spreading influence of nonviolent direct action as developed by Mahatma Gandhi, MARTIN LUTHER KING JR., and Cesar Chavez, and with renewed biblical study recovering more of the breadth of peacemaking themes in both Testaments, and especially in the Jesus material of the Gospels.

Modern Peace Movement

The modern peace movement began in Europe and North America in the second half of the nineteenth century, and Protestants have been an integral part of it. Protestants have joined in peace organizations that had no particular religious grounding (e.g., Peace Action, The International Peace Bureau, The Women's International League for Peace and Freedom [WILPF]), and have joined ecumenical Christian peace groups that include not only Protestants, but Orthodox and Catholics (e.g., Church and Peace, Christian Peacemaker Teams, Evangelicals for Social Action, Every Church a Peace Church). They have also created denominationally oriented peace groups (e.g., The Anglican Pacifist Fellowship, The Lutheran Peace Fellowship, Methodists United for Justice and Peace, The AMERICAN FRIENDS SERVICE COMMITTEE, the Baptist Peace Fellowship of North America). Protestants have also founded ecumenical Christian groups that have evolved into interfaith groups (e.g., the Fellowship of Reconciliation [FOR, http://www.forusa.org]) or no longer have any specific religious ties in theory, even though Protestants continue to form a large part of the organization in practice (e.g., Witness for Peace, The Center for Conscience and War). Sometimes a person is even motivated by a strong Protestant faith to found a peace organization that is deliberately open to persons of all faiths or no faith, as when Mubarak Awad, a Palestinian Baptist, founded Nonviolence International to promote the use of nonviolence in global struggles for justice, no matter the religion of the groups involved.

The purposes of these groups differ, and their differing relation to Protestantism reflects their different orientations. Denominational peace groups usually have as one purpose bringing together like-minded peacemakers who may feel isolated and powerless,

especially if their denomination does not have a long history of peacemaking (e.g., most Protestant denominations other than the "historic peace churches" of MENNONITES, the CHURCH OF THE BRETHREN, and the Religious SOCIETY OF FRIENDS [Quakers]). Another purpose of denominational peace fellowships (e.g., The Episcopal Peace Fellowship or the Lutheran Peace Fellowship) is to increase "peace education" among CLERGY and LAITY, explicitly connecting the history, doctrinal teachings, and/or LITURGY of that denomination to issues of peacemaking. In this way it hopes to increase the number of active peacemakers in that DENOMINATION and to have a "leavening" effect on the denomination itself. To the extent that this purpose succeeds, the grassroots denominational peace fellowship may find some of its peace education tasks taken up or supplemented by official agencies within the denominational leadership itself. Thus the United Church of Christ FOR (formerly the United Church Peace Fellowship) remains a grassroots peace fellowship explicitly connected to the Fellowship of Reconciliation, but the United Church of Christ Justice and Peace Action Network (UCC-JPAN) is an official program of the UNITED CHURCH OF CHRIST. Likewise, the Presbyterian Peace Fellowship's efforts are complemented by the PRESBYTERIAN CHURCH, USA's Peacemaking Program, and the Methodist Peace Fellowship's grassroots work is complemented by the Peacemaking Program of the UNITED METHODIST CHURCH's Board of Church and Society.

A third purpose of the denominational peace fellowship is often to link peacemakers in that denomination with wider, more ecumenical (or even interfaith) peace groups (see ECUMENISM). In the United Kingdom, almost all the denominational peace fellowships are affiliated with the British chapter of the Fellowship of Reconciliation and with the Network of Christian Peace Organizations. In Europe the International Fellowship of Reconciliation (IFOR) and the "historic peace churches" have, since 1949, combined efforts in the Church and Peace movement. In the UNITED STATES, again, almost all the denominational peace fellowships are connected with the U.S. branch of the Fellowship of Reconciliation. Just as grassroots denominational peace fellowships often spawn official efforts by denominational agencies, so these wider ecumenical and interfaith grassroots efforts stimulate parallel work by conciliar ecumenical bodies. The National Council of Churches of Christ, USA (most of whose member bodies are Protestant) has a Subcommittee on Peace, Security, and Disarmament, and the WORLD COUNCIL OF CHURCHES has a program promoting the first decade of the Twenty-First Century as a Decade to Overcome Violence.

Development and Change

Peace organizations sometimes have quite specific foci and their scope and constituency can change over time. For example, Every Church a Peace Church (ECAPC, http://www.ecapc.org) grew out of New Call to Peacemaking, the program to renew and strengthen the peace witness of Mennonites, Quakers, and the Church of the Brethren, plus World Peacemakers, a ministry of Church of the Savior in Washington, D.C. Working with the historic peace churches, the FOR, denominational peace fellowships in mainline churches, and individuals, ECAPC seeks to provide resources for congregations and denominations to become more faithful disciples of the living Christ, by becoming peace churches.

For another example, World War I broke out in 1914 at the end of an era that saw forms of Christian PACIFISM growing in most mainline Protestant groups both in Europe and North America. To take the example of the United States, however, the law at the time allowed *conscientious objection* (refusal of military service based on principled objection to war) only for the "historic peace churches." The National Interreligious Service Board for Conscientious Objectors (NISBCO, http://www.nisbco.org) was founded to protect the rights of conscientious objectors in other denominations, almost exclusively mainline Protestants at the time. As the nation became more pluralistic, NISBCO found itself also defending conscientious objectors who were Catholic, Orthodox, Jewish, Muslim, Buddhist, or of no particular faith whatsoever, and renamed itself the Center for Conscience and War. It also supports the *Campaign for a Peace Tax Fund* and gives assistance to war tax resisters. The *Campaign* pushes to create a law allowing conscientious objectors to designate the portion of their taxes earmarked for the military (most years around 50 percent) to go to nonmilitary purposes such as EDUCATION, environmental protection and cleanup, health care, and so forth. War tax resisters are also supported by the *National War Tax Resistance Coordinating Committee* (NWTRCC, http://www.nwtrcc.org) in Ithaca, New York.

Another peace organization with a very specific focus is Pastors for Peace. It began in the early 1970s as an organization of Protestant clergy challenging the continued U.S. embargo of Cuba. Although retaining its name, Pastors for Peace has involved more laity, and has recruited Catholic and Jewish members. They have become most well known for their "peace caravans" of food, medical supplies, and medical technology to Cuba—breaking U.S. law to do so. They have also taken up the cause of peace throughout Central America, especially where U.S. foreign policy is understood as a factor contributing to oppression or unrest.

Crossing Religious Boundaries

Some organizations change both their constituency and their understanding of peace and peacemaking. The classic example is the International Fellowship of Reconciliation (IFOR, http://www.ifor.org) and its various national branches. It began as a specifically Christian organization, founded in 1914 on the very eve of the First World War by a British Friend (Quaker), Henry Hodgin, and a German Lutheran minister, Friedrich Sigmund-Schultze, pacifist chaplain to the German Kaiser. Believing that the bonds of Christian love transcended all national boundaries, they vowed that they would refuse to sanction war between their two countries and that they would sow seeds of peace no matter what the future would bring. Hodgin founded the British FOR at Trinity College, CAMBRIDGE UNIVERSITY and Sigmund-Schultze founded the German branch, *Versöhnungsbund*. In 1915 Hodgin visited the United States and founded the U.S. branch. At its beginning, the FOR was entirely Protestant. In the mid-1930s Dorothy Day and a few other American Catholics joined. In the 1960s Catholics formed Pax Christi, the highly active Catholic Peace Fellowship. Orthodox participation came still later.

After World War II the FOR realized that one of the contributing factors to the HOLOCAUST was that even Christians who did not hold to anti-Jewish theologies seldom had contacts or ties with Jews and were ignorant of contemporary JUDAISM. Therefore, in the United States and international branches of the FOR, the explicitly Christian basis of membership was dropped but the religious motivation for pacifism, nonviolence, and peacemaking was retained. (In the United Kingdom and some other branches, the FOR has retained an explicitly Christian identity.) This led to Jewish members joining the U.S. FOR and IFOR and, eventually, the formation of The Jewish Peace Fellowship, modeled after the Christian denominational peace fellowships. The interfaith nature of the IFOR and U.S. FOR has continued to expand to include especially Buddhists, Bahais, Hindus, and, most recently, Muslims. (In the United States there is a Buddhist Peace Fellowship and a Muslim Peace Fellowship that are both branches of the FOR. The International Network of Engaged Buddhists, a peacemaking group, has created explicit ties to IFOR.) The FOR and peace organizations have increasingly understood peace not only as the absence of war, but the presence of justice, becoming increasingly involved in nonviolent direct action for human rights issues.

Other organizations having no explicit religious connection have, nevertheless, had strong faith-group connections. For example, Peace Action (http://www. peace-action.org), the largest grassroots peace organization in the United States, grew out of a merger of the Nuclear Weapons Freeze campaign of the 1980s and the Committee for a SANE Nuclear Policy. The Freeze was deliberately organized to be as wide a coalition as possible and thus officially secular, but it grew out of efforts by the U.S. FOR and by the peacemaking programs of the Church of the Savior's World Peacemakers and the Sojourners Community's Peacemaker Program. All this gave the Freeze strong church connections, especially with ecumenical mainline Protestants. Toward the end of the 1980s the Freeze merged with SANE to become SANE/Freeze. After the Cold War it changed its name again to Peace Action, retaining its emphasis on eliminating nuclear arms, but broadening to include peace education efforts and the promotion of human rights. It has come to embrace major practices of the new peacemaking ethic of *Just Peacemaking Theory,* with its emphasis on the need for a democratic foreign policy, HUMAN RIGHTS, cooperation with the United Nations and international organizations, and reductions in offensive weapons and weapons trade. The connection to churches, especially mainline Protestant ones, remains unstated but strong, and Peace Action's orientation continues to focus on grassroots organization to transform U.S. policies. Peace Action's national headquarters is in Washington, D.C., although its grassroots emphasis allows local affiliates in various cities and states freedom to adopt somewhat different emphases according to the perceived concerns of the local context. Some affiliates are strongly connected with churches.

Likewise, Witness for Peace (WFP, http://www. witnessforpeace.org) was deliberately founded to be "secular" but always had strong ties to U.S. churches and a smattering of synagogues. As its name "witness" indicates, WFP was founded by people of faith and they continue to form its largest percentage of members. It was founded in 1983 as a nonviolent intervention of U.S. citizens to prevent the U.S.-funded *Contra* terrorists from killing civilians in Nicaragua and to prevent a U.S. invasion of Nicaragua. Upon returning from their peace witness in accompanying the people of Nicaragua and thus nonviolently guarding many against violence by the Contras, they spread their witness in the United States to the truth of realities they experienced in Nicaragua. This contributed to the growing opposition of the people of the United States against U.S. funding for the Contra war, which persuaded Congress to terminate funding for that war. After 1988 WFP broadened to focus on peace and justice throughout LATIN AMERICA. Because the term "witness" is associated with JEHOVAH'S WITNESSES in Latin America, the Spanish version of the group's name is *Accion Permanente para la Paz* ("Permanent Action for Peace").

Other organizations began outside the churches and grew to forge stronger Christian connections. The Argentine sculptor and human rights activist, Adolfo Perez Esquivel, founded SERPAJ (*Servicio Paz y Justicio* or "Service for Peace and Justice," http://www. nonviolence.org/serpaj) to coordinate grassroots nonviolent movements for justice across Latin America. Although Esquivel (who won the 1980 Nobel Peace Prize) was and is a faithful Catholic, Latin America's Catholics were divided between those who supported the ruling powers (often including military dictatorships) and those whose "liberation theologies" were, at least in the popular mind, strongly connected to armed guerilla movements (see LIBERATION THEOLOGY). Hence SERPAJ was founded without a specifically religious orientation, but it quickly drew the support of the historic peace churches (especially the Mennonite Central Committee, the American Friends Service Committee, and the Brethren Volunteer Service) and IFOR. As the Catholic peace movement grew in the 1980s, SERPAJ also forged strong connections to Pax Christi, International—the largest grassroots Catholic peace organization. Today, many of SERPAJ's national branches are also branches of IFOR and sometimes also branches of Pax Christi. Where these ties are not official, there are usually strong informal ties and one quickly notices an overlap in members and officers (sometimes even working out of the same office space).

Churches for A Middle East Peace (http://www. cmep.org) is a Washington-based program of the American Friends Service Committee, Christian Church (DISCIPLES OF CHRIST), Church of the Brethren, CHURCH WORLD SERVICE, EPISCOPAL CHURCH, EVANGELICAL LUTHERAN CHURCH IN AMERICA, Franciscan Mission Service, Friends Committee on National Legislation, Maryknoll Missioners, Mennonite Central Committee, National Council of the Churches of Christ in the USA, Presbyterian Church (USA), Reformed Church in America, United Church of Christ, and the United Methodist Church, among others. Committed to nonviolence and to a two-state solution to the conflict between Israel and Palestine, human rights and the security of all in the region, and strengthening the role of the United Nations, it seeks to change the policy of the United States to promote a lasting peace with justice.

Evangelicals for Middle East Understanding seeks to involve more Evangelicals in peacemaking in the Middle East. It gives tours; makes connections to ancient Christian groups in the Middle East; works to combat hyper-Zionist theologies; educates on the history of Jewish–Muslim–Christian relations in Medieval and Modern history; encourages members to push their churches and legislators to work for a just two-state solution; and publishes a journal.

Christian Peacemaker Teams (CPT) was founded by Mennonites and the Church of the Brethren, and is also supported by Friends United Meeting. Like Witness for Peace, it seeks to make peace with justice in an unjust world by "getting in the way" between forces that otherwise are likely to do violence to each other, and thus persuading them actively to refrain from violence. It accepts volunteers from any Christian denomination who are committed to nonviolence. It has long-term workers in Hebron, in the Palestinian occupied territories; in Haiti, Columbia, Guatemala, the Chiapas region of MEXICO; and other global "hot-spots."

Ministries and Resources

Following are some examples of Protestant church peacemaking ministries and organizations with their vision statements.

- The Baptist Peace Fellowship of North America (http://www.bpfna.org) states its purpose as "to unite and enable Christians to make peace with justice in a warring world. Peace, like war, is waged. Those who wage war train for the battle, lift banners, and shout slogans. Those who would wage peace must also train for the battle, lift banners, and shout slogans."
- The Brethren Peace Fellowship (BPF) is part of the CHURCH OF THE BRETHREN, which is one of the "historic peace churches" whose members are all encouraged strongly to be pacifist and refuse military service. The BPF exists to strengthen the peacemaking witness of the Church of the Brethren and to connect members with other pacifists. It is a member organization of the Fellowship of Reconciliation.
- The Episcopal Peace Fellowship (EPF, http://www.episcopalpeacefellowship.org) describes its mission as "To aid and encourage all Episcopalians to strive for justice and peace among all people and to bear nonviolent witness to Christ's call to peace."
- The British Network of Christian Peace Organizations (NCPO, http://www.ncpo.org.uk) gives links to many church peace organizations in Great Britain and information on their joint projects.

The Religious Society of Friends has two action arms for peace and justice advocacy: The American Friends Service Committee (http://www.afsc.org), and The Friends Committee on National Legislation (FCNL), which seeks to bring the concerns, experiences, and testimonies of the Religious Society of Friends to bear on policy decisions in the nation's capital. Its multi-issue advocacy connects historic Quaker testimonies on peace, equality, simplicity, and truth with peace and social justice matters.

The Lutheran Peace Fellowship (http://www.lutheranpeace.org) is an international community of peacemakers, grounded in Christ, who seek peace according to the biblical vision of shalom, peace with justice; who pray and work to eliminate violence, oppression, and militarism; and who are committed to nonviolence in efforts to bring about justice and reconciliation. It offers resources for peace worship services, youth work, advocacy, workshops, and much else.

Mennonite Church, USA, Peace and Justice Support Network (http://www.mennolink.org) combines the work of the Mennonite Church's Peace and Justice Committee with the General Conference Mennonite Church's Peace and Justice Resources of its mission agency. Grassroots Mennonite peacemaking tends to work through the Christian Peacemaker Teams (see above). See also the Mennonite Central Committee (MCC, http://www.mcc.org), a relief, service, and peace agency of the North American Mennonite and Brethren in Christ churches. MCC reflects the biblical call to care for the hungry and thirsty, the stranger, the sick, and those in prison.

The Pentecostal Peace Fellowship (www.pentecostalpeace.org) "encourages, enables, and sustains peacemaking as an authentic and integral part of PENTECOSTALISM. It provides resources to help local churches and denominations in their faithfulness to the Way of Jesus, and serves as a source for education about conflict resolution, biblical and theological support for concerns about justice and peace, pamphlets and other works with practical guidelines regarding racial and gender issues. It also facilitates participation in peacemaking activities and training in conjunction with other peace fellowships."

The Presbyterian Peacemaking Program (http://www.pcusa.org/peacemaking) was created in 1980 when the General Assembly of the former United Presbyterian Church in the United States of America adopted *Peacemaking*: *The Believers' Calling*. The work of the Presbyterian Peacemaking Program is guided by three affirmations outlined in *Peacemaking*:

The Believers' Calling: (1) The church is faithful to Jesus Christ when it is engaged in peacemaking. (2) The church is obedient to Jesus Christ when it nurtures and equips God's people as peacemakers. (3) The church bears witness to Christ when it nurtures the moral life of the nation for the sake of peace in the world. The website for the Presbyterian Peace Fellowship is http://www.presbypeacefellowship. faithweb.com.

The United Church of Christ Justice and Peace Action Network (http://www.ucc.org/justice/jpan. htm), formerly known as the Justice and Peace Ministry, is the denomination's grassroots advocacy network, composed of individual members and local UCC congregations across the country. The UCC Justice and Peace Action Network "engages its members in shaping public policy and advocating systemic change in keeping with God's vision of a just and loving society. Our work is grounded in General Synod teachings, consonant with historic UCC witness, and formed by a biblical understanding of prophetic ministry." The Network collectively advocates justice and peace in a wide variety of areas, including economic justice, civil and human rights, environmental justice, peace issues, racial and gender justice, international/global concerns, and media ethics and advocacy. These are resourced by national staff of the Justice and Witness Ministries and Wider Church Ministries who work with local UCC advocates to shape coordinated strategy on our common witness.

References and Further Readings

Peace Ministry: A Handbook for Churches by Daniel L. Buttry Valley Forge, PA: Judson Press, 1995.

GLEN STASSEN

PEALE, NORMAN VINCENT
(1898–1993)

American preacher. Peale was a remarkable phenomenon in American religious life in the middle years of the twentieth century. *Life* magazine named him one of "Twelve Great American Preachers" in 1953, and he was the subject of a movie, *One Man's Way,* in 1963.

The son of a Methodist preacher, Peale was born May 31, 1898. He grew up in Ohio and graduated from Ohio Wesleyan University in 1920. He chose a career in journalism and worked at it briefly until he changed direction and began to study for the Christian ministry. The Methodist Episcopal Church ordained him in 1922, and he graduated from Boston University School of Theology two years later.

Peale showed great enthusiasm for the parish ministry, and had brief but successful appointments at St.

Mark's Methodist Church in Brooklyn and the University Church in Syracuse, New York. It was in Syracuse that he met his lifetime partner, Loretta Ruth Stafford. In 1932 he accepted a call from Marble Collegiate Church in New York City, a congregation of the REFORMED CHURCH IN AMERICA. He joined that DENOMINATION and remained at Marble Collegiate for the rest of his long career.

Marble Collegiate was a church in trouble when he arrived. Near despair, he concluded that he needed to focus on the possibilities for ministry and subsequently developed his lifelong conviction that positive thinking could lead to a richer spiritual life and material success. Seeking to bring the insights of psychology and religion together, he teamed up with psychiatrist Smiley Blanton and created the Religio-Psychiatric Clinic at Marble Collegiate Church. It later became the American Federation for Religion and Psychiatry.

The classic statement of his point of view was *The Power of Positive Thinking,* which he wrote in 1952. Atop the best-seller list for more than three years, it extended his audience and brought him much criticism. Liberal and conservative theologians joined in criticizing him for what they considered to be a shallow, self-help faith. The Reformed Church in America nonetheless elected him its president in 1969.

With the help of his wife he began distributing his sermons in 1943. That modest effort led to the widely circulated *Guideposts* magazine and an inspirational devotional called *Daily Guideposts.* He died December 24, 1993. His wife has carried on his work through numerous publications and through the Peale Center for Christian Living in Pawling, New York, where information about Peale and his manuscripts are available.

References and Further Reading

Primary Source:

Peale, Norman Vincent. *The True Joy of Positive Living: An Autobiography.* New York: Foundation for Christian Living, 1984.

Secondary Sources:

George, Carol V. R. *God's Salesman: Norman Vincent Peale and the Power of Positive Thinking.* New York: Oxford University Press, 1993.

Meyer, Donald. *The Positive Thinkers: A Study of the Quest for Health, Wealth, and Personal Power from Mary Baker Eddy to Norman Vincent Peale.* Garden City, NY: Doubleday, 1965.

JOHN PIPER

PEDERSEN, JOHANNES PEDER EJLER (1883–1977)

Danish theologian. Pedersen, Danish professor and Semitic philologist, advanced biblical scholarship through his lectures and publications on ancient Israelite CULTURE, Old Testament texts, and Hebrew grammar. Born in Illebølle, DENMARK on November 7, 1883, Pedersen attended Sorø Academy and studied Protestant THEOLOGY and Semitic languages in Copenhagen, Leipzig, Leiden, Budapest, and Cairo. In 1923 he succeeded Frants Buhls as professor at Copenhagen and taught there until 1953. He died in Copenhagen on December 22, 1977.

Pedersen's most acclaimed contribution to biblical scholarship is his four-volume *Israel: Its Life and Culture* (Copenhagen, 1920–1934; London, 1926–1940), which applied Grönbech's psychological model to Israelite society and argued that strength of community emanates from holiness of soul, which is sanctified by religious observance. For ancient Israelites everything formed a dynamic whole: soul and body, individual and group, inhabitants and land. Although criticized for overgeneralization, Pedersen's volume highlighted the cohesive function of the cult and centrality of the Passover (Exodus 1–15) ("Passahfest und Passahlegende [Passover Feast and Passover Legend]" (*Zeitschrift für die Alttestamentliche Wissenschaft* 52 [1934]: 161–175).

Noteworthy contributions include a description of oaths, *Der Eid bei den Semiten* (*The Oath among the Semites*) (Strasburg, 1914); critique of source criticism, "Die Auffassung vom Alten Testament [The Concept of the Old Testament]" (*Zeitschrift für die Alttestamentliche Wissenschaft* 49 [1931]: 161–181); a Hebrew grammar (Copenhagen, 1926, 1968); and a history of *The Arabic Book* (Copenhagen, 1946; New Jersey, 1984).

References and Further Reading

Lemche, Niels Peter. "Pedersen, Johannes Peder Ejler." In *Theologische Realenzyklopädie*, edited by S. Schwertner, vol. 26, 162–164. Berlin and New York: Walter de Gruyter, 1996.

Nielsen, Eduard. "Johannes Pedersen's Contribution to the Research and Understanding of the Old Testament." *Annual of the Swedish Theological Institute* 8 (1970/71): 4–20.

FRANK RITCHEL AMES

PENN, WILLIAM (1644–1718)

Quaker statesman. Born in London on October 14, 1644, the son of a prominent naval commander, Penn became a Quaker in 1667 and quickly became one of the most prominent leaders of the SOCIETY OF FRIENDS as a missionary, traveling speaker in local meetings, arbitrator of disputes among Friends, and especially as a writer defending Quakers against theological attacks and presenting Quaker principles and practices in systematic form. Educated as a lawyer as well as a theologian, Penn argued in law courts and in toleration tracts that religious liberty was a logical implication of Protestantism, as well as a fundamental right of Englishmen. Using his family's influence, he secured land in the New World so that he could found Pennsylvania as a "holy experiment," a society governed by Quaker principles. After 1682 Penn spent much of his time defending the colony, his proprietary rights, and even himself against charges of treason. He continued to write substantial Quaker treatises in the 1690s, in part to convince Englishmen that Quakers were orthodox Protestants and hence legal under the terms of the Toleration Act of 1689. He died in 1718.

Penn's understanding of the relationship between Quakerism and Protestantism was complex and not altogether consistent. On the one hand, he understood Quakerism to be *Primitive Christianity Revived...* (1696), and stressed the incompleteness of the Continental and English Reformations. Penn believed that the Quakers had received a measure of the same kind of anointing by the Spirit as the Apostles of Christ, at times arguing that the Quakers had gone beyond even the dispensation of the Apostles to begin a third era in the history of SALVATION marked by dispensing with such "outward" forms of religion as creedal doctrinal formulas, ordained ministry, sacraments, and even the gathering of bodies in a CHURCH.

On the other hand, in his treatises on TOLERATION Penn was more likely to present Quakerism as the purest form of Protestantism, completing the movement begun by the sixteenth-century reformers. When questioned about the Quakers' objections to the traditional understandings of the Trinity, substitutionary ATONEMENT, JUSTIFICATION by FAITH through imputed righteousness, and the SACRAMENTS, and about their deemphasis on the person and work of the historical or incarnate Christ in favor of the eternal Christ known to all human beings through the "inner light," Penn could argue that the Quakers simply preferred to stick to Scriptural statements about such matters and understood the traditional creeds as attempts by misguided Christians to claim a more adequate understanding of the eternal mysteries than was available to humanity. At times he even argued that the Quakers alone stuck to the essence of the REFORMATION, that is, the understanding that salvation was by GRACE alone, given that only the Quakers excluded all human means to salvation and simply waited passively for the Spirit to speak and act in them.

References and Further Reading

Dunn, Mary Maples, and Richard S. Dunn, eds. *The World of William Penn*. Philadelphia: University of Pennsylvania Press, 1986.

Endy, Melvin B. Jr. *William Penn and Early Quakerism*. Princeton, NJ: Princeton University Press, 1973.

MELVIN B. ENDY JR.

PENTECOSTAL ASSEMBLIES OF THE WORLD

Founded in 1919, this primarily African American denomination traces its roots to meetings held in Los Angeles from 1906, called the AZUSA STREET REVIVAL, in which leaders attempted to coordinate the fledgling Pentecostal movement (see PENTECOSTALISM). With the decreased prominence of the Azusa Street Mission, leaders scattered across the country. The leadership of what became the Pentecostal Assemblies of the World (PAW) then moved to Portland, Oregon. During the early period no organizational structures were established.

Most of the leadership of this tradition embraced "Oneness" theology. Sometimes called "Jesus Only" or erroneously "Pentecostal Unitarians," this tradition is radically monotheistic, believes in baptismal regeneration, and adheres to the more traditional Pentecostal liturgical and theological structures such as glossolalia (or speaking in TONGUES). From 1906 to 1919 the PAW was a loose fellowship of church leaders but with no governance structure.

The DENOMINATION owes its form to Garfield Thomas Haywood (1880–1931) of Indianapolis. When it was decided that the ASSEMBLIES OF GOD would not include black clergy and churches, Haywood converted to "Oneness" theology and entered the orbit of the PAW. He attended a meeting in Eureka Springs, Arkansas in 1918, called to explore the future structures of the PAW, but the results were inconclusive. In January 1919 he hosted a meeting in Indianapolis that drew several thousand delegates. It was Haywood's dream that the denomination be multiracial, active for civil rights, supportive of holiness, aggressive in EVANGELISM, and a promoter of MISSIONS. He drafted the constitution and bylaws and was elected executive secretary of the new denomination. He published the denominational periodical, *Voice in the Wilderness,* as well as a number of "best-seller" theological treatises that formed the intellectual structures of the PAW. Most of these have remained in print.

Almost immediately his leadership was contested, primarily orchestrated by Bishop Robert C. Lawson of New York, who could not tolerate Haywood's support of the right of WOMEN to preach, the money spent on international missions, and his acceptance of divorced persons into membership. All of these remain con-

tested issues. Next, the European American CLERGY decided to develop their own denominations, some of which merged to become the United Pentecostal Church, a white denomination. Other schisms have followed, grounded in concerns over ECUMENISM, personality, race, leadership style, and assorted theological issues. The PAW has remained determinedly multiracial and is primarily urban and Northern. It has been very active in the CIVIL RIGHTS MOVEMENT, and for that reason it has had less of a presence in the Old South. Governance is accomplished through annual national conventions and state conventions.

Foreign missions were undertaken to CHINA beginning in 1919. Missions to the CARIBBEAN, AFRICA, and Europe as well as to other areas of Asia followed. Although the church outside North America remains small, that in the UNITED STATES has grown quickly. In 2000 there were about 2,000 congregations and about 1.5 million members/adherents. Aenon Bible College, Indianapolis, Indiana, offers a variety of opportunities for residential and distance education. It annually enrolls as many as 10,000 students, mostly in distance education courses.

References and Further Reading

Bundy, David. "G. T. Haywood: Religion for Urban Realities." In *Portraits of a Generation: Early Pentecostal Leaders,* edited by J. Goff and G. Wacker, 237–253, 410–411. Fayetteville: University of Arkansas Press, 2002.

Golder, Morris E. *History of the Pentecostal Assemblies of the World.* Indianapolis: 1973.

Reeder, Hilda. *A Short History of the Foreign Missionary Department of the Pentecostal Assemblies of the World.* Indianapolis: c. 1939.

Tyson, James L. *The Early Pentecostal Revival.* Hazelwood, MO: World Aflame Press, 1992.

DAVID BUNDY

PENTECOSTAL CHURCH OF GOD

The Pentecostal Church of God (PCOG) is a Protestant, Pentecostal fellowship with offices in Joplin, Missouri (see PENTICOSTALISM). It was established in 1919 as the Pentecostal Assemblies of the U.S.A. Significant characteristics of the PCOG include its lack of a creedal statement and its "finished work" understanding of the doctrine of SANCTIFICATION. Although the denomination does not emphasize church membership, in 2001 they reported a constituency of 102,000 in the UNITED STATES and 600,000 outside the United States. In 2003 there were over 1,200 local congregations in the United States, with 5,200 churches and ministry stations outside the United States.

Founding a Fellowship

Many of the ministers that constituted the PCOG had been affiliated with the ASSEMBLIES OF GOD (AOG). Although many early Pentecostal ministers were independent minded, some saw the need to network and organized the General Council of the Assemblies of God in 1914. When the AOG faced internal doctrinal differences with those who did not accept the Trinity, believing the only name for the one God is Jesus, the AOG adopted a doctrinal statement in 1916, which was used to exclude the "Oneness" people. However, the adoption of any statement of faith as a tool for excluding ministers troubled some such as George C. Brinkman of Chicago.

Brinkman was the pastor of the Pentecostal Herald Mission in Chicago and published *The Pentecostal Herald*—a periodical that many AOG ministers read. Brinkman became frustrated that AOG leadership discouraged ministers from reading *The Pentecostal Herald* in favor of the AOG periodical *The Christian Evangel*. Brinkman called a meeting on November 5, 1919 to select trustees for *The Pentecostal Herald*. Attendees declared that *The Pentecostal Herald* was the official paper of the "Pentecostal Assemblies of the United States and Canada" and requested the AOG to recognize it as such, calling for another meeting of the ministers.

Delegates to the December 29–30, 1919 meeting in Chicago established an alternative fellowship to the AOG that they considered free from a creedal statement and based instead on the BIBLE alone. They adopted the name "The Pentecostal Assemblies of the United States" and a constitution for a fellowship with a congregational form of government. The delegates elected John Sinclair as chairman and Brinkman as general secretary. The name of the fellowship was changed to the Pentecostal Church of God in 1922, and for a brief period was the Pentecostal Church of God of America.

Although the PCOG rejected creeds as a standard for fellowship, it did promote evangelical and Pentecostal doctrines. Refusing to take a stand on a baptismal formula, which had been a point of controversy between the AOG and Oneness Pentecostals, the PCOG affirmed the Trinity, speaking in TONGUES as the evidence of Spirit baptism, and a baptistic understanding of sanctification, which had also divided the Pentecostal movement.

The Pentecostal movement had been an heir to the HIGHER LIFE MOVEMENT that swept North America in the nineteenth century. Founders such as Charles Fox Parham in Topeka, Kansas, and William Joseph Seymour at the AZUSA STREET REVIVAL and Mission in Los Angeles were products of the radical wing of the WESLEYAN HOLINESS MOVEMENT, and understood sanctification as a second crisis experience of GRACE in the life of the believer. Like the AOG, however, the PCOG followed William H. Durham in their understanding of sanctification. Durham rejected the idea that sanctification was a subsequent work of grace in the life of the believer. He taught that sanctification began at the time of CONVERSION and was appropriated over one's lifetime. This came to be called the "Finished Work at Calvary" doctrine and was generally adopted by Pentecostals from Presbyterian and Baptist backgrounds.

Developing a Structure

The PCOG has always desired to furnish fellowship without a controlling structure. Consequently there has been little emphasis on membership or "belonging" to an organization. Yet, over the years the need for cooperative ministry has gradually led to the formation of various departments and agencies.

PUBLISHING has always been a significant arm of Pentecostal movements because the printed page was the chief means of connecting networks of ministers, disseminating news of CAMP MEETINGS and REVIVALS, and standardizing acceptable DOCTRINE. At the founding meeting in 1919, ministers agreed to adopt *The Pentecostal Herald* as their official paper. Books and other publications were occasionally printed under the name Herald Publishing Company. In 1927 *The Pentecostal Messenger* was selected as the national publication. The denomination began to publish its own SUNDAY SCHOOL literature in 1938 and today operates Messenger Publishing House.

Throughout the twentieth century the PCOG developed a number of specialized ministries at the national level. These include Youth Ministries (1928), World Missions (1929), Indian Ministries (1949), Christian Education Department (1953), Women's Ministry Department (1957), King's Men Fellowship (1975), Home Missions/Evangelism Department (1981), and Senior Christian Fellowship (1982).

Early educational opportunities included Herald Correspondence Bible School in 1921. Beginning in 1946 there was an ongoing call for a central college, and the movement supported regional colleges including Pentecostal Bible Institute (later renamed Evangelical Christian College) and Southern Bible College. These two colleges were later combined into Messenger College, which opened in Joplin, Missouri in 1987.

Today the fellowship participates in organizations such as the NATIONAL ASSOCIATION OF EVANGELICALS, the PENTECOSTAL/CHARISMATIC CHURCHES OF NORTH AMERICA, the International Pentecostal Press Association, and the PENTECOSTAL WORLD FELLOWSHIP. Of special interest is the willingness of the PCOG to ordain WOMEN. Indeed, the first person ordained by the fellowship was the Reverend Ida Tribett (see WOMEN CLERGY). The headquarters of the denomination, previously in Ottumwa, Iowa, and Kansas City, Missouri, moved to Joplin in 1951.

See also Anti-Trinitarianism; Bible Colleges and Institutes; Keswick Movement

References and Further Reading

http://www.pcg.org/
Pentecostal Church of God. *General Constitution and Bylaws.* Joplin, MO: Messenger Publishing House, 2003.
Wilson, Aaron. *Basic Bible Truth: A Doctrinal Study of the Pentecostal Church of God.* Joplin, MO: Messenger Publishing House, 1987.
———. *Our Story: The History of the Pentecostal Church of God, 1919–2001.* Joplin, MO: Messenger Publishing House, 2001.

DAVID G. ROEBUCK

PENTECOSTAL WORLD CONFERENCE

See Pentecostal World Fellowship

PENTECOSTAL WORLD FELLOWSHIP

The Pentecostal World Fellowship (PWF), known as the Pentecostal World Conference until 2001, is an international coalition of Pentecostal denominations and local churches. Moving beyond the divisions that previously had existed among Pentecostals, it was established in 1947 for the purpose of spiritual fellowship without regard to denominational affiliation. The PWF sponsors a world conference every three years.

A Divided Movement

From its beginning Pentecostalism was MISSIONS oriented. One of its primary theological emphases was an eschatological emphasis that Christians were living in the last days and that Jesus would return soon (see ESCHATOLOGY). Indeed, Charles Fox Parham taught that the purpose of speaking in tongues was to be able to supernaturally preach in unlearned human languages. Although most Pentecostals came to reject Parham's idea regarding speaking in tongues, they continued to emphasize the need for worldwide EVANGELISM. Consequently Pentecostalism quickly spread to other parts of the world through the efforts of an army of missionaries and local believers who heard the Pentecostal message.

In North America, Pentecostals soon divided over race, DOCTRINE, and POLITY. Although the Azusa Street Revival and some early Pentecostal denominations were interracial, as Pentecostalism developed, it divided along racial lines. By the 1920s Pentecostals had succumbed to Jim Crow segregation laws and other social pressures of the first half of the twentieth century.

Both the doctrine of SANCTIFICATION and the doctrine of the Trinity were areas of major division among Pentecostals. Those in the Wesleyan Holiness Movement emphasized sanctification as a postconversion work of GRACE. Those in the Higher Life Movement saw sanctification as occurring at the time of JUSTIFICATION and then being appropriated throughout the life of the believer. Following William F. Durham, this Higher Life view was called the "Finished Work of Calvary" doctrine of sanctification. Regarding the doctrine of the Trinity, "Oneness" or "Jesus Only" Pentecostals emphasized that there is only one God and God's name is Jesus. They rejected the concept of a Trinity and insisted that every Christian be baptized in the name of Jesus according to Acts 2:38.

Furthermore, many Pentecostals were independently minded in terms of church polity—believing in a radical CONGREGATIONALISM and fearing that organization would quench the work of the Holy Spirit. For theological, mission, and financial reasons, a large number of these joined together to form the General Council of the Assemblies of God in 1914, but they considered themselves to be a fellowship of ministers rather than a DENOMINATION. Although they increasingly adopted the structures and practices of a denomination, they continued to place a great deal of emphasis on the liberty of the local church and minister. Moreover, even though loose networks have regularly developed, many Pentecostals have never identified with a denomination or organization of any kind.

Some of these distinctions may have seemed unimportant to outsiders, but they were of major importance to participants in a movement that saw itself as restoring the apostolic church and preparing the way for the second coming of Jesus Christ. In the minds of many Pentecostals, having the right understanding on doctrinal and polity matters would make the difference between the growth of the KINGDOM OF GOD and the ultimate return of Jesus Christ for his church.

These divisions occurred within a theological system that saw two world wars and attempts to unify nations as real expressions of a cosmic battle between God and Satan (see DEVIL) at the end of the age. Pentecostals loathed and feared unifying and ecumenical agencies such as the League of Nations, the United Nations, the Federal Council of Churches, and the WORLD COUNCIL OF CHURCHES because they represented vehicles that could be appropriated by the Roman Catholic Church and by the ANTI-CHRIST to thwart the kingdom of God. Thus differences in theology and polity were accentuated by a radical Eschatology and by fears of both a "one-world government" and an ecumenical church.

Ecumenical Efforts

Although racial, doctrinal, and polity differences among the various Pentecostal denominations led to isolationism in North America until World War II, this was not the case for Pentecostals in Europe. A few representative efforts illustrate both the efforts and hindrances to ecumenical progress among Pentecostals. As early as 1911, Norwegian pastor Thomas Ball Barratt issued "An Urgent Plea for Charity and Unity" in which he recommended an organic union that would express the spiritual unity among Pentecostals. In 1921, Pentecostals from several European groups gathered in Amsterdam, but differences among the participants over the use of visions and prophecies dissuaded them from further meetings. A more national attempt to encourage unity occurred in May 1939 and January 1940 when various British Pentecostal groups met together in London. Twenty European groups met in Stockholm for a Unity Conference in June 1939.

Without making any recommendations regarding mergers, these and other such meetings did provide fellowship, discussion, and shared worship opportunities. Those who participated had to be careful not to raise fears of compromise and merger among their various constituencies, however. With the outbreak of World War II, further conversations about unity meetings were set aside during the hostilities.

The isolationism among Pentecostals in the United States began to subside when denominational leaders came together with other evangelicals to form the NATIONAL ASSOCIATION OF EVANGELICALS (NAE). By this time Pentecostal denominations were more settled, the movement was experiencing significant growth so that it could no longer be ignored by the rest of Christianity, leaders and many adherents were on the cusp of becoming middle class, and fears of a "one-world government" and an ecumenical church drove Pentecostals to be more open to like-minded conservative and evangelical Christians. Thus, Pentecostals participated in the National Conference for United Action among Evangelicals in St. Louis in 1942 and in the constitutional meeting of the NAE in Chicago the next year. The results of this fellowship and cooperation raised the possibilities of a national meeting of Pentecostals as well as an international conference.

European leaders continued to lead the conversation regarding a national meeting, however. Key figures in Europe were Britain's Donald Gee (AOG), SWEDEN'S Lewi Pethrus (Filadelfia Church), and SWITZERLAND'S Leonard Steiner (Swiss Pentecostal Movement). In May 1946 a prayer conference was held in Basel. At that meeting delegates determined to call a world conference of Pentecostals in Zurich one year later using the theme "For by one Spirit we are all baptized into one body" (I Corinthians 12:13).

Most major Pentecostal denominations sent delegates to the 1947 meeting in Zurich. Leonard Steiner acted first as organizing secretary and then as chairman of the conference, and delegates represented twenty-two different nationalities, although the meeting was filled with tension. Differences in purpose and polity prohibited the adoption of any rationale for unity as delegates disagreed over whether they were meeting for spiritual or for practical cooperation. The Scandinavian delegation particularly opposed any form of organization other than that of the local church. One lasting result was that delegates agreed to form an international center in Basel to help in efforts to rebuild Europe after the War. Steiner supervised the center, which was funded by American and European Pentecostals.

Delegates to the Zurich conference also agreed to begin a publication named *Pentecost*, and appointed Donald Gee as the editor. Gee was one of the best-known Pentecostal statesmen and the author of numerous books. The magazine's purpose was to report Pentecostal missionary and revival activities. It was expected that Gee would not favor any particular Pentecostal group over another. Soon Gee became particularly known for his insightful editorials on the state of Pentecostalism. He edited the periodical until his death in 1966, at which time publication ceased. In 1971 the PWF introduced a new publication under the name *World Pentecost* with Percy S. Brewster as the editor. Other editors have been Eric C. Dando and Jakob Zopfi. The publication ended in 1998, in part because of the possibilities of publishing on the World Wide Web.

A second world conference was held in Paris in 1949. By then there was less tension among the delegations because they were assured that each denomination and independent congregation would remain autonomous. A major debate at the conference centered on what structure an international organization ought to have, but delegates did agree to several proposals. These included having a conference every three years in a different nation to strengthen fellowship, selecting a secretary and an advisory committee to serve between conferences, recognizing that the purpose of the conference was for spiritual fellowship rather than impinging on the autonomy of any denomination or local congregation, and encouraging fellowship and cooperative effort of Pentecostals throughout the world.

A Viable Fellowship

Elected officers of the PWF include a chairman, vice chairman, and secretary who along with four others constitute a Presidium. The Presidium plans each meeting's location, speakers, and theme in consultation with an Advisory Committee that is representative of the Pentecostal movement.

Except for one occasion since 1949, the conference has met every three years in major cities around the world. These have been London (1952), Stockholm (1955), Toronto (1958), Jerusalem (1961), Helsinki (1964), Rio de Janeiro (1967), Dallas, Texas (1970), Seoul (1973), London (1976), Vancouver, British Columbia, Canada (1979), Nairobi (1982), Zurich (1985), Singapore (1989), Oslo (1992), Jerusalem (1995), Seoul (1998), Los Angeles (2001), and Johannesburg (2004). Until 1958 the conference used the name World Pentecostal Conference. From 1961 to 2001 it went by the name Pentecostal World Conference. Then in 2001 the name was changed to Pentecostal World Fellowship to more accurately reflect the ongoing nature of the organization.

Denominations, local churches, or other organizations that wish to be members of PWF must agree to both a doctrinal statement and a statement of purposes. Following recommendation from a member of the advisory committee, the applicant must be approved by the entire committee. The Statement of Faith is:

We believe:

1. The Bible to be inspired, the only infallible, authoritative Word of God;
2. That there is one God, eternally existent in three persons: Father, Son, and Holy Spirit;
3. In the deity of our Lord Jesus Christ, in His virgin birth, in His sinless life, in His miracles, in His vicarious atoning death through His shed blood, in His bodily resurrection, in His ascension to the right hand of the Father, and in His personal return in power and glory;
4. That for the salvation of lost and sinful man regeneration by the Holy Spirit through faith in Jesus Christ is absolutely essential;
5. In the baptism of the Holy Spirit with the evidence of speaking in other tongues as the Spirit gives the utterance according to Acts 2:4, and in the operation of the spiritual gifts and ministries;
6. In the ministry of the Holy Spirit by whose indwelling the Christian is enabled to live a godly life;
7. In the resurrection of both the saved and the lost; they that are saved to eternal life and they that are lost unto the resurrection of damnation;
8. In the church of Jesus Christ and in the unity of believers;
9. In the practical application of the Christian faith in everyday experience and the need to minister to people in every area of life, which includes not only the spiritual, but also, the social, political, and physical.

The purposes of the PWF are to:

1. Encourage missions partnerships among participating Pentecostal groups.
2. Speak to governments and nations on behalf of Pentecostal believers everywhere and especially in countries where persecution exists or where individual rights and freedoms are compromised for the sake of the gospel.
3. Share as a Pentecostal World Fellowship in humanitarian aid through its various Pentecostal members by sharing information of assistance given and where possible to cooperate in humanitarian efforts worldwide.
4. Serve as a cooperative fellowship whereby educational institutions approved by individual Pentecostal members of the Pentecostal World Fellowship would be recognized by other member groups.
5. Pursue the fulfillment of the Lord's command to evangelize the lost in the shortest possible time, providing them the opportunity to hear and respond to the gospel in all of its fullness, by encouraging and assisting one another, promoting harmonious relationships, and seeking the most effective means of its accomplishment under the dynamic leadership of the Holy Spirit.
6. Emphasize worldwide prayer networks and coordinated prayer.

Although the PWF is the most diverse Pentecostal organization in the world, it does not represent all Pentecostals. Some groups, such as Oneness Pentecostals, are excluded by the Statement of Faith. Further PWF leaders have tended to be North American or European, and since 1967 have been from either the AOG or the COG in the United States. This has brought stability to the PWF but may have limited its participation on the world stage as well as narrowed its agenda. Conference attendees are most often either from the host nation or those who can afford international travel. Consequently the PWF has tended to be conservative and to oppose participation in movements such as the Charismatic Renewal and ecumenical expressions of Christianity. Thus, although the PWF has moved many Pentecostal groups out of isolation from other Pentecostals, it has yet to find ways in which it can involve the diversity that exists within Pentecostalism, speak in a unified voice for Pentecostalism, or serve as a prophetic witness to the concerns of a global community.

See also Anti-Trinitarianism; Biblical Inerrancy; Ecumenism; Pentecostal/Charismatic Churches of North America

References and Further Reading

Gee, Donald. *The Pentecostal Movement: Including the Story of the War Years (1940–1947)*. Revised and enlarged edition. London: Elim Publishing Company, 1949.

Nichol, John Thomas. *Pentecostalism: The Story of the Growth and Development of a Vital New Force in American Protestantism*. New York: Harper & Row, 1966.

Robeck, C. M. "Pentecostal World Conference." In *The New International Dictionary of Pentecostal and Charismatic Movements*. Revised and expanded edition. Edited by Stanley M. Burgess and Eduard M. van der Maas, 971–974. Grand Rapids, MI: Zondervan, 2002.

Synan, Vinson. *The Holiness-Pentecostal Tradition*. Grand Rapids, MI: Wm. B. Eerdmans, 1997.

Wacker, Grant. *Heaven Below: Early Pentecostalism and American Culture*. Cambridge, MA: Harvard University Press, 2001.

http://pentecostalworldfellowship.org

DAVID G. ROEBUCK

PENTECOSTAL/CHARISMATIC CHURCHES OF NORTH AMERICA

The Pentecostal/Charismatic Churches of North America (PCCNA) is the successor organization to the Pentecostal Fellowship of North America (PFNA). The Pentecostal Fellowship was founded in 1948 to promote fellowship and unity among Pentecostal movements. Because the organization was made up of denominations that were primarily white, the PFNA chose to disband in 1994 to allow for the formation of the interracial PCCNA.

Fellowship in the PFNA

PENTECOSTALISM is a Protestant movement considered to have begun in the UNITED STATES at the beginning of the twentieth century among adherents in the WESLEYAN HOLINESS MOVEMENT and HIGHER LIFE MOVEMENT. Most historians point to Charles Fox Parham's Bethel Bible College in Topeka, Kansas, where Agnes Ozman spoke in tongues on January 1, 1901 and to the 1906 AZUSA STREET REVIVAL in Los Angeles led by William Joseph Seymour as the beginnings of the Pentecostal movement in the United States. As a result of the Pentecostal revival, some existing denominations such as the CHURCH OF GOD IN CHRIST (COGIC) adopted the Pentecostal message, and new denominations such as the ASSEMBLIES OF GOD emerged. Doctrinal differences led to isolationism among Pentecostals until World War II, however. After the organization of the NATIONAL ASSOCIATION OF EVANGELICALS and the inaugural meeting of the PENTECOSTAL WORLD FELLOWSHIP, many Pentecostal denominations recognized a need to get together for fellowship and shared ministry.

On May 7, 1948, twenty-four representatives from eight denominations met in Chicago to discuss an association of Pentecostals. A second Chicago meeting chose the name PFNA and a committee to draft articles of fellowship. This committee consisted of J. Roswell Flower (Assemblies of God), H. L. Chesser (CHURCH OF GOD), E. J. Fulton (Open Bible Standard Churches), and Herman D. Mitzner (INTERNATIONAL CHURCH OF THE FOURSQUARE GOSPEL).

Organization of the PFNA took place October 26–28, 1948 in Des Moines, Iowa. Delegates adopted the Statement of Faith of the National Association of Evangelicals with the addition of the following paragraph: "We believe that the full gospel includes holiness of heart and life, healing for the body and the baptism in the Holy Spirit with the initial evidence of speaking in other tongues as the Spirit gives utterance." John C. Jernigan (Church of God) was elected chair and Flower was elected secretary.

Charter members included the AOG; the COG; the Pentecostal Holiness Church, International (PHCI); the International Church of the Foursquare Gospel; and the Open Bible Standard Church. Other Pentecostal denominations quickly joined. The Trinitarian paragraph in the Statement of Faith excluded Oneness groups, and black Pentecostals were not invited to participate in the PFNA.

An Interracial Organization

Although the Azusa Street revival and some early Pentecostal movements were interracial, as Pentecostalism developed into denominations it divided along racial lines. Pentecostals succumbed to Jim Crow laws and other social pressures of the first half of the twentieth century.

Toward the end of the twentieth century the racial climate in the United States had changed dramatically. Segregation was no longer legal, and African Americans were increasingly involved in public life. Under the leadership of Bishop Bernard E. Underwood (PHCI), who was elected as chairperson in 1991, the

PFNA began to discuss the inclusion of all races. The theme for its October 17–19, 1994 meeting in Memphis, Tennessee was "Pentecostal Partners: A Reconciliation Strategy for 21st Century Ministry." Memphis had been the site of a great deal of racial unrest, including the assassination of Martin Luther King Jr., and was the headquarters city of the largest black Pentecostal denomination, the COGIC. The meeting was cochaired by Bishop Ithiel Clemmons (COGIC) and Underwood. Day sessions included presentations by Pentecostal scholars on racial separation. Worship services were held each evening. After a dramatic washing of feet on October 18 (see Feet, Washing of) the PFNA held its final business meeting during which it dissolved itself.

On October 19 a constitution was adopted to form a new interracial organization. The governing board included an equal number of black and white members. At the suggestion of Billy Joe Daugherty, pastor of Victory Christian Center in Tulsa, Oklahoma, the term "Charismatic" was added to the name. The term charismatic is used to refer to those who testify of a Pentecostal "Spirit-baptism" but do not belong to a classical Pentecostal church. Additionally, delegates adopted a "Racial Reconciliation Manifesto," which pledged to prophetically oppose racism and to seek opportunities for reconciliation. The new PCCNA selected Clemmons as its chairperson, and before the meeting ended, delegates were calling it the "Memphis Miracle."

According to its constitution, the purposes of the PCCNA are:

1. To relate to one another as members of the one Body of Christ throughout the world.
2. To demonstrate the essential unity of Spirit-filled believers in answer to the prayer of Jesus in John 17:21 "That all may be one."
3. To foster the evangelization of the world through the preaching of the Gospel with signs and wonders and the demonstration of the gifts of the Holy Spirit by presenting Jesus Christ as the only Savior, Baptizer in the Holy Spirit, Healer, and Coming King. (Mark 16:19–20)
4. To promote and encourage the Pentecostal/Charismatic revival and renewal in North America and throughout the world.
5. To serve as a forum of spiritual unity, dialogue, and fellowship for all Pentecostal and Charismatic believers in North America that crosses all cultural and racial lines based on mutual equality, love, respect, and sound doctrine. (Acts 2:42)
6. To preserve mutual love and respect for each member group, maintaining "the unity of the Spirit in the bond of peace." (Ephesians 4:1)

Membership in the PCCNA is open to denominations, fellowships, ministries, parachurch organizations, and local churches who subscribe to the Statement of Faith, principles, purposes, and objectives as set forth in the constitution. The PCCNA meets annually.

See also Anti-Trinitarianism

References and Further Reading

Synan, Vinson. *The Holiness-Pentecostal Tradition.* Grand Rapids, MI: Wm. B. Eerdmans, 1997.

Warner, W. E. "Pentecostal Fellowship of North America." In *International Dictionary of Pentecostal and Charismatic Movements,* edited by Stanley Burgess and Eduard Van der Maas, 968–969. Grand Rapids, MI: Zondervan Publishing, 2002.

http://www.pctii.org/pccna

David G. Roebuck

PENTECOSTALISM

The Pentecostal Movement dates to the beginning of the twentieth century, and arose among Protestants who sought a baptism in the Holy Spirit. It takes its name from events described in the first two chapters of the New Testament book of Acts. St. Luke links spiritual power, evangelism, Spirit baptism, and Speaking in Tongues: "You shall receive power after the Holy Ghost is come upon you. . . . And they were all filled with the Holy Ghost and spoke in tongues as the Spirit gave them utterance."

Beginnings

Pentecostalism emerged out of the fascination for holiness that many late–nineteenth-century Protestants expressed. Among John Wesley's followers were Holiness people who urged believers toward a second definite work of Grace that had dual implications of purity and power. Premillennialists echoed the call for purity and power in their summons to holiness and Evangelism in preparation for Christ's imminent return. Keswick Movement proponents urged consecration as a means to full Salvation. Some advocates of divine healing anticipated a return of spiritual gifts to the end-times church. The era's many mission enthusiasts craved power to save the world. These interests and others united the faithful in nondenominational networks sustained by Camp Meetings, popular speakers, and inexpensive publications. Sets of connections often overlapped. Among the Protestant churches there existed informal networks, as well as some intentional clusters that formally separated from denominations. This informal Protestant world nurtured the impulses that gave birth to American Pentecostalism.

Although speaking in tongues occurred in various nineteenth-century American religious groups from SHAKERS to SEVENTH-DAY ADVENTISTS to Mormons (see MORMONISM), no one advanced the notion that speaking in tongues was the "uniform initial evidence" of the baptism with the Holy Spirit. The well-publicized tongues speaking in the 1830s in the Scottish Presbyterian Church in London's Regent Square brought notoriety, but also prompted theologian HORACE BUSHNELL to ruminate on spiritual gifts. But even the considerable publicity at the time did not yield a conclusion about uniform evidence for Spirit baptism. Wesleyans sometimes used the phrase "baptism with the Holy Spirit" to refer to the second blessing or entire SANCTIFICATION. Such people, following the lead of holiness advocates like William Arthur (*Tongues of Fire*, 1858), assigned to the second blessing both purifying and empowering roles. By the end of the nineteenth century, Benjamin Irwin's followers in the Fire-Baptized Movement identified a series of baptisms beyond the second blessing. Non-Wesleyan revivalistic Protestants like evangelist DWIGHT L. MOODY and his colleague, REUBEN A. TORREY, understood the baptism with the Holy Spirit to be an empowerment for Christian service. In 1898, Torrey wrote an influential book, *The Baptism With the Holy Ghost,* that urged every would-be Christian worker to stop everything and pray earnestly for this baptism. He taught that believers should claim the experience by FAITH; its evidence would be manifested in all kinds of effective Christian service.

Some yearned for concrete assurance that they had been baptized with the Holy Spirit. Among these, Charles Parham, a young independent-minded Methodist preacher (see METHODISM, NORTH AMERICA), rose to prominence when he began teaching—based on Acts 2:4—that an authentic baptism with the Holy Spirit would be evidenced immediately by speaking in tongues. He believed that tongues would be known languages and that the restoration of the gift of tongues would facilitate an end-times missionary harvest.

Born in Iowa but reared in Kansas, Parham briefly attended the Methodist-sponsored Southwestern Kansas College in Winfield. He left in 1893 and, though barely twenty, sought a PREACHING appointment in the Methodist Church. For the next two years, Parham supplied pulpits in Eudora and Linwood. In 1895, impatient with "the narrowness of sectarian churchism," Parham withdrew from Methodist supervision and became an itinerant evangelist. His under-

standing of Christianity was shaped by his conversations in the many country homes in which he boarded. He came to believe in the annihilation of the wicked. Shortly after his 1896 marriage to Sarah Thistlewaite, a Kansas Quaker (see FRIENDS, SOCIETY OF), he became desperately ill and renounced medical help to pray for healing. When he regained strength, he began preaching healing in the ATONEMENT and praying for the sick.

In 1898, Parham established in Topeka the Bethel Healing Home, a city mission, and a magazine called the *Apostolic Faith*. Its early issues revealed his growing fascination for restorationist thought (see RESTORATIONISM). By 1900, he was teaching a baptism with the Holy Spirit, an experience that he understood to "seal the bride" for the prophesied marriage supper of the lamb. Only those so sealed could hope to escape "the power of the DEVIL before this age closes." Parham thought this was the only essential baptism, so for a time he stopped practicing water BAPTISM. He had long been unsettled about water baptism, vascilating between triple and single immersion. He eventually made up his mind to offer only single immersion. He endorsed AngloIsraelism and gained local repute for his costumed lectures in support of a Jewish homeland (see PHILO-SEMITISM). A tour of ministries that shared his interest in God's plan for the end times brought him to Shiloh (near Lewiston), Maine, a community led by Frank Sandford. Among its several institutions was The Holy Ghost and Us Bible School, a place where the curriculum "gave way to the Holy Ghost's latest." Impressed with the flexibility and potential of this setting, Parham returned to Topeka and opened his own small Bible school in a rented property on the edge of the city (see BIBLE COLLEGES AND INSTITUTES).

With the Bible as the only text and Parham as the sole teacher, the school muddled through a few months before Parham advanced the idea that the Bible evidence of Spirit baptism was tongues speech. During the first days of 1901, Parham and various students spoke in tongues. The school disintegrated, and Parham did not regain a following until 1903, when the dramatic healing of a woman in Galena gave him an audience. Over the next few years, he attracted growing crowds in southern Kansas, southwestern Missouri, eastern Oklahoma, and Texas. The Houston area seemed particularly promising, and Parham opened another Bible school there in 1905.

Among several African Americans in Parham's following was William J. Seymour. In January 1906, Seymour left Houston to pursue preaching opportunities in Los Angeles. He had not yet spoken in tongues, but he had embraced Parham's insistence that tongues always evidenced Spirit baptism. Two more African Americans traveled from Parham's Houston center to join Seymour. First in a mission, then in a house, then in an abandoned Methodist church on AZUSA STREET, the three proclaimed what Parham had taught was the Apostolic Faith. It was nothing new, they assured; rather, it was New Testament Christianity restored. Seymour spoke in tongues in April, as did others, black, white, and Latino, who "tarried" with him for Spirit baptism. People from the local networks that pursued holiness soon discovered these eager advocates of a baptism with the Holy Spirit marked by specific uniform evidence. Before long, Seymour found himself the central personality in a movement that promised to exceed Parham's efforts. Parham's views, developed and tested in the country's rural heartland, now took their place in the religious mix of one of the country's growing cities. The urban context brought new issues into focus—ETHNICITY, GENDER, class—and offered an impersonal backdrop. In Galena, Kansas, or Joplin, Missouri, speaking in tongues brought public notice. In Los Angeles, tongues speakers took their place among other practitioners of unusual religious practices. The urban context brought immigrants into the mix, which facilitated the spread of the movement even as it forced adherents to address racial issues.

Los Angeles and Beyond

Between 1906 and 1908, the curious and the earnest mingled at the Apostolic Faith mission at Azusa Street. The Los Angeles area was home to various groups intrigued by spiritual empowerment and practical holiness. Formal Holiness associations, the large congregation of Joseph Smale's revival-seeking New Testament Church, the supporters of the maverick Phineas Yoacum, and members of the World's Faith Missionary Association were a few of those attracted by the Apostolic Faith claims. Popular religious periodicals carried reports of the emotion-packed, ecstasy-filled meetings, and people from elsewhere arrived to see for themselves. By September 1906, when the mission began publishing a monthly paper, *The Apostolic Faith,* the movement, billed as "Pentecost," claimed widely scattered devotees. It was old-time revivalism with a difference: a combination of premillennialism, spiritual gifts, and yearning for holiness framed the view that this restored Apostolic Faith was a sure sign of the imminent return of Christ.

By all accounts, the changing crowds at the Azusa Street mission did not come for the preaching. Rather, they arrived to decide about the movement's validity and perhaps to stay and seek the baptism with the Holy Spirit. Some tongues speakers thought themselves gifted with specific languages and promptly set off to do missionary evangelism, confident that God would supply their needs. People constantly came and went, and the convinced spread the message and modeled the behavior in the places they visited along the way. Convinced that the supernatural regularly invaded the natural, such people tended to see all of life through spiritual lenses. They understood themselves to be part of the cosmic struggle between good and evil. What they did, and, more importantly, what they were, mattered in the grand scheme of things. The vast majority of the convinced were working people without much financial security. The Apostolic Faith transformed their identity by making these ordinary people channels of powerful spiritual gifts that promised the global progress of God's kingdom.

Among the many who visited the Azusa Street Mission were a few who influenced the emergence of a revival of a Pentecostal Movement from the chaos. New networks built on already established connections. Some Azusa Street enthusiasts—whether they visited the REVIVALS or were convinced from afar—sent personal letters to far-flung Christian workers offering detailed descriptions of revival scenes and sharing the teaching that they heard. They also corresponded with family and friends. Others quickly targeted a larger audience and submitted their testimonies and accounts to the popular press, raising the possibility of new networking. In such ways, Azusa Street added yet another layer to the intertwined contacts that already characterized the conservative evangelical American religious landscape. Azusa Street attracted its share of people with restless pasts who had an experience and promptly traveled wherever opportunity offered to advocate the Apostolic Faith. But with the restless devout and the curious onlookers mingled some who represented existing or emerging networks and ministries. Their experiences reveal how the Pentecostal movement built on established associations.

One such person was Charles Harrison Mason, a gifted black preacher whose evangelism concentrated in Mississippi, Tennessee, and Arkansas. One of a group of black BAPTISTS whose interest in holiness forced them from the Arkansas Negro Baptist Convention, Mason was a founder of the CHURCH OF GOD IN CHRIST, the first of the sanctified churches in the African-American religious tradition. In March 1907, Mason and two associates visited Azusa Street and spoke in tongues. Their enthusiasm about the Apostolic Faith separated them from others in the Church of God in Christ who ultimately left the group and assumed another name. Mason remade the part of his old network that embraced Pentecostalism the nucleus of a new association that he built into a large Pentecostal denomination.

Gaston Barnabas Cashwell had a considerable following among white Holiness people in North Carolina. Reports in the popular religious press set him on a six-day rail journey to Los Angeles where he embraced the message and spoke in tongues. His enthusiasm for the Apostolic Faith proved contagious. In 1907, Cashwell won such small Southern holiness associations as the Fire-Baptized Holiness Church, the Pentecostal Holiness Church, and the FREE WILL BAPTIST CHURCH to the new movement. From his first base in Dunn, North Carolina, Cashwell toured the South and won recruits to the Movement. His visit to Cleveland, Tennessee brought the ambitious, impressionable founder of the small Church of God, Ambrose Jessup Tomlinson, into the Pentecostal Movement.

For two years, Azusa Street offered an inspirational environment. People newly committed to the Apostolic Faith needed a practical theology to establish boundaries for their movement and apply its teachings to their lives. The small Southern holiness associations that identified with the emerging movement had already established their identities and relationships to other communities of faith. They added to their existing doctrinal statements a crisis experience of baptism with the Holy Spirit evidenced by tongues. Charles Mason, too, had a framework to which to add his new views. Many others followed the advice of two gifted Chicago Pentecostal preachers, William Durham and William Piper, who dedicated their considerable energies to clarifying the implications of Pentecostalism for life and practice. They accomplished this by preaching, traveling to the network of conventions that sustained the far-flung movement, and, most importantly, by editing new publications that quickly gained national circulation.

William Durham, pastor of a congregation on Chicago's busy North Avenue, concerned himself with two primary tasks, both under a general determination to define the movement's core by drawing its boundaries. First, he built a case for tongues as initial evidence of Spirit baptism; second, he articulated an alternative to WESLEYAN HOLINESS teaching on sanctification. He used his paper, *The Pentecostal Testimony* (published "as the Lord provides") to make his case for these and other matters. His congregation stood on a busy thoroughfare in the heart of a neighborhood peopled by German, Swedish, and Norwegian immigrants. Italians and Persians also found Durham's mission, and these associations made Durham a participant in the planting of Pentecostalism in ITALY and BRAZIL, as well as in the evangelistic efforts of Chicago Persian settlers in their homeland.

On the city's South Side, William Piper edited *The Latter Rain Evangel* and preached at a church known as The Stone Church. More irenic than Durham, Piper cultivated for Pentecostalism the network he had served earlier as an overseer of John Alexander Dow-

ie's Christian Catholic Apostolic Church. By 1907, Dowie's now disenchanted following were ripe for Pentecostal CONVERSION. Before his downfall, Dowie had told them to anticipate a restoration of apostolic ministries and spiritual gifts to the church, and some of Dowie's erstwhile followers concluded that Pentecostalism fulfilled Dowie's expectations. Piper published countless sermons, testimonies, and accounts of Pentecostal conventions and camp meetings. The sermons that he provided gave the movement's faithful a simple theological framework in which to understand their experiences. Piper's sermons also exposed unacceptable teaching and practice, and, like Durham's writings, made the case for boundary setting. People who could not attend conventions at these two Chicago "Pentecostal powerhouses" could share the riches by reading the texts. These Chicago papers circulated the same words to people who never met and began to establish a common set of expectations and beliefs among scattered independent Pentecostals.

Beliefs

In the Pentecostal Movement's formative years after 1906, adherents shared certain beliefs. At Azusa Street, people identified generally with orthodox Christianity. They regarded the movement not as a departure, but rather as a fulfillment or realization of prophecy in the last days. The *Apostolic Faith* insisted that no sectarian controversies marred the religious excitement. This was simply the restoration of experience that predated any division of the church: it was, therefore, for every Christian. The Los Angeles mission did not embrace Charles Parham's annihilationism or the fine print of his ESCHATOLOGY.

That said, certain reigning assumptions must be clarified. One became Pentecostal by experiencing the baptism with the Holy Spirit marked by speaking in tongues. People prayerfully "tarried" or "waited on God" for this experience for varying lengths of time. But repeated exhortations encouraging seekers to pursue purity as a prerequisite to power made it amply evident that the governing views were traditional revivalistic notions of human sinfulness and salvation by faith, and that the leaders subscribed to the Holiness Movement's understanding of sanctification. Azusa Street advocated two works of grace (justification and sanctification) followed by a crisis enduement with power (Spirit baptism). Before long, people began to quibble about the timing of tongues. Might one have an assurance of Spirit baptism but not speak in tongues until later, if at all? Was it right to single out one gift over others? Suppose that one manifested another spiritual gift but never spoke in tongues? Disagreements about tongues, although not immediately widespread, have been a persistent challenge to the Pentecostal Movement.

Azusa Street attendees heard much about divine healing. Early Pentecostals taught that physical healing was "in the atonement" and was to be appropriated in the same way that one accepted forgiveness of Sin. They opted for faith instead of medicine. Prayer cloths and anointing with oil were common as the believing community agonized in prayer for the sick. Christ's second coming also figured prominently in sermons, songs, testimonies, and interpretation of messages in tongues. The absolute certainty of imminent judgment permeated the community. The faithful rejoiced in their readiness for the Rapture and saw in their religious movement a "sign of the times."

Pentecostals often embraced the view that one could rely on God for temporal needs. They called this "living by faith," and accounts of miraculous provision in the nick of time stirred others on to relinquish earthly security and devote themselves to propagating their faith. Charles Parham taught that any true Pentecostal minister must embrace faith living. The gainfully employed enabled this practice by generous giving.

The grand task of world evangelization animated their worldview and provided purpose and identity. Just as the Pentecostal Movement was the "latter rain" of biblical prophecy, so its devotees were God's end-times ambassadors. Some believed that tongues speech enabled proclamation, but more understood the defining moment of Spirit baptism as an enduement with power for service. Their certainty of an imminent end, as well as their reading of the biblical text (especially Acts 1:8) convinced them to equate "service" with evangelism, both domestic and overseas. Pentecostals both exploited and created opportunities to proclaim their message. Their new worldview allowed ample space for their entrepreneurial instincts.

Once the initial fervor that birthed the movement subsided, clarifications of doctrine and practice continued. Experience taught most Pentecostals that speaking in tongues did not replace the study of foreign languages. Unreserved commitment to faith living sometimes brought hardship, whereas untracked freewill offerings carried a potential for inequities and dishonesty. And Holiness teaching on sanctification failed to satisfy everyone. New revelations of doctrine threatened to separate the faithful decisively from orthodox Christianity. Some saw a need for boundaries and worked to provide them.

Among the revelations was one that proved particularly divisive. By 1913, influential Pentecostal preachers were proclaiming the Oneness of the Godhead (focusing this oneness in Christ) and the need for rebaptism "in the name of Jesus" rather than under a Trinitarian formula. The resulting controversy dragged on for several years and resulted in the emergence of a cluster of black and white "Jesus Only" non-Trinitarian associations (see Anti-Trinitarianism).

The attack on Holiness teaching resulted in another rift. The energetic Chicago evangelist William Durham proclaimed "the finished work of Calvary" and denied the need for a second definite work of grace. In Durham's view, sanctification was progressive rather than instantaneous. Like many early Pentecostals, Durham worked best when he felt most embattled, and he maximized the possibilities of the Holiness Movement as enemy. By World War I, Pentecostals had taken sides and divided into factions defined by Wesleyan and non-Wesleyan understandings of sanctification.

Race

Some scholars have made much of the interracial character of early Pentecostalism. The Azusa Street Mission, headed by the African American William Seymour, informally assisted by a group of women and men, some black, some white, seems to suggest an intrinsic racial and gender equality at the movement's core. In one of his many books, Frank Bartleman, a Pentecostal enthusiast, gushed that "the color line had been washed away in the blood" at Azusa Street. Accounts testify to the mingling of the races and to some reservations about this.

Yet African Americans found it impossible to coexist with the Latinos who soon found the Azusa Street Mission, and blacks forced a separation. Charles Parham, the self-styled progenitor of Pentecostalism, found it impossible to endorse the racial mingling he saw at Azusa Street when he visited in the fall of 1906. When people left Azusa Street, evidence suggests that they did not manifest markedly different racial attitudes than they had before they went. White Pentecostals enjoyed hearing the black Charles Mason preach, and during World War I interracial audiences were not unknown. Because Mason's Church of God in Christ was registered with the state, Mason may have permitted some white workers to be credentialed under its name, but no cooperation followed. In the 1920s, evidence suggests that the Church of God in Christ unsuccessfully attempted to create a "white branch." By then, most emerging Pentecostal denominations, Oneness and Trinitarian, were divided by race.

Evangelist Aimee Semple McPherson seemed to be an exception. A Canadian with ties to the Salvation Army, McPherson became the first Pentecostal evangelist of note in the larger world of American revivalism. Known as "Sister," she made much of her identification with the ordinary people who flocked to her services. Her homespun sermons and easy mingling with people everywhere won her a national following, though she established her base in Los Angeles. Her travels around the country brought her into contact with many people on the margins. She evangelized as diligently among Southern cotton pickers as she did in front of the thousands who crammed tents and auditoriums to hear her. A black preacher immersed McPherson's daughter; the gypsy population named her an honorary queen; and Mexicans in the Los Angeles area responded with gratitude to her attention to their needs. Yet she accepted money from the KU KLUX KLAN, as did other Pentecostal preachers in the 1920s.

The racial picture is at best foggy. It is safe to say that for the most part, Pentecostals mirrored the racial attitudes of their cohorts of similar race, class, and gender.

Reception

The Pentecostal Movement evoked several distinct responses, including ridicule, opposition, and indifference. The ridicule is most readily apparent in the press. Pentecostal behavior and claims offered ample entertainment for reporters hungry for stories. They published purported handwriting in tongues ("chicken scratch") and vivid descriptions of bizarre emotional behavior. They belittled Pentecostal claims of miraculous ability in foreign languages and, along with serious reporting, occasionally featured moments that emphasized the movement's contrasts to orderly WORSHIP. The first story to appear in Los Angeles papers told readers of "weird howlings" that "make the night hideous." Indianapolis reporters, referencing tongues speech, nicknamed Pentecostals the "gliggybluks people." Some reports were more serious. Readers of the Des Moines papers followed suggestions of child abuse occasioned by crowded surroundings and emotional ecstasy.

Opposition took several forms. Outright persecution—vandalism, arson—expressed the anger of some. At times, Pentecostals seemed to invite such response. Vehemently anti-Catholic and intent on denouncing sin (strictly construed), they made many enemies. They did not often mince their words: enemies were necessary to their self-understanding. If none appeared, then they talked of spiritual warfare. They charged their universe and their personal activities with spiritual significance. Some chose to leave the "dead" or "carnal" churches that resisted Pentecostal views. Others were asked to leave when their new enthusiasms clashed with church expectations.

Some opposition assumed thoughtful forms. Although their attacks on Pentecostals were virulent, the evangelicals closest in background to Pentecostals offered written reasons for their objections. Sometimes theological, sometimes sociological, these reasons revealed much about both Pentecostals and their evangelical opponents. For Holiness people, Pentecostalism precipitated family strife. From non-Wesleyans interested in the baptism with the Holy Spirit, Pentecostalism elicited a flood of texts expanding on the cessation of spiritual gifts, the vagaries of a handful of Pentecostal leaders (Charles Parham was arrested on an accusation of sodomy in San Antonio in 1907), and the excesses of their behavior. A few psychologists attempted explanations of tongues speech.

Most people proved indifferent. In 1906 *The Apostolic Faith* envisioned a great restoration to which the Christians would flock. It presented the Pentecostal Movement not as a denomination, but rather as an eschatological sign. By 1908, it was evident that the religious, cultural, and intellectual elites had not noticed. The Pentecostal Movement would not immediately focus on unity across Protestantism; in fact, its initial enthusiasm about unity foundered on internal divisions.

Meanwhile, around the world, some established Western missions also found it advisable to respond directly to Pentecostals. China Missionaries of the CHRISTIAN AND MISSIONARY ALLIANCE, a faith mission, complained that Pentecostals disrupted missionary work by targeting missionaries rather than working among the Chinese. In INDIA, the Women's Christian Missionary Union, citing the mission's commitment to avoid divisive teaching, forbade their missionaries from participating in tarrying meetings. A Congregationalist missionary in Hong Kong and a Swedish Baptist missionary in Brazil declared that Pentecostals had abused hospitality and taken over congregations of hard-won converts.

Organization

The first Pentecostal denominations had been formed as small regional associations before the Pentecostal Movement emerged. Mostly Southern, they included the Pentecostal Holiness Church, the Church of God (Cleveland), the Church of God in Christ, and the Free Will Baptist Church. Charles Parham's loosely organized Apostolic Faith Movement also began before the Pentecostal Movement emerged in 1901 among its small following. Its hub followed Parham, settling finally with the Parham family in Baxter Springs, Kansas. Another Apostolic Faith Movement under the leadership of Florence Crawford, a Holiness advocate and early worker at Azusa Street, established its headquarters in Portland, Oregon.

The principal Oneness groups are the United Pentecostal Church and the PENTECOSTAL ASSEMBLIES OF THE WORLD. A large contingent of the African-American congregations known as "Apostolic" subscribes to Oneness theology.

Among non-Wesleyan American Pentecostals, the ASSEMBLIES OF GOD, organized in 1914, with headquarters in Springfield, Missouri, claims the largest membership. The INTERNATIONAL CHURCH OF THE FOURSQUARE GOSPEL, with headquarters in Los Angeles, incorporated in 1927 to organize McPherson's following. The Pentecostal Church of God, located in Joplin, Missouri, also identifies with this wing of the Movement.

Many early Pentecostals resisted any organization beyond the local church, claiming that the Movement would soon devolve into "dead denominations." Opting instead for the "freedom of the Spirit," they gathered in independent churches or loose associations held together by entrepreneurs, publications, camp meetings, itinerant preachers, faith homes, and Bible schools. This independent sector has played a significant—although often ignored—role in the larger Movement. Its vigor became especially apparent after World War II with the emergence of the charismatic renewal. Prominent Pentecostals like ORAL ROBERTS, Gordon Lindsay, T. L. and Daisy Osborne, and A. A. Allen became the leading edge of a throng of media and platform personalities who thrived outside Pentecostal denominations and played a role in shaping the Charismatic Movement.

After World War II, Trinitarian white American Pentecostals began meeting annually in the Pentecostal Fellowship of North America. In the 1990s, the group reorganized and, for the first time, embraced African-American Trinitarian Pentecostals, especially the Church of God in Christ, as well as some charismatics. The resulting association took the name PENTECOSTAL/CHARISMATIC CHURCHES OF NORTH AMERICA. Representatives of some Trinitarian Pentecostal groups worldwide gather every three years in the Pentecostal World Conference (see PENTECOSTAL WORLD FELLOWSHIP). Both the U.S. and the world fellowships convene representatives of a small fraction of the total constituency.

Education

The Pentecostal Movement supported ministerial training schools almost from its inception. The understanding of Spirit baptism that defined the Movement emerged in a Bible school setting. The early Movement sponsored numerous similar schools offering no diplomas and featuring a few—sometimes only one—teacher. A few of the early Movement's most outspoken voices rejected even these informal schools as inappropriate for ministerial training. Instead, they advocated training for pulpit ministry by apprenticing to a preacher and serving in a congregation. Advocates of schools gained ascendancy, however. The larger Pentecostal denominations supported Bible institutes that eventually became accredited Bible Colleges. Others remained unaccredited and offered shorter courses. The largest Pentecostal-sponsored liberal arts colleges are Lee University in Cleveland, Tennessee and Evangel University in Springfield, Missouri.

Both the Assemblies of God and the Church of God sponsor accredited SEMINARIES, and the Church of God in Christ is a partner in the Interdenominational Theological Center in Atlanta.

The Charismatic Movement

In post–World War II America, several factors contributed to the emergence of wide interest in the Holy Spirit. Ambitious Pentecostal evangelists used modern media to reach new audiences. In the early 1950s, more than 1,000 evangelists registered with the Dallas-based Voice of Healing, a cooperative clearing house headed by Gordon and Freda Lindsay. Across America, these people preached divine healing wherever they could find an audience. They announced "signs and wonders evangelism," believing that miracles confirmed the immediate availability of answers to personal prayer. They spoke in tongues, but also gave prominent places to other New Testament gifts like words of wisdom, healing, and prophecy. Moreover, they charged Pentecostal denominations with choosing bureaucracy and programs instead of the power of Pentecost. The FULL GOSPEL BUSINESSMEN'S FELLOWSHIP INTERNATIONAL had the support of evangelist Oral Roberts. Over the next decades, this Fellowship sponsored large meal events that featured testimonies and spiritual gifts in nonthreatening environments. People reluctant to attend a Pentecostal church learned about spiritual gifts at such events. The women's counterpart came to be known as Women Aglow.

During the 1950s, leaders of the NATIONAL COUNCIL OF THE CHURCHES OF CHRIST, USA (NCCCUSA) noticed an exploding interest in Protestantism beyond the mainstream in LATIN AMERICA. JEHOVAH'S WITNESSES, Seventh-day Adventists, Mormons, and Pentecostals thrived in places where mainstream Protestant efforts languished. In a June 9, 1958, article in *Life Magazine,* Union Theological Seminary President

HENRY PITNEY VAN DUSEN posed the question, "Is There A Third Force in Christendom?" Recent events had brought United States Pentecostals to the attention of Van Dusen and his cohorts. For the most part, Pentecostals existed beyond the purview of urban Protestant elites. Early in the 1950s, a white South African Pentecostal, DAVID DU PLESSIS, arrived unannounced at the Manhattan offices of the NCCCUSA to share his Pentecostal testimony. The resulting interest transformed the unassuming Du Plessis into a leader among a growing interdenominational constituency interested in the baptism with the Holy Spirit. Du Plessis soon ran afoul of his friends in the Pentecostal Movement, because he did not insist that people abandon mainline denominations before praying for the baptism with the Holy Spirit. Whereas the Pentecostal Movement understood Spirit baptism in the context of verbally inspired scripture as part of a sequence that began with an evangelical new birth, Du Plessis assured members of historic faith traditions that the Holy Spirit stood ready to energize their spiritual lives where they were.

In 1960, both *Time* and *Newsweek* carried the story of a tongues-speaking Episcopal priest at St. Mark's Church in Van Nuys, California. National publicity surfaced of other members of mainline Protestant congregations who practiced spiritual gifts. In the 1960s, large numbers of Catholics began speaking in tongues, and huge summer rallies at Notre Dame Stadium gave visibility to a growing national movement. These new tongues speakers tended not to be evangelical in theology, usually had more education and greater professional standing than adherents of the older Pentecostal Movement, and often testified that they found their commitments to their historic traditions deepened by their Spirit baptisms. Intrigued as well by other New Testament spiritual gifts, charismatics within and across traditions relished spontaneous worship interrupted by tongues, interpretations, prophecies, words of knowledge, and words of wisdom. They found simple, repetitive worship choruses useful in their corporate gatherings. In the turbulent 1960s, some so-called "Jesus People" found charismatic informality appealing.

Despite opposition from many Pentecostals, the Charismatic Movement attracted many adherents and began producing its own literature and music. Some denominations created offices to coordinate renewal activities. Over time, the renewal found its niche, and some participants, disappointed by the renewal's domestication, chose to leave their denominations. Those who left sometimes mingled with disaffected Pentecostals in independent settings associated with well-known personalities, schools, or publications. During the 1970s and 1980s, Jim and Tammy Faye Bakker's PTL network modeled forms of charismatic piety and drew tens of thousands to their hub in Charlotte, North Carolina. On the West Coast, Paul Crouch's TBN network catered to a similar audience. Presidential aspirant PAT ROBERTSON presided over an East Coast media outreach and directed Regent University in Virginia Beach.

The Charismatic Movement spawned a variety of teachings that claimed center stage until displaced. The "health and wealth" gospel or "name it and claim it" teaching guaranteed specific this-worldly benefits from God. The Vineyard Movement and its leading figure, one-time rock musician John Wimber, emphasized worship, and they exerted a strong influence on popular evangelical song. The Kansas City Prophets stressed prophetic ministry. In the late 1980s, the Toronto Airport Vineyard unexpectedly came into the limelight, featuring emotional behavior—laughter, tears, "slayings in the Spirit," prophetic words—that came to be known as the Toronto Blessing. Thousands traveled from Europe and AUSTRALIA seeking personal renewal. In the 1990s, the focus shifted south to the Brownsville Assembly of God in Pensacola, Florida, where an emotion-packed revival displaced congregational life, incorporated behaviors associated with Toronto, drew an international audience, and spawned imitators. The progress of such parts of the charismatic movement can be glimpsed in the monthly magazine, *Charisma*.

Western Pentecostalism and World Christianity

Starting in 1906, Pentecostal movements emerged in many parts of the world. Mexicans joined the earliest throngs at the Azusa Street Mission in Los Angeles. Small, interrelated Pentecostal groups in Northern Europe maintained loose ties to the United States but were also shaped by local concerns. In Britain, for example, the CHURCH OF ENGLAND's identification with the government during World War I effectively transferred the organizing center of Pentecostalism from a Church of England parish into the hands of nonconformist conscientious objectors, many of whom spent the war years in confinement (see NONCONFORMITY). The Scandinavian Pentecostal movement worked outward from the tiny Methodist presence in Oslo and a small group of pietistic Swedish Baptists in Stockholm. A Pentecostal movement emerged in Italy after Italian immigrants who had embraced the movement in Chicago began traveling the globe to share their testimonies in extended family networks. Nowhere in Europe did Pentecostalism seriously challenge the religious establishment.

The growth of Pentecostalism outside the West has been far more dramatic than in the United States and Europe. News of the movement's first stirrings in Los Angeles quickly traveled through missionary networks and reached places like KOREA and India, where revivals in progress helped shape small, receptive constituencies. The Western movement's earliest ambassadors targeted missionaries and won a handful of influential converts, Western and native, among established Christian groups in CHINA and parts of AFRICA.

For decades in most places, Western Pentecostal denominations experienced at best modest growth abroad. In the last quarter of the twentieth century, indigenous movements (especially in the Southern Hemisphere) that often featured healing, exorcisms, prophecy, and ecstasy saw explosive growth. A wide range of Christian movements in places like Korea, BRAZIL, China, and sub-Saharan Africa often embrace charismatic style, if not outright Western Pentecostal THEOLOGY. Millions of Latin Americans belong to Pentecostal churches, both missionary and indigenous. Millions more participate in either Catholic charismatic worship or in historic Protestant congregations that have embraced Pentecostal-style worship. The Pentecostal Movement's emphasis on miracles, spiritual empowerment, healing, and exorcism give it wide appeal in places attentive to the supernatural. Traditionally MISSIONS oriented, the Western Pentecostal movement easily raises millions of dollars every year to fund evangelism. Pentecostal constituencies around the world share the missionary vision and scatter evangelistic endeavors around the globe, exploiting modern communications capabilities for anti-modern ends.

By any reading, from modest beginnings, the Pentecostal Movement has become a force in world Christianity. The Charismatic Movement also has international reach, and together these impulses have influenced the story of modern Christianity, at least as it is told from the West. Westerners—especially Pentecostals and Charismatics—readily label much of contemporary Christianity outside the West as "Pentecostal." Especially in the Southern Hemisphere, its preoccupation with the Holy Spirit and the supernatural seems to Western minds to be phenomenologically (and therefore essentially) similar. Yet unnuanced use of the label "Pentecostal" for large segments of burgeoning indigenous Christianity may mask the particularities of indigenous movements that are grounded in much that is local while sharing the universals of Christian faith. African historians Ogbu Kalu and Inus Daneel are among those who propose that the rich historical and theological variety indigenous groups manifest suggests that these groups may use other identity markers besides those typically associated with Western Pentecostalism.

References and Further Reading

Anderson, Robert Mapes. *Vision of the Disinherited.* New York: Oxford University Press, 1979.

Blumhofer, Edith L. *Aimee Semple McPherson: Everybody's Sister.* Grand Rapids, MI: Eerdmans, 1993.

Blumhofer, Edith L. *Restoring the Faith.* Chicago, IL: University of Illinois Press, 1993.

Cox, Harvey. *Fire from Heaven.* Reading, MA: Addison-Wesley, 1995.

Dempster, Murray, et. al. *The Globalization of Pentecostalism: A Religion Made to Travel.* Irvine, CA: Regnum Books, 1999.

Harrell, David Edwin. *All Things Are Possible.* Bloomington, Indiana University Press, 1976.

Martin, David. *Pentecostalism: The World Their Parish.* Malden, MA: Blackwell, 2002.

Quebedeaux, Richard. *The New Charismatics II.* San Francisco, Harper & Row, 1983.

Robert, Dana. "Shifting Southward: Global Christianity Since 1945," *International Bulletin of Missionary Research*, April (2000): 50–58.

Stoll, David. *Is Latin America Turning Protestant?* Berkeley, University of California Press, 1990.

Wacker, Grant. *Heaven Below.* Cambridge, MA: Harvard University Press, 2001.

EDITH BLUMHOFER

PERIODICALS, PROTESTANT

Periodicals that publish articles that have a direct impact on the thought and practice of Protestant denominations or Protestant adherents are manifold. Periodical literature provides a unique window into the life and thought of the many kinds of Protestant endeavors, a window that allows readers to peer into the unfolding present and explore the literary past. Although Protestantism has used periodical literature across the past two centuries to advance its cause, the identification of a periodical as Protestant is presently not an easy matter. The denominational publishing houses, an obvious source for Protestant periodicals, have seen declining subscriptions, whereas nonaffiliated or nondenominational independent publishers continue to grow. Academic journals from affiliated SEMINARIES and institutions of higher learning, along with learned societies and international Protestant organizations, provide access to theoretical and practitioner-oriented Protestant periodical publications. In an age of ecumenical dialogue, inter-religious understanding, and scholarly exchange of ideas, one must examine the scope and content of a periodical, as well as identify the author and/or editor, rather than assume a periodical does or does not have an impact on the thought and practice of Protestant Christians.

Dual Role of Periodical Literature

Periodical literature provides readers with access to the contemporary discourse and current thinking of a corporate body. Periodical articles emerge from many contributors; thus over time a large number of voices add to the discourse particular to any periodical. When collected over many decades, past volumes of a periodical document the issues and trends encountered by the corporate body that produced the volumes and reveal the perspectives and terminology used to address those issues. In this sense the printed periodical, in all of its various formats and frequencies, is a powerful medium for expressing current matters and for discovering past tendencies. Thus periodicals have a dual role: charting the contemporary scene as it unfolds and preserving for future investigation the historical pathways articulated by many voices. Protestantism's core themes cast in the journalistic forms of its periodical publications, coupled with a multiplicity of contributing voices and religious expressions, make the periodical literature an important resource for contemporary insight and historical study.

Protestant periodical literature, issued with some frequency (for instance, weekly, bimonthly, monthly, quarterly, semiannually, or annually, hence the name periodical) takes such forms as newspapers, newsletters, popular magazines, and professional and scholarly journals. Periodicals vary widely depending on their stated purpose and mission; the process of soliciting, receiving, and evaluating submissions; and the editor's inclusion and assessment of those contributions. The articles that appear in a periodical may be the products of an editorial staff, solicited from experts, or refereed (selected by qualified experts or passed through a rigorous blind peer review process).

As a type of communication media, periodicals tend to commit to print ideas that often are not typically expressed in other scholarly print-based media like books and specialized dictionaries or encyclopedias. Because books and encyclopedias often take many months, sometimes years, to create, there is less spontaneity to the ideas expressed than in the periodical literature. This means that periodical literature provides significant access to the contemporary discourse on important issues or treatments of recurring topics, given that the amount of time between the writing of an article and its appearance in print is considerably shortened—and may be as quickly corrected or criticized.

Periodical literature may also be distinguished from the host of religious tracts and brochures, World Wide Web pages, and other popular writing that is quickly consumed and then vanishes. The printed periodical relies on a critical editorial process on which many periodicals depend to protect and maintain their reputations as official publications of a corporate body or as reliable sources of scholarly expression. A library's bound collection of periodicals or microfilm collections are an invaluable resource because they preserve and archive periodical discourse for generations to come.

Finding Protestant Periodicals

What exactly a Protestant periodical is and how one can be identified as such, are not easy questions to answer. There are innumerable periodicals that publish articles that exert a direct impact on the thought and practice of Protestant denominations or Protestant adherents, ranging from the obvious to the obscure. Identifying such articles requires some recognition of the stylistic and formal features of periodicals, as well as skill in knowing where and how to search for them.

An important resource for identifying periodicals is *Ulrich's International Periodicals Directory* (New Providence, New Jersey: R. R. Bowker), published annually. This directory provides the most complete listing of periodicals currently being issued. In addition to an index of journal titles, many Protestant titles are listed under the general heading "Religions and Theology" and a large number of periodicals are listed under the heading "Religions and Theology—Protestant." While Ulrich's directory is indeed helpful, the list is neither fully accurate nor complete, and thus cannot be taken as definitive.

Library catalogs identify periodical titles that are held in library collections, and thus are an important resource for identifying current periodicals as well as those that have ceased publication. Despite the effort to use controlled subject heading access in library catalogs, searchers can find Protestant periodicals under the headings "Protestants—Periodicals," "Protestantism—Periodicals," and "Protestant Churches—Periodicals." Additional titles may be listed under the subject headings "Evangelicalism—Periodicals" and "Reformed Churches—Periodicals." One may also try searching under the more general subject heading "Christianity—Periodicals." The more specific headings like "Bible—Periodicals," "Preaching—Periodicals," or "Theology—Periodicals" are as apt to retrieve periodicals published by Roman Catholic, Eastern Orthodox, or Jewish presses as well as Protestant ones, so additional scrutiny is needed.

Denominational Periodicals

Readers looking for "Protestant" periodical literature might start with known denominational publications. Newsletters, general interest magazines, missionary magazines, and devotional literature focus on grass-roots issues confronting the DENOMINATION. These usually contain current news and human interest stories demonstrating how or where the denomination engages the larger world. Denominational magazines treat the practical expressions of religious life and church work often aimed at specific church functions like MISSIONS and ministry. Often, historical anecdotes related to the denomination or church history are treated. Denominational publications may also serve as platforms to advance doctrinal concerns. These magazines provide insight into the popular culture, current thinking, and dominant issues facing a particular denomination, its leaders, and its constituents. Some examples of denominational periodicals include *The Lutheran* from the EVANGELICAL LUTHERAN CHURCH IN AMERICA, *The Mennonite* from the Mennonite Church USA (see MENNONITES), and THE SALVATION ARMY'S *War Cry*.

One way to identify denominational periodicals in a library catalog is to look for a subject heading under the name of a particular denomination, for example, "Lutheran Church—Periodicals" or "Baptists—Periodicals" (a librarian may be able to help identify the appropriate subject heading). A search using a denominational name in the author field (as corporate author) or as words entered in the title field of a library catalog may retrieve periodical titles as well. Periodical titles change over time and many titles cease publication. Changes in information sharing technologies, like the Internet, and declining subscriptions have reduced the number of general denominational magazines over the past decade (LeBlanc 1992:74; Case 2001:23).

Independent Protestant Periodicals

Although denominational periodicals have been losing strength over the past decade, the independently published general interest magazine continues to have a significant place among Protestant readers. Two well-known and widely available Protestant periodicals, *The Christian Century* and *Christianity Today*, are produced by independent publishing corporations and between them represent a wide spectrum of Protestant issues, from traditionally liberal to traditionally conservative.

Published by the Christian Century Foundation, *The Christian Century* originated in 1884 as a denominational publication of the Christian Church (DISCIPLES OF CHRIST) (Toulouse 2000:80). It received its present name in 1900, and became a nondenominational journal with a decidedly liberal Protestant stance under the editorship of CHARLES CLAYTON MORRISON in 1908. Because of its longevity, *The Christian*

Century has been the subject of a number of historical reflections and dissertations (Marty 1978:939).

Christianity Today, established in 1956 under the editorial command of CARL F. H. HENRY, began with and maintains a clearly articulated conservative evangelical perspective. That publishing venture has grown into the publishing conglomerate Christianity Today International, a nonaffiliated corporation that publishes nearly a dozen titles with decidedly conservative evangelical interests including *Christianity Today, Campus Life, Leadership, Books & Culture, Christian History, Christian Parenting Today, Christian Reader, Marriage Partnership, Men of Integrity, Today's Christian Woman, Your Church*.

Periodicals from Affiliated Historical Societies

Many Protestant denominations have organized commissions on history or host official historical agencies that specifically focus on the collection, preservation, and publication of related histories. Articles in historical journals cover a wide range of the denomination's past: explorations on the founding figures, lives of famous preachers, assessments of theological ideals, reassessments of social roles, reporting on regional or local churches, and oral histories. Some examples include *Anglican and Episcopal History,* published by the Historical Society of the EPISCOPAL CHURCH; *The Mennonite Quarterly Review,* produced by the Mennonite Historical Society, Goshen College, and the Associated Mennonite Biblical Seminary; *Methodist History,* published by the General Commission on Archives and History of the UNITED METHODIST CHURCH; and *The Journal of Presbyterian History,* published by the Presbyterian Historical Society (see PRESBYTERIAN CHURCH, U.S.A.). Clearly these kinds of Protestant periodicals continuously advance the historical scholarship peculiar to Protestant people, places, ideas, and events.

Affiliated Schools of Theology and Seminary Periodicals

Journals published by theology schools and seminaries having denominational affiliations provide access to the ideological currents and intellectual history of Protestant academe. These periodicals tend to be forums for advancing the scholarly discourse particular to the school; thus readers should not presume that the content or the authors are Protestant. Where the journal is published by the faculties, these periodicals favor peer-reviewed scholarly articles or invited contributions from recognized experts in the theological disciplines. Some typical examples include *The As-*

bury *Theological Journal, The Calvin Theological Journal, Harvard Theological Review, Lexington Theological Quarterly, The Princeton Seminary Bulletin,* and *Sewanee Theological Review*—journals whose titles reflect the names of their parent institutions.

Theology schools can be a rich source of Protestant thinking from an international perspective. Some examples of this are such periodicals as *Communio viatorum,* a theological journal published by the Protestant Theological Faculty of Charles University in the Prague, Czech Republic; *Theological Review of the Near East School of Theology,* published by the school of that name in Beirut, Lebanon; and *Taiwan Journal of Theology,* issued from Taiwan Theological College and Seminary in Taipei, Taiwan. These journals reflect regional interests and often exhibit extensive cooperation with academic colleagues from other religious traditions.

Theology schools and seminaries also sponsor a variety of special topics journals treating THEOLOGY and biblical studies. For instance, *Horizons In Biblical Theology* is a publication of Pittsburgh Theological Seminary; *Journal of Theology* is a joint publication of the Methodist Theological School and United Theological Seminary, both of which are in Ohio; and *Interpretation: A Journal of Bible and Theology* is published by Union Theological Seminary and the Presbyterian School of Christian Education. These examples demonstrate the commitment to a critical study of theology and the BIBLE and the dissemination of that research to an educated ministry and interested laity.

Scholarly Societies and Professional Associations

Periodicals published by scholarly societies, professional associations, and religious orders serve an important function of advancing scholarship and provide an outlet for members to express their expertise. Biblical studies, church history, MISSIOLOGY, liturgics, pastoral ministry, theology, and other communities of practice organized around topics of particular concern for Protestant organizations are replete—although even these are not exclusively Protestant domains. Many scholarly organizations seek members with a variety of perspectives to enrich the scholarly treatment of topics and enhance inter-religious dialogue. Some examples include *Doxology: A Journal of Worship,* an annual journal of The Order of Saint Luke published for its members who are largely involved in Protestant WORSHIP; and *Missionalia,* the journal of the Southern African Missiological Society based in the University of South Africa, which represents a

broad range of perspectives on mission work in AFRICA with a predominantly, although not exclusively, Protestant orientation. More clearly Protestant are journals from those societies whose purpose or mission statements specify the journal's scope. For instance, *The Scottish Bulletin of Evangelical Theology* allows for free expression of its contributors "within the broad parameters of historical evangelicalism," and *The Journal of the Wesleyan Theological Society* expresses its social scope by stating that it is published by "a fellowship of Wesleyan-Holiness scholars." Many periodicals issued by scholarly societies are circumscribed by a mission statement or statement of purpose; statements such as these are useful for determining the scope and content of a journal.

European Protestant Periodicals

A wide variety of periodical literature is published by European Protestant endeavors; these may be identified in library catalogs using the resources and techniques outlined above or searched using the journal article indexing services described below. Many European periodicals published in German, French, Dutch, Italian, or Spanish receive wide distribution in academic and theological libraries worldwide, making them accessible for a large readership.

Protestantism's global reach is expressed and experienced through the periodical literature emerging from various countries and languages. European Protestant periodicals tend to use Protestant-specific terminology like "evangelical" and "reformed" (or their cognates) in the titles or to identify the corporate body sponsoring the periodical. For instance, *Reformatio: Zeitschrift für Kultur Politik Religion* is published in Zurich and offers a European Protestant perspective on the intersections of CULTURE and religion. Another example, *Zeitschrift für Evangelische Ethik,* seeks to publish manuscripts that advance a dialog on ethical issues with a distinctly European as well as Protestant point of view.

The same rubrics as those outlined above apply for identifying European Protestant periodicals; that is, one can seek by denomination, historical societies, affiliated schools of theology and seminaries, and scholarly societies and professional organizations. Many European periodicals treat the writings, history, and thought of the sixteenth-century reformers. For example, a search using MARTIN LUTHER's last name as a word in the title of a journal leads one to the journal *Luther: Zeitschrift der Luther-Gesellschaft,* a periodical published by the Luther Society in Hamburg, GERMANY. Research on the writings, history, and thought of Swiss reformer HULDRYCH ZWINGLI is published in the periodical *Zwingliana: Beiträge zur ge-*

schichte Zwinglis der Reformation und des Protestantismus in der Schweiz, by the Institute of Swiss Reformation History at the University of Zurich.

One other option for finding European Protestant periodicals is to look under the terminology of national origin reflecting the period of established churches in Scandinavia, for example *Studia Theological: Scandinavian journal of theology.* Other titles reflecting this history include DENMARK: *Dansk Teologisk tidsskrift;* the NETHERLANDS: *Nederlands theologisch tijdschrift;* NORWAY: *Norsk teologisk tidsskrift;* and SWEDEN: *Svensk teologisk Kvartalskrift.*

Periodical Indexing and Abstracting Services

There are two primary article indexing services that are valuable resources for identifying subjects in religion and the periodicals that treat those subjects. For scholarly works, the *ATLA Religion Database,* produced by the American Theological Library Association, provides indexing and some online full-text access to scholarly and international periodicals, many of which, although not exclusively, emerge from Protestant sources. The *Christian Periodical Index,* produced by the Association of Christian Librarians, focuses more particularly on conservative evangelical periodicals, exclusively English language and overwhelmingly North American in origin. Abstracts of articles may be found in *Religious and Theological Abstracts,* a service which regularly surveys over 400 titles in religion.

Additional indexing and abstracting coverage for journals in theology can be found in *Theology in Context,* produced by the Institute of Missiology in Germany. This print-only resource offers indexing of selected periodicals in theology (not just Protestant) by global region (Africa, Asia, Oceana, and LATIN AMERICA) and provides some brief summaries of selected articles. These summaries are useful for identifying the interests of the individual contributors and for determining the perspectives of the journals that advance their work. *Index Theologicus* (formerly *Zeitschrifteninhaltsdienst Theologie* [ZID] now published by Mohr Siebeck) regularly indexes over 640 titles, predominantly those of European origin. The *Australasian Religion Index,* produced by Australian and New Zealand Theological Library Association and Centre for Information Studies, Charles Sturt University, covers journals published in AUSTRALIA and NEW ZEALAND.

In addition, some denominations produce annual volumes of periodicals specific to the denomination, for instance, the Southern Baptist Periodicals Index or the Latter Day Saints Periodicals Index; these may be useful for intradenominational research.

See also Higher Education

References and Further Reading

Banman, Christina A. "The Study of Religion: Nineteenth Century Sources and Twentieth Century Misconceptions." *Method and Theory in the Study of Religion* 1 (1989): 160–185.

Case, Patricia R. "Parting Words of Advice: Never Stop in a Threshold." *The Disciple* (January/February 2002): 23–24.

"The End of an Era in Religious Journalism" (editorial). *Christian Century* 92 (April 9, 1974): 348.

Herb, Carol Marie. *The Light Along the Way: A Living History Through United Methodist Women's Magazines.* A special report to the Women's Division, General Board of Global Ministries, The United Methodist Church, Nashville, Tennessee, 1994.

LeBlanc, Doug. "The Decline of Two Historic Magazines." *Christianity Today* 36 (September 14, 1992): 74.

Marty, Martin. "Editorial Comment: Appropriating Morrison's Legacy." *Christian Century* 95 (October 11, 1978): 939–941.

Suiter, David E. Review of *Woman's Work for Woman,* 1871–1885; *Woman's Work: A Foreign Missions Magazine,* 1885–1924; *Women and Missions,* 1924–1946; and *Home Mission Monthly,* 1886–1924. In *Microform Review* 24 (Fall 1995): 188–189.

Switzer, Les. "Reflections on the Mission Press in South Africa in the 19th and Early 20th Centuries." *Journal of Theology for Southern Africa* 43 (June 1983): 5–14.

Toulouse, Mark. "The Origins of the *Christian Century,* 1884–1914." *The Christian Century* 117 (January 26, 2000): 80–83.

DAVID E. SUITER

PERKINS, WILLIAM (1558–1602)

Puritan theologian. Perkins, the most influential Elizabethan theologian, was born in Marston Jabbett, Warwickshire in 1558. Educated in Christ's College, CAMBRIDGE UNIVERSITY, he gained his M.A. in 1584. A fellow until 1595, he became lecturer at Great St. Andrews in 1584, notable both as a preacher and as a pastor. Perkins was formidably erudite, on the basis of wide reading of contemporary theologians, as well as of Fathers and Schoolmen, and helped by a retentive memory. He reflected carefully on method, hermeneutics, and communication, and sought to show how THEOLOGY aided living well. Uninterested in party or POLITY, he had a sharp eye for troubling issues.

Perkins's first book, *Antidicsonus* (1584), was on logic and was followed by a refutation of astrology and popular almanacs in 1585, given that he was concerned at the limitations of popular piety when measured against the BIBLE. In 1588, his *Foundation of the Christian Religion* sought to correct that piety more effectively than the official CATECHISM. In addition, he set out the foundations and signs of authentic piety in ways that strongly influenced the seventeenth-century CONVERSION narrative and Puritan COVENANT theology. European Pietist theological writers also drew on his insights into practical divinity and his resolution of the problems of assurance, which were troubling in many of the Reformed churches. The Dutch and German churches were especially influenced by his writings, which were sold in large numbers in translation.

As well as writing popular books with a large circulation, Perkins was an influential expositor of second-generation CALVINISM. In *Armilla aurea* (1590), translated as *Golden Chain,* he set out the connections between more learned writers and the concerns of ordinary Christians and working CLERGY. Cambridge and the CHURCH OF ENGLAND saw sharp debates in the 1590s over ELECTION and damnation because some, like Peter Baro (1534–1599), attempted to find alternatives to overly strict readings of the Augustinian heritage, to lessen anxieties about SALVATION. By contrast, Perkins saw the most consoling pastoral care growing from a theology of radical GRACE. In a major book *Concerning the manner and order of predestination* (1598), Perkins sought to demonstrate the essential rationality of the divine order. The work sparked a fierce debate in THE NETHERLANDS, where Arminius attempted to counter Perkins's approach, leading to the Synod of Dort and a split in the Reformed Church, the reverberations of which lasted into the nineteenth century.

Perkins was not interested in the debates on polity that divided the British churches, although he rejected separatist claims and was close to some in the classical movement. Content to leave such issues to individual conscience, he was more interested in building networks of the godly LAITY and informing their use of conscience to guide their daily life. *A discourse of conscience* (1596) and *On vocation* (1603) mapped some of the terrain. That discussion was enlarged by Perkins's discussion of cases of conscience. He adopted a very different method than that used by Roman Catholic casuists, and inspired a number of other English writers during the seventeenth century to work the subject more fully. Perkins aimed to foster discernment in living a responsible Christian freedom. *Christian Oekonomis* (1609) set out the foundations of Christian family life, creating another widely read genre.

Although very critical of contemporary Roman Catholicism, Perkins had a strong sense of catholicity. *A reformed Catholike* (1597) sought to show how English Christians should inwardly transform the Church of England. Expositions of the Lord's Prayer, the Apostles' Creed, and the first Protestant patrology in English underscored his commitment to reconstructing the Catholic heritage and encouraging others to draw from the wisdom of the Fathers. His historical perspective was more narrowly focused than RICHARD HOOKER's, but was nonetheless influential in keeping mainstream PURITANISM in touch with patristic theology, as well as with the Bible. His commentaries grew out of his preaching. He judiciously resolved contemporary disputes, but never obscured the scope of the whole book or let his audience forget that the message was to be lived. They show how theological reflection and life intersect, and were influential in shaping the directions of Puritan exegesis well into the seventeenth century, as well as helping to form the mainstream of Puritan spirituality.

Perkins's earnest and searching style of ministry provided a model for many entering parishes and lectureships. To assist them he wrote *The arte of prophecying,* translated from the Latin of 1592 in 1606. It was a deliberate departure from rhetorical patterns, designed to let the message of the Bible make its own impact, because the language was plain and simple, but based on the most careful preparation. Ramist categories clarified the logic of his method, leading readers to the order of the Divine mind. The pattern of DOCTRINE, reason, and use reappeared in the Westminster *Directory,* which influenced Presbyterian WORSHIP until the nineteenth century. *Of the calling of the ministry* (1605) was the first practical handbook for ministers since the introduction of the REFORMATION into ENGLAND. Its counsel was influential, even after the Puritan movement fractured, helping to shape a Protestant mindset that powerfully influenced British religion and society.

Perkins had married in 1595 and left his wife Timothye with a modest inheritance with which to rear their four children, after he died of complications attributed to a kidney stone. His influence lived on in people such as WILLIAM AMES and others whose lives had been powerfully shaped by his personal influence and writing. He was one of the most important sources of Reformed theology in the English and Irish established churches, in New England Puritanism, and in the English Dissenting bodies (see DISSENT).

See also Salvation

References and Further Reading

Primary Source:

Perkins, W. *The Workes.* 3 vols. Cambridge, UK: Legatt, 1616–1618.

Secondary Sources:

Augustine, J. H., ed. *Commentary on Hebrews.* New York: Pilgrim, 1991.

Breward, I., ed. *The Work of William Perkins.* Appleford, UK: Sutton Courtenay, 1970.

Malone, M. T. "The Doctrine of Predestination in the Thought of William Perkins and Richard Hooker." *Anglican Theological Review* 52 (1970): 103–117.

McKim, D. *Ramism in William Perkins*. New York: Lang, 1987.

Muller, R. A. "Perkins' A golden chaine." *Sixteenth Century Journal* 60 (1978): 69–81.

Sheppard, G. J., ed. *Commentary on Galatians*. New York: Pilgrim, 1989.

Spinks, B. D. *Two Faces of Elizabethan Anglican Theology*. London: Scarecrow, 1999.

IAN BREWARD

PETERS, THOMAS (c. 1738–1792)

African-American abolitionist. Peters was kidnapped into SLAVERY in 1760, marched to the African coast, and placed aboard a slave ship. A member of the Egba branch of the Yoruba, he was about twenty-two years old at the time. Taken to French Louisiana, he was sold to an English master, who probably gave him the name that he would carry for the remainder of his life. About 1770 he became the property of a Scottish immigrant in Wilmington, North Carolina. Here he learned and practiced the trade of a millwright, found a wife, and began a family. Peters escaped from slavery in 1776. He and other runaway slaves from the Cape Fear region of North Carolina were soon organized into a company of Black Pioneers who fought for the British side in the American Revolution.

When the war ended in 1783, Peters was one of nearly three thousand black loyalists evacuated from New York City and eventually settled in Nova Scotia and New Brunswick. In spite of British promises, they never obtained citizenship rights, tools, provisions, or tillable land. Peters soon emerged as their leader. In 1791, after petitioning colonial officials numerous times, he took their case to ENGLAND, where abolitionists helped him gain a hearing from the British government. He returned home with a promise that Britain would transport blacks to the new African colony of SIERRA LEONE if they wished, and provide better land for those who chose to remain. Peters recruited nearly 1,200 migrants. After reaching Sierra Leone in 1792 he continued to speak for his fellow settlers in the face of sickness, inadequate supplies, slow land distribution, and the paternalism of British officials. He and his fellow black Methodists in the colony called for a popularly elected government. Peters died some four months after arriving home in the continent of his birth.

See also Africa; Methodism, Global; Slavery, Abolition of

References and Further Reading

Fyfe, Christopher H. "Thomas Peters: History and Legend." *Sierra Leone Studies* 1 (1953): 4–13.

Gibson, Ellen. *The Loyal Blacks*. New York: G. P. Putnam's Sons, 1976.

ROY E. FINKENBINE

PETRI, LAURENTIUS (1499–1573)

Swedish Lutheran reformer. Laurentius Petri, like his older brother Olaus, was born in Orebro, SWEDEN, and educated in the local Carmelite Monastery. Eventually he matriculated at the University of Wittenberg, where he came under the strong influence of MARTIN LUTHER. Little is known of Laurentius's student career, but upon his return to Sweden in 1527 he was immediately appointed to the faculty of the University of Uppsala. Four years later the king, Gustav Vasa, declared the archbishopric to be vacant after a ten-year hiatus. A national assembly of CLERGY gathered in Stockholm and elected Laurentius by a margin of 150 to 20 to be the archbishop of Uppsala, making him the first evangelical archbishop in Sweden. The Erasmian reform-minded bishop of Vasteras, Petrus Magni, who himself had been ordained by Pope Clement VII in 1524, performed the ordination. Thus the historic episcopate was preserved in the Church of Sweden, unlike in DENMARK and NORWAY where a parish priest, JOHANNES BUGENHAGEN of Wittenberg, ordained seven "superintendents" for the two churches.

During the 1530s, Laurentius, together with his brother, slowly introduced a conservative evangelical renewal in the face of Catholic opposition. After the death of his brother in 1552, Laurentius continued the slow ecclesiastical transformation of the Church of Sweden. During the reign of Erik XIV (1560–1568) Laurentius successfully opposed the royal pressure that sought to turn Sweden into a Calvinist nation. In 1571 Laurentius reached the pinnacle of his reforming career when his *Church Ordinance* was adopted as the law of the land during the reign of John III (1568–1592). However, it was not until the Church Assembly of Uppsala in 1593 that the Church of Sweden officially adopted a Lutheran confessional subscription.

See also Lutheranism; Lutheranism, Scandinavia

References and Further Reading

Ahlberg, Bo. *Laurentius Petris nattvards uppfatning*. Lund, Sweden: Gleerup, 1964.

Yelverton, Eric. *An Archbishop of the Reformation: Laurentius Petri Nericius Archbishop of Uppsala 1531–1573*. London: Epworth Press, 1958.

TRYGVE R. SKARSTEN

PETRI, OLAUS (1493–1552)

Swedish Lutheran reformer. Sometimes called the "Luther of Sweden," Olaus Petri was born in Orebro, SWEDEN, the older brother of Laurentius Petri. He matriculated at the University of Wittenberg in 1516, where he heard Luther lecture on Galatians and Hebrews and witnessed the Indulgence Controversy with John Tetzel firsthand. In 1518 Olaus returned to Sweden as a zealous advocate of the new reform movement. There was no thought of a break with Rome as yet. The Leipzig Debate and the DIET OF WORMS were still off in the future.

Upon his return to Sweden, Petri preached and taught in Strengnas for five years. In 1523 Gustav Vasa was crowned king of Sweden in Strengnas after his successful revolt from DENMARK after the "Stockholm Bloodbath" of 1520. The new king became acquainted with the evangelical preacher, and the following year Olaus was appointed to the prestigious pulpit of Saint Nicholas in Stockholm, where he continued to preach and advocate a conservative, evangelical REFORMATION. In 1526, the year after his marriage, Olaus published a short CATECHISM and a Swedish translation of the New Testament wherein he outlined in a Preface his *sola scriptura* principle that undergirded his reforming work (see BIBLE TRANSLATION). In 1529 he published a Swedish Manual and two years later a Swedish Mass that enabled the CLERGY to conduct WORSHIP in an evangelical manner. Together with his brother Laurentius he introduced a slow ecclesiastical transformation into Sweden during the sixteenth century that culminated in the Church Assembly of Uppsala in 1593 declaring that Sweden and its royal house were to be Lutheran.

See also Lutheranism; Lutheranism, Scandinavia

References and Further Reading

Primary Source:

Hesselman, Bengt, ed. *Samlade skrifter af Olavus Petri.* Uppsala, 1914–1917.

Secondary Sources:

Bergendoff, Conrad. *Olavus Petri.* Philadelphia, PA: Fortress Press, 1965.

Ingebrand, Sven. *Olavus Petris reformatoriska askadning.* Lund, Sweden: Almquist, 1964.

Jäger, Tobias. *Olavus Petri, Reformator in Schweden und andere skandinavistische Beiträge.* Bonn, Germany: Wiksell, Verl. für Kultur und Wiss., 1995.

Yelverton, Eric. *The Manual of Olavus Petri, 1529.* London, 1953.

TRYGVE R. SKARSTEN

PHILANTHROPY

Philanthropy is the disposition to love humankind and the will to act accordingly. Jesus commanded that this love was superseded only by love for God. WILLIAM JAMES called CHARITY a shift of the "emotional center" that brings "tenderness for fellow-creatures." Protestant reformers looked to Scripture as a guide to a person's motive for charity. They saw that Jesus's teachings went beyond law when he advised a rich young man to sell his possessions and give the proceeds to the poor. Protestant agencies to ease poverty had their roots in biblical, classical Greek-Roman, and later Jewish and Christian practice. After glancing at the etymology of "philanthropy," we will look at historical biblical, classical, medieval, and Protestant-era charities.

Etymology of Philanthropy

The Hebrew word *chesed* describes God's loving-kindness as being far beyond human comprehension. Hosea 6:6 says that God expects us to respond to his mercy by being merciful: "for I desire mercy, and not sacrifice." In Greek, *philanthropia* marries two words: *philia* (love) and *anthropos* (mankind). In the New Testament (NT) *philanthropia* occurs twice, in Titus 3:4 and Acts 28:2. Paul says that when *philanthropia*, "the goodness and the love to men of God our Savior appeared, it was not by works wrought in righteousness, which we ourselves had done, but by his own mercy that he saved us." He advises those who put their faith in God to "plan how to practice fine deeds" (Titus 3:4,8). Classical Greek used *philia* and *agape* interchangeably as a fondness for doing good. Christian usage ennobled *agape* to mean universal love for friend and foe alike. The Greek *charis*, from which we get charity, means grace, charm, and loveliness. It is kindness done with grace and received with gratitude. In classical Greece *charis* was an offering to three *Charites*—goddesses who conferred grace. The Latin word *beneuolentia*, beneficence in English, means well wishing, and is synonymous with *philanthropia*.

In English, philanthropy means charity, almsgiving, and social concern. In 1567 philanthropy was first defined in the *Oxford English Dictionary* (*OED*) as a "disposition or active effort to promote the active happiness and well-being of one's fellow men." In 1693 English poet John Dryden said that English adopted the Greek word because "we have not a proper word in English to express a sentiment of love for mankind." In 1827 Edward Lytton mused that "while I felt aversion for the few whom I knew, I glowed with *philanthropy* for the crowd which I knew not." The *OED* found in 1869 that "enlightened philanthropism of ENGLAND [had come to mean] the formation of charitable societies, district-visiting, distribution of tracts, and teaching in charity schools." Philanthropy had become more institutionalized. The *OED*'s second meaning, "the love of God to man," draws on scripture, the basis for sixteenth-century Protestant authority.

Judaic, Classical, Early Christian, and Islamic References to Philanthropy

Mediterranean culture valued gifts. Roman emperors gave *donatives* (gold) to the army and civil servants. *Sportulae* were special-occasion gifts to high officials; seldom were gifts given to commoners. Thus Greeks and Romans saw philanthropy as a civic duty that demonstrated one's community standing. Patrons gave to clients, not to the poor, although stoics saw justice as piety and advocated fair treatment of the poor on whom a beneficent judge would have mercy. Cynics reveled in poverty; it brought virtue to the soul. The Roman bread dole aimed at maintaining peace in cities, not to aid the destitute as a philanthropic act.

At first Christians resisted gifts, even those presented to the church, because humans could not hope to replicate God's gift of the Holy Spirit; however, cultural forces seized the church. Pope Boniface (619–625) sent Queen Aelthelburh a silver mirror and a gold and ivory comb to gain Northumbrian king Eadwin's CONVERSION. Gregory of Nazianzus exchanged books at Easter with Christian friends. Cyril of Alexandria sent gold "blessings" to the Emperor in Constantinople. Constantine sent gifts to his cathedral in Rome for popes from whom he had received gifts. In the late Roman period voluntary sharing was an ideal in Roman, Greek, Byzantine, Jewish, and Christian utopian communities. Christian views of philanthropy increasingly mirrored that of general Mediterranean culture as the church became the dominant voice in the civilization.

JUDAISM regarded almsgiving as an obligation that God rewarded. Jews made gifts to the poor in private. Priests set aside a chamber in the temple where donors secretly deposited gifts, and individuals could draw from this treasury without shame. Jews cared for the poor in an organized way (Deuteronomy 14:28–29), an obligation that continued into the Christian era, when Jewish leaders distributed alms from community food chests.

Early Christians adopted Judaism's view of alms as an obligation. The New Testament urged provision for the poor, especially widows and orphans, but also prisoners, strangers, and the sick. The postapostolic church encouraged almsgiving, along with fasting and prayer, as acts of penance. Church Fathers cast wealth in positive terms when it enabled giving. After Constantine legalized the church, it organized leper colonies, hospitals, and orphanages. Bishops became civic patrons of the poor, and several church fathers declared that all excess wealth belonged to the poor. Almsgiving could remit small sins and benefit the souls of the departed. For early Islam, giving alms, *zakat* in Arabic, meant to be pure in heart. *Zakat* appears thirty-two times in the Qur'an as an obligation and a form of purification. The central mosque gathered and distributed alms, as in Judaic and Christian practice.

Medieval Philanthropy

Churches of the Middle Ages vested bishops and Monasteries (see MONASTICISM) with philanthropic responsibilities. Hospices offered food and shelter to the poor and hospitals cared for the sick before 400 CE, first in Byzantine churches and then in the Roman West. From the twelfth century, the increasingly wealthy and powerful Roman church, including even Franciscans, paid less attention to the condition of the poor and more to ecclesiastical and theological debates in cathedral schools, universities, and church councils. Preaching orders, such as Augustinians and Dominicans, fought heresy and paid little heed to the deprivation of rural peasants and the urban poor. Later, eighteenth-century ENLIGHTENMENT thinkers charged that church-run hospitals were inefficient because they were more concerned with a patient's SALVATION than with their cure. As science matured, increasing concern for clinical observation did not eliminate the moral concern for a patient's well-being that was embedded in the hospital's early Christian history.

Protestant Reformers and Sixteenth-Century Philanthropy

First-generation Protestant reformers accepted charity precedents set by Old Testament prophets, Jesus, and Church Fathers, as well as ideas of contemporary renaissance humanists. Although their zeal focused on religious reform, concern for exploited peasants and the urban poor only sporadically matched their focus on THEOLOGY and church POLITY. MARTIN LUTHER and JOHN CALVIN eloquently addressed Jesus's theme of two loves—for God and humanity (Matthew 22:37, Luke 10:27). When reformers appropriated Roman Catholic lands and buildings, they also assumed state-funded charities. In the REFORMATION's wake the Statute of Charitable Uses (1601) passed into Anglo-Saxon law to provide government aid to the poor, aged, orphans, hospitals, universities, and schools. The new Protestant civic rulers acted through state churches. For Luther the theology of the PRIESTHOOD OF ALL BELIEVERS translated into a social system in which all vocations were equal and the surplus from economic activity belonged to the poor.

Society of Friends (Quakers), Seventeenth Century

After the Reformation there was no central Protestant ecclesiastical authority (no pope), and philanthropic activity lodged in reformed churches, foundations, and governments. Several reforming groups deserve attention. Among seventeenth-century Protestant reformers the SOCIETY OF FRIENDS (Quakers) led the way in philanthropy. As advocates of WOMEN's equality, they offered a voice and vote to every church member. They embraced PACIFISM and the ABOLITION OF SLAVERY. In 1796 they opened the first asylum in England, and in 1813 ELIZABETH FRY began to reform the treatment of prisoners. She also opened homeless shelters (1820) and libraries for seamen. Into the twenty-first century Friends Service Committees remain as sources of innovative philanthropy.

Methodists, Eighteenth to Nineteenth Centuries

In the mid-eighteenth century JOHN WESLEY's Methodists (see METHODISM) formed a social creed that the U.S. Federal Council of Churches adopted in 1912. Wesley's charismatic leadership, his brother Charles's hymns, and an inclusive Arminian (see ARMINIANISM) theology of salvation formed a democratic working-class society with a multileveled governance system that produced a mass reform movement. Along with Congregationalists (see CONGREGATIONALISM), Presbyterians (see PRESBYTERIANISM), and BAPTISTS, Methodists founded colleges, a focus of eighteenth-century philanthropic activity, including schools for freedmen after the American CIVIL WAR. While they saved souls, they also condemned habits that made life miserable, particularly drunkenness (see TEMPERANCE and Methodist FRANCIS ELIZABETH WILLARD). When ABOLITION OF SLAVERY divided Wesleyans, many left the Methodist Episcopal Church. Wesleyan Methodists opposed SLAVERY, PRIMITIVE METHODISTS battled for women's right to preach, and FREE METHODISTS fought for free pews. Although reformers lost the battle for women's pulpit equality in the nineteenth century, the conflict revived in the 1950s with success in nearly every Protestant sect. Church schism in Britain and America in the nineteenth century grew out of Methodists' passion for democracy and liberty.

Christian Socialism and the Social Gospel, Mid-Nineteenth Century

In the mid-1800s Protestantism spawned CHRISTIAN SOCIALISM and the SOCIAL GOSPEL. Reacting to mid-century ideas of Karl Marx, Chartists, Henry George and others, John Malcolm Ludlow, CHARLES KINGSLEY, and FREDERICK DENISON MAURICE in England, and WASHINGTON GLADDEN and WALTER RAUSCHENBUSCH in America strove to create an economic/social order that enhanced character and aided the rural and urban poor. They sought to do what Jesus would have done in the nineteenth century. Liberal reformers saw progress as inevitable. A wide spectrum of Evangelicals and Modernists (see EVANGELICALISM, MODERNITY) modified Protestantism's singular focus on soul-salvation and embraced the idea that the environment of the poor must change as a precondition to and an outcome of their conversion. Young Men's and Young Women's Christian Associations (see YMCA, YWCA); Boy and Girl Scouts; the SALVATION ARMY; home and foreign MISSIONS; and the institutional churches sought to uplift the homeless, jobless, and sick, as well as drunkards, prostitutes, prisoners, and those who needed schooling. Generous gifts of rich and poor donors supported the work of Protestant institutions in spite of just criticism that their motives were paternalistic and imperialistic, and that they administered their charitable enterprises unscientifically. Yet, even when mixed with dross, their philanthropic motives often paid off in gold.

Foundations, Eighteenth to Twenty-First Centuries

From the eighteenth to the twenty-first centuries rich industrialists organized foundations for charitable giving. Benjamin Franklin had set up a fund in 1790 to aid worthy young men, and in 1829 English philanthropist James Smithson created the Smithsonian Institution. After the U.S. Civil War John D. Rockefeller, Andrew Carnegie, Henry Ford, and others set up foundations to distribute assets from their huge untaxed fortunes efficiently. Many entrepreneurs were Protestants who responded to Jesus's command to love one's neighbor as oneself. By 2000 there were 53,000 U.S. foundations making well over $16 billion in annual grants, mainly to 220,000 religious and secular nonprofit service providers. In all there were over 700,000 U.S. charities. A third of the foundations, worth more than $1 million each, controlled 90 percent of foundation assets of over $230 billion. For reasons not easy to identify, philanthropy has not been as pronounced in Europe as it is in North America. In the early twentieth century, most philanthropy in Germany came from Jewish donors.

Church and State

The U.S. government did not superintend the integrity of religious bodies that received grants because of

First Amendment separation of state and church (see CHURCH AND STATE, OVERVIEW), whereas the British government established controls. In 1969, however, Congress began to regulate foundations, both by taxing their invested income and by scrutinizing their benefactors' tax deductions. Congress was also concerned that foundation donations to politicians and political causes might affect public policy in a self-serving manner. Whereas the motives of donors ranged from humane to self-serving, foundations provided essential support to Protestant social agencies, churches, and colleges.

Community-based Philanthropy

Around 1900, nonsectarian community-based groups formed to raise money and distribute funds to local charities, including Protestant service agencies. These joint ventures operated as Associated Charities, Charity Organization Societies, Community Chests, the United Way, and community foundations. Other agencies formed to monitor the efficiency of charities. The American Institute of Philanthropy, National Charities Information Bureau, Better Business Bureau, and the Evangelical Council for Financial Accountability set standards for fund-raising costs (not over 40 percent of a budget) versus money spent on programs (at least 60 percent). They called for audits by external accountants, a board of directors composed of persons not in the employ of the charity, and modest executive salaries and overhead.

Late Twentieth-Century Developments

An article in *The New York Times* (July 6, 2000) reported a Deutsche Bank survey in which 112 donors worth at least $5 million each were interviewed. Responses indicated that donors were moving away from writing checks to traditional charities and toward giving to global charities that produced measurable results. New philanthropists preferred giving through their own charitable trusts to gain personal involvement. The report of the survey indicated that principal areas of concern were: (1) education; (2) "poverty, inequality, hunger, affordable housing and health care for the uninsured"; (3) arts and culture, listed by less than a third; and (4) "family stability and economic growth."

In the 2000 U.S. presidential race, both major party candidates argued for giving more government aid to the poor through "faith-based" social agencies. Congress had written "charitable choice" into the 1996 Welfare Reform Act that required government agencies to consider equally grant applications from faith-based and non–faith-based social services for senior citizen care, child welfare, housing, and substance abuse prevention, for instance. Religious groups applauded the idea. Groups that favored church–state separation opposed it preferring nonsectarian welfare administered by the state. Sixteenth-century Protestant reformers, who followed a medieval model where governments aided social services and schools of state churches, would applaud faith-based philanthropy. However, church–state separation, fostered in the United States in the 1780s, has inhibited state support for church-run social programs when they propagate sectarian theologies. Church control over local philanthropy weakened during the depression of the 1930s, when church coffers quickly ran dry. Moreover, historians claimed that the Protestant era of U.S. history was ending in the mid-twentieth century, when the government or foundations increasingly funded Protestant social programs once financed by church members. Meanwhile Europe's state churches declined in membership and in influence in the public square.

References and Further Reading

Bremner, Robert H. *American Philanthropy*. Chicago: University of Chicago Press, 1988.

Cragg, Gerald R. *The Church and the Age of Reason, 1648–1789*. Hammonsworth, Middlesex: Penguin, 1970.

Curti, Merle. "American Philanthropy and the National Character." *American Quarterly* 10 (1958): 420–437.

Cutler, Anthony. "Gifts & Gift Giving." In *Late Antiquity*, edited by G. W. Bowersock, et al., 287–288. Cambridge: Belnap Press, 1999.

Harvey, Susan. "Almsgiving." In *The Oxford Companion to Classical Civilization*, edited by Simon Hornblower and Antony Spawforth. New York: Oxford University Press, 1998.

Keck, L. E. "Poor." In *The Interpreter's Dictionary of the Bible*, supplemental volume, edited by Keith Crim. Nashville, TN: Abingdon, 1962.

Küng, Hans. *Christianity: Essence; History; Future*. New York: Continuum, 1995.

Lebowitz, Holly J. "Charitable Choice." *Sojourners* July–August (2000): 28–33.

Monsma, Stephen V. *When Sacred and Secular Mix*. Lanham, MD: Rowman and Littlefield, 1996.

Moore, George F. *Judaism*. Cambridge: Harvard University Press, 1927.

Southern, R. W. *Western Society and the Church in the Middle Ages*. New York: Penguin Books, 1970.

Spiker, Paul. *Social Policy: Themes and Approaches*. New York: Prentice Hall, 1995.

NORMAN H. MURDOCH

PHILIP OF HESSE (1504–1567)

German ruler. Born November 13, 1504, Philip was the offspring of Wilhelm II (1468–1509), scion of the Hessian House of Brabant, and Anna (d. 1525), daughter of Magnus II of Mecklenberg. He became the major lay leader of Protestantism during the early period of the REFORMATION. Philip ruled from 1518 to 1567, except during his imprisonment by the emperor (1547–1552), when he ruled with the help of his son Wilhelm IV. Although the Hessian court became a center of Lutheran sympathies in the early 1520s, Philip personally converted to LUTHERANISM IN 1524, after a fortuitous meeting with PHILIPP MELANCHTHON. He then played the roles of main political protector of Protestantism and secular counterpart to MARTIN LUTHER.

Philip's foreign and internal religious policies reveal his importance as a Protestant. Until 1547, Philip's foreign policy discouraged the emperor and anti-Protestant princes from using force to restore Catholicism and thus secured the future of Protestantism. His domestic religious policy created a territorial church that was based on the theology of the Lutheran AUGSBURG CONFESSION but was singularly tolerant of dissenters and committed to dialogue. In the War of Schmalkald, Philip was taken prisoner (1547–1552). Upon his death on March 31, 1567, Philip left Hesse religiously united under a common church synodal structure and university but politically decentralized under his four legitimate sons: Wilhelm, Ludwig, Philip, and Georg.

Philip's Protestant Foreign Policy

Philip engaged in a Protestant foreign policy based on the likelihood that Catholic opponents would try to use force to end the Lutheran "problem." But not all Lutherans shared Philip's assumptions. Beginning in 1524, Philip worked to unite the Protestants in a powerful preventative alliance. Philip went to great lengths to convince the reluctant Saxons to join. In 1528, based on the dubious revelations of Roman Catholic preparations for war against the Protestants, he proposed a preventative war. He held the MARBURG COLLOQUY in 1529, hoping to remove the religious reservations of the Saxons. To overcome political reservations, Philip and his advisors developed a constitutional argument for resisting the emperor's authority.

Philip gained Saxon support only after the emperor threatened to attack the Protestants (1530). Mostly under Philip's leadership, the SCHMALKALDIC LEAGUE protected Protestants from 1531 until the Schmalkaldic War (1547). During this period, Philip and MARTIN BUCER achieved the Württemberg (1534) and Wittenberg (1536) Concords. These theological agreements between the Upper German and Saxon theologians made the League more acceptable to the north Germans. In 1534, Philip unilaterally strengthened the Protestant position by ousting the Catholic Hapsburgs from Württemberg, denying them a land that connected their territories, and spread Lutheranism to Württemberg. The Braunschweig War (1542), arranged by Philip, removed the main anti-Protestant state under Duke Heinrich from Lower Germany and spread Lutheranism to Braunschweig-Wolfenbüttel.

Philip's Protestant Domestic Policy

Following the DIET OF SPEYER (1526), Philip undertook to settle the religious and church–state issues in Hesse. He called an extraordinary synod to consider the issues at Homberg in Hesse (October 1526), involving representatives of the New and Old Doctrines. He employed Franz Lambert of Avignon (1487–1530) to draw up the articles for debate. The synod produced a constitution for the immediate reformation of Hesse following Luther's teaching (*Reformatio ecclesiarum Hassiae*), characterized by a territorial church with a synodal structure and a significant princely role. Historians have disputed whether its provisions were Lutheran, democratic, and unique (meaning alien to Hesse). The *Reformatio* is probably best understood as a mixture of Philip's belief that dialogue best resolves religious matters and his assumption that its details were Lutheran. Based on Luther's advice, the details of the *Reformatio* were implemented gradually.

Philip worked to bring concord between Protestants domestically. Rather than denying the ministry to Zwinglians, the Landgrave insisted that Lutherans and Zwinglians not reproach one another from their pulpits. He commanded them to teach the uneducated LAITY only the use value of the LORD'S SUPPER and not to discuss the nature of the Christ's presence therein. In Philip's view, the theologians (including HULDRYCH ZWINGLI) were only disputing semantics. All believed in a salutary presence of Christ in the sacrament. For Philip, the Augsburg Confession was the theological standard.

Philip's belief in dialogue and TOLERATION was also seen in his policy toward ANABAPTISM in Hesse. Whereas radical reformers faced execution elsewhere, Philip employed Bucer to conduct discussions with jailed dissidents aimed at CONVERSION. Some were expelled, but no one was executed for religious reasons. Likewise, Philip tried to tolerate Jews in his lands, and rejected demands for severe persecution of Jews by Bucer and other theologians. Unfortunately, he capitulated to pressure with acts in 1539 and 1543 that discriminated against Jews and placed intolerable limitations on the practice of their religion. However, Jews were not denied the ability to earn a living in Hesse.

Philip's Motivation

The most controversial point regarding Philip as a Protestant involves his motives. Some have dubbed him a "realpolitiker," implying that his foreign and domestic policy were motivated by a desire for greater political power. This is a convenient view when one confronts his notorious bigamy (1541), which embarrassed Luther and his Wittenberg colleagues who had advised him. He misled the theologians into believing he would keep the bigamy secret and personal. But if Philip was a realpolitiker, then why did he abandon Cleves to the emperor in 1541, surrender to imprisonment, and divide the secular leadership of his territory in his last testament? Nor is it clear, as some historians have thought, that weakened by the bigamy and imprisonment, Philip lost interest in the Protestant cause thereafter. Less action was required in foreign affairs after the Augsburg Peace (1552), allowing Philip to concentrate on domestic affairs.

See also Anti-Semitism; Catholic Reactions to Protestantism; Catholicism, Protestant Reactions; Dialogue, Inter-Confessional; Judaism

References and Further Reading

Hauswirth, Rene,. *Landgraf Philipp von Hessen und Zwingli, 1526–1531.* Tübingen, Germany and Basel, Switzerland: Osiander, Balilea, 1968.

Hillerbrand, Hans J. *Landgrave Philipp of Hesse, 1504-1567: Religion and Politics in the Reformation.* St. Louis, MO: Foundation for Reformation Research, 1967.

Rommel, Dietrich Christoph von. *Philipp der Grossmüthige, Landgraf von Hessen; ein Beitrag zur genaueren Kunde der Reformation und des sechzehnten Jahrhunderts, nebst einem Urkunden-Bande.* 3 vols. Giessen, Germany: G. F. Heyer, 1830.

Rudersdorf, Manfred. *Ludwig IV. Landgraf von Hessen-Marburg, 1537–1604. Landestum und Luthertum in Hessen.* Mainz, Germany: Philipp von Zabern, 1991.

Wright, William J. "Philip of Hesse's Vision of Protestant Unity and the Marburg Colloquy," in *Pietas et Societas: New Trends in Reformation Social History. Essays in Memory of Harold J. Grimm.* Edited by Kyle C. Sessions and Phillip N. Bebb, 163-180. Kirksville, MO: Sixteenth Century Studies, 1985.

WILLIAM J. WRIGHT

PHILIP, JOHN (1775–1851)

Scottish missionary. Born in Kirkaldy, Scotland, on April 14, 1775, Philip was a weaver who was converted during the Haldane revival in SCOTLAND. After training in ENGLAND he became the minister of Belmont Congregational Church in Aberdeen. A very powerful evangelical preacher, he was soon much in demand throughout the northeast of Scotland, where he influenced many students and other young people. A supporter of overseas mission, Philip became a director of the London Missionary Society (LMS). Philip died in Hankey, Cape Colony (SOUTH AFRICA) on August 27, 1851.

In 1819 the LMS sent him to the Cape Colony to investigate the problems that had arisen in the LMS

missions there. When he decided what were the necessary reforms he remained to implement them as superintendent. For eighteen months in 1826–1828 he was in Britain and visited FRANCE and GERMANY, when he also wrote *Missionary Researches in South Africa,* published in 1828.

He was instrumental in bringing the Paris Evangelical Mission to work in southern AFRICA. He persuaded them to work with Moshweshwe and his following, the rising power among the Sotho people who created the kingdom of Lesotho. He also persuaded the Rhenish Missionary Society to begin their work in southern Africa.

Philip was one of the leading proponents of that brand of Protestant EVANGELICALISM that believed that the Gospel demanded not only personal CONVERSION but also seeking justice in this world for all of God's children. In 1828 he influenced the British government to enforce in the colony, where the population was one third white, one third free black, and one third slave, the legal equality of "all his Majesty's subjects," irrespective of color. As a result, when the slaves were freed in 1833 they gained this legal equality, as Philip intended.

See also Missionary Organizations; Missions

References and Further Reading

Macmillan, W. M. *Bantu, Boer and Briton.* Oxford, UK: Clarendon Press, 1963.

Ross, Andrew C. *John Philip: Missions, Race and Politics in South Africa.* Aberdeen: Aberdeen University Press, 1986.

ANDREW C. ROSS

PHILIPPINES

Part of the Malay Archipelago, the Philippine Islands are located northeast of Borneo and south of JAPAN between the China Sea and Pacific Ocean. The arrival of the explorer Ferdinand Magellan in 1521 began the period of Western "discovery" of the islands, and led to the Spanish claim and colonization. Because political control has decisively shaped the history of Christianity in the Philippines, this article divides the history and development of Protestantism in this country into the Spanish colonial period, the American colonial period, and the era of independence.

The Spanish Period (1565–1898)

Because of the Patronato Real (the Spanish king's patronage of the church) and the Catholic Church's status as part of the colonial administration, Protestant missionaries were not allowed into the Philippines under Spanish rule, which began in 1565. Hence, before the Philippine Revolution of 1896–1898, the only active Protestants in the archipelago were those from countries at war with Spain, such as the Dutch raiders of the early seventeenth century or the British who sacked Manila in 1762, or those who were surreptitiously distributing Spanish Bibles.

In the late nineteenth century, wealthy Filipino mestizos of Malay, Chinese, and/or Spanish descent began to encounter FREEMASONRY and then Protestantism when they traveled to Spain for their education. Through some of these returning Filipinos and the reading of a few smuggled Bibles, there emerged some Filipinos committed to Protestantism and even underground congregations before the arrival of the American military in 1898.

During the Revolution, Gregorio Aglipay, the Filipino military vicar general and Catholic priest who was later excommunicated, sought to form a Filipino National Catholic Church that would acknowledge papal authority but not Spanish rule. After Rome refused to recognize their nationalist aspirations, and later, after conversations with Protestant missionaries led nowhere, Isabelo de los Reyes, a prominent layman and labor leader, announced in 1902 the separation from Rome and the formation of the Iglesia Filipina Independiente (IFI, also referred to as the Philippine Independent Church, or PIC). Although not consulted on this move, Aglipay later agreed to it and became the church's Supreme Bishop in early 1903. Although their polity and liturgy resembled Catholicism, the official theology of the church became, for a while, Unitarian.

The American Period (1898–1946)

The transition from Spanish to UNITED STATES rule opened the doors to Protestant missionaries, Bible translators, and diverse Christian associations. The American missionaries, many of whom had encouraged the acquisition of the islands and who began arriving in 1899, were optimistic about the prospects of establishing a Christian nation in Asia. Freedom of religion became established by law, and the Catholic church lost all state support and faced severe financial crises and a shortage of priests. Many Catholics seemed to be only nominally attached to Rome, and the IFI was loosening the loyalties of others. Missionaries brought with them the gifts of Protestant civilization and the Gospel. Although more men than WOMEN were official missionaries, many women spread their faith informally as teachers, nurses, or supportive spouses.

Having learned from experiences in China and elsewhere of the disastrous effects of competing churches on MISSIONS, representatives of several major churches formulated a comity agreement in 1901 to divide mission fields among them. Manila was open to all churches, and other areas were assigned as follows: major portions of northern Luzon, the main island located in the north, to the Methodist Mission; southern portions of Luzon and parts of the centrally located Visayan islands to the Presbyterian Mission; sections of northern Luzon to the United Brethren; remaining parts of the Visayans to the Baptist Mission; and the large southern island of Mindanao, which contained Muslim areas that had defied Spanish rule for centuries, to the American Board Mission (see AMERICAN BOARD OF COMMISSIONERS FOR FOREIGN MISSIONS) and the Congregational Mission. The members of this Evangelical Union, which included the AMERICAN BIBLE SOCIETY and the YMCA, also agreed to share a common name, the Evangelical Church of the Philippines, followed by the name of the particular denomination in parenthesis. Although the DISCIPLES OF CHRIST did not agree to restrict themselves, they did concentrate in Manila and portions of northern Luzon. Similarly, the CHRISTIAN AND MISSIONARY ALLIANCE generally remained friendly with the Evangelical Union.

The Episcopal Church (see ANGLICANISM; EPISCOPAL CHURCH, UNITED STATES) led by Bishop Charles Henry Brent, refrained from joining the comity agreement because they had no interest in evangelizing good Catholics. Consequently, Episcopal missionaries concentrated their efforts on the mountainous areas of northern Luzon that had never been converted to Catholicism and that remained animist, on portions of Mindanao (some Muslim, some still animist), and on the ethnic Chinese community.

One of the major sources of conflict between the Catholic Church and Protestants was the school system. Although the American government sought to provide Catholic teachers for the public school system they established, the overwhelming majority of teachers from the United States were initially Protestants, and many of the Filipino teachers shared anticlerical sentiments. The erection of rival Protestant and Catholic dormitories for the large student population of Manila similarly signaled a struggle for the religion of the youth. Protestants established hospitals and colleges as well, hoping to provide medical care and education while also providing ways of reaching more Filipinos with the Gospel. Early Filipino converts to Protestantism, both women and men, served as important evangelists. The appeal of Protestantism varied greatly from one town or region to the next. Often members of the middle class converted, but itinerant workers or whole villages might also embrace the new faith.

Despite their initial confidence for the Christianization of this Catholic country, and despite a remarkable number of converts relative to other missions in Asia, missionaries soon learned that the vast majority of Filipinos were remaining Catholic. By 1918 only a little over one percent of the Christian population were worshipping in non-Catholic or non-IFI churches. This figure rose to about 3 to 4 percent of the total population and has remained there. Protestants, who never had an adequate number of missionaries, underestimated Filipino loyalty to folk Catholicism and its relationship to Filipino social identity. Perhaps most important, the missionaries did not recognize the extent to which aspirations for an independent Philippines inhibited Filipinos from accepting a faith associated with new colonial rulers.

Some Filipino Protestants resented the ways in which American missionaries and churches, believing that many years of tutelage would be needed, restricted Filipino leadership in their churches. (This had also been a complaint against the Catholic Church.) Schools such as Union Theological Seminary, founded jointly by Presbyterians (see PRESBYTERIANISM, PRESBYTERIAN CHURCH, U.S.A.) and Methodists (see METHODISM; METHODISM, NORTH AMERICA) in 1907, did prepare Filipinos for ordination, but missionaries retained administrative control of the churches. Nicholas Zamora, the first ordained Filipino Methodist, led a split from the METHODIST EPISCOPAL CHURCH and formed the Iglesia Evangelica Metodista en las Islas Filipinas (IEMELIF) in 1909. Another split formed the Philippine Methodist Church in 1933, and other churches experienced similar divisions. There were also, however, church unions. In 1929 the United Brethren, Congregational (see CONGREGATIONALISM), and Presbyterian churches united as the United Evangelical Church. Similarly, six smaller indigenous and independent churches joined as the Iglesia Evangelica Unida de Christo in 1932.

Because the IFI was able to combine elements of Catholic tradition with Filipino leadership and a nationalist message, and because they had taken possession of many impressive church buildings (sometimes violently), it was initially the most successful of the new churches, claiming perhaps as many as one and a half million adherents, or one quarter of the Catholic population. Although a Supreme Court decision in 1906 compelled them to return church properties to Rome, greatly weakening their stature, they remained a significant church. As of 1918 they could claim 13 percent of the total population. A hastily ordained and poorly trained clergy, however, and internal disputes over ORTHODOXY prevented them from developing beyond two million members, even as the population would undergo a sixfold increase by the 1970s. Thus by 2000 they claimed about 4 percent of the nation.

Another important indigenous church is the Iglesia ni Kristo (INK, or Church of Christ in Filipino),

founded by Felix Manalo in 1914. Attracted to Protestantism at a debate between a Catholic priest and a Protestant minister, he joined the Methodist Episcopal Church in 1904. Subsequently, he studied under Presbyterians, and joined the Disciples of Christ and then the SEVENTH-DAY ADVENTISTS before deciding that he was the angel arising from the East as foretold in Revelation 7:2 and founding the INK. He led the church until his death in 1963, when his son Eraño Manalo assumed the leadership. Because of their strong organization, the general belief that their claim of voting as a block under their leaders' directions sometimes determined national and local elections, their reputation for taking care of their own, and the consistent design for their distinctive church buildings, they have over the decades established a strong presence in Philippine public life.

The main contributions of Protestantism to the country as a whole include the promotion of English and literacy as well as the establishment of schools such as Silliman University, Central Philippine University, and Philippine Christian University; the founding of clinics and hospitals such as St. Luke's; and the support for cooperatives and credit unions. In addition to encouraging women to enter various professions, Protestants also claim to have helped develop a professional ethic throughout the society as a whole and to have fostered the spread of democratic values in an oligarchic nation. Finally, the need to meet the Protestant challenge helped prompt the striking reform of the Catholic Church in the early decades of the twentieth century and helped invigorate Catholic schools, youth movements, and lay associations.

Two Protestant missionaries achieved international recognition: Bishop Brent for his efforts against the use of opium and narcotics in Asia and for his ecumenical leadership at the world conference on Faith and Order in Lausanne in 1927; and Frank Laubach, a missionary of the American Board of Commissioners for Foreign Missions, who while learning a Philippine language developed an innovative method for teaching literacy to be used in over one hundred other countries.

The Era of Independence (1946–present)

During World War II the brief but devastating Japanese occupation of the country from late 1941 to 1944 promoted Filipino control of their churches. Missionaries from the Allied countries were imprisoned, and Filipinos assumed crucial leadership positions. The problem for many Filipino Protestant leaders has been how to assert their churches' equality with the foreign churches that founded them. They have sought to establish themselves as neither Catholic nor American.

After independence in 1946, the trend toward ecumenical cooperation between the more established churches increased (see ECUMENISM). In 1948 the Philippine Methodist Church, the United Evangelical Church, most of the remaining members of the Evangelical Church, and some congregations of the IEMELIF, the Unida de Christo, and the Disciples merged to form the United Church of Christ in the Philippines (UCCP), the largest of the churches with ties to American missionaries. Although the Baptists and other Methodists did not join the new church (these Methodists remain a part of the United Methodist Church), they did join the National Council of Churches in the Philippines (NCCP). The NCCP, formed in 1963, also includes the UCCP, the Philippine Episcopal Church, IEMELIF, and Unida de Christo. It provides a vehicle for the minority Protestant community to assume greater public prominence on social and political issues.

Although the IFI had been officially Unitarian, the laity had remained essentially Trinitarian. After the war, a split between Unitarians and Trinitarians led to the eventual triumph of the latter, and their bishops were finally brought into the historic episcopate through reconsecration by Episcopalians in 1948. In 1961 they entered into full communion with the Philippine Episcopal Church, and they share St. Andrew's Theological Seminary in Quezon City. The IFI has also joined the NCCP.

After World War II "faith missions" and various evangelical churches began to appear in the Philippines, led in some cases by missionaries who had been expelled from China. Many of these are now part of the Philippine Council of Evangelical Churches (PCEC). In contrast to the ecumenical orientation of the churches of the NCCP, the more conservative churches of the PCEC are less interested in ecumenism and public issues and more oriented toward church planting and personal EVANGELISM. Similarly, whereas the PCEC churches exhibit greater acceptance of foreign missionaries and funds, which now come from other Asian countries such as KOREA, NCCP churches assert greater independence and have sought reduced financial and missionary support.

The last decades of the twentieth centuries have seen numerous significant developments for the Protestant churches. A great number of indigenous quasi-Christian churches and sects of varying sizes have arisen. The student movements of the 1960s helped promote important youth organizations such as INTER-VARSITY CHRISTIAN FELLOWSHIP, Campus Crusade for Christ, and the Navigators. Whereas many Protestants cautiously welcomed the beginning of martial law in the early 1970s, by the end of the decade the UCCP and the United Methodists were calling for the end of military rule. Restrictions during Ferdinand Marcos's martial law years, which ended in 1986, limited the ability of the churches to protest, but some church leaders worked through informal Protestant channels to protect the lives and families of some of those wanted by the government. In the 1990s charismatic and Pentecostal groups (see PENTECOSTALISM), such as Jesus Is Lord and the Bread of Life Fellowship, have become prominent, even as some perceive a decline or perhaps only modest growth for the older, more established churches.

One sign of the vigor of some Protestants is that since the 1950s the Philippines has been sending missionaries abroad. Some go with financial support provided by churches from other countries, whereas others are able to spread the Gospel in other lands because they have been hired abroad. In fact, one social issue facing the churches is the great number of overseas contract workers and the difficulties they and their families face. Of ongoing concern to Filipino theologians and church leaders has been the problem of ministering and proclaiming in a country in which well over half the population lives in poverty. The removal of U.S. military bases, completed in 1992, and the liberation of the Philippines from ongoing economic exploitation, have been causes championed by some politically active Protestants. Finally, Filipino laity and clergy have also been active in international theological education and conferences.

References and Further Reading

Anderson, Gerald H., ed. *Studies in Philippine Church History.* Ithaca: Cornell University Press, 1969.

Bautista, Lorenzo C. "The Church in Philippines." In *Church in Asia Today: Challenges and Opportunities,* edited by Saphir Athyal, 169–195. Singapore: Asia Lausanne Committee for World Evangelization, 1996.

Clymer, Kenton J. *Protestant Missionaries in the Philippines, 1898–1916: An Inquiry into the American Colonial Mentality.* Urbana: University of Illinois Press, 1986.

Deats, Richard L. *Nationalism and Christianity in the Philippines.* Dallas: Southern Methodist University Press, 1967.

Elesterio, Fernando G. *The Iglesia Ni Kristo: Its Christology and Ecclesiology.* Quezon City: Loyola School of Theology, 1988.

Gowing, Peter G. *Islands Under the Cross: The Story of the Church in the Philippines.* Manila: National Council of Churches in the Philippines, 1967.

Kwantes, Anne C. *Presbyterian Missionaries in the Philippines: Conduits of Social Change (1899–1910).* Quezon City: New Day, 1989.

Sitoy, T. Valentino, Jr. *Several Springs, One Stream: The United Church of Christ in the Philippines.* 2 vols. Quezon City: United Church of Christ in the Philippines, 1992–1997.

DAVID KECK

PHILO-SEMITISM

Philo-Semitism might best be defined as support and admiration for Jews by non-Jews. Because of the persistence and virulence of its opposite, ANTI-SEMITISM (hostility to Jews by non-Jews), it has always been overshadowed as an element in Jewish–Gentile relations and, indeed, more often than not virtually ignored by scholars and others, although it has been a significant factor in the relationship of Christianity and JUDAISM. Protestant philo-Semitism, and other forms of Christian philo-Semitism, constitute one strand within the wider heading of philo-Semitism. Other nonreligious strands, stemming from political liberalism and radicalism, from gentile support for Zionism, and from a type of political conservatism that admired Jews as part of a historical elite, may also be distinguished. Nevertheless, Christian philo-Semitism has arguably been the most important single strand, with most of its impetus coming from Protestantism rather than from Catholicism or Eastern Orthodoxy.

Although medieval Christianity tolerated Jews and Judaism—indeed, Jews were the only tolerated non-Christian minority in Europe—and, to a certain extent protected them, Jews were chiefly tolerated as money-lenders and tax collectors among peoples to whom "usury" was forbidden and who frequently lacked the financial skills and expertise of the Jews. In contrast Jews were almost always pilloried and demonized as "Christ-killers," liable to certain damnation unless converted to Christianity, subject to frequent expulsions from many medieval European countries (most famously, perhaps, from England in 1290 and Spain in 1492), and often (although not invariably) forced to live in ghettos, found in various parts of Catholic Europe from the thirteenth century.

The Protestant REFORMATION had many positive effects for the Jews of predominantly Protestant states in Europe. By removing the ban on "usury" and other forms of capitalism, Protestant Europe quickly witnessed the emergence of highly successful native capitalists and businessmen, whose existence removed much of the close association in the popular mind between Jews and moneymaking. Indeed, one of the most famous of all sociological theories, the so-called Weber Thesis, propounded by the German theorist MAX WEBER (between 1904 and 1905), postulated a causal connection between Protestantism and capitalism. (Anti-Semites such as Werner Sombart have, indeed, criticized Weber for ignoring the connections between Judaism and capitalism.) Protestantism also removed much of the Roman Catholic imagery and ceremonials that were particularly inimical to Jews, especially the centrality of the Crucifixion and ac-

counts of Christians allegedly murdered by Jews, such as St. Hugh of Lincoln, the supposed victim of a Jewish "ritual murder" at Lincoln, England, in 1255 (recounted in the "Prioress's Tale" in Chaucer's *Canterbury Tales*). The religious wars that emerged after the early sixteenth century between Protestantism and Catholicism reoriented religious hostility away from the Jews. Indeed, much of the lurid anti-Catholicism that emerged in Protestant Europe bore many resemblances to anti-Semitism, but with the pope, the Jesuits, and the Catholic church as the progenitors of evil, not the Jews. There was also a growing relationship (but certainly not an invariable one) between Protestantism and a secular definition of civil society, which increasingly viewed religion as a private matter and all religions as equal before the law. This bore fruit most strikingly in the United States Constitution and BILL OF RIGHTS, which forbade the establishment of any religion by the government, and placed all religions, including Judaism, on an equal legal footing. One might also observe a growing strand in the thought of Protestants and of thinkers in Protestant countries to view history as consisting of a continuous evolution toward universal improvement, in which the Catholic church (in particular) was viewed as an obstacle to progress and the symbol of medieval obscurantism, especially in its supposed persecution of Jews (and Protestants) on religious grounds. By the mid-nineteenth century, the situation of Jews in largely Protestant countries, especially in the English-speaking world, was categorically better than in other parts of the European world or elsewhere.

There was, to be sure, another side to the coin. The sixteenth-century Protestant reformer MARTIN LUTHER may be taken as representative of Christian anti-Judaism. After speaking favorably of the Jews in 1523, he was disappointed by their failure to be attracted to his reformed Christianity, and he turned against them with a virulence that inspired many subsequent anti-Semites. Much Protestant philo-Semitism was also "conversionist" in nature, that is, aimed at eventually converting Jews to Protestantism after befriending them and helping them to ameliorate their plight. Christian conversionists, even those who genuinely sympathized with the suffering of Jews, came to be feared by many Jews. Indeed, only when Christianity itself recognized Judaism as a divinely inspired religion, worthy of full respect and acknowledgment, rather than as the "old" Covenant made obsolete by the mission of Jesus, were Jews fully able to recognize Christian philo-Semites as their genuine allies. Individual Protestants also exhibited as much in the way of anti-Semitism as anyone else, through such means as excluding Jews from elite universities and social clubs (as was common in the United States until 1945) or limiting their number by quota. Extremist Protestant groups such as the KU KLUX KLAN numbered Jews as one of their principal enemies, although in the English-speaking world seldom with the virulence found in continental Europe. Nevertheless, it is certainly true that Protestant-majority countries have exhibited less anti-Semitism than that of other societies, a fact recognized by Jews in their mass migrations after the mid-nineteenth century. (The "New Diaspora," above all in the United States, where the majority of Jews live today, is overwhelmingly in the Protestant world, with a number of Catholic Latin American societies such as Argentina providing the chief exception.)

Much of the force behind Protestant philo-Semitism came from a sense of affinity between Protestants and the descendants of the ancient Hebrews, an affinity based in large measure in the intimate knowledge of the BIBLE common to many Protestants and the internalization of the history of the ancient Hebrews as a component of their own identity. This was also the case among Puritans and Calvinists, who often sought out Jews as living embodiments of the events in the Bible. In Germany a number of seventeenth-century religious outsiders, such as PAUL FELGENHAUER, wrote most positively about Jews. Jews were legally readmitted to England in 1656 by the Puritan leader OLIVER CROMWELL. Later, American Puritans continuously identified with the Jews, often viewing America as a new Israel. "The Puritans accepted Jewish history as their own, identified themselves in many respects with the Jewish people and gave their children Hebrew names," Solomon Rappaport has noted. Some Puritans (such as Cromwell) believed that the Messiah would come when Jews were "scattered to every country," and thus facilitated the entry of Jews into their countries. What has been termed the "Judaization" of Protestant England and America, through the internalization of the Old Testament, was (and still is) a feature of a major strand in conservative Protestantism.

Many of these elements came together in the response of significant numbers of Protestants to outbursts of anti-Semitic crises in the Jewish world in modern times. During an outburst of anti-Semitism in Germany in 1880, for example, Henry Ward Beecher, the famous American minister, suggested sending a protest to Bismarck, whereas Christian philo-Semites were notable in protesting on behalf of Jews during the czarist pogroms of the 1880s, the Dreyfus affair of the 1890s, the Beilis case in Russia (a famous "ritual murder" accusation in 1913), and other notorious instances of anti-Semitism. Contrary to widespread popular belief, the record of the Protestant churches in protesting against Nazi persecution of the Jews was often remarkably good. The much-maligned archbishop of Canterbury, Cosmo Gordon Lang, had a particularly worthy record, repeatedly denouncing Nazi persecution of the Jews from 1934. In November 1938, just after *Kristallnacht* (a violent night of destruction against synagogues and Jewish businesses in Germany), the Conference of the Clergy and Laity of the Anglican Church adopted a resolution (moved by Hensley Henson, the bishop of Durham) that "the Conference . . . desires to express the disgust and horror with which it has heard of the recent anti-Semite outrages in Germany." In 1939 the General Assembly of the CHURCH OF SCOTLAND passed a resolution "urging the Government to spare no effort to come to the rescue of refugees," whereas one speaker, Rev. Dr. James Black, stated that "I have seen this people actually stretched on a cross, and I have heard with my own ears tales of incredible injustice and persecution that almost make me despair of the human race" (cited in W. D. Rubinstein). During the Second World War, Protestant churches throughout the English-speaking world repeatedly went on record as supporting greater generosity toward Jewish refugees, although, obviously, the Nazi regime took no heed of any plea for mercy. In Germany the record of the Protestant churches was notably worse, with the exception of individual activists. In particular, the record of the racialist, pro-Nazi German Christian Movement has been highlighted as notably bad. There seems clearly to have been a dichotomy between the English-speaking world and continental Europe in this.

Although nearly all Protestant denominations in the English-speaking world produced notable examples of outspoken philo-Semitism, probably the most biblically oriented sects on the one hand, and the most liberal sects on the other, were most visible in their support for the Jews, especially the Unitarians and the Quakers. The record of the SOCIETY OF FRIENDS toward Jewish suffering has been especially impressive, a component of their wider humanitarianism. Until after the Second World War, the record of Protestantism was certainly much more positive to Jews than that of Roman Catholicism, even if the pre-1960 record of Catholicism was itself more positive and complex than is often appreciated.

A number of especially notable philo-Semites ought to be highlighted particularly. In the tradition of the seventeenth-century MILLENARIANS, who saw the Jews' acceptance of Christianity as the necessary prelude to the Second Coming of Jesus, was Anthony Ashley Cooper, seventh earl of Shaftesbury (1801–1885), the famous factory reformer. He was an Evangelical, and president of the London Society for Promoting Christianity Amongst the Jews from 1848 until his death. Breaking out from this mold was another prominent Evangelical, the novelist Charlotte Elizabeth Tonna (1790–1846). She edited several religious periodicals, most notably, from 1836 to 1846, the influential and widely circulating *Christian Lady's Magazine*. She blazed a trail by advocating Judaism as an alternative path to salvation, denouncing conversionism, and calling for the removal of anti-Jewish references from Christian hymns and prayer books. An archfoe of Roman Catholicism, she campaigned vigorously on behalf of oppressed Jewries and was an early "gentile Zionist."

Another who renounced his earlier conversionist efforts was the London-based Welsh Calvinistic Methodist minister John Mills (1812–1873), who was among the small group of Jews and gentiles who in 1852 founded the Association for Promoting Jewish Settlement in Palestine, and wrote *The British Jews* (1853, updated 1862), a groundbreaking analysis.

Outstanding among twentieth-century British philo-Semites were Sidney Dark (1874–1947), editor of the Anglican *Church Times,* and Rev. James Parkes (1896–1981), an Anglican clergyman who wrote several books championing the Jewish people.

A similar tradition has been apparent in the United States, featuring such individuals as the millenarian William Blackstone, initiator of two noteworthy pro-Zionist memorials (1891 and 1916), and the mainstream Protestant clergyman John Haynes Holmes, an unswerving defender of Jews and Zionism.

In recent decades, the position of Protestantism and its denominations toward the Jews has undergone something of a transformation. On the one hand, there are certainly today more interfaith bodies and efforts than before the Second World War, such as the Council of Christians and Jews. There is also certainly less in the way of conversionist efforts by Protestant denominations aimed at Jews. Although these still exist, there is a general post-Holocaust awareness among Christians that Jews ought to be left alone and that the Covenant made by God with the Jewish people continues to run parallel with that created by the mission of Jesus, and was not superseded by it. As well, since 1945 anti-Semitism of any kind has certainly diminished, and its manifestations are often illegal in many Western countries. On the other hand, however, the creation of the State of Israel in 1948, the first Jewish state since biblical times, together with the inability of Israel and the Arabs to reach a resolution of their conflict that provides for an independent Palestinian state, has led to continuing difficulties between Jews and some Protestant denominations. In a historical reversal of the pre-1948 situation, by and large it has been "left-wing" and liberal-universalist denominations within Protestantism that have been most critical of Israeli policy (and hence mistrusted by most Jews), in part because Israel is seen by these elements as the oppressor of the Palestinians (in part because of a wider hostility to America and the West, of which Israel is seen as a staunch supporter). Resolutions passed by allegedly left-dominated bodies such as the WORLD COUNCIL OF CHURCHES have been consistently (and, in the eyes of many Jews, unfairly) hostile to Israel in the Middle East conflict. As well, links between Western Protestants and Arab Christian groups have also been seen as a source of hostility to Israel. On the other hand, many conservative and fundamentalist Protestant denominations and activists, such as those associated with the "Moral Majority" in the United States, have become strong supporters of Israel and, indeed, of right-wing Israeli governments. Jewish opinion has been divided on whether this support is helpful or not. In another historic reversal of traditional attitudes, since Vatican II the Roman Catholic church has discarded all vestiges of anti-Semitism from its doctrine, and has made great efforts to achieve reconciliation with the Jews. Many Jews believe that the Catholic church, especially under Pope John Paul II, is now friendlier to Jews than are the Protestants, a situation not readily imaginable two generations ago. What Yehuda Bauer has termed "the Jewish emergence from powerlessness" since the Second World War has also made dialogue and dealings between Jews and Christians one of equals, whereas in the past it was clear that Jews were often supplicants in avowedly Christian societies.

See also Bible; Calvinism; Confessing Church; Fundamentalism; Holocaust; Puritanism; Unitarian Universalist Association; German Christians; Conversion

References and Further Reading

Edelstein, Alan. *An Unacknowledged Harmony: Philosemitism and the Survival of European Jewry.* Westport, CT: Greenwood Press, 1982.

Katz, David S. "The Phenomenon of Philosemitism." *Studies in Church History* 29 (1992): 327–361.

Kobler, Franz. *The Vision Was There: A History of the British Movement for the Restoration of the Jews to Palestine.* London: Lincolns-Praeger for the World Jewish Congress, British Section, 1956.

Merkley, Paul Charles. *The Politics of Christian Zionism 1891–1948.* London: Frank Cass, 1998.

Rappaport, Solomon. *Jew and Gentile: The Philo-Semitic Aspect.* New York: Philosophical Library, 1980.

Rubinstein, Hilary L. "A Pioneering Philosemite: Charlotte Elizabeth Tonna (1790–1846) and the Jews." *Jewish Historical Studies: Transactions of the Jewish Historical Society of England* 35 (1996–1998): 103–118.

Rubinstein, W. D. *A History of the Jews in the English-Speaking World: Great Britain.* London: Macmillan, 1996.

———, and Hilary L. Rubinstein. *Philosemitism: Admiration and Support in the English-Speaking World for Jews, 1840–1939.* London: Macmillan, 1999.

Schoeps, Hans Joachim. *Philosemitism in the Baroque.* Tübingen: Mohr, 1952.

Vereté, Meir. "The Restoration of the Jews in English Protestant Thought, 1790–1840." *Middle Eastern Studies* 8 (1972): 3–50.

WILLIAM D. RUBINSTEIN

PIERSON, ARTHUR TAPPAN (1837–1911)

American missionary activist. A. T. Pierson was the leading American promoter of foreign MISSIONS in the late nineteenth century, and his reputation as a BIBLE expositor and preacher extended to both sides of the Atlantic. Editor of the leading missions journal of the era, *The Missionary Review of the World,* Pierson wrote more than fifty books and thousands of articles. He popularized the phrase "the evangelization of the world in this generation," the watchword of the student missions movement and a symbol of the activistic, pre–World War I generation. An original editor of the SCOFIELD REFERENCE BIBLE (1909), he was one of the significant figures in the movement of premillennial DISPENSATIONALISM.

Born in New York City in 1837, Pierson rose to prominence as a preacher, Bible teacher, and leader in urban ministry and ecumenical causes (see ECUMENISM) while serving leading Presbyterian churches in Detroit, Indianapolis, and Philadelphia. He became a premillennialist in 1878 in answer to questions about the relationship between biblical interpretation and the seemingly negative, antievangelical direction of urban America in the late 1800s. His books on missions, Bible study, EVANGELISM, and spirituality began appearing in the mid-1880s, the most famous of which were *The Crisis of Missions* and *Many Infallible Proofs.* In 1886, at a summer Bible conference for college YMCA leaders, he gave the speech on missions that motivated the "Mt. Hermon 100" to become missionaries, thereby beginning the Student Volunteer Movement. From the late 1880s onward, Pierson was a freelance author and lecturer at missions and spirituality conferences in North America and Great Britain, including succeeding CHARLES SPURGEON as preacher at the Metropolitan Tabernacle. He died in 1911 in Brooklyn, New York.

See also Millenarians and Millennialism

References and Further Reading

Primary Sources:

Pierson, Arthur T. *The New Acts of the Apostles, or the Marvels of Modern Missions.* New York: Baker & Taylor, 1894.

———. *"Many Infallible Proofs:" The Evidences of Christianity. Or, the Written and Living Word of God.* New York, Chicago: F. H. Revell, 1886.

———. *The Inspired Word: A Series of Papers.* New York: Garland Pub., 1988, 1888.

———. *The Gospel: Its Heart, Heights, and Hopes.* Grand Rapids, MI: Baker Books, 1978, c. 1890s.

———. *God and Missions Today.* Chicago: Moody Press, 1955.

———. *The Keswick Movement in Precept and Practice.* New York & London: Funk & Wagnalls Co., 1903.

———. *Outline Studies of Great Themes of the Bible.* Grand Rapids, MI: Baker Book House, 1973.

Secondary Sources:

Pierson, Delavan L. *Arthur T. Pierson.* New York: Fleming Revell, 1912.

Robert, Dana L. "Arthur Tappan Pierson and Forward Movements of Late Nineteenth-Century Evangelicalism." Ph.D. dissertation, Yale University, 1984.

DANA L. ROBERT

PIETISM

A religious renewal movement centered in seventeenth- and eighteenth-century GERMANY, Pietism profoundly shaped modern Protestantism. In contrast to the sixteenth-century Protestant REFORMATION, Pietism stressed religious experience and active lay participation. It established new forms of biblical devotion and made serious efforts at organized missionary activity. Its distinctive characteristics include regeneration, CONVERSION, CONVENTICLES, and millennialism. Pietists remained, however, theologically heterogeneous. Originally Pietism referred to the movement associated with PHILIPP JAKOB SPENER and AUGUST HERMANN FRANCKE within German LUTHERANISM. Since the nineteenth century, it has come to refer to a range of piety movements in European and North American Protestantism. There is no scholarly consensus on the meaning of the term. Some historians apply Pietism broadly to contemporaneous Protestant renewal movements across Europe including English PURITANISM and the Dutch *nadere reformatie* (further Reformation). Others understand Pietism more narrowly and concentrate on movements arising out of German Protestantism. This article focuses on the German context of Pietism with reference to cognate movements in other countries.

Origins

The origins of Pietism can be traced to several impulses within German Protestantism around 1600. Lutherans had succeeded in defining their doctrine authoritatively in the Formula of Concord (1577) and established their CONFESSION firmly in many Germany territories, but during the last decades of the sixteenth century, many Lutherans perceived an increasing gulf between THEOLOGY and personal piety, in which the key Reformation doctrine of JUSTIFICATION no longer addressed their religious needs and experiences. For the Reformed the disjuncture between piety and DOCTRINE was less pronounced, but the lack of recognition by the Imperial authorities contributed to growing unease at the end of the century. The crisis of piety that emerged was one of a series of crises faced by German Protestants at the end of the sixteenth and seventeenth centuries. These included crop failures, climatic changes, epidemics, and political instability alongside broader spiritual doubts about the Protestant project. The crisis of piety marked a break with earlier forms of Protestant practice, and signaled the introduction of a new wave of devotional literature that would shape Protestantism in the seventeenth century.

Typical of the new kind of piety were devotional writers such as Philipp Nicolai, whose *Joyous Mirror of Eternal Life* (1599) sought to comfort readers in the midst of epidemics in Germany by redirecting their attention away from pestilence and suffering to the joys of eternal SALVATION. The new piety was reflected in the rich hymnody of the period, which reached its apogee in the works of PAUL GERHARDT. Often seen in opposition to a sclerotic Protestant ORTHODOXY, the new piety is best understood as parallel and complementary to it. Even Johann Gerhard, the greatest Lutheran orthodox systematician of the era, wrote devotional works that fit the paradigm of the new literature.

The most prominent representative of the new piety and most important figure for later Pietism was JOHANN ARNDT (1555–1621). Arndt became one of the best-selling devotional writers of the seventeenth century, and his *True Christianity* (1605) remained a spiritual classic into the nineteenth century. *True Christianity* focused on the inner life of Protestants, who identified themselves as Christians, attended to the church's rituals, and yet appeared to deny Christianity with their immoral lives and lack of repentance. Through Arndt and devotional writers like him, mystical sources found a prominent place in Protestant devotional literature. In *True Christianity,* Arndt drew on Johann Tauler, Thomas a Kempis, Angela of Foligno, as well as the theosophist VALENTIN WEIGEL. Despite his indebtedness, Arndt carefully avoided contradicting Lutheran doctrine in his use of these sources.

Arndt's mystical inclinations and emphasis on the inner life of the Christian was not without controversy. After his death the Tübingen theologian Lucas Osiander the Younger challenged his orthodoxy. Although unease remained, overt attacks on Arndt remained isolated and his influence steadily grew. Within Lutheran orthodoxy an Arndtian school of theologians developed. The most popular devotional writers of the mid-seventeenth century, including

Joachim Lütkemann, Heinrich Müller, and Christian Scriver, all revered Arndt and consciously reflected his emphases on the inner life and personal piety in their works.

The crisis of piety and criticism of contemporary Protestantism by Arndt and others also led to a series of proposals for church reform within seventeenth-century German Lutheranism. Across Germany a wide spectrum of theologians proposed more effective CHURCH DISCIPLINE, rigorous Sunday observance, and better clerical training. The reform proposals within Lutheran orthodoxy reached their pinnacle with Theophil Großgebauer and his *Watchmen's Voice out of the Ravaged Zion* (1661). Großgebauer advocated greater inclusion of the LAITY, stricter church discipline, stronger emphasis on pastoral care and training, and a reconfiguration of WORSHIP services. Many orthodox CLERGY welcomed the diagnosis but viewed the proposed reforms suspiciously. In most cases rulers opposed the reforms, in large part because they challenged the AUTHORITY of the civil administrators in religious matters.

The development of the piety movement in Germany has distinct parallels to the Puritan movement in ENGLAND and the *nadere reformatie* (further Reformation) in the NETHERLANDS. All three represent an intensification of Christian life and emphasized themes of repentance, SANCTIFICATION, and the *imitatio*. Puritan devotional literature deeply influenced German Protestantism. However, historians disagree on the relationship between these movements. Scholars of Puritanism and *nadere reformatie* have generally emphasized their distinctiveness from German Pietism. Further elucidation of the mutual influences, similarities, and differences awaits additional research.

Emergence of Pietist Movements

The new piety represented by Arndt remained primarily a literary phenomenon. Pietism as a distinct movement emerged separately in Reformed and Lutheran areas during the 1660s and 1670s with a new emphasis on the gathering of the pious in conventicles. Rather than coming from above, reform would emanate from small circles of the pious to transform the larger church. This new emphasis is seen in Theodor Untereyck (1635–1693), Jean de Labadie (1610–1674), and Philipp Jakob Spener (1635–1705).

Theodor Untereyck began holding devotional gatherings in the Reformed city of Mühlheim/Ruhr at least as early as 1665. Through his studies in Utrecht and later Leiden, Untereyck was shaped by the *nadere reformatie*'s emphasis on strict CALVINISM and personal religious renewal as well as the federal theology of JOHANNES COCCEJUS (1603–1669). Called to Bremen in 1670, he established conventicles, stricter church discipline, and intensive catechesis in the city. Under his leadership Bremen and the Lower Rhine, including Mühlheim, became the center of a modest Pietist movement within the Reformed German churches.

A more radical movement emerged in Reformed Protestantism under Labadie. A former Jesuit, Labadie left FRANCE for Reformed Geneva and later the Netherlands, where he came under the influence of Gisbert Voetius (1589–1676) and the *nadere reformatie*. He served as a Reformed minister in Middleburg but his growing emphasis on lay conventicles and CHILIASM led to charges of heterodoxy in 1668. Labadie and his followers left for Amsterdam, where they formed a house church based on the early apostolic community. Among his followers was Anna Maria van Schurman. Forced from Amsterdam, the Labadists settled in Herborn, Germany in 1670, where they experienced a powerful revival. Expelled from Herborn, they moved to Altona in 1672. After Labadie's death they eventually returned to the Netherlands. Labadie's radical views on conventicles, chiliasm, and separation from the established church prefigured many of the controversies in later Pietism. His followers corresponded with a number of German Pietists, although the extent of his influence remains debated.

Often considered the founder of Pietism, Spener was the most important figure for the movement in this period. As leader of conventicles in Frankfurt/Main, author of the *Pia Desideria* (1675), correspondent, and public advocate of moderate Pietist causes, Spener became one of the best known and most influential theologians in Germany since MARTIN LUTHER.

The movement in Frankfurt/Main began when two laymen in 1670 approached Spener, the senior pastor in the city, about meeting outside of regular worship for their mutual edification. A year earlier Spener had suggested devotional gatherings on Sunday afternoons, but the decisive initiative for the establishment of the conventicles or *collegia pietatis,* as they were known in Frankfurt, came from the laity. Spener led the small gatherings in his parsonage. After song and prayer the conventicles focused on readings from devotional works.

The gatherings grew in size and, alongside academics and prominent citizens, they came to include artisans and servants, WOMEN as well as men. Around 1674 the understanding of the Frankfurt *collegia pietatis* evolved a step further as Spener and others, possibly under the influence of Labadie, came to understand the conventicles as the apostolic form of the early gatherings described in I Corinthians 14. It was out of these experiences that Spener developed the distinctive notion of the *ecclesiola in ecclesia,* or little church within the church, in which the gathered pious would themselves become a catalyst for reform within the larger CHURCH. By 1675 the *collegia pietatis* regularly included over fifty participants drawn from a cross section of Frankfurt's inhabitants.

In the spring of 1675 Spener first published his famous *Pia Desideria (Pious Wishes)* as a foreword to a collection of Johann Arndt's sermons. Within a few months the *Pia Desideria* were reprinted separately, and Spener's reform proposals became the chief programmatic document of the emerging Pietist movement. The *Pia Desideria* marked a departure from the earlier ideas of reform within Lutheran orthodoxy. Spener's criticisms of contemporary Christianity largely corresponded with earlier Arndtian piety literature and reform proposals, although—as Johannes Wallmann has argued—Spener's optimistic understanding of the in-breaking of better times, advocacy of *collegia pietatis* (conventicles), and emphasis on lay encounter with the entire BIBLE set his Pietist proposals apart from other reform programs within German Lutheranism.

The initial public reception of the *Pia Desideria* was strong, even among some who would later become opponents of the Pietist movement. Some theologians voiced reservations about Spener's predictions of the coming conversion of the Jews and especially about gatherings outside of regular worship, in which women and the unlearned took active roles. Spener defended the right of women to participate on the basis of their common priesthood in his *Spiritual Priesthood* (1677). The same year he also published an open letter *(Sendschreiben)* in which he explicitly defended the gatherings in Frankfurt.

In the 1670s the Frankfurt *collegia pietatis* inspired similar conventicles in a number of other urban areas, especially the Free Imperial cities. In the late 1670s several of Spener's allies published tracts supporting the widespread establishment of additional *collegia pietatis*. The conventicles, however, proved to be fleeting and susceptible to separatist tendencies. In Frankfurt itself earlier followers of Spener began their own gatherings, which acquired a more radical character than the approved *collegia pietatis*. The members of these gatherings distanced themselves from the Lutheran Church and established connections to radical Protestants elsewhere in Europe including Labadie and WILLIAM PENN.

During most of the 1680s the Pietist movement engendered only occasional public controversy and grew modestly. Through his correspondence and publications Spener sought to create a network of clergy and laity willing to support the kinds of reforms he proposed. He was, however, discouraged with the progress in Frankfurt, and in 1686 accepted a position as the senior court preacher in Dresden. This marked the end of the Frankfurt phase of the Pietist movement. Most early conventicle movements had disbanded or were tightly restricted as they had become in Frankfurt. Spener and his *Pia Desideria* had called forth a new wave of reform literature, but gains were modest. In the following years a more clearly defined and consequently polarizing movement would erupt.

Conflict and Expansion of the Pietist Movement

The Pietist movement took on a new character in Germany in the late 1680s. Earlier, the lines between supporters and opponents of the new movement were fluid and difficult to draw. However, the dramatic events of the late 1680s and early 1690s forced individuals to identify with one party or another. For the first time the terms Pietist and Pietism were applied consistently to the new movement. The events also signaled the arrival of a new generation of leaders, who extended the scope and impact of Pietism, most notably August Hermann Francke.

As a young lecturer at the University of Leipzig, Francke initiated colloquia devoted to biblical study in 1686. Originally, the *collegium philobiblicum,* as it was known, differed from the Frankfurt gatherings in its strict academic focus and Latin language. Its direction gradually shifted under a number of pietistic influences. Spener visited Leipzig in 1687 and urged Francke and his associates to focus on the devotional aspects of biblical studies. That same year Francke also experienced a powerful religious conversion, an experience that would become the paradigmatic conversion for many Pietists and energize Francke to redouble his efforts to achieve religious reform.

During 1688 the attendance at *collegium philobiblicum* grew as Francke and others concentrated on issues of piety and devotion alongside exegetical concerns. Other colloquia developed as well, drawing lay people to the movement. The theology faculty, which had previously encouraged the *collegium philobiblicum,* became increasingly alarmed at the new developments and forbade Francke to hold further colloquia. The gatherings continued, and a religious fervor gripped many students and townspeople in Leipzig. The Electoral Saxon authorities ordered an investigation into the disturbances. In response Francke published his *Apology* (1689), justifying the events in Leipzig theologically. His ally CHRISTIAN THOMASIUS sent a legal opinion defending the Leipzig Pietists to the Electoral government. Their responses inflamed matters and further publicized the Pietist cause. Francke left the city in the fall of 1689. Thomasius and others were expelled in 1690 after the government prohibited all conventicles.

Pietist disturbances were not limited to Leipzig. In Hamburg the clergy and parishioners divided into Pietist and anti-Pietist parties and the conflict nearly toppled the city council. In cities across middle and northern Germany from Erfurt to Lübeck, Pietist movements emerged often in close association with Francke. Ecstatic experiences and visions accompanied many of these. A series of prophetesses appeared in Pietist circles in Erfurt, Halberstadt, Quedlinburg, and Lübeck. The "extraordinary circumstances," as they were known, deepened the divide between the Pietists and their opponents and spawned a furious exchange of tracts on all sides. The polemics between the Pietists and their Orthodox opponents reached a pitch in the 1690s unseen in Lutheranism since the days of the Reformation. At stake were issues of religious enthusiasm, chiliasm, and conventicles. Numerous supporters of the Pietist cause lost their positions, including Francke who had been appointed preacher in Erfurt in 1690.

Many urban and territorial governments suppressed the Pietist movement, but in the territories of elector Friedrich III of Brandenburg (later king Friedrich I of Prussia) Pietists found refuge and qualified support for their aims. Friedrich saw the emergence of the Pietists as a convenient means of achieving his goals of religious TOLERATION and weakening the entrenched local interests in his territories that were closely allied with Lutheran orthodoxy. After Thomasius was dismissed from Leipzig the electoral government installed him at the academy in HALLE. Through Spener's intervention Friedrich offered Francke a professorship at Halle and a position as pastor just outside the city. Electoral patronage insulated Francke from the attacks of the anti-Pietist clergy. The electoral authorities appointed other leading Pietists to the theological faculty in Halle, making the city and its university—officially established in 1694—the intellectual center of ecclesial Pietism in Germany.

In Halle, Francke's views moderated, and he distanced himself from more radical Pietist visionaries and prophets. His characteristic emphases on powerful experiences of repentance, GRACE, and conversion became hallmarks of Halle Pietism. In 1695 Francke founded the famous orphanage in Halle, which grew into the most important Pietist institution in Germany. By 1714 the Halle foundations had over 1,850 pupils in its various schools. Alongside the pedagogical endeavors, the foundations produced pharmaceuticals and developed a large-scale printing house, whose revenues would substantially support their work. Francke's foundations were active in sending the first Protestant missionaries to INDIA and supported the first Protestant mission to the Jews (see JUDAISM).

In other areas of Brandenburg-Prussia, Pietists found widespread support from the government of Friedrich. In 1691 Spener became a leading church prelate in Berlin, where he developed close relationships with a number of government officials and was able to use his influence to secure church appointments for Pietist clergy across Hohenzollern territories. In Königsberg the theology faculty became increasingly pro-Pietist in the early 1700s. Pietist-trained students from Halle came to dominate the military chaplaincy, itself an important route to higher church office in Friedrich's territories. The advances of Pietism in Brandenburg-Prussia frequently encountered opposition from Lutheran orthodoxy, but as many historians have noted, the growth of Pietism played a significant role in the rise of the Prussian state.

Outside of Brandenburg-Prussia, Pietist success was much more uneven at the end of the seventeenth and beginning of the eighteenth centuries. Electoral Saxony became a bulwark against Pietism. The universities of Wittenberg and Leipzig were vehemently anti-Pietist, and the influential Dresden superintendent, Valentin Ernst Löscher (1673–1749), became one of Pietism's ablest opponents. In other territories Pietists found varying degrees of acceptance. In Hessen-Darmstadt Pietists garnered strong support at court. In Württemberg, despite continued opposition from the theology faculty in Tübingen, support for moderate Pietism grew within the territorial church.

Bremen, under the influence of Untereyck and later Cornelius de Hase (1653–1710) and Friedrich Adolph Lampe (1683–1729), became the center of Reformed Pietism in Germany and influenced the Reformed territories of the lower Rhine and East Friesland. Pietism there developed in close association with the COVENANT theology of Coccejus, and generally Pietism did not lead to the same level of conflict as it did in Lutheran areas. Although wary of separatism and the influence of the Labadists, the Reformed synods in the Lower Rhine endorsed conventicles so long as the clergy exercised a level of oversight. In SWITZERLAND, however, the development of a Pietist reform movement in Bern directly influenced by Spener and Francke was suppressed in 1699.

Radical Pietism

Other Pietist currents ran outside of and often opposed to the established Lutheran and Reformed churches. These radical Pietists, as they have come to be known, emphasized many of the same things as other Pietists: the practice of piety, regeneration, hopes for better times, conventicle formation. However, their criticism of the established churches was far more intense and often resulted in the rejection of the existing church as Babel and their separation from established Protestantism. The advocacy of heterodox ideas such as the authority of the inner word, imminent 1,000-year reign of Christ, and UNIVERSALISM placed many radicals outside the limits of orthodoxy. Much more than ecclesial Pietists, radicals drew on mystical spiritualist sources, which included medieval mystics but also theosophists like Weigel and JAKOB BOEHME. The lines between radical and ecclesial Pietism are fluid, however, and where older scholarship tended to dismiss the radicals as aberrations and fanatics, in recent decades they have been integrated more fully into the broader narrative of Pietism.

The interrelation of mainstream and radical Pietism is evident in one of the founders of the Frankfurt *collegia pietatis,* Johann Jacob Schütz. A wealthy lawyer, Schütz was one of Spener's most ardent early supporters and a leader within the gatherings. Early in the 1670s he established connections with the separatist Labadist community—including Anna Maria van Schurman—and was responsible for introducing Labadist ideas to Spener's circle. He gradually distanced himself from Frankfurt *collegia pietatis* and established separate gatherings in the Saalhof with Maria Baur von Eyseneck. By 1682 he broke with Spener and the Lutheran church, having become convinced that the true Christian church could be realized only in small communities of believers.

Johanna Eleonora von Merlau (1644–1724) came out of the Saalhof circle and became one of the most important figures for early radical Pietism. Influenced by both Spener and Schütz, she had renounced court life and found a spiritual calling in Frankfurt leading devotional gatherings and instructing young girls. Eventually, however, she married Johann Wilhelm Petersen (1649–1726), a protege of Spener's. The couple developed a collaborative intellectual relationship, and von Merlau influenced her husband's move toward radical Pietist views. Petersen was dismissed from his position as Lüneburg's superintendent in 1692 for his defense of chiliasm. They found refuge in Brandenburg, where sympathizers at the electoral court were able to secure a state pension for Petersen. Without ministerial obligations, he and his wife further developed their millennial views and, influenced by JANE WARD LEADE, advocated the doctrine of the return of all things. They became key figures in radical Pietism but never separated themselves fully from the Lutheran church.

One of the most important radical Pietists to emerge in the 1690s was the historian and theologian, Gottfried Arnold. Initially drawn to moderate Pietism, by the late 1690s Arnold had come to reject the established church entirely, embrace CELIBACY, and sought to combine older mystical theology with the theosophy of Boehme. His most important work, *An Impartial History of the Church and Heresy* (1699/1700), sought to turn the tables on the "orthodox" in Christian history and accused them of exacerbating error through their persecutions of the heterodox. His work on church history put him squarely in the camp of radical Pietists who had rejected established religion. Consequently Arnold confounded many when he married in 1701 and accepted a clerical position in the Lutheran church. Arnold's decision to moderate his views illustrates the permeable boundaries between radical and ecclesial Pietism.

Other radical Pietists never reconciled themselves to any form of established Christianity. JOHANN CONRAD DIPPEL (1673–1734), one of Arnold's most ardent followers, vehemently criticized the confessional churches throughout his life and developed a highly spiritualized ECCLESIOLOGY and understanding of the SACRAMENTS. His overt criticisms and NONCONFORMITY earned him frequent imprisonment and banishment. Like Dippel, the itinerant preacher Ernst Christoph Hochmann von Hochenau (1670–1721) rejected all formal church organizations and urged his followers to form only loose associations between conventicles.

For some radical Pietists the road to separation led not just to the rejection of the state churches but to the formation of new religious societies. One of the earliest—and most notorious—was the communal society around Eva von Buttlar (1670–1721), which emerged out of radical Pietist circles in Hesse around 1700. The group eventually settled in Wittgenstein in 1704, a territory known for its Toleration of religious dissenters. The society's bizarre sexual practices, derived from Buttlar's peculiar reading of theosophical and Philadelphian sources, shocked the German public, and led to the arrest of the group's leaders and eventual dissolution of the society. Although atypical, the "Buttlar Mob" as they came to be known, became a cautionary tale that was used by opponents to discredit radical Pietist sects.

One of the most enduring associations in radical Pietism was the formation of the New Baptists (Dunker, Schwarzenau Brethren) in 1708. Led by Alexander Mack, a follower of Hochmann von Hochenau, the New Baptists began instituting adult rebaptism in Schwarzenau in the territory of Wittgenstein. A number of radical Pietists had criticized infant BAPTISM, but Mack and his circle were the first to institute adult baptism as a communal practice in Pietism. The New Baptists grew in number and eventually emigrated to Friesland and later Pennsylvania, where their descendants formed the Brethren churches (see BRETHREN, CHURCH OF THE).

At the same time other radical Pietist sects formed in the religiously tolerant territories of Wittgenstein and the Wetterau. The Inspirationists, for instance, believed their leaders to be true instruments of God and thus able to speak authoritatively as prophets. They combined radical German Pietism with the prophecies and visions of the French Camisards and began establishing communities in Marienborn and Wittgenstein around 1715. Descendants of the Inspirationists emigrated to North America in the nineteenth century, eventually forming the AMANA CHURCH SOCIETY.

Later Pietism

After 1740 the strength of Pietist movements in Germany, both ecclesial and radical, waned. In Brandenburg-Prussia, where Pietists had enjoyed privileged positions at court and in the church, Friedrich II showed little sympathy for the Pietist cause. The University of Halle, previously a bastion of ecclesial Pietism, now became the leading exponent of theological Rationalism in Germany under JOHANN SALOMO SEMLER. In the face of new ENLIGHTENMENT challenges to traditional Protestantism, the differences that appeared to separate Pietists and their orthodox opponents seemed far less pressing. Pietist thought and practice continued in many parts of German Protestantism but often in an attenuated form. Against this broader trend of decline, Pietism flourished in the mid-eighteenth century in two contexts: the Duchy of Württemberg and the Moravians under NIKOLAUS LUDWIG VON ZINZENDORF. Both of these established enduring Pietist traditions that remain until the present day.

In no other territory in Germany did Pietism take deeper root than in Württemberg. Initially, however, Pietists found little support in the duchy. Theologians in Tübingen were among the most vocal opponents of Johann Arndt in the seventeenth century, and despite the reform proposals of Johann Valentin Andreae in the first half of the century or the presence of radical spiritualists in the second half, the ideas of Spener and other Pietists gained acceptance only slowly. By the 1690s, however, moderate Pietism had attained a limited level of recognition in Württemberg. Acceptance grew within the church throughout the early eighteenth century, and in 1743—in part to compete with the growing influence of the Moravians—the Württemberg church explicitly authorized conventicle gatherings, thereby institutionalizing a key Pietist practice in the congregations. A distinctive Württemberg Pietism within the territorial church emerged under the biblical scholar and millennialist thinker, JOHANN ALBRECHT BENGEL (1687–1752), and his pupil Friedrich Christoph Oetinger (1702–1782), whose speculative theology took him beyond Bengel's biblicism toward theosophy and the Kabbalah. Württemberg Pietism established itself first among the middle classes but eventually came to powerfully influence folk piety in Württemberg. Even today Pietist influences continue to shape Protestantism in Württemberg.

Another distinctive variant of Pietism emerged under the leadership of Zinzendorf, who had been raised in a thoroughly Pietist milieu. Beginning in 1722 he began settling religious refugees on his estate in Upper Lusatia. The refugees came from Moravia, Bohemia, Silesia, and other parts of central Europe and represented a number of confessions including descendants from the pre-Reformation Hussite church, the *Unitas Fratrum*. The community grew quickly and despite early dissension among the refugees, Zinzendorf was able to forge an agreement among nearly all the Brethren to establish a new communitarian life in 1727. Combining Spener's notion of the *ecclesiola in ecclesia* with the elements of the older *Unitas Fratrum*, Zinzendorf established HERRNHUT as an *ecclesiola* or little church within the established Lutheran church of Saxony.

Pietism profoundly shaped Zinzendorf and the early Herrnhut community. Zinzendorf came to reject, however, Francke's emphasis on the repentance struggle in the conversion process, and he dismissed Bengel's millennialism, leading to deep rifts between Zinzendorf and ecclesial Pietists in Halle and Württemberg. Increasingly Zinzendorf turned toward Luther's theology of the cross, out of which the distinctive themes of the blood and wounds of Christ and mystical "encounter with the Savior" developed. Zinzendorf also drew heavily on the Philadelphian ideas of the radical Pietists and sought to unite Christians in an ecumenical society that transcended confessional divisions. The Herrnhut community was extraordinarily dynamic and led to the establishment of sister communities across Europe and North America. Particularly active as preachers and missionaries, Zinzendorf's followers were responsible for the transmission of many Pietist ideas to Protestants beyond Germany, including JOHN WESLEY and English METHODISM. Despite Zinzendorf's ecumenical ideals, he eventually formed a separate free church, known in the English-speaking world as the MORAVIAN CHURCH. Because of its distinct identity, older narratives tended to treat Zinzendorf and the Moravians separately from other Pietist groups, but more recently they have been incorporated into the larger context and historiography of Pietism.

Additional Pietist impulses reemerged during the late eighteenth century. The establishment of the *Deutsche Christentumgesellschaft* in Basel in 1780 marked a neo-Pietist development within German Protestantism modeled on the SOCIETY FOR PROMOTING CHRISTIAN KNOWLEDGE. Within a few years sister societies were established across Protestant Germany and Switzerland. Unlike many earlier Pietist organizations, which retained their confessional identities, from the outset the *Christentumgesellschaft* was conceived as a joint Protestant project. The *Christentumgesellschaft* established a Bible society in 1804 and a mission society in 1815 (see BASEL MISSION), which became one of the leading Protestant missionary societies in Europe.

The late eighteenth century also saw a series of neo-Pietist figures such as JOHANN KASPAR LAVATER (1741–1801), JOHANN HEINRICH JUNG-STILLING (1740–1817), and JOHANN FRIEDRICH OBERLIN (1790–1824), all of whom drew consciously on elements of Pietism but also sought to come to terms with challenges presented by the Enlightenment. Jung-Stilling, in particular, provides a bridge to the revival movements of the nineteenth century.

Scholars disagree whether the term Pietism can be profitably extended into the nineteenth and twentieth centuries. Without question, Pietist currents continued in the revival movement (*Erweckungsbewegung*) in German-speaking lands during the nineteenth century. Pietism influenced HANS NIELSEN HAUGE in NORWAY and the Mission Covenant Church in SWEDEN (1878). In North America the legacy of Pietism continued among the existing Moravian and Brethren churches, in various Lutheran and Reformed denominations, as well as among new formations such as Johann Georg Rapp's Harmony Society and the EVANGELICAL UNITED BRETHREN CHURCH. The diversity of these groups, however, also illustrates the heterogeneity of movements inspired by Pietism and the problem of applying a single historical concept to them. Later Pietism bears a number of similarities to EVANGELICALISM and HOLINESS MOVEMENTS, but firm connections between them require further comparative research.

See also Millenarians and Millennialists

References and Further Reading

Brown, Dale. *Understanding Pietism*. Rev. ed. Nappanee, IN: Evangel Publishing, 1978.

Brecht, Martin, ed. *Der Pietismus vom siebzehnten bis zum frühen achtzehnten Jahrhundert. Geschichte des Pietismus*. Vol. 1. Göttingen: Vandenhoeck & Ruprecht, 1992.

———, and Klaus Deppermann, eds. *Der Pietismus im achtzehnten Jahrhundert. Geschichte des Pietismus*. Vol. 2. Göttingen: Vandenhoeck & Ruprecht, 1995.

Erb, Peter C., ed. "Pietists: Selected Writings." In *Classics of Western Spirituality*. New York and Mahwah, NJ: Paulist Press, 1983.

Gäbler, Ulrich, ed. *Der Pietismus im neunzehnten und zwanzigsten Jahrhundert. Geschichte des Pietismus.* Vol. 3. Göttingen: Vandenhoeck & Ruprecht, 2000.

Gawthrop, Richard. *Pietism and the Making of Eighteenth-Century Prussia.* Cambridge: Cambridge University Press, 1993.

Lehmann, Hartmut, ed. *Glaubenswelt und Lebenswelt des Pietismus. Geschichte des Pietismus.* Vol. 4. Göttingen: Vandenhoeck & Ruprecht, 2003.

Martin, Lucinda. "Women's Religious Speech and Activism in German Pietism." Ph.D. dissertation, University of Texas–Austin, 2002.

Pietismus und Neuzeit (1974–). [An international yearbook of Pietist studies, which includes a comprehensive annual bibliography of Pietism and related topics.]

Spener, Philipp Jacob. *Pia Desideria.* Translated and edited by Theodore Tappert. Philadelphia: Fortress Press, 1964.

Stoeffler, F. Erenst. *The Rise of Evangelical Pietism.* Leiden: Brill, 1965.

———. *German Pietism During the Eighteenth Century.* Leiden: Brill, 1973.

———, ed. *Continental Pietism and Early American Christianity.* Grand Rapids, MI: Wm. B. Eerdmans, 1976.

Strom, Jonathan. "Problems and Promises of Pietism Research." *Church History* 71 (2002): 536–554.

Wallmann, Johannes. *Der Pietismus. Die Kirche in Ihrer Geschichte.* Vol. 4/O1. Göttingen: Vandenhoeck & Ruprecht, 1990.

Ward, W. Reginald. *The Protestant Evangelical Awakening.* Cambridge: Cambridge University Press, 1992.

JONATHAN STROM

PILGRIM FATHERS

When King James I would not reform the CHURCH OF ENGLAND along Calvinist lines, disaffected Puritans (see PURITANISM) in northern Nottinghamshire and adjacent regions separated around 1605, forming independent congregations led by JOHN SMYTH at Gainsborough Hall, and by Richard Clifton at Scrooby Manor, the home of Elder William Brewster. JOHN ROBINSON, former dean of Corpus Christi College, Cambridge, then deposed "teacher" (assistant pastor) at St. Andrew's parish in Norwich, joined them around 1607–1608. Pursued, fined, and jailed, these Separatists fled in the summer of 1608 to Amsterdam, where they joined the group led by Francis Johnson. Their arrival caused Amsterdam's English Reformed to organize a distinct, contrasting congregation. It still uses the Begijnhof Chapel.

Influenced by Amsterdam MENNONITES, John Smyth rebaptized himself and some followers, forming the first English Baptist congregation and branding Clifton and other former friends who had not joined as heretics. In early 1609, to avoid further controversies, John Robinson moved with about a hundred adults to Leiden. Establishing a "congregational" church, they attracted new members from East Anglia, Kent, London, and elsewhere, including Walloon (Huguenot) refugees already in Leiden, and some Dutch. By 1620,

when resumption of the Dutch war with Spain made their future uncertain, the Leiden congregation had around 400 families ready to go to America.

Significance beyond their numbers was achieved by Brewster's printing Puritan and Separatist propaganda, smuggled into ENGLAND but also sold at the Frankfurt Book Fair. Befriended by Leiden's anti-Arminian (see ARMINIANISM) professor Johannes Polyander, Robinson debated with Simon Episcopius and grew toward a "semi-Separatist" position, open to collaboration with other congregations. Away from home, his members attended French and DUTCH REFORMED churches. WILLIAM AMES and Henry Jacob were among visitors to Robinson's congregation. Jacob returned to London, where in Southwark he set up England's first sustained Separatist congregation, along the same lines.

Plymouth Colony (now southeast Massachusetts) began in 1620 when the ship *Mayflower* transported Leiden Separatists and a smaller number of others from England. Before landing, the colonists drew up the "Mayflower Compact," a civil contract by which everyone including the "Strangers" (probably meaning the non-English HUGUENOTS) agreed to abide by English law and any new bylaws passed by the colonists. This applied congregational church polity (itself derived from Dutch Mennonite example) to civil society. It marks the beginning of town-meeting democracy in New England. Migration to Plymouth from Leiden continued for more than a decade. John Robinson, with the majority still in Leiden, died there in 1625. Without an ordained minister, the colonists introduced civil marriage registration, citing Dutch legal precedent.

The colony's independent history (1620–1691) is notable for peace treaties with local natives lasting fifty years, and for a court that recognized native sachems as the true proprietors of land. Governor William Bradford's nostalgic memoire, *Of Plimouth Plantation,* is the prime historical source for the early years. In the second half of the century, the congregation in the colony's largest town, Scituate, split over the combined issues of the exclusivity of the covenant and consequences for suffrage and the distribution of common lands. Plymouth colony, predominantly congregationalist, was comparatively tolerant of BAPTISTS and Quakers (see FRIENDS, SOCIETY OF); there was no witchcraft hysteria. Puritan theologian JOHN COTTON reported that the Pilgrims' CONGREGATIONALISM inspired imitation in Massachusetts Bay Colony. Since the nineteenth century, however, this has been rejected sarcastically with appeals to "common sense" but not to contradictory evidence. Eventually overshadowed numerically and economically by the Massachusetts Bay Colony to its north, at mid-century Plymouth was still considered important enough for its third governor, Edward Winslow, to be appointed by England's OLIVER CROMWELL and the Dutch parliament to act as chairman of an international committee to settle outstanding disputes after the First Anglo-Dutch War (1654).

Cast as heroes of romantic fiction in the nineteenth century, the Plymouth Separatists acquired the name "Pilgrims" and were excessively praised as paragons of civic and personal virtue who perfected the REFORMATION and founded DEMOCRACY in the American empire. An equally unscholarly debunking reaction followed in the twentieth century, and now the Pilgrims are ironically the focus of the American Indian Movement's "Day of Mourning" held on Thanksgiving Day.

See also Dissent

References and Further Reading

Primary Sources:

Arber, Edward, ed. *The Story of the Pilgrim Fathers, 1606–1623 A.D., as told by Themselves, their Friends, and their Enemies.* London: Ward & Downey; Boston and New York: Houghton Mifflin, 1897.

Ashton, Robert, ed. *John Robinson's Works.* 3 vols. Boston: Doctrinal Tract and Book Society, 1851.

Bangs, Jeremy Dupertuis. *Indian Deeds, Land Transactions in Plymouth Colony, 1620–1691.* Boston: New England Historic Genealogical Society, 2002.

Bradford, William. *Bradford's History "Of Plimoth Plantation."* [From the Original Manuscript]. Boston: Wright & Potter, 1901.

Shurtleff, Nathaniel B., and David Pulsifer, eds. *Records of the Colony of New Plymouth in New England.* 12 vols. Boston: William White, 1855–1861.

Secondary Sources:

Dexter, Henry Martyn, and Morton Dexter. *The England and Holland of the Pilgrims.* Boston and New York: Houghton Mifflin, 1905.

George, Timothy. *John Robinson and the English Separatist Tradition.* Macon, GA: Mercer University Press, 1982.

Harris, J. Rendell, and Stephen K. Jones, with D. Plooij, *The Pilgrim Press*, with new contributions by R. Breugelmans, J. A. Gruys, and Keith L. Sprunger. Nieuwkoop: De Graaf, 1987.

Langdon, George. *Pilgrim Colony, A History of New Plymouth, 1620–1691.* New Haven and London: Yale University Press, 1966.

Stratton, Eugene Aubrey. *Plymouth Colony, Its History & People, 1620–1691.* Salt Lake City: Ancestry Publishing, 1986.

JEREMY BANGS

PILGRIM'S PROGRESS, THE

The Pilgrim's Progress is one of the most widely read Christian texts of the English-speaking world, apart from the BIBLE, and is the best-known example of seventeenth-century English Nonconformist literature. Written while its author JOHN BUNYAN, the son of a tinker, was imprisoned for unlicensed PREACHING, it became a best-seller in its own time, was swiftly translated and disseminated throughout the world, and continues to be published and adapted by mainstream and evangelical presses.

The Pilgrim's Progress From This World To That which Is To Come, published in 1678, is a verse allegory of an individual's search for the way to SALVATION. It opens with the author's recollection of a dream in which a man, Christian, with a great burden on his back and a book in his hand, is crying "What shall I do to be saved?" Then follows his journey from the City of Destruction to the Celestial City. Vividly drawn figures and locations such as Mr. Worldly Wiseman, Giant Despair, the Slough of Despond, and Vanity Fair, add drama and social realism to a text that narrates the tensions of predestinarian CALVINISM as experienced by an individual.

The Pilgrim's Progress, Part Two, published in 1684, follows the journey of Christiana, Christian's wife, and her family, as they follow his path to salvation, guided by an ideal pastor, Mr. Great-heart. This focus on a group rather than an individual is often linked with Bunyan's later experience as minister of his Bedford congregation, but it also reflects the gradual consolidation of Nonconformist communities in the period and their own problems.

The Pilgrim's Progress is celebrated for its acute observations of spiritual and psychological states and social realities. Its wide readership has always been attributed to its lively colloquial language, dramatic scenes, and memorable characters that make the process of learning the theological lessons of Calvinism a pleasure.

References and Further Reading

Bunyan, John. *The Pilgrim's Progress.* Oxford and New York: Oxford University Press, 1984.

Hill, Christopher. *A Tinker and a Poor Man: John Bunyan and His Church, 1628–1688.* New York and London: W. W. Norton, 1988.

Keeble, N. H. *The Literary Culture of Nonconformity in Later Seventeenth-century England.* Leicester, UK: Leicester University Press, 1987.

TAMSIN SPARGO

PILGRIMAGES

See Travels and Pilgrimages

PILKINGTON, GEORGE LAWRENCE (1865–1897)

English missionary leader. Pilkington was born in Tyrrellspass, County Westmeath, IRELAND in 1865, and he died at Luba's Fort, Uganda, December 12, 1897. He was educated at Uppingham School and attended Pembroke College, CAMBRIDGE UNIVERSITY as a scholar when evangelical student activism was at its height. After a CONVERSION experience he became imbued with evangelistic zeal and with the teaching on holiness associated with the KESWICK MOVEMENT. Caught up in the enthusiasm for MISSIONS engendered by the Cambridge Seven, he offered his services to the CHINA INLAND MISSION, but bowed to his parents' entreaty to defer missionary service. The delay enabled him to achieve high academic success in classics on graduating in 1887.

After a short stint of teaching at Harrow and at Bedford Grammar School, he was appointed in 1890 by the (Anglican) CHURCH MISSIONARY SOCIETY to Buganda, where the Protestant missionary movement had recently seen its first major East African success. An active new bishop, A. R. Tucker (1849–1914), was consecrated for Eastern Equatorial Africa that year to oversee the consolidation of the church. Pilkington was one of several young men appointed for that purpose.

Buganda was in flux. Protestant and Catholic missions, led respectively by British and French missionaries, had arrived almost simultaneously, and each had a following among the Ganda. Muslim activity had preceded them. British, French, and German competition in AFRICA was intensifying. Conservative traditionalists were seeking to maintain and revive the power of the sacral monarchy. Buganda was full of complex power struggles, where political and religious loyalties inevitably interpenetrated.

Pilkington's brief service was significant in two respects. With Tucker's encouragement, he devoted his scholarly gifts to work on the Luganda vernacular. Early preaching and Scripture reading had been in Swahili, the current lingua franca. Pilkington was the key figure in the production—in a remarkably short time and at a remarkably high standard—of the BIBLE in the Luganda language, making use of the existing *de facto* oral translations arising from the work of Ganda preachers. Christianity and reading were closely identified in Buganda, and the printed Bible was soon in widespread use (see BIBLE TRANSLATION). A vernacular literature in Luganda followed.

Pilkington and his colleagues, as British Evangelicals, distinguished between "real" and "nominal" Christianity. Despite their best efforts, "nominal" Christianity was as manifest in Buganda as in Britain. Pilkington, with his Keswick views and impatience with anything he regarded as unspiritual, was especially distressed by the weight given by church members to political factors. He rejected an overture from the king to come over to the Protestant side because he saw no sign of "real" Christianity in him. Late in 1893, depressed and unwell, he took a solitary retreat on a lake island. There he received an experience of renewal that he described as "the baptism of the Holy Ghost." His colleagues responded enthusiastically, and in the meetings that followed, the renewal spread through much of the Ganda church, with all the marks of "real" Christianity clearly evident. On leave in 1896, Pilkington took the message about revival to the huge Liverpool conference of the Student Volunteer Missionary Union. On return to East Africa he surprised colleagues by cycling from the coast to Buganda, taking three weeks en route but arriving five weeks ahead of the rest of the party who were traveling by more conventional means.

Despite his unworldly outlook, Pilkington took for granted the desirability of British colonial overrule in East Africa. When in 1897 Ganda forces were called in to assist British officials to quell a mutiny by Sudanese troops, he readily went with them, and was mortally wounded in the battle.

The Ganda church was pivotal in the development of Protestant Christianity in East Africa. Ganda preachers brought about the evangelization of much of what is now Uganda, and the biblical and revival movements facilitated by Pilkington were important elements in that achievement. East African Protestantism has been overwhelmingly Biblicist; and the revival movement (Balokele), the most powerful element in Protestant spirituality throughout East Africa, acknowledges Pilkington as a forerunner.

See also Evangelicalism; Missionary Organizations; Missions, British; Revivals; Studd, Charles T.

References and Further Reading

Church Missionary Society Register of Missionaries. London: CMS, 1896.

Harford Battersby, C. F. *Pilkington of Uganda.* London: Marshall, 1898.

Pirouet, Louise. *Black Evangelists: The Spread of Christianity in Uganda 1891–1914.* London: Rex Collings, 1978.

Stock, Eugene. *History of the Church Missionary Society.* Vol. 3. London: CMS, 1899.

Taylor, J. V. *The Growth of the Church in Buganda.* London: SCM, 1958.

Tucker, A. R. *Eighteen Years in Uganda and East Africa.* London: Arnold, 1911.

ANDREW F. WALLS

PLURAL MARRIAGE (POLYGAMY)

Polygamy literally means "plural marriage." Though there are isolated instances of polyandry (multiple husbands), such as in Nepal, the overwhelming number of polygamous groups or societies throughout history have been polygynous (more than one wife). This is reflected in the fact that modern English speakers tend to use the term polygamy and its cognates when technically they are referring to polygyny. To avoid pedantry, the terms will be used interchangeably in this article.

Early Christian Views

Almost from the beginning, the dominant Christian view of plural marriage has been one of opposition and proscription. As with other religions, Christians often defined themselves in contradistinction to those around them. From an organizational-behavior perspective, this can be understood as "boundary maintenance" and identity formulation. As part of the effort to disengage from JUDAISM, for instance, Christians distanced themselves from contemporary Jewish polygamy and even from patriarchal polygyny. Justin Martyr's (c. 100–c. 165) repudiation of polygamy in his *Dialogue with Trypho the Jew* is an example of this. However, because Christians inherited the Hebrew Bible (Old Testament) as their Scripture, they felt compelled to explain how many of its leading men could have practiced polygyny and still enjoyed Yahweh's favor. In the context of an emerging patristic abhorrence of sex (even marital sex in some cases), justification for patriarchal polygamy was only possible by viewing it first as a special primordial "dispensation" from God in order to multiply and replenish the earth, and second, by stripping the patriarchs of any passion or pleasure in the process of fulfilling that dispensation.

During the patristic period, when Christianity was tilting toward ASCETICISM, the ideal was "no marriage" or at least no procreatively active marriage, rather than prolific plural marriage. If a man "had" to marry rather than burn, according to the early church evangelist (Paul), he should still work toward overcoming sexual desire, even toward his own wife. A concomitant of the patristic fear of sexual longing was a rather unflattering view of women as basically purveyors of male-corrupting temptation. Given such attitudes (which continued into the Middle Ages—Aquinas called women "misbegotten males"), why would any God-fearing Christian man wish to compound his problems by desiring more than one wife? The idea was to pull man out of the sexual mire, not push him in.

Still, allowances were made for the less spiritual, including toleration of "concubinage." In Roman society, certain classes of people could not legally be married, so they simply lived together. In other instances, married or unmarried men kept a mistress. Children born of concubinage, called "natural children," were accorded a status inferior to children of the lawfully wedded wife, and they received a lesser inheritance or, at times, none at all. Clerical toleration of concubinage was a begrudging concession to a fallen world. Elevating concubinage to polygamy, by giving it the status of legal marriage with all the concomitant rights and restrictions, was out of the question. The inconsistency of sanctioning one while condemning the other, however, was not lost on polygamy's supporters. Later defenders of polygyny would often point to the hypocrisy of society's tolerating promiscuity and prostitution while being scandalized by the prospect of socially stable, legalized polygamy.

Protestant Reformation

The Protestant REFORMATION challenged Roman Catholic teachings on various points with regard to marriage and sexuality, but not on polygamy. The Reformers adopted a more positive attitude toward sex within marriage, but they could see little good in reviving plural marriage. Among the rare exceptions was the occasional concession to royalty in need of an heir. MARTIN LUTHER (1483–1546) and PHILIP MELANCHTHON (1497–1560), for instance, justified polygamy as an acceptable way around the indissolubility of marriage for both HENRY VIII (1491–1547) and PHILIP OF HESSE. In cases such as these, where issues of inheritance were absolutely crucial and DIVORCE virtually impossible, polygamy was considered as a practical, even pious, alternative to adultery or concubinage. There is evidence that Pope Clement VII briefly pondered a polygamy dispensation for Henry but ultimately decided against it. His close advisor Cardinal Cajetan argued that because polygamy violated neither divine nor natural law, it was a viable emergency option. In Lutheran GERMANY, Philip of Hesse followed the pastoral advice of Luther, Melanchton, and MARTIN BUCER (1491–1551) and took a second wife.

Supporters of polygamy were literally anathematized by the Catholic Council of Trent in 1563, but throughout the sixteenth and seventeenth centuries, a steady, if minority, stream of Protestants continued to defend it as appropriate under certain circumstances. It was proposed, for instance, as a solution where a wife was barren or mentally ill, or where a husband had been taken captive in a foreign country. It was also advanced as the answer to localized imbalances in the sex ratio. Despite antagonists' lurid descriptions of the lustful theocrats who led the brief Anabaptist rebellion in Munster, polygyny appears to have been implemented there primarily as an interim welfare measure to provide protection for the large number of women left behind when their husbands departed or were expelled from the city. Similarly, following the Thirty Years War, the regional council in Nuremberg reportedly proposed a season of polygamy to care for the widows and fatherless and to replenish the stock of males in the population, though this has not been verified in any surviving contemporary records.

One of the most famous advocates of plural marriage in early modern Europe was the English poet JOHN MILTON (1608–c. 1674), whose marriage was sufficiently strained that his wife left him and returned to her childhood home. In his *Treatise on Christian Doctrine* (not discovered and published until the 1800s), Milton, on pragmatic as well as scriptural grounds, urged polygamy as a way around the virtual impossibility of divorce. On the continent a few years later, the German Lutheran John Leyser became the primary public proponent of polygamy. His *Political Discourse on Polygamy* (1676) was more elaborate than Milton's work, but followed the same dual format of defending polygamy based on the Bible and proposing it as a socially progressive possibility in select situations. Supporters of polygamy, always a tiny minority, were widely lampooned as lechers in the pamphlet wars of the day. For their part, in good Reformation tradition, they claimed only to be calling for the further restoration of legitimate biblical practices.

As polygamy apologetics continued sporadically throughout the eighteenth century, polygamy came to be seen as a panacea for yet other problems. One of the most significant examples was the work of the Methodist hospital chaplain, Martin Madan (1726–1790). In his multivolume work *Thelyphthora* (1780), Madan proposed a full-scale return to the laws of the Hebrew Bible as the solution to the sorry plight of seduced and abandoned young women like the ones he routinely dealt with in the hospital. According to Madan, if biblical laws were followed, then a man who seduced an unmarried woman would have to marry her and provide for her, and this would be possible for men already married because polygamy would be legal. Madan saw polygamy as the "divine law" of the Old Testament and argued that it had not been abrogated by Christ; only when uninspired churchmen in the post-apostolic period modified or overturned divine Old Testament practices like polygamy did society begin to deteriorate. In addition to reiterating many of the previously recognized special circumstances in which polygamy would be a viable alternative to extramarital liaisons, Madan acknowledged that some men would satisfy their lusts regard-

less of the consequences; polygamy became a way to make them pay the price for their indulgences. On the other hand, Madan gave little attention to how female victims or first wives would feel about this arrangement.

The Luthers, Miltons, and Madans notwithstanding, support for polygamy has been extremely limited throughout Christian history both in terms of numbers and scope. Until the nineteenth century, that support was almost always a response to the difficulties imposed by the prevailing view of the indissolubility of monogamous marriage. Monogamy was assumed to be the norm; plural marriage only filled in the dysfunctional gaps. Such, however, was not the case with Mormon polygamy in mid–nineteenth-century America, a phenomenon unique in the Western world, both in its scope and its nature. Though thousands of Mormons would eventually enter plural marriages, the Church of Jesus Christ of Latter-day Saints did not count polygamy as one of its founding principles. Plural marriage was added more than a decade after the church's 1830 organization and was not publicly proclaimed until the 1850s. After nearly four decades of openly practicing and defending "the principle," as Mormons called it, in the face of severe persecution, church president Wilford Woodruff (1807–1898) issued a formal statement in 1890 indicating the Latter-day Saints' intention to comply with the federal laws prohibiting plural marriages. Within Christendom, the uniqueness of the Mormon experience makes it worth discussing at some length.

Mormonism and Polygamy

Despite all that has been written about Mormon polygamy, no satisfactory explanation for its inauguration has emerged. It was not part of a conscious effort to reform marriage and divorce laws. It did not grow out of obvious social dysfunction within the community. Indeed, there is no clear background for its inception other than the fundamental Mormon commitment to biblical restorationism, which is apparent in the very wording of the revelation: "Verily, thus saith the Lord unto you my servant Joseph [Smith], that inasmuch as you have inquired of my hand to know and understand wherein I, the Lord, justified my servants Abraham, Isaac, and Jacob, as also Moses, David, and Solomon, my servants, as touching the principle and doctrine of their having many wives and concubines. Behold, and lo, I am the Lord thy God, and will answer thee as touching this matter. Therefore, prepare thy heart to receive and obey the instructions which I am about to give unto you . . . an appointment [to] restore all things" (Doctrine and Covenants 132:1–3, 40).

When the revelation came, Victorian Mormons were caught completely by surprise. Even BRIGHAM YOUNG (1801–1877), long regarded in popular stereotype as the quintessential Mormon polygamist, remarked that when the concept was first presented to him, he "desired the grave" rather than embrace the practice. Despite such initial hesitations, the Latter-day Saints pressed forward with the implementation of plural marriage. The biblical patriarch Abraham was their explicit model. Not only was he a polygamist and paragon of piety fully in favor with God, but the Saints could identify with Abraham's poignant (and painful) willingness to proceed with God's command to sacrifice Isaac even when his natural feelings recoiled. Appropriately, the revelation inaugurating plural marriage contained this injunction: "go ye, therefore, and do the works of Abraham; enter ye into my law and ye shall be saved" (Doctrine and Covenants 132:32).

The only other revealed rationale for Mormon polygamy was that it would aid in "raising up" a people to God. Again, Abraham was paradigmatic: "the promise [of numerous posterity] was made unto Abraham; and by this law [polygamy] is the continuation of the works of my Father, wherein he glorifieth himself" (Doctrine and Covenants 132:31). The Book of Mormon endorsed monogamy as its norm, except in special circumstances: "For if I will, said the Lord of Hosts, raise up seed unto me, I will command my people; otherwise they shall hearken unto these things" (Jacob 2:30). From the Latter-day Saints' perspective, plural marriage enabled God to "jump start" a latter-day covenant people because polygamist parents, representing the pinnacle of faithfulness, would raise in righteousness a large posterity. This is reminiscent of how earlier Christian apologists justified patriarchal polygamy. The Mormon revelation also reflects the sense of divine dispensation with regard to plural marriage rather than human initiation and indiscriminate implementation.

During the fifty years that "the principle" was in force, about twenty to thirty percent of the Latter-day Saints lived in polygamous families. This would place them at the upper end of the scale of participation when compared with the non-Western polygamous groups who have been studied by twentieth-century social scientists. Contrary to popular perception, monogamous marriages always outnumber polygamous ones in polygamous societies. According to data collected a generation ago, three out of every four tribes in sub-Saharan AFRICA considered polygamy the preferred form of marriage. In only one third of them, however, did the incidence of plural marriage exceed twenty percent. The incidence of polygamy in Mormon Utah in the second half of the nineteenth century closely parallels these findings. As George P. Murdock (1897–1985) the eminent twentieth-century cataloger of ethnographic information, explained, a society is said to be polygamous "wherever the culture permits, and public opinion encourages, a man to have more than one wife at the same time, whether such unions are common or comparatively rare, confined to men of outstanding prestige or allowed to anyone who can afford them" (Hillman 1975:88).

Another similarity between the African and the Mormon experience is the number of wives married by polygamists. In Africa a generation ago the mean number of wives per husband was 2.5; in Mormon Utah it was 2.3. These data reflect economic realities. Only a minority of males in any given society have the personal resources to expand their household in this manner. Polygamy has almost always been confined to the wealthy and/or the powerful in any place where it has been practiced. Today, people influenced by sex-saturated Western culture may view plural marriage as little more than plural sex, but to those who actually engage in the practice, it means plural families, with all the corresponding obligations and responsibilities. For those interested in multiple sex partners, there have always been less costly and consequential ways to achieve that goal. Though added responsibilities and burdens accompany the practice of polygamy, so often does enhanced prestige. As with other polygamous societies, studies show a high degree of correspondence between leadership standing within the Latter-day Saints community and the practice of plural marriage.

Although Latter-day Saints pointed primarily to revelation as the reason for practicing plural marriage, a strident and widespread antipolygamy campaign by contemporary Christians compelled them to develop elaborate justifications for the practice. Many of these were openly derived from earlier Protestant defenses of polygamy. For instance, Latter-day Saints knew of, and quoted, Luther, Milton, and Madan. Like Madan, they viewed plural marriage as protective of women. Polygamy would provide for the widow, the spinster, and the orphan. It would make promiscuity and its attendant health-care ills a thing of the past. As Mormons were fond of pointing out, there were no brothels in Zion. Plural marriage also ensured a God-fearing spouse to every woman who desired one. Some even argued that it offered a kind of spiritual version of Lycurgus's vision for ancient Sparta, where children were to be born not just to "first comer" wives but to all who wished to have a child fathered by the "best men." As George Bernard Shaw would later quip, "Women will always prefer a tenth share of a first-rate man to the exclusive possession of a third-rate one" (Cairncross 1974:221).

PLURAL MARRIAGE (POLYGAMY)

To the surprise of their contemporaries, Latter-day Saints women were as aggressive and vocal in their support of polygamy as the men. They argued that polygamy was progressive, the means to freedom, respect, and personal development. Leading Mormon Emmeline B. Wells (1828–1921) wrote that Latter-day Saints teachings in general and polygamy in particular made Utah women "real, genuine, rational beings," rather than a "glittering and fragile toy, a thing without brains or soul, placed on a tinseled and unsubstantial pedestal" as was common elsewhere in Victorian America (*Woman's Exponent,* July 15, 1872, 29). Shared domestic responsibilities enabled women to pursue what education and professional training was open to them at the time. Mormon women became doctors, midwives, merchants, and politicians. They aligned themselves with some of the foremost advocates of women's rights in their day. Susan B. Anthony (1820–1906), for instance, joined Wells and colleagues in 1879 to deliver a protest memorial against antipolygamy legislation. Reading the Latter-day Saints *Woman's Exponent* for this time period provides ample testimony that polygamous wives were far from the servile "pawns of the priesthood" their opponents claimed them to be.

Popular misunderstanding of Mormon polygamy led opponents in the United States to support the 1870 extension of the voting franchise to women in the Utah Territory on the assumption that if Latter-day Saints women could vote, they would naturally overturn the oppressive polygamic theocracy that held them in thralldom. When Mormon women turned out to be vocal defenders of plural marriage, regularly staging "indignation meetings" against meddling Easterners, opponents spent the 1880s trying to pass legislation to not only disenfranchise polygamist men but their wives as well. The Edmunds Act of 1882 disenfranchised polygamists, attached a misdemeanor penalty to cohabitation, and sent convicted practitioners to the penitentiary. When it became apparent that polygamist Latter-day Saint leaders would resist "the Raid" by going "on the underground" (Latter-day Saints Church President John Taylor died in 1887, while in hiding on the underground), the Edmunds-Tucker Act was passed. This not only perpetuated the provisions of the previous act but attacked the Latter-day Saints church itself. It dissolved the corporation of the church and escheated to the federal government its properties, valued over fifty thousand dollars. In 1890 the Supreme Court upheld the constitutionality of the Edmunds-Tucker Act as well as an Idaho statute disenfranchising *all* Mormons.

At this juncture, the destruction of the church and especially the desecration of its holy temples seemed imminent. Just before issuing his 1890 "Manifesto" calling for the cessation of plural marriage among the Mormons, church president Wilford Woodruff remarked "I have arrived at a point . . . where I am under the necessity of acting for the temporal salvation of the church" (Wilford Woodruff Journal, September 25, 1890). It took a period of years for the practice to be stopped completely. Some Mormons assumed the Manifesto was only a concession to the present power of the enemy, not an expression of what God really wanted his Saints to do. In time, Mormons came to realize that polygamy and its defense had indeed served the purpose of raising up a unified people to God. God's will for the Saints in the twentieth century was to follow the normal practice of monogamy. Today, the Church of Jesus Christ of Latter-day Saints openly condemns plural marriage and goes to considerable lengths to distance itself from break-off groups who still practice it. Such groups, usually labeled "Mormon Fundamentalists," have no official affiliation with the church, nor do Latter-day Saints presently lobby for the legalization of polygamy in the United States or elsewhere so that they can restore the practice. Indeed, in the intervening century, they have become as ardent in their endorsement of the ideal of monogamous marriage as they were in their support of plural marriage during the nineteenth century.

As cultural relativism came to philosophic prominence in the twentieth century, toleration of polygamy increased. In the second half of the century, a number of Christian churches with missions and congregations in the Third and Fourth World reevaluated their stance and abandoned the longstanding requirement that polygamists divorce all but one wife in order to receive baptism. Where plural marriage was deeply embedded in a group's pre-Christian culture, it came to be ecclesiastically countenanced in varying degrees. On the other hand, the same relativistic perspectives undercut the possibility that polygamy could any longer be seriously proposed as a universal panacea for world social problems. The "sexual revolution" of the 1960s both reflected and reinforced this erosion of an undergirding Judeo-Christian value system within which previous arguments for polygamy were elaborated. The revolution also removed the need for polygamy as a socially and religiously acceptable alternative to dyadic discontents. Tolerance for unmarried cohabitation and easy divorce procedures are pervasive in the Western world today. In this postmodern age, fringe forays into polygamy will be tolerated and will likely continue, but it is not likely that the West will again witness an institutionalized Christian experiment in polygamy.

References and Further Reading

Arrington, Leonard J, and Davis Bitton. *The Mormon Experience: A History of the Latter-day Saints.* New York: Knopf, 1979.

Brundage, James A. *Law, Sex, and Christian Society in Medieval Europe.* Chicago: University of Chicago Press, 1987.

Cairncross, John. *After Polygamy Was Made a Sin: The Social History of Christian Polygamy.* London: Routledge and Kegan Paul, 1974.

Embry, Jessie L. *Mormon Polygamous Families: Life in the Principle.* Salt Lake City: University of Utah Press, 1987.

Hardy, B. Carmon. *Solemn Covenant: The Mormon Polygamous Passage.* Chicago: University of Illinois Press, 1992.

Hillman, Eugene. *Polygamy Reconsidered: African Plural Marriage and the Christian Churches.* Maryknoll, NY: Orbis Books, 1975.

Miller, Leo. *John Milton Among the Polygamophiles.* New York: Lowenthal Press, 1974.

GRANT UNDERWOOD

PLYMOUTH BRETHREN

The Brethren movement consists of several lay-led Protestant evangelical groups. It originated in the 1820s in IRELAND and ENGLAND and from 1848 onward was broadly divided into the "Open Brethren," which became the largest section, and the "Exclusive Brethren," which subsequently fragmented further. The most distinctive contribution of Brethrenism to Protestant FUNDAMENTALISM was the eschatological scheme of DISPENSATIONALISM. The movement is widely dispersed throughout the world because of emigration and the Brethren enthusiasm for foreign missions. It explicitly rejected the use of denominational names, although adherents may call themselves "Christian Brethren" and in North America "Plymouth Brethren" is most commonly applied to it.

History

The first congregation was formed in Dublin in 1829 by the uniting of small groups of radical evangelical Anglicans and Dissenters who were searching for Christian unity and a more primitive church. A seminal influence was a candidate for the CHURCH MISSIONARY SOCIETY, Anthony Norris Groves, later an independent missionary in Baghdad and INDIA, and the nascent movement attracted another Anglican, the curate JOHN NELSON DARBY. The latter spread the new ideas among students at Oxford, attracting several individuals who were to be influential in the growth of the movement, among them Benjamin Wills Newton. Darby and Newton helped form an assembly (as they termed their congregations) in Plymouth in 1831 and other important early centers were formed in southwest England and London. In Bristol another early pioneer, GEORGE MÜLLER, founded an orphanage and promoted the notion of "living by faith": that Christian workers should be unsalaried, being dependent on God to supply them directly, a concept that influenced the interdenominational "faith missions."

Darby itinerated tirelessly and became of central importance to Brethren development. Tensions between him and Newton over ESCHATOLOGY and the control of the Plymouth assembly led to a formal split in 1845. The schism was widened when Newton made heretical christological statements, and in 1848 Darby maintained that the Bristol assembly had not distanced itself from his heterodoxy. This was the origin of the division into "Exclusive Brethren," who followed the leadership of Darby, and "Open Brethren." The latter was a movement of independent assemblies that maintained the evangelical ecumenicity of the early movement (see ECUMENISM). Because of mid-Victorian revivalism it grew into the larger section but, especially outside of southern England, sectarian isolation also intensified among its assemblies. In 1892–1894 many of the stricter individuals seceded to form the Churches of God, a separate body governed by a hierarchy of elders' councils.

A more introverted sectarianism continued within the Open Brethren and spread to other parts of the English-speaking world through emigration. Their assemblies in North America, for example, were principally planted through emigrants from northeast SCOTLAND, where the movement had been spontaneously founded after 1871 by a group of evangelists led by Donald Ross. The Open Brethren are enthusiasts for overseas MISSIONS and can be found in many countries, constituting a significant proportion of the Protestant population in places such as Angola, Chad, the Faroe Isles, Romania, and Argentina. The Exclusive Brethren grew in continental Europe, where Darby's itinerancy welded the movement together, and they spread to North America through European immigrants whom Darby also visited. They had adopted the principle of assemblies being united in judgment and during Darby's lifetime suffered divisions, something that accelerated after his death in 1882.

Beliefs, Practices, Issues

The Brethren are conservative Evangelicals in theology who readily identified with Protestant fundamentalism in the 1920s. In all sections of the movement (apart from some Open Brethren) there was an acceptance of Darby's dispensationalism, an eschatological scheme that divides salvation history into several distinct epochs culminating in an imminent private premillennial RAPTURE of Christians and a physical return of Christ to rule on earth over a restored Israel. Darby spread this thinking among conservative Protestants in

North America, where it has become influential outside Brethrenism. Also important across the movement is the celebration of the LORD'S SUPPER, or the "breaking of bread," during which the men (most usually) contribute spontaneously and stress is laid on communion with Christ. The Exclusives were not restorationists and did not try to reinstate the offices of the early CHURCH, their assemblies being governed by the unanimous decisions of the brethren, although the autonomous assemblies of most Open Brethren adopted rule by elders who are normally appointed by co-option. All sections of the movement are lay-led, rejecting the concept of ordination, although they do have full-time Christian workers. Their adherents tend to be ascetic in lifestyles.

After 1970 the main body of Exclusives fragmented further when their then leader, James Taylor Jr., a New York linen merchant, was involved in an alleged sexual scandal in northeast Scotland. They are an increasingly introverted sect; other Exclusive connections can be more moderate. In many countries since the 1950s the Open Brethren have seen a widening polarization between progressives, who have modified or rejected various aspects of traditional Brethrenism, and a more conservative element. One of the deepest of these *de facto* divisions exists in North America. Because of its zealous piety the Brethren movement has had an influence on conservative Protestant EVANGELICALISM that is out of all proportion to its size.

See also Millenarians and Millennialism

References and Further Reading

Baylis, Robert. *My People: The Story of those Christians Sometimes Called Plymouth Brethren.* Wheaton, IL: Harold Shaw Publishers, 1995.

Callahan, James Patrick. *Primitivitist Piety: The Ecclesiology of the Early Plymouth Brethren.* Lanham, MD: The Scarecrow Press, 1996.

Coad, F. Roy. *A History of the Brethren Movement: Its Origins, Its Worldwide Development and Its Significance for the Present Day.* 2nd edition. Exeter, UK: Paternoster Press, 1976.

Dickson, Neil T. R. *Brethren in Scotland 1838–2000: A Social Study of an Evangelical Movement.* Carlisle, UK: Paternoster Press, 2002.

Rowdon, Harold H. *The Origins of the Brethren 1825–1850.* London: Pickering & Inglis, 1967.

Sandeen, Ernest R. *The Roots of Fundamentalism: British and American Millenarianism 1800–1930.* Chicago: The University of Chicago Press, 1970.

Stunt, Timothy C. F. *From Awakening to Secession: Radical Evangelicals in Switzerland and Britain 1815–1835.* Edinburgh: T. & T. Clark, 2000.

NEIL T. R. DICKSON

POISSY, COLLOQUY OF

The Colloquy of Poissy, held near Paris in 1561, is generally recognized as the last great attempt at a theological reconciliation between Protestants and Catholics in the sixteenth century. The colloquy was organized by Catherine de Médici, the regent of FRANCE and mother of the young king Charles IX. Catherine sought to avert an impeding clash between the French Protestants, known as HUGUENOTS, and their Catholic counterparts, who were led by the powerful Guise family. The colloquy began on September 9, 1561, with the Protestants led by THEODORE BEZA, the theologian and lawyer who would become the leader of Geneva after the death of JOHN CALVIN. Béza was accompanied by the noted theologian Peter Martyr Vermigli. The Catholic contingent included numerous French prelates and was led by the wealthy and powerful Cardinal de Lorraine, later joined by representatives from the Council of Trent.

As had been the case in previous irenic gatherings, the aims of those who gathered at Poissy to promote Christian unity were thwarted most stubbornly by disagreements over the LORD'S SUPPER. The Colloquy dissolved in mid-October of 1561, having produced only two vaguely worded and largely insignificant pronouncements. Its failure was followed in January 1562 by Catherine's Edict, which granted limited religious freedom to the Huguenots. Soon thereafter came the March massacre of Protestants near Vassy, which began the first of France's Wars of Religion. The Colloquy of Poissy has been interpreted as a microcosm of the REFORMATION, in which reconciliation of theological differences among Christians, although championed by several prominent figures such as Erasmus and MARTIN BUCER, ultimately proved impossible.

References and Further Reading

Evans, G. R. *Problems of Authority in the Reformation Debates.* Cambridge: Cambridge University Press, 1992.

Nugent, Donald. *Ecumenism in the Age of the Reformation: The Colloquy of Poissy.* Cambridge, MA: Harvard University Press, 1974.

DEBORAH K. MARCUSE

POLAND

Beginnings of the Reformation Movement

The Kingdom of Poland and the Grand Lithuanian Princedom were related by union (1386 and 1569). This Commonwealth of the Two Nations stretched over an immense territory (around 900,000 kilometer^2) and included numerous nations and religions. Various confessions cohabited next to each other:

Roman Catholicism, Orthodoxy, Armenian Church, JUDAISM, Islam, with some relics of paganism existing in Lithuania until the sixteenth and seventeenth centuries.

The dominant role of the Roman Catholic Church was threatened by Hussitism, which had been finally silenced. Nevertheless it left durable influences, particularly in the northern regions of Poland (Great Poland) in Utraquism. Critics of the Polish church were also found in the writings of the Polish Humanists. Their works and those of other European humanists played an important role in shaping the political consciousness of the Polish gentry. In the fifteenth and even more in the sixteenth century, the gentry gained decisive influence over the destiny of the Polish kingdom to the detriment of the religious and lay aristocracy (in Lithuania the aristocracy was still important). The gentry was also the main guarantor and patron of the REFORMATION movement.

Echoes of MARTIN LUTHER's teachings reached Poland, and in 1520 King Sigismund I the Old (1506–1548) issued an edict forbidding the import of the works of the German reformer under the penalty of property confiscation and expulsion. In 1522 the monarch recommended respect of the edict and observed that many heretical books were being read and sold in Krakow, the Lutheran faith being publicly proclaimed. In 1536 Sigismund issued another strict edict, which threatened the penalties of death and property confiscation for the followers and propagators of the writings of Luther and other reformers. These edicts, as well as those issued in 1534 and 1540 forbidding trips and studies in Protestant countries, were not carried out because there were numerous matriculations of Polish students at Protestant universities. More important and paradoxically, Sigismund reinforced new religious trends even though he never purposely encouraged them. In 1525, guided by his understanding of "raison d'état," he agreed to secularize the state of the Teutonic Order and make it a Lutheran vassal state under the rule of his cousin Albrecht of Hohenzollern. Soon thereafter Ducal Prussia became an important center of Lutheran propaganda, spreading to Lithuania and Poland through various publications written in Polish and Lithuanian (CATECHISMS, hymnals, translation of the New Testament, etc.). Many Poles studied at the University of Konigsberg (now Kaliningrad) founded in 1544, and enthusiasts of new religious trends sought support at the court of the prince.

During Sigismund's reign, Anabaptist sentiment also reached Poland. Anabaptists who settled in the delta of Vistula near Gdansk, Malbork, and Elblag were considered to be great farmers. In 1535 and 1536 a Moravian Anabaptist group found refuge in Krasnik near Lublin. Some settled in Great Poland despite Sigismund's severe edict.

Development of the Reformation Movement

Only after Sigismund I's death did the development of the Reformation movement in Poland finally intensify. His successor, Sigismund II August (1548–1572), was deeply interested in reform, especially LUTHERANISM, even though he remained a Catholic. Lutheranism developed in the northern regions of Poland, in Great Poland, and Royal Prussia (western boundaries of the Teutonic Order under Polish rule after 1466) and found many adherents among Polish and German townspeople and gentry. The new religion adopted by Germans put an end to the Polonization process and created the roots for future national conflicts.

The Czech Brethren played an important role in Great Poland. Expelled from their motherland, they settled in Great Poland in the early 1560s thanks to the protection of wealthy aristocratic families. They soon established numerous parishes, schools, and a print house.

In Southern Poland (Poland Minor), after a short period of Lutheran fascination, the Swiss form of reform became more popular, even though we cannot precisely determine its precise doctrinal profile. The Church of Poland Minor started with a meeting in Pinczow in 1550 and was looking for organizational models, which explains its interest in the Czech Brothers in Great Poland. After their alliance a union of both churches was proclaimed in Kozminek in 1555, but it had never been realized. In opposition to the Unity of Czech Brethren, which did not participate in political controversy, patrons of the Polish Minor Church represented the elite of the reform gentry and aimed at calling a national council to set the religious issues. The final blow that pulled down the Unity was JAN LASKI's return to Poland in 1556. Laski became head of the Polish Minor Church and had misgivings about some of the concepts of the Unity (for example, Christ's presence during the LORD'S SUPPER). As a partisan of the Reformed Church, he also rejected the traditional LITURGY, which he believed was a papist heritage.

Laski's authority influenced prince Mikolaj Radziwill the "Black" (1515–1565)—the protector of the Calvinists—to join Lutheranism. The Lithuanian Reformed Church owes much to his protection and generosity. He also initiated cooperation with the Polish Minor Church, not exempt from conflicts. Radziwill authorized several printshops, which published many reform writings, among others an important translation of the Bible (1563) (see BIBLE TRANSLATION).

The late 1550s and 1560s represent the apogee of the Reformation movement in Poland and Lithuania. Decisions of the Sejm, the Polish diet of 1563—at which the jurisdiction of the Catholic CLERGY was abolished (this had been already achieved at the Sejm of 1552) and the clergy was exempted from taxation—were particularly important. However, weaknesses were visible in the Reformation movement, in particular in its Calvinist branch. It was not strong in cities and almost nonexistent in the countryside, peasants sticking to their old faith. Moreover, there was conflict between aristocratic patrons and Reformed clergy of low background, the latter complaining about low wages and unequal treatment. Dogmatic conflicts also perturbed the young Reformed Church, first the conflict about the character of Christ's intercession, triggered by Francesco Stancaro, then debates over the Trinity, which led to a division and the creation of a distinct Antitrinitarian Church (see ANTI-TRINITARIAN-ISM). This division halted the expansion of Polish CALVINISM in its most successful period when many well-educated pastors and wealthy patrons left the Reformed Church.

The Catholic Church constituted a serious opponent of Protestantism at the end of the 1560s, launching an active offensive against "heretics." The threat of Catholic claims was among the reasons for a group of pastors and patrons from the Unity of Czech Brethren and the Reformed Church to call the synod of Sandomierz. In addition to the representatives of those two confessions, representatives of the churches adhering to the AUGSBURG CONFESSION (Lutheran) took part in it, whereas Antitrinitarians were excluded. A common CONFESSION was promulgated that did not satisfy the orthodox Lutherans. The ecumenical character of the Agreement of Sandomierz (Consensus Sandomiriensis) triggered interest in part of European Protestant circles. It helped, to some extent, in Poland, to cool down the explosive relations between the Unity of Czech Brethren and the Reformed Church on one side and the "Augsburg Church" on the other.

Thanks to the efforts of Polish Protestants—above all members of the Lutheran Church—the gentry issued a bill intended to guarantee peace after Sigismund II's death at the meeting in Warsaw in 1573 (the so-called Confederation of Warsaw). Religious and political freedom of all "disagreeing within the Christian faith" (dissidentes in religionis Christiana) was guaranteed in the bill. It focused on the gentry but also included townspeople, even though future Catholic bishops and clergy insisted that the Confederation of Warsaw did not mention towns. A special section was addressed to peasants, reconfirming the superior authority of the lay and ecclesiastical gentry over their serfs. Despite those limits, the Confederation of Warsaw has to be recognized as one of the most important legal acts defending tolerance and religious freedom in sixteenth-century Europe. Sharply opposed by the Roman Catholic Church (only one bishop signed the Confederation of Warsaw), it represented a legally binding document, formally recognized by the Sejm of the republic and therefore often referred to by Protestants.

From the mid-1570s, the Reformation lost its vigor and became defensive. The activity of Jesuits—supported by two kings, Stefan Batory (1575–1586) and Sigismund II Waza (1587–1632)—played an important role in reinforcing the activities of the Catholic camp. Raids on Protestant centers, often inspired by Catholic clergy, started at the end of the sixteenth century.

The general assessment of the sixteenth century is positive. It is often referred to as the "golden age of Polish culture." The Reformation developed an important part of this culture. Thanks to the Reformation, literature developed, not only in Polish; schools were established, some with a high level of education (as for example the Calvinist gymnasium in Pinczow or the Lutheran Academy in Toruń). A closer relationship was also established with more important academic centers in other Protestant countries. Religious tolerance in Poland, which attracted many religious refugees persecuted in their own countries, triggered dissatisfaction and criticism from Catholics and Protestants alike, above all from theologians. In their opinion, sixteenth-century Poland was an asylum for heretics, Catholics referring to Protestant confessions and Protestants to Antitrinitarians.

Period of Limitations of Religious Freedoms and their Annihilation

From the last decade of the sixteenth century to the 1660s, the COUNTER-REFORMATION, increasingly supported by Polish gentry, succeeded in limiting Protestantism in Poland and Lithuania. Parliamentary sessions and deliberations of the Confederation during the *interregnum* represented the main field of their activities. During those sessions, anti-Protestant decisions were prepared, violating the resolutions issued by the Confederation of Warsaw. Catholic pressures were diverse according to place and time, but were reinforced in the second half of the seventeenth century. Until that time Protestantism could develop and defend itself in Poland.

The most attractive situation was in Lithuania, where the resolutions of the Confederation of Warsaw represented an integral part of the Third Lithuanian Statute—the latter serving as a legal basis for administration of justice in the Lithuanian Duchy until the end of the Polish–Lithuanian Commonwealth. Lithuanian churches enjoyed legal prerogatives and the guarantees of the Third Statute.

Major changes occurred in the second half of the seventeenth century, during the Swedish War, when some Polish Protestants sought protection from Swedish forces. The Counter-Reformation, putting forward the argument that the state was betrayed by Protestants, ingeniously exploited this fact. The expulsion of Socinians (see SOCINIANISM) from Poland in 1658 was a direct consequence of these accusations. The attempts to equalize the rights of Socinians with the followers of the Reformed Church (used for "Calvin-Arianism") represented another example of the rising anti-Protestant climate. In 1668 the rejection of Catholic confession was prohibited and the decision was made that Polish kings had to be Catholics.

As a result, by the end of the seventeenth century the Protestant state of affairs declined dramatically. The number of Reformed churches shrank from 140 to fifty; the Unity of Czech Brethren lost five churches out of fifteen. In Poland Minor only fifteen Reformed churches existed in 1691.

Discrimination intensified in the seventeenth century. In 1717 non-Catholics could not acquire royal goods, offices, or titles; in 1726 the jurisdiction of the Court in Lublin was enlarged to issues related to HERESY. In 1733 non-Catholics were deprived of the right to take part in parliamentary deliberations and tribunals. At the beginning of the ENLIGHTENMENT, the Polish–Lithuanian Commonwealth was widely perceived as intolerant and backward. The affair of Toruń was particularly notorious in Europe. In 1724 riots took place in Toruń after a conflict between Jesuit students and Lutheran townsmen, and the Jesuit College was ransacked. Extremely strict repression followed, with ten sentenced to death, including the mayor of the town.

This situation was carefully observed by RUSSIA and Prussia, who looked for a pretext to intervene in Poland. This reality also confirmed Catholics in their opinion that Protestants represented a fifth column, acting against the interests of the state.

Reforms implemented at the end of the seventeenth century granted many of the freedoms that Protestants had previously lost. The partitions of Poland (1772, 1793, 1795) that followed completely changed confessional relations in this country.

Protestantism during Times of Partitions

The final loss of independence of the Polish–Lithuanian state after the third partition (1795) triggered fundamental changes in the political, legal, and social situation of Protestantism. The Russian Empire annexed the biggest part of the Commonwealth with territories lying on the east side of the Niemen–Bog line. Lutheran parishes became part of the Evangelical Lutheran Russian Church. In the Polish Kingdom a General Evangelical Consistory was established that included both Lutherans and Reformed. The czar chose the superintendent from two candidates. In 1849 bills regulating the activities of both confessions were issued, which remained operative until the end of World War I. The structure of the Evangelical Augsburg Church was consistorial—named by the czar or the governor-general, the CONSISTORY was the administrative organ. Synods did not have the authority to issue legislative acts. The faithful could choose only pastors and clerical colleges. A general superintendent was the head of the church, responsible for four (from 1902, five) provinces.

The Reformed Church had a synodial-presbyterian structure consistent with its tradition. The superintendent in Warsaw dealt with common issues. Bills issued by the synod had to be confirmed by the state, which could suspend their execution. Members of the Reformed Church living in the Western provinces managed to obtain a more convenient regulation, which gave them a synodial structure guaranteeing much autonomy. Here bills issued by synods did not need to be approved by public authorities.

The Roman Catholic Church and the Unity Church were the main opponents of the czarist authorities, which often played the role of patrons or protectors of Protestants. On the other hand, they persecuted Protestants who emphasized their relation to Poland and proclaimed independence slogans. Russian authorities tried to prevent the "Polonization" of Protestants with German origins, who settled in the Polish Kingdom during INDUSTRIALIZATION at the end of the nineteenth century. At the end of the nineteenth century the Polonization process reached German Protestants, particularly in Warsaw. Protestants of German origin were among the independence leaders, participants of the January Uprising (1863), outstanding intellectuals, and molders of Polish CULTURE. General superintendents of the Evangelical-Augsburg Church in Poland were not opposed to the Polonization process, as were Russian Lutherans.

On the other hand, as the census of 1879 shows, Germans dominated the Protestants in the Polish Kingdom. Of the 400,000 Germans in the Polish Kingdom, 370,000 were Protestants and 30,000 were Catholics. There were 31,500 Polish Lutherans and 5,500 Reformed (1,150 Poles). The German majority was generally hostile toward the patriotic and independentist attitudes of Polish Protestants, the latter referring to the Polish Reformation movement of the sixteenth century. Pastors Lepolold Otto (1819–1882) and Juliusz Bursche (1862–1942)—the general superintendent of the Reformed Augsburg Church from 1904—were among the leaders of this trend, called Polish Evangelicalism. Bursche was unpopular among his German cobelievers in all formerly Polish areas in Russia and Germany; Catholics also attacked him for being a representative of German interests.

The situation in the Prussian partition (Grand Duchy of Poznan) was different. In 1815 some 200,000 Evangelicals were regrouped among 101 parishes dominated by German-speaking populations. "A few thousands Polish speaking Lutherans occupied the Southern part of the Duchy with a border to Silesia, a small group of Polish gentry belonged to the few Reformed communities" (Kiec 2002:17). One has to remember that German Evangelicals made up only 27 to 33 percent of the population of the Duchy and represented immigrants who had settled in areas inhabited by Poles and Catholics after migrations at the end of the seventeenth century and in the eighteenth and nineteenth centuries.

Protestant churches, which enjoyed autonomy in the Duchy, were under tight control of public authorities in the Prussian partition. In 1815 the creation of a centralized German State Church started. In 1827, under the pressures of the Prussian monarchy, a union of the Lutheran (Augsburg) Church with the Reformed Church was initiated. It led to the creation of the Evangelical Church of Nine Older Prussian Provinces (Die evangelische Kirche der neun älteren Provinzen Preussens), after 1922 the Evangelic Church of the Old Prussian Union (Die evangelische Kirche der Altpreussischen Union), despite the resistance of the so-called Old Lutherans. The Evangelical Union Church was its common name.

Living in areas where Poles and Catholics were in the majority and treated German neighbors as occupants and heretics (although examples of friendly religious coexistence did exist), German Protestants tried to reinforce their influence through various economic, social, and cultural initiatives. The latter were intended to testify about the great mission of German Protestantism—a bastion of superior civilization and culture. The loss of the Great Duchy of Poznan to Poland after World War I ended those aspirations. In this situation many Germans did not accept the new reality and accepted a belief about the transitory character of the Polish state because that was spread by Berlin after 1933.

In the Austrian partition Polish gentry belonged to the weak Reformed Church. Only in the 1780s did a sizable increase in the number of Evangelical followers occur, arising from German colonization with the support of Austrian authorities. In 1789 two seniorities were created, one in Biala and one in Teschen (Cieszyn, Tesin), with 100,000 Augsburg Evangelicals, most of them Polish. In 1804 Galicia was separated from Cieszyn Silesia, creating a superintendent office of Galicia-Bukovina with headquarters in Lwow.

The so-called Protestant Patent, issued by the emperor Franz Joseph I in 1861, gave the same legal treatment to Galician Evangelicals as to Catholics. It also established the regime of the Evangelical Church federating Augsburg Evangelicals and Reformed Evangelicals while keeping full doctrinal autonomy. The internal statute of the Augsburg and Helvetic Confession Church, finally issued in 1891, guaranteed the superintendence over clerical administration to the state.

After the autonomy of Galicia in 1867, with its own Sejm and local assembly, Polish became the official language and was taught in schools. Evangelical schools with German as the language of instruction were not subsidized any longer. After these changes reinforcing the Polish community at the end of the nineteenth century and in the beginning of the twentieth century, a massive reflux of German populations from Galicia took place (in 1880 there were 277,223; in 1890, 76,064; and in 1910, 64,845). Most of them were German Catholics. Mainly thanks to the efforts of their clergy, Evangelicals managed to keep their possessions (between 1880 and 1890, 40,000 people; and 1910, 30,186). Strong Polonization processes, particularly in Galicia at the end of the nineteenth century, enfolding many German Evangelicals, also deserve to be noticed.

Protestantism during the Second Republic

The end of World War I brought independence to Poland and represented the beginning of fundamental changes in Polish Protestantism. After the war clerical structures destroyed or seriously impaired during the war had to be rebuilt. Codifications in the field of confessional law were also foremost on the agenda. They were different in all three partitions and required rapid clarification. Additional difficulties related to the fact that communities of Polish Evangelicals were outside the new country, in Eastern Prussia and Silesia.

The most serious problem was that of nationalism—dividing German adherents of the Evangelical Augsburg Church (making up the majority of the population with 75 percent) and Polish adherents of the same church. The Evangelical Union Church in the area of Poznan (300,000 believers in 1933), supported by the same church in Polish Upper Silesia and the German Evangelical Augsburg Church in the territories of the Polish Kingdom, was opposed to the unification tendencies of the Polish government and

Polish Evangelicals (with regard to the legal system and administration). The Evangelical Union Church was only indirectly recognizing the existence of the Polish state, asking for the recognition of its relations with the Supreme Clerical Council in Berlin. The Polish government disapproved of these separatist tendencies (which were not expressed by the highly apolitical Old Lutheran Church), and it did not accept a bill regulating clerical matters proposed by the Union Church in 1929. The project of the Augsburg and Helvetic Evangelical Church in Poland Minor was also rejected because of political reasons. This Church, counting 33,000 members in 1936, was active among Ukrainians.

The Evangelical-Augsburg Church also launched legislative initiatives. German believers in Poland and Germany were incessantly accusing Juliusz Bursche—the superintendent of this church—of Polonization of the Lutheran Church in Poland. These initiatives were conducted in a tense atmosphere, boycotted by German Evangelicals. Polish national-Catholic parties also criticized them, identifying Protestantism with expansionist Germanization. Finally the work ended in 1936 with a decree of the president of the Republic of Poland. This decree gave the Evangelical-Augsburg Church a synodial-consistorial structure, public authorities retaining the right to influence personnel decisions. The decree introduced the office of bishop assumed by Bursche and ten dioceses replacing seniorities. In a sign of protest German delegates from the four largest dioceses boycotted the synod in 1937. The danger of a formal split in the Evangelical-Augsburg Church was real.

Despite these difficulties, the Evangelical-Augsburg Church intensively worked on the reinforcement of its position in the social and religious life in Poland. At its initiative a Faculty of Evangelical Theology was founded in 1920 at the University of Warsaw. In 1919 Lutheran and soon thereafter Reformed military chaplaincies were created.

In general the cooperation between the Evangelical-Augsburg Church and Reformed Church during a period of twenty years was good.

In those years the so-called Free Churches developed their activities in Poland, some of which had already started missions at the time of the partitions. The presence of BAPTISTS (around 14,600 believers), Evangelical Christians (around 10,000 believers), Whitsuntides (around 20,000 believers), Methodists (2,500 believers), Adventists (1,500 believers), and MENNONITES (around 1,000 believers) must be noted. Several smaller religious organizations and groups were represented as well.

World War II

German aggression on Poland on September 1, 1939 was assisted by the attack of Soviet troops and occupation of the eastern border of Poland on September 17. After the Soviet–German agreement of November 1939, the German population, in majority Evangelical, was moved to the Polish areas occupied by Germans.

From the beginning of the German occupation in the areas annexed to the Reich (Pomorze, the so-called Land of Warta, Upper Silesia, Cieszyn Silesia), religious organizations with a Polish character were not recognized and "the existence of Polish Evangelicals in Evangelic Churches was passed into silence. . . . The population of Silesia was not treated as Polish. . . . Polish activists, Silesian insurgents were sent to concentration camps or were sentenced to be shot" (Gatspary 1981:167).

Polish Evangelical parishes could exist only in the territories of the General Government (including voivodes of Kielce, Tarnpol, and parts of the voivodes of Warsaw and Lodz and from 1941 also voivodes of Stanislawow and Lwow). Pastor Waldemar Krusche replaced Juliusz Bursche, who was arrested by the Gestapo and died in a concentration camp on February 20, 1942. Many Polish pastors and activists from the Evangelical-Augsburg Church were arrested, accused of hostility toward Germans. Many of them were killed. The Evangelical-Augsburg Church and the Reformed Church endured severe repression. The latter fell on Poles with German origin who refused to sign the national German list (Volksliste), and many were sent to concentration camps. Other churches, and particularly the Roman Catholic Church, also endured extreme hardship. The Nazi authorities, opposed to religion, did not support the activities of the most loyal German Evangelicals. The Union Church in the Land of Warta was not recognized in public law; nor was its relation with the Clerical Council in Berlin. Similarly, in the so-called General Government no independent Evangelical Church was registered, even though appropriate documents had been sent to Berlin.

Protestantism after World War II

Destruction without precedent triggered by the war, human losses, territorial changes, and related substantial migration movements, as well as political changes brought Poland into the sphere of influence of the Soviet Union, and all these factors impacted confessional issues.

Important Protestant Churches with large membership progressively disappeared after voluntary or compulsory migrations of its members to Germany. This process lasted some twenty years, with the climax in the late 1940s and 1950s. Many Evangelicals acknowledging their Polish roots (living mainly in German territories before World War II in Eastern Prussia) emigrated, discouraged by discriminatory measures of the Communist government.

Even though the policy of public authorities toward Protestant Churches between 1945 and 1948 did not take aggressive forms—the main enemy being the Roman Catholic Church—in successive years (from 1956) their activities were subject to tight control and infiltration. These actions were aimed at subordinating and finally liquidating churches as a dangerous relic that slowed social development. These plans were implemented in a triangle—made up of the activities of the administration agendas, partisan activities, and secret police activities. Methods used included playing churches and confessional communities against each other, dividing clergy and lay activists into "progressive" and " reactionary." Clerical activists backed by the administration often reached high positions, becoming submissive tools in the hands of the government.

Churches that were perceived as dangerous because of international relations they had developed (considered contacts with "American imperialism") were in a particularly difficult situation. Through a skillful fomenting of internal conflicts in the Methodist Church and in the Union of Seventh-day Adventists, the government disrupted their ecclesial activity, and churches lost many of their members. The situation of Baptist-Evangelical Churches, accused in 1950 of espionage against the Soviet Union and national independent movements in the eastern part of the country in the 1920s and 1930s, was also difficult; 200 people were arrested, and many received lengthy sentences.

After the so-called October Breakthrough in 1956, the situation of all churches and confessional groups improved, even though they remained under tight control of the Office for Confessional Issues and the secret police. The Roman Catholic Church was the main target of this control. During this time Protestant Churches reestablished relations with foreign counterparts, taking part in the international ecumenical movement. The Christian Theological Academy in Warsaw, founded in 1954 with the participation of Old Catholic Churches, was developed. This led to establishing a department of Evangelical Theology and Old Catholic Theology, and from 1957 a department of Orthodox Theology.

Only with Poland's independence from the Soviet Union in 1989 did a full normalization of the situation of all churches and confessional groups take place. Articles 25, 48, and 53 of the Constitution of the Republic of Poland from April 2, 1997 and the bill regulating the relationship of the state with confessional groups from May 30, 1998 guarantee religious freedoms and equal treatment.

As of July 31, 2000, 157 churches and confessional groups were registered in Poland. The main Protestant denominations and their membership are listed below. It should be noted that membership figures differ substantially in different sources.

Name of Church	Membership
Evangelic-Augsburg Church	around 80,000
Evangelic-Reformed Church	around 4,000
Evangelic-Methodist Church	around 4,300
Church of Christian Baptists	around 3,000
Church of Evangelic Christians	around 2,500
Church of Adventists of the Seventh Day	around 10,000
Christ's Communities Church	around 3,600
Whitsuntide Church	around 18,000
Church of Christians of Evangelic Confession	around 4,000
Christ's Church	around 4,000

References and Further Reading

Alabrudzińska, Elżbieta. *Kościoły ewangelickie na kresach wschodnich II Rzeczypospolitej.* Toruń, Poland: Wydawnictwo Uniwersytetu Mikołaja Kopernika, 1999.

Dworzaczkowa, Jolanta. *Bracia Czescy w Wielkopolsce w XVI i XVII wieku.* Warsaw, Poland: Wydawnictwo Naukowe Semper, 1997.

Fox, Paul. *The Reformation in Poland. Some Social and Economic Aspects.* Baltimore, MD: Johns Hopkins Press, 1924.

Gastpary, Woldemar. *Historia protestantyzmu w Polsce od połowy XVIII w. do I wojny światowej.* Warsaw, Poland: Chrześcijańska Akademia Teologiczna, 1977.

———. *Protestantyzm w Polsce w dobie dwóch wojen światowych.* Część I: 1914–1939. Warsaw, Poland: 1978. Część II: 1939–1945. Warsaw: 1981.

Hubatsch, Walther. *Geschichte der Evangelischen Kirche Ostpreussens.* vols. I–III. Göttingen, Germany: Vandenhoeck & Ruprecht, 1968.

Jørgensen, Kai Eduard Jordt. *Ökumenische Bestrebungen unter den polnischen Protestanten bis zum Jahre 1645.* Copenhagen, Denmark: Forlag Arnold Busck, 1942.

Kiec, Olgierd. *Protestantyzm w Poznańskiem 1815–1918.* Warsaw, Poland: Wydawnictwo Naukowe Semper, 2001.

Kowalska, Halina. *Działalność reformatorska Jana Łaskiego w Polsce 1556–1560.* Warsaw, Poland: Wydawnictwo Neriton, 1999 [1st edition, Wrocław, 1969].

Krasiński, Walerian. *Historical Sketch of the Rise, Progress and Decline of the Reformation in Poland.* vols. 1 and 2. London: Murray, 1838–1840.

Lubieniecki, Stanislas. *History of the Polish Reformation and Nine Related Documents.* Translated and interpreted by George Huntston Williams. Minneapolis, MN: Fortress Press, 1995.

Maciuszko, Janusz T. *Konfederacja warszawska 1573 roku.* Warsaw, Poland: Chrześcijańska Akademia Teologiczna, 1984.

———. *Kościół luterański w Polsce od XVI do XX wieku* (in print); Michalak, Ryszard. *Kościoły protestanckie i władze partyjno-państwowe w Polsce (1945–1956).* Warsaw, Poland: Wydawnictwo Naukowe Semper, 2002.

Rhode, Arthur. *Geschichte der evangelischen Kirche im Posener Lande.* Würzburg, Germany: Holzner, 1956.

Schramm, Gottfried. *Der polnische* Adel *und die Reformation 1548–1607.* Wiesbaden: Franz Steiner Verlag, 1965.

Tazbir, Janusz. *The State without Stakes. Polish Religious Toleration in the Sixteenth and Seventeenth Centuries.* Translated by A. T. Jordan. New York and Warsaw, Poland: Kościuszko Foundation, 1973.

———. *Reformacja w Polsce. Szkice o ludziach i doktrynie.* Warsaw, Poland: Książka i Wiedza, 1993.

LECH SZCZUCKI

POLITICAL PARTIES

While less so than Roman Catholicism, Protestantism, too, has inspired a number of political parties. These wield a variety of banners and perform a variety of functions. They are now found not just in traditionally Protestant northern Europe, but also in the Americas, AFRICA, Asia, and Australasia, reflecting the recent global expansion of Protestantism and of multiparty democracies. One cannot talk today of Protestant parties without mentioning countries as diverse as NORWAY, Latvia, NEW ZEALAND, INDONESIA, Zambia, and Nicaragua. In 2003 there were about fifty such parties, in nearly thirty countries.

To call a party "Protestant" does not imply a confessional label or links to church hierarchies or religious tests for membership. Rather, it implies a party that, in its self-definition, is based on the CONFESSION of Protestant faith and principles. Usually, the founders of such parties are active Protestants who regard the party as a political expression of their faith.

Such parties are not the only way that Protestants get involved politically. Protestantism was more ready than Catholicism to embrace the competitive party model, with its adherents spread out along the party spectrum. There have been three waves of Protestant party creation. The *first wave,* from the 1870s to the early twentieth century, was restricted to the NETHERLANDS. The *second wave* was largely Scandinavian, with parties founded between the 1930s and early 1970s. The *third wave,* in the 1980s and 1990s, extended the model to LATIN AMERICA and southern Africa, the former communist world, parts of Asia and the Pacific, and even to Britain and its former "white dominions." Most of these parties are small, but some are respectable phenomena, and a few have experience in government. Of the third wave, parties in Fiji and Latvia have achieved instant success. But the most successful have been the Dutch and Scandinavian parties of the first and second waves.

Circumstances favoring the rise of political parties include ease of party registration and, especially, proportional representation with closed electoral lists. Parties usually depend on practicing rather than nominal Protestants. Perceived marginalization in the religious field or society also encourages parties. Among theological currents, those which develop full Christian worldviews are more favorable. A key factor is the perception of insufficient space in existing parties. Parties are often not supported by church hierarchies, because they represent rival power structures.

The recent surge in Protestant parties has been helped by the rise of identity politics in the West, the turmoils of postcommunism, and rapid Protestant growth and democratization in the third world. Parties can represent a range of "projects," from mere defense of (legitimate or illegitimate) ecclesiastical interests, to the idea of divine right to rule, to identity politics around issues of lifestyle and the family, to ethnic defense (see ETHNICITY), to broad political and economic concerns. Some parties are anti-Catholic, others are not; some are enthusiastically democratic, others not; some defend a secular state, others do not; some are neoliberal, others preach a "social market," and a few are slightly anti-capitalist. Many talk of "strengthening the family," but policy recommendations for doing so vary.

Parties evolve, typically incorporating broader concerns and losing the hard edges of confessional identity. Many countries have rival Protestant parties, because of tensions between doctrinnaire purity and political realism, and because Protestantism is itself socially and denominationally diverse.

In the Netherlands, the Anti-Revolutionary Party (ARP) was founded in 1879 and entered government in 1888. It can claim to be the first "Christian Democratic" party, and it governed for much of the first half of the twentieth century. Weakened by secularization, it merged in 1980 with another Protestant party and a Catholic party to form the CDA, which was in power in 2003. Three small Protestant parties were also in parliament at the turn of the century.

Protestant parties have also been successful in Scandinavia. Centered on pietist Lutherans and nonconformists, they began with narrow concerns and have evolved into strong supporters of third world aid and environmental protection. The Norwegian KrF party has held the prime-ministership three times, and the other Scandinavian parties have all been junior coalition partners.

The traditionally Protestant postcommunist countries of Estonia and Latvia have seen several Protestant parties since the late 1980s. Latvia's First Party was founded in 2002 by Lutheran and Baptist pastors and immediately won 9.6 percent of the vote, entering a coalition government.

Britain's "first-past-the-post" system is unfavorable to religious parties, but there are two types of Protestant parties: anti-Catholic ones in Ulster (and previously in SCOTLAND and Liverpool), such as the Democratic Unionist Party; and small anti-secular ones benefitting from the introduction of some elements of proportional representation. The Christian Peoples Alliance (founded 1999) is multiracial and exemplifies the contribution of Christian immigrants to European parties.

There are small parties in CANADA, AUSTRALIA, and New Zealand that are broadly "religious right." A partial exception is United Future New Zealand, more centrist, which erupted into parliament and almost into government in 2002. In Fiji, religion has reinforced the ethnic divide between indigenes and Indians. A Christian-ethnic party with strong support from the Methodist hierarchy, Soqosoqo Duavata ni Lewenivanua, stormed to power in 2001.

In Asia, Indonesia has the most Protestant parties. The oldest, Parkindo, dates back to 1945, but seven were formed after redemocratization in 1998.

Africa has few Protestant parties. The main instances refer to one country (SOUTH AFRICA) going through rapid secularization from the top, and another country (Zambia) going through "Christianization" of the nation by declaration, provoking Christian parties as a critique of this process. The African Christian Democratic Party is now the most genuinely multiracial party in South Africa.

Latin America became a major region for Protestant parties in the 1990s. Most have been personalistic, some corrupt, and none have become consolidated. They mobilize only a fraction of the Protestant community and are a sign of political marginalization rather than strength. The most successful has been the Camino Cristiano Nicaragüense, which placed third in the 1996 presidential elections. Most current parties in Latin America are unlikely to survive long.

References and Further Reading

Fogarty, Michael. *Christian Democracy in Western Europe, 1820–1953*. South Bend, IN: University of Notre Dame Press, 1957.

Freston, Paul, ed. *Evangelical Christians and Democracy in Latin America*. Forthcoming.

———. *Protestant Political Parties: A Global Survey*. Forthcoming.

Karvonen, Lauri. "Christian Parties in Scandinavia: Victory Over the Windmills?," in *Christian Democracy in Europe: A Comparative Perspective*. Edited by David Hanley, 121–141. London: Pinter, 1994.

Lucardie, Paul, and Hans-Martien ten Napel. "Between Confessionalism and Liberal Conservatism: The Christian Democratic Parties of Belgium and the Netherlands," in *Christian Democracy in Europe: A Comparative Perspective*. Edited by David Hanley, 51–70. London: Pinter, 1994.

Madeley, John. "The Antinomies of Lutheran Politics: The Case of Norway's Christian People's Party," in *Christian Democracy in Europe: A Comparative Perspective*. Edited by David Hanley, 142–154. London: Pinter, 1994.

———. "Reading the Runes: The Religious Factor in Scandinavian Electoral Politics," in *Religion and Mass Electoral Behaviour in Europe*. Edited by David Broughton and Hans-Martien ten Napel, 28–43. London: Routledge, 2000.

Van Holsteyn, Joop, and Galen Irwin. "The Bells Toll No More: the Declining Influence of Religion on Voting Behaviour in the Netherlands," in *Religion and Mass Electoral Behaviour in Europe*. Edited by David Broughton and Hans-Martien ten Napel, 75–96. London: Routledge, 2000.

PAUL FRESTON

POLITICAL THEOLOGY

Although theology and politics can never be completely separated, political theology has become a prominent movement in the twentieth century. In its various forms political theology resists both the modern separation of religion and politics and the confusion of the two.

The themes of political theology emerged in GERMANY after World War II, under the impression of the Third Reich and of the HOLOCAUST. The most pressing question for political theology was why the churches, both Protestant and Roman Catholic, had for the most part been silent in the face of these happenings. Why did THEOLOGY and the CHURCH even after the end of the war continue this silence, not only refusing to own up to what had happened but also failing to deal with the dangers of the Cold War between the superpowers of the East and West? In the UNITED STATES political theology took shape, raising questions in the context of the CIVIL RIGHTS MOVEMENT and the excesses of the free market economy.

The various political theologies on both sides of the Atlantic are based on two different assumptions. On the one hand it is noted that theology has often followed the increasing privatization of religion since the ENLIGHTENMENT and needs to reclaim its impact on the political. On the other hand it has been observed that theology, whether aware of it or not, is always political and is simply in need of owning up to its political affiliations. Although political theologies often combine both observations in one way or another, what has priority is weighted differently. Some of the early work of German political theologians focuses on the privatization of religion. Religion, seen as a private matter, is forced to leave politics to its own devices. In this situation, theology simply becomes irrelevant. The Protestant theologian Dorothee Sölle's early work exemplifies this position when she defines religion in terms of ideology—understood as "a system of propositional truths independent of the situation, a superstructure no longer relevant to praxis, to the situation, to the real questions of life" (Sölle 1974:23). Similar questions are raised in the early work of one of the Roman Catholic founders of political theology, Johannes Baptist Metz. Both Sölle and Metz, supported by the early work of JÜRGEN MOLTMANN, insist that critical theological thinking, focused heavily on existentialist thinking at the time, needs to be expanded to include the political realm.

Developing a North American perspective at the time of the civil rights movement and the Vietnam War, the Protestant theologian Frederick Herzog pursues a different line of argument: In the North American context theology first needs to understand how everything is politicized already. New Testament notions of justice, freedom, and peace are important, but do not sufficiently explain why the political dimensions have become so central. The task of political theology is to liberate the church from its political captivity to open the way for true political responsibility (Rieger 1999:73–79). Religion in this assessment appears to be ideological no longer in terms of being an irrelevant appendage to political power but in terms of supporting the status quo, often without being aware of it.

In the German context, Metz and Moltmann soon also deal with the unconscious identifications of theology and politics. In the United States, M. Douglas Meeks has pursued these issues in regard to the economy, pointing out that economic structures are more and more determining our world and theology. Other Protestants working on political theology in the United States include John B. Cobb Jr., who makes more sustained use of political theory and introduces questions of ECOLOGY; J. Deotis Roberts, who develops political theology from an African American perspective; and Alistair Kee in Great Britain. On the Roman Catholic side there are Helmut Peukert and Edmund Arens in Germany, Matthew Lamb in the United States, and Charles Davis in CANADA.

In response to the analysis of the relation of religion and politics, political theology has begun to focus more on the contributions of theology to politics. This process has been led on the Protestant side by Moltmann, whose basic concern is not to "politicize the church" but to "Christianize church politics and the political involvement of Christians" (Moltmann 1984: 99). Based on his earlier work on a theology of hope, Moltmann finds a new impulse for political theology in the expectation of the coming reign of God, in Christian ESCHATOLOGY. Such hope for God's coming is rooted in what God has already done. It does not merely wait for a better future but calls into question the powers that be and invites participation in God's reign here and now.

In sum, political theology pays attention to political structures that are often taken for granted, thinking through Christian symbols, traditions, and "dangerous memories" of God's work from this angle, and developing alternative ways of thinking and acting.

Implications

Various issues merit further consideration. Because theology is never done in isolation from political, economic, and other realities, what is the relation of theory and praxis? Moltmann has reminded us that "theological hermeneutic is abstract as long as it does not become the theory of practice" (Moltmann 1969: 98). It is becoming ever clearer, of course, that the problem is more than abstraction. If theology fails to pay attention to the ways in which it is always already shaped by political, economic, and other practices, it cannot but help perpetuating the way things are, no matter what it proclaims.

Despite various disagreements it has been claimed that political theology can be seen as an ally to LIBERATION THEOLOGY. Sölle, for instance, has moved from political to liberation theology, claiming that listening to the voices from the margins helped clarify her initial approach. Moltmann sees political theology as a tool that helps to further the liberation of those in power, understanding how the misuse of power distorts their own lives as well. In drawing out these connections, however, a closer understanding of the relations between the powerful and the powerless, the rich and the poor, and the oppressors and the oppressed will need to be developed, which includes a closer look not only at the coming God but God present in the political and economic tensions of our age.

See also Economics; Politics; Political Parties; Theology, Twentieth Century

References and Further Reading

Meeks, M. Douglas. *God the Economist: The Doctrine of God and Political Economy.* Minneapolis, MN: Fortress Press, 1989.

Metz, Johannes Baptist. *Theology of the World.* Translated by William Glen-Doepel. New York: Herder and Herder, 1969.

Moltmann, Jürgen. *Religion, Revolution, and the Future.* Translated by M. Douglas Meeks. New York: Charles Scribner's Sons, 1969.

———. *On Human Dignity: Political Theology and Ethics.* Translated by M. Douglas Meeks. Philadelphia, PA: Fortress Press, 1984.

Rieger, Joerg, ed. *Theology from the Belly of the Whale: A Frederick Herzog Reader.* Harrisburg, PA: Trinity Press International, 1999.

Sölle, Dorothee. *Political Theology.* Translated by John Shelley. Philadelphia, PA: Fortress Press, 1974.

JOERG RIEGER

POLITICS

In its most basic sense, politics (from the Greek word *polis*) is the activity of governing a discrete people and territory. Historically in the West those who governed came to their positions by conquest, custom, or consent, by inheritance, election, or appointment. Some polities were organized as monarchies, some as oligarchies, some as democracies, most as a mixture of the same. Their officers could be emperors, monarchs, or dukes, popes, bishops, or abbots, tribal chieftains, manorial princes, or feudal lords. Their regimes ranged from extended households, to bishoprics, to tribal lands, to cities, nations, and empires. Whatever their origin, organization, and orbit of influence, political officials in the West have generally engaged in a common set of activities that constitute the heart of politics. They protect and preserve the community and its welfare, make and enforce law, broker and resolve disputes, punish crime and civil offenses, negotiate diplomacy, collect taxes, raise armies, wage war, and engage in numerous activities that are necessary and proper to this office.

To be effective and enduring, political activity requires a balance of the political virtues and attributes of power, authority, coercion, persuasion, piety, charisma, justice, equity, clemency, courage, moderation, temperance, force, faithfulness, and more. Religious officials have long been essential political allies in striking this balance—lending sanctity, legitimacy, and pageantry to the political office; counsel, comfort, and commodities to political officials. Strong Western Christian leaders over the centuries have also served variously as critics or condoners of political abuse, as agents or opponents of political reform and revolt. Strong Christian CLERGY over the centuries have also seized their own political power and established powerful polities to rival the civil powers.

Today most Western nations have constitutions that define the powers and provinces of political authorities without much direct involvement from religious officials and with detailed provisions to govern the tender moments of political reform, transition, or expansion. Most Western nations now make formal distinctions among the executive, legislative, and judicial powers of government and functions of law, each designed in part to check and balance the other. Most have sophisticated rules and procedures to facilitate the legal transactions and interactions of their citizens and subjects and to resolve disputes between and among citizens and political authorities. Most recognize multiple sources of law and political power—constitutions, treaties, statutes, regulations, judicial precedents, customary practices, and a growing body of private and public international laws.

Protestants have made important and diverse contributions to the development of Western political ideas and institutions, often reshaping Classical, Patristic, Scholastic, and ENLIGHTENMENT traditions in so doing. This article reviews selectively (1) some of the early modern European models of politics born of the Protestant REFORMATION; and (2) the transplantation and adaptation of some of these Protestant models in American history.

Protestant Political Models of Early Modern Europe

The sixteenth-century Protestant Reformation was in part an attack on the political power and structure of the medieval Catholic Church. Since the twelfth century the church had been organized as an autonomous political corporation in Western Christendom. The church claimed a vast jurisdiction—personal jurisdiction over clerics, pilgrims, students, heretics, and the poor; subject matter jurisdiction over doctrine and liturgy, church property and polity, marriage and family, inheritance and trusts, education and charity, contracts and oaths, and sundry moral and ideological crimes. Although the church could not make good on all these jurisdictional claims, particularly as papal power waned in the fourteenth and fifteenth centuries, many clerics held enormous political power.

By the fifteenth century the church had developed an elaborate system of laws, called canon laws, that prevailed throughout Western Christendom. Canon lawyers licensed by the church collated the early apostolic constitutions and Christianized Roman law, which were then heavily supplemented by new papal and conciliar laws and legal commentaries. A vast hierarchy of church courts and officials administered this canon law in accordance with sophisticated new rules of procedure and evidence. A vast network of church officials discharged the church's executive and administrative functions. The medieval church was, in F. W. Maitland's famous phrase, "the first modern state in the West," its canon law the first modern international law.

The Protestant Reformation began as a call for freedom from this ecclesiastical regime—freedom of the individual conscience from canon laws and clerical controls, freedom of political officials from ecclesiastical power and privilege, freedom of the local clergy from central papal rule and revenue collection. "Freedom of the Christian" was the rallying cry of the early Reformation. Catalyzed by MARTIN LUTHER's posting of the Ninety-Five Theses in 1517 and his burning of the canon law books in 1520, the Reformation leaders denounced church laws and authorities with unprecedented alacrity and urged radical political reforms on the strength of the new Protestant theology.

The Reformation broke the unity of Western Christendom and thereby laid the foundation for the modern Western system of political and religious pluralism. The Reformation broke the superiority of clerical Au-

THORITY and canon law, and thereby vested new power in civil authorities and civil law. The Reformation broke the primacy of corporate Christianity, and thereby laid new emphasis on the role of the individual in the economy of SALVATION and the individual rights that should attach thereto. Lutherans, Anabaptists, and Calvinists forged the three main Protestant political models, with Anglicans striking something of a *via media* among them.

Lutheranism

The Lutheran Reformation territorialized the Christian faith and gave ample new political power to the local Christian magistrate (see LUTHERANISM). Luther replaced medieval teachings with a new two-kingdoms theory. The "invisible" church of the heavenly kingdom, he argued, was a perfect community of saints, where all stood equal in dignity before God, all enjoyed perfect Christian liberty, and all governed their affairs in accordance with the Gospel. The "visible" church of this earthly kingdom, however, embraced saints and sinners alike. Its members still stood directly before God and still enjoyed liberty of conscience, including the liberty to leave the visible church itself. Unlike the invisible church, however, the visible church needed both the Gospel and human law to govern its members' relationships with God and with fellow believers. The clergy must administer the Gospel. The magistrate must administer the law.

Luther insisted that the church was not a political or legal authority. The church had no sword, no jurisdiction, no daily responsibility for the administration of law and politics. To be sure, church officers and theologians must be vigilant in preaching and teaching the law of God to magistrates and subjects alike, and in pronouncing prophetically against injustice and tyranny, although formal legal authority lay with the state not with the church, with the magistrate not with the cleric.

Luther and his followers regarded the local magistrate as God's vice-regent called to elaborate natural law and to reflect divine justice in his local domain. The best source and summary of NATURAL LAW was the Ten Commandments and its elaboration in the moral principles of the BIBLE. The magistrate was to cast these general principles of natural law into specific precepts of human law, designed to fit local conditions. Luther and his followers also regarded the local magistrate as the "father of the community" (*Landesvater, paterpoliticus*). He was to care for his political subjects as if they were his children, and his political subjects were to "honor" him as if he were their parent. Like a loving father, the magistrate was to keep the peace and to protect his subjects in their persons, properties, and reputations. He was to deter his subjects from abusing themselves through drunkenness, sumptuousness, gambling, prostitution, and other vices. He was to nurture his subjects through the community chest, the public almshouse, the state-run hospice. He was to educate them through the public school, the public library, the public lectern. He was to see to their spiritual needs by supporting the ministry of the local church and encouraging attendance and participation through civil laws of religious worship and tithing.

These twin metaphors of the Christian magistrate—as the lofty vice-regent of God and as the loving father of the local community—described the basics of Lutheran political theory for the next three centuries. Political authority was divine in origin, but earthly in operation. It expressed God's harsh judgment against SIN but also his tender mercy for sinners. It communicated the Law of God but also the lore of the local community. It depended on the church for prophetic direction but it took over from the church all jurisdiction. Either metaphor of the Christian magistrate standing alone could be a recipe for abusive tyranny or officious paternalism, although both metaphors together provided Luther and his followers with the core ingredients of a robust Christian republicanism and budding Christian welfare state.

Accordingly Lutheran magistrates in early modern Germany, Scandinavia, and SWITZERLAND replaced traditional Catholic canon laws with new Lutheran civil laws on religious DOCTRINE and WORSHIP, church administration and supervision, MARRIAGE and family life, EDUCATION and poor relief, public morality, and discipline for each local polity. Many of these local Lutheran legal reforms found constitutional protection in the principle of *cuius regio, eius religio* guaranteed in the Peace of Augsburg (1555) and again in the Peace of Westphalia (1648). Under this principle each local magistrate was authorized to establish by civil law the appropriate forms of religious doctrine, worship, LITURGY, CHARITY, and education for his polity—with religious dissenters granted the right to worship and educate their children privately in their homes or to emigrate peaceably from the polity. This new constitutional policy rendered the German region of the Holy Roman Empire, with its 350-plus polities, a veritable honeycomb of religious and political pluralism.

Anabaptism

Contrary to Lutherans, Anabaptists advocated the separation of the redeemed realm of religion and the church from the fallen realm of politics and the state (see ANABAPTISM). In their definitive SCHLEITHEIM CONFESSION (1527), the Anabaptists called for a return to the communitarian ideals of the New Testament and the ascetic principles of the apostolic church. The Anabaptists eventually splintered into various groups of AMISH, German Brethren, HUTTERITES, MENNONITES, Swiss Brethren, and others. Some of these splinter groups were politically radical or utopian, particularly those following the tradition of THOMAS MÜNSTER of Germany; however, most Anabaptist communities by the later sixteenth century had become Christian separatists.

Anabaptist communities ascetically withdrew from civic life into small, self-sufficient, intensely democratic communities. When such communities grew too large or too divided, they deliberately colonized themselves, eventually spreading the Anabaptist communities from RUSSIA to IRELAND to the furthest frontiers of North America. These communities were governed internally by biblical principles of discipleship, simplicity, charity, and nonresistance. They set their own internal standards of worship, liturgy, diet, discipline, dress, and education. They handled their own internal affairs of property, contracts, commerce, marriage, and inheritance without appeal to state law.

The state, most Anabaptists believed, was part of the fallen world, which was to be avoided so far as possible. Although once the perfect creation of God, the world was now a sinful regime beyond the perfection of Christ and beyond the daily concern of the Christian believer. God had allowed the world to survive through his appointment of state magistrates who were empowered to use coercion and violence to maintain a modicum of order and peace. Christians should thus obey the political authorities, so far as Scripture enjoined, such as in paying their taxes or registering their properties, although Christians were to avoid active participation in and interaction with the world. Most early modern Anabaptists were pacifists (see PACIFISM), preferring derision, exile, or martyrdom to active participation in war. Most Anabaptists also refused to swear oaths, or to participate in political elections, civil litigation, or civic feasts and functions. This aversion to political and civic activities often triggered severe reprisal by Catholics and Protestants alike. Anabaptists suffered waves of bitter repression throughout the early modern era.

Although unpopular in its genesis, Anabaptist theological separatism ultimately proved to be an influential source of later Western political arguments for separation of religion and politics and for protection of the civil and religious liberties of religious minorities. Equally important for later political developments was the new Anabaptist doctrine of adult BAPTISM. This doctrine gave new emphasis to religious voluntarism as opposed to traditional theories of birthright or predestined faith. In Anabaptist theology, the adult individual was called to make a conscious and conscientious choice to accept the faith—metaphorically, to scale the wall of separation between the fallen world and the realm of religion to come within the perfection of Christ. Later Free Church followers, both in Europe and North America, converted this cardinal image into a powerful platform of liberty of conscience and free exercise of religion not only for Christians but eventually for all peaceable believers.

Calvinism

The Calvinist Reformation charted a course between the Erastianism of Lutherans that subordinated the church to the state, and the ASCETICISM of Anabaptists that withdrew the church from the state and society (see CALVINISM). Like Lutherans, Calvinists insisted that each local polity be an overtly Christian commonwealth that adhered to the general principles of natural law and that translated them into detailed positive laws of religious worship, Sabbath observance, public morality, marriage and family life, social welfare, public education, and more. Like Anabaptists, Calvinists insisted on the basic separation of the offices and operations of church and state, leaving the church to govern its own doctrine and liturgy, polity and property, without interference from the state. However, unlike both groups, Calvinists insisted that both church and state officials were to play complementary roles in the creation of the local Christian commonwealth and in the cultivation of the Christian citizen.

Building on the work of the Genevan reformer JOHN CALVIN, Calvinists emphasized more fully than other Protestants the educational use of the natural and positive law. Lutherans stressed the civil and theological uses of the natural law—to deter sinners from their sinful excesses and to drive them to repentance. Calvinists emphasized the educational use of the natural law as well—to teach persons both the letter and the spirit of the law, both the civil morality of human duty and the spiritual morality of Christian aspiration. Although Lutheran followers of PHILIPP MELANCHTHON had included this educational use of the natural law in their theology, Calvinists made it an integral part of their politics as well. They further insisted that not only the natural law of God but also the positive law of the state could achieve these three civil, theological, and educational uses.

Calvinists also emphasized more fully than other Protestants the legal role of the church in a Christian commonwealth. Lutherans, after the first two generations, left law largely to the Christian magistrate. Anabaptists gave the church a strong legal role, but only for voluntary members of the ascetically withdrawn Christian community. Calvinists, by contrast, drew local church officials directly into the enforcement of law for the entire Christian commonwealth and for all citizens, regardless of their church affiliation. In Calvin's Geneva this political responsibility of the church fell largely to the CONSISTORY, an elected body of civil and religious officials, with original jurisdiction over cases of marriage and family, charity and social welfare, worship and public morality. Among most later Calvinists—French HUGUENOTS, Dutch Pietists (see PIETISM), Scottish Presbyterians (see PRESBYTERIANISM), German Reformed, and English and American Puritans—the Genevan-style consistory was transformed into the body of pastors, elders, deacons, and teachers that governed each local church congregation, and played a less-structured political and legal role in the broader Christian commonwealth, although local clergy still had a strong role in advising magistrates on the positive law of the local community. Local churches and their consistories also generally enjoyed autonomy in administering their own doctrine, liturgy, charity, polity, and property and in administering ecclesiastical discipline over their members.

Anglicanism

ANGLICANISM struck something of a middle way among these competing Lutheran, Anabaptist, and Calvinist political models. The sixteenth-century English Reformation pressed to extreme national forms the Lutheran model of a unitary Christian commonwealth under the final authority of the Christian magistrate. Building in part on Lutheran and Roman law precedents, King HENRY VIII severed all legal and political ties between the CHURCH OF ENGLAND and the pope. The Supremacy Act (1534) declared the monarch to be "the only Supreme Head in Earth of the Church of England," with final spiritual and temporal authority in the Church and Commonwealth of England. Thus the Tudor monarchs, through their Parliaments, established a uniform doctrine and liturgy and issued the BOOK OF COMMON PRAYER (1559) and Authorized (King James) Version of the Bible (1611) (see BIBLE, KING JAMES VERSION). They also assumed final legal responsibility for poor relief, education, and other activities that had previously been carried on under Catholic auspices. Communicant status in the Church of England was rendered a condition for citizenship status in the Commonwealth of England. Contraventions of royal religious policy were punishable both as HERESY and as treason. A whole battery of apologists rose to the defense of these unitary Anglican political forms and norms, most notably THOMAS CRANMER, RICHARD HOOKER, and Robert Filmer.

The Stuart monarchs moved slowly, through hard experience, toward greater TOLERATION of religious pluralism and greater autonomy of local churches. From 1603 to 1640, King James I and Charles I persecuted Protestant nonconformists with a vengeance, driving tens of thousands of them to the Continent and often from there to North America. In 1640 those who remained led a revolution against the English Crown, and ultimately deposed and executed King Charles I. In 1649 they passed laws that declared England a free Christian commonwealth under the protectorate of OLIVER CROMWELL. Royal rule was reestablished in 1660, however, and repression of Protestant dissenters renewed (see DISSENT). However, when the dissenters again rose up in revolt, Parliament passed the Bill of Rights and Toleration Act of 1689 that guaranteed freedom of association, worship, self-government, and basic civil rights to all peaceable Protestant churches. Many of the remaining legal restrictions fell into desuetude in the following decades, although Catholicism and JUDAISM remained formally proscribed in England until the Emancipation Acts of 1829 and 1833.

Protestant Political Influence in America

These early modern Protestant political experiments were transmitted across the Atlantic to the Americas during the great waves of colonization in the sixteenth to eighteenth centuries (see COLONIALISM), and great waves of immigration in the nineteenth and twentieth centuries. In the colonial period European Catholic, Anglican, Lutheran, and Calvinist rulers alike, eager to extend their political and religious regimes, chartered hundreds of colonial companies in the New World under the rule of the distant mother country and mother church. At the same time numerous Protestant dissenters (along with Catholics, Jews, and others) flocked to America to escape hardship at home. They escaped not only from the repression of seventeenth-century ENGLAND but also from Germany and the Lowlands that were wracked with religious warfare from 1618 to 1648, and from FRANCE, whose monarchy had grown increasingly hostile to Protestants and then banned them in the EDICT OF FONTAINEBLEAU (1685).

The American colonies and later states featured a fantastic variety of Protestant (among other) political forms and norms—some in emulation of European models, many products of ample local innovation and experimentation. Two Protestant political formulations had the most innovative and enduring influence on American political life: (1) the Reformed models born in New England; and (2) the evangelical models born of the Great Awakenings.

Reformed Models

The fullest American adaptation and amplification of European Protestant political theory came in the New England colonies and their successor states. New England writers—ultimately composed of Puritans, Calvinists, Reformed, Congregationalists (see CONGREGATIONALISM), Huguenots, and Presbyterians—repeated Calvinist and classical commonplaces, but they also refashioned this inheritance, especially through the doctrine of COVENANT.

The New England Puritans (see PURITANISM) described the relationship between the person and God primarily as a covenant, an exchange of solemn promises about GRACE and works. Initially the Puritans viewed this covenant as something of a divine adhesion contract, with God setting all the terms and even dictating through PREDESTINATION who could enter the covenant and enjoy its promise of salvation. By the turn of the nineteenth century, however, Puritans described the covenant more as a bargained contract of salvation—each person choosing to reach his or her own conclusions about the duties owed to God, neighbor, and self based on reason, conscience, experience, and biblical meditation. This understanding of private religious liberty for all theistic religions figured very prominently in the religious liberty provisions in the charters of later colonial New England, and in the New England state constitutions of 1777–1818.

The New England Puritans also used the doctrine of covenant to describe the relationships among persons. The Puritans distinguished: (1) social covenants—the Mayflower Compact (1620) and its hundreds of colonial progeny; (2) political covenants—colonial charters and state constitutions as well as oaths for political office; and (3) church covenants—the Cambridge Synod and CAMBRIDGE PLATFORM (1648) and the hundreds of church charters and covenants that followed. The social covenant created the society or commonwealth as a whole. It defined each community as "God's elect nation," a "city on a hill," a "light to the nations." It also set out in detail the virtues of piety, justice, moderation, temperance, industry, frugality, and more that the law should protect and that persons should respect, on pain of divine and human sanction. The political and ecclesiastical covenants created the two chief seats of authority within that community, the state and the church. The Puritans emphasized that church and state were two independent covenantal associations within the broader covenantal community. Each was called to discharge discrete covenantal duties, as adumbrated in the laws of God and nature, and elaborated in the covenant by which they were formed. Each was to be separate from the other in their forms and functions, offices and officers, but mutually responsible to see that all served the common good in accordance with the terms of the social covenant.

Although the offices of church and state were divinely ordained, their officials were invariably sinful. Left to their own devices, church and state officials would invariably convert their offices into instruments of self-gain. Such official arbitrariness and abuse would inevitably lead to both popular insurrection and divine sanction. The Puritans thus advocated and adopted a variety of constitutional safeguards against autocracy and abuse within both church and state.

- First, church and state officials must have as "godly" a character as possible, notwithstanding their inherent sinfulness. Officials were to be models of spirituality and morality for the community. Political officers were to be professing members of a locally preferred if not established church and to swear oaths of allegiance to God and the Bible.
- Second, both church and state officials must occupy their offices only for limited tenures. Life tenures were too dangerous because they afforded the official the opportunity slowly to convert his office into an instrument of self-gain and self-aggrandizement. It was safer to limit the official's tenure and require periodic election and rotation of officers.
- Third, the Puritans advocated the development of self-limiting "republican" forms of government for both the church and the state. Rather than consolidate all forms of authority in one person or one office, they insisted on separate forms or branches of authority, each checking the sinful excesses of the other. Church authority was divided among the pastors, elders, and deacons of the consistory; state authority among executive, legislative, and judicial branches, each with a measure of responsibility and control over the other.
- Fourth, the Puritans adopted what they called a federalist (from *foedus*, "covenantal") structure of government for both the church and the state. The church was divided into semiautonomous congregations, but each loosely conjoined and democratically represented in a broader synod or presbytery. The state was divided into semiautonomous town governments but conjoined in a broader colonial and (later) state government.
- Fifth, the Puritans advocated the development of legal codes and clear statutes in the state, and clear confessions and canons in the church, so that officials were limited in their discretion.
- Sixth, the Puritans advocated regular popular meetings for officials to give account of them-

selves, and for their subjects to have occasion for discussion of important issues. In the church this took the form of congregational meetings; in the state, the form of town meetings and popular referenda.

- Seventh, the Puritans advocated regularly held democratic elections of both church and state officials.

The early American Reformed tradition provided an important source and resource, alongside many others, for the growth of American constitutionalism. Many of the basic ideas and institutions of the social, ecclesiastical, and political covenants were written directly into the constitutions of the New England states and openly advocated for the nation by Puritan sermonizers and political conservatives such as John Adams and JOHN WITHERSPOON. Moreover, several fundamental Puritan ideas found parallels, if not progeny, among other schools of American politics in the later 1700s and 1800s. Various "liberal" writers found in the Puritan ideas of a social covenant and a political covenant prototypes for their theories of a social contract and a governmental contract. They found in the doctrine of church covenants and separation of church and state a foundation for their ideas of disestablishment of religion and free exercise for both religious individuals and religious groups. They found in the doctrine of popular meetings and periodic elections important prototypes for the freedom of press and assembly and the right to vote. Various "republican" writers, by contrast, transformed the Puritan idea of the elect nation into a revolutionary theory of American NATIONALISM. They recast the Puritan ideal of the covenant community into a theory of public virtue, discipline, and order. They translated the Puritans' insistence on spiritual rebirth and reformation into a general call for "moral reformation" and "republican regeneration."

Moreover, basic Puritan constitutional institutions survived within the new federal and state constitutions of the young American republic. Political rulers were still required to manifest a moral, virtuous, and godly character. Most officials were required to stand for democratic elections to their offices. Political offices usually had limited tenures. Political authority was distributed among executive, legislative, and judicial branches, each with authority to check the others. Federalism was constitutionally prescribed. Liberties of citizens were copiously enumerated. Church and state were separated, yet allowed to cooperate.

New Evangelical Accents

Although Reformed political models and rhetoric continued to dominate American politics for the next century and a half, evangelical political models became increasingly prominent in the nineteenth and early twentieth centuries (see EVANGELICALISM).

The rise of evangelical political influence was in part a function of simple demography. American Evangelicals had their roots in small colonial Baptist and Anabaptist communities, many clustered in Roger Williams's Rhode Island. Their small size and separatist leanings kept them from exercising much political influence at first. The First Great AWAKENING (c. 1720–1770), however, led by GEORGE WHITEFIELD, JOHN WESLEY, JONATHAN EDWARDS, and others, divided many Protestant denominations into traditional Old Light and evangelical New Light groups. It also sparked the rise of Baptist and Methodist churches, whose leaders ISAAC BACKUS and John Leland joined others to secure constitutional guarantees of religious liberty. The Second Great Awakening (c. 1810–1860) splintered and stunted traditional Calvinist, Anglican, and Lutheran denominations still further, and led to the explosive growth of Baptists and Methodists, which together constituted some two-thirds of all Protestant churches by 1900.

The rise of evangelical political influence was also in part a function of theological innovation. Even though nineteenth-century American Evangelicals did not work out a detailed new political theology, they added accents to the Protestant inheritance that helped shape American politics. Evangelicals emphasized Christian CONVERSION, the necessary spiritual rebirth of each sinful individual. On that basis they strongly advocated the liberty of conscience of each individual and the free speech and press rights and duties of the missionary to proselytize, both on the American frontier and abroad. Evangelicals had a high view of the Christian Bible as the infallible textbook for human living. On that basis they celebrated the use of the Bible in chapels, classrooms, prisons, and elsewhere, and they castigated Jews, Catholics, Mormons (see MORMONISM), and others for their use of partial, apocryphal, or surrogate Scriptures. Evangelicals emphasized SANCTIFICATION, the process of each individual becoming holier before God, neighbor, and self. On that basis they underscored a robust ethic of spiritual and moral progress, education, and improvement of all.

Many Evangelicals coupled this emphasis on personal conversion and sanctification with a concern for social reform and moral improvement of the community. Great numbers of Evangelicals joined the national campaign and CIVIL WAR to end SLAVERY—although this issue permanently divided Methodists (see METHODISM) and BAPTISTS, as well as Presbyterians and Lutherans. Nineteenth-century Evangelicals were more united in their support for successive campaigns against dueling, FREEMASONRY, reservations for Indians, lotteries, drunkenness, Sunday mails, Sabbath-breaking, and more. In the later nineteenth century, many evangelical leaders also joined the struggle for the rights and plights of emancipated African Americans, poor workers, WOMEN suffragists, and labor union organizers—none more forcefully and successfully than WALTER RAUSCHENBUSCH, the leader of the SOCIAL GOSPEL MOVEMENT, although on these issues, too, evangelical camps were often bitterly divided.

On occasion, nineteenth-century Evangelicals became actively involved in national party politics, albeit with little success. At the turn of the nineteenth century, for example, many Evangelicals joined the Federalist Party to oppose the suspect religious and biblical views of Republican nominee THOMAS JEFFERSON in favor of the more traditionally religious incumbent President John Adams. At the close of the twentieth century Evangelicals flocked to the support of three-time Democratic nominee WILLIAM JENNINGS BRYAN, attracted by his public views on the inerrancy of Scripture (see BIBLICAL INERRANCY) and on the need for a sober Christian America that cultivated its own moral virtues and curbed its imperialist ambitions around the world.

Most evangelical groups, however, were suspicious of the national government and were staunch believers in the virtues of federalism and in no formal state establishments of religion. Many Evangelicals further believed that the individual congregation and the voluntary association were the more essential sources of governance and improvement. Churches, schools, clubs, charities, businesses, unions, corporations, learned societies, and other voluntary associations were essential buffers between the individual and state and essential brackets on state power.

The Rise and Fall of Public Protestantism

These evangelical and Reformed political models together gave a distinctive cast to American law and politics in the nineteenth and early twentieth centuries. Although there were endless local variations, most American states balanced the freedom of all peaceable private religions with the patronage of a public Protestant religion.

By 1833 every state constitution had formally disestablished religion, and guaranteed liberty of conscience and free exercise of religion for all. At the same time many government officials patronized biblical Christianity. "In God We Trust" and similar confessions appeared on currency, stamps, state seals, and government stationery. The Ten Commandments and favorite Bible verses were inscribed on the walls of court houses, public schools, and other public buildings. Crucifixes and other Christian symbols were erected in state parks and on state house grounds. Flags flew at half mast on Good Friday. Christmas, Easter, and other holy days were official holidays. Sundays remained official days of rest. Government-sponsored chaplains were appointed to Congress, the military, and various governmental asylums, prisons, and hospitals (see CHAPLAINCY). Prayers were offered at the commencement of each session of Congress and of many state legislatures. Thanksgiving Day prayers were offered by presidents, governors, and other state officials.

Government officials subsidized Christian missionaries and schools on the frontier. States and municipalities underwrote the costs of Bibles and liturgical books for poorer churches and donated land and services to them. Property grants and tax subsidies were furnished to Christian schools and charities. Special criminal laws protected the property, clergy, and liturgy of the churches. Tax exemptions were accorded to the properties of many churches, clerics, and charities. Tax revenues supported the acquisition of religious art and statuary for museums and other public buildings.

Government officials predicated some of their laws and policies directly on the moral and religious teachings of the Bible and the Christian church. The first public schools and state universities had mandatory courses in religion and compulsory attendance in daily chapel and Sunday worship services. Employees in state prisons, reformatories, orphanages, and asylums were required to know and to teach basic Christian beliefs and values. Polygamy (see PLURAL MARRIAGE), PROSTITUTION, pornography, and other sexual offenses against Christian morals and mores were prohibited. Blasphemy and sacrilege were still prosecuted. Gambling, lotteries, fortune-telling, and other activities that depended on fate or magic were forbidden. It was a commonplace of nineteenth-century American legal thought that "Christianity is a part of the common law."

This state patronage and participation in a general Protestant public religion worked rather well for the more religiously homogeneous times and towns of the American republic. The public religion confirmed and celebrated each community's civic unity and confessional identity. It also set natural limits to both political action and individual freedom—limits that were enforced more by communal reprobation than by constitutional litigation. To be sure, religious dissenters, who resisted or criticized the local public religion, fared poorly under this system. New England states remained notably inhospitable to dissenting Quakers (see FRIENDS, SOCIETY OF) and Methodists. New Jersey and Pennsylvania dealt churlishly with Unitarians and Catholics. Virginia and the Carolinas were hard on conservative Episcopalians and upstart Evangelicals alike. Few legislatures and courts anywhere showed much respect for the rights of Jews or Muslims, let alone those of NATIVE AMERICANS or African Americans.

Nonetheless, the saving assumption of this system was the presence of the frontier and the right to emigrate thereto. Religious dissenters did not stay long to fight the local establishment as their European counterparts had done. They moved—sometimes at gunpoint—to establish their own communities on the frontier, often on the heels of missionaries and schoolmasters who had preceded them. Mormons (see MORMONISM) moved from New York to Ohio, to Missouri, to Illinois, before finally settling in Utah and surrounding states. Catholics moved to California, the Dakotas, Illinois, Louisiana, Montana, Nevada, and New Mexico. Experimental Baptists and Methodists poured into the southern states from Georgia and Tennessee to Mississippi and Missouri. Free spirits escaped to the open frontiers of Wyoming, Montana, Washington, and Oregon.

The right—sometimes the duty—to emigrate was a basic assumption of the American political experiment, which even the most churlish establishmentarians respected. Many first-generation Americans had left their European faiths and territories to gain their freedom. Accordingly, they embraced the right to leave—to exit their faith, to abandon their blood and soil, to reestablish their lives, beliefs, and identities afresh—as a veritable sine qua non of freedom. It was this right of the religious dissenter to emigrate and to start anew that provided the release valve for this Protestant model of religion and politics to function so long and so effectively in America.

As the American populace became more pluralized and the American frontier more populated, however, this political system became harder to maintain. The Second Great Awakening not only sparked the explosion of Baptists and Methodists, but also introduced to the American scene a host of newly minted faiths—Adventists, Christian Scientists, Disciples, Holiness Churches, JEHOVAH'S WITNESSES, Mormons, Pentecostals, Unitarians, and more (see CHRISTIAN SCIENCE; DISCIPLES OF CHRIST; HOLINESS MOVEMENT; PENTECOSTALISM; SEVENTH DAY ADVENTISTS; UNITARIAN UNIVERSALIST ASSOCIATION). The American Civil War and Reconstruction Amendments not only outlawed Slavery but also liberated a host of long-cloaked African beliefs and rituals, some in pure African or Muslim forms, many inculturated with various Christian traditions (see AFRICAN AMERICAN PROTESTANTISM; SLAVERY, ABOLITION OF). The great waves of immigration after the 1860s brought strong new concentrations and forms of Catholics, Jews, Eastern Orthodox, Buddhists, Confucians, Hindus, and other Eastern religions. Materialism, Marxism, atheism, and various liberal and secular beliefs were also emerging (see CATHOLICISM, PROTESTANT REACTIONS TO; ORTHODOXY, EASTERN).

This radical reconfiguration of the American religious landscape required a new model of religion and politics. In particular, state policies of patronizing a public Protestant religion became increasingly difficult to maintain. A number of Baptists and Methodists, returning to their separatist roots, insisted that states adhere more firmly to principles of disestablishment of religion. Religious minorities in many communities also began to ally themselves in opposition to this system, particularly the patronage of a common Protestantism within the public schools. Some of these minority religious and secular communities refused to conform or to assimilate. Others refused to live or leave quietly. Still others began to crusade actively against the system.

When neither assimilation nor accommodation policies proved effective, state and local legislatures began to clamp down on these dissenters. In the early twentieth century local officials began routinely denying Roman Catholics their school charters, Jehovah's Witnesses their preaching permits, Eastern Orthodox their canonical freedoms, Jews and Adventists their Sabbath accommodations. As state courts and legislatures turned an increasingly blind eye to their plight, religious dissenters began to turn to the federal courts for relief, often supported by new or nonreligious groups.

In the landmark cases of *Cantwell v. Connecticut* (1940) and *Everson v. Board of Education* (1947), the United States Supreme Court applied the First Amendment religion clauses to state and local governments. In its early application of the free exercise clause, the Court set out to protect the rights of newly emergent religious groups against recalcitrant local officials. Jehovah's Witnesses, the Court held repeatedly, could not be denied licenses to preach, parade, or pamphleteer just because they were unpopular. Public school students could not be compelled to salute the flag or recite the pledge if they were conscientiously opposed. Other parties, with scruples of conscience, could not be forced to swear oaths before receiving citizenship status, property tax exemptions, state bureaucratic positions, or social welfare benefits.

In its early application of the establishment clause, the Court sought to outlaw state patronage of public religion altogether, particularly in the schools. On the one hand, the Court banned religion from public schools. Public schools could not offer prayers or moments of silence, could not read Scripture or religious texts, could not house Bibles or prayerbooks, could not teach theology or creationism (see CREATION SCIENCE), could not display Decalogues or crèches, could not use the services or facilities of religious bodies. On the other hand, the Court removed religious schools from state support. States could not provide salary and service supplements to religious schools, could not reimburse them for administering standardized tests, could not lend them state-prescribed textbooks, supplies, films, or counseling services, could not allow tax deductions or credits for religious school tuition.

In *Lemon v. Kurtzman* (1971) the Court held further that every federal or state law and policy would survive constitutional scrutiny only if it had: (1) a secular purpose; (2) a primary effect that neither advances nor inhibits religion; and (3) minimal entanglement between church and state. This test rendered the establishment clause a formidable obstacle to many traditional forms of state patronage of public Protestant religion. Legislatures and courts alike used this new test to outlaw all manner of government subsidies for religious charities, social services, and mission works, government use of religious services, facilities, and publications, government protections of Sundays and Holy Days, government enforcement of blasphemy and sacrilege laws, government participation in religious rituals and religious displays. It often did not take lawsuits to effectuate these reforms. Particularly local governments, sensitive to the political and fiscal costs of constitutional litigation, often voluntarily ended their prayers, removed their Decalogues, and closed their coffers to religion long before any case was filed against them. Although federal and state cases at the end of the twentieth century began to relax some of these holdings, they remained the basic law.

These strong constitutional challenges, together with the rapid liberalization of their theologies and defection from their churches, drove many Protestants from active political life and learning in the post–World War II period. Whereas individual luminaries such as REINHOLD and H. RICHARD NIEBUHR charted provocative new political pathways, American Protestants did not develop an authentic political model and program on the order of Roman Catholicism after the Second Vatican Council. Some Protestants repeated old political formulas, and often nostalgically recounted Protestant progress and prowess in American history. Other Protestants focused their attention on single political issues—PRAYER in public schools, the eradication of ABORTION, the protection of the traditional family—often mobilizing ample political support for these causes. However, a comprehensive Protestant political platform, faithful to the cardinal convictions of historical Protestantism and responsive to the needs of an intensely pluralistic polity, did not emerge.

A notable exception to the recent pattern of Protestant political quietism in America was the CIVIL RIGHTS MOVEMENT of the 1950s and 1960s, led by the Baptist preacher MARTIN LUTHER KING JR., that helped to bring greater political and civil equality to African Americans in a series of landmark statutes and cases. Another exception was the rise of the MORAL MAJORITY and Christian Coalition in the 1980s and early 1990s led by JERRY FALWELL, PAT ROBERTSON, and others—a broad political and cultural campaign to revitalize public religion, restore families, reform schools, reclaim unsafe neighborhoods, and support faith-based charities (see CHRISTIAN RIGHT). A still further exception has been the very recent coalition of Protestant and other religious and academic groups that have led campaigns for the greater protection of international religious freedom. Whether these movements are signposts for a vibrant new Protestant political mission and ministry remains to be seen.

See also Church and State, Overview; Democracy; Human Rights; Political Parties; Political Theology

References and Further Reading

Ehler, Sidney Z., and John B. Morrall. *Church and State Through the Centuries: A Collection of Historic Documents with Commentaries*. Westminster, MD: Newman Press, 1954.

Fowler, Robert Booth, Allen D. Hertzke, and Laura R. Olsen. *Religion and Politics in America: Faith, Culture, and Strategic Choices*. 2nd edition. Boulder/New York/Oxford: Westview Press, 1999.

Friedman, Robert. *The Theology of Anabaptism*. Scottdale, PA: Herald Press, 1973.

Hutson, James H., ed. *Religion and the New Republic: Faith in the Founding of America*. Lanham, MD: Rowman & Littlefield, 2000.

Klaassen, Walter. *Anabaptism in Outline: Selected Primary Sources*. Scottdale, PA: Herald Press, 1981.

LeCler, Joseph. *Toleration and the Reformation*. Translated by T. L. Westow. 4 vols. New York: Association Press, 1960.

Marty, Martin E. *Religion and Republic: The American Circumstance*. Boston: Beacon Press, 1987.

McLoughlin, William C. *New England Dissent, 1630–1833*. 2 vols. Cambridge, MA: Harvard University Press, 1971.

Noll, Mark A. *One Nation Under God? Christian Faith and Political Action in America*. San Francisco: Harper & Row, 1988.

O'Donovan, Joan Lockwood. *Theology of Law and Authority in the English Reformation*. Atlanta: Scholars Press, 1991.

Skinner, Quentin. *The Foundations of Modern Political Thought*. 2 vols. Cambridge: Cambridge University Press, 1978.

Stokes, Anson P. *Church and State in the United States*. 3 vols. New York: Harper and Bros., 1950.

Tinder, Glenn. *The Political Meaning of Christianity: The Prophetic Stance.* San Francisco: HarperSanFrancisco, 1991.

Walzer, Michael. *The Revolution of the Saints: Study in the Origins of Radical Politics.* Cambridge, MA: Harvard University Press, 1965.

West, John G. Jr. *The Politics of Revelation and Reason: Religion and Civic Life in the New Nation.* Lawrence: University Press of Kansas, 1996.

Witte, John. *Law and Protestantism: The Legal Teachings of the Lutheran Reformation.* Cambridge: Cambridge University Press, 2002.

———. *Religion and the American Constitutional Experiment.* Boulder/New York/Oxford: Westview Press, 2000.

Wuthnow, Robert, ed. *The Encyclopedia of Politics and Religion.* Washington, D.C.: Congressional Quarterly, Inc., 1998– .

JOHN WITTE

POLITY

Polity is the structure and form of governance of an organization or community, including its constitution, assignments and limitations of powers, offices, lines of AUTHORITY and amenability, and procedures of membership, participation, and representation. Like its companion term "POLITICS," polity derives from the Greek *politeia,* referring to the governance and citizenship of the *polis,* the city or state.

One of the structures central to polity and political practices in the Greek *polis* was the *ekklesia,* the public assembly of citizens meeting to address and resolve issues of the common good. That Christians took the name *ekklesia* for their own assemblies is surely no coincidence. Like the original *ekklesia,* Christian assemblies were called together (*kaleo,* the Greek verb "to call," is the root of *ekklesia*), responding to the summons of witness and service in Christ's name. They were public, inclusive of everyone who sought to participate. They aimed at the common good of their own community and of the human community whose greatest well-being would be realized in the Reign of God.

Protestantism itself has been as much a movement for reform in polity as in DOCTRINE. Much of the "protest" in Protestant groups has focused on structures of authority and governance in the churches. Just as Protestant disputes over church teachings have regularly been couched as a search for the original and pure truth of the Word of God, so Protestant struggles over polity have been framed as a striving to achieve an original and unadulterated form of Christian community. If "Scripture alone" (a central claim of the REFORMATION) contained everything necessary for SALVATION, then "Scripture alone" ought to be the basis for church order. In contrast with Roman Catholicism, in which polity can be authentic only in continuity with the church's practices across the cen-

turies, the test of Protestant polity has generally been its discontinuity with previous (corrupted) practice as it seeks to embody the original or "primitive" New Testament church.

Protestantism's break with Roman Catholic continuity, and its impulse to create new COVENANT communities, is captured in its language about polity. With the exception of the Anglican communion, most Protestant groups have avoided the term "canon law" for their written polity because of its overtones of organic legal tradition and precedent. They have chosen to speak either of church law and church order, in the sense of a constitution binding people together in covenant (typical of Reformed traditions), or of CHURCH DISCIPLINE, referring to the disciplined, common practices of seeking growth in the Christian life and sanctioning those who do not remain faithful (typical of Methodist and Pietist traditions). For example, the PRESBYTERIAN CHURCH USA titles its polity book *The Book of Order,* and the UNITED METHODIST CHURCH titles its *The Book of Discipline.*

The Protestant instinct to distrust existing forms and seek the original church polity in Scripture has produced far less unity than diversity, dispute, and schism. The hundreds of church groups that fall under the general label of Protestant are explicit testimony to a lack of consensus about what the original polity is. More than 250 distinct denominations that are not part of Orthodox (see ORTHODOXY, EASTERN) or Roman Catholic traditions persist in the UNITED STATES alone, and the impulse to generate entirely new ecclesial forms based on fresh readings of scripture continues to thrive. The flourishing of newly organized independent congregations, particularly those appealing to the Holy Spirit as guide and guardian of their communal life, virtually explodes comprehensive categories such as Protestantism. The denominations grouped under the canopy of Protestantism themselves appear to indicate that independent congregations seek to supersede with appeal to Scripture and Spirit.

For much of Protestantism, however, denominations continue to represent forms of polity consistent across multiple congregations. Denominations are literally the name (denominators) of various traditions of church teaching and polity. Many denominations bear in their name an explicit claim about their polity or the political reasons for their organization (e.g., Episcopal, Presbyterian, Covenant, Congregational, United). Denominations also demonstrate that polity is a creature of social context. This, too, is embodied in such names as AMERICAN BAPTIST, Swedish Covenant, AFRICAN METHODIST EPISCOPAL, and Korean Presbyterian.

The extent to which polity is embedded in national, ethnic, and local cultures has been a major source of controversy in Protestantism. The language, symbols, norms, and assumptions evident in church polity and its practice are inevitably shaped to a greater or lesser extent by the societies from which churches draw their participants. CLERGY AUTHORITY, for example, often mirrors wider cultural assumptions about GENDER roles, such as paternal dominance, or parallels other social positions, such as tribal chief or village patriarch.

Polity is also affected by the context of religious freedom in particular societies, the degree of regulation by the state, and the presence and degree of dominance of a national church. Because the rise of Protestantism was coincident with the emergence of modern nation-states, some Protestant churches (e.g., CHURCH OF ENGLAND, Church of Sweden) have functioned as national bodies with parish systems embracing the entire territory of the nation. Other Protestant churches have had to struggle for freedom to assemble for worship and governance of their own affairs, placing themselves in a separatist or sectarian position.

The diversity of Protestant churches makes generalizations about polity almost impossible. However, one continuum that may be useful in comprehending polity is the dynamic of *authority,* ranging from congregational, where most or all powers reside in the self-constituted local church congregation, to connectional, where significant powers in ministry and mission reside in regional judicatories, such as SYNODS or CONFERENCES, and/or in offices of oversight, such as executive presbyter, superintendent, or bishop. Even within such a continuum, forms of governance may differ greatly. Connectional assemblies are constituted variously by delegates, representatives, or messengers from local church congregations and the body of clergy, and have varying degrees of power to mandate actions by congregations. Bishops have diverse roles as legislators, administrators, and sacramental figures, with varying powers over assignment of clergy and connectional mission.

Given the diversity of polities and the enormous range of local and connectional practices that make up the distinct organizational culture of congregations and denominations, polity generally embraces five essential elements:

1. A common discipline for church membership.
2. A common discipline for congregational or local church ministry and mission.
3. A procedure for testing the call; assessing the preparation; authorizing, commissioning, or ordaining; and placing pastors, ministers, and others set apart for leadership of the community.
4. Organization of ministry and mission shared by congregations of a region or carried forward nationally or internationally.
5. A constitution, structures, and procedures governing the work of the denomination as an association or connectional organization, including its offices and forms of participation and representation.

Protestant congregations independent of any denominational affiliation must tend to the first three of these essential elements of polity, and often develop commitments in the fourth area as well. Thus these elements largely embrace the life and work of Protestant churches and merit further exploration.

Disciplines of Church Membership

At its most basic, local level, polity begins with the criteria for initiating and sustaining church membership (see also ECCLESIASTICAL ORDINANCES). Many of the reform movements involved in Protestantism began as efforts to address four disciplines of membership. Differences and disputes over these disciplines have accounted for numerous schisms and enduring controversies.

First of these is the understanding of BAPTISM, including questions of the appropriateness of infant baptism, proper preparation for initiation into the Christian life, and the standard of doctrine and practice required for adult or believer baptism. Positions on such questions are rooted in a sacramental theology of the nature of God's GRACE and the balance of divine initiative and human response. But theological stances are inseparable from practical ecclesiologic understandings of the formation of Christian community or, in polity terms, how the church members constitute the church. For national churches that understand themselves as comprehensive of the population, infant baptism symbolizes God's grace over the whole of human life and the breadth of the church to include all persons. For sectarian churches of Anabaptist character (see ANABAPTISM), baptism symbolizes the particularity of Christian faith and its acceptance by adult believers who then constitute the congregation of the faithful.

Second, for churches that practice infant baptism, adult CONFIRMATION of the vows taken on one's behalf before the age of conscious decision is a second significant discipline of membership. Again, the criteria for readiness and participation in a rite of confirmation present both theological issues of divine and human agency and practical issues of catechesis. Whereas administration of the baptismal sacrament is for most churches an act normally reserved to the ordained, catechesis is more widely the responsibility of lay as well as ordained officers.

Third, for all baptized members of churches, particularly adult believers, every church needs to provide the means to sustain faithful living and grow in the Christian life. These means, which are widely called "spiritual disciplines," include participation in public WORSHIP and the SACRAMENTS, PRAYER, Bible study, fasting, and giving to the poor. For many groups expressive of Pietist or Puritan movements beginning in the seventeenth century (see PIETISM; PURITANISM), these means have constituted a rule of life to which persons have been held accountable through membership in small groups within the larger church (*ecclesiola in ecclesia*). The relationship of these *collegia* or societies to the parishes of national churches stirred bitter polity disputes for groups such as the seventeenth-century Pietists of northern GERMANY or the eighteenth-century English Methodists (see METHODISM). Some separated from the national church and its pastors or priests on the grounds that their group life was not supported by the parish or that the pastor or priest did not meet the standard of belief and holy living expected of members of the movement. Such movements were under constant challenge as to whose ecclesiastical authority they recognized and to whom they were answerable. Most became independent churches in nations outside the sway of European national churches.

Fourth, every church discipline needs to create procedures for calling baptized persons to account for their behavior and sanctioning them in appropriate and effective ways. Pastors and priests, as well as boards of lay persons designated to uphold congregational discipline, seek means of confronting persons whose actions do not accord with Christian practice or morality as the church understands it, to call them back into the community with appropriate repentance and amends, or, in intractable cases, to expel them. Understandably, many disputes arise in such situations, particularly when sanctions are considered too harsh or ineffective. Moreover, churches may have to decide whether the scope of discipline extends only to behavior in the church or to members' lives in the wider community. They may have to determine whether to seek civil support from a local magistrate or to invoke civil laws that might affect the member's citizenship (in serious cases, such as sexual misconduct or financial malfeasance).

Many branches of Protestantism have become less stringent in examining members' lives than they were in founding generations. Whereas most Protestant denominations make provision for bringing formal charges against a church member and conducting a trial that might result in expulsion, such procedures are rarely invoked. Informal sanctions through which other members may convey disapproval or exclusion are not uncommon, however.

Discipline of Congregations

Every local church congregation must have structures for governing its own affairs. Protestant churches, grounded in teachings of "the PRIESTHOOD OF ALL BELIEVERS," commonly assume a significant role for LAITY. Although the scope of local control varies among denominations, governing bodies of congregations have some degree of authority in four basic areas.

First, they carry out functions related to the disciplines of church membership described earlier, such as electing persons into membership, affirming their confirmation, or stating expectations for participation and growth in Christian life. They examine church rolls, seek out inactive members, and authorize removal of persons who no longer desire membership.

Second, local church governing bodies create and manage forms of ministry and mission and provide the staff, volunteer or paid, to support those ministries. Oversight of personnel decisions and policies is usually the domain of lay committees in some form of consultation with the pastor or priest, who in many traditions is understood as head of staff or even chief executive officer. A lay committee, in many churches chaired by the priest or pastor, nominates persons to assume administration of programs and resources as volunteers, and provides training and support for those persons in their ministries.

Third, every local church congregation must manage its financial resources, raising the funds needed to operate and expending money in accord with the expectations and desires of the members. Although customs and standards for raising and handling money differ widely across Protestantism, each church also must account for the uses of its money. Regular audits, multiple signatures on checks, secure means of making bank deposits, and public financial statements are among the rules often stated in church law to prevent malfeasance and ensure trust among church members.

Fourth, most local church congregations also must manage tangible properties, such as land and buildings. Every church has a board or committee specifically charged with purchasing, maintaining, renovating, or expanding church facilities under the guidance of the church's governing body. Church law normally is at pains to require accountable management of properties and sound legal practices, such as proper deeds and contracts.

Protestant churches vary in their understanding of the control of church property, however. In more connectional polities, all property is held by deed in trust for the denomination so that if a congregation becomes inactive, then its buildings revert to a denominational judicatory. The trust clause also prevents a congregation from voting to take its property and leave its denomination. Major renovations, expansions, or purchases must be approved by a denominational body. In less-connectional churches, local property remains in the hands of local trustees or governing boards. Whatever the polity, however, churches generally expect that their facilities will be used for PREACHING, teaching, or ministry in accord with their own doctrines and traditions. Churches with congregational polities are self-constituted as congregations. They normally write their own constitution and by-laws, create and elect their own officers and governing bodies, employ their own pastor and staff, and own their own property. They take full responsibility for the four areas of congregational discipline described ealier.

Churches with connectional polities normally devise a framework of congregational discipline for all the local churches of the denomination to follow. Although local practice may vary, of course, a common terminology along with common designation of governing bodies and assignment of powers and duties is established in the book of order or discipline. Church law mandates structures and procedures that establish a local church congregation as an organization within the framework of civil law, including election of officers and corporate ownership of property. In the United States, many congregations are registered with the state as not-for-profit corporations to protect individual officers from liability in civil suits and to limit property taxes.

Ministry

Protestant churches advocate the ministry of the whole people of God. They provide for lay participation and leadership in varied ministries, both local and denominational, and expect members to extend Christian witness and service into everyday life in their workplaces, homes, schools, civic involvement, commerce, and other activities. Most Protestant efforts to advance christian EDUCATION, social services, and MISSIONS have been organized and governed by associations composed of and largely led by lay persons (see MISSIONARY ORGANIZATIONS; VOLUNTARY SOCIETIES).

Protestantism has also expected that the whole people of God will be able to discern spiritual gifts of persons to be set apart for authorized or ordained offices in the church. For this discernment the churches turn to Scripture, church traditions, and current statements of qualifications and preparation affirmed in church law. Yet the nature and practice of ordained offices has been the source of sharp controversies and lasting divisions in Protestantism.

Three church offices to which the New Testament letters refer have provoked immense debate in Protestantism about the translation of their Greek names, not to mention their function. The Greek *presbyteros* has been variously translated into English as "presbyter," "priest," or "elder." Each of these terms expresses authorization to guide and administer the church. Yet Protestants differ in their understanding of the office as lay or clergy. For the more presbyteral and congregational churches of Reformed traditions, the elder is an office in the local church to which lay persons are ordained. Elders constitute church governing bodies and participate in administration of the sacraments. The pastor is differentiated from these elders ("ruling elders" in the Presbyterian Church USA) with election by a presbytery to ordination for the Word and sacraments ("teaching elder" in the Presbyterian Church USA). For the more connectional and episcopal churches of Anglican (see ANGLICANISM) and Methodist traditions, the elder or priest is an office to which persons are ordained to serve as clergy, with specific and usually exclusive authorization to preach the Word, administer the sacraments, and guide the order and administration of the church.

The Greek *diakonos* has been translated as "deacon" or "diaconate" (see DEACONESS, DEACON). Extending the work of Stephen and others described in the New Testament, deacons are commonly expected to lead the service of the Christian community to those in need of help, especially the poor and sick, as well as to assist the presbyter, priest, or elders in worship and sacrament. In the more presbyteral and congregational churches of Reformed Protestantism, the diaconate is considered a lay office to which persons are ordained for service. Depending on the polity, deacons (usually organized as a group or board) may exercise significant authority in assisting pastoral offices, governing the congregation, and even calling or dismissing a pastor. In more connectional and episcopal churches, the diaconate has been a far less consistent office than the priesthood. In Anglican and Methodist traditions, ordination to deacon has been understood to be a step of preparation for ordination as elder or priest. Provision for the diaconate as a permanent clergy office is becoming more common, with many persons ordained as deacons to serve as educators, musicians, social service workers, or social action organizers.

Of the three church offices, the *episkopos* has led to perhaps the sharpest divisions among Protestant churches. Coming into English as bishop, overseer, or superintendent, the term has been understood as everything from a description of a pastoral function to a specific and permanent ordained office with a significant role in church governance (see BISHOP AND EPIS-COPACY). For many Protestants, the episcopal function of oversight applies mainly to the pastor's duties. Many churches find support for this stance in New Testament descriptions of the episcopate, and a number of local church pastors have taken the title of "bishop" and sought ordination from their congregation to capture this comprehensive pastoral role.

Reformed Protestants typically absorb the oversight function into pastoral or supervisory offices, but do not adopt the title of bishop even for roles of regional or judicatory ministers overseeing the work of pastors and congregations. They argue that Protestantism arose partly in resistance to the hierarchical power of episcopal office to control the churches and to influence civil polity.

Still other Protestant churches, such as Lutheran (see LUTHERANISM) and Methodist bodies, use the title of bishop for offices of preaching and administration in a region or judicatory. They elect bishops, often for life, to ordain priests, pastors, or elders; to be a pastor to pastors *(pastor pastorum)*, either to appoint or to oversee the call of pastors and priests to their congregations; and to encourage local churches to work together in connectional endeavors. To this understanding of the office, the Anglican communion of Protestantism adds liturgical functions such as the bishop's role in confirming new members into the church and a more symbolic place of bishop as head of the church in a diocese, ritualized by ordination into the episcopacy. The continuity of bishops with the episcopacy of the early church, termed the "apostolic succession," is a central historical and theological claim undergirding the authority of the office and legitimizing episcopal ordinations. Yet this, too, may be understood either literally as a tangible, continuous historical chain or figuratively as a succession to the roles and practices of apostolic office.

Protestant polities institute offices of ministry, including definitions of their scope and limitations of powers, their duties and responsibilities, and the standards of conduct expected of persons holding these offices. Polities also provide means of testing the call of persons to ordained ministries and define the steps by which persons may seek ordination. The twentieth century brought an increasing emphasis on formal education of clergy and other church leaders. In company with rising standards in parallel fields such as law, medicine, social work, and teaching, many churches have insisted on advanced preparation for ministry such as a professional master's degree (usually the Master of Divinity). This trend, too, has brought controversy among Protestants. For many churches, the test of call is seen in the fruits of the person's ministry as evidence of the Spirit. Education

is considered secondary, irrelevant, or even deceitful if it leads a person to cease teaching the doctrines of the home church.

As educational standards have changed, so in general have expectations of personal conduct and emotional maturity. In the nineteenth and twentieth centuries, the standards for ministerial conduct focused on avoidance of tobacco and alcohol and insistence on behavior governed by good manners and proper decorum. Late in the twentieth century, attention shifted, particularly in Western societies, to questions of SEXUALITY. By the 1990s, many Protestant churches had adopted statements of church law defining sexual harassment and abuse, child abuse, and sexual misconduct of clergy, along with procedures and remedies for addressing such behavior and its consequences. Psychological testing became a standard step in ordination processes, along with criminal background checks.

Governance of clergy matters, like the profession itself, has been assumed in many Protestant churches to be a male domain. Since the 1950s, however, several Protestant bodies, including the United Methodist Church, the Presbyterian Church USA, the EPISCOPAL CHURCH, the UNITED CHURCH OF CHRIST, and the EVANGELICAL LUTHERAN CHURCH IN AMERICA, have provided for ordination of WOMEN to pastoral offices (see WOMEN CLERGY). The actual place of women in ministry continues to be shaped, whatever formal polity may say, by local church attitudes and acceptance by male clergy peers. Many Protestant churches, like Roman Catholicism and Orthodoxy, reject ordination of women based on interpretation of scripture and TRADITION.

Many churches have similarly been caught up in debates over the ordination of homosexual persons (see HOMOSEXUALITY). In some cases, churches have formally banned such persons from ordained ministry, but then have struggled to state in clear legal definitions exactly what behaviors they are excluding. A few Protestant churches, such as the United Church of Christ, have chosen to leave sexuality issues to the discernment of regular ordination processes, at least in principle accepting persons of whatever sexuality who demonstrate gifts for ministry.

Just as Protestant polities have provided for discipline of church members, including in worst cases their exclusion from the church, so polities include standards of discipline of clergy and procedures for their removal from ministry. Malfeasance, misconduct, ineffectiveness, or teachings inconsistent with the doctrines of a particular church, all may be grounds for discipline or removal, though the latter two are difficult to prove. Church law must define offenses carefully and set up fair procedures through which a person may be charged, examined, and disciplined with opportunity for self-defense, explanation, and growth in mutual understanding within the Christian community.

Organization for Mission

Protestantism has exhibited a strong missionary impulse throughout its history. Many Protestant churches themselves are the offspring of missions planted by Christians from another country or continent, and in turn, most sponsor mission work beyond their own land or region. Mission, like ministry, is a broad-ranging term that eludes definition. Certainly for Protestants, it has included not only preaching and teaching of Christian faith, but also education, health care, economic development, social justice, and advocacy for the powerless. In some cases, mission has stirred churches to political action (see POLITICS; POLITICAL PARTIES).

Church law and discipline organizes, authorizes, and controls mission work. In churches with congregational polity, authorization of mission may be a relatively simple matter of building consensus and support to undertake certain initiatives in ministry. Authorization may expand to include forms of cooperation with other congregations, sharing financial and human resources, building a school or health clinic together, or pooling money to support the salary of a missionary.

In churches with connectional polities, the governance of missions may be considerably more complex. A DENOMINATION may require a self-incorporated body to act as a board of trustees overseeing multiple properties or managing endowments and cash flows in the hundreds of millions of dollars. Denominations with a longer heritage of mission work will bear responsibility for many different institutions, such as schools, hospitals, or homes, that have been built up over generations and continue to seek effective ministry. Some denominations have hundreds or even thousands of persons commissioned to do mission work, laboring under the administration and oversight of persons authorized through church polity.

In general, the principles of polity governing church mission are designed to build and maintain trust: trust between the many church members who give time and money to mission efforts and the persons carrying out and administering that mission; trust between institutions and congregations in different parts of the world trying to support and learn from each other; and trust in a more fiduciary sense of properly managing, distributing, and preserving the considerable resources that the churches pour into mission work and have accumulated over time. To strengthen and enhance that trust, most churches authorize oversight bodies that include lay persons and clergy, to work with paid staff. These bodies may be regional, national, or international in scope. Churches mandate regular detailed reporting on mission activities to congregations and donors. Denominational mission is usually amenable and accountable to the highest governing body of the denomination, such as a general council, synod, assembly, or conference, which alone can authorize administrative units for mission, define their duties and powers, and structure procedures for their accountability.

Constituting Denominations

All Protestant churches, congregational or denominational, are self-constituted. Having broken away from the organic continuity of Roman Catholicism or Orthodoxy, they have had to constitute themselves as independent entities with a name and constitutive elements such as members, councils, synods, or conferences. Normally Protestant churches have a written constitution and procedural by-laws delineating their governing bodies, assigning, limiting, and balancing powers, and providing for amendment.

For Protestant churches organized as denominations, particularly the more connectional churches, their constitutions embody a covenant of association and cooperation expressing some degree of unity in organization and purpose. These constitutions define the bodies with powers to govern denominational ministry and mission and constitute those bodies through forms of representation and delegation. They balance the powers of various entities, such as regional or general assemblies and local churches, clergy, and laity, as well as administrative offices and the assemblies that create and authorize them.

Protestant constitutions provide for the basic legislative, executive, and judicial functions of government, but do so in various ways depending on tradition and social location. For example, in more democratic societies, the churches expect and depend on governance through assemblies composed of persons who bring the assumptions and experience of citizens accustomed to the work of town councils, school boards, and other manifestations of public life. Such assemblies may be open to all or may be representative, that is, democratic or republican in nature. Their powers may be balanced by the administrative or episcopal authority of bishops and judicatory officials, who may also be organized as a council or legislative house with certain oversight responsibilities.

To these dynamics must be added the influential model of business corporations, growing throughout the twentieth century, that advocates executive entrepreneurialism and control, with assemblies functioning more like stockholder meetings. This is manifested in Protestant congregations that understand the pastor to be chief executive officer, in some cases even holding church property as proprietor, as well as in Protestant churches that give executives or bishops the major responsibility in management and initiative of mission. The tension between this commercial corporate model and the democratic political model is as evident in the churches as it is in societies more generally.

Protestant churches have wrestled continually with constitutional issues of participation. In Western societies granting universal suffrage, for example, churches likewise have moved from male assemblies to governing bodies composed of both women and men. Language inclusive of both genders has replaced the male pronouns and terms of earlier generations in many books of church order. Yet, although women usually exhibit higher levels of participation in church activities, in many churches men continue to hold the majority of offices and to predominate in assemblies. Churches have also struggled over the balance of lay and clergy authority in denominational matters. Normally clergy have powers at least equal to those of laity, even though the latter vastly outnumber the former. This reflects traditional deference to clergy office, historically pertaining especially to matters of ordination and clergy discipline.

Protestant denominations vary in their constitutional self-definitions as entities. Some name the denomination itself as a corporate entity, thus making it capable of owning property and functioning as a unit in civil law. Others specifically disclaim the existence of the denomination as a corporate entity to avoid liability in civil actions. In these polities, all property and legal functions are the responsibility of regional or missional units, and the denomination exists as a common tradition only.

In summary, Protestant churches elude generalization in terms of denominational organization and in polity. Yet for the most part, their forms of governance address the five elements discussed here, which together constitute what is usually encompassed by the term "polity." Any movement toward greater unity among Protestants, or among Protestants, Roman Catholics, Orthodox, or other branches of Christianity, will have to seek reconciliation of differences within these five elements.

References and Further Reading

Braaten, Carl E., ed. *The New Church Debate: Issues Facing American Lutheranism.* Philadelphia, PA: Fortress Press, 1983.

Doe, Norman. *Canon Law in the Anglican Communion: A Worldwide Perspective.* New York: Oxford University Press, 1998.

Frank, Thomas Edward. *Polity, Practice, and the Mission of The United Methodist Church.* Nashville, TN: Abingdon Press, 2002.

Gray, Joan S., and Joyce C. Tucker. *Presbyterian Polity for Church Officers.* 3rd ed. Louisville, KY: Westminster/John Knox Press, 1999.

Johnson, Daniel L., and Charles Hambrick-Stowe, eds. *Theology and Identity: Traditions, Movements, and Polity in the United Church of Christ.* Cleveland, OH: United Church Press, 1990.

Long, Edward Leroy, Jr. *Patterns of Polity: Varieties of Church Governance.* Cleveland, OH: Pilgrim Press, 2001.

Maring, Norman H., and Winthrop S. Hudson. *A Baptist Manual of Polity and Practice.* Rev. ed. Valley Forge, PA: Judson Press, 1991.

Miller, Donald E. *Reinventing American Protestantism: Christianity in the New Millennium.* Berkeley: University of California Press, 1997.

Schenck, Robert L. *Constitutions of American Denominations.* Buffalo, NY: William S. Hein, 1984.

THOMAS EDWARD FRANK

POLYGAMY

See Plural Marriage

PORVOO

See Ecumenical Agreements

POSTCOLONIALISM

The era of European imperialism introduced significant populations around the world to Protestant theologies, institutions, and social networks, and the establishment of an extensive Protestant missionary infrastructure in colonial territories converted millions of people to Western forms of Christianity. Although many embraced the religion of the colonizers, others rebelled against the imposition of foreign religions. In the twentieth century, as independence movements forced imperial governments out of AFRICA, Asia, and the Americas, Protestants in former colonial territories rallied around postcolonial ideologies to build a viable Christianity that was free from the taint of imperial violence and that spoke to indigenous needs and historical experiences.

Postcolonial Theory and Practice

The historical notion of postcolonialism is rooted in the belief that societies victimized by colonialism—be it directly or indirectly political, economic, or cultural—actively challenge imperial paradigms of power. This is crucial, to be certain that hegemonic colonial power is not replicated informally after independence. Postcolonialism therefore seeks to engage the historical and contemporary experiences of colonial subjects to forge an understanding of the suffering wrought by imperialism, rather than provide a glorified, Eurocentric narrative of imperial history. Because of its diffuse and universal character, postcolonialism is understood and expressed differently throughout the formerly colonized world. For most postcolonial theorists, however, a difficult balance must be struck: Eurocentrism must be rejected, yet the native CULTURE should not be glorified unduly. Instead, a hybrid culture, one that recognizes the interdependence of both cultures in the postcolonial world, yet breaks down the unequal power structures developed through imperialism, is the goal. In the case of Protestantism, postcolonialism has been expressed communally and theologically by activists eager to maintain their faith but also conscious of its colonial, and often violent, experience in their societies.

Many Protestants in areas largely converted by missionaries in the colonial era have looked to reinterpret the BIBLE in ways that resonate with indigenous cultural values, and that divorce the text from the Eurocentrism expressed by many mission organizations. A move toward vernacular hermeneutics, in which translations of the Bible refer to and make comparisons between biblical practices and indigenous traditions, have been useful for maintaining interest in Christianity independent of its association with the colonial powers (see BIBLE TRANSLATION). In tandem with this are postcolonial readings of the Bible that seek out instances of imperial oppression in the text and then analyze them against modern lived experiences of the disenfranchised. In this way Protestants may find inspiration to resolve remnant problems of imperial decadence, patriarchal oppression, economic disparity, and other social ills attributed to the trauma of empire. At the same time, postcolonial theologians also interrogate biblical interpretations and hermeneutics that have been promoted by theologians from the imperial Metropole. By this act postcolonial readers of Christianity's most sacred text can challenge biblical justifications for imperialism, as well as wrestle with the violence of the Bible.

Theologians have not only theorized a postcolonial Protestantism. Communal practice has been integral in developing Christian hybridity, too. In many countries of postcolonial Africa, for example, there has been a strong emphasis on indigenous Protestant churches independent from the missions of the West. Often referred to as AFRICAN INSTITUTED CHURCHES (AIC), these institutions largely reject Western missionary attempts to expel native traditions. Instead they fuse indigenous ideas about the spirit world with literal interpretations of the Bible to create theologies that,

for their adherents, feel more African and more historically in touch with the biblical era at the same time. AIC believers often see traditional African practices—such as FAITH HEALING, polygamy (see PLURAL MARRIAGE), and appeals to nature through PRAYER—legitimated in biblical events. AICs have been very successful in countries such as Kenya and NIGERIA, where Western missionaries worked to divorce people from their cultural heritage and embrace Westernization during the colonial period. Literal readings of the Bible appear to AIC believers to confirm cultural norms such as exorcisms and prayers for rain. Also, whereas Western missionaries usually rejected traditional African spirits as mere figments of the imagination, AIC Christians often interpret them as existing evil forces. In this way AIC believers often separate themselves from others in their societies, distinguishing themselves by clothing, diet, and even living in separate communities. Aladura Christians in Nigeria, Zionists in Southern Africa, and Kimbanguists in Zaire are but a few of the AICs that emerged as a postcolonial reaction against Western missionaries.

One of the most dramatic postcolonial movements of Protestantism to emerge was LIBERATION THEOLOGY. Working both independently and in concert with Catholics, Protestant liberation theologians in newly independent nations throughout the world sought to create theological frameworks that were historically localized and that emphasized social justice. Focusing on the commonplace and how the sacred and profane were experienced jointly in everyday life, liberation theologians read Christianity as a blueprint for social revolution. By interpreting the message of Jesus as a call for the deliverance of the poor and oppressed, they rejected ideas of spiritual transcendence and promoted ethnic and class equality within a contemporary social framework. Rejecting European Protestant ideals of INDIVIDUALISM and capitalism, liberation theologians emphasized wide-scale social movements and solidarity among oppressed peoples, merging a hermeneutical belief in the triumph of the subjugated with a strong commitment to overturning the remnants of the tyrannical colonial social order in favor of indigenous expressions of religion and AUTHORITY.

Liberation Theology and Postcolonialism

Liberation theology developed in LATIN AMERICA as a response to the desperate conditions of poverty spawned by the economic policies of the independent populist governments. As rural communities saw their economic power collapse in the face of rapid INDUSTRIALIZATION and import substitution programs, widespread social movements against the establishment emerged that called for more egalitarian distribution of wealth and power. In MEXICO, Argentina, BRAZIL, and other nations, Protestant and Catholic CLERGY and lay people established theologies glorifying the triumphant social justice message of Jesus, often merging ideologies of Marxism and social revolution formulated by theologians such as Uruguay's Emilio Castro of the Methodist Church and the Brazilian Ecumenical activist Rubem Alves. Throughout the 1960s and 1970s liberation theologians in Latin America such as Julio de Santa Ana and José Míguez Bonino inspired Protestants not only in their own societies, but throughout the world, to reject Christian leaders who claimed that earthly suffering was just. Instead, they and their followers sought to fight for social equality in the name of Christianity, and they hoped to complete the anti-imperial struggle by toppling corrupt postindependence governments.

Perhaps the most potent postcolonial Liberation Theology movement to come out of the Protestant tradition came from SOUTH AFRICA. The South African Contextual Theology Movement had a tremendous impact on world attitudes toward the racist legal system of Apartheid, and transformed theological ideals among millions of Christians. Protestants of many sects, as well as Roman Catholics, worked together to formulate Christian arguments against the Apartheid system. Inspired by the Anglican monk TREVOR HUDDLESTON's *Naught For Your Comfort* (1955), white and black South Africans spent the 1960s and 1970s developing Christian-based strategies for overthrowing institutionalized racism. One of the most charismatic and effective Anglican voices against Apartheid belonged to archbishop DESMOND TUTU (1931–). As the first black dean of Johannesburg's Anglican Cathedral, Tutu worked with like-minded reformers to draw international attention to the plight of black South Africans, calling for an international boycott of South African coal in 1980, which resulted in the government seizing his passport. Tutu's message, however, could not be contained, and he won the Nobel Peace Prize in 1984.

Tutu's compatriot, the Nederduitse Gereformeerde Kerk in Zuid Afrika minister ALAN BOESAK, was also instrumental in the development of South African liberation theology. After years of pressure the WORLD ALLIANCE OF REFORMED CHURCHES (WARC) revoked the membership of Afrikaner churches supportive of Apartheid in 1982. Boesak had led the campaign against them, and developed a theology, adopted by the WARC, that declared the racism of Apartheid a Christian HERESY. For the next four years Boesak developed a new CONFESSION of faith for South Africans. Finally published in 1986, the Belhar Confession explicitly tied the message of Christian redemption to the unity and equality of all people regardless of race, declaring that "the credibility of [Christianity] is seriously affected and its beneficial work obstructed when it is proclaimed in a land which professes to be Christian, but in which the enforced separation of people on a racial basis promotes and perpetuates alienation, hatred and enmity. . . . Therefore, we reject any ideology which would legitimate forms of injustice and any doctrine which is unwilling to resist such an ideology in the name of the gospel." With this confession Protestant South Africans were armed with a theological weapon with which to challenge the Apartheid machine.

A year earlier, in 1985, over thirty lay and ordained Protestants connected to the Institute for Contextual Theology in Johannesburg drafted another document that grounded the anti-Apartheid movement in Protestant resistance. The Kairos Document rejected Afrikaner claims that Apartheid was legitimated by the Bible, and also decried calls for nonviolent resistance by white South African churches living outside the context of the violent state oppression of black communities. Declaring the Kairos, or "moment of truth," had arrived, the 156 signatories representing over twenty denominations called for the church to actively oppose the regime and not to interfere with civil disobedience against it. Declaring that "God sides with the oppressed," the Kairos Document created a theology in which active participation of Christians in the anti-Apartheid movement was a religious duty. In this way, the church was to "move beyond a mere 'ambulance ministry' to a ministry of involvement and participation."

With the end of Apartheid in 1994, the National Unity government led by Nelson Mandela established the Truth and Reconciliation Commission. Convened in 1996 and directed by Desmond Tutu, contextual theologians worked with other activists to heal the deep wounds festering at every level of South African society by the Apartheid system. The Commission was shaped by a strong belief in the redemptive quality of repentance by perpetrators of human rights crimes committed, with the ultimate goal of widespread forgiveness among the repatriated victims, and social unification throughout South African society. From the outset, Tutu called on all South Africans— Christians, Jews, Muslims, Hindus, and others—to participate in the Commission, using the redemptive language of liberation theology and its emphasis on spiritual equality and social justice to motivate skeptics and supporters alike. As the Commission's investigations and subsequent amnesties continued on into the new century, the impact of South African contextual theology garnered accolades around the world.

Another postcolonial liberation theology movement rooted in Protestant thought emerged among the
Palestinians, the Sabeel Ecumenical Liberation Theology movement. Based in Jerusalem and founded in
1989, the Sabeel movement emerged from the Intifada
against Israeli occupation of the West Bank and Gaza
Strip. By highlighting the life of Jesus under Roman
occupation and the message of justice and reconciliation in the Christian message, the Sabeel movement
combined grassroots action with a fiercely anti-impe-
rialist message of nonviolent resistance to Israeli oppression of Palestinians. With members from the Palestinian Protestant, Catholic, Latin, and Orthodox
Christian communities in its ranks, Sabeel's liberation
theology sought to challenge Christian Zionist rhetoric
that the State of Israel was proof of the End Times and
Second Coming of Jesus. In response, Sabeel's theological understanding of Jesus promoted the ideals of
equality and social justice inherent in Jesus's message,
but rejected the idea that Jesus could be defined as
either Jew or Gentile. Instead Sabeel's Christian vision stressed the importance of securing a peaceful
resolution to the Israel–Palestine conflict that protected the human rights of all people in the Holy Land
and that preached the Gospel of Jesus parallel to the
Palestinian struggle.

Conclusion

The case of Sabeel is instructive for understanding the
way postcolonial theory has influenced Protestant
readings of the Bible. Colonial settler movements
often used the story of the Exodus as inspiration for
their political and economic displacement of indigenous populations. The Zionist movement is the most
obvious case, but European expansion into the Americas, AUSTRALIA, and Southern Africa provide other
examples of this rhetoric. However, for the Palestinians and other groups marginalized by such interpretations, the story of the Exodus can also be read from
the perspective of the Egyptians, as Sabeel's founder,
the Palestinian Episcopal Minister Naim Ateek, has
argued. In this way the destruction of the Egyptians in
the wake of the glory of the Israelites may serve as a
reminder of the dispossession and violence of the
colonial encounter. By reading the Bible as a story of
imperial conquest and liberation simultaneously and
employing postcolonial theories of power and hybridity, Protestants in the postcolonial world—both in the
former empires and their metropolitan centers—may
be able to reconcile their beliefs in a compassionate,
redemptive deity, and their lived experience of colonial displacement and trauma, often justified by colonial theologians.

References and Further Reading

Hastings, Adrian. *The Church in Africa: 1450–1950.* Oxford:
Clarendon Press, 1994.
Isichei, Elizabeth. *A History of Christianity in Africa from
Antiquity to the Present.* London: SPCK, 1995.
Smith, Christian. *The Emergence of Liberation Theology: So-
cial Religion and Social Movement Theory.* Chicago: Uni-
versity of Chicago Press, 1991.
Sugirtharajah, R. S. *The Bible and the Third World: Precolo-
nial, Colonial and Postcolonial Encounters.* Cambridge:
Cambridge University Press, 2001.
Young, Robert J. C. *Postcolonialism: An Historical Introduc-
tion.* Oxford, UK: Blackwell, 2001.

NANCY L. STOCKDALE

POSTMODERNITY

The term *postmodernity,* and its related expression
postmodernism, require as their definitional counterpoint the terms *modernity* and *modernism,* respectively. Before definitions are provided, however, it is
necessary to make some important and salutary distinctions. Following Marshall Berman, we need to
distinguish between modernity, modernization, and
MODERNISM. *Modernity* is a periodization, referring
generally to the time after the classical age, the time of
industrialization, or the time after the demise of traditional societies (each of these is of course related in
more or less complex ways to the others). *Modernization,* by contrast, refers to the process(es) whereby the
transition is made from a premodern to a modern
society or culture. *Modernism,* on the other hand, is
the aesthetic ideology and its affiliated movements
associated with the onset of modernity. Each of these
terms has its postmodern counterpart. Thus *postmodernity* refers to the period after the age of the modern,
postmodernism is the aesthetic ideology related to this
newly emergent period, and the processes of modernization have in principle to be completed in order for
postmodernity to emerge. Sometimes conflated with
these is the term *poststructuralism.* Poststructuralism,
however, usually designates a specifically philosophical position that transcends or negates its complement, *structuralism* (i.e., the theory whose basic principle, associated with the thought of Ferdinand de
Saussure, Roman Jacobson, and Claude Lévi-Strauss,
is that consciousness has a structure whose basic form
is that of the code), so that poststructuralism is the
theory that undermines or problematizes the notion
that consciousness, and the production of meaning
that constitutes its *raison d'etre,* functions as a code or
assemblage of codes. As such poststructuralism has
nothing necessarily to do with postmodernism or postmodernity, though they are lumped together in many
taxonomies of postmodernism, so that an exemplary
poststructuralist thinker like Jacques Derrida is often
(and sometimes misleadingly) called a postmodernist.

(It should also be noted that poststructuralism, though it happens to refer to a grouping of mainly French thinkers, is in fact an American invention: the designation is not typically used in France, and even when it is, it is usually made clear that the term is borrowed from the United States.)

The term "modernism," signifying an aesthetic movement, was first used by the Nicaraguan poet Rubén Darío, who referred in 1890 to a *modernismo* in a "declaration of cultural independence" from Spain (Anderson 1998:3). The term *postmodernismo* was first used in 1934 by the Spanish literary historian Frederico de Onís, who used it to refer to a conservative tendency within modernism itself, which favored irony and privileged textual detail, in contrast to an *untramodernismo,* which represented a radical tendency within modernism, which according to de Onís, quickly supplanted the ornamentalizing and ultimately trivial *postmodernismo* through the creation of a "rigorously contemporary poetry" (4).

It took another two decades for the term and its cognates to appear in anglophone circles. In 1954 the historian Arnold Toynbee published the eighth volume of his *Study of History,* in which he used the term the "post-modern age" to designate the period that began with the Franco-Prussian War (1870). Toynbee identified this age with the decline of the middle class and the concomitant rise of the proletariat, and also with the emergence outside the West of intellectual elites who would use resources afforded by modernity itself in order to challenge the West. Toynbee cited as examples of this challenge Meiji Japan, Bolshevik Russia, Turkey under Mustapha Kemal, and Maoist China (6).

Three years before the publication of Toynbee's volume, in 1951, the American poet Charles Olson wrote to his friend and fellow poet Robert Creeley and declared that "the first half of the twentieth century [was] the marshalling yard on which the the modern was turned to what we have, the post-modern or post-West" (7). As Perry Anderson points out in his illuminating conspectus of the the notion of the postmodern (to which this article is much indebted), Olson's "aesthetic theory was linked to a prophetic history, with an agenda allying poetic innovation with political revolution in the classic tradition of the avant-gardes of Europe" (12). Olson's legacy, focused as it was on the need for a literature divested of its humanistic impulses, became dormant until the early 1970s. In the 1970s the notion of a postmodern resurfaced in the journal *boundary 2* and in the writings of the literary theorist Ihab Hassan. The term now started to have the resonance currently associated with it, that is, a complex and heterogeneous amalgam containing a number of key indicators and themes: the critique of previous systems of rationality and especially of the project of the ENLIGHTENMENT, the possibility of a politics not constituted by liberal (and hence modern) notions of the political subject, and the emergence of radically new and different standpoints for the constitution of knowledges. The two most important theorists of these developments have been the late Jean-François Lyotard (1924–1998) and Fredric Jameson (1934–).

The Analysis of Postmodernity: Lyotard and Jameson

Lyotard's book *The Postmodern Condition* (originally published in 1979) described the postmodern not simply as an object of attention for literary theorists but as a problem posed for the legitimation of knowledge stemming from the collapse of the so-called "grand narratives" (MARXISM, Enlightenment rationality, Christianity, etc.). These "grand narratives," many embodying the myths that shaped modernity, and involving such notions as truth, reason, and progress have, in Lyotard's eyes, been displaced by a situation, typical of postindustrial societies, in which knowledge is no longer warranted by an overarching system of generally accepted norms and principles, but is instead validated in some way by a plethora of not always commensurable "language games" (a notion Lyotard borrowed from Ludwig Wittgenstein, 1889–1951). Truth is operationalized in this new epoch and reduced to "performativity" because language game is legitimated by its own "little narrative" and has no applicability outside the sphere of that particular little narrative. Lyotard also believes that postmodern social relations reflect this epochal shift: our interactions are now marked by contingency, temporal limits, and an essential revisability. Nothing in postmodernity possesses any finality, and all totalities and totalizations have effectively been discredited by the uncontainable heterogeneity of language games. *The Postmodern Condition* quickly acquired a notoriety out of all proportion to its actual intellectual merits. Many commentators, and later Lyotard himself, regarded it as a hodge-podge of ideas not very coherently put together. In fact, it was quickly pointed out that Lyotard had violated his own thesis of the demise of grand narratives by providing what looked suspiciously like a grand narrative (namely, the one regarding the emergence of the postmodern condition).

Fredric Jameson wrote the foreword to the English edition of *The Postmodern Condition,* and it is perhaps ironic that he should be a leading contemporary proponent of one of the grand narratives alleged by Lyotard to be discredited by postmodernity, namely, Marxism. Two essays in his collection *The Cultural*

Turn (1998) are important for any understanding of Jameson's theses concerning postmodernity and post-modernism. "Postmodernism and Consumer Society" defines postmodernism as "a periodizing concept whose function is to correlate the emergence of new formal features in culture with the emergence of a new type of social life and a new economic order—what is often euphemistically called modernization, post-industrial or consumer society, the society of the media or the spectacle, or multinational capitalism" (Jameson 1998:3). Postmodernity on this Marxist account is thus the "cultural logic" of "late capitalism." Jameson views the postmodern cultural logic as being marked by a number of distinctive features: pastiche replaces modernist parody, the subject of bourgeois individualism has died or else is now known never to have existed as the subject it is purported to be; nostalgia is its operative mode; reality collapses into images; and time is decomposed into a series of perpetual presents. The other essay from *The Cultural Turn* that is of interest to us, "Theories of the Post-modern," identifies a number of positions that can be taken with regard to this new cultural logic. One, which generally welcomes the new term, can be identified with the work of Ihab Hassan, and celebrates postmodernism from an antimodernist standpoint (22); another position, which also uses the new term, apotheosizes modernism in order to displace an "unacceptable" postmodernism (the cultural conservative Hilton Kramer). Yet another, while using modernism to dethrone this unacceptable postmodernism, nevertheless does so from a generally left perspective (Jürgen Habermas, who also uses the new term). Jameson also identifies two other positions on postmodernism: one, that of Jean-François Lyotard, which sees post-modernism as an offshoot of high modernism (albeit with one key difference, namely, that for Lyotard, postmodernism does not succeed high modernism, but precedes a new and revitalized high modernism for which it is paving the way); the second, identified with the work of the Italian architectural historian Man-fredo Tafuri, is anti-postmodernist without seeing anything of positive value in high modernism itself (on the contrary, for Tafuri, postmodernism simply reexpresses certain baneful tendencies already to be found in high modernism).

Jameson's many writings on postmodernism analyze its many dimensions. As a cultural logic the postmodern subtends all forms of present-day cultural production—architecture, art, film and other visual media, literature, music, philosophy, politics, and religion. Each (and he has written illuminatingly on all of these) is seen by him as an amalgam of cultural symptoms, to be deciphered ("transcoded" is Jameson's preferred term) by the appropriately deployed Marxist hermeneutical apparatus. The symptoms are historicized, a process that renders visible the sharpened or blunted political impulses contained within them. It is common in less well-informed circles to fault Jameson for being himself a postmodernist. This is simply not the case; if anything he is its most intractable critic: what he wants to do is present a phenomenology of it as a cultural object, to register the full range of its characters, and to provide a political critique of it. However, because he insists that thought be historicized, the very intellectual instruments used by him and others to analyze postmodernism are inflected by its widely ramifying cultural logic, and the thought that has postmodernism as its object, if properly constituted, must have a metatheory of this inflection. This gives Jameson's critique of postmodernity a subtlety lacking in other similar critiques (for example, the trenchant critique provided by Terry Eagleton in his *The Illusions of Postmodernism* [1996]).

There are other accounts and critiques of postmodernity (David Harvey's *The Condition of Postmodernity* [1990] being notable among these), but none has the quality of a definitive intellectual intervention that marks the work of Lyotard and Jameson. The fact of the matter is, the intellectual agendas and especially the theoretical armatures developed by Jameson have provided the terms of reference for much of the subsequent discussion of the postmodern and its appurtenances.

Theology and Postmodernity

Theologians have sought to respond to the intellectual agendas and conceptual frameworks devised by theorists of postmodernity. Two main strands of this theological response can be identified. One is affiliated with an appropriation of the writings of Derrida and his followers (but also of Martin Heidegger), and has two wings: (1) an atheological approach, exemplified by the work of Mark C. Taylor and others published primarily in Taylor's University of Chicago Press "Religion and Postmodernism" series; and (2) a resolutely theological approach, identified with such figures as Jean-Luc Marion, using the deconstruction of the Heideggerian-Derridean metaphysics of being to furnish a new framework that seeks to think "godhood" without recourse to the categories of being. The other main approach is the "radical orthodoxy" school of British theology, whose more prominent members include John Milbank, Catherine Pickstock, Graham Ward, Gerard Loughlin, and Phillip Blond. Several exponents of radical orthodoxy use the Heideggerian-Derridean critique of the metaphysics of being, but radical orthodoxy's paradigm relies on very much more than this critique (which it shares with those theologians influenced by Heidegger and Derrida such as Jean-Luc Marion). Radical orthodoxy also happens to have a wider-angled critique of the secular order; its exponents derive their philosophical inspiration not just from Heidegger, Derrida, and Emmanuel Levinas, but also Thomas Aquinas, Giambattista Vico, and Friedrich Jacobi, among others, and they also take their approach into other domains such as political theology and theological metaethics. Radical orthodoxy is also more concerned with the quest for a new basis for postsecular theological reason, a concern obviously not shared by the postmodern atheologians and one less explicitly evident in the thought of theologians whose focal point is (almost exclusively) the Heideggerian-Derridean critique of the metaphysics of being. It is perhaps too early to make more than a provisional assessment of the significance of the postmodern theologies and atheologies—a great deal will depend on the trajectory taken by postmodernity and the retrieval of those traditions, banished in the name of a "skeptical" modernity, it now makes possible. Postmodernity will not last for ever, and its successor dispensation will proffer other and alternative conditions for theological reflection. Postmodernity is closely (some would say exclusively) bound up with the character of the so-called advanced societies, and a great deal will hinge on the course taken by these societies and the relation they have to societies not currently functioning as vehicles of postmodernity. The societies outside the purview of the postmodern constitute postmodernity's "outside," and one senses that what comes after the postmodern will depend crucially on the transformations brought about by this ubiquitous "outside" and the images of thought generated by it and its as yet unknown sequelae. Another consideration in deciding what may come after postmodernity must be the propensity within the intellectual elites of advanced industrial societies to declare, as rapidly as possible, the supersession of a previous "post," so that one now hears declarations of the emergence of a "post-postmodernity." This haste is to be resisted: complex issues and powerfully entrenched practical and intellectual movements constitute the core of phenomena like modernity and postmodernity. The stakes in these issues must be ascertained, and the trajectories of these movements analyzed, before they can be consigned to the past of a present that seems to find its future in endless recyclings of the past and its images—a symptom of the postmodern that seemingly has pervaded the very attempts to reflect on it.

References and Further Reading

Anderson, Perry. *The Origins of Postmodernity.* London: Verso, 1998.

Berman, Marshall. *All That is Solid Melts into Air: The Experience of Modernity.* London: Verso, 1993.

Blond, Phillip, ed. *Post-Secular Philosophy: Between Philosophy and Theology.* London: Routledge, 1998.

Eagleton, Terry. *The Illusions of Postmodernism.* Oxford: Basil Blackwell Publishers, 1996.

Harvey, David. *The Condition of Postmodernity: An Enquiry into the Origins of Cultural Change.* Oxford: Basil Blackwell, 1990.

Jameson, Fredric. *Postmodernism, or, the Cultural Logic of Late Capitalism.* Durham: Duke University Press, 1991.

Jameson, Fredric. *The Cultural Turn: Selected Writings on Postmodernism, 1983–1998.* London: Verso, 1998.

Lyotard, Jean-François. *The Postmodern Condition: A Report on Knowledge.* Translated by Geoff Bennington and Brian Massumi. Minneapolis: University of Minnesota Press, 1984.

Milbank, John, Catherine Pickstock, and Graham Ward, eds. *Radical Orthodoxy: A New Theology.* London: Routledge, 1999.

Sim, Stuart, ed. *The Routledge Critical Dictionary of Postmodern Thought.* London: Routledge, 1999.

KENNETH SURIN

PRAETORIUS, MICHAEL (1571–1621)

German composer. Praetorius was born at Creutzburg an der Werra, GERMANY, February 15, 1571, and died February 15, 1621 at Wolfenbüttel. He was among the most versatile musicians of his day and is also notable for his theoretical writings. He produced over one thousand settings of Protestant hymns, many of which were published in a nine-volume collection, *Musae Sioniae,* 1605 (four volumes of miscellaneous hymn settings, two volumes of liturgically ordered works for from two to seven voices, and three volumes of liturgically ordered simple four-part harmonizations).

A notable feature of his works is the inclusion of congregational settings within his polychoral motets. His most ambitious works based on Protestant chorales (published in *Polyhymnia cauduceatrix et panegyrica* [1619]) display a mature assimilation of Venetian polychoral techniques. Three collections from 1611 contain his settings of Latin LITURGY and include four substantial organ hymn settings that present each cantus firmus in the pedals. In his comprehensive work on church music, *Syntagma musicum* I (1615), he published a unique account by Johann Walter (a colleague of his father at the Latin school at Torgau) about Walter's collaboration with MARTIN LUTHER and Luther's proposed musical reforms. *Syntagma musicum* II (1619) (dealing with instruments) contains particularly valuable and detailed information on the organ. Praetorius's prefaces to his musical collections are particularly sensitive to the exigencies of church performance, and give detailed instructions on their practical adaptation to a variety of performing forces, as well as much information of liturgical interest.

See also Hymns and Hymnals

Further Reading and Listening

Blume, Friedrich. *Protestant Church Music: A History*. London: Gollancz, 1975.

McCreesh, Paul, conductor, and Gabrieli Consort. *Michael Praetorius: Lutheran Mass for Christmas morning: as it might have been celebrated around 1620*. Hamburg: Archiv Produktion, 1994 (439 250-2 Archiv Produktion).

WILLIAM FLYNN

PRAYER

Protestant practices of prayer vary from one tradition to another, but Protestants can agree that prayer is a means of communication with God. God is addressed in words spoken or sung by individuals or communities, and a word from God is awaited in silent meditation. Protestants might further agree that Christian prayer should be informed by the Word of God and that it is inspired by the Holy Spirit. For some Protestants, such as JOHN WESLEY (1703–1791), prayer has been considered a third means of GRACE after BAPTISM and the LORD'S SUPPER.

Protestants have believed that prayer should be addressed only to God, not to SAINTS or to Mary (see MARY, VIRGIN). Forms of invocation of the saints practiced in the Middle Ages were suppressed in the REFORMATION. Protestants have also emphasized the high priestly mediation of Christ ("our only mediator and advocate") before the throne of God, where he pleads the merits of his atoning sacrifice on behalf of his brothers and sisters, as in the Epistle to the Hebrews. More informal or pietistic prayer may be addressed to Jesus rather than to God the Father. Less frequently in Protestant practice, prayer may be addressed to the Holy Spirit, but the Holy Spirit is more usually understood to be the enabler of prayer, according to Romans 8:26–27. In the last third of the twentieth century, liberal Protestants have striven to find ways of making the names and images of God in prayer more GENDER-inclusive by exploring other names and images in the biblical record and liturgical tradition (see LIBERAL PROTESTANTISM AND LIBERALISM).

Prayer may be done with others or alone. Prayer with others occurs in the CHURCH or liturgical assembly, in the family or household, or in prayer meetings. This article first treats prayer in public WORSHIP, then household prayer, and finally individual prayer.

Public Worship

Protestant public worship, like all Christian worship, includes such elements of prayer as adoration and praise, confession of SIN, intercession and supplication, and thanksgiving. Adoration and praise has been expressed in Protestant worship, especially in canticles and hymns sung by the congregation. A CONFESSION of sins became a part of Protestant worship by transforming the celebrant's preparatory prayers in the sacristy or at the foot of the ALTAR before the celebration of mass into a congregational act. Lutheran, Reformed, Anglican, and Methodist liturgies have included prayers of confession said by the congregation followed by an absolution or declaration of grace given by the minister. The lack of a practice of individual confession and sacramental absolution in Protestantism have raised these prayers of confession to a position of high regard in Protestant piety. Intercession and supplication achieved an important role in Protestant worship in the general pastoral prayers in which concerns for all human need were voiced by the preacher. The antecedent of the pastoral prayer is the intercessions offered from the pulpit in the medieval preaching office of Prone in conjunction with parish announcements. MARTIN LUTHER (1483–1546) revised the Great Litany, which is pure supplication, and it has had a place in Lutheran prayer and in the Anglican BOOK OF COMMON PRAYER through the translation of THOMAS CRANMER (1489–1556), archbishop of Canterbury (1534–1553). Thanksgiving for God's goodness has also had a place in Protestant prayer. Except for Lutherans, who focused on the Words of Institution as an act of consecration, Protestant Reformation celebrations of the Lord's Supper included new prayers of thanksgivings. There has been a prodigious production of new eucharistic prayers in the last third of the twentieth century in Episcopal, Lutheran, Presbyterian, and United Methodist worship books.

In addition to Sunday morning worship in word and sacrament, the church has had daily prayer services since the fourth century. In his *German Mass and Order of Service* (1526), Luther laid the groundwork for replacing the daily masses (unless there were communicants) with forms of morning and evening prayer based on the historic Roman and monastic prayer offices (Matins and Vespers). These services included psalms, an office hymn, Scripture readings, a gospel canticle (Benedictus or Te Deum at Matins, Magnificat or Nunc dimittis at Vespers), and various forms of prayer (collects, litanies, suffrages). Because PREACHING was included in all Lutheran public worship, the sermon eventually overshadowed the elements of praise and prayer that had characterized the traditional prayer offices. During the Age of ENLIGHTENMENT these daily prayer offices fell out of use. They were revived in the nineteenth century by Theodore Kliefoth (1818–1895) in northern GERMANY and WILHELM LÖHE (1808–1872) in southern Germany, especially for use in the DEACONESS mother houses. Their use in congregations has remained occasional (e.g., on retreats) or seasonal (e.g., during Advent and Lent) more than daily.

In the Edwardian ancestors of *The Book of Common Prayer* (1549 and 1552), Cranmer followed the Lutheran model of combining Matins and Lauds into one office of Morning Prayer and Vespers and Compline into one office of Evening Prayer. Cranmer provided a course of psalmody in which the entire psalter was recited in one month rather than choosing psalms appropriate to the time of the day. The old offices of Prime and Compline had included prayers of confession and absolution, and Cranmer prefixed Morning and Evening Prayer with a penitential rite, drawing inspiration from the Church Orders of Cologne and Strassburg prepared by MARTIN BUCER (1539, 1543). Over the course of four centuries many composers have provided fine musical settings of the psalms and canticles. Morning and Evening Prayer has served as the living heart of Anglican worship and devotion for four centuries.

The Anglican priest, JOHN WESLEY, expected his Methodist followers to attend worship in their parish church, their class meetings being supplementary to this (see METHODISM, METHODISM, ENGLAND). He provided an abridged form of the prayer offices in his Sunday Service (1784) for Methodists in America. In both America and Britain, Morning and Evening Prayer fell into disuse as a regular practice. The Methodist practice of spontaneous prayer in the class meetings was blended in America with the Puritan patterns of lay leadership in prayer, extempore prayer, and weekday prayer meetings. The prayer meetings were less formal than Sunday worship and were often lay-led. Methodists, like Episcopalians, preferred kneeling for prayer, but usually knelt facing the pew rather than the table or pulpit.

The major controversy over prayer in Protestantism has been between the use of written prayers and extempore prayer. Those traditions known as "FREE CHURCH" really mean free of the obligatory use of prayer books. Anabaptist communities in the sixteenth century practiced spontaneous prayer as well as periods of silent meditation (see ANABAPTISM). Anabaptist practice influenced both English Puritans (those within the CHURCH OF ENGLAND who sought a more thorough Reformation along Reformed lines) and Separatists who encountered Anabaptist practice in their expatriate communities in THE NETHERLANDS.

If the earlier Reformation traditions were content to have worship that did not conflict with Scripture as the "sole rule and norm" of faith and practice, the Puritans required worship and prayer that was completely biblical, although agreement on what the Bible required was not easy to achieve (see PURITANISM). Should the Lord's Prayer be recited as a text or does it serve as a model for prayer? Speaking in TONGUES (glossolalia) is clearly allowed in I Corinthians 14, but the Puritans were not interested in that practice. They were agreed, however, that decisions about worship and prayer should be made at the lowest ecclesiastical level, the congregation. This allowed prayers to be more relevant to local need than fixed forms in a prayer book, although printed prayers could be used if the congregation so decided. Because the real concerns of real people should be paramount in prayer, however, extempore prayer ("from the heart") was preferred to written prayers. In typical Puritan practice, following the "directions" given by the apostle in I Timothy 2:1, public worship began with thanksgiving and intercession led by the pastor, teacher, and others while all stood for prayer with the arms lifted above their heads in the manner enjoined in I Timothy 2:8. Prayer concerns could be written down on notes, but the prayers had to be extemporaneous. Until the eighteenth century not even the Lord's Prayer was recited in Puritan worship in Boston.

Puritan practice also influenced the Presbyterians (see PRESBYTERIANISM). In the Reformed tradition emanating from Geneva, prayers were read by the pastors from the pulpit with the people following the words in their hearts. The Presbyterian *Westminster Directory of Public Worship* (1645) prescribed an outline of the content of public prayer but not the exact wording. Because the Directory encouraged extempore rather than written prayers, public prayers came to reflect the personality and interests of the preacher and local interests.

In the Reformed/Presbyterian tradition, public praying was done by ministers. Puritans and Separatists not only permitted lay prophesying and praying, but encouraged it. BAPTISTS detested "hireling ministers," although they had their nonstipendiary pastors. Puritans and Baptists also held Sunday night weekday prayer meetings that ministers did not always attend.

Quakers (see FRIENDS, SOCIETY OF) had no clergy at all. Contemporary reports from the seventeenth century indicate that Quaker meetings were anything but quiet. Quaker WOMEN were allowed to prophesy and pray in public meetings as well as men, and this often created a public furor. In Quaker worship set forms were entirely eschewed lest the Spirit be quenched; however, as Quaker worship quieted down in the eighteenth century, the discipline of not praying audibly without the "motion of the Spirit" was adopted by the Society of Friends. Quaker prayer, more than other forms of Protestant prayer, includes a silent waiting on God.

Emerging from the frontier revival tradition, and infused with the experience of African American worship, Pentecostal practice moved in the direction of ecstatic utterance rather than a silent waiting on God (see PENTECOSTALISM). Although prayer may be led by a minister, other worshipers freely enter into prayer as the Spirit gives them utterance, often in the ecstatic speech of glossolalia. In both African American and Pentecostal worship, worshipers feel free to voice their "Amens," "Yes, Jesus," "Praise the Lord," "Halleluia," and often accompany oral prayer with the physical prayer of raising one or both arms in the air. Prayer for healing with the laying on of hands is often a part of Pentecostal worship, but may also be witnessed in Anglican worship.

Household Devotions

Martin Luther provided a foundation for household prayer in his *Small Catechism* (1529). The appendix to the Catechism includes little morning and evening offices and meal graces (see CATECHISMS). In both his *Little Prayer Book (Betbüchlein)* of 1522 and in the Catechisms, Luther sets out the Lord's Prayer as the model of all Christian praying as well as a text to be recited upon getting out of bed in the morning, at meals, and before retiring, along with the Apostles' Creed in the morning and evening, and optionally a hymn based on the Ten Commandments in the morning. Luther himself provided simple morning and evening prayers in the Catechism and revised the monastic meal graces with their psalmody for use in the household. As hymnody developed for evangelical worship in the congregation, it was also brought into the home. Many hymns written during the sixteenth to eighteenth centuries were actually intended for use in households and were sung by families in their devotions before they were incorporated into liturgical services. One noteworthy example is "Now thank we all our God" by Martin Rinkhart (1586–1649), which has been called the Protestant Te Deum. The Reformed also cultivated household devotions, although the exact forms of prayer are unknown. Psalm singing was done in the household as in the church, often in more elaborate musical arrangements than those used in public worship.

Private Prayer

Anglican spirituality also assumes that private and corporate prayer need each other (see ANGLICANISM). The private devotions of Bishop LANCELOT ANDREWES (1555–1626) assumes that LITURGY shapes the prayer of the private closet. The masterpiece of the poet and country priest GEORGE HERBERT (1593–1633), *The Temple,* portrays the spiritual journey of the individual within sacred space from the "church porch" to the gates of heaven.

Edification literature has provided material for both household and individual devotions since the middle of the sixteenth century, but these books tended to loosen the ties between household prayer and the corporate prayer of the church by providing prayers for various life situations and spiritual conditions. Some of these prayer books became encyclopedic. One of the classic prayer book traditions that grew out of PIETISM is the *Moravian Daily Texts,* still used worldwide. Under the leadership of Count NIKOLAUS VON ZINZENDORF (1700–1760), Moravians developed a tradition of daily texts or "Watchwords" *(Losungen)* for each day of the year (see MORAVIAN CHURCH). Originally chosen by Zinzendorf, since 1788 the "watchwords" have been drawn by lot from a collection of several thousand suitable texts. In the twentieth century devotional booklets for use by families and individuals have been published in serial form in mass quantity. One successful example is *The Upper Room,* published every two months by the UNITED METHODIST CHURCH since 1935. Its format of a brief Scripture text, meditation, and brief prayer has served as a model for devotional booklets published by other denominations.

Finally, we not only have the teachings of great Protestant reformers and teachers on prayer, but a record of their personal prayers that shows the relationship between prayer and belief. Luther's prayers express a simple trust in a loving heavenly Father, whereas JOHN CALVIN's prayers display a regenerating moral energy in response to the will of a majestic God. Toward the end of the sixteenth century the mysticism represented by Bernard of Clairvaux and Johann Tauler was integrated with Lutheran thinking in Philip Nicolai's *Mirror of Joy* (1598), JOHANN ARNDT's *True Christianity* (1606–1609), JOHANN GERHARD's *Sacred Meditations* (1606), and, in the eighteenth century, in the hymns and prayers of the Reformed poet Gerhard Tersteegen (1697–1769). A more rational relationship with God is evident in JOHN DONNE's *Devotions Upon Emergent Occasions* (1624) and Lancelot Andrewes's *Private Devotions* (published posthumously in 1675), whereas a spiritual self-discipline is found in the prayers in JOHN BUNYAN (1628–1688) and in WILLIAM LAW's *A Serious Call to a Devout and Holy Life* (1729). A sturdy willingness to engage God in the concerns of life is evident in the prayers of SØREN KIERKEGAARD (1813–1855) and JOHN BAILLIE's *A Diary of Private Prayer* (1949). Confidence in the power of prayer to change life and events was affirmed in their books on prayer by George A. Buttrick (1942) and Frank C. Laubach (1946).

See also Hymns and Hymnals

References and Further Reading

Althaus, Paul. *Forschung zur evangelischen Gebetsliteratur.* Hildesheim, Germany: 1966.

Buttrick, George A. *Prayer.* New York and Nashville, TN: Abingdon-Cokesbury Press, 1942.

Gallen, John, ed. *Christians at Prayer.* Notre Dame, IN: UND Press, 1977.

Heiler, Friedrich. *Prayer: History and Psychology of Religion.* Translated and edited by Samuel McComb. New York: Oxford University Press, 1932, 1958.

Laubach, Frank C. *Prayer. The Mightiest Force in the World.* Westwood, NJ: Fleming Revell, 1946.

Senn, Frank C., ed. *Protestant Spiritual Traditions.* Mahwah, NJ: Paulist Press, 1986.

White, James F. *Protestant Worship: Traditions in Transition.* Louisville, KY: Westminster John Knox Press, 1989.

FRANK C. SENN

PREACHING

The Continental Reformation

Jesus came preaching the Gospel (Mark 1:14). Nothing is more characteristic of Protestantism that its strong emphasis upon preaching—the oral proclamation of the Good News. Though a quite diverse movement, one thing has united Protestantism through the ages—a conviction that Christ is vividly present in preaching. The Reformation did not make preaching an important aspect of Christian life—it already was. The contribution of the reformers was to champion two particular sorts of preaching: expository and catechetical. Although the preaching of sermons has been a distinctive means of Christian communication from the beginning of the church, the REFORMATION made preaching the theological foundation of the CHURCH, the human result of a God who speaks. Although reformer PHILIPP MELANCHTHON admitted that he was not much of a preacher himself, in the 1530 AUGSBURG CONFESSION (Art. 7) he defines the church for Lutherans as "the congregation of the saints in which the Gospel is rightly preached and the sacraments are rightly administered." Shortly thereafter, JOHN CALVIN proclaimed in the INSTITUTES OF THE CHRISTIAN RELIGION that "where the word is heard with reverence and the sacraments are not neglected there we discover. . . an appearance of the Church" (IV.1.10). These statements typify the Protestant inclination to make preaching a principal mark of the faithful church. Faith comes as an auditory phenomenon (MARTIN LUTHER loved to quote Romans 10:17). The church is dependent on the freedom of the Word that gives rise to the church and also is the church's most severe critic. Thus Luther called the church building a *Mundhaus* (mouth-house).

A pastor is, for Luther, *minister verbi divini* (servant of the Word of God). For all of the reformers, preaching is the primary ministerial function. In his introduction to his 1526 *German Mass,* Luther described the round of services at Wittenberg. Three services were held every Sunday with sermons from the Epistles for the earliest service, from the Gospel at the main morning service, and from the Old Testament at Vespers. It was Luther's practice to preach through an entire book of the BIBLE in successive sermons, Sunday after Sunday. At the Monday and Tuesday services, the sermons were expositions on parts of the CATECHISM, the Decalogue, the Creed, the SACRAMENTS, or the Lord's Prayer. The morning midweek service on Wednesday contained a sermon always from the Gospel of Matthew. Thursday and Friday sermons were on the Epistles. At Vespers on Saturday, the Gospel of John was preached. Luther urged similar disciplines on those congregations that were under his influence.

Whereas medieval preachers tended to look for a fourfold meaning of scripture (the literal, allegorical, moral, and eschatological meanings), Luther (who had a doctorate in biblical interpretation) claimed to be bound only by the plain sense of the text and the text's disclosure of Christ. Lutheran sermons tended to see Christ at the heart of all scripture, looking for a christological meaning in almost every text. Theologically, every Lutheran sermon attempted to stress law and Gospel as the principal means of presenting the Gospel. Hearing the law is a prelude to reception of the Gospel word of GRACE and forgiveness, through the power of the Holy Spirit. The basic theological content of the Lutheran sermon is the forgiveness of sins because even the saved do not cease sinning; we are all *simul Justus et Peccator.*

Luther's preaching style tended to be expository, paraphrasing a biblical text, interspersed with commentary that included theological and moral observations. He shared his own personality in his preaching, often showing a quaint, mundane style that was lively and engaging. His sermons usually followed a predictable structure: a brief introduction and contextualization of the biblical text; an exposition of the text in which Luther exposited what he believed to be the "kernel" or "point," the *Herzpunkt* of the passage; and, finally, suggestions for putting the text into practice in daily life. While on exile in Wartburg Castle, Luther wrote his *Postil Sermons* to give Reformation preachers copious of examples of biblically based preaching. He published the first of these *postils,* a collection of Advent and Christmas sermons, in 1522. The *postils* were quite influential for generations of Lutheran preachers. Approximately 2,000 of Luther's sermons were published, many in edited and condensed form.

The other key reformers were also committed preachers, although none equaled the style and power of Luther. Biblical exposition was the engine driving most Protestant preaching. HULDRYCH ZWINGLI, inspired by the example of Chrysostom, preached through the Gospel of Matthew, verse by verse, *lectio continua,* commenting on subjects as diverse as superstition, military service, clerical CELIBACY, and, of course, JUSTIFICATION BY FAITH. Zwingli's sermons tended to be dry and intellectual. It took HEINRICH BULLINGER, the successor of Zwingli in Zurich, just over fifteen years to preach through the entire Bible, verse by verse. JOHANNES OECOLAMPADIUS, also inspired by the Chrysostom, pioneered grammatical-historical exegesis, or explanation, abandoning the allegorical exegesis that had been so popular with medieval preachers. John Calvin preached daily and twice on Sundays, interpreting biblical texts extemporaneously, holding a Bible in his hand. Calvin's sermons often began with PRAYER, specifically a prayer for the inspiration of the Holy Spirit who makes the preacher's words the Word of God for the congregation, followed by a brief recapitulation of the previous sermon, then a consideration of the biblical text, followed by an application of the meaning of the text to the present context, then an exhortation for the congregation to obey the text, closing with a prayer that summarized the main points of the sermon. The sermons in Calvin's extant fourteen volumes of published sermons show Calvin to be a preacher with a deep knowledge of the Bible, particularly the nuances of the original biblical language, a clear communicator who eschews verbal ornamentation and who rarely illustrates a given point. Calvin's sermons today sound distant and abstract, though he was known as a comforting, pastoral preacher. MARTIN BUCER, although an equally committed expository preacher, was noted for his rambling, long-winded style.

Nearly all Protestant preachers saw the catechism as a valid basis for sermons, particularly sermons at weekday services that focused on the instruction of the LAITY. Johannes Zwick devised a series of catechetical sermons for children that cover a wide range of theological topics. In their interest in catechesis, they had medieval precedents, but their zeal to educate the laity in the most complex of DOCTRINES was one of their most notable contributions to the history of preaching—a zeal that does not seem to have continued in many contemporary Protestant congregations.

Protestant preachers in the hinterland were urged to use sermons that were written by the masters, to memorize them if they could and, if they could not, to read them aloud from the pulpit. Many volumes of sermons were printed throughout the Reformation. Among the most popular was a book of sermons for specific pastoral occasions written by Urbanus Rhegius of Augsburg. On many occasions, the scholarly leaders of the Reformation lamented the sorry state of preaching among their followers. Luther repeatedly stressed the need for educated preachers. Schools were founded to train Protestant clergy, but rarely did these schools specifically concern themselves with homiletical training. Zwingli organized regular meetings *(Prophezei)* for his fellow Protestant CLERGY in Zurich in which scripture was read and explained for the purpose of use in sermons. Most of the reformers seemed to assume that if a pastor mastered the art of biblical interpretation and theological exposition, then the ability to preach would naturally follow. Yet a Protestant, Andreas Gerhard Hyperius, published the first real textbook on homiletics in 1533. Impressed as they were with the general ignorance of the laity, early Protestant preachers tended to see a sermon primarily as an occasion to instruct and to correct rather than to convert or to inspire.

In the sixteenth century, it was not unusual for a sermon to last for as long as three hours. Luther was opposed to long sermons, saying that he was always concerned about the limitations of "little Hans and little Else." He pioneered in the art of simple, vernacular, direct discourse in preaching, enlivened with charming illustrations from daily life. Luther left us these directives for a good sermon:

> First of all, a good preacher must be able to teach correctly and in an orderly manner. Second, he must have a good head. Third, he must be able to speak well. Fourth, he should have a good voice, and, fifth, a good memory. Sixth, he must know when to stop. Seventh, he must know his stuff and keep at it. Eighth, he must be willing to risk body and soul, property and honor. Ninth, he must let everyone vex and ridicule him.

Protestants tended to stress that "the preaching of the Word of God is the Word of God," an extremely high view of preaching indeed. Luther and Zwingli had quite different notions of just how preaching was the Word of God for the church, mainly having to do with their different doctrines of the Holy Spirit. Rejecting the spiritual enthusiasts *(Schwärmer)* who presumed that the Spirit was the immediate gift to each believer independent of the means of Word or Sacrament, Luther linked the Spirit to the Word. Zwingli rejected the Lutheran binding of Word and Spirit, insisting that preaching was a simple human witness to Christ that helped the believer to seek the true, inner Word of God that can be given only by the Spirit. Zwingli distinguished between the "external word of God" (i.e., human preaching) and the "internal word of God" (i.e., self-communication of the Holy Spirit).

Calvin appeared to take a somewhat mediating position between Luther and Zwingli on the issue of preaching as the Word of God. Calvin taught that although preachers are human, God graciously elects to use preaching, through God's gift of the Holy Spirit, to address congregations (*Institutes* 4.1.5). Through the Holy Spirit, God's Word accomplishes what God's word promises, effecting that which it proclaims. Preaching empowered by the Holy Spirit, admitted Calvin, is a double-edged sword, provoking among hearers both acceptance and rejection, according to God's election. Through preaching, Christ is present in and rules over the church. Preachers succeed at communicating the Word of God to their listeners only because God graciously wills that God's Word be spoken here, now, through them.

Whereas Luther was intent on restoring the sermon to its rightful, historic position within the Sunday mass (a position that had been lost in the Middle Ages), Zwingli and Calvin tended toward a separation of preaching from the mass in their adoption of a simple preaching service *(Pronaus).* Luther's purified mass embodied his conviction that Word and Sacrament are inseparable means of God's self-communication, although later Protestants have tended, in practice if not in theology, to exalt the sermon as the supreme means of grace.

Zwingli's radical views (compared with those of Luther or Calvin) did not go far enough, said the Anabaptists of the so-called Radical Reformation. The Anabaptists (see ANABAPTISM) tended to be as suspicious of preaching as a corrupted human practice, as they were suspicious of the mass. Their worship stressed informal teaching, prayer, and mutual exhortation rather than contrived sermons, with many worshippers taking an active role in impromptu speaking. The Anabaptists considered careful composition of new sermons a sign of sinful pride. Their proclamation consisted of the public reading of sermons from the past combined with extemporaneous exhortation to the congregation by any member who was so moved by the Holy Spirit.

Europe

Although the centrality of expository and catechetical preaching was slow to impact the English Reformation, when the power of the crown got behind the Reformation during the reign of Edward VII, preaching became a principal means of bringing the English into the Protestant realm of thought. Archbishop THOMAS CRANMER'S *The Book of Homilies,* a collection of elegantly stated topical sermons, were to be read to their congregations by less well-trained clergy. The Baroque period gave rise to some distinctively

English contributions to homiletics. LANCELOT ANDREWES and JOHN DONNE became the ecclesiastical counterparts to Shakespeare in their masterful literary sermons that were indebted to the classical rhetorical tradition.

In Germany, FRIEDRICH SCHLEIERMACHER'S sermons attempted to counter the rationalism and skepticism of an age in which DEISM was on the rise. PIETISM, of the sort that influenced Schleiermacher, took Protestant preaching away from its historical concerns with doctrinal and biblical exposition, focusing pietistic preaching on inward religious experience. This development ushered in a great revival in England with the preaching of JOHN WESLEY and in the North American colonies with the preaching of GEORGE WHITEFIELD. On Whitefield's 1739 trip to America, his dramatic, extemporaneous preaching fanned into flame the Great Awakening (see AWAKENINGS). Along with Puritans (see PURITANISM) like JONATHAN EDWARDS, whose preaching in Northampton, Massachusetts elicited "Surprising Conversions," Whitefield preached a distinctly American mix of pietism and CALVINISM that stressed Christianity as an experiential faith.

Nineteenth-century EVANGELICALISM tended to be centered on proclamations that linked the inner CONVERSION of the individual believer with the conversion of society. Scotland's THOMAS CHALMERS not only established a church in the slums of Glasgow, but also preached through the Gospel of John while organizing social work among the poor of the city. CHARLES HADDON SPURGEON spoke directly to the common people, stressing God's power to transform individual lives. One of the nineteenth-century's greatest preachers, Spurgeon was a careful biblical preacher who, like most of that century's preachers, generally ignored the troubling questions being raised by the fledgling field of historical-critical biblical study (see HIGHER CRITICISM).

North America

Evangelicalism in America changed forever the nature of Protestant preaching. CHARLES G. FINNEY (1792–1875) was full of evangelistic zeal for the religious needs of a growing nation. Finney was impatient with the historic Protestant concerns for both expository and catechetical preaching, finding such preaching ill-suited to his great invention—the frontier REVIVAL. Among his innovations were the anxious bench, the inquiry room, and the protracted meeting. Finney preached dramatic, personal conversion mixed with calls for the abolition of SLAVERY and the practice of TEMPERANCE, that is, a mix of personal and social transformation that became typical of American Protestant preaching well in to the twentieth century.

Finney's stirring call for conversion undermined the earlier Calvinism of preachers like Whitefield. In planning a protracted meeting, in using an array of means to beckon sinners to repentance and conversion, Finney's "new measures for revivals" side-stepped Calvinistic notions of double PREDESTINATION in a new stress on SALVATION as dependent on the decision of the repentant sinner rather than the eternal decree of a God who predestines some to salvation and some to damnation. Finney's sermons were carefully reasoned arguments in which the Bible was presented as a sort of legal contract where God clearly set out what was required for salvation and what was expected of humanity. The preacher, in Finney's sermons, was a lawyer persuading a guilty client to confess and thus to be vindicated.

DWIGHT L. MOODY (1837–1899) and BILLY SUNDAY (1862–1935), lay heirs of Finney, perfected the city-wide revival meeting and emotional, transformative preaching that tended to take one biblical text and use it for the purpose of emotional conviction of the listeners. Moody sounded like a businessman making a sales pitch, keeping things short, simple, and interspersed with sentimental, homely anecdotes. Moody presented a good product to a self-interested customer. The goal of his preaching was to "get the customer to sign on the dotted line"—a small card given to those who wished to make personal commitments to Christ. Potentially divisive doctrinal issues like the sacraments or predestination were avoided rather than expounded on by evangelists like Moody. The Gospel message tended to be limited to a word that causes dramatic change in the listeners. Ex-baseball player Billy Sunday was America's first Protestant evangelist celebrity. He made preaching into mass entertainment, a style that was to be developed in later twentieth-century television preachers.

Preachers in predominately African-American churches, overwhelmingly Protestant in their traditions, tended to be heavily influenced by the fervent preaching of the Great Awakening, when great numbers of African-American slaves were converted to the religion of their white masters (see AFRICAN AMERICAN PROTESTANTISM). The chanted sermon, a distinctively African-American style of preaching, has its roots in the Second Great Awakening. A number of scholars have also pointed to African musical and speech pattern elements, the dialogical, responsive relationship between preacher and congregation, and the "hum" in African-American homiletical styles as distinctly African-American contributions to the practice of preaching that persist into the present. Theologically, African-American preachers participated in the great theological movements of American Protestantism, while also stressing themes of exodus and deliverance, hope, and redemptive suffering, thus contextualizing their sermons to the particular challenges of being black in America (see BLACK THEOLOGY).

In the 1960s, many Americans who had known nothing of the vital African-American preaching tradition were introduced to it through the preaching of MARTIN LUTHER KING, JR. in his "I Have a Dream" speech at the March on Washington (August 1963) and heard in that speech a call to become a more righteous nation.

By the beginning of the twentieth century, HARRY EMERSON FOSDICK led a wing of American Protestantism into liberalism (see LIBERAL PROTESTANTISM AND LIBERALISM). Fosdick's radio sermons were immensely popular. His straightforward language, everyday life illustrations, and unchecked optimism became characteristics of what could be called the "American school" of preaching that dominated mainline Protestant preaching until the later half of the century. In an a July 1928 article in *Harper's Magazine* titled "What Is the Matter With Preaching?," Fosdick charged that too much preaching (and by preaching he meant Protestant preaching) had lost touch with the real concerns of real people. Fosdick championed what he called "life-situation" or "problem-centered" preaching, in which every sermon began not with a biblical text, but rather with some current human dilemma or concern, then moved toward an engaging address of that concern based on both biblical and secular materials. Whereas the Protestant Evangelicals and fundamentalists tended to see the modern world, with its domination by the thought of science, as a threat and regularly preached against it, Fosdick sought conciliatory accommodation with modernity in his sermons, sermons that tended to quote from learned contemporary secular authorities on various matters far more than citing Scripture.

The Second Vatican Council (1962–1965) laid great emphasis upon preaching in the context of the mass, thus leading to a renewal of preaching in Catholicism and blurring one of the characteristics that Protestants had thought of as distinctively their own (see CATHOLICISM, PROTESTANT REACTIONS TO). Vatican II led to a widespread ecumenical rediscovery of the centrality of preaching, particularly biblically based preaching, that enervated many Protestant preachers and congregations. Many Protestant preachers discovered the lectionary as a resource for preaching after the Vatican II revision of the Catholic lectionary. Numerous preaching resources, interpretative materials keyed to the lectionary, were published. There were now more biblical preaching aids available to Protestant and Catholic preachers than at any time in the history of the church.

Contemporary Challenges

Protestant preaching at the beginning of the twenty-first century is building on its vital past and is continuing to wrestle with some of its historic challenges. Much of Protestantism, particularly that with its roots in reformers such as Calvin and Zwingli, continues to struggle with the severance of Word from Sacrament. Perhaps the continental reformers never intended to make BAPTISM and the Eucharist (LORD'S SUPPER) subservient to preaching, but that was the practical result of their reformation of Christian worship. Protestant Pietists and Evangelicals tended to stress personal experience of the Gospel through preaching, prayer, and personal devotional exercises as more important than acts of public, corporate worship. Finney advised his crusade planners to avoid potentially divisive and unproductive liturgical and doctrinal issues and to concentrate exclusively on the sermon and its response. ENLIGHTENMENT thought elevated words over symbols. For all of these reasons and others, Protestantism became noted for its elevation of the sermon as the supreme act of worship. Such elevation is biblically, as well as historically, theologically, and anthropologically, indefensible. There is a growing ecumenical consensus that the Eucharist is the normative shape for Sunday morning worship; word and table belong together. As the sermon is the preached Word, the Eucharist is the enacted Word. The revelation of God is not limited to the sermon or even to the reading of Scripture. Therefore, for many Protestant congregations, the restoration of a proper linkage between Word and sacrament is a pressing need.

Protestant preachers, from the beginning, offered commentary on extra-ecclesial events. Luther developed a theology of "two kingdoms," the one of God and the other of humanity, each with separate, God-ordained responsibilities. Yet he did not shrink from offering strong words (and, alas, often terribly misguided advice) to the secular authorities on how to manage their side of the equation. Reformers like Zwingli and Calvin saw themselves as having God-given responsibilities for the care and maintenance of civil order through their preaching. English preachers like Cranmer and Donne thought it their duty to provide theological support for the authority of the crown. The Great Awakenings, as well as the frontier revivals in America, unleashed a great wave of social reform among Protestant preachers in such national political issues as slavery, temperance, immigration, and organized labor. Finney seamlessly interwove concern for the salvation of souls with radical social reform. In the twentieth century, great preachers like Fosdick and REINHOLD and H. RICHARD NIEBUHR were also political activists. Thus the joint vocation of preacher and prophet is a time-honored Protestant tradition. A few generations ago, politically charged preaching was the province of more liberal Protestant preachers, who saw themselves as heirs of WALTER RAUSCHENBUSCH and Reinhold Niebuhr. They saw themselves as continuing the project of christianizing America, applying Christian judgments to social issues, usually from the political left. Today, many of the most politicized of Protestant clergy seem to be political conservatives, Christians on the political right.

Although African-American preachers continue to exercise the African-American church's historic office of the prophetic preacher that was so well embodied in such preachers as Martin Luther King, Jr., or the Harlem Congressman and pastor Adam Clayton Powell, so-called "prophetic preaching" seems to be on the wane among Protestants. Perhaps the issues that ought to be addressed seem less clear. Perhaps preachers feel that parochial congregational concerns are more pressing on their homiletical attention than larger political and social matters. Perhaps many Protestants have lost that old Protestant optimism that America is a basically Christian country whose preachers have both the vocation and the means to make it even more Christian.

Protestants also placed WOMEN in the pulpit. Although women sometimes preached among the Methodists, and women played a large role in some Pentecostal churches in the early part of the last century, women began to be ordained in large numbers by Protestant churches only in the last quarter of the twentieth century (see WOMEN CLERGY). The presence of women in the pulpit is itself a prophetic witness against conventional social arrangements, as well as against the infidelity of the church itself in not recognizing the spiritual gifts of women. Various theologies of liberation, a Catholic gift to some Protestant theologians, and WOMANIST and FEMINIST THEOLOGIES, would-be successors to the prophetic tradition, appear to have failed to capture the imagination of Protestant preachers and their congregations. The challenge for any prophetic preacher is to have not only the sense of pastoral authority and the God-given obligation to speak out on controversial issues (commodities that seem in short supply among many Protestant pastors today), but also the challenge of speaking a peculiarly, specifically Christian word to controversial social and political issues. Protestant theology today is not known for its self-confidence and coherence, or for its energy and zeal, so perhaps a renewal of Protestant prophetic preaching awaits a renewal of Protestant theology. Or perhaps Protestant theology languishes because it awaits a revival of Protestant proclamation. Historically, in the story of Protestant Christianity, theology and proclamation ascend on mutually rising tides.

The various Awakenings that so determined American religious life were distinctly Protestant phenomena. They ensured that an evangelical, missionary approach to preaching would typify the American homiletics. The purpose of preaching is more than to edify believers, to nurture those already within the fold; it is also to reach out, to convict, and to win unbelievers to the Gospel. Preachers like Finney, Sunday, and Moody pioneered preaching with this dominating evangelistic intent; BILLY GRAHAM perfected it for the twentieth century. Graham's first big evangelistic "crusade" was in Los Angeles in 1949. Electronic amplification meant that his voice could easily accommodate crowds of more than 100,000. His "Hour of Decision" radio ministry demonstrated the adaptability of a simple, direct evangelistic appeal. Through his preaching, well over one million people were said to have made a "decision for Christ." Most of today's "televangelists" owe their ministries to Graham's half-century of much-praised preaching (see TELEVANGELISM; MASS MEDIA). His simple, oft-repeated message, designed to culminate in a decision by the hearer to be converted to the Gospel, became the dominant form for Protestant preaching in the more conservative and evangelical churches.

Protestant preaching is biblically based preaching. Although Protestantism was in great part a rediscovery of the centrality and freedom of Scripture for the church and against the church, Protestant preaching has also been a long struggle over just how the preaching is to be biblical. Is "biblical preaching" limited to verse-by-verse exposition of Scripture—a rather wooden form of preaching that does not seem congruent with the rather dramatic, narrative, literary form of Scripture itself? Or does biblical preaching mean that the sermon's message, shape, form, and intention be congruent with the message, shape, form, and intention of Scripture? In the late twentieth century, Protestant preachers like Fred Craddock and Eugene Lowry rediscovered the essentially narrative shape and purpose of Scripture, the predominance of narrative over abstract propositions in the way that the Bible presents the truth of the Gospel. This rediscovery, embraced by many preachers in the mainline, more liberal Protestant denominations, called into question some historic Protestant methods of proclamation. Rather than being the explication of a set of abstract ideas and principles with an exhortation to live better lives, preaching, among the practitioners of narrative preaching, was seen as a story, a movement of a drama through time, something that is experienced rather than explained. Inductive preaching is a mode of proclamation linked with narrative preaching.

Inductive preachers stress that a sermon is not only what the preacher is saying, but also what and how the listeners are hearing. A sermon consists not simply in the correct assertion of right thoughts, but also in the listener's faithful embrace of the Christian life. Is narrative preaching just another form of the old Protestant pietistic concern with the individual's inner life, a forsaking of the historic Protestant concern with doctrine, theology, and faithful thinking, or does it represent a more creative, more truly biblical way of thinking? At present there seems to be some critical questioning of the enthusiasm for narrative and inductive preaching that perhaps signals a return to historic Protestant concerns about the theological content of preaching, a realization that faithful biblical preaching requires a mix of interpretive and homiletical strategies that are as rich as the mix of communicative forms with the Bible itself.

Fosdick once spoke of preaching as "counseling on a group scale." His *therapeutic* approach to preaching fit well with the new twentieth-century American orthodoxy: psychology. Many Protestant preachers, building on their pietistic background, refashioned Christian proclamation into a form of pastoral care. Preaching became a means whereby people received helpful psychological advice, personal care, and support. NORMAN VINCENT PEALE'S "power of positive thinking" was embraced by millions as a creative, caring approach to contemporary human dilemmas, but was condemned by others as mere popular psychological platitudes with only a thin Christian veneer. California pastor Robert Schuller, although nurtured in the conservative Reformed tradition, packaged his preaching into a television format designed for maximum appeal to, as he once said, "the unchurched who. . . are not at all prepared to listen to someone with God talk," preachers who are obsessed with sin and guilt delivered in "scolding sermons from angry pulpits." Television preachers like Schuller enthusiastically embraced technology, making their sermons a mirror of American cultural values. They have frequently argued that television is a neutral medium, that the medium does not force an alteration of the message, and that Jesus would have undoubtedly used television rather than the pulpit had it been available to him. Yet their sermons tend to be more influenced by the communicative techniques and the mass entertainment values of television than they may know. In their preaching, the religion of the self-sacrificial, suffering love of the cross tends to be transformed into just another sensible, practical strategy for personal success. Although Schuller's messages (he refuses to use the word "sermon" to describe his preaching) are seen on television by millions, perhaps more listeners than to any other preacher in history, his message seems to be mostly about mental health and self-esteem and only incidentally about the Gospel of Jesus Christ—a perfect theological justification for a North American culture of abundance.

Luther's focus on reaching the common people through simple speech, along with Finney's conviction that acceptance of the Gospel is the result of well-planned homiletical strategies, appear to have produced theologically questionable fruits. The result has been a homiletic that elevates a concern for the feelings in and response of the listener over concerns about the theological and biblical content of the sermon, combined with a focus on the presentation of the messenger rather than the divine source of the message. As contemporary Protestant preachers attempt to be faithful to the evangelical thrust of the Gospel all around the world, as they attempt to speak a Word that can be accepted by those who have not yet heard, they will continue to struggle with issues of biblical fidelity. Graham's evangelistic preaching for decision, and Schuller's preaching as entertainment meant to help people with their problems, provide the antecedents for much of the preaching in the so-called "MEGA-CHURCHES" that were the late twentieth century's most dramatic contribution to Protestant ECCLESIOLOGY. In these churches, vast congregations gather to hear a Gospel proclaimed unashamedly in a decidedly contemporary, secularized idiom, often augmented by slick technological sounds and images. The traditional vocabulary of Christianity, along with the historic images of the faith like the cross and sacraments, are downplayed or even ignored by many mega-church preachers. Whereas most of these preachers think of themselves as within the evangelical tradition, their preaching sometimes seems more indebted to the "therapeutic life-situation" preaching of the liberal Fosdick than to the "come down to the altar and be saved" EVANGELISM of Graham. Cut off from the wellsprings of the liturgy of the church, devoid of orthodox Christian vocabulary, and without explicit ties to creed, denominational tradition, or sustained, extensive dialogue with Scripture—traditional Protestant means of keeping a sermon grounded in the historic Christian faith—these preachers face a great challenge. When does their preaching drift from proclamation of the Gospel into pop-psychological therapy or right-wing political advocacy? How does a preacher utilize the media of the consumer culture without having his or her message tainted or irrevocably diverted by those media? When the listener's alleged ability or inability to accept the message becomes the criterion for what is said in a sermon, Protestant preachers are right to be troubled by the possibility that they may have jettisoned their historic homiletical birthright for that which is merely thera-peutic, merely moral, or merely entertaining—a Word that cannot be heard as well elsewhere by more congenial means than a sermon.

These challenges and others will continue to perplex the homiletical tradition known as Protestant. At this juncture in the history of the Reformation, it is not known whether Protestantism will continue as a set of distinct homiletical practices or whether it shall eventually come full circle and merge into some new assimilation of the Catholic tradition. Yet the experience of Protestant preaching affirms that the Word of God is infinitely resourceful, indomitable, and a fire inextinguishable, that this Word of God is sharper than a double-edged sword, and that the church, reformed and ever reforming, is bound to be the recipient of even greater Gospel-induced reformations. Although empires wax and wane, and all of our human aspirations come to dust, the Word of the Lord is forever.

References and Further Reading

Crocker, Lionel. *Harry Emerson Fosdick's Art of Preaching; An Anthology.* Springfield, IL: Thomas. 1971.

Davies, Horton. *Worship and Theology in England from Cranmer to Hooper, 1534–1603.* Princeton, NJ: Princeton University Press, 1970.

Fant, Clyde F. *Twenty Centuries of Great Preaching.* 13 vols. Waco, TX: Word Books, 1971.

Hunter, Edwina, and David Farmer. *And Blessed Is She: Sermons by Women.* Valley Forge, PA: Judson Press, 1994.

Leith, John H. "Calvin's Doctrine of the Proclamation of the Word and Its Significance for Today." In *John Calvin and the Church: A Prism of Reform.* Edited by Timothy George. Louisville, KY: Westminster/John Knox Press, 1990. 206–229.

Lischer, Richard. *The Company of Preachers: Wisdom on Preaching, Augustine to the Present.* Grand Rapids, MI: Eerdmans, 2002.

———. *The Preacher King: Martin Luther King Jr. and the Word that Moved America,* New York: Oxford University Press, 1995.

McNeill, John T., ed. *John Calvin. Institutes of the Christian Religion.* Translated by Ford Lewis Battles. 2 vols. Philadelphia, PA: Westminster Press, 1960.

Meuser, Fred W. *Luther the Preacher.* Minneapolis, MN: Augsburg, 1983.

Miller, R. M. *Harry Emerson Fosdick: Preacher, Pastor, Prophet.* New York: Oxford University Press, 1985.

Old, Hughes Oliphant, *The Reading and Preaching of the Scriptures in the Worship of the Christian Church: Vol. 4. The Age of the Reformation.* Grand Rapids, MI: Eerdmans, 2002.

Parker, T. H. L. *Calvin's Preaching.* Edinburgh, UK: T. & T. Clark, 1992.

Willimon, William H. *Pastor: The Theology and Practice of Ordained Leadership.* Nashville, TN: Abingdon, 2002.

Willimon, William H., and R. Lischer, eds. *Concise Encyclopedia of Preaching.* Louisville, KY: Westminster/John Knox Press, 1995.

WILLIAM H. WILLIMON

PREDESTINATION

The word *predestination* comes from the Latin *"praedestinatio,"* meaning "a determining beforehand." Theologically the term primarily refers to God's ELECTION or choice of those who will receive SALVATION, although it has also been used for aspects of providence. "Single" predestination applies the word only to God's gracious choice of those who will be saved, attributing reprobation to causes in the damned themselves. "Double" predestination refers to God's free choice to save some and God's free choice to damn others. To some, predestination is based on God's foreknowledge of people's merit or faith, whereas to others predestination is a choice solely within God's will.

The doctrine of predestination has been a subject of contention throughout the history of the church, and particularly within Protestantism. Churches of the Reformed tradition are known for concern with this DOCTRINE more than any other.

Pre-Reformation

The Greek verb "προοριζω", meaning "to decide upon beforehand" or "to predetermine," appears in the New Testament, particularly in Romans 8:29–30, and Ephesians 1:5 and 11. This was translated in the Vulgate as *"praedestinare"* and into English by the verb "to predestine." These texts present an apparent conflict with passages like I Timothy 2:4, which proclaim God's desire that all be saved.

In the early Church predestination was interpreted as God's foreknowledge of people's good works. The earliest exception was the fourth-century theologian Athanasius. In his "Second Oration against the Arians," Athanasius supported his argument for the eternal divinity of the Word with Paul's claim that those who will be saved are predestined in Christ and by Christ.

More influentially, in the fifth century, Augustine made predestination the defense of the primacy of God's GRACE in salvation. The Pelagians insisted that people were able to obey God and live holy lives. Augustine believed that this made salvation depend on human works. In Augustine's understanding, humanity is weakened by SIN, unable to seek salvation or persevere in holiness without God's gracious intervention. Predestination is God's free gracious choice to save some, but not others, from the mass of guilty humanity. All are guilty, so condemnation of the non-elect is just.

These views were immediately controversial and rarely fully accepted. However, Augustine's general influence and clarity of argument ensured that these views were never fully abandoned. "Semipelagians"

in European monastic circles soon argued that neither Pelagian reliance on works nor Augustinian reliance on grace was sufficient. Salvation required both effort at holiness and grace. The Council of Orange (529) formally rejected semipelagianism, affirming Augustine's teaching on predestination and grace but softening its harder edges by rejecting predestination to evil or damnation.

By the thirteenth century the consensus view was a type of single predestination. According to Thomas Aquinas, God predestined individuals to receive grace. Empowered by grace they would do good works, which would be meritorious. God foreknew their works and merit, thus predestining them to glory. In the fourteenth century alternate views arose, with Peter Aureol teaching general election to life and Gregory of Rimini teaching double predestination.

Lutheran

For the first Lutheran and Reformed theologians, predestination affirmed God's grace as the source of salvation and gave assurance to believers. In his preface to Romans, MARTIN LUTHER wrote that faith and forgiveness, as well as their absence, proceed from God's eternal predestination (see LUTHERANISM). In *The Bondage of the Will* (1525) Luther taught that God's will is twofold. Scripture shows God working for people's salvation; however, in a hidden mysterious sense, God works out the damnation of the rest. Still, Luther did not develop a prominent doctrine of double predestination.

In the *Loci Communes* of 1521, Luther's colleague PHILIPP MELANCHTHON held a fairly strong doctrine of predestination, but by the 1543 edition his view had softened: Although Christ is the cause of our election and JUSTIFICATION, the Gospel offers salvation to all. Finally he moved explicitly away from double predestination: the idea that God's decree caused damnation implied human passivity, removing ethical responsibility. One must participate in justification, at least by accepting the promise, a view that came to be known as "synergism."

The GNESIO- (or "true") LUTHERANS of the next generation sought to follow Luther's position, opposing the synergism of the "Philippists" who followed Melanchthon. The Formula of Concord of 1577 settled the debate, distinguishing clearly between predestination and mere foreknowledge. The Formula attributed salvation to predestination, but argued that damnation was justice for people's own sins.

Since the REFORMATION, the Lutheran Churches have not been immune from change or controversy on this topic. In the seventeenth and eighteenth centuries Lutheran ORTHODOXY taught that predestination was based on God's foreknowledge of those who would respond to the gospel with persevering faith. In 1877 in the United States, LUTHERAN CHURCH–MISSOURI SYNOD theologian C. W. F. Walther pointed out that this was in conflict with the Formula of Concord because it placed a cause of election in human beings. The ensuing controversy divided the Missouri Synod from other American Lutheran Churches, a division that has not healed although the conflict has passed.

Reformed: Sixteenth Century

The Zurich reformer HULDRYCH ZWINGLI also taught predestination in opposition to meritorious works. In his *Commentary on True and False Religion* (1525) he linked predestination to providence, with providence as the "mother" of predestination. God's providence directs all things; within the category of all things, God's providence predestines those who will be saved. Election is from God's goodness, apart from any actions of those elected. Zwingli's focus was on election to life, although God's will also plays a role toward the damned. Faith proceeds out of election, and those with faith have good evidence of their election.

Genevan reformer JOHN CALVIN is the name most associated with predestination (see CALVINISM). For Calvin predestination is God's choice of some for eternal life and God's choice of others for damnation. He believed that the plain teaching of scripture, and the obvious implications of that teaching, led to double predestination. His pastoral sensibility led him to frame it differently than did Zwingli. In the authoritative 1559 edition of his INSTITUTES OF THE CHRISTIAN RELIGION, Calvin did not treat predestination as a part of providence. Instead he added it to the discussion of justification and faith. In this position the doctrine assures the worried believer that salvation depends solely on God's gracious choice, not on personal holiness. If one is in Christ, responding to Word and Sacrament with faith in obedience, then one is surely elect. It was, to Calvin himself, a terrifying mystery, acknowledged as part of revelation but not to be explored. The reasons are hidden in the secret counsel of God. The doctrine can, however, be of benefit. It explains why not all hear the Gospel and fewer still respond in faith. It also should keep believers trusting in God's grace alone, humbly glorifying God.

Calvin's teaching on predestination gave rise to significant controversy during his life. Even HEINRICH BULLINGER, Zwingli's successor at Zurich, objected to the double decree as presented by Calvin, believing that this made God the author of sin. Bullinger favored the view that election was by grace but reprobation was by justice.

Peter Martyr Vermigli took another distinctive approach to predestination among the sixteenth-century Reformed theologians. With similarities to Gregory of Rimini, Vermigli taught that election is in the eternal will, not the foreknowledge, of God and is exclusively to eternal life. Reprobation also is in the eternal will of God, but actual condemnation is worked out in time as justice for human sin.

THEODORE BEZA, Calvin's successor in Geneva, looked more closely into the order of the divine decrees than Calvin had, arguing that the decree to save some and damn others was logically before the Fall, a position known as "supralapsarianism." In some works Beza linked predestination to providence, portraying all of salvation history as the outworking of God's decrees. However, in more systematic works such as his *Confession de la foi chrétienne* (1559), predestination is not presented as part of providence, but rather as part of the assurance of salvation. Taking Beza's work as a whole, predestination is not the organizing principle it was once thought to be.

Reformed: Post-Reformation

In Reformed theology after the sixteenth century there was a shift toward an "infralapsarian" view. In infralapsarianism, God's decree predestining the elect to salvation logically follows after the Fall, removing the implication that God intended sin. In DUTCH REFORMED CHURCHES this teaching is found in the Canons of the Synod of Dort (1618–1619) (see DORT, CANONS OF).

The Synod of Dort was primarily concerned with the teachings of JACOBUS ARMINIUS, a Dutch theologian who argued that predestination by divine decree is inconsistent with God's grace and human freedom. Arminius taught that predestination is God's foreknowledge of those who will believe and persevere in faith. The Synod decided against ARMINIANISM, affirming predestination as a decree of God's will to salvation and reprobation. The Arminians were nevertheless able to form churches after 1625.

In the nineteenth century, ABRAHAM KUYPER sought to renew Calvinism in the NETHERLANDS and elsewhere. Although he saw predestination as a central Reformed doctrine, he did not emphasize it, being more concerned with God's common grace working in the world. Some of the Dutch Churches abroad have held the doctrine firmly, although they have also faced problems. The CHRISTIAN REFORMED CHURCH IN NORTH AMERICA faced protests against the doctrine of reprobation, both in the writings of Harold Dekker of Calvin Theological Seminary in 1962 and in an official grievance by missionary theologian Harry R. Boer in 1977. In both cases the church maintained its traditional doctrinal stance. The most tragic misuse of the doctrine of predestination was in the South African Church, where from the mid-nineteenth century to the late twentieth it was used to give credence to white racial superiority and apartheid.

In ENGLAND, double predestination was affirmed in the WESTMINSTER CONFESSION of 1646, long the doctrinal standard of Presbyterians in SCOTLAND and America (see PRESBYTERIANISM). The Westminster Confession placed the double decree of predestination in the doctrine of God as the first expression of the decrees by which God governs all things, much as Zwingli had done.

In the UNITED STATES a number of forces, including REVIVALS and the ENLIGHTENMENT, have led to a general decline of predestinarian teaching in the Reformed tradition. In the early nineteenth century, under the leadership of WILLIAM ELLERY CHANNING, the Congregationalists of New England suffered the loss of their liberal party (which became the AMERICAN UNITARIAN ASSOCIATION), partly out of the liberals' objections to predestination (see CONGREGATIONALISM). Presbyterians have been reshaped by Arminianism structurally and theologically. The 1810 birth of the CUMBERLAND PRESBYTERIAN CHURCH was attributed in part to the Arminianism of revivalistic ministers who were forced out of the larger Presbyterian Church. The split between Old School and New School Presbyterians in 1837 was also influenced by the New School's embrace of revivalistic methods. These seemed to assume Arminian doctrinal positions, and in CHARLES FINNEY and other leaders Arminianism was explicit. Presbyterian confessions still teach predestination, but the doctrine is not prominent in the churches. It has been officially softened or removed in some cases. The Cumberland Presbyterian Church developed its own confession to avoid Westminster's predestinarian teaching, and in 1903 the PRESBYTERIAN CHURCH IN THE U.S.A. added a moderating "declaratory statement" to the Westminster Confession.

Some major Reformed theologians since the Reformation have defended the doctrine, and some have adapted it. American JONATHAN EDWARDS in *Freedom of the Will* (1754) defended predestination against Wesleyan Arminianism, and Charles Hodge did the same in response to the Arminianism of the Second Great Awakening (see AWAKENINGS). FRIEDRICH SCHLEIERMACHER rooted predestination in God's good pleasure rather than foreknowledge, but he held to a universal predestination to life and none to reprobation. KARL BARTH saw election as the sum of the gospel, but did not view predestination as a pair of opposite choices, to life or to damnation. Drawing on Athanasius he argued that Christ is both the elect human being, and the electing God. Because he taught that all people find themselves elect in Christ, Barth has been accused of UNIVERSALISM, although he denied this was a necessary conclusion.

Anglican

In England theologians taught predestination as early as during the reign of HENRY VIII. The THIRTY-NINE ARTICLES (1571) proclaim a mild doctrine of single predestination, and the Lambeth Articles (1595) approved double predestination by God's will, not foreknowledge. At the end of the sixteenth century Anglican theologians such as RICHARD HOOKER and Puritans such as WILLIAM PERKINS taught predestination, although with some differences (see ANGLICANISM; PURITANISM). Perkins denied that predestination was at all based on foreknowledge. Hooker claimed that, although this is true of election, reprobation is based on foreknowledge of people's rejection of God's gracious offer. In the reign of James I, the High Church party, under the leadership of WILLIAM LAUD, supported Arminianism in their struggle against the Calvinists. They argued that predestination, despite its presence in the Thirty-Nine Articles, was contrary to the free promise of the Gospel as embodied in the LITURGY. After the 1626 York House Conference they were able to ban the teaching of predestination, first at Cambridge and then throughout England, and to place Arminians in most bishoprics.

The EPISCOPAL CHURCH in the United States in the nineteenth century tolerated both predestinarian and Arminian interpretations of the Thirty-nine Articles. In the latter part of the century the dominant view was "ecclesiastical election," by which God elects individuals to the visible church but salvation is still subject to human free will.

Wesleyan

Anglican priest JOHN WESLEY was a convinced Arminian, believing that Calvinist predestination was a blasphemous teaching portraying God as unjust, arbitrary, and in fact worse than the DEVIL (see WESLEYANISM). Throughout his remarkably successful evangelistic and organizational career Wesley engaged in a public struggle against the doctrine. His 1739 sermon "Free Grace" was the first of several written works on the subject, and his steady teaching against predestination led to an acrimonious public parting with his friend and colleague, the Calvinist GEORGE WHITEFIELD. The influence of METHODISM in the United States has contributed to the pervasive assumption of Arminian views there.

References and Further Reading

Armstrong, Brian G. *Calvinism and the Amyraut Heresy: Protestant Scholasticism and Humanism in Seventeenth-Century France.* Madison: The University of Wisconsin Press, 1969.

Baker, Frank. "Whitefield's Break with the Wesleys." *Church Quarterly* 3 (1970): 103–113.

Bray, John S. *Theodore Beza's Doctrine of Predestination.* Nieuwkoop, The Netherlands: B. De Graaf, 1975.

Busch, Edward. "The Predestinarian Controversy 100 Years Later." *Currents in Theology and Mission* 9 no. 3 (1982): 132–148.

James, Frank A. III. *Peter Martyr Vermigli and Predestination: The Augustinian Inheritance of an Italian Reformer.* Oxford, UK: Clarendon Press, 1998.

Kendall, R. R. *Calvin and English Calvinism to 1649.* Oxford: Oxford University Press, 1979.

Klooster, Fred H. *Calvin's Doctrine of Predestination.* 2nd ed. Grand Rapids, MI: Baker Book House, 1977.

Muller, Richard A. *Christ and the Decree: Christology and Predestination in Reformed Theology from Calvin to Perkins.* Durham, NC: The Labyrinth Press, 1986.

———. *God, Creation, and Providence in the Thought of Jacob Arminius: Sources and Directions of Scholastic Protestantism in the Era of Early Orthodoxy.* Grand Rapids, MI: Baker Book House, 1991.

GARY NEAL HANSEN

PRE-RAPHAELITES

Pre-Raphaelitism was a mid- and late-Victorian movement in ART and poetry. The seven young men of the Pre-Raphaelite Brotherhood (P.R.B.) sought to restore to British painting sincerity, high purpose, and earnest scrutiny of visible facts. After the P.R.B. disbanded, a second group of Pre-Raphaelite artists coalesced around Dante Gabriel Rossetti. The artistic agenda of this second phase of Pre-Raphaelitism was distinct from the earlier project and led to the Aesthetic Movement in British art and LITERATURE of the 1880s and 1890s.

The Pre-Raphaelite Brotherhood

The P.R.B. was formed in London in 1848 with Rossetti, John Everett Millais, and William Holman Hunt as founding members and central figures. Rossetti (poet and painter), although lacking the artistic training and proficiency of Millais and Hunt, through genius and force of personality became the natural leader of the brotherhood. Hunt was the theoretician of the group and invented their detailed, glowing painting technique. Millais was a brilliant painter who commanded virtuoso technical skill. The brotherhood was completed by Thomas Woolner (sculptor), James Collinson (painter), F. G. Stephens (painter and later art critic), and William Michael Rossetti (art and literary critic and the memoirist of the movement). Other close associates were the painters Ford Madox Brown, Walter Deverell, and Charles Allston Collins, and Rossetti's sister, the poet CHRISTINA ROSSETTI.

In 1850 the P.R.B. established a journal, *The Germ: Thoughts toward Nature in Poetry, Literature, and Art,* as an organ to expound its views. *The Germ* contained treatises on art, short stories, critical reviews, and a substantial body of verse, most notably by Rossetti, Christina Rossetti, and Coventry Patmore. Although it survived for only four issues, it set themes and motifs characteristic of later Pre-Raphaelite poetry.

Early Paintings

The Pre-Raphaelite visual style was instantly recognizable, with its clarity of outline, vivid coloration, and natural lighting effects brought to bear on historical, literary, or religious subjects. The P.R.B. shared the conviction that English painting was feeble, conventional, and stagnant, mainly through its reliance on academic conventions codified in the time of Raphael, hence their self-characterization as "Pre-Raphaelite." Rejecting Joshua Reynolds (calling him "Sir Sloshua") and the Royal Academy, they sought to reestablish an earlier artistic spirit of individuality and freedom. Their canvases were heavily symbolic and moralistic, minutely detailed yet at the same time suggestive of spiritual meanings beyond exterior realities.

The earliest paintings were exhibited anonymously, signed only with the mysterious signature "P.R.B.," and were notable for deliberate archaism and medieval flavor, presented with scrupulous fidelity to fact. Hunt's *Rienzi Vowing to Obtain Justice for the Death of His Brother* (1849), Millais's *Lorenzo and Isabella* (1849), and Rossetti's *The Girlhood of Mary Virgin* (1848–1849) were greeted with critical favor. In 1850 and 1851, however, the meaning of the secret signature became generally known, and the P.R.B. came under serious attack, particularly for their unconventional representation of religious subjects. Charles Dickens led the bitter criticism, calling Millais's *Christ in the House of His Parents* (1850) "mean, odious, repulsive, and revolting." The crisis passed when, in 1851, famous art critic John Ruskin wrote two letters to *The Times* supporting the P.R.B.'s artistic practice.

Pre-Raphaelite paintings evince Protestant influences of both evangelical and High Anglican flavors. The P.R.B. certainly attempted to develop a new style of religious art for the contemporary age, one that was modern, historically accurate, and—some would argue—distinctly Protestant in its use of figural methods as described by Ruskin in *Modern Painters.* In their subject matter and typological figural mode, many of the paintings and poems also showed the influence of the OXFORD MOVEMENT and its sacramentalism and ritualism. Various Pre-Raphaelite paintings make pictorial references to ANGLO-CATHOLICISM and its newly introduced Catholic rituals and ornaments, particularly Rossetti's *The Girlhood of Mary Virgin* and *Ecce Ancilla Domini!* (1849–1850), Collinson's *The Renunciation of St. Elizabeth of Hungary* (1850), Millais's *Christ in the House of His Parents,* Collins's *Convent Thoughts* (1850–51), and Hunt's *The Light of the World* (1851–1853). In poetry, the influence is evident as well: Rossetti gathered early versions of his poems, including "The Blessed Damozel," "Ave," and "My Sister's Sleep," titling the manuscript collection *Songs of the Art Catholic* (1847). Rossetti, however, made used of religious symbolism without having any definite spiritual commitment himself.

By 1853 internal differences had broken up the P.R.B. Millais eventually joined the establishment that the P.R.B. opposed, becoming a member of the Royal Academy and its president, and later a baronet. Hunt throughout his life remained committed to the laborious method and spiritual intent of the P.R.B. In 1854 he made the first of three journeys to the Holy Land to paint biblical events with strict historical and geographic accuracy. The paintings produced, most notably *The Scapegoat* (1854), baffled Hunt's English audiences. The verdict that *The Scapegoat*'s symbolism was incomprehensible, that it particularly failed to impress on viewers a correspondence between the scapegoat and Christ, signaled the failure of the P.R.B.'s attempt to revitalize in mid–nineteenth-century ENGLAND a sacramental religious art.

Later Pre-Raphaelites

Pre-Raphaelitism continued to develop, with a new set of artists forming around Rossetti, including William Morris, Edward Burne-Jones, Arthur Hughes, Algernon Charles Swinburne, and Richard Watson Dixon. The soft-edge painting of this second group differed dramatically from the style of Hunt and Millais between 1848 and 1858. This second generation turned away from both the moral earnestness and the careful exactitude of the first period, taking their inspiration from art rather than from NATURE.

Rossetti's own style changed, with his symbolism becoming more private and esoteric, and his paintings more enigmatic. His wife, poet and painter Elizabeth Siddal, whom he had envisioned as Beatrice to his Dante, had been his early muse. After her death in 1862 Rossetti depicted a new and influential ideal of female beauty—a large and loosely dressed woman, with full and red fleshy lips, masses of hair, and soulful eyes—an embodiment of a secular religion of beauty and spiritualized femininity.

The Pre-Raphaelite movement enjoyed successes in poetry with Morris's *The Defence of Guenevere* (1858), Christina Rossetti's *Goblin Market and Other Poems* (1862) and *The Prince's Progress and Other Poems* (1866), and Swinburne's *Poems and Ballads* (1866). Finally, and only after he had the unique manuscript of his compositions exhumed from Siddal's grave, Rossetti published *Poems* (1870), which included his important sonnet sequence, *The House of Life*. However, this poetic achievement was blighted by "The Fleshly School" controversy, which began in 1871 when Robert Buchanan accused Rossetti and fellow Pre-Raphaelite poets of lewd sensuality. Rossetti suffered a breakdown from which his recovery was only partial, although he continued to write and paint, especially pictures of his new muse, Morris's wife Jane.

Pre-Raphaelitism continued to confront prevailing aesthetic norms in various aspects of Victorian life. The "Arts and Crafts Movement" was inspired by Morris and the firm he founded in 1861 with various other Pre-Raphaelites. Valuing craftsmanship and design, they provided architecture, furniture, fabrics, tiles, wallpaper, stained glass, church decoration, book design, and illustration to meet a purified, more medieval, aesthetic. Morris, always prodigiously energetic, continued to write prolifically in a variety of genres; he also ardently supported Socialism and was a founder of the Socialist League (1884). Rossetti turned toward Aestheticism and the "art for art's sake" movement, which valued intensity in the experience of art. Although the original impulse of Pre-Raphaelitism was diffused, to the end the movement retained an opposition to convention and to mainstream bourgeois Victorian culture.

See also Aesthetics; Architecture, Church

References and Further Reading

Bentley, D. M. R. "The Pre-Raphaelites and the Oxford Movement." *Dalhousie Review* 57 (1977): 525–539.

Marsh, Jan. *Dante Gabriel Rossetti: Painter and Poet*. London: Weidenfeld and Nicolson, 1999.

Prettejohn, Elizabeth. *The Art of the Pre-Raphaelites*. London: Tate Publishing, 2000.

Rossetti, Dante Gabriel. *The Correspondence of Dante Gabriel Rossetti*. Edited by William E. Fredeman. 9 vols. Woodbridge, UK: Boydell and Brewer, 2002–.

Sambrook, James, ed. *Pre-Raphaelitism: A Collection of Critical Essays*. Chicago: University of Chicago Press, 1974.

Sussman, Herbert. *Fact into Figure: Typology in Carlyle, Ruskin, and the Pre-Raphaelite Brotherhood*. Columbus: Ohio State University Press, 1979.

Wood, Christopher. *The Pre-Raphaelites*. London: Weidenfeld and Nicolson, 1981.

MARY ARSENEAU

PRESBYTERIAN CHURCH U.S.A.

The Presbyterian Church in the United States of America (PCUSA) identifies itself with the one, holy, catholic, apostolic church, and accepts the Hebrew and Christian Scriptures as its "rule of faith and life" as well as the Apostles and Nicene (325) creeds of the early church. It traces its origins especially to JOHN CALVIN (1509–1564) of Geneva. Calvin's influence spread, especially through his INSTITUTES OF THE CHRISTIAN RELIGION (1536) to FRANCE, Holland, GERMANY, HUNGARY, and to the British Isles under the leadership of JOHN KNOX (1513–1572) of SCOTLAND. During the Puritan Revolution (1642–1660), Presbyterians, Anglicans, and Congregationalists produced the WESTMINSTER CONFESSION OF FAITH, the Larger and Shorter Catechisms, and a Directory for the Public Worship of God. The leaders of the various churches could not resolve issues of church POLITY, as indicated by their denominational titles. Presbyterians adopted the offices of CLERGY and lay elders (presbyters) and DEACONS, who preached, taught, governed, and cared for the welfare of congregations. Numerous Scots along with Presbyterians from Northern Ireland began to emigrate to America, many to settle in the middle colonies in the eighteenth century.

Early History in America

There they founded churches and the first PRESBYTERY in Philadelphia (1706) under the leadership of Irishman Francis Makemie (c. 1658–1708). This body grew into a Synod (1716) under clergy and lay elders. The SYNOD adopted the Westminster doctrinal standards in 1729 with reservations about its Erastian references. To build an indigenous leadership, William Tennent Sr. (1673–1746), another Irishman, began to educate his sons and others at a "log college," which later became the College of New Jersey (1747) and Princeton University. Influenced by GEORGE WHITEFIELD, Tennent and his two sons, William and GILBERT (1703–1758), stimulated the Great AWAKENING, joined by JONATHAN EDWARDS and SAMUEL DAVIES (1723–1761). Awakening "enthusiasm" caused a "New Side–Old Side" division in 1740. The Old Side accused the New Siders of stirring up uncontrolled emotionalism. In 1758 the two Sides reunited, agreeing to preserve in religious matters a balance between ardor and order. They formed the Synod of New York and Philadelphia with ninety-four ministers and approximately 200 congregations. United, Presbyterians joined the British in fighting the French and Indian War on the Frontier.

Presbyterians were alienated from the mother country during the debate over American political rights in the 1760s and 1770s. Led by JOHN WITHERSPOON

(1723–1794), called from Scotland to the presidency of Princeton College, Presbyterians in general supported the American Revolution. Witherspoon was the only clergyman to sign the DECLARATION OF INDEPENDENCE (1776). Numerous clergy and LAITY provided leadership during the conflict, including ELIAS BOUDINOT (1740–1821), a Philadelphian who served as president of the UNITED STATES (1782–1783) as well as presided over the AMERICAN BIBLE SOCIETY. With his SCOTTISH COMMON SENSE REALISM, Witherspoon made a profound impact on his student, JAMES MADISON, an Episcopalian, who became a chief architect of the United States Constitution (1788–1789) and the BILL OF RIGHTS (1791) with its First Amendment, guaranteeing religious and civil rights and defining church–state relations in the new nation. Presbyterian clergy and elders organized the General Assembly of the Presbyterian Church in the United States of America, which met for the first time in Philadelphia in 1789. The commissioners adopted the Westminster creedal standards and developed a Directory for Worship and a Form of Government and Discipline based on "general principles" of the PCUSA. These affirmed that "God alone" is the "Lord of Conscience," that "Truth is in order to goodness," that all church pronouncements are only "ministerial and declarative" and do not bind the conscience or impair civil rights. These statements, among others, still guide the denomination.

Western Migration and Expansion

Along with other Christians, Presbyterians pressed westward. With Congregationalists, such as TIMOTHY DWIGHT, they entered a Plan of Union (1801) to plant churches across the nation. They also cooperated with others to form VOLUNTARY SOCIETIES—educational societies (e.g., to publish and distribute Bibles, tracts, and to form SUNDAY SCHOOLS), reforming societies (e.g., to promote peace, TEMPERANCE, and to oppose SLAVERY or to colonize freed slaves in AFRICA), and home and foreign missions (e.g., the AMERICAN BOARD OF COMMISSIONERS FOR FOREIGN MISSIONS). Influenced by CAMP MEETING revivals under James McGready, some Presbyterians in Kentucky formed the CUMBERLAND PRESBYTERIAN CHURCH (1810), modifying strict standards for the ordination of ministers and doctrine with Arminian overtones (see ARMINIANISM). New York revivalist CHARLES GRANDISON FINNEY (1792–1875) promoted "New Measures" (e.g., "protracted meetings" and "anxious benches"), offensive to the more conservative. Finney helped cause a division between New School (NS) and Old School (OS) Presbyterians (1838) who thought "Presbygationalists," as they were called, had diluted Calvinist doctrine, lowered qualifications for ministers, and promoted the antislavery cause (see SLAVERY, ABOLITION OF). African-American Presbyterian Samuel Cornish (1795–1858), pastor of the First Black Presbyterian Church in New York, promoted that cause in his *Freedom's Journal,* the first Black American periodical.

In the meantime the PCUSA founded theological SEMINARIES, such as Princeton (1812), Union, Virginia (1812), and Union, New York (1835); produced national leaders, for example, John Holt Rice (1771–1831), Archibald Alexander (1772–1851), and LYMAN BEECHER (1775–1863); and prominent theologians, for example, James Henley Thornwell (1812–1862), Henry Boynton Smith (1815–1877), and Charles Hodge (1797–1878), whose *Systematic Theology* (3 vols., 1872–1873) was widely used. Believing in a well-educated citizenry, Presbyterians promoted public education, along with a few private schools, assisted by William McGuffey (1800–1873) through his widely used MCGUFFEY READERS. They also planted numerous institutions of HIGHER EDUCATION, colleges and universities for women and men.

Tension and Division

Increasingly the PCUSA had to deal the national debate over slavery, which intensified after the passage of the Compromise of 1850 and the Fugitive Slave Law. These laws prompted Beecher's daughter HARRIET BEECHER STOWE to write *Uncle Tom's Cabin* (1851), a widely read novel that brought greater attention to the situation. In 1858 the NS in the South withdrew from its party, and in 1861 the OS, South and North, split over issues such as state sovereignty, slavery, and the responsibilities of the church in public affairs. Under the presidency of ABRAHAM LINCOLN, the nation fought a bloody fratricidal conflict. After the CIVIL WAR hostilities, the PCUSA failed to heal the church's divisions. Southerners organized the Presbyterian Church in the United States (PCUS) (1865), holding among other things to the "spirituality of the Church." In the North the OS and NS reunited in 1870. It could not establish fraternal relations with the PCUS until later in the century. In the meantime the denomination continued to plant churches, even in Alaska, under the leadership of such leaders as SHELDON JACKSON. In 1870 the PCUSA numbered 446,564 members, 4,526 churches, and 4,238 ministers.

To help meet its responsibilities, the PCUSA established church boards, which had headquarters in Philadelphia and New York. Church officials, under the General Assembly, continued to meet the pastoral, educational, and mission needs of members. Presbyterians, many in the middle and upper classes, had to deal with the growth of an industrialized and urban-

ized society with its inequalities and injustices. They did so by proclaiming a "Social Creed," to awaken the conscience, and by supporting institutions, such as the Labor Temple in New York, which championed the cause of working people. The PCUSA also helped found the Federal Council of Churches (1908), an ecumenical body concerned about such matters (see ECUMENISM). Presbyterians had to deal with the rising women's rights movement, led by ELIZABETH CADY STANTON, who grew up Presbyterian. The PCUSA sponsored women's organizations and over the years admitted women to the diaconate in the 1890s, the eldership (1930), and finally to the ordained ministry (1954) (see WOMEN CLERGY). Presbyterians also had to deal with racism, the legacy of slavery. Supreme Court justice, elder John Marshall Harlan, showed the way by being the lone dissenter in the "separate-but-equal" *Plessy v. Ferguson* (1896) decision. The PCUSA developed special denominational programs for African Americans, and supported the CIVIL RIGHTS MOVEMENT of MARTIN LUTHER KING JR. in the 1950s and 1960s.

With regard to War the PCUSA officially supported armed conflict on "just and necessary" occasions. Presbyterians were divided over the Spanish-American War, but generally supported as "just" World War I, World War II, and the Korean War. They were divided again over the Vietnam War. Presbyterian presidents WOODROW WILSON (1856–1925) and Dwight D. Eisenhower (1890–1969), and Secretary of State John Foster Dulles (1888–1959) gave national leadership during many of these years. The PCUSA supported the League of Nations and the United Nations Organization (UNO). Because of worldwide MISSIONS work, Presbyterians helped to establish self-governing, self-supporting, and self-propagating churches in various regions of the world. After World War II the denomination redefined its role as a "partner in obedience" with these new bodies to transcend the paternalism of the early mission enterprises. In these efforts, elder ROBERT E. SPEER (1867–1947) provided executive leadership and ecumenical vision.

Modern Times

After the Civil War the PCUSA faced with other Christians the intellectual ferment of the times, including DARWINISM, HIGHER CRITICISM, and calls for confessional revisions. Some proposed new confessional standards to replace the Westminster documents, but only managed amendments that emphasized the work of the "Holy Spirit" and the "Love of God and Missions" (1903), which reflected the interests of the DENOMINATION at the time. Some prominent Presbyterians, including revivalist BILLY SUNDAY and politician WILLIAM JENNINGS BRYAN, opposed evolution. The PCUSA continued to affirm Christian belief in a Creator, the uniqueness of human life, and underscored that in the struggle for human existence might does not make right. The denomination dealt with the critical study of the BIBLE, during the HERESY trial of Charles Briggs (1841–1913) over the authorship of the biblical books. In this connection they faced the controversy between FUNDAMENTALISM and MODERNISM, not only over the "inerrancy" of Scripture (see BIBLICAL INERRANCY), but doctrines, such as the "virgin birth" of Jesus, "miracles," the "substitutionary atonement," and the "bodily resurrection" of Christ. Led by moderates such as Speer and HENRY SLOANE COFFIN (1877–1954), the PCUSA affirmed the Westminster doctrinal statements of the denomination and allowed presbyteries to decide on a case by case basis what were "essential and necessary" articles of faith. This did not satisfy conservatives, such as biblical scholar J. GRESHAM MACHEN (1881–1937). He was further angered by the mission board that seemed to support the liberalism of prize-winning novelist Pearl S. Buck, a teacher under the board in the 1930s. Machen withdrew to form the Orthodox Presbyterian Church in 1936.

During this latter period, Presbyterian theologians began to draw insight from European thinkers, such as KARL BARTH, EMIL BRUNNER, and others, including Americans REINHOLD NIEBUHR and H. RICHARD NIEBUHR, whose works shaped the NEO-ORTHODOXY MOVEMENT. This theological renewal also led them to draw more insight from theologians of the Ancient and Reformation churches. With assistance of these sources the PCUSA adopted a *Book of Confessions* (1967), which included the familiar Apostles and Nicene Creeds, together with the Reformation's HELVETIC CONFESSION (1566), HEIDELBERG CATECHISM (1563), the Westminster Confession and Short Catechism, and BARMEN DECLARATION (1934) of the German Confessing Church, and a new Confession of 1967. The latter was based on the theme of reconciliation found in II Corinthians 5:18f. The PCUSA spoke in an ecumenical spirit, while emphasizing the need for the reconciling love of Christ to help deal with contemporary issues such as relations among nations and races, between rich and poor, and within the family. The PCUSA has continued to wrestle with these issues especially with regard to conflicts over MARRIAGE, HOMOSEXUALITY, same-sex marriages, and ABORTION.

During the early part of the nineteenth century, with a new taste for the past, the PCUSA began to revisit its liturgical legacy and its WORSHIP needs. For example, Charles W. Baird (1828–1888) published

Eutaxia, or the Presbyterian Liturgies: Historical Sketches (1855), which explored the worship ideas and practices of Calvin and Knox before the rise of PURITANISM in the seventeenth century. Clergymen Louis Benson (1855–1930) and Henry Van Dyke, assisted by laity, organized the Church Service Society (1897) to enhance public and private worship. Despite some resistance the PCUSA recommended a *Book of Common Worship* (1906) for "voluntary use" only. The liturgical movement grew. This earlier volume was revised and adopted officially by the church. Recently the denomination adopted a new *Directory for Worship* and the *Book of Common Worship* (1933), a rich historical, ecumenical, and liturgical treasure for use by clergy and laity. Benson published *The Hymnal* (1895), which set the model for later volumes, and deepening Presbyterian praise leading to the *Presbyterian Hymnal, Hymns, Psalms, and Spiritual Songs* (1990) representing the praise of the whole Christian family.

Ecumenism and International Connection

Over many decades the PCUSA has been engaged in the ecumenical movement beginning in the nineteenth century. Historian PHILIP SCHAFF (1819–1893) gave impetus to this cause with the publication of *Creeds of Christendom* (3 vols., 1877) and through his efforts in organizing the WORLD ALLIANCE OF REFORMED CHURCHES (1876) and the Evangelical Alliance (1870), which led to cooperation among all Protestants. The PCUSA helped shaped these organizations as well at the Federal Council of Churches (1908), the NATIONAL COUNCIL OF CHURCHES (1950), the WORLD COUNCIL OF CHURCHES (1948), and the CONSULTATION ON CHURCH UNION (COCU, c. 1960) embracing Presbyterians, Episcopalians, and Congregationalists among others. In addition to Speer, JOHN A. MACKAY (1889–1983), HENRY P. VAN DUSEN (1897–1975), and EUGENE CARSON BLAKE (1897–1975) gave support and leadership to these efforts. Blake served as general secretary of the World Council of Churches (1966–1972). The PCUSA joined with the United Presbyterian Church of North America (1854) to form the United Presbyterian Church in the United States of America (1954). It reunited with many Cumberland Presbyterians in 1906, and with the PCUS in 1983, healing the Civil War wound. The Rev. J. Randolph Taylor (1930–2002), a southern Presbyterian, took the leadership in this reunion and presided over the PCUSA as its first moderator in 1982–1983.

The PCUSA moved its headquarters to Louisville, Kentucky. During recent years the church elected its first black moderator, Edler Hawkins (1908–1977) in 1964; its first woman moderator, Lois Stair (1923–1981) in 1972; and its first Korean moderator, Syngman Rhee (1931–) in 2001. It carries on dialogue and cooperates not only with other Protestants worldwide, but with Roman, Orthodox, and Evangelical churches, Jews, Muslims, and other religions (see DIALOGUE, INTER-CONFESSIONAL). The PCUSA has been emphasizing the denomination's responsibilities for peacemaking throughout the world, and keeps an office at the United Nations Organization in New York City. Because of the aging American population and other reasons, the PCUSA has been losing membership. In 2000 the denomination counted 2,525,330 members, 11,178 churches, and 21,065 ministers. In 1984 the denomination added the Scots Confessions (1560) to its Book of Confessions, along with the Westminster Larger Catechism, and in 1991 a Brief Statement of Faith. In the latter, Presbyterians continued to express belief in the Scriptures, the triune God, and the conviction that in life and death Presbyterians belong to God and commit to God's love, the grace of the Lord Jesus Christ, and the communion of the Holy Spirit.

References and Further Reading

Armstrong, Maurice W., Lefferts A. Loetscher, and Charles S. Anderson, eds. *The Presbyterian Enterprise.* Philadelphia, PA: Westminster Press, 1956.
The Book of Confessions. Louisville, KY: Office of the General Assembly, 1991.
Boyd, Lois A., and R. Douglass Brackenridge. *Presbyterian Woman in America.* Westport, CT: Greenwood Press, 1983.
Coalter, M. J., John W. Mulder, and Louis B. Weeks, eds. *The Presbyterian Presence, The Twentieth Century Experience.* 7 vols. Louisville, KY: Westminster/John Knox Press, 1990–1992.
Loetscher, Lefferts. *The Broadening Church.* Philadelphia: University of Pennsylvania Press, 1954.
Murray, Andrew E. *Presbyterian and the Negro—A History.* Philadelphia: Presbyterian Historical Society, 1966.
Smylie, James H. *A Brief History of Presbyterians.* Louisville, KY: Geneva Press, 1996.
Sweet, William Warren. *The Presbyterian 1783–1840, A Collection of Source Materials.* New York: Harper & Brothers, 1936.
Trinterud, Leonard. *The Forming of an American Tradition.* Philadelphia, PA: Westminster Press, 1949.

JAMES H. SMYLIE

PRESBYTERIANISM

Presbyterianism emerged during the REFORMATION, a protest beginning in the fifteenth century against Roman Catholicism. The word derives from the Greek for elder *(presbuteros).* Presbyterians were associated with the Reformed Movement, as distinguished from Lutherans and Anabaptists, mainly on the European continent, and from Anglicans, or Episcopalians, and Congregationalists who emerged in the British Isles. It also spread in the following centuries to North America and to much of the rest of the world to form a

global Presbyterian and Reformed family. This religious movement also influenced educational, economic, political, and cultural shifts that emerged at the time of the Reformation. *The Reform Family Worldwide* (1999), compiled and edited by Jean-Jacques Bauswein and Lukas Visher, provides a detailed overview of this subject.

Presbyterianism was influenced mainly by French-Genevan JOHN CALVIN (1509–1564), through his biblical commentaries, the INSTITUTES OF THE CHRISTIAN RELIGION (1st ed. 1536), essays, and correspondence. His influence spread to FRANCE, GERMANY, HUNGARY, NETHERLANDS, and other places where Protestantism is found. These Christians adopted the BIBLE as the rule of faith and life, asserted a PRIESTHOOD OF ALL BELIEVERS, with simpler forms of WORSHIP, involving the preaching of the Word, the SACRAMENTS OF BAPTISM, (child and adult), and the LORD'S SUPPER. They accepted the Apostles and Nicene Creeds as well as regional doctrinal statements such as the BELGIC CONFESSION (1561), HEIDELBERG CATECHISM (1563), HELVETIC CONFESSION (1566), and later, the Dutch decrees of the Synod of Dort (1610) (see DORT, CANONS OF). This latter favored a view of unconditional ELECTION over JACOBUS ARMINIUS'S view that humans may resist God's grace (see ARMINIANISM). The Reformed adopted a nonhierarchical form of church government, with General Assemblies, SYNODS, Presbyteries, and Sessions, composed of elders—clergy and lay, who preached, taught, and exercised CHURCH DISCIPLINE—along with DEACONS who cared for the welfare of congregations. Hungarians, it should be noted, developed an office of bishops-in-presbytery. Now most Presbyterian churches admit WOMEN to all these offices. Further the Reformed contributed to the rise of public and theological EDUCATION, DEMOCRACY and representative government, and a middle class, INDUSTRIALIZATION, and capitalism. It also contributes to women's rights.

Presbyterianism in the British Isles

The Reformation in Britain was often marked by turmoil and bloodshed in its earliest years beginning with John Wycliffe (c. 1330–1384) and lasting to the end of the seventeenth century. MARTIN LUTHER'S influence was felt in Britain, but HENRY VIII, interested in ENGLAND'S independence from Rome, took reform in his own direction. THOMAS CRANMER (1489–1556) sympathized with Reformed influences. In the THIRTY-NINE ARTICLES (1536–1563), adopted under ELIZABETH I (1533–1603), Anglicans attempted to restate ORTHODOXY with Catholic, Calvinist, and Anabaptist elements. In the meantime SCOTLAND fell under Genevan influence also. JOHN KNOX (c. 1514–1571) composed a Scottish Confession (1560) and encouraged Reformation in Scotland. Scots, such as ANDREW MELVILLE (1545–1622), continued reform. The Reformation ebbed and flowed during the age of the Stuarts, whose reigns were interrupted by the bloody Puritan Revolution under OLIVER CROMWELL (1599–1658). During this period the WESTMINSTER ASSEMBLY (1643–1648) was called. Scots joined Anglicans, Congregationalists, Presbyterians, and Erastians to revise the Thirty-nine Articles. Instead they produced a *Directory of Church Government* (1644), *A Directory of Public Worship* (1645), and the WESTMINSTER CONFESSION with the *Larger and Shorter Catechisms* (1647). The church government tended toward Presbyterianism, and the worship was simple. Presbyterians were Psalm singers, but they were and still are influenced by dissenter ISAAC WATTS (1674–1748), who believed Psalms should be modernized with a Christian focus and that believers could sing hymns of human composition (see HYMNS AND HYMNALS).

The doctrinal statements drew on Augustine Scholastics as well as Calvin. They acknowledged God sovereign, a sovereignty as manifested in the "light of nature," the works of creation and providence, and also emphasized the Bible as the inspired rule for Christian faith and life. They went on to confess God as Trinity, as "wise and holy" in "decrees" and the "COVENANT" made with Adam and all human beings. They confessed human sinfulness, and also God's work of forgiveness, SANCTIFICATION, and SALVATION through Christ's ATONEMENT. They recognize that Christians become members of Christ's body, the CHURCH, through the rite of baptism and are nurtured at the Lord's Supper. Much of these doctrinal statements are devoted to the life of Christians as citizens and civil magistrates in council with one another. Christians look forward to the resurrection and the KINGDOM OF GOD. The Shorter Catechism's first question and answer underscores the purpose of human life:

Q 1. What is the chief end of man?
A 1. Man's chief end is to glorify God and enjoy him forever.

These documents still shape Presbyterianism.

The Assembly could not resolve all questions, especially about PREDESTINATION, which was raised by Arminians, and about church POLITY. These contentions remained and were carried on after the restoration of the Stuarts. With the bloodless GLORIOUS REVOLUTION (1688), William III and Mary of Holland established a Bill of Rights and Settlement, which curbed royal power and brought Scotland and IRELAND under English control with limited TOLERATION.

After 1689, Presbyterianism in England remained in some disarray, at first because of debates over relations with Congregationalists and Unitarians (see UNITARIAN, UNIVERSALIST ASSOCIATION). Later, however, Congregationalists joined with Scottish settlers in north England to form an autonomous Presbyterian Church in 1836. Other such Presbyterian bodies organized, eventually to unite in the Presbyterian Church of England (PCE) in 1876, uniting those who were English, Welsh, Scottish, and Irish by birth. The denomination produced noted scholars such as John Oman (1860–1939). In 1972 the PCE united with other Congregationalists to form the United Reformed Church, embracing most of their members. In 1980 the Reformed Association of Churches of Christ joined this body, which confesses the Apostles and Nicene Creeds, a Statement of Faith adopted at the union in 1972. It ordains women as elders, and numbers approximately 102,600 members. It has been unable recently to keep up its ecumenical concerns to unite with other bodies. The Presbyterian Church of Wales was originally known for its Calvinistic Methodist connection in 1894. It has nearly 53,900 members and close ties to the Reformed family.

The established CHURCH OF SCOTLAND remained in place when England and Scotland united in 1707, although the Westminster Parliament allowed patrons to name ministerial candidates to churches. This act caused a number of eighteenth-century divisions, Seceders and Covenanters, who opposed patron control and oath taking. Presbyterians suffered a major split over patronage in 1843, resulting in the Free Church of Scotland. Over the years denominations were drawn together. In 1929 the FREE CHURCH reunited with the Church of Scotland under Declaratory Articles that defined the new body as both *national* and *free*. The church worship is guided by a Book of Common Order, which emphasizes the reading and interpretation of Scripture, singing, especially Psalms, and which encourages celebration of the Lord's Supper on a monthly basis. It accepts the Apostles and Nicene Creeds, and the Westminster Standards. During the early days of Reform, Scots rejected the episcopal office, but instituted superintendents, ministers, exhorters, and readers. The polity was not fixed, and the church is now governed by a General Assembly and presbyteries, with pastors, elders, and deacons, including women ordained to all offices (see WOMEN CLERGY). During the eighteenth century, layman ROBERT RAIKES (1735–1811) started SUNDAY SCHOOLS, which spread throughout Protestantism. The church promoted MISSIONS worldwide with enthusiasm, DAVID LIVINGSTONE and ROBERT MOFFAT being only two examples of Scottish international reach. Intellectual ferment gave rise to SCOTTISH COMMON SENSE REALISM. DAVID HUME's experimental philosophy stimulated skepticism, Adam Smith's *Wealth of Na-*

tions (1776) advanced industrial capitalism, whereas W. ROBERTSON SMITH helped introduce biblical criticism in the nineteenth century. All had Presbyterian backgrounds. In 2000 the Church of Scotland numbered approximately 1,220,000 members.

Although Roman Catholicism dominated Ireland, Presbyterian ministers founded churches under William and Mary, especially in ULSTER, where they organized an Irish Presbytery (1642). Growing in number, mainly in the North, they were able to organize the Presbyterian Church in Ireland (PCI), confessing the Apostles and Nicene Creeds and Westminster Standards in 1840. Early in the eighteenth century some Presbyterians, dissenting from English rule, began to support home rule in cooperation with Catholics. Because Ireland was divided in 1922 into the Republic of Ireland and Northern Ireland, Ulster Scots Presbyterians and other Protestants have grown anxious about violence involving attempts to unite north and south. Many, however, have attempted to develop common interests among all Christians. The PCI numbers about 308,000 members and cooperates with other Presbyterians in a BRITISH COUNCIL OF CHURCHES founded in 1942.

Presbyterians in North America

During British exploration and colonization of the New World, Presbyterian immigrants began to settle and grow in number (see COLONIALISM). Anglicans and Congregationalists settled first, in Virginia and New England, beginning in the seventeenth century, thus bringing the Reformed movements to the colonies. Presbyterians arrived in force in the eighteenth century, settling mainly in the Middle and Southern colonies. Most were Scotch-Irish. Under the leadership of Francis Makemie (1658–1708) they organized the first Presbytery (1706) and then a Synod (1716), so steady was the migration. They began to develop an indigenous leadership, especially at a log college presided over by William Tennent (1673–1746), finally located in Princeton, New Jersey. The Synod divided, 1741–1758, during the Great AWAKENING, led by JONATHAN EDWARDS (1703–1758) and SAMUEL DAVIES (1723–1761), over the nature of CONVERSION and pastoral leadership. Later, Scot JOHN WITHERSPOON, called to the presidency of the College of New Jersey (later Princeton University), gave leadership to the American Revolution (1776) as the only clergyman to sign the Declaration of Independence. He trained a number of laymen who engaged in writing the American Constitution adopted in 1788. The Synod organized the General Assembly of the PRESBYTERIAN CHURCH in the United States of America (PCUSA) in 1787–1789 with Witherspoon presiding and John Rodgers (1727–

1811) as first moderator. The denomination adopted an American *Directory of Worship,* the *Westminster Standards,* and adopted a *Form of Government and Discipline,* rejecting the establishments of the British Isles. Presbyterians have lived under these documents, with modifications, for over two centuries. During this period they had to deal with ecclesial, national, and international challenges.

As Americans pressed westward, Presbyterianism grew. Presbyterians experienced conflicts within for various reasons. In 1810 some left the denomination to form the CUMBERLAND PRESBYTERIAN CHURCH, differing with others over ordination requirements for frontier ministry and over ARMINIAN sympathies. This division was partially healed in 1906. The Old School (OS)–New School (NS) divided over a Plan of Union (1801), encouraging Presbyterian–Congregationalist cooperation. The Old School held that New Schoolers, many in northern states, were too liberal theologically and were opposed to SLAVERY. After the CIVIL WAR, OS and NS were able to reunite in 1870. Southerners organized the Presbyterian Church in the United States (PCUS) to champion the "spirituality of the church," opposing entanglement in civil affairs. In 1858 Scottish immigrants from the covenanter tradition organized the United Presbyterian Church of North America, which joined resources with the PCUSA in 1958. Finally with the diminishing of racism and sectionalism, the PCUSA and the PCUS reunited in 1983. Korean Presbyterians, it should be noted, have a sizable presence in the United States and have been organizing their own denominations.

Although these various entities differed on some points, they shared some basic agreements. With regard to worship, directories focused on biblical PREACHING, free and liturgical PRAYER, with the baptism of infants and adults, and with celebrating the Lord's Supper at times on a monthly basis. In the liturgical revival of the nineteenth century, the PCUSA began to use a *Book of Common Worship* (1906) for voluntary use. Enlarged in 1993, it is more ecumenical in character and uses inclusive language. Whereas in the Old World, Presbyterians first sang metered Psalms, often ISAAC WATTS paraphrases, they now may also sing hymns of various contemporary poets and musicians. With regard to DOCTRINE, these denominations affirmed the Apostles and Nicene Creeds and the Westminster Standards. However, in 1967 PCUSA adopted a Book of Confessions that, in addition to those mentioned, now includes the SCOTS CONFESSION, Heidelberg Catechism, Second Helvetic Confession, BARMAN DECLARATION of the German CONFESSING CHURCH, a Confession of 1967, and an added Brief Statement of Faith in 1983. Presbyterianism is governed by a General Assembly with Synods and Presbyteries. All offices are open to women, and more and more of them exercise leadership in the denomination. It carries on a global mission in cooperation with Reformed and other Christians. It has been deeply involved in seeking economic justice and civil rights for women and racial minorities worldwide. The PCUSA numbers about 3,644,000 members with about 12,700 congregations. In recent years its membership has aged. It has been losing membership, and has been disrupted with debates over human SEXUALITY and confessing the faith in the twenty-first century.

Because of differences over liberalism involving evolution, HIGHER CRITICISM, and FUNDAMENTALISM, J. GRESHAM MACHEN led an exodus from the PCUSA in the 1930s. In 1973 some conservative bodies, joined by adherents of the PCUS, formed the Presbyterian Church in America. It focuses on ancient ORTHODOXY and the Westminster Standards, and does not ordain women. It numbers nearly 278,000 members.

Although French Catholics first explored and began to settle CANADA, the English took over the area in 1763, and French Protestant (HUGUENOT) immigrants also began to settle there. Immigrants from Scotland and Ireland, joined later by Loyalists from the United States, organized Presbyterianism, shaped by conflicts inherited from the Old World. Secessionists who opposed the patronage laws were among the first to organize in 1817. The Church of Scotland soon founded a Synod in 1833, whereas the Free Church organized in 1843. Then in 1875 these bodies came together to form the Presbyterian Church of Canada in time to meet continuing mission challenges of the west. Neo-Orthodox in theology in recent years, the church affirms the Apostles and Nicene Creeds along with the Heidelberg Catechism, Helvetic Creed, and Westminster Standards. It ordains women to all offices of the denomination. It is the largest Presbyterian body in Canada, with about 267,000 members. Like other denominations it is declining in membership, attributed in part to lack of interest by younger Canadians. In 1925 about 70 percent of its members merged with Congregationalists and Methodists in the UNITED CHURCH OF CANADA, preserving much of the Presbyterian tradition.

Presbyterians of the PCUSA and PCUS, among others, began to converge on MEXICO when it gained independence as a nation from Spain in 1857, beginning a postcolonial life. The educator Melinda Rankin (1811–1888) of the PCUSA crossed the border and helped prepare indigenous pastors and leaders, such as Arcadio Morales (1850–1888), for young churches. The mission spread rapidly and by 1883, through much cooperation, converts were able to organize the National Presbyterian Church in Mexico (NPCM) in 1901. Reconstruction of Mexico after the Revolution (1917) stimulated indigenization of Presbyterianism, although conservative Christians grew in numbers. The NPCM adheres to the Westminster Standards, Confession of Dort, Belgic Confession of 1561, and the Heidelberg Catechism. It is a multilingual community. Women engage in much church work, but are not ordained.

Presbyterianism Worldwide

The Reformed tradition spread globally, from Albania to ZIMBABWE, through European and American colonization and missionary endeavors on a world frontier, beginning in earnest in the eighteenth century. Missionary efforts often went hand in hand with explorers, traders, and settlers to spread the Gospel, especially in connection with the growth of the British Empire. Missionaries carried on their work through VOLUNTARY SOCIETIES, for example, the AMERICAN BOARD OF COMMISSIONERS FOR FOREIGN MISSIONS (ABCFM) founded in 1810, and by denominational boards and agencies of various denominations led by clergy and laity. American Presbyterian layman Robert E. Speer (1867–1947) emerged as a world statesman. These leaders engaged not only in EVANGELISM and conversion but also in education, founding schools at every level, including seminaries, building hospitals, and engaging in other works of PHILANTHROPY and nation-building. This effort by various Presbyterian denominations caused some confusion among indigenous populations. Therefore, even before the postcolonial age, indigenous ecumenical endeavors and theologies emerged in various countries. Furthermore, Presbyterian emphasis on the priesthood of all believers, an educated ministry and membership, and participation in church governance fostered education, DEMOCRACY, and HUMAN RIGHTS along with economic ferment in host countries. Bauswein and Vischer demonstrate how widespread this development was. An early study *Rethinking Missions* (1932), edited and written by WILLIAM ERNEST HOCKING, aided by laymen Speer and Methodist JOHN R. MOTT, underscored the breadth of this development.

Reformed Christians began to evangelize in the Middle East in the middle of the eighteenth century. They found ancient Eastern Orthodox churches there and aimed to reform them, a purpose the Orthodox did not always appreciate (see ORTHODOXY, EASTERN). The ABCFM sent Congregationalists to the area in the early nineteenth century. They were followed by Presbyterians. American Henry H. Jessup (1823–1910) went to Syria where he helped to establish what is now the University of Beirut; his ministry reached all the way to Iran. He spent over fifty-three years in the area, became a missionary statesman, and was offered a diplomatic post by President Chester Arthur, a position he did not take. The UPCNA missionaries built the largest Presbyterian presence in Egypt, beginning with an attempt to revitalize the Coptic church there in 1854. They organized the first Presbyterian Church in Cairo in 1863, and started educational and medical institutions in later years. In 1858 the Coptic Evangelical Church–Synod of the Nile became independent. It holds the Apostles and the Westminster Standards, and claims about 300,000 members. It ordains women to all church offices, and it works for better relations with the Coptic Christians.

Dutch Reformed colonists settled in SOUTH AFRICA as early as 1652 and began to dominate the area. They were followed by English-speaking Presbyterians of the United Presbyterian Church of Scotland, which founded a mission in 1829. In 1897 mission stations around the country founded the Presbyterian Church of Southern Africa, integrated now with about 90,000 adherents living under the Apostles Creed. Scot Robert Moffat took the Gospel north into Rhodesia, now called Zimbabwe. The Presbyterian Church of Africa, an all-black denomination, was started under the leadership of Pamboni Mzimba in 1898. The denomination now claims 927,000 members. It lives under the Apostle's Creed and the Westminster Standards, and ordains women to all offices of the church.

Central Africa was colonized first by FRANCE and then by Belgium, which exploited its resources. PCUS missionaries began to found churches there in 1891 whose influence spread through the Kasai. In the first decade of the twentieth century missionaries William H. Sheppard, an African American, and William M. Morrison won Congolese hearts and minds by protesting the brutal exploitation of Africans by King Leopold. They exposed his company's injustices to natives for not making their rubber quotas. The Presbyterian Community of Kinshasa founded a Synod in 1955, subscribes to the Apostles Creed and Westminster Standards, and ordains women to all church offices. It claims 1,250,000 members, is a member of the Church of Christ in Zaire, and is deeply concerned about civil rights not only in Central Africa but elsewhere. The Presbyterian Church of NIGERIA began in 1846 under the leadership of freed slaves from Jamaica sent out by the Church of Scotland. Later, missionary MARY SLESSOR (1848–1915) carried on work as a teacher, preacher, and health provider—and promoted reform in this Muslim country. Through her work, along with that of others, the church grew and became autonomous in 1954. It accepts the Apostles and Nicene Creeds and the Westminster Standards, and ordains women to all offices of the church. It has almost 124,000 members and is engaged in extended

medical work throughout the country. It should be noted that freed American slaves sent out by the AMERICAN COLONIZATION SOCIETY in 1822 helped found LIBERIA and assisted in building a Presbyterian Church there. There is a strong Reformed place in countries such as Ghana and Cameroon.

Presbyterians also traveled down under to Oceania and built churches in AUSTRALIA and NEW ZEALAND as well as INDONESIA. Although the Dutch touched base in the area in the sixteenth and seventeenth centuries, Scottish Presbyterians and Congregationalists settled there early in the nineteenth century. In 1840 Presbyterians established the Synod of Australia connected with the Church of Scotland. Even though they experienced disagreements over the years, they were able to unite as the Presbyterian Church in Australia in 1901. In 1977 many went into the UNITING CHURCH IN AUSTRALIA with Methodists, holding to a presbyterial structure. The denomination holds to a range of Reformed Confessions as well as JOHN WESLEY *Sermons* as its affirmation of faith. It has a membership of about 1,386,000. About 70,000 adherents continue in the Presbyterian Church in Australia.

British settlement of New Zealand began as early as 1814. By 1840 Presbyterians were able to form congregations as Scots of various denominations continued to move down under. They were able to unite in 1901. The Presbyterian Church of Aotearoa, New Zealand adheres to the Apostles Creed, Westminster Standards, and a New Zealand Statement of Faith. Australian and New Zealand Presbyterians carry on a number of ministries in a variety of indigenous languages.

Portuguese Roman Catholics planted Christianity in South America. Later Calvin himself sent pastors to BRAZIL to serve Huguenot settlers encouraged by the French government to move there. Later Reformed and Presbyterian missionaries planted churches in various countries on the continent, for example, Argentina, Chile, and Peru. When the Brazilian government broadened its religious toleration in the nineteenth century, Scot Robert Reid Kalley (1809–1882), a Presbyterian physician, founded a congregation in 1858. A year later Ashbel Green Simonton of the PCUS arrived in Rio de Janeiro to spread the Word and organized a presbytery in 1865. The PCUSA missionaries joined this effort and, together with the PCUS, built the strong Presbyterian Church of Brazil (PCB) in the 1880s. Others with a sense of Brazilian enterprise organized an indigenous Independent Presbyterian Church (IPCB) in 1903 under the leadership of Eduardo Pereira. The PCB adheres to the Apostles Creed and Westminster Standards. It has approximately 480,000 members, with no women officers. The IPCB also adheres to the Apostles Creed and

Westminster Standards and ordains women ministers. A number of ethnic churches have emerged. Over the years Brazilians have strengthened bonds of the Reformed family in the nation. JOHN A. MACKAY, another Scot who had studied in Spain, served as educator in Peru. There is still a Peruvian Presbyterian presence.

Presbyterians also spread to Asian lands, such as, CHINA, KOREA, and JAPAN. Although Christianity had been planted in the area earlier by Roman Catholics, Scottish missionaries arrived in China as early as 1807. They were followed by other Presbyterians from Britain and the United States who translated the Bible and spread the Gospel (see BIBLE TRANSLATION). They believed, as did other Christians, that if China could be won to Christianity, the whole world would be converted. By 1906 Presbyterian churches, joined by the Reformed Church in America, formed a Council of Presbyterian Churches. By 1927 this body, in a spirit of cooperation, joined other Christians to form the Church of Christ in China. Western interest in China and the Chinese was stirred by author Pearl S. Buck, a missionary educator of the PCUSA. Her novel *The Good Earth* (1931) awakened the world to the struggles of Chinese peasants. The Church of Christ centers its attention on the Bible, and adheres to the person and work of Christ and the Apostles Creed. It holds to the Presbyterian form of government. After the repression of churches under the Peoples Republic of China, Presbyterians in the postcolonial and post-denominational age cooperate with the China Christian Council and affirm the Three-Self Formula popularized by Presbyterian John L. Nevius (1829–1893), that is, the call to build self-governing, self-supporting, and self-propagating churches to serve the whole Christian community (see POST-COLONIALISM).

Presbyterianism has grown fastest over the years in Korea, often ruled by its neighbors through the centuries. Jesuits first planted the Gospel in Korea in the eighteenth century and were persecuted. Later a layman, Suh Sang-Yoon, was converted in 1876 while in Manchuria by Scottish missionaries, and helped to translate the New Testament in Korean. He brought it home and formed a small Christian community. PCUSA missionaries, Horace Allen, a physician, and Horace G. and Lilias Underwood, also a physician, arrived with others to evangelize, establish schools and seminaries, and offer medical care. They began to build the Korean church. In a Revival Movement of 1907, led by Presbyterian Sun-Joo Kim (1869–1935), Presbyterianism spread with the use of the Three-Self Formula. The Korean Presbyterians seemed to flourish in difficult times under Japanese domination and Korea's authoritarian governments, protesting such oppression in a Theological Declaration (1973). Although Korean Presbyterianism is divided into a

bewildering number of denominations, there are four large bodies. The Presbyterian Church of Korea (Hap Dong) numbers around 2,160,000 members, the Presbyterian Church of Korea (Dong Hap) records 2,095,300 adherents, the Presbyterian Church in the Republic of Korea (Ki Jang) has 326,000 supporters, and the Presbyterian Church in Korea (Ke Shin), ministers to 363,000 Koreans. Some of these bodies are more liberal than others; some are fundamentalists. Most hold to the Apostles Creed and Westminster Standards, and the largest ordain women to all offices of the church. Korean Presbyterians have spread across the world to build congregations and denominations, to carry on EVANGELISM, and to make contributions to their adopted countries. For example, Syngman Rhee, with roots in North Korea, served as moderator of PCUSA in 1999. He encourages and works for the unification of North and South Korea, and for contacts with other Christians of the area. Presbyterian missionaries established churches in Japan, and many converts belong to the United Church of Christ in Japan (Kyodan), founded in 1941. Presbyterians motivated Toyohiko Kogawa, noted Japanese reformer.

The Dutch also planted the Reformed tradition in INDIA as early as the seventeenth century. In the nineteenth century Scottish Presbyterians sent Alexander Duff (1806–1878) to India. He and others began to established churches, schools, and hospitals. Presbyterians tended to identify with untouchables, challenge the caste system, and tried to impart a sense of dignity to India's masses. Later American Presbyterians, such as layman Sam Higginbotton (1874–1959), and the PCUSA mission introduced modern agricultural methods to Indians and founded Allahbad University (1932). His wife, Lilias, cared for India's lepers. Over the years Presbyterians joined other Protestant denominations to form the CHURCH OF SOUTH INDIA (1947) and the CHURCH OF NORTH INDIA (1970). The Presbyterian Church of India (PCI), in Northeast India, began under Welch mission efforts in 1841. The first presbytery was organized in 1867, followed by a Synod formed in 1896 and a General Assembly. This is the largest such body in the area. The church allows Synods much freedom. The PCI adheres to the Apostles Creed and Westminster Confession, and ordains women as ministers. It carries on a multilingual mission and counts almost 798,000 members. Presbyterianism has been at work in Pakistan as early as 1849 in Lahore.

As already indicated, the ecclesiastical bodies mentioned here represent only a few of the larger Presbyterian bodies founded by the British and North Americans, and more recently by mission efforts of younger churches. They do not embrace the accomplishments of the larger Reformed family. Over centuries these efforts have shaped the worldwide community of independent bodies of diverse ETHNICITY. They have given rise to cultural revivals in various parts of the world and to indigenous theologies and programs. As also suggested, Presbyterians have had their differences and divisions, although they have continued to confess belief in the one, holy, catholic, and apostolic church, and they have cooperated, mended divisions, and still seek the unity of the whole Christian community. In 1875 they joined other Reformed bodies to organize the WORLD ALLIANCE OF REFORMED CHURCHES throughout the world holding to the Presbyterian system (WARC), headquartered first in Knox's Scotland, now in Calvin's Geneva. American Presbyterian PHILIP SCHAFF (1819–1893), born in SWITZERLAND, played a leading role in founding this body. In 1970 WARC merged with the International Congregational Council to found WARC (Presbyterian and Congregational), with 211 denominational affiliates, and numbering an estimated 70,000,000 members.

Presbyterians have also fostered ecumenical endeavors in their own countries, such as the NATIONAL COUNCIL OF CHURCHES and Churches Uniting in Christ in the USA, and world conferences, such as the EDINBURGH MISSION CONFERENCE (1910) and the LAUSANNE CONFERENCE (1927) to promote theological consensus among Christians. They were present at the founding of the WORLD COUNCIL OF CHURCHES (1948) in Geneva, often led by Presbyterians, such as Scot JOSEPH H. OLDHAM (1874–1969) and American EUGENE CARSON BLAKE (1906–1985). They have promoted INTERCONFESSIONAL DIALOGUE, not only with other Protestants but also with Roman Catholic and Orthodox churches, and built bridges to non-Christians, Jews, Muslims, and others, while still holding to the transforming power of Christ. They have also supported the CHURCH WORLD SERVICE, the United Nations, and defended human rights as a witness to Christian life as well as faith.

See also Anabaptism; Anglicanism; Congregationalism; Lutheranism; Methodism

References and Further Reading

Agbiti, J. Kofi. *West African Church History, 1886–1991.* Leiden, The Netherlands: Brill, 1991. [passim M414A264]

Bauswein, Jean-Jacques, and Lukas Vischer, eds. *The Reformed Family Worldwide, A Survey of Reformed Churches, Theological Schools, and International Organizations.* Grand Rapids, MI: Wm. B. Eerdmans, 1999.

Benedetto, Robert, Darrell L. Guder, and Donald K. McKim. *Historical Dictionary of Reformed Churches.* Landham, MD: Scarecrow Press, 1999. [Especially Bibliography, 359–482, and appendices.]

Bolam, C. Gordon, Jeremy Goring, H. L. Short, and Roger Thomas. *The English Presbyterians, from Elizabethan Puritanism to Modern Unitarianism.* Boston: Beacon Press, 1996.

Brooke, Peter. *Ulster Presbyterianism: The Historical Perspective, 1610–1970.* 2nd ed. Belfast, Northern Ireland: Athol Book, 1994.

Brown, Arthur Judson. *One Hundred Years: A History of the Foreign Missionary Work of the Presbyterian Church in the U.S.A.* New York: Fleming H. Revell, 1936.

Brown, G. Thompson. *Earthen Vessels and Transcendent Power: American Presbyterians in China, 1837–1952.* Maryknoll, NY: Orbis Books, 1997.

———. *Not by Might: A Century of Presbyterians in Korea.* Atlanta, GA: General Assembly Mission Board, Presbyterian Church (U.S.A.), 1984.

Coalter, Milton J., John Mulder, and Louis B. Weeks, eds. *The Presbyterian Experience.* 7 vols. Louisville, KY: John Knox, 1991–1995.

Drury, Clifford M., ed. *Four Hundred Years of World Presbyterianism.* San Francisco: Privately published, 1961. [Microfilm]

Elder, Earl E. *Vindicating A Vision: The Story of the American Mission in Egypt, 1854–1954.* Philadelphia, PA: United Presbyterian Board of Publication, 1958.

Isichei, Elizabeth. *A History of Christianity in Africa.* Grand Rapids, MI: Wm. B. Eerdmans, 1995.

Moir, John S. *Enduring Witness: A History of the Presbyterian Church in Canada.* Toronto, Canada: Presbyterian Publications, 1975.

Pierson, Paul E. *A Younger Church in Search of Maturity: Presbyterianism in Brazil from 1910 to 1959.* San Antonio, TX: Trinity University, 1973.

Scrimgeour, Robert J. *Some Scots Were Here: A History of the Presbyterian Church in South Australia, 1839–1977.* Adelaide, Australia: Lutheran Publishing House, 1994.

Singh, D. V., ed. *History of Christianity in India.* 6 vols. Bangalore: Church History Association of India, 1982–.

Smylie, James H. *A Brief History of Presbyterians.* Louisville, KY: Geneva Press, 1996.

———, ed. "American Presbyterians in India/Pakistan, 150 Years." *Journal of Presbyterian History* 62 no. 3 (Fall 1984): 198–281.

Thompson, Ernest Trice. *Presbyterians in the South.* 3 vols. Richmond, VA: John Knox, 1963–1973.

JAMES H. SMYLIE

PRESBYTERIAN CHURCH GOVERNMENT

The theological premise that the will of God must be sought in community is the foundation of Presbyterian POLITY. With historical roots in the Scottish reformation, PRESBYTERIANISM has developed a form of government distinctly different from episcopal and congregational polities. LAITY and CLERGY together make decisions under this polity. Different levels of governing bodies interact to create mutual accountability. At its best, Presbyterian government allows the delicate balance between the wisdom of the community and the prophetic voice of the individual to work together toward discerning the will of God. When this balance has not been maintained, however, Presbyterian polity has been particularly susceptible to schism and denominationalism.

The origins of polity in Presbyterian churches, like their THEOLOGY, lie in the Scottish Reformation of JOHN KNOX, and before that, in JOHN CALVIN's Geneva. From these sources Presbyterians derived the ordained offices of their polity, as well as their hierarchical structure of governing bodies. The adoption of the WESTMINSTER CONFESSION of Faith in the seventeenth century as the sole confessional standard of Presbyterian denominations until the mid-twentieth century brought to these churches a tension between the ORTHODOXY of the community and the individual right of conscience. Ongoing disputes as to the degree of adherence to the Westminster Confession required of ordained offices, particularly in the Presbyterian denominations in the UNITED STATES, reflected this tension, and deeply shaped the balance of AUTHORITY within the Presbyterian form of government.

Theologically, Presbyterian polity rests on a Reformed concern that leaving decision making in the church to individual church leaders, particularly in a hierarchical structure, has the potential to corrupt the CHURCH, given humanity's fallen nature. On the other hand, with the bywords "all things decently and in order," Presbyterians, consistent with their Reformed roots, place a high priority on orderly governance. Presbyterians thus believe that decisions made in community reflect God's covenant with humanity, and that seeking to discern God's will in this way imitates the communion of the triune God.

Presbyterians recognize the ordained offices of DEACON, elder, and minister of Word and Sacrament, tracing the roots of each to the New Testament church. Deacons do not have specific governing responsibilities but rather carry out ministry to persons in need or distress. Both elders (in some traditions called "ruling elders") and ministers (in some traditions called "teaching elders") are presbyters (from the Greek word *presbuteros* or elder) responsible for the government of the church at all levels. At all levels above the congregation, elders and ministers are typically represented in as equal a number as possible in all decision-making bodies.

Governing Bodies

Although hierarchical in appearance, governing bodies in Presbyterian denominations have a more complex interrelationship. Sessions, consisting of elders elected for a term and the minister or ministers serving a congregation, govern individual congregations. Presbyteries oversee the work of local congregations and carry out mission within their bounds. Synods and general assemblies (some Presbyterian denominations have both; other smaller denominations either call their highest governing body a SYNOD or have a general assembly without synods) care for the broader mission of the church and resolve disputes as to DOCTRINE and practice.

Deacons and elders are elected and ordained by local congregations. Ministers are ordained only by the presbyteries. The reservation of these rights to congregations and presbyteries serves as a check on what could otherwise become the dominating power of a general assembly (or in some Presbyterian denominations, the SYNOD) to control the church. In addition, all powers not specifically delegated to other bodies are reserved to the presbyteries.

A core component of Presbyterian polity is expressed in the Westminster Confession of Faith: "God alone is Lord of the conscience, and hath left it free from the doctrines and commandments of men which are in anything contrary to his Word, or beside it, in matters of faith or worship." Thus, although the elders on a session are elected by the congregation, and members of higher governing bodies are elected by lower governing bodies, Presbyterian polity is not a representative DEMOCRACY. Rather, members of governing bodies are commissioned to seek God's will in their decision making. This obligation to faithfully seek the will of God can allow a fruitful tension between the prophetic voice of the individual and the collective wisdom of the community. However, when a persistent minority concludes that the majority has not found God's will, the high value placed on individual conscience tends to lead to schism, as evidenced by the fractious history of Presbyterian denominations both in SCOTLAND and the United States.

Presbyterian polity differs from episcopal polity in its distrust of vesting power in individual religious leaders, particularly bishops, and by relationships between its various levels of governing bodies that are based on mutual accountability, rather than a hierarchical structure. On the other hand, Presbyterian polity rejects the autonomy vested in local congregations under congregational polities based on the view that the lack of mutual accountability between different levels of church government makes each more likely to err.

Presbyterian polity has been troubled in recent years by conflicting tendencies toward more hierarchical vesting of power in national governing bodies and a local tendency toward CONGREGATIONALISM. This tension is compounded by growing consumerism among church members, which makes obtaining commitments to lay leadership difficult on a consistent basis. On the other hand, in a period of community breakdown and resulting alienation, Presbyterian polity offers a model of community decision making in which the will of God is sought together, and the body of Christ built up and renewed.

See also Bishop and Episcopacy

References and Further Reading

Chapman, William E. *History and Theology in the Book of Order: Blood on Every Page.* Louisville, KY: Witherspoon Press, 1999.

Gray, Joan S., and Joyce C. Tucker. *Presbyterian Polity for Church Officers.* 3rd ed. Louisville, KY: Geneva Press, 1999.

Loetscher, Lefferts A. *A Brief History of the Presbyterians.* 4th ed. Philadelphia, PA: Westminster Press, 1983.

JAMES A. WILSON

PRIESTHOOD OF ALL BELIEVERS

Although formulated for a narrower historical range, the title of Hans von Campenhausen's magisterial study, *Ecclesiastical Authority and Spiritual Power in the Church of the First Three Centuries,* describes a definitive tension in the larger Christian tradition. Priest and prophet, apostle and charismatically endowed congregation, duly called pastor and energized LAITY confront one another uneasily in the church's sources and history, commonly contending over leadership, sometimes coming together in mission and service. The phrase "priesthood of all believers," historically associated with MARTIN LUTHER and the REFORMATION, arises from the side of spiritual power. It has been used as a critical principle over against perceived clerical domination; positively, to describe the vocations of the faithful in everyday life. In Protestantism the priesthood of all believers has been invoked for more democratic forms of church governance.

The Sources

Appealing to a prior authority of the Scripture, Protestant theories of the priesthood of all believers have emerged out of conversation with the Old and New Testaments. Whatever the disclaimers, though, TRADITION has also played a significant part in the discussion.

In the Old Testament, priesthood is generally associated with rituals of sacrifice. So, for example, in Leviticus and Numbers, priestly codes are spelled out, defining both the quality and quantity of the appropriate sacrifices in circumstances that demand them. The priests' office derives its authority from this sacrificial service, which is understood to maintain the community's standing in relation to the divine COVENANT.

Embedded deeply within the Old Testament narrative, however, lies a trenchant critique of priestly claims, predating the emergence of the sacrificial cultus and accompanying it. As the definitive priest, responsible for prescribing ritual by mediating God's law, Moses is also the original prophet, setting standards for its authenticity (Numbers 12:6–8). Also a priest, Samuel has a standing defined by the spiritual power with which he has been endowed—he is a charismatic judge, overseeing the legitimate functions of authority in the community (I Samuel 8:10–22). Later prophets, like Hosea and Amos, evidence greater distance from the priestly cultus. "I hate, I despise your festivals . . ." God says in the hearing of Amos, "Even though you offer me your burnt offerings and grain offerings, I will not accept them" (5: 21). If the priest's authority is defined by association with sacrifice, the prophet's arises exclusively out of the divine word, with which he has been entrusted as speaker.

With the distinction in forms of authority, the prophets also set out a different standard for the covenant community. The ritual cleanliness required for sacrifice gets replaced by justice and righteousness, defined in terms of particular forms of service—to the widow, the alien, and the poor, for example. It is in this sense that the people of Israel are spoken of as a "nation of priests" or a "priestly kingdom" (Exodus 19:2). God has made covenant with Israel for the sake of the other nations of the world, a theme struck resoundingly in the books of Ruth, Jonah, and Isaiah.

Apocalyptically charged, shaped by Christ's death and resurrection, the New Testament emerges out of the prophetic tradition of ministry and radicalizes it accordingly. The tension between official authority and spiritual power is tipped so decisively in favor of an outpouring that offices survive only at the margins, in emergent forms. There are several factors in this tipping.

One factor is historical origins. Identified with Nazareth in Galilee, Jesus comes from the Diaspora, where the normative form of WORSHIP was not sacrifice but the PREACHING and teaching services of the synagogue. The Gospels report various visits to the temple in Jerusalem, where the rituals of sacrifice continued to be practiced, but they are fraught with conflict—whether in the report of a child prodigy confounding the elders (Luke 2:41–52), more spectacularly in an onslaught on the money changers and temple profiteers (Matthew 21:12–17), or in the quiet prophecy before the passion, "Do you see these great buildings? Not one stone will be left upon another" (Mark 13:2).

A second factor involves Jesus's mission. Baptized by John, Jesus from the beginning identifies himself with sinners in need of renewal and promises the transcending of such moral overhaul in a BAPTISM of the Spirit (Luke 3:15–22). He travels through the countryside as a wandering rabbi, gathering adherents—twelve disciples, formally identified as such, and untold others, including among them women who take a critical role in the narrative, crucially identified with the passion and the resurrection. Breaking moral and GENDER boundaries, Jesus presses at the geographic borders of the sacred as well, reaching out to those excluded by ETHNICITY: among the tax collectors and prostitutes there are also Roman soldiers (as well as their terrorist counterpart, zealots), Syro-phoenicians, and Samaritans.

However, the decisive factor in this tipping from the official is the cross and the resurrection. For the community that he gathered, the death of Jesus was a disaster of such proportions that not even the Easter accounts could negate it. "We had hoped he would be the redemption of Israel," Cleopas and his companion say, speaking in the past perfect without knowing the identity of the one to whom they speak (Luke 24:21). Jesus appears as both the crucified and the risen one, bearing the marks of his death even as he appears from beyond it.

The sacrificial tradition of Israel plays a critical part in the church's interpretation of the death of Jesus. Although the terminology is different, the conceptuality of the sacrificial tradition serves as a container for the Christ hymn of Philippians 2:5–11, one of the earliest Christian creeds: "he emptied himself, taking on the form of a servant, becoming obedient unto death, even death on a cross." Speaking specifically against Israel's sacrificial cultus, the Letter to the Hebrews describes Jesus's sacrifice as "once for all" (Hebrews 7:27), the ultimate fulfillment, and therefore completion and end. In effect the death of Jesus is the final manifestation of his own words, familiar from the prophetic tradition but now enacted, "I desire mercy, not sacrifice" (Matthew 9:13).

Once Jesus's cross has torn open the temple curtain (Mark 15:38), the resurrection follows as apocalyptic outpouring. Manifesting him as Lord, God in the flesh (Romans 1:4), Easter also reveals a new condition of life, in which the gifts of the end time—forgiveness of sins, deliverance from death and its allied powers—are present realities. As such, the resurrection places every earthly power, whether official or unofficial, in question, and turns loose a divine flood in the everyday.

The Apostle Paul declares the negation, most emphatically in I Corinthians 15. Risen from the dead, Christ is presently undermining "every ruler, and every authority and power," and will complete this mission when death itself is suborned (vss. 23–25). A present reality among believers, this hope delayed the development of offices in the Christian community for

virtually a century. "Call no man on earth your father," Jesus is quoted as saying, "you have one father, who is in heaven" (Matthew 23:9). The apostles, so important in the Gospel accounts and in the early mission of the church, are told in the midst of self-promotion that the first will be last (Mark 9:35) and exposed again and again in the narratives for their foolishness. Peter can only be "the rock" (Matthew 16:13–28) when he is also identified as three times the betrayer. In fact, the office of apostle is so closely associated with Jesus's historic presence that it is restricted to the first generation. Thus Paul describes himself as the "least of the apostles" or "afterbirth" (I Corinthians 15:8).

Given the political necessities of communal life—such as "waiting on tables," in Acts—some official function would be demanded, no matter how powerful the critique. In fact, the two congregations that appear in the New Testament—in Jerusalem and Corinth—both show some movement in this direction. In Jerusalem, Luke, considered the author of both the Gospel and the Acts of the Apostles, is particularly concerned to show the divine origin of the apostolate and describes the election of deacons, called to other forms of service while the apostles preach. Confronted by the claims of Corinthians who believe that the resurrection has carried them beyond all earthly limits, Paul is at some pains to move beyond a merely personal to a more public authority. In the Pastoral Epistles, toward the end of the New Testament period, three offices are developing: with the deacons there are also bishops and presbyters. However, as Ernst Schweizer observed conclusively, "there is no theory of church order in the New Testament." Jesus's lordship leaves every human office in shards, which have value only in their connection with him.

Terminating the sacrificial, undermining the official, with the cross the resurrection of Jesus is also an outpouring. In Luke's account this happens at Pentecost. The Spirit of the risen Christ, sent to the church after his ascension into heaven, breaks out in wind and flame. In the process the ethnic and linguistic borders that have divided the human community are blown, burned away like so many leaves—"they all heard the word, each in his own language" (Acts 2:8). With this, through the apostolic preaching, the Spirit assaults a host of other impediments, be they economic, social, political, or immunological. Christ's resurrection has released the Spirit of life in a world previously under the uncontested control of death.

In a passage beloved of various Protestant traditions, Paul defines "GRACE" or *charis* in the Greek, in terms of the resurrection: "the wages of sin is death but the free gift of grace is eternal life in Christ Jesus our Lord" (Romans 6:23). As the power of the resurrection, grace manifests itself in the life of the believer as well as the larger community in the shape of particular gifts, given for service—*charis*—at the same time that it carries those so possessed by the Spirit beyond death, also producing *charismata,* specific endowments given for service in the mundane relations of everyday. So endowed, those graced by the Spirit of the risen Christ become *charismatic*—the Spirit has invested its particular gifts, whether prophecy or administration or otherwise, in the continuing reclamation of a rebellious world that was begun in Christ's death.

Not surprisingly, given deep rootage in the prophetic tradition, in Paul's language the Spirit's outpouring results in a reorientation of the language of sacrifice. "Present your bodies as a living sacrifice, holy and acceptable to God," he writes when he turns to the earthly dimensions of grace, "which is your spiritual worship" (Romans 12:1–2). Justifying the godless, the triune God turns sacrifice away from ritual qualification and appeasement, taking hold of the body—the self in all of its concrete dimensions and relationships—to make believers useful to the divine purpose of the Creator, in the creation and with other creatures. The self-seeking, heaven-storming, religious person, intent on gaining control over the powers of death, in being released from such bondage is turned back to the creation in the confidence that bringing in the new creation, the Holy Spirit can make even such a creature some earthly good.

Whether in Luke's historicizing account or Paul's more theological treatment, their vision of the outpouring opened by Christ's death and resurrection is shared by all the New Testament. "All authority, in heaven and earth, has been given to me," Jesus says in Matthew 28:19–20. On this basis the community is called to "go and make disciples of all nations" by baptizing and preaching. When the work is complete, in the authority and power of the risen Christ, the whole creation—in Ephesians and Colossians, the whole cosmos—will have been restored. Then, according to Revelation 21, there will be no temple, neither any church. Both ecclesiastical authority and spiritual power will have been transcended by the presence of God.

Given the historic tension between ecclesiastical office and spiritual authority, it is to be expected that even having been overwhelmed in the defining events of the New Testament, the official side would reassert itself soon. The lack of a comprehensive theory of church order left an opening to be filled; the disorder of the Pauline congregations, seemingly in constant conflict, and the press of community maintenance combined with other factors to move the church in this direction. So in the post-Apostolic fathers, as traditionally named, what began in the later reaches of the New Testament continues to develop. Ignatius of Antioch, for example, reflecting regional theories of leadership, can make the presence of the bishop, or someone appointed by him, necessary to the gathering of the church.

Ignatius's employment of local Antiochene tradition points to the ongoing influence of nonbiblical, nontheological factors in the development of church order. The various traditions within the Christian faith—Orthodox, Catholic, or Protestant—commonly appeal to the Scripture for ratification of a particular theory, whether for official authority or spiritual power. In fact the appeal is generally cloaked in terms of necessity with claims to the eternally proper or only correct form, although communal leadership, no matter what the scale, is also a political matter. Thus transient factors such as traditional leadership patterns, local circumstance, and current need have a dramatic way of affecting what is said to be eternal.

The office of BISHOP becomes particularly strategic with the growth of the church, the bishops being effectively senior pastors in larger parishes, served in turn by presbyters or priests and deacons. Occasionally, there is a minority voice from the other side—Tertullian, in North Africa, for example—and the laity may retain the power of election in various communities, as they did with such legendary bishops as Ambrose and Augustine. By the second century, however, the New Testament balance has changed, ecclesiastical office claiming the ascendancy.

Two events are critical in subsequent developments of church order. One is the Constantinian and Theodosian settlement, in the fourth century, in which Christianity became established as the religion of the Roman Empire. As it joined the state, sharing the coercive power necessary to maintaining a common order, the church bureaucratized its ministry. The bishop is now a regional official, on par with a magistrate, enforcing ORTHODOXY, overseeing a staff of ministers. Another signal event is the fall of Rome and the later loss to militant Islam of safe passage through the Mediterranean. With public life atomized, reduced to its smallest components, the local bishop and under him the parish priest became the local embodiment of the church.

The office that benefited most significantly from these developments is the papacy. Into the fifth century the bishop of Rome is one office holder among others, advancing the same ultimate claims for himself as bishops in Alexandria, Antioch, or Constantinople. However, a series of dramatically powerful popes—Leo I, Gregory I, and later Gregory VII, with or without the theorizing of Pope Damasus and Gelasius—consolidated the powers of the Roman bishopric, making it the one workable international office in early medieval Europe. Thirteenth-century figures like Innocent III and Boniface VIII completed the process, describing the papacy in sacerdotal terms as the physical embodiment of Christ's rule on earth. Such a sacerdotalism makes any talk of a tension between ecclesiastical authority and spiritual power an abstraction.

Luther and the Reformation

Traditionally Protestants have told the story of the Reformation as a narrative of biblical recovery—Luther leading the way back to the Scripture. In fact, there is an element of truth to the old account. With a newly minted doctorate Luther was a professor of biblical studies, working his way particularly through the Psalms and Paul's letters, especially to the Romans. Sometime late in the teens of the sixteenth century, the date perennially disputed, Luther came to what for the later Middle Ages was an unusual way of reading the texts, in terms of their apocalyptic meaning, with a particular emphasis on the cross. The result was an exegetical revolution.

Revolutions, no matter how radical, are generally not driven by exegesis alone. A maelstrom of historic causes gathered around his early protest, swirling, accelerating, propelling his initial complaints into a protest as wide as Northern Europe. Some of the factors were regional, particularly a long-standing hostility to Mediterranean dominance. Other were socioeconomic, the most important being population growth and a developing cash economy that combined to force migration from farm to city. A powerful Moslem military threat, sporadic outbursts of plague, and a pervasive disgust with public morality all fed a profound sense of the nearness of the end times.

In this mix Luther's appeal to the priesthood of all believers proved catalytic. As he himself worked with it, the argument moved in both of the directions set classically in the New Testament. Initially it was a critique of an ECCLESIOLOGY dominated by office, restoring what von Campenhausen called the "spiritual power" side of the tension, even if such language would be strange to Luther. As such, the critique did not develop into a full-blown doctrine of church governance in either Luther or the Lutheran confessions, definitive for the church that still bears his name. With its critical edge, however, the priesthood of believers was also linked to what has been called "the doctrine of vocation," which for Luther specified the place of Christian service.

In the view of Luther as well as the humanist reformers gathered around Erasmus—HULDRYCH ZWINGLI, JOHANNES OECOLAMPADIUS, MARTIN BUCER,

and others—the medieval papacy was predicated on the sacrifice of the mass (see LORD'S SUPPER). This dogma, officially defined by the Fourth Lateran Council in 1215, held that in presenting the transubstantiated elements of the sacrament—the bread and wine having become the actual historic body and blood of Jesus of Nazareth—the priest performing the sacramental action was effectively re-presenting Christ's sacrifice to God. Just as the authority of the Old Testament priesthood derived from the sacrificial act, the authority of the pope as *sacerdos,* physically embodying Christ on earth, derived from the sacrament. Through the bishops, the papacy controlled both those who administered the sacrament, legitimizing ordination, and those allowed to participate and therefore benefit, through the sacrament of communion. The cutting edge of papal authority was in excommunication, exclusion from the sacrament or in its greater form, membership in the larger community.

The Upper Rhine reformers, students of Erasmus concentrated in Southwest GERMANY and SWITZERLAND, attacked this theory of authorization of the papacy by denying the connection between the historic body of Christ and his Eucharistic presence, in the elements. So doing, they set footings for much of modern Protestantism, in which the sacrament has historically been interpreted as a memorial meal.

Luther went a different direction. Reaching back into the prophetic tradition of the Old Testament as interpreted in the New, he argued that the means of Christ's presence is God's word, whether in its preached or sacramental form. As the vehicle or means of God's presence, the word is at the same time God's power at work in the human community to affect the divine purposes. Thus "priesthood" and "sacrifice" have both been reoriented—instead of humankind's service to God, they are exercised in proclamation of the word that bespeaks God's presence in Christ for the restoration of the creation. Instead of simply communicating information, which must then be understood by reason and applied by the will, the word in its preached and sacramental forms actually accomplishes God's intentions among the faithful for the larger world.

Early on in what became the Reformation, Luther did not spell out some of the more radical consequences of his interpretation. However, as the papal bureaucracy moved to quell what was becoming a major uprising in Germany, Luther became more and more specific about the implications. Two of the great treatises of 1520, *The Babylonian Captivity of the Church* and *To the German Nobility,* set benchmarks in his critique of the medieval church. "Therefore," he writes in the former, analyzing the medieval sacramental system, "I can have mass every day. For I can set before me the word of God." Then, having broken the papal sacramental lock on God's grace, he called on the German nobility to put its hands to the reformation of the church. Because the means of God's activity in the human community is the word, it can be both held over and against those who claim it and spoken by all who hear it. "The Word of God is incomparably superior to the church," he can write.

As the Wittenberg reform unfolded, Luther continued to use the concept of the priesthood of all believers critically. So, for example, in *The Right and Power of a Christian Congregation or Community to Judge all Teaching and to Call, Appoint and Dismiss Teachers, Established and Proved from Scripture,* he argued that the word's authorization of the community gives it a basis to challenge unfaithful CLERGY. Similarly, in *Concerning the Ministry,* Luther wrote to a congregation of Hussites who were without a properly ordained pastor that given the presence of the word, they could elect one of their own, setting that person aside for preaching and the administration of the SACRAMENTS.

As tellingly as he brought the critique, however, Luther did not develop the priesthood of all believers into a formal DOCTRINE or theory of church order. Neither did the Lutheran confessors. The concept of the priesthood of believers is altogether absent from the AUGSBURG CONFESSION, an absence lamented by some—including Regin Prenter, a critically important interpreter in twentieth-century Luther studies—and rejoiced in by others, such as Arthur Carl Piepkorn, seeking to establish a more official theory of ministry in American Lutheranism. The Formula of Concord of 1577 in its tenth article identifies circumstances that require resistance to the impositions of ecclesiastical authority, but again with little more than passing reference.

There have been attempts, among both European and American Lutherans, to develop Luther's and other confessional statements into a theory of church order, some of them emphasizing office, others the congregation. However, as Edgar Carlson, a Swedish-American Luther scholar of a prior generation argued, the sources themselves rest with a dialectic: God's continuing presence in the word requires a human office set aside for its speaking but limits the authority of the office to the speaking, whether in preaching or the sacraments; God's word establishes the congregation that therefore has a right to word and sacrament but at the same time limits the authority of the congregation accordingly. It is von Campenhausen's tension, both ecclesiastical authority and spiritual power being constitutive of the church and its ministry.

The priesthood of all believers takes a more positive turn in the doctrine of VOCATION. Luther did not directly employ the Pauline progression of grace and

graces, *charis, charism, charismata,* although he followed the same down-to-earth movement of grace in everyday life. So in *On Christian Liberty,* the third of the great treatises of 1520, he argued a dialectic: "The Christian is the perfectly free lord of all, subject to none"; just so, the Christian is also "the perfectly dutiful servant of all, subject to all." In the contemporaneous *Sermon on Two Kinds of Righteousness,* another classical source, he spoke of Christ's righteousness being realized in a provisional but nevertheless actual righteousness of the believer, realized in everyday service. In later essays of the 1520s, particularly *On Monastic Vows* and *Concerning Married Life,* he located this service in the vocations or callings of the daily round—the formative relations of work and family, citizenship, and the life of the Christian community. Providing a platform for a relentless critique of either clericalism or congregationalism, the priesthood of all believers is realized in service of the word and the neighbor.

Later Protestantism

In the Reformation and after, the Lutheran willingness to leave church order in a dialectic proved an invitation to others seeking more precise definition. Protestant reformers were in general more careful, filling out more complete theories, although when Europeans began immigrating to America, the priesthood of believers found fresh and compelling grounds.

Losing significant allegiances in South, West, and even Northern Germany toward the end of the Reformation and later in the Thirty Years War, LUTHERANISM maintained its hold in Eastern Germany and the Scandinavian countries. The Peace of Augsburg in 1555, followed by the Peace of Westphalia in 1648, ratified a relationship already developing in the Reformation, whereby political officials provided a rudimentary structure for the church. Generally, actual governance of the church fell to consistories, gathering of pastors under the leadership of a superintendent who in function, though with rare exceptions not in title, replaced the bishops (see CONSISTORY). In the Scandinavian folk churches, citizenship and church membership came together. The priesthood of all believers became a rallying cry for various renewal movements that swept the nations, seeking to activate or "awaken" fidelity in the citizenry.

JOHN CALVIN was not one to rely on chance. Considering himself to be completing what Luther began, he resolved the Lutheran dialectic into a theory of church order intended to transform Geneva into the "beacon on the hill" of Jesus's Sermon on the Mount. For this purpose he took over the language of the Pastoral Epistles, although without the title "bishop" so compromised by late medieval Catholicism. The pastors, the elders, and the deacons worked together in a system of check and balance, each of them theoretically subject to "the glorious company"—the assembled laity who as object of ministry also had the power of a vote. Although eventually contained in FRANCE, Calvin's homeland and first objective, CALVINISM spread to Western and Northern Germany and with some roots in ENGLAND, eventually established itself in SCOTLAND.

That which was predictable in Europe became unpredictable in America. In the old European order, established churches could rely on the states' coercive powers, just as the early church following the Constantinian settlement. Where they were established by the state, Protestant churches accepted definitions of ministry focused on office, although as Sidney Earl Mead, longtime dean of American church historians pointed out, in the United States the churches surrendered access to coercion. Initially the surrender was geographically enforced—dissenters, like ROGER WILLIAMS, simply moved, finding an open frontier. The disestablishment clause of the constitution made the geographical reality legal as well. Those churches that had relied on coercion in Europe were forced in America to accept persuasion as the means to the desired end: voluntary association.

Even on the western side of the Atlantic, established European churches did not always surrender easily. There were attempts to replicate the old patterns, some of them—such as folk church Lutheranism—proving surprisingly enduring. Generally, however, the communities of faith best prepared for religious freedom were those that in Europe had already had some experience with supporting themselves through appeal. The various renewal movements that had moved through the state churches, the dissenters and heirs of the radical Reformation, had learned through hard experience how to survive as minorities, dependent on appeal, and they put the experience to good use. It did not take long for previously established churches to follow their lead, adopting the anxious bench, the crusade, and other paraphernalia calculated to move the will to acceptance of God's proffered grace.

The priesthood of all believers was conceptually made to order for the American situation. In historic churches that had defined themselves and their ministry top-down, it had been a critical principle. In churches building themselves bottom-up, seeking adherents, the priesthood of all believers became a *de facto* necessity of church order. So, for example, High Church Episcopalians, deriving the authenticity of the church through the succession of the bishops, were soon forced to put candidates up for popular vote,

thereby emplacing in practice another form of authorization. The clergy learned quickly to adapt. As ALEXIS DE TOCQUEVILLE noticed in a famous observation, "everywhere in America where one expects to meet a priest, one finds a politician"—a pastor who had learned the power of the annual meeting, and therefore the necessity of getting along with the congregation.

Denominationalism and congregationalism are two important consequences. Neither has European, not to speak of earlier roots in the life of the church; both are adaptations to voluntary association. The DENOMINATION bands congregations of similar background and purpose in a common effort; congregationalism gives the priesthood of all believers a political form, so that those who have joined the congregation have the last word in its governance. No matter what form the theory of ecclesiastical authority may take, power—be it spiritual or otherwise—tells the tale.

References and Further Reading

Brunotte, Wilhelm. *Das Geistliche Amt bei Luther*. Berlin, Germany: Lutherisches Verlagshaus, 1959.

Campenhausen, Hans von. *Ecclesiastical Authority and Spiritual Power in the Church of the First Three Centuries*. Stanford: Stanford University Press, 1969.

Carlson, Edgar. "The Doctrine of the Ministry in the Confessions." *The Lutheran Quarterly* XV no. 2 (May 1963): 118–131.

Eastwood, C. Cyril. *The Priesthood of All Believers*. Minneapolis, MN: Augsburg, 1962.

———. "Luther's Conception of the Church." *The Scottish Journal of Theology* 11 (1958): 22–36.

Ebeling, Gerhard. "The Protestant Idea of the Priesthood." In *The Word of God and Tradition: Historical Studies Interpreting the Divisions of Christianity*. Philadelphia, PA: Fortress Press, 1964.

Haendler, Gert. *Luther on Ministerial Office and Congregational Function*. Philadelphia, PA: Fortress Press, 1981.

Kasemann, Ernst. "Ministry and Community in the New Testament." In *Essays on New Testament Themes*. London: SCM Press, 1964.

Mead, Sidney Earl. *The Lively Experiment The Shaping of Christianity in America*. New York: Harper & Row, 1963.

Piepkorn, Arthur Carl. *Profiles in Belief*. San Francisco: Harper & Row, 1978.

Prenter, Regin. *Das Bekenntnis von Augsburg: eine Auslegung*. Erlangen, Germany: Martin-Luther Verlag, 1980.

Schweizer, Eduard. *Church Order in the New Testament*. London: SCM Press, 1961.

von Rad, Gerhard. *The Theology of the Old Testament*. New York: 1962.

Wingren, Gustaf. *Luther on Vocation*. Philadelphia, PA: Muhlenberg Press, 1957.

JAMES ARNE NESTINGEN

PRIESTLEY, JOSEPH (1733–1804)

English theologian and scientist. Priestley was born on March 13, 1733, a few miles southwest of Leeds, where his father was a Yorkshire weaver at Fieldhead in the parish of Birstall. His mother died when he was seven and shortly afterward he was adopted by an aunt, Sarah Keighley, at Heckmondwike. He attended various schools nearby and at an early age began to learn Greek, Latin, and then Hebrew. His proficiency at these and other languages led his aunt to abandon her intention to place him in commerce. His family having had a long history of DISSENT, Priestley was unable to proceed to either of the English universities. Accordingly, in 1752 he began studies at a new Dissenting Academy at Daventry. Here Priestley began studies in science, encouraged by a local Dissenting minister who was well versed in Newtonian science and philosophy. He encountered modern chemistry in the influential *Elementa Chemiae* of Boerhaave. He also read widely in THEOLOGY and began a long career of writing. A manuscript from this period, *Institutes of Natural and Revealed Religion,* although actually published seventeen years later, signaled a growing interest in natural theology. At Daventry he encountered Hartley's *Observations on Man,* which became crucially important for introducing him to the philosophical ideas of JOHN LOCKE and extending his early grasp of the science of ISAAC NEWTON.

In 1755 Priestley left Daventry to become assistant minister at Needham Market in Suffolk. Three years later he moved to Nantwich in Cheshire, an important center for the extraction of salt, serving the church there and opening a school where pupils could learn science as well as the more conventional subjects. In 1761 he accepted the post of tutor at the famous Warrington Academy, and a year later married Mary Wilkinson, sister of the future iron-master John Wilkinson. During this period he wrote books ranging from *Rudiments of English Grammar* and a *Chart of Biography* to *The History and Present State of Electricity.* This last volume appeared just after his election as FRS (Fellow in the Royal Society). By now he had become ordained and in 1767 became minister of Mill Hill Chapel in Leeds. More books poured from his pen during the six years in his native Yorkshire, some thirty in all, and his lively interest in science led to the invention of "soda water" (in which carbon dioxide is dissolved in water under pressure).

In 1767 he accepted an invitation from the Earl of Shelburne to become his librarian, and to act as tutor to his two sons, chiefly at Bowood House, near Calne in Wiltshire. Offering in effect part-time employment in a congenial place, the post left him ample time for scientific research (as had been the Earl's intention). For another six years Priestley labored intensively in his laboratory, developing techniques for manipulating some of the gases that were being discovered by him and others, and obtaining a highly reactive gas

that kindled glowing splints, which we know as oxygen but which he could never recognize as such. By now he was clearly one of Europe's leading chemists.

His final, and longest, appointment in England saw him again as a minister, to the New Meeting congregation in Birmingham. Here he met many leading men of science (in the famous Lunar Society), and developed not only his science but also his political ideas. A series of broadsides against the establishment, including the CHURCH OF ENGLAND, brought him into disrepute and, in 1791, a crowd burned down several chapels and Priestley's own house in the notorious "Church and King" riots. Forced to flee to London, Priestley found himself so unpopular that, in 1794, he emigrated to America, where he died on February 6, 1804.

Theologically Priestley moved from the most conservative to the most liberal form of Christianity. Turning from the strict CALVINISM of his youth, he had accepted Arianism by the 1750s, and by 1767 enthusiastically embraced SOCINIANISM, the thought of Laelio So. His rejection of the Trinity stemmed partly from his reading of scripture (where the actual term is not used), partly from his expressed desire to secure the CONVERSION of Jews and Muslims, and probably from his inherited tradition of radical dissent in which Unitarianism had often been an element of differentiation from the hated Established Church. His views were so extreme—and so clear—that he even opposed orthodox Dissenters, and in his final years was sadly despised by unbelievers and by orthodox Christians. His theology accepted the AUTHORITY of scripture, provided it be interpreted by rational means, but rejected Calvinist ideas of ATONEMENT and double PREDESTINATION.

Politically he detested SLAVERY, sympathized with the French Revolution, and expressed his views without inhibition. However, the revolution he sought was primarily in the mind, for he believed that rational thought would inevitably lead to reform in state and church. So in education the function of teacher was to eliminate prejudices and myths. His science, theology, and politics were inextricably linked by this fundamental belief. One such error in his sight was the notion of "spirit." Opposing a theological dualism he denied spirits, which in chemistry (he thought) had exerted a retarding effect. Inert matter, with its attractions and repulsions, was the object of his concern.

Priestley did not believe in "arbitrary" divine interventions in either personal SALVATION or the natural world, which was grounded in God's own creativity. Hence arose the laws of NATURE, so facts rather than hypotheses were the goal of science. Above all he wanted to establish a system of nature. His refusal to recognize the existence of oxygen was partly at least attributed to his mistrust of hypothetical schemes, like those invented by his rival Antoine Lavoisier. His devotion to the old idea of phlogiston was far from unusual at that time. To his many enemies he was wrong in all three areas: politics, theology, and chemistry. To posterity he was a most gifted man of science and a notable warrior for ENLIGHTENMENT Rationalism.

References and Further Reading

Brooke, J. H. " 'A sower went forth': Joseph Priestley and the Ministry of Reform." [Paper presented at the Third BOC Priestley Conference of the Royal Society of Chemistry, 1983, London.]

Gibbs, W. *Joseph Priestley, Adventurer in Science and Champion of Truth.* New York: Nelson, 1965.

"Joseph Priestley." Commemorative Issue of *Enlightenment and Dissent* no. 2 (1983).

Kieft, L., and R. R. Willeford, eds. *Joseph Priestley, Scientist, Theologian and Metaphysician.* Lewisburg, PA: Bucknell University Press, 1980.

COLIN A. RUSSELL

PRIMITIVE BAPTIST

Primitive Baptist is a general term referring to Baptist churches that have roots in the antimission movement of the antebellum era in the UNITED STATES, specifically those churches that interpret Calvinist doctrine to require opposition to missionary means (including MISSIONARY ORGANIZATIONS, Bible and tract societies, and the like) to spread the gospel. "Primitive" in this context comes from the nineteenth-century usage of the term, meaning "original," and carrying with it the connotation of restoring the ancient faith of Christians dating back to apostolic times from the corruption of modern innovations. Primitive Baptist churches are scattered throughout the United States, and a few exist overseas, although the bulk of their strength is in the Southeast and Appalachian regions. Primitive Baptist churches represent the decentralized, small-scale, traditionalist world of rural Protestantism.

Origins of Primitive Baptists

From their early days the BAPTISTS practiced a congregationalist system and BAPTISM by immersion, the two beliefs that have characterized virtually all Baptists through their history. However, very few doctrines have united what historically has been a disputatious tradition that has spread by division. Primitive Baptists emerged from one of these splits. In the 1820s in North Carolina, the Kehukee Association of Baptists became a leading advocate for the "Hardshell" or "Old School" Baptists, those known for their strict adherence to Calvinist doctrines of limited ATONEMENT. They made known their opposition to the entire benevolent project of mission societies that were beginning to become prominent in American Protestantism.

In the fall of 1832, Baptists in Baltimore county, Maryland, called a meeting at the Black Rock Church. Attendees included Old School Baptists from all over the young country. The "Black Rock address" of 1832 set the agenda for the theology and practice of Primitive Baptists very largely down to the present day. In the doctrinal polemic the Primitive brethren explained their opposition to tract societies, SUNDAY SCHOOLS, BIBLE SOCIETIES, missions organizations, SEMINARIES, and protracted meetings (REVIVALS). All were contrary to God's sovereign will; all encouraged the expansion of man's wisdom and the diminution of God's sovereignty. The difference, as they saw it, came down to this: missionary Baptists "declare the gospel to be a system of means; these means it appears they believe to be of human contrivance. . . . But we believe the gospel dispensation to embrace a system of faith and obedience." Those who honestly reflected on biblical commands "must be, like us, convinced that this religion must remain unchangeably the same at this day, as we find it delivered in the New Testament. . . . And if persons who would pass for preachers, will come to us, bringing the messages of men, &c., a gospel which they have learned in the schools, instead of that gospel which Christ himself commits unto his servants, and which is not learned of men, they must not be surprised that we cannot acknowledge them as ministers of Christ."

Primitive Baptist Theology and Structure

The Primitives uphold the total depravity of natural man; personal and unconditional ELECTION; special atonement; irresistible GRACE; and preservation of the SAINTS. Primitive Baptists historically have eschewed larger denominational structures above the level of associations, that is, groupings of churches in local areas that meet annually for fellowship. DENOMINATIONS were seen as human contrivances that lacked any justification from the New Testament. In the twentieth century, however, groups such as the Progressive Primitive Baptists and the NATIONAL PRIMITIVE BAPTIST CONVENTION (the black Primitive Baptists) accepted into their organizations Sunday schools, denominational organizations, and a paid CLERGY.

Although in agreement on opposition to "means," Primitive Baptists have been just as susceptible to schism as were other groups. Theological and social controversies—over issues as serious as the exact province of PREDESTINATION, and as seemingly trivial as the advent of indoor plumbing to the simple and spare meeting houses that characterize Primitive Baptist CHURCH ARCHITECTURE—have wracked Primitive Baptists virtually from their origins. After World War II, Primitive Baptists have gone into some decline, largely because of the exodus of population from the rural and Appalachian South where the Primitives historically were at their strongest. Nevertheless some contemporary Primitives have shown a greater ability than their predecessors to adopt to some of the mechanisms of modernity, including websites and radio broadcasts.

Primitive Baptist Practices

Aside from their theological insistence on predestinarian views of SALVATION and their opposition to organized and monied organizations to win CONVERSION from others, Primitive Baptists are best known for carrying on older traditions of WORSHIP; indeed, the most conservative Primitive Baptist churches are virtual time capsules of Baptist church practice from the late eighteenth and early nineteenth century. Historically, most Primitive Baptist churches have been pastored by lay elders, men (never WOMEN) who feel called to preach and have no expectation of making a living doing it. Primitive Baptist sermons, especially those in Appalachia, are usually long and chanted in a high-pitched, rhythmic, nasal-sounding whine, punctuated by grunts of "ha" as the preacher catches his breath between long and poetic discourses on the nature and sovereignty of God and the "sweet hope" of salvation. Most Primitive Baptists oppose instrumental church music, believing that nowhere in the New Testament are believers commanded to play instruments in sacred worship, and that instrumentalists call attention to themselves and thus draw proper focus away from the sovereignty of God. Generally, the more conservative the church, the more likely that church is to sing in the time-honored way with extremely slow tempos, a DEACON or elder lining out the hymn, and mournful minor keys being predominant. Primitive Baptists also typically practice foot-washing (see FEET, WASHING OF) as an ordinance. Although the Primitives see it as an ancient "landmark," in fact the practice seems to have arisen mostly in the early twentieth century, as the Primitives sought to distinguish themselves more from mainline missionary Baptist practice. Washing feet often climaxes services, as the brethren and sisters tearfully bond over the powerfully affecting ritual.

Primitive Baptists carry out the faith once delivered to the saints, in highly decentralized organizations that uphold TRADITION over innovation, a stalwart trust in the sovereignty of God over the inroads of new theologies or SCIENCE, and what they see as a simple apostolic form of Christianity over hyperorganized and efficient church organizations.

See also Baptists, United States; Calvinism; Congregationalism

References and Further Reading

Brackney, William. *The Baptists*. Westport, CT: Greenwood Press, 1988.
Crowley, John G. *Primitive Baptists of the Wiregrass South*. Gainesville: University Press of Florida, 1998.
Dorgan, Howard. *Giving Glory to God in Appalachia*. Knoxville: University of Tennessee Press, 1988.
Lambert, Cecil Byron. *The Rise of the Antimission Baptists: Sources and Leaders, 1800–1840*. New York: Arno Press, 1980.
"Primitive Baptist Net." http://www.pb.net (Accessed May 20, 2002).

PAUL HARVEY

PRIMITIVE METHODIST CHURCH

The Primitive Methodist Church's roots lie in an early nineteenth-century English revival movement led by Methodist lay leaders HUGH BOURNE and William Clowes, who espoused CAMP MEETING revivalism as promoted by Methodist revivalist Lorenzo Dow (see REVIVALS). An 1807 camp meeting held at Mow Cop in Northern Staffordshire became the rallying point of the movement. In 1812, after its leaders were rejected by the more staid English Wesleyan Methodist Connexion (see METHODISM, ENGLAND), they organized The Primitive Methodist Connexion popularly known as "Camp Meeting Methodists" or "Ranters." The church's advocacy for the laity and its simplicity of worship made it an attractive home for the struggling members of the rising British working class, some of whom became leaders of the British labor movement. By century's end it was the second largest Methodist body in England. The British Primitive Methodists united with the British Wesleyan Methodist Church in 1932.

In 1829 the Primitive Methodist church had sent missionaries to the UNITED STATES. Churches were founded across the country, but only in the northeastern part, among coal miners of Pennsylvania, in any significant concentration. The mission churches organized as the American Primitive Methodist Church in 1840. "American" later was dropped from the name. In 1889 the several conferences united under a common general conference, and in 1975 both the annual and the general conferences were united as the Primitive Methodist Church in the United States of America. The church has missions in Spain and Guatemala.

It is affiliated with the National Association of Evangelicals and as a WESLEYAN HOLINESS body associates with The Christian Holiness Partnership.

See also Wesleyan Holiness Movement; Methodism; Revivals Holiness Movement

References and Further Reading

Acornley, John H. *A History of the Primitive Methodist Church in the United States of America from Its Origin and The Landing of the First Missionaries in 1929 to the Present Time.* Fall River, MA: B. R. Acornley, 1909.

Kendall, H. B. *The Origin and History of the Primitive Methodist Church.* London: Edward Dalton, n.d.

Werner, J. S. *The Primitive Methodist Connexion: Its Background and Early History.* Madison, WI: University of Wisconsin Press, 1984.

MELVIN E. DIETER

PROCESS THEOLOGY

Process theology depends on philosophies that have replaced the substance categories, dominant in the Western tradition, with events and processes. There are both scientific and philosophic reasons for this shift, and process theologians believe there are also theological advantages. Although it can include theologies influenced by GEORG WILHELM FRIEDRICH HEGEL and Henri Bergson, the term refers chiefly to those influenced by WILLIAM JAMES, John Dewey, C. S. Peirce, Alfred North Whitehead, and CHARLES HARTSHORNE. Of these, Whitehead and Hartshorne have been most important for theologians.

Distinctive Teachings

Process theology claims to recover a more biblical understanding of God from the overlay of Greek philosophy in the tradition. Traditional THEOLOGY depicts God as ideal substance. It thereby accents God's immutability, denying that God is genuinely affected by human joy and sorrow. Process theology argues, in contrast, that God, as love, is perfectly responsive to every occurrence.

Traditional theology has emphasized God's all-controlling power. Because of the arbitrary rendering of El Shaddai as God Almighty, many Christians suppose that such omnipotence is a biblical teaching. Process theology points out that this denies that human beings have any power at all. Instead of explaining the history of the interaction between God and creatures characteristic of the biblical story, this doctrine implies that God unilaterally determines all that occurs, including human responses to divine calls. Some back away from this implication, affirming that God freely limits the exercise of divine power so as to leave decisions to human beings. Process theologians argue, instead, that the true nature of divine power is persuasive, empowering, and liberating rather than controlling, and that this is the kind of power revealed in Jesus and celebrated by Paul, when he speaks of divine power as manifest in the "weakness" of Christ crucified (cf. I Corinthians 2:21–25).

The doctrine of God's all-controlling power raises doubts about God's goodness. If God causes or allows the terrible events of history, it is hard to believe that God is good. Process theologians hold that, if we understand God's power as it is revealed in Jesus, the goodness of God is clear. God is working in all situations for the good of creatures, calling people to join in this work, and empowering them to do so.

Substance thinking teaches that relations are external to the things that are related. That is, these things would be just what they are even if their relationships were different. Process thinkers teach, instead, that relations largely constitute the events that make up the world. This is the doctrine of internal relations. God is internal to creaturely experiences, and creatures are internal to the divine experience. The latter is the doctrine of panentheism—all in God. Its clearest biblical expression is in Paul's speech at the Areopogus: in God "we live, and move, and have our being" (Acts 17:28). This differs from pantheism, which affirms that God and the world are the same reality viewed in two ways.

Process theology affirms the classical doctrine that God was in Jesus, participating in constituting Jesus's existence. God is in all humans in this way. Its Christological task is to clarify what is distinctive about the way God was in Jesus and what was accomplished through his life, death, and resurrection.

The doctrine of internal relations also applies to relations among God's people. We humans are deeply formed by our natural environment and especially by the human communities in which we live. We become persons only in community and are truly "members one of another" (Ephesians 4:25).

Because so much of the natural and social sciences, especially economics, is based on substance thinking, which excludes these constitutive relations, process theologians try to reformulate these sciences and the policies that follow from them. They believe that Christian thinking should be informed by what can be learned from others and should, in turn, challenge others to consider different interpretations of their data.

Criticism and Influence

Criticism comes from diverse directions. The philosophy employed by process theologians is metaphysical or speculative at a time when many believe that such philosophy is outdated. It affirms the independent reality of the nonhuman world at a time when many limit reality to the sphere of human experience or human language. Process theology overrides disciplinary boundaries at a time when many believe that theology should be a self-contained academic discipline largely independent of other sources of knowledge and should respect their independence. Process theology engages in extensive revision of the TRADITION at a time when many take that tradition as normative. Process theology denies that God's power is the sort that can determine what happens, when many believe that only such controlling power can evoke our worship.

The adoption of this philosophic view leaves much of theological importance open. There are Roman Catholic, Unitarian, and Jewish process theologians who formulate the beliefs of their respective traditions in ways influenced by process thought. Much of Western process thought resembles insights attained by Buddhists more than two thousand years ago, and today there are Buddhists who find this thought useful.

Nevertheless, process theology has been largely Protestant. This is partly by historical chance. Much of it developed out of the sociohistorical school that flourished at the University of Chicago Divinity School from the end of the nineteenth century to World War II. Henry Nelson Wieman, Bernard Meland, Bernard Loomer, and Daniel Day Williams were among the early shapers of process theology there. It retained a foothold at Chicago, but it has also spread, largely through Chicago graduates, to other seminaries and graduate schools. Quite independently of Chicago, Norman Pittenger made a large contribution to the literature and influence of the school. Among Catholics, the major center for the study of process theology has been the University of Leuven. It has attracted significant attention in East Asia and AUSTRALIA as well.

References and Further Reading

Cobb, John B., Jr. and David Ray Griffin. *Process Theology: An Introductory Exposition.* Philadelphia: Westminster Press, 1976.

Hartshorne, Charles. *Omnipotence and Other Theological Mistakes.* Albany: State University of New York Press, 1984.

Ogden, Schubert. *The Reality of God and Other Essays.* New York: Harper & Row, 1963.

Suchocki, Marjorie. *God Christ Church: A Practical Guide to Process Theology.* New Rev. ed. New York: Crossroad, 1993.

Williams, Daniel Day. *The Spirit and the Forms of Love.* New York: Harper & Row, 1968.

JOHN B. COBB, JR.

PROGRESSIVE NATIONAL BAPTIST CONVENTION

The Progressive National Baptist Convention (PNBC) emerged in 1961 from a break with the parent body, the NATIONAL BAPTIST CONVENTION U.S.A., Incorporated (NBCI), over two principle points: tenure of convention officers and strategies for civil rights. Headquartered in Washington, D.C. the convention has almost 2,000 churches in some forty-six states and the District of Columbia. The membership of approximately 1.8 million is mainly northeastern and urban, far less strong in Southern and rural areas. It has missions in at least two west African countries, LIBERIA and NIGERIA, as well as the Caribbean nation of Haiti. The *Baptist Progress* is the official organ of the convention, published on a bimonthly basis; the convention owns no publishing press. Its motto, somewhat revised from the original, is "Unity, Service, Fellowship, and Peace."

There are a few white congregations holding dual alignments with the PNBC but far more black Baptist churches dually aligned with predominantly white bodies, such as the SOUTHERN BAPTIST CONVENTION and the AMERICAN BAPTIST CHURCHES. Officers serve for two years, but the president of the convention has a term limit of eight years, resulting in a more frequent turnover of presidents than in other black Baptist groups. The PNBC has boards and commissions typical of Baptist conventions, including those for pensions, civil rights, foreign MISSIONS, WOMEN, and youth. The convention is organized in four major geographic regions: the East, Midwest, South, and Southwest.

Founded in 1895, the National Baptist Convention U.S.A. has had relatively few convention presidents, given that these officers tended to serve long terms. Early in the 1950s some Baptists had grown increasingly concerned about such long tenures. Joseph Harrison Jackson, a Chicago pastor, was elected in 1953 in part with the promise that he would serve a limited number of terms. However, in 1956 Jackson refused to stand down for reelection, insisting that a convention rule limiting presidential terms had been enacted in an irregular fashion. The courts agreed. In addition to the issue of tenure, some convention members believed that the NBC should be more aggressively involved in the direct action, mass demonstrations approach to civil rights. Jackson had supported the Montgomery Bus Boycott and was a lifelong supporter of the NAACP and civil rights, although he believed that continued mass demonstrations and acts of civil disobedience adversely affected race relations. Rather, Jackson placed greater emphasis on the pursuit of civil rights through the courts and legislatures and economic development of the black community. His philosophical opponents backed the Reverend Gardner Taylor, a prominent Brooklyn pastor in his electoral challenge to Jackson in 1960. Jackson succeeded in outmaneuvering his opponents in the convention meeting and secured the federal court's decision that the group that had "elected" Taylor was indeed a nonofficial meeting. After another defeat in 1961, this one supervised by the courts, the Taylor faction conceded to Jackson but the latter proceeded to eliminate Taylor's allies from their convention offices.

At that point the Reverend L. Venchael Booth, who for years had voiced need for the formation of a "progressive" convention, issued a call for interested Baptists to assemble at his Zion Baptist Church in Cincinnati, Ohio in November 1961. At least thirty-three Baptists from fourteen states answered the call and formed the PNBC. Along with Taylor and Booth the new group included MARTIN LUTHER KING JR., Martin Luther King Sr., Ralph Abernathy, and Benjamin Mays. T. M. Chambers served as the first convention president until 1967, when Gardner Taylor succeeded him. Over the years the group sought to live up to its "progressive" title by being more directly involved in the CIVIL RIGHTS MOVEMENT, taking public stances against the Vietnam War, giving support to the black power movement, and fostering job training, education, and support for the black family. Interestingly it has taken no official, convention-wide position regarding women's ordination (see WOMEN CLERGY).

In the first decade of the twenty-first century, decades after the civil rights movement and the subsequent defeat of Jackson as NBC president, the two Baptist groups have had no serious, continuous, public conversations regarding a reunion. Although the PNBC held steady and growing membership strength, it appeared unlikely to command the majority of African American Baptists' allegiance, although many churches were dually aligned with the PNBC and one of the other black groups.

References and Further Reading

Bruce, M. C. "National Baptists." In *Dictionary of Christianity in America.* Edited by Daniel G. Reid, et al., 794–795. Downers Grove, IL: InterVarsity Press, 1990.

Fitts, Leroy. "Baptists." In *Encyclopedia of African-American Culture and History,* edited by Jack Salzman, David Lionel Smith, and Cornel West. vol. 1, 255–261. New York: Simon & Shuster Macmillan, 1996.

Lincoln, C. Eric, and Lawrence H. Mamiya. *The Black Church in the African American Experience.* Durham, NC: Duke University Press, 1990.

Mamiya, Lawrence H. "Progressive National Baptist Convention, Inc." In *Encyclopedia of African and African-American Religions,* edited by Stephen D. Glazier, 248–250. New York: Routledge, 2001.

Newsome, Clarence G. "A Synoptic Survey of the History of African American Baptists." In *Directory of African American Religious Bodies.* 2nd ed. Edited by Wardell J. Payne, 20–31. Washington, D.C.: Howard University Press, 1995.

SANDY DWAYNE MARTIN

PROSTITUTION

Prostitution is often described, somewhat jokingly, as the "world's oldest profession," and there have certainly been individuals who traded sex for money in most of the world's cultures. Recently historians have questioned the appropriateness of labeling all exchanges of sex for money as "prostitution"—a word that was devised in the commercial economy of Western cultures in the nineteenth century—and have encouraged greater attention to the context of such exchanges. In the era of imperialism, for example, although European authorities generally labeled the relationships between European men and indigenous women "prostitution," they were often understood differently by indigenous people, who saw them as temporary MARRIAGE or concubinage, both practices that were respectable forms of sexual relationships to them. Whether labeled "prostitution" or not, however, Protestant CLERGY and lay people have generally opposed the trading of sex for money, along with all other forms of sexual relationships other than monogamous marriage.

The Middle Ages and the Reformation

Christian opinion about prostitution during the Middle Ages was more tolerant. During the late Middle Ages, many cities and towns throughout Europe opened official municipal houses of prostitution or designated certain parts of the city as places in which selling sex would be permitted. Generally this was done with little recorded discussion, but sometimes authorities justified their actions, usually with reference to St. Augustine, who regarded prostitution as a necessary evil that protected honorable girls and women from the uncontrollable lusts of young men. Prostitutes—or at least those who lived in municipal brothels—were integrated fairly well into urban society, appearing as a group at city festivals and publicly welcoming visiting dignitaries; in some cities brothels were owned by bishops.

The integration of prostitutes into urban society was never complete, however, and during the later fifteenth century many cities, particularly in northern Europe, began to restrict prostitutes' movements and appearance more sharply, requiring them to wear clothing that distinguished them from "honorable" women and to stay in the brothel at all times. This process of marginalization culminated in the closing of official brothels. During the period from 1520 to 1590 almost all cities in GERMANY closed their municipal brothels, sometimes quietly and sometimes with great fanfare and proclamations against "whoredom" *(Hurerei)* and "procuring" *(Kuppelei).* In ENGLAND the Bankside brothels, the only legal and protected brothels in the country, were closed by royal statute in 1546. Until very recently scholars linked this wave of closings to fears about syphilis, which first entered Europe in 1493, and to the Protestant REFORMATION. Intensive study of city records has shown that leaders were much more concerned about moral issues than about disease, however. Although Protestants may have been more harsh in their criticism of brothels, both Protestants and Catholics in central and northern Europe increasingly regarded prostitutes as worse than other criminals because they seduced other citizens from the life of moral order that authorities regarded as essential to a godly city.

The language used by reformers about prostitutes was often very harsh. MARTIN LUTHER called them "stinking, syphilitic, scabby, seedy, and nasty" tools of the DEVIL and accused them of bewitching students and other unmarried men; he shared the common sixteenth-century opinion that women were more sexual than men and so regarded prostitutes as responsible for their own situation. Luther and many other reformers also used the word "whore" metaphorically to describe their religious opponents; English anti-Catholic writers in the 1680s were particularly vituperative, terming the Catholic Church "a foul, filthy, old withered harlot . . . the great Strumpet of all Strumpets, the Mother of Whoredom."

Women charged with prostitution were most often so poor that punishment by fine was impossible, so they were imprisoned, punished corporally, and then banished; by the seventeenth century in England this banishment occasionally included deportation to the colonies. By contrast, Catholic cities in southern Europe generally favored regulation over suppression, although they did support the establishment of conventlike institutions (often termed "Magdalene houses") for women who wished to give up prostitution.

The closing of municipal brothels and the increasingly harsh punishments did not, of course, end prostitution, and the religious wars brought about by the Reformation may have actually led to an increase in the number of women—and occasionally men—who made their living at least in part by selling sex. By the seventeenth century some Protestant cities followed the example of Catholic cities such as Florence and Venice and either permitted prostitution or did not enforce laws against it. In Amsterdam houses termed *speelhuizen* combined dancing, nightlife, and the sale of sex; they were the favorite haunts of the thousands of sailors from the East and West India companies who came to Amsterdam every summer.

Similar establishments could be found in Protestant colonial cities such as New York, where large numbers of soldiers and sailors provided a steady customer base and official prohibitions were enforced only sporadically. In the Asian and African regions of the Dutch and British Empire, the number of European women was very small, and most trading of sex for money involved indigenous women, which was generally tolerated by colonial authorities.

Moral Reform Movements

Such tolerance (or indifference) came under increasing attack in the middle of the eighteenth century, when Protestant evangelicals in both Europe and colonial areas began a series of reform campaigns that lasted more than a century, designed to eradicate or lessen "vice" and convince people to lead more moral lives. Reforming prostitutes was an important part of these campaigns because their moral salvation and personal redemption were emblematic of those of all sinners, and their activities a symbol of the moral disintegration of society, the worst of the "social evils." Clergymen such as the Presbyterian minister Ezra Stiles Ely of New York and politicians such as the British prime minister WILLIAM GLADSTONE ventured into poor neighborhoods in search of "fallen" women to "rescue." Their aims were shaped by a different attitude toward female sexuality than that prevalent in the sixteenth century; although non-white and working-class white women might still have strong sexual drives, middle-class women were supposed to be pure and asexual, and even lower-class women might not be responsible for their own abject situation. Thus most prostitutes merited sympathy rather than punishment and were often portrayed in the pamphlets and speeches of reformers as the innocent victims of male seducers.

Reformers organized groups such as the London Society for the Rescue of Young Women and Children and the New York Magdalene Society; first in London and other cities around Britain, and then in New York and Philadelphia, they opened hospitals or smaller refuges and asylums for penitent prostitutes. These reform institutions sought to bring women to physical and moral health and provide them with occupational training that would allow them to support themselves once they left the hospital; religious instruction was a major part of daily life in such asylums.

Attempts at encouraging women to reform voluntarily were accompanied in the middle of the nineteenth century by coercive measures; in an effort to combat venereal disease, prostitutes in many parts of Europe were required to be examined regularly by government doctors and forced to enter special locked prison hospitals if they were found to be infected. In 1864 Britain went further than this and passed a series of "Contagious Diseases Acts," through which women in the port cities of Britain who were simply suspected of being prostitutes could be arrested and sent to a lock hospital. Men who frequented prostitutes were not detained or examined, however, so such measures were completely ineffectual against venereal disease. The unfairness of these laws was recognized by many reformers, most prominently JOSEPHINE BUTLER—the wife of a clergyman—who founded the Ladies National Association for the Repeal of the Contagious Diseases Acts. This group held prayer meetings, sent petitions to Parliament, and applied continual pressure; in the 1880s it was successful in having the Contagious Diseases Acts repealed and the age of consent raised from twelve to sixteen.

Along with efforts at reforming prostitutes and repealing unfair laws, Protestant evangelical reformers also sought to end prostitution by preventing young women from becoming prostitutes in the first place. In Britain, for example, there were over one hundred local Ladies Associations for the Care of Friendless Girls by the 1880s, which sought to provide occupational training (usually in household service) and moral instruction to young working-class women. This double purpose continued among such groups into the twentieth century; an advertisement in the English magazine *Punch* in 1926 for the London Female Guardian Society for the Rescue of Young Women and Girls pled "for help to maintain its large family of young girls rescued from the danger of the streets" and noted, "the Society's chief aim [is] to lead them to Christ for true reformation."

Another aim of moral reformers was the encouragement of male chastity and the end of the sexual double standard. Prostitution, they argued, would never be ended unless men could be convinced to restrain themselves. Organizations such as the White Cross Army, the Church of England Purity Society, and the National Vigilance Association in England, and the Seventh Commandment Society and Female Moral Reform Society in the UNITED STATES, worked to hold men to a higher moral standard and demanded punishment for men who frequented prostitutes or had other "licentious habits." They argued—usually not very successfully—that such men were to be excluded from respectable society and kept out of public office. As in Butler's National Association, middle- and upper-class women were often prominent leaders in these groups; their experiences in such groups and in those involved in other social reforms such as abolition and prison improvement often provided them important skills for their later work in women's rights groups (see SLAVERY, ABOLITION OF).

Reformers often conceived of their efforts at moral reform in the cities of Europe and North America as missionary work, and they also carried their moral campaigns into the mission fields of Asia, AFRICA, the Pacific, and AUSTRALIA. Male and female missionaries in Hawaii, for example, discouraged traditional dancing and dress styles (the muu-muu was a missionary invention), and labeled as "prostitution" any relations between indigenous women and American or European men in which goods or money were exchanged. Missionaries in many areas objected to company and government policies that allowed only unmarried men to serve as colonial officials, employees, and soldiers, arguing that these encouraged prostitution; such objections were largely ineffective in lifting the marriage ban, although European companies and governments often came to favor long-term concubinage over short-term prostitution in imperial settings. These policies changed once more European women were allowed in the colonies in the early to mid-twentieth century and marriage became permissable and possible for a larger share of the European male population. At this point prostitution reemerged as the most common type of sexual relationship between European men and indigenous women, although again Protestant clergy both in the colonies and in the home countries decried this.

Protestant opinion about prostitution—as about so much else—became more diverse after the First World War. Conservative Protestants tended to view prostitution as a moral issue and encouraged the reform of prostitutes and their customers, whereas liberals and later those influenced by LIBERATION THEOLOGY and FEMINIST THEOLOGY viewed it more as an issue of ECONOMICS and the exploitation of women. These two views both influenced government policies toward prostitution in countries that were predominantly Protestant; they generally restricted prostitution along with other activities judged harmful to morality (such as pornography) to certain districts, but enforced these restrictions—which targeted the women involved rather than their customers—only sporadically and selectively.

References and Further Reading

Bartley, Paula. *Prostitution: Prevention and Reform in England, 1860–1914.* London: Routledge, 2000.

Brock, Rita Nakashima, and Susan Brooks Thistlethwaite. *Casting Stones: Prostitution and Liberation in Asia and the United States.* Minneapolis, MN: Fortress Press, 1996.

Hobson, Barbara Meil. *Uneasy Virtue: The Politics of Prostitution and the American Reform Tradition.* Chicago: University of Chicago Press, 1987.

Jolly, Margaret, and Martha MacIntyre, eds. *Family and Gender in the Pacific: Domestic Contradictions and the Colonial Impact.* Cambridge: Cambridge University Press, 1989.

Nash, Stanley D. *Prostitution in Great Britain, 1485–1901* Metuchen, NJ: Scarecrow Press, 1994.

Roper, Lyndal. "Discipline and Respectability: Prostitution and the Reformation in Augsburg." *History Workshop* 19 (1985): 3–28.

Schuster, Beata. *Die freien Frauen: Dirnen und Frauenhaüser im 15. und 16. Jahrhundert* (Free Women: Whores and Brothels in the Fifteenth and Sixteenth Centuries). Frankfurt, Germany: Campus, 1995.

Whiteaker, Larry. *Seduction, Prostitution, and Moral Reform in New York, 1830–1860.* New York: Garland, 1997.

MERRY E. WIESNER-HANKS

PROTESTANT ETHIC

See Ethics

PRUSSIAN UNION

During the preparations for the festivities surrounding the 300th anniversary of the posting of MARTIN LUTHER's theses on October 31, 1517, the Prussian king Friedrich Wilhelm III proclaimed on September 27, 1817 that he desired a "truly religious unity" of the two Protestant faiths in his country (Lutheran and Calvinist/Reformed). On the forthcoming Reformation day, Lutherans and Reformed Christians were to celebrate the LORD'S SUPPER together. This notion was on one hand the realization of a long-held wish of the Hohenzollern dynasty, who had reigned as Reformed Christians over a predominantly Lutheran populace. At the same time, PIETISM, ENLIGHTENMENT, and revival movements (see REVIVALS) had erased many of the confessional discrepancies in Protestantism to the extent that such distinctions appeared meaningless to most contemporaries. The unions that had been established in a number of German territories provided the evidence—for example, in Nassau, Baden, and in the Palatinate. Finally the political and administrative reconfiguration of Prussia after the Vienna Congress (1815) increased Prussia's role, where unified church authorities were integrated in the eight Prussian provinces (Brandenburg, Pomerania, Western Prussia, Eastern Prussia, Saxony, Silesia, Westphalia, and the Rhineland).

The idea of unification met with approval in the churches, particularly in the West. It was the king who held up its implementation because he tried starting in 1822 to impose a uniform LITURGY on this new church. Confessional Lutheran groups, however, voiced their opposition, because—as did for example FRIEDRICH W. SCHLEIERMACHER—they were not ready to tolerate the absolutist intervention of the crown into church matters. As the king increased his pressure in 1830, some resolute Lutherans (the so-called Old-Lutherans) decided to split off in Silesia and later in Pomerania; many of them later emigrated to AUSTRALIA and the UNITED STATES. Although the king declared in 1834 that he wished only for an administrative union, the limits on the imposition of a confessional union (consensus union) were rather fluid.

Even though the successor to the throne, Friedrich Wilhelm IV, initially gave the impression in 1840 that he wanted to dissolve the union, it continued to exist and won increasing approval in Prussia. Although it experienced only limited opposition in Prussia from small groups of confessional Lutherans, Lutherans in other states—especially in Hannover, Mecklenburg, Saxony, and Bavaria—attacked it vigorously and uncompromisingly. Objections in theology, church polity, and massive political opposition to the hegemony of Prussia blended together. Bismarck took such sentiment into account insofar as he did not incorporate the Lutheran churches of the areas Prussia annexed in 1864 and 1866 (among them Schleswig-Holstein, Hesse-Kassel, and Hannover) into the Council of the Prussian Church. The Prussian Union was limited to the eight old provinces (see above). From then on it was called the Evangelical Church of the Old Prussian Union (Altpreussische Union or APU).

The dispute surrounding the union order of worship, especially the reaction that it entailed in 1817, blocked the expansion of a church constitution. Restorative forces within the APU worked toward that same goal in the 1850s. In 1835 the Church Order of Rhineland Westphalia may have been introduced and combined the Presbyterian-synodal expansion of the congregation with consistorial supervision; however, a church constitution existed in the provinces of the APU beginning only in 1876. This constitution organized the church along the same lines all the way to the general synod. Confessional differences continued to play a role in German Protestantism, but they were increasingly overcome by the comprehensively effective actions of the church leadership, as well as by the activities of the Inner and Foreign Mission that focused on all of German Protestantism, and especially, around the turn of the century, by an expanding sense of a national Protestant mentality.

The strength of the Prussian Union became visible in 1918. The fall of the House of Hohenzollern and the end of the sovereign church regiment was in way an end of the APU. It gave itself a new constitution in 1922 and in May 1933 concluded a treaty with the State of Prussia. In the church elections of May 23,

1933 the "Germanic" Christians emerged overwhelmingly victorious—just as in most German territorial churches—and they took over the leading committees. The controversy between churches that ensued was especially bitter in the APU. In addition to Berlin, the church provinces of Brandenburg, Rhineland, and Westphalia were at the center of an intense dispute and under growing pressure by the Nazi government. The first confessional synod of the new APU took place on May 29, 1934 in Barmen, just two days before the confessional synod of the German Evangelical Church that would adopt in the same town the famous Theological Declaration. The twelfth and last confessional synod of the APU was held on October 16–17 in Breslau.

At the end of World War II, the Church of the APU lost about one third of its territory with the loss of East and West Prussia, large parts of Pomerania and Silesia to POLAND and the Soviet Union. Confessional Lutherans inside and outside of the APU now pressed for a dissolution of the Union and for confessionally constituted churches. That did not happen. However, individual church provinces—starting with Rhineland and Westphalia—split off from the Evangelischen Ober Kirchenrat (EOK) in Berlin and organized autonomous regionally organized churches, although there existed great hesitancy to sacrifice the unity of the APU. A special general synod legitimized this development in February 1951.

Because the German Democratic Republic (East Germany) did not recognize the decisions of that synod and raised objections to the use of the word "Prussia" in the name of the church, the APU renamed itself the Evangelical Churches of the Union (Evangelische Kirchen der Union or EKU) after 1953. In principle, with this name, the limitation to the formerly Prussian areas was lifted and hence the Evangelical Churches of Anhalt joined the EKU in 1960. Pressure from the GDR did not lead to a separation, but it did result in a breakdown into an Eastern and Western region. This arrangement was in place until January 1, 1992.

Currently, a process of integration of the EKU is taking place with the churches that cooperated with the Arnoldshain Conference. This conference was formed in 1967 as an organization that encompasses those churches that do not belong to the United Evangelical-Lutheran Church (Vereinigte Evangelisch-Lutherische Kirche Deutschlands or VELKD). Once the merger of the EKU and the Arnoldshain Conference succeeds as planned in the summer of 2003, only the church in Oldernburg and Württemberg will belong to neither the VELKD or UEK within the Evangelical Church of Germany (EKD).

References and Further Reading

Gerhard Goeters, J. F., and Joachim Rogge, eds. *Die Geschichte der Evangelischen Kirche der Union.* 3 vols. Leipzig, Germany: Evangelische Verlagsanstalt, 1992–1999.

MARTIN GRESCHAT

PUBLISHING

Before the invention of the printing press in the fifteenth century, religious publishing was a tedious business. From the advent of Christianity to the Middle Ages, the audience for published material was very small. Literacy rates rose significantly between the first and the fourteenth centuries, but the financial means that allowed individuals to own manuscripts did not accompany this rise in literacy. Even by the fourteenth century, European society was so deeply divided by economics and education that reading and owning manuscripts was the province primarily of a wealthy elite class and the church. Those manuscripts owned by the church were transmitted primarily through the work of monastic communities, whose task was primarily preservation. The reproduction of manuscripts in these communities was performed by hand, with members copying and recopying one manuscript after another.

The invention of the printing press brought the new profession of publishing. Not only was it now possible to produce more copies of manuscripts than ever before, but there was also demand for people to run these presses. Close on the heels of the introduction of the press was the Protestant REFORMATION, and one of the first books to be published on the press was MARTIN LUTHER's translation of the BIBLE. Although before the late sixteenth century the church controlled its congregations by controlling manuscripts and the language in which those texts were written, suddenly there was a proliferation of books written in the language of the people. Because the literacy rate had been increasing, some peasants for the first time could read a copy of the Bible that they owned in a language that they could understand. In many ways, then, publishing and the rise of Protestantism go hand in hand.

By the seventeenth century, Protestant publishing in England was flourishing. Sermons, pamphlets, devotional manuals, essays, and didactic works were the mainstays of publishers during these years. Patronage was still the primary manner in which an author could advance his or her career, so publishers that were devoted to producing particular kinds of books had not yet developed as a distinct private industry. Even though the new publishing industry now made religion books available to a wider audience, the audience consisted primarily—as it had a century earlier—of

CLERGY. The colonial experiment in the New World helped broaden the audience for the books, but most of those living in the colonies had brought their books with them from ENGLAND. It was not until the eighteenth century and Benjamin Franklin's introduction of the printing industry to the colonies that publishing began to flourish on American soil.

By 1792, religious publishing had experienced both a decline and a revival. Printing presses in the eighteenth century were occupied more with producing political and social pamphlets than with devotional manuals. In addition, writers like Richard Steele, Joseph Addison, and SAMUEL JOHNSON were instrumental in producing some of the first newspapers in the English world, the *Tatler* and *The Spectator*. Such papers reported gossip and attracted a large readership in local taverns and pubs, but they contained little religious content. The papers were moralistic and didactic, but they approached morality from the standpoint of philosophy rather than religion. In general, religion in the eighteenth century found itself in decline and was replaced by an emphasis on classical LITERATURE and humanistic values. Even though religion publishing and religion experienced a decline in the eighteenth century, by century's end JOHN BUNYAN's *PILGRIM'S PROGRESS* had gone through 160 editions.

Publishing in the New World

In the colonies, Franklin's printing presses focused on producing newspapers (the first published in the American colonies in Philadelphia), books of moral instruction, and political pamphlets. The bookstalls of the cities were also flooded with revolutionary essays and pamphlets, such as Thomas Paine's "The Rights of Man" and "Common Sense." At the same time, Puritans had access to a number of readers that they had published and used to teach their children about their faith (see PURITANISM). Children would learn their alphabet by reading verses like "In Adam's fall, we sinned all."

Succeeding generations of American seekers have sought to reshape their faith to incorporate or reflect the cultural forces of the times. By the nineteenth century, the desire of European immigrants to hold onto their indigenous religions as safe havens in a new world resulted in the rise of American denominationalism. During these years, religious publishing was a largely sectarian enterprise, with church-owned presses like the Methodist Book Concern (founded in 1789 and later known as the United Methodist Publishing and Abingdon Press), Augsburg (founded in 1848), and Broadman House (then a trade division of the Sunday School Board of the SOUTHERN BAPTIST CONVENTION, founded in 1898) publishing devotional books, curriculum resources, and hymnals for a niche audience of clergy and LAITY.

By the 1960s, many Americans had become disenchanted with traditional institutional religious authority, turning away from what they perceived as rigid authoritarianism and moving toward religious expressions that fostered introspection, individuality, and creativity. Trade publishers like Macmillan, Bobbs-Merrill, Harper & Row, and New Directions began to release titles that appealed to disaffected churchgoers. Macmillan scored big with Harvey Cox's *The Secular City* (1965), while Bobbs-Merrill released Thomas Altizer's *The Death of God* in 1966. New Directions, the preeminent publisher of the modernist poetry of Ezra Pound and William Carlos Williams, poured out a steady stream of Thomas Merton's protest writings, Zen poems and essays, while Harper & Row published the writings of Dorothy Day, as well as Sam Keen's celebratory paean to the body and its role in Christian faith and worship, *To a Dancing God* (1965).

After the religious and spiritual ferment of the 1960s, Americans seemed to go through much of the 1970s and 1980s seeking not so much spiritual renewal as individual gratification, with unparalleled consumption of material goods and a focus on the self (the so-called "me generation"). A turn from God-centeredness to self-centeredness and individual experience in religion could be seen during this period in movements as diverse as LIBERATION THEOLOGY and the JESUS MOVEMENT in the 1970s. The self-help and recovery movements of the 1980s eventually became a significant influence on religion publishing through such titles as *The Road Less Traveled* by M. Scott Peck and *When Bad Things Happen to Good People* by Harold Kushner.

One of the great surprises of religious publishing in the 1970s was the growth of evangelical Christian publishing. Driven by the popularity of new forms of Christianity among young people, publishers like Tyndale House and Zondervan began to publish books to appeal to this new generation. Tyndale's *Living Bible* (1971) sold three million copies in its first year, and Zondervan hit the jackpot with Hal Lindsey's apocalyptic thriller *The Late Great Planet Earth* (1972).

In 1984, Robert Bellah and colleagues published *Habits of the Heart,* a now-classic book that acknowledged the problems and promises of INDIVIDUALISM for society and religion. That same year, Harvard theologian Harvey Cox's *Religion in the Secular City: Toward a Postmodern Theology* surveyed the resurgence of religion in CULTURE and predicted that religious grassroots movements like political FUNDAMENTALISM and liberation theology would shape the religion of the 1990s and beyond. Bellah's and Cox's books played a pivotal role in gauging the spiritual temperament of America by opening new conversations about the role of religion and spirituality in American life.

Contemporary Trends

The baby boomers who were formed by the 1960s, 1970s, and 1980s today constitute the largest segment of book-buying consumers, and as they enter middle age and begin to confront their own mortality, their spiritual search has intensified. If religion appeared to be absent or marginal in the 1970s and 1980s, it has returned to the American landscape in the 1990s with a vengeance. Popular culture is filled with references to religion and spirituality, from the reverential depiction of angels on prime-time television ("Touched by an Angel") to the quirky lyrics of Joan Osbourne's pop song "What If God Was One of Us?" Polls in 1997 indicated that 96 percent of Americans believed in God or a universal spirit. But how does such a statistic translate into practice? How are Americans religious in the early twenty-first century? Where do they find their religion, and how are their religious questions shaped? Is there an "American religion," and, if so, what is it?

In his *The Index of Leading Spiritual Indicators* (1996), researcher George Barna characterized 1990s religion in America as "a personalized, customized form of faith views which meet personal needs, minimize rules and absolutes, and which bear little resemblance to the pure form of any of the world's major religions." The syncretism, relativism, and individualism that Barna points to reflect the central ways Americans reinvented their religion in the 1990s, and the striking commercial success of trade books about spiritual and religious topics, may be both the clearest indicator and the most central facilitator of that approach to religion.

Who could have guessed that a simple and sentimental little inspirational book called *Chicken Soup for the Soul* would sell millions of copies in trade bookstores and spawn a whole series of books for various kinds of "souls," including women, teenagers, Christians, and so on (not to mention a rash of book titles with the word "soul," many having only the most tenuous connection to anything spiritual)? Who could have known that a biography of God, written by journalist-turned-academic Jack Miles, would win the Pulitzer Prize? The enormous popularity of books like these, which thirty years ago likely would have been published (if at all) by a sectarian religious publisher or an academic press and found only small audiences, reflects not only the unexpected resurgence of religion in American culture, but also the transformation of the trade publishing of religion.

The success of Jack Miles's *God: A Biography*, Harold Bloom's *Omens of Millennium*, and Walter Wangerin's *The Book of God* provided a signpost for the way things will be in commercial publishing about religion. Not only are people finding religion in its various forms a fascinating topic, they are also engaged in their own varied quests to fill the spiritual void that rampant consumerism and greed have left in their personal lives. The success of books like Kathleen Norris's *The Cloister Walk*, the Jesus Seminar's *The Five Gospels*, and Karen Armstrong's *A History of God*, demonstrated the publishing industry's new willingness to release books that popularized esoteric subjects like monastic disciplines and New Testament theology.

Of course, as Protestant religion publishing has been reshaped by our history, over the past thirty years it has also examined that history through a number of key books. The most popular and comprehensive may be Sydney Ahlstrom's monumental *A Religious History of the American People* (1972), which after more than thirty years is still in print. Edwin Gaustad's *A Religious History of America*, first published in 1966 and now in its third edition, is still in print and selling steadily. The dean of American church historians, Martin Marty, recently completed the third volume of an anticipated four-volume work, *Modern American Religion,* and brought his study of American religious history into the 1960s. And in 1992, cultural critic Harold Bloom declared in *The American Religion: The Emergence of a Post-Christian Nation* that American religion was a kind of gnosticism, a religious system emphasizing the possession of secret knowledge and practices of religious exclusivism.

Challenges and Possibilities

American Protestants have been reinventing their religion since the Puritans first built their "city upon a hill" in the New World, and that process continues into this new millennium. The religion publishing industry continues to experience exciting successes and dismal failures. The success of evangelical Protestant publishers with fiction and Bible translations has been mirrored by the disappointing performances of denominational publishers' with trade books. Just as the printing press offered a new technology for publishers to use to disseminate writings more widely, so has the advent of the Internet and electronic books provided the same opportunities for religion publishers in the twenty-first century. More and more readers will now have an opportunity to read books that are readily available in a variety of affordable formats. How such technology will affect American Protestant publishing over the next fifty years is anyone's guess. One thing is certain—the floodgates have opened, and books will continue to play a leading role in shaping the uniquely American Protestant religious quest.

See also Best Sellers in America, Religious; Bible Translation; Mass Media; Periodicals, Protestant

References and Further Reading

Ahlstrom, Sidney. *A Religious History of the American People.* New Haven, CT: London, 1972.

Aue, Pamela Willwerth, and Henry L. Carrigan, Jr., eds. *What Inspirational Literature Do I Read Next?* Detroit, MI: Gale, 2000.

Carrigan, Henry L. Jr. "Reinventing American Religion." *Publishers Weekly,* 245: no. 11 (1998).

Gaustad, Edwin. *A Religious History of America.* San Francisco: Harper and Row, 1966.

Herberg, Will. *Protestant, Catholic, Jew.* New York: Doubleday, 1955.

HENRY L. CARRIGAN, JR.

PUFENDORF, SAMUEL (1632–1694)

German Lutheran philosopher. Pufendorf was born in Saxony in 1632, the son of a Lutheran minister, and was originally bound for the ministry himself. He pursued an education in THEOLOGY at the University of Leipzig, a center of Lutheran learning, but eventually he abandoned the study of theology in order to study law. He was a professor at the universities of Heidelberg (1661) and Lund (1670).

Pufendorf is famous for his contribution to the philosophy of moral, civil, and NATURAL LAW, and for his arguments regarding the relationship between church and state. In his treatise *The Whole Duty of Man According to the Law of Nature* (1673), Pufendorf argued that moral law was the result of revelation, civil law was the jurisdiction of the state, and natural law was necessary for the functioning of society. God wills each individual to live a social life, which is the moral obligation of all humans.

In *Of the Nature and Qualification of Religion in Reference to Civil Society* (1687) Pufendorf argued for religious tolerance. He concluded that by making religion a private matter rather than a public one, societies will achieve religious tolerance. Pufendorf originally wrote the treatise as a reaction to Louis XIV's oppression of the French HUGUENOTS. Later the treatise influenced debates elsewhere regarding the separation of church and state.

See also Church and State, Overview; Enlightenment; Toleration

References and Further Reading

Primary Sources:

Brett, Thomas. *A Review of the Lutheran Principles: Shewing How They Differ from the Church of England, and that Baron Puffendorf's Essay for Uniting of Protestants, was not Design'd to Procure an Union Between the Lutherans and the Church of England, as is Insinuated in the Title of the Late Edition of that Book. In a Letter to a Friend. . . .* London: Henry Clements, 1714.

Pufendorf, Samuel. Gesammelte Werke. Schmidt, Wilhelm, ed. 5 vols. Berlin: Akademie, 1996–1999.

Pufendorf, Samuel von. *The Whole Duty of Man According to the Law of Nature.* Translated by Andrew Tooke and edited by Ian Hunter and David Saunders. Indianapolis, IN: Liberty Fund, 2002.

———. *Of the Nature and Qualification of Religion in Reference to Civil Society.* Translated by Jodocus Crull and edited by Simone Zurbuchen. Indianapolis, IN: Liberty Fund, 2002.

The Morality of the Fallen Man: Samuel Pufendorf on Natural Law. Saastamoinen, Kari Helsinki: SHS, 1995.

Zurbuchen, Simone. "From Denominationalism to Enlightenment: Pufendorf, Le Clerc, and Thomasius on Toleration." In *Religious Toleration,* 191–209. New York: St Martin's Press, 1999.

JAY LAUGHLIN

HENRY PURCELL (1659–1695)

English composer. Working in England's politically and religiously tumultuous seventeenth century, Henry Purcell is considered among the greatest English composers. Purcell was born into a family of court musicians in London in 1659, just after the restoration of the monarch and the reestablishment of ANGLICANISM. As a boy he sang as a chorister in the King's Chapel Royal, and later studied composition with John Blow and Christopher Gibbons.

In 1677 Purcell began his lifelong career as a composer and musician for church and court when he was appointed to write pieces for the violins of Charles II's court. He became organist at Westminster Abbey in 1679 and at the Chapel Royal in 1682. While serving the court, Purcell wrote dozens of church anthems, the *Service in B-flat minor,* the *Burial Service,* and *Te Deum.*

In 1685 a Catholic king, James II, ascended the English throne. Purcell and other musicians serving the Anglican Church met with hardship as a result. Although Purcell did not lose his position, the Chapel Royal's status was greatly diminished. His career hardly benefited when Anglican-friendly William and Mary claimed the throne in 1689. Their court lacked a focus on music and Purcell was forced to supplement his income by writing more music for the theater. His operas include *Dido and Aeneas* and *The Fairy-Queen.* Purcell died in London in 1695 and was buried in a plot near the organ at Westminster Cathedral.

Purcell's compositional style developed within the context of great political and religious change in England. Charles II's Anglican sympathies and devotion to the French music he encountered during his exile spurred a reinvigoration in church music upon his return in 1660. The new king's support of church music stood in direct contrast to the period of decline under OLIVER CROMWELL's rule. Under Charles II, Purcell and his contemporaries brought back some older forms of polyphonic, or many-voiced music. However, they also experimented with dramatic solo vocal lines in their music for the church.

Purcell's particular contribution to this experimentation came in the form of word painting, or pictorialisms. Purcell used a variety of musical gestures to dramatize individual words of the text. His anthems, including *O Give Thanks unto the Lord* and *Blessed are They that Fear the Lord,* exemplify his ability to vivify hymn texts through music. His devotional songs include emotional settings of penitential texts and solo versions of the traditional form of biblical dialogue. Purcell's innovative settings of English texts, both for church and theater, have made him renown among composers working in the English language.

See also Hymns and Hymnals; Music, English Church

References and Further Reading

Holman, Peter, and Robert Thompson. "Henry Purcell." In *New Grove Dictionary of Music and Musicians.* 2nd ed. Edited by Stanley Sadie. Vol. 20, 604–630. London: Macmillan Publishers Limited, 2001.

Van Tassel, Eric. "Music for the Church." In *Purcell Companion.* Edited by Michael Burden, 101–199. Portland: Amadeus Press, 1994.

Zimmerman, Franklin B. *Henry Purcell: A Guide to Research.* New York: Garland, 1989.

JENNIFER GRABER

PURITANISM

Any description of the Puritan movement must begin by acknowledging that in sixteenth- and seventeenth-century England, the very word *puritan* was a term of abuse that contemporaries applied indiscriminately to anyone who was critical of the CHURCH OF ENGLAND or, even more indiscriminately, to persons of a certain temperament. London stage plays of the late sixteenth century caricatured the "puritan" as ridiculously over-zealous and yet hypocritical. Politically, the monarchy and church treated the term as synonymous with sedition and schism, a strategy based on the assumption that any challenge to the authority of the officers of the church (the bishops) was also a challenge to the authority of the monarchy. None of these contexts tells us much about the real thing. Not until the early seventeenth century did some English men and women begin to use the word in a positive sense, although "the godly" was probably a more prevalent self-reference. In the nineteenth and twentieth centuries, puritanism came to stand for mental narrowness and a moral authoritarianism. Again, none of these uses of the term informs us about Puritanism as a religious movement in its own time and place, except that it was always controversial.

Puritanism was a movement of religious reform that arose within the Church of England during the reign of ELIZABETH I (1558–1603). Summoning Christians to intensify their level of religious practice, and calling also for changes in worship and church government, the movement could not avoid becoming entangled in politics in a country where, as a consequence of the REFORMATION, the head of the civil state was also head of a single, comprehensive state church. Never supported by Elizabeth or her successors James I (1603–1635) and Charles I (1625–1649), the movement unexpectedly came into power in the early 1640s after Parliament asserted its authority and its army defeated the king in a CIVIL WAR (1643–1645). This moment of triumph was short-lived because the moderates and conservatives who dominated Parliament were alienated by the ascendancy of left-wing puritanism in the army under the leadership of OLIVER CROMWELL. The radicals had their way with the execution of Charles I in 1649, and a Commonwealth was established with Cromwell as its head (1653–1658). After Cromwell's death and the restoration of Charles II to the throne in 1660, the new government enacted stringent rules of "conformity" that thousands of clergy and lay people could not accept. Leaving the Church for good, these "Nonconformists" or "Dissenters" (see NONCONFORMITY, DISSENT) practiced their faith under conditions of great difficulty. The presence of Puritans in America began in the 1620s and 1630s, when a significant number of emigrants founded the colonies of Plymouth, Massachusetts, Connecticut, and New Haven in New England. There they were able to implement distinctive patterns of ministry, worship, and church organization and to maintain these patterns well beyond the close of the seventeenth century. Beginning with a common parent and continuing to share many of the same ideas, Puritanism in America enjoyed a hegemony that puritans in England never achieved.

Like many other reformers, Puritans did not agree among themselves on means and ends. The movement encompassed a spectrum that ranged from radicals impatient with the "corruptions" of the church to conservatives who preferred unity and order to schism or sectarianism. During the reign of Elizabeth I, some reformers agitated for replacing the office of bishop, or episcopacy, with a ministry of equals, and for transforming the rituals of worship in the BOOK OF COMMON PRAYER by eliminating all "remnants" of Catholic practice. Such Puritans were influenced by the example of Reformed churches in GERMANY, SWITZERLAND, FRANCE, and the NETHERLANDS. Leaders of the Reformed tradition—JOHN CALVIN but also HEINRICH BULLINGER, MARTIN BUCER (who came to ENGLAND in 1549 and taught briefly at Cambridge University), and THEODORE BEZA—provided the core ideas that were publicized in the 1560s and 1570s by a small group of English clergy, some of whom had encountered the Reformed model during their years as exiles on the Continent during the reign of Mary Tudor (1553–1558). These ideas included the following: (1) that the "lawful" form of church government was prescribed in the New Testament, which contained rules that must be followed exactly; (2) that Catholic forms of worship were "idolatrous" violations of the Second Commandment, and that Protestant worship should eliminate all vestiges of Catholicism; (3) that the proper relationship between CHURCH AND STATE was not to allow one to dominate the other, as the monarchy in England did the church, but to regard them as constituting two distinctive realms or kingdoms, the first spiritual, the other temporal, each independent of each other yet conjoined under God; and (4) that the visible church should be a purified, ethical community that administered the SACRAMENTS of BAPTISM and the LORD'S SUPPER only to persons who could demonstrate their worthiness. "Forward" reformers in England, chief among them THOMAS CARTWRIGHT and John Field, brought most of these ideas together in a manifesto that others within the movement regarded as too extreme, *An Admonition to the Parliament* (1572).

Everyone within the movement agreed, however, on the imperative to elevate the quality of the ministry and to demand much more of the LAITY. From a puritan perspective the average English person was too ignorant and uncaring to qualify as a "real" Christian. Nor were the mass of the CLERGY considered much better. The founding of Emmanuel College, Cambridge (1584) was undertaken expressly to train a different kind of minister for the church, men devoted to PREACHING and to practicing a rigorously disciplined lifestyle. Another aspect of the puritan program was to address such problems as poverty, drunkenness, violence, unrestrained sexuality, and illiteracy. This concern for "social discipline" was in keeping with a widely held principle—vigorously renewed in the second phase of the Protestant Reformation and, in the wake of the Council of Trent, within the Catholic COUNTER-REFORMATION—that the church was responsible for supervising the moral and social health of a Christian society. Puritanism thus became a factor in the social life of English communities as reformers, often with the support of local magistrates or notables, encouraged the regulation of social behavior, stricter observance of the Sabbath (Sunday), or SABBATARIANISM, more schooling to promote literacy, and better care of the disabled and disadvantaged.

Puritanism as a Devotional Movement

The deeper goal was to bring about a deeper, more systematic piety among lay people and clergy, a piety expressed in practices such as prayer, meditation, attending sermons, reading the BIBLE and other "godly" books, maintaining an orderly household, and, above all, constant, routinized self-examination. The ministers who described this piety insisted that religious practices were useless if they were performed only mechanically, out of a sense of obligation. Anyone who did so was a hypocrite or formalist, someone trapped in the externals of religion. The true Christian was someone whose "heart"—the spiritual center of the self—was stirred up to seek after Christ. Self-examination taught the fundamental lesson that humans were sinners entirely without merit, and that SALVATION was solely theirs thanks to divine mercy. Self-examination also taught the imperative of repentance: the true Christian mourned with a broken heart the condition of being a sinner. Only then was it possible to respond in faith to the gospel promise of free GRACE, a promise conveyed through preaching. By about 1600 or 1610, a handful of preacher-theologians, most notably WILLIAM PERKINS (1558–1602), who taught at Cambridge, had expanded this description of the spiritual life into a well-rehearsed "practical divinity," a description of what the would-be Christian must do to experience his or her election, that was widely reiterated by a "spiritual brotherhood" of like-minded ministers within the church.

Preaching was the principal means of propagating this way of life, but preaching was seconded by a lively market in printed books. One important publication was a translation of the Bible that became known as the "Geneva Bible" (1560) because most of the work on it was done by English clergy in exile on the Continent during the reign of Mary Tudor. (Not until the publication in 1611 of the "King James version" was the Geneva Bible replaced, at least for official purposes.) Another of great significance, although too bulky and expensive for most persons to own, was JOHN FOXE's deeply anti-Catholic and apocalyptic retelling of the history of the Christian church, and especially the most recent century of English history, *The Acts and Monuments* or *Book of Martyrs* (1559). By the early seventeenth century, manuals or guides on how to be a true Christian were being frequently reprinted in response to reader demand; among the more popular or influential was Arthur Dent's *The Plain Mans Pathway to Heaven* (1610) and Richard Rogers's *Seven Treatises*.

The theological framework of these manuals was broadly Calvinist, although always a CALVINISM titled toward the practical divinity. During the reigns of Elizabeth and James I, much of the church leadership shared with the reformers the concept of an all-sovereign God who determined which of humankind were destined to be saved; whether God also elected others to a state of reprobation (damnation) was more controversial. That is, the Church of England officially supported certain aspects of Calvinism. A wide spectrum of clergy followed St. Augustine in always rejecting Pelagianism, or salvation through works-righteousness. Yet differences also emerged; for example, William Perkins has been termed a "hyper-Calvinist" for his emphasis on double predestination; that is, God decided that much of humankind was "reprobate" and others were of the elect without regard in either instance to their actions in the world. Nonetheless, the order of salvation endorsed in sermons and manuals encompassed a voluntarism that the clergy justified on the basis of certain scholastic or philosophical truisms, and also on their own role as means of grace, intermediaries between Christ and humankind who pleaded with sinners to acknowledge and accept the gospel promise. For some of the clergy, this voluntarism was linked to an idiom of a "COVENANT" between God and humankind, with faith and repentance as conditions to be fulfilled on the part of humans in response to the promise of free grace (see COVENANT THEOLOGY).

A Movement Beset by Tensions

This description of the "practical divinity" poses anew the question as to what was distinctive about Puritanism. The anti-Catholicism of Foxe's *Book of Martyrs* was the meat and drink of popular Protestantism in early seventeenth-century England. Many Puritans who taught or practiced the order of salvation accepted some version of episcopal church government; William Perkins conformed to the rules of the church. Nor were "forward" Puritans committed to the "Presbyterian" form of church government that most of the Reformed churches on the Continent had adopted (see PRESBYTERIANISM, PRESBYTERY, CHURCH GOVERNMENT). Although a substantial number of clergy and laity were uncomfortable with Catholic "remnants," an un-

disciplined clergy, and the "mixed" or unpurified nature of church membership, the Puritan movement of the early seventeenth century cannot be neatly summarized, in part because it contained an incipient radicalism and a de facto "CONGREGATIONALISM" that grew up within Puritan-controlled towns and parishes, especially in the counties of Essex and Suffolk. Any movement founded on a vision of the "true" church, and wielding also the categories of "unlawful" and "idolatrous," was bound to spawn purists who rejected any accommodation with the "corruptions" of the Church of England. A leading example of this purism was "Separatism," or secession from the Church of England on the grounds that, having violated the law of God, it was no longer a true church. The most important of the early Separatists was the clergyman ROBERT BROWNE, who laid out this argument in a brief, illicitly published pamphlet entitled *Reformation without Tarying for Anie* (1582). Other Separatists followed him in denouncing the church as untrue and in acting out of "conscience" to form independent congregations in which they experimented with covenants and lay-centered governance. Facing heavy fines, imprisonment, or execution, most of the Separatists moved to the Netherlands. One such group of exiles, originating as a congregation in Yorkshire under the leadership of JOHN ROBINSON, settled in Amsterdam and afterward in Leiden (1609); some of this group sailed on the *Mayflower* in 1620 and founded the colony of Plymouth in New England.

Those clergy who rejected schism and remained within the church faced another set of tensions. Should they work vigorously to exclude the ignorant and the scandalous in their parishes from the sacraments of baptism and the Lord's Supper? To attempt such a process of discipline in local churches was to risk arousing anger and conflict within a town or parish. Yet to accept everyone was to admit pollution into the church. No less perplexing was the dilemma of whether to practice some aspects of nonconformity, as in refusing to wear the vestments of a priest or omitting the sign of the cross in the service of baptism, irregularities that appealed to many members of the spiritual brotherhood. The fundamental tension, present within the Reformed tradition but exacerbated in the English context, was theological, whether to understand the visible church as comprehensive or as selective. Every puritan-minded minister also faced the moral dilemma of whether schism was preferable to conformity.

When the authority of the crown collapsed in the early 1640s and Parliament assumed control of the church, these tensions made it impossible for the reformers to agree on how to reorganize the church. At the WESTMINSTER ASSEMBLY, a gathering of English and Scottish clergy commissioned in 1643 by Parliament to prepare a new scheme of church order, the great majority favored some version of presbyterianism. A minority insisted that the true apostolic model was "independency" or congregationalism, that is, a church order centered on the authority of each autonomous (and selective) congregation. The Assembly did, however, prepare the widely acknowledged WESTMINSTER CONFESSION and a CATECHISM. As this debate was taking place, thousands of lay men and women, together with some clergy, were rethinking the relationship between Scripture and the Holy Spirit, the place of the "law" in the order of salvation, the timing of the coming kingdom, and the proper basis for church and state. Out of this period of confusion and innovation emerged three enduring religious communities in England, each with puritanism as its parent: the Independents or Congregationalists; the BAPTISTS, who repudiated infant baptism and who, like the Independents, favored the autonomy of local congregations; and the SOCIETY OF FRIENDS, or Quakers, a group that began to take shape in the early 1650s and that rejected all external "forms" (ministry, sacraments, instituted church) in favor of an indwelling of the Holy Spirit. Not surprisingly, these groups challenged the authority of the civil state over the church. Certain radicals such as JOHN MILTON, Oliver Cromwell, and ROGER WILLIAMS (who published in England even though he lived in New England) began to argue for a wider liberty of conscience and the toleration of Jews and Protestants.

This extraordinary period came to an end in 1660 with the restoration of the monarchy. The 1662 Act of Conformity forced those clergy and laity who still wanted to pursue the puritan program to leave the Church of England and to practice their faith under conditions that sometimes approached those of persecution. Many Nonconformists, and especially Quakers, were jailed; all were excluded from major institutions such as Parliament and the universities. Slowly, the several groups of Nonconformists built up a system of alternative institutions: first and foremost, churches, congregations, or societies, but also educational and charitable institutions, together with systems of publishing. During this period the Baptist lay minister JOHN BUNYAN wrote the greatest masterpiece of Puritan prose, *The Pilgrim's Progress from This World, to That Which Is to Come* (Pt. 1, 1678; Pt. 2, 1684). At the beginning of the reign of William III, who overthrew James II in the "Glorious Revolution" of 1688, moderates on both sides proposed that the church find ways of accommodating the presbyterian and congregational wings of Nonconformity. For political and other reasons, no such accommodation occurred. Nor were the Presbyterians and Congregationalists able to overcome their own differences and combine into a single denomination, in part because some of the Presbyterians were turning away from Reformed orthodoxy as defined by the Westminster Confession. This liberalizing trend is one sign that the Puritanism of the late sixteenth century was winding down. However, a more important sign is that by the mid-1690s Nonconformists no longer aspired to reform the entire Church of England. That is, they gave up on their historical goal of attaining comprehensiveness. A movement dedicated to transforming a national church had given way to denominations or sects and to an acceptance of pluralism in place of uniformity.

Puritanism in New England

The chief motive behind the migration to New England in the 1630s of some 15,000 English men and women was their wish to worship as they pleased, although many may have also hoped to improve their economic situation. The emigrants, most of whom came as families, included a large contingent of clergy whose authority helped to ensure that the colonists were spared most of the confusion that undermined the English movement in the 1640s and 1650s. Compared to the situation in England, Puritanism in New England may seem remarkably coherent, as in certain respects it was. Yet no culture is static or completely homogeneous, and so change and conflict also figure in the New World side of the story.

The emigrants experimented in various ways with how to reorganize church, ministry, and worship. By 1636 a normative pattern was taking shape, a pattern described in a document drafted and approved by a "synod" of ministers that met in Cambridge, Massachusetts, in 1646 and 1648 and subsequently approved by individual churches and the Massachusetts civil government. Published in 1649 in Cambridge and London under the title *A Platform of Church Discipline Gathered Out of the Word of God,* but familiarly known as the CAMBRIDGE PLATFORM, this document defined the true church as covenanted and selective in its membership; declared that such membership was confined to "visible saints," that is, adults who could make a profession of the "work of grace," together with their children; asserted that each congregation was autonomous—hence, "Congregationalism"; democratized the structure of church government by specifying that the "power of the keys" (Matthew 18:17) rested with the entire congregation (although the right to vote on church affairs was limited to men); and provided a new basis for church and state, the "two-kingdom" theory that was favored within the Reformed tradition.

The Platform was at once radical and moderate, uncompromising and flexible. Although it seemed firmly to reject the idea of the visible church as comprehensive in favor of a highly selective standard for admitting members, in several places it urged that congregations exercise the "judgment of charity." Empowering the laity in a manner akin to the experiments of the Separatists, it also insisted that God had mandated a clerical "office" with privileges and powers unique to those who were called to this vocation. Moreover, although it affirmed the autonomy of each congregation, it also permitted interchurch synods and sanctioned a role for the civil magistrates as guardians of church order.

The flexibility of the Platform and the new-found hegemony of puritan practices, however, did not prevent radical critics from attacking the new church order. Roger Williams, an ordained clergyman in the Church of England who emigrated in 1631 and was briefly attached to the church in Salem, felt that the "Congregational Way" erred in sanctioning a religious role for the civil magistrate and, Separatist-like, accused the emigrants of not fully renouncing the corruptions of the Church of England. Williams was banished from the colony in 1635, and moved to unclaimed territory to the south that became the town of Providence in a new colony, Rhode Island. The most dramatic reliving of old tensions was a controversy that arose in 1636 and 1637 over matters of doctrine, style, Biblical interpretation, and church membership. The majority of the ministers were dismayed to find themselves being criticized as "legal preachers" and "popish factors" (i.e., claiming too much authority) by some of the laity. Especially outspoken was ANNE HUTCHINSON, an articulate, self-confident woman member of the Boston church in her early forties, whose father had been a nonconformist clergyman in the Church of England and whose husband was a substantial merchant. The ministers were further dismayed to discover that their colleague JOHN COTTON, a minister in the Boston church and a man of great personal authority, was questioning some aspects of their preaching. Together, Cotton and Anne Hutchinson complained that the other ministers were resting assurance of salvation on evidence that tilted in the direction of "SANCTIFICATION," or "works." Rhetoric quickly overtook reality. The majority riposted by equating Hutchinson and her followers with ANTINOMIANISM and by warning that social and religious order would be turned "upside down" if WOMEN were allowed to assert themselves in public, as Hutchinson seemed to be doing. Cotton eventually yielded to the pressure put on him to disavow Anne Hutchinson and to cease criticizing his colleagues. Hutchinson, who asserted a role as prophetess and veered off into murky waters, theologically, was banished from the colony in 1638. A number of persons, most of them members of the Boston church, were also banished or penalized in other ways.

Historians continue to debate whether John Cotton and the "legal" preachers, of whom the most important were Thomas Shepard, THOMAS HOOKER, Richard Mather, and Peter Bulkeley, were at odds with each other or out of step with Reformed ORTHODOXY. Regardless of any such differences, the Westminster Shorter Catechism became the catechism of choice among the colonists by the end of the seventeenth century, and the clergy affirmed the Westminster Confession (technically in its "congregational" version, known as the Savoy Declaration of 1658) as their doctrinal standard.

Uniformity, Change, and Identity

The "Congregational Way" fulfilled the longstanding ambition of the Puritan movement to restore the apostolic model of the church, in their eyes the only "lawful" system of church governance. Christian primitivism—that is, the goal of eliminating all "humane inventions" and restoring the purity of the "first times"—also shaped the earliest compilations of "laws and liberties" (1641; 1648) in Massachusetts and New Haven. The rules and practices that governed civil society were consistent in other ways with the Puritan program. The colonists substituted numbers for the customary "pagan" names of the months and days of the calendar, eliminated all of the holidays and feast days of the traditional liturgical calendar, restricted the sale of alcohol, and required families to teach their children to read. More unusual, even unexpected, was the restricting of freemanship, a legal status that entitled those admitted to it to vote in civil affairs, to men who were church members. In the two colonies (Massachusetts and New Haven) where this law was enacted, its purpose was to protect the churches from unwarranted intrusions, not of giving the churches authority over civil affairs. Simultaneously, although informally, the colonists resolved to exclude the clergy from holding civil office, a means of safeguarding the civil state from undue influences. Yet the underlying assumption was that the two "kingdoms," the one "spiritual," the other "temporal," constituted a harmonious whole grounded on the principle that God wanted both forms of government to enforce the moral law and defend truth against heresy. Yet the extent to which everyday life was regulated by a strict moral code or families by patriarchy is often exaggerated, as it was by Nathaniel Hawthorne in *The Scarlet Letter* (1850).

The consolidating of this social and religious system was abetted by institutions that dated back to the beginnings of settlement. In 1636 a group of ministers initiated the founding of a college, shortly to be named Harvard after a minister who died in 1638 and left half of his estate to the new institution. Its leading purpose was to provide a ministry fully literate in the classical languages and in the "arts" of thinking and writing, as then understood, to take the place of the men who emigrated in the 1630s. Because it was also assumed that truth—that is, a Reformed Protestant understanding of God's Word—was clearly revealed to anyone who honestly sought it, differences of opinion were regarded as inappropriate, possibly subversive of good order, and potentially as sins against the divine will. The well-being of the godly commonwealth depended, therefore, on preventing any such differences of opinion, which the magistrates and ministers likened to infectious disease. The colonists acknowledged a "liberty of conscience" that could be exercised privately, aside from civil obligations. Otherwise, they assumed that the civil state was responsible for suppressing religious dissent.

The colonists' policy of uniformity was put to the test in the 1640s, when it attracted the attention of English radicals, but more severely so in the late 1650s when the first Quaker missionaries arrived in Massachusetts, and again in the 1660s when a small group of Congregationalists renounced infant baptism and organized a Baptist church (1665). Whippings, fines, and imprisonment proved ineffective; and the execution of four Quakers in Massachusetts between 1659 and 1661 led the English government to order that no more such executions take place. When the civil government in Massachusetts was reorganized in 1691 on the basis of a charter granted by William III in place of the original charter of the Massachusetts Bay Company, the crown mandated a certain measure of toleration.

Meanwhile the Congregational system had been evolving in several respects. The Cambridge Platform left unresolved a question that eventually had to be addressed: were the children of a parent who had been baptized as an infant entitled to the sacrament themselves? Strictly speaking the answer was no because baptism belonged only to the children of persons who qualified for membership on the basis of describing the work of grace. In the 1630s and 1640s, the original system worked well enough to incorporate at least half, and perhaps closer to three-quarters, of the colonists and their children within the church. However, as those children came of age and had families of their own, a much smaller percentage of them came forward as adults to offer the customary testimony. Were all those who were simply members by virtue of their baptism entitled to remain as members, and to pass the privilege of membership on to the next generation? First in 1657, then in 1662, two councils of ministers answered this question affirmatively. In authorizing what was later nicknamed the "half-way covenant," they ended up creating two categories of visible saints: "full" members, entitled to vote in church affairs and participate in the Lord's Supper, and members in the "external" covenant, entitled mainly to have their children baptized. Schisms and ongoing conflict followed upon the decisions of 1662, for some congregations and a handful of ministers resisted any deviation from the original rules, labeling them "humane inventions." Gradually the second category of members surpassed the first in size. As this happened, the Congregational Way became a hybrid: selective or gathered in one respect, but very nearly a parish church system in another. Moreover, local practice varied from one town to the next, with towns and churches in the Connecticut River Valley always a little out of step with those along the coast.

From the beginning, the Puritan colonists puzzled over the meaning of their venture across the Atlantic. The framework of Christian primitivism served them well in some respects. Another framework was providence, a framework the colonists shared with most other Christians of their day. The answer to a great many questions (e.g., why safe passage across the Atlantic, why that drought or storm or illness) was the intention (and attention) of a God who watched over and arranged every event in human life. Discerning the signs of God's providence, and deciphering their significance, was an ongoing challenge that engaged the ministers, the civil leaders, and a great many ordinary people. Most of these people also assumed that the colonists had entered into a national covenant with God, a sequel to the great prototype in Deuteronomy. A covenanted people were obligated to obey God's rules and persist in holiness; if they faltered, then God was sure to indicate his anger. As early as the late 1630s, the ministers were beginning to warn that the colonists were losing some of their fervor, and by the 1660s and 1670s these warnings had coalesced in a sermon form known as the JEREMIAD. INCREASE MATHER, a second-generation colonist and longtime minister in Boston, became perhaps the most persistent preacher of jeremiads. He was also drawn to APOCALYPTICISM, or the expectation that the final events foretold in Revelation were beginning to occur. It has often been suggested that the Puritans in New England were millenarians who thought of themselves as distinctively "chosen" and their land as the site of the New Jerusalem of the end times, although the prevailing world view was closer to primitivism and providentialism (see MILLENARIANS AND MILLENNIAL-ISM).

Well into the eighteenth century the "Congregational Way" remained the dominant system of church government in the New England colonies, and the "practical divinity" that can be traced back to William Perkins reigned as well. Given these continuities, and given the thorough implementing in New England of the Reformed program with respect to worship, doctrine, ministry, church and state, sacred space, and time, dating the "end" of Puritanism in New England is almost an artificial exercise. Yet the hegemony of Puritanism in New England can easily mislead historians and interpreters in the twenty-first century into exaggerating its importance. Much of the intellectual baggage of the colonists, together with the social rules they employed about such matters as property distribution, child rearing, and inheritance, drew on far more complex sources: custom, humanism, and the English common law, to name but three. Separating out these influences from those that originated within the Puritan movement of the late sixteenth century is crucial, as is recognizing that Puritanism modified its tone or coloring in response to changing historical circumstances and in its multiple local settings.

Puritanism and Modernity

In the twentieth century, Puritanism attracted a great deal of attention as a likely source of MODERNITY. The German social theorist MAX WEBER advanced the most influential argument in this regard. He proposed that Protestants, but especially the Puritans, had transformed the "other-worldly asceticism" of the Catholic system as practiced by monastics into a "this-worldly asceticism," that is, a disciplined approach to time and work that drew its energy from anxieties about being one of the elect. In turn, this "work ethic," or making work normative and regular, had been a critical agent in the making of capitalism, which incorporated this self-discipline and transmuted it into an unrelenting urge to work and therefore to acquire. The American sociologist Robert Merton complemented Weber's broad argument by proposing that English Puritans had played a distinctive role in the scientific revolution of the seventeenth century (see NATURE). More recently, social historians of early modern England have proposed that Puritans took the lead in suppressing the communal and morally extravagant modes of "traditional popular culture" with a proto–middle-class culture of discipline centered on the FAMILY and the individual (see INDIVIDUALISM). Historians of Puritanism in America have followed a different path in suggesting that the movement served as a source of democracy. The equivalent argument among British

historians, now generally rejected, is that Puritans advocated the authority of Parliament and "the people" over against the authority of the monarchy. To this day, Puritanism is an irresistible "x" that historians, social theorists, and cultural critics interpret in light of the ever-changing shape of modernity.

References and Further Reading

Bozeman, Theodore Dwight. *To Live Ancient Lives: The Primitivist Dimension in Puritanism*. Chapel Hill: University of North Carolina Press, 1988.
Collinson, Patrick. *The Elizabethan Puritan Movement*. Berkeley: University of California Press, 1968.
———. *The Religion of Protestants: The Church in English Society 1559–1625*. Oxford: Oxford University Press, 1982.
Foster, Stephen. *The Long Argument: English Puritanism and the Shaping of New England Culture, 1570–1700*. Chapel Hill: University of North Carolina Press, 1991.
Gura, Philip. *A Glimpse of Sion's Glory: Puritan Radicalism in New England, 1620–1660*. Middletown, CT: Wesleyan University Press, 1983.
Hall, David D. *Worlds of Wonder, Days of Judgment: Popular Religious Belief in Early New England*. New York: Knopf, 1989.
Hambrick-Stowe, Charles. *The Practice of Piety: Puritan Devotional Disciplines in Seventeenth-Century New England*. Chapel Hill: University of North Carolina Press, 1982.
Hill, Christopher. *The World Turned Upside Down: Radical Ideas during the English Revolution*. New York: Viking Press, 1972.
Lake, Peter. *Moderate Puritans and the Elizabethan Church*. Cambridge: Cambridge University Press, 1982.
Lamont, William. *Godly Rule: Politics and Religion, 1603–1660*. London: Macmillan, 1969.
Watts, Michael R. *The Dissenters: From the Reformation to the French Revolution*. Oxford: Clarendon Press, 1978.
Weber, Max. *The Protestant Ethic and the Spirit of Capitalism*. Translated by Talcott Parsons. London: Allen & Unwin, 1930.

DAVID D. HALL

PUSEY, EDWARD BOUVERIE (1800–1882)

English scholar and church leader. Pusey was born August 22, 1800 and died September 16, 1882. He was educated at Eton and Christ Church (Oxford) and was elected a fellow of Oriel College in 1823. Urged by his teachers to become versed with the new intellectual movements coming out of GERMANY so that they might be refuted, he studied at Göttingen, Berlin, and Bonn between 1825 and 1827. There he encountered J. G. Eichhorn and FRIEDRICH SCHLEIERMACHER, and established friendships with FRIEDRICH THOLUCK and JOHANN AUGUST NEANDER.

During this period Pusey, expressing sympathy with some of the German religious trends, published *An Historical Enquiry into the Probable Causes of the Rational Character lately Predominant in the Theol-*

ogy of Germany (1827). He was later to repudiate this sympathetic account and become an archcritic of the ENLIGHTENMENT theologies. As a result of his scholarship he was appointed Regius professor of Hebrew at Oxford and canon of Christ Church. He was ordained to the priesthood in the CHURCH OF ENGLAND in 1828.

Pusey's religious and political sympathies moved to the right as liberal criticism of the religious establishment grew, and by 1832 he had become convinced that the Church of England was being threatened by the growing liberal agenda. In 1833 he formally associated himself with the OXFORD MOVEMENT and its defense of the traditional tenets of the church. His first contribution to the Tracts for the Times—Tract XVIII ("Thoughts on the Benefits of the System of Fasting")—was signed with his initials (EBP). Pusey's signature to what had been theretofore anonymous publications associated both Pusey with the movement and the movement with Pusey. His academic and social standing gave status to the fledgling movement, which frequently came to be labeled "Puseyism."

During 1836 he published a series of tracts on BAPTISM that appealed to early church teachings and emphasized the seriousness of postbaptismal sins. His interest in SIN and GRACE led him to be an advocate of priestly CONFESSION. His interest in the early church also led him to organize the republication of much of the literature in the *Library of the Fathers*. Also during the late 1830s he served as an important apologist for the Oxford Movement and published his *Letter to the Bishop of Oxford* (1839).

After 1841, and JOHN HENRY NEWMAN's withdrawal from active participation in the movement on account of the negative reactions toward Tract XC, Pusey became its most important leader. In 1843 he published *The Holy Eucharist: A Comfort to the Penitent,* which emphasized the doctrine of the real presence. The vice chancellor of Oxford and six faculty of divinity condemned the sermon as heretical (see HERESY), and he was suspended from the university pulpit for two years. The harshness and questionable legality of the decision, however, earned Pusey a large degree of public sympathy.

With Newman's secession to Rome in 1845, Pusey's leadership assumed even more importance and he gave the Catholic revival within ANGLICANISM new themes. One was the focus on parish ministry. He underwrote the rebuilding of St. Saviour's, Leeds, as a memorial to his wife, and this church became a ministerial model for later Catholic-revival parishes. He participated (and financially supported) the move to

reestablish religious orders within Anglicanism. He continued to emphasize the importance of priestly confession. Although not a Ritualist himself, he strongly defended the movement among members of the Catholic revival to restore traditional ritual and ceremony in Anglican worship. Finally in the decade of the 1860s he worked to advance the cause of reunion with Rome. He argued that popular devotions and beliefs, not official doctrines, separated the two churches. The First Vatican Council and its definition of papal infallibility disappointed him profoundly.

Throughout the latter decades of his career Pusey actively assumed the role of defender of the traditional teachings of the Church of England against liberal threats. He attacked the attempt by men such as BENJAMIN JOWETT to reform (and declericize) the education at Oxford; he criticized the publication of *Essays and Reviews* (1860) and its advocacy of an historical critical approach to the BIBLE; he vigorously supported the retention of the Athanasian Creed in the Anglican BOOK OF COMMON PRAYER; he defended the belief in eternal punishment; and he fought those who wished to reconceptualize the miracles of the gospels to make Christianity more palatable to modern science.

Pusey died September 16, 1882 and was buried in the nave of Christ Church (Oxford). His library (purchased by followers of his) became the foundation of Pusey House in Oxford, an institution that continues to be a memorial and study center dedicated to his principles.

See also Anglo-Catholicism

References and Further Reading

Primary Sources:

Pusey, E. B. *Selections from the Writings of Edward Bouverie Pusey.* London: Rivingtons, 1885.
———. *The Church of England a Portion of Christ's Holy Catholic Church: and a Means of Restoring Visible Unity.* New York: Appleton, 1979.

Secondary Sources:

Butler, Perry, ed. *Pusey Rediscovered.* London: SPCK, 1983.
Forrester, David. *Young Doctor Pusey.* London: Mowbrays, 1989.
Liddon, H. P. *The Life of Edward Bouverie Pusey.* 4 vols. London: Longman, Green, 1893–1897.
Prestige, Leonard. *Pusey.* London: Philip Allen, 1933.
Rowell, Geoffrey. *The Vision Glorious: Themes and Personalities of the Catholic Revival in Anglicanism.* Oxford and New York: Oxford University Press, 1983.

ROBERT BRUCE MULLIN

Q

QUAKERS

See Friends, Society of; Society of Friends in North America

R

RADE, MARTIN (1857–1940)

German theologian. Rade was born at Rennersdorf/Oberlausitz April 4, 1857, and died at Frankfurt/Main April 9, 1940. His father was a Lutheran pastor, and he studied THEOLOGY in Leipzig, a stronghold of LUTHERANISM. His most important theological teacher was ADOLF VON HARNACK. After a brief tenure as a private tutor he became a pastor in Schoenbach/Oberlausitz in 1882, serving there for ten years. From 1892 to 1899 Rade served as minister at the Paulskirche in Frankfurt/Main.

While he was serving in his first parish, Rade also began to work as a journalist. In 1886 he founded the journal *Christliche Welt* together with theologians Wilhelm Bornemann, Paul Drews, and Friedrich Loofs. Until 1931 he remained editor and publisher of this magazine, which represented the voice of "culture Protestantism" (*Kulturprotestantismus*) in GERMANY. Rade supported the politics of national liberals. As did his brother-in-law FRIEDRICH NAUMANN, Rade later became a liberal theologian and politician. Theological and political liberalism were decisive for his religious engagement.

To devote himself to publishing the *Christliche Welt,* Rade left his parish in 1898 and began to teach at the University of Marburg. Marburg became the center of his political and journalistic work.

As a liberal theologian Rade supported the *Evangelisch-sozialer Kongreß,* which was founded in 1890. In various controversies with conservative church leaders he afforded critical voices the opportunity to publish in his journal.

Early on Rade supported the demands for a democratic Germany. After 1918 he supported the Weimar republic. Together with other liberal theologians he was active in the liberal *Deutsche Demokratische Partei.*

After 1933 Rade did not belong to the "CONFESSING CHURCH" (*Bekennende Kirche*). Despite his distance from National Socialism and his personally courageous support of individual persecuted Jews, Rade did not perceive the unjust character of the Nazi regime.

See also Cultural Protestantism; Liberal Protestantism and Liberalism

References and Further Reading

Primary Sources:

Barth, Karl, Martin Rade, and Christoph Schwobel. *Ein Brief-wechsel.* Gütersloh, Germany: Gütersloher Verlagshaus, 1981.

Rade, Martin. *Ausgewählte Schriften.* Edited by Christoph Schwoebel. 3 vols. Gütersloh, Germany: Gütersloher Verlagshaus, 1983–1988.

———. *Glaubenslehre.* Gotha, Germany: F. A. Perthes, 1924–1927.

———. *Die Stellung des Christentums zum Geschlechtsleben.* Tübingen, Germany: J. C. B. Mohr (P. Siebeck), 1910.

Secondary Sources:

Nagel, Anne Ch. *Martin Rade—Theologe und Politiker des Sozialen Protestantismus. Eine politische Biographie.* Gütersloh, Germany: Gütersloher Verlagshaus, 1996.

Rathje, Johannes. *Die Welt des Freien Protestantismus. Ein Beitrag zur deutsch-evangelischen Geistesgeschichte. Dargestellt am Leben und Werk von Martin Rade.* Stuttgart, Germany: Klotz, 1952.

NORBERT FRIEDRICH

RADIO EVANGELISM

See Mass Media

RAGAZ, LEONHARD (1868–1945)

Swiss theologian. Ragaz was born to Bartholome and Luzia Ragaz, a farming family, in Tamins in the

Grisons of SWITZERLAND on July 28, 1868. Familiar with economic hardship, and marked by his rural mountain community's cooperative movement and common ownership of the surrounding forests and meadows, Ragaz early embraced democratic socialism. After theological study in Basel, Jena, and Berlin, and ordination in 1890, he served three different congregations of the Swiss Reformed Church. The plight of the poor, problems related to alcoholism, peace, and—as a result of his marriage to Clara Nadig—WOMEN's rights claimed much of his energy alongside PREACHING. In 1908 he was called to the University of Zürich to teach systematic and practical theology. He resigned from that position in 1921, moved to the city's workers' district, and attempted to establish a settlement house there. He sided with the strikers in the highly political Swiss strikes of 1903, 1912, and 1918. A card-carrying socialist, he fought the Bolshevik and Nazi ideologies, and engaged in efforts to bring their victims into Switzerland. Ragaz died December 6, 1945.

At the heart of his religious socialism was the theology of the "KINGDOM OF GOD." For Ragaz this kingdom was a vision of the Christian revolution. The recovery of New Testament ESCHATOLOGY and its teaching of God's present and coming reign caused Ragaz to renounce the individual-focused faith of culture Protestantism. Interpreting Jesus's death and resurrection as events of a revolution that both judges the world and propels it toward its own coming resurrection, Ragaz preached a double hope: one that awaits the great change at the end of time and one that expects and works for change even now in the present. He saw such latter changes in renewal movements like democracy and socialism, and in the work for peace and women's rights while never identifying them with God's kingdom.

See also Cultural Protestantism; Socialism, Christian; Theology

References and Further Reading

Primary Sources:

Signs of the Kingdom. A Ragaz Reader. Edited and translated by Paul Bock. Grand Rapids, MI: Wm. B. Eerdmans, 1984.
Ragaz, Leonard. *Israel, Judaism, and Christianity.* London: V. Gollancz, 1947.
———. *Von Christus zu Marx, von Marx zu Christus: ein Beitrag.* Wernigerode am Harz, Germany: H. Harder, 1929.
———. *Eingriffe ins Zeitgeschehen: Reich Gotles und Politik. Texte von 1900–1945.* Luzern, Switzerland: Edition Exodus. 1995.

MARTIN RUMSCHEIDT

RAIKES, ROBERT (1735–1811)

English social reformer. Born in Gloucester, ENGLAND on September 14, 1735, Robert Raikes was the son of a printer who founded a local newspaper. Succeeding to the editorship of the paper after his father's death in 1757, Raikes became known for his local benevolence. In 1768, for example, he appealed in the paper for reform of abuses in the local jail's treatment of prisoners, gaining the notice of leading English philanthropists in the process. His initiative, his access to the press, and the attention he had received set the stage for his most notable achievement, the creation of four small schools to educate poor children of Gloucester, the first of which opened in July 1780. In November 1783, his newspaper mentioned the success of these schools, attracting considerable attention and encouraging similar initiatives elsewhere. Thus, Robert Raikes became known as the creator of the SUNDAY SCHOOL.

However, Raikes cannot be credited with originating educational programs for children. There is an extensive history of Christian initiative in this respect, especially programs under evangelical sponsorship in the mid-eighteenth century. But Raikes drew together several previously disparate themes: the necessity of basic Christian education for children, the possibilities inherent in education for poor children, and the role of independent, lay-led programs to supplement the churches. Initially Sunday schools functioned as ecumenical agencies (see ECUMENISM). But by the mid-nineteenth century, they became aligned with denominational programs and were subject to CLERGY oversight. Raikes found support for his own work from influential Anglican bishops. He retired from business in 1802 and died in Gloucester on April 5, 1811.

See also Education, Overview; Denomination

References and Further Reading

Booth, Frank. *Robert Raikes of Gloucester.* National Christian Education Council, 1980.
Cliff, Philip B. *The Rise and Development of the Sunday School Movement in England, 1780–1980.* National Christian Education Council, 1986.
Laqueur, Thomas W. *Religion and Respectability: Sunday Schools and Working Class Culture, 1780–1850.* New Haven, CT: Yale University Press, 1976.

WILLIAM SACHS

RAMABAI, PANDITA (1858–1922)

Indian educator and Christian activist. Ramabai was born April 23, 1858 in rural INDIA and died April 5, 1922 in Kedgaon, India. The daughter of an aging

Hindu holy man and his young second wife, Ramabai learned from her parents to read and write. From her father she gained remarkable familiarity with Hindu sacred texts. The family's religious pilgrimages took them across India. By 1881 Ramabai alone had survived the poverty and famines that decimated her family.

In 1878 Ramabai had come to fame in Calcutta where the faculty of the University of Calcutta recognized her abilities by bestowing on her the coveted titles, Pandita and Sarasvati, distinctions generally not attained by WOMEN. She began her lifelong agitation for social reform, especially as it pertained to Indian women. An ardent champion of female education, Ramabai testified on behalf of Indian women before a British Commission in 1883. Shortly thereafter she sailed for ENGLAND. There, under the auspices of an Anglo-Catholic religious order (see ANGLO-CATHOLI-CISM), she converted to Christianity. In 1886 she arrived in the UNITED STATES, intent on studying education and raising support to accomplish her dream of educating high-caste Hindu widows.

Between 1886 and 1888 Ramabai traveled in the United States, often under the auspices of the Women's Christian Temperance Union. In December 1887 Edward Everett Hale chaired a large meeting in Boston's Channing Hall at which a Ramabai Association was formed. PHILLIPS BROOKS, George A. Gordon, FRANCES WILLARD, and Mary Hemenway joined him on its board. The Association pledged the support of leading American Protestants in the task of creating a residential school in Bombay for high-caste Hindu widows. Over the next ten years Ramabai more than fulfilled this dream. Her efforts for social change soon assumed a distinctive Christian cast and drew larger numbers of evangelically minded Protestants to her support. Within a decade she had established two institutions, the larger of which housed nearly 2,000 widows and orphans in a community she called "Mukti," or "Salvation." She maintained close ties to American and British Protestants and welcomed various missionaries to assist in her efforts. She undertook a translation of the BIBLE into colloquial Marathi, with study notes included to enable Indian women to work as village evangelists.

For two decades, Ramabai captured the hearts of American Protestants. She affiliated with no American DENOMINATIONS, but most of them supported her. She carried on her work as an Indian venture in which missionaries could be partners, although Indians retained control. A TEMPERANCE advocate and ardent supporter of the "uplifting" of India's women, she seized a critical moment and has been recognized since as a precursor of feminism whose efforts inspired not only Anglo-American Protestants but also the builders of modern India.

See also Bible Translation; Education, Overview

References and Further Reading

Primary Sources:

Ramabai, Pandita. *The High-Caste Hindu Woman*. Philadelphia, PA: JB Rodgers, 1888.
———. *A Testimony of Our Inexhaustible Treasure*. Kedgaon, India: Pandita Ramabai Mukti Mission, 1992.
Ramabai, Pandita, and Shamsundar Manohar Adhav. *Pandita Ramabai*. Madras, India: Christian Literature Society, 1979.
Ramabai, Pandita, and Meera Kosambi. *Pandita Ramabai Through Her Own Words: Selected Works*. New Delhi, India; New York: Oxford University Press, 2000.
———. *Pandita Ramabai's American Encounter: The Peoples of the United States (1889)*. Bloomington: Indiana University Press, 2003.

Secondary Source:

Adhav, Shamsundar Manohar. *Pandita Ramabai*. Madras, India: Christian Literature Society, 1979.

EDITH BLUMHOFER

RAMSEY, ARTHUR MICHAEL (1904–1988)

Archbishop of Canterbury. A biblical theologian, archbishop, and keen ecumenist, Ramsey saw the need for the church to hold together the extremes of catholic sacramental TRADITION and reformed concern for scriptural AUTHORITY.

Arthur Michael Ramsey was born November 14, 1904 in Cambridge, ENGLAND and died April 25, 1988 in Oxford. He was brought up within a Congregationalist heritage, of Anglo-Catholic formation, and educated at CAMBRIDGE UNIVERSITY. Ramsey was ordained in the CHURCH OF ENGLAND in 1928. He served in parochial ministry and lectured in THEOLOGY at the universities of Lincoln and Durham. In 1950 he was appointed Regius professor of divinity at Cambridge. Two years later he was elevated to bishop of Durham, and archbishop of York. He was archbishop of CANTERBURY from 1961 to 1974.

Despite a liberal political instinct, Ramsey was theologically conservative, and maintained that gospel truth is recognized through the CHURCH and sacramental participation. This ignored the contribution of theologians outside ecclesiastical structures. Ramsey would have struggled to engage with later feminist and liberation theologians. Influenced by KARL BARTH's commentary on the book of Romans, his most significant work, *The Gospel and the Catholic Church*, stresses the cross as the starting point for theological truth, with the BIBLE as the living word that opens the heart to Christ's living presence. Reading FREDERICK DENISON MAURICE, Ramsey became increasingly unimpressed by Protestantism's lack of creational and incarnational appreciation in its focus on a gulf between God and the world.

Once at Canterbury, Ramsey established dialogue, declarations, and papers with Eastern Orthodox and Roman Catholic Churches. By conviction a disestablishmentarian, he worked, unsuccessfully, toward reunification with the Methodist church, and closer ties with LUTHERANISM. Criticized by liberals for not being radical enough, and by fundamentalists for encouraging Catholic rites and ritual, Ramsey would have been gladdened by the increased engagement by Protestants with the ascetical tradition (such as retreats), and by Catholics with biblical theology. His primacy was made difficult by his producing reactionary defenses of ORTHODOXY, poor administration, and disinterest in the appointment of bishops.

See also Catholicism, Protestant Reactions; Dialogue, Interconfessional; Ecumenism; Fundamentalism; Methodism, England; Orthodoxy, Eastern; Neo-Orthodoxy

References and Further Reading

Primary Source:

Ramsey, Arthur Michael. *The Gospel and the Catholic Church.* London: Longmans, Green and Co., 1936.

Secondary Sources:

Chadwick, Owen. *Michael Ramsey: A Life.* Oxford, UK: Clarendon Press, 1990.

Gill, Robin, and Lorna Kendall, eds. *Michael Ramsey as Theologian.* London: Darton, Longman and Todd, 1995.

JAMES CHAPMAN

RAPTURE

The term "rapture" comes from the Latin *raptus* or *rapio,* denoting "caught up." This derives from St. Paul's description of the Second Advent: "For the Lord himself shall descend from heaven with a shout, with the voice of the archangel, and with the trump of God: and the dead in Christ shall rise first: Then we which are alive and remain shall be caught up [*harpagesometha*] together with them in the clouds, to meet the Lord in the air: and so shall we ever be with the Lord" (I Thessalonians 4:16–17, King James Version). Now although this "catching away" was understood throughout most of the history of the church as referring to what would happen to the people of God at the return of Christ, during the nineteenth century a

more specific understanding was formulated whereby the rapture of the church by Christ was distinguished from the second coming of Christ with the church. This development itself produced a variety of eschatological scenarios associated with whether the rapture would occur before, during, or after the tribulational period understood to precede the second coming and millennial reign of Christ.

The Rapture as Distinct from the Second Advent

The emergence to prominence of the specific notion of the rapture from the more general doctrine of the second coming must be understood against developments in eschatological ideas during the seventeenth through nineteenth centuries. Given developments in the new world, the amillennial view of Augustine dominant during the Middle Ages was gradually displaced initially by a growing acceptance of a postmillennialism (of not necessarily 1,000 literal years) thought to be ushered in by the church. However, the FRENCH REVOLUTION and the Second Great AWAKENING and associated REVIVALS at the turn of the nineteenth century precipitated a more apocalyptic perspective resulting in British and American mid-century Millenarian movements like MORMONISM, SEVENTH-DAY ADVENTISM, Irvingism (followers of Edward Irving), and PLYMOUTH BRETHRENISM. The RESTORATIONISM of these groups led to a literalistic and futuristic reading of biblical prophecies, especially Revelation chapters 6–19, and a retrieval of what might be called the historic premillennialism of the early (pre-Constantinian) church whereby the second advent would inaugurate the 1,000-year reign of Christ.

This set of premillennialist ideas were forged into a system known as DISPENSATIONALISM by JOHN NELSON DARBY (1800–1882). Central features of Darby's dispensationalism included a distinction between scriptures addressed to and regarding the two ages of Israel (the former preceding Christ and the future millennium) and scriptures regarding the parenthetical age of the church (present) and addressed to the church. This dispensationalist reading of the BIBLE concluded that the future literal millennial reign of God would fulfill all the prophecies concerning the "Day of the Lord" made to Israel; that there would be a transition period between this present age of the church and the future millennium of about seven years (derived from various interpretations of the frequent references to three and a half years made in the books of Daniel and Revelation); that this transitional period would be one of "great tribulation" (Matthew 24:21) upon the earth; and that the church would be removed or raptured secretly and suddenly (see also I Corinthians 15:52

and Matthew 24:40–41), thereby releasing the tribulational forces and inaugurating this "hour of temptation" (Revelation 3:10, KJV). In this way, it was thought, the scriptural teachings regarding the imminent return of Christ on the one hand and the Second Advent as preceded by signs on the other could be reconciled. The former referred to the secret rapture for the church and the latter to the second coming of the Messiah with the church.

Theological Perspectives and Debates

Darby's dispensationalism in general and pretribulationist rapture theory in particular gained a following across large segments of conservative North American Protestantism through the Bible Conference movement of the late nineteenth and early twentieth centuries. The publication of the widely distributed SCOFIELD REFERENCE BIBLE (1909, improved edition 1917) both popularized and further solidified this pretribulationist and premillennialist ESCHATOLOGY. By the mid-twentieth century, however, sufficient questions had been raised about the pretribulationist theory to result in a variety of premillennialist scenarios.

Posttribulationists, for example, called attention to the many scriptural texts that indicated the church would endure rather than be exempt from persecution, thus questioning the function of the rapture to preserve the saints. Further, they were unconvinced that the two-stage return of Christ—*for* the Church first and then *with* the Church—could be sustained exegetically, thus affirming the historic premillennialist understanding of a single Second Advent. Finally, and perhaps more subtly decisive, posttribulationists are neither staunch dispensationalists nor biblical literalists.

Midtribulationalism, by far the minority of the three positions, describes the attempt of those who responded to the posttribulationist questions by distinguishing between a "milder" tribulational period during the first half of the seven years and the more "wrathful" tribulational period during the last three and a half years. Whereas the church will endure the tribulation, she will be saved "from the wrath to come" (I Thessalonians 1:10; cf. I Thessalonians 5:9) at the sounding of the seventh trumpet (Revelation 11:15–19). Finally, the partial-rapture view is advocated by those who wish to acknowledge the call of the New Testament texts to vigilance and faithfulness. Those like the five virgins with oil in their lamps (Matthew 25:1–13) will be taken whereas the rest will be saved, but only through enduring the tribulation.

See also Millenarians and Millennialism

References and Further Reading

Gundry, Robert H. *The Church and the Tribulation*. Grand Rapids, MI: Zondervan, 1973.

Ladd, George Eldon. *The Blessed Hope: A Biblical Study of the Second Advent and the Rapture*. Grand Rapids, MI: Wm. B. Eerdmans, 1956.

Prosser, Peter E. *Dispensationalist Eschatology and Its Influence on American and British Religious Movements*. Lewiston, NY: The Edwin Mellen Press, 1999.

Reiter, Richard R., Paul D. Feinberg, Gleason L. Archer, and Douglas J. Moo. *The Rapture: Pre-, Mid-, or Post-Tribulational?* Grand Rapids, MI: Academic Books/Zondervan Publishing House, 1984.

Sandeen, Ernest R. *The Roots of Fundamentalism: British and American Millenarianism, 1800–1930*. Chicago and London: The University of Chicago Press, 1970.

Walvoord, John F. *The Rapture Question*. Rev. and enlarged. Grand Rapids, MI: Zondervan, 1979.

AMOS YONG

RAUSCHENBUSCH, WALTER (1861–1918)

The leading exponent of the American social gospel movement. Rauschenbusch was admired for the clarity and passion of his speaking and writing. Considered a social prophet in church circles, he was known to the public through books, magazine, and newspaper articles in which his social and religious thought appeared. Rauschenbusch both contributed to and was swept along by the multifaceted Progressive movement of the early twentieth century. Like many progressives, his views were informed by a mild form of socialism, belief in progress in history, the importance of democratic freedom, and American MANIFEST DESTINY. He believed the KINGDOM OF GOD would come in America if the church could be motivated to join the social movement already underway in society.

Rauschenbusch, who spent part of his childhood and his high school years in GERMANY, was fluent in German and English. He was born October 4, 1961 to August and Caroline Rauschenbusch in Rochester, New York, where his father had joined the German department at Rochester Theological Seminary (RTS) after serving as a German Baptist missionary to the Missouri frontier. They eventually returned to Germany. A graduate of the Free Academy of Gütersloh, Germany (1884), the University of Rochester (1884), and RTS (1886), he later returned to Europe four times to visit relatives, for independent study in Germany, and to observe the effects of social Christianity in ENGLAND. In 1893 he married Pauline Rother, a German Baptist born in Silesia. They had five children.

Rauschenbusch served as the pastor of a German-speaking Baptist immigrant congregation on the edge of "Hell's Kitchen" in New York City for eleven years before becoming a professor of the New Testament in the German Department at RTS in 1897. While still a pastor he published German translations of gospel hymns with IRA D. SANKEY (1840–1908) and a life of Jesus in German. A move to the English Department of the seminary in 1902 as professor of church history marked the beginning of his remarkable career as a social prophet to American Protestants. Although dozens of pastors and professors were associated with the Social Gospel, Rauschenbusch attracted a national following as a platform speaker, lecturer, and writer after the publication of *Christianity and the Social Crisis* in 1907. After that he crisscrossed the country speaking at public forums, in college, seminary, and YMCA lecture series, and at Baptist and ecumenical church gatherings. Among his favorite topics were "The New Evangelism," "What About the Woman?" and "The Freedom of Spiritual Religion."

In addition to *Christianity and the Social Crisis,* he wrote seven other books in English. The best known were *Christianizing the Social Order* (1912); *The Social Principles of Jesus* (1916), written as a study book for the YMCA; and *A Theology for the Social Gospel* (1917). *A Theology for the Social Gospel,* his only sustained engagement with theological reflection, is an important link in the development of modern American theology and social ethics.

As the young pastor of an immigrant congregation, Rauschenbusch was deeply disturbed by the traumatic effect of city life on the poor, and the sudden economic fluctuations and social unrest marked by the labor problems, riots, strikes, and boycotts of the late 1880s. Many of his views about the church and social issues were formed at that time through his study of writers such as the Christian economist Richard Ely (1854–1943), the social theorist Henry George, the utopian visionary Edward Bellamy, and English social Christians like FREDERICK D. MAURICE (1805–1872) and Frederick W. Robertson. He refers to German theologians like FRIEDRICH SCHLEIERMACHER (1768–1834) and ALBRECHT RITSCHL (1822–1889) in his later writing, but his approach to "the social question" and theology was shaped by the American context of his ministry, Anglo-American social Christianity, and the theology of HORACE BUSHNELL (1802–1876).

Rauschenbusch was a founding member of The Brotherhood of the Kingdom, a group of Social Gospel leaders who met annually from 1893 to about 1912 for study, discussion of position papers, prayer, and communion. The goal of his ministry was the same as the stated purpose of the brotherhood, to reestablish the idea of the Kingdom of God in the thought of the church and to assist in its practical realization in the world. This meant using every available means of communication to influence and change public opinion.

Rauschenbusch continued to write and speak until a year before his death from cancer at the age of fifty-seven. As Europe moved toward war in 1914, there were growing allegations that he was a German sympathizer. The loneliness he had experienced as a young pastor stricken by serious hearing loss returned to haunt his final years. When he died, Social Gospel and seminary colleagues set aside political and theological disagreements and acknowledged him as the most influential figure in the development of the social gospel in America. Harry F. Ward (1873–1966), a Methodist social gospeler, predicted that future leaders of religion would continue to find guidance and inspiration in his writing.

The Social Gospel, a Movement and a Theology

Theologians are usually associated with a school of theology, but the Social Gospel is both a movement and a theology. A leading propagandist for the movement, Rauschenbusch had an extensive network of people across the country who corresponded with him, received copies of his books, and invited him to speak. Although many social gospelers published books with a similar combination of social and religious thought, only those by Rauschenbusch continue to move and impress readers. With the exception of *A Theology for the Social Gospel,* his theological convictions were rarely stated directly, a characteristic that made it possible for him to address several audiences simultaneously.

Although social gospel theology was one of several new theologies written to defend the credibility of Christian beliefs seriously challenged by DARWINISM and biblical criticism, social gospelers always gave priority to social problems and social ethics. In his quest for a new synthesis, Rauschenbusch incorporated theories from Bushnell about moral law, language, and the progressive unfolding of truth with social theory, popular science, and political economy. Emboldened by a belief that revelation is always mediated through personal contact between God's spirit and the human spirit, he was highly selective in his use of the BIBLE, drawing most often on the Old Testament prophets and the life and ministry of Jesus for inspiration. He regarded parts of the Bible as outmoded, even harmful to modern moral principles.

The theme of unity and social cooperation pervades Rauschenbusch's thought. He had observed the reactionary response of doctrinal denominations like the Baptists to social and intellectual change, and was convinced that theological conflict and competition between denominations worked against God's Kingdom on earth. Because he believed that metaphysical issues and the language of orthodox theology were also divisive, he expressed himself in noncreedal, nondoctrinal language. For similar reasons he participated in ecumenical organizations like the EVANGELICAL ALLIANCE and the Federal Council of Churches.

In the first paragraph of *A Theology for the Social Gospel,* Rauschenbusch writes that the church needs a theology large enough to match the social gospel and vital enough to back it. He was well aware of the difficulty of consolidating "the old faith" with the new aim of social salvation, but felt constrained to respond to a growing chorus of detractors who said the social gospel had no theology. His use of the term "social gospel" was ambiguous. His earlier books appealed to an amorphous Protestant public associated with American manifest destiny, and relied on phrases like the Fatherhood of God and the brotherhood of man, slogans with religious overtones also frequently used by politicians.

A Theology for the Social Gospel, written originally for a Yale University lecture series, reflects the knowledge of a professor of New Testament and church history. In each chapter Rauschenbusch contrasted old and new theology, describing differing interpretations of doctrines like sin, salvation, eschatology, and atonement. He critiqued old ways of thinking, then offered a new social approach to each doctrine. Saying that the social gospel had already become orthodox, he clearly believed theology was behind the times.

Christianity and the Social Crisis, written during a period of Protestant cultural hegemony, challenged readers to recognize and respond to the changing social order. Rauschenbusch urged Christians to recover the social purpose of Jesus's ministry and make it their own. He argued that the Kingdom would come if Christians accepted their social responsibility. Otherwise, society could regress or worse, fall into social chaos, a powerful argument at a time when early twentieth-century optimism was tempered by constant fear of social disorder.

In *Christianizing the Social Order,* Rauschenbusch claimed that God was acting through a social awakening already underway to create a new social order that would fulfill the highest ideals of democratic freedom. Describing family, church, education, and politics as already Christianized, he urged Christians to give their attention to the economic order, which he regarded as the primary source of social unrest and individual moral failure. He outlined the ways Christians could contribute to or even hasten the coming Kingdom, consigning women to "the home" while calling men to social amelioration in the world of business and politics.

Always alert to the impact of religious language and ideas, Rauschenbusch chose his words carefully, more like an evangelist than a classical theologian. He was critical of the negative impact of older theologies on both church and culture. In 1894 he presented a paper to a Baptist congress in which he explained that using language inappropriate to the age to represent God would retard progress. He almost always referred to God as Father, a familial reference to the love, justice, and brotherhood that characterize the Kingdom of God, but deplored references to God as Judge as too individualistic to inspire and undergird modern social faith.

Rauschenbusch prized the freedom of American democracy because he considered freedom essential to moral development. He evaluated the social maturity of nations, historical periods, religions, and social groups according to the extent to which they were capable of living a moral life in an immoral society. Although his ideal was a society in which moral maturity for all was a possibility, he never expected social perfection due to the fluctuating nature of society. He regularly cited the freedom of American women as a sign of progress, but gave limited support to women's suffrage, saying that women lacked the moral maturity needed to participate in politics.

Legacy to American Protestantism

Walter Rauschenbusch longed for a faith to give unity to the whole of life, and found it in the Kingdom of God. It was the grand overarching vision through which he saw his own work as unifying theology and ethics, sacred and secular, church and state. He used the phrase to signify God's coming Kingdom on earth, the importance of doing God's will, personal union with Christ and God, unity in the church, nation, and world. It was important to him that Jesus introduced the Kingdom idea to his followers, died for the Kingdom, and instructed his followers to sacrifice themselves for it.

During his lifetime some critics regarded his theology as heretical. By the 1920s, early fundamentalists declared him an enemy of the church and orthodoxy. Yet as the most kindly, collegial apologist of the Social Gospel, Rauschenbusch played a major role in the restoration of historic Protestant concern for civic order and justice in American denominations. Never before in American church history had so many pastors, professors, and church members been caught up in the social issues, politics, and practical reform measures of their time.

Rauschenbusch participated in limited civic reform in Rochester, but his primary social ministry was his work as a scholar seeking social change by changing minds. His understanding of the potential of human nature for goodness and the reality of social change

RAUSCHENBUSCH, WALTER

was overly optimistic. Scientific theories of social evolution widely accepted at the time led him to believe there would be far less need for government and laws to protect people from each other as capitalism was gradually replaced by a cooperative social order. In the meantime, he challenged the churches to replace the old individual motive with the new social motive essential to moral and social progress. In his gradualist, noninterventionist understanding of progress there would always be a place for religion as the source and safeguard of moral progress in society.

A moralist at heart, the legacy of Rauschenbusch to Protestantism is mixed. The ethicist and theologian REINHOLD NIEBUHR (1892–1971) was an articulate critic of Rauschenbusch's optimism about human nature, history, and social progress; yet without Rauschenbusch it is unlikely that Niebuhr would have written a book like *Moral Man in Immoral Society.* While Rauschenbusch undoubtedly laid foundations for a Christian social ethic, in their haste to attack his theology, his critics often fail to notice the extent to which his social ethic incorporated nineteenth-century popular science, psychology, and biological dualism.

Rauschenbusch's political agenda was far more conservative than his theology due to his belief that by the early twentieth century, laissez-faire capitalism had been contained, making the moral development and maturity of the American people a real possibility. He opposed the use of legislation as an instrument of social change, holding that a new law should represent an existing consensus of public opinion. He objected to the Sherman antitrust law, saying it worked against the law of progress by association. He opposed any idea or action that interfered with the potential of every individual for moral development through the use of the faculty of moral sense. In the final analysis his social ethic depended on a utopian vision of a society in which, as he liked to say, "good men can be good."

Walter Rauschenbusch, first-generation American, social theorist, and theologian, laid the foundations for a pragmatic theological ethic based on a rational view of the world. The power of his vision was matched by his ability to express his concern about the future of church and society through engaging writing and speaking. A seminary professor who never lost touch with church people, Rauschenbusch addressed the public at a moment in history when church and state came together around a very Protestant belief in American manifest destiny.

See also Baptist: Biblical Interpretation; Church and State; Manifest Destiny; Social Gospel.

References and Further Reading

Primary Sources:

Hudson, Winthrop S., ed. *Walter Rauschenbusch, Selected Writings.* New York: Paulist Press, 1984.
Rauschenbusch, Walter. *Christianity and the Social Crisis.* New York: Macmillan, 1907.
———. *Christianizing the Social Order.* New York: Macmillan, 1912.
———. *The Social Principles of Jesus.* New York: Association Press, 1916.
———. *A Theology for the Social Gospel.* New York: Macmillan, 1917.

Secondary Sources:

Fishburn, Janet Forsythe. *The Fatherhood of God and the Victorian Family: The Social Gospel in America.* New York: Fortress Press, 1981.
Handy, Robert T., ed. *The Social Gospel in America: Gladden, Ely, Rauschenbusch.* New York: Oxford University Press, 1966.
Jaehn, Klaus Juergen. *Walter Rauschenbusch. The Formative Years.* Valley Forge, PA: Judson Press, 1976.
Minus, Paul M. *Walter Rauschenbusch. American Reformer.* New York: Macmillan, 1988.

JANET F. FISHBURN

REFORMATION

The Reformation of the sixteenth century with deep medieval roots and variegated fruits affected every aspect of early modern life. Its evangelical sprouts not only hardened into many of the contemporary branches of Protestantism, but also intertwined with the growth of early modern Catholicism. The taxonomy of the Reformation focuses on the reformers with the supposition that without them there would have been no Reformation. At the same time, to carry our garden image a bit further, it is clear that any analysis of growth must take into account the soil and environment.

Interpretations of the Reformation

How one sees the Reformation depends on one's commitment and vantage point. Interpretations now range far beyond the stock church-historical categories of "magisterial" (led by academics—*magistri*—and supported by magistrates: Anglican, Lutheran, Calvinist); "radical" (or "left wing," dissidents and Anabaptist movements); and "Catholic" (in pre-ecumenical days, "Counter") Reformations. Political and social historians have provided a multitude of new perspectives informed by political history, Marxism, psychology, sociology, and anthropology. Older interpretations formulated by the great German scholars Leopold von Ranke (1795–1886), ERNST TROELTSCH

(1865–1923), and KARL HOLL (1866–1926) were, in one way or another, efforts to relate the modern German identity and state to the Reformation. For Ranke, the Reformation was a unique epoch of history bracketed by MARTIN LUTHER's "Ninety-Five Theses" (1517) and the "Religious Peace" of the Diet of Augsburg (1555). Troeltsch, on the other hand, viewed the magisterial Reformation, especially in its Lutheran form, as the last gasp of the Middle Ages. For Troeltsch, the break from the unified, authoritarian medieval culture and the initiation of the modern world came with the Calvinist, but even more so the Anabaptist decoupling of CHURCH AND STATE, and in the quest for individual freedom of conscience and faith. Holl strove to refute Troeltsch's position by concentrated research on Luther's theology and ETHICS as key to the integration of German CULTURE.

Marxist historians, informed by Friedrich Engels' (1820–1895) study of the Peasants' War (1524–1525), interpreted the Reformation as an early bourgeois revolution against feudalism that facilitated the next stage of social formation, capitalism. The Marxist interpretive model stimulated social-historical interests that have greatly increased knowledge of the social, economic, and theological bases of the Reformation. Informed by constructs such as "social disciplining," "CONFESSIONALIZATION," and "popular religion," there has been a growing sense that "the Reformation" consists of a number of messily intertwining movements with such labels as "princes' Reformation," "urban Reformation," "communal Reformation," and "peoples' Reformation" that extend back to medieval renewal movements and into the early modern period. While the debate over the plurality of Reformations and their interpretations shows no sign of slackening, some scholars remind us that there would not have been a Reformation without reformers. The reformers themselves were driven by the question that Luther posed in a 1524 letter to Strasbourg, "What makes a person a Christian?"

In continuity with the early church, the reformers sought answers to this question in the praxis of the worshipping community: *lex orandi, lex credendi.* Hence, although the Reformation is traditionally dated from Luther's posting of the "Ninety-Five Theses," it is important to remember that this formal academic disputation focused on the sacrament of penance and its associated issues of justification, indulgences, purgatory, and ecclesiastical authority. Sharply put, the Reformation began with a focus on the central pastoral praxis of the church. Luther and his colleagues brought THEOLOGY out of the academic closet with vernacular sermons and devotional writings addressed to the fundamental issues of the religious life: the need for God's love and acceptance, personal anxiety before DEATH, and guidance in life.

A constant Reformation refrain was the recovery of biblical PREACHING and pastoral theology. The reformers benefited in this task by the works of their humanist predecessors and contemporaries such as Jacques Lefèvre d'Etaples (c. 1460–1536) and Desiderius Erasmus (1469–1536). The former promoted a unified reading of Scripture by a spiritual, christological vision in his biblical prefaces, Pauline commentaries, Psalm comparisons, and French lectionary and homilies. The latter promoted textual advances in biblical understanding by his edited version of the Greek New Testament (first edition in 1516), as well as hermeneutical perspectives in his many other writings. Preachers now became translators, and translators became preachers. The conviction that theology serves proclamation is succinctly expressed in Erasmus' rendering of the opening verses of the Gospel of John: "In the beginning was the *sermon.*"

The Reformation in Germany

The theological and pastoral problem that plagued Luther was whether SALVATION is achieved or received. The medieval scholastic answer, that it is both, did not resolve the issue for him, because the necessity of even the smallest human contribution to salvation threw the burden of proof back on the person. Luther's teaching responsibilities at the recently founded (1502) University of Wittenberg, as well as his own quest for certainty of salvation, led him to intensive study of the BIBLE. Here he discovered that righteousness before God is not what the sinner achieves, but rather what the sinner receives as a free gift from God. Thus salvation is no longer the goal of life, but rather the foundation of life. Luther reversed the medieval piety of achievement: Good works do not make the sinner acceptable to God, but rather God's acceptance of the sinner prompts good works.

The Reformation motif of FAITH active in love energized innovative approaches to a broad range of early modern social issues including reform of social welfare, literacy and public EDUCATION, and political issues of AUTHORITY and the right to resistance. The reformers rejection of mandatory clerical CELIBACY not only struck at church authority, but also "civil"-ized the clergy in the sense that they became citizens with homes, families, and a stake in civil responsibilities. Scholars such as MAX WEBER noted that this liberation from "otherworldly asceticism" released human energy and material resources for this-worldly activities.

While Luther referred to the early evangelical movement in Wittenberg as "our theology," fissures among erstwhile colleagues began appearing by the early 1520s. ANDREAS BODENSTEIN VON KARLSTADT (1486–1541), sometimes referred to as the forerunner of PURITANISM, insisted that evangelical insights must be instituted without tarrying for anyone. One effect of this, paralleled in other centers of reform such as Zurich, was an outbreak of ICONOCLASM during efforts to sweep out the old faith. Luther's response was that to coerce people into Gospel perspectives by forced reform was only to revert back to a religion of laws, and thus undermine the insight that JUSTIFICATION is a free gift.

Tensions and conflicts between the German reformers escalated in relation to the Peasants' War (1524–1525) as THOMAS MÜNTZER (c. 1490–1525) joined the late phase of the war with the rallying cry that "the godless have no right to live." The extremely volatile mix of late medieval APOCALYPTICISM, oppressive social and economic conditions, coupled with the Reformation motifs of the "freedom of the Christian" and theological critiques of canon law and papal authority fueled the peasants' social and religious expectations but horribly misfired at their disastrous defeat at Frankenhausen in 1525.

The Emperor Charles V's (1500–1558) military preoccupations with FRANCE (the Habsburg-Valois Wars, 1521–1559) and the Ottoman Empire (Sultan Süleyman I the Magnificent, r. 1520–1566) continually frustrated Charles's efforts to eliminate the Reformation movements in his realm apart from his hereditary lands, the Low Countries. Charles needed the support of the Protestant princes (the pejorative term "Protestant" arose from the protest by evangelical princes against imposition of the EDICT OF WORMS outlawing the evangelical movement at the 1529 DIET OF SPEYER) in his military campaigns. The Protestant princes presented an irenical confession of their faith to the Emperor at the 1530 Diet of Augsburg. Composed by Luther's colleague, PHILIPP MELANCHTHON (1497–1560), the AUGSBURG CONFESSION did not sway the Catholic Emperor to rescind the Edict of Worms, but it did become the foundational document for Lutheran churches up to today (see LUTHERANISM).

The rejection of the Augsburg Confession led the Protestants to form a military alliance, the SCHMALKALDIC LEAGUE, that managed to protect the Protestant movement until its defeat by imperial forces in 1547. By this time, however, the evangelicals had gained sufficient strength that a series of settlements led finally to their TOLERATION in the 1555 Peace of Augsburg.

The Reformation in Switzerland

The Reform movement in SWITZERLAND under the leadership of HULDRYCH ZWINGLI (1484–1531) proceeded along roughly parallel lines in Zurich, and then under the leadership of JOHN CALVIN (1509–1564) in Geneva. Unlike Luther, these Reformers lacked the protection of a benevolent and supportive prince and thus had to develop and implement their movements in cooperation (and tension) with their respective town councils.

Influenced by Humanism, Zwingli's intensive biblical study and preaching led to his 1518 appointment by the city government to the major preaching post in Zurich. His commitment to the Reformation principle, *sola scriptura*, was evident immediately. His sermons, no longer based upon the church's lectionary, methodically exposited book after biblical book. By 1525 he had established "prophesyings," weekly Bible studies for the Zurich CLERGY and advanced students. A similar practice was established in Geneva in 1536 under Calvin and GUILLAUME FAREL. All of life, personal and communal, was to be normed by Scripture.

Controversy, however, soon erupted on multiple fronts. At home, Zwingli and his colleagues found themselves in a double-fronted conflict with those who wanted to halt reforms and those who wanted to expand and radicalize them. The former were led by Hugo, the bishop of Constance, whose diocese included Zurich; the latter were led by CONRAD GREBEL (1498–1526), the reputed founder of ANABAPTISM. The Anabaptists (i.e., "re-baptists"), in applying biblical norms to faith and life, understood BAPTISM to be contingent on a mature confession of faith rather than a sacrament administered to infants who neither understood nor evidenced a Christian life. The Anabaptist confession of faith, the SCHLEITHEIM CONFESSION (1527), also rejected what most of their contemporaries assumed were normal obligations of citizenship: oaths, tithes, and military service.

Added to these challenges facing Zwingli was the years-long dispute with Luther over the correct interpretation of the LORD'S SUPPER. The German Lutheran prince, PHILIP OF HESSE, hoping for a united Protestant front, brought Luther and Zwingli to the negotiating table in Marburg in 1529. At the MARBURG COLLOQUY, the Lutherans and Zwinglians agreed on 14 of 15 articles. They repudiated TRANSUBSTANTIATION and the belief that the mass is a sacrifice for the living and the dead, and they insisted on communion in both kinds. The two evangelical parties however remained apart on whether the Lord's Supper is primarily an act of thanksgiving for the Gospel (Zwingli's symbolic and memorial view) or a concrete offer of the Gospel (Luther's sacramental emphasis on Christ's real presence). The differing Protestant theologies of the Eucharist continued to divide the church despite Calvin's later ecumenical efforts informed by his own emphasis on the gift character of the sacrament. Calvin did achieve agreement with Zwingli's successor, HEINRICH BULLINGER (1504–1575). In 1549 they signed the Consensus Tigurinus, but by this time many second-generation Lutherans suspected that this was more Zwinglian than Lutheran.

Unable to achieve recognition at the Diet of Augsburg in 1530, Zurich was vulnerable to Catholic pressures. In 1531 the Zurich forces were routed at the Second Battle of Kappel, during which Zwingli was killed. The consequent political resolution that divided Switzerland by confessional allegiance foreshadowed the fate of Europe. In 1555 the Peace of Augsburg ratified confessional divisions with the faith of the ruler. This arrangement was later summarized by the motto *cuius regio, eius religio,* "whose reign, his religion."

At the time of Zwingli's death, Geneva had not yet adopted the Reformation and neither had its future reformer John Calvin, who was just completing his legal studies in France. Sometime in 1533–1534, Calvin experienced his so-called "unexpected CONVERSION." Trained in law and imbued with humanist learning, Calvin echoed Luther's fundamental understanding of salvation. In his INSTITUTES OF THE CHRISTIAN RELIGION, Calvin described justification by faith in terms of God's acquittal of the guilty sinner.

In early 1535 Calvin sought refuge in Basel from the intensifying persecution of Protestants in his native France. Here he completed and published the first edition of his *Institutes,* prefaced by a masterful appeal to Francis I for a fair hearing of the evangelical faith. Calvin then settled his affairs in France and set out for the free imperial city of Strasbourg, where he hoped to settle down to a life of evangelical scholarship. Forced to detour through Geneva, Calvin was confronted by his compatriot, Guillaume Farel (1489–1565), who had been preaching reform in Geneva since 1532. Only months before Calvin's arrival in July 1536, Geneva had finally achieved independence, with the aid of its neighbor Bern, from the Duchy of Savoy and its imposed Episcopal rule. The citizens voted to adopt the Reformation and to expel all clergy who disagreed. Faced by the enormous task of institutionalizing reform in Geneva, Farel made it clear in no uncertain terms to Calvin that God had sent Calvin to Geneva for precisely this task. Furthermore, he told Calvin that to shirk this duty would incur his damnation; thus Calvin stayed!

The reforming colleagues' emphasis on CHURCH DISCIPLINE and authority soon alienated the Geneva council and many of its citizens. Exiled in 1539,

Calvin now finally made it to Strasbourg, where he spent the next years learning about institutional reform and church organization from that city's reformer, MARTIN BUCER (1491–1551). Here, too, he married. Geneva, now concerned about faltering reform, appealed to Calvin to return. Not without misgivings, but with the promise that he could develop a reformed order for the church, Calvin returned in 1541. Within six weeks of his return, Calvin completed and submitted to the magistrates of Geneva his *Ecclesiastical Ordinances.* Soon ratified, the *Ordinances* organized the Genevan church according to four categories of ministry: doctors, pastors, deacons, and elders. The doctors were to maintain doctrinal purity through theological study and instruction. Pastors were responsible for preaching, administering the SACRAMENTS, and admonishing the people. Deacons were responsible for the supervision of poor relief and the hospitals. Elders, laymen, were responsible for maintaining discipline within the community. The institutional organ for church discipline was the CONSISTORY, a kind of ecclesiastical court that included the pastors and elders. The Consistory was a bone of contention through most of Calvin's career in Geneva due to its supervision of public morality and its power to excommunicate.

Challenges to Calvin's authority came not just from those who resented what they considered meddling by the Consistory. Two doctrinal debates threatened to unravel the fabric of "the most perfect school of Christ," as Scottish reformer JOHN KNOX called Geneva. The first of these was a sharp public attack on Calvin's doctrine of PREDESTINATION by Jerome Bolsec, who claimed that it was unbiblical. The charge that the Genevan reformers were unclear about a point of Scripture was not a narrow theological challenge, because the reform movement rested on popular confidence in its biblical basis. Calvin's response was to reiterate that PREDESTINATION is an expression of unconditional GRACE: God chooses the sinner, not vice versa. Bolsec himself was banished from Geneva for life.

The second controversy was the trial and execution of MICHAEL SERVETUS (c. 1511–1553) for his denial of the DOCTRINE of the Trinity (see ANTI-TRINITARIANISM). Already notorious throughout Europe for his written attacks on the Trinity, Servetus escaped execution in France (where the Catholics had to be satisfied with burning him in effigy) and ended up in Geneva, where the Protestants did the "honor." From a political perspective, the Genevans were in a bind if they did not try and execute Servetus, because the city had gained a reputation as the haven for heretics, but the operative motive was theological. It was this to which the Genevan schoolmaster exiled by Calvin, SEBASTIAN CAS-

TELLIO, responded when he wrote: "To burn a heretic is not to defend a doctrine, but to kill a person." Castellio's 1554 *Concerning Heretics, Whether They Are to be Persecuted* is one of the most well-known early modern pleas for religious toleration.

Calvin's Protestant contemporaries did not view Geneva as a vengeful theocracy; large numbers of religious refugees flocked to Geneva. Thousands of refugees came from nearly every province in France as well as from ENGLAND, SCOTLAND, Holland, ITALY, Spain, GERMANY, POLAND, and Bohemia. When they returned home, they took CALVINISM with them.

The Reformation in France

Once Calvin's leadership was established in Geneva, he and the French exiles living there directed an effective evangelization program toward France. Although French evangelicals were called "HUGUENOTS," these Calvinists preferred the term "Reformed." By 1567, more than 100 pastors sent from Geneva were organizing Reformed congregations patterned on the Geneva church. In 1559 the first national SYNOD of the Reformed church in France met in Paris. Calvin himself provided the first draft of its CONFESSION of faith, the GALLICAN CONFESSION. It was modified at the Synod of La Rochelle in 1571 and continues to inform French Reformed churches to this day.

As in England, the crown played a major role in the course of the Reformation in France. Until the late 1520s, reform-minded humanists and reformers found shelter under Francis I's enthusiasm for Renaissance humanism. But the Gallican tradition of "one king, one law, one faith," plus the crown's considerable power over the church guaranteed by the Concordat of Bologna (1516), precluded state endorsement of Reformation ideas. By 1516, Francis I had everything that HENRY VIII broke with the church to get. Thus as Reformation ideas began to take root not only in the "middle class," but also in the nobles of the Bourbon (next in line for the throne after the ruling Valois) and Montmorency houses, the crown began a policy of persecution designed to root out Protestantism.

The resulting civil strife prompted the crown's call for a public Protestant–Catholic debate. Any hope that the COLLOQUY OF POISSY (1561) would contribute to peace was dashed when THEODORE BEZA (1519–1605), Calvin's heir apparent in Geneva and leader of the Huguenot delegation, unequivocally rejected transubstantiation in his opening address. To Beza and his colleagues, the Catholic belief that the Mass was the community's supreme good work of offering and receiving the corporeal Christ was no more than idolatry and rejection of the gospel. The Catholic rage against such blasphemy was not merely a reaction to theological disputation, but also reflected the offenses visited on their faith by a generation of iconoclasts who had desecrated churches and holy objects including the consecrated sacramental bread.

The crown's effort to overcome the failure at Poissy by an Edict of Toleration (January 1562) lasted barely two months before armed attacks on Huguenot congregations occurred, and the country sank into decades of barbarity fueled by religious hatred. The most infamous event in the French Wars of Religion was the St. Bartholomew's Day Massacre (August 24, 1572), when thousands of Huguenots were massacred in a frenzy of state terrorism. A generation later, weary of bloodshed and assassinations, the Protestant Bourbon, Henry of Navarre, became king as Henry IV, converted to Catholicism ("Paris is worth a Mass"), and set forth a policy of limited toleration in the EDICT OF NANTES (1598) that lasted until its revocation by Louis XIV in 1685.

The Reformation in England

Henry VIII, whose drive for a male heir, among other things, prompted his break with Rome, informed the traditional view of the English Reformation as an act of state. Indeed, the top-down imposition of ECCLESIOLOGY continued in his heirs: Protestantism with Edward VI, Catholicism with Mary Tudor, and Protestantism with ELIZABETH I. Yet, without gainsaying the significant roles of the various Tudors, the Reformation in England benefited from a residual Lollard anticlericalism, humanist interest in reform, and Continental Reformation influences spread by young CAMBRIDGE UNIVERSITY scholars, pamphlets, BIBLE TRANSLATIONS, the return of English students studying in the centers of Switzerland, and then the influx of Protestant refugees fleeing the 1548 AUGSBURG INTERIM imposed by Charles V after his victory over Protestant forces. Later, of course, with the accession of Elizabeth I (1558), the Marian exiles returned from such Protestant centers as Frankfurt and Geneva and began to radicalize reforms in England in the direction of Puritanism.

Translations of the Bible into English were significant means of introducing Reformation ideas. WILLIAM TYNDALE (c. 1494–1536), one of the most influential translators, carried out most of his work in exile on the Continent. His translation of the New Testament (first printed in 1525) used Luther's translation and included many of the prefaces to Luther's Bible. MILES COVERDALE (1488–1568) assisted Tyndale in translating the Old Testament, and was responsible for the first complete English translation of the Bible (1535). Largely through the influence of THOMAS CROMWELL (c. 1485–1540), Henry VIII's chief minister in state and church, and Archbishop THOMAS CRANMER (1489–1556), the king was persuaded to put the Bible in all the churches.

Theological ideas, both home-grown and imported, were not however the source for the English break with Rome, but rather the king's "great matter." Henry's marriage to his brother's widow, Catherine of Aragon, arranged to continue the alliance with Spain, necessitated a papal dispensation because Leviticus 18:6–18 prohibited marriages within close relationships. The only child to survive from the marriage was Mary Tudor. Henry wanted a male heir and hoped that Anne Boleyn would do the honors. He appealed to Pope Clement VII for an annulment on the biblical basis that one should not marry a brother's widow (Leviticus 20:21). Henry's demand put Clement in an ecclesiastical and political bind. If he granted an annulment, then he would undermine papal authority by reversing a previous pope's action. The political problem was that Clement was virtually a prisoner of the emperor Charles V (the Sack of Rome, 1527), who as Catherine's nephew was adamantly opposed to Henry's plan to divorce her. Henry's solution, after a very long and convoluted process, was to get satisfaction through the English court. To free himself from papal interference, Henry declared himself and his successors head of the CHURCH OF ENGLAND (Act of Supremacy, 1534). Henry wanted Rome, but not Catholicism, out of his realm. Hence the Act of Six Articles (1539) reaffirmed pre-Reformation ORTHODOXY.

Reformation theology—oriented to the Swiss Reformed—came to the fore during the reign of the child king, Edward VI (1547–1553). Cranmer provided the Prayer Book (1549, revised 1552) and a statement of faith, the Forty-Two Articles (revised to the THIRTY-NINE ARTICLES under Elizabeth). The tide was reversed with the accession of the ardent Roman Catholic Mary to the throne (1553–1558). Ironically, her efforts to restore Catholicism strengthened Protestant resolve. Her marriage to Philip of Spain linked her faith to foreign influence; her efforts to restore church properties alienated their present owners; her persecution of Protestants created the host of martyrs celebrated by JOHN FOXE's martyrology (see ACTS AND MONUMENTS); and through the flight of hundreds of leading Protestants, she exposed English Protestants to Continental theology that they eagerly brought back on her death.

The pendulum of reform swung to the middle with Elizabeth whose long reign (1558–1603) facilitated the establishment of English Protestantism. Elizabeth's *via media* retained traditional VESTMENTS and liturgy now in English with sermon and prayers informed by a Reformed COVENANT theology and normed by the Thirty-Nine Articles. The theology of Eucharist, a perennial focal point of dispute, denied transubstantiation on the one hand and Zwinglian symbolism on the other while remaining open to a range of Lutheran and Calvinist interpretations. The Scriptures were affirmed to be the source and norm of faith, and the Creeds were accepted as expressions of Scripture. As "Supreme Governor" of the church (1559 Act of Supremacy), Elizabeth proceeded to appoint moderate clergy who conformed to her program. Significant support came from such apologists as JOHN JEWEL (1522–1571; *Apology for the Anglican Church*) and RICHARD HOOKER (c. 1554–1600; *Treatise on the Laws of Ecclesiastical Polity*). Elizabeth resolved the challenge from Mary Stuart, Queen of Scots, with her French Catholic connection, by executing Mary in 1587, and destroying the Spanish Armada in 1588. The challenge from Calvinists of varying persuasions was a continual bother with "Presbyterians" rejecting Episcopal polity and "Puritans" striving to purify the church of all vestiges of Catholicism (see PURITANISM). Elizabeth charted a course between Catholicism and Calvinism, because the former denied her legitimacy and the latter rejected the episcopacy she believed supported monarchy. To rule the Church of England through her bishops, Elizabeth had to reject the decentralized polity of European Reformed churches and of Scottish PRESBYTERIANISM. Her successor, James I, agreed with his succinct phrase: "No bishop, no king."

Scandinavia and Eastern Europe

Humanism and Catholic reform movements prepared the ground for the introduction of the Reformation in DENMARK, which at that time included NORWAY, ICELAND, a number of provinces in present-day SWEDEN, and the associated duchies of Schleswig and Holstein, where the Danish king was duke. Lutheran influences were evident in Schleswig already in the early 1520s, and King Christian III (r. 1534–1559) officially established the Lutheran Reformation in Denmark in 1537. The king's own evangelical commitment may have begun when he saw Luther at the Diet of Worms; he later married a Lutheran; corresponded extensively with Luther, Melanchthon, and JOHANNES BUGENHAGEN (1485–1558) on theological subjects; and provided economic support to the Wittenberg reformers. Christian appointed Luther's colleague Bugenhagen, known as the "Reformer of the North" for his introduction of the Wittenberg reforms throughout northern German cities and his native Pomerania, to lead the reform of the Danish church. Stationed in Copenhagen from 1537–1539, Bugenhagen led the reorganization of the church, ordaining seven new Lutheran bishops, thus ending apostolic succession, and reforming the University of Copenhagen according to the model of the University of Wittenberg. Influential Danish theologians, such as the bishops Peder Palladius, HANS TAUSEN, and Niels Palladius, were trained at Wittenberg. In 1538 the Augsburg Confession was made the theological foundational document of the Danish church.

Luther's theology was brought to Sweden and FINLAND by OLAUS PETRI and his brother LAURENTIUS, both of whom had studied in Wittenberg. The Swedish king Gustavus Vasa (r. 1523–1560) established the Reformation there in 1527. One consequence in Finland was the sending of Finnish students to Wittenberg, the most famous of these being MICHAEL AGRICOLA (c. 1510–1557). Agricola is known as the father of written Finnish through his prayer book (1544) and New Testament translation (1548). In Eastern Europe, the Reformation was established in Prussia and Livonia but remained a minority movement in other areas.

Early Modern Catholicism

Well before Luther came on the scene, reform movements found personal expression in corporate devotional movements such as the Beguines and Beghards (twelfth century), the Brethren of the Common Life or Devotio Moderna (late fourteenth century), and institutional expression in the conciliar movement (fourteenth century on) that called for reform of the church "in head and members." By the eve of the Reformation, Catholics, Humanists, and theologians were exploring and translating the Bible, preachers (e.g., Girolamo Savonarola, d. 1498) were endeavoring to instill piety and ethics, and confraternities and oratories provided vehicles for lay spirituality and CHARITY. The continuation of medieval monastic reforming movements may be seen in the person and work of Ignatius Loyola (1491–1556), whose interest centered on the promotion of pastoral and mission work rather than the reform of doctrine.

On the other hand, the late medieval papacy's antipathy toward conciliarism was a major factor in Roman foot-dragging in response to repeated Protestant calls since 1520 for a council to deal with the issues raised by the Reformation. When the council finally began in 1546 in Trent, a generation of strife had hardened positions. By the eve of the Council, various mediating efforts (e.g., Cardinal Contarini and Philipp Melanchthon at the COLLOQUY OF REGENSBURG in 1541) had been rejected by both sides as unacceptable compromises of the "truth."

The Council of Trent, meeting in three distinct assemblies (1545–1547, 1551–1552, and 1561–1563), focused on both the moral, spiritual, and educational renewal of the Catholic Church and the refutation of Protestantism. The latter goal found expression in the Council's repudiation of *sola Scriptura* by the elevation of TRADITION to an equal source of revelation; the supplementation of *sola gratia* with human cooperation; and reaffirmation of the seven sacraments and the doctrine of transubstantiation. Papal authority, although not officially established in the modern sense until Vatican I (1870), was reaffirmed at the conclusion of the Council of Trent by the papal bull *Benedictus Deus* that reserved authentic interpretation of conciliar decrees to the pope.

References and Further Reading

Brady, Thomas A. Jr., Heiko A. Oberman, and James D. Tracy, eds. *Handbook of European History 1400–1600. Late Middle Ages, Renaissance and Reformation*. 2 vols. Leiden, The Netherlands: E. J. Brill, 1994.

Cameron, Euan. *The European Reformation*. Oxford, UK: Clarendon Press, 1991.

Dickens, A. G., and John M. Tonkin with Kenneth Powell. *The Reformation in Historical Thought*. Cambridge, MA: Harvard University Press, 1985.

Dixon, C. Scott, ed. *The German Reformation: The Essential Readings*. Oxford, UK: Blackwell, 1999.

Edwards, Mark U. Jr. *Printing, Propaganda, and Martin Luther*. Berkeley, CA: University Of California Press, 1994.

Gordon, Bruce, ed. *Protestant History and Identity in Sixteenth-Century Europe*. 2 vols. Aldershot, UK: Scholar Press, 1996.

Greengrass, Mark. *The Longman Companion to the European Reformation c. 1500–1618*. London: Longman, 1998.

Gregory, Brad S. *Salvation at Stake: Christian Martyrdom in Early Modern Europe*. Cambridge, MA: Harvard University Press, 1999.

Hillerbrand, Hans J., editor-in-chief. *The Oxford Encyclopedia of the Reformation*. 4 vols. New York: Oxford University Press, 1996.

Lindberg, Carter. *The European Reformations*. Oxford, UK: Blackwell, 1996.

——, ed. *The Reformation Theologians*. Oxford, UK: Blackwell, 2001.

O'Malley, John W. *Trent and All That: Renaming Catholicism in the Early Modern Era*. Cambridge, MA: Harvard University Press, 2000.

Muller, Richard A. *The Unaccommodated Calvin: Studies in the Foundation of a Theological Tradition*. New York: Oxford University Press, 2000.

Pettegree, Andrew, ed. *The Reformation World*. London: Routledge, 2000.

Wiesner, Merry E. *Women and Gender in Early Modern Europe*. Cambridge: Cambridge University Press, 1993.

Williams, George H. *The Radical Reformation*, 3rd ed. Kirksville, MO: Sixteenth Century Journal Publishers, 1992.

CARTER LINDBERG

REFORMED CHURCH IN AMERICA

The Reformed Church in America (RCA) is a Protestant denomination with roots in the Reformed Church in THE NETHERLANDS. It is presbyterian in church government (see PRESBYTERY, CHURCH GOVERNMENT) and holds as standards of faith the ecumenical creeds, the BELGIC CONFESSION, the HEIDELBERG CATECHISM, and the CANONS OF DORT. Currently there are 300,000 baptized and confirmed members and 950 churches in the UNITED STATES and CANADA.

Origins

The Reformed Church is the state church of the Netherlands and was shaped by the THEOLOGY and practices of JOHN CALVIN in Geneva in the sixteenth century. In the 1620s the Dutch West India Trading Company established a community in New Amsterdam (Manhattan). People emigrated primarily for economic reasons, but the Classis of Amsterdam wanted to establish a religious presence there. The RCA officially began in April 1628 when the Rev. Jonas Michaelius arrived in Manhattan and held the first communion service. The Dutch settlers had previously attended worship services led by *krankenbezoekers* [visitors of the sick] who held the office of deacon and were authorized to lead WORSHIP and read Dutch sermons.

The Reformed Protestant Dutch Church (RPDC), as it was called until 1867, grew slowly where Dutch immigrants settled in Manhattan, Long Island, New Jersey, along the Hudson River to Albany, and west along the Mohawk River. Worship services were held in Dutch, which meant that few non-Dutch people joined, and that children who spoke more English than Dutch often left for English-speaking churches. The British took over New Netherlands in 1664 but allowed Dutch churches and CULTURE to continue.

The Classis of Amsterdam supervised the Reformed churches and expected ministers to be trained and ordained in the Netherlands. It assumed the right to make most decisions concerning the colonial churches. New initiatives were rare because letters traveled slowly over the ocean. A rift developed in the eighteenth century between those who wanted to develop an independent American body called a Coetus, and those of the Conferentie group who preferred a minimal structure that would submit most decisions to Amsterdam. The conflict was complicated by the fact that the Coetus advocated contemporary religious practices such as revivalism (see REVIVALS), and the Conferentie opposed such innovations and preferred formal piety and worship. Theodorus Frelinghuysen was a pastor and a controversial advocate of revival in the 1720s and 1730s. He stirred his congregations in central New Jersey to conflict as much as to piety. He also became a strong advocate of the Coetus after two of his sons drowned en route from education and ordination in the Netherlands.

Dutch Reformed congregations also disagreed about the Revolutionary War. Some pastors and clergy emphasized Romans 13 and the need to obey the current government. Others insisted on the need for liberty. Rev. John Henry Livingston helped unite the factions by drafting a new constitution in 1792 that made the RPDC into a DENOMINATION separate from Amsterdam. In 1784 he had been chosen to offer formal theological education at what would become New Brunswick Theological Seminary. The church had already founded Queens (Rutgers) College.

During the nineteenth century the Reformed Church cooperated with other Protestant denominations in missions and benevolent societies. The RPDC became Americanized, although the Dutch influence continued. Because the Reformed Church required such extensive education for CLERGY, it never had enough ministers and did not experience growth on the frontier as did the BAPTISTS and Methodists (see METHODISM, NORTH AMERICA).

In the Netherlands during the 1830s some pietist Reformed Church members criticized the state church and eventually separated from it. The ensuing conflict as well as poverty sparked a desire to emigrate. Rev. Albertus Van Raalte led a group to Holland, Michigan in 1847 and Rev. Hendrik Scholte led a group to Pella, Iowa. The RPDC gave financial aid to Van Raalte and invited the new Dutch congregations to join the denomination, which they did. As more immigrants arrived during the next few decades a number of them decided that the Reformed Church was too Americanized because it used hymns in addition to Psalms, and permitted Freemasons to be church members (see FREEMASONRY). Schisms in 1857 and 1882 resulted in the formation of the CHRISTIAN REFORMED CHURCH in North America.

The eastern branch of the RCA was larger until the middle of the twentieth century when many congregations lost members because of suburbanization. Dutch immigrants and their children settled in western Michigan, Chicago, Wisconsin, and northwest Iowa. The RCA formed a college and seminary in Holland, Michigan and two colleges in Iowa. It started a number of new churches in Florida, Colorado, and California. Conflicts occasionally arose because the churches in the East tended to be more ecumenical and Americanized whereas those in the Midwest emphasized piety, purity, and ethnic identity (see ETHNICITY). The RCA considered merger with the Reformed Church in the United States (German) in 1893, with Northern Presbyterian groups in 1930 and 1949, and with the Presbyterian Church in the United States (Southern) in 1969 (see PRESBYTERIAN CHURCH U.S.A.). All failed, largely because of midwestern resistance. The RCA was a founding member of the Federal Council of Churches in 1908, the WORLD

COUNCIL OF CHURCHES in 1948, and the NATIONAL COUNCIL OF CHURCHES in 1950.

The RCA established MISSIONS in CHINA, JAPAN, INDIA, Arabia, MEXICO, and AFRICA. Its most notable missionaries were Samuel Zwemer in Arabia and Dr. Ida Scudder in India. Missions were both evangelistic and institutional, and the RCA helped to build schools and hospitals in the belief that missions should affect the whole person and not simply the soul.

References and Further Reading

Balmer, Randall. *A Perfect Babel of Confusion: Dutch Religion and English Culture in the Middle Colonies.* New York: Oxford University Press, 1989.

Bratt, James. *Dutch Calvinism in Modern America.* Grand Rapids, MI: Wm. B. Eerdmans, 1984.

DeJong, Gerald. *The Dutch Reformed Church in the American Colonies.* Grand Rapids, MI: Wm. B. Eerdmans, 1978.

Harmelink, Herman III. *Ecumenism and the Reformed Church.* Grand Rapids, MI: Wm. B. Eerdmans, 1968.

LYNN JAPINGA

REFORMED THEOLOGY

See Theology

REGENSBURG COLLOQUY

The Regensburg Colloquy of 1541 was a discussion between Protestant and Catholic theologians convened by Emperor Charles V in conjunction with the Diet of the Holy Roman Empire. Charles's quest for political and religious unity within the empire matched the theological agendas of moderate theologians on both sides, such as MARTIN BUCER of Strasbourg. At an earlier colloquy at Worms at the end of 1540, Bucer and reform-minded Catholic Johann Gropper of Cologne had drawn up a set of compromise articles, which now served as basis for the Regensburg discussions. Two other major participants in the discussion, Protestant PHILIPP MELANCHTHON and Catholic John Eck, were skeptical of what they saw as the utopian proposals of their colleagues. The imperial chancellor Granvella and other important political figures were also present at the discussion, whereas behind the scenes stood the papal legate Gasparo Contarini, charged with protecting papal interests but also sympathetic to evangelical doctrine.

After initial rejection of the Worms article on JUSTIFICATION by both Eck and Melanchthon, a slightly altered formula found acceptance from both sides. In this theory of "double justification," inherent righteousness of the individual believer is essential, but initial and final justification both depend on the imputed righteousness of Christ received by FAITH. Further agreement proved elusive, however. The discus-

sion of ECCLESIOLOGY broke down over the question whether councils can err, and a fatal impasse arose over the Eucharist (see LORD'S SUPPER). Gropper and his Catholic colleague Pflug were ready to compromise, but Contarini insisted on the term "TRANSUBSTANTIATION" to avoid Protestant evasiveness. This marked the effective end of any hope of reunion, though discussion continued on the sacrament of penance. The emperor and Granvella tried unsuccessfully to bring the theologians to a partial agreement, based on the sixteen articles on which agreement had been reached. In July, both the Catholic and Protestant Estates rejected the Regensburg Book as a whole. Even the colloquy's major achievement, the compromise on justification, did not in the end find favor with either Rome or Wittenberg. Although religious colloquies continued to be held during the 1540s and 1550s, none of them came close to reaching agreement.

References and Further Reading

Primary Source:

Martin Bucers Deutsche Schriften, Vol. 9.1, Religionsgespräche, 1539–1541. Gütersloh, Germany: Gütersloher Verlagshaus, 1995.

Secondary Source:

Matheson, Peter. *Cardinal Contarini at Regensburg.* London: Oxford University Press, 1972.

EDWIN TAIT

REIMARUS, HERMANN SAMUEL (1694–1768)

German biblical scholar. Reimarus was born in Hamburg on December 22, 1694, and died there March 3, 1768. He studied philosophy, THEOLOGY, and philology at Jena in 1714 and Wittenberg in 1716, where he completed a postdoctoral thesis and became an outside lecturer in philosophy in 1719. Appointed headmaster at Wismar (1723) and Hamburg (1727), Reimarus was professor of Hebrew and Oriental Languages at the *Akademisches Gymnasium* of Hamburg. He was strongly influenced by his teacher at Hamburg, who was also his father-in-law, the important classical philologist J. A. Fabricius, who was responsible for Reimarus's meticulous research methods. Reimarus also influenced the rather rationalistic philosophy of GOTTFRIED WILHELM LEIBNIZ and CHRISTIAN WOLFF. Reimarus acquired an excellent knowledge in oriental studies, mainly through self-education.

A research trip at the end of his studies led him to Holland and ENGLAND where he first encountered the works of the English Deists (see DEISM) such as MAT-THEW TINDAL, JOHN TOLAND, and Thomas Morgan who were critical with regard to the BIBLE and revelation. This explains why Reimarus was, on the one hand, a convinced representative and committed vindicator of the concept of "natural religion" solely based on reason, and why, on the other hand, he became a tough-minded critic of any kind of belief based on revelation (as exemplified in the Old and New Testament Scriptures). Reimarus's rejection of any kind of revealed religion was not disclosed to the public until his death. Rather, he was known to be an acknowledged thinker and scholar who spoke up for a natural and reasonable religion by emphasizing its fundamental importance with regard to moral behavior and human existence as such.

This conviction is echoed throughout one of his works, entitled *Die vornehmsten Wahrheiten der natürlichen Religion* (The Noblest Truths of Natural Religion) (1791; reprint 1985), first published in 1754 and reprinted several times. To his contemporaries, this study represented an excellent description and successful vindication of all those religious truths that could be accounted for by reason alone. Just two years later, an essay on logic, entitled *Die Vernunftlehre* (The Doctrine of Reason) (1790; reprint 1979) followed. His devout, yet rationally based attitude manifests itself in another work written in 1760 (1798; reprint 1982), which contained several treatises on animal instinct and was clearly dominated by a scientific yet theological discourse that relied heavily on the concept of a divine world order ruled by wise Providence.

Soon after 1735, however, Reimarus secretly drafted the first outline of a work that he would constantly remodel throughout the years that followed and finally leave behind in a state ready for publication. The first rendition was entitled *Gedancken von der Freyheit eines vernünftigen Gottesdienstes*; the final version was *Apologie oder Schutzschrift für die vernünftigen Verehrer Gottes* (Apology or Defense of the Reasonable Worshipers of God). The entire work—from which Lessing, without disclosing the author's name, culled certain parts between 1774 and 1778 that were critical of the concept of revelation and published them as "Anonymous Fragments"—went unprinted until 1972! The fact that Reimarus, even at an early age, had already turned his back on the then dominant, explicitly theological methods of biblical exegesis and hermeneutics has been verified by Peter Stemmer in his study.

In his *Apologie* Reimarus now took radical logical steps. His plea to practice a "Toleration of the De-ists"—thus the title of the first fragment published by Lessing in 1774 and taken from an early rendition of *Apologie*—is connected to a devastating historical cri-

tique of the foundational testimonies of both JUDAISM and Christianity: on the one hand, the narrative of the Exodus, especially of "The Israelites' [miraculous] procession through the Red Sea"; and on the other, the narratives concerning the resurrection of Jesus crucified. By means of intricate meticulousness and expert historical criticism, Reimarus deconstructed these biblical testimonies and shattered their credibility. Especially in *Von dem Zwecke Jesu und seiner Jünger*—the last of the fragments that Lessing ascribed to the "Anonymous Author of Wolfenbüttel" (it was not until 1814 that Reimarus's authorship was publicized)—the Christian creed was interpreted as a cunning deception and intentional web of lies on the disciples' part. This work may be considered a prelude to the research on the life of Jesus (see JESUS, LIVES OF) that dominated the nineteenth century.

References and Further Reading

Primary Source:

Schmidt-Biggemann, Wilhelm. *H.S.R. Handschriftenverzeichnis und Bibliographie*. Göttingen, Germany: Vandenhoeck & Ruprecht, 1979.

Secondary Sources:

Lötzsch, Frieder. *Was ist "Ökologie"? H.S.R. Ein Beitrag zur Geistesgeschichte des 18. Jahrhunderts*. Cologne, Germany/Vienna, Austria: Böhlau, 1987.
———. *H.S.R. (1694), ein "bekannter Unbekannter" der Aufklärung in Hamburg. Vorträge gehalten auf der Tagung der Joachim-Jungius-Gesellschaft der Wissenschaften Hamburg am 12. und 13. Oktober 1972*. Göttingen, Germany: Vandenhoeck & Ruprecht, 1973.
Stemmer, Peter. *Weissagung und Kritik. Eine Studie zur Hermeneutik bei H.S.R.* Göttingen, Germany: Vandenhoeck & Ruprecht, 1983.
Wolfgang, Walter, and Ludwig Borinski, eds. *Logik im Zeitalter der Aufklärung. Studien zur "Vernunftlehre" von H.S.R.* Göttingen, Germany: Vandenhoeck & Ruprecht, 1980.

ARNO SCHILSON

REINDORF, CARL CHRISTIAN (1834–1917)

Ghanaian clergy. Reindorf was a first-generation Ghanaian Protestant pastor and historian who worked for the BASEL MISSION in the Gold Coast (now Ghana). His parents were traders from Accra, Ghana who had a Danish background. He was a product of the Basel Mission school at Christiansborg, Osu, and Abokobi (after 1854). He became a teacher, church organizer, and a pastor under the auspices of the Basel Mission church in Ghana. The training that Reindorf received from the Mission, which emphasized the use of the mother tongue in mission work, as well as the influence of his colleague J. G. Christaller, enabled him to publish the important book *The History of the Gold Coast and Asante* originally in Ga language and later translated into English by the author and published in SWITZERLAND. This book has been acknowledged as ground breaking for the use of oral history; Reindorf interviewed more than 200 people in writing his work. This achievement made Reindorf the first African to publish a remarkably substantial and systematic history that conforms to standard Western academic tradition. His experience with the Basel Mission's characteristic style of integrated mission helped him to see Christian mission as holistic, involving such aspects as church organizing, language learning, EDUCATION, industrial training, and agriculture.

Reindorf was a man of varied achievements; his peers described him as "very gifted," and he was respected for his deep spirituality, particularly his gift of healing. He was able to assert himself as an independent thinker even if he had to differ from the Mission whenever the need arose. Reindorf's students displayed self-confidence and clear self-consciousness as African Christians who saw it as their task to contribute to the religion and intellectual tradition of their society.

See also Africa; Missions; Missionary Organizations

References and Further Reading

Primary Sources:

Reindorf, Carl Christian. *The History of the Gold Coast and Asante* (1895, 1966).
Reindorf, C. D. *Remembering Rev. Carl Reindorf* (1984).

Secondary Sources:

Jenkins, Paul, ed. *The Recovery of the West African Past: African Pastors and African History in the Nineteenth Century, C. C. Reindorf and Samuel Johnson.* Basel, Germany: Basler Afrika Bibliographien, 1998.
Jenkins, Raymond. "Gold Coast Historians and Their Pursuit of the Gold Coast Pasts, 1882–1918" (Ph.D. dissertation, University of Birmingham, 1985).

CEPHAS N. OMENYO

REMONSTRANTS

After theologian JACOBUS ARMINIUS died in 1609, the defense of his views against misrepresentations by professors Sibbrandus Lubertus and FRANZ GOMAR was taken up by Johannes Uytenbogaert. With the support of forty-four Arminian CLERGY (see ARMINIANISM) of the DUTCH REFORMED CHURCH, and after consultation with Holland's official chief legal advisor Johan van Oldenbarnevelt, in 1610 Uytenbogaert presented a "Remonstrance" to the States of Holland and West Friesland (the provincial parliament) to obtain continued protective toleration within the Reformed Church for the Arminian theological position, which was summarized in five points contained in the document. A reply by anti-Arminian opponents—called the "Contra-Remonstrance"—followed at the Hague Conference in 1611. The two parties in the ongoing conflict between the Arminians and the adherents of Gomar's rigid interpretation of THEODORE BEZA's reduction of CALVINISM thus acquired their names. Eventually, the Arminian clergy and their followers would be known as the Remonstrant Brotherhood, forming a separate DENOMINATION that continues to exist.

Enjoying the support of factions of Holland's urban leaders, the Arminians requested a national synod that was expected to supervise and adjudicate the theological dispute. The Arminians also suggested that the BELGIC CONFESSION and the HEIDELBERG CATECHISM should be subjected to biblical critique and, where necessary, modified. Such a synod was opposed by the GOMARIANS, who wanted the authority of the government subordinate to that of the clergy and who attributed the binding AUTHORITY of Scriptural revelation to the Confession and Catechism. The jurist Hugo Grotius went to ENGLAND to explain the controversy from an Arminian point of view. Contra-Remonstrants, however, spread rumors that Remonstrants were more than sympathetic to SOCINIANISM. Despite the Arminian agreement with the principles by which a king could properly be superior to the bishops, the rumors reached King James I of England who intervened against the appointment of Conrad Vorstius, nominated to be successor to Arminius, ultimately preventing him from taking up his duties in Leiden. The traditional balance in Leiden's theology faculty was restored when the Arminian Simon Episcopius was appointed professor in 1612, as successor to Gomar. Episcopius continued the public disputes with the Gomarian Johannes Polyander.

In 1618 Prince Maurits, hired by the States General to lead the army in the war against Spain, used military force to eject Arminians from city governments throughout the country, replacing them with Gomarians willing to support his coup, and maneuvering himself into a position of control over his former employer, Parliament. This coup ensured a return to war with Spain, as desired by many Calvinistic refugees from the southern Low Countries. Military victory might enable them to return. Arminians had been associated with the politics of peace, which would have left boundaries as they were when the war was interrupted by the Twelve Years' Truce in 1609. Arminian politics represented a logical outcome of their view of the role of choice in personal acceptance of the means of GRACE. (If choice were involved, Catholics might be converted through peaceful contact and education, best furthered by expanded trade.) Van Oldenbarnevelt was tried on trumped-up charges of treason and executed. Rombout Hoogerbeets, Hugo Grotius, and others were sentenced to life imprisonment. Uytenbogaert fled to Antwerp. Remonstrant ministers were removed from their duties. Assured of dominance, the Gomarians then called for a national synod, the Synod of Dordrecht (Dort), to which foreign observers from other Reformed countries including England were invited. The Remonstrant clergy were summoned to appear and were treated as if accused before an ecclesiastical court, which in 1619 found them guilty of HERESY. They were dismissed from the Reformed Church and banished. Laws suppressing DISSENT were passed by Parliament, marking the end to Holland's famed TOLERATION.

Exile and Return

In exile the Remonstrant clergy immediately organized their brotherhood, secretly sending pastors on brief visits to care for Arminian congregations that continued to exist despite persecution. The most famous was Passchier de Fyne who often narrowly escaped capture, even preaching while on ice skates. Some congregations lacking pastors formed collegial meetings. The meeting at Warmond later moved to nearby Rijnsburg, where people who attended were known as the Rijnsburger Collegiants. Spinoza and other thinkers were attracted to the undogmatic and egalitarian gatherings in which all were allowed to "prophesy."

After the death of Prince Maurits in 1625, his brother Frederik Hendrik succeeded him. Toleration was revived and exiled Remonstrants returned. The Remonstrant Seminary was established in Amsterdam in 1634; Episcopius became its first professor, well known for his Institutiones Theologicae. He continued Erasmus's philological emphasis in exegesis. This approach was to be a characteristic of Remonstrant biblical study, seen also in the works of Grotius and C. P. Tiele (nineteenth century). After Episcopius's death (1643), Etienne de Courcelles (Steven Curcellaeus) became the Remonstrant professor. A friend and translator of Descartes, Curcellaeus developed further Episcopius's tendency to emphasize the role of reason in assessing revelation. From 1668 to 1712 the Remonstrant professor was Philippus van Limborch. His friendship and influence among the CAMBRIDGE PLATONISTS is well known. From a Remonstrant perspective, Van Limborch championed toleration in various writings. He was author of a widely read study of the Inquisition, *Historia Inquisitionis cui subjungitur*

Liber Sententiarum Inquisitionis Tholosonae ab anno Christi 1307 ad annum 1323. This was based on a manuscript made available to Van Limborch by his Rotterdam friend, the Quaker Benjamin Furly (see FRIENDS, SOCIETY OF). Through this contact Van Limborch's ideas must have reached WILLIAM PENN, a guest of Furly's. Both Van Limborch and Furly were friends and hosts of JOHN LOCKE during his exile in Holland. Locke acknowledged Van Limborch's influence on his ideas on religious toleration. Van Limborch's involvement in the liberal Mennonite Galenus Abraham de Haan's projects to coordinate relief, both material and diplomatic, to MENNONITES persecuted in SWITZERLAND and the Palatinate is indicated by Van Limborch's inclusion of a letter (February 14, 1660) from the city of Rotterdam to the city of Bern. This letter, arguing for toleration of Protestant dissenters, appears in Van Limborch's monumental third edition (1704) of collected letters of contemporary theologians *Praestantium ac Eruditorum Virorum Epistolae Ecclesiasticae et Theologicae* (by Uytenbogaert, Vorstius, Vossius, Grotius, Episcopius, Barlaeus, et al.). Van Limborch's theological works, translated as *Christian Theology,* became a standard text for the CHURCH OF ENGLAND.

Similar to Van Limborch's publication of source materials contributing to a history beyond the official Reformed point of view (or contrary Catholic versions) was Gerard Brandt's four-volume *History of the Reformation,* also published in English. Brandt supported his narrative, which demonstrated that the Remonstrants represented the continuation of a broadly tolerant stream that had existed from the beginnings of the Dutch Reformation, with numerous original documents published in extenso. This dominated English views of the Dutch Revolt until the works of John Motley in the nineteenth century.

Later Developments

During the eighteenth century, Remonstrants were significant in ENLIGHTENMENT societies for social improvement, natural science research, contemporary literature, and drama. At mid-century, Remonstrant theologian Cornelis Nozeman, also an important ornithologist, was one of the last who needed to write against Dutch Reformed antagonists, in defense of toleration. Toleration was becoming a generally accepted enlightened social virtue. When the Dutch Reformed Church lost its privileged status in 1795, Remonstrants participated in the new democratic government of the Batavian Republic. Membership dwindled, however, and the organization contemplated abolishing its seminary under the influence of rationalism. In the nineteenth-century romantic reaction, the oratory of preacher and professor Abraham des Amorie van der Hoeven attracted new converts. His students Martinus Cohen Stuart and Johannes Tideman were notable for abolitionist activity and historical research, respectively. Tideman, professor from 1855 to 1872, applied the modern historical research methods of the period to a study of the origins of the Remonstrant Brotherhood *De Stichting der Remonstranse Broedershcap, 1619–1634*. Tideman was succeeded by C. P. Tiele, who oversaw the move of the seminary to Leiden. Tiele was not only Remonstrant professor; he also became the first Dutch professor of comparative religion. His broad comparative and contextual approach was augmented by association with the Dutch Reformed professor Abraham Kuenen, a pioneer in the application of historical criticism to Old Testament studies. The Remonstrants, having been associated with the Enlightenment in the eighteenth century, became adherents of nineteenth-century MODERNISM, the combination of historical, contextual study of the BIBLE and religion generally, with a belief in scientific progress.

WOMEN were welcomed into the Remonstrant clergy in 1921, having been allowed to preach since 1915 (see WOMEN CLERGY). Also in 1921 Professor G. J. Heering reconceived the task of the CHURCH in his paper "The Church as Social Conscience." Like many others reacting to the scientific progress embodied in the First World War, he wanted to move the church beyond late romantic INDIVIDUALISM with its characteristic emphasis on personal experience. Typically, the Remonstrant Brotherhood continued to debate the question of whether the church should be society's conscience for the next sixty years and longer, without arriving at any conclusion for fear of infringing on its principle of not allowing dogma to become binding on individual conscience. After the Second World War, the Remonstrant Brotherhood, despite steadily decreasing membership, reached out to ever-expanding international contacts through the WORLD COUNCIL OF CHURCHES and with CONGREGATIONALISTS and UNITARIANS. Church leaders including Professors H. J. Heering and G. J. Hoenderdaal developed an emphasis on church and secular social and moral issues such as nuclear disarmament and ethical aid to developing countries, as well as the concern for liturgical art in contemporary society.

At the beginning of the twenty-first century, Remonstrants were experiencing declining membership (c. 7,000) in a society that has adopted many of its principles of toleration. Although Arminian emphasis on personal responsibility underlay support for ending SLAVERY in the nineteenth century (a condition that could be justified as part of God's predestined plan), in the twentieth century Arminian responsibility was a

basis for involvement with existentialist philosophy. However, Dutch society was largely secular, with secularized Calvinist PREDESTINATION theory justifying the Dutch status quo. The selection of government officials predominantly by co-optation leads to general apathy.

References and Further Reading

Bangs, Carl. "Regents and Remonstrants in Amsterdam." In *het Spoor van Arminius*. Nieuwkoop, Netherlands: Uitgeverij Heuff, 1975.

Brandt, Gerard. *The History of the Reformation and Other Ecclesiastical Transactions in and about the Low Countries From the Beginning of the Eighth Century, Down to the Famous Synod of Dort*. Translated by John Chamberlayne from the Dutch of 1671–1704. 4 vols. New York: AMS Press, 1979.

Calder, Frederick. *Memoirs of Simon Episcopius*. London, 1838.

Colie, Rosalie. *Light and Enlightenment: A Study of the Cambridge Platonists and the Dutch Arminians*. Cambridge: Cambridge University Press, 1957.

Harrison, A. W. *Arminianism*. London: Duckworth, 1937.

Hoenderdaal, G. J., and P. M. Luca. *Staat in de Vrijheid, De Geschiedenis van de Remonstranten*. Zutphen, Netherlands: Walburg, 1982.

van Holk, L. J. "From Arminius to Arminianism in Dutch Theology." In *Man's Faith and Freedom: The Theological Influence of Jacobus Arminius*, edited by G. O. McCulloh. New York and Nashville, TN: Abingdon, 1962.

JEREMY DUPERTUIS BANGS

RESTITUTION, EDICT OF

Issued by the Holy Roman Emperor Ferdinand II in March 1629 the Edict of Restitution sought to reestablish the religious and territorial settlement achieved by the Peace of Augsburg some seventy-five years earlier in 1555. The declaration came after the opening decade of bitter fighting in the Thirty Years' War (1618–1648). Bolstered by a series of military and diplomatic gains, the Catholic imperial government saw an opportunity to fortify Catholicism and weaken significantly the Protestant position. The Edict aimed at a general realignment of the religious and political balance in the German world. The specific goal was the return of church lands that Protestants, principally Lutherans, had seized from Catholics during the preceding three-quarters of a century. The Edict also meant to strengthen the political position of Catholic ecclesiastical princes and bar the practice of CALVINISM, whose followers were a growing presence within the empire. Yet the measure was difficult to enforce and provoked considerable opposition. Accordingly the emperor was obliged to suspend the Edict by 1635 and eventually abandoned the initiative completely.

Ferdinand initially claimed to be doing no more than reinstating the status quo of 1555 and insisting on proper observance of imperial law. Protestants had illegally usurped, according to the emperor's interpretation, land belonging to Catholic archbishoprics, bishoprics, monasteries, and endowments. The property, which these Catholic entities had possessed as of the Treaty of Passau of 1552, the moment stipulated by the Peace of Augsburg, must be returned to them. In addition prelates who had left the Catholic Church could not continue to hold imperial church lands. Finally ecclesiastical rulers would have the same rights as secular princes in compelling confessional uniformity among their subjects. As imperial commissioners set out to enforce the Edict, it quickly became the most contentious political issue in Germany.

The decree caused enormous disruption, especially in northern and central Germany. Implementation meant adjustment of borders and threatened Protestant princes who had prospered from the confiscation of ecclesiastical possessions. A number of bishoprics and perhaps 500 former monasteries or similar church properties were affected. The duke of Württemberg stood to lose land that had once belonged to fourteen large monasteries and thirty-six convents. The duke of Wolfenbüttel, to take another example, held considerable property from the bishopric of Hildesheim as well as from thirteen former convents. The electors of Brandenburg and Saxony were also decidedly ill-disposed toward the new arrangement. Although both governments had secularized ecclesiastical assets long before 1552, they feared that their position might nonetheless be jeopardized by the Catholics' uncompromising stand and the possibility of additional legislation. Experiences elsewhere, particularly in the cities, suggested that imperial commissioners were exceeding the terms of the Edict and reclaiming church lands confiscated by Lutherans before the Peace of Augsburg.

The free imperial cities were understandably alarmed. Many found themselves required to return properties secularized before 1552. More serious was the situation for cities that had been Catholic at the time of the Augsburg settlement. By the seventeenth century some had, at best, a handful of Catholics within their walls. Lutheran Magdeburg, for instance, had technically been Catholic in 1552. By 1628 Catholics numbered no more than a few hundred of the city's 30,000 inhabitants. One small monastery remained in Catholic hands, whereas the city government had confiscated the cathedral and other churches. Dortmund had only thirty Catholics and all the churches were Protestant.

If, furthermore, the Peace of Augsburg's principle of *cujus regio, ejus religio* (roughly, "he who rules, his is the religion") and the right of the territorial princes to impose religious uniformity on their subjects were maintained, and expanded to include ecclesiastical principalities, Protestants residing in lands restored to Catholic authorities would soon find themselves forced to conform or emigrate. In short the Edict of Restitution menaced property rights that dated to mid-sixteenth century, and earlier in some cases. Furthermore, it meant the reduction of political and social clout among the Protestant feudal nobles and urban burghers. The Edict caused unease even among some Catholics. The elector Maximilian of Bavaria, who had his own political aspirations, had reservations regarding the increase in land and power that the Edict promised the imperial Habsburg family.

In all of this the commissioners and other officials executed the Edict in heavy-handed and unpleasant fashion. The emperor stood ready to deploy soldiers toward installation of a Catholic bishop at the Lutheran town of Magdeburg. Even Augsburg, long a Lutheran stronghold and, equally important, a free imperial city with a time-honored tradition of municipal self-governance, to include religious affairs with the arrival of the REFORMATION, was obliged to submit to Ferdinand's will. It was situated in the center of a Catholic bishopric and had been officially Catholic in 1552. Thus Lutheran worship was forbidden, the pastors were expelled, and thousands of Protestant townspeople sought refuge elsewhere.

Ultimately Swedish entrance into the war with a formidable army under the command of King GUSTAVUS ADOLPHUS altered the dynamics of the conflict and frustrated the emperor's plans. To meet the new challenge Ferdinand needed broad military and political support. Although papal diplomats and William Lamormaini, the emperor's Jesuit confessor, opposed any compromise on the Edict, Ferdinand had little choice. In 1635 imperial officials suspended enforcement and by the 1640s, in the negotiations leading to the Peace of Westphalia of 1648, abrogated the Edict. The entire project was, in retrospect, ill-fated. Apart from obvious military and political obstacles, confessional identity among Protestants had set deep roots and was not amenable to the facile transformations implicit in the Edict. The endeavor to return church lands and, more broadly, recatholicize Protestant regions proved impossible.

See also Adolphus, Gustavus; Calvinism; Lutheranism, Germany; Reformation

References and Further Reading

Bireley, Robert. *Religion and Politics in the Age of the Counterreformation: Emperor Ferdinand II, William Lamormaini, S.J., and the Formation of Imperial Policy.* Chapel Hill: University of North Carolina Press, 1981.

Lundorp, Michael Caspar, ed. *Acta publica* (Frankfurt, 1668). vol. 3, 1048–1054. [Text of the edict]

Parker, Geoffrey. *The Thirty Years' War.* London and New York: Routledge and Kegan Paul, 1984.

Wedgwood, C. V. *The Thirty Years War*. London: Jonathan Cape, 1938.

RAYMOND A. MENTZER

RESTORATIONISM

Restorationism is an often overlooked and yet foundational concept in the religious world. Synonymous with primitivism, restorationism as manifested in BIBLE-based movements seeks to restore in present society a perceived ideal based on biblical times. Restorationism assumes a departure from the original ideal; therefore, the original must be brought about anew. This is different from a reformation, which seeks to change or reform an institution already present. For restorationists, the original is no longer present; therefore, the need to restore, to bring it into being again. Because of this aspect restorationists usually consider themselves out of step with classical Protestantism. Nevertheless traces of restorationism can be found throughout Protestantism as well.

Restorationism has been a motivating concept throughout the centuries in many Bible-related movements that appear quite different from each other. Under the broad category designated "Christianity," the initial impulse of restorationism manifested between differing bodies may not be immediately obvious. For Mormons, restorationism seeks to restore the office and AUTHORITY of the original apostles. For Pentecostal and Holiness traditions, restorationism seeks to restore the New Testament gifts and power of the Holy Spirit. For Anabaptists, restorationism appears as a focus on New Testament lifestyle and piety. For Churches of Christ, restorationism seeks to re-create the apostolic pattern of New Testament church organization and member initiation. These, and other differences, come about as each group focuses on one aspect or another in need of restoration. Yet the central defining characteristic throughout these differing expressions of restorationism judges the present times by standards of the past and not vice versa.

Restorationism can be further defined and clarified as it is seen in contrast with FUNDAMENTALISM. These two systems of belief in particular have many similarities; yet there are major differences that must not be confused or overlooked. Fundamentalism seeks to remake the political and social world according to a combination of origins, traditions, and present-day CULTURE. Restorationism seeks to remake the personal and communal world strictly from origins. Fundamentalism is present and future oriented, whereas restorationism re-creates the past in the present. Changes from the original are often perceived as developments by fundamentalists and departures by restorationists. One may say that fundamentalism is preoccupied with modernity, or MODERNISM, and as such uses current means—for example, social and political structures—to create society according to its own design. Restorationism sees modernity as a hindrance, or at best as offering no help. Yet both in a sense are seeking to change society, one by working directly on society, and the other by changing individuals who will then make up the society that is changed. Ultimately restorationism seeks to recover an accurate perception of the "original" and use that model to restore a foundational, primeval ideal.

See also Anabaptism; Christian Churches, Churches of Christ; Holiness Movement; Mormonism; Pentecostalism

References and Further Reading

Hughes, Richard T., ed. *The Primitive Church in the Modern World*. Urbana: University of Illinois Press, 1995.
Wentz, Richard E. *Religion in the New World: The Shaping of Religious Traditions in the United States*. Minneapolis, MN: Fortress Press, 1990.

DAVID L. LITTLE

RÉVEIL

The word *réveil* (awakening) is used to describe a French-speaking evangelical movement that began in SWITZERLAND in the early nineteenth century. With Pietist and Moravian roots, but also significantly influenced by British Evangelicals like Thomas Erskine and Robert Haldane, those identified with the *réveil* rejected much of the rationalism of the ENLIGHTENMENT and embraced many of the attitudes of the romantic movement. In their emphasis on spiritual experience (particularly that of CONVERSION) and a recovery of REFORMATION dogma they were reverting to the Augustinian worldview to which the Enlightenment had taken exception.

In the aftermath of the FRENCH REVOLUTION, the Genevan Church had effectively muted any public expression of distinctively Protestant dogma, preferring a conservative system of morality that shunned any sort of "enthusiasm." Although many of the early protagonists of the *réveil* were not separatists by choice, they found themselves effectively silenced or excluded by the Genevan establishment. Candidates for the ministry like Henri Louis Empaytaz, Henri Pyt, and Émile Guers established the *petite église* at Bourg-de-Four in 1817, and although some ordained ministers, who were sympathetic to the *réveil*, retained their positions, others like Ami Bost and the Rochat brothers in the canton of Vaud chose to secede. Another such seceder was Henri Abraham César Malan whose *Église du Témoignage* in Geneva attracted a considerable following. A typical product of the Swiss movement was the missionary Samuel Gobat, who later became the second Anglican bishop of Jerusalem.

When in 1830 ministers like Louis Gaussen and JEAN HENRI MERLE D'AUBIGNÉ established the *Société Évangélique* (with its services at the Oratoire and its *École de Théologie*) the "'neo-Protestant" ecclesiastical authorities suspended them from the ministry. The continuing reluctance of the establishment to accommodate the *réveil* (which was stigmatized as foreign, fanatic, and exclusive), and the hostility of radical politicians led others who were associated with the movement, like Alexandre Vinet, to advocate more strongly the separation of CHURCH AND STATE. With the political upheavals of the 1840s, the *réveil*, encouraged by the example of Scottish secessionists in 1843, found institutional expression in the *Églises Évangeliques Libres* in Geneva and Vaud.

The response among French Protestants to the *réveil* varied. Thanks to the enthusiasm of JOHANN FRIEDRICH OBERLIN, the respected pastor from Alsace, many Protestants in the Midi welcomed the establishment of Bible and Tract Societies (see BIBLE SOCIETIES). In several parishes the consistories (see CONSISTORY) were prepared to cooperate and harness the enthusiasm and dedication of evangelists like Félix Neff and of pastors like Fréderic and Adolphe Monod, although elsewhere there was opposition to the perceived separatist tendencies of the movement. In the seminary at Montauban there were a number of sympathetic professors, and the activities of the English Methodist missionary Charles Cook gave the *réveil* further impetus. In Paris the movement gained support both among Lutherans and in the Reformed Church and for a while the *réveil* was associated with the salons of Madame de Stael's daughter, the Duchesse de Broglie, whose husband was a minister in the government from 1830. Indeed in the early 1840s when the Protestant François Guizot was the effective head of the government, a wave of optimism characterized the outlook of many supporters of the *réveil* in FRANCE. By 1850, however, the exclusive tendencies latent in the movement, aggravated by the extreme position taken by separatists like Comte Agénor de Gasparin and Fréderic Monod, led to a break with the traditional Protestant churches and the establishment of the *Églises libres françaises*.

The *réveil* must not be treated in isolation from the flowering evangelical movement in English-speaking countries or its contemporary counterpart, the German *Erweckung* associated with the BASEL MISSION (founded in 1815) and with men like FRIEDRICH AUGUST THOLUCK OF HALLE. There was an international dimension to nineteenth-century EVANGELICALISM and part of the strength of the *réveil* lay in its links with the wider movement.

References and Further Reading

Dubief, H. "Réflexions sure quelques aspects du premier Réveil et sure le milieu où il se forma." *Bulletin de la Société de l'Histoire du Protestantisme Français.* cxiv (1968): 373–402.

Fatio, O., ed. *Genève Protestante en 1831.* Geneva: Labor et Fides, 1983.

Maury, Leon. *Le Réveil religieux dans les Églises réformées de Genève et en France.* Paris: Fischbacher, 1892.

Robert, Daniel. *Les Églises Réformées en France (1800–1830).* Paris: Presses Universitaires de France, 1961.

Stunt, Timothy C. F. *From Awakening to Secession: Radical Evangelicals in Switzerland and Britain 1815–35.* Edinburgh: T. & T. Clark, 2000.

Wemyss, Alice. *Histoire du Réveil 1790–1849.* Paris: Les Bergers et les Mages, 1977.

TIMOTHY C. F. STUNT

REVIVALS

Religious revivals are periods of religious fervor characterized by repentance among Christians and numerous conversions. MARTIN LUTHER and JOHN CALVIN laid the groundwork for revivals by teaching JUSTIFICATION by FAITH and by calling for ongoing reform in the CHURCH. By the seventeenth century many Christians believed that the REFORMATION had bogged down in formalism, doctrinal disputes, and political controversy. In response, Lutheran Pietists such as PHILIPP JAKOB SPENER and AUGUST HERMANN FRANCKE promoted individual CONVERSION, Bible study, and social reform. One of Francke's students, Count NIKOLAUS LUDWIG VON ZINZENDORF, organized refugees from Moravia into a Pietist Christian community (see PIETISM). Traveling bands of Moravians spread the doctrine and experience of conversion throughout Europe and America (see MORAVIAN CHURCH).

Meanwhile English-speaking Calvinists increasingly called for a pure church of converted "saints." Like the Pietists, these Puritans gathered the most fervent believers into household religious meetings (see PURITANISM). They preached against the evils in church and society and called for a "revival of religion." In SCOTLAND, Calvinist clergymen held outdoor communion festivals that drew hundreds of participants and produced numerous conversions.

These religious precedents combined with cultural changes like the industrial revolution, the expansion of international trade, and the ENLIGHTENMENT to produce the full flowering of revivals in the eighteenth century. Revivals proved to be a popular alternative to the economic insecurity, vice, and rationalism of the era. Taking advantage of new methods of communication and transportation, an international network of Calvinists, Methodists, and Pietists spread the stories, beliefs, and methods of revival (see CALVINISM; METHODISM). With the encouragement of Moravian missionaries, Anglican clergyman JOHN WESLEY experienced his own "new birth" in 1738. He preached revival to the common people of ENGLAND and formed them into Methodist religious societies. Other revival participants like CHARLES WESLEY, John Newton, and ISAAC WATTS wrote HYMNS that transformed Protestant WORSHIP in this era. In the American colonies a dramatic period of revival, later called the First Great AWAKENING, began around 1720. The high point came in 1740 when English Calvinist GEORGE WHITEFIELD toured the colonies and preached to massive crowds. Congregationalist minister JONATHAN EDWARDS provided a key theological defense of the movement.

Later Revivals

Beginning at the turn of the nineteenth century a new wave of revivals called the Second Great Awakening transformed the UNITED STATES. On the frontier Americans gathered for religious CAMP MEETINGS. One of the most famous of these took place at an 1801 communion festival in Cane Ridge, Kentucky. Thousands of participants experienced conversion and many displayed behaviors like fits of shouting, muscle jerks, and falling. Culturally marginalized individuals like slaves, WOMEN, and children spontaneously preached to the crowds. This camp meeting tradition heightened the emotional element in revivals and revealed their democratizing potential.

Similar frontier and urban revivals between 1800 and 1850 contributed to the dramatic growth of the Methodist and Baptist denominations in America and led to the founding of numerous new denominations and sects. This period also saw the large-scale Christianization of the African American population. Slaves and free blacks created their own version of revivalism that emphasized the liberating power of the Christian message.

Presbyterian clergyman CHARLES GRANDISON FINNEY aroused controversy with the use of "new measures" in his revival meetings in upstate New York in the 1830s. Finney allowed women to pray in mixed gatherings, called on sinners by name to repent, and called seekers forward to sit on the "anxious bench." Finney also taught Arminian and holiness doctrines (see ARMINIANISM; HOLINESS MOVEMENT) and claimed that a revival was "not a miracle" but the result of correct application of God's appointed means. Converts in these revivals led campaigns against alcohol, slavery, PROSTITUTION, and other vices. They established MISSIONARY ORGANIZATIONS, homes for the poor, hospitals, and colleges. This period of revivalism came to a close with the 1857–1858 Businessmen's Revival.

In the 1880s DWIGHT L. MOODY and his musical partner IRA SANKEY led revival meetings in Britain and North America. This era saw the publication of numerous new "gospel songs," which functioned as the music of revivalism for the next seventy-five years. These revivals also produced social service agencies like WILLIAM BOOTH's SALVATION ARMY in England and rescue missions in American cities. Others converted through organizations like the Student Volunteer Movement and the CHRISTIAN AND MISSIONARY ALLIANCE devoted themselves to foreign MISSIONS.

Contemporary Expressions

The twentieth century saw the globalization of revivals. Word of the Welsh revival of 1903–1904 spread throughout the world, sparking revivals in KOREA, CHINA, SOUTH AFRICA, INDIA, Scandinavia, and the United States. Participants in the Welsh revival influenced the Pentecostal revival of 1906–1909 that spread around the world from its center in the AZUSA STREET MISSION in Los Angeles. The East African Revival of 1933–1935 spread to Rwanda (formerly Ruanda), Uganda, Kenya, Tanzania, and Burundi under the leadership of Simeoni Nsibambi and Blasio Kigozi. Between 1965 and 1970 massive revivals broke out in INDONESIA. In LATIN AMERICA, evangelical and Pentecostal revivals doubled the number of Protestants between 1970 and 1990. Indigenous leadership increasingly characterized revivals in AFRICA, Asia, and Latin America.

Beginning with his highly publicized Los Angeles Crusade of 1949, BILLY GRAHAM became an international leader in EVANGELISM and revival. In the late 1960s and early 1970s the Jesus People movement combined the hippie youth culture with revival (see JESUS MOVEMENT). At the same time the charismatic movement brought the Pentecostal experiences of Holy Spirit baptism, healing, and speaking in TONGUES to millions of Protestants and Roman Catholics around the world. The resulting revivals of the 1970s led to the widespread acceptance of praise choruses and more exuberant styles of worship.

Influences

Although the causes and impact of revivals have been much disputed, several patterns have emerged. First, revivals have produced both renewal and schism in the Christian churches. Second, social and economic instability enhance receptivity to revivals, and help explain their appeal among the middle and lower rungs of society. Third, revival converts often establish educational, social service, and missionary organizations that transform society. Fourth, revivals have significant yet complex political consequences. Finally, although key innovations took place in North America, revivals have most often been international in origin and scope.

References and Further Reading

Blumhofer, Edith, and Randall Balmer, eds. *Modern Christian Revivals*. Urbana: University of Illinois Press, 1993.

Carwardine, Richard. *Trans-atlantic Revivalism*. Westport, CT: Greenwood Press, 1978.

Hatch, Nathan. *The Democratization of American Christianity*. New Haven, CT: Yale University Press, 1989.

McLouglin, William G. *Revivals, Awakenings, and Reform*. Chicago: University of Chicago Press, 1978.

Orr, J. Edwin *The Flaming Tongue: The Impact of Twentieth Century Revivals*. Chicago: Moody Press, 1973.

Riss, Richard M. *A Survey of Twentieth-Century Revival Movements in North America*. Peabody, MA: Hendrickson Publishers, 1988.

Ward, William R. *The Protestant Evangelical Awakening*. New York: Cambridge University Press, 1992.

THOMAS E. BERGLER

RICHARDSON, HENRY HOBSON (1838–1886)

American architect. Born in Louisiana of well-to-do parents, Richardson was educated at Harvard and the Ecole des Beaux-Arts in Paris. He returned to the United States in 1865, practicing first in New York before relocating his office and family to Brookline, Massachusetts, in 1874, where he remained until his death.

Although Richardson's work was predominantly secular, institutional, and domestic, his Trinity Church in Boston remains an outstanding contribution to nineteenth-century Protestant architecture. Completed in 1878, following three earlier, more conventional, churches (also in Massachusetts), it immediately established Richardson as an architect of exceptional power and sophistication. The exterior is essentially southern French Romanesque (a style admired by Richardson), while the tower draws freely upon Salamanca's former cathedral. The overall effect is not eclectic pastiche, but, with its pervasive rock-faced cladding, is of genuine monumentality. The large, cruciform interior consciously fuses Romanesque liturgical space (with comprehensive polychrome decoration) with both the historic "auditorium" tradition of New England Protestantism and the famed oratorical skills of Trinity's first incumbent, PHILLIPS BROOKS. Richardson's other potential masterpiece—his 1883 competition design for an Episcopal cathedral at Albany, New York, again in the Romanesque style—was, unfortunately, deemed too complex and expensive to secure the commission.

In retrospect, it is clear that both Richardson's religious outlook and his architecture were shaped by his Unitarian roots (his mother was the granddaughter of chemist JOSEPH PRIESTLEY, 1733–1804), his membership of Boston's Unitarian elite, and the normative transcendentalism of his own professional and social circle. If Ruskin's strong impact ("all art must be based on truth"), and the architect's own formative encounters with the Romanesque are also taken into account, then what one contemporary called Richardson's "power to appreciate the value both of ancient forms consecrated by persisting sentiment and of practical modern needs, and to put one without violence to the service of the other" becomes both convincing and self-evident.

References and Further Reading

Hitchcock, H. R. 1966. *The Architecture of Henry Hobson Richardson and His Times*. Cambridge, MA: MIT Press, 1966.

Meister, M., ed. *H. H. Richardson: The Architect, His Peers and Their Era*. Cambridge, MA: MIT Press, 1999.

Van Rensselaer. *Henry Hobson Richardson and His Works*. New York: Dover, 1969

GRAHAM A. K. HOWES

RICHER, EDMOND (1559–1631)

French political theorist. Richer was born September 15, 1559 at Chesley, near Chaours, FRANCE and died November 29, 1631 at Paris. A student at the College du Cardinal Lemoine in the University of Paris and at the Sorbonne, he received the doctorate in THEOLOGY around 1592, became (1595) grand master and principal of the College du Cardinal Lemoine, and then syndic of the Parisian theology faculty. That position he held until 1612 when he was forced out of office by the hostility of the papal nuncio the cardinal du Perron to the views expressed in his celebrated *Libellus de ecclesiastica et politica potestate* (1611). Having in earlier years been a supporter of the Catholic Ligue and an admirer of Cardinal Bellarmine's high papalist views, he later rallied to the cause of Henri IV and emerged as a proponent both of the divine right of the French monarchy and of Gallican views.

While making common cause with the politique Gallicans of the Parlement de Paris, Richer's central aim was to reinvigorate the theological heart of the Gallican tradition by reviving the knowledge of the great conciliarist doctors of Paris and by promulgating, among other things, their advocacy of the jurisdictional subordination of the pope to general council. He realized that aim through an extensive array of editions, treatises, and works of compilation, notably the *Libellus* of 1611, his influential 1606 edition of the works of Jean Gerson (d. 1429), and his reprinting of the conciliarist tracts of Jean de Paris (d. 1306), Pierre d'Ailly (d. 1420), Jacques Almain (d. 1505), and John Mair (d. 1550). Herein—as disseminator to future generations of the old tradition of conciliarist constitutionalism in the church, rather than as the alleged (if shadowy) precursor of far more radical and supposedly heterodox views smacking of what in the eighteenth century was labeled as *richerisme, multitudinism, presbyterianisme,* and *parochisme*—lies his historical significance.

References and Further Reading

Primary Sources:

Richer, Edmond. *Joannes Gersonii . . . Opera omnia.* 2 vols. Paris: 1606.
———. *Apologia pro Joanno Gersonii, pro ecclesiae et concilii generalis aucoritate.* [n.p.], 1607; Lyons: 1676.
———. *Libellus de ecclesiastica et politica potestate* (1611). Printed in Melchior Goldast, *Monarchia S, Romani Imperii.* vol. 3, 797–806. Frankfurt: 1611–1613.
———. *Defensio libelli de ecclesiastica et politica potestate.* 2 vols. Cologne: 1701.

Secondary Sources:

Cottret, Monique. "Edmond Richer (1559–1631): La politique et le sacre." In *L'état baroque: Regards sur la pensée politique de la France au première XVIIe siècle,* edited by Henry Mechoulin, 159–177. Paris: 1985.
Oakley, Francis. "Bronze-Age Conciliarism: Edmond Richer's Encounters with Cajetan and Bellarmine." *History of Political Thought* 20 (1999): 65–86.
Preclin, E. "Edmond Richer (1559–1631): Sa vie, son oeuvre et le Richerisme." *Revue d'histoire moderne* 5 (1930): 241–269, 321–336.
Puyol, Edmond. *Edmond Richer: Etude historique et critique sur la rénovation du Gallicanisme au commencement du XVIIe siècle.* 2 vols. Paris: 1876.

FRANCIS OAKLEY

RITSCHL, ALBRECHT BENJAMIN (1822–1889)

German theologian. Ritschl was born in Berlin on March 3, 1822. His father was a Protestant theologian as well as the Pomeranian general superintendent of the Prussian regional church with the title of bishop. After studying in Bonn, HALLE, Heidelberg, and Tübingen, Ritschl received his doctorate and qualified to teach at a university. He became a lecturer in church history in 1864 and later in systematic theology at the University of Bonn. In 1865 he was appointed professor of systematic theology in Göttingen and eventually known as the most important scholar of systematic theology in Protestant GERMANY in the last third of the nineteenth century. He died on March 20, 1889 in Göttingen.

Development of Thought

Ritschl's THEOLOGY takes as its starting point the branch of scholarship known as *Vermittlungstheologie,* or mediating theology. After a short-lived turn toward the speculative theology of Richard Rothe, Ritschl joined the school of thought from Tübingen dominated by FERDINAND CHRISTIAN BAUR. This school combined strict criticism of historical sources with the interpretation of church history formulated by the German philosopher GEORG W. F. HEGEL, which understood history in terms of a dialectically unfolding process of thesis, antithesis, and synthesis. The systematic clarity of this approach impressed Ritschl, but it also caused him to grow less convinced of its treatment of source materials. In the second edition of his study *Entstehung der altkatholischen Kirche (Origins of the Early Catholic Church,* 1857), Ritschl broke with Baur. From then on he advocated a more sober positivism based on close readings of texts.

The principal work that made Ritschl well known and famous initiated a turning point in theology when it was published from 1870 to 1874 in three volumes under the title *Die christliche Lehre von der Rechtfertigung und Versöhnung (The Christian Doctrine of Justification and Reconciliation,* 3d edition, 1889, English translation 1966). In 1875 an abbreviated synopsis of the larger work was published as *Unterricht in der christlichen Religion (Instruction in the Christian Religion).* Given the realities of the industrial age and the overwhelming power of SCIENCE and technology, Ritschl wanted to safeguard the irreducibility of the individual and especially the religious experience of the individual.

The theological concept that Ritschl formulated to this end began with the knowledge and experience found in a community of believers, the basis of which is the revelation of God. Ritschl sought to raise what is in the BIBLE to a truth attested to by history. His attempt to support this approach by turning to IMMANUEL KANT's theory of cognition convinced few, however, and Ritschl's students felt obliged to look for other solutions. By following this path, however, Ritschl could exclude any natural theology.

Ritschl described the love of God as the content of Christian revelation and argued that this love seeks to find a form as the self-revelation of God. SIN hampers movement toward this goal and so must be eliminated, which, according to Ritschl, occurs by doing the work of Christ. Although Ritschl uses common theological terminology, his approach does not refer to traditional CHRISTOLOGY or soteriology. Christ communicates to a community of believers because God is love. They know from this that God forgives sins and confers a state of peace. In this respect Ritschl's theology focuses strictly on Christ, although in doing so, it is a more intellectually sober position that leaves no room for religious emotion. It makes no sense, then, to speak of the Catholic church mediating SALVATION. According to Ritschl the forgiveness of sins and reconciliation with God supply all the information needed to assure a congregation.

This knowledge offers a devout community the possession of a special value. Behind it is the notion that in contrast to the natural sciences, religion concerns not judgments of fact but judgments of value. The value of a religion rests in the extent to which it promotes morality, and the religion of greatest value is the one that enables the greatest morality. That such a statement holds true only for Christianity was a central message in Ritschl's theology.

He demonstrated this contention as follows: Reconciliation with God brings one a freedom understood as independence and detachment from the world. Christ is thus not bound to the laws of rational logic, but stands in spiritual contrast to them. This is precisely the fundamental condition that allows the individual to develop as a moral person.

Concern for the Kingdom

In addition to the notion of individual, subjective growth, Ritschl's theology included a notion of the whole. True morality endures only in service, and for Ritschl this meant that Christ participates in establishing the KINGDOM OF GOD in the world. In this respect, Ritschl broadened the doctrines of JUSTIFICATION and reconciliation to include an ethical imperative.

His theological program, like an ellipsis, had two focal points. Forgiveness of sin and reconciliation with God form one, and the kingdom of God understood as an ethical imperative forms the other. For Ritschl it is essential that ethics have no specific Christian content. What matters most is living up to the demands of the everyday in the place in which one is situated: family, profession, country.

Ritschl insisted on this notion of the Christian's relationship to the world with enormous sobriety and emphasized its distinction from Catholicism and PIETISM. Catholicism falsely identified the kingdom of God with the CHURCH; Pietism divided in a fateful way the kingdom of God from the world. From 1880 to 1886 Ritschl composed a massive three-volume *Geschichte des Pietismus* (*History of Pietism*). The work—parts of which are so rich in their use of source materials that no other work has yet surpassed them—sets out to prove that Pietism constituted not a further

development of the REFORMATION but an eruption of late-medieval Catholic mysticism into Protestantism.

Assessment

Ritschl's theology had an enormous impact for two reasons. On the one hand Ritschl focused little on fundamental concepts in theology; on the other hand his theology represented not only a cognitive theoretical approach but also a study in positivism—a method that corresponded well to the conscious self-understanding of the period. Ritschl conceived and developed a combination of religious transcendence and strict fulfillment of duty that to a great degree met the expectations of the Protestant bourgeoisie in late 19th century Germany.

It was no coincidence that this theology dominated Germany and affected instruction in the schools through World War I. Ritschl influenced not only various representatives of systematic theology—for example, Wilhelm Herrmann, MARTIN RADE, and ERNST TROELTSCH—but also church historians and interpreters such as Julius Wellhausen and ADOLF VON HARNACK.

References and Further Reading

Jodock, Darrell, ed. *Ritschl in Retrospect. History, Community, Science.* Minneapolis, MN: Fortress, 1995.
Kuhlmann, Helga. *Die theologische Ethik Albrecht Ritschls.* Munich, Germany: Kaiser, 1992.
Schäfer, Rolf. *Ritschl: Grundlinien eines fast verschollenen Systems.* Tübingen, Germany: Mohr, 1968.

MARTIN GRESCHAT

ROBERTS, GRANVILLE ORAL (1918–)

American evangelist. Roberts was born on January 24, 1918, in Pontotoc County, Oklahoma. Reared in the parsonage of a Pentecostal minister (see PENTECOSTAL-ISM) he experienced the hardships of poverty during the Depression era. At age seventeen Roberts collapsed on the basketball court. Diagnosed with tuberculosis he spent five months in convalescence. He claimed complete healing when attending a service conducted by George Moncey. He entered the ministry in 1935, having been ordained by the Pentecostal Holiness Church. For eleven years he pastored churches in Oklahoma. By 1946 he was serving one of his DENOMINATION's largest churches, teaching classes at Southwest Bible College and taking coursework at Phillips University.

In 1947 he abruptly changed course. Influenced by the recent success of evangelist William Branham, Roberts resigned his pastorate and launched an interdenominational healing and evangelistic ministry (see

FAITH HEALING). He set up headquarters in Tulsa, Oklahoma, started a magazine titled *Healing Waters,* published a book, *If You Need Healing, Do These Things,* and began a weekly radio broadcast. He began crisscrossing the UNITED STATES, holding tent REVIVALS on the outskirts of America's largest cities. Thousands attended every meeting with scores claiming healing in every crusade.

He helped found the FULL GOSPEL BUSINESS MEN'S ASSOCIATION in 1951. The Association's impact, together with Roberts's ecumenical crusades, laid much of the groundwork for the Charismatic Movement that burst on mainline North American Christianity in the 1970s. With three hundred crusades behind him, he returned to Tulsa to start a university in 1967. Oral Roberts University gained full accreditation within six years and had over 4,000 students at the turn of the century.

Roberts's move to establish a medical school proved to be the most controversial decision of his ministry. The City of Faith Medical and Research Center failed to gain financial solvency, closing within ten years of its 1981 opening.

References and Further Reading

Primary Sources:

Roberts, Oral. *God is a Good God; Believe It and Come Alive.* Indianapolis, IN: Bobbs-Merrill, 1960.
———. *The Baptism with the Holy Spirit: and the Value of Speaking in Tongues Today.* Tulsa, OK: 1964.
———. *The Call: An Autobiography.* Garden City, NY: Doubleday, 1972.
———. *The Miracles of Christ and What They Mean to You for All Your Needs in the Now.* Tulsa, OK: Pinoak Pub., 1975.
———. *3 Most Important Steps to Your Better Health and Miracle Living.* Tulsa, OK: Oral Roberts Evangelistic Assn., 1976.
———. *How to Get Through Your Struggles: or, You Can Walk on the Stormy Waters of Your Life.* Tulsa, OK: Oral Roberts Evangelistic Assn., 1977.
———. *Don't Give Up!: Jesus Will Give You That Miracle You Need.* Tulsa, OK: Oral Roberts Evangelistic Assn., 1980.
———. *God Still Heals Today: and Here's How He Heals You.* Tulsa, OK: O. Roberts, 1984.
———. *How I Learned Jesus Was Not Poor.* Altamonte Springs, FL: Creation House, 1989.
———. *Expect a Miracle: My Life and Ministry; An Autobiography.* Nashville, TN: T. Nelson, 1995.

Secondary Sources:

Harrell, David Edwin. *Oral Roberts: An American Life.* Bloomington: Indiana University Press, 1985.
Robinson, Wayne A. *Oral: The Warm Intimate Unauthorized Portrait of a Man of God.* Los Angeles: Acton House, 1976.

D. WILLIAM FAUPEL

ROBERTSON, FREDERICK WILLIAM (1816–1853)

English clergyman. Robertson was born in London on February 3, 1816, and died in Brighton, Sussex, ENGLAND, on August 15, 1853. He received his B.A. in 1840 and his M.A. in 1841, both from Brasenose College, Oxford. After a rather undistinguished six years of ministry Robertson became minister at Trinity Chapel, Brighton, and made Trinity Chapel one of the most famous churches in England by his PREACHING. At Brighton he helped establish the Working-Man's Institute, which was a library, reading room, and cultural center.

Robertson was a brilliant BIBLE expositor and an outstanding pastoral preacher. Although he believed that Jesus Christ was divine, he stressed his humanity in sermons such as "The Sympathy of Christ," "The Loneliness of Christ," and "The Sinlessness of Christ." He was sympathetic to Christian Socialism as was illustrated in his sermons "The Message of the Church to Men of Wealth" and "Christ's Moral Judgment Respecting Inheritance." Robertson insisted that Christianity is the revelation of the love of God and a demand of our love by God. Christianity is the revelation of forgiveness and a requirement that we should forgive each other.

Robertson was very effective in telling biblical stories. Sermons such as "Jacob's Wrestling," "Triumph Over Hindrances—Zaccheus," and "The Doubt of Thomas" were vivid in detail and undoubtedly captured the hearers' attention. Thus he observed about Thomas: "The faith of Thomas was not merely satisfaction about a fact; it was trust in a person."

See also Christology; Socialism, Christian

References and Further Reading

Primary Sources:

Robertson, Frederick W. *Sermons Preached at Brighton.* New York and London: Harper & Brothers, Publishers, n.d.
———. *Sermons and Outlines on the Seven Words.* Grand Rapids, MI: Baker Book House, 1953.
———. *Sermons by Frederick W. Robertson.* London, New York: J. M. Dent & Co., E. P. Dutton & Co., 1906, 1909.

Secondary Sources:

Blackwood, James Russell. *The Soul of Frederick W. Robertson, the Brighton Preacher.* New York and London: Harper & Brothers, 1947.
Brooke, Stopford Augustus, ed. *Life and Letters of Frederick W. Robertson.* 2 vols. London: Kegan Paul, Trench, Trubner & Co., 1891.
Henson, Henley. *Robertson of Brighton, 1816–1853.* London: Smith, Elder, 1916.

DONALD S. ARMENTROUT

ROBERTSON, PAT (1930–)

American evangelist. Marion Gordon Robertson (known as Pat) was born on March 22, 1930, in Lexington, Virginia, the son of Absalom Willis Robertson and Josephine Ragland Willis. Robertson's father was an attorney who served terms in the Senate of Virginia, the U.S. House of Representatives, and in the U.S. Senate.

Robertson graduated from Washington and Lee University *summa cum laude* and in 1955 received a law degree from Yale University. After a series of disappointing career moves, Robertson underwent a religious conversion, including a tongues-speaking experience, and enrolled in the conservative Biblical Seminary in New York City. After a brief period of ministering in the slums, Robertson purchased a run-down UHF television station in Portsmouth, Virginia, to which he gave the grandiose name "the Christian Broadcasting Network." By the mid-1960s CBN had a solid core of supporters and in 1966 the station began broadcasting a program hosted by Robertson, the "700 Club." That show became one of the longest-running television programs in the history of the industry. Robertson's network was unashamedly religious, although it also promoted a conservative political and economic agenda.

The expansion of CBN was an unbroken success story. In 1979 a newly constructed headquarters building housed two state-of-the-art television studios and recording facilities. A year earlier Robertson unveiled plans to build a graduate university; the opening of Regents University (originally called CBN University) vastly expanded the reach of Robertson's ministry. At the end of the twentieth century Regents was the most prestigious education institution associated with the Pentecostal/charismatic movement. In 1988 CBN took the name "The Family Channel" and the network became one of the nation's leading cable systems. The prosperity of the ministry's television enterprise threatened its tax-exempt status and in 1997 it was sold, producing large endowments for Regents and the ministry.

Robertson was a natural to lead the political awakening of American evangelicals in the 1970s. Well-known to and trusted by the millions of Americans who had embraced the Pentecostal/charismatic movement, he was also equipped by upbringing and education to discuss political and economic issues. He became one of the most visible leaders of the religious right in the last quarter of the twentieth century. In 1988 Robertson entered the primaries as a Republican candidate for the presidency and surprised many by winning the Iowa caucus. After his presidential campaign faltered, he placed his brand on the conservative political agenda by founding the Christian Coalition of America.

Robertson is the author of ten books, several of them best-sellers. His ministry is presently housed on a 700-acre complex in Virginia Beach, Virginia. The elegant Williamsburg-style buildings symbolize the success and patriotism of Pat Robertson. In addition to its educational activities, the ministry has a major presence on television in America and in about fifty other countries, and through Operation Blessing International is one of the largest private relief organizations in America. The ministry's annual budget exceeds $200 million and CBN employs about one thousand people.

See also Pentacostalism; Evangelicalism; Televangelism

References and Further Reading

Primary Source:

Robertson, Pat, and Jamie Buckingham. *Shout It From the Housetops.* Plainfield, N.J.: Logos International, 1972. http//www.cbn.com/

Secondary Source:

Harrell, David Edwin, Jr. *Pat Robertson: A Personal, Political and Religious Portrait.* San Francisco: Harper & Row, 1987.

DAVID EDWIN HARRELL JR.

ROBINSON, HENRY WHEELER (1872–1945)

English biblical scholar. Robinson was an Old Testament scholar, theologian, English Baptist clergyman, historian, and educator. Born in Northampton, ENGLAND, February 7, 1872, he and his mother lived with his mother's uncle. He left school at an early age and worked in the leather business.

He became associated with College Street Baptist Church where he was baptized in 1888. Attracted to the Christian ministry he began attending Regent's Park College in London. A year later he moved to Edinburgh University where he graduated in 1895. He completed his university studies at Mansfield College, Oxford with a concentration in Old Testament studies.

Brief pastorates at Baptist churches in Pitlochry and Coventry led to a call to be a tutor at Rawdon Baptist College. His lectures attracted considerable attention as did his books, in particular *Deuteronomy and Joshua* (1907) and *The Religious Ideas of the Old Testament* (1913).

In 1920 Robinson was appointed principal of Regent's College, a post he held until 1942. His career blossomed with the new responsibilities. He became a member of the London Society for the Study of Religion and a major figure in the Society for Old Testament Study. He participated in the planning and editing of the "The Library of Constructive Theology." He wrote *The Christian Experience of the Holy Spirit* (1928). He was active in the Baptist Historical Society, serving as president, and he published important books in Baptist history, including *The Life and Faith of the Baptists* (1927).

The great achievement of his career was his role in moving Regent's College from London to Oxford. In Oxford he became a well-known theological lecturer and a reader in biblical criticism. In 1937 he became the chairman of the board of the faculty of theology, the first Free Churchman so honored. Robinson died May 12, 1945.

See also Baptists

References and Further Reading

Payne, E. A. *Henry Wheeler Robinson.* 1946.

JOHN PIPER

ROBINSON, JOHN ARTHUR THOMAS (1575 OR 1576–1625)

English Separatist and Pilgrim pastor. Robinson was born in Sturton-le-Steeple, Nottinghamshire. He entered Corpus Christi College, CAMBRIDGE UNIVERSITY, in 1592, was awarded a B. A. in 1596 and an M. A. in 1599; in 1598 he became a fellow of the college but resigned his fellowship in 1604 and married Bridget White. At Cambridge, the CALVINISM of WILLIAM PERKINS (1558–1602) influenced him. Early in 1604 he was appointed curate of St. Andrews, Norwich, although he had already disclosed his Puritan sympathies (see PURITANISM) by denouncing church courts and unlearned ministers; no later than 1606 he was suspended for his dissident views. Robinson joined the Separatist circle of English nonconformist JOHN SMYTH (1554–1612) and affiliated with the Separatist congregation gathered in Scrooby, Nottinghamshire, which included William Brewster (1566–1644) and William Bradford (1590–1657), both later leaders of the Plymouth colonists in New England. Troubled by the local ecclesiastical courts, the Scrooby group moved to the NETHERLANDS, settling in Amsterdam in August, 1608, where they chose Robinson their pastor and came in contact with English Separatists led by Francis Johnson and Henry Ainsworth (1571–1622). By April 1609 they had moved to Leiden.

Robinson's 1610 treatise *A Justification of Separation* proves him by then a Separatist who believed that the CHURCH OF ENGLAND was so corrupt that the godly should no longer remain within it. Identifying with the earlier Separatist tradition of Henry Barrow, he argued that a true visible CHURCH was a disciplined community of gathered SAINTS, covenanted together for mutual edification (see COVENANT). But he modified his Separatism, probably as a result of contact with such non-Separatist Congregationalists as WILLIAM AMES (1576–1633) and Henry Jacob, to the extent of allowing that one could have spiritual fellowship with godly persons within the Church of England and even hear sermons in its parish churches. When Smyth rejected infant BAPTISM, Robinson defended it against him and other Baptists. Robinson also attacked Smyth for denying original SIN, and in 1624 he defended PREDESTINATION against the Baptist John Murton; earlier, in 1613, he had assisted the Dutch Calvinists' assault upon ARMINIANISM by publicly debating Simon Episcopius (1583–1643).

In 1620 part of Robinson's Leiden congregation left for Plymouth in New England, and though he planned eventually to join them, he died before doing so, though his wife and children later settled in New England. His reported exhortation to the departing Pilgrims that "the Lord had more truth and light yet to break forth out of his holy word," has been taken to indicate the tolerant tenor of his thought, but he remained a committed Separatist and Calvinist.

References and Further Reading

Ashton, R., ed. *The Works of John Robinson.* 3 vols. London: John Snow, 1851.
Brachlow, Stephen. *The Communion of Saints: Radical Puritan and Separatist Eccesiology 1570–1625.* Oxford: Oxford University Press, 1988.
Burgess, W. H. *The Pastor of the Pilgrims: A Biography of John Robinson.* New York: Harcourt, Brace and Howe, 1920
George, Timothy. *John Robinson and the English Separatist Tradition.* Macon, GA: Mercer University Press, 1982

DEWEY D. WALLACE, JR.

ROMAN CATHOLICISM

See Catholic Reactions to Protestantism; Catholicism, Protestant Reactions

ROMANIA

The modern state of Romania in southeastern Europe emerged after the 1920 Treaty of Trianon at the end of the First World War. The vast majority of those living in the provinces of Moldavia and Wallachia belong to the Eastern Orthodox Church. In Transylvania and counties to the west of the Carpathian mountains, Romanians mostly adhere to EASTERN ORTHODOXY or the Greek Catholic Church. The German and Hungarian communities of Transylvania belong to a range of churches, including the Lutheran, Reformed, and Unitarian churches. Many German and Hungarian communities in Transylvania have remained faithful to Protestantism since the middle decades of the sixteenth century.

The Reformation in Transylvania

At the beginning of the sixteenth century Transylvania and the lands between the river Tisza and the Carpathians were part of the Hungarian kingdom. In 1526 the armies of Sultan Suleiman "the magnificent" won a decisive victory at the battle of Mohács over the Hungarian king, Louis II. The Ottomans were able to consolidate control over southern and central HUNGARY during the middle decades of the sixteenth century. The remainder of the medieval Hungarian kingdom was divided in two. To the north and west, the Habsburgs became kings of Royal Hungary, which stretched from the Adriatic coast to the mountains of modern Slovakia. To the east native nobles were elected as princes over Transylvania proper and the Hungarian *Partium* beyond the river Tisza. This Transylvanian principality had a diet of three estates: the Hungarian nobility, the German towns, and Szekler people.

REFORMATION ideas spread first to the German or Saxon towns during the 1540s. Johannes Honter gained acceptance for Lutheran reforms from the urban magistrates of Braþov (Kronstadt), and Braþov's example was quickly followed in other Saxon towns. The fledgling Transylvanian state authorities took advantage of growing support for reform to bring all church property under princely control in 1556. Having bolstered his position, Prince János Zsigmond Zápolyai then accepted the diet's demand for the legal recognition of Protestantism, and in 1557 the Saxon towns received approval for the free practice of LUTHERANISM. Although communication linkages with GERMANY helped establish loyalty to Lutheranism in the German-speaking community, Hungarian speakers were also at first influenced by Lutheran PREACHING.

However, from the late 1550s Hungarian nobles and towns moved to embrace Reformed religion. Debates were held between German and Hungarian clergy over understanding of the SACRAMENTS, and especially the Eucharist, or LORD'S SUPPER. Reformed or Calvinist clergy could not agree with Lutherans that Christ was "really present" in the sacrament, and their statements on DOCTRINE argued that the Eucharist was merely a sign and pledge of SALVATION by faith. In 1564 the diet recognized two Protestant churches in Transylvania, one for Germans and the other for Hungarians. The doctrine of the emerging Reformed Church was clearly established by a CONFESSION drawn up by Péter Méliusz Juhász at Debrecen in 1567, and Reformed clergy also recognized the Second HELVETIC CONFESSION.

Transylvanian Protestantism split again in the 1560s over understanding of the doctrine of the Trinity. FERENC DÁVID led a group of anti-Trinitarian clergy, whose message that "God is one" received some support from prince János Zsigmond Zápolyai. In 1568 the diet met at Turda (Torda) and reached the remarkably tolerant decision to devolve to ministers the responsibility of preaching the word of God "according to their understanding of it." The diet described FAITH as a gift from God that could not be compelled against conscience. Legal status was therefore granted to the Catholic, Lutheran, Reformed, and anti-Trinitarian (or Unitarian) churches, and ownership of church buildings was decided by the majority in each parish (see UNITARIAN UNIVERSALIST ASSOCIATION).

By the 1570s the Catholic Church had virtually ceased to exist in many areas. German-speaking towns remained Lutheran, whereas the Reformed and Unitarian churches were dominated by Hungarian speakers. Although a sense of linguistic and ethnic community may have made some contribution to the outcome of the Reformation in this region, the role of the socially privileged elite of nobles and urban magistrates was generally decisive in establishing the form of religion in each locality. The Romanian peasantry in Transylvania remained mostly Orthodox, although attempts were made by both the Lutheran and Reformed churches to stimulate reform, and a Romanian Reformed Church was established in southwestern Transylvania in the seventeenth century.

Support for ANTI-TRINITARIANISM in Transylvania was badly disrupted by internal divisions. Some anti-Trinitarians moved toward non-adorantism of Christ in the 1570s, despite a 1572 law preventing any further religious innovation. Although outlawed, a minority, so-called Sabbatarian strain of anti-Trinitarianism, which denied the divinity of Christ and adopted Mosaic laws, persisted in eastern Transylvania into the seventeenth century (see SABBATARIANISM). In the 1620s the range of legal religions expanded still further with princely approval for a settlement of Anabaptists (see ANABAPTISM).

The Protestant Churches

The Lutheran, Reformed, and Unitarian churches each adopted a hierarchical form of government, governed by superintendents who were confirmed in their offices by the prince. All the Protestant churches recognized the importance of improving the standards of the CLERGY and made efforts to develop their EDUCATION. Local schools were established in many towns, and in the early seventeenth century a princely academy was established at the capital, Alba Iulia (Gyulafehérvár). However, because the principality did not have a university of its own, many Protestant student ministers were sent abroad to foreign universities. Saxon Lutherans attended German universities, particularly Wittenberg. Reformed students traveled to Heidelberg university toward the end of the sixteenth century, and later to Dutch universities and to ENGLAND.

Protestant ideas spread throughout Transylvania through preaching and printed literature (see PUBLISHING). Printing presses were established in major towns, producing Protestant creeds, statements of doctrine, sermons, CATECHISMS, school books, and HYMNALS. The first complete translation of the BIBLE into Hungarian was available from 1590 thanks to the work of Gáspár Károlyi, minister at Vizsoly in northeastern Hungary (see BIBLE TRANSLATION). In the early seventeenth century Reformed clergy were inspired by contact with western Calvinist centers, and especially the Dutch Republic and England, to produce practical theological literature for their communities. These so-called Puritan clergy aimed to improve popular piety and moral discipline and also supported the development of presbyteries to enforce higher standards of morality (see PURITANISM). Although the formation of presbyteries received some support, the traditional form of church government by a clergy hierarchy was upheld by a national SYNOD at Satu Mare (Szatmár) in 1646. At the beginning of the eighteenth century Pietist Lutheran clergy also appealed for moral discipline and spiritual renewal (see PIETISM).

From 1568 the legal freedoms of the Protestant churches in the Transylvanian principality were clearly established. However, the Habsburg kings of Royal Hungary sought to restore Catholicism across Hungary and to gain control over Transylvania. Attempts in 1604 by Rudolf II to close down the Lutheran church in Košice (Kassa) in Upper Hungary provided one of the sparks of rebellion against Counter-Reformation in the region. A Reformed noble, István Bocskai, led his forces to victory over Habsburg armies in eastern Hungary. By February 1605 Bocskai had been elected as the first of a series of Calvinist princes in Transylvania. Under these princes Transylvania remained largely unaffected by the COUNTER-REFORMATION in the seventeenth century. Princes Gábor Bethlen and György I Rákóczi intervened in the Thirty Years' War against the Habsburgs, claiming that they were defending Hungarian constitutional freedoms and Protestant liberties. They supported Protestant nobles in Royal Hungary who complained that church buildings were being seized by Catholics. This period of Transylvanian autonomy under Calvinist princes saw the Reformed Church become in effect the public church of the principality.

However, Reformed-dominated Transylvania was gravely weakened by the attempted invasion of POLAND by György II Rákóczi in the late 1650s, with a subsequent loss of territory to the Ottomans.

Protestantism in Habsburg Transylvania

Toward the end of the seventeenth century the Habsburgs extended their territory at the expense of the Ottomans. In 1686 the Transylvanian diet appealed to Leopold I for protection and in 1691 agreed to the Diploma of Leopold I, which brought the principality under Habsburg sovereignty. This Diploma maintained the privileges of the Lutheran, Reformed, and Unitarian churches. Although the Habsburg court supported Catholic interests, the Protestant churches retained their legal privileges throughout the eighteenth century. The old political and religious order came under increasing challenge in the late eighteenth and early nineteenth centuries, with the rise in Hungarian and Romanian nationalist politics. The continuing inequalities that Protestants faced in Hungary formed part of their agenda for reform, and the inequalities facing Transylvania's Romanians, both Orthodox and Greek Catholic, formed part of their reform proposals.

Hungarian-speaking Protestants in Transylvania enthusiastically supported the 1848 revolution in Hungary, and the declaration of Hungarian independence in April 1849 took place at the Reformed college chapel in Debrecen, announced by the Lutheran Lajos Kossuth. After the 1848 revolution had been crushed Habsburg rule was restored, but by the 1867 Compromise, Transylvania was returned within the governmental structures of Hungary. In 1881 the Reformed Church held its first national synod at Debrecen, including clergy from Transylvania. This synod was able to lay down the foundations of a national church, with a synod to meet every tenth year to decide on church laws, and a council that represented the church between these synods. The late nineteenth century saw increased educational and publishing activity from all the Protestant churches, and concern for domestic mission from the 1880s in the face of some decline in church numbers.

In 1895 the Hungarian parliament passed a law declaring the free practice of religion. The full benefit of these laws was offered to the traditional churches: Catholic, Calvinist, Lutheran, Unitarian, Jewish, and Orthodox. These churches and their schools could all gain state subsidies, their clergy were offered a minimum salary, and their religious teachers were given a state salary. A second category of religions, including a Baptist Church that had emerged in the nineteenth century, enjoyed full legal freedoms but could not claim state subsidies (see BAPTISTS, EUROPE). Finally small tolerated denominations were allowed to function under rights of free association.

Protestantism in Twentieth-Century Romania

After Hungary's defeat in the First World War, Hungarian territory was reduced by two-thirds by the 1920 Trianon peace treaty. Transylvania and parts of eastern Hungary to the west of the Carpathian mountains were brought within the Romanian state. The Hungarian minority complained of mistreatment by the Bucharest government and sought to overturn the terms of the Trianon peace treaty. The churches provided key means of expressing the identity of the ethnic minority communities in Romania. The Lutheran Church had long been closely linked with the German community, and the Reformed, Unitarian, and Catholic churches played a similar role for the Hungarian minority. Militant NATIONALISM increased in the interwar period, and none of the Christian churches had a distinguished role in opposing the rise of fascism and ANTI-SEMITISM in Romania in the 1930s (see JUDAISM). During the Second World War both Romania and Hungary were allied to the fascist powers, partly aiming to secure German support for rival territorial claims. In 1940 Hungary temporarily regained control over northern Transylvania as part of their agreement with Germany. In 1944 Romania switched to join the Allies, and the Trianon border was restored at the end of the Second World War.

In the postwar period the churches found themselves increasingly marginalized under the new Communist regime (see COMMUNISM). This was particularly the case for the churches of ethnic minorities, including the Protestant churches. By far the largest Protestant church, the Reformed Church had around 700 ministers in Romania, supported by around 12,000 active presbyters. However, the ability of these clergy and presbyters to carry out their functions was increasingly restricted by the government. In 1949 new laws required all churches to be registered with the Department of Cults, which gained administrative and financial control over the churches. In 1950 the small communities of BAPTISTS, Pentecostals (see PENTECOSTALISM), and SEVENTH-DAY ADVENTISTS were forced to unite into a Federation of Protestant Cults. The larger Protestant churches were forced to accept a united seminary college, which was attended by Reformed, Lutheran, and Unitarian students at Cluj (Kolozsvár) and by Lutheran students in Sibiu (Hermannstadt). The state restricted the numbers of students who could attend these colleges, and as a result by 1989 there

were 70 unfilled parishes in the Transylvanian Reformed province alone.

After the 1956 Hungarian Revolution the churches of the Hungarian minority in Transylvania came under particular oppression from the Bucharest regime. Some clergy, students, and teachers were imprisoned, connections between the churches and foreign countries were cut, publishing activity curtailed, and no Bibles could be produced. The Protestant church hierarchies were emasculated by state officials, and the appointment of parish ministers was influenced by the state. Ministers who were deemed to be beyond official control could face forced retirement or arrest. Opposition to a move to a remote village enforced on the Timișoara (Temesvár) Reformed minister, László Tőkés, became one of the sparks of the revolutionary movement that ended the dictatorship of Nicolae Ceaușescu in 1989.

In the period after the downfall of the Ceaușescu regime, the Orthodox Church has come to dominate the public culture of the Romanian state. Overall 85 percent of the Romanian population are claimed to belong to the Eastern Orthodox Church. The largest Protestant church remains the Reformed Church with between 800,000 and 900,000 members. The Unitarian church has around 80,000 members in 140 churches, mostly located in eastern Transylvania. There are also around 30,000 Hungarian Lutherans. However, the rapid decline of the German community in Romania from 800,000 to a very few thousand has meant the reduction of the Lutheran Church to small numbers of active congregations. In addition there are perhaps up to 100,000 other Protestants across Romania, including both Hungarian and Romanian-speaking Baptists and Pentecostals. The churches have again become a prime means of expressing the identity of ethnic minorities in Romania, which has invited suspicion and hostility from Romanian nationalist politicians. Efforts to regain church property have been slow, but vacant parishes have received new ministers, contact has been reestablished with Western Protestants, and some new schools have opened. The historic Protestant churches of Transylvania face many challenges in post-Communist Romanian society, including competition from some new Protestant groups.

References and Further Reading

Binder, Ludwig. *Grundlagen und Formen der Toleranz in Siebenbürgen bis zur Mitte des 17. Jahrhunderts.* Cologne, Germany/Vienna, Austria: Böhlau, 1976.

Dán, Róbert, and Antal Pirnát, eds. *Antitrinitarianism in the Second Half of the Sixteenth Century.* Budapest, Hungary: Akadémiai kiadó, 1982.

Evans, Robert. "Calvinism in East Central Europe: Hungary and her Neighbours." In *International Calvinism, 1541–1715.* Edited by Menna Prestwich. Oxford, UK: Clarendon, 1985.

Murdock, Graeme. *Calvinism on the Frontier, 1600–1660. International Calvinism and the Reformed Church in Hungary and Transylvania.* Oxford, UK: Clarendon Press, 2000.

Révész, Imre, ed. *History of the Hungarian Reformed Church.* Translated by George Knight. Washington, D.C.: Hungarian Federation of America, 1956.

Wilbur, Earl. *A History of Unitarianism in Transylvania, England and America.* Cambridge, MA: Harvard University Press, 1952.

GRAEME MURDOCK

ROMANTICISM

European Romanticism has been described in many ways, ranging from a narrowly defined historical period to metaphors of a "boiling" or "fermentation-point" producing a fundamental change of state. For some we are still in a Romantic age; for others, a post-Romantic one. For those involved, however, one strikingly common characteristic was a feeling of *loss*. In many poets, this longing—at once personal and cultural—for something lost, unattainable, or incomplete, was an obsession amounting to a personal reinvention. In both the *Immortality Ode* and the autobiographical *Prelude* WILLIAM WORDSWORTH displays nostalgia for a state of childhood ecstasy that cannot quite be recalled or re-created, but remains liminal, just *beyond* the threshold of consciousness. Similarly SAMUEL TAYLOR COLERIDGE's *Ancient Mariner* is haunted by the idea of a state of innocence that is the more desirable because unrecoverable. John Keats's *Odes* hanker after health as much psychological as physical. Even Lord Byron's mockery has a hint of whistling in the dark. Perhaps most startling of all is WILLIAM BLAKE's discovery that to recapture the prophetic sense of meaning in current events, he has to invent a completely new mythology of history.

Above all, what had been lost was religion. Not in the popular evangelical sense of a relationship with a personal God, but rather a general and collective world picture in which there was no boundary between the sacred and the secular, in which supernatural or divine power was everywhere apprehended through type, symbol, and sacrament. Although in their own idiosyncratic ways, Blake, Wordsworth, and Coleridge were devout Protestants, unlike their predecessors; to be devout, they *had* to be idiosyncratic. The union of personal piety and collective sensibility of the Metaphysical poets was no longer viable. If, as some claim, this progressive separation of the sacred and the secular began with the REFORMATION, the conflicts of the sixteenth century still belonged to a world where religious belief was an instinctive part of life. In contrast, however much the newer forms of eighteenth-century religious revival may have differed, they had in common a perceived sense of loss—often expressed in the new Evangelical terminology as "a sense of sin."

In the first enthusiasm for the French Revolution, the language of politics merged with that of religious revival. Hailing the dawn of this new age, Richard Price (1723–1791), a nonconformist preacher (see NONCONFORMITY), saw political and spiritual freedom as inseparable:

> Be encouraged, all ye friends of freedom, and writers in its defence! The times are auspicious. Your labors have not been in vain. Behold kingdoms, admonished by you, starting from sleep, breaking their fetters, and claiming justice from their oppressors! Behold, the light you have struck out, after setting AMERICA free, reflected to FRANCE, and there kindled into a blaze, that lays despotism in ashes, and warms and illuminates EUROPE! (Price 1789:49)

Echoes of Acts 12:7 and 16:23–33 are obvious, as is Christian's release from Despair in JOHN BUNYAN's PILGRIM'S PROGRESS, and CHARLES WESLEY's famous lines on conversion from "And can it be":

> Long my imprisoned spirit lay
> Fast bound in sin and nature's night;
> Thine eye diffused a quickening ray—
> I woke, the dungeon flamed with light;
> My chains fell off, my heart was free,
> I rose, went forth, and followed Thee.

However, political disillusion, after 1793 and the Terror, only increased hunger for revolution that was spiritual and aesthetic.

In FRANCE and GERMANY, ravaged by Revolutionary and Napoleonic wars, immediate exhilaration was counterbalanced both by loss and a quest not just for new religious experience, but to reinvent religion rather than accept established forms. Paradoxically the conservative Catholicism of R. F. A. de Chateaubriand (1768–1848) draws him into a quite new romantic religious synthesis in *The Genius of Christianity* (1802): "What particularly distinguishes Christian eloquence from the eloquence of the Greeks and the Romans is, in the words of La Bruyère, *that evangelical sadness which is the soul of it,* that majestic melancholy on which it feeds" (his italics) (Chateaubriand 1856:438). Novalis (Friedrich Von Hardenberg 1772–1801) invokes "the infinite sadness of religion." FRIEDRICH SCHLEIERMACHER (1768–1834) has a similar sense of what he calls a "holy sadness" in religious feeling "which accompanies every joy and pain" (Schleiermacher, 1988:217). All sought a quite new relationship with a past where, it was felt, such a loss had not yet occurred. W. H. Wackenroder (1773–1798) turned back to the Italian Renaissance as an imaginary golden age for his *Confessions from the Heart of an Art-Loving Friar* (1797). Novalis turned to the seventeenth-century world of JAKOB BÖHME, and beyond that other-worldly mysteries of Gnosticism and Neoplatonism, but nevertheless proclaimed that "true religion" had not yet arrived (Forstman 1977: 47–63). This attempt to return to a unified world picture made a deep impression on his friend Friedrich Schlegel (1772–1829), who was with him when he died at the age of 29. Partly under his posthumous influence, Schlegel and his wife converted to Catholicism in 1808. "If only because it is so ancient," wrote Dorothea Schlegel, "I prefer Catholicism. Nothing new is of any use" (Eichner, 1970:106–111). Schleiermacher and the Schlegels shared a distaste for contemporary LUTHERANISM, and the evangelical Protestantism of his *Speeches on Religion* almost amounts to a re-created Romantic Christianity of his own.

The background to this almost universal desire to reinvent religion lies both in the general temper of eighteenth-century DEISM and, more specifically, in new near-Eastern scholarship. In 1791 the former aristocrat Constantin-François Chasseboeuf de Volney (1757–1820) presented the Revolutionary French National Assembly with a monograph entitled *Les Ruines, ou méditation sur les revolutions des empires*. Despite its gothic-sounding title, it was less a "meditation" than a polemic on the origins of religion—particularly Christianity. Not merely all Indo-European and Semitic religion, Volney argued, but even astrology could be traced back to ancient Egypt at least 17,000 years ago. All supernatural and revealed religions were nothing more than the misplaced products of primitive nature-worship, time, and the accidents of historical diffusion. The gods of ancient Egypt, through the Aryans, had been eventually reduced by the sixth century B.C. in Persia to a single deity. This new syncretistic monotheism was then appropriated by the Israelites during their Babylonian and Persian captivities, transmitted to the Christians, and thence in the sixth century A.D. to the Arabs. To any historian the conclusion was clear: "Jews, Christians, Mahometans, howsoever lofty may be your pretensions, you are in your spiritual and immaterial system, only the blundering followers of Zoroaster" (Volney, 1881:83).

Following ENLIGHTENMENT assumptions, Volney attributed miracles to imagination, gods to forces of nature, and moral codes to natural law and self-love (14–15:93). His dazzling erudition, ranging from Hindu cosmology to the esoteric doctrines of the Essenes (83-5), together with his revolutionary and anticlerical bias, made for immediate popularity. At least three English and one Welsh translation appeared by 1800 (eleven by 1822) and extensive summaries appeared in radical magazines. Both Shelley's *Queen Mab* and *Ozymandias* show his influence, as does Blake's *Marriage of Heaven and Hell*. In 1817 Mary Shelley gave the *Ruins* further mythopeoeic status by making the Monster read it in *Frankenstein*.

Worse even than Volney's refusal to separate Christianity from other near-Eastern religions, was the claim for pre-Biblical texts 17,000 years old—contrary to Archbishop Ussher's date of 4004 B.C. for the Creation—and that the Old Testament was not the earliest writing. Many still assumed that Hebrew was the oldest language—containing elements of the original unfallen Adamic speech where words stood in an essential rather than a contingent relationship to what they described (Aarsleff, 1982:58–60). Thus J. G. Herder (1744–1783), in his *Spirit of Hebrew Poetry* (1782), took it for granted that Hebrew poetry "expresses the earliest perceptions, the simplest forms, by which the human soul expressed its thoughts, the most uncorrupted affections that bound and guided it."

Yet, for all its ICONOCLASM, there is a "gothick," even mystical, quality to *The Ruins* that often seems to prelude a new religion than demolish old ones. This suggestion (never quite substantiated) that readers, far from passing from superstition into the light of Reason, were to be initiated into the mysteries of a new age, differentiated Volney from other Enlightenment skeptics and points toward the more psychological questioning of later critics, such as Schleiermacher and LUDWIG FEUERBACH. Comte's transformation of Volney's key to all mythologies into a positivist religion of humanity was, as GEORGE ELIOT saw, not a perversion but a logical extension of qualities implicit in *The Ruins*.

Thus even as Christianity's historical origins were challenged, many of its central ideas were being re-appropriated. Biblical typology was recycled as poetic "symbolism." Blake supports his radical and antinomian ideas with a personal mythology, which includes "conversations" with the prophets Isaiah and Ezekiel in *The Marriage of Heaven and Hell* (1793). Coleridge and Wordsworth, although more orthodox Protestants, both attach greater importance to personal experience than to either "evidences" of Christianity (such as arguments from design) or history. Despite obvious philosophic differences, all use reconstituted religious imagery in their poetry. Shelley, who was expelled from Oxford University for writing *The Necessity of Atheism*, nevertheless uses in *Mont Blanc* a range of language previously belonging to religion to describe nature as a vast organic process now inseparable from the psychology of the perceiver, concluding with:

And what were thou, and earth, and stars, and sea,
If to the human mind's imaginings
Silence and solitude were vacancy? (142-4)

Similarly, the posthumous *Defence of Poetry* subsumes both Jesus and the Old Testament prophets into Shelley's tradition of poets "as the unacknowledged legislators of mankind."

In Germany the "Jena" Romantics, centering around the Schlegel brothers in the late 1790s, which included Fichte, Hölderlin, Hegel, Novalis, Schleiermacher, and Schelling, explicitly cast religion in aesthetic terms. "Belief in God," insists the young Schleiermacher, "depends on the direction of the imagination" (Schleiermacher 1988:138). A similar secular blending of the aesthetic and religious lay at the heart of Friedrich Schlegel's strategy for creating a theoretical basis for Romanticism itself:

> Feeling that is aware of itself becomes spirit; spirit is inner conviviality, and soul, hidden amiability. But the real vital power of inner beauty and perfection is temperament. One can have a little spirit without having any soul, and a good deal of soul without much temperament. But the instinct for moral greatness which we call temperament needs only to learn to speak to have spirit. It needs only to move and love to become all soul; and if it is mature, it has a feeling for everything. Spirit is like a music of thoughts; where soul is, there feelings too have outline and form, noble proportions, and charming coloration. (Schlegel 1991:69)

Here "spirit" (*Geist*) has a secular force never achieved by its feebler English equivalent, and with Hegel the word was to infuse history with an extraordinary religious dynamic.

Significantly, the full implications of the radical subjectivity of the English romantics come to fruition only in Schleiermacher, who disproves the cliché that French Romanticism was radical, but German conservative. His *On religion: Speeches to its Cultured Despisers* (1799) challenged not merely the dominant Kantian philosophy, but also his own circle of Romantic friends (the "cultured despisers"). Whereas Volney's historical and evolutionary theory of the origins of religion shows little sense of interpretational problems, Schleiermacher saw that the problems lay less in the history than on our relationship to it. For him there is an almost infinite range of possible interpretation. Hermeneutics was less a matter of a "correct" understanding of the past, still less of decoding a fixed and universally valid content, but of a much subtler and less determinate process of bringing author and reader into a relationship that made understanding and interpretation possible. No simple key would unlock the Scriptures, no formula bared a final transhistorical meaning; for the true reader "understanding is an unending task."

What was clear for British, French, and German romantics alike was that although religion was essential for any wholeness of life, there was no return to a collective age of faith. For all their backward glances to a mythical and timeless middle ages, they are firmly historical, recognizing that belief could now only be personal, internalized, and subjective—to the point where it is often difficult to distinguish in practice between orthodoxy, pantheism, and naturalism. In this sense Chateaubriand is often as "Protestant" as Blake, Coleridge, Schleiermacher, Shelley, or Wordsworth. "I must create my own system, or be enslaved by another's," wrote Blake. There remained a yawning gulf between the immediacy of personal experience and that acquired on trust from other authorities—the difference between what Newman (one of the last true romantics) was to call "real" and merely "notional" assent. For Schleiermacher such authority was ultimately fatal to true religious experience:

> What one commonly calls belief, accepting what another person has done, wanting to ponder and empathize with what someone else has thought and felt, is a hard and unworthy service, and instead of being the highest in religion, as one supposes, it is exactly what must be renounced by those who would penetrate into its sanctuary. To want to have and retain belief in this sense proves that one is incapable of religion; to require this kind of faith from others shows that one does not understand it. (Schleiermacher 1988:134)

Such a statement of Romantic religion does not merely leave space for individual experience; it makes the foundation stone. However, Schleiermacher, no more than Newman, urges the *sole* sufficiency of personal experience because, as the context makes clear, this is less an evangelical *credo* as a psychological observation about the nature of human belief. The age of passive acceptance is gone. From henceforth, "real assent" is inevitably a matter of imagination and engagement. As such it is also part of a debate about aesthetic theory belonging as much to the English Romantic tradition of Wordsworth and Coleridge, Blake and Shelley, as it does to the German.

See also Blake, William; Böhme, Jakob; Bunyan, John; Coleridge, Samuel Taylor; Deism; Eliot, George; Enlightenment; Feuerbach, Ludwig; Iconoclasm; Lutheranism; Pilgrim's Progress; Reformation; Schleiermacher, Friedrich; Wesley, Charles; Wordsworth, William

References and Further Reading

Aarsleff, Hans. *From Locke to Saussure: Essays on the Study of Intellectual History.* Minneapolis: University of Minnesota Press, 1982.

Chateaubriand, René François Auguste de. *The Genius of Christianity.* Translated by Charles White. Baltimore: 1856.

Eichner, Hans. *Friedrich Schlegel.* New York: Twayne, 1970.

Forstman, Jack. *A Romantic Triangle: Schleiermacher and Early German Romanticism.* Missoula, MT: Scholars Press, 1977.

Herder, J. G. *The Spirit of Hebrew Poetry* (Dessau 1782–1783), 3d edition. Marburg: 1822. Translated by James Marsh. Burlington, VT: Edward Smith, 1833.

Mueller-Vollmer, Kurt, ed. *The Hermeneutics Reader.* Oxford: Blackwell, 1986.

Price, Richard. *Discourse on the Love of our Country.* London: 1789.

Schlegel, Friedrich. *Philosophical Fragments.* Translated by Peter Firchow. Minneapolis: University of Minnesota Press, 1991.

Schleiermacher, Friedrich. *On Religion: Speeches to its Cultured Despisers.* Translated by Richard Crouter (1799). Cambridge: Cambridge University Press, 1988.

Shelley, Percy Bysshe. "A Defence of Poetry (1819)." In *Prose Works,* edited by Mary Shelley, 1840.

Volney, Constantin-François Chasseboeuf de. *The Ruins: or a Survey of the Revolutions of Empires.* Introduction by Charles Bradlaugh. London: Freethought Publishing Co., 1881.

STEPHEN PRICKETT

ROSSETTI, CHRISTINA (1830–1894)

English poet. Christina Rossetti was a major Victorian poet and author of a substantial body of devotional prose. The youngest in an exceptionally artistic and literary English-Italian family (her brother was poet and painter Dante Gabriel Rossetti), Rossetti was closely associated with the pre-Raphaelite movement in ART and poetry. Born on December 5, 1830, Rossetti's religious tendencies were stimulated by the THEOLOGY and poetics of the OXFORD MOVEMENT, which reached London in the 1840s. A devout Anglo-Catholic and longtime resident of London, she died there on December 29, 1894.

Rossetti established her poetic reputation with *Goblin Market and Other Poems* in 1862, followed by *The Prince's Progress and Other Poems* (1866), *Sing-Song: A Nursery Rhyme Book* (1872), *A Pageant and Other Poems* (1881), and *Verses* (1893). Her lyric poetry is exquisite in its simple diction, pure tone, and suggestive symbolism; the inconstancy of human love, the vanity of earthly pleasures, renunciation, individual unworthiness, and the perfection of divine love are recurring themes.

Rossetti also wrote several prose volumes, including the fictional works *Maude* (published posthumously in 1897), *Commonplace and Other Short Stories* (1870), and *Speaking Likenesses* (1874) as well as six volumes of devotional prose, the composition of which occupied Rossetti's creative energies for the last decades of her life: *Annus Domini* (1874); *Seek and Find* (1879); *Called to Be Saints* (1881); *Letter and Spirit* (1883); *Time Flies* (1885); and *The Face of the Deep* (1892). Often structurally complex, these volumes include meditations on NATURE, commentary on SAINTS and scripture, personal reflection, and poetry. Rossetti is considered the most significant poet to

develop out of the literary tradition of the Oxford Movement.

See also Anglo-Catholicism; Bible; Keble, John; Pre-Raphaelites

References and Further Reading

Primary Sources:

Rossetti, Christina. *The Complete Poems of Christina Rossetti: A Variorum Edition.* Edited by R. W. Crump. 3 vols. Baton Rouge and London: Louisiana State University Press, 1979–1990.

———. *The Letters of Christina Rossetti.* Edited by Antony H. Harrison. 4 vols. Charlottesville: University Press of Virginia, 1997.

———. *Selected Prose of Christina Rossetti.* Edited by David A. Kent and P. G. Stanwood. New York: St. Martin's Press, 1998.

Secondary Source:

Marsh, Jan. *Christina Rossetti: A Literary Biography.* London: Jonathan Cape, 1994.

MARY ARSENEAU

ROTHMANN, BERNARD (1495–1535)

Anabaptist reformer. Rothmann was born in or near Stadtlohn to the west of the Münster diocese in GERMANY about 1495. He attended schools in Münster, Deventer, and Alkmar, became a teacher in Warendorf near Münster, and studied at the University of Mainz, receiving a master's degree in 1524. After his ordination to the priesthood he became chaplain at the church of the monastery of St. Mauritz near Münster. To enhance his theological studies, the canons sent him to Cologne. It is not known whether it is here or elsewhere that Rothmann came in contact with reform ideas. After his return he advocated Lutheran doctrines in his sermons and gained followers among the tradesmen who financed a study trip for him in 1531. After a visit with Lutherans in Marburg (Buschius, Schnepf), in Wittenberg (PHILIPP MELANCHTHON, JOHANNES BUGENHAGEN), and in Strasbourg (WOLFGANG CAPITO, CASPAR SCHWENCKFELD) Rothmann returned to St. Mauritz in the summer of 1531. He declined to practice or participate in church rituals (e.g., requiem masses) that had no biblical mandate. In August of 1531 this resulted in denunciations by Catholic townsmen, but also in higher attendance on the part of Lutheran sympathizers. Rothmann had to set up his pulpit in the churchyard to accommodate the crowd.

Because Rothmann ignored the prohibition of his church authorities (both the bishop and cathedral chapter of Münster) not to preach, his opponents pressed for an order by emperor Charles V to bishop

Friedrich von Wied (1522–1532) to restore peace and quiet and to expel the unwanted preacher. Before the order issued on December 28, 1531 in Brussels was received in Münster, the citizens had called on the authorities (city council and guild leadership) to protect Rothmann and to allow his teachings, the main features of which were clear, to be preached in Münster. Anticipating the impending expulsion order, Rothmann sought the protection of the city of Münster and took up residence in the house of the Merchants Guild.

With the support of preachers sent by the Protestant Landgrave of Hesse, Münster became an evangelical, or reformed, city. In August of 1532 Rothmann was PREACHING at the church of St. Lamberti, the main Münster church, while other Lutheran clergy preached at five other parish churches in the city.

A year later, in April of 1533, Rothmann introduced a new church order which the city council had commissioned. Because some of the theologians from Marburg had reservations about it, Rothmann received the help of five preachers who had been banished from Wassenberg in Jülich. Rejecting in principle all non-biblical customs, they denounced infant BAPTISM. Rothmann followed them, as his writings of October and November showed: He declared that the introduction of infant baptism had brought about the beginning of the desolation of faith and the apostasy of the Roman Catholic church from the truth of Christ. On the basis of the date and duration of the apostasy that Paul (II Thessalonians 2:3–4) had described, numerous calculations had been made for the imminent return of Christ and the Last Judgment. Rothmann and others such as MELCHIOR HOFMANN and Michael Stiefel had determined that the time of Christ's return would be the end of 1533. A postponement of the date by three and a half months to Easter of 1534 had been initiated by JAN MATHIIS in Amsterdam, whose "apostles" arrived in Münster at the beginning of 1534. They baptized Rothmann and the preachers from Wassenberg, a practice that was derided by its opponents as "rebaptism."

While the town of Münster was besieged by troops of the neighboring counts for its Anabaptist orientation, Rothmann developed his ideas of the regeneration (or restitution) of the true church of Christ that should take shape in Münster as the "New Jerusalem." When Jon von Leiden took over leadership from Jan Mathiis, who was killed in a skirmish, Rothmann was given the rank of "enunciator of the word" whose responsibility included defining new forms of communal living (joint property, polygamy) and new forms of church worship in theological terms, and communicating that to the outside world through letters and announcements. Rothmann probably did not survive the occupation of Münster on June 24, 1535, but his body was never found.

From the earliest texts that have been handed down (1531), Rothmann's theological positions are clear: he was convinced that the Catholic church had moved away from the teachings of Christ and that it had introduced human fabrications (such as purgatory, requiem masses, intercession of the SAINTS, fasting, holy water, last rites, forgiveness of sins through CONFESSION) not mentioned in the Scriptures. He believed the end of times and Last Judgment were near; thus all Christians had to be brought back to the right faith before these events. These changes were required to bring an end to papal HERESY and abuses.

The main works of Rothmann's doctrine were first (at the beginning of January 1531) formulated (Stupperich, pp. 78–86) by his followers and then published extensively by Rothmann himself (epitome, Druck: Ibid., pp. 64–77). A list of "Miβbräuche der römischen Kirche" ("Abuses of the Roman Church") was done in August of 1532 (Ibid., pp. 58–59). After a successful defense (Ibid., pp. 94–118) Rothmann printed in October of 1532 his first main work "Bekenntnis von beiden Sakramenten" ("Confession of both Sacraments") (Ibid., pp. 138–194). In the months during the siege (starting in February of 1534) four further treatises followed, among them the "Restitution," a programmatic piece on the reinstatement of a "rechten und gesunden Lehre" ("just and healthy Christian doctrine") (Ibid., pp. 208–283). A final essay, written in May of 1535, has survived only in a fragmentary copy (Ibid., pp. 372–404).

See also Anabaptism; Capito, Wolfgang

References and Further Reading

Bakker, Willem J. de. "De vroege theologie van Bernhard Rothmann. De gereformeerde achtergrond van het Munsterse Doperrijk," in: *Doopsgezinde Bijdragen 3* (1977), 9–20.

Bakker, Willem J. de, "Bernhard Rothmann. Civic Reformer in Anabaptist Münster," in: *Dutch Dissenters. A Critical Companion to their History and Ideas.* With a Bibliographical Survey of Recent Research Pertaining to the Early Reformation in the Netherlands, ed. by Irvin Buckwalter Horst (Kerkhistorische Bijdragen 13), Leiden: E.J. Brill 1986, pp. 105–116.

Bakker, Willian John De. Civic Reformer in Anabaptist Münster: Bernhard Rothmann. 1495–1535, Diss. o. O. 1987.

Brecht, Martin. Die Theologie Bernhard Rothmanns. *Jahrbuch für Westfälische Kirchengeschichte,* 78, (1985), 8. 49–82.

Detmer, Heinrich. *Bilder aus den religiösen und sozialen Unruhen in Münster während des 16.Jahrhunderts.* 2. Band: Bernhard Rothmann, Münster 1904.

Haller, Bertram. Bernhard Rothmanns gedruckte Schriften. Ein Bestandsverzeichnis. *Jahrbuch für Westfälische Kirchengeschichte,* 78, 1985, S. 82–102.

Porter, Jack Wallace. *Berhard Rothmann 1495–1535.* Royal Orator of the Münster Anabaptist Kingdom. (Phil. Diss.), Univ. of Wisconsin 1964.

Rothert, Hugo. Bernhard Rothmann. *Westfälische Lebensbilder.* 1. Band, Münster 1930, S. 384–399.

Stupperich, Robert, ed. *Die Schriften der münsterischen Täufer und ihrer Gegner.* Teil I: Die Schriften Bernhard Rothmanns, Münster 1970.

Wray, J. Bernhard Rothmann's Views on the Early Church. *Reformation Studies.* Essays in Honor of Roland H. Bainton, ed. by F. H. Littell, Richmond 1962, S. 229–238.

KARL-HEINZ KIRCHHOFF

ROUSSEAU, JEAN-JACQUES (1712–1778)

French philosopher. Rousseau was born into a Protestant family descended from French HUGUENOTS exiled in Geneva on June 28, 1712. Raised by an aunt and uncle, he ran away from Geneva at age sixteen to nearby Savoy (1728). Here, as he later said, for reasons of expediency and in ignorance of Catholicism, he quickly renounced his Protestantism, and converted to the Catholic Church. He made his way to FRANCE where he spent many years and achieved fame because of two of his writings, *Discours sur les arts et sciences* (1750) and *Discours sur l'origine et les fondements de l'inégalité parmi les hommes* (1753). He returned to Geneva in 1754 and, now in his early forties, reconverted to Protestantism and regained Genevan citizenship. Two of his most famous works, *Emile, ou de l'éducation* and *Du contrat social* (both 1762), were condemned by the parliament of Paris and burned by the government of Geneva. He then, in his early fifties, renounced his Genevan citizenship (1763), although not specifically his Protestantism, and spent most of his remaining years at no fixed address in France. His *Les Confessions* (written by 1770, published posthumously in 1782) depicted his life in an autobiographical genre. Rousseau died at Ermenonville, near Paris, July 2, 1778.

Both during his lifetime and continuously since, Rousseau's interpreters have represented him in quite opposite ways, whether as Genevan Protestant, French Catholic, exponent of new civil religion, ENLIGHTENMENT rationalist and deist, French proto-revolutionary, or pristine romantic.

In spite of the severe rejection of Rousseau's works in Geneva, later interpreters have sometimes detected Protestant motifs in certain of his writings, especially the controversial *Emile* and *Contrat social,* written while a Genevan citizen, and *Confessions,* recalling the tradition of intimate self-disclosure linked to St. Augustine. The "profession of faith of a Savoyard vicar" found in *Emile,* commonly assumed to suggest Rousseau's own beliefs, had a self-acknowledged Protestant ring in its approval of dogmas contrary to the Church of Rome, its low esteem for the ceremonies of WORSHIP, and its attention to the promptings of the heart. The civil society displayed in *Contrat social* seemed more like Calvinist Geneva than anything French, Catholic, or secularist. In *Confessions* he characterized Catholics as people who accept decisions made for them, and associated himself with the trait of Protestants who learn to think for themselves.

See also Deism; Enlightenment; Huguenots; Romanticism

References and Further Reading

Masson, Pierre Maurice. *La religion de Jean-Jacques Rousseau.* 3 vols. Paris: Hachette, 1916; reprint 1970.

McEachern, Jo-Ann E. *Bibliography of the Writings of Jean Jacques Rousseau to 1800.* Oxford, UK: Voltaire Foundation, 1993.

University of Geneva Rousseau website: http://rousseau.unige.ch

C. T. MCINTIRE

ROYCE, JOSIAH (1855–1916)

American philosopher. Born in 1855 in Grass Valley, California, Royce grew up in a home where a pious and devout father was frequently absent, searching for jobs that would provide a living for the family. Royce's mother ensured that he received an education, and after his promising work as a high school student, he attended the University of California at Berkeley. After postgraduate study in GERMANY he moved to Johns Hopkins University and began an auspicious career in philosophy. While at Hopkins he met WILLIAM JAMES, who later was instrumental in securing Royce a position at Harvard.

Although many observers often place Royce in the school of American Pragmatism that developed under James and others at Harvard in the late nineteenth century, Royce developed his ideas about philosophy and religion from the standpoint of the idealism of GEORG W. F. HEGEL and German philosophy. He also incorporated Darwin's notion of evolution (see DARWINISM) into his philosophy in ways that James and others did not, thus building a philosophical system that incorporated the insights of SCIENCE and religion, which he believed were compatible.

In his first book, *The Sources of Religious Insight* (1885), Royce put his idealism into practice as he tried to offer a rational basis for religion, as opposed to the pragmatic and instrumental version that James was offering. In his later work on Christianity, Royce built on this early study and his work in *The Philosophy of Loyalty* to construct what he called a "religion of loyalty." Transcending the tension between morality and religion, Royce argued that devotion to a cause, which results in a loyal life, directs the individual's will to the common good. Such devotion takes on a religious character because the cause is an object that comes from outside the individual. The cause is a unique form of reality—a "real spiritual unity"—that binds many different people into one community. Members of this beloved community share a common faith and a common hope.

Royce believed that religion emphasized the social rather than the individual. His Beloved Community represented his ideal community in which his ideas of loyalty and devotion would be the hallmarks of the religious life.

References and Further Reading

Primary Source:

Royce, Josiah. *The Problem of Christianity*. Chicago: The University of Chicago Press, 1968.

Secondary Source:

Smart, Ninian, John Clayton, Partrick Sherry, and Steven T. Katz, eds. *Nineteenth-Century Religious Thought in the West*. 3 vols. Cambridge: Cambridge University Press, 1988.

HENRY L. CARRIGAN JR.

RUSSELL, CHARLES TAZE (1852–1916)

American religious figure. Russell was born on February 16, 1852 in Pittsburgh, Pennsylvania to Scottish-Irish parents. His mother died when he was nine years old, and his father raised him as a Presbyterian. Although religious as a young boy, by age sixteen Russell had repudiated his Presbyterian background and rejected all religion. As a teenager he went into business with his father operating a chain of successful clothing stores. He accumulated a substantial fortune from these business interests, much of which he ultimately used to support his religious activities. In 1879 Russell married Maria Francis Ackley, who contributed to Russell's work until their contentious divorce seventeen years later. Through his adult life "Pastor Russell," as he was called by his followers, was a prolific writer (Barbour and Russell 1877). He produced tens of thousands of pages of written work, his writings were published in thousands of newspapers, and many millions of his books were distributed internationally. Russell was the founder of the Bible Students movement, which ultimately became the JEHOVAH'S WITNESSES, and by the end of his life the movement had gained several thousand members

around the world. Russell died unexpectedly on October 31, 1916 in Pampa, Texas.

Theology

Russell developed a distinctive THEOLOGY based on his own scriptural study and liberal borrowing from both the Adventist and contemporary American Protestant traditions. His major theological tenets include the following: (1) There was no biblical basis for the trinity. (2) The DEATH of Christ was the ransom price for humanity, but humans had been ransomed from death rather than eternal hell. (3) Christ was not part of a trinity but rather a lesser god who had been created by his father. (4) The dead will remain unconscious in their graves until the resurrection. (5) Christ was resurrected in spirit but not in the flesh in 1874 as the first step in a two-stage coming (parousia). (6) The church and all of its constituent branches lost their legitimacy after the death of the apostles. Although Russell initially rejected Adventist date setting, he soon became caught up in the practice. He set a number of dates for the end time—1874, 1878, 1881, and 1914—and each time offered a reassessment and new date. Russell taught his followers that they should be prepared for the climactic events when his followers would be transformed into spirits and taken to HEAVEN. The remainder of humanity, Russell preached, would achieve SALVATION during the millennium and form a "Great Company" that would live on an Edenlike earth.

Organization

It is clear that when he began his religious career Russell did not intend to establish a church but rather slowly adopted more formal organization over several decades. When he was sixteen Russell formed his own BIBLE study group that initially consisted of a small group of friends and his father. The following year he attended a religious meeting led by Jonas Wendall, an Adventist preacher who ignited his religious passion. In 1876 Russell met another Adventist, Nelson Barbour, who was the editor of *The Herald of the Morning,* and the two worked together for three years before parting company over doctrinal differences. Russell then founded his own competing magazine, *Zion's Watch Tower and Herald of Christ's Presence* to disseminate his theological message. Beginning with the single congregation that Russell established in the late 1870s, new congregations formed quickly, and by 1880 congregations existed throughout the eastern and central states. Russell gradually created formal organizations to administer his growing movement. In 1884 he founded the Zion's Watch Tower

Tract Society, and he was installed as its first leader. In 1889 he established the Bible House in Pittsburgh as headquarters; in 1909 the headquarters were moved to Brooklyn, New York and a second corporation, The People's Pulpit Association, was established.

As Russell gradually created a congregational style of organization, he emphasized voluntaristic, democratic governance. "Ecclesias," as congregations were termed, were loosely linked to Russell through "pilgrims," representatives from each ecclesia. Congregational leaders were to be elected, collections were not taken during services, and members were free to express their own conscience but could not dispute fundamental doctrinal tenets. Dissidents were free to form separate ecclesias. However, Russell clearly was the dominant influence within the Bible Students movement. His personal wealth was a major source of movement funding, his writings were the primary source of movement theology, and he administered Zion's Watch Tower Tract Society. As time went on he directed the topics of Bible study of each ecclesia. Bible Studies members began referring to Russell as the "faithful and wise servant" (referred to in the book of Matthew), the "Laodicean Messenger" (referred to in the book of Revelations), or "the man with the inkhorn" (referred to in the book of Ezekiel). Whichever title was used, there is little doubt that Russell was viewed within the movement, and regarded himself, as a prophetic figure.

Russell's unexpected death in 1916 produced a period of tumult within the movement. For many members the failure of Russell's last prediction was disillusioning. In the wake of his death the movement was weakened by defections, struggles for power among potential successors, and schisms. Russell was succeeded by Joseph Franklin Rutherford, who led the movement through a period of schism and persecution and renamed the group the Jehovah's Witnesses. Over time the Witnesses' doctrines changed significantly, and a number of the schismatic groups have claimed to be the legitimate heirs to the original Russell tradition.

References and Further Reading

Barbour, Nelson, and C. T. Russell. *Three Worlds and the Harvest of This World*. Rochester, NY: Office of the Herald of the Morning, 1877.

Beckford, James. *The Trumpet of Prophecy: A Sociological Study of Jehovah's Witnesses*. Oxford, UK: Basil Blackwell, 1975.

Bergman, Jerry. *Jehovah's Witnesses and Kindred Groups: A Historical Compendium and Bibliography*. New York: Garland Publishing, 1984.

Harrison, Barbara. *Visions of Glory: A History and Memory of Jehovah's Witnesses*. New York: Simon and Schuster, 1978.

Penton, M. James. *Apocalypse Delayed: The Story of Jehovah's Witnesses*, 2d edition. Toronto: University of Toronto Press, 1997.

Primary Sources:

Russell, C. T. *Studies in the Scriptures*. East Rutherford, N.J.: Dawn Bible Students Association, 1953–1959.

———. *The Battle of Armageddon*. Edison, NJ: Divine Plan, 1978, 1897.

———. *Harvest Gleanings*. Chicago: Chicago Bible Students' Book Republishing Committee, 1980.

Russell, C. T., Clayton J. Woodworth, and George H. Fisher. *Studies in the Scriptures. Series I–[VII]*. Brooklyn, London: International Bible Students Association, 1924.

DAVID G. BROMLEY

RUSSIA

Terminology

In Russian, the term "Protestantizm" serves in general as a designation for all of those Christian churches and congregations that come out of the Reformation. Specifically, the term is applied to all of the denominations (BAPTISTS, evangelical Christians, Adventists, etc.) that have had a footing in Russia since the nineteenth century. Lutherans have been resident in Russia since the sixteenth century and in general are referred to as "ljuteranskij," the reformists that settled in Russia a bit later than the Lutherans are designated as "reformatskij" or "kalvinskij."

Current Statistics

The number of Protestants in Russia is currently estimated to be about 1 million, which corresponds to about 0.6 percent of Russia's total population (147,307,000). As a result of the Law on Religion, a law that took effect in 1997 and that mandated registrations for all new religious institutions in Russia, it is apparent that with about 3,800 institutions, Protestantism (after the Russian Orthodox Church with 10,912 and before Islam with 3,048) is the second largest statistically. Within Protestantism, the Pentecostal Christians represent the largest group (1,323), followed by Evangelical Christians-Baptists (975), Evangelical Christians (612), and Adventists (563). Lutherans represent a relatively small group, with 213 registered institutions.

History, An Overview

Historically, Protestantism in Russia goes back to immigrants from various countries, people that emigrated to Russia at the behest of Russian czars, already in the sixteenth and seventeenth centuries and later, especially after the manifests of the year 1763 by Catherine II (1762–1796) and similar statements by

Alexander I (1801–1825). (Between 1763 and 1769 about 25,000 and between 1804 and 1824 about 54,000 immigrants settled in Russia.) Russia is dependent on the technical know-how of immigrants and requires the agricultural migrants to settle virgin soil or the territories around the Black Sea that have been depopulated after wars. The motives of the immigrants are economic, political, and/or religious. (For example, religious are the motives of the tide of settlers at the beginning of the nineteenth century, people who, motivated by the apocalyptic speculations of JOHANN ALBRECHT BENGEL and JOHANN HEINRICH JUNG-STILLING, tried save themselves from the impending disaster.) In general, there have been three big migrant tides: in the eighteenth century coming from the Rhineland, the Electorate Trier, and the Hessian possessions (to the Volga region); at the beginning of the nineteenth century especially from parts of Southern GERMANY, but also from Prussia, Saxony, and HUNGARY (to Southern Russia and the Caucasus); and finally in the mid-nineteenth century from the area of interior POLAND (to Volhynia). At the end of the twentieth century, there were migrant movements out of this area. From the migrant community of the Lower Volga alone, more than 90 dependent communities were formed in the years 1772–1909.

During the Czarist system, compared to the Russian Orthodox Church, Protestant congregations, if recognized at all, faced legal restrictions, for example, the prohibition to convert a Russian-Orthodox believer of Slavic origin to Protestantism. However, they also received specific privileges, including tax relief and exemption from military service.

For Protestant congregations, the time after the October Revolution of 1917 brought a certain period of religious freedom, because antireligious state terror at that time was directed primarily at the Russian Orthodox Church as the former state church (see ORTHODOXY, EASTERN). But with the regulations "concerning all religious communities" in the year 1929, all of the elements were in place for the systematic elimination of all religious institutions, a move that resulted in the persecution, ban, and often the obliteration of Protestant congregations.

World War II marked a break insofar as from then on, congregations were not so much exposed to persecution. But a positive turn of events occurred only in the aftermath of the political changes of the 1980s and 1990s. The current legal basis for religious institutions is the Law on Religions of 1997. The Law on Religions guarantees the general freedom of religion; but nevertheless, among others, Protestant churches and congregations are discriminated against, because the preamble of the Law on Religions offers the Russian Orthodox Church a special role with regard of the Russian CULTURE, before Islam and before other religious institutions.

Characteristics

Protestantism in Russia is characterized by a diaspora-like situation: Protestantism represents a widely dispersed minority composed largely of ethnic minorities (German, Swiss, Dutch, Estonian, Lithuanian, Latvian, Finnish, Swedish, and others) in a society that is shaped mainly by Orthodox Christianity, but increasingly also by Islam. This situation has had three major effects. First, the Protestant congregations are strongly shaped by the respective countries of origin, and church services are performed in multiple languages (in the mother tongue of the members of the congregation and in Russian). Second, because they are in the minority, the congregations are faced with defection of its members to the Russian Orthodox Church, just as the Russian Orthodox Church perceives Protestant congregations as a threat. (Historically, such conversions can be proven in one direction: Protestant believers have converted to the Orthodox Church—often during a mixed marriage or for the sake of a better education. Inversely, in the 1860s, the influence of revivalists among the German settlers in Southern Russia led to the creation of the Russian free-church movement, the so-called "Stundists.") Third, to this day, the diaspora situation has forced congregations to concentrate their efforts primarily on basic preservation of their existence. Under these circumstances, the development of a specific theological science has not been possible. And, hence, unlike in Germany or in SWITZERLAND, Protestantism has not become a source of cultural influence.

Yet, before 1917, (especially German-speaking) Protestantism did have some influence in different areas: through the agriculturally influenced (Mennonite) congregations in agricultural production and in the agricultural craft, through the Protestant elites in the palaces of the rulers (Alexander I, for example, was greatly influenced in a revivalist sense after his meeting with Jung-Stilling, the baroness BARBARA VON KRÜDENER, and others), through the participation of the Russian Bible Society (1812–1826) and then the Evangelical Bible Society (1831–1902), through various missionary services (for example, the reformist-inspired Bale Mission at the beginning of the nineteenth century), and through the German Protestant theology that allowed advances in the education and development of a scientific Orthodox theology in Russia during the nineteenth and twentieth centuries.

Protestant Churches and Congregations

Lutherans

The first German-Lutheran congregation was founded in 1576 in Moscow (see LUTHERANISM). Since 1704, evangelical congregations (Franco-German, German-Swedish, and German-Dutch) emerged in the newly created capital of St. Petersburg. Between 1734 and 1832, the Justice Council, set up under Peter the Great (1682/89–1725), was in charge of dealing with all matters pertaining to evangelical congregations. In 1832, a new Church Order was passed that was closely modeled on the Swedish Church Order and thus was more strongly geared toward a Lutheran understanding than other evangelical congregations in Russia as a whole with regard to matters of organization and church service. (Consistories were created, where members are not elected, but were appointed by the czar in consultation with the general CONSISTORY. The same applies to the secular president and the spiritual vice president of the general consistory, thus practically eliminating any influence on the part of congregations and synods.) The church that emerges is partly a state church; it is in charge of maintaining the registry of civil unions and adjudicates divorces. On the other hand, it is a free church with limited rights, because it is restricted by law from recruiting converts from the Orthodox faiths. Internally, the church is subjected to tensions between the need for independence on the part of congregations that are often separated by a great distance and the need for unity with regards to intercongregational matters. In 1850, the foundation of a "Support Fund for Evangelical Lutheran Congregations in Russia" helps further the desire, held over the course of the nineteenth century, to go beyond particularized congregations and towards transcongregational awareness. The church was characterized by a high degree of heterogeneity, both in terms of its social structure (engineers, tradesmen, merchants, farmers) and its ethnic makeup (in 1914, 1.3 million Latvians, 1.1 million Estonians, 1.1 million Germans, and 150,000 Finns belonged to the Evangelical Lutheran Church).

After 1917 (with the Decree of January 23, 1918 separating CHURCH AND STATE), the church's operation was impeded and its assets confiscated ("nationalized"). Thus it becomes necessary to reorganize the church, a task that the general synod meeting of 1924 in Moscow tackled. Until the end of the 1920s, the church enjoyed a degree of freedom (in 1925, the preacher's seminar was founded, and publication of church publications, such as the magazine *Our Church*, was allowed). After 1929, the church lost a large number of pastors and active members. Churches and chapels had to close and were converted to production or repair shops. The Petri Paul Church in Moscow was the last Lutheran church to be closed in the Soviet Union. The situation grew worse with the deportations that begin in 1941, a move that resulted in the destruction of a number of congregations. Even though the outer structure of the church was dissolved, there remained a loose organization of local congregations ("Brotherly Circles"). The experiences in incarceration camps contributed to a spirit of community.

After World War II, the collection and support for congregations continued under Harald Kalnins, the pastor of the Latvian Jesu Church in Riga, who was appointed bishop in 1988. The appointment was recognized by the state, thus resulting in the official recognition of the Lutheran Church in Russia. At the general synod that took place on September 27–29, 1994 in St. Petersburg, the former deputy Georg Kretschmar became Kalnins' successor. From then on, the official name of the church became the Evangelical Lutheran Church in Russia and Other Countries (ELKRAS). Not all Lutheran Churches in the CIS countries are part of the German-inclined ELKRAS. With more than 600 congregations, the ELKRAS constitutes the most important Lutheran church in the current CIS countries.

In 1992, the Finnish congregations Ingermanlands and Karelias created the Evangelical Lutheran Church of Ingermanlands, an organization under the leadership of Bishop Leino Hassinen, then led by Bishop Aarre Kuukauppi since 1995. In December 2000, the Belarus Evangelical-Lutheran Church was created against the efforts of the ELKRAS to incorporate Lutheran and reformed teachings, but with the help of the Missouri synod and the theological institute in Fort Wayne, Indiana. Its goal is to establish an Evangelical Church in Belarus that is decidedly confessional. (According to its constitution, the organization confers membership only to churches that reject the ordination of WOMEN (see WOMEN CLERGY), applies the justification doctrine, teaches real presence, and advocates that HOMOSEXUALITY is a sin.) Similar tendencies can be observed in Siberia, where the creation of a third Lutheran church organization in Russia (in addition to ELKRAS and the Evangelical-Lutheran Church Ingermanlands) hints at an unmitigated Russian profile.

Reformed

The first Reformed congregation in Russia was founded in 1632 by Dutch and French immigrants in Tula. Among the settlers that streamed into Russia over the coming centuries, the Reformed represented about one-sixth. Their share was further reduced over time, because they were absorbed into what were counted as Lutheran congregations. Prohibited initially during the seventeenth and eighteenth centuries (in 1714, Thomas Ivanov, a surgeon major in the Moscow Infantry Regiment, was executed in public for his commitment to Reformist teachings), the position of the Reformed congregations was incorporated into Evangelical Lutheran consistories in the form of a "Reformed caucus" in charge of the matters pertaining to Reformed congregations. Like the Lutheran church, the Reformed congregations were faced with the antireligious policies of the Soviet government, and in 1991 the Union of Evangelical Reformed Churches in Russia was founded, leading in 1992 to the establishment of the Reformed Fundamentalist Church in Tula.

Mennonites

After the manifesto by Catherine the Great, a few thousand (Flemish and Friesian) MENNONITES settled in the area around Danzig, first near Dnepr (west of the Dnepr island Chortica) and then around the region north of the Crimea (near the small stream of Molocnaja). In the nineteenth century, dependencies were formed in Sibiria. Before World War I, Mennonites in Russia counted a population of around 120,000 (approximately 10 percent of all Germans in Russia).

With the clemency of Czar Paul I (1796–1801) in 1800, the Mennonites received special privileges, including free trade and commerce, exemption from military service, and the right to open distilleries. In 1874, as the exemption from military service was lifted, 18,000 Mennonites emigrated to North America. Subsequently, the Russian government offered a kind of civil service. Because of their tradition (Baptist) and their dialect, Mennonites were considered distinct from other German congregations in Russia. From an economic standpoint, they were reputed to be exemplary. For their spiritual development, the revivalist movement (especially through Pastor Eduard Wüst and the "separate" congregations he shaped) was of special importance; the repercussions resulted in a split between the so-called "Mennonite Brother Congregation" and the traditional "churchly" Mennonite congregation. Other smaller secessions occurred. Because the Mennonites were considered "Kulaks," they were subjected to even more repression on the part of the Soviet government than other Germans. (Between 1922 and 1926, 21,000 Mennonites emigrated from the Soviet Union; from 1926 on, emigration was made more difficult.) In the 1930s, the Mennonites were subject to widespread persecution; in 1941, this persecution took the form of deportation and incarceration in camps. In addition, after 1945, among some 35,000 Mennonite refugees, 23,000 were affected by

"repatriation," the forced return to the Soviet Union. In 1963, the Mennonites were forced to join the ALL UNION COUNCIL OF EVANGELICAL CHRISTIANS-BAPTISTS.

Baptists

Starting in the mid-nineteenth century, continental Baptists expanded into all areas where evangelical Christians in Russia settled, probably through Memel. While German-speaking Baptist congregations gained state recognition in 1879, and while the conference of the Federation of the Faithful and Baptized Christians and So-Called Baptists of Southern Russia and the Caucasus took place in 1884 in Novo-Vasil'evka, the czarist government sought to avoid Baptist-inspired free-church groups, having gained an organizational structure in 1884. In 1907, however, a break occurred between Baptists who were committed to a strong order within the congregations and those who were open to an open federation of evangelical Christians. After the "golden" 1920s, after persecution and banishment in the 1930s, the two Baptist federations were accorded legal status in 1944. For better monitoring, they had to join the All-Union Council of Evangelical Christians-Baptists, the same organization that Pentecostals (in 1945) and Mennonites (in 1963) were forced to join. In 1961, about half of the congregation members left the All-Union Council (because of the initiatives against the Soviet leadership of the All-Union Council called "Initiativniki") and joined the underground Council of Congregations.

In 1991, the All-Union Council was renamed the Russian Federation of Evangelical Christians. Since 1990, a number of new groups have emerged. Among them is the Union of Brotherly Congregations that grew out of the circle of the Initiativniki, the socially oriented Association of Evangelical Christians (1992; also called Prochanov supporters), the Missionary Federation of Evangelical Christians (1996) that originated from the All-Union Council and the Council of Congregations with a strongly missionary aim, and the Association of Congregations of Evangelical Christians (1998), which emerged with support of the American organization East-West-Missionaries.

Adventists

The Adventists began to expand in the Russian Empire starting around 1880, almost exclusively under German influence. As in the case of other FREE CHURCH movements, for the Adventists the 1920s represented "golden years" of unprecedented freedom and progress in the life of the congregation: All-Unions Congresses with representatives of the entire Soviet Union were held yearly. In 1926, 600 Adventist congregations could be counted in Russia. But for

Adventists, the 1930s brought persecution and obliteration of their congregations. After World War II, Adventists were allowed to build an organization, but they had to submit to the control of the All-Union Council. Since 1997, a number of Adventist institutions have been registered.

Pentecostals

Active since the beginning of the 1920s, the Pentecostals (see PENTECOSTALISM) formed the Union of Christians of Evangelical Beliefs (Pentecostals) in 1924. After 1945, a small number of Pentecostals were represented by the All-Union Council. Most congregations opted to exist in the underground. Of these congregations, the United Church of Pentecostals was formed in 1961. The Federation of Christians of Evangelical Beliefs/Pentecostals was recognized by the state in 1989, while the nonregistered United Church continued to exist. In the meantime, the Federation of Christians and the United Church cooperate. In addition, there are charismatic groups, including the New Generation movement, founded with the participation of the influential American missionary Bob Winer; the Word of Life missionary movement, created under the influence of the former Lutheran pastor Ulf Eckman; and the rapidly expanding Church of God and the Russian United Church of Christians of Evangelical Belief/Pentecostal. Tensions often arise between the "traditional" Pentecostal Christians and the charismatic groups over such issues as the composition of the church service and the assessment of ecstatic phenomena. Common to both groups is their strong social and missionary commitment.

Advisory Council

In 2002, the leaders of the most important free-church movements (Baptists, Adventists, and Pentecostals) formed the Advisory Council of the Leaders of Protestant Organizations. This council is meant to represent a large share of evangelical adherents in Russia.

See also Lutheranism; Orthodoxy, Eastern

References and Further Reading

Bauswein, Jean-Jacques, and Lukas Vischer, eds. *The Reformed Family Worldwide: A Survey of Reformed Churches, Theological Schools, and International Organizations.* Grand Rapids, MI: Eerdmans, 1999, pp. 438–440.
Diedrich, Hans-Christian. *Ursprünge und Anfänge des russischen Freikirchentums.* Erlangen, Germany: Oikonomia, 1985.
Felmy, Karl Christian. "Die Auseinandersetzung mit der westlichen Theologie in den russischen theologischen Zeitschriften zu Beginn des 20. Jahrhunderts." *Zeitschrift für Kirchengeschichte* 94 (1983): 66–82.
Kahle, Wilhelm. *Evangelische Freikirchen und freie Gemeinden im Russischen Reich, in der Sowjetunion und den Nachfolgestaaten. Ein kleines Lexikon der Gestalten, Geschehnisse und Begriffe.* Zollikon, Germany: G2W-Verlag, 1995.
———. *Wege und Gestalt evangelisch-lutherischen Kirchentums: Vom Moskauer Reich bis zur Gegenwart.* Erlangen, Germany: Martin Luther-Verlag, 2002.
Kretschmar, Georg, and Heinrich Rathke. *Evangelisch-Lutherische Kirche in Rußland, der Ukraine, Kasachstan und Mittelasien (ELKRAS)* (Evangelical-Lutheran Church in Russia, the Ukraine, Kazakhstan, and Middle Asia). St. Petersburg, Russia: Der Bote, 1995.
Lunkin, Roman. "Die euphorischen neunziger Jahre: Pfingstler und Charismatiker in Rußland" ("The Euphoric Nineties: Pentecostals and Charismatics in Russia"). *Glaube in der 2. Welt* 30 no. 1 (2002): 26–31.
Schneider, Harry. *Schweizer Theologen im Zarenreich (1700–1917): Auswanderung und russischer Alltag von Theologen und ihren Frauen.* Zurich, Switzerland: Verlag Hans Rohr, 1994.
Sticker, Gerd. "Russische Freikirchen im Rückblick. Wichtige Entwicklungsschritte von ihren Anfängen bis zur Perestroika" ("Russian Free Churches in Retrospect. Important Developments from the Beginnings to Perestroika"). *Glaube in der 2. Welt* 30 no. 1 (2002): 13–18.
Wisotzki, Elisabeth. "Die Überlegensstrategien der rußlanddeutsche Mennoniten" ("The Survival Strategies of Russian-German Mennonites"). Dissertation, Rheinische Friedrich-Wilhelms-Universität Bonn, 1992.
http://mcdonald.southern.edu/churches (Adventists Churches Online).
http://www.ebf.org (European Baptist Federation).
http://www.cec-kek.org (Conference of European Churches).
http://www.elkras.org (Evangelical-Lutheran Church in Russia and in other countries).
http://www.mwc-cmm.org (Mennonite World Conference).
http://www.reformed-online.org (Reformed online).

JENNIFER WASMUTH

RUSSWURM, JOHN BROWN (1799–1851)

African American church leader. Russwurm was born in Jamaica in 1799, the son of an English merchant and his African slave. After receiving his early education in Quebec he taught for several years at the African School in Boston, Massachusetts. He graduated from Bowdoin College in 1826, becoming only the second black to earn a degree from an American college. From 1827 to 1829 he edited *Freedom's Journal* in New York City, the first black newspaper in the UNITED STATES. This made him a controversial figure. When he announced his growing support for African colonization, the voluntary relocation of African Americans to the African continent, black leaders in the northern United States were outraged. However, Russwurm had come to believe that blacks would never achieve equality with whites in the United States. After earning a master's degree from Bowdoin in 1829 he immigrated to LIBERIA.

After arriving in Monrovia Russwurm assumed the post of superintendent of schools for the colony and actively participated in colonial politics. He founded the *Liberia Herald* in 1830 and served as editor for its first half-decade, a role that made him the most prominent black advocate of African colonization. In 1836 officials of the Maryland Colonization Society appointed him as governor of their Maryland-in-Liberia colony at Cape Palmas. As the first black governor of an African colonial administration Russwurm promoted actions that were often viewed as confirmation of black capacity for self-government. He provided exemplary leadership, in spite of continued challenges, encouraging agricultural development and trade, organizing a militia, establishing a judiciary and uniform legal code, and negotiating relatively peaceful relations with indigenous Africans. Despite occasional conflict with Protestant missionaries he established a setting in which missionary efforts could flourish. Before his death in 1851 he began working for the annexation of the colony by the newly independent Republic of Liberia.

References and Further Reading

Borzendowski, Janice. *John Russwurm*. New York: Chelsea House Publishers, 1989.

Campbell, Penelope. *Maryland in Africa: The Maryland Colonization Society, 1831–1857*. Urbana: University of Illinois Press, 1971.

ROY E. FINKENBINE